Portugal

THE ROUGH GUIDE

There are more than two hundred Rough Guide titles
covering destinations from Alaska to Zimbabwe and subjects from
Acoustic Guitar to Travel Health

Forthcoming travel guides include

Dordogne & the Lot • Menorca • Tenerife • Vancouver • Malta & Gozo

Forthcoming reference guides include

100 Essential Latin CDs • Videogaming • Personal Computers
Pregnancy & Birth • Trumpet & Trombone

Rough Guides online
www.roughguides.com

ROUGH GUIDE CREDITS

Text editors: Lisa Nellis, Polly Thomas and Claire Saunders
Series editor: Mark Ellingham
Editorial: Martin Dunford, Jonathan Buckley, Jo Mead, Kate Berens, Amanda Tomlin, Ann-Marie Shaw, Paul Gray, Helena Smith, Judith Bamber, Orla Duane, Olivia Eccleshall, Ruth Blackmore, Sophie Martin, Geoff Howard, Claire Saunders, Gavin Thomas, Alexander Mark Rogers, Polly Thomas, Joe Staines, Lisa Nellis, Andrew Tomičić, Claire Fogg, Richard Lim, Duncan Clark, Peter Buckley (UK); Andrew Rosenberg, Mary Beth Maioli (US)
Production: Susanne Hillen, Andy Hilliard, Link Hall, Helen Ostick, Julia Bovis, Michelle Draycott, Katie Pringle, Robert Evers, Neil Cooper, Niamh Hatton

Cartography: Melissa Baker, Maxine Repath, Nichola Goodliffe, Ed Wright
Picture research: Louise Boulton, Sharon Martins
Online editors: Kelly Cross, Loretta Chilcoat (US)
Finance: John Fisher, Gary Singh, Edward Downey, Mark Hall, Tim Bill
Marketing & Publicity: Richard Trillo, Niki Smith, David Wearn, Jemima Broadbridge (UK); Jean-Marie Kelly, Myra Campolo, Simon Carloss (US)
Administration: Tania Hummel, Charlotte Marriott, Demelza Dallow

ACKNOWLEDGEMENTS

Individually the authors would like to thank:

Matthew Hancock: Matthew would like to thank Mandy for her support and ideas; Alex for checking out kids' facilities; Luke, Paula and Marianna for their Anglo-Portuguese hospitality; Agostinho for use of his fantastic flat; Bob Taylor, Nicky Bailey and Sapphire Flash for checking out the nightlife; Vítor Carriço, José Aragão, Mário Carneiro, Wilden Fonseca, Lucila Travassos and the Setúbal regional tourist office for supplying information; Dr Manuel Duarte Fernandes and ENATUR for their hospitality; and everyone at Rough Guides, particularly those mentioned below.

Jens Finke would like to thank Maria Helena for many things, but specifically for dragging him up mountains and through spiny thickets in search of

elusive "rock art"; the funny old carver near Torre de Moncorvo who now only makes spoons but continues to play his harmonica beautifully in spite of his wife's hectoring; and those in the turismo offices who were as helpful as ever.

Mark Mann: Zainem Ibrahim for her invaluable assistance.

Thanks also to those at Rough Guides, particularly Amanda Tomlin, Paul Gray, Lisa Nellis, Polly Thomas, Claire Saunders and Demelza Dallow. Thanks also to Maxine Repath and Kingston Presentation Graphics for Cartography, Neil Cooper for typesetting, Gillian Armstrong for proofreading, and Robert Mackey and Alistair McDermott for US and Australian Basics.

PUBLISHING INFORMATION

This ninth edition published March 2000 by Rough Guides Ltd, 62–70 Shorts Gardens, London, WC2H 9AH. Reprinted October 2000 & June 2001.
Distributed by the Penguin Group:
Penguin Books Ltd, 27 Wrights Lane, London W8 5TZ
Penguin Putnam Inc., 375 Hudson Street, New York 10014, USA
Penguin Books Australia Ltd, 487 Maroondah Highway, PO Box 257, Ringwood, Victoria 3134, Australia
Penguin Books Canada Ltd, 10 Alcorn Avenue, Toronto, Ontario, Canada M4V 1E4
Penguin Books (NZ) Ltd, 182–190 Wairau Road, Auckland 10, New Zealand
Typeset in Linotron Univers and Century Old Style to an original design by Andrew Oliver.
Printed in England by Clays Ltd, St Ives PLC
Illustrations in Part One and Part Three by Edward Briant.

Illustrations on p.1 by Andrew Harris and on p.491 by Helen Manning
© Mark Ellingham, John Fisher & Graham Kenyon 2000
No part of this book may be reproduced in any form without permission from the publisher except for the quotation of brief passages in reviews.
560pp – Includes index
A catalogue record for this book is available from the British Library
ISBN 1-85828-516-x

Portugal

THE ROUGH GUIDE

written and researched by

Mark Ellingham, John Fisher
and Graham Kenyon

this edition updated by

Jens Finke, Matthew Hancock, Mark Mann
and Charles Young

THE ROUGH GUIDES

THE ROUGH GUIDES

TRAVEL GUIDES • PHRASEBOOKS • MUSIC AND REFERENCE GUIDES

 We set out to do something different when the first Rough Guide was published in 1982. Mark Ellingham, just out of university, was travelling in Greece. He brought along the popular guides of the day, but found they were all lacking in some way. They were either strong on ruins and museums but went on for pages without mentioning a beach or taverna. Or they were so conscious of the need to save money that they lost sight of Greece's cultural and historical significance. Also, none of the books told him anything about Greece's contemporary life – its politics, its culture, its people, and how they lived.

So with no job in prospect, Mark decided to write his own guidebook, one which aimed to provide practical information that was second to none, detailing the best beaches and the hottest clubs and restaurants, while also giving hard-hitting accounts of every sight, both famous and obscure, and providing up-to-the-minute information on contemporary culture. It was a guide that encouraged independent travellers to find the best of Greece, and was a great success, getting shortlisted for the Thomas Cook travel guide award,

and encouraging Mark, along with three friends, to expand the series.

The Rough Guide list grew rapidly and the letters flooded in, indicating a much broader readership than had been anticipated, but one which uniformly appreciated the Rough Guide mix of practical detail and humour, irreverence and enthusiasm. Things haven't changed. The same four friends who began the series are still the caretakers of the Rough Guide mission today: to provide the most reliable, up-to-date and entertaining information to independent-minded travellers of all ages, on all budgets.

We now publish more than 150 titles and have offices in London and New York. The travel guides are written and researched by a dedicated team of more than 100 authors, based in Britain, Europe, the USA and Australia. We have also created a unique series of phrasebooks to accompany the travel series, along with an acclaimed series of music guides, and a best-selling pocket guide to the Internet and World Wide Web. We also publish comprehensive travel information on our web site:

www.roughguides.com

THE AUTHORS

Mark Ellingham set up Rough Guides in 1981, writing the first title in the series on Greece, and the original edition of this book the following year. He has updated various editions of the Portugal guide since then but is currently doing time developing Rough Guides new ventures. He claims he'd be a lot happier back in Portugal, roaming around Trás-os-Montes, hanging out in Lisbon's bars or watching a Benfica match. He lives in London with his partner, Natania Jansz (editor of the *Women Travel* Rough Guide special), and their toddler, Miles.

John Fisher has also been involved with Rough Guides from the start and has been inextricably involved with the series and with Portugal ever since. The author of several other Rough Guide titles, John can normally be found at Rough Guide HQ in London, where work takes up far too much good travelling time. He lives in South London with his wife and two young sons.

Graham Kenyon became involved in the *Rough Guide to Greece* during a year off after studying classics at Oxford. He went on to co-write the Rough Guides to Spain and Portugal before retiring from travel writing to pursue a career in information technology. He now works in the City of London, specializing in business systems development. He still travels widely and his interest in ancient civilizations continues to provide a focal point to trips.

READERS' LETTERS

Caroline Anderson, Peter Archer, J.H. Aston, Mark Austin, Toby Ayer, Angela Ayling, Cindi Beckman & Benno Oude Veldhuis, Ari Biernoff, David Birchall, Mark Bolton, Graham Breeze, John Buckwell, Katinka Buters, Pauline Chester, Val Clark, Pauline Clendening, Alessandro Colombo, Angela Crew, Simon Dadd, Adam Davis, John Drabble, Phil Dunk, Peter Ekamper, Gary Elflett, Mervyn Evans, Kate Falloon, Nichola Farr, Philippe Fontana, Polly Gardiner, Stuart Gay, Mark Godber, Jonathan Greetham, Colin Hazelton, Richard Heaton, Alan Hickey, M. Hoath, Margit Huber, Andrew James, Maya Kar, Terence Kimber, Uschi Koster, Maggie & Simon Krabbendam, Betty Krantz, Suzanne Lampl & Stephan Carriglio, B. Levitt, Matthew Leys, Isla Lohman, Susan Luici, Stephen & May Lutman, Dan & Amy Marcus, Fernando Marquis de Silva, Bill Martin, S. & J. Matthews, Chris Melia, Dolores Mita, D.W. Money, Gillian Moore, Rosemary Morlin, F. Morris, Liz Naylor, Philippa Nicholson, Fleur Nooteboom & Lea Lemans, Jack Nouwes & Helen Snoerwang, Marian Pattison, Michael Pipe, Ventura Pobre, Stephen Potter, D.R. Pownall, John Prest, Roderick Pryde, Rudi Raterink, Nick Read, Yizhar Regev, W. Richardson, Heather & John Roberts, Dan Rowley, Stewart Russell, Birgitta Schnell & Nicholas Wickens, M. Scofield, Ewald Schröder, Jeannette Seale, Tim Shirley, Nicholas Simon, Lesley Skinner, Jo Slater, Ann Smith, Al Spicer, Gary Spinks, Dominic Stanger, Ian Stuart & Katja Storz, Philip Stubbins, C. Sutcliffe, John & Julie Till, S.J. Thearle, Helen Thomas, J.J.R. Turnbull, Jos van Beek, Hanneke van Nieuwenhuyzen, Jacqueline van Otterloo, Paul & Maroa van Snol, Rene van der Vleuten, Fran Vickers, André Violette, Sandy & Anne Webster, Howard Wells, Peter Wetterhäll, Steven Widdowson, John Wilkis, Rachel Whiffen, Peter Whiteley, Susan Willis, Meryl Williams, Craig Wright.

CONTENTS

Introduction x

● CHAPTER 3: COIMBRA AND THE BEIRA LITORAL 179–216

● CHAPTER 4: MOUNTAIN BEIRAS 217–247

● CHAPTER 5: PORTO AND THE DOURO 248–303

● CHAPTER 6: THE MINHO 304–363

● CHAPTER 7: TRÁS-OS-MONTES 364–395

● CHAPTER 8: ALENTEJO 396–438

PART THREE CONTEXTS 491

LIST OF MAPS

MAP SYMBOLS

▭▭	Railway	⚶	Viewpoint
▭	Motorway	⬇	Waterfall
▭	Road	Δ	Campsite
▬	Pedestrianized roads	ⵌ	Lighthouse
-----	Path	✕	Airport
— —	Ferry route	★	Bus stop
~~	Waterway	Ⓜ	Metro station
– – –	Chapter division boundary	ⓘ	Tourist office
▬·▬·	International boundary	Ⓒ	Telephone
◆	General point of interest	⊠	Post office
✡	Synagogue	⬤	Swimming pool
⅄	Church (regional maps)	▨	Building
+	Chapel (regional maps)	⊞	Church (town maps)
∴	Ruins	⊞	Cemetery
⌓	Cave	▨	Park
▲	Peak	▨	National Park
⌁	Mountains	▨	Beach

INTRODUCTION

I am very happy here, because I loves oranges, and talks bad Latin to the Monks, who understand it as it is like their own. And I goes into society (with my pocket pistols) and I swims in the Tagus all across at once, and I rides on an ass or a mule and swears Portuguese, and I have got a diarrhoea, and bites from the mosquitoes. But what of that? Comfort must not be expected by folks that go a-pleasuring.

Byron in Portugal, July 1809.

Portugal is an astonishingly beautiful country, the rivers, forests and lush valleys of the north are a splendid and complementary contrast to its contorted southern coastline of beaches, cliffs and coves. If you've come from the arid plains of central Spain, Portugal's dry southern Alentejo region doesn't promise any immediate relief, but – unlike Spain – you don't have to travel very far to witness so total a contrast that it's hard, at first, to take in. Suddenly the landscape is infinitely softer and greener, with flowers and trees everywhere. Life also seems easier-paced and the people more courteous; the Portuguese themselves talk of their nation as a land of *brandos costumes* – gentle ways.

For so small a country, Portugal sports a tremendous cultural diversity. There are highly sophisticated resorts along the coast around Lisbon and on the well-developed Algarve in the south, upon which European tourists have been descending for around thirty years. Lisbon itself, in its idiosyncratic, rather old-fashioned way, has enough diversions to please most city devotees; the massive development projects that accompanied the 1998 Lisbon Expo firmly locking it into modern Europe without quite jettisoning its most endearing, ramshackle qualities. But in the rural areas – the Alentejo, the mountainous Beiras, or northern Trás-os-Montes – this is often still a conspicuously underdeveloped country. Tourism and European Union membership have changed many regions – most notably in the north, where new road building scythes through the countryside – but for anyone wanting to get off the beaten track, there are limitless opportunities to experience smaller towns and rural areas that still seem rooted in the last century.

In terms of population, and of customs, differences between the **north and south** are particularly striking. Above a roughly sketched line, more or less corresponding with the course of the Rio Tejo (River Tagus), the people are of predominantly Celtic and Germanic stock. It was here, in the north at Guimarães, that the "Lusitanian" nation was born, in the wake of the Christian reconquest from the North African Moors. South of the Tagus, where the Roman, and then the Moorish, civilizations were most established, people tend to be darker-skinned (*moreno*) and maintain perhaps more of a "Mediterranean" lifestyle (though the Portuguese coastline is, in fact, entirely Atlantic). **Agriculture** reflects this divide as well, with oranges, figs and cork in the south, and more elemental corn and potatoes in the north. Indeed, in the north the methods of farming date back to pre-Christian days, based on a mass of tiny plots divided and subdivided over the generations.

More recent events are also woven into the pattern. The 1974 **Revolution**, which brought to an end 48 years of dictatorship, came from the south – an area of vast estates, rich landowners and a dependent workforce – while the later conservative backlash came from the north, with its powerful religious authorities and individual smallholders wary of change. But more profoundly even than the Revolution, it is

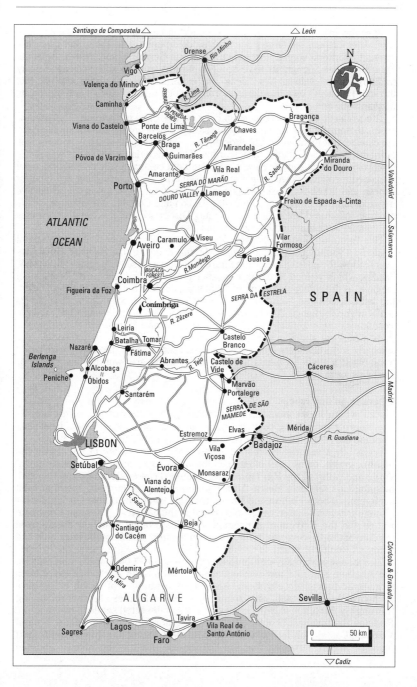

emigration that has altered people's attitudes and the appearance of the country-side. After Lisbon, the largest Portuguese community is in Paris, and there are migrant workers spread throughout France, Germany and North America. Returning, these emigrants have brought in modern ideas and challenged many traditional rural values. New ideas and cultural influences have arrived, too, through Portugal's own **immigrants** from the old African colonies of Cape Verde, Mozambique and Angola.

The greatest of all Portuguese influences, however, is **the sea**. The Atlantic seems to dominate the land not only physically, producing the consistently temperate climate, but mentally and historically, too. The Portuguese are very conscious of themselves as a seafaring race; mariners like Vasco da Gama led the way in the discovery of Africa and the New World, and until comparatively recently Portugal remained a colonial power, albeit one in deep crisis. Such links long ago brought African and South American strands into the country's culture: in the distinctive music of fado, blues-like songs heard in Lisbon and Coimbra, for example, or the Moorish-influenced Manueline, or Baroque "Discovery", architecture that provides the country's most distinctive monuments.

This "glorious" history has also led to the peculiar national characteristic of *saudade*: a slightly resigned, nostalgic air, and a feeling that the past will always overshadow the possibilities of the future. The years of isolation under the dictator Salazar, which yielded to democracy after the 1974 Revolution, reinforced such feelings, as the ruling elite spurned "contamination" by the rest of Europe. Only in the last decade or so, with Portugal's entry into the European Union, have things really begun to change. A belated industrial revolution is finally underway, and the Portuguese are becoming increasingly geared toward Lisbon and the cities. For those who have stayed in the countryside, however, life remains traditional – disarmingly so to outsiders – and social mores seem fixed in the past. Women still wear black if their husbands are absent, as many are, working in France, or Germany, or at sea.

Where to go and when

Since Portugal is so compact, it's easy to take in something of each of its elements – northern river valleys, southern coast, and mountains – even on a brief visit, whether you rent a car or make your own way by public transport.

Scenically, the most interesting parts of the country are in the north: the **Minho**, green, damp, and often startling in its rural customs; the sensational gorge and valley of the **Rio Douro**; the remote **Trás-os-Montes**; and the wild, mountainous *serras* of **Beira Alta**. For contemporary interest, spend at least some time in both **Lisbon** and **Porto**, the only two cities of real size. And if it's monuments you're after, the whole centre of the country – above all **Coimbra**, **Évora** and the **Estremadura** region – retains a faded grandeur dating from the Age of the Discoveries in the sixteenth century and from the later gold and diamond wealth of Brazil.

The **coast** is virtually continuous beach – some 800km of it – and only on the **Algarve** and in a few pockets around Lisbon and Porto has there been large-scale tourist development. Elsewhere, a number of beach areas have seen casual development on a relatively small scale, these resorts remaining thoroughly Portuguese, with great stretches of deserted sands between them. Perhaps the loveliest beaches are along the northern **Costa Verde**, around Viana do Castelo, or, for isolation, the wild stretches of **southern Alentejo**. It must be added, however, that the Portuguese coast is the Atlantic and can often be windswept and exposed. If you like your swimming warm, the only area where the water approaches Mediterranean temperatures is the **eastern Algarve**, where a series of sandbank islands, the *ilhas*, protect the shore.

Swimming aside, **when you go** matters little. The entire country is warm from **April to October**, if slightly erratically so in the rainy north, while the Algarve is amazingly mild throughout the year – it hardly has a winter and January can be delightful when the almond blossom is out. The **Serra da Estrela**, in contrast, features winter snow for skiers, while further north winter is wet and the wind bitingly cold – this is no time for extended journeys around Trás-os-Montes. Throughout the year, escaping the crowds, outside the Algarve and Lisbon, is little problem. Especially on the Algarve, booking accommodation is essential in high season; elsewhere, however, you should find rooms with little difficulty throughout the year except at festival times when even the smallest towns and villages can fill up quickly.

DAYTIME TEMPERATURES (°C) AND AVERAGE MONTHLY RAINFALL (MM)						
	JAN	MARCH	MAY	JULY	SEPT	NOV
LISBON						
Max °C	14	18	22	27	25	17
Min °C	8	10	13	17	16	12
Rainfall	111	109	44	3	33	93
PORTO (Costa Verde)						
Max °C	13	15	19	25	24	17
Min °C	5	7	10	15	14	8
Rainfall	159	147	87	20	51	148
FARO (Algarve)						
Max °C	15	18	22	28	26	19
Min °C	9	11	14	20	19	13
Rainfall	70	72	21	1	17	65

PART ONE

THE

BASICS

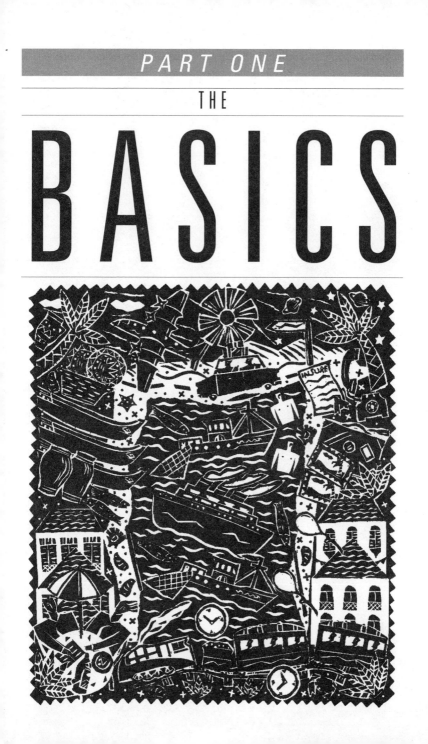

GETTING THERE FROM BRITAIN

It takes at least thirty hours to travel overland from Britain to Portugal, so the majority of visitors find flying is the most viable option. There are scheduled year-round flights to Lisbon, Porto and Faro (in the Algarve) from London and from several regional British airports, including Birmingham, Edinburgh, Glasgow, Manchester and Newcastle. Numerous package companies also sell significantly cheaper charter flights (mostly to Faro) from a variety of British regional airports. Alternatively, if time isn't the most important factor, you can approach Portugal overland from Spain, to which there are many more, and often cheaper, charter deals.

Road or rail alternatives are worth considering if you plan to visit Portugal as part of an extended trip through Europe. There is no direct ferry from Britain to Portugal but drivers can knock off much of the journey by taking the ferry from Plymouth to Santander in northern Spain or the Motorail from Paris to Madrid.

BY AIR

Most of the cheaper flights to Portugal are **charter** deals, sold either with a package holiday or as a flight-only option. They have fixed and unchangeable outward and return dates, and allow a maximum stay of one month. Obviously the more flexible you can be about departure dates, the better your chances of a rock-bottom fare. Last-minute summer flights go for as little as £120 return, occasionally even less, though more realistically you'll pay around £160.

Travel agents throughout Britain sell charter flights to Portugal (see the box on p.4 for agents' addresses) and even the major high-street chains frequently promote "flight-only" deals, or heavily discount their all-inclusive holidays. The greatest number of flights, however, tends to be from the **London airports to Faro**; there are fewer charters to Lisbon and Porto. Flying from other **British regional airports**, you'll find flights often have a connection in London. However, the independent Portuguese airline, Portugália, has daily flights (except Sat) from **Manchester** to both Porto and Lisbon, and a Saturday flight from Manchester to Faro; all these flights cost from £207 low season, and £213 high season, and are for standard returns. British Midland fly twice-weekly (Thurs & Sun) to Faro from **East Midlands** airport, with low season fares starting at a very competitive £138 return, though prices rise considerably in high season.

Student/youth charters are also available sporadically to Lisbon, though it's usually easier (and cheaper) to pick up flights to Madrid or Málaga (see below). The main student/youth operator for charters is Usit Campus (see p.4 for address).

Scheduled flights (with British Airways, British Midland, Go, or, the Portuguese national airline TAP) are generally more expensive than charters, but can be booked well in advance and remain valid for three months, sometimes longer. There are various classes of scheduled ticket and occasional special offers, but with most of the cheaper tickets you'll have to stay at least one Saturday night and you won't be allowed to change your flight once it's booked. As with charters, discount deals are available from high-street travel agents, as well as specialist flight and student/youth agencies. Currently the cheapest scheduled option is **Go** who offer flights from London Stansted to Lisbon from £90 (all year), and to Faro from £140 (all year; Oct–Mar only on Sat) depending on the availability of tickets – in general the further ahead you book the cheaper the seat. Unsurprisingly, these flights fill up quickly and you'll need to book a couple of months ahead for the summer.

Pricier alternatives include **TAP** flights from London (Heathrow) to Lisbon, Porto and Faro;

AIRLINES, AGENTS AND SPECIALIST OPERATORS

AIRLINES

British Airways, (☎0345/222111; www.british-airways.com).

British Midland, (☎0870/607 0555; www.iflybritishmidland.com).

EasyJet, (☎01582/702 900, 0870/600 0000; www.easyjet.com).

Go (☎0845/6054321; www.go-fly.com).

Iberia (☎020/7830 0011; www.iberia.com).

Portugália Airlines (☎0990/502 048; www.pga.pt/atrio/).

TAP (☎0845/6010932; www.tap-airportugal.pt/)

FLIGHT AGENTS

Avro Vantage House, 1 Weir Rd, London SW19 8UX (☎020/8715 0000). Good-value flight-only deals to Lisbon (summer only) and Faro.

Eclipse Direct First Choice House, Peel Cross Rd, Salford, Manchester M5 2AN (flights ☎08702/329 326; packages ☎08705/010 203). Discount fares from Gatwick to Faro, and packages to Lisbon and the Algarve.

Flightbookers 177–178 Tottenham Court Rd, London W1P 0LX (☎020/7757 2444; www.flightbookers.com). Low fares on an extensive selection of scheduled flights and tailor-made holidays. Discounted TAP tickets.

North South Travel Moulsham Mill Centre, Parkway, Chelmsford, Essex CM2 7PX (☎01245/492 882, fax 356 612). Friendly, competitive travel agency, offering discounted fares to all destinations – profits are used to support projects in the developing world.

Portugalicia 110b Ladbroke Grove, London W10 5NE (☎020/7221 0333). Discounted scheduled flights (BA/TAP from Gatwick and Heathrow; Portugália from Manchester).

STA Travel (☎0870/160 6070; www.statravel.co.uk).

Usit Campus, (☎0870/240 1010; www.usitcampus.co.uk).

British Airways services to Lisbon from London (Heathrow), and to Lisbon, Porto and Faro from London (Gatwick). Fares vary widely depending on time of year and length of stay; economy-class return **fares** range from £153 to £177 low season and from £250 to £493 high season. If there are two of you travelling, TAP will give you a small discount on two tickets.

An alternative is to **fly to Spain** and travel on to Portugal from there. You can pick up scheduled flights by budget airlines such as EasyJet, Virgin and Go throughout the summer to Madrid, Bilbao or Málaga from as little as £80 return (depending on availability). Train and bus connections from these Spanish cities on to Portugal are simple enough (Internorte to northern Portugal, EVA to the south) – see the box "Train connections in Spain" on p.6 for more details.

Besides the operators above, you can try the classified sections of newspapers like *The Independent* and *The Guardian*, *The Sunday Times* and *The Observer* or, in London, *Time Out*, the *Evening Standard* or *TNT*. On the **Internet** there are several sites for cheap flights and last minute deals. Two of the best are imaginatively called www.cheapflights.co.uk and www.lastminute.com.

PACKAGE HOLIDAYS

Although **package holidays** tend to concentrate on the Algarve, there is a fair range of other possibilities as well. In addition to beach-and-villa or beach-and-hotel holidays, there are companies which arrange rooms in manor houses and *pousadas* (see p.33) and others which operate weekend breaks to Lisbon or organize sporting (mainly tennis and golf) holidays.

Standard villa/hotel breaks to the Algarve start at around £320 per person (including flights) for a week in high season, although some companies will take only two-week bookings at this time; in winter, you can get some very good deals and may pay around £60 less than this. **Specialist holidays** come a little pricier, from around £450 for a week's golfing holiday based in a four-star hotel; though a three-night **weekend break** in Lisbon can be had for as little as £180 in winter, more like £300 to £350 in high season. With package deals most companies will be quite flexible, and a week or two's extension to the flight – allowing you to indulge in some independent travel – shouldn't usually be a problem.

SPECIALIST OPERATORS

Abreu Travel 109 Westbourne Grove, London W2 4UW (☎020/7229 9905). Portuguese-run agency – always worth a call for flights or accommodation.

Caravela Tours 38–44 Gillingham St, London SW1V 1JW (☎020/7630 9223). Tour-operator wing of TAP. Offers stays in manor houses in the north, *pousadas* throughout the country and a multitude of package holidays.

Destination Portugal Madeira House, 37 Corn St, Witney, Oxfordshire OX8 7BW (☎01993/773 269; *www.destination-portugal.co.uk*). This agent claims to accommodate any Portuguese needs, including discount flight-only deals, car rental, villa and manor house lets, bird-watching, sailing and national park hiking holidays. Highly recommended.

Explore Worldwide 1 Frederick St, Aldershot, Hants GU11 1LQ (☎01252/319 448; *www.explore.co.uk*). Hiking specialist that offers small group tours in the Douro, Gerês and the Azores.

Latitude 40 13 Beauchamp Place, London SW3 1NQ (☎020/7581 3104). Flights, car rental, hotels and villas.

Mundi Color 276 Vauxhall Bridge Rd, London SW1V 1BE (☎020/7828 6021). Specializes in a range of holidays, from city breaks in Lisbon and Porto to tailor-made stays in *pousadas* and manor houses. Also offers special fly/drive deals between Spain and Portugal.

Something Special 10 Bull Plain, Hertford, Herts SG14 1DT (☎01992/552 231; last-minute deals ☎01992/557 755; *somethingspecial.co.uk*). Algarve and Costa Verde villas.

Sunvil Holidays Sunvil House, Old Isleworth, Middlesex TW7 7BJ (☎020/8568 4499; *www.sunvil.co.uk/discovery*) Tailor-made tineraries to suit most budgets, including fly-drive options and stays in *pousadas* and manor houses.

Travel Club of Upminster 54 Station Rd, Upminster, Essex RM14 2TT (☎01708/225 000; *www.Travelclub.org.uk*). Long-established operator specializing in villas and four/five star hotels.

Travelscene 11–15 St Ann's Rd, Harrow, Middlesex HA1 1LQ (☎020/8427 4445). Weekend breaks in Lisbon, Porto and elsewhere.

There's a list of recommended specialist operators in the box above, most of which are smaller companies, whose holidays tend to be directed towards individuals; all should be able to arrange flights and car rental. For further details of companies offering holidays in Portugal, contact the Portuguese National Tourist Office (see p.23 for addresses).

There are two main **routes into Portugal**: from Paris via Irún, Salamanca, Fuentes de Onoro, Pampilhosa and Guarda to Porto, Coimbra and Lisbon; and alternatively to Madrid from Irún via Valladolid and then through Cáceres to Marvão-Beirã, Abrantes and Entroncamento (where the line splits to Lisbon, or to Coimbra and Porto).

BY TRAIN

To get **from London to Lisbon** by train is quicker now thanks to the Channel Tunnel, but the journey still takes at least thirty hours. All inexpensive tickets, however, still route you via the ferries; setting out from Charing Cross station, crossing the Channel at Dover–Calais, changing trains in Paris (and transferring stations, from Nord to Austerlitz via Metro line #5) and again at the Spanish border (at Hendaye/Irún), takes closer to forty hours. It's a good way to travel if you want to stop off in France or Spain on the way. But even if you qualify for under-26 or over-65 discounts, you are likely to pay more than you would for a charter flight. For full details and information on fares, call Connex for tickets using the ferry, or Rail Europe for tickets using the tunnel (see box opposite).

TRAIN INFORMATION

Connex Rail Customer Services Centre (☎08706/030 405).

Eurostar EPS House, Waterloo Station, London SE1 8SE (reservations ☎0345/303 030; *www.eurostar.com/eurostar/*).

Eurotrain Usit Campus Travel, 52 Grosvenor Gardens, London SW1W 0AG (☎020/7730 3402).

Le Shuttle Customer Services Centre (☎0990/353535).

Rail Europe 179 Piccadilly, London W1V 0BA. (European line ☎08705/848 848; *www.raileurope.co.uk*).

Wasteels Victoria Station (by platform 2), London SW1V 1JT (☎020/7834-7066; fax 7630 7628).

TRAIN CONNECTIONS FROM SPAIN

Flying to **Madrid** or **Málaga** may well work out cheaper than flying to Portugal, and from these places train connections west are routine, with rewarding stops en route.

From Madrid, the most direct trains leave from the Estación Atocha, reaching **Lisbon** (Santa Apolónia Station) ten hours later. The fastest route is **via Badajoz**, the "gateway to Portugal", a close neighbour of Elvas (see p.412), the first stop the train makes in Portugal. Other stops along this line, such as the lofty towns of Portalegre (p.416) and Abrantes (p.170), make this the recommended route through the country.

From Málaga you are well placed to head for the **Algarve** and, if you have the time, you could take in a loop through the great Andalucian cities

of Granada, Córdoba and Seville (though note that the Málaga–Granada and Granada–Córdoba journeys are quicker and easier by bus). At Córdoba, you're back on the main train line to Seville from where buses run to the Portuguese border at Ayamonte–Vila Real de Santo António and along the coast to Albufeira. Alternatively, you can get off at the Portuguese border town of Vila Real, where you can join the Algarve train line, towards Faro and Lagos, or catch one of the frequent local buses.

If you want to explore central Portugal, the line **from Salamanca**, which enters Portugal at Vilar Formoso, has useful connections to Guarda and Coimbra. From northern Spain, trains connect **from Vigo** in Galicia (3hr to Porto, 9hr to Lisbon).

The current standard, return **fares** from London **using the ferry** to Lisbon are £195 via Salamanca and £207 via Madrid; youth fares (under-26) on the same routes cost £166 and £176 respectively. Tickets are available from Connex or any of their agents; phone Connex for your nearest outlet (see p.5). On the Paris–Hendaye/Irún leg you'll also have to pay for either a reclining seat (£7.50) or couchette (£10.50), which needs to be booked at Paris Nord – they'll charge an extra £2.50 to make the reservation.

Tickets from Rail Europe, all **via the tunnel**, are £278 for either route, with a youth discount of about £20 on the Salamanca route but no discount on the Madrid route – tickets from Rail Europe already include the cost of a couchette from Paris to Irún. For trains to Faro, in the Algarve, you'll have to go via Lisbon and the standard return fare is £26 more; it will almost certainly be cheaper, and quicker, to buy a ticket to Lisbon, then get an express coach on to Faro, which would cost £10 one way. All the above quoted train tickets are valid for two months and stops are allowed anywhere along the way on a pre-specified route.

If you intend to travel a lot around France and Spain on your way to Portugal, you may consider buying an **InterRail** pass, available from Rail Europe, travel agents or any UK train station, which sells international tickets. If you're under-26, a two-zone pass covering all countries between the UK and Portugal will cost you £209 for one month, and gives discounts in Britain and on various ferry services. The 26-and-over version costs £279. Alternatively an under-26 one-zone ticket (covering only Portugal, Spain and Morocco) costs £159 (under-26) and £229

(26 and over) for 22 days. To qualify for an InterRail pass, you have to have been resident in Europe for six months; if you haven't been resident in the UK for longer than six months you can purchase a **Eurail pass** (see p.12 for details).

Senior citizens holding a British Rail Senior Card can buy a **Rail Europe Senior Card** for £5, which gives a thirty percent discount on rail travel between – but not within – 25 European countries, and includes Eurostar and rail-connected sea crossings (see also opposite for further details).

Note, for all these passes, however, that rail travel in Portugal itself is very cheap (about a quarter of the equivalent journeys in the UK), and you may find it better value to purchase tickets as you make individual journeys within Portugal. There are Portugal-only passes such as the **Eurodomino pass** (see p.29) but you would need to travel intensively within the country to get the best value from them.

BY BUS

If you can tolerate the long journey (40–45hr depending on your destination), **Eurolines**, the foreign travel wing of National Express, operates a service three times weekly from London to Coimbra, Fátima and Lisbon, and another to Faro and Lagos. The current fare to Lisbon is £139 return (£83 for under-12s); there are no student discounts. Tickets are available in Britain from any National Express or Eurolines agent (in effect most travel agents), or from the Eurolines office at 52 Grosvenor Gardens, London SW1W 0AU (☎0990/143 219), opposite Victoria Station. You have to change buses in Paris, where there's a wait of around three hours between connections. Alternatively, if you make your own way to **Paris**, there are buses six days a week (not Mon) to Lisbon, and fairly regular services to most other towns in Portugal. Coming back, providing you've made bookings in advance, you can join these buses at any stage. In Paris, tickets are sold at the Porte de Charenton terminus.

Tiring though these journeys are, they're comfortable enough, and broken by frequent rest and meal stops. As long as you take plenty to eat, drink and read, as well as a certain amount of French and Spanish currency to use along the way, you should emerge relatively unscathed.

BY CAR, FERRIES, LE SHUTTLE AND MOTORAIL

Driving through France, your route obviously depends on what you want to see along the way. The quickest route is to take the coast road via Nantes and Bordeaux, entering Spain at Irún. This can be approached from the standard **Channel ports** (Calais, Boulogne or Dieppe) or, further to the west, off the **ferries** from Portsmouth–Cherbourg (5hr; P&O); Poole–Cherbourg (4hr 15min; Brittany Ferries); Portsmouth–Caen (6hr; Brittany Ferries); Portsmouth–St Malo (8hr 45min; Brittany Ferries); or Plymouth–Roscoff (6hr; Brittany Ferries).

Ferry costs vary enormously and depend on the size of car, number of passengers and, especially, the season – from October to March there are very good deals on all the longer crossings. From the Channel ports you're looking at around £140 to £320 standard return (two weeks) for a car and up to five passengers, depending on the season – with an extra £50 to £100 for an open ticket. Fares from Portsmouth, Poole, or Plymouth range from £200 to £335 for a car and two adults open return. For all of the above options, full details can be obtained from travel agents, the ferry companies (see box below), or on the Internet (*www.seaview.co.uk*).

Another alternative is to take your car on **Le Shuttle**, the freight trains which carry coaches, cars and motorbikes in the Channel Tunnel. Le Shuttle runs every 15–30 minutes and the journey takes 35 minutes. Fares start at £149 for a car and up to five passengers, rising to £199 at peak times. Call Le Shuttle Customer Services Centre (see box) for further information. Making advance bookings is unnecessary, although if you have a motorcycle, caravan or motor-caravan it would be advisable.

FERRY COMPANIES, LE SHUTTLE AND MOTORAIL
Brittany Ferries ☎0990/360 360;
    www.brittanyferries.com
Hoverspeed ☎0990/240 241;
    www.hoverspeed.co.uk
Le Shuttle ☎0990/353 535;
    www.eurostar.com
P&O European Ferries ☎0990/980 555;
    www.poef.com/portsmouth/
P&O Stena Line Ferries ☎0990/707 070;
    www.posl.com
SNCF (Motorail service) ☎(00 33) 836.35 35.39;
    www.sncf.fr

The only other ways of substantially cutting down on the driving time to Portugal is to take the **ferry to northern Spain** or the **Motorail from Paris to Madrid**. The **ferry** – run by Brittany Ferries – sails from Plymouth (twice weekly Feb–Oct; 24hrs) or Poole (weekly Nov–Jan; 31hrs) to Santander – although this still leaves you a long day's drive before you reach Portugal itself. Passenger-only prices for a one-way trip cost £50 to £80. Return fares for a car with two adult passengers range from £197 to £359 low season, £312 to £569 mid-season and £352 to £644 high season (mid-July–Aug); prices also depend on the duration of the ticket. All passengers are obliged to book some form of accommodation on the ferry itself, seats cost £4 to £6 and berths £19 to £24. In addition, from Portsmouth to Bilbao, P&O runs a ferry though it takes a whopping 33–34 hours and is more expensive. Details and tickets are available from most travel agents or direct from the ferry companies. Note that prices for motorcyclists are significantly cheaper – especially if you can find one of the frequent discounted fares advertised in motorcycling publications.

SNCF operates the very useful **Motorail** service. Cars or motorbikes are loaded onto the special daily train at Paris – which departs Paris 10.50pm and arrives in Madrid at 8.05am the next day. From here you can drive to Lisbon in about six to seven hours. For a small car (such as a Fiat Uno) the single fare is FF1200 (£120), plus FF809 per adult (FF647 for under-26s), although prices rise around fifty percent in July and August. Information and bookings can be made only by contacting SNCF direct in France (see box); they have English-speaking operators and accept most credit cards.

GETTING THERE FROM IRELAND

Summer charter flights to Faro are easy to pick up from either Dublin or Belfast, while year-round scheduled services operate to Lisbon, usually via London or Manchester.

TAP run a direct **scheduled flight** on Saturdays, from Dublin to Lisbon, starting from around £IR250. Most BA flights to Portugal (daily services to Lisbon, Porto and Faro) use Aer Lingus to Gatwick – except the BA flight from Belfast to Heathrow – with fares from between £IR270 to £IR290 depending on season. British Midland flights are twice weekly from Dublin to Faro via East Midlands airport with prices ranging between £IR180 and £IR240 also depending on season – though fares are discounted for over-60s, under-12s, and students if booked through STA or USIT NOW. You can expect to pay around £IR200 to £IR220 return for summer **charters** from Dublin to Faro, and around IR£250 return from Belfast to Faro. Taking a **package holiday** may cut costs, with one week's villa or hotel holiday in the Algarve costing from £IR300 to £IR500 (from Dublin) or around £500 (from Belfast). If you book for two weeks, it can work out cheaper.

If you're really trying to get there in the cheapest way possible, you might find budget flights from Dublin (with Ryanair, Aer Lingus and British Midland) or from Belfast (British Airways and British Midland) to London, plus a last-minute London–Faro charter flight, will save you a few pounds, but don't count on it. Buying a Eurotrain ticket from Dublin to London will slightly undercut the plane's price, but by this time you're starting to talk about a journey of days and not hours.

USEFUL ADDRESSES IN IRELAND

AIRLINES

Aer Lingus Northern Ireland reservations (☎0645/737 747); 40–41 O'Connell St, Dublin 1; 13 St Stephen's Green, Dublin 2; 12 Upper St George's St, Dun Laoghaire (centralized reservations at Dublin airport ☎01/886 8888); 2 Academy St, Cork; 136 O'Connell St, Limerick. *www.aerlingus.ie.*

British Airways 1 Fountain Centre, College St, Belfast BT1 6ET (reservations ☎0345/222 111).

BA does not have a Dublin office; Aer Lingus acts as their agent (reservations ☎1800/626 747).

British Midland Northern Ireland (reservations ☎0870/607 0555; *www.iflybritishmidland.com*).

Ryanair Phoenix House, Conyngham Rd, Dublin 8 (☎01/609 7800, flight information ☎1550/200 200; *www.ryanair.com*).

TAP (Air Portugal) 1st Floor, 54 Dawson St, Dublin 2 (☎01/679 8844).

SPECIALIST AGENTS AND TOUR OPERATORS

Abbey Travel 34 Lower Abbey St, Dublin 1 (☎01/804 7100; *abbeytvl@indigo.ie*). Charter flights, accommodation and packages, as well as city breaks to Lisbon.

Joe Walsh Tours 69 Upper O'Connell St, Dublin 2 (☎01/872 2555); 8–11 Baggot St, Dublin 2 (☎01/676 3053); 117 St Patrick St, Cork (☎021/277 959); General budget fares agent (*joewalshtours.ie*).

Neenan Travel 12 South Leinster St, Dublin 2 (☎01/676 5181; *admin@neenantrav.ie; www.neenantrav.ie*). City breaks, packages and flights.

Selective Travel 146 Lisburn Road, Belfast BT9 6AJ (☎028 32 663 303). Specialists in charter flights from Belfast.

Trailfinders 4–5 Dawson St, Dublin 2 (☎01/677 7888). Competitive fares out of all Irish airports, as well as deals on hotels, insurance, tours and car rental worldwide.

Co-op Travel Care 35 Belmont Rd, Belfast (☎028 90 471 717). Offers packages and charter flights (summer only) to the Algarve and direct scheduled flights, as well as city breaks to Lisbon.

USIT NOW Now Fountain Centre, College St, Belfast BT1 6ET (☎028 32 324 073); 10–11 Market Parade, Patrick St, Cork (☎021/270 900); 4 Shipquay Place, Derry (☎01504/371 888); 19 Aston Quay, Dublin 2 (☎01/602 1600 or 679 8833); Victoria Place, Eyre Square, Galway (☎091/565 177); Central Buildings, O'Connell St, Limerick (☎061/415 064); 36–37 Georges St, Waterford (☎051/872 601). *www.usit.ie* (for Eire and N.Ireland); *www.usitworld.com* (international site). Student and youth specialists for flights and the only Irish outlet for rail passes.

GETTING THERE FROM NORTH AMERICA

Flying to Portugal directly from the US is more feasible than it used to be. TAP (the Portuguese national airline) has a range of flights available, while other deals and routes have opened up in general. However, at present, there are no direct scheduled flights from Canada to Portugal.

Until quite recently, travellers from North America were better off buying a flight to Spain and then making their own way to Portugal by train or bus. But with more competition on the US to Portugal route, this is no longer the case. Similarly, where once you might have made substantial savings (particularly on flights from Canada) by taking a scheduled flight to London and picking up a British charter flight to Portugal, there are now competitive charter carriers serving the US (Azores Express and Suntrips) and Canada (Sata Express, Lawson Tours and Munditravel).

If you're making Portugal part of a longer European trip, you may want to check out details of the Eurail pass, which must be purchased in advance of your arrival and can get you by train to Portugal from anywhere in Europe (see "European rail passes" on p.12 for details).

SHOPPING FOR TICKETS

Discounted tickets aside, the cheapest way to go is with an **Apex** (Advance Purchase Excursion) ticket, although this carries certain restrictions: you'll most likely have to book – and pay – 21 days before departure, be restricted as to the time you spend abroad (minimum seven days, maximum three months, must include a Saturday

night, etc) and face penalties if you change your schedule. There are also winter **Super Apex** tickets, sometimes known as "Eurosavers" – slightly cheaper than an ordinary Apex, but limiting your stay to between 7 and 21 days. Some airlines issue **Special Apex** tickets to those under 24, often extending the maximum stay to a year. It's worth looking in the newspapers – check your local listings paper such as *Time Out* for New York – for any limited offers from the major carriers. The catch with these, apart from the usual Apex restrictions, is that you often have only a small window of time to make your bookings, which may be several months before departure.

The discount outlets advertised in Sunday newspaper travel sections, such as that in the *New York Times*, can usually do better than any Apex fare. They come in several forms. **Consolidators** buy up large blocks of tickets that airlines don't think they'll be able to sell at their published fares, and sell them at a discount. Besides being cheap, consolidators normally don't impose advance purchase requirements (although in busy times you'll want to book ahead to be sure of getting a ticket), but they do often charge very stiff fees for date changes. Also, these companies' margins are tiny, so they make their money by dealing in volume – don't expect them to entertain lots of questions. **Discount agents** also wheel and deal in blocks of tickets offloaded by the airlines, but they typically offer a range of other travel-related services such as travel insurance, rail passes, youth and student ID cards, car rental, tours, and the like. These agencies tend to be most worthwhile to students and under-26s, who can often benefit from special fares and deals. **Travel clubs** are another option for those who travel a lot – most charge an annual membership fee, which may be worth it for discounts on air tickets and car rental.

Regardless of where you buy your ticket, the fare will depend on the season. **Fares** to Portugal are highest from June to mid-August; they drop during the "shoulder" seasons (mid-Sept to Oct and mid-March to May and the ten days or so before Christmas), and you'll get the best deals during the low season, November to early December and just after Christmas to mid-March. Note that flying on weekends ordinarily adds $50–70 to the return fare.

AIRLINES, AGENTS AND TOUR OPERATORS IN NORTH AMERICA

AIRLINES

Air Canada (☎1-800/776-3000; in Canada call ☎800/555-1212 for local toll-free number; *www.aircanada.ca*). Flights from Toronto, Montréal and Vancouver to Lisbon (via London, Frankfurt or Zurich, with code-shares on European carriers).

Air France (☎1-800/237-2747; *www.airfrance.com*). Flies from many North American cities to Paris and then on to Lisbon and Porto.

British Airways (☎1-800/247-9297; in Canada, ☎800/668-1059; *www.british-airways.com*). Flies from many North American cities to London, with connections to Lisbon, Faro and Porto.

Continental Airlines (☎1-800/231-0856; *www.continental.com*). Daily flights from Newark to Lisbon.

Delta Airlines (☎1-800/241-4141; *www.delta-air.com*). New York to Lisbon, code-sharing on a TAP flight with connections from many North American cities.

Iberia (☎1-800/772-4642; *www.iberia.com*). Flights from many North American cities to Madrid, with connections to Lisbon, Porto and Spanish cities.

KLM (☎1-800/374-7747; *www.klm.com*). Flights from many North American cities – some in conjunction with Northwest – to Amsterdam, with connections to Lisbon and Porto.

Lufthansa (☎1-800/645-3880; *www.lufthansa.com*). Flights from many North American cities to Lisbon, Porto and Faro, all via Frankfurt.

Sabena (☎1-800/955-2000; *www.sabena-usa.com*). Flights from East Coast cities to Brussels and on to Lisbon and Porto.

TAP (Air Portugal) (☎1-800/221-7370; *www.TAP-AirPortugal.pt*). Daily flights from New York (JFK) or Newark to Lisbon with connections to Porto, Faro, Madeira and the Azores. Twice weekly flights from Boston to Lisbon.

TWA (☎1-800/221-2000; *www.twa.com*). Flights daily from New York to Lisbon with connections from many US cities.

CHARTER CARRIERS
Note that some charter companies will accept bookings only through a travel agent.

Azores Express (☎1-800/762-9995). All year round from Boston to the Azores and on to Lisbon in the summer.

Lawson Tours (☎416/977-3000). Year round flights from Toronto and Montréal to Lisbon, Porto, Faro and the Azores.

Sata Express (☎1-800/387-0365; 416/515-7188). From Toronto and Montréal (in summer).

CONSOLIDATORS, DISCOUNT AGENTS AND TRAVEL CLUBS

Council Travel Head Office, 205 E 42nd St, New York, NY 10017 (☎1-800/226-8624 or 212/822-2700; *www.counciltravel.com*). Other branches at: 530 Bush St, Suite 700, San Francisco, CA 94108 (☎415/421-3473); 10904 Lindbrook Drive, Los Angeles, CA 90024 (☎310/208-3551); 1138 13th St, Boulder, CO 80302 (☎303/447-8101); 3300 M St NW, 2nd Floor, Washington, DC 20007 (☎202/337-6464); 1153 N Dearborn St, Chicago, IL 60610 (☎312/951-0585); 273 Newbury St, Boston, MA 02116 (☎617/266-1926). Nationwide US organization, specializing in student travel.

Encore Travel Club 4501 Forbes Blvd, Lanham, MD 20706 (☎1-800/444-9800). East coast travel club.

Interworld 800 Douglass Rd, Miami, FL 33134 (☎1-800/468-3796; *www.interworldtravel.com*). Southeastern US consolidator.

Moment's Notice 7301 New Utrecht Ave, Brooklyn, NY 11204 (☎718/234-6295 or 212/486-0500; *www.moments-notice.com*). Discount travel club.

New Frontiers/Nouvelles Frontières 12 E 33rd St, New York, NY 10016 (☎1-800/366-6387 or 212/779-0600; *www.nouvelles-frontieres.com*); 1001 Sherbrook East, Suite 720, Montréal, PQ H2L 1L3 (☎514/526-8444). French discount travel firm. Other branches in LA, San Francisco and Quebec City.

Now Voyager, 74 Varick St, Suite 307, New York, NY 10013 (☎212/431-1616; *www.nowvoyagertravel.com*). Courier flight broker and consolidator.

STA Travel 10 Downing St, New York, NY 10014 (☎1-800/781-4040 or 212/627-3111; *www.sta-travel.com*); 7202 Melrose Ave, Los Angeles, CA 90046 (☎323/934-8722); 51 Grant Ave, San Francisco, CA 94108 (☎415/391-8407); 297 Newbury St, Boston, MA 02115 (☎617/266-6014); 429 S Dearborn St, Chicago, IL 60605 (☎312/786-9050); 3701 Chesnut St, Philadelphia, PA 19104 (☎215/382-2928); 317 14th Ave SE, Minneapolis, MN 55414 (☎612/615-1800). Worldwide specialists in independent travel; particularly student travel, although they offer many other services for non-students, including insurance.

Travac 989 6th Ave, New York, NY 1001 (☎1-800/872-8800; *www.thetravelsite.com*). Consolidator and charter broker. If you have a fax machine you can have a list of fares faxed to you by calling toll-free: ☎1-888/872-8327.

Travelers Advantage 3033 S Parker Rd, Suite 1000, Aurora, CO 80014 (☎1-800/548-1116; *www.travelersadvantage.com*). Discount travel club; annual membership of $59.95 required.

Travel Avenue 10 S Riverside, Suite 1404, Chicago, IL 60606 (☎1-800/333-3335; *www.travelavenue.com*). Discount travel agent.

Travel Cuts 187 College St, Toronto, ON M5T 1P7 (in Canada, ☎1-800/667-2887; in US, ☎416/979-2406; *www.travelcuts.com*), and other branches all over Canada, including: 180 MacEwan Student Centre, University of Calgary, Calgary, AB T2N 1N4 (☎403/282-7687); 10127-A 124th Street, Edmonton, AB T5N 3K5 (☎780/488-8487); 1613 Rue St Denis, Montréal, PQ H2X 3K3 (☎514/843-8511); 555 W 8th Ave, Vancouver, BC V5Z 1C6 (☎604/822-6890); University Centre, University of Manitoba, Winnipeg, MB R3T 2N2 (☎204/269-9530). Canadian student travel organization.

Unitravel 11737 Administration, St Louis, MO 63146 (☎1-800/325-2222; *www.flightsforless.com*). Consolidator.

Worldwide Discount Travel Club 1674 Meridian Ave, Miami Beach, FL 33139 (☎305/534-2082). Discount travel club.

TOUR OPERATORS

Abercrombie and Kent 1520 Kensington Rd, Oak Brook, IL 60523 (☎1-800/323-7308; *www.abercrombiekent.com*). Upmarket tours of Portugal and Spain.

Abreu Tours 25 W 45th St, New York, NY 10036 (☎1-800/223-1580; *www.abreu-tours.com*). Pousada bookings, tailor-made holidays and set land/air packages.

American Express Vacations PO Box 1525, Fort Lauderdale, FA 33301 (☎1-800/241-1700). Land/air packages, hotel stays.

Backroads 816 Cedar St, Berkeley, CA 94710 (☎1-800/462-2848; *www.backroads.com*). Combined Portugal/ Spain cycling tours.

Contiki Holidays 300 Plaza Alicante, Suite 900, Garden Grove, CA (☎1-800/266-8454; *www.contiki.com*). Spain and Portugal coach tours for 18- to 35-year-olds.

Elderhostel 75 Federal St, Boston, MA 02110 (☎1-877/426-8056; *www.elderhostel.com*). Specialists in educational and activity programmes, cruises and homestays for senior travellers.

Euro-Bike Tours PO Box 990, De Kald, IL 60115 (☎1-800/321-6060; *www.eurobike.com*). Cycling tours of Portugal and Spain.

Europe Through the Back Door 120 4th Ave N, PO Box 2009, Edmonds, WA 98020 (☎425/771-8303; *www.ricksteves.com*). Excellent travel club which publishes a regular newsletter packed full of travel tales and advice, sells its own guides and travel accessories, Eurail passes, and runs good-value bus tours to Spain and Portugal.

Globus and Cosmos 5301 South Federal Circle, Littleton, CO 80123 (☎1-800/221-0090; *www.cosmostours.com*). Offers motor-coach sightseeing tours, including the twelve-day "Portugal Indepth" tour and others that combine Spain and Portugal. Bookable through travel agents only.

Gogo Worldwide Vacations 69 Spring St, Ramsey, NJ 07446 (☎201/934-2996). City breaks, fly-drives, *pousada* holidays all over Portugal. Bookings through travel agents only.

Golf International 275 Madison Ave, New York, NY 10016 (☎800/833-1389). Customized golfing holidays and packages.

Homeric Tours 55 E59th St, New York, NY 10022 (☎800/223-5570 or 212/753-1100; *www.homerictours.com*). Customized tours and packages. Lisbon city breaks.

Magellan Tours 100 East Broad St, Palmyra, NJ 08065 (☎1-888/962-4355 or 609/786-6969; *www.magellantours.com*). City breaks, fly-drives, *pousadas*, manor houses, spas, cruises and open hotel vouchers.

Maupintour 1421 Research Park Drive, Lawrence, KS 66049 (☎1-800/255-6162; *www.maupintour.com*). Fifteen-day *pousadas* and *paradors* tour of the western Iberian peninsula; countryside tour of Portugal and Spain.

Odyssey Adventures 537 Chestnut St, Cedarhurst, NY 11516 (☎1-800/344-0013, *odysseysny@aol.com*). Customized tours and a wide range of packages featuring trekking, fishing, surfing, historical and religious programmes.

Petrabax Tours 9745 Queens Blvd, Rego Park, NY 11374 (☎1-800/634-1188; *www.petrabax.com*). Customized tours plus a variety of set packages.

Portuguese Tours 321 Rahway Ave, Elizabeth, NJ 07202 (☎1-800/526-4047). Customized tours.

Prices quoted in the sections below assume midweek travel, exclude taxes and are subject to change.

FLIGHTS FROM THE US

TAP (the Portuguese national airline), **Delta** (in a code-sharing agreement with TAP), **TWA** and **Continental** are the operators of direct scheduled flights to Lisbon. TAP also offers flights to Porto, Faro, Madeira and the Azores (all via Lisbon). In addition it has a scheduled service between Boston and Lisbon, with a stop at Ponta Delgada in the Azores.

Iberia flies to Lisbon and Porto (via Madrid); this slight diversion can be worthwhile, with shoulder season fares from New York to Lisbon as low as $378. They also fly from many North American cities to Santiago de Compostela in northwestern Spain, just a couple of hours by car or train from the Portuguese border. Several other European carriers fly, via their respective capitals, to Lisbon and on to Porto and Faro. However, given the competitive nature of the business, you'll find little if any difference in fares.

FROM EASTERN AND CENTRAL USA

At the time of writing, TAP's cheapest return Apex fare **from New York** to Lisbon is $298 in low season, $580 in shoulder season and $900 in high season; fares to Porto and Faro (via Lisbon, but allowing no stopovers) are $60 to $65 more. **From Miami or Chicago** you can expect to pay an extra $100 and **from Houston** $160 (these charges are the same for any season). If you book through a discount agent, you may be able to get even lower fares. The **flight time** from New York/Newark to Lisbon is 6 hours 40 minutes and from Lisbon to Porto or Faro, between 30 and 45 minutes.

FROM THE WEST COAST

All flights to Portugal from the West Coast involve changing planes, either in New York or somewhere in Europe. **From Los Angeles**, **San Francisco** or **Seattle**, TAP (using feeder flights on other carriers to get to New York) adds about $250 onto its fares from New York (see above). **From Denver** the extra cost is $200. A discount agent may find you a low-season Los Angeles to Lisbon fare for around $598.

FROM CANADA

There are no direct flights from Canada to Portugal, but Air Canada will fly you to Lisbon in conjunction with one of several European airlines, connecting in London, Paris or Frankfurt. Air Canada fares **from Toronto** and **Montréal** range from CDN$1100 (low season) to CDN$1540 (high season); **from Vancouver** CDN$1230 (low) to CDN$1700 (high). A discount travel agent, however, might be able to find you a lower fare.

EUROPEAN RAIL PASSES

Train travel in Portugal is extremely cheap and rail passes are only really worth looking into if you're intending to visit Portugal as part of a longer trip to Europe. The passes, which must be purchased before arrival in Europe, allow unlimited free train travel for specified periods of time in seventeen European countries and come in various forms.

The Eurail **Youthpass** (for under-26s) costs $388 for 15 days, $499 for 21 days, or $623 for 1 month; if you're 26 or over you'll have to buy a first-class pass, available in 15-day ($554), 21-day ($718), and 1-month ($890) versions. You stand a better chance of getting your money's worth out of a **Eurail Flexipass**, which is valid for a certain number of travel days in a two-month period. This, too, comes in under-26/first-class versions: 10 days, costing $458/$654 and $599/$862 for 15 days.

Alternatively, the more specific **Portuguese Railpass** (see "Getting around" p.29) allows four days' travel out of fifteen ($105, all ages). All these passes can be purchased through Rail Europe (see box) or youth-oriented travel agents (see p.10).

RAIL CONTACTS IN NORTH AMERICA

CIT Tours, 342 Madison Ave, Suite 207, New York, NY 10173 (☎1-800/223-7987; *www.fs-on-line.com*).

DER Travel, 9501 W. Divon Ave, Suite 400, Rosemont, IL 60018 (☎1-800/421-2929; *www.dertravel.com*).

Rail Europe, 226 Westchester Ave, White Plains, NY 10604 (☎1-800/438-7245 in USA; ☎1-800/361-7245 in Canada; *www.raileurope.com*). Official Eurail Pass agent in North America.

GETTING THERE FROM AUSTRALIA & NEW ZEALAND

There are no direct flights to Portugal from Australia or New Zealand, but changing planes a couple of times can get you there within 24 hours, via stopovers in Europe, Asia or the Pacific.

Currently, the cheapest scheduled flights to Lisbon are via Asia, with Garuda and Alitalia/KLM offering the best price. For a little more, there are the options of Air France, Singapore Airlines and Aeroflot, all of which fly via their home bases. Alternatively, you can find a rock-bottom fare to Amsterdam, London and other European hub city and then either pick up a cheap charter flight (see p.3) or travel overland by road (see p.7) or rail (see "European rail passes" on p.12). However, with the high living and transport costs in northwestern Europe, this rarely works out any cheaper in practice. **Round-the-World** (RTW) tickets (valid for a year) are a better choice; they are usually priced according to the number of stopovers you make, but extras are not always expensive. Cathay Pacific-UA's "Globetrotter", Air New Zealand-KLM-Northwest's "World Navigator" and Qantas-BA's "Global Explorer" all offer six stopovers worldwide (including Lisbon), limited backtracking, and additional stopovers (around A$140 each/NZ$160), from A$2200–3200/NZ$3100–3700.

Fares to Portugal vary according to the **seasons** which break down as follows: high season (mid-May to end-Aug and Dec to mid-Jan); shoulder season (March to mid-May & Sept); and low season (rest of the year). However, seasons vary slightly depending on the airline, and there are high and low shoulder times too. You can expect to pay about A$400–600

more for high-season fares. Tickets purchased direct from the airlines tend to be expensive; you'll get much better deals on fares from your local travel agent (see box on p.15) as well as the latest information on limited specials, fly-drive, accommodation packages, stopovers en route and round-the-world fares. Some of the best discounts are through Flight Centres and STA, who can also advise on visa regulations. Seat availability on most international flights out of Australia and New Zealand is often limited so it's best to book at least three weeks ahead.

FROM AUSTRALIA

All the fares quoted below are from eastern Australian cities. Flights from Perth and Darwin are A$200–400 less.

Currently the lowest scheduled return fares to Lisbon are offered by Garuda flying three times weekly via Jakarta and London, Amsterdam or Frankfurt, at around A$1700 (low season) to A$2100 (high season). This is a very long flight taking up to thirty hours, however, free stopovers in several Asian cities such as Jakarta, Denpasar, or Bangkok are possible. Other good options are KLM, which flies daily via Singapore and Amsterdam for A$1700–2410, and Aeroflot via Singapore, Hong Kong or Bangkok and Moscow for A$1800–2200. Alternatively, you could consider the Japan Airlines deal which takes you as far as Madrid (from where you continue overland), with an overnight stop in Tokyo or Osaka included for A$1850–2400. For a little more, daily Air France flights code-sharing with Qantas or Singapore Airlines via Singapore or Hong Kong and Paris start from A$2200.

More expensive (starting at AS$2400) but offering extras such as stopovers en route are Qantas/British Airways flying via Bangkok or Singapore and London, and Cathay Pacific flying via Hong Kong and Paris.

Another option is to look around for a bargain fare to a European hub city from where you can shop around for a cheap charter flight to Portugal. Currently the cheapest are to London – Britannia Airways flies several times a month during its charter season (Nov–April) via Singapore and Abu Dhabi. Low-season fares start at A$1100, going up to A$1900 in high season.

Via the US the best deals to Lisbon are with United Airlines–TAP which offers a through connecting service via LA and New York for A$2300–2900.

AIRLINES IN AUSTRALIA AND NEW ZEALAND

AIRLINES

Aeroflot 24/44 Market St, Sydney (☎02/9262 2233). Flights to Lisbon from Sydney via Singapore, Hong Kong or Bangkok, and Moscow.

Air France 64 York St, Sydney (☎02/9244 2100); 229 Queen St Auckland (☎09/308 3352). Air France do not fly direct from Australia or New Zealand, but code-share with Qantas or Singapore Airlines for flights to Singapore or Hong Kong, which then connect with Air France daily flights from these cities on to Lisbon, via Paris.

Air New Zealand, Australia (☎132 476); New Zealand (☎0800 737 000). Daily flights from Sydney and Auckland to London via LA. No code-share agreement exists with any European airline for the onward flight to Portugal.

Alitalia, Australia (☎1300/653 757); 229 Queen St, Auckland (☎09/379 4457). Three times a week (from Sydney, Melbourne, Brisbane and Perth) to Lisbon via Rome or Milan; code-share with Qantas/Cathay Pacific for the first leg.

British Airways, Level 4, 50 Franklin St, Melbourne (☎03/9603 1133); 70 Hunter St, Sydney (☎02/8904 8800, 1300/653 757); 154 Queen St, Auckland (☎09/356 8690). Daily to London from Sydney, Perth or Brisbane with onward connections to Lisbon.

Cathay Pacific, Level 3, 31 Queen St, Melbourne (☎131 747), Level 12, 8 Spring St, Sydney (☎131 747); Floor 11, 205 Queen St, Auckland (☎09/379 0861). Several flights a week from major Australasian cities to Paris via Hong Kong, with onward connections to Lisbon.

Garuda, 45 Bourke St, Melbourne (☎03/9654 2522, 1300/365 330); 55 Hunter St, Sydney (☎1300/365 331); 120 Albert St, Auckland (☎09/366 1855). Three times a week from Brisbane, Sydney, Perth and Auckland to Paris and twice weekly to Paris via Rome with a transfer in Jakarta or Denpasar. Links with Alitalia for onward travel to Lisbon from Rome.

Japan Airlines (JAL), Level 6, 250 Collins St, Melbourne (☎03/ 9654-2733); Floor 14, Darling Park, 201 Sussex St, Sydney (☎02/9272 1111); Floor 12, Westpac Tower, 120 Albert St, Auckland (☎09/379 9906). Flies several times a week from Sydney, Brisbane, Cairns and Auckland to Tokyo and then on to Madrid (with overland connection to Lisbon); includes an overnight stop in Tokyo or Osaka.

KLM, Nauru House, 80 Collins St, Melbourne (☎03/9654 5222, 1800 500 747); 5 Elizabeth Street, Sydney (☎02/9231 6333, 1800/500 747); 369 Queen St, Auckland (☎09/309 1782). Twice weekly to Faro and daily to Lisbon via Amsterdam from Sydney.

Lauda Air/Lufthansa 7th Floor, 84 William St, Melbourne (☎03/9600 4000, 1800/642 438); Level 11, 143 Macquarie St, Sydney metro area (☎02/9251 6155 toll free (outside Sydney metro) ☎1800/642 438); 36 Kitchener St, Auckland (☎09/303 1529). Several flights a week from Sydney, Brisbane and Melbourne to Vienna with onward connections to destinations in Portugal.

MAS Malaysian Airlines, Level 114, 388 George St, Sydney (☎1300/656 566; 1800 269 9988); Floor 12, Swanson Centre, 12–26 Swanson St, Auckland (☎09/373 2741). Twice weekly to Madrid via Kuala Lumpur and Istanbul, from Brisbane, Sydney, Melbourne, Perth and Auckland.

Qantas, Australia (☎131 313); 154 Queen St, Auckland (☎09/357 8900, 0800/808 767). Daily from capital cities with code-sharing arrangements giving connections to Lisbon.

Singapore Airlines, Australia (☎131 011); West Plaza Building, cnr Fanshawe and Albert streets, Auckland (☎09/303 2129). Code share with TAP to provide daily service to Lisbon via Singapore and Frankfurt from Sydney, Melbourne, Brisbane, Perth and Auckland.

TAP Air Portugal 64 York St, Sydney (☎02/9244 2344). No New Zealand office. TAP do not fly from Australia or New Zealand. Connect with TAP flights from the European gateway cities to Lisbon and other destinations in Portugal.

DISCOUNT AGENTS AND SPECIALIST OPERATORS

DISCOUNT AGENTS

Anywhere Travel, 345 Anzac Parade, Kingsford, Sydney (☎02/9663 0411;*anywhere@ ozemail.com.au*).

Budget Travel, 16 Fort St, Auckland; other branches around the city (☎09/366 0061; toll-free 0800/808 040; *www.budgettravel.co.nz*).

CIT, 422 Collins St, Melbourne (☎03/9650 5510); 263 Clarence St, Sydney (☎02/9267 1255), as well as Brisbane, Adelaide and Perth.

Destinations Unlimited, 3 Milford Rd, Milford, Auckland (☎09/373 4033).

European Travel Office (ETO), 122 Rosslyn St, West Melbourne (☎03/9329 8844); 20th Floor, 133 Castlereagh St, Sydney (☎02/9267 7727).

Flight Centre, Australia: branches nationwide, 24 hours a day (☎131 600) for your nearest office. New Zealand: National Bank Towers, 205–225 Queen St, (☎0800/354 448); plus branches nationwide (*www.flightcentre.com*).

Northern Gateway, 22 Cavenagh St, Darwin (☎08/8941 1394).

STA Travel, Australia: Australia-wide (☎1300/360 960); 256 Flinders St, Melbourne (☎03/9654 7266); 855 George St, Sydney

(☎02/9212 1255; toll-free 1800/637 444); other offices in state capitals and major universities. New Zealand: Travellers' Centre, 10 High St, Auckland (☎09/309 0458); 90 Cashel St, Christchurch (☎03/379 9098); 130 Cuba St, Wellington (☎04/385 0561); other offices in Dunedin, Palmerston North, Hamilton and major universities. (*www.statravelaus.com.au*).

Thomas Cook, Australia: 257 Collins St, Melbourne (☎03/9282 0222, 131 771); 175 Pitt St, Sydney (☎02/9231 2877, 1800/801 002); branches in other state capitals. New Zealand: 159 Queen St, Auckland (☎09/379 3924, 0800/353535) plus branches. Travellers' cheques, bus and rail passes.

Topdeck Travel, 65 Glenfell St, Adelaide (☎08/8232 7222).

Trailfinders, 8 Spring St, Sydney (☎02/9247 7666).

Travel.com, 80 Clarence St, Sydney (☎02/9290 1500; *www.travel.com.au*).

Tymtro Travel, 428 George St, Sydney (☎02/9223 2211).

SPECIALIST OPERATORS

Adventure Specialists 69 Liverpool St, Sydney (☎02/9261 2927). Offers a selection of adventure holidays in Portugal.

Adventure World 73 Walker St, North Sydney (☎02/9956 7766 or 1800/221 931), plus branches in Brisbane and Perth; 101 Gt South Rd Remuera Auckland (☎09/524 5118 *www.adventureworld. co.nz*). Agents for rambles through "Vinho Verde" country.

CIT, 422 Collins St, Melbourne (☎03/9650 5510); 263 Clarence St, Sydney (☎02/9267 1255), as well as Brisbane, Adelaide and Perth. City tours and accommodation packages.

European Travel Office (ETO), 122 Rosslyn St, West Melbourne (☎03/9329 8844); 20th Floor, 133 Castlereagh St, Sydney (☎02/9267 7727). A wide selection of tours and accommodation from hotels to country inns, palaces and monasteries.

Peregrine 258 Lonsdale St, Melbourne (☎03/9662 2700; *www.peregrine.net.au*), plus offices in Brisbane, Sydney, Adelaide and Perth. Guided and independent walking and cycling holidays in Portugal.

Ya'lla Tours, 661 Glenhuntly Rd Caulfield (☎03/9523 1988, outside metro area 1300/362 844). Holidays to Portugal and other European destinations.

FLIGHTS FROM NEW ZEALAND

The prices of flights to Lisbon quoted below are out of **Auckland** (with fares from Christchurch and Wellington being NZ$150–300 more). The cheapest fare currently on offer is with Garuda–Alitalia, flying via Jakarta or Denpasar and Rome, for NZ$2300–2600. Singapore Airlines and TAP also fly several times a week from Auckland for around NZ$2600–3250. British Airways and Air New Zealand fly daily to Lisbon via LA and London for NZ$2800–3500.

Alternatively, you can pick up a rock-bottom flight to another European city and then look around for a cheap charter flight to Lisbon – one of the best deals is offered by Britannia Airways which runs several times a month from Auckland to London during its charter season (Nov–April) for NZ$1450–2250.

As with Australia the best deals to Lisbon via the US are with United Airlines starting at NZ$2600–3000.

EUROPEAN RAIL PASSES

If you're planning to visit Portugal as part of an extensive European trip it's worth looking into one of a variety of **Eurail** passes, which are valid in seventeen European countries. The **Eurail Youthpass** (for under-26s) costs A$485/NZ$580 for 15 days; A$635/NZ$856 for 21 days; A$785/NZ$932 for one month, or, A$1110/NZ$1259 for two months. If you're 26 or over you'll have to buy a **first-class pass**, available in 15-day A$695/NZ$829, 21-day A$905/NZ$1077, one-month A$1115/NZ$1331, two-month A$1585/NZ$1795, and three-month A$1955/NZ$2165 increments.

Eurail Flexipass is good for a certain number of travel days in a two-month period and also comes in an under-26 version: 10 days cost A$575/NZ$685 and 15 days costs A$755/NZ$902; and a first-class version: 10 days cost A$820/NZ$978, and 15 days costs A$1085/NZ$1289. A scaled-down version of the Flexipass, the **Europass**, allows travel in France, Germany, Italy, Spain and Switzerland for (youth/first-class) A$280/420, NZ$334/502 for 5 days in 2 months, up to A$665/980, NZ$794/1169 for 15 days in 2 months with the option of adding Portugal as an "associate" country.

All the above passes have to be bought before leaving home (see box below for outlets), but, as rail travel is very cheap in Portugal, they are unlikely to prove good value unless you were to use it as part of an intensive spin around Europe.

> ### RAIL CONTACTS IN AUSTRALASIA
>
> **CIT**, 422 Collins St, Melbourne (☎03/9650 5510); 263 Clarence St, Sydney (☎02/9267 1255), as well as Brisbane, Adelaide and Perth. No New Zealand office; all enquiries via Australian offices (*www.cittravel.com.au*).
> **Thomas Cook Direct** Australia (☎1800/801 002, 1300/728 747; *www.thomascook.com.au*) New Zealand (☎09/263 7260, 0800/353 535).

RED TAPE AND VISAS

Citizens of the European Union need only a valid passport or identity card for entry to Portugal, and can stay indefinitely. Australian and New Zealand nationals can stay up to ninety days but Australians must have a visa. The visa is valid for all European Schengen Treaty countries (which also includes Belgium, France, Germany, Luxembourg, the Netherlands and Spain). Application forms for visas are available from the embassy or consulates or off the Web sites listed below. American and Canadian nationals can stay up to sixty days without a visa. Visa requirements do change and it is always advisable to check the current situation before leaving home.

PORTUGUESE CONSULATES AND EMBASSIES ABROAD

A full list can be found on the Internet at www.Portugal.org/geninfo/missions/missions.html

Australia Embassy: 23 Culgoa Circuit, O'Malley ACT (☎02/6290 1733). Consulates: Level 9, 30 Clarence St, Sydney NSW (☎02/9262 2199; *www.consulportugalsydney.org.au/*); 15 Colster Crs, Wagaman NT (☎08/8927 1956); Floor 14, 379 Queens Street, Brisbane QLD (☎07/3229 2233); Floor 3, 25 Peel St, Adelaide SA (☎08/8212 1666); 846 Toorak Rd, Hawthorn VIC (☎03/9822 7140); 22 Cliff St, Fremantle WA (☎08/9335 9458).

Canada Embassy: 645 Island Park Drive, Ottawa, K1Y 0B8 (☎613/729-0883, fax 729-4236; *www.Portugal.org/geninfo/missions/canada.html*); for enquiries related to tourism call ☎416/360-8260. Consulates in Vancouver, Montréal and Toronto: 700 West Pender Street, Ste.904, Vancouver, B.C V6C-353 (☎604/688-6514, fax 685-7042); 2020 Rue de L'Université, 17th Floor, Montréal, QUEBEC H3A 2A5 (☎514/499-0359, fax 499-0366); 121 Richmond Street West, 7th floor, Toronto, Ontario M5H 2K1 (☎416/360-8260, fax 360- 0350; *www.consulportugaltoronto. com/home.htm*)

France Embassy: 3 Rue de Noisiel, 75116 Paris (☎01/47.27.35.29, fax 47.55.00.40). Consulates in Bordeaux, Clermont-Ferrand, Lille, Lyon, Marseille, Nancy, Nantes, Orléans, Reims, Rouen, Strasbourg, Toulouse, Tours, and Versailles.

Ireland Embassy: Knock Sinna House, Fox Rock, Dublin 18 (☎031/2894416, fax 2892849).

Spain Embassy: Calle del Pinar 1, 28006 Madrid (☎01/5617800, fax 4110172). Consulates: Paseo del General Martinez Campos 11-1, Madrid 10

(☎01/4454600, fax 4454608); Ronda de S. Pedro 7-1, Barcelona 10 (☎03/3188150, fax 3185912); Calle Marques de Valladares 23-1, 32601 Vigo (PO Box 247; ☎086/436911, fax 433064); Avenue de Francia, NR.2-1.C, San Sebastian (Guipuzcoa) (PO Box 3115; ☎043/276859, fax 277547); Avenue del Cid, NR.1, 41004 Seville (☎05/4231150, fax 4236013).

United Kingdom Embassy: 11 Belgrave Square, London SW1X 8PP (☎020/7235 5331, fax 7245 1287). Consulate: Silver City House, 62 Brompton Rd, London SW3 1BJ (☎020/7581 8722, fax 7581 3085).

USA Embassy: 2125 Kalorama Rd NW, Washington, DC 20008 (☎202/328-8610, fax 4623726; *www.Portugal.org/geninfo/missions/states.html*). Consulates in Newark, New York, Boston, San Francisco, New Bedford Mass, and Providence: 1180 Raymond Boulevard – Suite 222, Newark, NJ 07102 (☎201/622-7300, fax 622-5655); 630 Fifth Avenue – Suite 310-378, New York, N.Y 10111 (☎212/246-4580, fax 459-0190); 899 Boylston Street, Boston, MA 02115 (☎617/536-8740, fax 536-2503); 3298 Washington Street, San Francisco, CA 94115 (☎415/921-1443, fax 346-1440); 628 Pleasant Street – Room 201, New Bedford, MA 02741 (☎508/997-6151, fax 508/992-1068); 56 Pine Street, Hanley Building – 6th Floor, Providence, RI 02903 (☎401/272-2003, fax 273-6247).

New Zealand Consulates: 33 Garfield Street, Parnell, Auckland (☎09/309 1454); Suite 1 1st floor, 21 Marion Street, Wellington (☎04/385 9639)

INFORMATION ON THE WEB

Information on the Web for visa requirements:

www2.travelocity.com/destg/content/PT/ess.html
travel.state.gov/passport_services.html
www.travisa.com/visa1.htm

travel.state.gov/visa_services.html
travel.state.gov/foreignentryreqs.html

An **extension** to your stay can be arranged once you're in the country. Extensions are issued by the nearest District Police headquarters or the Foreigner's Registration Service (Rua Conselheiro José Silvestre Ribeiro 4, 1600 Lisbon; ☎217 141 027) which has branch offices – Serviço de Estrangeiros e Fronteiras – in most major tourist

centres. You should apply at least a week before your time runs out and be prepared to prove that you can support yourself without working (for example by keeping your bank exchange forms every time you change money). Extended stay visas are also available through any Portuguese Consulate abroad; see above for addresses.

HEALTH AND INSURANCE

No inoculations are required for Portugal, though, as throughout southern Europe, it's a sensible precaution to have a typhoid shot and an up-to-date polio booster. A hepatitis jab may also be worth considering, as there have been outbreaks in the past along parts of the coastline around Porto.

Whatever you might hear from hypochondriacs, water is drinkable from the tap anywhere in the country, and from some freshwater sources, too. Be wary, however, of pools and streams in the south of the country. Otherwise, Portugal poses few health problems. **Mosquitoes** can be an intolerable menace at certain times of year and in certain areas, but there seems to be no pattern to this, though the north and the Lisbon coast are often cited as being particularly bad. December and January are usually mosquito-free. Mosquito-repellent lotion and coils are widely sold in towns and resorts.

MEDICAL MATTERS

For minor health complaints in Portugal you should go to a **farmácia** (pharmacy), which you'll find almost every village; in larger towns there's usually one where English is spoken. Pharmacists are highly trained and can dispense many drugs that would be available only with a prescription in Britain or North America.

In the case of serious illness, you can get the address of an **English-speaking doctor** from a British or American consular office or, with luck, from the local police or tourist office, or a major hotel. There's a British Hospital in Lisbon (see "Listings", p.109). In an **emergency** dial ☎112 (free).

TRAVEL INSURANCE

As an EU country, Portugal has free reciprocal health agreements with other member states on production of your passport. You don't need a form E111 (available from main post offices) unless you're emigrating. Reassuring as the EU health agreements may sound, however, some form of travel insurance is still worthwhile – and essential for North Americans and Australasians, who must pay for any medical treatment in Portugal.

In many parts of Portugal public health care lags behind much of northern Europe and you may well prefer to get private treatment. With insurance you have to pay on the spot, but will be able to claim back the cost – along with any drugs prescribed by pharmacies. Be sure to keep all your receipts. Travel insurance usually provides cover for your **baggage, money and tickets**, too, should they be stolen, though to reclaim from your insurance company you must register any theft with the police within 24 hours.

Before you buy your policy, however, be aware of the cover offered by various **credit card companies** for holidays bought on their account; Visa, Barclaycard and American Express offer some medical and theft coverage on items and travel arrangements paid for with their cards. The level of cover varies considerably from card to card, so check with your card-issuer or bank, but should at least include travel accident cover up to £50,000.

If you plan to participate in water sports, or do some hiking, you'll probably have to pay an extra premium; check carefully that any insurance policy you are considering will cover you in case of an accident.

EUROPEAN COVER

In Britain and Ireland, travel insurance schemes are sold by almost every travel agent or bank, and by **specialist insurance companies** (see box). For standard cover, you can expect to pay around £16 for a basic two-week policy covering Portugal, and around £28 for a month. Cover varies, but a standard policy will include the cost of cancellation and curtailment of flights, medical expenses, travel delay, accident, missed departures, lost baggage, lost passport, personal liability and legal expenses.

Some insurance companies refuse to cover travellers over 65, or stop at 69 or 74 years of age,

TRAVEL INSURANCE COMPANIES

UK

USIT Campus (☎0870/240 1010; www.usit campus.co.uk).

Endsleigh Insurance Cranfield House, 97–107 Southampton Row, London WC1B 4AG (☎020/7436 4451, fax 7637-3132; *www.end-sleigh.co.uk*).

Marcus Hearne & Co Ltd 65–66 Shoreditch High Street, London E1 6JL (☎020/7739 3444, fax 7739-7888).

STA Travel (☎0870/160 6070; www.statravel.co.uk

US and CANADA

Carefree Travel Insurance PO Box 9366, 100 Garden City Plaza, Garden City, NY 11530 (☎1-800/323-3149, fax 516/294-1096).

Desjardins Travel Insurance (Canada only, ☎1-800/463-7830).

STA Travel Insurance (☎1-800/781-4040; *www.sta-travel.com*).

Travel Assistance International 1133 15th St NW, Suite 400, Washington, DC 20005 (☎1-800/821-2828; *www.worldwideassitance.com*).

Travel Guard 1145 Clark St, Stevens Point, WI 54481 (☎1-800/826-1300; in Canada, ☎715/345-0505, call collect from abroad; *www.noelgroup.com*).

Travel Insurance Services 2930 Camino Diablo, Suite 200, Walnut Creek, CA 94596 (☎1-800/937-1387; *www.travelinsure.com*).

AUSTRALASIA

Cover More Level 9, 32 Walker St, North Sydney (☎02/9202 8000; *www.covermore.com.au*).

Ready Plan 141 Walker St, Dandenong, Melbourne (☎03/9771 4000, or, 1300/555 018, fax 03/9771 4003) and 63 Albert St, Auckland (☎09/300 5333, fax 09/307 0035).

Travel.com *www.travel.com.au*

and most that do charge hefty premiums. The best cover for **older travellers**, with no upper age limit, is offered by Age Concern (☎01883/346 964; fax 834 002) with policies costing between £16–29 (depending on age) for two weeks.

NORTH AMERICAN COVER

North Americans should check on existing cover (including bank and charge card benefits) before buying special travel insurance. For example, **Canadians** are usually covered for medical expenses by their provincial health plans. Holders of **ISIC** student identity cards are entitled to accident coverage and sixty days of hospital in-patient benefits for the period during which the card is valid. **University students** will often find that their student health coverage extends for one term beyond the date of last enrolment. **Company** plans may take care of most contingencies, and **homeowners' or renters'** insurance may cover overseas theft or loss of documents, money, and valuables.

If, after exhausting the above possibilities, you feel you still need additional travel insurance, your travel agent can recommend a policy. The best **premiums** are usually to be had through student/youth travel agencies – such as

STA Travel Insurance who offer cover for travellers under the age of 60. Coverage is worldwide and comes in packages covering 7 days ($35); 15 days ($55); 1 month ($115); 45 days ($155); 2 months ($180); and 1 year ($730) – add an extra $35–50 for each additional month on longer stays.

It's worth knowing that policies offered through student/youth agencies are often available to everyone. If you are travelling for some length of time in Europe, or if you are stopping en route in Britain, it is worth considering taking out a British travel insurance policy, which routinely covers thefts – sometimes excluded from the more health-based American policies.

AUSTRALASIAN COVER

Travel insurance is available from most travel agents or direct from insurance companies, for periods ranging from a few days to a year or even longer. Most policies are similar in premium and coverage. A typical policy covering medical costs, lost baggage and personal liability for Portugal will start at about: A$100/NZ$110 for two weeks, A$170/NZ$190 for one month.

TRAVELLERS WITH DISABILITIES

Portugal is slowly coming to terms with the needs of travellers with disabilities, but you should not expect much in the way of special facilities. That said, the Portuguese themselves always seem ready to help and people will go out of their way to make your visit as straightforward as possible.

Facilities that do exist include adapted WCs and wheelchair facilities at airports and main train stations; a "dial-a-ride" system for wheelchair users in Lisbon (call ☎213-632-044; two days' notice required); and reserved disabled parking spaces in main cities, where the Orange Badge will be recognized. Portuguese national tourist offices abroad can supply a list of wheelchair-accessible hotels and campsites. Once there, your first port of call in any town should be the local turismo, which will invariably find you a suitable hotel and, in smaller towns, may be able to organize your needs. It's worth bearing in mind that many of the cheap hotels in towns are located on the first floor, and often don't have lifts. All official buildings tend to have good wheelchair access and bars and restaurants do not usually present much of a problem.

For other **information**, contact one of the organizations listed in the box below.

USEFUL ADDRESSES (continued)

Mobility International USA, PO Box 10767, Eugene, OR 97440 (☎541/343-1284; *www.miusa.org*). Information and referral services, access guides, tours and exchange programmes. Annual membership $35 (includes quarterly newsletter).

Society for the Advancement of Travel for the Handicapped (SATH), 347 5th Ave, Suite 610, New York, NY 10016 (☎212/447-7284 or 0027; *www.sath.org*) Non-profit travel-industry referral service that passes queries on to its members as appropriate; allow plenty of time for a response.

Travel Information Service, Moss Rehabilitation Hospital, 1200 West Tabor Rd, Philadelphia, PA 19141 (☎215/456-9603; *www.mossresourcenet.org*). Information and referral service.

Twin Peaks Press, Box 129, Vancouver, WA 98666; (☎1-800/637-2256 or 360/694-2462; *www.pacifier.com/twinpeak*). Publisher of the *Directory of Travel Agencies for the Disabled* ($19.95), listing more than 370 agencies worldwide; *Travel for the Disabled* ($14.95); the *Directory of Accessible Van Rentals*; and *Wheelchair Vagabond* ($14.95), loaded with personal tips.

AUSTRALIA

Barrier Free Travel, 36 Wheatley St, North Bellingen, NSW 2454 (☎02/66551 733).

Wheelchair Travel 29 Ranelagh Dr, Mt Eliza VIC 3930 (☎1800/674 468 or 03/97878861; *www.travalability.com*)

NEW ZEALAND

DPA (Disabled Persons Assembly) NZ
Level 4 Wellington Trade Centre, 173-175 Victoria St or PO Box 27-524 Wellington (☎04/801 9100)

INFORMATION AND MAPS

You can pick up a wide range of brochures and maps, for free, from the Portuguese National Tourist Office in your home country (see p.23 for addresses). Though some of their descriptions are best taken with a pinch of salt, it is well worth contacting one of their offices for information before you leave home.

In Portugal itself you'll find a tourist office, or **turismo**, in almost every town and village of any size. Most are detailed in the guide and are usually helpful and friendly. Aside from the help they can give you in finding a room (some will make bookings, others simply supply lists), they often have useful local maps and leaflets that you won't find in the national offices. **Opening hours** are given after each office in the text but don't be surprised if you find them closed when they should be open – times of opening are often totally dependent on staff available, especially in small towns and villages.

For all tourist queries, there's now an excellent **freephone telephone number** (*Linha Verde Turista*: ☎800 296 296) – that you can call when you arrive in Portugal – whose operators can give you information about museums and their opening times, transport practicalities and timetables, and provide lists of hotels and restaurants, hospitals, and police stations, for example. It operates Monday to Saturday from 9am to midnight, and Sundays and holidays from 9am to 8pm. The operators speak Portuguese, English, French and Spanish.

PORTUGAL ON THE INTERNET

The following sites have English language versions unless otherwise stated.

Budget Travel
www.budgettravel.com/portugal.htm

Good links to more or less everything, with helpful site-by-site descriptions.

Feiras e Romarias
www.rede-almanaque.pt/feiras

Lists of most of the country's *feiras* and *romarias* (in Portuguese), organized by districts. Read this before you go.

ICEP (Investments, Trade and Tourism of Portugal)
www.portugal.org/ or *www.portugalinsite.pt*

Run by the government agency responsible for promoting Portugal abroad. Information on tourist attractions, sport and culture, and links to accommodation agencies, businesses and directories. Look up *www.dgt.pt* for the official ministry of tourism Web site.

Instituto Português de Museus
www.ipmuseus.pt/html/inetdex1.html

Stylish site containing detailed information and "guided visits" to 29 museums, plus links to others.

Music
www.ed.ac.uk/~ptr/music/Musica.html

Bibliography on modern and ethnological Portuguese music.

Newspapers
The only English-language online paper is
The Electric News
(*www.nexus-pt.com/news/index.hts*), a cut above the usual Algarve-based expat rags. The Portuguese press is well represented:

Correio da Manha: *correiomanha.pt/*

Diário de Notícias: *www.dn.pt/*

Jornal de Notícias: *www.jnoticias.pt/*

Público: *www.publico.pt/*

National parks
www.di.uminho.pt/~esteves/turismo/parques1.html

Pages and links to all Portuguese national and natural parks, with maps, info and practicalities. Similar pages in Portuguese at *www.infocid.pt/areas/* which also contains the Portuguese constitution among other delights.

Portuguese National Geographic Information Infrastructure (GEOCID)
www.geocid–snig.cnig.pt

High resolution satellite and aerial topographic images, and innumerable maps of almost all of Portugal – which may be useful for hiking. An in-depth site which also includes useful information on beaches, heritage and even weather reports.

Portuguese Pedestrian
www.iut-orsay.fr/~guet/Pietons.html

Bizarre ethnological study of the wonderful world of Lusitanian traffic signs – look out for the chameleon crossing and the x-rated pedestrian.

Postcard from Portugal
www.tntmag.co.uk/travel/p/portugal_post.htm

Lively collection of feature articles from the UK free magazine.

Portugal Travel and Hotels Guide
portugal-hotels.com/

The largest Portuguese hotel list on the web, with phone numbers, address and some prices, but no descriptions.

Portugal Virtual
www.portugalvirtual.pt/

Links site with extensive hotel listings (including prices), restaurants and bars – each inconveniently arranged on a separate page, which makes it useful only for checking out specific places in specific cities.

Solares de Portugal (formerly Turihab)
www.turihab.pt or *www.solares-de-portugal.com*

On-line brochure with photographs and details of over ninety properties belonging to the scheme (see p.33 for further details), ranging from simple farmhouses to former palaces. Full booking details.

Town Net
www.townnet.com/world/europe/portugal.html

The Portugal section of Town Net, with general info links, newspapers, weather and exchange rates.

Turista Virtual Português
tvp.ua.pt/ One of the best for links to regional and city Web sites organised by territorial divisions. Browse by map or list.

PORTUGUESE TOURIST OFFICES ABROAD

A full list can be found at www.Portugal.org/geninfo/abouticep/about9.html

Australia The Web site:
www.consulportugalsydney.org.au/ can offer information on Portugal for Australians and New Zealanders. Otherwise, there are no Portuguese Tourist Offices in Australia or New Zealand.

Canada 60 Bloor St West, Suite 1005, Toronto, Ontario, M4W 3B8 (☎416/921 7376, fax ☎921 1353, *iceptor@idirect.com*).

France 7 Rue Scribe, 75009 Paris (☎01/47.42.55.57, fax 42.66.06.89, *icepar@world-net.sct.fr*).

Germany Schäfergasse 17, 60313 Frankfurt Main (☎069/234094, fax 231433, *icepfra@portugal.f.eunet.de*).

Ireland 54 Dawson Street, Dublin 2 (☎01/670 9133, fax 670-9141, *info@icep.ie*).

Netherlands Paul Gabriëlstraat 70, 2596 VG Den Haag (☎070/326 4371, fax 328 0025).

New Zealand There are no offices in New Zealand, see Web site: *www.consulportugalsydney.org.au/* for information.

Spain Gran Via 27-1ª, 28013 Madrid (☎01/522 4408, fax 522 2382, *opthm@super.medusa.es*); Calle Bruc 50-4a, 08010 Barcelona (☎03/301 4416, fax 318 5068); c/Asunción 84–11°D, Edificio Presidente Portal B1, 41011 Seville (☎05/428 4910, fax 428 4793).

United Kingdom 2nd Floor, 22/25a Sackville Street, London W1X 1DE (☎020/7494 1441, fax 7494 1868, *iceplond@dircon.co.uk*).

USA 590 Fifth Avenue, 4th Floor, New York, NY 10036-4785 (☎212/719 3985, fax 764 6137, *jfcosta@portugal.org*); 1900 L Street NW, Suite 310, Washington, DC 20036 (☎202/331 8222, fax 331 8236).

MAPS

The Portuguese National Tourist Office and the turismos in larger towns can provide you with a reasonable **map** of the country (1:600,000), which is fine for everything except mountain roads. If you're doing any real exploration, however, it's worth investing in a good **road map**. The best maps available abroad are Michelin's 1:400,000 Portugal (#440); or Geo Centre's Euro Map *Portugal and Galicia* at 1:300,000. Geo Centre also produces a 1:200,000 map of the Algarve and a 1:250,000 map of the Lisbon area; *Bartholomew's Algarve Holiday Map* 1:100,000 is good, too. If you're planning on spending more than a day or two in Lisbon, the German *Falk Plan* of the city is unequalled. The new Geocid Web site is certainly worth a visit at: *www.geocid–snig.cnig.pt* the site offers high

resolution satellite and aerial topographic images, and innumerable maps of almost all of Portugal.

More detailed topographic **maps for walkers** are produced by the Instituto Geográfico do Exercito, Avenida Dr. Alfredo Bensaúde, Olivais Norte (☎218 520 063, fax 218 532 119, *igeoe@igeoe.pt*, *www.igeoe.pt*). You can also find them at the Instituto Geográfico e Cadastral by the Basilica da Estrêla in Lisbon, and in Porto at Porto Editora, Praça Filipe de Lancastre 42 (☎222 007 681). Many of these topographic maps are disastrously out of date, although a major updating programme began in 1996: the new versions (scale 1:25,000, so-called Serie M888) are now available for some regions, and are invaluable for hiking.

Most general and regional Portuguese maps can be ordered through one of the map suppliers in Britain and North America detailed below.

MAP OUTLETS IN THE UK

Glasgow John Smith and Sons, 57–61 St Vincent St, G2 5TB (☎0141/221 7472). Specialist map department in long-established booksellers; full range of foreign maps; mail order service.

London Daunt Books, 83 Marylebone High St, W1M 3DE (☎020/7224 2295), and 193 Haverstock Hill,

NW3 4QL (☎020/7794 4006); National Map Centre, 22–24 Caxton St, SW1H 0QU (☎020/7222 2466); Stanfords, 12–14 Long Acre, WC2E 9LP (☎020/7836 1321; maps by mail or phone order are available on this number); The Travel Bookshop, 13–15 Blenheim Crescent, W11 2EE (☎020/7229 5260).

MAP OUTLETS IN IRELAND

Belfast Waterstone's, Queens Bldg, 8 Royal Ave, Belfast BT1 1DA (☎028 32 247 355).

Cork Waterstone's, 69 Patrick St, Cork (☎021/276 522).

Dublin Easons Bookshop, 40 O'Connell St, Dublin 1 (☎01/873 3811); Fred Hanna's Bookshop, 27–29 Nassau St, Dublin 2 (☎01/677 1255); Hodges Figgis Bookshop, 56–58 Dawson St, Dublin 2 (☎01/677 4754); Waterstone's, 7 Dawson St, Dublin 2 (☎01/679 1415).

MAP OUTLETS IN NORTH AMERICA

Chicago Rand McNally, 444 N Michigan Ave, Chicago, IL 60611 (☎312/321-1751). Note: Rand McNally now has more than 20 stores across the US; call ☎1-800/333-0136 (ext 2111) for the address of your nearest store, or for direct mail maps.

Montréal Ulysses Travel Bookshop, 4176 St-Denis, H2W 2M5 (☎514/843-9447).

Los Angeles Distant Lands, 56 S Raymond Ave, Pasadena, CA 91105 (☎626/449-3220).

New York The Complete Traveler Bookstore, 199 Madison Ave, NY 10016 (☎212/685-9007); Rand McNally, 150 E 52nd St, NY 10022 (☎212/758-7488).

San Francisco The Complete Traveler

Bookstore, 3207 Fillmore St, CA 92123 (☎415/923-1511); Rand McNally, 595 Market St, CA 94105 (☎415/777-3131).

Santa Barbara Map Link Inc, 30 S La Patera Lane, Unit 5, CA 93117 (☎805/692-6777).

Seattle Elliot Bay Book Company, 101 S Main St, Seattle, WA 98104 (☎206/624-6600).

Toronto Open Air Books and Maps, 25 Toronto St, Toronto, M5R 2C1 (☎416/363-0719).

Vancouver International Travel Maps and Books, 552 Seymour St V6Z 1G3 (☎604/687-3320).

Washington DC Rand McNally, 7988 Tysons Corner Center, McLean, VA 22102 (☎703/556-8688).

MAP OUTLETS IN AUSTRALIA AND NEW ZEALAND

Adelaide The Map Shop, 16a Peel St, Adelaide, SA 5000 (☎08/8231 2033).

Auckland Speciality Maps, 58 Albert St, Auckland (☎09/307 2217).

Brisbane Worldwide Maps and Guides, 187 George St, Brisbane (☎07/3221 4330).

Melbourne Map Land, 372 Little Bourke St, Melbourne (☎03/9670 4383).

Perth Perth Map Centre, 884 Hay St, Perth (☎09/9322 5733).

Sydney Map World, 371 Pitt St, Sydney (☎02/9261 3601). Travel Bookshop, Shop 3, 175 Liverpool St, Sydney (☎02/9261 8200).

COSTS, MONEY AND BANKS

The cost of living in Portugal has been edging up ever since entry into the EC in 1986 but, for tourists, it remains one of the cheapest places to travel in Europe. Accommodation, transport, food and drink are still cheaper than in northern Europe – or North America – and, on the whole, better value than in Spain. The only things that are markedly more expensive are phone calls and petrol.

A **European Under-26 card** (Euro<26; £7 in the UK) is well worth having if you're eligible – it'll get you free or reduced admission to many museums and sights, discounts on bus and train tickets, as well as reductions in numerous shops and restaurants (sometimes even hotels). Of much less use is the **International Student Identity Card** (ISIC), which is rarely accepted, even if you attempt an explanation in Portuguese. Both are available through STA and Usit Campus in Britain and Ireland, Council Travel in the US and Travel CUTS in Canada (see the relevant "Getting there" sections for addresses). You will also find the Euro<26 card on sale in Portugal at post offices and banks – ask for a *Cartão Jovem*.

COSTS

Costs for a **double room** in the cheaper pensions work out at about £10–20/$15–30, rising to around £20–40/$30–60 in two- or three-star hotels, £50–170/$75–265 in four- and five-star places, and upwards of £60/$96 in *pousadas*. **Campsites** are a bargain at around £2–4/$3–6 a night per person, tent included, in all but the fanciest coastal sites.

You should always be able to get a substantial basic **meal** for around £5/$7.50; even dinner in the smarter restaurants is unlikely to cost more than £20/$30 a head. **Drink** costs are more than reasonable, too – a bottle of house wine rarely comes to more than £3/$5, a glass of the local brew in a bar around 40p/60¢. Even **transport** is hardly going to break the bank, especially since most distances you'll travel are fairly short and fares (especially on trains) low. A second-class train journey from Porto to Lisbon, or Lisbon to the Algarve, for example, costs around £12/$18.

To sum up, then, in most places you can get by on a budget of **around £30/$45 a day**, which will get you a room for the night, picnic lunch, dinner with drinks in a restaurant, a bus or train ride, and a beer or two. By camping and being a little more frugal, you could reasonably expect to survive on much less than this; while on £35–40/$50–60 a day you'll be living pretty well. It's worth noting that prices in Lisbon and the Algarve are higher than anywhere else in the country; expect things to cost up to twenty percent more in all the main tourist resorts.

CURRENCY

The Portuguese currency unit is the **escudo ($)**; 1000 escudos is called a **conto**. Prices are written with the $ sign in the middle: thus 2$50 is two escudos and fifty centavos, and 1000$00 is a thousand escudos or one conto. For the last few years, exchange rates have been edging up in the visitor's favour, currently around 305$00 to the pound sterling, 185$00 to the US dollar. You can buy escudos in advance at most European, US and Canadian banks. **Notes** come in denominations of 500$00, 1000$00, 2000$00, 5000$00 and 10,000$00; **coins** as 1$00, 2$50, 5$00, 10$00, 20$00, 50$00, 100$00 and 200$00.

You will often find that shops round up bills to the nearest 5$00 or 10$00, so don't feel you've been short-changed. When travelling in rural areas, avoid getting stranded without **small notes and change**: a 10,000$00 note can be hard to change on a bus or at a small village market.

BANKS AND EXCHANGE

You'll find a **bank** in all but the smallest towns. Standard **opening hours** are Monday to Friday 8.30am to 3pm. In Lisbon and in some of the Algarve resorts they may also open in the evening to change money, while some banks have installed **automatic exchange machines** for various currencies and denominations. Changing **cash** in banks is easy, and shouldn't attract more than 600$00 commission. As ever, it's unwise to carry all your money as cash, so consider the alternatives.

By far the easiest way to get money in Portugal is to use a **credit or debit card** to withdraw cash from any of the large number of **ATM cash machines** (called Multibanco). You'll find them in even the most out-of-the-way small towns and you can withdraw up to 40,000$00 per day. Any card using the Cirrus or Eurocheque system will work, as will all major credit cards (Visa, American Express, Mastercard and Eurocard), though you'll be charged a hefty cash advance fee with the credit and charge cards, in addition to the usual currency conversion fee. Most Portuguese banks will give cash advances on cards over the counter and will also charge a currency conversion fee. **Credit cards** are also accepted for payment in many hotels and restaurants.

Most British banks can issue current-account holders with a **Eurocheque** card, with the option of cheques, too, with which you can pay for things in some shops and get cash from the majority of Portuguese banks; you'll pay around £7.50 to £10 service charge a year but only small currency conversion fees on each transaction. In fact, Portuguese banks are not supposed to charge you commission at all on Eurocheques but many do. For all cards, keep a copy of the issuing bank's telephone helpline in a safe place away from the card: blocking cards, if stolen, can be a nightmare otherwise.

Watch out if using **travellers' cheques**, as banks charge an outrageous **commission** for changing them (upwards of 2500$00 per cheque in some cases). However, more reasonable fees can be had in *caixas* – savings banks or building societies – and larger hotels are sometimes willing to change travellers cheques at low commission. It's probably worth taking a supply in case your plastic is lost, stolen or swallowed by an ATM. You can buy them at most banks (even if you don't have an account), or from offices of Thomas Cook and American Express. They are accepted by all Portuguese banks and by exchange bureaux (*câmbios*) at airports and major train stations.

GETTING AROUND

Portugal is not a large country and you can get almost everywhere easily and efficiently by train or bus. Trains are often cheaper, and some lines very scenic, but it's almost always quicker to go by bus – especially on shorter or less obvious routes. Approximate times and frequencies of most journeys are given in the "Travel details" section at the end of each chapter; local connections and peculiarities are pointed out in the text. Car rental is also worth considering if time is limited and you want to cover a lot of ground, though you may find you need nerves of steel to drive on some Portuguese roads.

TRAINS

CP, the Portuguese railway company, operates all trains. Most are designated *Regional*, which means they stop at most stations en route and have first- and second-class cars. *Inter-regional* are faster, stopping only at major stations. On both of these, night trains can be populated with some dodgy characters – stay awake or get someone you trust to keep an eye on your luggage. The next category up, *Intercidades*, are twice as fast and twice as expensive, and you should reserve your seat in advance if using them. The fastest, most luxurious and priciest services are the *Rápidos* (known as "Alfa"), which speed between Lisbon, Coimbra and Porto – sometimes they have only first-class seats. Both these latter classes charge supplements for rail-pass holders (see below).

Always turn up at the station with time to spare since long queues often form at the ticket desk. On certain trains, even with a rail pass, you'll need to queue up for seat reservations, too. If you end up on the train without first buying a ticket you could be liable for a huge supplement, payable to the ticket controller, or be kicked off the train by the guard at the next stop. However, smaller regional stations are sometimes unmanned, in which case just hop on and pay the ticket inspector on board.

Complete **train timetables** (600$00) and timetables for individual lines are available from information desks at main stations, as well as on the Internet (*www.cp.pt/*). These can also supply information about taking a **car train** (Auto-express), a service available on the main Lisbon to Porto, Faro, Guarda and Mangualde routes.

Sadly, several of the old narrow-gauge **mountain railways** of the north have been phased out, with the Tâmega, Corgo, Tua Valley and Douro lines terminating, respectively, at Amarante, Vila Real, Mirandela and Pocinho. Several other minor lines have been closed, too, though some have at least been replaced by buses operated by CP. Regular train tickets and passes are valid on these bus lines.

Lastly, it's as well to note that train stations can be some miles from the town or village they serve – Portalegre station and town are 12km distant, for example – and there's no guarantee of connecting transport.

TICKETS AND PASSES

Train travel is relatively inexpensive and most visitors simply buy a ticket every time they make a journey; **children** under four go free, under-12s pay half price. **Senior citizens** (over-60s) can get thirty percent off travel if they produce their passport (or other form of ID proving their age) and ask for a *Bilhete Terceira Idade* (third-age ticket). On main lines it's cheapest to travel on the so-called "Blue Days" – ie: avoiding Friday afternoons, Sunday afternoons, Monday mornings, national holidays and the day preceding a national holiday.

If you're planning a lot of train travel, using a **rail pass** might save you money, though note that pass holders pay **supplements** and **reservation fees** on *Intercidades* and *Rápidos*. With

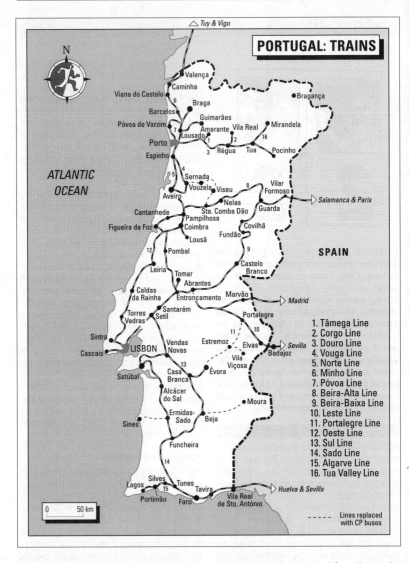

△ Tuy & Vigo

PORTUGAL: TRAINS

N

ATLANTIC OCEAN

SPAIN

Valença
Caminha
Viana do Castelo
Braga
Barcelos
Póvoa de Varzim
Porto
Espinho
Guimarães
Amarante Vila Real
Lousado
Régua Tua
Bragança
Mirandela
Pocinho
Sernada
Vouzela Viseu
Aveiro
Nelas
Sta. Comba Dão
Cantanhede
Pampilhosa
Figueira da Foz
Coimbra
Lousã
Pombal
Leiria
Tomar
Abrantes
Caldas da Rainha
Santarém
Torres Vedras
Setil
Entroncamento
Sintra
LISBON
Cascais
Vendas Novas
Setúbal
Casa Branca
Alcácer do Sal
Ermidas-Sado
Sines
Beja
Funcheira
Silves
Lagos
Portimão
Tunes
Faro
Tavira
Vila Real de Sto. António
Vilar Formoso
Guarda
Covilhã
Fundão
Castelo Branco
Marvão
Portalegre
Estremoz
Elvas
Badajoz
Vila Viçosa
Évora
Moura

▷ Salamanca & Paris
▷ Madrid
▷ Sevilla
▷ Huelva & Sevilla

1. Tâmega Line
2. Corgo Line
3. Douro Line
4. Vouga Line
5. Norte Line
6. Minho Line
7. Póvoa Line
8. Beira-Alta Line
9. Beira-Baixa Line
10. Leste Line
11. Portalegre Line
12. Oeste Line
13. Sul Line
14. Sado Line
15. Algarve Line
16. Tua Valley Line

0   50 km

- - - - Lines replaced with CP buses

though, you are only liable for the latter. CP sells its own **Bilhete Turistico** rail pass (valid for first-class travel on all trains except the Lisbon–Madrid Talgo) for 18,200$00 (£65/$104) for 7 days, 36,000$00 (£130/$208) for 14 days, and 54,000$00 (£195/$312) for 21 days. There's also a CP family card (*cartão de familia*) and group tickets (*bilhetes de grupo*), which offer varying

reductions on tickets – more information can be obtained from local stations.

Both **InterRail** (see p.6) and **Eurail** passes (see p.12) are valid on Portuguese trains, though unless you're planning to travel extensively by train you're unlikely to be able to make them pay on a short trip just to Portugal. The following passes covering Portugal only (all of which must be purchased in your home country) may not give you your money's worth either, given that the journey from Porto to Faro costs only 2000$00 (£7/$11) and takes the best part of a day. The **Eurodomino** pass allows three to eight days rail travel in one calendar month within Portugal; under-26 and over-26 fares are £39/£49 for 3 days, £49/£69 for 5 days and £69/£89 for 8 days. With this pass, though, you'll still have to pay reservation fees. Alternatively, the **Portugal Explorer** pass entitles you to 7, 14 or 21 days of consecutive travel on the Portuguese rail network for £48, £81, and £120 respectively. Both are available in Britain from Eurotrain or Wasteels (see p.5). North Americans are eligible to purchase the **Portuguese Railpass**, allowing 4 days' travel out of 15 ($99 all ages). The Portuguese Railpass is obtainable through Rail Europe, 226 Westchester Ave, White Plains, NY 10604 (☎800/438-7245) or youth-oriented travel agents (see p.10).

BUSES

Buses shadow many of the main train routes as well as linking most of the country's smaller towns and villages. It's almost always quicker to go by bus if you can, though you'll pay slightly more than for the equivalent train ride. Comfortable express buses operate on longer routes, for which you'll usually have to reserve tickets in advance – certainly for the Lisbon–Algarve routes in summer.

All bus services are privatized, though a national network of express coaches (Rede Expressos) has been maintained, combining services from a number of different companies (there's a map of their routes on the Internet at *www.rede-expressos.pt/index_uk.htm*). Although the competition brought on by privatization has meant an increase in the number of buses on certain routes, it has also led to the inevitable reduction or phasing out of many local services. The variety of companies can also be a cause of confusion, as two buses going to the same destination may leave from different terminals (in the case of Porto almost all of the twenty companies operate out of different terminals) and companies may be unwilling to volunteer information about rival bus operators.

Local bus stations (detailed wherever possible in the text) are the place to pick up timetables and reserve seats on long-distance journeys but, as companies, addresses and routes change every year, it's advisable to check first with the local turismo – they can usually advise on where to book or catch specific buses. It's as well to be aware that bus services

are considerably less frequent – occasionally non-existent – at weekends, especially on rural routes; while at other times, you'll find that departures can be frighteningly early in the morning. This is because bus services are often designed to fit around school and market hours.

DRIVING, CAR RENTAL AND TAXIS

With car rental rates among the lowest in Europe, driving around Portugal is an option worth thinking about, even for just a part of your travels. **Petrol** (*gasolina*), however, is not so cheap, at around 170$00 (about 57p/$1) a litre for both unleaded (*sem chumbo*) and Super, and around 110$00 a litre for diesel (37p/0.66¢). Most rental cars run on unleaded. **Driving licenses** from most countries are accepted, so there's no need to get an international one.Before you set out, bear in mind that Portugal has one of the highest **accident** rates in Europe.

Road surfaces are improving, but even major roads are often potholed, narrow and full of dangerous bends. But it's not so much the quality of roads but the driving that is lethal – reckless overtaking being the main problem. Even on motorways, you'll need to check your mirror every few seconds to make sure someone isn't right up your exhaust pipe. August is especially dangerous, with Portuguese emigrant workers returning home in fast cars to show off to relatives.

A massive EU-funded **road construction programme**, now in its final stages, has made previously remote areas of the country such as Trás-os-Montes and Beira far more accessible, via a network of main highways (numbers prefixed "IP"), similar in speed to motorways. The **motorway network** itself (numbers prefixed with "A") is privately owned by BRISA and is a network of toll roads gradually expanding outwards from a central spine that links Setúbal and Lisbon with Porto. Heading east, stretches are now complete between Porto and Amarante, and from Lisbon to Montemor-o-Novo in Alentejo. In the south, a motorway connects Lisbon to Ourique in Alentejo, but the long-delayed completion of the link into the Algarve, where the IP1 sweeps east to the Spanish border at Vila Real, appears to have been put on hold indefinitely. Be warned, though, that the **tolls** can add significantly to the cost of your journey – as an indication, the stretch from Lisbon to Porto will set you back £10/$15. The advantages, as usual, are less traffic and a faster journey time.

Traffic on the **smaller roads** will be much heavier: slow journeys stuck behind trucks are common. In addition, as car ownership has increased massively over recent years, towns can no longer cope with the traffic. Travelling by car, you'll have endless problems finding central parking spaces. Only the top hotels have car parks; otherwise you can expect to spend ages looking for a space, often ending up on the outskirts of town and having to walk to the centre. Coimbra is notoriously bad, and has pioneered a park-and-ride scheme in response.

Traffic drives on the right: **speed limits** are 50kph in towns and villages; 90kph on normal roads; and 120kph on motorways and inter-regional highways. At road junctions, unless there's a sign to the contrary, vehicles coming from the right have priority – a rule that wreaks havoc at roundabouts, effectively giving anyone cutting in the right of way. If you're **stopped by the police**, they'll want to see your documents – carry them in the car at all times and be courteous to the officers (see "Police and trouble", p.46).

When **parking** in cities, you're likely to see men pointing to empty spaces – invariably alcoholics or drug addicts, most drivers will tip them (50$00 is enough), if only to avoid a key being scraped along the side.

Many **car insurance policies** cover taking your car to Portugal; check with your insurer while planning your trip. However, you're advised to take out extra cover for motoring assistance in case your car breaks down. Look into the RAC's European Cover (☎0800/455 0055; *www.rac.co.uk*) or the AA's Five-Star Europe cover (☎0800/444 4500; *www.theaa.co.uk*).

Alternatively, you can get assistance from the Automóvel Clube de Portugal which reciprocal arrangements with foreign automobile clubs. The head office is at Rua Rosa Araújo 24, Lisbon (☎219-425-095); in the north, phone their Porto service on ☎228-340-001.

CAR RENTAL

Car rental agencies can be found in all the major towns and at the airports in Lisbon, Porto and Faro. Local agencies usually charge less than the big three – Hertz, Avis and Europcar – and we've listed addresses and phone numbers for some of them in the Lisbon, Porto and Algarve chapters; tourist offices can give details of others.

Rates are reasonable, from around £100–120/$150–180 a week for the cheapest category car with unlimited mileage, though prices are inflated on the Algarve in high season. It's often a much better deal to **arrange rental before setting out**. In Britain, several of the specialist holiday companies detailed on p.5 will arrange car rental in conjunction with flights; or call one of the major car rental outfits listed in the box above. In the US, you can get cheaper deals (as low as $120 a week) by booking your car through a wholesaler, such as Auto Europe or Europe by Car (see box opposite). However, you must reserve and pay for the car in advance, before you leave the US.

When picking up your car, check such important details as brakes and, if you're renting locally, **insurance coverage**. As you might have gathered, collision insurance is a good idea and unless you pay a separate supplement the initial several thousand *escudos'* worth of damage may be on your head; if you're given the option of collision damage waiver, take it. Keep the receipts of any repairs you make along the way – you may be able to get some money back from the company.

Finally, it can't be stressed enough that hire cars are especially prone to **theft**. If at all possible detach any tell-tale stickers – the company might complain but at least the car and your belongings won't be a sitting target. And, obviously, don't leave anything of value in an unattended car.

TAXIS

Travelling **by taxi** in Portugal is relatively cheap by European standards. It is worth considering for trips across major towns and for shorter journeys in rural areas where other means of transport may be limited. Generally, taxis are metered, with a minimum fare of 250$00. Additional charges are made for carrying baggage and fares are slightly higher between 10pm and 6am and at weekends. Outside major towns, you can also negotiate specific fares if you want to hire a taxi for a few hours. Unsurprisingly, they're more expensive in the Algarve.

BIKES, MOPEDS AND MOTORBIKES

Bicycles are a great way of seeing the country, though everywhere north of Lisbon is hilly and you'll find pedalling hard work in mountainous Beira Alta or across the burned plains of southern Alentejo. The bicycle-carrying service on trains is efficient, if expensive: prices are unpredictable, varying between 800$00 and 2000$00. Ask in advance which train to take, as not all take bicycles and it's advisable to arrange it in advance with the baggage office. On long-distance international trains, allow three days for the bike to arrive.

Although it's a hassle taking your own **bike by plane**, it really is worth it to have a decent machine with gears and brakes you can trust. Standard **spares**, such as tyres and inner tubes, are easy enough to get hold of but it's still worth taking your own, especially if you have a modern, specialized model. Good practical informationand tips on cycling in Portugal can be found on the Internet (*www-math.science.unitn.it/Bike/Countries/Portugal/*).

If all that legwork is not to your taste, you can rent **mopeds** and low-powered (80cc) **motorbikes** in many tourist areas, especially on the Algarve. Go easy and check all the cables before setting off. A helmet and valid licence are obligatory.

CAR RENTAL AGENCIES

BRITAIN

Avis	☎0990/900 500;	www.avis.com
Budget	☎0800/418 1181;	www.budget.com
Europcar/InterRent	☎0345/222 525;	www.europcar.com
		www.interrent.com
Hertz	☎0990/996 699;	www.hertz.com
Holiday Autos	☎0990/300 400;	www.holidayautos.co.uk
National Car Rental	☎0990/365 365;	www.nationalcarrentals.com

NORTH AMERICA

Auto Europe	☎1-800/223-5555;	www.autoeurope.com
Avis	☎1-800/331-1084;	www.avis.com
Budget	in US, ☎1-800/527-0700;	
	in Canada ☎1-800/268-8900;	www.drivebudget.com
Dollar	☎1-800/800-6000;	www.dollar.com
Europe by Car	☎1-800/223-1516 or	
	212/245-1713;	www.europebycar.com
Hertz	in US, ☎1-800/654-3001;	
	in Canada, ☎1-800/654-3001;	www.hertz.com
Holiday Autos	in US, ☎1-800/422-7737;	
	in Canada ☎1-800/678-0678;	www.kemwel.com
National	☎1-800/CAR-RENT;	www.nationalcar.com
Thrifty	☎1-800/367-2277;	www.thrifty.com

AUSTRALIA

Avis	☎1800/225 533, 13 6333;	www.avis.com
Budget	☎1300/362 848;	www.budget.com.au
Hertz	☎1800/550 067, 13 3039;	www.hertz.com

NEW ZEALAND

Avis	☎09/526 2847;	www.avis.com
Budget	☎09/375 2222;	www.budget.co.nz
Hertz	☎09/309 0989, 0800/655 955;	www.hertz.com

ACCOMMODATION

In almost any Portuguese town you can find a *pensão* (pension) offering a double room for around 4000$00–5000$00 (£12–15/$20–25) and singles for around 2500$00 (£8/$13). The only accommodation that you're likely to find cheaper than this is rooms in a private home; most turismos have lists of those available in the area. You can expect to pay more in Algarve resorts in high season, or in Lisbon. If you have the money to move upmarket, you're often spoilt for choice, with some wonderful manor houses and a network of state-run *pousadas* scattered about the country, and at prices that beat the rest of Europe hands down.

Even in high season you shouldn't have much of a problem finding a bed in most Portuguese regions. However, parts of the Algarve are often a very different matter, with all rooms booked up for days ahead. Try and reserve in advance where you can, especially if you're arriving late in Faro.

ROOMS, PENSÕES AND RESIDENCIAIS

Other than youth hostels and camping (see p.34), the cheapest accommodation consists of **rooms** (**quartos** or **dormidas**) let out in private houses. Most commonly available in the seaside resorts, these are sometimes advertised, or more often hawked at bus and train stations. The local turismo may also have a list of rooms available. Rates should be a little below that of a *pensão*, say 3000–4000$00 for a double (£10–13/$16–22), though on the Algarve, in high season, you can expect to pay up to twice as much. It's always

worth haggling over prices, especially if you're prepared to commit yourself to a longish stay, but don't expect too much success in high season. And always ask where the room is before you agree to take it – in the resorts you could end up miles from the town centre or beach.

The main budget travel standby is a room in a **pensão** (plural, *pensões*) – which are officially graded from one to three stars (often, it seems, in a quite random fashion). Many serve meals, but they rarely insist that you take them. *Pensões* that don't serve meals are sometimes called **residenciais** (singular *residencial* or *residência*), though in price and all other respects they are virtually identical, and many establishments use both definitions. Similar to *pensões*, and generally at the cheaper end of the scale, are **hospedarias** or **casas de hóspedes** – boarding houses – which can be characterful places.

Pensão **prices** for a double room range from around 4000–8000$00 (£13–26/$22–44), depending on the season, their location and facilities. Always ask to see the room before you take it, and don't be afraid to ask if there's a cheaper one (rooms without private showers or bathrooms are often considerably less) – especially if you're travelling alone, in which case you'll frequently be asked to pay more or less the full price of a double. *Tem um quarto mais barato?* ("Do you have a cheaper room?") is the relevant phrase.

HOTELS AND POUSADAS

A one-star **hotel** usually costs about the same as a three-star *pensão*, though quirks abound in the

---

ACCOMMODATION PRICE CODES

Nearly all the accommodation prices in this book have been coded using the symbols below. The symbols represent the lowest prices you can expect to pay for a **double room in high season**. Effectively this means that most rooms in places with a ① or ② category will be without private bath or shower, though there's usually a washbasin in the room. In places with a ③ category and above, you'll probably be getting private facilities; while many of the cheaper places may also have more expensive rooms with bath/shower if you ask.

Price codes are not given for youth hostels and campsites (see p.34 for the rates at those).

① Under 4000$00	② 4000$00–7000$00	③ 7000$00–11,000$00
④ 11,000$00–15,000$00	⑤ 15,000$00–20,000$00	⑥ 20,000$00–25,000$00
⑦ 25,000$00–30,000$00	⑧ 30,000$00–40,000$00	⑨ Over 40,000$00

official grading systems, and establishments classified as one-star hotels often don't show any notable differences from *pensões*. Tourist offices sometimes downgrade hotels to *pensão* status, although it is rare for the hotel to change its sign accordingly. Indeed, it's not uncommon to find a two- or three-star *pensão* offering much better quality rooms than a one-star hotel. Prices for two- and three-star hotels, though, see a notable shift upscale, with doubles running from 8000$00 (£27/$44) upwards.

There's a further and more dramatic shift in rates as you move into the four- and five-star hotel league, where you'll pay anything from 15,000–50,000$00 (£50–170/$82–274) for a double. The very fanciest places, on the Algarve and in Lisbon, can pretty much charge what they like. **Estalagems** and **albergarias** are other designations of hotels in the same range.

One fairly surprising bargain is the chain of 44 government-run **pousadas**, often converted from old monasteries or castles, or located in dramatic countryside settings. They're rated in four categories, and charge different prices in low, middle and high season; in summer, a double room in a historical *pousada* costs around 31,000$00 (20,300$00 in winter), whilst other *pousadas* average out at 14,300–16,300$00 in winter and 22,500–24,600$00 in summer. Some have a *quarto pequeno* (small room), which goes for sixty percent of the price of a standard double room, but these are not bookable in advance. Look out for seasonal promotions, however, especially for over-60s, who can receive discounts of around forty percent. We've detailed most of the *pousadas* in the guide but for a full list, contact the Portuguese National Tourist Office in your home country (see the box on p.23), or ENATUR, Av. Santa Joana Princesa 10A, 1749 Lisbon (☎218-442-001, fax 218-442-085; *info@pousadas.pt, www.pousadas.pt*).

COUNTRY AND MANOR HOUSES

An increasingly popular alternative in the three- to four-star hotel price range is to stay in one of the many properties throughout Portugal promoted by the tourist board as **country and manor houses** – phrases commonly used are *Turihab, turismo no espaço rural*, and *turismo rural*. Rivals to the *pousadas*, there are now upwards of 150 of them, all of which have had their facilities and accommodation inspected and approved by the government tourist office. In terms of atmosphere and luxury,

they are often unbeatable and their equivalent in other European countries would command in excess of double the price. The properties vary from simple farmhouses (*casas rústicas*) offering just two or three rooms on a bed-and-breakfast basis to country manors (*quintas*) and estate houses (*herdades*) and even palaces (*casas antigas*) owned by Portuguese aristocrats who have allowed their ancient seats to become part of the scheme. Their facilities have to conform to certain standards, categorized on a scale of A–C. Rates are currently the same throughout the year: category A doubles are around 18,500$00; B 14,000$00; and C 10,600$00. In high season in certain areas you might find that stays are for a minimum of three nights. Facilities can vary from a simple room in a rustic house to a suite or annexe of a manor house with its own gardens and swimming pool. All properties which have been approved under this scheme are entitled to display a **green tree symbol**, although there are some unauthorized houses displaying their own symbols.

In general the scheme has given a new lease of life to properties which had begun to fall into decline through changing patterns of economics and lifestyles. The appeal – or not as the case may be – lies in the chance to stay with the owners of the properties. Many will provide typical dinners made from local ingredients, sometimes accompanied by wine and other produce made on the estate, and almost all are founts of advice and information about local matters. Even if dinner is not available – or you prefer not to eat with the family – large breakfasts are invariably included.

Once a property has passed the government inspection, its owners can choose to join one of the private marketing organizations, of which the first and best known is **Solares de Portugal** (formerly known as *Turihab*), based in Ponte de Lima where the scheme originated (Praça da República, 4990 Ponte de Lima; ☎258-741-672, fax 258-741-444, *turihab@mail.telepac.pt, www.turihab.pt* or *www.solares-de-portugal.com*). It has some amazing country houses on its books as well as simpler, more basic properties. The success of Solares de Portugal has prompted the formation of similar marketing associations such as Privetur, Largo das Pereiras, 4990 Ponte de Lima (☎258 743 923, fax 258 741 493, *privetur@mail.telepac.pt, www.manorhouses.com*), and ANTER, Quinta do Campo, Valado dos Frades, 2450 Nazaré (☎262 577 135, fax 262 577 555). All three can provide you with brochures detailing their properties; bookings can be made through the offices listed above or with the individual properties directly. It's also possible to book in advance with several of the specialist holiday operators detailed on p.5, 8, 11 or 15, who can make arrangements for you, or the Portuguese National Tourist Office who can send you the short *Guide to Country and Manor Houses*. The full listing, with colour pictures, is a hefty book (updated annually) available from the Direcção-Geral do Turismo in Lisbon at Av. António Augusto de Aguiar 86, 1069-021 Lisbon (☎213 575 086, fax 213 575 220, *dgtu@mail.telepac.pt*), or in Porto at Praça Dom João I 25-4° (☎222 005 805).

VILLAS

Holiday and tour operators are also the best sources if you want to rent a **villa** for your stay in Portugal. Summer sees most places booked solid months in advance, especially on the Algarve, but either side of the peak period you should be able to turn up in more out-of-the-way resorts like Tavira or Sagres and bag a self-catering apartment. The local turismo will probably be able to help. In winter, prices can be very reasonable indeed.

YOUTH HOSTELS

There are twenty-eight **youth hostels** (*pousadas de juventude*) in Portugal, most open all year round. The price for a dormitory bed runs from 1200–2900$00 a night, depending on the location and season; doubles cost between 3500$00 and 6000$00. Add on a little extra if you need to hire sheets and blankets. The most expensive hostels are in Lisbon, Porto and on the Algarve.

Most have a curfew (usually 11pm or midnight) and all require a valid Hostelling International (HI) card – available from your home-based youth hostel association (see box). In Portugal, the head office of the **Portuguese Youth Hostel Association** (*Movijoven*) is at Av. Duque de Ávila 137, 1069-017 Lisbon (Mon–Fri 9.30am–12.45pm & 2–5.45pm; ☎213 558 820, fax 213 528 621, *movijovem@mail.telepac.pt*).

Among the best hostels in Portugal are those at Vilarinho das Furnas (in the Gerês National Park), Penhas de Saúde (in the Serra de Estrêla), São Martinho do Porto, Areia Branca, Oeiras (on the seafront near Lisbon), Coimbra, Alcoutim (northeastern Algarve) and Leiria (perhaps the best of the lot).

YOUTH HOSTEL ASSOCIATIONS

Australia Australian Youth Hostels Association, Level 3, 10 Mallett St, Camperdown, 2050 NSW (☎02/9565 1699; *www.yha.org.au*).

Canada Canadian Hostelling Association, Suite 400, 205 Catherine St, Ottawa, ON K2P IC3 (☎613/237-7884; *www.hostellingintl.ca*).

England and Wales Youth Hostel Association (YHA), Trevelyan House, 8 St Stephen's Hill, St Albans, Herts AL1 2DY (☎01727/845 047, *customerservices@yha.org.uk*, *www.yha.org.uk*). London membership desk and booking office: 14 Southampton St, London WC2 7HY (☎020/7836 8541). Annual membership £11, (£5.50 under-18).

Ireland An Oige, 61 Mountjoy St, Dublin 7 (☎01/830 4555; *www.irelandyha.org*).

New Zealand Youth Hostels Association of New Zealand, PO Box 436, Christchurch (☎03/379-9970; *yha.co.nz*).

Northern Ireland Youth Hostels Association of Northern Ireland (YHANI), 22 Donegall Rd, Belfast BT12 5JN (☎01232/324 733; *www.hini.org.uk*).

Scotland Scottish Youth Hostels Association, 7 Glebe Crescent, Stirling, FK8 2JA (☎01786/890 400; *www.syha.org.uk*).

USA American Youth Hostels (AYH), 733 15th Street NW, Suite 840, Washington, DC 20005 (☎202/783-6161; *www.hiayh.org*).

CAMPING

Portugal has more than a hundred authorized **campsites**, many of them in very attractive locations and, despite their often large size (over five hundred spaces is not uncommon), can get extremely crowded in summer. Charges are per person and per tent, with showers and parking extra; even so, it's rare that you'll end up paying more than 600–800$00 a person. Some are even cheaper than this, while those operated by the Orbitur chain are usually a little more expensive. For details of their sites, contact Orbitur, Rua Diogo Couto 1-8°, 1100 Lisbon (☎218 117 070, fax 218 148 045, *info@orbitur.pt*, *www.orbitur.pt*). The most useful campsites are detailed in the text (unless otherwise stated they are open all year) but you can get a fairly complete list from any Portuguese tourist office, or a detailed booklet

(700$00) called *Roteiro Campista* (with prices, exact locations, facilities, etc) from Portuguese bookshops or direct from Guia de Parques de Campismo, Apartado 3168, 1304 Lisbon Codex (☎213 642 374, fax 213 642 370).

There are only a few sites in Portugal for which you will have to produce an **international camping carnet**, but if you want to be on the safe side they are available from home motoring organizations, or, in Britain, from the Camping & Caravanning Club of Great Britain, Greenfields House, Westwood Way, Coventry CV4 8JH (☎01203/694 995, fax 694 886), in the US from the Family Campers and RVers (FCRV), 4804 Transit Rd, Building 2, Depew, NY 14043 (☎1800/245-9755; *www.fcrv.org*) and in Canada from FCRV, 51 W 22nd St, Hamilton, Ontario, LC9 4N5 (same phone as US). They serve as useful identification and cover you for third party insurance when camping.

Camping outside official grounds is legal, but with certain restrictions. You're not allowed to camp :"in urban zones, in zones of protection for water sources, or less than 1km from camping parks, beaches, or other places frequented by the public". What this means in practice is that you can't camp on tourist beaches, but with a little sensitivity you can pitch a tent for a short period almost anywhere in the countryside. That said, in recent years a number of Portugal's natural parks have banned unofficial camping in an attempt to reduce littering and fire damage. Check first with the relevant park office as to whether it is permitted or not.

The **Algarve** is another exception, having banned freelance camping altogether. When staying on one of the region's campsites, be warned that thefts are a regular occurrence – over most of the rest of the country the locals are extremely honest and you can leave equipment without worrying.

EATING AND DRINKING

Portuguese food is excellent, inexpensive and served in quantity. Virtually all cafés, whatever their appearance, will serve you a basic meal for around 1500$00 (£5/$8), while for 1600–3000$00 (£5.50–10/$9–16) you have the run of most of the country's restaurants. Only a handful of top-class restaurants in Lisbon and the Algarve will cause a credit card crisis. Do beware, however, of eating anything you haven't explicitly asked for and expecting it to be free, or included: it won't be.

BREAKFAST, SNACKS AND SANDWICHES

For **breakfast** it's best to head for a café or *pastelaria* (pastry shop) for a croissant or pastry of some kind washed down with a coffee. The latter is usually taken espresso-style (ask for *uma bica* in the south, or simply *um café* in the north), though the milky version (*um galão*) served in a glass, is also popular at breakfast time.

You'll often find a whole range of dishes served at a café, but classic Portuguese **snacks** include *rissóis* (deep-fried meat patties); *pastéis de bacalhau* (cod fishcakes); and *prego no pão* (steak sandwich), which when served on a plate with a fried egg on top is called a *prego no prato*, while the same with sliced ham is a *prego no fiambre*. In the north you may also find *lanches* (pieces of sweetish bread stuffed with ham) and *pastéis de carne* or *pastéis de chaves* (puff pastries stuffed with sausage meat). If cafés cook in a big way you'll probably see blackboard lists of dishes, or perhaps just a sign reading *Comidas* (meals).

Among **sandwiches** (*sandes*) on offer, the most common fillings include *queijo* (cheese), *fiambre* (ham), *presunto* (smoked ham) and *chouriço* (smoked sausage). *Sandes mistas* are

PORTUGUESE FOOD GLOSSARY

BASICS

Acepipes	Hors d'oeuvres	*Ovos*	Eggs	*Pimenta*	Pepper
Arroz	Rice	*estrelado*	fried	*Piri-piri*	Chilli sauce
Azeitonas	Olives	*mexido*	scrambled	*Sal*	Salt
Batatas fritas	French fries	*cozido*	boiled	*Salada*	Salad
Legumes	Vegetables	*Pão*	Bread	*Queijo*	Cheese
Manteiga	Butter				

IN THE RESTAURANT

Almoço	Lunch	*Ementa*	Menu	*Jantar*	Dinner
Colher	Spoon	*Faca*	Knife	*Mesa*	Table
Conta	The bill	*Garfo*	Fork	*Pequeno almoço*	Breakfast
Copo	Glass	*Garrafa*	Bottle		

SOUPS (SOPAS)

Caldo verde	Cabbage/potato broth	*Sopa de feijão verde*	Green bean soup
Canja de galinha	Chicken broth with rice	*Sopa de grão*	Chickpea soup
	and boiled egg yolks	*Sopa de legumes*	Vegetable soup
Gaspacho	Chilled vegetable soup	*Sopa de marisco*	Shellfish soup
Sopa à alentejana	Garlic/bread soup with	*Sopa de peixe*	Fish soup
	poached egg on top		

FISH (PEIXE) **AND SHELLFISH** (MARISCOS)

Ameijoas	Clams	*Lulas*	Squid
Anchovas	Anchovies	*Mexilhões*	Mussels
Atum	Tuna	*Ostras*	Oysters
Camarões	Shrimp	*Pargo*	Sea bream
Caranguejo	Crab	*Peixe espada*	Swordfish (often confused
Carapau	Mackerel		with the more common
Cherne	Sea bream		*espadarte*)
Chocos	Cuttlefish	*Perceves*	Goose barnacles
Enguia	Eel	*Pescada*	Hake
Espadarte	Scabbard fish (a long, thin	*Polvo*	Octopus
	fish, black or white in	*Robalo*	Sea bass
	colour)	*Salmão*	Salmon
Gambas	Prawns	*Salmonete*	Red mullet
Garoupa	(Like) bream	*Sarda*	Mackerel
Lagosta	Lobster	*Sardinhas*	Sardines
Lampreia	Lamprey (similar to eel)	*Truta*	Trout
Linguado	Sole		

MEAT (CARNE), **POULTRY** (AVES) **AND GAME** (CAÇA)

Almondegas	Meatballs	*Costeleta*	Chop	*Pato*	Duck
Borrego	Lamb	*Dobrada*	Tripe	*Perdiz*	Partridge
Cabrito	Kid	*Fiambre*	Cooked ham	*Perú*	Turkey
Carne de porco	Pork	*Fígado*	Liver	*Presunto*	Smoked ham
Carneiro	Mutton	*Frango*	Young chicken	*Salsicha*	Sausage
Coelho	Rabbit	*Galinha*	Chicken	*Tripas*	Tripe
Cordoniz	Quail	*Lombo*	Loin of pork	*Vitela*	Veal

SPECIALITIES

Açorda (*de marisco*)	Bread-based stew (cooked with shellfish and spices)	*Cataplana*	Shellfish or fish cooked with strips of ham, pepper and onion
Arroz de marisco	Seafood paella	*Chanfana*	Casserole of lamb or kid
Bacalhau	There are reputedly 365 ways of cooking dried salt cod, including *com batatas e grão* (with boiled potatoes and chickpeas), *à brás* (with egg, onions and potatoes), *na brasa* (roasted with sliced potatoes), *à Gomes de Sá* (sliced, with boiled eggs and potatoes), and *à minhota* (with fried potatoes)	*Cozido à portuguesa*	Boiled casserole of chicken, lamb, pork, beef, sausages, offal and beans, served with rice and vegetables
		Espetada mista	Mixed meat kebab
		Frango no churrasco	Barbecued chicken, nearly always superb; eat with the *piri-piri* (chilli) sauce provided
		Leitão assado	Roast suckling pig
		Porco à alentejana	Pork cooked with clams, an oily and salty dish from the Alentejo
Bife à Portuguesa	Beef steak, topped with mustard sauce and a fried egg	*Tripas à moda do Porto*	Tripe stewed with beans and vegetables
Caldeirada	Fish stew, with a base of onions, tomatoes and potatoes		

SOME TERMS

Assado/no espeto	Roasted/spit-roasted	*Guisado*	Stew
Cozido	Boiled/stewed	*Molho*	Sauce
Ensopado de…	Soup or stew of…	*Na brasa*	Charcoal-grilled
Frito	Fried	*No forno*	Baked
Fumado	Smoked	*Piri-piri*	With chilli sauce
Grelhado	Grilled	*Salteado*	Sautéed

VEGETABLES (LEGUMES) AND SALAD (SALADA)

Alcachofra	Artichoke	*Espargos*	Asparagus
Alface	Lettuce	*Espinafre*	Spinach
Alho	Garlic	*Favas*	Broad beans
Batatas	Potatoes	*Feijão*	Beans
Cebola	Onion	*Grão*	Chickpeas
Cenoura	Carrot	*Pepino*	Cucumber
Cogumelos	Mushrooms	*Pimenta*	Pepper
Ervilhas	Peas	*Salada*	Salad

FRUIT (FRUTA)

Ameixas	Plums	*Maçã*	Apple
Ananás	Pineapple	*Melão*	Melon
Cerejas	Cherries	*Morangos*	Strawberries
Figos	Figs	*Pêra*	Pear
Laranja	Orange	*Pêssego*	Peach
Limão	Lemon	*Uvas*	Grapes

usually a combination of ham and cheese; grilled, they're called *tostas mistas*. If there's food displayed on café counters and you see anything that looks appealing, just ask for *uma dose* (a portion). *Uma coisa destas* (one of those) can also be a useful phrase.

Markets – often held in indoor covered sites – are always good hunting grounds for snacks. At many of them you'll find stands serving complete meals, or at least some local delicacy. In the north, especially, the most delicious standby is a chunk of *broa* (corn/rye bread) with local cheese and *marmelada* (thick quince – *marmelo* – spread).

MEALS AND RESTAURANTS

Even those on the tightest of budgets won't need to depend exclusively on snacks and picnics. The country is awash with accessible and affordable **restaurants** and, in addition, servings tend to be huge. Indeed, you can usually have a substantial **meal** by ordering a *meia dose* (half portion), or *uma dose* between two. Meals are often listed like this on the menu and it's normal practice; you don't need to be a child.

It is worth checking out the **ementa turística**, too – not a "tourist menu", but the set meal of the day, sometimes with a choice of two starters and two main courses, plus beer or wine. It can be very good value, particularly in *pensões* that serve meals, or in the cheaper workers' cafés. Smarter restaurants, however, sometimes resent the law that compels them to offer the *ementa turística*, responding with stingy portions, excessive prices, or, where there's any deviation from the set fare, declaring your meal to be *à lista* (à la carte) and consequently twice as expensive. If you feel strongly enough to want to make a formal complaint, ask for the *livro de reclamações* (complaints book) – every restaurant, however humble, is obliged to keep one.

Otherwise, the one thing to watch for when eating out in Portugal – especially if you've grown happily complacent in Spain on a regular intake of free *tapas* – is the plate of **starters** usually placed before you when you take a table and before you order. These can be quite elaborate little dishes of olives, cheese, sardine spread and *chouriço*, or can consist of little more than rolls and butter, but what you eat is counted and you will be charged for every bite. Each item should be itemized on the menu, so you can see what you're spending.

Apart from straightforward restaurants – **restaurantes** – you could end up eating a meal in one of several other venues. A **tasca** is a small neighbourhood tavern; a **casa de pasto**, a cheap, local dining room usually with a set three-course menu, mostly served at lunch only. A **cervejaria** is literally a "beer house", more informal than a restaurant, with people dropping in at all hours for a beer and a snack. In Lisbon they are often wonderful old tiled caverns, specializing in seafood. Also specializing in seafood is a **marisqueria**, occasionally very upmarket, though as often as not a regular restaurant with a superior fishy menu.

Meal times are earlier than in Spain, with lunch usually served from noon–3pm, dinner from 7.30pm onwards; don't count on being able to eat much after 10pm outside the cities and tourist resorts. Simple cafés and restaurants don't charge for service, though you'll have paid a **cover charge** for bread and appetizers if you had any. People generally leave just small change as a **tip** in these places, though in more upmarket restaurants, you'll either be charged, or should leave, around ten percent.

DISHES AND SPECIALITIES

It's always worth taking stock of the *prato do dia* (dish of the day) if you're interested in sampling **local specialities**. They're often considerably cheaper than the usual menu fare as well. Some of the more common dishes are detailed in the food lists on p.36.

Soups are extraordinarily inexpensive (though few restaurants are happy with people only ordering soup), and the thick vegetable *caldo verde* – cabbage and potato broth sometimes with pieces of ham – is as filling as dishes come. The other soup served everywhere is *sopa à alentejana*, a garlic and bread soup with a poached egg in it. Otherwise, fish and shellfish soups are always worth sampling.

On the coast, **fish and seafood** are pre-eminent: crabs, prawns, crayfish, clams and huge barnacles are all fabulous, while fish on offer always includes superb mullet, tuna and scabbard fish. The most typical Portuguese fish dish is that created from **bacalhau** (dried, salted cod), which is much better than it sounds. It's virtually the national dish with reputedly 365 different ways of preparing it. Running a close second are **sardines** (*sardinhas*), which – when grilled or barbecued outside – provide one of the country's most familiar and appetizing smells. Normally very cheap (a few hundred escudos a kilo), the price can increase tenfold on the eve of São João (on June 23), when seemingly everyone gets out the barbeque. On the coast, you shouldn't miss trying a **cataplana** – pressure-cooked seafood and strips of ham, named after the copper vessel in which it's cooked – or **arroz de marisco**, a bumper serving of mixed seafood served with a soupy rice. These are nearly always served for a minimum of two people, though.

On the whole, **meat** dishes are less special, though they're often enlivened by the addition of a fiery *piri-piri* (chilli) sauce, either in the cooking or provided on the table. Simple grilled or fried steaks of beef and pork are common; while **chicken** is on virtually every menu – at its wonderful best when barbecued (*no churrasco*); certain restaurants specialize in this and little else. Other, more exotic, specialities include smoked hams (*presunto*) from the north of the country (especially Chaves), and the ubiquitous and extremely tasty **porco à alentejana** (pork cooked with clams) – perhaps Portugal's most enterprising contribution to world cuisine – which originated, as its name suggests, in the Alentejo. However, steel yourself for a couple of special dishes that local Portuguese people might entice you into trying: Porto's **tripas** (tripe) dishes incorporate beans and spices but the heart of the dish is still recognizably chopped stomach-lining; while **cozido à portuguesa**, widely served in restaurants on a Sunday, is a stomach-challenging boiled "meat" stew in which you shouldn't be surprised to turn up a pig's ear or worse. And it's worth paying good money to avoid eating the unspeakable **papas de sarrabulho** (a blood- and bread-based dish).

Accompanying most dishes will be potatoes (generally fried so ask if you want them boiled) and/or rice – calorific overkill is a strong feature of Portuguese meal times. Other **vegetables** rarely make an appearance, though you might find sliced fresh tomato served with your fish, and boiled carrots or cabbage and the like accompanying meat stews.

If you've had enough rich food, any restaurant will fix a **salada mista** (mixed salad), which usually has tomatoes, onions and olives as a base, and you can ask for it to be served *sem óleo* (without oil), though it's nowhere near as tasty if you do. Otherwise, strict **vegetarians** are in for something

of a hard time outside Lisbon and the Algarve, where there's a bigger choice of non-Portuguese food. Eggs are mostly free-range in Portugal, but out in the sticks you'll soon tire of omelettes or fried eggs, chips and salad – though every restaurant will be happy to prepare this for you if you ask.

PASTRIES, SWEETS AND CHEESES

Pastries (*pastéis*) and cakes (*bolos*) are usually at their best in *casas de chá* (tearooms), though you'll also find them in cafés and in *pastelarias*, which themselves often serve drinks, too. Here, pastries are serious business and enthusiasts won't be disappointed. Among the best are the Sintra cheesecakes (*queijadas de Sintra*), *palha de ovos* (egg pastries) from Abrantes, *bolo de anjo* (angel food cake), *pastéis de nata* (delicious little custard tarts), and a full range of marzipan cakes from the Algarve. The incredibly sweet, egg-based *doces de ovos* – most infamously from Aveiro – are completely over-the-top.

Unfortunately, few of these delicacies are available in restaurants as **desserts**. Instead, you'll almost always be offered either fresh fruit, the ubiquitous Olá ice cream price list, *pudim flan* (crème caramel), *arroz doce* (rice pudding) or *torta da noz* (almond tart). **Cheese** is widely available in restaurants, the best being the *queijo da Serra* (from the Serra da Estrela). *Cabreiro* or *queijo de cabra* is a goat's cheese like a dry Greek *feta*; and also worth looking out for are the soft cheeses of Tomar and Azeitão. Travelling in remoter areas, you're also in for a treat – the cheeses of northern Beira and southern Trás-os-Montes being especially worth a mention.

ALCOHOLIC DRINKS

Portuguese table wines are dramatically inexpensive and of a good overall quality. Even the standard *vinho da casa* that you get in the humblest of cafés is generally a very pleasant drink. But it's fortified port, of course, and Madeira that are Portugal's best-known wine exports – and you should certainly sample both.

Beer choices are far less varied, with just two or three brands available country-wide, while the typical Portuguese measure of spirits is equivalent to at least two shots in Britain or North America, making drunkenness all too easy. Low prices, too, are an encouragement, as long as you stick to local (*nacional*) products.

WINES

Modern wine-making techniques are making fast inroads into Portugal's traditional wine-growing regions, with a corresponding growth in the number of internationally recognized and reputed Portuguese labels, such as **Bairrada**, from the region between Coimbra and Aveiro, and **Ribatejo**, **Arruda** and **Liziria** from the Ribatejo. Some of the best-known Portuguese table wines are reds from the **Dão** region, a roughly triangular area between Coimbra, Viseu and Guarda, around the River Dão. Tasting a little like burgundy, and produced mainly by local co-operatives, they're available throughout the country. Among other smaller regions offering interesting wines are **Colares** (near Sintra), **Bucelas** in the Estremadura (crisp, dry whites), **Valpaças** from Trás-os-Montes, **Reguengos** from Alentejo and **Lagoa** from the Algarve.

The light, slightly sparkling **vinhos verdes** – "green wines", in age not colour – are again produced in quantity, this time in the Minho. They're drunk early as most don't mature or improve with age, but are great with meals, especially shellfish. There are red and rosé *vinhos verdes*, though the whites are the most successful. The region was officially demarcated in 1908, and producers are now entitled to use the European VQPRD label. Worth seeking out are the *vinhos verdes de quinta*, which are produced solely with grapes from one property (*quinta*), along the lines of the French chateaux wines: look for labels saying "Engarrafado Pelo Viticultor (or Produtor)" and "Engarrafado Na Propriedade (or Quinta)".

Otherwise, Portuguese **rosé wines** are known abroad mainly through the spectacularly successful export of Mateus Rosé. This is too sweet and aerated for most tastes, but other rosés – the best is Tavel – are definitely worth sampling.

Portugal also produces an interesting range of sparkling, champagne-method wines, known as **espumantes naturais**. They are designated *bruto* (extra dry), *seco* (fairly dry), *meio seco* (quite sweet) or *doce* (very sweet). The best of these come from the Bairrada region, north of Coimbra, though Raposeira wines are the most commonly available.

Even the most basic of restaurants usually has a decent selection of wines, many of which are available in half-bottles, too. The *vinho da casa* (house wine) is nearly always remarkably good value, but even ascending the scale and choosing from the wine list, you'll be surprised at the quality wines on offer at very moderate prices. Most **wine lists** don't just distinguish between *tinto* (red) or *branco* (white); they'll also list wines as either *verdes* (ie, young and slightly sparkling) or *maduros* (mature) – choose from the latter if you're after a red with a kick or a white with no bubbles.

FORTIFIED WINES: PORT AND MADEIRA

Port (*vinho do Porto*) – the famous fortified wine – is produced from grapes grown in the valley of the Douro and stored in huge wine lodges at Vila Nova de Gaia, facing Porto across the Rio Douro. You can visit these for tours and free tastings; see p.265 for all the details. Alternatively, you can try any of three hundred types and vintages of port at the *Instituto do Vinho do Porto* (Port Wine Institute) bars in Lisbon (p.100) and lodges Porto (p.265). But even if your quest for port isn't serious enough to do either, be sure to try the dry white aperitif ports, still little known outside the country.

Madeira (*vinho da Madeira*), from Portugal's Atlantic island province, has been exported to Britain since Shakespeare's time – it was Falstaff's favourite tipple, known then as sack. Widely available, it comes in three main varieties: Sercial (a dry aperitif), Verdelho (a sweeter aperitif) and Bual or Malmsey (sweet, heavy dessert wines). Each improves with age and special vintages are greatly prized and priced.

SPIRITS (*LICOR*)

The national **brandy** is arguably outflanked by its Spanish rivals – which are sold almost everywhere – but the native spirit is available in two varieties (Macieira and Constantino), each with loyal followings. It's frighteningly cheap. Portuguese **gin** is weaker than international brands but again ridiculously inexpensive.

Local **firewaters** – generically known as *aguardente* – are more impressive. They include Bagaço (the fieriest), Figo (made from figs, with which it shares similar qualities when drunk to excess), Ginginha (made from cherries; watch out for the cherry, however, soaked in alcohol for years it has an incredible bite), and the very wonderful Licor Beirão (a kind of cognac with herbs).

BEER

The most common Portuguese **beer** (*cerveja*) is Sagres in the south or Super Bock in the north, but there are a fair number of local varieties. If you're curious, they can all be tasted at the Silves Beer

Festival, held in the town's castle for a week every June. For something unusual (and not recommended on a hot afternoon) try the Sagres Preta, which is a dark beer, resembling British brown ale.

When **drinking draft beer** order *um imperial* (or *um fino* in the north) if you want a regular glass; *uma caneca* will get you a half-litre. And when **buying bottles**, don't forget to take your empties back: they can represent as much as a third of the price!

COFFEE, TEA AND SOFT DRINKS

Coffee (*café*) comes either black, small, and espresso-strong (*uma bica* or simply *um café*); small and with milk (*um garoto* or *um pingo* in some parts of the north); or large and with milk but often disgustingly weak (*um galão*). For white coffee that tastes of coffee and not diluted warm milk, ask for "*um café duplo com um pouco de leite*".

Tea (*chá*) is usually plain; *com leite* is with milk, *com limão* with lemon, but *um chá de limão* is hot water with a lemon rind. *Chá* is a big drink in Portugal (which originally exported tea-drinking to England) and you'll find wonderfully elegant *casas de chá* dotted around the country.

All the standard **soft drinks** are available. Tri Naranjus is a good local range of fruit drinks (excellent *limão*, lemon), and the fizzy Sumol is extremely fruity and appetizing. Fresh orange juice is *sumo de laranja* – add the word *fresca* to ensure you get the real thing. Lastly, **mineral water** (*água mineral*) is available almost anywhere in the country, either still (*sem gás*) or carbonated (*com gás*).

COMMUNICATIONS : POST AND PHONES

POSTAL SERVICES

Portuguese postal services are reasonably efficient. Letters or cards take three or four days to arrive at destinations in Europe, and a week to ten days to North America. The Correio Azul system guarantees delivery in two or three days but, naturally, you pay for it – 350$00 for a letter to Europe (20g) compared to the standard 100$00.

Post offices (*correios*) are normally open Monday to Friday 8.30am–6pm, larger ones sometimes on Saturday mornings, too. The main Lisbon and Porto branches have much longer opening hours; see "Listings", p.110 and p.278. **Stamps** (*selos*) are sold at post offices and anywhere that has the sign of a red horse on a white circle over a green background and the legend *Correio de Portugal – Selos*. To send a card to Europe or the USA costs 90$00, 180$00 to anywhere else.

You can have **poste restante** (general delivery) mail sent to you at any post office in the country. Letters should be marked *Poste Restante*, and your name, ideally, should be written with your surname first, in capitals and underlined. To collect, you need to take along your passport – look for the counter marked *encomendas*. If you are expecting mail, ask the postal clerk to check for letters under your first name and any other initials (including Ms, etc) as well as under your surname – filing can be erratic. Mail is held until the end of the month after the receiving date, and there's a 60$00 charge per item.

TELEPHONES

All calls, whether local or international, are most easily made using **card-operated public phones** called *credifones*, which you'll find in all but the most remote villages. Cards come in denominations of 50 and 120 units (*impulsos*), costing 875$00 and 2100$00 respectively, and are available from post offices, newsagents, tobacconists and kiosks. One oddity, though, is that there are two different kinds of phone cards – the ones that are inserted horizontally are currently being phased out. The few coin-operated phones remaining are often broken.

You'll also find **pay phones** in bars and cafés (and, increasingly, in turismo offices and newsagents), usually indicated by the sign of a red horse on a white circle over a green background and the legend *Correio de Portugal – Telefone*. If you need quieter surroundings you'd

be better off in one of the phone cabins found in most main post offices – simply tell the clerk where you want to phone, and pay for your call afterwards. Except in Lisbon and Porto, most telephone offices are closed in the evening. The **cheap rate for international and national calls** is between 9pm and 9am Monday to Friday, and all day weekends and holidays.

Reverse charge (collect) calls (*chamada cobrar ao destinatório*) can be made from any phone, dialling ☎099 for a European connection, ☎097 for North America, and ☎098 for the rest of the world. If you encounter difficulties, call ☎090.

TELEPHONE CODES AND USEFUL NUMBERS

To phone abroad from Portugal
Dial 00 + country code (given below) + area code (minus initial zero) + number

Country Codes

Australia	61	France	33	Ireland	353	UK	44
Canada	1	Germany	49	New Zealand	64	USA	1

To phone Portugal from abroad
Dial the international access code (see below) + 351 (country code) + number (nine digits)

International Access Code

Australia	0011	Ireland	00	UK	00
Canada	001	New Zealand	00	USA	001

Portugal's international dial code for mobile phones is 268

Useful Telephone Numbers

Directory enquiries	118	Operator (rest of the world)	098
Emergency services	112	Speaking clock	151
Operator (Europe and North Africa)	099	Tourist enquiries (freephone)	800 296 296
Operator (USA and Canada)	097 then dial 1		

As from October 1999 area codes are no longer in use in Portugal. You may, however, still see old leaflets and brochures with the old codes on. If you have a number with an old code try substituting the initial 0 in the code for a 2, the number should then be nine digits long and should connect. If the number is still not correct call the excellent freephone service *Linha Verde Turista*: ☎800 296 296.

THE MEDIA

The two most established Portuguese daily newspapers are the Lisbon-based *Diário de Notícias* and the *Jornal de Notícias* from Porto (see p.22 for newspaper Web sites). They have their uses for listings information, even if you have only a very sketchy knowledge of the language. The stylish *Público* has good foreign news and regional inserts as well as fairly easy-to-read listings. For an interesting view of the country's culture, try *JL* (*Jornal de Letras*).

The *International Herald Tribune*, and most British **newspapers**, can be bought in the major cities and resorts, usually a day late. One or two domestic English-language magazines and newspapers pop up from time to time on the Algarve, none of them especially informative but occasionally useful for finding work.

Portuguese **television** imports many American and British shows – nearly always subtitled rather than dubbed. Increasingly, too, European **satellite TV** stations are spawning their dishes around the country; sports channels are popular in bars, showing televised bullfights among other things. You also get *telenovelas* – soaps – often from Brazil, and compelling, if trashy, viewing even if you don't understand a word.

On the **radio**, you can pick up the BBC World Service, with hourly news, on 648 KHz medium wave and 15.07 MHz short wave; Voice of America is sporadically audible on 6040 on the 49m short wave band.

OPENING HOURS AND PUBLIC HOLIDAYS

Like Spain, Portugal has held onto the institution of the siesta. Most stores and businesses, plus smaller museums and rural post offices, close for a good lunchtime break – usually from around 12.30pm to 2.30 or 3pm.

Banks are a rare exception, opening Monday to Friday 8.30am to 3pm. **Shops** generally open around 9am, and upon re-opening after lunch keep going until 7 or 8pm; except in larger cities, they tend to close for the weekend at Saturday lunchtime. Larger shopping centres, however, stay open seven days a week, often until midnight. **Museums, churches and monuments** generally open from around 10am to 12.30pm and 2 to 6pm, though the larger ones stay open through lunchtime. Almost all museums and monuments, however, are closed Mondays (or Wednesdays for palaces). **Restaurants** tend to be closed on Sundays. The other thing to watch out for are national **public holidays** (see box) when almost everything is closed and transport services reduced. There are also **local festivals** and holidays (see p.44), when entire towns, cities and regions grind to a halt: for example June 13 in Lisbon and June 24 in Porto.

PUBLIC HOLIDAYS
January 1 New Year's Day
Good Friday
April 25 Liberty Day, commemorating the 1974 Revolution
May 1 Labour Day
Corpus Christi Usually early June
June 10 Dia de Camões e das Comunidades – Camões day: the community part was added after the Revolution
August 15 Feast of the Assumption
October 5 Republic Day
November 1 All Saints' Day
December 1 Celebrating independence from Spain in 1640
December 8 Immaculate Conception
December 25 Christmas Day

FESTIVALS, BULLFIGHTS AND SPORTS

Portugal maintains a remarkable number of folk customs which find their expression in local carnivals (*festas*) and traditional pilgrimages (*romarias*). Some of these have developed into wild celebrations lasting days or even weeks and have become tourist events in themselves; others have barely strayed from their roots.

Every region is different, but in the north especially there are dozens of village festivals, everyone taking the day off to celebrate the local saint's day or the harvest, and performing ancient songs and dances in traditional dress for no one's benefit but their own. Look out, too, for the great **feiras**, especially at Barcelos (p.323). Originally they were markets, but as often as not nowadays you'll find a combination of agricultural show, folk festival, amusement park and, admittedly, tourist bazaar.

The festival list is potentially endless and only the major highlights are picked out below. For more **details** on what's going on around you, check with the local turismo or buy either of the annual *Borda d'Água* or *Seringador* booklets, which are old-style almanacs detailing saints' days, star signs, eclipse predictions, gardening tips and, most importantly, all the country's annual fairs – available from stationers or tobacconists. It is often the obscure and unexpected event which turns out to be the most fun.

Among major national celebrations, **Easter Week** and **St John's Eve** (June 23/24) stand out. Both are celebrated throughout the country with

MAJOR POPULAR FESTIVALS

Among the biggest and best known of the country's **popular festivals** are:

MAY
Queima das Fitas, celebrating the end of the academic year in Coimbra (mid-May).
Fátima (May 13), Portugal's most famous pilgrimage; also in October; see p.163.

JUNE
Feira Nacional at Santarém lasts for ten days (starting on the first Fri). Dancing, bullfighting and an agricultural fair; see p.174.
Festa de São Gonçalo in Amarante (1st weekend); see p.287.
Santos Popularos (Popular Saints) in Lisbon – celebrations in honour of St Anthony (June 13), St John (24) and St Peter (29). Festival, too, in Porto for St John on the same date.

JULY
Festa do Colete Encarnado in Vila Franca de Xira, with Pamplona-style running of bulls through the streets (first two weeks); see p.176.

AUGUST
Romaria da Nossa Senhora da Agonía in Viana do Castelo (third weekend); see p.331.

SEPTEMBER
Romaria de Nossa Senhora dos Remédios in Lamego (pilgrimage from Sept 6–8, though events start in last week of Aug and run through to mid-Sept); see p.298.
"New Fairs" in Ponte de Lima (2nd and 3rd weekend); see p.245.

OCTOBER
Feira de Outubro in Vila Franca de Xira (first two weeks); more bull-running and fighting.
Fátima (Oct 13); second great pilgrimage of the year; see p.163.

NOVEMBER
Feira Nacional do Cavalo (National Horse Fair) in Golegã; see p.171.

religious processions. The former is most magnificent in Braga, where it is full of ceremonial pomp, while the latter tends to be a more joyous affair. In Porto, where St John's Eve is the highlight of a week of celebration, everyone dances through the streets all night, hitting each other over the head with plastic hammers.

BULLFIGHTS

The Portuguese **bullfight** is neither as commonplace nor as famous as its Spanish counterpart, but as a spectacle it's marginally preferable. In Portugal the bull isn't killed, but instead wrestled to the ground in a genuinely elegant, colourful and skilled display. After the fight, however, the bull is usually injured and it is always slaughtered later in any case.

If you choose to go – and we would urge visitors not to support the events put on simply for tourist benefit on the Algarve – these are the basics.

A **tourada** opens with the bull, its horns padded or sheared flat, facing a mounted *toureiro* in elaborate eighteenth-century costume. His job is to provoke and exhaust the bull and to plant the dart-like *farpas* (or *bandarilhas*) in its back while avoiding the charge – a demonstration of incredible riding prowess. Once the beast is tired the *moços-de-forcado*, or simply *forcados*, move in, an eight-man team which tries finally to immobilize it. It appears a totally suicidal task – they line up behind each other across the ring from the bull and persuade it to charge them, the front man leaping between the horns while the rest grab hold and try to subdue it. It's as absurd as it is courageous, and often takes two or three attempts, the first tries often resulting with one or more of the *forcados* being tossed spectacularly into the air.

The great Portuguese bullfight centre is **Ribatejo**, where the animals are bred. If you want to see a fight, it's best to witness it here, amid the local aficionados, or as part of the festivals in Vila Franca de Xira and Santarém. The season lasts from around April to October. Local towns and villages in the Ribatejo also feature **bull-running**, through the streets, at various of their festivals; see Chapter Two for further details.

SPORTS

Soccer is the Portuguese national sport, with a long and often glorious tradition of international and club teams. Portugal will host the European Football Championships in 2004; an event that will surely lead to the upgrading of some of the country's stadiums and possibly the building of a totally new stadium. The leading clubs, inevitably, hail from Lisbon (Benfica and Sporting) and Porto (FC Porto). Just about every Portuguese supports one of these two teams, paying scant attention to the lesser, local teams. Of these, F.C. Guimarães are the most consistent challengers to the big-league boys, though Académicia de Coimbra are worth watching too, if only for their metronomic cycle of promotion-and-relegation. If you want to see a league match, the season runs from September through to May. Tickets are inexpensive, and matches given due prominence in the local press. The spectacle of a packed capacity football stadium puts bullfights somewhat in the shade.

Participatory sports on offer in Portugal include windsurfing, golf and tennis – all of which are promoted mainly on the Algarve. **Windsurf boards** are available for rent on most of the Algarve beaches and at the more popular northern and Lisbon coast resorts. The biggest windsurfing (and surfing) destination is **Guincho**, north of Lisbon (see p.115), though the winds and currents here require a high level of expertise.

Tennis courts are a common feature of most larger Algarve hotels – their attraction being that you can play year-round. If you want to improve your game, the best intensive coaching is under the instruction of ex-Wimbledon pro Roger Taylor at the **Vale do Lobo** resort complex. Arguably the country's best **golf course**, designed by Frank Penninck, is just up the road from here at **Vilamoura**, and several others are within reach.

Anyone interested in **fishing** should head to the trout streams of the Minho and other northern regions; licences are available from local town halls. For further information – and addresses of operators promoting **sporting holidays** – contact the Portuguese National Tourist Office for a copy of their *Sportugal* brochure.

TROUBLE, POLICE AND SEXUAL HARASSMENT

By European standards, Portugal is a remarkably crime-free country, though there's the usual petty theft in larger tourist resorts. Although Lisbon is one of the safer European capitals, you should take care in the Alfama and parts of the Bairro Alto after dark; if you are robbed, whatever you do, don't resist. Hand over your valuables and run. Watch out also for pickpockets on public transport, something for which Lisbon is developing a bit of a reputation. Rental cars, too, are always prey to thieves: remove any rental company stickers and wherever you park, don't leave anything visible in the car – preferably, don't leave anything in the car at all.

WHAT TO DO IF YOU ARE ROBBED

If you do have anything stolen while in Portugal, you'll need to go to the **police** – primarily to file a report, which your insurance company will require before they'll pay out for any claims made on your policy. Police stations in Lisbon and other major towns are detailed in the various "Listings" sections throughout the guide.

You can't count on English being spoken by most of the local police personnel you may have occasion to meet, and since tourists can usually muster only a few basic words of Portuguese, confusion can easily arise. To this end, showing deference to a police officer is wise: the Portuguese still hold respect dear, and the more respect you show a figure in authority, the quicker you will be on your way.

In an emergency, dial ☎112 for the police.

THE POLICE

There are three different authorities with which you might come into contact, though in an emergency, the first policeman you see will be able to point you in the right direction. In Porto and Lisbon, the police force most likely to be of assistance will be the blue-uniformed **PSP** (*Polícia de Segurança Pública*), responsible among other things for incidents involving tourists. Outside these cities, you will have to rely on the **GNR** (*Guarda Nacional Republicana*) for help: they police the rural areas, patrol the motorways, and are responsible for overseeing all ceremonial occasions, like state visits, at which time they deck themselves out in magnificent dress uniforms. Ordinarily, though, they wear blue-grey uniforms and highly polished knee-length boots. If you require specialist help – work permits and the like – the local office of the **Serviço de Estrangeiros e Fronteiras** is the place to go.

SEXUAL HARASSMENT

The ruralism and small-town life of Portugal make it one of the most relaxed of the Latin countries for **women travellers**. Which is not to say that the Portuguese *machismo* is any less ingrained than in Spain or Italy: simply that it gets rather less of an outlet.

Portugal is rarely a dangerous place for women travellers, and only in the following few areas do you need to be particularly wary: parts of Lisbon (particularly around Cais do Sodré and the Bairro Alto by night), streets immediately around train stations in the larger towns (traditionally the red-light districts), and some of the Algarve resorts, where aggressive males congregate on the pick-up.

On the whole it's a rural country, intensely traditional and formal to the point of prudishness. People may initially wonder why you're travelling on your own – especially inland and in the mountains, where Portuguese women rarely travel unaccompanied – but once they have accepted that you are a crazy foreigner you're likely to be welcomed, adopted, and even offered food and lodging in their homes.

As far as transport goes, **hitching** is reasonably safe as long as there are two or more of you – but absolutely not recommended for lone women travellers. If you are on your own, you should be able to get around at night by **taxi**, which are very cheap anyway outside the Algarve. By day **public transport** is good and quite safe; but remember to take the usual precautions at night on Lisbon's Metro and on the Cais do Sodré–Cascais coastal train line.

WORKING IN PORTUGAL

Portugal has employment problems of its own, and without a special skill you're unlikely to have much luck finding any kind of long-term work. One realistic option though is *teaching English*. For this a TEFL certificate is a distinct advantage, though you may find work without one. The biggest demand nowadays is for teaching English to children, probably in the smaller provincial towns. If you're already in Portugal you could just apply to individual schools or advertise your services privately, but even EU citizens should register with the Serviço de Estrangeiros e Fronteiras. Non-EU passport holders must apply for a work permit before they enter Portugal.

WORKING ON THE ALGARVE

As far as temporary jobs go, the only real opportunities are in tourist-related work **on the Algarve**, which offer a range of ways of getting money, all of them dependent to some extent on your self-confidence and/or lack of scruples. Most obvious of the jobs is **bar work**. This is not easy to find –

you'll stand the best chance in one of the many British-owned places – and even when you do, it often brings in barely enough money to live on. Better, at least in terms of time involved, is to try your hand walking the streets at night **handing out nightclub invitations** to holiday-makers. This work is available in most major resorts and is paid solely on a commission basis, but it does leave you free during the day – and much of the night – to seek your own entertainment.

Which leads nicely into the biggest scam in the country – perhaps in Europe – of **selling time shares**. Here possibilities exist for making really big bucks, though not everyone, of course, strikes it rich. The work involves walking the streets in the major resorts inviting British tourist couples to view time-share resorts and villas. It is extremely tiring, soul-destroying, and, at its most successful, pretty disreputable work, but earnings are on a commission basis and this can add up to a fair living if you're the type who enjoys selling your own grandmother. Just ask the people who are already doing the job on the street what to do. They'll tell you how to find work and how depressing it is.

One last option is to head for the huge yacht marina at **Vilamoura**, which holds around a thousand craft and is slowly being surrounded by trendy bars, boutiques and cafés. You could try some of these, but it's even better to approach the yachties themselves. Almost all boat owners have hundreds of little tasks that need doing and, given the opportunity, will pay a few thousand escudos to anyone presenting themselves as a handyman/woman. Mostly it's **painting** or **scrubbing down** decks – hardly skilled labour – but if you can convince someone you know what you're doing the quality of work you'll be given may improve. Between late September and early November, however, there's the chance of **crewing** to the Canaries or the Caribbean; for this sort of angle try the local bars as well as word of mouth. For the more menial odd jobs you just need persistence and a thick skin: spend a couple of days asking around and something should turn up.

If you do decide to stay on in the Algarve to work, note that non-EU visitors can no longer simply hop over to Spain to get a visa extension, but must leave all European Schengen Treaty countries, and will not be permitted to return until six months after the start of your first stay. The only way to renew your visa, if reliable long-term employment beckons, is to go to one of the Serviço de Estrangeiros offices in Portimão, Albufeira or Faro.

DIRECTORY

ADDRESSES Most addresses in Portugal consist of a street name and number followed by a storey number, eg, Rua de Afonso Henriques 34-3°. This means you need to go up to the third floor of no. 34 (US, fourth floor). An "esq" or "E" (standing for *esquerda*) after a floor number means you should go to the left; "dir" or "D" (for *direita*) indicates the apartment or office you're looking for is on the right. *Esquina* means corner or junction.

BAGGAGE You can often leave bags at a train or bus station for a small sum while you look for rooms. On the whole the Portuguese are highly trustworthy, and even shopkeepers and café owners will keep an eye on your belongings for you. Or try the local turismo, which may agree to look after your bags for a while.

BEACHES Beware of the heavy undertow on many of Portugal's western Atlantic beaches and don't swim if you see a red or yellow flag. The EU blue flag indicates that the water is clean enough to swim in – sadly, not always the case at many of Portugal's resorts. The sea is warmest on the eastern Algarve (ie the beaches east of Faro).

CHILDREN Portugal is child-friendly and families should find it as easy a place to roam as any other country. Cheap hotels and *pensões* will only rarely charge extra for children in their parents' room and many of the more upmarket hotels give a fifty percent discount for children under eight or twelve. In restaurants small portions and extra plates are absolutely the norm for all who require them. Lastly, museums and most sights don't usually charge for small children.

CONTRACEPTION Condoms – *preservativos* – are widely available from street vending machines, as well as in pharmacies and supermarkets. In more rural, traditional places, you may have to ask and the pharmacist will set out an array on the counter, in the best formal Portuguese manner.

DRESS Churches often require "modest dress" – which basically just means you shouldn't wear shorts or very flimsy tops.

EMERGENCIES Phone ☎112 for the emergency services. If you're involved in a road accident, use the nearest roadside orange-coloured SOS telephone – press the button and wait for an answer.

FILM Going to the movies in Portugal is extremely cheap, and films are often shown with the original (usually English-language) soundtrack with Portuguese subtitles. Listings can be found in the local newspaper or on boards, invariably placed somewhere in the central square of every small town. Screenings are cheap, with reduced prices at matinées and at all Monday shows.

GAY LIFE The gay scene isn't especially prominent, or commercialized, though there's a fair sprinkling of clubs, and a gay beach, in Lisbon and one or two places to meet in Porto and the

Algarve. Attitudes in the capital are fairly tolerant; elsewhere a gay consciousness has yet to make much impact. There is no explicit law against homosexuality.

LAUNDRY There are very few self-service launderettes, but loads of *lavandarias*, where you can get your clothes washed, mended, and ironed (overnight) at a fairly low cost. Some of these offer only a dry-cleaning service.

SWIMMING POOLS Every sizeable town has a swimming pool, usually outdoors, but you'll find that they are often closed from September to May.

TIME Portugal now follows "British" time, ie GMT in winter and one hour ahead in summer. Clocks go forward one hour at the end of March and back an hour at the end of October.

TIPPING Hotels and restaurants include a service charge but porters and maids expect something; cab drivers don't.

TOILETS "Ladies" often charge and are clean, "Gentlemen" may look more aesthetic (lots of ironwork) and are free, but are usually pretty unattractive inside. A sign that says *Retretes*, *Banheiro*, *Lavabos* or WC will head you in the right direction, then it's *homens* or *cabalheiros* for men and *senhoras* for women. Ask for "*um banheiro*" if in doubt.

WOMEN'S MOVEMENT There are relatively few women's organizations in Portugal. The best contact points are the IDM centre and the feminist bookshop Editora das Mulheres, both in Lisbon (see p.110). Also of interest is the Comissão para a Igualdade e para os Direitos das Mulheres (Avenida da República 32-1°, 1000 Lisbon; ☎217 983 000), which maintains a watching brief on all aspects of women's lives in Portugal; members organize conferences and meetings, are very active in areas of social and legal reform, and are linked with other feminists throughout the country.

PART TWO

THE

GUIDE

CHAPTER ONE

LISBON AND AROUND

There are few cityscapes as startling and eccentric as that of **Lisbon** (Lisboa). Built on a switchback of hills above the broad **Tejo** estuary, its quarters are linked by an amazing network of cobbled streets with outrageous gradients, up which crank trams and funiculars. Down by the river, you are lured across towards the sea by a vast, Rio-like statue of Christ, arms outstretched, whose embrace encompasses one of the grandest of all suspension bridges and a fleet of cross-river ferries. For visitors, it's hard not to see the city as an urban funfair: a sense heightened by the castle poised above the Alfama district's medieval, whitewashed streets; the fantasy Manueline architecture of Belém; the mosaics of the central Rossio square, and the multitude of Art Nouveau shops and cafés.

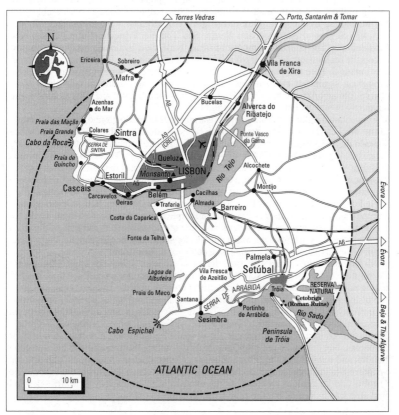

To Americans, San Francisco is an obvious counterpart: a city that exhibits parallels not only in its physical appearance but also in its fault-line location – Lisbon's Great Earthquake of 1755 levelled most of the old lower town. The two cities stand further comparison as Lisbon, too, is immediately likeable, gentler than any port or capital should expect to be, almost provincial in feel and defiantly human in pace and scale. For much of the present century, the city stood apart from the European mainstream, an isolation that ended abruptly with the 1974 Revolution, and still more so with Portugal's integration into the European Community (now the European Union) just over a decade later.

Over the past hundred years, central Lisbon's population has more than doubled to over a million, one tenth of all Portuguese, with numbers boosted considerably after the Revolution by the vast influx of **refugees** – *retornados* – from Portugal's former African colonies of Angola, Cabo Verde, São Tomé e Principe, Guinea-Bissau and Mozambique. The *retornados* imposed a heavy burden on an already strained economy, especially on housing, but their overall integration is one of the chief triumphs of modern Portugal. Like the city's Brazilian contingent, the Portuguese Africans have also brought a significant **cultural** buoyancy. Alongside the traditional fado clubs of its Bairro Alto and Alfama quarters, Lisbon now has superb Latin and African bands, and a panoply of international restaurants and bars.

Conventional sights and monuments are arguably thin on the ground, largely as a result of the 1755 earthquake. The Romanesque **Sé** (cathedral) and the Moorish walls of the **Castelo de São Jorge** are fine early survivors, though hardly unique in Portugal. But there is one building from Portugal's Golden Age – the extraordinary **Mosteiro dos Jerónimos** at Belém – that is the equal of any in the country. Two museums demand attention, too: the **Fundação Calouste Gulbenkian**, a combined museum and cultural complex with superb collections of ancient and modern art, and the **Museu Nacional de Arte Antiga**, effectively Portugal's national art gallery. The latest highlight, however, is the **Oceanarium** – Europe's largest – at the former Expo site of Parque das Nações. Beyond these sights, it's the central streets, avenues and squares, and their attendant comings and goings, that keep the interest level well topped up; watch out, too, for some adventurous contemporary architecture, such as Tómas Taveira's shopping complex at **Amoreiras**.

All of this makes for a city that demands at least a few days out of anyone's Portuguese itinerary. Better still, make the capital a base for a week or two's holiday, taking day-trips and excursions out into the surrounding area. The sea is close by, with the beach suburbs of **Estoril** and **Cascais** just half an hour's journey away to the west by train; while to the south, across the Tejo, are the miles of dunes along the **Costa da Caparica**. Slightly further south lies the port of **Setúbal**, featuring one of the earliest Manueline churches, and nearby is the resort of Sesimbra – a popular day-trip for Lisboetas. Northwest of the city, again easily reached by train, lie the lush wooded heights and royal palaces of **Sintra**, Byron's "glorious Eden". And should you develop an interest in Portuguese architecture, there are the Rococo delights of the **Palácio de Queluz** and its gardens en route, or the extraordinary monastery of **Mafra** – a good first step into Estremadura, the region immediately to the north.

LISBON

Physically, **LISBON** is an eighteenth-century city: elegant, open to the sea and carefully planned. The description does not extend to its modern expanse, of course – there are suburbs here as poor and inadequate as any in Europe – but remains accurate within the old central boundary of a triangle of hills. This "lower town", the **Baixa**, was the product of a single phase of building, carried out in less than a decade by the dictatorial minister, the Marquês de Pombal, in the wake of the earthquake that destroyed much of central Lisbon in 1755.

The **Great Earthquake**, which was felt as far away as Jamaica, struck Lisbon at 9.30am on November 1 (All Saints' Day) 1755, when most of the city's population was at Mass. Within the space of ten minutes there had been three major tremors and the candles of a hundred church altars had started fires that raged throughout the capital. A vast tidal wave swept the seafront, where refugees were seeking shelter, and, in all, 40,000 of the 270,000 population died. The destruction of the city shocked the continent, prompting Voltaire, who wrote an account of it in his novel *Candide*, into an intense debate with Rousseau on the operation of providence. For Portugal, and for the capital, it was a disaster that in retrospect seemed to seal an age. Previously, eighteenth-century Lisbon had been arguably the most active port in Europe.

Indeed, the city had been prosperous since **Roman**, perhaps even Phoenician, times. In the Middle Ages, as **Moorish** Lishbuna, it thrived on its wide links with the Arab world, while exploiting the rich territories of the Alentejo and Algarve to the south. The country's reconquest by the Christians in 1147 was an early and dubious triumph of the Crusades, its one positive aspect being the appearance of the first true Portuguese monarch **Afonso Henriques**. It was not until 1255, however, that Lisbon took over from Coimbra as capital.

Over the following centuries Lisbon was twice at the forefront of European development and trade, on a scale that is hard to envisage today. The first phase came with the great Portuguese **discoveries** of the late fifteenth and sixteenth centuries, such as Vasco da Gama's opening of the sea route to India. The second was in the opening decades of the **eighteenth century**, when the colonized Brazil was found to yield both gold and diamonds. These phases were the great ages of Portuguese patronage. The sixteenth century was dominated by the figure **Dom Manuel I**, under whom the flamboyant national architectural style known as Manueline developed. Lisbon takes its principal monuments – the tower and monastery at Belém – from this era. The eighteenth century, more extravagant but with less brilliant effect, gave centre stage to **Dom João V**, best known as the obsessive builder of Mafra, which he created in response to Philip II's El Escorial in Spain.

The city in the nineteenth and early twentieth centuries was more notable for its political upheavals – from the assassination of Carlos I in 1908 to the Revolution in 1974 – than for any architectural legacy, though the **Art Nouveau** movement made its mark on the capital. In the last two decades, however, Lisbon has once more echoed to the sounds of incoming money and reconstruction on a scale not seen for two hundred years. After the influx of EU cash for economic regeneration in the 1980s came the recognition of Lisbon as **European City of Culture** in 1994, with new arts facilities giving the city a higher European profile. Even more dramatic was **Expo** in 1998, when almost every monument was spruced up and a major new transport infrastructure put into place, including the construction of Europe's longest bridge, new rail and metro lines and a road network encircling the capital. If this activity helped in some ways to diminish the provincial feel of the city, it also injected a wave of excitement and optimism that has made Lisbon one of Europe's most happening cities.

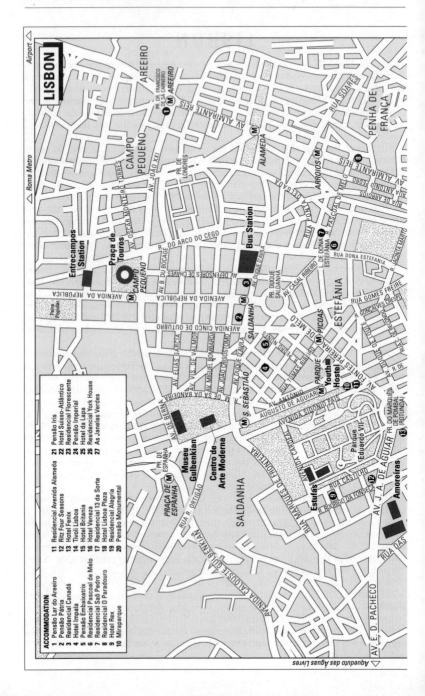

LISBON

△ Airport
△ Roma Metro

▽ Aqueduto das Águas Livres

ACCOMMODATION

1 Pensão Lar do Areeiro
2 Pensão Pátria
3 Residencial Canadá
4 Hotel Impala
5 Pensão Embaixatrix
6 Residencial Pascoal de Melo
7 Residencial São Pedro
8 Residencial O Paradouro
9 Hotel Rex
10 Miraparque
11 Residencial Avenida Alameda
12 Ritz Four Seasons
13 Hotel Fenix
14 Tivoli Lisboa
15 Hotel Britania
16 Hotel Veneza
17 Residencial 13 da Sorte
18 Hotel Lisboa Plaza
19 Residencial Alegria
20 Pensão Monumental
21 Pensão Iris
22 Hotel Suisso-Atlântico
23 Residencial Florescente
24 Pensão Imperial
25 Hotel da Lapa
26 Residencial York House
27 As Janelas Verdes

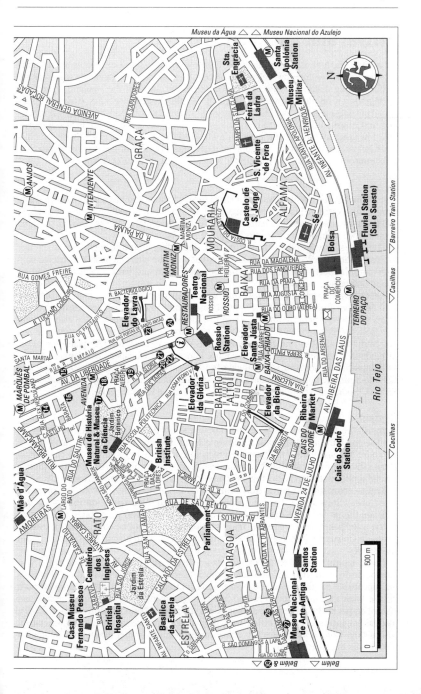

Arrival and information

On **arrival**, the first place to head for is Rossio, which is easily accessible from all points of arrival, either on foot, by metro, bus or taxi. Most of the city's pensions (*pensões*) are within walking distance of the square. On the eastern side of the adjoining Praça dos Restauradores on Rua Jardim do Regedor 50, the English-speaking **turismo** (daily 9am–1pm & 2–6pm; ☎213 433 672) can provide you with accommodation lists, bus timetables and **maps** of the city. You can arrange car rental here, too. There is also a tourist board in Restauradores in the Palácio da Foz (daily 9am–8pm; ☎213 463 314), which is more helpful in providing information on destinations outside of Lisbon. For **departure information**, by air, bus and train, refer to the relevant sections of "Listings".

By air

The **airport** is just twenty minutes north of the city centre and has a tourist office (daily 6am–1am), exchange bureau, exchange machines and an information desk that can help you find accommodation (see p.62). There are also car rental agencies at the airport, full details of which appear in "Listings" on p.109.

The easiest way into the centre is by **taxi**, depending on traffic conditions a journey to Rossio should cost 1500–2000$00. Note that you'll be charged 300$00 extra for baggage, and that fares are slightly higher between 10pm and 6am, at weekends and on public holidays.

Alternatively, catch the #91 **Aerobus**, which departs every twenty minutes between 7am and 9pm from outside the terminal, and runs to Praça do Marquês de Pombal, Praça dos Restauradores, Rossio, Praça do Comércio and Cais do Sodré train station. The **ticket**, which you buy from the driver, gives you one day's travel on the city's buses and trams for 450$00 (available free from the Welcome Desk for TAP passengers), or three days' for 1050$00 – see p.59 for more information. Cheaper **local buses** (#44 or #45) leave from the main road outside the terminal to Praça dos Restauradores and Cais do Sodré station every ten to fifteen minutes between 4am and 1.40am and cost 160$00, though these are less convenient if you have a lot of luggage.

By train

Long-distance trains from Coimbra, Porto and northern Portugal, as well as from Madrid and Paris, arrive at **Santa Apolónia train station** (☎218 884 142), from where it's about fifteen minutes' walk west to Praça do Comércio, or a short metro or bus ride (buses #9, #39, #46 or #90 for Praça dos Restauradores or Rossio). At the station there's a helpful information office (Mon–Sat 9am–7pm) and an exchange bureau.

Trains from the Algarve and south take a slightly more convoluted approach. The railway lines from the south terminate at the **Barreiro train station** (☎212 073 028), on the far bank of the river, from where you catch a ferry (included in the price of the train ticket) to the **Fluvial train station** (also known as Sul e Sueste), next to Praça do Comércio. Buses #9, #39, #80 and #90 run up from Fluvial to Rossio, through the Baixa.

Local trains – from Sintra or Queluz – emerge right in the heart of the city at **Rossio train station** (☎213 465 022), a mock-Manueline complex with train platforms an improbable escalator-ride above street-level entrances. The station is complete with shops, bank exchange counters and left-luggage cabins. Services from Cascais and Estoril arrive at the other local station, **Cais do Sodré train station** (☎213 470 181), also fairly central – you can either walk the half a kilometre east along the waterfront to Praça do Comércio or take any of the buses heading in that direction. The station also has its own metro stop.

By bus

Various bus companies have terminals scattered about the city, but the main terminal is at **Avenida João Crisóstomo** metro Saldanha; ☎213 545 775), north of the centre, which has an information office that can help with all bus arrival and departure details. This terminal is also where most **international bus services** arrive. You can usually buy tickets if you turn up half an hour or so in advance, though for the summer express services to the Algarve it's best to book a seat (through any travel agent), a day in advance. See "Listings" for other bus terminals in the city, and check with the turismo for the latest details.

By car

Driving into Lisbon can take years off your life, and if it's the beginning or end of a public holiday weekend should be avoided at all costs. Heading to or from the south on these occasions, it can take over an hour just to cross the Ponte 25 de Abril, a notorious traffic bottleneck that the new Vasco da Gama bridge has done little to alleviate. **Parking** is also very difficult in the centre. Pay-and-display bays get snapped up, and many unemployed people earn tips for guiding cars into any available space (give a tip – 50$00 is enough – to avoid finding any unpleasant scratches on your car when you return).

You'd be wise to head straight for an official **car park**: central locations include the underground one at Restauradores; Parque Eduardo VII; the underground car parks around the Gulbenkian such as Parking Berna on Rua Marquês de Sá da Bandeira; and the Amoreiras complex on Avenida Eng. Duarte Pacheco. Wherever you park, do not leave valuables inside as the break-in rate is extremely high.

If you are **renting a car** on arrival, for touring outside Lisbon, the best advice is to wait until the day you leave the city to pick it up; you really don't need your own transport to get around Lisbon. See "Listings" on p.109 for car rental companies if you remain undeterred, and remember to leave plenty of time if returning your car to the airport; bus transfers from the special car-rental car parks and paperwork is time-consuming.

City transport

Most places of interest are within easy walking distance of each other, but for those that are further away transport connections by tram, bus or metro are outlined in the relevant accounts. Taxis are among the cheapest in Europe and a useful complement at all hours. Although Lisbon ranks among one of the safer European cities it too has its share of **pickpockets**, so take special care over your belongings when using the metro and buses, and when walking around the main squares.

Apart from taxis and the metro, **public transport** in the city is operated by Carris (☎213 632 044). If you want to do some intensive sightseeing, it may be worth getting a **Lisboa Card** (1900$00 for one day, 3100$00 for two days or 4000$00 for three days), which entitles you to free bus and metro rides and entry to 25 museums, plus discounts of around 20 to 50 percent for other main sites. The card is available from the turismo on Rua Jardim do Regedor 50, the Mosteiro dos Jerónimos and the Museu Nacional de Arte Antiga. The **Passe Turístico** (1680$00 for four days, 2380$00 for seven days) might also be worth considering. It's valid on the metro, trams, buses and *elevadors*, and is obtainable, on production of a passport, at kiosks next to the Elevador Santa Justa, in Praça da Figueira and in Restauradores' metro station, among other places. Otherwise, just buy a ticket each time you ride: all the details are given below.

The metro and local trains

Lisbon's **metro** – the Metropolitano – was radically restructured for Expo 98 and is now the slickest way to reach outlying sights including the Gulbenkian museum, the zoo and the Oceanarium. The most central metro stations are those at Praça dos Restauradores and Rossio. The **hours of operation** are from 6.30am to 1am and **tickets** cost 100$00 per journey or 800$00 for a ten-ticket *caderneta* – sold at all stations. Consider buying a one-day pass (260$00) if you plan to make several journeys in one day.

There is a **local train** line originating from Cais do Sodré station, which runs west along the coast through Belém (see p.85), to Estoril (see p.112) and Cascais (see p.113). Tickets to Estoril and Cascais are currently 200$00 one way. The other local train line you're likely to use is the service to Queluz (see p.124; 175$00 one way) and Sintra (see p.116; 200$00 one way), which departs from the central Rossio station.

Trams, elevadors and buses

At the slightest excuse you should ride one of the city's **trams** (*eléctricos*). Ascending some of the steepest gradients of any city in the world, Lisbon's five tram routes are worth taking for the sheer pleasure of the ride alone. The best route is **#28**, which runs from Largo Martim Moniz to Prazeres, though the most interesting stretch is from São Vicente to the Estrela gardens, passing through Rua da Conceição in the Baixa – possibly the best public transport ride in the city. Other useful, and interesting, routes include the **#12** which circles the Castelo de S. Jorge via the Alfama, Praça da Figueira and Largo Martim Moniz; and the new modern "supertram" **#15** from Praça da Figueira to Algés via Belém. Tram **#18** runs from Rua da Alfândega via Praça do Comércio and Cais do Sodré to the Palácio da Ajuda; and the remaining route, **#25**, runs from Rua da Alfândega to Campo Ourique via Praça do Comércio, Cais do Sodré, Lapa and Estrela.

The three funicular railways and one street lift – each known as an **elevador** – are also exciting forms of transport and offer quick access up to Lisbon's highest hills and the Bairro Alto (see box below for their routes). Otherwise, **buses** (*autocarros*) run just about everywhere in the Lisbon area and can prove valuable for getting to and from the more outlying attractions. Most of the trams, buses and *elevadors* run every ten to fifteen minutes throughout the day, from around 6.30am to midnight: stops are indicated by a sign marked *paragem*, which carries route details.

Individual **tickets** for a bus, tram or *elevador* bought on board cost 160$00, although it is much cheaper to buy a ticket in advance from a kiosk as the same amount buys two journeys (or one trip over two transport zones, say out to Belém). There are also one-day (450$00) or three-day (1050$00) **passes** – also bought from kiosks – which you validate by punching in the machine beside the driver the first time you ride; it's then valid for 24 or 72 hours.

ELEVADORS

Elevador da Bica: funicular linking Calçada do Coimbro in Barrio Alto to Rua da Boavista near Cais do Sodré station.

Elevador da Glória: a funicular linking the Bairro Alto with the west side of Praça dos Restauradores.

Elevador de Santa Justa: a lift, rather than a funicular, taking you from Rua do Ouro, on the west side of the Baixa, up to a walkway by the ruined Carmo church; due to reopen shortly.

Elevador do Lavra: funicular linking Rua São José, just off Avda da Liberdade, to the back of the Institute of Medicine and Hospital de São José.

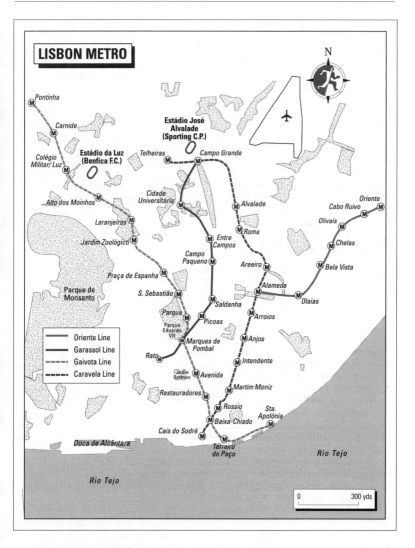

A couple of **tram and bus tours** run during the summer months, departing from Praça do Comércio; for more information see "Listings".

Taxis

Lisbon's cream or (older) black-and-green **taxis** are inexpensive, so long as your destination is within the city limits; there's a minimum charge of 250$00 and an average ride will run to around 600$00. Fares are higher from 10pm to 6am, at weekends and on public holidays. All taxis have meters, which should be switched on, and tips are not expected. A green light means the cab is occupied. They can be found quite easily by day at the **ranks** in Rossio and Praça da Figueira, at the southern end of Avenida da Liberdade, by Fluvial and Cais do Sodré. At night, however, when going home from a bar or restaurant, it's usually best to **phone** (which entails an extra charge of 150$00): try Rádio Taxis (☎218 155 061), Autocoope (☎217 932 756) or Teletaxi (☎218 152 076).

Ferries

Finally there are the **ferries**, which cross the Tejo at various points and are worth taking for the terrific views of Lisbon alone. From **Praça do Comércio** (Fluvial), there are crossings to Cacilhas (daily 6am–10.30pm; 105$00, one way), Barreiro (daily 6am–10.30pm; 200$00, one way) and Montijo (daily 6am–10.30pm; 300$00). From **Cais do Sodré**, ferries also cross to Cacilhas (24-hour service, every 20–30min during day, 40–50min at night; 105$00, one way). From **Belém** there are services to Trafaria (Mon–Sat 6.30am–11.30pm, Sun 7.30am–11.30pm, every 30 min–1hr; 150$00, one way), from where you can catch buses to Caparica.

Accommodation

The **airport information desk**, facing you as you pass through customs, or any of the turismos in town will establish whether or not there's space at a city *pensão* or hotel, they won't reserve the room for you but will supply telephone numbers if you want to phone yourself. For more information on the various types of accommodation available see "Basics" p.32.

Lisbon has scores of small, inexpensive **pensões**, often in tall tenement buildings, in all the central parts of the city. The most obvious and accessible areas, with dozens of possibilities, are around Rossio, Praça dos Restauradores and Praça da Figueira. Among cheaper *pensões*, the most likely to have space during busy times of the year are those on streets parallel to Avenida da Liberdade, such as Rua das Portas de Santo Antão and Rua da Glória. The Baixa grid, to the south, has a fair selection of places, too, with a couple of more upmarket choices in the Chiado's shopping streets. Bairro Alto is the best place to stay to be in the thick of the nightlife, though rooms in its few *pensões* can be both hard to come by and noisy. If you want to stay in the most atmospheric part of town there are a few attractive places on the periphery of the Alfama, climbing up towards the castle. Finally, a number of more expensive places are located outside of the historic centre: in the prosperous streets in the suburb of Lapa; around Parque Eduardo VII and Saldanha, where many places are geared to the business traveller; or to the east, towards the airport, in the area around Avenida Almirante Reis – in particular the streets between Anjos and Arroios metro stops.

When doing the rounds, be warned that the *pensões* tend to be on upper storeys (leaving one person with all your bags is a good idea if you're in company). **Addresses** – written below as 53-3° and so on – refer to the street number followed by the storey number. Don't be unduly put off by some fairly insalubrious staircases, but do be aware that rooms facing onto the street can be unbearably noisy.

METRO STOPS

Metro stops are given in these reviews only when they are the most convenient way to reach the hotel, restaurant or bar. Otherwise, for places that are central, taking a bus or one of the *elevadors*, or walking, is probably the best option.

At Easter, and even more so in midsummer, room **availability** is often stretched to the limit, with artificially inflated prices. At these times, be prepared to take anything vacant – within reason – and, if need be, look around the next day for somewhere better, or possibly cheaper. Fortunately, for most of the year you should have little difficulty finding a room, and can even try knocking the price down at quieter times, especially if you're able to summon up a few good-natured phrases in Portuguese.

Lisbon has two **youth hostels**, one in the city centre and one out at Oeiras, overlooking the sea. For details of these, and the city's **camping** possibilities, see p.67.

Rossio and Praça da Figueira
All the hotels and pensões listed below are marked on the Baixa map on p.69.

Pensão Arco da Bandeira, Rua dos Sapateiros 226-4° (☎213 423 478). Friendly pension with half a dozen comfortable rooms, some overlooking Rossio. The separate bathrooms are spotless. The entrance is just through the arch at the southern end of the square. ③.

Hotel Avenida Palace, Rua 1° de Dezembro (☎213 460 151, fax 213 422 884). Lisbon's grandest downtown hotel, tucked away between Rossio and Praça dos Restauradores. Elegant nineteenth-century style, recently renovated, and very comfortable rooms sporting high ceilings, traditional furnishings and marble bathrooms. ⑦.

Pensão Beira Minho, Praça da Figueira 6-2° (☎213 461 846). Rooms (with and without bath) are small but clean and some have fine views, though the cheaper ones without windows may dissuade some. There are rooms on the fourth floor, too. ④.

Pensão Coimbra e Madrid, Praça da Figueira 3-3° (☎213 421 760, fax 213 423 264). Large, decently run (if faintly shabby) *pensão*, above the *Pastelaria Suíça*. Superb views of Rossio, Praça da Figueira and the castle beyond from – street-honkingly noisy – front-facing rooms, which come with shower or bath. Best choice on the square. Breakfast included. ④.

Pensão Estação Central, Calçada do Carmo 17-2° (☎213 423 308). To the side of Rossio station; climb the flight of stairs and head up the road to the left. Small, musty rooms, some with cubby-hole bathrooms, but you get what you pay for. ②.

Pensão Ibérica, Praça da Figueira 10-2° (☎218 867 026). Central location and lots of rooms, most with TVs, but it's a bit ramshackle and has gloomy, uninspiring decor. The rooms overlooking the Praça are the best, if the noisiest. There's a breakfast room and a 24hr reception for those planning a late night out. ③.

Hotel International, Rua da Betesga 3 (☎213 466 401, fax 213 478 635). You know this is a smart central choice as soon as you see the red-carpeted lift, and if you get one of the rooms with a balcony overlooking the town, you won't be disappointed. Rooms have air-conditioning, TV and a safe. ⑤.

Hotel Metrópole, Rossio 30 (☎213 469 164, fax 213 469 166). Comfortable rooms in historic building overlooking Rossio with airy lounge bar; buffet breakfast included in the price ⑤.

Hotel Mundial, Rua Dom Duarte 4 (☎218 863 101, fax 218 879 129). Central four-star hotel with nearly 300 plush rooms. Rooftop pool, restaurant, disabled access and all mod cons. Buffet breakfast included. ⑤.

Hotel Portugal, Rua João das Regras 4 (☎218 877 581, fax 218 867 343). An amazing old hotel that has suffered from an appalling conversion; the high decorative ceilings upstairs have been chopped up under wall partitions. For all that, there are comfortable rooms, a lovely ornate TV room and fine *azulejo*-lined stairs. ④.

Residencial do Sul, Praça Dom Pedro IV 59 (☎213 422 511, fax 218 132 697). Entered through a small shop, this is very close to the station, and a good first choice if you want a view of Rossio itself. It's very clean and there are quieter back rooms, though some are windowless. ②.

The Baixa and Chiado
All the hotels and pensões listed below are marked on the Baixa map on p.69.

Hotel Borges, Rua Garrett 108 (☎213 461 951, fax 213 426 617). Nice position near the *Brasileira* café in Chiado's main street, though the rooms are very ordinary and the hotel itself often filled with tour groups. Breakfast included. ④.

Hotel Duas Nações, Rua da Vitória 41 (☎213 460 710, fax 213 470 206). Classy, pleasantly faded, nineteenth-century hotel in the Baixa grid with a secure entrance and friendly reception. Rooms with bath are more attractive but cost quite a bit more.③.

Pensão Galicia, Rua do Crucifixo 50-4° (☎213 428 430). The entrance is through a shoe repair stall, which you may be in need of once you've been up and down the steep stairs a few times. Small rooms – the best have sunny balconies and wooden floors – but surly owners and dodgy drains. ②.

Residencial Insulana, Rua da Assunção 52 (☎ and fax 213 427 625). Reached by a series of underwear shops, this has smart rooms, each with its own bath. The bar overlooks a quiet pedestrianized street. English-speaking staff. Good breakfasts, too. ③

Pensão Moderna, Rua dos Correeiros 205-4° (☎213 460 818). The stairwell is offputting but rooms are big, clean and crammed with old furniture. Some have (rickety) balconies overlooking the pedestrianized street. Communal bathrooms. ②.

Residencial Nova Silva, Rua Vítor Cordon 11 (☎213 424 371, fax 213 427 770). A clean, friendly option, which is also good value. Make sure you get a back room, ideally on the top floor, for a stunning view over the Tejo. ②.

Pensão Prata, Rua da Prata 71-3° (☎213 468 908). You need mountaineering experience to climb the stairs to this place, which offers small rooms in a welcoming, family-run apartment with TV lounge. Some rooms have showers, others share a clean bathroom. It's in a handy location for Praça do Comércio. Book in advance as it's popular. ②.

Bairro Alto and Principe Real

All the pensões listed below are marked on the Bairro Alto map on p.72.

Residencial Camões, Trav. do Poço da Cidade 38-1° (☎213 467 510, fax 213 464 048). Small, pretty rooms, some with balcony and the more expensive ones with private bathroom. Situated right in the midst of the Bairro Alto action (which can up the noise level). Breakfast is served in a nice, light room. ②–③.

Casa de São Mamede, Rua da Escola Politécnica 159 (☎213 963 166, fax 213 951 896). Superb seventeenth-century town house with period fittings, bright breakfast room and even a grand stained-glass window. Rooms are rather ordinary but come with private bathrooms and TVs. ⑤.

Pensão Duque, Calçada do Duque 53, (☎/fax 213 463 444). Near São Roque church, down the steps off the square. Fairly basic rooms with separate bathrooms. ②.

Pensão Globo, Rua do Teixeira 37 (☎213 462 279). Up Travessa da Cara from the Elevador da Glória and first right. Located in an attractive house, the rooms are simple but clean and reasonably large (though those at the top are a little cramped). It's in a good location, near the clubs but in a quiet street. Cheaper rooms are without shower or windows, more expensive ones have showers and views. ②–③.

Pensão Londres, Rua Dom Pedro V 53 (☎213 465 523). Great old building with high ceilings and pleasant enough rooms spread across several price ranges and floors. Some rooms come with cubby-hole bathrooms. Breakfast included. ③.

Pensão Luar, Rua das Gaveas 101-1° (☎213 460 949). Calm, polished interior and decently furnished rooms (with and without shower), which are somewhat noisy. Some are much larger than others, so ask to see. ③.

Hotel Principe Real, Rua da Alegria 53. (☎213 460 116, fax 213 422 104.) Four-star hotel reached via steps off Praça Principe Real, in a characterful street by the lower entrance to the botanical gardens. Small but comfortable rooms with balconies, though the only decent views are from the rooftop restaurant, which is open to non-residents. ⑥.

Lapa

To reach these superb hotels (marked on the general map of Lisbon on p.56), take bus #40 or #60 from Praça do Comércio. Booking in advance is recommended.

As Janelas Verdes, Rua das Janelas Verdes 47, Lapa (☎213 968 143, fax 213 968 144, *heritage.hotels@mail.telepac.pt*). This discreet eighteenth-century town house, where novelist Eça de Queiróz wrote *Os Maios*, is just metres from the Museu Nacional de Arte Antiga. Well-proportioned rooms with marble-clad bathrooms, period furnishings, and a delightful walled garden with a small fountain. Top-floor rooms have river views. Breakfast is served in the garden. ⑦.

Hotel da Lapa, Rua do Pau de Bandeira 4 (☎213 950 005, fax 213 950 665, *reservas@hotelapa.com*). A stunning nineteenth-century mansion with dramatic vistas over the Tejo. Rooms are luxurious, particularly within the Palace Wing, where stylish rooms are themed from Classical to Art Deco. In summer, grills are served in the gardens by the outside pool. Disabled access ⑨.

Residencial York House, Rua das Janelas Verdes 32 (☎213 962 435, fax 213 972 793). Installed in a sixteenth-century convent, rooms come with rugs, tiles and four-poster beds. The best rooms are grouped around a beautiful interior courtyard, where drinks and meals are served in summer. The restaurant is highly rated and is also open to non-residents. ⑧.

Alfama and Castelo

All the hotels and pensões listed below are marked on the Alfama and Castelo map on p.76.

Pensão Beira-Mar, Largo do Terreiro do Trigo 16 (☎ 218 871 528). A 10min walk east of Praça do Comércio, at the foot of the Alfama. Reasonable top-floor rooms (communal showers and toilets), some with balcony facing the main street and others with bathrooms but no windows. ③.

Pensão Ninho das Águias, Costa do Castelo 74 (☎218 867 000). Beautifully sited in its own view-laden terrace-garden on the street looping around the castle. Climb up the staircase and past the bird cages. Rooms are bright, white and light; management capricious. Book in advance. ⑥.

Pensão São João de Praça, Rua de São João de Praça 97-2° (☎ 218 862 591, fax 218 881 378). Located immediately below the cathedral in a beautiful town house with street-facing balconies. It's a clean, quiet and friendly choice. Rooms vary from en-suite to sharing a shower. Dinner can be provided. ②.

Sé Guest House, Rua São João de Praça 97-1° (☎218 864 400, fax 063 271 612). In the same building as the *Pensão São João de Praça*. Wood floors and bright, airy rooms, but communal bathrooms. ③.

Albergaria Senhora do Monte, Calçada do Monte 39 (☎218 866 002, fax 218 877 783). Comfortable, modern hotel in a beautiful location, close to Largo da Graça, with lovely views of the castle and Graça convent from its south-facing rooms – the more expensive rooms have terraces. Breakfast is included. Parking available or tram #28 passes close by. ⑥–⑦.

Avenida da Liberdade, Restauradores and Rua das Portas de Santo Antão

All the hotels and pensões listed below are marked on the general map of Lisbon on p.56.

Residencial 13 da Sorte, Rua do Salitre 13 (☎ /fax 213 531 851). Translates as 'lucky 13', it's certainly an attractive option in a good location. Rooms have TVs and bathrooms, but book ahead as it is often full. ③.

Residencial Alegria, Praça Alegria 12 (☎213 475 522, fax 213 478 070); metro Avenida. Great position, facing the leafy square, with spacious, spotless rooms with TVs. Those with bath are more expensive than shower-only rooms. ②.

Hotel Britania, Rua Rodrigues Sampaio 17 (☎213 155 016, fax 213 155 021, *heritage.hotels@mail.telepac.pt*); metro Avenida. A smart three-star hotel, just to the east of the Avenida, with good-sized rooms and classic 1940s' Deco interior designed by Cassiano Branco. Buffet breakfast included. Children under 12 stay free. ⑥.

Residencial Florescente, Rua das Portas de Santo Antão 99 (☎213 426 609, fax 213 427 733). One of this pedestrianized street's best-value establishments, whose best rooms are spick-and-span and come with TV and small bathroom (others are windowless and less appealing). Breakfast not included. ③.

Pensão Imperial, Praça dos Restauradores 78-4° (☎213 420 166). This *pensão* has a fine blue-tiled facade and is situated in a sunny position at the bottom of the avenue (by Rua Jardim Regedor). Enter through an optician's and climb to the top floor for small rooms, some with showers and a view up the avenue. ②.

Pensão Iris, Rua da Glória 2a-1° (☎213 423 157). Extremely off-putting entrance but has English-speaking proprietors and large, clean, if shabby rooms (triples available), some have showers and a couple overlook the main avenue. The ones at the side are a bit too close to the clanking street funicular for comfort. ②.

Hotel Lisboa Plaza, Trav. Salitre 7 (☎213 463 922, fax 213 471 630, *heritage.hotels@mail.telepac.pt*); metro Avenida. Just off the Avenida, and in front of a theatre park, this bright, polished, four-star hotel has marble bathrooms, bar, restaurant and botanical garden views from rear rooms. Good breakfast included. Disabled access. ⑦.

Pensão Monumental, Rua da Glória 21 (☎213 469 807, fax 213 430 213). A backpackers' favourite with a mixed bag of rooms in a rambling old building; the hot water supply is a little erratic, but it's handy if you fancy a night out at the *Ritz Club* up the road. ③.

Hotel Suisso-Atlântico, Rua da Glória 3–19 (☎213 461 713, fax 213 469 013). Tucked around the corner from the *elevador*, just off the Avenida, this is a clean and modern hotel in a central location. Standard mid-range accommodation; rooms with shower and and some with a balcony overlooking the seedy Rua da Glória. The intriguing mock-baronial bar is the best bit. ④.

Hotel Veneza, Avda da Liberdade 189 (☎213 522 618, fax 213 526 678); metro Avenida. Tastefully converted town house with period furniture and plush rooms, each with a mini bar and en-suite bathroom. ⑥.

Tivoli Lisboa, Av. da Liberdade 185 (☎213 198 900, fax 213 198 900, *htlisboa@mail.telepac.pt*); metro Avenida. Flash hotel with cavernous lobby-lounge. Three hundred sound proofed rooms, outdoor pool, tennis courts, garden and a top-floor grill-restaurant with superb city views. Breakfast included. Disabled access. ⑨.

Praça Marquês de Pombal to Saldanha

All the hotels and pensões listed below are marked on the general map of Lisbon on p.56.

Residencial Avenida Alameda, Sidónio Pais 4 (☎213 532 186, fax 213 526 703); metro Parque or Rotunda. Very pleasant three-star *pensão* with air-con rooms, all with bath and park views. Breakfast included. ④.

Residencial Canadá, Av. Defensores de Chaves 35-1–4° (☎213 521 455, fax 213 542 922); metro Saldanha. Excellent value for money, largish, airy rooms with private bathrooms (and satellite TV). Sunny breakfast room and lounge area. Very handy for bus station. ④.

Pensão Embaixatrix, Rua Pedro Nunes 45-2° (☎213 531 029); metro Picoas. Welcoming management make this a perennially popular place. Hardly luxurious but inexpensive (even less for a room with a shower instead of a bath), clean and respectable. ②.

Hotel Fenix, Praça do Marquês de Pombal 8 (☎213 862 121, fax 213 860 131, *h@fenixip.pt*); metro Marquês de Pombal. Large four-star hotel on the Rotunda, with double-glazed rooms to keep out the noise. Popular with tour groups, some rooms overlook Rotunda or the park. ⑥.

Hotel Impala, Rua Filipe Folque 49 (☎213 148 914, fax 213 575 362); metro Picoas. Interesting choice if you want a longer Lisbon stay, offering small and simple apartments for one, two or three people. *Pensão*-standard bedrooms attached to small kitchen/living rooms with TVs. There are also laundry facilities. ④.

Miraparque, Av. Sidónio Pais (☎213 524 286, fax 213 578 920, *miraparque@isoterica.pt*); metro Marquês de Pombal or Parque. An attractive building with a traditional feel overlooking Parque Eduardo VII. The reception can be a bit brusque, but there's a decent bar and restaurant. All rooms come with TV. ⑤.

Pensão Pátria, Av. Duque d'Ávila 42-5–6° (☎213 150 620, fax 213 578 310); metro Saldanha. Situated close to the main bus station; plenty of nice little rooms with clean bathrooms in a cheerful establishment. Some rooms with rooftop views, others with small, glassed-in verandahs. ②.

Hotel Rex, Rua Castilho 169 (☎213 882 161, fax 213 887 581, *rex@rex.pt*); metro Marquês de Pombal. Modern hotel with good facilities; best are the front rooms with large balconies overlooking Parque Eduardo VII. ⑥.

Ritz Four Seasons, Rua Rodrigo da Fonseca 88 (☎213 832 020, fax 213 831 783, *ritzfourseasons@mail.telepac.pt*); metro Marquês de Pombal. On the west side of Parque Eduardo VII, this vast modern block is one of the grandest – and most expensive – hotels in Lisbon. Huge airy rooms, terraces overlooking the park, and public areas replete with marble, antiques, old masters and overly attentive staff. The restaurant is highly regarded. ⑨.

Around Avenida Almirante Reis

All the hotels and pensões listed below are marked on the general map of Lisbon on p.56

Pensão Lar do Areeiro, Praça Dr. Francisco de Sá Carneiro 4-1° (☎ 218 493 150, fax 218 406 321); metro Areeiro. Respectable, old-fashioned, and well-run *pensão*, whose rooms all come with a bath. It's right on the Praça, which means it's noisy; ask for a room at the back. Breakfast included. ③.

Residencial O Paradouro, Av. Almirante Reis 106-7° (☎218 153 256, fax 218 155 445); metro Arroios. Smart, English-speaking establishment in a residential neighbourhood, opposite the fine *Portugalia* restaurant. All rooms with TV, some with balconies. Breakfast included. ③.

Residencial Pascoal de Melo, Rua Pascoal de Melo 127–131 (☎213 577 639, fax 213 144 555); metro Arroios or Saldanha. Spotless and airy, this three-star *residencial* is characterful, with an *azulejo*-lined entry hall. Rooms have bathrooms, TVs and balconies. ②.

Residencial São Pedro, Rua Pascoal de Melo 130. (☎213 578 765, fax 213 578 865); metro Arroios or Saldanha. Lots of dark wood and heavy furniture gives this a rather sombre feel, but rooms are clean and comfortable. ③.

Youth Hostels

Pousada de Juventude de Catalazete, Estrada Marginal, Oeiras (☎214 430 638). A small attractive hostel, overlooking the beach at Oeiras, between Belém and Cascais. To reach it take any train from Cais do Sodré, followed by a taxi from Oeiras station (or it's a 2km walk), or alternatively bus #44 from the airport. Reception is open from 6pm to 11pm; midnight curfew. Phone before setting out. Pleasant double rooms are ②, dorm beds from 1500$00.

Pousada de Juventude de Lisboa, Rua Andrade Corvo 46 (☎213 532 696), metro Picoas. This is the main city hostel, with 200 beds, good facilities and no curfew; reception is open at all times. There are doubles as well as hostel beds. The price includes breakfast; lunch and dinner are served at bargain prices. Dorm beds from 2900$00; doubles ②.

Campsites

Parque Municipal de Campismo, Parque Florestal de Monsanto (☎217 609 620). The main city campsite – well-equipped with a swimming pool and shops – is 6km west of the city centre, though buses run every 15min or so. The entrance is on Estrada da Circunvalação on the park's west side. Either take a train from Cais do Sodré to Algés, then bus #50 to the campsite; or bus #43 from Praça da Figueira or Belém. Take care in the park after dark.

Costa da Caparica, There are several small and lively campsites here, 30–50min away by bus from the Praça de Espanha terminal, or by ferry from Cais do Sodré to Cacilhas and then local bus on from there. See p.127.

Guincho. Attractive Orbitur campsite set among pine trees close to Guincho beach, just up from Cascais (see p.116). The well-equipped site also has bungalows and caravans for hire.

The City

Eighteenth-century prints show a pre-quake Lisbon of tremendous opulence and mystique, its skyline characterized by towers, palaces and convents. There are glimpses of this still – the old Moorish hillside of Alfama survived the destruction, as did Belém – but these are isolated neighbourhoods and monuments. It is instead Pombal's perfect Neoclassical grid that covers the centre. Giving orders, following the earthquake, to "Bury the dead, feed the living and close the ports", the king's minister followed his success in restoring order to the city with a complete rebuilding. The **Baixa** – still the heart of the modern city – was rebuilt according to Pombal's strict ideals of simplicity and economy; individual streets were assigned to each craft and trade and the whole enterprise was shaped by public buildings and squares.

One of the legacies of this visionary town planning is a city centre in which it could hardly be easier to get your bearings. At the Baixa's southern end, opening onto the Rio Tejo, is the broad, arcaded **Praça do Comércio** (also known as Terreiro do Paço), with its ferry stations for crossing the river, tram terminus for Belém, and grand triumphal arch. At the Baixa's northern end – linked to the Praça do Comércio by almost any street you care to take – stands Praça Dom Pedro IV, popularly known as **Rossio**, the main square since medieval times and the only part of the rebuilt city to remain in its original place, slightly off-centre in the symmetrical design. Rossio merges with

Praça da Figueira and **Praça dos Restauradores** and it is these squares, filled with cafés and lively with buskers, business people, and streetwise hawkers and dealers, that form the hub of Lisbon's daily activity. At night the focus shifts to the **Bairro Alto**, high above and to the west of the Baixa, and best reached by funicular (the Elevador da Glória) or by the great street elevator, the Elevador de Santa Justa. Between the two districts, halfway up the hill, **Chiado** is Lisbon's most elegant shopping area, largely rebuilt after being severely damaged in the fire that swept through the Baixa in 1988. East of the Baixa, the **Castelo de São Jorge**, a brooding landmark, surmounts a still taller hill, with the **Alfama** district – the oldest, most fascinating part of the city with its winding lanes and anarchic stairways – sprawled below.

From Rossio, the main, tree-lined **Avenida da Liberdade** runs north to the city's central park, **Parque Eduardo VII**, beyond which spreads the rest of the modern city: the **Gulbenkian** museum is to the north; the **Amoreiras** shopping complex to the west; and mundane shopping streets to the east. No stay in Lisbon should neglect the futuristic **Oceanarium** in the Parque das Nações, 5km to the east, or the waterfront suburb of **Belém**, 6km to the west, which is dominated by one of the country's grandest monuments, the **Jerónimos** monastery. En route to Belém lies Lisbon's other main museum, the **Museu de Arte Antiga.**

However, it should be remembered that Lisbon's contemporary interest lies as much in the everyday aspects of the city as in any specific sights. The cafés, markets, trams, ferries across the Tejo: all these are sufficient stimulation for random wanderings; the most rewarding areas being, as you'd expect, the oldest – the aforementioned lower and upper towns of Baixa and Bairro Alto, and the Alfama district.

The Baixa

The lower town – the **Baixa** – is very much the heart of the capital, housing many of the country's administrative departments, banks and business offices. Europe's first great example of Neoclassical design and urban planning, it remains an imposing quarter of rod-straight streets, cobbled underfoot and much of it given over to pedestrians, street performers and pavement artists. This area was also the site of Lisbon's first settlers; building work on the Banco Comercial Português at Rua dos Correeiros 21 revealed Roman walls and a mosaic floor, which can be viewed from the tiny **Núcleo Arqueológico** museum (tours Thurs 3–5pm & Sat 10am–noon, 3–5pm, max 15 people; free). A major appeal of the Baixa is the survival of tradition. Many of the streets in the grid maintain their crafts and businesses as Pombal devised: in Rua da Prata (Silversmiths' Street), Rua dos Sapateiros (Cobblers' Street), Rua do Ouro (Goldsmiths' Street), Rua do Comércio (Commercial Street). These, along with the mosaic-sidewalked squares, are a visual delight, with tiled Art Deco shopfronts and elaborately decorated *pastelarias* still surviving here and there. Note, too, that in the upper reaches of the Baixa, from the western end of Rua de Santa Justa, the restored **Elevador de Santa Justa** (see p.72) provides easy access to the Bairro Alto; its upper exit should reopen once work on the new metro lines is complete.

At the southern, waterfront end of the Baixa, the **Praça do Comércio** was the climax to Pombal's design, surrounded by classical buildings and centred on an exuberant bronze of Dom José – the reigning monarch during the earthquake and the capital's rebuilding. The metro station is named **Terreiro do Paço**, after the original royal palace that once stood here (its steps still lead up from the Tejo). Ironically, Portugal's royals came to a sticky end in the Praça; in 1908, alongside what was then the Central Post Office, King Carlos I and his eldest son were shot and killed, clearing the way for the declaration of the Republic two years later. Plans are currently afoot to pedestrianize the area between the river and the Baixa, sinking road traffic into a tunnel next to the metro station; which would free this elegant space to host cultural and political functions once more; however, it is unlikely to occur much before 2010. At present the

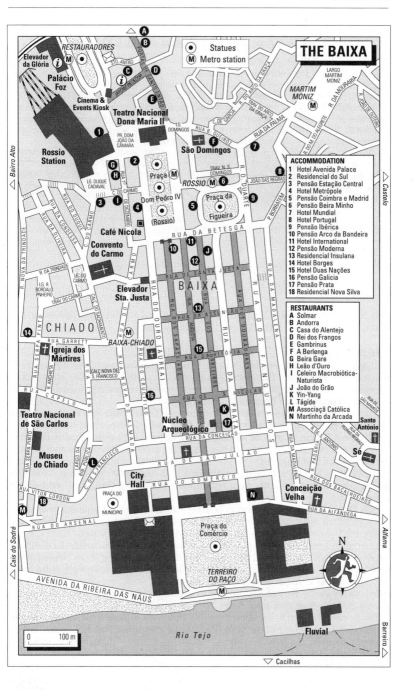

THE BAIXA

● Statues
Ⓜ Metro station

ACCOMMODATION
1 Hotel Avenida Palace
2 Residencial do Sul
3 Pensão Estação Central
4 Hotel Metrópole
5 Pensão Coimbra e Madrid
6 Pensão Beira Minho
7 Hotel Mundial
8 Hotel Portugal
9 Pensão Ibérica
10 Pensão Arco da Bandeira
11 Hotel International
12 Pensão Moderna
13 Residencial Insulana
14 Hotel Borges
15 Hotel Duas Nações
16 Pensão Galicia
17 Pensão Prata
18 Residencial Nova Silva

RESTAURANTS
A Solmar
B Andorra
C Casa do Alentejo
D Rei dos Frangos
E Gambrinus
F A Berlenga
G Beira Gare
H Leão d'Ouro
I Celeiro Macrobiótica-Naturista
J João do Grão
K Yin-Yang
L Tágide
M Associaçã Católica
N Martinho da Arcada

DEVELOPMENT AND DESTRUCTION

In recent years Lisbon has experienced some of the most radical **redevelopment** since the Marquês de Pombal rebuilt the shattered capital after the 1755 earthquake. This phase began with Portugal's relative economic stability – and extensive grants – in the wake of joining the European Community in 1986, when foreign investment poured into the capital. The building boom accelerated in preparation for Expo 98, which saw further chunks of old Lisbon disappearing under new transport links while tramlines were removed to provide space for faster roads. Ironically, it is beyond Pombal's statue at Rotunda that most of the redevelopment work is being done.

Meanwhile, complicated **rent laws** have meant that landlords get insufficient income to maintain properties, making the option of selling up to property developers a tempting one. As a result, many of the city's beautiful pre-war mansions and tenement buildings are either in a state of decay, or have been demolished to make way for office buildings – while new property in Lisbon is some of the most expensive in Europe.

But not all of old Lisbon is lost and at least the **city centre** retains its elegance. EU funding continues to help with the restoration work of many historic buildings, including Lisbon's oldest quarter, the **Alfama**. However, the most obvious sign of renovation is in the streets of the **Chiado**, burned out in the 1988 fire and now beautifully restored to their original design.

---

only refreshment spot on the square is the old-world café of *Martinho da Arcada*, one of the poet Pessoa's old haunts.

Rossio and around

Perhaps the most interesting places in the Baixa are the squares, of which **Rossio** – at the northern end of the Baixa grid – is the liveliest. The square itself is modest in appearance, but very much a focus for the city, sporting several atmospheric and popular cafés, most of which have outdoor seating.

The square's single concession to grandeur is the **Teatro Nacional de Dona Maria II**, built along the north side in the 1840s. Here, prior to the earthquake, stood the Inquisitional Palace, in front of which public hangings, *autos-da-fé* (ritual burnings of heretics) and even bullfights used to take place. The nineteenth-century statue atop the central column is of Dom Pedro IV (after whom the square is officially named), though curiously it's a bargain adaptation: cast originally as Maximilian of Mexico, it just happened to be in Lisbon en route from France when news came through of Maximilian's assassination.

São Domingos church, immediately to the east in Largo São Domingos, was where the Inquisition read out its sentences. It was blackened and gutted by a fire in the 1950s, but has now been fully restored. The road and square outside the church, at the bottom of Rua das Portas de Santo Antão, is a popular meeting place – the local African population hangs out on the street corner; businessmen get their shoes cleaned at the rank of little metal booths; and Lisbon's lowlife frequent the various **ginginha bars**, which specialize in lethal measures of cherry brandy. Resist the urge to eat the proffered cherry itself – they've been soaked in alcohol for years and provide a kick usually only available from expensive drugs.

South, past the church, the street runs into **Praça da Figueira**, the square adjacent to Rossio. It contains one of the main city bus and tram stops, and, like Rossio, is centred on a fountain and lined with shops, though there is less through traffic making it an altogether more relaxing spot to enjoy the cafés with outdoor seating.

Chiado

On the west side of the Baixa, stretching up the hillside towards the Bairro Alto, the area known as **Chiado** – the nom de plume of the poet António Ribeiro – suffered great damage from a fire that swept across the Baixa in August 1988. It destroyed all but the facade of the Grandella department store and many old shops in Rua do Crucifixo, though most buildings are now fully restored. Restoration is very much in keeping with the Chiado's traditions; new, soaring marble facades consciously mimic those destroyed in the fire, though they now shelter designer shops and the new Baixa-Chiado metro station.

Chiado remains one of the city's most affluent quarters, focused on the fashionable shops and old café-tearooms of the Rua Garrett. Of these, **A Brasileira**, Rua Garrett 120, is the most famous, having been frequented by generations of Lisbon's literary and intellectual leaders – the very readable Eça de Queiroz and Portugal's greatest twentieth-century poet, Fernando Pessoa (see box on p.75), among them. While on Rua Garrett, take a stroll past **Igreja dos Mártires** (Church of the Martyrs), which occupies the site of the Crusader camp during the Siege of Lisbon. As its name suggests, the church was built on the site of a burial ground, created for the English contingent of the besieging army. Music recitals are often held in the church; check the local press for details.

Just beyond, Rua Serpa Pinto veers steeply downhill to the **Museu do Chiado** (Wed–Sun 10am–6pm, Tues 2–6pm; 400$00). Opened in 1994, this stylish building, with a pleasant courtyard café and rooftop terrace, incorporates the former Museum of Contemporary Art, whose original home was damaged in the Chiado fire. The new museum was constructed around a nineteenth-century biscuit factory, which explains the presence of the old ovens. The three floors display the work of some of Portugal's most influential artists since the nineteenth century. Highlights include the beautiful sculpture *A Viúva* (The Widow) by **António Teixeira Lopes** and some evocative Lisbon area scenes by Carlos Botelho and José Malhoa. Look out also for the wonderful decorative panels by **José de Almada Negreiros**, recovered from the San Carlos cinema. There is also a small collection of French sculpture, including Rodin's *The Bronze Age*.

Around Cais do Sodré

Ten minutes' walk west of the Baixa grid, along the riverfront or the parallel **Rua do Arsenal** (a road packed with shops selling dried cod, cheap wines, port and brandies) is **Cais do Sodré** station, from where trains run out to Estoril and Cascais, and ferries cross to Cacilhas. It's not the most elegant, or inviting, of areas, but its various **markets** are wonderful, particularly the informal **fish market** (Mon–Sat) behind the station, which starts at dawn. Here you can still see *varinas*, fishwives from Alfama, who were joined a few years ago by groups from Cabo Verde, bargaining for and carting off great baskets of wares on their heads.

Take a look inside the **Ribeira market**, too, located in the domed building on Avda 24 de Julho, just beyond Cais do Sodré. Even if you're not tempted by the food – least of all perhaps by the gruesome slabs of flesh and innards – the fruit, flower, spice and vegetable displays on the upper storey are impressive.

A short walk behind the market, with its entrance on Rua de São Paulo, is the precipitous **Elevador da Bica** (160$00 one way), an atmospheric funicular railway leading up to the foot of the Bairro Alto.

Bairro Alto

High above the central city, to the west of the Baixa, **Bairro Alto**, the upper town, is the natural place to wind up at night – in its fado houses, bars, excellent restaurants, or even in the refined and somewhat dauntingly named *Instituto do Vinho do Porto* (Port Wine Institute). By day, the quarter's narrow seventeenth-century streets have a very

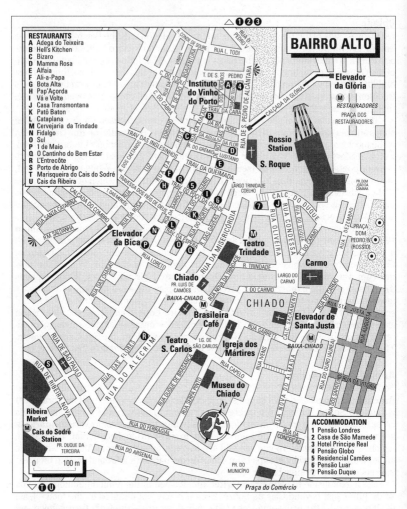

△❶❷❸

BAIRRO ALTO

RESTAURANTS
A Adega do Teixeira
B Hell's Kitchen
C Bizaro
D Mamma Rosa
E Alfaia
F Ali-a-Papa
G Bota Alta
H Pap'Açorda
I Vá e Volte
J Casa Transmontana
K Patô Baton
L Cataplana
M Cervejaria da Trindade
N Fidalgo
O Sul
P 1 de Maio
Q O Cantinho do Bem Estar
R L'Entrecôte
S Porto de Abrigo
T Marisqueira do Cais do Sodré
U Cais da Ribeira

ACCOMMODATION
1 Pensão Londres
2 Casa de São Mamede
3 Hotel Príncipe Real
4 Pensão Globo
5 Residencial Camões
6 Pensão Luar
7 Pensão Duque

Elevador da Glória
RESTAURADORES
PRAÇA DOS RESTAURADORES
Rossio Station
S. Roque
Instituto do Vinho do Porto
Elevador da Bica
Teatro Trindade
Chiado
Carmo
Brasileira Café
Elevador de Santa Justa
CHIADO
Teatro S. Carlos
Igreja dos Mártires
Museu do Chiado
Ribeira Market
Cais do Sodré Station
PRAÇA DOM PEDRO IV (ROSSIO)

0   100 m

▽ Praça do Comércio

different character, with children playing and the elderly sitting in doorways. It is well worth a morning or afternoon's exploration, with two of the city's most interesting churches – Carmo and São Roque – on the fringes and a few approaches to the quarter that are a treat in themselves.

Approaches by Elevador

Raul Mésnier's **Elevador de Santa Justa**, just off the northern end of Rua do Ouro (also known as Rua Aurea) on Rua de Santa Justa, is the most startling approach to the Bairro Alto. Built in 1902, it is one of the city's most extraordinary and eccentric structures, whisking you up through metal latticework, and depositing you on a platform high above the Baixa. Its upper exit is due to reopen when work is completed on a new metro line; until then, the lift (daily 7am–11.45pm; 160$00, one way) takes you up to a rooftop café with great views over the Baixa. Alternative – though hardly more conventional – feats of engineering, are the two funicular-like trams, originally powered by water displacement, and then by steam, until electricity was introduced. One, the **Elevador da Glória**, (7am to 1am; 160$00 one way) built in 1885, links the quarter directly with Praça dos Restauradores, from where it takes off just behind the tourist office on the left. The other, **Elevador da Bica**, (Mon–Sat 7am–10.45pm, Sun 9am–10.45pm; 160$00 one way) climbs up to Rua Loreto (west of Praça Luis de Camões) from Rua de São Paulo/Rua da Moeda, northwest of Cais do Sodré. Our account below follows a route from the disembarkation point of the Elevador da Glória, and enables you to take in the main highlights of the area.

From the Elevador da Glória to São Roque
The Elevador da Glória drops you at the top of the hill on Rua de São Pedro de Alcântara, from whose adjacent **gardens** there's a superb view across the city to the castle. Immediately across the road is the **Instituto do Vinho do Porto**, a good place to stop and taste Portugal's finest tipple (see p.100), while a turn to the left from the *elevador* takes you downhill and round the corner to the **Igreja de São Roque** (daily 8.30am–6pm; free), in Largo Trindade Coelho. From the outside, this looks like the plainest church in the city, its bleak Renaissance facade (by Filipo Terzi, architect of São Vicente) having been further simplified by the earthquake. Neither does it seem impressive when you walk inside. But take a look at the succession of side chapels, each lavishly crafted with *azulejos* (some emulating reliefs), multicoloured marble, or Baroque painted ceilings.

However, the highlight of a visit is the **Capela de São João Baptista**. This chapel is estimated to be the most expensive ever constructed, for its size, and was certainly one of the most bizarre commissions of its age. It was ordered from Rome in 1742 by Dom João V to honour his patron saint, and, more dubiously, to requite the pope, whom he had persuaded to confer a patriarchate upon Lisbon. Designed by the papal architect, Vanvitelli, and using the most costly materials available, including ivory, agate, porphyry and lapis lazuli, it was actually erected at the Vatican for the pope to celebrate Mass before being dismantled and shipped to Lisbon. The cost, then, was about £250,000 sterling, which is perhaps its chief curiosity. But there are other eccentricities; take a close look at the four "oil paintings" of John the Baptist's life and you'll discover that they are in fact mosaics, intricately worked over what must have been years rather than months.

Next to the church, the associated **Museu de São Roque** (Tues–Sun 10am–7pm; 150$00, free Sundays) displays sixteenth- to eighteenth-century paintings and the usual motley collection of vestments, chalices and bibles bequeathed to the church over the centuries, including treasure from the Capela de São João Baptista.

Convento do Carmo
Further south, it's a couple of minutes' walk down to the pretty, enclosed **Largo do Carmo**, with its outdoor café. From here you can return to the Baixa by using the Elevador de Santa Justa (see above) whose entrance lies up an alley to the side of the ruined Gothic arches of the **Convento do Carmo**. Once the largest church in the city, this was half-destroyed by the earthquake but is perhaps even more beautiful as a result. In the nineteenth century its shell was adapted as a chemical factory but these days it houses the splendid **Museu Arqueológico do Carmo**, whose miscellaneous collection is one of the joys of the city. At the time of writing, however, both the top entrance of the Elevador and the museum were closed for work on a new metro line, but they are due to re-open shortly.

Assuming the convent will be much the same as it was, the entire nave is open to the elements, with roses growing up the aisle, columns and tombs and with statuary scattered in all corners. Inside, on either side of what was the main altar, are the main exhibits, centering on a series of **tombs** of great significance. Largest is the beautifully carved, two-metres-high stone tomb of **Ferdinand I**; nearby, the tomb of **Gonçalo de Sousa**, chancellor to Henry the Navigator, is topped by a prone statue of Gonçalo himself, his clasped arms holding a book to signify his learning. Other noteworthy pieces include a jasper sculpture of the Virgin Mary, from Brazil, with cherubs clinging to the stand for dear life; more alarmingly, two pre-Columbian **mummies** lie curled up in glass cases, alongside the preserved heads of a couple of Peruvian Indians. Elsewhere there are flints, arrowheads, prehistoric ceramics, coins dating back to the thirteenth century, Roman inscriptions, church architecture and much more, all well labelled in English and endearingly positioned cheek-by-jowl with little thought of thematic progression.

The Museums of Natural History and Science and the Jardim Botânico

A pleasant ten-minute walk uphill from the top of Elevador da Glória, past the attractive Praça do Principe Real, and along Rua Escola Politécnica, leads you to the classical building housing both the **Museu de História Natural** and the **Museu da Ciência**; alternatively take bus #15 or #58 from Cais do Sodré station. The Museu de História Natural (Mon–Fri 10am–noon & 1–5pm; closed Aug; free), exhibits a rather sad collection of stuffed animals tracing the evolution of Iberian animal life; while the adjoining Museu da Ciência (Mon–Fri 10am–1pm & 2–5pm, Sat 3–6pm; closed Aug; free), includes an imaginative interactive section amongst its geological displays. Neither museum, however, is particularly inspiring.

Beyond the museums lies the entrance to the enchanting **Jardim Botânico** (summer Mon–Fri 9am–8pm, Sat–Sun 10am–8pm; winter Mon–Fri 9am–6pm; Sat–Sun 10am–6pm; 200$00). Laid out in 1873, the gardens are almost completely invisible from the surrounding streets, and form an oasis of twenty thousand exotic plants from around the world – each one neatly labelled.

Estrêla

Situated on another of Lisbon's hills, the district of **Estrêla** lies 2km west of Bairro Alto – a thirty-minute walk or a short ride on tram #28 from Praça Luís de Camões in Chiado, or bus #13 from Praça do Comércio. Its main point of interest for the visitor is the **Basílica da Estrêla** (Mon–Sat 8am–7pm, Sun 9am–7pm; free), a vast domed church and *de facto* monument to late-eighteenth-century Neoclassicism. Below the church is the **Jardim da Estrêla**: Lisbon takes its gardens seriously, even the small patches amid squares and avenues, and these are among the most enjoyable in the city, a quiet refuge occasionally graced with an afternoon band. There's a pool of giant carp, too, and a café with outside tables.

Through the park and on Rua de São Jorge is the gate to the post-Crusader **Cemitério dos Ingleses** (English cemetery; ring loudly for entry) where, among the cypresses, lies Henry Fielding, author of *Tom Jones*, whose imminent demise may have influenced his verdict on Lisbon as "the nastiest city in the world".

A little uphill from here at Rua Coelho da Rocha 16 is the **Casa Museu Fernando Pessoa** (Mon–Wed & Fri 10am–6pm, Thurs 1–8pm; free), home to Portugal's best-known poet for the last fifteen years of his life (see box below). The building is now a cultural centre containing **Almada Negreiros'** famous painting of the writer, a few of Pessoa's personal belongings, such as his glasses and diaries, and exhibits of artists who have been influenced by Pessoa.

FERNANDO PESSOA

In common with many other great artists, **Fernando Pessoa** was largely unrecognized until after his death, but he is now Portugal's most celebrated modern poet. Born in Lisbon in 1888, Pessoa spent most of his childhood in South Africa with his mother, and subsequently wrote many of his poems in English. When he returned alone to Lisbon aged 17, he lived mostly in spartan rented rooms, contributing poetry to literary magazines. With his distinctive gold-rimmed glasses, bow tie and hat, the quirky poet was a conspicuous figure in the Baixa cafés where he wrote and soon became known as a modernist, influenced by the European avant-garde, Cubists, Futurists and others.

Unfortunately, his need to smoke and drink while he worked led to his premature death in 1935, a year after the appearance of *Mensagem*, his only work to be published during his lifetime. Since his death, researchers have unearthed several other previously unpublished works, many written under pseudonyms: Alberto Caeiro, Alvaro de Campos, Ricardo Reis and, for his prose, Bernardo Soares. Each of these pseudonyms represented a different persona and a different literary style, but each was equally learned and inspired, embodiments of the different personalities that the enigmatic Pessoa believed we all possess.

From the tram stop in front of the Basílica da Estrêla you can catch #25 down the steep Rua de São Domingos à Lapa, getting off where the tram veers left into Rua Garcia de Orta. Here, you're only a five-minute walk from the Museu Nacional de Arte Antiga (see p.84); staying with the tram takes you to Praça do Comércio and back into the Baixa.

From Praça do Comércio to the Sé and Castelo

A couple of blocks east of Praça do Comércio, along Rua da Alfândega, is the church of **Conceição Velha**, severely damaged by the earthquake but still in possession of its flamboyant Manueline doorway, an early example of the style and hinting at the brilliance that later emerged at Belém. It once formed part of the Misericórdia (almshouse) – you'll find one of these impressive structures in almost every Portuguese town or city. Five minutes' walk further east, at Campo das Cebolas, stands the curious **Casa dos Bicos**, set with diamond-shaped stones and again offering an image of the richness of pre-1755 Lisbon. The building is not routinely open, though it sees fairly regular use for cultural exhibitions.

The Sé
Lisbon's cathedral – the **Sé** (daily 8.30am–6pm; free) – stands stolidly above the Baixa grid. Founded in 1150 to commemorate the city's reconquest from the Moors, it has a suitably fortress-like appearance, similar to that of Coimbra, and in fact occupies the site of the principal mosque of Moorish Lishbuna. Like so many of the country's cathedrals, it is Romanesque – and extraordinarily restrained in both size and decoration. The great rose window and twin towers form a simple and effective facade, but inside there's nothing very exciting: the building was once splendidly embellished on the orders of Dom João V, but his Rococo whims were swept away by the earthquake and subsequent restorers. All that remains is a group of Gothic tombs behind the high altar and the decaying thirteenth-century **cloister**.

You need to buy tickets for admission to the cloister (Mon–Sat 10am–5pm; 100$00) and the Baroque Sacristia (same hours; 400$00) with its small **museum** of treasures, including the relics of Saint Vincent, brought to Lisbon in 1173 by Afonso Henriques in a boat piloted by ravens. For centuries the descendants of these birds were shown to

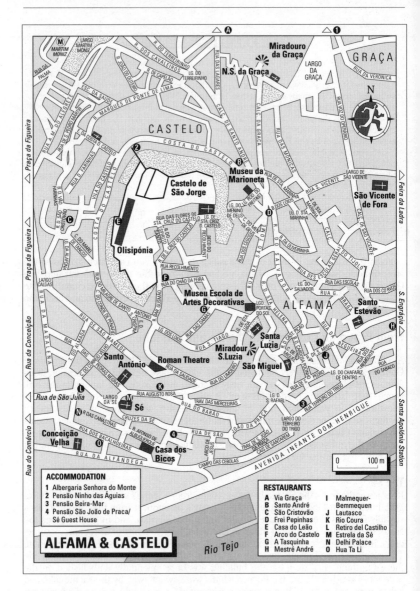

ALFAMA & CASTELO

ACCOMMODATION
1 Albergaria Senhora do Monte
2 Pensão Ninho das Águias
3 Pensão Beira-Mar
4 Pensão São João de Praca/
  Sé Guest House

RESTAURANTS
A Via Graça
B Santo André
C São Cristovão
D Frei Pepinhas
E Casa do Leão
F Arco do Castelo
G A Tasquinha
H Mestré André
I Malmequer-
  Bemmequen
J Lautasco
K Rio Coura
L Retiro del Castilho
M Estrela da Sé
N Delhi Palace
O Hua Ta Li

0   100 m

Rio Tejo

visitors but the last one died in 1978, despite receiving great care from the sacristan. Nevertheless, ravens are still one of the city's symbols.

Opposite the Sé is the church of **Santo António**, said to have been built on the spot where the city's adopted patron saint was born. His life is chronicled in the neighbouring **museum** (Tues–Sun 10am–1pm & 2–6pm; 175$00, free on Sun).

Up to the Castelo

From the Sé, Rua Augusto Rosa winds upward towards the castle, past sparse ruins of a **Roman theatre** (57 AD), set behind a grille just off to the left at the junction of ruas de São Mamede and Saudade. Further up the hill you reach the well-positioned **Igreja da Santa Luzia** and the adjacent **Miradouro da Santa Luzia**, from where there are fine views down to the river.

Just beyond, at Largo das Portas do Sol 2, is the Espírito Santo Silva Foundation, home of the **Museu Escola de Artes Decorativas** (Tues–Sun 10am–5pm; 900$00), a seventeenth-century mansion stuffed with what was once the private collection of banker Ricardo do Espírito Santo Silva, who offered it to the nation in 1953. On display are unique pieces of furniture, major collections of silver and porcelain, paintings, textiles and *azulejo* panels – in short, some of the best examples of seventeenth- and eighteenth-century applied art in the country. The museum, which promotes traditional crafts, also contains a café and restaurant.

Over the road from the **terrace-café** in Largo das Portas do Sol, the views are tremendous – a solitary palm rising from the stepped streets below, the twin-towered facade of Graça convent, the dome of Santa Engrácia, and the Tejo beyond. Catch your breath here for the final push up to the castle, higher up the hill to the northeast. You can enter the grounds from a couple of points and signposts keep you on the right track as the roads wind confusingly ever higher.

Incidentally, **tram** #28 runs from Rua da Conceição in the Baixa, past the Sé and Santa Luzia, to Largo das Portas do Sol; coming from Rossio, **bus** #37 from Praça do Comércio follows a similar route, cutting off at Santa Luzia and climbing to one of the castle entrances.

The Castelo de São Jorge

A small statue of Afonso Henriques, triumphant after the siege of Lisbon, stands at the main entrance to the **Castelo de São Jorge.** An important victory, leading to Muslim surrender at Sintra and throughout the surrounding district, this was not, however, the most Christian or glorious of Portuguese exploits. A full account of the siege survives, written by one Osbern of Bawdsley, an English priest and Crusader, and its details, despite the author's judgmental tone, direct one's sympathies to the enemy.

The attack, in the summer of 1147, came through the opportunism and skilful management of Afonso Henriques, already established as "King" at Porto, who persuaded a large force of French and British Crusaders to delay their progress to Jerusalem for more immediate goals. The Crusaders – scarcely more than pirates – came to terms and in June the siege began. Osbern records the Archbishop of Braga's demand for the Moors to return to "the land whence you came" and, more revealingly, the weary and contemptuous response of the Muslim spokesman: "How many times have you come hither with pilgrims and barbarians to drive us hence? It is not want of possessions but only ambition of the mind that drives you on." For seventeen weeks the castle and inner city stood firm but in October its walls were breached and the citizens – including a Christian community coexisting with the Muslims – were forced to surrender.

The pilgrims and barbarians, flaunting the diplomacy and guarantees of Afonso Henriques, stormed into the city, cut the throat of the local bishop and sacked, pillaged and murdered Christian and Muslim alike. In 1190 a later band of English Crusaders stopped at Lisbon and, no doubt confused by the continuing presence of Moors, sacked the city a second time.

The Castelo

The **Castelo** (winter 9am–6pm, summer 9am–9pm; free) is perhaps Lisbon's most splendid monument, as much through its impressive location as anything else. Beyond the main gates stretch gardens and terraces, walkways, fountains and peacocks, all lying within the old Moorish walls which were scrubbed raw in an over-zealous clean-up operation for Expo 98. At first the Portuguese kings took up residence within the castle – in the *Alcáçova*, the Muslim palace – but by the time of Manuel I this had been superseded by the new royal palace on Terreiro do Paço. Of the *Alcáçova* only a much-restored shell remains. This now houses **Olisipónia** (daily 10am–6pm; 600$00), a multi-media exhibition detailing the history of the city. On entry you are given portable headsets which deliver a 35-minute commentary at four booths presenting aspects of Lisbon's development through film, sounds and images. The presentations overlap somewhat and gloss over some of the less savoury chapters of the past – such as slavery and the Inquisition – but are a useful introduction to the city's make-up nonetheless.

The rest of the castle is an enjoyable place to spend a couple of hours, wandering amid the ramparts looking down upon the city. Built into the ramparts, the Tower of Ulysses holds a **Câmara Escura** (daily every half hour, weather permitting, 10am–4.30pm; 300$00), a periscope focusing on sights round the city with English commentary –though the views are almost as good from the neighbouring unadorned towers.

Crammed within the castle's outer walls is the tiny medieval quarter of **Santa Cruz**, still very much a village in itself. This area, despite a few grand old houses, is largely in decay, though currently undergoing substantial redevelopment.

Just below the castle's eastern entrance sprawls the old **Mouraria** quarter, to which the Moors were relegated on their loss of the town. At the top of the quarter, at Largo Rodrigues de Freitas 19a, is the **Museu da Marioneta** (daily 10am–1pm & 2–7pm; 500$00, under 10s free), housing historical, satirical-style puppets. The museum itself is of limited interest, but the occasional weekend puppet shows are worth catching; ask at the museum for details. From the Museu da Marioneta, Calçada da Graça leads up to the Graça district and the **Miradouro da Graça** from where the views across the city are stunning.

Alfama

The oldest part of Lisbon, stumbling from the walls of the castle down to the Tejo, **Alfama** was buttressed against significant damage in the 1755 earthquake by the steep, rocky mass on which it is built. Although none of its houses dates from before the Christian conquest, many are of Moorish design and the kasbah-like layout is still much as Osbern described it, with "steep defiles instead of ordinary streets… and buildings so closely packed together that, except in the merchants' quarter, hardly a street could be found more than eight foot wide".

In Arab-occupied times Alfama was the grandest part of the city, and continued to be so after the Christian reconquest, but following subsequent earthquakes the new Christian nobility moved out, leaving it to the local fishing community. Today, it is undergoing some commercialization, with its cobbled lanes and "character", but although antique shops and an increasing number of fado restaurants are moving in, they are far from taking over. The quarter retains a largely traditional life of its own: you can eat at local prices in the cafés; the flea market (see below) engulfs the periphery of the area twice a week, and this is very much the place to be during the June "Popular Saints" festivals (above all on June 12), when makeshift cafés and stalls appear on every corner.

The steep defiles, alleys and passageways are known as *becos* and *travessas* rather than *ruas*, and it would be impossible (as well as futile) to try and follow any set route. At some point in your wanderings around the quarter, though, head for the **Rua de São Miguel** – off which are some of the most interesting *becos* – and for the (lower) parallel **Rua de São Pedro**, the main market street leading to the lively **Largo do Chafariz de Dentro**, right at the bottom of the hill. Along all these streets and alleys, life continues much as it has done for years: kids playing ball in tiny squares and chasing each other up and down precipitous staircases; people buying groceries and fish from hole-in-the-wall stores; householders stringing washing across narrow defiles and stoking small outdoor charcoal grills; and elderly men idling away the hours on decrepit wooden benches.

The Feira da Ladra

The **Feira da Ladra**, Lisbon's rambling and ragged flea market, fills the Campo de Santa Clara, at the eastern edge of Alfama on Tuesdays and Saturdays (7am–6pm). Though it's certainly not the world's greatest – "you will find stalls with shabby ready-made clothes" advises the cautious turismo pamphlet – it does turn up some interesting things: oddities from the former African colonies, old prints of the country, and army-surplus gear. Out-and-out junk – broken alarm clocks and old postcards – is spread on the ground above Santa Engrácia, and half-genuine antiques at the top end of the *feira*.

To get here, tram #28 runs from Rua da Conceição in the Baixa to São Vicente (see below), and bus #12 runs between Santa Apolónia station and Praça Marquês de Pombal.

Santa Engrácia and São Vicente de Fora

While at the flea market, take a look inside **Santa Engrácia** (Tues–Sun 10am–6pm; closes at 5pm in winter; free), the loftiest and most tortuously built church in the city. Begun in 1682 and once a synonym for unfinished work, its vast dome was finally completed in 1966. If you ask nicely, you may be allowed to take the elevator to the dome, from where you can look down on the empty church and out over the flea market, port and city.

More interesting, architecturally, is the nearby **São Vicente de Fora**, whose name – "of the outside" – is a reminder of the extent of the sixteenth-century city. It is also where Afonso Henriques pitched camp during his siege and conquest of Lisbon. Built during the years of Spanish rule by Philip II's Italian architect, Felipe Terzi, its severe geometric facade was an important Renaissance innovation. Through the **cloisters**, decorated with *azulejos*, you can visit the old monastic refectory, which since 1855 has formed the **pantheon of the Bragança dynasty** (Tues–Sun 10am–5.30pm; 400$00). Here, in more or less complete (though unexciting) sequence, are the bodies of all Portuguese kings from João IV, who restored the monarchy, to Manuel II, who lost it and died in exile in England in 1932. Among them is Catherine of Bragança, the widow of Charles II and (as the local guide points out) "the one who took the habit of the fifth o'clock tea to that country". You can enjoy tea and other beverages at the monastery café, which has a roof terrace commanding superb views over the Alfama and the Tagus.

Further east: the Museu Militar, Museu da Água and Museu Nacional do Azulejo

There's not much call to head east beyond the Alfama, unless you're leaving by train from **Santa Apolónia station** or visiting the dockside nightclubs (see p.100). However, there is a trio of museums of varying interest. Opposite the station, on Largo Museu da Artilharia, a couple of blocks south of Santa Engrácia, is the imposing Corinthian facade of the city's military museum, the **Museu Militar** (Tues–Sun 10am–5pm; 300$00, free on Wed), though this is very traditional in layout – old weapons in old cases – and lacks much appeal. However, some ten minutes' walk beyond Santa Apolónia station, or a ride on bus #105 from Praça da Figueira, off Calçada dos Barbadinhos at Rua do Alviela 12, stands the **Museu da Água** (Mon–Sat 10am–6pm; 300$00), a moderately engaging museum devoted to the evolution of the city's water supply. It is housed in an attractive old pumping station, built in 1880 to pump water up Lisbon's steep hills, and is complete with working nineteenth-century steam engines. While here, you can arrange a visit to the Aqueduto das Águas Livres (see p.81).

PORTUGUESE AZULEJOS

Fans of *azulejos* – tiles – have plenty to enjoy in Lisbon which displays some 500 years of different styles both on the interior and exterior of various houses, shops, monuments and even metro stations. Though influenced by Moorish and Spanish glazed tiles – the early sixteenth-century tiles in the Palácio Nacional in Sintra, typify Moorish geometric patterns – Portuguese **azulejos** developed their own style around the mid-sixteenth century when tile-making techniques were improved. A new Italian method allowed images to be painted onto the clay, and those in the Igreja de São Roque reflect the religious imagery and the new Italian method favoured at this time. By the seventeenth century, decadent and colourful images were all the rage and the wealthy commissioned large *azulejo* panels displaying battles, hunting and biblical scenes. Soon, new Dutch techniques came to the fore, but they produced tiles in blue and white only; those on the Palácio dos Marquêses de Fronteira (see p.84) and São Vicente de Fora (see p.79) are representative of this time. This fervent competition with Dutch ceramics, however, meant that the Portuguese tile business had to turn professional in order to survive. As a result the early eighteenth century saw trained artist "masters" producing highly decorated ceramic mosaics, culminating in Rococo themes as seen in Madre de Deus, now the tile museum (see below). After the Great Earthquake, more prosaic tiled facades, often with Neoclassical designs, were considered good insulation devices, as well as protecting buildings from rain and fire.

By the mid-nineteenth century, *azulejos* were being produced in factories to decorate shops and industries: the tiles on the front of the Fábrica Viúva Lamego, for example (see p.107) date from 1865. The end of the century saw the appearance of figures on tiles, typified by the work in the *Cervejaria da Trindade* (see p.93). The nineteenth century also heralded the arrival of individualists such as Rafael Bordalo Pinheiro (see p.83). One of many popular styles of the twentieth century was Art Deco, which took hold in the 1920s. Interestingly, more modern, contemporary works can be admired in Lisbon's underground stations, such as Campo Pequeno, Colégio Militar, Cidade Universitária.

About 1.5km east of Santa Apolónia (bus #104 from Praça do Comércio, bus #105 from Praça da Figueira), at Rua Madre de Deus 4, is the **Museu Nacional do Azulejo** (Tues 2–6pm, Wed–Sun 10am–6pm; 400$00, free on Sun). Installed in the church and cloisters of Madre de Deus, whose own eighteenth-century tiled scenes on the life of Saint Anthony are among the best in the city, it contains an impressive collection of *azulejos* from the fifteenth century to the present day. The highlight, however, is Portugal's longest *azulejo* – a wonderfully detailed 36-metre panorama of Lisbon, completed in around 1738. Don't miss out on the opportunity of a drink in the lovely garden café here.

Avenida da Liberdade, Parque Eduardo VII and Amoreiras

To the north of the Baixa is the city's principal park – the Parque Eduardo VII. The easiest approach is by metro (to Marquês de Pombal or Parque) or bus (to Marquês de Pombal), though you could take an energetic twenty-minute walk up the main **Avenida da Liberdade**, which would give you the chance to make a couple of stops along the way. The bottom end of Avenida da Liberdade, just above the new metro interchange at Restauradores, has some of the city's nicest outdoor **cafés**, with esplanade tables in the green swathes that split the avenue. Running parallel, to the east, the pedestrianized **Rua das Portas de Santo Antão** is well known for the seafood restaurants that line it; their waiters lurk by every doorway attempting to entice you in. Despite the obvious tourist trappings, you can still have a good, reasonably inexpensive meal here (see p.92). If here on a Monday or Friday, take a look inside the **Geographical Society** at number 100 (tours at 11am & 3pm Mon, Wed and Fri; free), a reminder of the exotic nature of Portugal's former colonies. There are snake spears, African instruments and other ethnographical relics from Africa and the east.

Parque Eduardo VII

At the top of the avenue, in the formal, elongated **Parque Eduardo VII**, the big attractions are the **Estufas** (daily 9am–4.30pm; 100$00). These are huge and wonderful hothouses at the park's northern end, and are filled with tropical plants, pools and endless varieties of palms and cacti. Rock and classical concerts and an antiques fair are occasionally held in the **Estufa Fria**. Just south of the Estufas, next to a children's play area, is a handy café with tables set up outside. You can walk uphill past the viewpoint, which affords fine views over the city, over the grassy hillock to the Gulbenkian museum (see below), or alternatively take bus #51, which runs from Belém to the museum via the top of the park near the Estufa Fria. Other useful **bus links** from the park are #27 and #49 west to Belém.

Amoreiras

Leading west of the park from Praça do Marquês de Pombal, Avenida J.A. de Aguiar becomes Avenida E. Duarte Pacheco, on which you will find Lisbon's Post-Modernist shopping centre, **Amoreiras**, still visible on the city skyline from almost any approach despite the growing number of high-rise blocks around it. The complex, designed by Tomás Taveira, is Portugal's most adventurous – and most entertaining – modern building: a wild fantasy of pink and blue, sheltering ten cinemas, sixty cafés and restaurants, 370 shops and a hotel. Most of the shops here stay open until midnight (11pm on Sun); the heaviest human traffic is on Sunday, when entire families descend on the complex for an afternoon out. To get here directly by bus, take the #11 from Rossio/Restauradores. While in the area, take a look in the Mãe d'Água water cistern at Rua das Amoreiras, close to Largo do Rato, a shimmering pool where water was stored from the Aqueduto das Aguas Livres (see below); it is now used for occasional art exhibits.

The Aqueduto das Águas Livres

Buses #11 and #23 pass Amoreiras and then continue on the kilometre or so west to the **Aqueduto das Águas Livres**. Opened in 1748, the aqueduct brought reliable drinking water to the city for the first time. It stood firm during the 1755 earthquake and later became notorious through one Diogo Alves, a nineteenth-century serial killer who threw his victims off the arches – a drop of 60m. If you'd like to visit it, enquire at the Museu da Água (see p.79), who can arrange walking tours over the aqueduct. Once inside and up, you can make the very scenic walk across the aqueduct to the **Parque Monsanto**.

The Fundação Calouste Gulbenkian

The **Fundação Calouste Gulbenkian** is the great cultural centre of Portugal – and it is a wonder that it's not better known internationally. Housed in a superb complex, a few minutes' walk north of Parque Eduardo VII, the foundation is set in its own park, and features a museum whose collections seem to take in virtually every great phase of Eastern and Western art – from Ancient Egyptian scarabs to Art Nouveau jewellery, Islamic textiles to French Impressionists. In a separate building, across the park, the **Centro de Arte Moderna** sports excitingly displayed and largely Portuguese works, which touch on most styles of twentieth-century art. The complex has its main entrance at Avda de Berna 45; to reach it, take **bus** #31 or #41 from Rossio, #51 from Belém, or the **metro** to Praça de Espanha or São Sebastião.

Astonishingly, all the main museum exhibits were acquired by just one man, the Armenian oil magnate **Calouste Gulbenkian** (1869–1955), whose legendary art-market coups included buying works from the Leningrad Hermitage after the Russian Revolution. In a scarcely less astute deal made during the last war, Gulbenkian literally auctioned himself and his collections to the European nations: Portugal bid security, an aristocratic palace home (a Marquês was asked to move out) and tax exemption, to acquire one of the most important cultural patrons of the century.

Today the Gulbenkian Foundation runs an orchestra, three concert halls and two galleries for temporary exhibitions, in the capital alone. It also finances work in all spheres of Portuguese cultural life – there are Gulbenkian museums and libraries in the smallest towns – and makes charitable grants to a vast range of projects. The admissions desk of the museum has a schedule of current activities.

Anyone travelling with children may be equally impressed to know that the Gulbenkian maintains a **Centro Artístico Infantil** in its gardens (entrance just off Rua Marquês de Sá de Bandeira), well-stocked with toys and offering free **childcare sessions** for four- to twelve-year-olds between 9.30am and 5.30pm.

The Museu Gulbenkian

The **Museu Gulbenkian** (main entrance on Avenida de Berna: Tues–Sun 10am–5pm; 500$00, free on Sun) is divided into two complete and distinct halves – the first devoted to Egyptian, Greco-Roman, Islamic and Oriental arts, the second to European art – and ideally you'll want to take them in on separate visits. The collections aren't immense in number but each contains pieces of such individual interest and beauty that you need frequent unwinding sessions – well provided for by the basement **café-bar and gardens**.

CLASSICAL AND ORIENTAL ART

It seems arbitrary to hint at highlights, but they must include the entire contents of the small **Egyptian room**, which covers almost every period of importance from the Old Kingdom (2700 BC) to the Roman period. Particularly striking are a carved ivory spoon from the time of Amenophis III and an extraordinarily lifelike sculpture *Head of a Priest* from the penultimate, Ptolomaic period. **Mesopotamia** produced the earliest forms of writing, and two cylinder seals – one dating from before 2500 BC – are on display here, along with architectural sculpture from the Assyrian civilization.

Fine **Roman** statues, silver, glass and intricate gold jewellery from ancient **Greece** come soon after. There's also a particularly extensive collection of Greek coins, followed by remarkable illuminated manuscripts and ceramics from **Armenia**, porcelain from **China**, and beautiful **Japanese** prints and lacquer-work. Islamic arts are magnificently represented by ornamented texts, opulently woven carpets, glassware (such as the fourteenth-century mosque lamps from Syria) and precious bindings from **Persia** and **India**.

EUROPEAN ART

In the **European art** section you'll find work from all the major schools, beginning with a group of French medieval ivory diptychs (in particular the six scenes depicting the *Life of the Virgin*) and a thirteenth-century version of Saint John's prophetic *Apocalypse*, produced in Kent and touched up in Italy under Pope Clement IX. From fifteenth-century Flanders, there's a pair of panels by van der Weyden, and from the same period in Italy comes Ghirlandaio's *Portrait of a Young Woman*. The seventeenth-century collection yields two exceptional portraits – one by Rubens of his second wife, *Helena Fourment*, and Rembrandt's *Figure of an Old Man* – plus works by van Dyck, Frans Hals and Ruisdael. Eighteenth-century works featured include a good Fragonard, and a roll-call incorporating Gainsborough, Sir Thomas Lawrence and – most impressively, with no fewer than nineteen paintings – Francesco Guardi. Finally Corot, Manet, Monet, Degas and Renoir supply a good showing from nineteenth- to twentieth-century France.

Sculpture is poorly represented on the whole, though a French sixteenth-century religious statue of *Mary Magdalene*, a fifteenth-century medallion of *Faith* by Luca della Robbia, a 1780 marble *Diana* by Jean-Antoine Houdon, and a couple of Rodins all stand out. Elsewhere, you'll find **ceramics** from Spain and Italy; **furniture** from Louis XV to

Louis XVI; eighteenth-century works from **French goldsmiths**; fifteenth-century Italian bronze **medals** (especially by Pisanello); and assorted Italian tapestries and textiles. An Art Nouveau collection with 169 pieces of fantasy jewellery by **René Lalique** is the best of the tail-end of this great collection.

The Centro de Arte Moderna

To reach the **Centro de Arte Moderna** (main entrance on Rua Dr. N. de Bettencourt; hours as main museum; 500$00, free on Sun) walk through the gardens, which are enlivened by some specially commissioned sculptures. The light and well-laid out centre features some big names on the twentieth-century Portuguese scene, including **Almada Negreiros** (1873–1970), the founder of *modernismo* (his portrait of Fernando Pessoa, now in the Casa Museu Fernando Pessoa, is particularly well known; see p.75), Amadeu de Sousa Cardoso and Guilherme Santa-Rita (both of Futurist inclinations), Vieira da Silva (whose distinctive painting style is a crisscross of lines) and **Paula Rego** (one of Portugal's leading contemporary artists, now resident in England). Next to the museum, don't miss the perennially popular self-service **restaurant** (see p.95).

North of the Gulbenkian

Few visitors explore anything of Lisbon **north** of the Gulbenkian, unless for a trip to the Sporting or Benfica football stadiums or the Campo Pequeno bullring. Out past the Cidade Universitária, though, are some mildly diverting **museums**, devoted to the city's history and to costume, plus a private **art collection**. They are all on the route of the #1 bus, which runs from Cais do Sodré via Rossio. Over to the northwest of the Gulbenkian, further peripheral attractions are provided by the **Jardim Zoológico** (the city's zoo), and by the nearby **Palácio dos Marquêses da Fronteira**. Buses #31 and #41 link Rossio with the Jardim Zoológico via Praça Marques de Pombal, or take the metro, to Jardim Zoológico.

The Museu da Cidade, Museu Rafael Bordalo Pinheiro and Museu do Traje

Some 2km north of the Gulbenkian, the **Museu da Cidade** (Tues–Sun 10am–1pm & 2–6pm; 350$00, free on Sun) is installed in the eighteenth-century Palácio Pimenta, in the northwestern corner of Campo Grande. Its principal interest lies in an imaginative collection of prints, paintings and models of pre-1755 Lisbon. A death-defying crossing of the road leads you to another lovely mansion housing the **Museu Rafael Bordalo Pinheiro** (Tues–Sun 10am–1pm & 2–6pm; 270$00), dedicated to the caricaturist and ceramicist. Upstairs exhibits include his amazing collection of ornate dishes crawling with crabs and lobsters, frogs and snakes. The paintings, cartoons and sketches downstairs are of less interest.

The **Museu do Traje** (Tues–Sun: summer 10am–6pm; joint ticket with Museu do Teatro 400$00; free on Sun) occupies another eighteenth-century palace, the Palácio do Monteiro-Mor, some 2km further north of the Museu da Cidade. The museum's extensive collections are drawn upon for temporary thematic exhibitions – excellent if costume is your subject, less gripping if you're not an aficionado of faded fabrics. For more casual visitors, the surrounding **park** is at least as big an attraction – one of the lushest areas of the city, open daily until 5pm and with a good restaurant and café. The small **Museu do Teatro** (Tues 2–6pm, Wed–Sun 10am–6pm; joint ticket with Museu do Traje 400$00, free on Sun), containing theatrical memorabilia, is also sited in the grounds but is of truly specialist interest.

The Jardim Zoológico

The **Jardim Zoológico**, on Estrada de Benfica 158–160 (daily Oct–March 10am–6pm; April–Sept 10am–8pm; 1600$00) has been spruced up but remains one of the least inspiring of European zoos, exhibiting overheated bears and other unhappy captives. On the other hand it's really as much a rambling garden as anything else and in this, and in its peculiarly Portuguese eruptions of kitsch (an extraordinary dogs' cemetery), makes for an enjoyable afternoon's ramble, with a small *téléférique* (daily from 11am), a reptile house and performing dolphins as further diversions. You can get there by metro, to Jardim Zoológico, or by bus #31, #41 and #46 from Rossio.

The Palácio dos Marquêses da Fronteira

Palace enthusiasts might like to visit the seventeenth-century **Palácio dos Marquêses da Fronteira**, Largo de São Domingos de Benfica 1, which is around twenty minutes' walk west from the zoo; bus #46 from Rossio (via the zoo) or bus #58 from Cais do Sodré pass nearby. After the view of the bland housing development on Rua de São Domingos de Benfica, the fantastic gardens of this small, pink country house feel like an oasis, complete with topiary, statues and fountains. Inside, there is period furniture along with more stunning *azulejos*. The allegorical panels on the lower level, taken from Camões' tale of the *Doze da Inglaterra*, mark an historic moment in the history of *azulejos* when, in the mid-seventeenth century, the Portuguese dropped the formal Moorish methods of design and turned to painting straight onto tiles.

Because the palace is still lived in, **visiting hours** are limited and by guided tour only (June–Sept Mon–Sat, tours at 10.30am, 11am, 11.30am & noon; Oct–May tours at 11am & noon; 500$00 gardens only or 1500$00 palace and gardens). Call ☎217 782 023 to check on the latest details.

The Museu Nacional de Arte Antiga

The **Museu Nacional de Arte Antiga** (Tues 2–6pm, Wed–Sun 10am–6pm; 500$00, free on Sun), Portugal's national gallery, certainly stands comparison with the Gulbenkian. The core of the museum – comprising fifteenth- and sixteenth-century Portuguese works by artists such as Nuno Gonçalves – is excellent and well displayed in a beautiful converted seventeenth-century palace; the garden and restaurant (hours as for museum, restaurant open till midnight) are worth a visit in their own right. It is situated at Rua das Janelas Verdes 95 in the wealthy suburb of **Lapa**, two kilometres west of Praça do Comércio. To get there, take bus #40 or #60 from Praça do Comércio, or bus #27 or #49 on the way to or from Belém.

Gonçalves and the Portuguese School

Gonçalves and his fellow painters of the so-called "Portuguese school" span that indeterminate and exciting period when Gothic art was giving way to the Renaissance. Their works, notably Gregório Lopes' *Martyrdom of São Sebastião*, and those by Frei Carlos, are exclusively religious in concept, and particularly interesting in their emphasis on portraiture – transforming any theme, even a martyrdom, into a vivid observation of local contemporary life. Stylistically, the most significant influences upon them were those of the Flemish, "Northern Renaissance" painters: Jan van Eyck, who came to Portugal in 1428, Memling and Mabuse (both well-represented here) and Rogier van der Weyden.

The acknowledged masterpiece, however, is Gonçalves' **Panéis de São Vicente** (Saint Vincent Altarpiece; 1467–1470), a brilliantly marshalled canvas depicting the saint, Lisbon's patron, receiving homage from all ranks of its citizens. On the two left-hand panels are Cistercian monks, fishermen and sailors; on the opposite side the Duke of Bragança and his family, a helmeted Moorish knight, a Jew (with book), a beggar, and a priest holding Saint Vincent's own relics (a piece of his skull, which is still possessed by the Sé). In the epic central panels the mustachioed Henry the Navigator, his nephew Afonso V (in green), and the youthful (future) Dom João II, pay tribute to the saint. Among the frieze of portraits behind them, that on the far left is reputed to be Gonçalves himself; the other central panel shows the Archbishop of Lisbon. **Later Portuguese**

painters – from the sixteenth to the eighteenth century – are displayed too, most notably António de Sequeira and Josefa de Óbidos (for more on whom, see p.145).

The rest of the collection

After Gonçalves and his contemporaries the most interesting works are by **Flemish and German** painters – Cranach, Bosch (represented by a fabulous *Temptation of St Anthony*) and Dürer – and miscellaneous gems by Raphael, Zurbarán, and, rather oddly, Rodin. But exhibits more likely to delay you are those in the extensive **applied art** sections. Here, on Level 1, you'll find **Portuguese furniture and textiles** to rival the European selection in the Gulbenkian and, on Level 2, an excellent collection of **silverware** and **ceramics**. Also on Level 2, the **Oriental Art** collection shows the influence of Indian, African and Oriental designs derived from the new trading links of the time. Other colonially influenced exhibits include inlaid furniture from Goa and a supremely satisfying series of late sixteenth-century **Japanese screens**, showing the Portuguese landing at Nagasaki, complete with Pinnochio-like noses.

Belém

It was from **Belém** in 1497 that Vasco da Gama set sail for India, and here too that he was welcomed home by Dom Manuel "the Fortunate" (*o Venturoso*). Da Gama brought back with him a small cargo of pepper, but it was enough to pay for his voyage several times over. The monastery subsequently built here – the **Mosteiro dos Jerónimos** – stands as a testament to his triumphant discovery of a sea route to the Orient, which amounted to the declaration of a "golden age". Built to honour the vow Dom Manuel made to the Virgin in return for a successful voyage, it stands on the site of the old Ermida do Restelo or Capela de São Jerónimo, a hermitage founded by Henry the Navigator, where Vasco da Gama and his companions had spent their last night ashore in prayer. The monastery was partly funded by a levy on the fruits of da Gama's discovery – a five percent tax on all spices other than pepper, cinnamon and cloves, whose import had become the sole preserve of the Crown.

The Rio Tejo at Belém has receded with the centuries, for when the monastery was built it stood almost on the beach, within sight of caravels moored ready for expeditions, and of the **Torre de Belém**, guarding the entrance to the port. This, too, survived the earthquake and is the other showpiece Manueline building in Lisbon. Both monastery and tower lie in what is now – despite the road and railway cutting it in half – a pleasant waterfront suburb, 6km west of the city centre, close to a small group of museums, and with some fine **cafés and restaurants**. Make time, in particular, for the *Antiga Confeitaria de Belém*, in Rua de Belém, by the tram stop, which bills itself as the "única fábrica de pasteis de Belém" – *pasteis de Belém* being delicious flaky tartlets filled with custard-like cream.

Belém is easily reached by **tram** (signed Algés) – the fast supertram #15 runs from Praça da Figueira via Praça do Comércio taking about twenty minutes – or by slow train from Cais do Sodré or bus #51 from the Gulbenkian museum. If you feel like escaping to a **beach** you can get a **ferry** across the Tejo from Belém to Trafaria, which is only 3km by bus from Costa da Caparica (see p.127); ferries leave on the hour and half hour (Mon–Fri 6.30am–11.30pm, Sun 7.30–11.30pm) from a terminus right by the train station (some five minutes from central Belém). Alternatively, **trains** from here continue to Cascais (see p.113). When planning your trip keep in mind that quite a few of the sights at Belém are closed on Mondays.

The Mosteiro dos Jerónimos

Even before the Great Earthquake, the **Mosteiro dos Jerónimos** (Tues–Sun: June–Sept 10am–6.30pm; Oct–May 10am–5pm; monastery free, cloister 500$00, 250$00

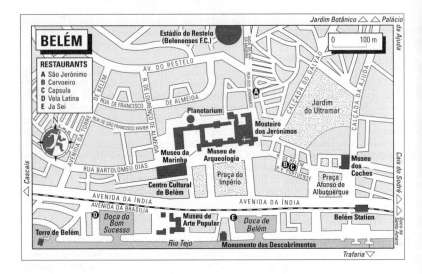

for students, free Sun morning) was Lisbon's finest monument: since then, it has stood quite without comparison. Begun in 1502 and more or less completed when its funding was withdrawn by João III in 1551, the monastery is the most ambitious and successful achievement of Manueline architecture. It is less flamboyantly exotic than either Tomar or Batalha – the great culminations of the style in Estremadura – but, despite a succession of master-builders, it has more daring and confidence in its overall design. This is largely the achievement of two outstanding figures, **Diogo de Boitaca**, perhaps the originator of the Manueline style with his Igreja de Jesus at Setúbal, and **João de Castilho**, a Spaniard who took over the construction from around 1517.

It was Castilho who designed the **main entrance** to the **church** (closed during Mass) a complex, shrine-like hierarchy of figures centred around Henry the Navigator (on a pedestal above the arch). In its intricate and almost flat ornamentation, it shows the influence of the then current Spanish style, Plateresque (literally, the art of the silversmith). Yet it also has distinctive Manueline features – the use of rounded forms, the naturalistic motifs in the bands around the windows – and these seem to create both its harmony and individuality. They are also unmistakably outward-looking, evoking the new forms discovered in the East, a characteristic that makes each Manueline building so new and interesting and so much a product of its particular and expansionary age.

This is immediately true of the church itself, whose breathtaking sense of space alone places it among the great triumphs of European Gothic. Here, though, Manueline developments add two extraordinary and fresh dimensions. There are tensions, deliberately created and carefully restrained, between the grand spatial design and the areas of intensely detailed ornamentation. And, still more striking, there is a naturalism in the forms of this ornamentation that seems to extend into the actual structure of the church. Once you've made the analogy, it's difficult to see the six central columns as anything other than palm trunks, growing both into and from the branches of the delicate rib-vaulting.

Another peculiarity of Manueline buildings is the way in which they can adapt, enliven, or encompass any number of different styles. Here, the basic structure is thoroughly Gothic, though Castilho's ornamentation on the columns is much more Renaissance in spirit. So too is the semicircular apse (around the altar), added in 1572, beyond which is the entrance to the remarkable double cloister.

Vaulted throughout and fantastically embellished, the **cloister** is one of the most original and beautiful pieces of architecture in the country. Again, it holds in balance Gothic forms and Renaissance ornamentation and is exuberant in its innovations, such as the rounded corner canopies and delicate twisting divisions within each of the arches. These lend a wave-like, rhythmic motion to the whole structure, a conceit extended by the typically Manueline motifs drawn from ropes, anchors and the sea. In this – as in all aspects – it would be hard to imagine an artistic style more directly reflecting the achievements and preoccupations of an age.

In the wings of the monastery are two museums. The **Museu de Arqueologia** (Tues 2–6pm, Wed–Sun 10am–6pm; 400$00, free Sun morning), to the west of the main entrance, seems sparse and, apart from a few fine Roman mosaics unearthed in the Algarve, thoroughly unexceptional. In contrast, the enormous **Museu da Marinha** (Tues–Sun: June–Sept 10am–6pm; Oct–May 10am–5pm; 400$00, free Sun morning), with its entrance opposite the Centro Cultural de Belém, is more interesting, packed not only with models of ships, naval uniforms and a surprising display of artefacts from Portugal's oriental trade and colonies, but also with real vessels – among them fishing boats and sumptuous state barges – a couple of seaplanes and even some fire engines. It also incorporates the **Museu das Crianças** (Sat–Sun 10am–5pm; 750$00, children 500$00), a children's museum, with imaginative interactive displays designed to raise children's awareness of themselves, other children and adults.

The Torre de Belém

Still washed on three sides by the sea, the **Torre de Belém** (Tues–Sun: June–Sept 10am–6pm; Oct–May 10am–5pm; 400$00) stands 500m west of the monastery, fronted by a little park with a café. Whimsical, multi-turreted and with a real hat-in-the-air exuberance, it was built over the last five years of Dom Manuel's reign (1515–20) as a fortress to safeguard the approach to Lisbon's harbour – before the Great Earthquake shifted its course, it stood virtually in the centre of the river. As such, it is the one completely Manueline building in Portugal, the rest having been adaptations of earlier structures or completed in later years.

Its architect, **Francisco de Arruda**, had previously worked on Portuguese fortifications in Morocco and the Moorish influence is very strong in the delicately arched windows and balconies. Prominent also in the decoration are two great symbols of the age: Manuel's personal badge of an armillary sphere (representing the globe) and the cross of the military Order of Christ, once the Templars, who took a major role in all Portuguese conquests. Though worth entering for the views from the roof, the tower's interior is unremarkable except for a "whispering gallery". It was used into the nineteenth century as a prison, notoriously by Dom Miguel (1828–34), who kept political enemies in the waterlogged dungeons.

Back towards the Monumento dos Descobrimentos

Walking back along the waterfront, towards the monastery, you'll pass the **Museu de Arte Popular** (Mon–Sat 10am–12.30pm & 2–5pm; 300$00), a province-by-province display of Portugal's still very diverse folk arts, housed in a shed-like building. Almost adjacent is the **Monumento dos Descobrimentos** (Monument to the Discoveries; Tues–Sun 9.30am–6.30pm; 330$00), an angular slab of concrete in the shape of a caravel which was erected in 1960 to commemorate the 500th anniversary of the death of Henry the Navigator. Henry appears on the prow with Camões and other Portuguese heroes. Within the monument is a small exhibition space, with interesting and changing exhibits on the city's history; the entrance fee also lets you climb right up to the top for some fine views of the Tejo and Torre de Belém.

The Centro Cultural de Belém and the Museu dos Coches

Across from the monument, on the western side of the Praça do Imperio, an underpass leads to the controversial modern **Centro Cultural de Belém** (daily 11am–8pm; ☎213

612400), which puts on regular cultural exhibitions and concerts as well as hosting some kind of live entertainment over the weekend – jugglers, mime artists and the like. For the best views of the surroundings, drop into the café, whose garden esplanade overlooks the river and the Monument dos Descobrimentos. The Centro Cultural's Exhibition Centre houses a **Design Museum** (daily 11am–8pm, last entry 7.15pm; 500$00, 250$00 for students; ☎213 612 400), which anyone with a passing interest in contemporary design will find highly enjoyable. The collection comprises of design classics including furniture, glass and jewellery spanning the period from 1937 to today, all amassed by former stockbroker and media mogul Francisco Capelo.

At the corner of Belém's other main square – Praça Afonso de Albuquerque, a few minutes' walk east from the monastery along Rua de Belém – you'll find the **Museu dos Coches** (Tues–Sun 10am–5.30pm; 450$00, free Sun), oddly one of the most visited tourist attraction in Lisbon. Housed in the attractive former riding school of the President's palace, it consists of an interminable line of royal coaches – baroque, heavily gilded and sometimes beautifully painted.

Palácio da Ajuda

Jump on bus #14, from central Belém or Calçada da Ajuda behind the Museu dos Coches, for the short ride uphill to the **Palácio da Ajuda** (half-hour tours 10am–5pm; closed Wed; 400$00, free Sun morning). The palace was built by those crashingly tasteless nineteenth-century royals, Dona Maria II and Dom Ferdinand, and like their Pena Palace folly at Sintra (see p.119) is all over-the-top aristocratic clutter. The **banqueting hall**, however, is quite a sight; likewise the lift, decked out with mahogany and mirrors. Tram #18 will get you back from the palace to Praça do Comércio, or take bus #14 or #60 to Praça da Figueira.

Parque das Nações

Now called **Parque das Nações** – the Park of Nations – (Sun–Thurs 9.30–1am, Fri–Sat 9.30–3am) the former Expo site, 5km to the east of the city, remains a huge attraction for Lisboans who pack out the 2km-long site especially at weekends. The main highlight is the world's second largest **Oceanarium**, one of Lisbon's most impressive landmarks. The **Virtual Reality Pavilion** is another key draw, while the educational exhibits in the **Centre of Live Science** are also highly rewarding. Other attractions include water gardens, a cable-car offering a stunning perspective over the site, a viewing tower, two of Lisbon's largest concert venues and a diverse array of bars, shops and restaurants, many with outdoor seating overlooking Olivais docks and the astonishing 17km-long Vasco da Gama bridge over the Tagus. The park is part of an area of three square kilometres along Lisbon's eastern riverfront, which is in the process of being transformed into a large-scale business and residential zone, complete with a mammoth riverside park. The main aim is of redirecting Lisbon's sprawling suburbs in a more planned fashion; completion is due in the next ten years.

Getting there

Stepping off Oriente metro, you arrive in the bowels of the **Estação do Oriente**, a stunning glass-and-concrete bus and train interchange designed by Spanish architect Santiago Calatrava; from the station, there are also connecting overland trains to Santa Apolónia station, as well as bus links to towns north and south of the Tagus. Turn right out of the station and the entrance to the Parque is on the left. A free toy train trundles anticlockwise round the whole site every 20 minutes or so, a fun chance to get an idea of what is on offer; there is also a less useful shuttle bus more geared to connecting the car parks. It is not too taxing, however, to walk to the principal attractions, especially if you take advantage of the cable car (see above). Within the Parque, there are automatic teller machines, a post office and countless bars and restaurants, the best of which are reviewed on p.96.

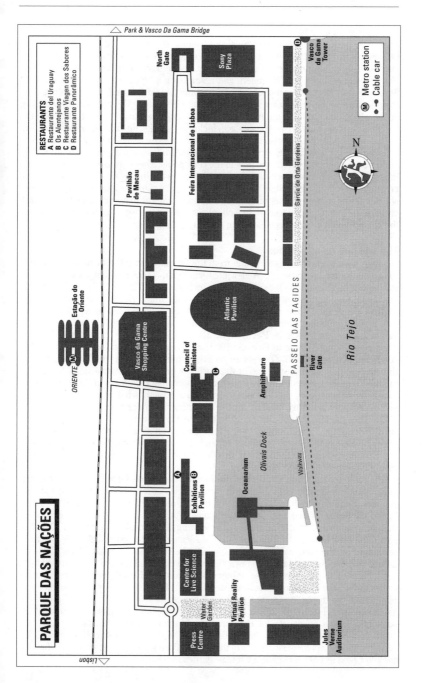

PARQUE DAS NAÇÕES

△ Park & Vasco Da Gama Bridge

△ Lisbon

RESTAURANTS
A Restaurante del Uraguay
B Os Alentejanos
C Restaurante Viagem dos Sabores
D Restaurante Panorâmico

ⓜ Metro station
•—• Cable car

N

ORIENTE ⓜ Estação do Oriente

Vasco da Gama Shopping Centre

Pavilhão de Macau

North Gate

Sony Plaza

Feira Internacional de Lisboa

Vasco da Gama Tower Ⓓ

Garcia de Orta Gardens

Atlantic Pavilion

Council of Ministers

Ⓒ

Amphitheatre

River Gate

PASSEIO DAS TAGIDES

Rio Tejo

Centre for Live Science

Ⓐ

Exhibitions Pavilion Ⓑ

Oceanarium

Olivais Dock

Walkway

Press Centre

Water Garden

Virtual Reality Pavilion

Jules Verne Auditorium

Oceanário de Lisboa

From the park's main entrance turn right along the waterfront and the futuristic **Oceanarium** (daily 10am–8pm; 1500$00), is only a five-minute walk. At weekends in particular, hour-long queues to get in are not uncommon, so it is worth getting here early. Designed by Peter Chermaeff, and resembling a typical set from a James Bond film, Europe's largest oceanarium contains some 25,000 fish and marine animals. Its main feature is the enormous central tank, the size of four Olympic-sized swimming pools, which you can look into from various different levels to get close-up views of the various creatures that live on the surface, including sharks, down to the rays which live on the sea-bed. Almost more impressive, though, are the recreations of various ocean ecosystems, such as the Antarctic tank containing frolicking penguins, and the Pacific tank, where otters bob about and play in the rock pools. These areas are separated from the main tank by invisible acrylic sheets, which gives the impression that all the marine creatures are swimming together in the same space. On the darkened lower level, smaller tanks contain shoals of brightly-coloured tropical fish and other warm water creatures. Find a window free of the school parties and the whole experience becomes the closest you'll get to deep-sea diving without getting wet.

The site and its attractions

Heading back towards Oriente station from the Oceanarium is the **Centro da Ciência Viva** (Centre for Live Science; Wed–Mon 10am–6pm; 600$00), which hosts temporary exhibitions on subjects such as cutting-edge technology and multimedia. Highly absorbing if twiddling knobs and clicking a mouse is your thing. Behind the centre lies the **Jardim da Água** (Water Garden), crisscrossed by ponds linked by stepping stones, with various fountains, water gadgets and pumps to keep kids occupied for hours. At the foot of the gardens stands the **Pavilhão da Realidade Virtual** (Virtual Reality Pavilion: Tues–Sun 1–7pm, Voyage to Oceania 1000$00, Voyage to Virtual Oceanarium 300$00, combined tickets 1200$00). Tickets go on sale at midday and it's worth getting here at this time as this has become one of the Parque's most popular attractions. The forty-minute simulation takes visitors through an imaginative recreation of the lost world of 'Oceania'. Alternatively, the Virtual Oceanarium is exactly what its name suggests, so you're probably better off heading for the real thing next door (see above).

On the riverfront side of the Virtual Reality Pavilion is the **Jules Verne Auditorium**, the Parque's main venue for classical music and opera. Beyond here, a narrow walkway leads across Olivais docks below the **cable car** (Mon–Fri noon–7pm; Sat–Sun 10am–8pm; 500$00) which shuttles you to the northern side of the Parque, giving commanding views on the way.

The cable car takes you just beyond the **Jardim Gardia de Orta** (Garcia de Orta garden), a leafy waterside strip displaying plant species collected from Portugal's former colonies. But the main draw on this side of the Parque is a lift ride to the top of the **Torre Vasco da Gama** (Vasco da Gama Tower; daily 10am–8pm; 500$00). A relic from its former incarnation as part of an oil refinery, the viewing platform at the top gives a 360 degree panorama over Lisbon, the Tejo and into the Alentejo to the south. There also a pricey restaurant on the summit (see p.96). Opposite the tower is the **Sony Plaza,** Lisbon's largest purpose-built outdoor arena which hosts concerts and sports events; there is also a giant screen showing live soccer or pop videos most evenings. Opposite here, Lisbon's trade fair hall, the **Feira Internacional de Lisboa** (FIL) hosts various events including a handicrafts fair displaying crafts from round the country (usually in July). To find out about events, call ☎218 917 420, or refer to the Web site: *www.parquedasnações.pt.* At the back of FIL, the mock-colonial **Pavilhão de Macau** (Pavilion of Macau; Tues–Sun 10am–6pm; 250$00) is the only international pavilion remaining from Expo 98, and displays traditional and modern aspects of the former Portuguese colony, which was handed back to China in 1999, including a Chinese garden.

Heading back towards Olivais Docks you'll pass the bulk of the impressive **Pavilhão Atlântico** (Atlantic Pavilion), officially Portugal's largest indoor arena and the venue for major visiting bands and sporting events. From here it is a short walk back to Oriente station, or to the waterfront cafés and restaurants of Olivais Docks.

Eating

Lisbon has some of the best-value **cafés and restaurants** of any European city, serving large portions of good Portuguese food at sensible prices. A set menu (an *ementa turística*) at lunch or dinner will get you a three-course meal for 1800–2500$00, though you can eat for considerably less than this by sticking to the ample main dishes and choosing the daily specials. **Seafood** is widely available – there's an entire central street, Rua das Portas de Santo Antão, as well as a whole enclave of restaurants across the Rio Tejo at Cacilhas, that specialize in it. This is the only time you'll need to be careful what you eat as seafood is always pricier than other menu items. Several traditional restaurants still survive in Lisbon, most notably beautifully tiled **cervejarias** (literally beer halls) where the emphasis is often as much on drinking as eating; while the capital, naturally, also features some of the country's best (and most expensive) restaurants – specializing for the most part in a hybrid French-Portuguese cuisine. If you tire of all this, Lisbon has a rich vein of inexpensive **foreign restaurants**, in particular those featuring food from the former colonies: Brazil, Mozambique, Angola, Cape Verde, Macão and Goa.

There are plenty of restaurants scattered around the Baixa, where a multitude of set lunches are on offer to office employees, and there are some good places, too, in all the other areas in which you're likely to be sightseeing, up in the Alfama and out in Belém. **By night** the obvious place to be is Bairro Alto, which hosts several of the city's trendiest restaurants, as well as other more basic venues that offer fine value for money. Metro stops are given for outlying restaurants if this is the best way to reach them.

Note that many restaurants are **closed on Sunday evenings or Mondays**, while on Saturday nights in midsummer you may need to book for the more popular places: phone numbers are given below where necessary, or pass by during the day to reserve a table. The following are open daily unless marked. Assume moderate **prices** at all the places listed below – around 2500$00 per person for a two-course meal including wine – unless otherwise stated.

You can get snacks and sandwiches in most cafés and bars (see the following section); for locations of **markets** and central **supermarkets**, see p.108.

VEGETARIAN RESTAURANTS

The following restaurants are reviewed in the geographical listings below. Not all of these are purely vegetarian, but all offer good meat-free options.

Celeiro Macrobiótico-Naturista, Rua 1° de Dezembro 65, Baixa.

Centro de Alimentaçao e Saúde Natural, Rua Mouzinho da Silveira 25, Avda da Liberdade.

Centro de Arte Moderna, Fundação Calouste Gulbenkian, Saldanha.

Espiral, Praça Ilha do Faial 14a, Estêfania.

Farah's Tandoori, Rua de Santana à Lapa 73.

Os Tibetanos, Rua do Salitre 117, Avda da Liberdade.

Yin-Yang, Rua dos Correeiros 14-1°, Baixa.

Baixa

The restaurants are marked on the Baixa map p.69.

Andorra, Rua das Portas de Santo Antão 82. Occupying a raised bit of the street, the *Andorra* specialises in *açorda* and *arroz de marisco*, plus fresh fish and steaks served at its well-positioned outdoor tables. Inside it's small and cosy. Good value. Closed Sun.

Beira Gare, Praça Dom João da Câmara. Long-standing snack-bar restaurant opposite Rossio station serving stand-up Portuguese snacks and cheap lunches and dinners in the back diner.

A Berlenga, Rua Barros Queiróz 29, behind São Domingos church. A *cervejaria*/restaurant with a window stuffed full of crabs and seafood. Early-evening snackers at the bar munching prawns give way to local diners eating meals chosen from the window dislays. *Ementa turística* at 2000$00 offers best value, otherwise 3000$00 and up.

Casa do Alentejo, Rua das Portas de Santo Antão 58. Extravagantly decorated building which is as much private club dedicated to Alentejan culture as mere restaurant. The courtyard is stunning, as is the period furniture. The house also holds cultural exhibits, giving a great ambience to the sound Portuguese food.

Celeiro Macrobiótico-Naturista, Rua 1° de Dezembro 65. Just off Rossio, this health-food supermarket with basement self-service restaurant offers tasty vegetarian spring rolls, quiches and the like. Open till 7pm; closed weekends.

Gambrinus, Rua das Portas de Santo Antão 15 (☎213 421 466). One of Lisbon's top seafood restaurants, serving up dishes like broiled eel with bacon, lobster and dessert crepes in a smart, wood-panelled interior. Expensive.

João do Grão, Rua dos Correeiros 220–228. Established Baixa restaurant with *azulejos*-covered interior, outdoor seats, and good, reliable Portuguese dishes and interesting salads.

Leão d'Ouro, Rua 1° de Dezembro 105 (☎213 469 495). Very attractive, *azulejo*-covered restaurant specializing in seafood and grilled meats. Get there early to get a table.

Martinho da Arcada, Praça do Comércio 3. Beautiful, traditional restaurant, in the arcade, little changed from the beginning of the century when it was frequented by writer Fernando Pessoa. Closed Sun. Expensive.

Rei dos Frangos, Trav. de Santo Antão 11–18. Also known as *Bom Jardim*, this place has branches on two sides of an alleyway connecting Restauradores with Rua das Portas de Santo Antão. It is the place for spit-roast chicken – whole ones with fries for about 1000$00.

Solmar, Rua das Portas de Santo Antão 108 (☎213 423 371). A vast showpiece seafood restaurant, with fountain and marine mosaics, though recent reports suggest its standards of service and cooking have gone down somewhat. Expensive.

Yin-Yang, Rua dos Correeiros 14-1°. Macrobiotic-vegetarian lunches (noon–1pm), including tofu dishes, fruit juices and crepes. Main dishes cost 600–1300$00, and it's open from 6–8pm for light snacks. Closed weekends.

Chiado

Unless stated the restaurants are marked on the Baixa map p.69.

Associação Católica, Trav. Ferragial 1. Go through the unmarked door and head to the top floor for this self-service canteen offering different dishes each day. The chief attractions are the low prices and the fine rooftop terrace with views over the Tejo. Open Mon–Fri noon–3pm.

L'Entrecôte, Rua do Alecrim 121. The place to eat steaks washed down with fine wines. Relaxed, informal atmosphere in a spacious, wood-panelled interior with soaring ceilings (see Bairro Alto map p.72).

Tágide, Largo Academia das Belas Artes 18–20 (☎213 420 720). One of Lisbon's priciest restaurants, serving superb regional dishes in a dining room with sweeping city views. Book ahead, especially for a window seat. At least 6000$00 per person. Closed weekends.

Around Cais do Sodré

The restaurants are marked on the Bairro Alto map p.72.

Cais da Ribeira, Armazem A, Porta 2 (☎213 463 611). Attractive converted warehouse with river views around the back of Cais do Sodré serving superior (and pricey) fish, meat and seafood dinners, straight from the market. Closed Sun and Sat, Mon and Tues lunch.

Marisqueira do Cais do Sodré, Cais do Sodré (☎213 422 105). Big, expensive seafood restaurant by the station, complete with bubbling fish tanks. Try the *caldeirada de tamboril* (monkfish stew), the *caril de gambas* (curried prawns) or the seafood *parrilhada*. Closed first two weeks in August.

Porto de Abrigo, Rua dos Remolares 16–18. Old-style tavern-restaurant serving market-fresh fish at reasonable prices. Closed Mon.

Bairro Alto

Unless stated, the restaurants are marked on the Bairro Alto map p.72.

1 de Maio, Rua da Atalaia 8. Buzzing *adega* at the Chiado end of the road; good-value dishes of the day and sizzling meat and fish dishes. Closed all day Sun and Sat evenings

Adega do Teixeira, Rua da Teixeira 39. The leafy, streetside outdoor terrace is unusual for this part of town and the main appeal of this tranquil restaurant; all the usual Portuguese dishes and good salads. Closed Sun.

Alfaia, Trav. de Queimada 18–24. Very good-value lunches and dinners in characterful haunt full of *azulejos*, barrels of wine and a mixed, lively crowd. Closed all day Sun and Mon lunch.

Ali-a-Papa, Rua da Atalaia 95. Rare Moroccan restaurant in attractive interior. Good-value couscous and tajine dishes. Closed Tues.

Bizarro Rua da Atalaia 133. Unpretentious spot with a limited, but tasty, menu and a TV in the corner. The *ementa turística* is a good deal. Closed all day Mon, and Sat lunch.

Bota Alta, Trav. da Queimada 37 (☎213 427 959). This attractive old tavern with quirky, boot-themed decor (its name means 'high boot') attracts queues for its large portions of traditional Portuguese food. The tables are crammed in cheek-by-jowl and it's always packed; try to get there before 8pm. Closed all day Sun and Sat lunch.

O Cantinho do Bem Estar, Rua do Norte 46. Friendly, authentic tiled Alentejan restaurant – get there before 9pm. Cheap and with a good-value tourist menu including local wine. Closed Mon.

Casa Transmontana, Calçada do Duque 39. Tiny place specializing in cuisine from nothern Portugal, mostly meat-oriented. Inexpensive.

Cataplana, Rua do Diário de Noticias 27. Quirky local where simple Portuguese food and speciality *cataplanas* are served in a room with bubbling fish tanks, wall-mounted guitars and occasional live music.

Cervejaria da Trindade, Rua Nova da Trindade 20. Huge, vaulted beer hall-restaurant, with some of the city's loveliest *azulejos* on the walls. It specializes in shellfish, though go for the experience rather than the food, which is overrated.

Comida de Santo, Calçada Engenheiro Miguel Pais 39. Rowdy, late-opening Brazilian restaurant serving cocktails and classic dishes. Off Rua das Escola Politécnica, opposite the entrance to the botanical gardens. Expensive.

Faz Frio, Rua Dom Pedro V 96. A beautiful, traditional restaurant, replete with tiles and distinctive private cubicles. Huge portions of *bacalhau*, seafood paella and daily specials at inexpensive prices. A five-minute-walk north of the Bairro Alto up Rua Dom Pedro V.

Fidalgo, Rua da Barroca 27 (☎213 422 900). This has long been a fashionable and cosy hang-out for artists and media types, who are rewarded with delicious seafood creations such as *arroz de tamboril com camarão*. Closed Sun.

Hell's Kitchen, Rua da Atalaia 176 (☎213 422 822). Fashionable place with unusual and good- value dishes such as falafels and creole salmon.

Mamma Rosa, Rua do Grémio Lusitano 14. Late-opening pizza and pasta restaurant popular with the student and gay communities; always bustling and good-value.

Pap'Açorda, Rua da Atalaia 57–59 (☎213 464 811). Famous restaurant attracting arty celebrities who enjoy the agreeable surroundings of a dining room converted from an old bakery, which is now hung with chandeliers. An *açorda* – the house speciality – is a sort of bread and shellfish stew, seasoned with fresh coriander and a raw egg. Reservations recommended. Expensive. Closed all day Sun and Mon lunch.

Patô Baton, Travessa dos Fiéis de Deus 28 (☎213 626 372). One of the most stylish interiors in Bairro Alto provides a backdrop for pleasant, French-inspired cooking. The *Bife Dijonais* is splendid. In summer there's terrace dining on the steps outside. Around 3500$00.

Sul, Rua do Norte 13. Idiosyncratic restaurant and tapas bar that serves all types of food from the South, ie southern Portugal/Spain/Italy, southern Africa and South America. Excellent Uruguayan steak dishes – don't ask for them well-done as the Belgian owner takes offence – and a wine list consisting of little-known Portuguese vintages. Open daily 12pm–2am.

Vá e Volte, Rua do Diário de Notícias 100. Family diner serving large plates of fried/grilled fish or meat; food is not spectacular but prices are thoroughly modest. Closed Mon.

Estrela and Lapa

Farah's Tandoori, Rua de Santana à Lapa 73. Between Lapa and Estrela, this is one of Lisbon's more reliable Indian restaurants and is good for vegetarians, with dishes such as vegetable *tikka massala* and *palak paneer*. Meat dishes are also fragrant and delicious. Closed Tues.

Flor da Estrela, Rua João de Deus 11. Neighbourhood restaurant around the back of the Estrela basilica, serving all the usual dishes and cheap wine. There are a few outdoor tables, but the interior is attractive. Try the *feijoada de marisco*. Closed Sun.

Sua Excelência, Rua do Conde 42 (☎213 903 614). Small, intimate restaurant in the heart of Lapa specializing in Mozambiquan tiger prawns. Marvellously inventive Portuguese cooking, worth the high prices. Reservations advised. Expensive. Closed Wed.

York House, Rua das Janelas Verdes 47, Lapa (☎213 968 143). Inside this sumptuous hotel is a surprisingly moderately priced restaurant serving delicious fish, meat, pasta and vegetarian options. In summer, you can dine in the tranquil courtyard. Closes at 9.30pm.

Around the Sé

The restaurants are marked on the Alfama and Castelo map p.76.

Delhi Palace, Rua da Padaria 18–20. Unusual Indian-run restaurant offering curries, pizza and pasta in traditional, *azulejo*-covered interior; full marks for innovation and pretty good marks for the cooking.

Estrela da Sé, Largo S. António da Sé 4. Beautiful, *azulejo*-covered restaurant serving inexpensive and tasty dishes like *alheira* sausage and salmon. Closed Sun.

Hua Ta Li, Rua dos Bacalhoeiras 115 (☎218 879 170). Highly rated Chinese restaurant, particularly popular at Sunday lunch when reservations are advised; good-value seafood along with usual Chinese dishes.

Retiro del Castilho, Rua da Padaria 34. Budget meals in a subterranean vault of paper-topped tables. Good for lunches, and soups are recommended.

Rio Coura, Rua Augusto Rosa 30. A couple of hundred metres up from the Sé, and despite the tourist trappings, this place offers good-value meals including rough house wine for around 2500$00, served in a traditional, tiled dining room.

Alfama and around the Castelo

Unless stated, the restaurants are marked on the Alfama and Castelo map p.76.

Arco do Castelo, Rua do Chão da Feira 25. Cheerful place specializing in Goan dishes; tempting shrimp curry, Indian sausage and spicy seafood. Closed Sun.

Casa do Leão, Castelo de São Jorge (☎218 875 962). Couldn't be better sited, within the castle walls and with outdoor summer terrace, offering a superb city view and slick service – which explains high but not too outrageous prices; tourist menu 4500$00, and main courses from around 2000$00.

Frei Pepinhas, Rua de São Tomé 13–21. Inexpensive, long, *azulejo*-covered bar-restaurant with checked blue tablecloths and decent Portuguese food; largely the haunt of locals. Closed Sun.

Lautasco, Beco do Azinhal 7. (☎218 860 173). Tucked just off the Largo do Chafariz de Dentro, this has a lovely courtyard with fairy lights, and is particularly good for *cataplana*s. One of the nicest outdoor options in the area; book ahead. Closed Sun and December. Expensive.

Malmequer-Bemmequer, Rua de São Miguel 23–25, at Largo de São Miguel. Charcoal-grilled meat and fish (try the sole) served up amidst cheery, flowery decor. Tourist menu 2250$00. Closed all day Sun and Tues evenings.

Mercado de Santa Clara, Campo de Santa Clara, east of São Vicente de Fora. Above the old market building, this offers award-winning cuisine and river views; specializes in beef and meat dishes with small fish selection. Closed all day Mon and Sun evening.

Mestré André, Calçadinha de Santo Estevão 4–6. A fine tavern with a bit of traditional colour about it, superb pork dishes and good *churrasco* (grills). Outdoor terrace seating in summer. Closed Sun.

Santo André, Costa do Castelo 91. Just down from the puppet museum, this is a very inexpensive local with a small terrace overlooking tram route #12; unexceptional but reliable meat and fish dishes, and salads.

São Cristóvão, Rua de São Cristóvão 28–30. Wonderful, titchy Cape Verdean restaurant which somehow squeezes in live African music on weekends, while serving dishes such as *galinha caboverdiana* (chicken with coconut milk).

A Tasquinha, Largo do Contador Mor 5–7. Considering its position, on the main route up to the castle, this lovely *tasca* has remained remarkably unaffected by tourism, with a few tables in its traditional interior and a fine outdoor terrace. Closed Sun.

Via Graça, Rua Damasceno Monteiro 9b (☎218 870 830). Unattractive new building but an interior offering stunning panoramas of Lisbon. Specialities include spider crab and duck with moscatel. Closed all day Sun, and Sat lunch.

Along and around Avenida da Liberdade

Casa da Comida, Trav. das Amoreiras 1 (☎213 885 376); metro Marquês de Pombal. One of the city's top French-Portuguese restaurants set in one of the city's nicest squares, under the aqueduct. Superb mansion surroundings, an outdoor patio and meals costing a good 6000$00 and upwards. Closed Sun.

A Casa de Pompeia, Rua da Alegria 23; metro Avenida. Well worth the uphill walk, for trendy Portuguese food, with good grilled meat dishes, and young, friendly staff. Closed Sun.

Centro de Alimentaçao e Saúde Natural, Rua Mouzinho da Silveira 25; metro Marquês de Pombal. Self-service restaurant with light, bright upstairs dining rooms and a summer courtyard. Serves good, inexpensive vegetarian options such as chickpea stew, pepper rice and natural fruit juices. Open Mon–Fri till 6pm.

Cervejaria Choupal, Rua do Salitre 9; metro Avenida. Rather gloomy backstreet *cervejaria*, just off the Avenida, but with tasty food and pleasant service. Try the *caril de marisco* (seafood curry). Inexpensive. Closed Sun.

O Manel, Parque Mayer, Av. da Liberdade; metro Avenida. The small group of theatres tucked off Trav. do Salitre also hides a cluster of restaurants, this one serving great *feijoada* and *bacalhau* in a log-cabin-style interior. There's even an open fire in winter. Closed Sun.

Os Tibetanos, Rua do Salitre 117; metro Avenida. Located in the Buddhist Centre, this stripped-pine restaurant has superb, unusual veggie food such as vegetarian paella. Closed Sat and Sun.

Restaurante 33, Rua Alex. Herculano 33; metro Marquês de Pombal. Fine old wood-beamed building where you can eat partridge stuffed with onions, duck rice, curried seafood and the like in some style but at moderate prices. Closed Sun.

Belém

Rua Vieira Portuense, a block back from the main Rua de Belém, off Praça Afonso de Albuqerque, is a terrace of little buildings housing a line of *tascas* and restaurants, all with outdoor seating. They're packed at lunchtime; expect to wait in line if you want to sit outside.

Càpsula, Rua Vieira Portuense 74. Cheap place with tiled interior, upstairs seating and outside tables catering to tourists tucking into tuna steaks, trout and the like.

Carvoeiro, Rua Vieira Portuense 66–68. An inexpensive little *tasca*, with good grilled fish and jugs of wine. A good-value choice with outdoor tables.

Ja Sei, Av. de Brasilia 202. Prowling waiters see to your every need in this modern place with great views over the Discoveries monument and prices to match. International and Portuguese dishes. Closed Mon evenings.

São Jerónimo, Rua dos Jerónimos 12 (☎213 648 797). Classic formal dining by the side of the monastery. High prices but worth it for excellent fish dishes. Closed all day Sun, and Sat lunch.

Vela Latina, Doca de Bem Sucesso. Trendy smart option overlooking the docks. Expensive Portuguese cooking and a late-night bar open till 2am. It has a cheaper self-service café round the corner. Closed Sun.

Saldanha, Estefânia, Campo Pequeno and Arroios

Centro de Arte Moderna, Fundação Calouste Gulbenkian, entrance by Rua Dr. N. de Bettencourt; metro São Sebastião. Join the lunchtime queues at the museum restaurant for good-value hot or cold dishes. There are excellent salads for vegetarians; you get a choice of four or six varieties. Open daily noon–4pm.

Restaurante Chimarrão, Campo Pequeno 79; metro Campo Pequeno. If you're looking for quantity, 3800$00 spent here gets you unlimited stabs at twelve types of barbecued meat and various salads – you'll need to pace yourself. There are also branches on Rua 1 de Dezembro 102, (Baixa), Avda Roma 90 and at Parque das Nações.

Espiral, Praça Ilha do Faial 14a, off Largo de Dona Estefânia; metro Saldanha or Arroios. Inexpensive, self-service macrobiotic restaurant downstairs (including vegetarian, Chinese and fish dishes) with adjacent snack bar and upstairs bookshop. The food isn't that great, but there's often live music at the weekend.

Cervejaria Portugália, Av. Almirante Reis 117; metro Arroios. Busy beer-hall-restaurant where you can either snack and drink at the bar or eat fine *mariscos* or steak in the dining room. A popular family outing and always busy. Open till 1.30am. Closed Sun.

Ser-Veja-Ria, Av. João XXI 80C; metro Campo Pequeno. As it sounds: a decent modern town *cervejaria*, with moderate food and drink.

Parque das Nações

Os Alentejanos, Cais dos Argonautas; metro Oriente. Great wooden barrels and a ceiling dangling with hams jolly up an otherwise dull building. Serves regional food from Alentejo district; tapas and thick red wines are the best bet. Closed Mon.

Restaurante del Uruguay, Cais dos Argonautas; metro Oriente. Chance to sample Uruguayan cuisine in modern restaurant near Water Gardens. *Picaña ala parrilla con papa paisana* (thin strips of beef with potatoes, garlic and salsa) is recommended. Closed Mon.

Restaurante Panorâmico, Torre Vasco da Gama (☎218 939 550); metro Oriente. Former oil refinery tower now an exclusive restaurant with fantastic views; decent Portuguese and international food at prices as high as the tower. Closed Mon.

Restaurante Viagen dos Sabores, Pavilhão de Portugal (☎218 918 617); metro Oriente. This attracts local politicians from the neighbouring Council of Ministers and is the closest you'll get to a culinary experience in the Parque; upstairs views over Olivais Dock, attentive service and expensive food such as *Alcatra da Terceira* (steak from the Azores). Closed Sun evenings and all day Mon.

Cafés, bars and clubs

Drinking, at its most prosaic level, is done in bars and cafés throughout Lisbon; some of the older **cafés** and *pastelarias* (specializing in cakes) in particular are worth dropping into at some stage during the day. For night-time drinking, there are a few good places in the **Alfama**, but the densest concentration of designer **bars and clubs** is found in the **Bairro Alto**, traditionally the centre of Lisbon's nightlife, with its cramped streets still sheltering around fifty or so of them, in addition to the fado houses and restaurants. As the night progresses, most Lisboetas seek out the nightlife along **Avenida 24 de Julho** and its surroundings, though this area is now less trendy than the docks a little further west at **Alcântara** and **Santo Amaro**, the latter right underneath the Ponte 25 de Abril.

Cafés

All the places listed below are good for breakfast, coffee and cakes or just a beer during the afternoon. Most stay open into the evening, too, with a few – like *A Brasileira* and *Cerca Moura* – also on the late-night bar-crawl circuit. All are open daily unless stated otherwise.

Académica, Largo do Carmo, Bairro Alto. Tables in one of the city's nicest, quietest squares, outside the ruined Carmo church. Also does light lunches – the grilled sardines are hard to beat.

Antiga Casa dos Pastéis, Rua de Belém 90, Belém. Excellent and cavernous, tiled pastry shop and café with scrumptious *pasteis de Belém*.

Bernard, Rua Garrett 104, Chiado. Superb cakes, ice cream and coffees, which you can sample on the outdoor terrace on Chiado's most fashionable street. Open Mon–Sat until 2am.

A Brasileira, Rua Garrett 120, Chiado. Marked by a bronze of Pessoa outside, this is the most famous of Rua Garrett's old-style coffee houses. Livens up at night with a more youthful clientele swigging beer outside until 2am, though the interior is its real appeal.

A Camponeza, Rua dos Sapateiros 155–157, Baixa. Yesteryear *leitaria* (dairy shop) with tiled walls, snacks and milk products. Closed Sun.

Casa Chineza, Rua Aurea 274, Baixa. Beautifully decorated pastry and coffee shop. Closed Sat evenings & Sun.

Cerca Moura, Largo das Portas do Sol, Alfama. Stunning views of the Alfama from its esplanade; a good resting place as you climb up and down the hilly streets. Open till 2am, 8pm on Sun.

Martinho da Arcada, Praça do Comércio 3, Baixa. Traditional, old, stand-up café with outdoor tables under the arches, call in for a coffee and *pastel de nata*. Closed Sun.

Nicola, Praça Dom Pedro IV 24. On the west side of Rossio, this grand old place is not quite what it was following restoration in the 1990s, but is still a good stop for breakfast. Outdoor seats are always at a premium. Closed Sat afternoon, and all day Sun.

Pastelaria São Roque, Rua D. Pedro V 57c, Bairro Alto. Relaxed, ornate corner café where you can enjoy coffee and croissants below a wonderfully high ceiling.

Suíça, Praça Dom Pedro IV 96, Bairro Alto. Famous for its cakes and pastries; you'll have a hard job getting an outdoor table here, though there's plenty of room inside – the café stretches across to Praça da Figueira where the best tables are.

Bars and clubs

Lisbon does not immediately strike visitors as a city for **nightlife**, largely because many of its clubs are somewhat discreet, get going late and are concentrated in select areas of the city. But once in the know, you'll find its clubs and bars hard to beat. The **Bairro Alto** hosts one of Europe's biggest weekly street parties, with up to 50,000 people descending on the maze of streets over the weekend, drifting from bar to club before heading out to those at Alcântara and around the docks for the small hours. Several Bairro Alto clubs are extremely low key, revealing their presence simply by a street-light and a slot in the door for the attendant to inspect customers. Don't be intimidated by this: just knock and walk in – and straight out, if you don't like the look of the place. Also in Bairro Alto, and on its periphery, around **Praça Principe Real** and Rato, is much of the city's gay scene. You'll be hard pushed to find a bar open late at night in the **Baixa**, though things are picking up further east in the **Alfama** and **Graça**, where a growing number of bars cater for the crowds leaving the excellent local restaurants.

Though some of the trendy action still takes place along **Avenida 24 de Julho**, around Santos station, a lot of the nightlife action has moved to the docks, in particular those at **Alcântara** and **Santo Amaro** under Ponte 25 de Abril, and – more recently – opposite Santa Apolónia station. Here, tastefully done-up warehouses heave with a wealth of bars and clubs. The shift is partly the result of the local authority's plan to encourage clubs to move out of Barrio Alto into non-residential areas where they can stay open until 6am or later without disturbing the neighbours. Once some of the hippest operators had made the move, the transformation gathered momentum and now the districts attract a largely young, upmarket crowd, who flit from bar to bar before hitting the clubs. Santa Apolónia is on the metro, but to get to the other docks, you'll need to hop in a taxi or catch a train to **Alcântara Mar** from **Cais do Sodré**, which has a growing number of riverside clubs and bars itself. Committed clubbers, drinkers and low-life enthusiasts might try one of a dozen places along the nearby Rua Nova do Carvalho, which range from atmospheric to downright seedy.

Drinks are uniformly expensive in all fashionable bars and clubs – from 600$00 for a beer – but the plus-side is that very few charge admission. Generally, where there is an **admission charge**, you can expect to pay around 3000$00, which usually includes a drink or two; if you're handed a ticket on entry, keep hold of it to claim your first drink. **Friday and Saturday nights** tend to be overcrowded and expensive everywhere; while on

Sunday, especially in Bairro Alto, places often close to sleep off the weekend excesses. Note that none of the places listed below **opens** much before 10pm unless otherwise stated; all are open until at least 2am, with most doing business much later than that, 3–4am is normal, 7am not unheard of. Unless stated otherwise, the following are open daily. Metro stops are given for places in outlying areas if this is the best way to reach the place.

Baixa and Chiado

A Ginginha, Largo de São Domingos 8. Everyone should try *ginginha* – Portuguese cherry brandy – once. There's just room in this microscopic joint to walk in, down a glassful and stagger outside to see the city in a new light.

A Licorista, Rua dos Sapateiros 218. Attractive, traditional tiled and brick interior bar, a good spot for a refreshment stop near the Baixa shops. At lunchtime tables are set for inexpensive meals. Closed Sat afternoon and all day Sunday.

Café Rosso, Galerias Garrett, Rua Ivens 57, entrance on Rua Garrett. Courtyard bar that also serves coffee and snacks in the renovated shop galleries off Rua Garrett, a relaxed spot with seats under huge square canopies. Downstairs there's a huge room with modernist seats and lighting.

Around Cais do Sodré

Armazém F, Armazém F, Cais do Sodré. Converted *armazém* (warehouse) has room for a bar, restaurant and club, though it still fills up after 1.30am when you may have to queue to get in; Thursday night is ballroom dancing night.

Irish Pub O'Gilins, Rua de Remolares 8. This was the first of a growing band of popular – if pricey – Irish bars with a pleasant, light wooden interior and live music from Thursday to Saturday. Pub quizzes too on Sundays too.

Jamaica, Rua Nova do Carvalho 8. Set on a seedy road this is a very characterful club thanks to a mixed bag of clientele from sailors to ex-pats and trendies; music is predominantly retro, with reggae on Tuesday nights. Open till 4am, closed Sundays.

Poisa Copos, Cais da Ribeira. Small bar in a converted warehouse by the river; handy for a pick-me-up at six in the morning; popular with students and a good place for drinks or snacks. Closed Sun.

Rock City, Rua da Cintura do Porto de Lisboa, Cais de Santos. Flash American-style bar and club just above Cais do Sodré station and next to the river – just head for the palm trees. As well as the outdoor esplanade, there's a restaurant and live – usually rock – music most nights. Open till 3am.

Bairro Alto

The map on p.99 shows the whereabouts of the bars and clubs listed below.

Apollo XIII, Trav. da Cara 8. Most nights, a young, boisterous student crowd stuffs itself into this hard-to-spot aluminium sweatbox, a likeable place for a drink until 3.30am. Closed Sun.

Arroz Doce, Rua da Atalaia 117–119. Nice, normal bar in the middle of otherwise frenetic nightlife. Friendly owners and a good spot for an early or late beer; or try "Auntie's" sangria. Closed Sun.

Bar Ártis, Rua do Diário de Notícias 95. A relaxed, mildly sophisticated bar wallowing in jazzy decor and music, with a fine range of snacks such as chicken toasties, too. Open til 2am (4am at weekends). Closed Mon.

Cafédiario, Rua do Diário de Notícias 3. Jazz and laid-back dance music in a basic bar with a heavy gay presence.

Catacumbas Jazz Bar, Trav. da Água da Flor 43. The 'catacombs' used to be a secretive hideaway for trendies in the know. Rebuilding work has opened it up, though, with occasional live music and it's now too obvious to be particularly trendy; still a decent spot for a drink. Closed Sun & Mon.

Cena de Copos, Rua da Barroca 103–105. Not a club to frequent unless you're under 25 and bursting with energy, though the cheap cocktails at least help anyone feel under 25. Don't turn up until after midnight.

Cervejaria Real Fábrica, Rua Escola Politecnica 277. A fifteen-minute-walk north downhill in Rato, this is famous for its own brewed beer, which you can enjoy at the long, curly wooden bar or at smart tables beneath huge mirrors. Good upstairs restaurant, too.

BAIRRO ALTO BARS & CLUBS

BARS & CLUBS

1 Snob	7 Apollo XIII	13 Frágil	19 Os Três Pastorinhos
2 Pavilhão Chinês	8 Instituto do Vinho do Porto	14 Catacumbas Jazz Bar	20 Bar Ártis
3 Cervejaria Real Fábrica	9 Sen Nom Bar	15 Arroz Doce	21 Cena de Copos
4 Bar Nova	10 O Tacão Grande	16 Portas Largas	22 Tertúlia
5 Harry's Bar	11 Independente	17 Incógnito	23 Café Targus
6 Lisboa	12 Keops	18 Sudoeste	24 Cafédiario

Frágil, Rua da Atalaia 126. An icon of trendiness for years before the owner opened *Lux* (see below). Partly gay, definitely pretentious, this continues to be a fashionable club belting them out from Thursday to Saturdays till 4am, slighly quieter on other days. Best after 1am. Ring bell to get in. Closed Mon.

Harry's Bar, Rua de São Pedro de Alcântara 57. A tiny front-room bar, with waiter service, bar snacks and an eclectic clientele – often including late-night, slighly older contingent from the nearby gay discos. Ring bell for admission. Closed Sun.

Incógnito, Rua dos Poiais de São Bento 37. Appropriately named as only indication is a pair of large metallic doors. The low-lit, plush dance floor downstairs bangs out various tunes. Tuesday nights feature pop classics, Thursday is big beat night. Closed Sun and Mon.

Independente, Trav. de Água da Flor 40. Fashionable metal and wood bar playing loud and catchy rock. Friendly English-speaking staff. Closed Sun.

Instituto do Vinho do Porto, Rua de São Pedro de Alcântara 45. This is firmly on the tourist circuit, with over 300 types and vintages of port, supposedly from around 200$00 a glass upwards, served at low tables in a comfortable old mansion. Waiters are notoriously snooty and the cheaper ports never seem to be in stock, but it's a good place to kick off an evening. Closed Sun.

Keops, Rua da Rosa 157–159. Small, friendly bar with a tiny dance floor. The house sangria will make you want to get down to the soul, jazz and funk which varies nightly depending on the resident DJ. Open till 3.30am; closed Mon.

Lisbona, Rua da Atalaia 196. Earthy, local bar with its share of quirky regulars, but its chequer-board tiles covered in soccer memorabilia, old film posters and graffiti also lure in Bairro Alto trendies. Catchy music and inexpensive beer, too. Closed Sun.

Bar Nova, Rua da Rosa 261. The club with matt-black frontage, hip rock and pop play out as you shuffle between the three rooms and terrace. 'Revival' nights on Sun and Mon.

O Tacão Grande, Trav. da Cara 3. Barn-like bar pulls in young crowd into thumping rock, beer and free popcorn. Closed Mon.

Café Targus, Rua do Diário de Notícias 40. Very much on the night-out circuit for clubbers, this bar gets lively at around midnight before the regulars move on to the clubs. Usually has a good mix of soul, funk and jazz.

Os Três Pastorinhos, Rua da Barroca 111. Another "in" place, which gets very busy after midnight: music varies between dance and easy listening, funk and soul. Open till 4am; closed Mon.

Pavilhão Chinês, Rua Dom Pedro V 89. A wonderfully decorated bar, completely lined with mirrored cabinets full of ludicrous and bizarre tableaux of artefacts from around the world, including a room full of old war helmets. Drinks include a long list of speciality cocktails.

Portas Largas, Rua da Atalaia 105. Atmospheric, black-and-white tiled *adega* with cheapish drinks, music from fado to pop and a varied, partly gay crowd, which spills out onto the street on warm evenings. Often a starting point for clubbers moving on to *Frágil* opposite.

Sem Nom Bar, Rua Diário de Noticias 132. Popular modern sounds and cheapish drinks make for a great atmosphere at the weekends. During the week, grab a seat by the door and watch the world go by. Open till 4am.

Snob, Rua do Século 178. Appropriately named upmarket bar-restaurant towards Principe Real, full of media people. A good spot for cocktails or a late-night light meal (steaks always good); open until 2am.

Sudoeste, Rua da Barroca 135. No longer the in-crowd's hangout but a friendly club with small dance floor and areas for chats. Ring for admission. Happy hour from 10pm–1am during the week; that's quite an hour. Closed Mon.

Tertúlia, Rua do Diário de Notícias 60. Laid-back café-bar, with inexpensive drinks, papers to read, background jazz and varied art exhibitions that change fortnightly. If you fancy the urge to play, there's a piano for customers too. Open till 4am; closed Sun.

Alfama, Graça and Santa Apolónia

Bar da Graça, Trav. da Pereira 43. Off the east side of Largo da Graça, this arty bar mixes live music with exhibitions, and serves a mean range of cocktails and snacks. Closed Sun.

Chapitô, Costa do Castelo 1/7. (☎218 878 225). Multimedia centre incorporating a circus school, an open-air bar and a marvellous river view. It's youthful, highly fashion-conscious and there's no charge for admission; the only problem is the notoriously fickle opening hours so phone before you trek up the hill. Closed Sun.

Costa do Castelo, Calçada do Marquês de Tancos 1B. Sunny terrace-café and bar with views over the Baixa and a long list of cocktails. Live music most Thursday and Friday evenings (usually African, Brazilian or jazz) and poetry readings during the week. There's a good-value restaurant, too, serving fine Mozambiquan dishes in the evenings. Open 3pm–2am. Closed Mon.

Graça Esplanado, Caraçol da Graça. Esplanade-bar underneath the Miradouro da Graça, with great views and, as it gets late, pumping music. Great place for a drink at sunset.

Lux, Rua Gustavo Matos Sequeira 42. This vast, green and blue concrete lump has surpassed *Frágil* (see p.99) as Lisbon's fashionable place to be seen and was the first place to venture into the docks opposite Santa Apolónia station. With its tasteful decor on three floors (the basement is the place to dance), fantastic lightshows, varied sounds, river views and beautiful people, it pretty much has the lot. Open 4–8pm on Sunday for those wanting a quiet drink, otherwise open 11pm–4am; closed Mon.

Sua Excelência O Marquês, Largo Marquês do Lavradio 1. Dark rock bar hidden away in a little square behind the Sé. Live music most nights. Closed Sun.

Tradicional, Rua Afonso de Albuquerque 4. Live Portuguese singing, viola playing and fado on Friday and Saturdays, with a decent range of drinks, including some extremely powerful local firewaters.

Avenida 24 de Julho and around

Indústria, Rua do Instituto Industrial 6. Increasingly popular club which attracts a varied crowd into a good time; the converted factory houses three bars and dancing area echoing to thumping sounds; best after 3am. Closed Sun and Mon.

Kapital, Av. 24 de Julho 68. Well-established trendy hotspot, with three sleekly designed floors full of *queques* (yuppies) paying high prices for drinks and listening to techno, but it's hard work getting past the style police on the door. There's a great rooftop terrace. Wednesday night is rock night. Open till 6am, until 4am on Sun and Mon.

Kremlin, Escadinhas da Praia 5. Another of the established fashionable nightspots, this is packed with flash, young, raving Lisboetas. Tough door rules, and don't bother showing up before 2am. Open till 7am; closed Sun & Mon.

Metalúrgica, Av. 24 de Julho 110. Fairly unpretentious, good-time club, cheaper than most, dishing out pop, blues and soul for a happy, mixed crowd till 4am.

Plateau, Escadinhas da Praia 3–7. This club, which was well-designed by nightclub mogul Pedro Luz, has remained pretty much unchanged over the last few years, the result of which is a gentle admission policy which makes it easy to get in. Good if you like pop, rock and 90s indie sounds Wednesday is considered the best night. Open till 6am; closed Sun.

A Última Ceia, Av. 24 de Julho 96. Rock and pop restaurant-bar where Thursday to Sunday is karaoke night with a vengeance. All the fun starts after midnight. Open till 4am; closed Mon.

Alcântara

Alcântara Café, Rua Maria Luísa Holstein 15. Expensive designer bar-restaurant blending industrial and modern architecture. One of the city's trendiest in decor and clientele. Most people have a drink here and move on to one of the neighbouring clubs. Open 8pm–3am.

Alcântara-Mar, Rua Cozinha Económica 11. Big, glitzy house-techno spot, attracting soccer stars, gays, executives and trendies amid the chandeliers, candelabras and country-house furnishings. Great fun. Daily from 11.30pm.

Benzina, Trav. Teixeira Junior 6. Smart chrome-and-wood interior. Disco and funk night on Tuesday, slipping into underground sounds on Wednesday and Thursday. Closed Mon.

Paradise Garage, Rua João de Oliveira Miguens 38–48. Extremely trendy café and club and also a major venue for bands. Wednesday night is rock night. Opens at midnight, closed Sun.

Pillon, Rua do Alvito 10. Cape Verdean disco sounds for a relaxed in-crowd. Best night is said to be Tuesday.

Rock Line, Rua das Fontainhas 86. Straight-down-the-line rock and roll in a small club. Tuesday night is ladies night when women get free drinks, a ploy which succeeds in turning the place into a cattle market. Open till 6am; closed Mon.

Doca de Alcântara

Blues Café, R. Cintura do Porto de Lisboa. Cajun food in the restaurant plus dancing till 4am in what is claimed to be Lisbon's only blues bar. Closed Sun.

Cais de Alcântara. One of a row of bar-restaurants on boats in the docks, this one with moderately priced food, a pool table and lively music. Closed Sun.

Indochina, R. Cintura do Porto de Lisboa. Large, eastern-influenced restaurant in a converted warehouse done up in the style of a 1930s colonial mansion, which becomes a "dance club" when the eating's over. Thursday nights are the most lively, with soul, jungle, Latin and classics spinning till the small hours. Closed Sun.

Doca de Santo Amaro

Unless otherwise stated, all of the following are clustered around the small Doca de Santo Amaro, beneath Ponte 25 de Abril.

Café da Ponte. Bills itself as Lisbon's craziest café, serving everything from croissants to cocktails plus meals until 11.30pm. Sunday night karaoke and live sounds on Thursday.

Cais S. Dancing till 4am combined with the chance to drink by the river in this minimalist bar decorated with giant metal insects.

Doca de Santo. Designed by nightclub mogul Pedro Luz, this large, palm-fringed club, bar and restaurant was one of the first places in the docks to attract – and keep – a late-night clientele. Closed Mon.

Doca 6 (☎213 957 905). Rated as one of the best bars in the docks and also has good – if pricey – food. Restaurant tables get snapped up so it is best to reserve. Closed Mon.

Zonadoca. Worth a visit for its ice creams, though you can also enjoy coffee or alcohol inside or outside this friendly, family-oriented café. Open till 4am.

Lapa

Foxtrot, Trav. de Santa Teresa 24r/c. The place to go for a relaxing drink on one of the comfy sofas or the outdoor patio. Lots of cocktails and snacks plus a snooker table.

Stones, Rua do Olival 1. Upmarket joint for good-time Sixties' and Seventies' rocking, pricey and endless list of drinks and grooving until 4am. Ring to enter. Closed Mon.

Belém

T-Clube, Edifício Espelho de Água, Av. Brasília. Politicians dine here and the jet-set dance here so not the place for your average clubber. High-spending, high-flying, thirty-something crowd strut their stuff to live music, house, or retro hits depending on the night (Thurs is the best dance night). Very pricey drinks and members-only policy though day membership is an option if you have the funds. Great riverside terrace, too. Closed Sun.

Gay and lesbian bars, clubs and discos

While the Lisbon **gay and lesbian** scene doesn't yet have the high profile common to some other European capitals, there are some lively goings-on around the borders of the Bairro Alto and the Rato quarter to its northwest. Unless stated, listings featured below are in this area.

Bric-a-Bar, Rua Cecílio de Sousa 82–84. Fairly cruisy gay disco with large dance floor, 'dark room' and various bars. Free entry.

Finalmente, Rua da Palmeira 38. A well-known and very busy place, with a first-class disco and lashings of kitsch. Weekend drag shows (at 2am) feature skimpily dressed young *senhoritas* camping it up to high-tech sounds. Free entry but minimum drinks consumption of 1000$00.

Katedral, Rua de Manuel Bernardes 22. Intimate, relaxed snooker bar attracting lesbian crowd; one of the better places for gay women.

Kings and Queens, Rua Cintura do Porto de Lisboa, Armázem H Naves A–B, Alcântara docks. Nightclub mogul Pedro Luz's latest offering is Lisbon's newest and most high-tech gay disco, though it attracts a large following of beautiful people of all sexual persuasions. Closed Sun.

Memorial, Rua Gustavo Matos Sequeira 42. One of the few clubs for lesbians, with floor shows some nights; otherwise low-key, with disco and 'romantic' sounds. Closed Sun.

Sétimo Ceu, Travessa de Espera 54. Real success story of recent years and obligatory stop for beers and *caipirinhas* served by Brazilian owner. Great atmosphere spilling out onto the street. Closed Sun.

Trumps, Rua da Imprensa Nacional 104b. Popular gay disco with a reasonably relaxed door policy. Packed from Thurs to Sat which sees a good lesbian turnout, a bit cruisy midweek. Drag shows on Sun and Wed.

Live music, the arts and other entertainments

Although tourist brochures tend to suggest that **live music** in Lisbon begins and ends with fado (see below) – the city's most traditional music – there's no reason to miss out on other forms. Portuguese **jazz** can be good (there's a big annual **International Jazz Festival** at the Gulbenkian in the summer), and **rock** an occasional surprise. For Lisboans, **African music** from the former colonies of Cabo Verde, Guinea Bissau, Angola and Mozambique is the happening sound, as is **Brazilian** music with artists touring frequently.

There's often a crossover between musical styles at many of the places listed below; it's always worth checking the listings magazines (see below) and posters around the city to see what's on. Note, too, that many of the bars listed in the previous section put on live bands on certain nights of the week. There's a charge to get into most music clubs, which usually covers your first drink, and most of them stay open until around 4am, often later. In addition, big American and British rock bands on tour – not forgetting the top visiting Brazilian singers – play at a variety of **local halls and stadia** (listed below); you can usually get advance tickets from the APEB kiosk (☎213 475 823) at the corner of Praça dos Restauradores (near the post office), which also has ticket and programme details for all the city's cinemas and theatres.

Most major **cultural events** in the city – including just about every classical music concert – are sponsored either by the Fundação Calouste Gulbenkian (p.81) or the Centro Cultural de Belém (p.87), both of which have a full annual programme. Classical music aside, there's a fair amount of other cultural entertainment in Lisbon: several **theatres**, countless **cinemas**, three top-flight **soccer** teams, summer season **bull-fights**, and a host of cultural and traditional **festivals**.

To find out **what's on**, pick up a schedule of exhibitions, concerts and events from the reception desks at the Gulbenkian and the Belém Cultural Centre. Most things are also listed, in English, in *What's On* and *Lisboa em*, free monthly magazines, or in the *Agenda Cultural* booklet (in Portuguese), published monthly by the city council. All are available from the tourist office. For other **listings and previews** of forthcoming events, concerts, bars, clubs and restaurants, get hold of the Friday editions of the *Diário de Notícias* or *O Independente* newspapers: both have pull-out listings magazines. You can also refer to Lisbon city hall's funky cultural Web site at *portugal.hpv.pt/lisboa/agenda/* with the all the low-down on upcoming events (arts and festivals) you'll need, plus info on museums and libraries.

Fado

Fado is often described as a kind of working-class blues, although musically it would perhaps be more accurate to class it as a kind of light operetta, sung to a viola accompaniment. Alongside Coimbra (which has its own distinct tradition), Lisbon is still the best place to hear it, in one of thirty or so nightclubs in the Bairro Alto, Alfama and elsewhere – either at a *casa de fado* or in an *adega típica*. There's no real distinction between these places: all are small, all serve food (though you don't always have to eat), and all open around 9 to 10pm, get going toward midnight, and stay open until 3 or 4am.

Their drawbacks are inflated minimum charges – rarely, these days, below 4000$00 – and, in the more touristic places, extreme tackiness. Uniformed bouncers are fast becoming the norm, as are warm-up singers crooning Beatles' songs, and photographers snapping your table. Ask around to discover which are the most authentic current experiences. For more on the roots of fado, see p.512. The following are open daily unless stated otherwise; metro stops are given when this is the best way to reach a place.

Adega do Machado, Rua do Norte 91, Bairro Alto (☎213 224 640). One of the longest-established Bairro Alto joints as photo portraits on the wall testify (heads of state included); the minimum consumption of 3000$00 isn't too hard to notch up; you'll end up paying more like 6000$00 a head for fine Portuguese cooking and several styles of fado from Lisbon and Coimbra. Closed Mon.

Adega Mesquita, Rua do Diário de Notícias 107, Bairro Alto (☎213 462 077). Another of the big Bairro Alto names, with better-than-average music and meals, air-conditioning and traditional dancing as well as singing.

Adega do Ribatejo, Rua do Diário de Notícias 23, Bairro Alto (☎213 468 343). Great little *adega*, with one of the lowest minimum charges and fado that locals describe as "pure emotion". Enjoyable also for its food, it remains popular with locals. The singers include a couple of professionals, the manager and – best of all – the cooks. There's a minimum charge of 2000$00. Closed Sun.

Parreirinha d'Alfama, Beco do Espírito Santo 1, Alfama (☎218 868 209). Just off Largo do Chafariz de Dentro, this place offers music by some renowned singers and food at reasonable prices; a fairly authentic experience. Closed Mon.

O Senhor Vinho, Rua do Meio à Lapa 18, Lapa (☎213 977 456). Famous Bairro Alto club sporting some of the best singers in Portugal, which makes the 4000$00 minimum charge (more like 8000$00 for a meal) pretty good-value. Good decor and relaxed atmosphere. Closed Sun.

A Severa, Rua das Gáveas 55, Bairro Alto (☎213 468 314). A city institution, named after a nineteenth-century gypsy singer who had an affair with a Count, with big fado names and big prices. Closed Thurs.

Taverna do Embuçado, Beco dos Cortumes 10, Alfama (☎218 865 078). Well-established *adega* with a nice feel. Gets some big-name visitors. Closed Sun.

Timpanas, Rua Gilberto Rola 24, Alcântara (☎213 972 431). This is one of Lisbon's most authentic options, away from the tourist scene. Minimum consumption is 2000$00. Closed Wed.

African music

B.leza, Largo Conde-Barão 50, Santos. Live music on most nights in this wonderful old venue; dance floor and table service. Closed Sun.

Keyanda, Rua Maria Luisa Holstein 11. Alcântara. (☎213 626 486). Fairly smart African club in a converted warehouse with live music on Tuesdays and Thursdays and dance music other nights; packed at weekends. Closed Mon.

Lontra, Rua de São Bento 157, Bairro Alto (☎213 691 083). You'll be hard pushed not to join in the animated dancing in this intimate African club with live music most nights; come after midnight. Closed Mon.

Ritz Club, Rua da Glória 57 (☎213 425 140); metro Avenida. Lisbon's largest African club occupies the premises of an old brothel-cum-music-hall, one block west of Av. da Liberdade. It's a great place, with a resident Cabo Verdean band, plus occasional big-name concerts. Closed Sun & Mon.

Brazilian music

Bipi-Bipi, Rua Oliveira Martins 6 (☎217 978 924); metro Roma. Uptown venue for Brazilian bands, exotic cocktails and dirty dancing. Closed Mon.

Chafarica, Calçada de São Vicente 81, Alfama (☎218 867 449). Tiny, pricey old Brazilian bar with live music till late most nights. Closed Sun.

Havana, Doca de Santo Amaro. (☎213 979 893). Cuban-themed bar-restaurant with wicker chairs and ornate stairway; live Brazilian sounds on Fridays.

Pê Sujo, Largo de São Martinho 6–7, Alfama. (☎218 865 629). The 'dirty foot' is just up from the Sé. There's an outdoor wooden terrace and live bands most nights which can result in massive table-banging sessions if the audience approves. Closed Mon.

Pintaí, Largo Trindade Coelho 22, across the road from the São Roque church. Bouncy Brazilian music and cocktails. Open till 3am; closed Sun.

Salsa Latina, Gare Marítima de Alcântara. A bar-restaurant just outside the docks offering salsa nights Thurs to Sat from midnight to 3am with riotous dancing to a live band serving up Brazilian rhythms, jazz, Dixieland and other sounds. Monday to Wednesday offers the chance to have salsa dance lessons, or just come and admire the terrace views. Food is moderate, but for the bar, minimum consumption is 5000$00.

Rock and pop

Álcool Puro, Av. Dom Carlos I 59, Santos (☎213 967 467). Different bands every night in this rock bar. Closed Sun.

Anos Sessenta, Largo do Terreirinho 21, Mouraria (☎218 873 444); metro Martim Moniz. This small club ("The Sixties") has different rock bands on Fridays and Saturdays; as you can guess, the music is retro. It's a few minutes' walk from Largo Martim Moniz, near the castle. Closed Mon.

Paradise Garage, Rua João de Oliveira Miguens 38, Alcântara (☎213 955 977). This club (see also p.101) hosts regular gigs, including foreign bands. Closed Sun.

Rock City, Rua da Cintura do Porto de Lisboa, Cais do Santos. (☎213 428 640). Live music most nights by the river in brash, American-themed warehouse conversion (see p.98).

Jazz

Café Luso, Trav. da Queimada 10, Bairro Alto (☎213 422 281). Touristy fado joint with regular weekend jazz sessions from 11pm. Closed Sun.

Hot Clube de Portugal, Praça de Alegria 39, off Av. da Liberdade (☎213 467 369); metro Avenida. The city's best jazz venue – a tiny basement club that hosts local and visiting artists. Closed Mon.

Speakeasy, Armazém 115, Cais das Oficinas, Doca de Alcântara. (☎213 957 308). Newish docklands jazz venue with some big and up-and-coming names; sets after 11pm. Food also served. Closed Mon.

Large venues

Atlantic Pavilion, Parque das Nações (☎218 918 409); metro Oriente. Big name stars play at Portugal's largest indoor venue which holds up to 17,000 spectators.

Aula Magna, Reitoria da Universidade de Lisboa, Alameda da Universidade (☎217 967 624); metro Cidade Universitaria. The student union venue, which feels like a lecture hall; seating only.

Coliseu dos Recreios, Rua das Portas de Santo Antão, Baixa (☎213 461 997 or 213 431 697). Main city centre indoor rock and pop venue set in a lovely old, domed building.

Estádio José Alvalade, (☎217 589 021); metro Campo Grande. The Sporting Lisbon soccer stadium stages concerts by huge international stars.

Estádio do Restelo, Restelo, next to Belém (☎213 010 461). Belenenses soccer stadium plays host to smaller rock and pop bands.

Sony Plaza, Parque das Nações (☎218 918 409); metro Oriente. The Parque's main outdoor venue, holds up to 10,000 people for summer concerts and New Year's Eve extravaganzas; also has big screen for soccer matches.

Classical music, theatre and opera

There are three **concert halls** (including an outdoor amphitheatre) at the Gulbenkian (see p.81), both a large and small auditorium at the Centro Cultural de Belém (see p.87), and two auditoriums in the enormous, modern Culturgest arts complex at Av. João XXI 63, near Campo Pequeno (☎217 905 454). In addition, regular **classical music** concerts take place at the Teatro Nacional de São Carlos, Rua Serpa Pinto 9, Chiado (☎213 465 914); the Teatro Municipal de São Luís, Rua António Maria Cardoso 40, Baixa (☎213 421 772); the Coliseu dos Recreios, Rua das Portas de Santo Antão, Baixa (☎213 461 997 or 213 431 697) and at the Jules Verne Auditorium, Parque das Nações (☎218 918 409). Tickets range from 500$00 to 5000$00, though there are also **free concerts and recitals** at the São Roque church in Bairro Alto (every Saturday night), the Sé, the Basílica da Estrela, São Vicente de Fora and the Igreja dos Mártires.

For **theatre**, there are performances of Portuguese and foreign plays at the Teatro Nacional de Dona Maria in Rossio (Aug–June); ☎213 422 210) and an **opera** season (Sept–June) at the Teatro Nacional de São Carlos (see above). For details of ballet refer to the home page of the renowned Lisbon-based ballet, **Companhia Nacional de Bailado**, at *www.cnb.pt/*.

Film

Lisbon and its environs have dozens of **cinemas**, virtually all of them showing original-language films with Portuguese subtitles, and ticket prices are low (around 800$00; cheaper on Mon). Sadly, however, most of the city's Art Nouveau and Art Deco palaces, often with original period bars, have given way to multiplex centres. The tourist office should be able to tell you what's on, or consult the kiosk at the corner of Restauradores.

Among the most interesting **art-house** venues are Quarteto, Rua das Flores Lima 16 (☎217 971 378), off Avenida Estados Unidos (metro Entre Campos), with four screens; and the Instituto da Cinemateca Portuguesa (☎213 546 279), Rua Barata Salgueiro 39 (metro Avenida), the national film theatre, with twice-daily shows, ranging from contemporary Portuguese films to anything from Truffaut to Valentino.

Mainstream movies are shown, most centrally at the Xenon, Praça dos Restauradores (☎213 468 446) and the São Jorge, Av. da Liberdade 174 (☎213 579 144). At the Amoreiras complex (see p.81; ☎213 831 275) there are no fewer than ten screens; all, unfortunately, are modest in size. Other large centres include the fourteen screens in the Edifício Monumental, Av. Praia da Vitória 71, Saldanha (☎213 531 859) and the ten screens at the vast Colombo Shopping Centre, Av. Lusíada Letras (☎217 113 200); metro Colégio Militar-Luz.

Sports

Soccer is the biggest game in Lisbon, and **Benfica** – Lisbon's most famous football team – have a glorious past (the great Eusébio played for the team in the 1960s), though they have been struggling of late to keep up with rivals Porto. Games take place at the huge Estádio da Luz, Av. Gen. Norton Matos (☎217 266 129), north of the city centre, and you can buy tickets in advance from the kiosk in Praça dos Restauradores (at a small commission), or at kiosks (not the turnstiles) at the ground on the night. The stadium will soon be upgraded for the European championships which will be held in Portugal in 2004. The best way to get to matches is on the metro – Colégio Militar-Luz is a short walk from the stadium. **Sporting Club de Portugal**, Benfica's traditional city rivals, play at the Estádio José Alvalade (☎217 589 021) – metro Campo Grande or bus #1 or #36; a new state-of-the-art stadium is due to open next door to the old one in 2003. Top-division action can also be caught at the Estádio do Restelo, home of **Belenenses** of Belém (☎213 010 461); a trip out to the small Estádio Estrela Praia to watch F.C. Estoril can also be fun. Details of all matches are printed in the daily papers, especially the sports paper *Bola* – most of the regular league fixtures take place on Sunday afternoons (Sunday evenings for a few big events).

Bullfights take place most Thursdays (April–Sept) at the principal **Praça de Touros do Campo Pequeno** (metro Campo Pequeno; ☎217 932 093), just off Avenida da República; tickets cost 3000–10,000$00, depending on where you sit, and the performances start at 10pm. There are less frequent fights at Cascais in summer; travel out of Lisbon to Vila Franca de Xira and surrounding towns and villages for more traditional events.

Golf is best enjoyed at the upmarket courses around Estoril (see p.112). Portugal's Formula One **Grand Prix** also takes place in Estoril though the race has been cancelled for the last few years, as the track was considered too dangerous. For those into **water sports**, good surfing opportunities can be found at Caparica and windsurfing at Guincho and Ericeira, both of which have previously held world windsurfing championships.

Festivals and events

Lisbon's main **popular festivals** are in June, with fireworks, fairground rides and street-partying to celebrate the **Santos Populares** – saints António (Anthony; June 13), João (John; June 24), and Pedro (Peter; June 29). Celebrations of each begin on the previous evening; Santo Antonio's is the largest, taking over just about every square in Alfama. Also in June, the **Festas da Lisboa** are a series of city-sponsored events, including free concerts, exhibitions and culinary contests.

On the cultural front, there's the annual **Sintra Music Festival** and **Estoril Festival**, which take place throughout July and August offering – sometimes adventurous – performances by internationally known orchestras, musicians and dance groups. There are also various summer events in Cascais, mostly held in the Parque Palmela. Again at Estoril, and a lot better than it sounds, is the state-run **Handicrafts Fair**; crafts of all kinds, from every region of the country, are on display – if you buy anything, though, bargain at length. The fair runs through July and August, from around 5pm until midnight, with foodstalls included in the attractions.

Other events in Lisbon include a low-key **carnival** celebration in February or early March, and more vibrant celebrations on **New Year's Eve**, with fireworks and all-night partying in Praça do Comércio, in Cascais and around the Sony Plaza at the Parque das Nações.

Shops and markets

The more interesting **shopping areas** are detailed in the preceding pages: the Chiado district (p.71); the markets around Cais do Sodré (p.71); the Amoreiras complex (p.81); and the Alfama flea market (p.79). Some of the better **shops** are picked out below, along with a handful of **markets**. The Bairro Alto is fast becoming a centre for designer clothes and furniture but the main shopping area for **clothes** is in the modern city, from Praça de Londres north along Avenida de Roma. Portuguese designers also have outlets in Amoreiras shopping centre, Chiado and various fashionable stores in the Bairro Alto, while international designer names are fast appearing along Avenida da Liberdade.

Other than traditional **ceramics and carpets**, perhaps the most Portuguese of items to take home is a **bottle of port**: check out the vintages at the *Instituto do Vinho do Porto* (see p.100), where you can also sample the stuff. Alternatively, buy port or the increasingly respected Portuguese **wines** from one of the specialist shops listed on p.108, or from any delicatessen or supermarket. Metro stops are given below when this is the best way to reach a place.

Antiques, arts and crafts

Cheapish antique/junk shops are concentrated along **Rua do Alecrim** in Chiado and **Rua Dom Pedro V** in the Bairro Alto. None stands out above the others, but most make for some good browsing. Other interesting shops throughout the city include:

Antiquíssimo, Rua São Tiago 8, Alfama. One of many antique shops close to the Miradouro Santa Luzia, for bric-a-brac, old toys, *azulejos* and other bits and bobs. Closed Sun.

Deposito da Marinha Grande, Rua de São Bento 243, São Bento; metro Rato. Portuguese glassware at affordable prices. Closed Sun.

Fábrica Sant'ana, Rua do Alecrim 95, Chiado. If you're interested in Portuguese tiles – *azulejos* – check out this factory-shop, which sells copies of traditional designs and a great range of pots and ceramics. Closed all day Sun and Sat afternoon.

Fábrica Viúva Lamego, Largo do Intendente 25; metro Intendente. Highly rated *azulejo* factory-shop producing made-to-order designs or reproduction antiques. Closed all day Sun and Sat afternoon.

Olaria do Desterro, Rua Nova do Desterro 14; metro Intendente. Old family firm that's been turning out excellent Portuguese pottery for over 150 years. Closed all day Sun and Sat afternoon.

Pessoa de Carvalho, Costa do Castelo 4, Alfama. Cool, old Alfama town house with candles, glassware, jewellery, carvings, umbrellas and the like. Closed Sun.

Ratton Cerâmicas, Rua Academia das Ciências 2c, São Bento. Expensive gallery-cum-shop displaying and selling some of the country's classiest ceramics and tiles. Closed weekends.

Books and maps

All the following shops are closed all day Sun, and Sat afternoon.

Livraria Bertrand, Rua Garrett 73, Chiado; Loja 1129, Amoreiras (metro Rato); and also Av. de Roma 13B (metro Roma). Good general bookshops with novels in English, plus a range of foreign magazines.

Livraria Britânica, Rua Luís Fernandes 14, Just up from the Bairro Alto. English-language bookshop, which caters mainly for the British Council nearby, and is well-stocked.

Livraria Buchholz, Rua Duque Palmela 4, off Av. da Liberdade; metro Marquês de Pombal. Good range of English-language books and very helpful staff.

Livraria Portugal, Rua do Carmo 70–74, Baixa. Excellent Portuguese bookshop that features – among other fine books – *Rough Guides*.

SHOPPING HOURS

Traditional **shopping hours** are Monday to Friday 9am to 1pm and 3 to 7pm or 8pm, Saturday 9am to 1am. However, many of the **Bairro Alto** shops are open afternoons and evenings only, usually 2 to 9pm or so, while the **Amoreiras** shops stay open daily 9am to 11pm. Many larger shops now open all day, some even on Sundays.

Markets

Feira da Ladra, Campo de Santa Clara, Alfama. Flea market (see p.79). Tues & Sat 7am–6pm.

Mercado 31 de Janeiro Rua Eng. Vera da Silva; metro Picoas or Saldanha. Once an outdoor affair, this is now housed in a smart new block on two floors. Features everything from fresh fish and flowers to arts and crafts. Mon–Sat 7am–2pm.

Mercado da Ribeira, Av. 24 de Julho. Just up from Cais do Sodré, one of Lisbon's most atmospheric covered markets; the fish hall is fascinating (see p.71). Mon–Sat 6am–2pm.

Numismatists' market, Praça do Comércio, Baixa. Old coins and notes from Portugal and its former colonies. Sun morning.

Praça do Chile, off Av. Almirante Reis; metro Arroios. An interesting, general market set in a large circular building. Mon–Sat 7am–2pm.

Rotunda do Aeroporto, The main rag-trade market, with complete wardrobes of clothing for a few thousand *escudos*. Take an airport bus to get there and follow the crowds. Sun morning.

Supermarkets and shopping centres

The following are all open daily.

Colombo Shopping Centre, Av. Colégio Militar-Luz, metro Colégio Militar-Luz. Iberia's largest shopping complex boasts four hundred international and national stores, restaurants, cinemas and kids' areas.

Libersil, Av. da Liberdade 38. Modest, central shopping centre catering to most consumer needs.

Lojas de Conveniência Extra. Central branches of this supermarket chain include those at Campo das Cebolas 25, Alfama; and Rua Joaquim António de Aguiar 35; metro Marquês de Pombal. Good for late-night shopping, open 7am–2am.

Monumental, by metro Saldanha. Modern shopping centre with international chain stores, cinemas and cafés.

Pão d'Açúcar. Branches of this Brazilian supermarket chain can be found in the Amoreiras centre; at Rua Luís de Camões 133, Bairro Alto, and throughout the city. Most stay open daily until 8pm; the huge branch in the Amoreiras centre stays open until midnight.

Wine and food

Casa Pereira da Conceição, Rua Augusta 102–104, Baixa. Fine Art Deco 1930s shop selling tempting coffee beans and teas. Closed Sun.

Instituto do Vinho do Porto, Rua de São Pedro de Alcântara 45, Bairro Alto. Over three hundred types of port, so you should find something to your taste (see p.100 for further details). Closed Sun.

Londrina, Rua das Portas de Santo Andrão 55, Baixa. One of several shops on this street that are crammed with ancient ports, cheeses, *bacalhau* and hams. Closed all day Sun and Sat afternoon.

Manuel Tavares, Rua da Betesga 1A, Baixa. On the edge of Rossio, this small, century-old shop has a decent selection of wine, chocolate and national cheeses. Closed all day Sun and Sat afternoon.

Napoleão, Rua dos Fanqueiros 70, Baixa, at the junction with Rua da Conceição. Great range of port and wine, with knowledgeable, English-speaking staff. Closed Sun.

Listings

Airlines Air France, Av. 5 de Outubro 206 (☎217 900 202); Alitalia, Praca Marquês de Pombal 1, 5° (☎213 536 141); British Airways, Avda da Liberdade 36–2° (☎213 217 900); Go (☎0808 204 204); Iberia, Rua Rosa Araújo 2 (☎213 558 119); KLM, Campo Grande 220B (☎217 955 018); Lufthansa, Av. da Liberdade 192 (☎213 573 722); Sabena, Av. da Liberdade 144 (☎213 465 572); Swissair, Av. da

Liberdade 38 (☎213 226 000); TAP, Praça Marquês de Pombal 3 (☎213 179 100); Varig, Praça Marquês de Pombal 1 (☎213 136 830).

Airport information ☎218 413 700.

American Express The local agent is Top Tours, Av. Duque de Loulé 108 (metro Marquês de Pombal ; Mon–Fri 9.30am–1pm & 2.30–6.30pm; ☎213 155 885).

Banks Most main branches are in the Baixa and surrounding streets. Standard banking-hours are Mon–Fri 8.30am–3pm. ATMs can be found throughout Lisbon, and, if you have a credit or debit card are the best way of obtaining escudos. English-language instruction options are usually available.

Bicycle rental You'd have to be insane to do it, but you can hire bicycles for the day from Velocipédica do Alto do Pina, Rua Carrilho Videira 7 (☎218 130 177; Arroios metro); and Biocicio-Apoios a Actividade Turística, Rua Prof. Egas Moniz, Lt1-Anexo A, Parede (☎214 351 503). For even shorter-term hire, the kiosk by the ferry terminal at Belém hires out bikes for 800$00 per hour (Tues–Fri 10am–5.30pm, Sat & Sun 10am–7.30pm).

Buses The main terminal is at Av. João Crisóstomo (metro Saldanha; ☎213 545 775/213 545 439) for international and most domestic departures, including express services to the Algarve. There are other bus services from Praça de Espanha (metro Praça de Espanha) and Av. 5 de Outubro 75 (metro Saldanha; ☎217 262 740) for Transportes Sul do Tejo departures to Caparica, Sesimbra and places south of the Tagus; Campo Pequeno (metro Campo Pequeno; ☎217 910 579) for AVIC services to the north-west coast and SolexPresso to the Alentejo and Algarve; Campo das Cebolas, at the end of Rua dos Bacalhoeiros, east of Praça do Comércio, for Renex services to the Minho and Algarve (☎218 874 871); and Campo Grande 5 (metro Campo Grande) or Rua Fernandes da Fonseca (metro Martim Moniz; ☎217 951 447), northeast of Rossio, for Empresa Barraqueiro services to Mafra and Ericeira. You can buy advance bus tickets from most of the major travel agents, one helpful agency is Marcus & Harting, Rossio 45–50 (☎213 469 271).

Camping Orbitur have 21 campsites throughout the country including two in the Lisbon region (see p.67). For membership and information contact Orbitur, Rua Diogo do Couto 1–8. (☎218 117 070, fax 218 148 045; *info@orbitur.pt*).

Car rental If you're not picking up a car at the airport, ask at the main tourist office, who can arrange car rental for you and have the car delivered to your hotel. The main agencies in Lisbon are: Alamo/Guerin, Av. Alvares Cabral 45b (☎213 882 724); Auto Jardim, airport (☎218 463 187); Avis, Av. Praia da Vitória 12c (☎213 561 176) and at the airport (☎218 499 947); Budget, Rua Castilho 167b (☎213 860 516) and at the airport (☎218 478 803); Eurodollar, airport (☎218 478 748); Europcar, airport (☎218 401 176) and Santa Apolónia station (☎218 875 472); Hertz, airport (☎218 492 722) and at Rua Castilho 72 (☎213 812 430); Nova Rent, Largo Monterroio Mascarenhas 9 (☎213 870 808).

Car trouble Automóvel Clube de Portugal, Rua Rosa Araújo 24–26 (☎219 425 095), have a reciprocal agreement with automobile associations in other EU countries.

Email You can send email from the otherwise sterile *Web Café*, Rua do Diário de Notícias 12 daily 4pm–2am, (☎213 421 181; *web1@mail.esoterica.pt*) or at *Ciber Chiado*, above the *Café No Chiado*, Largo do Picadeiro 11, (Mon–Fri 11–1am, Sat 2pm–midnight; ☎213 466 722; *info@cnc.pt*). Larger outlets, which charge for sending email, include Espaço Agora (daily 3pm–2am), a student resource at Pavilhão 2, Av. Ribeira das Naus by Cais de Sodré ferry terminal; and the Forum Telecom building (Mon–Fri 9am–5pm), Av. Fontes Pereira de Melo 38, by metro Picoas.

Embassies Canada, Av. da Liberdade 144–3° (metro Avenida; ☎213 474 892); Ireland, Rua da Imprensa à Estrela 1–4° (tram 28 to Estrela; ☎213 929 440); Netherlands, Av. Infante Santo 43, 5° (tram 28 to Estrela; ☎213 961 163); South Africa, Av. Luís Bivar 10 (metro São Sebastião or Saldanha; ☎213 525 618); UK, Rua São Bernardo 33 (tram 28 to Estrela; ☎213 961 191); USA, Av. das Forças Armadas (metro Jardim Zoológico; ☎217 273 300).

Emergencies ☎115.

Fairs There's a permanent fairground, the Feira Popular, opposite the Entrecampos metro station: eats, rides and a thoroughly Portuguese night out (rides Mon–Fri 7pm–midnight, Sat & Sun 3pm–1am; restaurants open daily noon–3pm & 8pm–midnight; entrance 300$00, rides extra).

Hospital British Hospital, Rua Saraiva de Carvalho 49 (☎213 955 067 or 213 976 329) has English-speaking staff. For an ambulance, call ☎213 017 777.

Language courses Portuguese lessons are given by the Cambridge School, Av. da Liberdade 173 (☎213 527 474), or the Centro Europeu de Línguas, Rua Joaquim A. Aguiar 43 (☎213 863 782).

Laundry Lava Neve, Rua de Alegria 37, Bairro Alto; or try the one at Rua Saraiva de Carvalho 117, a little west of Rato (bus #9 from Rossio). Lavandaria Sous Ana, in the Centro Comércial da Mouraria, Largo Martim Moniz, does service washes for around 2000$00 (Mon–Sat 9.30am–8pm).

Left luggage There are lockers at the airport, at Rossio, Cais do Sodré and Santa Apolónia stations, and a left-luggage office at the bus terminal on Av. João Crisóstomo.

Lost property The police lost property office is at Rua dos Anjos 56a (metro Anjos). The metro office is at Restauradores metro (☎213 427 707); the Carris office is at Rua de Santa Justa 11 (☎213 427 944).

Newspapers There are several newsstands around Rossio and Restauradores – such as the one attached to the ABEP ticket kiosk – which sell foreign-language papers, as do the lobbies of many of the larger hotels.

Pharmacies and contraception Open Mon–Fri 9am–1pm & 3–7pm, Sat 9am–1pm. Local papers carry information about 24-hour pharmacies and the details are posted on every pharmacy door. Contraceptives – and even, in some areas, hypodermic syringes – are available from automatic vending machines outside pharmacies.

Police 24-hour office at Rua Capelo 13 (☎213 466 141), west of the Baixa near the Teatro de São Carlos. You need to report here in order to make a claim on your travel insurance.

Post Office The main post office is on Praça dos Restauradores 58 (Mon–Fri 8am–10pm, Sat & Sun 9am–6pm), from where you can send airmail and *correio azul* (express mail – the fastest service). There's a 24-hour post office at the airport. Stamps can also be purchased from some – but not all – newsagents.

Public toilets There are very few of these in the street. However, nearly all the museums and main tourist sights have a public toilet (*casa de banho, retrete, banheiro, lavabos* or WC), and it is not difficult to sneak into a café or restaurant if needs be. Gents are usually marked H (*homens*) or C (*cabalheiros*), and ladies M (*mulheres*) or S (*senhoras*).

River cruises Two-hour return trips down the Tejo depart from the Estação Fluvial (daily April–Oct 11am & 3pm; 3500$00) and go as far as the Ponte 25 de Abril. Prices include a drink and commentary, though the views are little different to the standard ferry crossings.

Students The Instituto da Juventude, Av. da Liberdade 194, 1000 Lisboa (9.30am–7pm; ☎213 151 955), offers practical advice and a library; or try Turismo Juvenil at Praça de Londres 9 (☎218 485 363, metro Alameda).

Swimming pools The most central option is the pool in the Atheneum club on Rua das Portas de Santo Antão, next to the Coliseu (Mon–Fri 3.30–4.30pm & 9–10pm; 500$00; Sat 3.30–7pm; 650$00).

Telephones For international calls, there's a telephone office next to the post office in Praça dos Restauradores (see above). There's a second office on the corner of Rossio (no. 65; 8am–11pm). You can also make international calls from any phone booth. Phonecards, available in denominations of 650$00, 1300$00 or 1900$00 from any post office, make calls from cabins a lot easier.

Tickets for football matches, films and other spectacles can be bought from ABEP, the kiosk at the corner of Praça dos Restauradores (☎213 475 823).

Tram and bus tours The Circuito Colinas ("Hills tour"; March–June & Oct, two daily; July, four daily; Aug, five daily; Sept, three daily; 2900$00, children under 10, 1600$00) takes you on a 90min tram ride from Praça do Comércio round the Alfama, Chiado and São Bento. The Circuito Tejo (May–Sept hourly 11am–4pm; 2500$00, children under 10, 1500$00) is an open-top bus tour around Lisbon's principal sites; a day ticket allows you to get on and off whenever you want. Tickets can be bought on board. For more information call ☎213 632 021.

Trains See "Arrival and information", p.58, for details of Lisbon's various stations. Timetables and train information are available at Rossio station information office (daily 10am–1pm & 2–6pm). For information about departures from any Lisbon station call ☎218 884 025 (daily 8am–11pm). Always check departure times and stations in advance: many intercity services require a seat reservation (particularly to Coimbra/Porto), which you can do prior to departure, though allow yourself plenty of time.

Travel agencies Specialists include Turismo Juvenil, Praça de Londres 9B (Mon–Sat 9am–1pm & 2.30–5.30pm; ☎218 485 363; metro Alameda); Tagus Travel, Rua Camilo Castelo Branco 20 (☎213 525 986), specializing in discounted student tickets. Transalpino, Av. Guerra Junqueiro 28 (☎218 482 279); and well-established charter agents Abreu, Av. da Liberdade 160 (☎213 476 441).

Walks The tourist office in Praça dos Restauradores (☎213 906 149; *jcabdo@ip.pt*) is the starting point for three-hour privately organized guided walks through Lisbon's historical and cultural areas. There are additional walks round the Alfama and Castle areas, beginning from Casa dos Bicos on Praça da Ribeira (Mon, Wed & Fri). Minimum groups of four people; two to three day's notice required.

Women's Movement The best contact points are: the Movimento Democrático das Mulheres, Av. Duque de Loulé 111–4°, 1110 Lisboa (☎213 527 853); Editora das Mulheres bookshop, Rua da Conceição 17, Baixa; and IDM (Informação e Documentação das Mulheres) at Rua Filipe da Mata 115a (metro Palhavã or bus #31 from Rossio to Praça de Espanha) – a women's centre incorporating a small library and café and very eager to welcome foreign travellers.

Youth hostels The central booking office for Portugal's Pousadas de Juventude is Movijovem, near metro Saldanha on Av. Duque D'Avila 137 (☎213 138 820, fax 213 528 621; *movijovem@mail.telepac.pt*).

AROUND LISBON

The most straightforward way to escape the city is to head for the string of beach resorts west along the coast from Belém, which can be reached by train from Cais do Sodré. At places like **Oeiras** and **Carcavelos**, and above all at **Estoril** and **Cascais**, the beaches are good even if the water quality isn't. For better sands and a cleaner ocean you'll have to head north to **Guincho**; or cross the Tejo by ferry to reach the **Costa da Caparica**, a thirty-kilometre expanse of dunes to the south of the capital. There's reasonably priced accommodation at all these places, as well as a youth hostel at Oeiras and campsites at Guincho and Caparica. But as you might imagine, all the beach resorts in the Lisbon area get very crowded at weekends and throughout August.

Basing yourself in Lisbon, you also could take in a fair part of the provinces of Estremadura (Chapter Two) and Alentejo (Chapter Eight) on day-trips. Indeed, some of those regions' greatest attractions lie within a fifty-kilometre or so radius of the capital – such as the palaces of **Queluz** or **Mafra** – and are best seen on a day-trip. The beautiful town of **Sintra**, the most popular excursion from Lisbon, demands a longer look, and reveals a different side if you stay overnight. However you decide to see them, bear in mind that most of the Sintra palaces are closed on Mondays, and those at Queluz and Mafra on Tuesdays. Further afield, south of the Tejo, the large town of **Setúbal** is noted for its Igreja de Jesus, the earliest of all Manueline buildings, while the coast to the south-west sports a succession of small resorts and beaches of varying degrees of popularity.

West to Estoril and Cascais

Stretching for over 30km west of Lisbon, the **Estoril coast** – from Oeiras to Cascais – makes for an enjoyable day out, drifting from beach to bar and strolling along the lively seafront promenades. Sadly, the water itself has suffered badly from pollution and though steps are being taken to clean it up, it remains something of a health hazard. Nonetheless, the coast retains its attractions and **Cascais**, in particular, makes a pleasant alternative to staying in Lisbon, and is well placed for trips to Sintra or to the wild Guincho beach.

Access to the resorts could hardly be easier. The Linha de Cascais train leaves every twenty minutes or so between 5.30am and 2.30am (185$00 one way) from **Cais do Sodré** station, stopping at Belém en route to Cascais. Beware, though, that some trains stop only at Alcântara, Oeiras and stations beyond. By road, the **N6** is the coastal highway, passing through most of the centres along the seafront, often as the Avenida Marginal; the faster **A5 motorway** (Auto-Estrada da Oeste) is an (inexpensive) toll road running from Lisbon to Estoril – drive west past Amoreiras and follow the signs.

Oeiras to São João

The first suburb of any size after Belém is **OEIRAS**, where the River Tejo officially turns into the sea. The **beach** here has recently been cleaned up, though most people swim in the Ocean Pool alongside the sands; riverside walkways are also being improved. Unless you're staying at the youth hostel (see p.67), however, the only reason for a stop here would be to see the **Palácio do Marquês de Pombal**, erstwhile home of the rebuilder of Lisbon. The house is now an adult education centre and the park is not technically open to visitors. However, if there's nothing special going on, the guard should be able to show you the gardens, or at least let you peer over the walls at its massive grotto.

Carcavelos

Next stop along the coast is **CARCAVELOS**, popular for its kilometre of beach, a great place for surfers, and its plethora of bars and cafés. The main motivation for a visit is the huge **market** that sprawls between the train station and town centre every Thursday – a great place to pick up cheap clothing.

São Pedro and São João

Along the last stretch of the Linha de Cascais, the beaches improve rapidly and you reach the beginning of an esplanade that stretches virtually uninterrupted to Cascais. **SÃO PEDRO** has a superb beach, just down from the station, and **SÃO JOÃO** is flanked by two lovely stretches of sand. The whole seafront here is pretty animated in the summer months, swarming with young surfers and Portuguese holidaymakers frequenting the numerous cafés and restaurants: *A Choupana* on the Estrada Marginal is a good choice.

Estoril

ESTORIL gained a postwar reputation as a haunt of exiled royalty and the idle rich, and it continues to maintain its pretensions towards being a "Portuguese Riviera", with grandiose villas and luxury hotels. It is little surprise, then, that the town's touristic life revolves around an exclusive **golf course** (golf passes are available from the tourist office) and **casino**. The latter – located within the attractive gardens of the **Parque do Estoril** – requires some semblance of formal attire to get in (daily 3pm–3am). Inside you'll find roulette, cards, slot machines, restaurants, shops, nightly shows at 11pm and even an art gallery.

Estoril also holds a yearly **Grand Prix**, which unfortunately has been cancelled in recent years because the course was considered too pot-holed; it usually takes place in September and should be repaired in time for 2001. At other times, unless you can afford one of the splendid sea-view hotels, the best move after a lounge on the pleasant sandy beach is out – following the **seafront promenade** through **Monte Estoril** to Cascais, a lovely walk that takes about twenty minutes.

Practicalities

The **train station** is on Estoril's through-road, with the beach accessible by underpass. Across the main road from the station, at the bottom of the park, you'll find the very helpful **turismo** (Mon–Sat 9am–7pm, Sun 10am–6pm; ☎214 680 113), which can give advice on private rooms and details of the area's various golf clubs. They can also point out where to catch the toy train which trundles round Estoril (daily 10am–7pm, every 30 minutes; 500$00).

Upmarket hotels aside, there are just a few **pensões**, of which *Pensão-Residencial Smart*, Rua José Viana 3 (☎/fax 214 682 164; ③), is perhaps the best, with pleasant rooms and breakfast included. It's east of the park – turn right out of the station, turning left when you reach Avenida Bombeiros Voluntarios, which runs up behind the *Hotel Paris*. If this is full, the *Pensão Maryluz*, Rua Maestro Lacerda 13 (☎214 682 740; ③), is just one block south, also off Avenida Bombeiros Voluntarios – breakfast is included here, too, and room prices drop considerably in winter.

For coffee and cake, a meal or just a late **drink**, it's nice to sit at the outdoor tables at *Frolic* (open till 2am), a restaurant, café and nightclub complex on Av. Clotilde 2765, overlooking the eastern side of the park. There are plenty of other **cafés and restaurants** around, none particularly worth singling out though the *English Bar*, Av. Sabóia 9 (just over the main road from Monte Estoril train station), is a bar-restaurant with sea views and a good local reputation, if on the pricey side. For **nightlife**, *Absurdo* on Praia do Tamaris is the current "in" place.

Cascais

At the end of the train line, and with three fairly good beaches along its esplanade, **CASCAIS** is now a major resort, with a new marina adding to its appeal. It is positively bursting at the seams in summer, especially at weekends, but despite its commercialism, it's not too large or difficult to get around and has a much younger, less exclusive, feel than Estoril, even retaining a few elements of its previous existence as a fishing village. There's a lively **market** every Wednesday on Rua do Mercado, to the right of Avenida 25 de Abril, and Sunday evening **bullfights** during summer in the Praça de Touros that draw a largely local crowd.

You'll find the main concentration of **bars and nightlife** – and consequently most of what makes Cascais tick as a town – on Rua Frederico Arouca, the main pedestrian thoroughfare on the east side of the Avenida Combatantes da Grande Guerra, which splits the town. Also in this area and worth a look is the **fish market** that takes place around 8am (Mon–Sat) between the Ribeira and Rainha beaches. For a wander away from the crowds, cross over Avenida Com. Grande Guerra, and stroll up beyond Largo 5 de Outubro into the old, and surprisingly pretty, west side of town, at its most delightful in the streets around the graceful **Igreja da Assunção**.

Cascais' other attractions are all to the west of the centre. Beyond the church lies the pleasant **Parque Municipal da Gandarinha** (daily 10am–5pm), in whose southern reaches stands the mansion of the counts of Guimarães, preserved complete with its nineteenth-century fittings as the **Museu Biblioteca Conde Castro Guimarães** (Tues–Sun 10am–5pm; 400$00); most days, there's someone around to give you a guided tour of the furniture, paintings and archeological finds housed here. On the north side of the park, opposite the Pavilhão de Cascais, signs point you to the modern **Museu do Mar** (Tues–Sun 10am–5pm; 400$00), an engaging little collection of model boats, sea-related artefacts, old costumes and pictures.

Taking the coastal road, it's about twenty minutes' walk or a short ride on the toy train (daily 10am–7pm, every 30 minutes; 500$00) west to the **Boca do Inferno** – the "Mouth of Hell" – where waves crash against caves in the cliff face. The viewpoints above are always packed with tourists (as is the very tacky market on the roadside) but, frankly, the whole affair is rather unimpressive except in stormy weather. En route, however, there's a little beach at **Praia de Santa Marta** with a nice café (see "Eating" below) on a terrace above. The beach sits next to Cascais' fort, closed to the public, but now guarding the entrance to the **marina**, with further shops, cafés and restaurants.

Practicalities

From the **train station** it's just a short walk across to Rua Frederico Arouca; **buses** to Guincho, Cabo da Roca and Sintra leave from the stands outside the station. Walk down Rua Frederico Arouca and cross the main avenue for the **turismo** (Mon–Sat 9am–7pm, Sun 10am–6pm; ☎214 868 204), set in an old mansion on Rua Visconde da Luz, where the staff can provide you with a map and will usually phone around on your behalf for private rooms. There are local bus timetables posted in here, too. They can also advise you on the best place to hop on the **tourist toy train** train that rattles from the station to Boca do Inferno (see above).

ACCOMMODATION

Prices in July and August are very high but most of the places listed below will drop room rates by up to forty percent out of season.

Hotel Albatroz, Rua Frederica Arouca 100 (☎214 832 821, fax 214 844 827; *albatroz@mail.telepac.pt*). Seaside hotels don't come much grander than this – one of the best in the region, with glorious views from rooms and restaurant, and top-of-the-range facilities. Around 45,000$00 in the height of the summer, half that in winter, but even more if you want a sea view. ⑨.

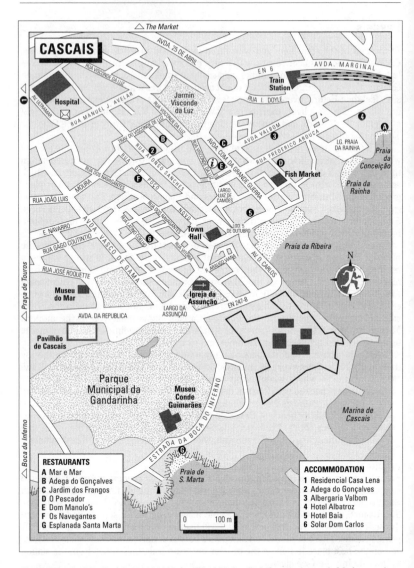

Hotel Baia, Av. Marginal (☎214 831 095, fax 483 10 95; *hotelbaia@mail.telepac.pt*). Modern seafront hotel overlooking the beach and harbour. Rooms are very good value out of season, and not bad in summer; it's worth booking ahead for a room with a sea view. ⑤.

Adega do Gonçalves, Rua Afonso Sanches 54 (☎214 831 519). Basic rooms above the restaurant; in a handy location but guaranteed to be noisy. ②.

Solar Dom Carlos, Rua Latina Coelho 8 (☎214 828 115, fax 214 865 155). A very attractive sixteenth-century mansion on a quiet backstreet with cool tiling throughout and a welcoming air. Bright, pretty rooms, garden and even an old royal chapel. Breakfast included. ④.

Albergaria Valbom, Av. Valbom 14 (☎214 865 801, fax 214 865 805). Modern, comfortable hotel between the station and the centre, furnished in the 1970s so now fashionably retro. Rooms with bath. Breakfast included. ④

EATING

Dom Manolo's, Av. Marginal 13. Busy grill house just down from the turismo, where the alley runs through to Largo Luís de Camões. Superb chicken and chips; add a salad, local wine and homemade dessert and you'll still pay only around 2000$00.

Esplanada Santa Marta, Praia de Santa Marta. Charcoal-grilled fish served on a tiny terrace overlooking the sea and little beach on the road out to the Boca do Inferno.

Adega do Gonçalves, Rua Afonso Sanches 54. Traditional *adega* not yet overwhelmed by tourists, serving huge portions of good food at moderate prices; the grilled fish is recommended.

Jardim dos Frangos, Av. Com. da Grande Guerra 66. Permanently buzzing with people and sizzling with the speciality, grilled chicken, which is devoured by the plateload at indoor and outdoor tables.

Mar e Mar, Praia da Conceição. Tiny kiosk serving beach-side grills, kebabs and salads on outdoor tables facing the waves.

Os Navegantes, Rua do Poço Novo 171. Splendid local *churrasqueria*; stick to the daily specials and you won't go far wrong. Closed Sun.

O Pescador, Rua das Flores 18. (☎214 832 054). One of several close to the fish market, this offers superior fish meals. Good food and service but pricey. Closed Sun.

DRINKING AND NIGHTLIFE

At night, Cascais shows itself off in the smart pubs, bars and cafés along **Rua Frederico Arouca**. More boisterous behaviour goes on in **Largo Luís de Camões**, down the steps on the west side of the main avenue. By day this is a suntrap, none of whose café-bar-restaurants serve particularly memorable meals but are pleasant (if expensive), places to sit and drink. However, on summer nights, the bars throw open their doors, turn up the music and, come closing time at 2am, the square is full of bleary-eyed drinkers dancing and shouting the words to tunes they never realized they knew.

Belbuerguer, Trav. do Visconde de Luz 20. American rock music and burgers, though on Friday and Saturday nights it does good business as a lively bar. Open till 2am.

Chequers, Largo Luís de Camões 7. Not quite as "legendary" as it would have you believe, but lively enough English-style pub, especially once the pumping rock music strengthens its grip.

Coconuts, Av. Rei Humberto II de Itália 7. Disco on the road to Boca do Inferno, attracting an odd mix of the trendiest locals and raving tourists. Theme nights include karaoke and male strippers on Wednesday nights.

John Bull, Praça Costa Pinto 31. Backing onto the Largo, another English-style pub which fills up early with a good-time crowd; serves meals, too.

Music Bar, Largo da Praia da Rainha. One of the few bars in town with decent sea views, which you can take in sitting at tables on the patio above the beach. Open till midnight. Closed Mon.

News, Estrada da Malveira da Serra. One of the "in" discos in the area, with a terrace and a lively night guaranteed, especially on Fridays. Open till 4am.

Van Gogo, Trav. da Alfarrubeira 9. Small, friendly and unpretentious disco. Open till 4am.

Praia do Guincho

There are hourly buses (Mon–Sat 7.45am–7.45pm, Sun 9am–7.15pm; 320$00 one way) from outside Cascais train station that run the 6km west to **PRAIA DO GUINCHO**, a great sweeping field of **beach** with body-crashing Atlantic rollers. It's a superb place for **surfing and windsurfing** – legs of the World Windsurfing Championships are often held here in August – but also a dangerous one. The undertow is notoriously strong and people are drowned almost every year. To add to that, there's absolutely no shade and on breezy days the wind cuts across the sands. Even if you can't feel the sun, you'll still burn to pieces unless you're careful.

The beach has become increasingly popular over the years and the coastal approach road is flanked by half a dozen large **terrace-restaurants**, and a couple of **hotels**, all with standard, fish-dominated menus and varying views of the breaking rollers. As nearly everyone comes here on day-trips, there's nowhere cheap to stay, except the campsite (see below). At the de luxe-class *Hotel de Guincho* (☎214 870 491, fax 214 870 431; ⑨), rooms are around 36,000$00 a night. Slightly more moderate is *Estalagem O Muchaxo* (☎214 870 221, fax 214 870 044; ⑤), showing signs of shabbiness but remaining a highly attractive place, with stone-flagged bar and picture windows looking out across the beach from the restaurant, which is rated as one of the best in the Lisbon area. Pop in for just a coffee or a beer if you don't want to spend around 4000$00 a head on a meal. Just below is a **public pool** (summer only), handy if the waves are too perilous. The well-equiped Orbitur **campsite** see (p.67) is about 1km back from the main part of the beach; follow the signs from the coast road.

Sintra and around

As the summer residence of the kings of Portugal, and the Moorish lords of Lisbon before them, Sintra's verdant charms have long been celebrated. British travellers of the eighteenth and nineteenth centuries found a new Arcadia in its cool, wooded heights, recording with satisfaction the old Spanish proverb: "To see the world and leave out Sintra is to go blind about". Byron stayed here in 1809 and began *Childe Harold*, his great mock-epic travel poem, in which the "horrid crags" of "Cintra's glorious Eden" form a first location. Writing home, in a letter to his mother, he proclaimed the village:

> *perhaps in every aspect the most delightful in Europe; it contains beauties of every description natural and artificial. Palaces and gardens rising in the midst of rocks, cataracts and precipices; convents on stupendous heights, a distant view of the sea and the Tagus …it unites in itself all the wildness of the Western Highlands with the verdure of the South of France.*

That the young Byron had seen neither of these is irrelevant: his description of Sintra's romantic appeal is exact – and still telling two centuries later. Move mountains and give yourself the best part of two full days here.

The Town

SINTRA loops around a series of green and wooded ravines making it a confusing place in which to get your bearings. Basically, though, it consists of three distinct and separate villages: the drab **Estefânia** (around the train station), **Sintra-Vila** (the attractive main town) and, 2km to the east, the functional but pleasant **São Pedro de Sintra**. It's a ten- to fifteen-minute walk from the station to Sintra-Vila and around twenty minutes from Sintra-Vila to São Pedro.

Before you head into the town centre, it's worth making a small detour 300m northeast of the station to visit the new **Museu de Arte Moderna** on Avenida Heliodoro Salgado (Wed–Sun 10am–6pm, Tues 2–6pm; 600$00, free on Thurs for under-18s), which is housed in a 1920s building formerly occupied by Sintra's casino. Among its highlights are works by Jackson Pollock, Hockney, Lichtenstein, and Warhol, including his Campbell's soup tin and a wonderful portrait of Judy Garland. Lovers of kitsch will enjoy Jeff Koons's sculpture of a poodle and Bobtail the sheepdog. The top floor contains a café and restaurant, with an outdoor terrace offering great views over the Pena Palace.

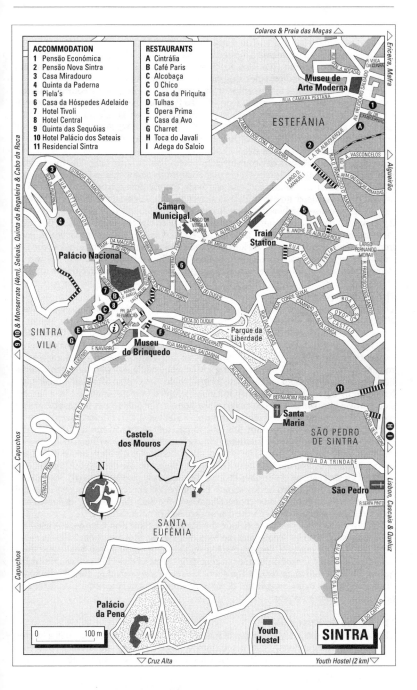

ACCOMMODATION
1 Pensão Económica
2 Pensão Nova Sintra
3 Casa Miradouro
4 Quinta da Paderna
5 Piela's
6 Casa da Hóspedes Adelaide
7 Hotel Tivoli
8 Hotel Central
9 Quinta das Sequóias
10 Hotel Palácio dos Seteais
11 Residencial Sintra

RESTAURANTS
A Cintrália
B Café Paris
C Alcobaça
C O Chico
C Casa da Piriquita
D Tulhas
E Opera Prima
F Casa da Avo
G Charret
H Toca do Javali
I Adega do Saloio

On the way into town you pass the fantastical **Câmara Municipal** (town hall), but it is the extraordinary landmark of the **Palácio Nacional**, distinguished by its vast pair of conical chimneys, that dominates the central square around which the town is gathered. Just downhill the turismo (see "Practicalities" on p.121) in Praça da República can help with accommodation and provides a useful map of the surroundings.

There's a daily **market** in the centre of Sintra-Vila, and a much larger **country market** – with antiques and crafts, as well as food – in São Pedro on the second and last Sunday of every month. The town's annual **festa** in honour of Saint Peter is held on June 28 and 29, and in July and August there's a **music festival**, with classical performances in a number of the town's buildings. The end of July also sees the Feira Grande in São Pedro, with crafts, antiques and cheeses on sale.

Getting around Sintra's environs involves a fair amount of travelling. The most useful **bus** service is #434, which takes a circular route from Sintra station to Sintra-Vila, the Castelo dos Mouros, Palácio da Pena and back (hourly departures from station from around 10am, last departure from Palácio at around 5pm, Tues–Sun; 500$00 return); tickets can be purchased on board. A **Day Rover Ticket** (1200$00) may also be worthwhile if you want to pack it all in; they are valid for one day on any Stagecoach bus. If you want to see some of Sintra's environs, the Day Rover ticket is also valid on #403, which goes from Sintra to Cascais via Cabo da Roca. For full details of buses and times, ask in the turismo. You might also want to make use of **taxis**, which cost roughly 1500$00 one way to Pena or Monserrate, though negotiate a fee beforehand as metres aren't always used.

The Palácio Nacional

The **Palácio Nacional** – or **Paço Real** (10am–12.30pm & 2–4.30pm; closed Wed; 400$00, free Sunday morning) – was probably already in existence under the Moors. It takes its present form, however, from the rebuilding and enlargements of Dom João I (1385–1433) and his fortunate successor, Dom Manuel, heir to Vasco da Gama's inspired explorations. Its style, as you might expect, is an amalgam of Gothic – with impressive roofline battlements – and the latter king's Manueline additions, with their characteristically extravagant twisted and animate forms. Inside, the Gothic-Manueline modes are tempered by a good deal of Moorish influence, adapted over the centuries by a succession of royal occupants. The last royal to live here, in the 1880s, was Maria Pia, grandmother of the country's last reigning monarch – Manuel II, "The Unfortunate".

Today the palace is a museum (it's best to go early or late in the day to avoid the crowds). You pass through the **kitchens** first, their roofs tapering into the giant chimneys, and then on to the upper floor. The first room on this floor is a gallery above the palace chapel, built perhaps on the old mosque. In a room alongside, the deranged Afonso VI was confined for six years by his brother Pedro II; he eventually died here in 1683, listening to Mass through a grid, Pedro having seized "his throne, his liberty and his queen". Beyond the gallery, a succession of state rooms climaxes in the **Sala das Armas**, its domed and coffered ceiling emblazoned with the coats-of-arms of 72 noble families.

Highlights on the lower floor include the Manueline **Sala dos Cisnes**, so-called for the swans painted on its ceiling, and the **Sala das Pegas**. This last room takes its name from the flock of magpies (*pegas*) painted on the frieze and ceiling, holding in their beaks the legend *por bem* (in honour) – reputedly the response of João I, caught by his queen, Philippa (of Lancaster), in the act of kissing a lady-in-waiting. He had the room decorated with as many magpies as there were women at court in order to satirize and put a stop to their gossiping.

The Museu do Brinquedo

The fascinating private toy collection of João Arbués Moreira is now housed in a former fire station, imaginatively converted into a high-tech toy museum (Tues–Sun 10am–6pm; 600$00) just round the corner from the Palácio Nacional on Rua Visconde de Monserrate. The museum comes complete with internal glass lifts, a café and video units. The huge array of toys over three floors are somewhat confusingly labelled, but look out for the 3000-year-old stone Egyptian toys on the first floor; the Hornby trains from the 1930s, and some of the first ever toy cars, produced in Germany in the early 1900s. Perhaps the most interesting section is that on early Portuguese toys, containing old cars made from papier-maché, tin-plate animals, wooden trams and trains, as well as a selection of 1930s beach toys, including beautifully painted buckets and the metal fish that appears on the museum brochure.

The Castelo dos Mouros and Palácio da Pena
From near the church of **Santa Maria**, towards São Pedro, a stone pathway leads up to the ruined ramparts of the **Castelo dos Mouros** (daily: June–Sept 10am–7pm; Oct–May 10am–5pm; free). Alternatively you can catch bus #434 from Sintra station. Captured with the aid of Scandinavian Crusaders by Afonso Henriques, the Moorish castle spans two rocky pinnacles, with the remains of a mosque spread midway between the fortifications. **Views** from here are extraordinary: south beyond Lisbon's bridge to the Serra de Arrábida, west to Cascais and Cabo da Roca (the westernmost point of mainland Europe), and north to Peniche and the Berlenga Islands.

The upper gate of the castle gives onto the road up to Pena, opposite the lower entrance to **Pena park** (daily: June–Sept 9am–7pm; Oct–May 10am–5pm; free), a stretch of rambling woodland, with a scattering of lakes and follies. At the top of the park, about twenty minutes' walk, rears the fabulous **Palácio da Pena** (Tues–Sun: July–Oct 10am–6pm; Sept–June 10am–5pm; 400$00, free Sunday morning), a wild fantasy of domes, towers, ramparts and walkways, approached through mock-Manueline gateways and a drawbridge that doesn't draw. A compelling riot of kitsch, it was built in the 1840s to the specifications of Ferdinand of Saxe-Coburg-Gotha, husband of Queen Maria II, and it bears comparison with the mock-medieval castles of Ludwig of Bavaria. The architect, the German **Baron Eschwege**, immortalized himself in the guise of a warrior-knight on a huge statue that guards the palace from a neighbouring crag. Inside, Pena is no less bizarre, preserved exactly as it was left by the royal family on their flight from Portugal in 1910. The result is fascinating: rooms of concrete decorated to look like wood, statues of turbanned Moors nonchalantly holding electric chandeliers – it's all here. Of an original convent, founded to celebrate the first sight of Vasco da Gama's returning fleet, a chapel and genuine Manueline cloister have been retained.

Above Pena, past the statue of Eschwege, a marked footpath climbs to the **Cruz Alta**, highest point of the Serra de Sintra. Another footpath (unmarked) winds down to the left from Pena, coming out near Seteais (see below).

Sights around Sintra

After the castle and Pena, a visit to **Quinta da Regaleira**, the palace of **Seteais** and luxuriant gardens of **Monserrate** are the other obvious goals of a Sintra walk. Enthusiastic hikers can make a circuit of these, via the **Convento dos Capuchos** "Cork Convent"; otherwise, to see everything, you're looking at a taxi-ride at least one way.

Quinta da Regaleira
Quinta da Regaleira lying just a five-minute-walk out of town on the Seteais/Monserrate road (June–Sept 10am–7.30pm; Oct–May 10am–5.30pm; visits last ninety minutes and must be booked by phone ☎219 106 650; 2000$00), is one of Sintra's most elaborate private estates and was declared a UNESCO World Heritage site in 1995.

The estate was designed by Italian architect and theatrical set designer Luigi Manini for wealthy landowner António Augusto Carvalho Monteiro at the turn of the century. The Italian's sense of the dramatic is obvious: a mish-mash of Gothic, Renaissance and

Manueline palaces, chapels and houses cloaked in dense woodland. The principal building, the mock-Manueline Palácio dos Milhões, sprouts turrets and towers and has superb views over the area. The surrounding gardens shelter fountains, terraces, lakes and grottoes, including the "Initiation Well", so-called after Freemasons-inspired initiation rights. A moss-strewn spiral stairway descends the well to an underground warren of grottoes, which eventually resurface at the edge of a lake.

The Palácio de Seteais

The **Palácio de Seteais** ("Seven Sighs") stands just to the right of the upper Colares road, fifteen minutes' walk west from the centre of town. It is one of the most elegant palaces in Portugal, completed in the last years of the eighteenth century and entered through a majestic Neoclassical arch. Maintained today as an immensely luxurious **hotel** (see "Accommodation" on p.121), it is one of the most expensive places to stay in Portugal. With more modest money to blow, make for the bar and terrace downstairs to the left, past a distinctly unwelcoming reception; its teas are also worth splashing out on.

Monserrate

Beyond Seteais, the road leads past a series of beautiful private *quintas* (manors or estates) until you come upon **Monserrate** (daily except on public holidays: June–Sept 10am–6pm; Oct–May 10am–5pm; 200$00) – about another forty minutes' walk away.

With its Victorian folly-like mansion and vast botanical park of exotic trees and subtropical shrubs and plants, Monserrate is one of the most romantic sights in Portugal. It would be easy to spend the whole day wandering around the paths laid out through the woods. The charm of the place is immeasurably enhanced by the fact that it's only partially maintained. The name most associated with Monserrate is that of **William Beckford**, author of the Gothic novel *Vathek* and the wealthiest untitled Englishman of his period. He hired the *quinta* here from 1793 to 1799, having been forced to flee Britain because of homosexual scandal – buggery then being a hanging offence. Setting about improving this "beautiful Claude-like place", he landscaped a waterfall and even imported a flock of sheep from his estate at Fonthill. In this Xanadu-like dreamland, he whiled away his days in summer pavilions, entertaining with "bevys of delicate warblers and musicians" posted around the grounds.

Half a century later, a second immensely rich Englishman, **Sir Francis Cook**, bought the estate. His fantasies were scarcely less ambitious, involving the construction of a great Victorian house inspired by Brighton Pavilion. Cook also spared no expense in developing the grounds and imported the head gardener from Kew to lay out succulents and water plants, tropical ferns and palms, and just about every conifer known. Fernando II, who was building the Pena Palace at the time, was suitably impressed, conferring a viscountcy on Cook for his efforts. **Cook's house** is closed but you can still admire the exterior, with its mix of Moorish and Italian decoration (the dome is modelled on Brunelleschi's Duomo in Florence), and peer into a splendid series of empty salons.

The Convento dos Capuchos

One of the best long walks in the Sintra area is to the **Convento dos Capuchos** (daily: June–Sept 10am–6pm; Oct–May 10am–5pm; 200$00), an extraordinary hermitage with tiny, dwarf-like cells cut from the rock and lined in cork – hence its popular name of the "Cork Convent". Philip II, King of Spain and Portugal, pronounced it the poorest convent of his kingdom, and Byron, visiting a cave where one monk had spent 36 years in seclusion, mocked in *Childe Harold*:

> Deep in yon cave Honorius long did dwell,
> In hope to merit Heaven by making earth a Hell.

Coming upon the place after a walk through the woods, however, it's hard not to be moved by the simplicity and seclusion of the place. It was occupied for three hundred years and finally abandoned in 1834 by its seven remaining monks, who must have found the gloomy warren of rooms and corridors too much to maintain. Some rooms – **penitents' cells** – can be entered only by crawling through 70cm-high doors; here, and on every other ceiling, doorframe and lintel, are attached panels of cork, taken from the surrounding woods. Elsewhere, you'll come across a washroom, kitchen, refectory, tiny chapels, even a bread oven set apart from the main complex.

To get there, the most straightforward approach is by the ridge **road from Pena** – a distance of 9km. There are other indistinct paths through the woods from Monserrate and elsewhere in the region, but without local advice and a good map, you'll be hard pushed to find your way. Whichever route you take, the surroundings, too, beg a startled reaction: the minor road between Sintra, the convent and Cabo da Roca sports some of the country's most alarming natural rock formations, with boulders as big as houses looming out of the trees.

Practicalities

Trains depart every 15 minutes for Sintra from Lisbon's Rossio station (200$00 one way). The **train station** in Sintra itself is fifteen minutes' walk from the centre of Sintra-Vila; **buses** stop across the street from the station, with services to and from Cascais, Colares, Cabo da Roca, the Sintra beaches, Estoril and Mafra. There are **taxis** outside the train station and in Praça da República, near the Palácio Nacional; check the price first for every journey since the meters aren't always used. You'll find a **post office** and **bank** on Praça da República, too.

Sintra is a popular resort and you should book ahead or turn up early in the day if you intend to stay, especially if you're here during one of the town's festivals (see p.106) when accommodation will definitely be scarce. On the spot, accommodation is best arranged through the efficient and helpful **turismo** (daily: June–Sept 9am–8pm; Oct–May 9am–7pm; ☎219 231 157), just off the central Praça da República. There is also a small turismo desk at Sintra station.

Accommodation

There's a fair range of **accommodation** available including: a network of private rooms (best booked through the turismo; usually ②), half a dozen **pensões** and **hotels**, and upmarket bed and breakfast in several local *quintas*, or manor houses; the best choices are reviewed below. In addition, there's an attractive **youth hostel** located in the hills above São Pedro de Sintra, while the nearest **campsite** is at Praia Grande (see p.122).

PENSÕES, QUINTAS AND HOTELS

Casa de Hóspedes Adelaide, Rua Guilherme Gomes Fernandes 11 (☎219 230 873). Welcoming and inexpensive place, midway between the train station and Sintra-Vila. ②

Casa Miradouro, Rua Sotto Mayor 55 (☎219 235 900, fax 219 241 836). Renovated turn-of-the-century mansion 500m beyond the Palácio Nacional, with terrific views of coast and castle. Five rooms with bath, terraced garden and good breakfast included. ⑥.

Hotel Central, Largo Raínha D. Amélia 35 (☎219 230 963). Characterful and comfortable nineteenth-century hotel, opposite the Palácio Nacional – polished wood and tiles throughout. Triple rooms available, too, and good off-season discounts. Breakfast included. ③.

Pensão Económica, Pátio de Olivença 6, off Av. Heliodoro Salgado (☎219 230 229). Interesting old building and handy for the station; clean, basic and friendly. ②.

Pensão Nova Sintra, Largo Afonso de Albuquerque 25 (☎&fax 219 230 220). Decent rooms and a convenient location on the square by the train station. Some rooms have fine views. ④.

Quinta da Paderna, Rua da Paderna 4 (☎219 235 053). Highly attractive accommodation in a lovely old house, just north of Sintra-Vila. ⑤.

Hotel Palácio dos Seteais, Rua Barbosa do Bocage 8 (☎219 233 200, fax 219 234 277). One of the most luxurious and expensive hotels in Portugal. Rooms at over 46,000$00 a night in a superb eighteenth-century building, surrounded by elegant gardens. Antique furnishings abound at every turn and there's a terrific restaurant too. ⑨.

Piela's, Rua João de Deus 70–72 (☎219 241 691). On the street behind the train station, this café-*pastelaria* has six simple but spotless double rooms available, presided over by a welcoming and informative proprietor. Serves food and there's a games room. ③.

Quinta das Sequóias (☎ 219 230 342, fax 219 230 342). Immaculate manor house with six rooms, out in the Sintra hills beyond Seteais – continue past the Palácio de Seteais for 1km and follow the signposted private road on your left. A lovely, antique-furnished place with superb views, gardens, sauna, jacuzzi and pool. Excellent buffet breakfast included. Recommended. ⑥.

Residencial Sintra, Trav. dos Alvares, São Pedro (☎219 230 738, fax 219 230 738). Big, rambling old *residencial* with a garden and swimming pool, and friendly, multilingual owners. You'll need to book ahead in summer. ⑤.

Hotel Tivoli, Praça da República (☎219 233 505, fax 219 231 572; *htsintra@mail.telepac.pt*). Sintra's largest, most central hotel – bang next to the palace – with fine views and comfortable rooms with bath. Rates drop in winter. ⑦.

YOUTH HOSTEL AND CAMPSITES

Pousada de Juventude de Sintra, Santa Eufémia, São Pedro de Sintra (☎/fax 219 241 210). The hostel is a 5km walk from the train station, less if you first catch a local bus to São Pedro. Meals served if you can't face the hike down into town and back. Closed noon–6pm.

Camping Praia Grande (☎219 290 581). Properly equipped site on the beach at Praia Grande, west of Sintra. Bus #441 runs from the train station.

Eating and drinking

There are some fine **restaurants** scattered about the various quarters of Sintra. With a couple of honourable exceptions the most mundane are in the centre, near the palace or around the train station; the best concentration is at São Pedro, a twenty-minute walk from town.

Local specialities include *queijadas da Sintra* – sweet cheese pastry-cakes. If you're out for the day, take a **picnic**: the only refreshments out of town are cold drinks from a stall below Pena park (summer only), or exorbitantly priced meals at Palácio dos Seteais.

SINTRA-VILA

Alcobaça, Rua das Padarias 7–11. The best central choice for a decent, straightforward Portuguese meal. Plain, tiled dining room with friendly service and large servings of grilled chicken, *arroz de marisco*, clams and steak for around 2500$00 a head.

Casa da Avo, Rua Visconde de Monserrate 46 (☎219 231 280). Basic eating house with few pretensions but the house wine is cheap enough and it's hard to fault dishes like the *caldeirada* (fish stew). There's a decent bar attached, too. Closed Mon.

Casa da Piriquita, Rua das Padarias 1. On the uphill alley across from the *Café Paris*. Quality tearoom and bakery, busy with locals queueing to buy *queijadas da Sintra* and the similarly sticky *travesseiros*. Closed Wed.

Café Paris, Largo Rainha D. Amélia (☎ 219 232 375). Highly attractive and highest-profile café in town, opposite the Palácio Nacional, which means steep prices for underwhelming food. Great place to sit and nurse a drink in the sun, though.

Charret, Rua Consiglieri Pedroso 20. Handicraft shop with a back room offering set teas of scones, cakes, etc for around 1000$00.

O Chico, Rua Arco do Teixeira 8. Standard Sintra prices (ie, fairly high) and food, but come on Thursdays in summer for the fado. It's off Rua das Padarias and has outdoor tables on the cobbles. Bar open till 2am.

Opera Prima, Rua Consiglieri Pedroso 2A. Late-opening, Belgian-owned bar restaurant with international food and live music most Thursdays varying from pop to jazz.

Tulhas, Rua Gil Vicente 4, behind the turismo (☎219 232 378). Imaginative cooking in a fine building, converted from old grain silos. The speciality is veal with Madeira at a reasonable 1500$00 or so. Closed Wed.

NEAR THE STATION

Cintrália, Largo Afonso de Albuquerque 1 (☎219 242 200). Attractively renovated *marisqueira* where you can try the specialities such as *arroz de lagosta* (lobster rice) under sparkling chandeliers. Moderate to expensive.

Piela's, Rua João de Deus 70–72. Budget meals and late-night drinks, as well as rooms (see above). Inexpensive. Closed Tues.

SÃO PEDRO DE SINTRA

Adega do Saloio, Trav. Chão de Meninos (☎219 231 422). A fine grill-restaurant with a standard Portuguese menu and notably hospitable owners. Does a good *arroz de marisco*. Closed Tues.

Toca do Javali, Rua 1º Dezembro 18 (☎219 233 503). Tables set up outside in summer amidst a lovely terraced garden; superb cooking at any time of year. Wild boar *(javali)* is the house speciality. Prices are fairly steep, though the set lunch is a great deal at around 2000$00. Closed Wed.

Further west: Colares, the beaches and Cabo da Roca

About 6km further west of Monserrate is **COLARES**, a hill village famed for its wine and boasting several much-prized vintages. It's easily reached on the Sintra–Cascais bus route #403, with **buses** leaving from outside the train station in both towns, and has a couple of mid-range hotels and country inns, such as the *Estalagem de Colares* (☎219 282 942, fax 219 282 983; ⑤), making it an attractive alternative base to Sintra. For food, there's a smart restaurant and teashop, *Colares Velho* on Largo Dr. Carlos Franca 1–4 (Tues–Sun 11am–11pm), or, if you have your own transport, it is worth making a detour to the excellent *Toca do Júlio* (Tues–Sun; ☎219 290 815) – take the Praia Grande road from the nearby village of Almoçageme.

Continuing west of Colares, the road winds around through the hills to the beach-resort of **PRAIA DAS MAÇÃS**. You can take bus #441 from Sintra train station or, in summer, there's a **tramline** running from Ribeira da Sintra, just outside Sintra, via Colares. Praia das Maçãs has two good *pensões* – *Oceano* (☎219 292 399, fax 219 292 123; ⑤) and *Real* (☎219 292 002; ③) – and a scattering of restaurants; *O Loureiro*, Esplanada Vasco da Gama has great-value seafood and overlooks the beach. Nearby **AZENHAS DO MAR**, to the north, is a picture-book cliff-top town with a small beach, while **PRAIA GRANDE**, to the south has an even better, certainly bigger, beach and a large **campsite** (see p.122). Both can be reached on bus #441 from Sintra.

Cabo da Roca

A major destination in this region is **CABO DA ROCA**, 14km southwest of Colares; regular buses (#403) from either Sintra or Cascais train stations make the run throughout the year. It's an enjoyable trip, though the cape itself comprises little more than a lighthouse – below which foamy breakers slam the cliffs – a couple of stalls selling shells, a café and a **tourist office**. In here, you can buy a certificate recording that you've visited the "Most Westerly Point in Europe" – which indeed you have. A **cross** at the cape carries an inscription by Luís Camões ("Here …where the land ends, and the sea begins"), whose muse, for once it seems, deserted him. The bleak, blustery, scrub-covered headland deserves more of a salute.

Palácio de Queluz

The **Palácio de Queluz** (10am–1pm & 2–5pm; closed Tues; 500$00, free Sunday morning) lies on the Sintra train line, making it easy to see either on the way out (it's just twenty minutes from Lisbon's Rossio station; 180$00 one way) or on the way back from Sintra. The station is called Queluz-Belas: turn left out of the station and walk down the main road for fifteen minutes, following the signs through the unremarkable town until you reach a vast cobbled square, Largo do Palácio, with the palace walls reaching out around one side. The Largo is also home to a local **turismo** (Fri–Wed 10am–12.30pm & 2–7pm; ☎214 350 039).

The Palace

The building is as perfect a counterpoint to Mafra (see p.105) as you could imagine: an elegant, restrained structure regarded as the country's finest example of Rococo architecture. Its low, pink-washed wings enclose a series of public and private rooms and suites, as well as rambling eighteenth-century formal gardens. Although preserved as a museum, it doesn't quite feel like one – retaining instead a strong sense of its past royal owners. In fact, the palace is still pressed into service for accommodating state guests and dignitaries, and hosts classical concerts in the summer months.

It was built by Dom Pedro III, husband and regent to his niece, **Queen Maria I**, who lived here throughout her 39-year reign (1777–1816), quite mad for the last 27, following the death of her eldest son, José. William Beckford visited when the Queen's wits were dwindling, and ran races in the gardens with the Princess of Brazil's ladies-in-waiting; at other times firework displays were held above the ornamental canal and bullfights in the courtyards.

Visitors first enter the **Throne Room**, lined with mirrors surmounted by paintings and golden flourishes. Beyond is the more restrained **Music Chamber** with its portrait of Queen Maria above the French grand piano. Smaller quarters include bed- and sitting rooms; a tiny oratory overwhelmed with red velvet; and a **Sculpture Room**, whose only exhibit is an earthenware bust of Maria. Another wing comprises an elegant suite of **public rooms** – smoking, coffee and dining rooms – all intimate in scale and surprisingly tastefully decorated. The **Ambassador's Chamber**, where diplomats and foreign ministers were received during the nineteenth century, echoes the Throne Room in style, with one side lined with porcelain chinoiserie. In the end, though, perhaps one of the most pleasing rooms is the simple **Dressing Room** with its geometric inlaid wooden floor and spider's web ceiling of radial gilt bands.

The formal **gardens** are included in the ticket price. Low box hedges and elaborate (if weatherworn) statues spread out from the protection of the palace wings, while small pools and fountains, steps and terracing form a harmonious background to the building. From May to October, there is a display of Portuguese horsemanship here every Wednesday at 11am (100$00). You can still enjoy a meal in the Palace's original kitchen, the **Cozinha Velha** (daily from 12.30–3pm & 7.30–10pm; ☎214 350 232), which retains its stone chimney, arches and wooden vaulted ceiling, and sports copper pots, pans and utensils in every niche and alcove. The food – classic French-Portuguese – is not always as impressive as the locale, and you're looking at around 5000$00 a head for a full meal (though there is a cheaper café in the main body of the palace). The kitchens are now part of the *Pousada Dona Maria I* (☎214 356 158, fax 214 356 180, *enatur@mail.telepac.pt* ;⑧), a **hotel** that gives you the chance to stay in an annexe of the palace itself. Its 26 rooms come equipped with satellite TV, but as you would expect, it isn't cheap.

Mafra and around

Moving on from Lisbon or Sintra, **MAFRA** makes an interesting approach to Estremadura. It is distinguished – and utterly dominated – by just one building: the vast **Palace-Convent** (10am–4.30pm; closed Tues and all December; 400$00), which João V – the wealthiest and most extravagant of all Portuguese monarchs – built in emulation of El Escorial in Madrid. Arrive at least an hour before closing time to be sure of getting a guardian to usher you round (which takes about one hour).

The Palace-Convent

Begun in 1717 to honour a vow made on the birth of a royal heir, **Mafra Convent** was initially intended for just thirteen Franciscan friars. But as wealth poured in from the gold and diamonds of Brazil, João V and his German court architect, Frederico Ludovice, amplified their plans to include a massive basilica, two royal wings and monastic quarters for 300 monks and 150 novices. The result, completed in thirteen years, is quite extraordinary and, on its own bizarre terms, extremely impressive.

In style the building is a fusion of Baroque and Italianate Neoclassicism, but it is the sheer magnitude and logistics that stand out. In the last stages of construction more than 45,000 labourers were employed, while throughout the years of building there was a daily average of nearly 15,000. There are 5200 doorways, 2500 windows and two immense bell towers each containing over 50 bells. An apocryphal story records the astonishment of the Flemish bellmakers at the size of the order: on their querying it, and asking for payment in advance, Dom João retorted by doubling their price and his original requirement.

Parts of the convent are used by the military but an ingenious cadre of guides marches you around a sizeable enough portion. The **royal apartments** are a mix of the tedious and the shocking: the latter most obviously in the **Sala dos Troféus**, with its furniture (even chandeliers) constructed of antlers and upholstered in deerskin. Beyond are the **monastic quarters**, including cells, a pharmacy and a curious infirmary with beds positioned so the ailing monks could see Mass performed. The highlight, however, is the magnificent Rococo **library** – brilliantly lit and rivalling Coimbra's in grandeur. Byron, shown the 35,000 volumes by one of the monks, was asked if "the English had any books in their country?" The **basilica** itself, which can be seen outside the tour, is no less imposing, with the multicoloured marble designs of its floor mirrored in the ceiling decoration.

The **Tapada de Mafra**, the palace's extensive hunting grounds, are also open for ninety-minute tours (Sat, Sun and public holidays at 10am and 3.15pm; 120$00). For further details, ask at the turismo (see below).

Practicalities

Hourly **buses** run from Largo Martim Moniz (metro Martim Moniz) or Centro Alvalade (by Alvalade stadium; metro Campo Grande) in Lisbon, stopping near the convent. The **town** of Mafra itself is dull, and with frequent buses heading on to the lively resort of Ericeira, 12km away (see p.138), there seems no point in lingering. Alternatively, you can see the palace as a day-trip **from Sintra**: there are hourly services from outside Sintra station.

If you need to stay, the **turismo** on Avda 25 de Abril (daily: July–Sept 9.30am–7.30pm; Oct–June 9.30am–6pm; Sat & Sun closed 1–2.30pm; ☎ 262 812 023) can give details of rooms; or try the modern *Hotel Castelão*, also on Avda 25 de Abril (☎262 812 050, fax 262 814 698; ④). For an inexpensive **restaurant** with good food try the *Solar d'El Rei*, Rua Detras dos Quintas, five minutes' walk from the palace.

Sobreiro

The small village of **SOBREIRO**, around 5km northwest of Mafra on the road to Ericeira (see p.138), is home to a **craft village** (daily 8am–8pm) – the Aldeia Típica – established by José Franco. As well as Franco's own work, the showroom sells other reasonably priced ceramics from all over the country, while children will enjoy looking round the traditional bakery, smithy, clockmaker, cobbler, schoolroom, distillery, wind- and water-mills and several other small museum shops, all displaying various tools, fur- niture and artefacts collected over many years. The *adega* makes a splendid stop for lunch, serving local wine, bread and meals; at weekends, there is also a restaurant.

The Lisbon–Mafra–Ericeira **bus** passes by every hour or so, and it's definitely worth a stop if you're driving on to Ericeira from Mafra. There is also a pleasant **campsite** should you wish to stay (☎261 813 333).

South of the Tejo: Costa da Caparica, Setúbal and its coast

As late as the nineteenth century, the southern bank of the Tejo estuary was an under- populated area used as a quarantine station for foreign visitors; the village of Trafaria here was so lawless that the police visited it only when accompanied by members of the army. The huge **Ponte 25 de Abril**, a suspension bridge inaugurated as the "Salazar Bridge" in 1966 and renamed after the 1974 Revolution, finally ended what remained of this sepa- ration between "town and country". Since then, Lisbon has spilled over the river in a string of tatty industrial suburbs that spread east of the bridge, while to the west the **Costa da Caparica** has become a major holiday resort. **Setúbal**, 50km south of the cap- ital, sustains one remarkable church and is a pleasant provincial base from which to explore the River Sado and the Parque Natural da Arrábida. Its **coastal** surroundings are particularly attractive, with one full-blown resort at **Sesimbra.**

Across the river: Cacilhas and the Cristo-Rei

The most enjoyable approach to the Setúbal peninsula is to take a **ferry** from Lisbon's Fluvial (Cais de Alfândega) station, by Praça do Comércio, to the suburb of **CACILHAS** (daily: every ten minutes from 6am until 10.30pm, 9.30pm at weekends; the crossing takes around ten minutes; 150$00 one way). **Late-night ferries** back to the capital go to, and from, **Cais do Sodré** (24 hour service: every 20 to 30 minutes during the day, every 40 to 50 minutes throughout the night; 105$00 one way). The blustery ride itself is fun, granting you wonderful views of the city, as well as of the enormous Ponte 25 de Abril bridge, though the **seafood** is as good a reason as any to go over for an evening. Cacilhas's main street – Rua Candido dos Reis – is one long line of reasonably priced **fish restaurants**, popular with Lisbon locals. *Arroz de marisco* is a speciality in most, particularly good in the *Escondidinho de Cacilhas* (closed Thurs), immediately on the right as you leave the ferry. More upmarket, but with better views, is the riverside *Cervejaria Farol* (closed Wed). Head towards the bridge along the waterside Cais do Ginjal to two other atmospheric riverside restau- rants, the pricey *Atira-te ao Rio*, with Brazilian cuisine, or the marginally cheaper *Ponto Final*, offering Portuguese staples.

Bus #101 (every 20 minutes; daily 8am–8pm) from Cacilhas climbs the hill to the prominent **Cristo-Rei**. Built in 1959, this relatively modest version of Rio's Christ-statue landmark has a lift inside (daily: summer 9am–7.30pm; winter 9am–6pm; 250$00), which shuttles you up the plinth above its church, via a souvenir shop, to a highly dramatic viewing platform, 80m up in the air. On a good day, Lisbon stretches like a map below you and you can catch the glistening roof of the Pena Palace at Sintra in the distance. Back at ground level, there is also a new **visitor centre** next to the Cristo-Rei, showing occasional art exhibits and with a handy bar should you need a pick-me-up.

From Cacilhas bus station, you can also catch regular **buses** to Costa da Caparica, Setúbal, Sesimbra and Vila Fresca de Azeitão, for all of which see the relevant sections that follow.

Costa da Caparica

Regular buses from Cacilhas (every 15–30min, express buses every 30 min; daily 7am–9pm), or from Praça de Espanha (every 30min; daily 7am–12.45am), run on to **Costa da Caparica**, half an hour from Cacilhas, around forty minutes (or 1hr in rush hour) from Praça de Espanha. Though anything but a pretty place, this is a thoroughly lively Portuguese resort, crammed with restaurants, summer bars and discos and it's here that most locals come if they want to swim or laze around on the sand: there are foreign tourists, too, but they're in a minority. In Caparica town itself, **Rua dos Pescadores** leads up from the central Praça da Liberdade (where you'll find the market, supermarkets and banks) to the beach and is lined on both sides by café-restaurants with outdoor seating.

The **beach** stretches north towards Lisbon and away south into the distance, its initial stretch backed by apartments and more cafés. A promenade with wooden shacks at intervals offering grilled sardines, fresh fish, ice cream and drinks lies alongside the **mini-railway** which runs along the 8km or so of dunes to Fonte da Telha (June–Sept; 580$00 to the end of the line) – if you're after solitude you need only take it this far and walk. However, it's useful to know that each of the twenty mini-train stops, based around one or two beach-cafés, has a very particular scene or feel. Earlier stops tend to be family-oriented, later ones are on the whole younger and more trendy, with nudity (though officially illegal) more or less obligatory, especially around Stop 18–19, which is also something of a gay area.

As far as sea and sand go the beaches are excellent, taking in coves and lagoons as they spread southwards. The water is of good quality, though watch out for dangerous undertows.

Practicalities
Buses in summer stop at the bus park in town near the beginning of the sands. In winter, buses go to the station in Praça Padre Manuel Bernades, in which case it is best to get off at the first stop in Caparica, on the edge of the leafy square, Praça da Liberdade, five minutes back from the beach. If you arrive here, walk diagonally across the square, turn right and at Av. da Liberdade 18 you'll find the **turismo** (Mon–Sat 9.30am–1pm & 2.30–6pm; ☎212 900 071).

There are a growing number of **hotels** in Caparica, though they are relatively pricey and often full in summer; *Pensão Real* on Rua Mestre Manuel 18 (☎212 901 713, fax 212 901 701; ④) is one of the more reasonable central options. Accommodation is hardly a problem though, given the frequency of the buses and ferries back to Lisbon. If you really want to stay, talk first to the turismo or aim for one of the string of **campsites**, all of which, again, are pricier than average and crowded in summer. Your best bet is also the nearest, the well-equipped *Orbitur* (☎212 900 661), complete with café and tennis courts – it's one of the only ones where camping club membership is not required.

Among the dozens of fish and seafood places, a couple of recommended **restaurants** are: *O Borbas*, Praia da Costa (☎212 900 163; closed Tues) at the northern end of the beach with window seats looking out over the sands and bubbling fish tanks inside; and *Primoroso*, further round the seafront towards Lisbon, which has excellent *cataplanas* and outdoor tables facing the beach (closed Mon).

Setúbal and around

Some 50km south from Lisbon, **SETÚBAL** is Portugal's third port and a major industrial centre. It was once described by Hans Christian Andersen as a "terrestrial paradise", and although most of its visual charm is long gone, it's a friendly, enjoyable enough place. If you're heading south and have time to break the journey, it's worth stopping at least for a look at the remarkable Igreja de Jesus and the views from the Castelo São Filipe. On a more prolonged visit, the town is a good base for going on local **boat trips**, or to explore some other local vantage points such as the series of excellent **beaches** nearby, or, the town of Palmela.

The Town

Setúbal's greatest monument is the **Igreja de Jesus** (Tues–Sun 9am–noon & 2–5pm; closed Mon and public holidays) designed by Diogo de Boitaca and possibly the first of all Manueline buildings. Essentially a late-Gothic structure, with a huge, flamboyant doorway, its interior design was transformed by Boitaca, who introduced fantastically twisted pillars to support the vault. The rough granite surfaces of the pillars contrast with the delicacy of the blue and white *azulejos* around the high altar, which were added in the seventeenth century.

Another place to head for is the **Castelo São Felipe**, half an hour's walk to the west of the town; head along Avenida Luísa Todi and keep following the signs, or take a taxi. Built on the orders of Spanish king Felipe II in 1590, it's a grand military structure, harbouring

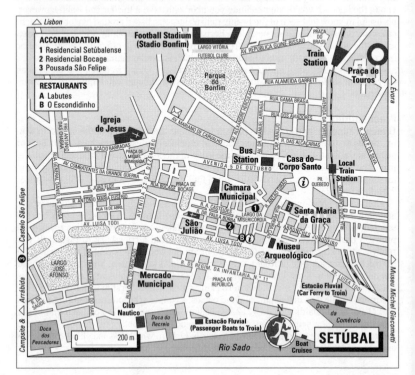

an *azulejo*-lined chapel and protected by sheer walls of overpowering height. Legend has it that a series of secret tunnels connect the castle with the coast, but any proof was lost in the great earthquake. Part of the castle is now a *pousada* (see p.130) but the ramparts and bar are open to non-guests and there are superb views over the mouth of the Sado estuary and the Tróia peninsula.

The rest of town has little to detain you, though the pedestrianized shopping streets in the **old town** around Rua A. Castelões are handsome enough, and there are gardens, a market and port to poke around as well. There's a certain amount of interest, too, in the central **Museu Arqueológico**, at Av. Luísa Todi 162 (Tues–Sat 9am–12.30pm & 2–5.30pm; closed Sun & Mon; free) where finds from the city's Roman age are displayed along with historical fishing boats and handicrafts. If you nip into the nearby turismo, too (see below), you can see the foundations of a Roman fish-preserving industry underneath the glass floor. A ten- to fifteen-minute-walk east along Rua Arronches Junqueiro brings you to the **Museu Michel Giacometti** at Largo Defensores da República (Tues–Fri & Sun 9am–noon & 2–5pm; free) a museum of work implements collected by Giacometti – a Corsican ethnologist who was particularly interested in Portuguese culture – in the 1970s. Historical agricultural implements from round Portugal complement exhibits of tools from traditional local trades such as blacksmiths, braziers, basket weavers and canners. Attractively housed in a large former canning factory, the museum is worth a detour for anyone interested in Portuguese enthnography.

Practicalities

You can reach Setúbal by **train**, though since it involves crossing to Barreiro by ferry and changing (see p.58), it's quicker to take the half hourly **bus** from Lisbon's Praça de Espanha, which takes around an hour; routes go via Ponte 25 de Abril and Vila Fesca de Azeitão or via Ponte Vasco da Gama. There are buses, too, from Cacilhas (hourly; 50min–1hr). Both routes are run by the bus company Setubalase (☎265 525 051). By **car**, the fast A2 from Ponte 25 de Abril whisks you to Setúbal in around forty minutes; it's about the same from Lisbon airport via Ponte Vasco da Gama. Trains from Lisbon drop you at Praça do Brasil, north of the centre; local trains use Setúbal's more central station at the eastern end of Avenida 5 de Outubro, along which the city turismo and bus station can also be found.

There are two **tourist offices** in Setúbal, the city one across from the local train station in the Casa do Corpo Santo, on Praça do Quebedo (Mon–Fri 9am–12.30pm & 2–5.30pm; ☎265 534 222) and the regional one, just off Avenida Luísa Todi at Travessa Frei Gaspar (June–Sept: Mon–Sat 9am–12.30pm & 2–7pm, Sun 9am–12.30pm; Oct–May: Tues–Fri 9am–6pm, Mon & Sat 9am–12.30pm & 2–6pm; ☎265 539 120),

---

BOAT TRIPS, DOLPHIN WATCHING AND ACTIVITY SPORTS

The tourist office can supply details of a range of privately organized tours and activity sports in the area including walking trips, jeep excursions, hot-air balloon flights and off-road driving. Highlights include the Cruzeiros – Galeões do Sal cruises up the Sado in sailing boats traditionally used to transport salt; organized by Troiacruze (☎265 228 482). The trips leave from the harbour, and departures are daily depending on both the weather and the number of people interested (minimum of ten passengers); phone ahead to check for next sailing. Trips costs 6000$00 per person. Vertigem Azul (☎265 238 000; *vertigemazul@mail.telepac.pt*) organize year-round trips to watch bottle-nosed dolphins in the Sado estuary (daily 9.30am and 3pm, dependent on weather; 5000$00 per person). Nautur (☎265 532 914; *nautur@mail.telepac.pt*) offer boat cruises to Arrábida and Sesimbra, including lunch and swimming stops (May–Oct; 7000$00 per person).

worth a visit for the remains of the Roman "fish condiments" factory under its glass floor. Both hand out maps and can help with finding rooms. If you want information on walking tours round Arrábida (see p.131), contact the **Parque Natural Da Arrábida** office on Praça da República (Mon–Fri 9am–12.30pm & 2–5pm; ☎265 524 032).

ACCOMMODATION
Accommodation is rarely a problem with plenty of hotels geared to business travellers. Among the **pensões** worth trying out are: *Residencial Bocage*, Rua de São Cristovão 14 (☎265 521 598; ③), offering small rooms with private bathrooms and TVs; or *Residencial Setubalense*, Rua Major Afonso Pala 17 (☎265 525 790, fax 265 525 789; ③), a good choice with smartish rooms and a friendly welcome in a quiet part of town. The extremely attractive **pousada**, the *São Filipe* (☎265 523 844, fax 265 532 588, *enatur@mail.telepac.pt*; ⑧) occupies the castle and the front rooms command superb views over the estuary, as does the surprisingly good-value restaurant, which is open to non-guests. A more basic option is *Toca do Pai Lopes*, the municipal **campsite**, on Rua da Praia Saúde(☎265 522 475), to the west of town on the shore beneath the castle.

EATING, DRINKING AND NIGHTLIFE
Good-value fish and seafood **restaurants** abound in the dock area and around the western end of Avenida Luísa Todi. A good option is *Labutes* (Setúbal backwards) Avenida 22 de Dezembro, out by Parque do Bonfim, which serves inexpensive, quality Portuguese dishes. *O Escondidinho*, Rua José António Januário da Silva 6, is another inexpensive option with outdoor tables. For a more expensive treat, however, head for the restaurant attached to *São Filipe* (see accommodation above). There are also plenty of places around the **market**; in midsummer, the market area is considerably expanded with clothes and touristy bric-a-brac.

Nightlife in Setúbal is lively; outdoor tables at the café-bars along Avenida Luísa Todi bustle with activity all evening. Other options include the *Cactus* bar on Largo Dr Francisco Soveral, the music bar and club *Absurdo* at the end of Avenida Luísa Todi, and the *Tropicalia* complex by the ferry terminal, which doubles as a club and restaurant. The best **clubs**, however, are situated out of town: *TGV*, at Estrada da Rasca 23 (Thurs–Sat); or the less pretentious *Leo Taurus*, 3km east along the N10 road. Alternatively, for a competely different scene, the *Teatro Luísa Todi* stages shows at weekends and often runs art-house movies during the week

Tróia
Setúbal's local **beaches**, reached by frequent ferries from the town, are on the **PENÍNSULA DE TRÓIA**, a large sand spit hemming in the Sado estuary. The peninsula was settled by the Phoenicians and subsequently by the Romans, whose town of Cetobriga appears to have been overwhelmed by a tidal wave in the fifth century. There are some desultory remains, including tanks for salting fish, on the landward shore. Originally a wilderness of sand and wild flowers, Tróia must once have been magnificent, but it's now a heavily developed resort with its own golf course. However, there are currently plans to demolish all but two of the high-rise blocks, although it remains to be seen whether the new upmarket complex, which will partially replace them, complete with marina and a casino, will be much of an improvement. To avoid the worst, and the crowds, be prepared to walk for twenty minutes or so south along the beach. Car **ferries** depart daily from Setúbal (every 15–30min, 6am–11pm; hourly during the night; 160$00 per person, cars 700$00); Passenger ferries (as above, no night service) avoid the long queues for cars in summer.

Palmela

The small town of **PALMELA**, around 10km north of Setúbal, is worth a quick visit for the views from its medieval **castle**, which on a clear day encompass Lisbon, Setúbal, the Sado estuary and Tróia. This is the centre of a wine-producing area, hence the town's major event in September: the Festa das Vindimas celebrating the first of the year's wine harvest, with processions, fireworks, grape-treading and running of the bulls.

A fabulous place to stay is the former church in the castle, which has been restored and extended into a *pousada*, the *Castelo de Palmela* (☎212 351 226, fax 212 330 404, *enatur@mail.telepac.pt*; ⑧). The castle also incorporates a row of handicraft shops selling *azulejos*, cheeses and the highly rated local wines; a café and a **museum** (Tues–Fri 10am–12,30pm & 2–5.30pm, Sat–Sun 10am–1pm & 3–5.30pm; free), which houses a small collection of archeological remains from the area dating back to Moorish times. Opposite the museum is Palmela's **turismo** (Mon–Fri 10am–12.30pm & 2–5.30pm, Sat–Sun 10am–1pm & 3–5.30pm; closes 8pm from June-Sept; ☎212 332 122), which can provide you with details of accommodation options in the area such as *O Moinho* (☎212 351 033; ④), a place which offers rooms in a converted windmill. During the week there are ten buses a day with four at weekends from Lisbon's Praça de Espanha, the ride takes forty minutes; and there are buses every twenty minutes, on the ten- to fifteen-minute-run, from Setúbal.

The Parque Natural da Arrábida

Between Setúbal and Sesimbra lies the **PARQUE NATURAL DA ARRÁBIDA**, whose main feature is the 500-metre granite ridge known as the Serra da Arrábida, visible for miles around and popular for its wild mountain scenery – home to wildcats, badgers, polecats, buzzards and Bonelli eagels. The twisted pillars of Setúbal's Igreja de Jesus were hewn from here. If you want to explore the area on foot, **walking guides** are available from the park's main office in Setúbal (see p.128).

Year-round public transport is limited to those **buses** from Setúbal to Sesimbra, which take the main road, well back from the coast. The bus passes through the town of **VILA FRESCA DE AZEITÃO** where the main highlight is the **José Maria da Fonseca wine vaults** (Mon–Fri 9am–noon & 2.30–5pm; 230$00; ☎212 198 940). A tour of the vaults, which lasts 45 minutes, includes free tasting, and provides an interesting introduction to the local Setúbal Moscatel. Vila Fresca de Azeitão can also be reached by bus from Lisbon's Praça de Espanha (hourly; 45min). Just south of Vila Fesca de Azeitão is **Quinta da Bacalhoa**, a privately owned fifteenth-century manor house, whose beautiful gardens (Mon–Sat 9am–1pm; free), complete with topiary, pools and *azulejos*, are open for visits. There is a **campsite**, *Picheleiros* (☎212 181 322), just outside town, which is the only site in the park area.

If you have your own transport, however, you should take the N379–1 from Vila Fresca to the **Convento da Arrábida**. Nestling in the cliffs – and signposted above this road – the sixteenth-century convent's crumbling white buildings have stunning ocean views. The convent is owned by the Fundação Orient; to make an appointment to look round, call in advance (☎213 527 002, or 213 474 702).

South of the convent, the N10 winds down to the coast and the tiny harbour village of **PORTINHO DA ARRÁBIDA**, which has one of the coast's best beaches – wonderful out of season and often quieter than Tróia. The harbour is guarded by a tiny seventeenth-century fort, now housing the **Museu Oceanográfico** (Tues–Fri 10am–4pm, Sat–Sun 3–6pm; 200$00), displaying marine animals from the region either live – in a small aquarium – or stuffed. At weekends, day-trippers head for the *Restaurant Beira Mar* (closed Wed) on the seafront, serving a good range of moderately priced fish and seafood. Pricey, but attractive, private rooms can be rented out above the diving school, the *Centro de Mergulho* (☎212 183 197, fax 212 183 656), with a couple of double rooms (③) or a self-catering apartment sleeping up to five (④). If you hold a diving certificate, the diving school can organize equipment.

As you continue along the coast towards Setúbal you come to **GALAPOS**, a beautiful stretch of sand with a beach café. Closer to Setúbal – and correspondingly more crowded – is the wide beach of **Figueirinha** and the small **Praia de Albarquel** whose main appeal is the beachside restaurant. In summer, the coast road is served by three daily buses from Setúbal; if driving, expect queues back into town at the end of the day in summer.

Sesimbra

If you get up early enough in **SESIMBRA**, you'll still see the fishermen mending their nets on the town's beach, but that's about the limit of this fishing town's tradition now that it's a full-blown resort, with apartment buildings and hotels mushrooming in the low, bare hills beyond the steep narrow streets of the old centre. It's largely a day-trip destination for residents of Lisbon, though the wealthier ones have bought second homes here for the summer, during which time Sesimbra is extremely busy. Nonetheless, it's still an admirable spot, with excellent swimming from the long **beach** and an endless row of **café-restaurants** along the beach road, each with an outdoor charcoal-grill wafting fine smells across the town. The beach splits into two, with a strand either side of the waterfront seventeenth-century **Forte do Santiago** (now a police office); offshore, jet skis and little ketches zip up and down the clear blue sea.

A **Moorish castle** sits above Sesimbra, a stiff half-hour climb from the centre. Within the walls are a church and various ruins, while a circuit of battlements gives amazing panoramas over the surrounding countryside and coastline. Back in the town, just off Avenida da Liberdade (take the steps by *Restaurante Xurrex*), the **Museu Municipal** (Mon–Fri 10am–12.30pm & 2–5.30pm; free) features archeological and historical finds from the area, while the best of the churches, the Manueline **Igreja da Mai**, is on nearby Rua João de Deus.

Give yourself time, too, to see the original fishing port, **Porto de Abrigo**, with its brightly painted boats, daily fish auctions, and stalls selling a superb variety of shellfish. Departing from the Naval Club are three-hour **boat cruises** to Cabo Espichel (Tues only, 9.30am; 3000$00), which stop at beaches en route and for snorkelling. On Saturdays, six-hour fishing trips depart at 7am (8000$00). It's a pleasant walk to Porto de Abrigo from the centre, along Avenida dos Náufragos – follow the signs towards the **Forte do Cavalo**, where the local anglers try their hand at sea fishing.

Practicalities

There are six **buses** a day from Lisbon's Praça de Espanha; and half-hourly services from Cacilhas and Setúbal. Coming from Lisbon in summer, it's usually much quicker to take the ferry across to Cacilhas (p.126) and pick up a bus there, as the main bridge road is often jammed solid with traffic.

In Sesimbra, you're dropped at the **bus station**, halfway up Avenida da Liberdade, a five-minute walk from the seafront. Walk down to the water, turn right past the fort, and the **turismo** (daily: June–Sept 9am–8pm; Oct–May 9am–12.30pm & 2–5.30pm; ☎212 235 743) is underneath the terrace, a step back from the seafront Avenida dos Náufragos.

ACCOMMODATION

Accommodation can be hard to come by in high season, with just a dozen or so *pensões* and pricey hotels. If you haven't booked in advance, your best bet is to try for private rooms through the turismo. Otherwise, head for the very central *Residencial Chic*, Trav. Xavier da Silva 2–6 (☎212 233 110; ③), just back from the sea on a corner with Rua Candido dos Reis. It has bright rooms, some with restricted sea views; ask in the pizza restaurant below. *Residencial Náutico*, Bairro Infante D. Henrique 3 (☎212 233 233; ③), is another comfortable place and a little more secluded. The *Hotel do Mar* (☎212 233 326, fax 212 233 888; ⑦) is an upmarket choice, high above the beach with over three hundred rooms and its own swimming pool. There's also a well-located **campsite** at Forte do Cavalo (☎212 233 905), just past the fishing port.

If you have your own transport, consider staying out of town at the *Casa da Terrina* (summer only, June–Sept; ☎212 680 264; ⑤), 3km inland at Quintola de Santana in the village of Santana; it's a white, nineteenth-century farmhouse with garden, pool and breakfast served on the terrace.

EATING, DRINKING AND NIGHTLIFE
At night, families crowd the line of **restaurants** east of the fort, along Avenida 25 de Abril. For a quality fish meal, the *Tony Bar* (☎212 233 199) in the little square, Largo dos Bombaldes, is hard to beat but expensive. The *Nova Fortaleza*, also on the square is another good option as is the extremely popular *Marisqueira Filipe* (closed Wed), further along. It's one of the more expensive places – 4000$00 and upwards – but serves great grilled fish, a bumper *arroz de marisco* and some decent wines. The attractive *O Farol*, opposite, can be good, though if you choose from the fish slab outside make sure you know what you're spending; it can be outrageously expensive here. *Santiago*, at Av. dos Náufragos 22, has some of the best sea views. Tucked behind Largo dos Bombaldes on Rua Plinio Mesquita 17, *A Tasca de Ratinho* (closed Wed) specializes in sword fish cooked in cream and port, and other moderately priced dishes, with a terrace overlooking the sea. Cheaper places (meals under 2500$00) abound in the backstreets on either side of the central spine, Avenida da Liberdade, though you'll sacrifice the outdoor seating and the views.

West of the fort along the avenue is also where most of the **music bars** and **cafés** are found. At some point in the evening, dip into *De Facto*, Av. dos Náufragos 26; the *Sereia* at no. 22, more of a hippy rock bar; *Bote Douro* at no. 10, a *cervejaria*-café; or the sleek and booming *Mareante* at no. 13, which sometimes has live music. *A Galé*, Rua Capitão Leitão 5, on a raised terrace overlooking the sea, next to the Safari surf shop, is that rare thing in Sesimbra, a proper local bar with no frills and extremely rough house wine.

Clubs with a bit of a summer reputation include *Belle Epoch*, off Largo do Calvario, and two places on Rua Prof. Fernandes Marques *Virtual* and the current in–place, *Bolina*; all stay open till 4am.

Cabo Espichel and beaches

Twice a day (both in the afternoon, making a day-trip by bus feasible if brief), buses make the eleven-kilometre journey west from Sesimbra to the **CABO ESPICHEL**, an end-of-the-world plateau where the road winds up at a wide church square. This is enclosed on three sides by ramshackle eighteenth-century pilgrimage lodgings, whose desolate air have made them a popular location for film directors. Beyond, wild and windswept cliffs drop almost vertically several hundred feet into the Atlantic; appropriately, dinosaur footprints have been found on the nearby Praia dos Lagosteiros.

Four buses a day travel from Sesimbra beyond Cabo Espichel to the southern **beaches** of the Costa da Caparica (see p.127 for the northern section). A few kilometres to the north of Cabo Espichel and up the surprisingly verdant and undeveloped coast is the village of **ALDEIA DO MECO,** with a particularly good **campsite** at Fetais (☎212 682 978), five minutes walk out of town. A path from here cuts down the superb beach of Praia do Meco. Like the other beaches on this coast, this is prone to overcrowding in July and August, but can be almost deserted out of season when the main drawback is the strong surf. The calmest strip of beach is by the lagoon at **Lagoa de Albufeira**: it is extremely clean and excellent for windsurfing.

travel details

Trains

Cais do Sodré to: Belém (every 15–30min; 7min); Cascais (every 15–30min; 30min); Estoril (every 15–30min; 25min).

Fluvial, via Barreiro, to: Albufeira (2-4 daily; 4hr–6hr 45min); Beja (3-4 daily; 2hr 30min-5hr 30min); Évora (change at Casa Branca, 2-4 daily; 2-6 hr); Faro (4-5 daily; 4hr–7hr 15min); Palmela (hourly; 40min); Loulé (5 daily; 4-7hr); Olhão (2-3 daily; 4hr 30min-7 hr); Setúbal (20 daily; 55 mins-2hr); Tavira (2-3 daily; 5–7hr 45min); Vila Real de Santo António (2-3 daily; 5hr 30min–8hr).

Rossio to: Queluz (every 15–20min; 20min); Sintra (every 15-20 min; 50 min). Change at Cacém for: Caldas da Rainha (8-10 daily; 2hr–5hr 30min); Leiria (4-5 daily, 4–6hr 45min); Mafra (11 daily; 50mins); Óbidos (10 daily; 1hr 55mins-5hr 20 min); Torres Vedras (8 daily; 1hr 10min).

Santa Apolónia to: Abrantes (4 daily; 1hr 50min–2hr 15min); Aveiro (2 daily; 4hr–7hr 45min; additional service from Oriente, 3 hours); Braga (2 daily; 5-6hr); Castelo Branco (4-5 daily; 3hr 20min–4hr); Coimbra (16 daily; 2hr–6hr 15min; additional service from Oriente, 2hr 15min); Covilhã (4 daily; 4hr 30min–5hr 30min); Elvas (change at Abrantes; 3 daily; 4hr 30min); Figueira da Foz (change at Cacém; 2 daily; 3hr 40min); Guarda (4 daily; 5hr 30min–7hr); Porto, for additional connections to Spain (12 daily; 3hr 30 min–6hr 40 min); Santarém (hourly; 50min–1hr 05 min); Tomar (13 daily, 1hr 45 min- 2hr).

International Trains

Santa Apolónia to: Biarritz (1 daily; 16hr 30min); Bordeaux (1 daily; 18hr 30min); Caceres (1 night train, 6 hr); Madrid (1 night train; 10hr 30min); Paris (1 daily; 23hr); Salamanca (1 daily; 8hr 30min); San Sebastián (1 daily; 14hr 30min).

Buses

Express buses run daily to all main towns throughout the country; see entries at the end of relevant chapters. Information from the main bus terminal at Avenida João Crisóstomo (see p.159). Other services depart from a variety of termini. Local services include:

Lisbon to: Costa da Caparica (every 15–30min; 30min–1hr); Mafra (10 daily; 1hr 30min); Ericeira (10 daily; 1hr 50min); Évora (6-12 daily; 2hr); Fátima (10 daily; 1hr 30min); Nazaré (hourly; 1hr 50min); Palmela (hourly, 40 mins); Peniche (9 daily; 1hr 45min); Sesimbra (7–9 daily; 1hr 30min–2hr); Setúbal (every 30min; 45min–1hr); Tomar (2-4 daily; 1hr 45); Torres Vedras (12 daily; 2hr); Vila Fresca Azeitão (hourly; 45min).

Domestic flights

There are **internal flights** of varying regularity from Lisbon to: Bragança, Chaves, Covilhã, Faro, Porto, Vila Real, Viseu and to Madeira and the Azores. Check current schedules at any travel agency.

CHAPTER TWO

ESTREMADURA AND RIBATEJO

T he **Estremadura** and **Ribatejo** regions have played a crucial role in each phase of the nation's history, and have the monuments to prove it. They are also comparatively wealthy regions, both having received substantial EU grants to help restructure agriculture. Although they encompass a comparatively small area, the provinces boast an extraordinary concentration of vivid architecture and engaging towns: **Alcobaça**, **Batalha**, and **Tomar** – comprising the most exciting buildings in Portugal – all lie within a ninety-minute bus ride of each other. Other attractions are equally compelling: ferries sail from Peniche to the remote **Ilha Berlenga**; **Óbidos** is a completely walled medieval village; spectacular underground caverns can be visited at **Mira d'Aire**; and there are tremendous castles at **Porto de Mós**, **Leiria** (itself an elegant town), and on **Almourol**, an islet in the middle of the Rio Tejo.

The Estremaduran coast – the lower half of the Costa de Prata – provides an excellent complement to all this, and if you're simply seeking sun and sand it's not a bad alternative to the Algarve. **Nazaré** and **Ericeira** are justifiably the most popular resorts but there are scores of less developed beaches. For more isolation, try the area around **São Martinho do Porto** or the coastline west of **Leiria**, backed most of the way by the pine forest of **Pinhal de Leiria**.

Virtually all of these highlights fall within the boundaries of Estremadura, which, with its fertile rolling hills, is perhaps second in beauty only to the Minho. Although the flat, bull-breeding lands of **Ribatejo** (literally "banks-of-the-Tejo") fade into the dull expanses of northwestern Alentejo, the Tejo river valley itself boasts some of Portugal's richest **vineyards**, while many of its towns host lively traditional **festivals**. The wildest and most famous of these is the Festa do Colete Encarnado of **Vila Franca de Xira,** with Pamplona-style bull-running through the streets.

ACCOMMODATION PRICE CODES

All the accommodation prices in this book have been coded using the symbols below. The symbols represent the lowest prices you can expect to pay for a **double room in high season**; for a full explanation, see p.32.

① Under 4000$00	④ 11,000$00–15,000$00	⑦ 25,000$00–30,000$00
② 4000$00–7000$00	⑤ 15,000$00–20,000$00	⑧ 30,000$00–40,000$00
③ 7000$00–11,000$00	⑥ 20,000$00–25,000$00	⑨ Over 40,000$00

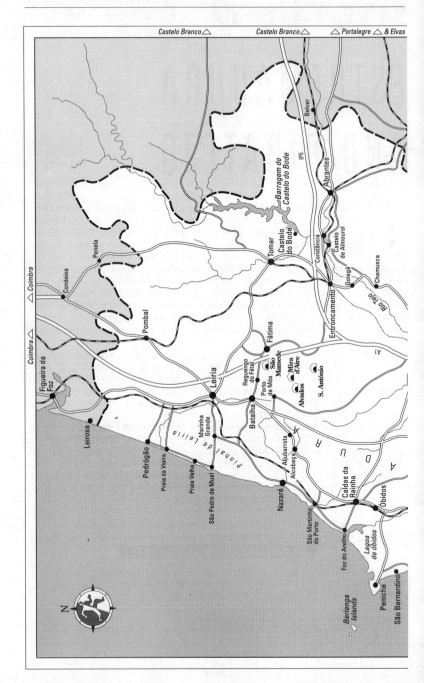

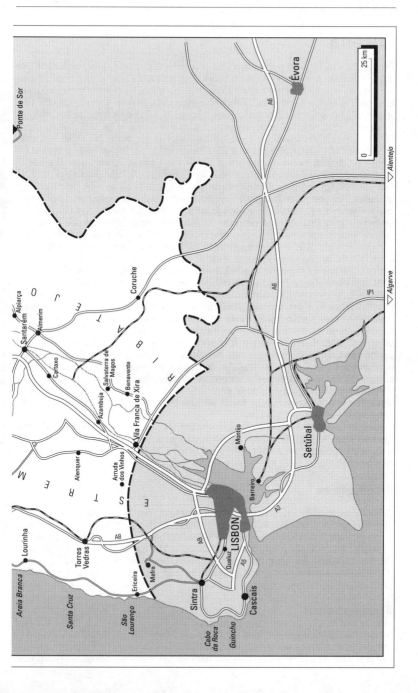

Ericeira

Perched on a rocky ledge thirty metres above a series of fine sandy beaches, **ERICEIRA** offers one of the few natural harbours between Cascais and Peniche. As a result, during the last century, the town became a major port, from where boats left to trade with countries such as Scotland and Brazil. The town's main claim to fame, though, is as the final refuge of Portugal's last monarch, Dom Manuel II – "The Unfortunate" – who, on October 5, 1910, was woken in his palace at nearby Mafra to be told that an angry Republican mob was advancing from Lisbon. Aware of the fate of his father and elder brother, he fled to the small harbour at Ericeira and sailed into the welcoming arms of the British at Gibraltar, to live out the rest of his days in a villa at Twickenham. Baedeker's guidebook, published the same year, described Ericeira as "a fishing village with excellent sea bathing" and recent development has done little to change the town's original character. The place is undeniably a busy resort – the main square has been pedestrianized and there are plans to build a *pousada* in the seventeenth-century fort (once used to protect the town from Algerian pirates) – but it remains an attractive town. It is especially lively on summer weekends, when people come up from Lisbon to enjoy the surprisingly buoyant nightlife, and is well known to the Portuguese for its seafood (particularly lobsters and crayfish) – its very name is said to derive from the words *ouriços do mar* (sea urchin). You can see the tanks in which the shellfish are reared at the foot of the cliffs.

At the centre of town **Praça da República**, the small main square, is busy with sidewalk cafés and wonderful *pastelarias*, while bars and restaurants are concentrated on Rua Dr. Eduardo Burnay, which leads from the southwestern corner of the praça towards the town's main beach, **Praia do Sul**. The most central of the beaches is the tempting one in the Porto de Pesca, but it's a working fishermen's beach and you're not allowed to swim there. To the north of town you'll find the **Praia do Norte** and the prettier, less crowded, **Praia do São Sebastião**, a fifteen-minute walk past the next headland and popular with surfers. Another option is to take the bus from Praça dos Navigantes to reach the series of untouched local beaches further to the north – the World Surfing Championships have been held at Praia da Ribeira d'Ilhas, 3km out of town. The best local beach, however, is perhaps the one at **São Lourenço**, a peaceful hamlet just 5km north of Ericeira.

Back in town, if the sea is too rough, you can use the pool in the *Hotel de Turismo* (1000$00) just beyond the pretty Parque Santa Marta, which has tennis courts. If you want to try surfing, equipment can be hired in town from *Ultimar* at Rua 5 de Outubro 37 (closed Sun).

Practicalities

Buses run virtually every hour to and from Mafra (see p.125) and Lisbon, making Ericeira a useful first or last stop in Estremadura, and there are also services to Sintra. If you arrive by bus, you will be dropped in town at the top of Rua Prudêncio Franco da Trindade, which leads down to the main square. The **turismo**, at Rua Dr. Eduardo Burnay 33a (daily: July–Aug 9am–midnight; Sept–June 9am–10pm; ☎261 863 122, fax 261 865 909), may help with finding **private rooms**, which are advertised throughout town above bars and restaurants.

Accommodation

Pensões and hotels are generally good value and pleasant (there's a list of the best below), though most are not open all year round; those that are should be a good deal cheaper in winter. There's an excellent, well-equipped **campsite** at Parque Mil Regos, just beyond Praia do São Sebastião (☎261 862 706), and a second at Sobreiro (see p.126).

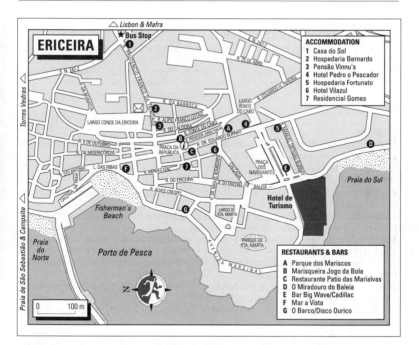

Hospedaria Bernado, Rua Prudêncio Franco da Trindade 17 (☎261 862 378). Spotless and attractive *pensão*, fairly close to the main square. ②.

Casa do Sol, Rua Prudêncio Franco da Trindade 1 (☎261 864 400). A small, but grand, house with shady gardens at the top end of the steep street into town. Rooms are small but some have attached bathrooms. ④.

Hospedaria Fortunato, Rua Dr. Eduardo Burnay 7 (☎261 862 829). Good views of Praia do Sul from the rooms, but a little noisy. There's a range of accommodation and prices; an annexe copes with the overflow. Breakfast included. ③.

Residencial Gomes, Rua Mendes Leal 11 (☎261 863 619). An old, rambling building with faded decor, but clean and fresh with friendly, if somewhat eccentric, staff. ②.

Hotel Pedro o Pescador, Rua Dr. Eduardo Burnay 22 (☎261 864 302). Elegant and friendly but a little run-down, with its own patio. The lively bar and club downstairs may disturb early-nighters. Closed Jan. ④.

Hotel Vilazul, Calçada da Baleia 10 (☎261 864 101, fax 261 862 927, *vilazul@ip.pt*). Just off Rua Dr. Eduardo Burnay, this plush, good-value hotel is popular with upmarket British tour operators. The rooms have private bathrooms and good views from the balconies. Serves great breakfasts. ④.

Pensão Vinnu's, Rua Prudêncio Franco da Trindade 25 (☎261 863 830). Close to the main square, this is clean, modern and airy with a lively bar to boot. Some rooms have small balconies. ③.

Eating

The lively *pastelarias* around Praça da República are recommended for lunch – or tea-time indulgences. In the **restaurants**, seafood is obviously the thing to go for; the local speciality is *açorda de mariscos*, a sort of shellfish stew with bread.

O Barco, Rua Capitão João Lopes 14 (☎261 862 759). Upmarket and expensive seafood restaurant overlooking the harbour; the *ementa turística* is around 3000$00 a head. Closed Thurs & Nov.

Marisqueira Jogo da Bola. Moderately priced seafood restaurant on the corner of Rua Provedor Jorge Fialho and Rua Fonte do Cabo.

Mar a Vista, Largo das Ribas. This popular place for locals has some tables with sea views; a full meal with wine will set you back 2500$00 a head. Closed Wed.

O Miradouro do Baleia, Praia do Sul. Great sea views and a wide range of reasonably priced seafood.

Restaurante Patio dos Marialvas, Rua Dr. Eduardo Burnay 29. A friendly place with outdoor tables, serving excellent *arroz de marisco* at moderate prices. Closed Mon.

Parque dos Mariscos, Rua Dr. Eduardo Burnay 27. Another good, moderately-priced seafood restaurant in the same street.

Nightlife

Ericeira after dark is surprisingly animated – its bars, clubs and proximity to the beaches attract an influx of young Lisboetas. In Ericeira itself, the bars are on or around Rua Dr. Eduardo Burnay, but most of the "in" places are to be found out of town. The following are recommended:

Bar Big Waves, Praça dos Navigantes 22. One of the happening bars on the square near Praia do Sul. The place where locals start off the evening.

Cadillac Bar, Praça dos Navigantes 21. Next door to *Big Waves* and easily recognized by the model Cadillac sticking out of the front. Lively rock and pop.

Limpicos, Foz do Lizandro. This is one of the best of a group of trendy bars in this small beach resort 8km south of Ericeira – part of the night-time circuit for those with their own transport.

Bar Neptuno, Trav. J. Mola. A good-time bar with a two-for-one Happy Hour and frequent live music.

Disco Ouriço, Rua Capitao João Lopes 10, next to *O Barco* restaurant. Currently the in-place for the trendies of Ericeira.

Hotel Pedro o Pescador, Rua Dr. Eduardo Burnay 22. The club below the hotel is a popular young hang-out.

Disco-Bar Pirata, attached to the *Hotel de Turismo*, Rua Porto de Revez, at the top of Praia do Sul. Biggest disco in town, slightly pricey and mainly frequented by tourists but always has a hectic buzz.

Saturday, Seixal, 8km south of Ericeira. A large and brash out-of-town venue which can be great fun on summer weekends but a big let-down at other times.

Torres Vedras

TORRES VEDRAS, 27km to the north and inland from Ericeira, took its name from the Duke of Wellington's famous defence lines (Linhas de Torres) in the **Peninsular War** against Napoleonic France. The "Lines" consisted of a chain of 150 hilltop fortresses, stretching some 40km from the mouth of the Rio Sizandro, directly west of Torres Vedras, to Alhandra, southeast of Torres Vedras, where the Tejo widens out into a huge lake. Astonishingly, they were built in a matter of months and without any apparent reaction from the French. Here, in 1810, Wellington and his forces retired, comfortably supplied by sea and completely unassailable. The French, frustrated by impossibly long lines of communication and by British scorching of the land north of the Lines, eventually retreated back to Spain in despair. Thus from a last line of defence, Wellington completely reversed the progress of the campaign – storming after the disconsolate enemy to effect a series of swift and devastating victories.

The Town

In view of this historical glory, modern Torres Vedras is somewhat disappointing. There are a few ruins of the old fortresses and a couple of imposing sixteenth-century churches, but all this is swamped by a dull sprawl of recent buildings. Yet, from the thirteenth to the sixteenth century, the **castle** (daily 9am–7pm; free) at Torres Vedras was a popular royal residence. It was here, in 1414, that Dom João I confirmed the decision to take Ceuta – the first overseas venture leading towards the future Portuguese maritime empire. The castle was eventually abandoned and then reduced to rubble by the earthquake of 1755.

Booklets and old maps can be read at the **turismo**, Rua 9 de Abril, off Praça 25 de Abril (Mon–Sat 10am–1pm & 2–6pm; ☎261 314 094); while across Praça 25 de Abril, in the old Convento da Graça, is the **Museu Municipal** (Tues–Sun 10am–noon & 2–6pm; 150$00), with a room devoted to the Peninsular War. Unless you get hooked on the local wine, there's not much else to keep you in the town.

However, if you decide **to stay**, try the clean but basic *Pensão-Restaurante 1° de Maio*, Rua 1° de Dezembro 3 (☎261 322 875; ②), or *Residencial Moderna*, opposite the cinema on Av. Tenente Valadim (☎261 314 146; ③). For a **meal**, *Gordo* in Rua Almirante Gado Coutinho 15 (☎261 323 079; closed Tues) and *Adega Tipica Manadinha*, Rua Capitão Luis Boto Pimental (☎261 324 294), are good options.

In general, however, you'd probably be better off taking one of the many buses on to Peniche, Óbidos, or the popular local resort of Praia de Santa Cruz. The **bus station** is just uphill from the **train station** which is located at the end of the central Avenida 5 Outubro.

Praia de Santa Cruz and other beaches

Most people at the modern resort of **PRAIA DE SANTA CRUZ** are locals from Torres Vedras, 13km to the east, and the place has a friendly, easy-going feel, as well as some excellent places to eat. There are two sandy beaches, **Praia Guincho** below the town, and the more secluded **Praia Formosa**, beneath cliffs to the south. In between is a "screaming rock" – partly covered by the tide – where air and water is forced through a hole in the rock at certain times to produce the distinctive sound. **Rooms** are available at the *Pensão-Restaurante Mar Lindo*, Trav. Jorge Cardoso (☎261 937 297; ④), some with sea views, and at the modern *Hotel de Santa Cruz*, Rua José Pedro Lopes (☎261 937 148; ④). There's a shady **campsite** north of the village, five minutes' walk from the sea but it fills up quickly in summer.

Quieter resorts – uncrowded outside public holidays or summer weekends – are to be found to the north of here and are easily reached on buses heading to Lourinhã or Peniche.

Praia de Porto Novo

Five kilometres north of Santa Cruz, **PRAIA DE PORTO NOVO** is just beginning to show signs of development, but the beach is still relatively unspoilt and there are good walking possibilities inland. In August 1808, British reinforcements were landed here, at the mouth of the River Maceira. They enabled Wellington, in his first serious encounter with the French, to defeat General Junot at the battle of Vimeiro, following which the French sued for peace. Should you want **to stay**, the reliable *Residencial Promar* (☎261 984 220; ④) is the best bet among the cluster of *pensões* and restaurants opposite the beach.

Areia Branca and Consolação

Further north on the Peniche road, 21km from Torres Vedras, lies **AREIA BRANCA** ("White Sand"), a small resort with a congenial campsite (☎261 412 199) and a good beachside **youth hostel** (☎261 422 127). Other **accommodation** options include *Estalagem Areia Branca*, Praia da Areia Branca (☎261 412 491; ⑤), near the beach, and *Residencial Restaurante D. Lourenço*, on the way out of town (☎261 422 809; ④); alternatively, ask at the **turismo** (Mon–Sat 10am–1pm & 2–6pm; ☎261 422 167) for a list of private **rooms**. The *Restaurante Dom Lourenço* is the best place for **food**.

Despite the attractive sands here, the sea at Areia Branca is not too clean and it's better to go north to **CONSOLAÇÃO**, just south of Peniche, with its great swathe of beach.

There's a rash of development behind the sand dunes, but it's relatively hidden. There are few places to stay the night but you're probably better off moving on to Peniche or Baleal for accommodation. For snacks and drinks, try *Bar Forte Club* in the old fort in the attractive old part of town.

Peniche and the Ilha Berlenga

PENICHE, impressively enclosed by ramparts and one of Portugal's most active fishing ports, is the embarkation point for the **Ilha Berlenga**. As late as the fifteenth century the town was an island but the area has silted up and is now joined to the mainland by a narrow isthmus with gently sloping beaches on either side. Unfortunately, Peniche has burst out of its natural confines and unsightly development now stretches along the coast, but inside the walled town there is more to appreciate. The main attraction is the fortress which dominates the south side of town, and there's also an enjoyable market on the *campo*, held on the last Thursday of the month.

The sixteenth-century **Fortaleza** (Tues–Sun 10.30am–12.30pm & 2–7pm; closes at 5pm in winter) was one of the dictator Salazar's most notorious jails. Greatly expanded in the 1950s and 1960s to accommodate the growing crowds of political prisoners, it later served as a temporary refugee camp for *retornados* from the colonies. Today it houses a **museum** (120$00), with the familiar mix of local archeology, natural history and craft displays, among which you can still see the old cells (on the top floor), the solitary confinement pens (*segredos*) and the visitors' grille (*parlatório*).

Just outside the city walls, off the fine **north beach** of the peninsula, there's a traditional boat yard. It's fascinating to watch the shipwrights here manoeuvring huge timbers into position to form the skeletal framework of a new fishing vessel. If you've got more time to spare, you can take a ninety-minute walk (though if you have a car it's a good idea to drive clear of the suburbs first) beyond the fortress – out to the tip of **Cabo Carvoeiro**, the

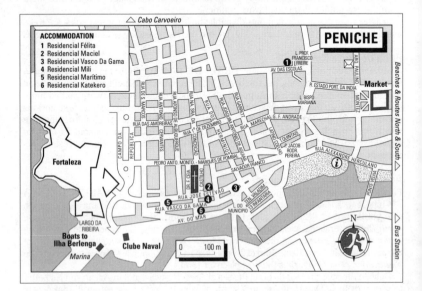

rugged, rock-pillared and lighthouse-topped peninsula, where there's a smart restaurant, the *Nau dos Corvos*, with a superb view and a tourist menu for around 2000$00. Another rewarding walk, a few kilometres to the north of Peniche, is to **BALEAL**, an islet-village, joined to the mainland by a narrow strip of fine sand. This would make a good base in its own right, with a fine beach, not too much development and a few **rooms** for rent. It has a small, but reasonably equipped **campsite** (☎262 769 333) or you could try *Hospedaria Baleal a Vista* on the main Peniche road (☎262 769 467; ③), *Pequena Baleia* (☎262 769 370; ③) or the wonderful *A Casa das Marés* (☎262 769 371; ⑥).

If you are in Peniche over the first weekend in August, you'll see the **festival** of Nossa Senhora da Boa Viagem (Our Lady of Good Journeys), during which the statue of the Virgin is brought to the harbour by boat to be greeted by candle-bearing locals. After the village priest has blessed the fleet, there are fireworks, bands and dancing in the street.

Practicalities

Buses arriving in Peniche pull in at the station on the isthmus just outside the town walls. It's a ten-minute walk into the centre across the Ponte Velha, which takes you to Rua Alexandre Herculano, where you turn left for the **turismo** (daily: summer 9am–8pm; winter 10am–12.30pm & 2–5pm; ☎262 789 571). Nearly all of Peniche's hotels, bars and restaurants are on or just back from Rua Alexandre Herculano and Avenida do Mar, which leads down to the harbour by Largo da Ribeira.

Accommodation

In summer (particularly in August), **accommodation** can be hard to find; you may be approached by people offering private rooms, but it's best to head for the turismo who can usually help you to find something. Out of season, or early in the day, try one of **residenciais** below. There's a municipal **campsite** (☎262 789 529) on the way into town, after you've crossed the Rio Lagôa, which is well placed for the bus station, and a fine private campsite, *Camping Peniche Praia* (☎262 783 460), complete with pool and restaurant, on the north shore of the peninsula.

Félita, Largo Prof. Francisco Freire (☎262 782 190). Fairly characterless but comfortable rooms in a modern building. ④.

Katekero, Av. do Mar 76 (☎262 787 170). Good-value, airy rooms with TVs, some with sea views. ③.

Residencial Maciel, Rua José Estêvão 38 (☎262 784 685). The best budget option in town, with excellent, spotless rooms and a central location. ③.

Marítimo, Rua José Estêvão (☎262 782 850). Set just back from the harbour, this *residencial* has simple rooms with private bathrooms. ②.

Mili, Rua José Estêvão 45 (☎262 787 107). Comfortable, well-located and efficient place with friendly owners. ④.

Vasco da Gama, Rua José Estêvão 23 (☎262 781 902). Good value and in a central position. Rooms come with TV and bathrooms and the price includes breakfast. ④.

Eating and drinking

There is a fine array of **restaurants** along Avenida do Mar – most of them good value, and serving huge portions. *Restaurante Gaivota* and *Restaurante Onda Azul*, both by the harbour on Largo da Ribeira, have inexpensive seafood and often set up outdoor barbecues. The wonderful **market snack bar** just off Arq. Paulino Montez is just the place for breakfast or picnic provisions; it's usually full of fishwives in knitted capes and socks, swinging plastic bags of fish as they sip *bicas* and exchange news. Your best bet for a lively drink and a view of the world going by is one of the harbourside **bars**.

Ilha Berlenga

The **ILHA BERLENGA**, 10km offshore and just visible from the cape, is a dreamlike place – rather like a Scottish isle transported to warmer climes. Just two-and-a-half square kilometres in extent, it is the largest island of a tiny archipelago, with a jagged coastline of grottoes, miniature fjords, and extraordinary rock formations. In summer the sea is calm, crystal clear, and perfect for snorkelling and diving – rare in the Atlantic.

The only people permitted to live here are a couple of dozen fishermen, as the whole island has been declared a **Natural Reserve**, the home of thousands upon thousands of seabirds, including gulls, puffins and cormorants, perched in every conceivable cranny and clearly plotting to leave their mark on every possible victim. Makeshift paths are marked out with stones, and guardians watch out for visitors straying into the prohibited areas and disturbing the birds.

The island

Human life revolves around the main **landing dock** with its colour-washed fishing boats and small sandy **beach**. It can get crowded and noisy down here at the height of the season – it takes very few people to make the place seem packed – though the only buildings are a cluster of huts, a rather basic shop and a lighthouse. If you want **to stay**, it's a choice between the nearby bar-restaurant *Pavilhão Mar e Sol* (☎262 750 331; ⑤) which offers somewhat pricey **rooms** or, for the tighter budget, the rudimentary **hostel** (☎262 785 263; ①) in the seventeenth-century Forte de São João Baptista, a short walk beyond the lighthouse, on an islet joined by the narrowest of causeways. You have to reserve in advance and bookings are for a minimum of one week – you'll need to bring your own food (the hostel has a kitchen) and sleeping stuff. There's also a **campsite** (500$00 per person), which clings to a strictly limited site on the rocky slopes above the harbour. If you want to stay here, you have to book at the turismo in Peniche – it's best to write in advance.

Rowing boats can be hired at the jetty to explore the intricacies of the coastline, though you may prefer to go in something with a motor if there's any motion on the sea (you can get a guided trip for a few hundred escudos). Don't miss the **Furado Grande**, a fantastic tunnel 75m long which culminates in the aptly named **Cova do Sonho** (Dream Cove) with its precipitous cliffs.

Getting there

The **ferry** from Peniche to Berlenga is operated by Viamar and takes one hour – longer if the sea is rough. The service operates from May 15 to September 15; currently, there are three ferries daily in July and August (9am, 11.30am and 5.30pm; return at 10.30am, 4.30pm and 6.30pm) and one daily in May, June and September (10am; return at 4.30pm). A return **ticket** costs 3000$00 and there's a limit of 300 tickets sold each day; one person can buy up to five at a time. In July and August the ticket office opens at 8pm to take bookings for the next day's ferry; if you want to be sure of a place, get there in good time. Outside these months, it's not usually a problem getting a ticket on the day of travel.

Two other companies, Turpesca (☎262 789 960) and Berlenga Praia (☎262 782 636), operate **boat trips** all year round except December (minimum four people). Tickets are 3000$00 return and the price includes a visit to the caves along the coastline. Both companies can arrange fishing or diving trips, for which equipment can be hired from the Clube Naval near the old harbour in Peniche (☎262 782 568 or 782 550). Note that you can use Turpesca for overnight stays on the island only between June and September; the rest of the year it will take only day-trippers. All boats to the island are booked from the jetty below the fort.

However, bear in mind that if the weather is difficult, times will change and boats may be cancelled. In any case, be sure to go without breakfast – it's a rough ride, as evinced by the grim collection of buckets under the seats!

Óbidos

ÓBIDOS, "The Wedding City", was the traditional bridal gift of the kings of Portugal to their queens. The custom was begun in 1282 by Dom Dinis and Dona Isabel, and the town can hardly have changed much in appearance since then. It is very small and completely enclosed by lofty medieval walls: streets are cobbled, houses whitewashed with bright blue and yellow borders, and at all points steep staircases wind up to the ramparts, where you can gaze across a lovely rural landscape.

It wasn't always like this. Five hundred years ago, when Peniche was an island, the sea also reached the foot of the ridge on which Óbidos stands and boats were moored below its walls. However, by the fifteenth century the sea had retreated, leaving a fertile green plain and the distant Lagoa de Óbidos with its narrow, shallow entrance to the sea.

The town is touristy, of course, and the area around it is becoming somewhat built up. However, you can walk right around the town along its perimeter **walls** – a narrow and at times hair-raising walkway with no handrails, and from this vantage point the town still seems to have a private life of its own. If you stay the night, the feeling is reinforced, as the town slowly empties to regain its charm.

The Town

The most striking building in town is Dom Dinis's massively-towered **Castelo**, which has been converted to a very splendid *pousada* (see "Accommodation" on p.146). Below the castle, the principal focus of the streets is the parish church, the **Igreja de Santa Maria**, in the central praça – chosen for the wedding of the ten-year-old child king, Afonso V, and his eight-year-old cousin, Isabel, in 1444. It dates mainly from the Renaissance period, though the interior is lined with seventeenth-century blue *azulejos* in a homely manner typical of Portuguese churches. On the left-hand wall is an elaborate tomb designed by Nicolas Chanterene, an influential French sculptor active in Portugal in the first half of the sixteenth century. The *retábulo* to the right of the main altar was painted by **Josefa de Óbidos**, one of the finest of all Portuguese painters – and one of the few women artists afforded any reputation by art historians. Born at Seville in 1634, Josefa spent most of her life in a convent at Óbidos. She began her career as an etcher and miniaturist and a remarkable handling of detail is a feature of her later full-scale religious works. Another of her paintings, a portrait, can be seen in the adjacent **museum** in the old town hall (daily 10am–12.30pm & 2–6pm; 250$00).

There's an annual **festival of ancient music** in October, held in various venues around the town, including the purpose-built **Casa da Música**, just inside Porta da Vila, the principal town gate at the far end of Rua Direita. The town is also busy on Tourist Day (one of the last two Sundays in August), when free wine is on offer. If you're on the lookout for things to buy, there's a range of **shops** on the main Rua Direita, from the Casa Mourisco (ceramics, paintings and carvings) to the worthy old people's **handicrafts centre**, which has a good variety of nicely made items.

Practicalities

Buses from Caldas da Rainha (6km to the north) and Peniche (24km west) stop outside the Porta da Vila. From here **Rua Direita** leads straight through the town to the **turismo** (Mon–Fri 9.30am–7pm, Sat & Sun 9.30am–1pm & 2–7pm; ☎262 959 231). The **train station**

is at the foot of the ridge; there is no ticket office here, so pay once you are on the train. If you are not too heavily laden, you can cross the tracks and climb the steps, which will bring you to the gate by the Castelo *pousada* – at the opposite end of Rua Direita. Otherwise, follow the road and the easier gradients to reach the Porta da Vila.

Accommodation

Accommodation is on the expensive side, unless you get one of the handful of private **rooms** (usually ③), advertised in the windows of a few houses and sometimes touted at the bus station. Try those at Rua Direita 40 (☎262 959 188). Of the **pensões and hotels** the following represent a good selection:

Casa do Poço, Trav. da Rua Nova (☎262 959 358). Downhill from the castle, this renovated house retains its Moorish foundations and a well in the courtyard. There are only four double rooms, all en suite, and there's fado in the bar at weekends. ④.

Casa da Relógio, Rua da Graça (☎262 959 282). Outside the walls, a former eighteenth-century mansion whose "clock" is in fact a stone sundial. Six double rooms available, all with bath. Real value for money. ④.

Pousada do Castelo (☎262 959 105). Relatively small but nevertheless one of the country's finest and priciest *pousadas* – visit for morning coffee or afternoon tea at the very least. Its size means it fills up quickly. ⑧.

Estalagem do Convento, Rua Dr. João de Ornelas (☎262 959 214). A minor convent, converted rather tastelessly into a hotel. Expensive patio dining in summer is the best feature. ⑤.

Albergaria Josefa de Óbidos, Rua Dr. João de Ornelas (☎262 959 228). A modern air-conditioned hotel, outside the walls. Rooms all have TVs and breakfast is included. ④.

Residencial Martim de Freitas, Estrada Nacional 8 (☎262 959 185). On the road to Caldas da Rainha, this has huge, simply furnished rooms, and is generally friendly. Breakfast is included. ③.

Albergaria Rainha Santa Isabel, Rua Direita (☎262 959 323). The carefully preserved facade hides a modern hotel with lounge and bar. Hearty breakfasts included. Some of the rooms have balconies overlooking the main street. ⑤.

Eating

Restaurants are geared towards day-trippers and are not generally high on atmosphere, but the quality of the cuisine is good as long as you don't mind paying above-average prices.

Restaurante Alcaide, Rua Direita, opposite the *Albergaria Rainha Santa Isabel* (☎262 959 220). Arrive early – or book – particularly if you want to eat on the balcony; pricey. Closed Mon & Nov.

Casa de Ramiro, Rua Porta do Vale. Just outside the walls in an old house, redesigned in Arabic style. It's noted for its aromatic grills and is moderately priced. Closed Thurs & Jan–Feb.

Restaurante O Conquistador, Rua Josefa de Óbidos, off Rua Direita. Near the Porta da Vila; try the soup and the duck, or eat from the *ementa turística* for around 1500$00.

Estalagem do Convento, Rua Dr. João de Ornelas. Excellent but expensive patio dining, though the *ementa turística* isn't outrageously priced at 2800$00.

Café-Restaurante 1° de Dezembro, Largo Sao Pedro, next to the church. The best bet for a cheap meal, although service can be slack.

Caldas da Rainha

Six kilometres north of Óbidos, **CALDAS DA RAINHA** ("Queen's Spa") was put firmly on the map by Dona Leonor. Passing by in her carriage, she was so impressed by the strong sulphuric waters that she founded a hospital here, initiating four centuries of noble and royal patronage. That was in 1484 but the town was to reach the peak of its popularity in the nineteenth century when, all over Europe, spas became as much social as medical institutions. The English Gothic novelist, William Beckford, stopping off on his journey to Batalha and Alcobaça (recorded in his *Travels in Spain and Portugal*), found it a lively if depressing place – "every tenth or twelfth person a rheumatic or palsied invalid, with his limbs all atwist, and his mouth all awry, being conveyed to the baths in a chair".

Disappointingly little remains of all the royal wealth poured into the spa, though it is still a pleasant stop on your way to Nazaré or Alcobaça. From the central **Praça da República**, which hosts a fruit market every morning, the **royal spa hospital**, still very much in use, is a short walk downhill. There is a museum (Tues–Sun 10am–12.30pm & 2–5pm; 200$00) but you can only bathe in the warm, sulphurous swimming pools under doctor's orders. Protruding from the back of the spa is the striking Manueline belfry of **Nossa Senhora do Pópulo**, the hospital church. There's a *Virgin and Child* by Josefa de Óbidos in the sacristry.

In the leafy Parque Dom Carlos I, the **Museu de José Malhoa** (Tues–Sun 10am–12.30pm & 2–5pm; 250$00, free Sunday morning) displays Malhoa's work and that of other late-nineteenth-century Portuguese painters. There are two other museums at the far edge of the park: the **Atelier Museu António Duarte** (Mon–Fri 9am–1pm & 2–6pm, Sat & Sun 10am–1pm & 2–6pm; 250$00), devoted to the eminent sculptor; and, alongside, the much better **Museu da Cerâmica** (Tues–Sun 10am–12.30pm & 2–5pm; 250$00), which contains some of the original work of local potter and caricaturist Rafael Bordalo Pinheiro – look for his series of life-sized ceramic figures representing the Passion. Indeed, Caldas remains famed for its traditional ceramics (including peculiar phallus-shaped objects) and the **Feira Nacional da Cerâmica** is held here during July or October in the *Expooeste*, an industrial part of town, northwest of the railway tracks.

Practicalities

It's a short walk from either the **bus** or **train station** to **Praça da República**, where you'll find the summer **turismo** (Mon–Fri 9am–7pm, Sat & Sun 10am–1pm & 3–7pm; ☎262 831 003); the main turismo (same hours & ☎) is open all year and is situated next to the town hall in Praça 25 de Abril.

Accommodation

Due to the presence of the spa, there's a fair amount of **accommodation** around town, most of it reasonably priced.

Caldas Internacional Hotel, Rua Dr. Figueirôa Rêgo 45 (☎262 832 307). The smartest option in town, if unexciting. ⑤.

Pensão Central, Largo Dr. José Barbosa (☎262 831 914). A pleasant choice and the birthplace of painter José Malhoa. Breakfast included. ③.

Pensão Residencial Estremadura, Largo Dr. José Barbosa 23 (☎262 832 313). Central, but somewhat rundown for the price. ③.

Residencial Europeia, Rua Almirante Cândido dos Reis 64 (☎262 831 508). Another central, smart choice with heavy wooden furniture, TVs and a bar. ④.

Residencial Rainha D. Leonor, Hermicício João Paulo II, 9 (☎262 842 171). A big, modern, soulless block but with satellite TV, private parking and all mod cons. ④.

Eating and drinking

For **food**, it's hard to beat the spit-roasts and grills at the *Zé do Barrete*, at Trav. da Cova da Onça 16–18 (☎262 832 787; closed Sun), midway down Rua Almirante Cândido dos Reis. There are several other good restaurants along this street. *Populus* (closed Mon), on the edge of the park at Rua de Camões, has lovely outdoor seating and serves up good salads and beef dishes at moderate prices. You may also be tempted to visit *Supatra* (☎262 842 920; closed Mon), 1km out on Rua General Amílcar Mota (the Óbidos road) – an unlikely setting for one of the country's most respected Thai restaurants. The cafés around Largo Rainha D. Leonor are a good bet for an evening **drink**, and also for sampling the local, rather sickly, sweets, such as *trouxas de ovos*.

North to Nazaré

Heading **north from Caldas**, buses and trains loop inland, touching the coast only at São Martinho do Porto, 13km south of Nazaré. However, if you have your own transport, you can bear northwest from Caldas along the N360, which takes you past the tranquil **Lagoa de Óbidos**, and then out along the coast via Foz do Arelho on a beautiful clifftop route – a much better option than the busy N8.

Foz do Arelho

At **FOZ DO ARELHO**, 9km from Caldas and the first resort you come to, there's a fine beach and a lagoon where you can swim. There is a **campsite** (☎262 979 197) plus a few decent **places to stay**: the modern *Penedo Furado* (☎262 979 610; ④); the upmarket but not always welcoming *Foz Praia* (☎262 979 413; ⑤), complete with pool, tennis courts and restaurant; and, 1km before the village and only 500m from the lake, the *Quinta da Foz* (☎262 979 369; ⑥) – a lovely sixteenth-century country house hotel with just five rooms. Good seafood **restaurants** can be found behind the beach, while *Frenetico* nightclub, at the northern end of the beach, is the place to head for after dark.

São Martinho do Porto

SÃO MARTINHO DO PORTO is the main resort between Peniche and Nazaré, and one of the more developed spots along the Estremaduran coast, though at least most of the new building is relatively low-rise. In high season, it's probably not worth the struggle to find a room – or even a place in the campsite.

The reason for São Martinho's tourist success is its **beach**: a vast sweep of sand which curls around a landlocked bay to form a natural swimming pool. This shelter makes it one of the warmest places to swim on the west coast, with the sands sloping down into calm, shallow, solar-heated water. For something more bracing – or less crowded – there's a good northern beach on the open Atlantic coastline beyond the bay. (Beware of the Atlantic beaches beyond the bay; they can be dangerous.)

Check with the **turismo**, at the far end of Avenida 25 de Abril (summer Mon–Fri 10am–7pm, Sat & Sun 9am–1pm & 3–6pm; winter Mon–Fri 10am–1pm & 3–6pm; ☎262 989 110), about the possibility of accommodation in **private rooms**. Alternatively, try one of the following: *Pensão Americana*, Rua D. José Saldanha 2 (☎262 989 170; ④), a popular place two blocks from the seafront, which also rents out mountain bikes; *Pensão Carvalho*, Rua Miguel Bombarda 6 (☎262 989 605; ④), slightly nearer to the beach and with a good restaurant; or *Residencial Concha*, Largo Vitorino Froís (☎262 989 220; ⑤), a comfortable place some of whose rooms have satellite TV and balconies. There's also a **campsite**, *Colina do Sol* (☎262 989 764), 2km to the north, off the Nazaré road (N242), and a **youth hostel** (☎262 999 506), 4km away and further inland at Alfeizerão, off the Caldas da Rainha/Alcobaça road (N8).

Eating is best done at the restaurants attached to the *Americana* or *Carvalho* pensões. Other good options include: *A Cave*, Rua Conde de Avalar (closed Wed); *O Largo* at Largo Vitorino Froís 21; or the *Café Baia*, Rua Vasco da Gama, behind the turismo. After that, look into the *Amnésia Club*, near the *Residencial Concha*, open every night from midnight and with a disco at weekends open until 6am.

Nazaré

After years of advertising itself as the most picturesque seaside village in Portugal, **NAZARÉ** has finally more or less destroyed itself in the process. In summer, the crowds are way too much for the place to cope with, and the enduring characteristics are not so much "gentle traditions" as trinket stalls and high prices. That said,

Train Station, Valado Campsite, Leiria & Alcobaça △   △ Campsite & Lisbon

AVENIDA DE OLIVENÇA

RUA DOS BARRANCOS

RUA MOUZINHO DE ALBUQUERQUE

ACCOMMODATION
1 Hotel de Nazaré
2 Pensão Central
3 Residencial Marina
4 Residencial Beira-Mar
5 Pensão Restaurante Ribamar
6 Residencial Cubata

RESTAURANTS & BARS
A Carlota e Catarina
B Pôr do Sol
C Aquário
D Casa Lazaro
E O Casalinho

Bus Station

△ Funicular to Sítio

△ São Martinho do Porto

RUA DO LEIRIA

LARGO DAS CALDEIRAS

PRAÇA SOUSA OLIVEIRA

TRAV DE ELEVADOR

PRAÇA DR MANUEL DE ARRIAGA

AVENIDA DA REPÚBLICA

NAZARÉ

0   100 m

local traditions are still just about managing to coexist with tourism – you'll see women weaving barefoot through the town bearing immense trays of fish on their heads, and a few fishermen sitting unperturbed on the beach, mending their nets beside brilliantly painted sardine boats. However, most of the boats have disappeared to a new harbour, fifteen minutes' walk from the village, where cranes have replaced the oxen once used to haul them in.

The village and beaches

The original settlement was not at Nazaré but at Sítio, 110m up the rock face above the present sprawl of holiday apartment buildings, a location that was, by most accounts, the legacy of pirate raids which continued well into the nineteenth century. However, legend has a different explanation, telling of a twelfth-century knight, Dom Fuas Roupinho, who, while out hunting, was led up the cliff by a deer. The deer dived off into the void and Dom Fuas was saved from following by the timely vision of **Nossa Senhora da Nazaré**, in whose name a church was subsequently built.

You can reach this church, and the surrounding Sítio district, by a **funicular**, which rumbles up and down almost continuously from 7am to midnight (85$00). There is an enjoyable *miradouro* at the top, though the shrine itself is unimpressive, despite an icon carved by Saint Joseph and painted by Saint Luke (a handy partnership active throughout Europe). The church does, however, host a well-attended **romaria** (Sept 8–10) with processions, folk dancing, and bullfights. The Sítio bullring also stages Saturday night *touradas* in summer.

Back down below, the area between the funicular and Praça Dr. Manuel de Arriaga retains an old-world charm which the seafront has all but lost. But the main disadvantage of staying in Nazaré is that its **beaches** – grand, tent-studded sweeps of clean sand, stretching out to the north beyond the headland of Sítio, and south across the narrow Alcôa estuary – are dangerous for swimming. The Atlantic can be fierce along the Estremaduran coast, so, for safety's sake, stick to the patrolled main beach where the bathers are packed in as tightly as the sardine boats. Alternatively, tramp southwards towards the village of Gralha, where you'll find a number of small coves and one sheltered beach isolated enough to be a popular spot for nude bathing.

Practicalities

Using public transport, it's simplest to arrive at Nazaré by bus. There are regular connections with most towns in the region, and the **bus station** is centrally located, halfway down Avenida Vieira Guimarães, which meets the main drag, Avenida da República, at right angles at the foot of the hill. The nearest **train station** is at Valado, 6km inland, on the Alcobaça road; buses from Alcobaça call there on the way into town.

Avenida da República runs the length of the beach, and this is where you'll find most of the hotels and restaurants, as well as the **turismo** (daily: July & Aug 10am–10pm; Sept–June 10am–1pm & 3–6pm; ☎262 561 194), near the funicular.

Accommodation

Pensões in Nazaré are heavily booked throughout the summer but rooms are plentiful and you'll be accosted by their owners at the bus station – expect to pay around 4500$00 in high season. If you have problems finding a place, consult the turismo, which has a list of available rooms. The more promising *pensão* and hotel possibilities are listed below. There's a campsite on the road to Valado (☎262 561 111; closed mid-Nov to mid-Jan), and another – the well-equipped *Vale Paraíso* (☎262 561 800, fax 262 561 900, *camping.vp.nz@mail.telepac.pt*) – nestling in pine woods 2km out of town on the road to Marinha Grande (N242), complete with pool and bikes for rent.

Residencial Beira-Mar, Av. da República 40 (☎262 561 358). Right on the beachfront and very pleasant, with large breezy rooms (some with sea views) and private bathrooms; the price includes breakfast. Closed Nov–Feb. ⑤.

Quinta do Campo, Valado dos Frades (☎262 577 135, fax 262 577 555). Situated in a tranquil setting 6km inland, this *quinta* was founded as an agricultural college by monks in the fourteenth century and makes an excellent base if you have your own transport. The building is set in extensive grounds and offers various sports facilities including a pool and tennis courts. ⑥.

Pensão Central, Rua Mouzinho de Albuquerque 85 (☎262 551 510). Old and well-managed; book in advance if you can. The rooms facing the courtyard are best. Breakfast included. ④.

Residencial Cubata, Avd. da República 6 (☎262 561 706). A great position and good value if you can get a sea view. It's between the turismo and the foot of the funicular. ④.

Residencial Marina, Rua Mouzinho de Albuquerque 6 (☎262 551 541). Down the street from the *Central*, this is a good-value, cheerful choice. ④.

Hotel de Nazaré, Largo Afonso Zuquete (☎262 569 030). Upmarket choice with small rooms, simply furnished. The views from the upper floors are splendid, and even better from the rooftop terrace. Closed Jan. ⑥.

Pensão Restaurante Ribamar, Rua Gomes Freire 9 (☎262 551 58). Across the road from the turismo, with some rooms overlooking the beach. The bathrooms are tiled with *azulejos* and breakfast is included in the price. ⑤.

Eating and drinking

The main concentration of **restaurants and cafés** is along Avenida da República and the several squares off the avenue. Places worth trying include:

Aquário, Largo das Caldeiras 13. Moderately priced and one of the best of a cluster of places in this pretty square with outdoor tables.

Carlota e Catarina, Rua Adrião Batalha 162. Good seafood served in an agreeable setting and at reasonable prices, but it's quite a climb to get there.

Casa Lazaro, Rua Adrião Batalho. Good-value seafood and excellent house wine in tiled surroundings by the seafront.

O Casalinho, Praça Sousa Oliveira 6. Popular with locals which is recommendation enough for its fish and meat dishes. Service is with a smile and prices are moderate.

Pôr do Sol, Av. da República 54. Expensive but top-quality seafood overlooking the beach.

Alcobaça

The Cistercian monastery at **ALCOBAÇA** was founded in 1153 by Dom Henrique to celebrate his victory over the Moors at Santarém six years earlier. Building started soon after, and by the end of the thirteenth century it was the most powerful monastery in the country. Owning vast tracts of farmland, orchards and vineyards, it was immensely rich and held jurisdiction over a dozen towns and three seaports. Its church and cloister are the purest and the most inspired creation of all Portuguese Gothic architecture and, alongside Belém and Batalha, are the most impressive monuments in the country. The church is also the burial place of those romantic figures of Portuguese history, Dom Pedro and Dona Inês de Castro.

Aside from the monastery, the only other point of interest in Alcobaça is the **Museu do Vinho** (summer Tues–Sun 9am–noon & 2–5.30pm; winter Mon–Fri, same hours; free), ten minutes' walk from the bus station out on the Leiria road, which gives a fascinating glimpse into the area's wine-making and agricultural past. There are free guided tours, which last about an hour, and you get the chance to purchase some of the local produce.

The Mosteiro de Alcobaça

The **Mosteiro de Alcobaça** (daily: April–Sept 9am–7pm; Oct–March 9am–5pm; 400$00; entry to church free), although empty since its dissolution in 1834, still seems to assert power, magnificence and opulence. And it takes little imagination to people it again with the monks, said once to have numbered 999. Mass was once celebrated here without interruption, but it was the residents' legendary extravagant and aristocratic lifestyles that formed the common ingredients of the awed anecdotes of eighteenth-century travellers.

Even William Beckford, no stranger to high living, found their decadence unsettling, growing weary of "perpetual gormandising. .. the fumes of banquets and incense. .. the fat waddling monks and sleek friars with wanton eyes, twanging away on the Jew's harp". Another contemporary observer, Richard Twiss, for his part found "the bottle went as briskly about as ever I saw it do in Scotland" – a tribute indeed. For all the "high romps" and luxuriance, though, it has to be added that the monks enjoyed a reputation for hospitality, generosity and charity, while the surrounding countryside is to this day one of the most productive areas in Portugal, thanks to their agricultural expertise.

The abbey church

The main **Abbey Church**, modelled on the original Cistercian abbey at Citeaux in France, is the largest in Portugal. External impressions are disappointing, as the Gothic facade has been superseded by unexceptional Baroque additions of the seventeenth and eighteenth centuries. Inside, however, all later adornments have been swept away, restoring the narrow soaring aisles to their original vertical simplicity. The only exception to this Gothic purity is the frothy Manueline doorway to the sacristy, hidden directly behind the high altar, and, as at Tomar and Batalha, encrusted with intricate, swirling motifs of coral and seaweed.

The church's most precious treasures are the fourteenth-century **tombs of Dom Pedro and Dona Inês de Castro**, each occupying one of the transepts and sculpted with phenomenal wealth of detail. Animals, heraldic emblems, musicians and biblical scenes are all portrayed in an architectural setting of miniature windows, canopies, domes and towers; most graphic of all is a dragon-shaped Hell's mouth at Inês's feet, consuming the damned. The tombs are inscribed with the motto "Até ao Fim do Mundo" (Until the End of the World) and in accordance with Dom Pedro's orders have been placed foot to foot so that on the Day of Judgement the pair may rise and immediately feast their eyes on one another.

Pedro's earthly love for Inês de Castro, the great theme of epic Portuguese poetry, was cruelly stifled by high politics. Inês, as the daughter of a Galician nobleman, was a potential source of Spanish influence over the Portuguese throne and Pedro's father, Afonso IV, forbade their marriage. The ceremony took place nevertheless – secretly at Bragança in remote Trás-os-Montes – and eventually Afonso was persuaded to sanction his daughter-in-law's murder. When Pedro succeeded to the throne in 1357 he brought the murderers to justice, personally ripping out their hearts and gorging his love-crazed appetite for blood upon them. More poignantly, he also exhumed and crowned the corpse of his lover, forcing the entire royal circle to acknowledge her as queen by kissing her decomposing hand.

The kitchen

From one highlight to another. Beckford – Romantic dilettante that he was – stood bewildered by the charms of these tombs when "in came the Grand Priors hand in hand, all three together. 'To the *kitchen*,' said they in unison, 'to the kitchen and that immediately.'" They led him past the fourteenth-century Chapter House to a cavernous room in the corner of the cloisters – a route that you can follow.

Alcobaça's feasting has already been mentioned but this **kitchen** – with its cellars and gargantuan conical chimney, supported by eight trunk-like iron columns – sets it in real perspective. A stream tapped from the River Alcôa still runs straight through the room: it was used not only for cooking and washing but also to provide a constant supply of fresh fish, which plopped out into a stone basin. At the centre of the room, on the vast wooden tables, Beckford continued to marvel at:

> *pastry in vast abundance which a numerous tribe of lay brothers and their attendants were rolling out and puffing up into a hundred different shapes, singing all the while as blithely as larks in a cornfield. "There," said the Lord Abbot, "we shall not starve. God's bounties are great, it is fit we should enjoy them."*

And enjoy them they did, with a majestic feast of "rarities and delicacies, potted lampreys, strange Brazilian messes, edible birds' nests and sharks' fins dressed after the mode of Macau by a Chinese lay brother"! As a practical test for obesity the monks had to file through a narrow door on their way to the **refectory**; those who failed were forced to fast until they could squeeze through.

The cloisters and Sala dos Reis

The **Claustro do Silencio** (Cloisters of Silence), notable for their traceried stone windows, were built in the reign of Dom Dinis, the "poet-king" who established an enduring literary and artistic tradition at the abbey. An upper storey of twisted columns and Manueline arches was added in the sixteenth century, along with, in its standard position opposite the refectory, a beautiful hexagonal lavatory.

The **Sala dos Reis** (Kings' Room), off the cloister, displays statues of virtually every king of Portugal up until Dom José, who died in 1777. Blue eighteenth-century *azulejos* depict the siege of Santarém, Dom Afonso's vow, and the founding of the monastery. Also on show here is a piece of war booty which must have warmed the souls of the brothers – the huge metal cauldron in which soup was heated up for the Spanish army before the battle of Aljubarrota in 1385 (for more of which, see "Batalha" on p.157).

The rest of the monastery, including four other cloisters, seven dormitories and endless corridors, is closed to the public; parts of it are currently occupied by an old people's home. For the best overall view of the monastery, make your way to the ruined hilltop **castle**, about five minutes' walk away.

Practicalities

Though Alcobaça itself is not a hive of activity, it's not a bad place to stay. A useful first stop is the **turismo** (daily: summer 10am–7pm; winter 10am–1pm & 3–6pm; ☎262 582 377) on the central Praça 25 de Abril, opposite the monastery. It can supply maps of the town and advise on accommodation and transport. The **bus station** is five minutes' walk from the centre of town, across the bridge; coming into town, bear right and head towards the abbey towers. There are reasonably frequent connections to Nazaré and Leiria.

Accommodation

Alcobaça has a scattering of inexpensive **pensões and hotels**, just off Praça 25 de Abril. The local **campsite** (☎262 582 265) is some ten minutes' walk north of the bus station, on Av. Manuel da Silva Carolina, near the covered market; there are some trees for shade, but the ground here is hard and barren.

Challet Fonte Nova Palacete, Estrada da Fonte Nova (☎262 598 300). This upmarket option is located in a restored palace built in 1861. ⑤.

Pensão Corações Unidos, Rua Frei António Brandão 39, just off the main square (☎262 582 142). Big but rather dark rooms, some overlooking an internal courtyard. The restaurant below is well thought of. ③.

Residencial Mosteiro, Av. João de Deus 1 (☎ & fax 262 581 836). On the corner of Rua Frei Estevão Martins and just up from the turismo, this has airy rooms, some with bathrooms and pleasant balconies. Price includes breakfast. It also has two restaurants – the one in the basement is a noisy *taberna típica* seating 180, which, nevertheless, fills up at weekends. ②.

Hotel Santa Maria, Rua Dr. Francisco Zagalo (☎262 597 395). A modern hotel facing the monastery and with all mod cons. Rooms at the front have good views. ④.

Eating

In addition to the **restaurants** at the various *pensões*, you could consider eating at the *Celeiro dos Frades* ("monks' barn"), on Arco de Cister under the arches alongside the abbey, where you can dine well for around 2000$00, or just enjoy a coffee in its atmospheric café. *Restaurante O Telheiro*, Rua da Lavadinha (closed Sat), up the road beyond the *Hotel Santa Maria*, is more expensive but has great views over the abbey. Also worth a try is the huge *Frie Bernardo* on Rua D. Pedro V 17–19, which seats 180 and serves the sort of meals you need to fast after, and at moderate prices – albeit geared to tourists.

Leiria

A royal castle hangs almost vertically above the large town of **LEIRIA**, whose graceful old town is a place of cobbled streets, attractive gardens, and fine old squares, once you penetrate its drab modern outskirts. If you are travelling around on public transport, you will probably want to make it your base for a couple of nights, as the three big sites of northern Estremadura – Alcobaça, Batalha and Fátima – all make easy day excursions by bus. Not so easy, but still quite feasible, are day-trips to Porto de Mós and the caves of Mira de Aire, Alvados and Santo António (see p.160); or to São Pedro de Muel and the

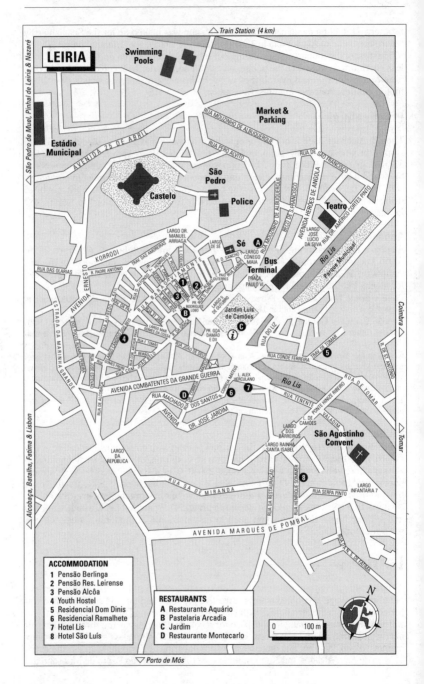

LEIRIA

Train Station (4 km)

Swimming Pools

Market & Parking

Estádio Municipal

São Pedro de Muel, Pinhal de Leiria & Nazaré

AVENIDA 25 DE ABRIL

RUA MOUZINHO DE ALBUQUERQUE

RUA PERO ALVITO

RUA DE SÃO FRANCISCO

Castelo

São Pedro

Police

Teatro

BECO D.S-FRANCISCO

RUA MOUZINHO DE ALBUQUERQUE

AVENIDA HERÓIS DE ANGOLA

RUA DR. AMÉRICO CORTES PINTO

LARGO DR. MANUEL ARRIAGA

LARGO DE SÉ

Sé Ⓐ

LARGO CÓNEGO MAIA

LARGO JOSÉ LÚCIO DA SILVA

KORRODI

RUA DAS OLARIAS

AVENIDA ERNESTO

ESTRADA DA MARINHA GRANDE

R. PADRE ANTÓNIO

RUA

TRAV. DAS AMOREIRAS

R. D. SANCHO I

R.D. DINIS

Bus Terminal

PRAÇA PAULO VI

Rio Lis

Parque Municipal

Coimbra

❶ ❷

❸

Ⓑ

LARGO 5 DE OUTUBRO

Jardim Luís de Camões

Ⓒ

ℹ

RUA DO LIZ

❹

LARGO MAR GOMES DA COSTA

RUA J. TOMÁS

RUA JOÃO DE DEUS

PR. GOA DAMÃO E DII

TRAV. DE TOMAR

❺

RUA CONDE FERREIRA

RUA DE TOMAR

R. DE ST. ANTÓNIO

AVENIDA COMBATENTES DA GRANDE GUERRA

RUA MACHADO DOS SANTOS

CORREIA MATEUS

L. ALEX HERCULANO

Ⓓ ❻ ❼

Rio Lis

RUA TENENTE

PONTE HINTZE RIBEIRO

VALADIM

AVENIDA DR. JOSÉ JARDIM

L. DE CAMÕES

LARGO DOS BARREIROS

LARGO RAINHA SANTA ISABEL

São Agostinho Convent

LARGO DA REPÚBLICA

RUA SÁ DE MIRANDA

RUA DA RESTAURAÇÃO

RUA HENRIQUE SOMMER

❽

RUA SERPA PINTO

LARGO INFANTARIA 7

Alcobaça, Batalha, Fátima & Lisbon

AVENIDA MARQUÉS DE POMBAL

Tomar

N

Porto de Mós

ACCOMMODATION
1 Pensão Berlinga
2 Pensão Res. Leirense
3 Pensão Alcôa
4 Youth Hostel
5 Residencial Dom Dinis
6 Residencial Ramalhete
7 Hotel Lis
8 Hotel São Luís

RESTAURANTS
A Restaurante Aquário
B Pastelaria Arcadia
C Jardim
D Restaurante Montecarlo

0   100 m

coast (see p.156). Leiria also has enough restaurants, bars and nightlife to keep the evenings occupied, with most of the bars being concentrated around the lively Largo Cândido dos Reis.

Leiria's **Castelo** (April–Sept Mon–Fri 9am–6.30pm, Sat & Sun 10am–6.30pm; Oct–March Mon–Fri 9am–5.30pm, Sat & Sun 10am–5.30pm; 135$00) was one of the most important strongholds in Moorish Portugal, reconquered by Afonso Henriques as he fought his way south in 1135. The actual building you see today dates mostly from the fourteenth and eighteenth centuries. Within its walls stands a royal palace, with a magnificent balcony high above the Rio Lis. Leiria was the main residence of Dom Dinis, who gave the town to his beloved Queen Isabel along with Óbidos, Abrantes, Porto de Mós and Trancoso. The walls also contain the **Church of Nossa Senhora da Penha**, erected by João I in about 1400 and now reduced to an eerie, roofless shell. If you have small children with you, beware: there are several precipitous, unguarded points among the buildings and staircases. Nearby, on Largo de Sé, is the town's sixteenth-century **Cathedral**, which was built under the reign of Dom João III and has three naves. It was designed by Afonso Alvares, who worked on the São Roque in Lisbon.

At the heart of the old town is **Praça Rodrigues Lobo**, surrounded by beautiful arcaded buildings and dominated by a splendidly pompous statue of the eponymous seventeenth-century local poet. In fact, Leiria's literary connections go back much further than this – in 1480, the town had one of Portugal's first printing presses, which was run by Jews who printed in Hebrew.

Practicalities

Arriving by **bus**, you'll be dropped at a modern terminal at the near end of Avenida Heróis de Angola, but with another entrance on Praça Paulo VI. Across the Jardim Luís de Camões, on Praça Goa Damão e Dio, is the very helpful **turismo** (summer: daily 10am–1pm & 3–7pm; winter daily 2–6pm; ☎244 814 748), which dispenses maps. The **train station** is 4km north of town – a cheap taxi ride away.

Accommodation

For **accommodation**, make your way to Praça Rodrigues Lobo and look around the restaurants and *pensões* both here and on the narrow side streets: try Rua Mestre de Aviz and Rua Miguel Bombarda. Other cheap rooms are to be found in Largo Paio Guterres and Largo Cónego Maia, both near the cathedral. There's also a very well-appointed **youth hostel** – one of the most enjoyable in the country – at Largo Cândido dos Reis 9 (☎244 831 868).

Pensão Alcôa, Rua Rodrigues Cordeiro 24–26 (☎244 326 90). Smallish but good-value rooms with TVs. Price includes breakfast. There's a good restaurant, too. ③.

Pensão Berlinga, Rua Miguel Bombarda 3 (☎244 823 846). Just off Praça Rodrigues Lobo; look for the sign in the corner of the square. A big, rambling, friendly place. ③.

Residencial Dom Dinis, Trav. de Tomar 2 (☎244 815 342). Across the bridge from the turismo and up a steep side road. A modern, popular place with a pleasant roof-terrace and parking. ④.

Pensão Residencial Leirense, Rua Afonso de Albuquerque 6 (☎244 823 054, fax 244 823 073). A firm favourite for some years that offers good value for money. It's very central and breakfast is included. ③.

Hotel Lis, Largo Alexandre Herculano 10–13 (☎244 814 017). Fairly central, near the bridge by the turismo. Good value, with breakfast included. ③.

Residencial Ramalhete, Rua Dr. Correia Mateus 30 (☎244 812 802). An efficiently run place; the rooms at the rear are quieter. ④.

Hotel São Luís, Rua Henrique Sommer (☎244 813 197). Good value and a good location, albeit out of the centre. Breakfast included. ④.

Eating and drinking

September is the best time to sample the region's cuisine, when the **Festival of Gastronomy** fills up the Mercado Santana with row upon row of food stalls. The best place for a **drink** and a snack is at one of the **cafés** or **bars** around Largo Cândido dos Reis which also give you the chance to take in Leiria's lively streetlife – try *Bar Estrebaria* at no. 23, or *Bar Santo Estevão* at Trav. da Paz 9. Alternatively, the *Galeria Bar*, Quinta de Santo António 43, is worth a visit. **Eating** options include:

Restaurante Aquário, Rua Mouzinho de Albuquerque 17, on a side street running off Jardim Luís de Camões. There's a good *ementa turística* here for around 2000$00 but you could eat for less, especially if you sit at the bar. Closed Thurs.

Pastelaria Arcadia, Praça Rodrigues Lobo. Under the arches in the main square and a good place to enjoy breakfast or a tea stop at the outdoor tables.

Jardim, Jardim Luís de Camões. Nice position overlooking the river and the park, serving inexpensive seafood and other specialities; popular with students. Closed Mon.

Restaurante Montecarlo, Rua Dr. Correia Mateus 32–34. The best on this street – you can eat for under 1000$00 if you have a *meia dose*, which should be sufficient.

Tromba Rija, Rua Professores Portelas 22 (☎244 855 072). Real Portuguese cuisine – expensive, but worth every penny – can be found out of town on the Marrazes road; go west under the N1 and take a left turning after the *Casa da Palmeira*. Closed Sun, Mon lunch & Aug.

The Pinhal de Leiria and its beaches

Some of the most idyllic spots on the stretch of coast west of Leiria are in the **Pinhal de Leiria** (or Pinhal do Rei), a vast 700-year-old pine forest stretching from São Pedro de Muel to Pedrógão. Although there were always trees here, the "Royal Pine Forest" was planned by Dom Dinis, a king renowned for his agrarian reforms, to protect fertile arable land from the menacing inward march of sand dunes. It has since grown into an area of great natural beauty, with sunlight filtering through endless miles of trees and the air perfumed with the scent of resin. The turismo at Marinha Grande, halfway between Leiria and the coast, can supply maps of the forest if you want to make your way through its grid-like tracks on foot.

The **beaches**, for the most part, are superb, and currently the sea is free of pollution from Paredes da Vitória, 12km south of São Pedro de Muel, to Leirosa, 11km south of Figueira da Foz.

São Pedro de Muel

The nearest beach to Leiria is at **SÃO PEDRO DE MUEL**, 22km to the west, where development has remained low-key. Many buildings have been renovated or built in the old style with attractive wooden balconies, making it a pleasant place to stay, though the town gets very busy in high season. If the sea is too fierce to swim in you can try one of the swimming pools situated surreally above the beach.

Buses from Leiria involve a change at Marinha Grande, about halfway. There are regular buses in summer, but the service is less frequent outside of the holiday season. If you wish to stay, **accommodation** – even in high season – should be no problem, since there are more than a dozen *pensões* and hotels. The seasonal **turismo** (☎244 599 152), at the top of the village by the post office, should be able to help. Otherwise, try *Residencial Perola do Oceano* (☎244 599 157; ③) in Trav. Antigos Armazens, which is virtually on the seafront; it has a large annexe up the hill, too. Next door, *A Fonte* restaurant (☎244 599 479; ③) also has good-value rooms. There are two **campsites**, north of the village. The nearer is the *Orbitur* site (☎244 599 168), which can get packed; further out but less expensive is the *Inatel* (☎244 599 289; closed mid-Dec to mid-Jan).

Excellent **restaurants** abound, among them the *Brisamar*, Rua Dr. Nicolau Bettencourt, and *A Fonte*, on Praçeta Afonso Lopes Vieira, both of which specialize in seafood, and the upmarket *A Concha*, Rua Duquesa de Caminha 16 (closed Thurs). However, for sunsets and sea views *Estrela do Mar* (closed Thurs in winter) is hard to beat, situated right above the town beach. For breakfast, try *Café Central* on Rua Dr. Alfonso Leitão, where you can relax on wicker chairs outside.

South of São Pedro, too, you can find sheltered stretches of beach – especially around **PAREDES DA VITÓRIA**, 6km to the south and popular with the Portuguese for camping wild – though here you're no longer in the forest. Another quiet spot is **AGUA DE MADEIROS**, 3km south, where the smart *Residencial Água de Madeiros* sits above the wild, often deserted beach (☎ 244 599 324; ⑤).

Praia Velha, Praia da Vieira and Pedrógoã

A couple of kilometres north of the lighthouse at São Pedro, **PRAIA VELHA** is a popular local beach – mainly because of the chance to swim in the small lake behind the beach – though it can get littered in summer. There's no accommodation here but the lone restaurant, *O Pai dos Frangos*, has won awards – try its amazing mixed kebabs.

Ten kilometres to the north of Velha, **PRAIA DA VIEIRA** and the main town of **VIEIRA DE LEIRIA** (the latter 3km inland) are on the estuary of the Rio Liz and are notable for their fish restaurants. Praia da Vieira is served by a patchy bus service from Marinha Grande and has grown into quite an unattractive modern resort, though it does have a great beach. Of the several *residenciais*, try first the *Ouro Verde* (☎244 695 931; ④) or the *Estrela do Mar* (☎244 695 762; ③). Alternatively, the seasonal **turismo** (☎244 695 230) can recommend places to stay. Among the resort's several **restaurants** is the excellent *Solemar*, on Rua José Botas (☎244 695 404). There's also a municipal **campsite** (June – mid-Sept; ☎244 695 354).

PEDRÓGOÃ, 6km further to the north, also has a rash of modern development spread around another fantastic expanse of beach, which is still used by fishermen to launch their high-prowed boats. There's a great **campsite** (☎244 695 403; closed mid-Dec to Jan) in the woods, while in town, there are several restaurants and a seasonal **turismo** (July & Aug Tues–Sun 10am–1pm & 3–7pm; ☎244 695 411), which can give information about private **rooms**.

Batalha and around

Eleven kilometres south of Leiria, the Mosteiro de Santa Maria da Vitória, better known as **BATALHA** (Battle Abbey), is the supreme achievement of Portuguese architecture – the dazzling richness and originality of its Manueline decoration rivalled only by the Mosteiro dos Jerónimos at Belém, with which it shares UNESCO world monument status. An exuberant symbol of national pride, it was built to commemorate the battle that sealed Portugal's independence after decades of Spanish intrigue.

With the death of Dom Fernando in 1383, the royal house of Burgundy died out, and in its wake there followed a period of feverish factional plotting over the Portuguese throne. Fernando's widow, Leonor Teles, had a Spanish lover even during her husband's lifetime, and when Fernando died she betrothed her daughter, Beatriz, to Juan I of Castile, encouraging his claim to the Portuguese throne. João, Mestre de Aviz, Fernando's illegitimate stepbrother, also claimed the throne. He assassinated Leonor's lover and braced himself for the inevitable invasion from Spain. The two armies clashed on August 14, 1385, at the **Battle of Aljubarrota**, which despite its name was actually fought at São Jorge, 10km northeast of Aljubarrota and just 4km south of present-day Batalha (see p.160). Faced with seemingly impossible odds, João struck a deal with the

Virgin Mary, promising to build a magnificent abbey in return for her military assistance. It worked: Nuno Álvares Pereira led the Portuguese forces to a memorable victory and the new king duly summoned the finest architects of the day.

Today, however, the abbey is rattled by the N1 highway from Lisbon to Coimbra which runs across an embankment perilously close to the abbey and is gradually altering the structure as vibrations and fumes take their toll. There is talk of "moving" the road, though no plans have yet been forthcoming. Furthermore, the abbey is showing its age: built largely of limestone, it's being increasingly affected by acid rain.

The Abbey

The honey-coloured **Abbey** (daily: April–Sept 9am–6pm; Oct–March 9am–5pm; main church free, cloisters 400$00; both free on Sunday morning) was transformed by the uniquely Portuguese Manueline additions of the late fifteenth and early sixteenth centuries, but the bulk of the building was completed between 1388 and 1434 in a profusely ornate version of French Gothic. Pinnacles, parapets, windows and flying buttresses are all lavishly and intricately sculpted. Within this flamboyant framework there are also strong elements of the English Perpendicular style. Huge pilasters and prominent vertical decorations divide the main facade; the nave, with its narrow soaring dimensions, and the chapter house, are reminiscent of church architecture in the English cathedral cities of Winchester and York.

The Capela do Fundador

Medieval architects were frequently attracted by lucrative foreign commissions, but there is a special explanation for the English influence at Batalha. This is revealed in the **Capela do Fundador** (Founder's Chapel), directly to the right upon entering the church. Beneath the octagonal lantern rests the joint tomb of Dom João I and Philippa of Lancaster, their hands clasped in the ultimate expression of harmonious relations between Portugal and England.

In 1373, Dom Fernando had entered into an alliance with John of Gaunt, Duke of Lancaster, who claimed the Spanish throne by virtue of his marriage to a daughter of Pedro the Cruel, king of Castile. A crack contingent of English longbowmen had played a significant role in the victory at Aljubarrota, and in 1386 both countries willingly signed the **Treaty of Windsor**, "an inviolable, eternal, solid, perpetual, and true league of friendship". As part of the same political package Dom João married Philippa, John of Gaunt's daughter, and with her came English architects to assist at Batalha. The alliance between the two countries, reconfirmed by the marriage of Charles II to Catherine of Bragança in 1661 and the Methuen Commercial Treaty of 1703, has become the longest-standing international friendship of modern times – it was invoked by the Allies in World War II to establish bases on the Azores, and the facilities of those islands were offered to the British Navy during the 1982 Falklands war.

The four younger sons of João and Philippa are buried along the south wall of the Capela do Fundador in a row of recessed arches. Second from the right is the **tomb of Prince Henry the Navigator**, who guided the discovery of Madeira, the Azores and the African coast as far as Sierra Leone. Henry himself never ventured further than Tangiers but it was a measure of his personal importance, drive and expertise that the growth of the empire was temporarily shelved after his death in 1460.

Concerted maritime exploration resumed under João II (1481–95) and accelerated with the accession of Manuel I (1495–1521). Vasco da Gama opened up the trade route to India in 1498, Cabral reached Brazil two years later and Newfoundland was discovered in 1501. The momentous era of burgeoning self-confidence, wealth and widening horizons is reflected in the peculiarly Portuguese style of architecture known (after the king) as Manueline. As befitted the great national shrine, Batalha was adapted to incorporate two masterpieces of the new order: the Royal Cloister and the so-called Unfinished Chapels.

The Claustro Real and Sala do Capítulo

In the **Claustro Real** (Royal Cloister), stone grilles of ineffable beauty and intricacy were added to the original Gothic windows by Diogo de Boitaca, architect of the cloister at Belém and the prime genius of Manueline art. Crosses of the Order of Christ and armillary spheres – symbols of overseas exploration – are entwined in a network of lotus blossom, briar branches and exotic vegetation.

Off the east side opens the early fifteenth-century **Sala do Capítulo** (Chapter House), remarkable for the audacious unsupported span of its ceiling – so daring, in fact, that the Church authorities were convinced that the whole chamber would come crashing down and employed criminals already condemned to death to build it. The architect, Afonso Domingues, could finally silence his critics only by sleeping in the chamber night after night. Soldiers now stand guard here over Portugal's **Tomb of the Unknown Warriors**, one killed in France during World War I, the other in the country's colonial wars in Africa. The **refectory**, on the opposite side of the cloister, houses a military museum in their honour. From here, a short passage leads into the **Claustro de Dom Afonso V**, built in a conventional Gothic style which provides a yardstick against which to measure the Manueline flamboyance of the Royal Cloister.

The Capelas Imperfeitas

The Capelas Imperfeitas (Unfinished Chapels) form a separate structure tacked on to the east end of the church and accessible only from outside the main complex. Dom Duarte, eldest son of João and Philippa, commissioned them in 1437 as a royal mausoleum but, as with the cloister, the original design was transformed beyond all recognition by Dom Manuel's architects. The portal rises to a towering fifteen metres and every centimetre is carved with a honeycomb of mouldings: florid projections, clover-shaped arches, strange vegetables; there are even stone snails. The place is unique among Christian architecture and evocative of the great shrines of Islam and Hinduism: perhaps it was inspired by the tales of Indian monuments that filtered back along the eastern trade routes. Although conveniently referred to as Manueline, it is really in a class by itself and illustrates the variety and uninhibited excitement of Portuguese art during the Age of Discovery.

The architect of this masterpiece was Mateus Fernandes, whose tomb lies directly outside the entrance to the Capela do Fundador. Within the portal, a large octagonal space is surrounded by seven hexagonal chapels, two of which contain the sepulchres of Dom Duarte and his queen, Leonor of Aragon. An ambitious upper storey – equal in magnificence to the portal – was designed by Diogo de Boitaca, but the huge buttresses were subsequently abandoned after a few years.

Practicalities

The Batalha stands alone, the huddle of cottages that once surrounded it swept away and replaced by a bare concrete expanse. There's a **turismo** (summer: daily 10am–1pm & 3–7pm; winter daily 2–6pm; ☎244 765 180), but not much else here except a sprinkling of tourist shops, bars and restaurants, which all do brisk business during the Fátima weekend in early October, when the place is packed. **Buses** stop on the central Largo 14 de Agosto de 1385.

Accommodation is limited and the best idea is to see Batalha on a day-trip from Leiria. If you do want to stay, try: *Casa do Outeiro*, Largo Carvalho 4 (☎244 765 806; ④), near the town hall, a charmingly converted small house with a swimming pool; *Residencial*

Batalha on Largo da Misericórdia (☎244 767 500; ④), a modern, comfortable option, or the cheaper *Residencial Gladius*, Praça Mouzinho de Albuquerque (☎244 765 760; ③). For leisured luxury, the *Pousada do Mestre Afonso Domingues*, Largo Mestre Afonso Domingues (☎244 766 168, fax 244 765 247; ⑥), is impossible to better. For good-value Portuguese **food**, try the restaurant in the *AutoSnack Bar* beside the petrol station, about 200m from the Abbey.

Around Batalha

The busy N1 highway carries heavy traffic from Batalha to the small town of **São Jorge**, 4km to the south and site of one of Portugal's most important battles. Just beyond here the quieter N243 branches off to **Porto de Mós**, with its distinctive castle and the added attraction of being the nearest base from which to visit the fabulous **underground caves** at Mira de Aire – which lie within the wild and craggy **Parque Natural das Serras de Aire e Candeeiros**, a good spot to do some **walking**. The N362 provides an alternative scenic route through the park, running from Porto de Mós in the north all the way to Santarém, though the caves themselves are located in the more wooded eastern half of the park.

São Jorge: the battle site
The Battle of Aljubarrota was fought on a plain 10km northeast of Aljubarrota itself, at the small hamlet of **SÃO JORGE**, just 4km south of Batalha. When the fighting was over a **chapel** was built and it still stands today. The battle lasted only one hour, but it was a hot day and the commander of the victorious Portuguese forces, Nuno Álvares Pereira, complained loudly of thirst; even today, a jug of fresh water is placed daily in the porch of the chapel in his memory. Legend has it that Aljubarrota itself was defended by its baker, Brites de Almeida, who fended off the Castilian army with her baking spoon. This fearsome weapon dispensed with seven soldiers, whom Brites then proceeded to bake in her oven.

Also in São Jorge, the **Museu Militar** (Tues–Fri 2–5pm, Sat & Sun 10am–noon & 2–5pm) deals with the battle itself and the contemporary political intrigue, while nearby there's a frieze commemorating the battle with carved blocks of stone representing, it is said, the archers and foot soldiers.

None of this is particularly any reason to come, though you can always break your journey here on the way to or from Porto de Mós (see below), 5km to the south; indeed, you may have to change buses in São Jorge anyway.

Porto de Mós
High above the expanding and uninspiring village of **PORTO DE MÓS**, 8km south of Batalha, a grandiose thirteenth-century **castle** stands guard. It was given to Nuno Álvares Pereira in 1385 by the grateful Dom João I in recognition of his victory at Aljubarrota – significantly, the Portuguese army had rested here on the eve of the battle – and was later turned into a fortified palace reminiscent in scale of that at Leiria. Severely damaged in the earthquake of 1755, the castle (Tues–Sun 8am–5pm; free) has been renovated piecemeal since then; four of its original five electric-green conical towers have been restored so far. Just below the castle is the town's small **archeology and geology museum** (Tues–Sun 10am–12.30pm & 2–5.30pm; free), which boasts locally collected dinosaur bones amongst its displays.

The town's bus terminal is on Avenida Dr. Francisco Sá Carneiro. On weekdays, there are around three **buses to Porto de Mós** from Leiria, via Batalha, and others from Alcobaça, Santarém and Nazaré (summer only), or from Batalha itself. At other times, you could catch one of the long-distance buses from Leiria or Batalha to Alcobaça or Caldas da Rainha and ask to be set down at São Jorge, just off the main N1, and take a local bus from there to Porto de Mós. The **turismo** (summer daily 10am–1pm & 3–7pm; winter Mon–Sat 10am–1pm & 3–6pm; ☎244 491 323) is in the Jardim Público, adjacent to the main Largo do Rossio. If you plan to stay, there are two **overnight** possibilities: the *Residencial O Filipe*, Largo do Rossio 41 (☎244 401 455; ③); and the *Quinta do Rio Alcaide* (☎244 402 124; ④), a converted mill around 1km out of the village on the road to the caves (the N243). Cafés and **restaurants** are grouped around the bus terminal.

The caves

The largest, most spectacular and most accessible caves in Portugal are the **GRUTAS DE MIRA DE AIRE** (daily: Oct–May 9.30am–5.30pm; June & Sept 9.30am–7pm; July & August 9.30am–8.30pm; 600$00; ☎244 440 322), ten minutes' walk from the bus stop in the drab textile town from which they take their name. There are three daily **buses** to Mira de Aire from Porto de Mós, at 12.05pm, 2.30pm and 5.20pm. The only return bus leaves from Mira de Aire town at 4.15pm. On weekends, there are buses at 12.05pm and 5.20pm, but no return service: a return trip by **taxi** from Porto de Mós should cost around 2500$00, including a two-hour wait while you visit the caves. Known locally for years but only open to the public since 1974, the caves comprise a fantasy land of spaghetti-like stalactites and stalagmites and bizarre rock formations with names like "Hell's Door", "Jelly Fish" and "Church Organ". Rough steps take you down and the excellent 45-minute guided tour (in

---

A WALK IN THE SERRAS DE AIRE E CANDEEIROS NATIONAL PARK

The **Serras de Aire e Candeeiros** is a small but scenic national park to the south of Porto de Mós, which contains a mix of rugged limestone hills, crags and upland farmland divided by ancient stone walls. This ten-kilometre circular trail – known as the **Algar do Pena** – is well-marked with yellow equal signs and begins at Vale da Trave on the southern boundary of the national park. To get there take the bus from Porto de Mós to Mira de Aire and ask the driver to let you off at the junction for Barreiras and Vale da Trave. A three-kilometre-walk from the junction brings you to Vale da Trave. You should bring along lots of water and a picnic, as no supplies are available along the route.

To begin the walk, take the gravel track that leads from a stone cross in the middle of Vale da Trave, ignoring signs for the Grutas da Pena and keep on the lane to the right. After half a kilometre, the trail forks; at a signpost for the Algar do Pena circuit keep right, following the route through cork and olive groves until you reach an olive tree to the right of the lane, marked with a red equal sign. Turn right here, and 20m down the path a second marked olive tree signals the point where the route threads down along a little-used track between two more prominent lanes. Although overgrown in parts, the trail is well-marked and easy to follow to the outskirts of the village of **Cortiçal**, 2km on from Vale da Trave. From here, it swings sharply uphill and to the left, passing a quarry and winding through a series of traditionally built farm buildings hewn from local limestone. Once on top of the barren plateau, **views** open out to the south. For the next 3km, the trail passes several quarries and an old well, eventually going over the brow of a hill and arriving at the **Grutas da Pena** – large caves, similar to the Grutas de Mira de Aire, but not open to casual visitors.

The broad track back from the caves to Vale da Trave leaves from behind the information centre, following a shallow valley downhill. Several less prominent paths strike off from the route, but you should ignore these and stick to the marked track. After a couple of kilometres, a marked post signals a smaller track off to the left, which leads 50m to a huge iron grate covering the entrance to a large **cavern** – Algar da Aderneira. Several of the bat species found in the park live inside, and a twilight visit may be rewarded with the sight of **bats** emerging for a night's hunting. From here, keeping to the same little track, it's only another kilometre to Vale da Trave, where you can purchase a cool drink at either of the village's two bars, one of which doubles as a barber.

French or Portuguese, or even English on occasion) culminates in an extravagant fountain display in a natural lake 110m underground. You might have to wait some time for a group of acceptable size to gather. At the end of the tour, you emerge beside an aquatic park (summer only; use of its pools and slides is included in the entry fee for the caves), a great place to cool off and admire the views.

Fátima and around

FÁTIMA is the fountainhead of religious devotion in Portugal and one of the most important centres of pilgrimage in the Roman Catholic world. Its cult is founded on a series of six **Apparitions of the Virgin Mary**, in the first of which, on May 13, 1917, three peasant children from the village were confronted, while tending their parents' flock, with a flash of lightning and "a lady brighter than the sun" sitting in the branches of a tree. According to the memoirs of Lúcia, who was the only one who could hear what was said – and the only one of the children to survive into her teens – the Lady announced, "I am from Heaven. I have come to ask you to return here six times, at this same hour, on the thirteenth of every month. Then, in October, I will tell you who I am and what I want."

News of the miracle was greeted with scepticism, and only a few casual onlookers attended the second appearance, but for the third, July 13, apparition, the crowd had swollen to a few thousand. Although only the three children could see the heavenly visitor, Fátima became a *cause célèbre*, with the anticlerical government accusing the Church of fabricating a miracle to revive its flagging influence, and Church authorities afraid to acknowledge what they feared was a hoax. The children were arrested and interrogated but refused to change their story.

By the date of the final appearance, October 13, as many as 70,000 people had converged on Fátima where they witnessed the so-called **Miracle of the Sun**. Eyewitnesses described the skies clearing and the sun, intensified to a blinding, swirling ball of fire, shooting beams of multicoloured light to earth. Lifelong illnesses, supposedly, were cured; the blind could see again and the dumb were able to speak. It was enough to convince most of the terrified witnesses. Nevertheless, the three children remained the only ones actually to see the Virgin, and only Lúcia could communicate with her.

To her were revealed the three **Secrets of Fátima**. The first was a message of peace (this was during World War I) and a vision of Hell, with anguished, charred souls plunged into an ocean of fire. The second was more prophetic and controversial: "If you pay heed to my request," the vision declared, "Russia will be converted and there will be peace. If not, Russia will spread her errors through the world, causing wars and persecution against the Church" – all this just a few weeks before the Bolshevik takeover in St Petersburg, though not, perhaps, before it could have been predicted. The **third secret** has never been divulged – it lies in a drawer of the pope's desk in the Vatican, read by successive popes on their accession but supposedly too horrible to be revealed, though the present incumbent has hinted that the day may not be far off when he will announce its contents. In 1984, an Irish priest tried to hijack an Aer Lingus plane in an attempt to persuade the Pope to reveal the secret, but the crisis was defused with no one any the wiser.

The Basilica and the Town

To commemorate the extraordinary events and to accommodate the hordes of pilgrims who flock here, a shrine has been built, which has little to recommend it but its size. The vast white **Basilica**, completed in 1953, and its gigantic esplanade are capable of holding more than a million devotees. In the church the **tombs of Jacinta and Francisco** – Lúcia's fellow witnesses, both of whom died in the European flu epidemic of 1919–20 – are the subject of constant attention in their chapels. Long Neoclassical colonnades flank the basilica and enclose part of the sloping esplanade in front. This huge area, reminiscent of an airport runway, is twice the size of the piazza of Saint Peter's in Rome. On its left-hand side the original oak tree in which the Virgin appeared was long ago consumed by souvenir-hunting pilgrims; the small **Chapel of the Apparitions** now stands in its place, with a new tree a few yards away.

Whatever your feelings about the place, there is an undeniable atmosphere of mystery around it, perhaps created by nothing more than the obvious faith of the vast majority of its visitors. It's all at its most intense during the great **annual pilgrimages** on May 12–13 and October 12–13. Crowds of up to 100,000 congregate, most arriving on foot, some even walking on their knees in penance. Open-air Mass is celebrated at 5am and an image of the Virgin is paraded by candlelight as priests move among the pilgrims hearing confessions. The fiftieth anniversary of the apparitions attracted one-and-a-half million worshippers, including Pope Paul VI and Lúcia – who is still alive, a Carmelite nun in the Convent of Santa Teresa near Coimbra. Lúcia was again part of the vast crowds that greeted John Paul II here in 1982 and 1991.

A multitude of hotels, car parks, hospices and convents have sprung up in the shadow of the basilica. Inevitably the fame of Fátima has resulted in its commercialization and some of the town's last surviving old houses and mansions are under threat of demolition to make way for further developments. (The latest plan is to build a covered area to shelter up to ten thousand people during open-air Mass.) As each year goes by, the grotesquely kitsch souvenirs on sale move into hitherto unexplored territories of tastelessness – look out for the Fátima ballpoint pens, which tilt to reveal the Virgin in Glory. Business is particularly brisk on Sunday, when thousands of local families converge by bus, car, lorry and cart, often just for a family picnic – yet the shrine itself is not yet swamped. Make sure you catch the daily torchlit procession at dusk, which can be uplifting whatever your religious feelings; the procession is largest on the twelfth day of each month.

The town's other attractions include the **Museu de Cera** (Wax Museum) on Rua Jacinta Marto (daily: April–Oct 9.30am–6.30pm; Nov–March 10am–5pm; 700$00), which relates the story of the miracle in 28 scenes filled with somewhat grotesque wax figures. There is also a pleasant walk from the Rotunda de Santa Teresa de Ourém, on the outskirts of town, up to the place of the **"Apparitions of the Angel"**, along which pilgrims follow the Stations of the Cross.

Practicalities

There are regular **bus services** to Fátima from Leiria (25km to the northwest) and Tomar (35km east) making it an easy day-trip. Coming **from Batalha** (20km west) on the N356, you'll pass Reguengo do Fétal, another pilgrimage site that's host to a torchlit procession (lit by burning oil carried in shells) up to a hilltop sanctuary around October 3. If you arrive **by train**, you'll need to get a local bus (there's not always an immediate connection) from Estação de Fátima, a hefty 25km east of town; the station is on the main Lisbon–Porto line. The **turismo** (daily: May–Oct 10am–1pm & 3–7pm; closes at 6pm in winter; ☎249 531 139) is just off the main esplanade and through-road, the Avenida D. José Alves Correia da Silva.

The basilica and it's huge esplanade cut the town in half; on the west side of the basilica is Rua Jacinta Marto, while to the east, the main street becomes Rua Francisco Marto. *Pensões* and restaurants abound in Fátima, but during the pilgrimages (when most accommodation is booked up months in advance), people camp all around the back and sides of the basilica. However, outside the major pilgrimages – and weekends – there's enough **accommodation** to go round, since many of the older boarding houses are built on monastic lines, with over a hundred rooms and private chapels; the huge modern hotels which abound can be bargains in low season. Otherwise, try

Residencial Santo Amaro, Rua Francisco Marto 59 (☎249 532 527; ②), with modern, comfortable rooms but away from the main area of restaurants and bars; *Residencial São Paulo,* Rua de São Paulo 10 (☎249 531 572; ②), another modern giant, but friendly and welcoming; or, best of all, *Irmãs Dominicanos,* Rua Francisco Marto 50 (☎249 533 317; ④), one of the few remaining attractive old buildings.

One of the best **restaurants** is *Santa Cruz,* on the corner of Rua Jacinta Marto and Rua de São José, with a pleasant outlook and reasonably priced dishes. Other possibilities are *O Zé Grande,* Rua Jacinta Marto 32, or *Restaurante O Truão* (☎249 521 542), 4km out of Fátima at Boleiros but worth the trip.

Grutas da Moeda

Six kilometres west of Fátima, the labyrinthine **Grutas da Moeda** (daily: April–Sept 9am–6pm; Oct–March 9am–5pm; 600$00; ☎244 704 302) at **SÃO MAMEDE** are well worth seeing, not least because one of the chambers has been converted into a bar with rock music, subtle lighting and stalactites nose-diving into your glass of beer. With haggling, you should be able to arrange a reasonably priced taxi, though you may have to wait for a group to form before you can enter the caves.

Ourém

If you have your own transport, you may prefer to visit Fátima from a base at **OURÉM**, 12km east, staying at *Pensão Ouriense,* Avd. D. Nuno Álvares Pereira (☎249 542 202; ②); plans are afoot to build a *pousada.* Although the new town, Vila Nova de Ourém, is nothing special, Ourém **castle**(no set hours; free) is just 2km above it, sitting on a hilltop within an impressive medieval walled town. The town's heyday was in the fifteenth century, when the fourth count of Ourém, Don Afonso, built several grand monuments and converted the castle into a palace. The castle was virtually destroyed by Napoleon's forces, but is now largely restored; walk around its parapet, and you'll get stunning views, with the basilica in Fátima to the west. The well-signed history trail round the old town will lead you to the **cisterns** (daily 3–6pm), which, according to local legend, have never run dry. Look out also for the fifteenth-century **fountain** by the town gates. The **turismo**, to your right as you enter the old town (Tues–Sun: May–Sept 10am–1pm & 3–7pm; Oct–April 2–6pm; ☎249 544 654), can provide maps and also arrange guides for visits to the small archeological museum (☎249 540 900; free).

Tomar

The Convento de Cristo at **TOMAR**, 34km east of Fátima, is an artistic *tour de force* which entwines the most outstanding military, religious and imperial strands in the history of Portugal. The Order of the Knights Templar and their successors, the Order of Christ, established their headquarters here and successive Grand Masters employed experts in Romanesque, Manueline and Renaissance architecture to embellish and expand the convent in a manner worthy of their power, prestige and wealth.

In addition, Tomar is an attractive town in its own right, well worth a couple of days of slow exploration. Built on a simple grid plan, it is split in two by the Rio Nabão, with almost everything of interest on the west bank. Here, Tomar's old quarters preserve much of their traditional charm, with whitewashed, terraced cottages lining narrow cobbled streets. This pleasing backdrop is seen to best effect during Tomar's famous **Festa dos Tabuleiros**, held at intermittent intervals (see box on p.166), when the entire town takes to the streets.

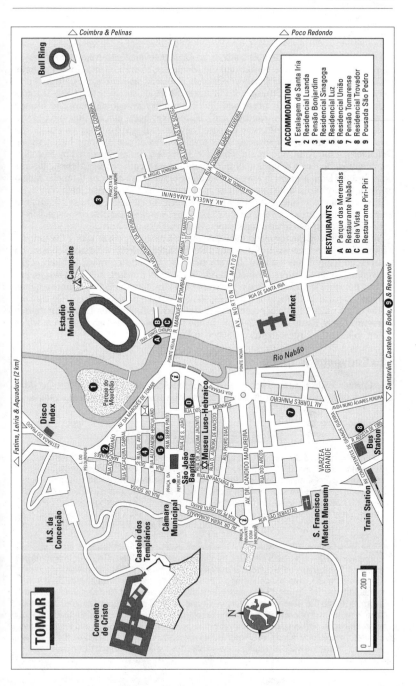

TOMAR

△ *Coimbra & Pelinas* △ *Poco Redondo*

Bull Ring

△ *Fatima, Leiria & Aquaduct (2 km)*

Campsite

Estadio Municipal

Disco Index

Parque do Mouchão

N.S. da Conceição

Castelo dos Templários

Convento de Cristo

Câmara Municipal

São João Baptista

Museu Luso-Hebraico

S. Francisco (Match Museum)

Train Station

Bus Station

Market

Rio Nabão

VARZEA GRANDE

▷ *Santarém, Castelo do Bode,* ❾ *& Reservoir*

200 m

N

ACCOMMODATION
1 Estalagem de Santa Iria
2 Residencial Luanda
3 Pensão Bonjardim
4 Residencial Sinagoga
5 Residencial Luz
6 Residencial União
7 Pensão Tomarense
8 Residencial Trovador
9 Pousada São Pedro

RESTAURANTS
A Parque das Merendas
B Restaurante Nabão
C Bela Vista
D Restaurante Piri-Piri

The Town

On the central Praça da República stands an elegant seventeenth-century town hall, a ring of houses of the same period, and the Manueline church of **São João Baptista**, remarkable for its octagonal belfry, elaborate doorway, and six panels attributed to Gregório Lopes (1490–1550), one of Portugal's finest artists. Nearby at Rua Joaquim Jacinto 73 is an excellently preserved fifteenth-century synagogue, now the **Museu Luso-Hebraico Abraham Zacuto** (daily 10am–7pm; free), named after the Spanish astronomer, Abraham Zacuto, who prepared navigational aids for Vasco da Gama. The museum is particularly interesting in a town dominated for so long by crusading Defenders of the Faith, and its stark interior, with plain vaults supported by four slender columns, houses a collection of thirteenth- to fourteenth-century Hebraic inscriptions. In 1496 Dom Manuel followed the example of the Reis Católicos (Catholic Kings) of Spain and ordered the conversion or expulsion of all Portuguese Jews. The synagogue at Tomar was one of the very few to survive so far south – there's another at Castelo de Vide in the Alentejo (see p.421). Many Jews fled northwards, especially to Trás-os-Montes where Inquisitional supervision was less hawk-eyed.

Midway between the town and the Convento de Cristo, it's worth taking the time for a look around the unassumingly beautiful Renaissance church of **Nossa Senhora da Conceição** (daily 11am–6.45pm). It is attributed to Diogo de Torralva, architect of the Convento's Great Cloisters. Also of interest is the town **market**, held on Fridays, just off Rua de Santa Iria, and the impressive seventeenth-century Pegões **aqueduct**, built to supply the convent with water; the best place to see it – or walk along it – is 2km out on the Leiria road. A touch of eccentricity is provided by the **Aguiles Lima Matchstick Museum** (daily 10am–noon & 2–4pm), inside the Convento de São Francisco, which claims to have the largest match collection in Europe.

The Convento de Cristo

The **Convento de Cristo** (Tues–Sun: June–Sept 9.15am–12.30pm & 2–6pm; Oct–May 2–5pm; 400$00) is set among pleasant gardens with splendid views, about a quarter of

---

THE FESTA DOS TABULEIROS

Tomar is renowned throughout the country for its **Festa dos Tabuleiros** (literally, the Festival of the Trays). Its origins can be traced back to the saintly Queen Isabel who founded the Brotherhood of the Holy Spirit in the fourteenth century, though some believe it to derive from an ancient fertility rite dedicated to Ceres. Whatever its origins, it's now a largely secular event, held at three- or four-yearly intervals. The next one is likely to happen in either 2002 or 2003, but check with the local turismo. It's a five-day affair, at the beginning of July, with the highlight – the parade of "trays" – on the final Sunday.

The **procession** (Procissão dos Tabuleiros) consists of four hundred or so young women wearing white, each escorted by a young man in a white shirt, red tie and black trousers. She carries on her head a tray with thirty loaves threaded on vertical canes, intertwined with leaves and colourful paper flowers, and crowned with a white dove – the symbol of the Holy Spirit. The resulting headdress weighs 15kg, and is roughly person-height – hence the need for an escort to lift and help balance it. As with other festivals, there's music and dancing in the streets, fireworks at dawn and dusk, and a bullfight the night before the procession. The day after the procession, bread, wine and beef are distributed to the local needy, following Isabel's injunction to "give bread to the poor" – needless to say, the bulls providing the beef have their own procession, three days before that of the *tabuleiros*.

an hour's walk uphill from the centre of town. Founded in 1162 by Gualdim Pais, first and grandest Master of the **Knights Templar**, it was the headquarters of the Order, and, as such, both a religious and a military centre.

One of the main objectives of the Templars was to expel the Moors from Spain and Portugal, a reconquest seen always as a crusade against the Dark Forces – the defence of Christianity against the Infidel. Spiritual strength was an integral part of the military effort and, despite magnificent additions, the sacred heart of the whole complex remains the **Charola** (also known as the Rotunda or Templars' Apse), the twelfth-century temple from which the Knights drew their moral conviction. It is a strange place, more suggestive of the occult than of Christianity. At the centre of the sixteen-sided, almost circular, chapel stands the high altar, surrounded by a two-storeyed octagon. Deep alcoves, decorated with sixteenth-century paintings, are cut into the outside walls. The Templars are said to have attended mass on horseback. Like almost every circular church, it is ultimately based on the Church of the Holy Sepulchre in Jerusalem, for whose protection the Knights Templar were originally founded. The Charola has been closed for restoration for some years and is slated to reopen in 2000; until it does, you can see it only from a distance.

Dom Manuel's additions

By 1249 the reconquest in Portugal was completed and the Templars reaped enormous rewards for their services. Tracts of land were turned over to them and they controlled a network of castles throughout the Iberian peninsula. But as the Moorish threat receded, the Knights became a powerful political challenge to the stability and authority of European monarchs.

Philippe-le-Bel, King of France, took the lead by confiscating all Templar property in his country, and there followed a formal papal suppression of the Order in 1314. In Spain this prompted a vicious witch-hunt and many of the Knights sought refuge in Portugal, where Dom Dinis coolly reconstituted them in 1320 under a different title: the **Order of Christ**. They inherited all the Portuguese property of the Templars, including the headquarters at Tomar, but their power was now subject to that of the throne.

In the fifteenth and sixteenth centuries, the Order of Christ played a leading role in extending Portugal's overseas empire and was granted spiritual jurisdiction over all conquests. Prince Henry the Navigator was Grand Master from 1417 to 1460, and the remains of his **Palace** in the Convento de Cristo can be seen immediately to the right upon entering the castle walls. Henry ordered two new cloisters, the **Claustro do Cemitério** and the **Claustro da Lavagem**, both reached via a short corridor from the Charola and attractively lined with *azulejos*.

Dom Manuel succeeded to the Grand Mastership in 1492, three years before he became king. Flush with imperial wealth, he decided to expand the convent by adding a rectangular **nave** to the west side of the Charola. This new structure was divided into two storeys: the lower serving as a chapter house, the upper as a choir. The **main doorway**, which leads directly into the nave, was built by João de Castilho in 1515, two years before Dom Manuel appointed him Master of Works at Belém. Characteristically unconcerned with structural matters, the architect profusely adorned the doorway with appliqué decoration. There are strong similarities in this respect with contemporary Isabelline and Plateresque architecture in Spain.

The crowning highlight of Tomar, though, is the sculptural ornamentation of the windows on the main facade of the **Chapter House**. The richness and self-confidence of Manueline art always suggests the Age of Discovery, but here the connection is crystal clear. A wide range of maritime motifs is jumbled up in two tumultuous window frames, as eternal memorials to the sailors who established the Portuguese Empire. Everything is here: anchors, buoys, sails, coral, seaweed and especially ropes, knotted over and over again into an escapologist's nightmare.

The windows can only be fully appreciated from the roof of the **Claustro de Santa Bárbara**, adjacent to the Great Cloisters, which unfortunately almost completely obscure a similar window on the south wall of the Chapter House.

A new style: João III

João III (1521–57) transformed the convent from the general political headquarters of the Order into a thoroughgoing monastic community, and he endowed it with the necessary conventual buildings: dormitories, kitchens and no fewer than four new cloisters (making a grand total of seven). Yet another, much more classical, style was introduced into the architectural melange of Tomar. So meteoric was the rise and fall of Manueline art within the reign of Dom Manuel that, to some extent, it must have reflected his personal tastes. João III on the other hand had an entirely different view of art..He is known to have sent schools of architects and sculptors to study in Italy, and his reign finally marked the much-delayed advent of the Renaissance in Portugal.

The two-tiered **Great Cloisters**, abutting the Chapter House, are one of the purest examples of this new style. Begun in 1557, they present a textbook illustration of the principals of Renaissance neoclassicism. Greek columns, gentle arches and simple rectangular bays produce a wonderfully restrained rhythm. At the southwest corner a balcony looks out on to the skeletal remains of a second Chapter House, begun by João III but never completed.

Practicalities

The **train** and **bus stations**, on Avenida Combatentes da Grande Guerra, are within easy walking distance of the centre. Head directly north and you'll soon hit Avenida Dr. Cândido Madureira, at the top end of which there's a **turismo** (daily: April–Sept 9.30am–8pm; Oct–March 9.30am–6pm; ☎249 322 427), which can give details of local walks round the Sete Montes National Forest. The turismo faces a fierce statue of Infante Dom Henrique and the gates of a park, which once formed the gardens of the Convento de Cristo. There's also a **regional tourist office** at the bottom of Rua Serpa Pinto (Mon–Fri 9.30am–12.30pm & 2–6pm; ☎249 329 000).

Accommodation

Tomar has a good range of **accommodation** and finding a room should be pretty straightforward. The only time when rooms will be hard to come by is during the Festa dos Tabuleiros (see box on p.166 for details). There's a pleasant municipal **campsite** (☎249 322 608), out towards the football stadium, and an even nicer site 14km out of town at Castelo do Bode (☎249 849 262, fax 249 849 244), served by two buses daily from Tomar. It's set amid pine woods by the reservoir and you can rent out boats to visit the islands in the lake. The pleasant campsite *Campismo Rural* (☎249 301 814), in the small village of Pelinos, 7km out of town on the road to Coimbra, rents out mountain bikes and can arrange canoeing trips; but beware that the sporadic buses here from Tomar can take up to two hours. There is another campsite – even further out – at Poço Redondo, 10km east of Tomar (☎249 376 421).

Pensão Bonjardim, Praçeta de Santo André (☎249 313 195). Basic but adequate, though some way out, across the river. ③.

Residencial Luanda, Av. Marquês de Tomar 15 (☎249 315 153). Modern and comfortable *pensão* facing the river. All the rooms come with bath. ④.

Residencial Luz, Rua Serpa Pinto 144 (☎249 312 317). Simple rooms but can be good value, especially those for four to six people. ③.

Estalagem de Santa Iria, Parque do Mouchão (☎249 313 326). In the park, by the river, Somerset Maugham once stayed here – but then he was rich. Its restaurant, however, is good value. ⑥.

Pousada São Pedro, Castelo do Bode (☎249 381 159, fax 249 381 176). Overlooking the reservoir, 13km from Tomar, this is a great place to unwind if you have the funds. ⑥.

Residencial Sinagoga, Rua Gil Avô 31 (☎249 323 083). Near the town hall, this smart place has air-conditioning and satellite TV in all rooms. ④.

Pensão Tomarense, Av. Torres Pinheiro 13 (☎249 312 948). Not a first choice, but cheap. Rooms are spartan and, at the front, noisy, but there are fine views of the convent from the rear rooms. Breakfast included. ②.

Residencial Trovador, Rua de Agosto de 1385 (☎249 322 567). Light and airy modern *residencial* facing the bus station. ④.

Residencial União, Rua Serpa Pinto 94 (☎249 323 161). Central and very popular; in July and August advance booking is essential. Nice rooms around a courtyard, all with private bath or shower. ④.

Eating, drinking and nightlife

Many of the *pensões* in Tomar have **restaurants** attached. Midday, the busiest **cafés and bars** are on Avenida Dr. Cândido Madureira and around the Varzea Grande; on a summer's evening there's more action on the riverside. The liveliest **dance venue** is *Index* on Estrada do Prado 2.

Bela Vista, Trav. Fonte Choupo 6. Justifiably the town's most renowned restaurant, by the river, with full meals for around 2000$00; try the chicken curry. Closed Mon evening, Tues & Nov.

Restaurante Nabão, Trav. Fonte Choupo 3. Standard Portuguese favourites at moderate prices and with a river view. Closed Wed.

Restaurante Parque das Merendas. Situated by the river, this has a somewhat limited menu, but it's cheap and in a lovely position, with a lively café attached.

Restaurante Piri-Piri, Rua dos Moinhos 54. Large portions of occasionally bland but reasonably priced food; the grilled trout is good. Closed Tues.

East along the Tejo to Abrantes

Eighteen kilometres south of Tomar, the N110 road and the railway both divide at the dull town of Entroncamento. From here, one branch of the railway swings east to follow the Rio Tejo past **Tancos** and the remarkable castle at **Almourol**, meeting the Rio Zêzere at **Constância**, one of the most attractive towns on the Tejo. By road, an alternative route to Constância is via Castelo do Bode, which will also take you across the dam (Barragem do Castelo do Bode). From Constância, the Tejo retains its rural hue for the 12km east to **Abrantes**, a town with a historic centre and the last significant stop on the river, beyond which road and rail routes branch out for Spain or north and south for the rest of the country.

Almourol and Tancos

As if conjured up by some medieval-minded magician, the **castle of Almourol** stands deserted on a tiny island in the middle of the Tejo. Built by the Knights Templar in 1171, it never saw military action – except in sixteenth-century romantic literature – and its double perimeter walls and ten small towers are perfectly preserved. It's military property but there's no objection to visitors, and once inside you'll be granted a beautiful rural panorama from the tall central keep.

The train line hugs the northern banks of the Tejo at this point and there are two convenient stations, Tancos and Almourol, thirty and fifteen minutes' walk respectively from the island. The latter is stuck in the middle of nowhere but **TANCOS** is actually a small village with a couple of bars catering for a nearby army barracks. To reach the castle from Tancos, take a taxi or strike out east along the railway tracks; the river banks are an impassable forest of eucalyptus trees, cacti and assorted bushes. For around 250$00 per person, a ferryman will row you around the island and deposit you on a miniature beach to explore the castle at leisure.

Constância

CONSTÂNCIA, 3km upstream from Almourol, is a useful place to stay the night after a visit to the castle. A sleepy, incredibly picturesque, whitewashed town, arranged like an amphitheatre around the Tejo and the mouth of the Rio Zêzere, it is best known in Portugal for its association with **Luís de Camões**, Portugal's national poet. In fact, Camões was here for only three years (1547–50), taking refuge from the court of Dom João III, whom he had managed to offend by the injudicious dedication of a love sonnet to a woman on whom the king himself had designs. Constância, however, is said to have remained dear to the poet's heart until the end of his life. In more troubled times, the town served the Duke of Wellington in 1809: he amassed his forces here and prepared for the Battle of Talavera in Spain. Nowadays, Constância is at its liveliest during the **Festa dos Barqueiros**, on Easter Monday, with parades and traditional boats on the Tejo.

For Constância, get off the **train** at Praia do Ribatejo-Constância, the stop after Almourol. If you want **to stay**, ask for *dormidas* in the central cafés or try one of the following: the spotless *Residencial Casa João Chagas*, on Rua João Chagas near the main square (☎249 739 403, fax 249 739 458; ③); the fantastic Privetur property, *Casa O Palácio* (☎249 739 224; ④), by the water's edge; or the *Quinta de Santa Bárbara* (☎249 739 214; ⑤), 1km out of town, off the road to Abrantes. There is a **campsite** (☎249 739 546) by the river beach, next to the Horto de Camões gardens, which are based on the gardens described in Camões' epic poem, *Os Lusíadas*. An alternative campsite is in an attractive lakeside setting at Castelo do Bode 9km to the north, up the Rio Zêzere (see p.168).

Abrantes

ABRANTES is perched strategically above the Tejo, 15km upstream of Almourol. The streets and praças here are pretty, especially when the spring and summer flowers on Rua da Barca and in the Jardim da República are in bloom; the views are also impressive. Additionally, the town has useful train connections linking up with the lower Beiras and the Alto Alentejo.

The high point – in all respects – is the town's battered **Castelo** (Mon–Fri 9am–noon & 1–5pm, Sat & Sun 10am–1pm & 2–6pm), constructed in the early fourteenth century. As at Santarém (see p.172), Romans and Moors established strongholds here, and the citadel was again sharply contested during the Peninsular War. The chapel of **Santa Maria do Castelo**, within the fort, houses a motley archeological museum, its prize exhibits being three tombs of the Almeidas, Counts of Abrantes. From the battlements there's a terrific view of the countryside and the rooftops of Abrantes and the gardens around its old town walls. The two large, whitewashed churches visible from here were both rebuilt in the sixteenth century.

Practicalities

The **turismo** (Mon 9am–noon & 2–6pm, Tues–Thurs 9am–6pm, Fri, Sat & Sun 10am–1pm & 2–6pm; ☎241 362 555) is on Esplanada 1 de Maio, next to the **bus station**. Tejo buses stop a kilometre or so down the hill, in a separate depot on the way to the IP6 highway. There are two local **train stations**, both out of town. The main one is 2km south, across the Tejo, and all trains stop there; you could walk into the centre from here, but it's uphill all the way – shared taxis aren't too expensive.

If you want **to stay**, there are three decent *pensões* in the old centre: first choice for atmosphere is the old and very pleasant *Pensão Central*, Praça Raimundo Soares 15 (☎241 362 422; ②); the *Pensão Aliança*, Largo do Chafariz 50 (☎241 362 348; ③), owned by the same proprietor, is slightly less characterful but has better facilities, with showers in some rooms. *Pensão Lírios*, Praça Barao da Batalha 31 (☎241 362 142; ③), is another reliable choice. A kilometre out of town, just off the road to the IP6 highway, is the more modern *Hotel de Turismo* (☎241 361 261; ④), with its own tennis courts and pool. Some 10km from Abrantes, the *Quinta dos Vales* (☎241 897 363; ⑤) sits on the southern bank of the Tejo at Tramagal (a 10min walk from Tramagal train station); horses are available for a hack along the river banks. Abrantes' nearest **campsite** is in Rossio ao Sul do Tejo (☎241 333 550), over the bridge on the south side of the Tejo.

There are a number of reasonable **restaurants** in Abrantes: one of the best in town is the *Pelicano* (☎241 362 317; closed Thurs) on Rua Nossa Senhora de Conceição 1, near the bus station, where a meal still shouldn't cost more than 2500$00. *Fumeiro* at Rua do Pisco 9 (closed Sun) serves good Portuguese staples, while *Nova Grelha*, Rua Montéiro de Lima, is the place for good-quality, chunky, grilled food. The locals' favourite is *Cascata* (☎241 361 011; closed Mon), 3km out of town, at Alferrarede, near the second train station. *Tasquinha Américo e Vera Cruz* (☎241 333 884), at Rossio ao Sul do Tejo, is highly recommended for those with transport, or if you're staying at the campsite.

Ribatejo: along the east bank

Seven kilometres south of Entroncamento, the attractive town of **Golegã** is one of the main crossing points to the east bank of the Rio Tejo – bull-breeding territory, full of rich plains and riverside marshes. This side of the river isn't as accessible by bus or train but, with your own transport, the N118 from here marks the most attractive route along the river, taking in several small historic towns, villages and *quintas* worth passing by en route to Lisbon or the Alentejo coast. Accommodation isn't particularly plentiful, but then you're unlikely to want to stop for any great length of time, except during their energetic annual **festivals**, when what accommodation there is may be fully booked in any case.

Golegã

GOLEGÃ, on the west bank of the Tejo, midway between Tomar and Santarém, is a very pleasant town, best known for its **Feira Nacional do Cavalo** (National Horse Fair), held during the first two weeks in November. The fair incorporates celebrations for St Martin's Day on November 11, when there's a a running of the bulls and a grand parade in which red-waistcoated grooms mingle with gypsies. Culinary diversions include roasted chestnuts and barbecued chickens, accompanied by *água-pé* (literally "foot water") – a light wine made by adding water to the crushed grape husks left after the initial wine production. During the evening, people crowd into the *Restaurante Central*, on Largo da Imaculada Conceição, both to eat and to mingle with haughty *cavaleiros* who have survived the bullfighting.

Golegã also boasts two museums: the **Museu Municipal de Pintura e Escultura Martins Correia** (Tues–Sun: June–Sept 11am–12.30pm & 3–5pm; Oct–May 10am–12.30pm & 3–6pm; free), opposite the Igreja Matriz, which houses an impressive collection of contemporary art and sculpture; and the amazing **Casa-Museu de Fotografia Carlos Relvas**, at the top of Rua José F. Relvas (same hours; free). Carlos Relvas was father of the Republican José Relvas (see below) and, ironically, godfather to King Carlos, who was assassinated by Republicans in 1908. The museum is an archive of Relvas's interest in the newly discovered art of photography and contains some thirteen thousand glass negatives. The house itself is worthy of being a museum piece; it's a fantastic fairy-tale building designed by Henrique Carlos Afonso and set in landscaped gardens. Other attractions in Golegã include the sixteenth-century **Igreja Matriz**, with its Manueline door, and the nearby Reserva Natural Parque do Paúl do Boquilobo, 5km out of Golegã off the road to Azinhaga, where you may be lucky enough to spot some otters.

If you want **to stay** in Golegã, *Restaurante Central* is your best bet, with a few rooms to rent, though they'll almost certainly be occupied during the fair. There's also a lovely **campsite** (☎249 976 222) very close to the Igreja Matriz. Otherwise, if you're continuing south along the west bank, you could stay at the *Casa de Santo António da Azinhaga*, Rua Nova de Santo António (☎249 957 162, fax 249 957 122; ⑤), in the attractive stream-side village of Azinhaga, 12km southwest from Golegã.

Chamusca

Across the Tejo from Golegã and 9km by road, **CHAMUSCA** is the most northerly of the east bank's bullfighting towns. Its **Festa da Ascensão** – six days of bull-running and bull-fighting – is held during the week incorporating Ascension Day (ie, forty days after Easter) and also features a craft fair. Outside these times, the town remains attractive enough for a brief stopover: the 1930s-style **Casa Rural Tradicional** – a country house reconstructed with traditional furnishings – and the municipal swimming pool, both in the park alongside Largo 25 de Abril, are the main attractions.

Alpiarça

ALPIARÇA, on the east bank 18km south of Chamusca (and just 10km east of Santarém), boasts the **Casa Museu dos Patudos** (Mon–Fri 10am–5.30pm, Sat & Sun 10am–1pm & 2–5.30pm; 500$00), on Rua José Relvas south of town, which was originally the home of José Relvas (1858–1929). Musician, art collector, landowner, bullfighter, diplomat and politician, José is best known as the man who proclaimed the Portuguese Republic in Lisbon in 1910. The exterior of the house, designed by Raul Lino, is striking, with a colonnade and outdoor staircases to the first floor. Inside, you'll find priceless collections of Portuguese paintings, porcelain, furniture, tapestries and over forty carpets from Arraiolos, including one embroidered in silk and dating from 1701. The **turismo** in the town hall may be able to help with renting **rooms**; otherwise, there's a **campsite** (☎243 557 040) beyond the museum and off the Almeirim road.

Almeirim and Salvaterra de Magos

Seven kilometres south of Alpiarça lies **ALMEIRIM**, whose golden days were during the reign of the House of Avis (1383–1580), when the royal family – ensconced at Santarém, just 7km to the northwest – hunted from a summer palace on the riverside here. Nothing remains of the palace today but the town does boast an **ethnographical museum** (Mon–Fri 9am–12.30pm & 2–4pm; free) with moderately interesting insights into local traditions. *Restaurante Tonçinho*, on Rua de Timor 2 (closed Thurs) is a good place both for lunch – the brick oven and open kitchen add a certain interest to mealtimes – and to sample the local wines, considered some of the best in the region. If you want to visit the **vineyards**, the eighteenth-century *Quinta da Alorna*, 1km from Almeirim on the Lisbon road, offers tours and tastings on Fridays and Sundays (call ☎243 570 700 for details).

SALVATERRA DE MAGOS, 29km south of Almeirim, retains rather more of its historical relics and has a fine, sandy river beach nearby. A palace built for the Bragança monarchs is long gone, but the palace **chapel** with its outstanding golden altarpiece still survives, as does the **Palácio da Falcoaria** (Falconry Palace), whose 310 niches once housed the royal falcons. In its eighteenth-century heyday, the palace contained a theatre and a bullring, though after the noble Count of Arcos was killed during a bull-fight here, Pombal banned the sport – it was only legally reinstated in 1920.

Santarém

SANTARÉM, capital of the Ribatejo, rears high above the Rio Tejo, commanding a tremendous view over the rich pasturelands to the south and east. It ranks among the most historic cities in Portugal: under Julius Caesar it became an important administrative centre for the Roman province of Lusitania; Moorish Santarém was regarded as impregnable (until

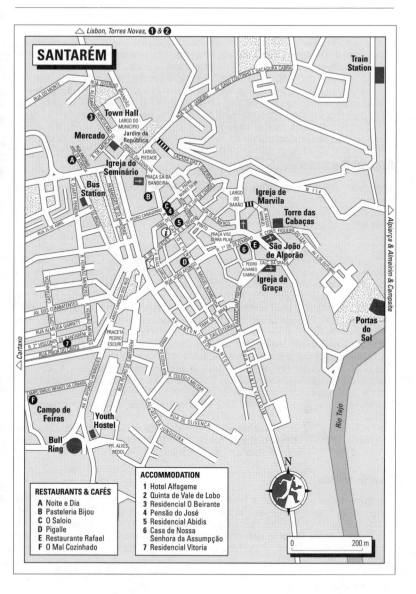

△ Lisbon, Torres Novas, ❶ & ❷

SANTARÉM

Train Station

RUA DO MONTE
RUA ZEFERINO BRANDAO
RUA ALEXANDRE HERCULANO

Town Hall
LARGO DO MUNICIPIO
Jardim da República

❸

Mercado

RUA JOSÉ ANDRADE
R. DE MERCADO
R. CIDADE DA COVILHÃ

AV. GAGO COUTINHO E SACADURA CABRAL
RUA 31 DE JANEIRO

CAÇADA DAS PADEIRAS

Ⓐ

Igreja do Seminário

LARGO PIEDADE

PRAÇA SÁ DA BANDEIRA

Bus Station

RUA DUARTE PEREIRA

Ⓑ

R. PEDRO CANAVARRO

PADRE NUNES SILVA
RUA LUÍS DE CAMÕES

LARGO DO BARÃO

Igreja de Marvila

N 114

Torre das Cabaças

Ⓒ ❹

R. DE S. MARTINHO
RUA SERPA PINTO

R. CONS. FIGUEIRA DO LEAL
R. PASSOS MANUEL

RUA 25 DE ABRIL

❺

PRAÇA VISC SERRA PILAR

ℹ

R. DR. TEIXEIRA GUEDES

R. 1° DE DEZEMBRO

❻ Ⓔ

São João de Alporão

RUA FERNÃO MENDES

RUA CAPITÃO DOS REIS
RUA SERPA PINTO
RUA JOÃO AFONSO

Ⓓ

R. MIGUEL BOMBARDA

CALÇ DA GRAÇA

L. PEDRO ALVARES CABRAL

Igreja da Graça

AV. DOS COMBATENTES

RUA ALMEIDA GARRETT

RUA 7° VISCONDE DE SANTARÉM

RUA PRIOR DO CRATO

PRACETA PEDRO ESCURO

AV. ANTÓNIO DOS SANTOS

TRAV. DE S. BRAZ

R. DAS ESTEIRAS

RUA DOM LUIS

CAMPO EMÍLIO INFANTE DA CAMARA

Ⓕ

Campo de Feiras

Youth Hostel

AV. AFONSO HENRIQUES
AV. PEDRO DE SANTARÉM

CALÇADA DA JUNQUEIRA

R. COVA DA PIA

R. COLÉGIO MILITAR

RUA DE OLIVENÇA

CALÇADA DA JUNQUEIRA

Bull Ring

PR. ALVES REDOL

Portas do Sol

Rio Tejo

△ Alpiarça & Almeirim & Campsite

△ Cartaxo

N

ACCOMMODATION

1 Hotel Alfageme
2 Quinta de Vale de Lobo
3 Residencial O Beirante
4 Pensão do José
5 Residencial Abidis
6 Casa de Nossa Senhora da Assumpção
7 Residencial Vitoria

RESTAURANTS & CAFÉS

A Noite e Dia
B Pasteleria Bijou
C O Saloio
D Pigalle
E Restaurante Rafael
F O Mal Cozinhado

0   200 m

Afonso Henriques captured it by enlisting the aid of foreign Crusaders in 1147); and it was here that the royal *Cortes* (parliament) was convened throughout the fourteenth and fifteenth centuries. All evidence of Roman and Moorish occupation has vanished but, with its two exquisite churches, modern Santarém remains a pleasant place to stay and a visit will also be rewarded by the famous view from the *miradouro* known as the **Portas do Sol**.

If you can, it's worth planning your stay to coincide with one of the many **festivals** held in the town. The thinly populated agricultural plain above which Santarém stands is the home of Portuguese **bullfighting**: here, the very best horses and bulls graze in lush fields under the watchful eyes of *campinos*, mounted guardians dressed in the traditional bright costume. Agricultural traditions, folk dancing (especially the fandango), and bullfighting all come together in the great annual **Feira Nacional da Agricultura**, held at Santarém for ten days starting on the first Friday in June, while dishes from every region in Portugal are sampled at the **Festival de Gastronomia** (10–12 days, ending on Nov 1). For a fixed price you can eat as much as you like during this event. There are also **street markets** on the second and fourth Sunday of every month.

Around the town

At the heart of the old town is **Praça Sá da Bandeira**, overlooked by the many-windowed Baroque facade of the Jesuit **Seminário** (1676), which serves as the town's cathedral. Rua Serpa Pinto or Rua Capelo e Ivens lead from here towards the signposted Portas do Sol, about fifteen minutes' walk, with the best of the churches conveniently en route.

First of these is the Manueline **Igreja de Marvila** (Tues–Fri 9.30am–12.30pm & 2–6pm, Sat & Sun open till 6.30pm) at the end of Rua Serpa Pinto, with its brilliant seventeenth-century *azulejos* and lovely stone pulpit comprising eleven miniature Corinthian columns. From here, Rua J. Araújo, at right angles to the side of the church, descends a few yards to the architectural highlight of Santarém: the early fifteenth-century **Igreja da Graça** (Tues–Sun 9.30am–12.30pm & 2.30–5.30pm). A spectacular rose window dominates the church and overlapping blind arcades above the portal are heavily influenced by the vertical decorations on the main facade at Batalha. Pedro Álvares Cabral, discoverer of Brazil in 1500, is buried within, but his rather austere tomb-slab is overshadowed by the elaborate sarcophagus of Pedro de Menezes, the first Governor of Ceuta, who died in 1437.

Continuing toward the *miradouro*, a third sidetrack is to the twelfth-century church of **São João de Alporão**, now an **archeological museum** (Tues–Sun 9.30am–12.30pm & 2–5.30pm; 200$00). Take a look at the flamboyant Gothic tomb of Duarte de Menezes who met his gruesome fate in 1464 – so comprehensively was he butchered by the Moors in North Africa that only a single tooth was recovered for burial. Avenida 5 de Outubro eventually finishes at the **Portas do Sol** (Gates of the Sun), a large garden occupying the site of the Moorish citadel. Modern battlements look down on a long stretch of the Tejo with its fertile sandbanks and, beyond, a vast swathe of the Ribatejo disappears green and flat into the distance.

Practicalities

The **train station** lies a couple of hundred metres below the town. There are half-hourly buses into the town centre, or you can take a taxi or walk. The **bus station** is more central, on Avenida do Brasil; and Rua Pedro Canavarro, across the gardens opposite, leads into Rua Capelo e Ivens, the main pedestrian street of the old town. Excellent free maps are available from the **turismo** at no. 63 (Mon–Fri 9am–7pm, Sat & Sun 9am–12.30pm & 2.30–5.30pm; ☎243 391 512).

Accommodation

Finding a place to stay can be hard during festival times, when your best bet is to turn up early and see if the turismo can find you a **private room**. There should be little problem at other times of year; try one of the **hotels or pensões** listed below. The cheapest beds are at the **youth hostel** (☎243 333 292 or 391 914) at Av. Afonso Henrique 109, near the bullring and fairground; while the nearest **campsite** is across the river, 9km to the east, at Alpiarça (☎243 557 040; see p.172).

Residencial Abidis, Rua Guilherme de Azevedo 4 (☎243 322 017). A slice of nineteenth-century style with close on thirty rooms, though only six have a bath. Highly recommended and excellent value, with breakfast included. ②.

Hotel Alfageme, Avd. Bernardo Santaremo 38, just off the Torres Novas road (☎243 370 870). Modern hotel whose rooms are all en suite, air-conditioned and double-glazed. Breakfast included. ⑤.

Residencial O Beirante, Rua Alexandre Herculano 5 (☎243 333 845). Moderately priced rooms, all with private bath. ③.

Casa de Nossa Senhora da Assumpção, Rua 1° Dezembro 55 (☎243 325 048). A beautiful old building right in the centre of town, but as it has only two rooms you'll need to book in advance. ④.

Pensão do José, Trav. do Frois 14 (☎243 323 088). A clean, basic *pensão*, on a quiet alleyway just off Rua Capelo e Ivens. ②.

Quinta de Vale de Lobo, Azóia de Baixo, 6km north of town on the Lisbon and Torres Novas road (☎243 429 264). This pleasant house (where the historian Alexandre Herculano spent the last years of his life) is surrounded by gardens and has a pool. ⑤.

Residencial Vitoria, Rua 2° Visconde de Santarém 21 (☎243 309 130, fax 243 328 202). Fifteen minutes' walk from the centre, with decent, if small, rooms – all with bath. Breakfast included. ④.

Eating

Santarém has a range of **restaurants**, especially around Rua Capelo e Ivens, behind the market, or near the bullring on the road to Cartaxo. Among local fish specialities look out for *fataça na telha*, mullet cooked on a tile.

Pastelaria Bijou, Praça Sa da Bandeira. Perfect croissant-and-coffee spot opposite the Seminário, with outdoor tables from where you can watch the world go by.

O Mal Cozinhado, Campo de Feiras (☎243 323 584). Small place where you may need to reserve a table, particularly on Friday, which is fado night. Some of the meat comes from bulls recently on duty in the nearby bullring – and, despite the odd restaurant name ("badly cooked"), dishes are good, if expensive.

Noite e Dia, Rua António José de Almeida 9. Reliable Portuguese cooking at moderate prices.

Pigalle, Rua Capelo e Ivens. Busy restaurant-cum-snack bar. Closed Sun.

Restaurante Rafael, Rua 1° Dezembro 3. Good tourist menu in a friendly, family-run place.

O Saloio, Trav. do Montalvo 11, off Rua Capelo e Ivens. Popular with local families, this cheap *tasca* is good value for money.

The west bank: wine towns and Vila Franca de Xira

The western bank of the Rio Tejo is highly developed south of Santarém, though away from the river it doesn't take long to get into the rolling hills and vineyards. It's around an hour's journey on the fast A1 motorway from Santarém to Lisbon, but if you have a passing interest in **wines**, there are several worthy detours on your way west including *quintas* and museums where you can sample the stuff. In addition, the west bank hosts two of Portugal's most distinctive festivals in the city of **Vila Franca de Xira**, which sits at the edge of the important wetlands of the **Reserva Natural do Estuario do Tejo**.

Wine towns

Some of the Ribatejo's finest vineyards are found on the west bank (see box on p.176) and a good place to start exploring the wine trade is **CARTAXO**, 14km south of Santarém. The town is uninspiring but it has a fine **Museu Rural e do Vinho** (Tues–Fri 10.30am–12.30pm & 3–5.30pm, Sat & Sun 9.30am–12.30pm & 3–5.30pm; 110$00), in a *quinta* on Rua José Ribeiro da Costa, with a couple of traditional houses where you can taste and buy the local, full-bodied, fruity wine.

AZAMBUJA, 13km to the south, is known for its great reds made from the Periquita grape, but the town itself only really comes alive with the bull-running during its Feira do Maio, held during the last weekend in May. The Marquês de Pombal built a 26-kilo-metre-long canal – the Vala de Azambuja – parallel to the river here, to drain the land when the Tejo was in flood – at its mouth are the ruins of the **Palácio das Obras Novas**, used as a staging post for the steamers plying from Lisbon north to Constância (see p.170) in the nineteenth century.

Perched on a hillside 17km to the southwest, **ALENQUER** sits in a major wine area; its refreshing, lemony-flavoured whites are particularly worth tasting. There is little else to delay you apart from the attractive upper town sprawling up a steep hillside and boasting a **Franciscan convent** as its most prominent building. Founded in 1222 by Dona Sancha, daughter of Dom Sancho I, the convent is the oldest Franciscan house in Portugal and was built during the lifetime of St Francis of Assisi. It features a fine thir-teenth-century doorway and Manueline cloisters, the latter added in 1557. Sadly it is open only on the first Sunday of the month between morning and evening Mass.

However, it is in the valleys below the windmill-topped hills around **ARRUDA DOS VINHOS**, 16km south of Alenquer, that the region's vineyards are at their most attractive. The fresh, beaujolais-style Arruda (also known as Arruta) red wines pro-duced here are known throughout Europe, and are one of the reasons why Lisboans come to the village in their droves on Sundays. Many have lunch at the *adega-restau-rante O Fuso* (☎263 975 121), where vast slabs of meat and *bacalhau* are grilled over crackling open fires – if you can't get in there, *Restaurante Nazareth* opposite is a good alternative.

Vila Franca de Xira

VILA FRANCA DE XIRA, 45km downriver from Santarém, makes a rival claim to be the capital of the Ribatejo, but it's largely a drab, industrial city – a poor second when it comes to cultural attractions. Its riverside location made it the favoured home for English Crusaders, who named it Cornogoa after Cornwall. Now Vila Franca is the central point of interest for aficionados of the Portuguese bullfight: the rearing of bulls and horses dominates the local economy. The two great annual events are the **Festa do Colete Encarnado** ("Red Waistcoat Festival", a reference to the costume of the *campinos*) held over several days in the first two weeks of July; and the **Feira de Outubro** (October Fair), in the first two weeks of the month. On both occasions there are bullfights and a Pamplona-style running of the bulls through the streets – leading to the usual casualties among the bold (and drunk). The town's other claim to fame is being home to **Imax** – Portugal's first 360-degree cinema screen – in the shopping centre opposite the railway station.

RIBATEJO WINES

Wine has been produced on the banks of the Tejo for around 2000 years, but it is only recently that modern wine-making techniques have ensured that the result is appreciat-ed not only in local *tascas* but throughout Europe. The highly respected wines from the five denominations in the Ribatejo region – Almeirim, Cartaxo, Chamusca, Coruche and Santarém – can now be found in supermarkets outside Portugal, marketed under labels such as Ribatejo, Arruda and Liziria. Ribatejan **whites** are typically from the Fernão Pires or Trincadeira-das-Pratas grapes, which give rise to a dry, lemon-coloured and fruity wine. **Reds** tend to be from the Periquita, Tincadeira Preta and Castelão Nacional grapes, though Cabernet Sauvignon produces some of the best-tasting wines.

Accommodation is difficult to find during festivals – its advisable to book well in advance or visit on a day-trip from Santarém or Lisbon; the **turismo**, Rua Dr. Manuel Arriaga 24 (☎263 260 43), may be able to help. Places to stay in town include the *Residencial Ribatejana*, Rua da Praia 2 (☎263 229 91; ②), next to the station, and the *Residencial Flora*, Rua Noel Perdigão 12 (☎263 271 272; ③), one block from the station and with a good restaurant. There's a shaded **campsite** (☎263 276 031) on the outskirts, near the municipal swimming pool, but it's only open in the summer months.

For **eating**, *O Copote* in the station square, on the first floor above a bar, is inexpensive; *Restaurante O Redondel*, Praça de Touros (near the bullring on the Lisbon side of town; closed Mon), is also recommended, though the full works here can cost around 3500$00 per person.

The Reserva Natural de Estuario del Tejo

South and southeast from Vila Franca de Xira, the banks of the Tejo are classified as the **Reserva Natural de Estuario del Tejo**, providing protection for the thousands of wild birds that gather in the estuary. It is Portugal's most important wetland, but has been somewhat disrupted by the construction of the enormous Vasco da Gama bridge (see p.88). The reserve's headquarters are 35km south of Vila Franca in **ALCO-CHETE**, right on the waterfront on the south side of the bridge at Av. Combatentes 1 (☎212 341 742), from where information and advice are dispensed. With your own transport, the best approach to the reserve is from Alcamé, south of the N10 Vila Franca–Porto Alto road, or – better still – from Pancas, west of the N118. Otherwise, take the ferry from Lisbon (hourly from Praça do Comércio) to Montijo, a fifty-minute journey. Once there, it's a five-kilometre bus or taxi ride to Alcochete.

Between October and April, you can book **tours** of the wetlands from the reserve's headquarters in Alcochete. This is the best time to see the migrating bird species such as flamingoes, teal and avocet. During the summer, you'll catch nesting species: such as black-winged stilt, purple heron and marsh harriers.

You can also arrange a tour of the reserve from the Tejo estuary itself by **renting a boat** (or a place in a boat). Contact either Domingos Chefe, (☎296 384 724), the boat owner (☎212 360 278) or his English-speaking guide, Victor Casalinho, a day in advance to agree on the timing; you'll also need to obtain permission to visit from the reserve headquarters. The boat can take up to nine people and trips are available on weekends only throughout the year.

travel details

Trains

Abrantes to: Castelo Branco (6 daily; 1hr 30min–2hr); Covilhã (5 daily; 3hr); Elvas (3 daily; 2hr 45min); Lisbon (6 daily; 1hr 40min–2hr); Portalegre (3 daily; 1hr 45min).

Caldas da Rainha to: Figueira da Foz (7 daily; 1hr 30min–2hr 20min); Leiria (8 daily; 45min–1hr); Lisbon (10 daily; 1hr 30min–2hr); São Martinho do Porto (8 daily; 25 min); Torres Vedras (11 daily; 35–50min).

Leiria to: Caldas da Rainha (8 daily; 45min–1hr); Figueira da Foz (7 daily; 1hr 20min); Lisbon (5 daily; 2–3hr); São Martinho do Porto (8 daily; 50min); Torres Vedras (8 daily; 1hr 40min–2hr).

Lisbon to: Caldas da Rainha (10 daily; 1hr 30min–2hr); Leiria (5 daily; 2hr–3hr); Torres Vedras (14 daily; 1hr 10min–1hr 30min).

Santarém to: Castelo Branco (6 daily; 2hr 30min–3hr); Covilhã (5 daily; 3hr 45min–4hr); Lisbon (every 30 mins; 50min–1hr); Tomar (hourly; 1hr).

Tomar to: Lisbon (16; 2hr 5min); Santarém (16; 1hr);

Torres Vedras to: Caldas da Rainha (11 daily; 35–50min); Figueira da Foz (4 daily; 2hr 20min); Leiria (8 daily; 1hr 40min–2hr); Lisbon (14 daily; 1hr 10min–1hr 30min).

Vila Franca de Xira to: Lisbon (every 20 min; 30–40min); Santarém (hourly; 40min); Tomar (hourly; 1hr 40min).

Buses

Abrantes to: Coimbra (1 daily; 2hr 45min); Fátima (3–4 daily; 1hr 30min); Leiria (1 daily; 2hr); Lisbon (10 daily, 1hr 45min–2hr 50min); Santarém (4 daily; 1hr 25min); Tomar (2–4 daily; 1hr 10min).

Alcobaça to: Batalha (10 daily; 30min); Leiria (4 daily; 45min); Lisbon (3–4 daily; 2hr); Nazaré (hourly; 35 min).

Batalha to: Fátima (4 daily; 25min); Leiria (5 daily; 15min); Lisbon (6 daily; 2hr).

Caldas da Rainha to: Foz do Arelho (9–10 daily, 25min); Leiria (4 daily; 1hr 55min); Lisbon (6 daily; 1hr 45 min); Nazaré (7 daily; 40min); Óbidos (6–12 daily; 20min).

Ericeira to: Lisbon (6–8 daily; 1hr 30min); Sintra (15 daily; 45min).

Fátima to Coimbra (5 daily; 1hr–1hr 30min); Leiria (9 daily; 25 min); Lisbon (7–8 daily; 1hr 45min–2hr 15min); Porto (4–5 daily; 2hr 30min–3hr 30min).

Leiria to: Abrantes (1 daily; 1hr 50min); Alcobaça (4 daily; 50min); Batalha (5 daily; 15min); Coimbra (10 daily; 50min); Fátima (9 daily; 25min); Lisbon (9 daily; 1hr –2hr 10min); Porto de Mós (3 daily; 35min); São Pedro de Muel (4 daily, change at Marinha Grande; 1hr 10min); Tomar (2 daily; 1hr 10 min–2hr).

Nazaré to: Alcobaça (12 daily; 20min); Caldas da Rainha (7 daily; 40min); Leiria (10 daily; 1hr 10min); Lisbon (6 daily; 2hr); Óbidos (3 daily; 1 hr); São Martinho do Porto (6 daily; 20 min).

Óbidos to: Caldas da Rainha (6–12 daily; 20min); Nazaré (6–7 daily; 1hr); Peniche (7–8 daily; 25–40min).

Peniche to: Areia Branca (6 daily; 30min); Caldas da Rainha (7 daily; 45min); Consolação (hourly; 15min); Lisbon (9 daily; 1 hr 45min); Óbidos (7–8 daily; 25–40min); São Martinho do Porto (3 daily; 1hr); Torre Vedras (9 daily; 50min).

Santarém to: Abrantes (6 daily; 1hr 25min); Fátima (9 daily, 1 hr 10min); Lisbon (12 daily; 1hr–1hr 15min); Ourem (1 daily; 1hr 10min); Tomar (2–4 daily; 1hr); Vila Franca (2–5 daily; 1hr 35min–2hr 20min).

Tomar to: Abrantes (2–4 daily; 1hr 10min); Coimbra (2 daily; 2hr); Fátima (2–5 daily; 45min); Leiria (2 daily; 1hr 10min–2hr); Lisbon (2–4 daily; 1hr 15min–2hr 30min); Santarém (2–4 daily; 1hr 5min).

Vila Franca de Xira to: Évora (1 daily; 2hr); Lisbon (15 daily; 50min); Santarém (2–5 daily; 40min–1hr 35min).

Alfama, Lisbon

Torre de Belém, Lisbon

Chiado's famous café, Lisbon

View of Monsanto from the castle

Elevador da Bica, Bairro Alto, Lisbon

Looking down from the Monumento dos Descobrimentos, Belém

The university buildings, Coimbra

Convento de Cristo, Tomar

Cabo Espichel

PETER WILSON

Dressed up for the Festa da Ria, Aveiro

PETER WILSON

Bacalhau shop

CHAPTER THREE

COIMBRA AND THE BEIRA LITORAL

T he province of **Beira Litoral** is dominated by the city of **Coimbra**, which, with Guimarães, Lisbon and Porto, forms the quartet of Portugal's historic capitals. Situated on a hill above the Rio Mondego, it's a wonderfully moody place, full of ancient alleys and lanes, spreading around the country's oldest university. As a base for exploring the region, the city can't be beaten, with Portugal's most extensive Roman site, **Conímbriga**, 16km to the southwest, the castle at **Montemor-o-Velho** 32km west on the road to Figueira da Foz, and the delightful spa town of **Luso** and ancient **forest of Buçaco** under an hour's journey to the north.

Beira's endlessly sandy coastline, from Figueira da Foz north as far as Porto, has been dubbed the **Costa de Prata** ("Silver Coast"). Although slowly succumbing to development, most noticeably around **Praia de Mira**, it remains one of the least spoiled coasts in Portugal, backed by rolling dunes and pine forests. The only resort of any real size is **Figueira da Foz** and even this remains thoroughly and enjoyably local in character. Inland, the villages and towns of the fertile plain have long been conditioned by the twin threats of floodwaters coming down from Portugal's highest mountains, and silting caused by the restless Atlantic. Drainage channels have had to be cut to make cultivation possible and houses everywhere are built on high ground. At **Aveiro**, positioned on a complex estuary site, a whole network of canals was developed to cope with the currents, and to facilitate salt production and the harvesting of seaweed – still the staple activities of the local economy.

The Beira region also hints at the river valley delights to come, in the Douro and Minho, further north. Following the delightful **Rio Mondego** upstream from Coimbra, you'll come to see why it has been celebrated so often in Portuguese poetry as the "Rio das Musas" – River of the Muses. An equally beautiful road journey trails the **Rio Vouga**, from Aveiro, up to the town of **Vouzela** and the spa of **São Pedro do Sul**.

ACCOMMODATION PRICE CODES

All the accommodation prices in this book have been coded using the symbols below. The symbols represent the lowest prices you can expect to pay for a **double room in high season**; for a full explanation, see p.32.

① Under 4000$00
② 4000$00–7000$00
③ 7000$00–11,000$00
④ 11,000$00–15,000$00
⑤ 15,000$00–20,000$00
⑥ 20,000$00–25,000$00
⑦ 25,000$00–30,000$00
⑧ 30,000$00–40,000$00
⑨ Over 40,000$00

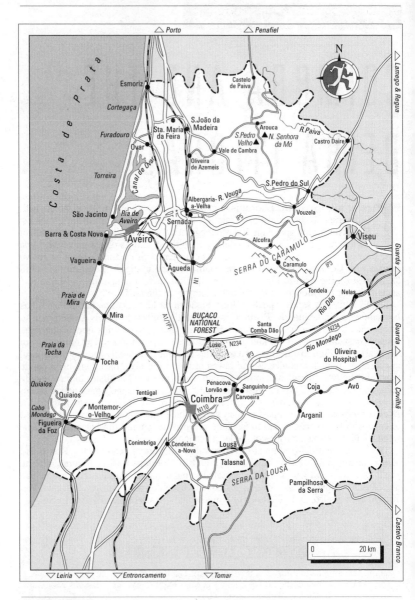

Coimbra

COIMBRA was Portugal's capital for over a century (1143–1255) and its famous **university** – founded in 1290 and permanently established here in 1537 after a series of moves back and forth to Lisbon – was the only one in Portugal until the beginning of this century. It remains highly prestigious (though Lisbon has far more students nowadays) and provides the greatest of Coimbra's monuments and buildings, most notably the renowned Baroque library. In addition, there are a remarkable number of other riches: two cathedrals, dozens of lesser churches, and scores of ancient mansions, one housing the superb **Museu Machado de Castro**.

This roll-call of splendours is promoted zealously by the inhabitants of what – when all is said and done – is little more than a small, provincial town. There's an air of self-importance that whistles through city and citizens, bolstered by Coimbra's long academic tradition and fed by shops, galleries and cafés that would sit easily in Lisbon. For visitors, this means that Coimbra can be a lot of fun: it's a very manageable size, with a population of under eighty thousand, its streets packed with bars and taverns, at their liveliest when the students are in town. The best time to be here is in May, when the end of the academic year is celebrated in the **Queima das Fitas**, with graduates ceremoniously tearing or burning their gowns and faculty ribbons. This is also when you're most likely to hear the genuine **Coimbra fado**, distinguished from the Lisbon version by its mournful pace and romantic or intellectual lyrics.

Arrival, information and city transport

There are three **train stations** – Coimbra A, Coimbra B and Coimbra Parque. Riverside **Coimbra A** (often just "Coimbra" on timetables) is right at the heart of things; express through-trains call only at **Coimbra B**, 3km to the north, from where you pick up a local train into Coimbra A – just follow everyone else across the platform (you don't need another ticket). **Coimbra Parque**, southeast of the centre, is for services to and from Lousã, to the south (see p.197).

The main **bus station** is on Avenida Fernão de Magalhães, about fifteen minutes' walk northwest of the centre. Almost all long-distance buses operate from here, as do international services to Spain, France and Germany. AVIC buses, operating along the Costa de Prata to and from Praia da Mira, stop at the station at Rua João de Ruão 18, on the way in from the main bus station. AVIC also runs buses to and from Condeixa-a-Nova (for Conímbriga), which also make a stop at the top of Avenida Emídio Navarro, just before Coimbra A station.

Drivers should beware that driving into Coimbra can be a nightmare, since most of the central streets are closed to cars. It's best to use one of the signposted car parks (also marked on the map on pp.182–183) or stay at a hotel with car parking and then walk into town.

Information and transport

For a free map, call in at the **turismo** on the triangular Largo da Portagem, facing the Ponte Santa Clara (summer: Mon–Fri 9am–7pm, Sat & Sun 10am–1pm & 2.30–5.30pm; winter: daily 9am–6pm; ☎239 855 930). There are also tourist offices on Praça Dom Dinis (☎239 832 591) and Praça da República (☎239 833 202), both open the same hours as the main office, and a small information kiosk on the platform of Coimbra B.

You'll get most out of **walking** around the old quarter of Coimbra; indeed, you'll have no choice given the complexity and inaccessibility of most of the hillside alleys and streets. Tickets for **town buses** (which include services out to the campsite and youth hostel; see p.185) are sold on board or more cheaply from kiosks in Largo da Portagem, Praça 8 de Maio and Praça da República. Even better value are the five- or ten-ticket strips (called *senhas*) which you buy from automatic machines dotted around town. There's one in front of the Bank of Portugal in Largo da Portagem, and they all have an English-language option. Cancel your ticket in the machine by the driver as you board. For a cheap bus **tour** of the city, #3 and #26 take in most of the sights. Information on bus routes and timetables is available from the riverside café in front of the *Hotel Astória*, or the kiosk a little further up.

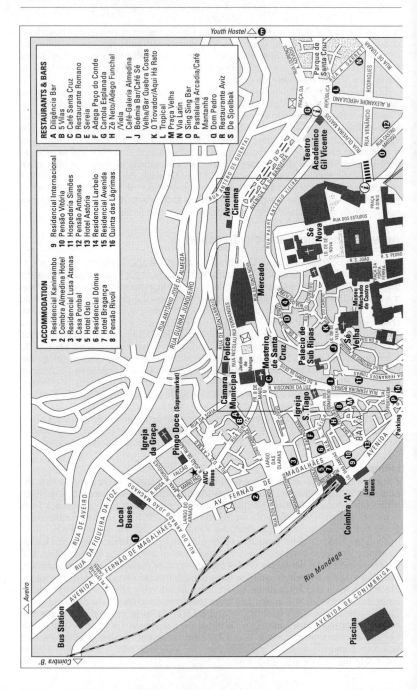

Youth Hostel △ **E**

RESTAURANTS & BARS
A Diligência Bar
B 5 Vilas
C Café Santa Cruz
D Restaurante Romano
E Sereia
F Adega Paço do Conde
G Cartola Esplanada
H Zé Neto/Adego Funchal /Viela
I Café-Galeria Almedina
J Boémia Bar/Café Sé Velha/Bar Quebra Costas
K O Trovador/Aqui Há Rato
L Tropical
M Praça Velha
N Via Latin
O Sing Sing Bar
P Pastelaria Arcadia/Café Mantanhã
Q Dom Pedro
R Restaurante Aviz
S De Sjoelbak

ACCOMMODATION
1 Residencial Kanimambo
2 Coimbra Almedina Hotel
3 Residencial Lusa Atenas
4 Casa Pombal
5 Hotel Oslo
6 Residencial Dómus
7 Hotel Bragança
8 Pensão Rivoli
9 Residencial Internacional
10 Pensão Vitória
11 Hospedaria Simões
12 Pensão Antunes
13 Hotel Astória
14 Residencial Larbelo
15 Residencial Avenida
16 Quinta das Lágrimas

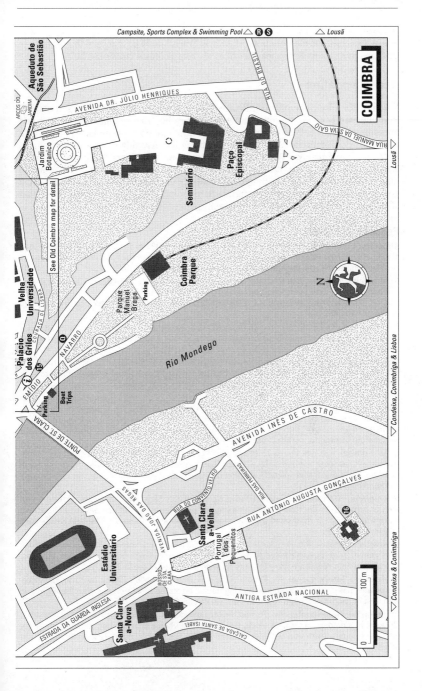

Campsite, Sports Complex & Swimming Pool △ Ⓡ Ⓢ

△ Lousã

COIMBRA

RUA DO BRASIL

RUA MANUEL DA SILVA GAIO

▷ Lousã

Aqueduto de São Sebastião

ARCOS DO JARDIM

AVENIDA DR. JÚLIO HENRIQUES

Jardim Botânico

See Old Coimbra map for detail

Seminário

Paço Episcopal

Velha Universidade

Palácio dos Grilos

PRAÇA DE LISBOA

NAVARRO

EMÍDIO

Parking

Boat Trips

PONTE DE ST. CLARA

Parque Manuel Bragã

Parking

Coimbra Parque

Rio Mondego

N

AVENIDA INÊS DE CASTRO

▷ Condeixa, Conimbriga & Lisboa

Estádio Universitário

Santa Clara-a-Nova

ESTRADA DA GUARDA INGLESA

ROSSIO DE STA. CLARA

AVENIDA JOÃO DAS REGAS

RUA DO CONVENTO VELHO

Santa Clara-a-Velha

Portugal dos Pequenitos

RUA DAS FIGUEIRAS

RUA ANTÓNIO AUGUSTA GONÇALVES

CALÇADA DE SANTA ISABEL

ANTIGA ESTRADA NACIONAL

▷ Condeixa & Conimbriga

100 m

0

Taxis are a cheap way of getting around, too, given the short distances involved. There are ranks outside Coimbra A station, at Praça 8 de Maio, opposite the *Santa Cruz* café, and in Praça da República. To call a cab, ring Politaxis (☎239 484 045).

Accommodation

Much of the city's **accommodation** is within a short walk of Coimbra A station. The cheaper *pensões* are concentrated in the rather sleazy Rua da Sota (left and immediately right out of the station) and the little streets between here and the central Praça do Comércio. More expensive places line Avenida Fernão de Magalhães (left and immediately left out of the station) and the riverside Avenida Emídio Navarro (directly ahead of the station). What you won't find is much choice in the hilly streets of the old town. Budget alternatives to the *pensões* and hotels include a **youth hostel** and **campsite**, though both are a fair way from the centre. Note that all accommodation reviewed below is marked on the map on pp.182–183.

Pensões and hotels

Almedina Coimbra Hotel, Av. Fernão de Magalhães 203 (☎239 829 161, fax 239 829 906). Situated next to a fire station on a race-track main road. Double-glazing keeps the noise down, but the rooms here lack charm. Nearby parking, though, and breakfast is included. ⑤.

Residencial Antunes, Rua Castro Matoso 8 (☎239 823 048, fax 239 838 373). Quiet, polished and good value – some rooms look across the river, and most are decently sized with bathrooms and TV. It's near Praça da República, a fair walk from the old town, though close to a couple of excellent bars. ④.

Hotel Astória, Av. Emídio Navarro 21 (☎239 822 055, fax 239 822 057). Perfectly placed (look for the landmark dome), classically upmarket choice exhibiting a strange blend of Art Nouveau and 1930s decor. The best rooms overlook the river. ⑥.

Residencial Avenida, Av. Emídio Navarro 37 (☎239 822 156, fax 239 822 155). On the riverside, a gorgeous (if slightly musty) Art Nouveau place with palatial rooms complete with broken chandeliers, sturdy old furniture and small, clean bathrooms. Bar, restaurant and TV lounge, too. ④.

Hotel Bragança, Largo das Ameias 10 (☎239 822 171, fax 239 836 135). If you were staying any nearer the train station, you'd be in it – which given the *Bragança*'s pseudo-Soviet brutalist exterior might be no bad thing. Things pick up inside, where rooms are inoffensively modern and spacious, with marble bathrooms; breakfast included. ⑤.

Casa Pombal, Rua dos Flores 18 (☎239 835 175, fax 239 821 548). Higgledy-piggledy Dutch-run town house near the university with lashings of atmosphere, a tiled dining room and small patio-garden. Breakfast is splendid and you can order good vegetarian meals, too. Thoroughly recommended. ④.

Residencial Dómus, Rua Adelino Veiga 62 (☎239 828 584). On the nicest of the narrow streets across from the train station, this homely place (entrance hidden next to a rug store) has a wide variety of rooms and friendly owners keen to show them off. The best rooms have shower and TV. ③.

Hospedaria Simões, Rua Fernandes Tomás 69 (☎239 834 638). Cheapest choice in the old town, with simple, clean, monastic lodgings on a cobbled street that climbs from the Arco de Almedina. The ground-floor rooms are noisy but cheaper than in the rest of the building. ①.

Residencial Internacional, Av. Emídio Navarro 4 (☎239 825 503). Facing the river, this once-grand hotel has divided up its rooms, making them a bit on the small side. But it's a friendly place, with a bit of character, though rooms at the front can be rather noisy. ③.

Residencial Kanimambo, Av. Fernão de Magalhães 484 (☎239 827 151, fax 239 828 408). Upstairs in a modern apartment block, this is the best choice near the bus station, with nicely furnished rooms (with and without shower) spread across two cool, dark, quiet floors and accessed by lift. ③.

Residencial Larbelo, Largo da Portagem 33 (☎239 829 092, fax 239 829 094). Close to the main turismo; you can't miss the lime green facade. It's simply furnished and has new bathrooms, but it's also rather gloomy and – for single travellers at least – rather overpriced. You'll pay more for a room with bath or shower. Rooms facing the Largo are noisy. ③.

Residencial Lusa Atenas, Av. Fernão de Magalhães 68 (☎239 826 412, fax 239 820 133). Clean, spacious rooms, with private bath and TV, in a once-grand building on the busy main road. Enthusiastic staff keep things running smoothly; try and avoid being put in the annexe at no. 191, which is not as good, or the balconied room on the street corner – it may look tempting but the pedestrian crossing, not four metres from your head, bleeps every thirty seconds. ③.

Hotel Oslo, Av. Fernão de Magalhães 25 (☎239 829 071, fax 239 826 014). Pleasant, modern hotel with a restaurant and bar on the top floor. Despite the Scandinavian style, the rooms facing the street feature traditional Portuguese late-night noise. ④.

Quinta das Lágrimas, off Rua António Augusta Gonçalves (☎239 441 615, fax 239 441 695). Situated across the river, this is possibly the most atmospheric choice in Coimbra. A plush stately house set in the infamous gardens and counting Wellington amongst its former guests. ⑥.

Pensão Rivoli, Praça do Comércio 27 (☎239 825 550). Excellent-value rooms (some with en-suite showers) in a splendid central, pedestrianized location. The quiet rooms are tucked away at the back of the building, approached along a plant-filled corridor. ③.

Pensão Vitória, Rua da Sota 9 & 19 (☎239 824 049). The best of the two or three cheap *pensões* on this street, close to the train station. ②.

OUTSIDE THE CITY

Casa dos Quintais, at Assarfage, 6km south of Coimbra (☎239 438 305). Small private house with a delightful garden and fine views of Coimbra; follow signs to Carvalhais de Cima and then signs for "Casa Rurale". There are just three double rooms with a common lounge area, and an excellent breakfast is served; call ahead to reserve a room. ⑤.

Hostel and campsite

Parque de Campismo Municipal, Praça 25 de Abril (☎239 701 497). The well-shaded campsite is at the municipal sports complex (open all year), and has the added attraction of the adjacent town swimming pool. Bus #5 runs there from Largo da Portagem, or, if you're coming from Lousã, get off at São José station, 250m from the campsite entrance. Reception open daily 9am–10pm (winter 6pm).

Pousada de Juventude, Rua Henrique Seco 14 (☎ & fax 239 822 955). Above the Parque Santa Cruz, this is a decent modern hostel with nice rooms, patio, kitchen and TV room: reception is open 9am–noon and 6pm–midnight. It's about twenty minutes' walk, or take buses #7, #8, #29 or #46 from Coimbra A.

The City

Old Coimbra straddles a hilly site, with the university crowning its summit, on the north bank of the Rio Mondego. Its slopes are a convoluted mass of ancient alleys around which the modern town has spread, and most of interest is concentrated on the hill itself or in the largely pedestrianized commercial centre at its foot. Chances are you'll get lost as soon as you start to climb past the remains of the city walls, but that's half the fun. It's probably best to start your exploration of Coimbra with the **Velha Universidade**, not least because it's the easiest place to find, and from its balcony the city is laid out below you like a map. You can see right across the river to the twin **Santa Clara** convents, a visit to which is the only time you need leave the confines of the old city. If you don't feel like walking, bus #1 takes you up to the Museo Machado de Castro and the university buildings.

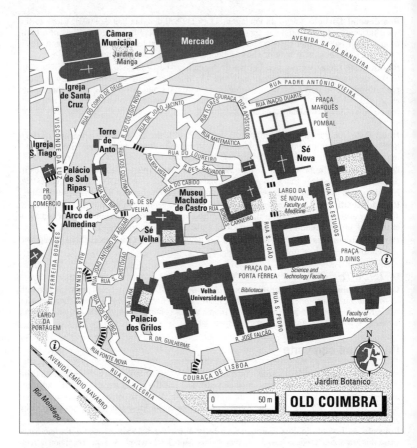

Into the old town

The old town is bounded on its western side by the pedestrianized main street which runs north from the café-filled Largo da Portagem to the Igreja de Santa Cruz. Here, in the **Baixa**, along **Rua Ferreira Borges** and its continuation **Rua Visconde da Luz**, are most of the fashionable shops and cafés; off to the west, the narrow rat-runs and alleys that cut down to the train station contain budget restaurants, canteens, grocery stores, workshops, butchers and bakers.

Heading up into the old town involves a steep climb, with perhaps the nicest approach being halfway along the main street, through the Arco de Almedina, an arch cut through the old city wall; the *Café-Galeria Almedina* bar here on the right (see p.190) actually burrows its way into the medieval wall. Stepped streets climb beyond into the heart of old Coimbra, with attractive alleys off to either side. Down Rua Sub Ripas, to the left, is the Palácio de Sub Ripas, sporting a fine Manueline doorway – the Renaissance windows and stone medallions are from the workshop of the French sculptor Jean de Rouen (João de Ruão), which used to be nearby. Almost any other turn you care to make reveals more interest: hidden courtyards, flower-decked balconies, cobbled dead-ends and glimpses of sky and lower town through unexpected gaps in the crumbling walls.

The Sé Velha

The **Sé Velha** (Mon, Thurs & Sat 10am–noon & 2–7.30pm, Fri 10am–2pm, Sun 10am–1pm), an unmistakable fortress-like bulk, squats about halfway up the hill in its own steeply shelving square. Begun in 1162, it's one of the most important Romanesque buildings in Portugal, little altered and seemingly unbowed by the weight of the years. The one significant later addition – the Renaissance Porta Especiosa in the north wall – has, in contrast to the main structure, almost entirely crumbled away. Solid and square on the outside, the cathedral is also stolid and simple within, the decoration confined to a few giant conch shells holding holy water and some unobtrusive *azulejos* from Seville around the walls. The Gothic tombs of early bishops and the low-arched cloister (100$00) are equally restrained.

The Velha Universidade

The main buildings of the **Velha Universidade** (daily 9.30am–noon & 2–5pm; 250$00 for university and library; another 250$00 for Sala dos Capelos) lie further up the hill, and date from the sixteenth century when João III declared its establishment at Coimbra permanent. The buildings are set around the **Pátio das Escolas**, a courtyard dominated by the Baroque clock tower nicknamed "A Cabra" – the goat – and a statue of the portly João III.

The elaborate stairway to the right of the main court leads into the administrative quarters and the **Sala dos Capelos**; tickets are sold here for visits to each of the main sections of the university. The hall itself – hung with portraits of Portugal's kings – is used for conferring degrees and has a fine wood-panelled ceiling with gilded decoration in the Manueline style. The highlight of this part of the building, though, is the narrow catwalk around the outside walls. The central door off the courtyard leads past the **Capela**, not the finest of Coimbra's religious foundations but one of the most elaborate – covered with *azulejos* and intricate decoration including twisted, rope-like pillars, a frescoed ceiling, and a gaudy Baroque organ.

To the left is the famous library, the **Biblioteca Joanina**, a Baroque fantasy presented to the faculty by João V in the early eighteenth century. Its rooms telescope into each other, focusing on the founder's portrait in a disconcertingly effective use of trompe l'oeil. The richness of it all is impressive, such as the expanse of cleverly marbled wood, gold leaf, tables inlaid with ebony, rosewood and jacaranda, Chinese-style lacquer work and carefully calculated frescoed ceilings. The most prized valuables, the rare and ancient books, are locked away out of sight and, despite their impressive multilingual titles, the volumes on the shelves seem largely chosen for their aesthetic value; no one seems likely to disturb the careful arrangement by actually reading anything.

Sadly, the other faculty buildings of the university are almost completely devoid of interest. Their lofty position atop the narrow, cobbled streets notwithstanding, too many are mere concrete excrescences dating from a modernization programme under Dr. Salazar. The wide spaces in between are tempered by modern sculpture of dubious quality, and only the lure of the student-frequented pavement cafés on **Praça da República** – down the steep steps from Praça Dom Dinis – merit the diversion. The **Parque de Santa Cruz**, stretching uphill from the praça, is best avoided after dark.

The Jardim Botânico

Just down the hill from Praça Dom Dinis, ten minutes or so to the south, the **Jardim Botânico** is worth a brief visit. Founded in the eighteenth century, these botanical displays once enjoyed a worldwide reputation and, even if they've seen better days, it's still very pleasant to stroll among the formally laid out beds of plants from around the world, but note that you're not allowed to picnic here. Nearby are the impressive remains of the sixteenth-century **Aqueduto de São Sebastião**.

The Museu Machado de Castro and Sé Nova

Back up on the hill, after the old university buildings, is the **Museu Machado de Castro** (Tues–Sun 9.30am–12.30pm & 2–5.30pm; 250$00; free Sun morning), just down Rua de São João. The museum, named after an eighteenth-century sculptor, is housed in the former archbishop's palace, which would be worth visiting in its own right even if it were empty. As it is, it's positively stuffed with treasures: sculpture (see especially the little medieval knight riding home with his mace slung over his shoulder), paintings, furniture, and ceramics. Underneath all this is the Roman **Cryptoportico**, a series of subterranean galleries probably used by the Romans as a granary and subsequently pressed into service for the foundations of the palace.

Across the way stands the unprepossessing **Sé Nova**, or New Cathedral (daily 9am–noon & 2–6pm; free), a seventeenth-century Jesuit foundation which replaced the Sé Velha as cathedral in 1772.

Igreja de Santa Cruz

The last old-town stop is right at the bottom of the hill, at the northern end of Rua Visconde da Luz, where restraint and simplicity aren't words that spring to mind when considering the **Igreja de Santa Cruz** (daily 9.30am–noon & 2–5.45pm; cloister 200$00), the church of the monastery that was founded on the site by São Teotónio. The church predates even the Sé Velha, but nothing remains that has not been substantially remodelled – its exuberant facade and strange double doorway setting the tone. In the early sixteenth century Coimbra was the base of a major sculptural school that included the French artists Nicolas Chanterene and Jean de Rouen (João de Ruão), as well as the two Manueline masters João de Castilho and Diogo de Boitaca, all of whom had a hand in rebuilding Santa Cruz.

These artists designed a variety of projects: **tombs** to house Portugal's first kings, Afonso Henriques and Sancho I; an elaborate **pulpit**; and, most famously, the **Cloister of Silence**. It is here that the Manueline theme is at its clearest, with a series of airy arches decorated with bas-relief scenes from the life of Christ. From the cloister a staircase leads to the raised *coro*, above whose wooden benches is a frieze celebrating the nation's flourishing empire.

Around the back of the church, the small **Jardim da Manga** faces the main road. More cloister than garden, it was at one time surrounded by orange trees, and today still retains a cupola and fountain; there's a handy café at the rear of the garden.

The Santa Clara convents

It was in Santa Cruz that the romantic history of Dom Pedro and Inês de Castro (see "Alcobaça", p.151) came to its ghoulish climax. Pedro, finally proclaimed king, had his lover exhumed and set up on a throne in the church, where his courtiers were forced to pay homage to the decomposing body.

Inês had originally lain in the **Convento de Santa Clara-a-Velha**, a twenty-minute walk away from the main town across the river, her tomb placed alongside the convent's founder and Coimbra's patron, the saint-queen Isabel. Isabel was married to Dom Dinis, whom she infuriated by constantly giving away his wealth to the poor. She performed one of her many miracles when, confronted by her irate husband as she smuggled out yet another cargo of gold, she claimed to be carrying only roses: when her bag was opened that was exactly its contents. The Gothic hall church she built, over time, became almost entirely covered by silt from the River Mondego, but the ruin is slowly being restored.

The two tombs have long since been moved away, Inês's to Alcobaça and Isabel's to the **Convento de Santa Clara-a-Nova** (Tues–Sun 8.30am– 6pm, Mon 8.30am–noon & 2–6pm), higher up the hill and safe from the shifting river. The new convent, built in 1650, doesn't have much of the charm of the old and the fact that the nuns' quarters now house a Portuguese army barracks doesn't help. Its two saving graces, which make the climb worthwhile, are **Isabel's tomb** – made of solid silver collected by the citizens of Coimbra

– and the vast **cloister** (100$00), heady with honeysuckle, which was financed by João V, a king whose devotion to nuns went beyond the normal bounds of spiritual comfort. The army's presence exerts itself in a small **military museum** (daily 10am–noon & 2–5pm; 100$00), displaying bits and bombs retrieved intact from World War II.

Portugal dos Pequenitos

Between the two convents extends the parkland site of **Portugal dos Pequenitos** (daily: summer 10am–6.30pm; winter 10am–4.30pm; 800$00), a 1950s' theme park where scale models of many of the country's great buildings are interspersed with "typical" farmhouses and sections on the overseas territories, heavy with the White Man's Burden. Historically and architecturally accurate it's not, but the place is great fun for kids who can clamber in and out of the miniature houses.

A short distance beyond is a somewhat more sombre little park, the **Quinta das Lágrimas** (Garden of Tears), in which, so legend has it, Inês de Castro was finally tracked down and murdered.

Eating

The city's **cheapest meals** are to be found in the dives along Rua Direita in the Baixa, where if you're not too bothered about your surroundings – basement saloons and rough tables – or your fellow diners (even rougher old men) you can eat for under 1000$00. For a tad more sophistication, search out the atmospheric little cafés and restaurants tucked into the tiny alleys between Largo da Portagem, Rua da Sota and Praça do Comércio – Rua das Azeiteiras, in particular, has several good possibilities. Local specialities to try out are *chanfana* – kid goat roasted in wine, a little fatty for some tastes – and Santa Clara pastries. For **breakfast**, the cafés and coffee houses in the Baixa are best; see p.186 for more details.

5 Vilas, Rua Direita 53. One of the more salubrious of the places on this street, with a clientele that looks as though it might eat the food rather than fight with it. Best at lunch time, where around 1000$00 gets you the works including the brutal home-made wine.

Restaurante Aviz, Rua do Brasil 185. Bustling good-time local eating place, a five-minute taxi ride east of the centre and serving later than most in town. Best-known for its seafood, though it also does great (and cheaper) steaks – try the *bifé Aviz*, cooked in cream and coffee. Around 2000–3000$00.

Dom Pedro, Av. Emídio Navarro 58. On the main road by the river, the decor (including a fountain) is attractive and the waiters attentive, but the food can sometimes disappoint. Around 3000$00.

Adega Funchal, Rua das Azeiteiras 18. Just off Praça do Comércio, this reasonably priced place serves generous helpings of chicken or mutton stew and the like in agreeable rustic surroundings. Under 2000$00.

Adega Paço do Conde, Rua Paço do Conde 1. Great, locally renowned *churrasqueiria* of cavernous proportions, with a dining room either side of a covered terrace. Under 1500$00 for grilled meat or fish, salad, wine and coffee. Closed Sun.

Restaurante Romano, Rua João Jacinto 18–20. Excellent pizzeria where everything is fresh and the chef is happy to conjure up special requests; you'll pay around 1000–1500$00. Open till 11pm.

Sereia, Rua Henriques Seco 1. Café-bar close to the youth hostel with a popular range of grills, egg dishes and stews at middling prices. Open till midnight.

O Trovador, Largo da Sé Velha 17. Next to the old cathedral, this lovely wood-panelled and ceramic-tiled restaurant is surprisingly good value – around 2500–3500$00 – if rather limited in choice. There are regular fado sessions here, too. Closed Mon.

Viela, Rua das Azeiteiras 35. Gloomy tiled dining room with good food, overseen by a friendly proprietor. The *carne de porco* is delicious and a gluttonous bargain at 1200$00 – splitting the enormous full portions means a meal shouldn't top 2000$00 or so.

Zé Neto, Rua das Azeiteiras 8–12. This provides a similar list of Portuguese grills and fries to that served up at *Adega Funchal* but at budget prices, washed down with some of the cheapest house wine in town. Last orders around 9.45pm.

Drinking and nightlife

At some stage of the day, you should visit one of the traditional **cafés** and **coffee houses** along Rua Ferreira Borges and Rua Visconde da Luz, filled with package-laden shoppers. Praça da República, across town by the Parque de Santa Cruz, is also surrounded by cafés, this time popular with students and staying open until 2am. Other trendy **bars** are scattered across old and new parts of town, and the best are reviewed below; all stay open until 2am unless otherwise stated. Coimbra's **clubs** remain open much later; in some, you can expect the music to keep going until 6am. As a rule, you'll pay a minimum entrance fee of around 500–800$00 in the clubs, and in bars where there's a DJ or live music.

You're most likely to catch **fado** during the student celebrations in May, though there are year-round performances in bars like *Diligência* (see below) and even in some restaurants; those around the Sé Velha are good bets. For up-to-the-minute news on **concerts** and events, watch for fly posters stuck up all over university buildings.

Cafés

Pastelaria Arcadia, Rua Ferreira Borges 144. A favourite old-time cake-shop just off Largo do Portagem.

Café Montanha, Largo da Portagem. Best-sited of the square's cafés with a good view of the passing parade and bridge traffic. There's live music or poetry some evenings.

Café Santa Cruz, Praça 8 de Maio. Occupying part of the monastery buildings, it's hard to say which is more attractive – the vaulted stone interior or the tables outside on the busiest downtown shopping stretch.

Café Sé Velha, Rua Joaquim António d'Aguiar 132. At the top of a particularly exhausting flight of steps a stone's throw from the cathedral, with outdoor terrace seating.

Praça Velha, Praça do Comércio. Tables outside in a veritable suntrap of a square, just down the steps from the main street.

Bars

Café-Galeria Almedina, Arco de Almedina 10. A sweeping vault-bar-cum-art-gallery in the bowels of the old city walls with live music at weekends. Open 8pm–4am.

Aqui Há Rato, Largo da Sé Velha 20. Bar with dance floor and DJ spinning pop-dance hits from 10pm until 4am.

Bar Quebra Costas, Rua Quebra Costas 47. Small, stylishly laid-back bar tucked away on the steps leading down from the Sé Velha.

Boémia Bar, Rua do Cabido 6. Upmarket wood-and-tile jazz/blues bar, which packs in the students at weekends; just off Largo da Sé Velha. Has fado on some Friday and Saturday nights. Closed Sun.

Cartola Esplanada Bar, Praça da República. Student favourite, next to the turismo, with esplanade seats, interior chrome fittings and boombox acoustics.

Diligência Bar, Rua Nova 30, between Rua Direita and Rua da Sofia. There's food, drink and fado every night in this atmospheric joint with cobblestone walls and candles, though the feelings of *saudade* (loss and longing), from which the music draws its spirit, will also be felt in your wallet.

Sing Sing Bar, Rua Castro Matoso 11. More peaceful than most of the late-night bars, with the chance of a seat and some conversation – provided you're not unlucky enough to coincide with karaoke night. Other nights it's a diet of alternative and underground sounds.

De Sjoelbak, Rua do Brasil 93. Out-of-town Dutch bar with lashings of lager and a boisterous crowd swinging to R&B and Sixties' classics; eat at the *Aviz* (see p.189) and pop in here afterwards. Closed Sun.

Tropical, Praça da República, corner of Rua Alexandre Herculano. Split-level bar packed with students at the weekends. The pavement tables soon get swamped, while the barman roves around with trays of ice-cold Super Bocks.

Clubs

States, Praça Machado de Assis 22a. Indie, rock and grunge; don't turn up until after midnight. Open till 4am; closed Sun.

Varadero, Quinta da Ínsua, Santa Clara. Lively disco-bar across the river, behind the Galp and Mobil stations. Predominantly dance and techno, with live music on Friday and Saturday nights; there's a café-snack bar here, too. Open till 6am.

Via Latina, Rua Almeida Garrett 1. Youthful, disco hi-jinks near Praça da República. Smaller than *Varadero*, but with a similar crowd. Open till 4am; closed Sun.

Listings

Banks and exchange Banks are grouped along the avenidas west and east of Coimbra A station, Avenida Emídio Navarro and Avenida Fernão de Magalhães. The *Hotel Astória*, Av. Emídio Navarro 21 (close to Largo da Portagem), will change currency outside bank hours, as will *Hotel Tivoli*, Rua João Machado.

Boat trips Basófias (☎239 404 135) runs 75min trips up the Rio Mondego (departing from beside Parque Dr. Manuel Braga), giving you a duck's-eye view of the old city. In summer, trips depart at 3pm, 4.30pm & 6pm, with additional 11.30am & 7.30pm services at weekends; in winter, 3pm & 4.30pm, additional 6pm service at weekends. There are no trips on Monday. O Pioneiro do Mondego also arrange downriver **kayak trips** from the nearby town of Penacova to Coimbra – for details, see p.196. More information is also available from the turismo in Coimbra.

Buses Most services use the main bus station at the top end of Av. Fernão de Magalhães (information on ☎239 855 270). AVIC, Rua João de Ruão 16 (☎239 823 769), runs to the Costa de Prata resorts, Figueira da Foz, Aveiro and Condeixa-a-Nova (for Conímbriga); Moisés Correia de Oliveira, Rua João Machado 23 (☎239 828 263), runs to Montemor-o-Velho and other villages on or close to the Coimbra–Figueira da Foz road (N11) and direct to Figueira itself.

Car breakdowns Automóvel Club de Portugal (ACP), Av. Emídio Navarro 6 (☎239 826 813).

Car rental Hertz, Rua João de Ruão 16 (☎239 837 491); Hervis, Rua João Machado 94 (☎239 824 062); Salitur, Rua da Sota 42 (☎239 820 594).

Cinema Cine Avenida, Av. Sá da Bandeira (☎239 822 131); also has a rooftop bar and great city views. Teatro Academico Gil Vicente, Praça da República (☎239 829 372), has an arts cinema as well as a gallery, café and occasional classical and jazz concerts.

Hospital Hospital da Universidade de Coimbra, Praça Professor Mota Pinto (☎239 400 400).

Internet Cybercafé *Egomundo*, Rua Antero de Quental 73 (Mon–Fri 10am–midnight, Sat 2pm–midnight, Sun 7pm–midnight; ☎239 841 025), has Internet and email facilities. To get there, head up Rua Laurenco a Azevedo from Praça da República and take the first left.

Markets The main food market is on Rua Nicolau Rui Fernandes, above the post office. On Saturday mornings, there's an open-air antiques market in Praça do Comércio.

Police Main HQ at Rua Nicolau Rui Fernandes, across from the post office (☎239 822 022).

Post office The main post office is at Av. Fernão de Magalhães 223, near Largo do Arnado (Mon–Fri 8.30am–6.30pm, Sat 9am–12.30pm); other central offices are on Rua Nicolau Rui Fernandes, across from the market, and on Praça da República (both same hours as main post office).

Swimming pool The Piscina Municipal (summer only 10am–1pm & 2–7pm) is at the Estádo Municipal São José sports complex, east of the centre: take bus #5 from Largo da Portagem.

Telephones The easiest way to make international calls is to buy a phone card (see p.41) and use a pay phone in the street. Otherwise you can call from the main post office or the branch across from the market.

Train information Coimbra A (☎239 834 998); Coimbra B (☎239 833 525).

Travel agencies Abreu, Rua da Sota 2 (☎239 827 011), and Intervisa, Av. Fernão de Magalhães 11 (☎239 823 873), both sell international bus and flight tickets. Or try Viagens Mondego, Rua João de Ruão 16 (☎239 822 025).

Conímbriga

The ancient city of **CONÍMBRIGA** (daily: March 16–Sept 30 10am–1pm & 2–6pm; rest of year 8am–1pm & 2–5pm; 400$00), 16km southwest of Coimbra, is by far the most important Roman site in Portugal. It was almost certainly preceded by a substantial Celto-Iberian settlement, dating back to the Iron Age, but the excavated buildings nearly all belong to the latter days of the Roman Empire, from the second to the fourth century AD. Throughout this period Conímbriga was a major stopping point on the road from Olisipo (Lisbon) to Bracara Augusta (Braga). Although by no means the largest town in Roman Portugal, it has survived better than any other – principally because its inhabitants abandoned Conímbriga, apparently for the comparative safety of Coimbra, and never resettled it. That the city came to a violent end is clear from the powerful wall thrown up right through its heart; a wall thrown up so hurriedly and determinedly that it even cut houses in two.

The site

It is the **wall**, with the **Roman road** leading up to and through it, that first strikes you. Little else, indeed, remains above ground level. In the urgency of its construction anything that came to hand was used and a close inspection of the wall reveals pillars, inscribed plaques and bricks thrown in among the rough stonework. Most of what has been excavated is in the immediate environs of the wall; the bulk of the city, still only part-excavated, lies in the ground beyond it.

What you can see is impressive enough, though. **Houses** with excellent mosaic floors (now covered to protect them from the elements), **pools** whose original fountains and water-ducts have been restored to working order, and a complex series of **baths** with their elaborate under-floor heating systems, have been revealed. In one part of the grounds, two skeletons lie partly exposed beneath the dust covering a Visigothic burial site. Beyond the wall, less work has been undertaken, but here, too, are evocative remains, particularly of the **aqueduct**, which fed the city with water, and the **forum**, with its shop entrances, and nearby **temple**. At the edge of the site, on a bluff above the steep valley below – for many years Conímbriga's main defence – the **public baths** (no set hours; free) enjoy a stupendous view.

There are some explanatory notes in English posted across the site, but to make sense of it all, it's worth investing in the official guidebook sold at the entrance. In the summer you may find students on site to explain the finer points.

The museum

The Conímbriga entrance fee (hang onto your ticket) includes entry to the excellent **Museo Monográfico de Conímbriga** (closed Mon), opposite the site entrance. On display are fascinating finds from the dig, presented thematically in cabinets detailing various trades (glass-making, ironmongery, weaving, even house-building) and aspects of daily life: in the section on health and hygiene, scalpels and needles wink wickedly in the light, while nearby is a lovely collection of carved jade rings. The other side of the museum shows how the finds relate to the site itself, by means of photographs and diagrams. Here, too, are displayed the larger spoils – statues of torsos, carved lintels, gargoyles from temples, monochromatic mosaics, remarkably bright mural fragments, and slabs, pillars and tombstones from the necropolis. The only drawback to this fascinating museum is that there's no English-language labelling whatsoever. Make sure you end up with a visit round the back, to the **café** with terrific views from its terrace down into the valley.

Practicalities

There are two **buses** direct to the site in the morning (9.05am & 9.35am) from the AVIC bus station in Coimbra (see p.181), returning from the site at 12.55pm and 5.55pm. At weekends, only the 9.05am (outward) and 12.55pm (return) buses operate. Alternatively, take one of the half-hourly buses (reduced service Sat & Sun) from the AVIC station to the small market town of **CONDEIXA-A-NOVA**, half an hour's walk north of Conímbriga. The bus drops you by the church at the edge of the main square, with the market directly opposite. It's a pleasant little place, with several cafés and bars around the square – try *O Joaquim*, next to the Banco Pinto & Sotto Mayor, a local diner with decent budget meals. For something more upmarket there's the restaurant in the elegant *Pousada de Santa Cristina* (☎239 941 286; ⑦).Condeixa is also the centre of the Beira's **hand-painted ceramics** industry and eight local factories are open for visits – you'll pass a couple on the walk out along the main road to the site.

Montemor-o-Velho

Thirty-two kilometres west of Coimbra, the **castle** (10am–12.30pm & 2–5pm; closed Mon; free) at **MONTEMOR-O-VELHO** broods over the flood plain of the Mondego. From the train, or driving along the N111, to Figueira da Foz (see p.203), its keep and crenellated silhouette rival that of Óbidos, as does its early history. First the Romans, then the Moors, fortified this conspicuous rocky bluff; finally taken from the Moors at the end of the eleventh century, it became a favoured royal residence. It was here in 1355 that Dom Afonso IV met with his council to decide on the fate of Inês de Castro, and here, thirty years later, that João of Avis received the homage of the townspeople on his way to Coimbra to be acclaimed king Dom João I.

Despite this royal attention, the town itself never prospered, and today there's little enough to see inside the castle walls either, though the views from the walkways, naturally enough, are stunning. The main attraction within the walls is the Manueline **Igreja de Santa Maria de Alcáçova**, said to have been designed by Diogo de Boitaca of Belém fame; it has a beautiful wooden ceiling, fine twisted columns and Moorish-style *azulejo* decoration.

If you can, aim to visit on the second or fourth Wednesday of the month, when Montemor's vast **market** spills across the plain in the lee of the castle. Families swarm in from the surrounding countryside, some still by donkey and cart, though most by car and scooter, which soon clog up the congested central streets.

Practicalities

The **train station** is a long, long walk from town and castle; **buses** from Coimbra drop you much more centrally. There's no particular reason to stay, given the proximity of Coimbra or indeed Figueira da Foz, just 13km further west. That said, the *Residencial Abade João*, Rua Combatentes da Grande Guerra 15 (☎239 689 458; ③), a beautiful, converted period town house, may persuade you to stop; it's just up the street to the left as you face the large, pink town hall in the central Praça da República. The **turismo**, on the first floor of the town hall (Mon–Fri 9am–12.30pm & 2–5.30pm; ☎239 689 114), could doubtless drum up more reasons to hang around, though there's no better excuse than a **meal** at the *Restaurante Ramalhão*, Rua Tenente Valadim 24 (closed Sun evening, Mon, and Oct), where all the dishes – eel stew, chicken with rice, duck or rabbit – use ingredients grown, reared or caught around the town. You'll get away with spending 2000–3000$00 depending on your appetite.

Lousã and the Serra da Lousã

Another popular day-trip from Coimbra is to **LOUSÃ**, 25km to the southeast, with its attractive ruined castle and surrounding Serra countryside. You can get there by train (Coimbra Parque station) or by bus (Mon–Fri). There are two train stations at Lousã: get off at the first, **Lousã A**. From here, take the road at right angles to the rail line and walk uphill to the centre. To reach the castle, you'll need to continue on past the church until you see a sign for "C.P. Prado", which you follow until reaching the *Café Lousanese* – at the fork here, it's left for the castle ("Castelo e Ermidas"), right for *A Cave* restaurant (see p.194).

The village

Development in the last few years has transformed Lousã from a diminutive village into the sprawling town of today, though the compact and attractive old centre remains fairly unchanged. Wandering around the older streets, you pass a succession of intricately decorated **chapels** and **casas brasonadas** (heraldic mansions), while in the handsome town hall, a little museum doubles as the **turismo** (daily 9am–12.30pm & 2–5.30pm; ☎239 990 370). Customarily helpful, this can supply you with a sketch map of the Serra da Lousã, vital if you want to explore the range, and useful, too, for the walk up to the castle.

Follow the path up from the village through the pine trees, and you pass springs midway, bubbling beautifully clear water that locals drive up to collect. After around 2km (30min), you emerge at a spot where a tributary of the Mondego curls around a narrow gorge between two splendid wooded hills. On one sits a miniature **castle**, whose stone keep provides views across the valley; on the other is a small hermitage dedicated to **Nossa Senhora da Piedade**. Pilgrims mingle with picnickers and the swimmers who come to bathe in the chilly river pool between the two. The *Burgos* **restaurant** (Easter–Sept only, closed Mon; ☎ & fax 239 991 162) has a lovely setting, with a dining room overlooking the river.

Practicalities

The village has two central **pensões**, both pleasant and moderately priced: the *Residencial Martinho*, Rua Forças Armadas (☎ & fax 239 991 397; ②), whose rooms all have bathrooms; and *Pensão Bem Estar* at Av. Coelho da Gama 11 (☎239 991 445, fax 239 993 915; ②), where the back dining room serves typical country dishes at reasonable prices – all rooms come with TV and telephone, though only some have bathrooms. There is also a **campsite** (☎239 991 052, fax 239 772 307; officially open March–Oct, ring to check at other times), ten minutes' east of the centre and signposted from the town hall.

Apart from *Burgos* by the castle, the best **eating** options are *Casa Velha*, a good, smart restaurant in the modern plaza behind the market, or the unlikely-looking *A Cave*, a modern building set among new housing fifteen minutes' walk from the centre in Barrio do Penedo, on the way to the local paper factory. It has a basement dining room dishing up huge portions of local cooking – the *leitão* (suckling pig) is excellent, though there's also lamb, *chanfana* and even *coq au vin*. During your stay, try the shockingly alcoholic **Licor Beirão** – herb-flavoured "firewater" – which is made locally from a secret recipe developed by a pharmacist from Lousã.

Upriver: Penacova and Lorvão

Northeast of Coimbra, the hilly, wooded valley of the **Rio Mondego** is a delight. The river is trailed by the minor N110 road, along which run regular buses from Coimbra, while for six months of the year it's possible to rent a **kayak** to travel downriver from Penacova to Coimbra. You must book in advance to do this; all the details are given below.

The drive is lovely, the **N110 road** keeping high above the river for the most part, affording the occasional sweeping view of glistening water and improbably perched hamlets. At Penacova, the road forks and drivers can make the most of the scenic surroundings by heading up the equally attractive **N235 to Luso** (see p.199). The **IP3**, meanwhile, sticks initially with the Mondego and forges on for Viseu, via Tondela (p.200), a roller coaster of a main road with some very fast sections and more fine views.

A HIKE AROUND THE SERRA DA LOUSÃ'S ABANDONED VILLAGES

This hike in the **Serra da Lousã** provides marvellous views and a sequence of eerie sights in the range's abandoned mountain villages, deserted in the 1950s as a result of rural emigration. It's quite an unsettling experience to wander through the empty streets and into the open rooms. In the first village you come to, Casal Novo, a few of the houses are being renovated as holiday homes and it's possible that you may be able to stay the night; check first with the turismo in Lousã. Beyond Casal Novo, at Talasnal, more houses are available to rent.

Intermittently marked with blue and yellow paint blazes, this three-hour, 8km circular hike begins at Lousã's ruined castle and climbs steeply through the woods to some of the villages. The 1:25,000 map (no.252) available from the IGeoE in Lisbon, or from Porto Editora in Porto (see p.277), covers this walk, but it's a bit out of date and you may also find the map handed out at Lousã's turismo helpful.

From the *Burgos* restaurant near the pools below the castle, walk up the stone steps to the end of the picnic area, and take steep, rocky path marked by paint blazes. After one kilometre, take the right-hand path at a junction; here, the landscape becomes barren, charred by regular forest fires. After 700m or so along the path, turn left at a dirt forestry track and continue uphill. The track changes from dirt to gravel as you reach a T-junction with another gravel track; ignore the latter and go straight ahead up a narrower rocky path until you reach **Casal Novo**. Turn right at the top of the village, then immediately left onto a dirt track. Take the left-hand turn at a dusty road 1km later to arrive at **Chiqueiro**. The village is still inhabited by shepherds and farmers and there's a drinking fountain here.

Leave the village on a stony track clearly marked with paint blazes, then turn right on joining a broad track which quickly peters out. Head steeply downhill to join the dusty road visible below, turn right on reaching it, and another kilometre brings you into **Talasnal**, probably the most beautiful of the range's villages with a harmonious mix of ruined and restored cottages amidst stunning mountain views. Continue through the village along an old stony path, and turn left when you join a track at the bottom of the village. Head over an old stone bridge and follow this good, easily navigable path all the way back to the river pools, keeping an eye out for occasional burnt-out logs blocking the path and the dizzy drop to your right. A well-earned dip in the pools below the castle make a refreshing end to the walk.

Penacova

PENACOVA, 22km northeast of Coimbra, is a small town of some antiquity set high above the river, with stunning views of the valley – spoiled only by the sweep of the motorway which cuts through on the opposite hillside. There is little enough to the place itself – a pint-sized square, a couple of cafés and restaurants, and the surrounding river and woods – though an oddity is the highly elaborate **toothpicks** (*palitos*) on sale. These are hand-carved from willow by local women and are beautiful artefacts; the more delicate ones are like feathered darts. You can inspect these – and buy them, too, if you wish – at the **turismo** (Mon–Fri 9am–5pm, Sat & Sun 10am–1pm & 2–5pm; ☎239 470 300) in the town hall in the main square.

If you fancy a night in these quiet surroundings, there are three **places to stay**: 100m uphill, past the town hall and turismo, is *Casa de Repouso* (☎239 477 137; ③), a lovely old house with a beautiful garden and the best views in town. Otherwise, try the friendly, traditional *Pensão Avenida*, Av. Abel Rodrigues da Costa (☎239 477 142; ②), on a bluff as you drive up into town, with a polished wood interior, sun-terrace and restaurant; or the newer *Residencial São João* (☎239 477 545; ③), a modern building across the road from the *Avenida*. For meals, the *O Panorâmico* **restaurant** – next to the town

A WALK AROUND PENACOVA

This leisurely 11km, three-hour stroll starts near the campsites on the outskirts of Penacova and threads through farmland, woodland and hamlets that remain peaceful and tourist-free even in July and August. You might want to take along a copy of the IGeoE 1:25,000 map (no. 231) available from the IGeoE in Lisbon (see p.23), or from Porto Editora in Porto (see p.277).

From the campsite to the right of the bridge in Penacova, turn left to walk down a tarmac road, turning right after 100m onto another paved but usually car-free road that follows a river valley to the tiny village of **Sanguinho**, 2km away. At the village, turn right to follow the cobbled road uphill, then left at the last house along a good, uphill forestry track that affords excellent views of Penacova and the Mondego valley. Two kilometres along, there's a pronounced fork in the track; turn right here. Take a right turn at a T-junction 100m later, and right again 50m further on. After heading downhill for 400m, you arrive at the hamlet of **Cume do Soito**; on joining a T-junction with a tarmac road, turn right, then immediately right again down a stony track. After 300m, this meets another paved road where you turn right. Another 300m and the road bends sharply to the left; take the right-hand forestry track 50m after this bend. Once the forestry track becomes paved and turns another left-hand bend, take the forestry track which strikes off to the right and you'll arrive back at the top of Sanguinho after a 1km walk through forest. The woodland here has been devastated in parts by indiscriminate logging, and monotonous swathes of pine and eucalyptus alternate with bare patches of badly eroded land.

Leave Sanguinho along the same road, but instead of following the road back to the campsite, turn left 150m after the village along a dirt track which follows the bottom of the valley, narrowing and eventually crossing over the stream via a small concrete bridge. An intricate network of tiny fields awash with sunflowers during the summer, the valley is also dotted year-round with bizarre scarecrows. Keep a lookout for birds of prey circling the fields for prey. The path emerges at the village of **Carvoeira** – a tiny, beautifully-preserved collection of narrow cobbled streets and stone archways with a bar and a small grocery shop. At the other end of Carvoeira, you'll reach a main road; turn right here and it's a 200m walk back to the campsite.

hall and turismo – has a glorious view down the valley; full meals cost around 2500–3300$00. The adjacent *Café Turismo*, behind the turismo at the back of the square, has a terrace with the same views and yet more carved toothpicks on display.

There's a municipal **campsite** 3km away at Vila Nova (☎239 477 946), where you can fish in the river. To get there, turn left after you cross the bridge below town; if you turn right instead of left after the bridge, you'll find a second campsite (☎239 477 464; closed Jan). From here, O Pioneiro do Mondego arranges downriver **kayak trips** to Coimbra (April to mid-Oct daily; 2500$00 per person), leaving Penacova at 11am. It's a 25km (3–4hr) trip back to Coimbra. You'll need to book in advance (English-speaking: call ☎239 478 385, 1–3pm & 8–10pm), and if you've reserved there's a free minibus from Coimbra at 10am to get you to Penacova in time for departure; more information is available from the turismo in Coimbra. O Pioneiro also rent out canoes and bicycles for the day (3000$00).

Lorvão

A side-trip from Penacova, or Coimbra, could also be made to the **Convento de Lorvão**, at the village of **LORVÃO**, accessible up a side road off the N110. By public transport, the best you can do is to take the RBL bus to Rebordosa, 3km before Penacova, and then walk the remaining 5km to the convent. This very ancient complex was founded by Benedictines in the ninth century, predating the arrival of the Arabs, and later taken over by Cistercian nuns. The abbesses are buried horizontally in the graveyard; the lesser sisters are buried vertically, in twos and threes.

Most of what remains of the convent is the product of heavy restoration in the eighteenth century. If you ring for admission, you can visit the **church**, which displays the skull of an Arab king in its treasury, and with luck climb up to the *zimbório*, or domed roof, with its splendid views over the village. The visit, however, is a disturbing one, as the convent still serves as a distressingly old-fashioned mental institution.

The Buçaco Forest and Luso

The **Buçaco Forest** is something of a Portuguese icon. The country's most famous and most revered woods were a monastic domain throughout the Middle Ages, and the site in the Peninsular War of a battle that saw Napoleon's first significant defeat. Today, they are a little uncared for and overvisited, but remain an enjoyable spot for rambling.

Benedictine monks established a hermitage in the midst of Buçaco Forest as early as the sixth century, and the area remained in religious hands right up to the dissolution of the monasteries in 1834. The forest's great fame and beauty, though, came with the **Carmelite monks** who settled here in the seventeenth century, building the walls which still mark its boundary.

In 1643 Pope Urban VIII issued a papal bull threatening anyone who damaged the trees with excommunication; an earlier decree had already protected the monks' virtue by banning women from entering. The monks, meanwhile, were propagating the forest, introducing varieties new to Portugal from all over the world. Nowadays there are estimated to be more than seven hundred different types of tree, but the most impressive remain some of the earliest – particularly the mighty Mexican cedars.

From Coimbra it is easy enough to visit the forest as a day-trip, or en route to Viseu. Entry is free during the winter (walls enclose the area and access is via a number of gates), but you pay 500$00 if you want to go in by car between May and September. All non-express buses from Coimbra to Viseu take a short detour from the spa town of **Luso** (40min from Coimbra), through the forest, stopping at the old royal forest lodge, now the swanky **Hotel Palace do Buçaco**, and again by the **Portas da Rainha**. Alternatively, if you have money to burn, you could stay overnight in the *Hotel Palace* itself (☎231 930 101, fax 231 930 509; ⑦), which was built on the site of the old Carmelite monastery as a summer retreat for the Portuguese monarchy. However, as it was completed only in 1907, three years before the declaration of the Republic, it saw little royal use. An enormous imitation Manueline construction, it charges upwards of 20,000$00 for a double room in low season and around 30,000$00 in high season, but anyone can stroll in and have a drink (their wine cellar is superb) or a meal. You can also view what remains of the **Mosteiro dos Carmelítas** (Mon–Thurs 10am–12.30pm & 2–5.30pm; 100$00), and admire the Afonso Mucha prints or the sequence of *azulejos* depicting the Portuguese conquest of Ceuta and the Battle of Buçaco (see below). If your budget won't stretch to the *Hotel Palace*, you can find less expensive accommodation in Luso itself (see p.199).

The Battle of Buçaco and the Museu Militar

The **Battle of Buçaco** (1810) was fought largely on the ridge just above the forest, and it marked the first serious reverse suffered by Napoleon in his campaigns on the Peninsula. The French under Massena launched a frontal assault up the hill on virtually impregnable Anglo-Portuguese positions, sustaining massive losses in what for the Duke of Wellington amounted to little more than a delaying tactic, which he exploited in order to give himself time to retreat to his lines at Torres Vedras. A small **Museu Militar** (Tues–Sun 10am–5pm; 200$00), outside the forest near the Portas da Rainha, contains maps, uniforms and weapons from the campaign. Just above it, a narrow road climbs to the **obelisk** raised as a memorial to the battle, with vistas inland right across to the distant Serra da Estrêla, from where the **Portas de Sula** leads back into the forest.

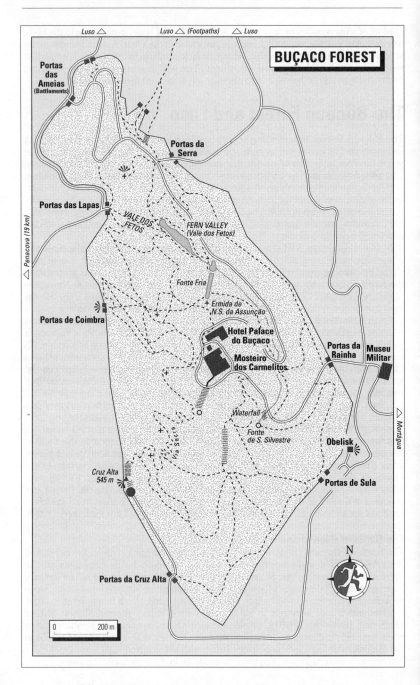

BUÇACO FOREST

Luso △   Luso △ (Footpaths)   △ Luso

Portas das Ameias (Battlements)

Portas da Serra

Portas das Lapas

△ Penacova (19 km)

VALE DOS FETOS

FERN VALLEY (Vale dos Fetos)

Fonte Fria

Ermida de N.S. da Assunção

Portas de Coimbra

Hotel Palace do Buçaco

Mosteiro dos Carmelitos

Portas da Rainha

Museu Militar

△ Mortágua

Waterfall

Fonte de S. Silvestre

Obelisk

Via Secca

Cruz Alta 545 m

Portas de Sula

Portas da Cruz Alta

N

0   200 m

Walks around the forest

Walks are laid out everywhere in Buçaco: along the **Vale dos Fetos** (Valley of Ferns) to the lake and cascading **Fonte Fria**, for example, or up Avenida dos Cedros to the **Portas de Coimbra**. But you can wander freely anywhere in the forest, and in many ways it's at its most attractive where it's wildest, away from the formal pathways.

The **Via Sacra**, lined with seventeenth-century chapels in which terracotta figures depict the stages of Christ's journey carrying the cross to Calvary, leads from the *Hotel Palace* to the **Cruz Alta**, a giant cross at the summit of the hill. From here, as from the Portas de Coimbra, there are magnificent panoramas of the surrounding country. It's a lovely place, if not always the haven of peace the monks strove to create – at weekends and holidays the woods are packed with picnicking Portuguese.

Luso

LUSO lies just 3km downhill from the forest. A spa town for the past hundred years or so, it still draws crowds of Portuguese, taking the waters as a cure for rheumatism and other complaints. As such places go, it's pretty enjoyable, with a series of elegant spa buildings, a wonderful nineteenth-century *salão do chá* – all white wicker, potted palms and Art Nouveau decor – and a casino along the main street.

Taking the waters can be fun, too. Massages, hydrotherapies and other treatments cost from 1100$00 to 2400$00 a go; the only serious expenditure is incurred if you see one of the spa's consultants. There's also a fine, Olympic-sized **swimming pool**, attached to the central *Grande Hotel das Termas* (see below), whose somewhat stiff admission fee (Mon–Fri 1000$00; Sat & Sun 1500$00) is more than recompensed by a few hours' basking. Most locals, though, are here to picnic in the surroundings, taking the opportunity to fill bottles and plastic containers for free with spa water from the outdoor **Fonte de São João** (which also has its own *casa do chá*).

PRACTICALITIES

There are regular **buses** to Luso from the bus station in Coimbra, which is much the easiest way to arrive; the bus drops passengers at the bottom of the central avenida. By **train** (on the Coimbra–Guarda line), there are currently two morning departures suitable for a day-trip – the 8.17am and 10.39am from Coimbra B – the single train back to town returns at 6.18pm (6.27pm in winter). Trains stop on the northern outskirts of Luso – walk down past the *Cesteiro* restaurant and into the centre along Rua Dr. António Granjo.

The **turismo** (summer: daily 10am–1pm & 2–8pm; winter Mon–Fri 10am-12.30pm & 2.30–6, Sat 10am–1pm, closed Sun; ☎231 939 133) is just up from the bus stop on Avenida Emídio Navarro, near the post office, and can help you find a **room** or provide a list of local accommodation.

The best of the budget **places to stay** is the friendly *Pensão Luso* (☎231 939 207; ②) on Rua Dr. Costa Simões above the town centre – from the bus stop, walk up and head right along Rua Dr. Francisco Diniz. Alternatively, there's the *Pensão Portugal*, Rua Marinha Pimenta (☎231 939 158; ②), quite a climb from the town centre – on the way to the turismo, turn left off Av. Emídio Navarro along Rua Alvaro Castelões; it's fairly unprepossessing but undeniably value for money. More expensive but still good-value are: *Pensão Astória*, Av. Emídio Navarro (☎231 939 182; ③), which has a certain faded charm and is located beyond the turismo, almost opposite the *Grande Hotel*; and *Pensão Alegre*, also on the avenida (☎231 930 256; ③), up past the *Hotel Eden*, an impressive building full of nineteenth-century style which was once the residence of the Conde Graciosa. Top-of-the-range is, of course, the *Grande Hotel das Termas de Luso*, Rua dos Banhos (closed Nov & Dec; ☎231 930 450, fax 231 930 350; ⑤), with its unmissable yellow exterior. Inside, it's splendidly furnished with a heated indoor pool. There's also a **campsite** about 2km out of town on the way to the football ground (☎231 930 916).

Most of the *pensões* and hotels have **restaurants** attached, one of the best being that of the *Pensão Central* on Avenida Emídio Navarro (between the *Eden* and the *Alegre*), which has a rooftop terrace. The restaurant at the *Pensão Luso* is good, too, while at the plain and popular *Cesteiro* on Rua Lúcio Pais Abranches, on the way out towards the train station, you can eat well for around 2500$00. *O Caracol*, Rua Dr Francisco A Dimiz 33 (the street behind the turismo), serves good cheap Portuguese food in the usual huge quantities.

The Dão Valley and the Serra do Caramulo

The route northeast from Coimbra to Caramulo leads through the **valley of the Rio Dão**, heart of the region where **Dão wines** – some of the country's finest and richest reds – are produced. Where they're not covered with vineyards, the slopes are thickly wooded with pine and eucalyptus trees, though all too often there are bare tracts where forest fires have raged. It's a fine ride and though there's no overwhelming point of interest en route, you might stop for coffee at least in the small market town of **SANTA COMBA DÃO**, a little over 50km from Coimbra.

Beyond here, the views from the main IP3 are of the spectacular **Serra do Caramulo**, breaking to the northwest. Tondela (see below) marks the eastern turn-off point for the mountains, accessed along the minor **N230** which winds tortuously through a succession of tiny villages at the heart of the mountain range, before descending to Águeda, from where the fast main road runs due south to Coimbra. With your own transport, you could describe the circle from Coimbra, seeing Luso and Buçaco Forest on the way. By **bus**, the same circuit is possible, though it's a much more complex affair and one which will entail a night in the mountains, at the pretty village of Caramulo – no great hardship.

The Serra do Caramulo

Most of the Serra villages are little more than hamlets, of interest principally for their environs, full of rhododendrons, brightly coloured azaleas and thick green shrubs growing wild on the hillside. If you feel like staying off the beaten track, places like **Cambarinho** and **Alcofra** have **rooms** to rent, but perhaps the best base is the main village, Caramulo, a twisting 19km from Tondela and the highway. Coming **from Coimbra**, there are three daily buses to Caramulo, via Águeda. **From Luso**, you need first to take the Viseu bus as far as **TONDELA**, where you should be able to pick up one of the two daily buses on to Caramulo/Águeda, a majestic if rather bumpy drive straight across the centre of the Serra do Caramulo. If you're detained by choice or necessity in Tondela, the *Pensão Ferrador* (☎232 822 559; ②), in the main square, is excellent value, as is the *Residencial Tondela de Severino Gonçalves* (☎232 822 411; ③), also in the main square. For **eating**, there's a good restaurant, *O Solar*, opposite.

An alternative approach to Caramulo, from the north, is **from Vouzela** (see below) in the Vouga valley. On weekdays, one bus a day runs between Vouzela and Caramulo. If you are approaching from the south, Vouzela is an obvious next destination after Caramulo.

Caramulo

Tucked beneath the peaks of the high Beiras Serra, **CARAMULO** is a great walking base – the loftiest Serra de Caramulo peak, **Caramulinho** at 1075m, is less than an hour's hike away. It's also a very striking village, a diminutive, rather ghostlike place, which makes an almost surreal setting for a couple of very fine museums.

At the **Museu do Caramulo** (daily 10am–1pm & 2–6pm; 600$00), the principal display is the **Museu de Arte**, a wonderfully jumbled art collection, with everything from primitive religious sculpture to sketches by the greatest modern masters – minor works by Picasso and Dalí among them. There's an exquisite series of sixteenth-century Tournai tapestries depicting the earliest Portuguese explorers in India, full of weird animals and natives based on obviously very garbled reports. A painting by British portraitist Graham Sutherland, donated to Portugal by the Queen, and symbolizing the long alliance with Britain, is accompanied by its letter of authenticity from Buckingham Palace. Elsewhere there's a large *John the Baptist*, painted by Grão Vasco, and quantities of beautiful furniture and jewellery. Next door, and even more incongruous, is the **Museu do Automóvel**, a collection of vintage cars and motorcycles, including a pack of chrome-plated American dream machines.

The **turismo** (☎232 861 437) is on the Tondela road, past the post office. Of **accommodation** choices, Caramulo has a fine *pensão*, the *São Cristovão* (☎232 861 394; ②) – call first to check it's open as it closes over winter. With more money to spend, first choice is the excellent *Quality Hotel*, Av. Dr. Abel Lacerda (☎232 860 100, fax 232 861 200; ⑥), with superb amenities (including Internet access, jacuzzi and hydrotherapy facilities on site), and unbeatable views over the plains towards the Serra da Estrela. You can also book mountain activities such as canyoning, canoeing and mountain-biking through Desafios Caramulo (☎232 860 155), which is based in the *Quality Hotel*. The six-bedroom **pousada**, *São Jerónimo* (☎232 861 291, fax 232 861 640; ⑥), a kilometre along the Tondela road, pales in comparison but is cheaper than most in the chain and has a swimming pool and great views. The *Café-Restaurante Marte*, on the main road through the village, has affordable **meals**; just up the hill, locals while away the hours under the trees at the *Café Avenida*.

Along the Rio Vouga

The **Rio Vouga** is one of the most beautiful, somnolent rivers in the country and a fine route to follow if you feel like taking in a little of backwater Portugal. The old Vouga train line along the river has been replaced by a bus service which stops at various rural spots en route. You probably won't want to get off until **Vouzela** (see below), though drivers will feel compelled to pause now and again to take in the views. Coming from Coimbra or Aveiro, you can get a train as far as **Albergaria-a-Velha**, where you change to a CP bus. Alternatively, you can approach from the south, from Caramulo, or from Viseu, to the east, from where the minor N337 makes a particularly memorable approach.

Vouzela

VOUZELA is one of the most immediately attractive of Beira towns, a small place with an almost palpable sense of civic pride. The locals boast of the peculiar sweet cakes, or *pasteis de Vouzela* (only for the most sweet-toothed), richly flavoured traditional dishes such as *vitela de Lafões*, and the heady local *vinho Lafões* (similar to *vinho verde*). Vouzela also has its own local paper, which is quite a feat for a town with little over two thousand inhabitants.

The old centre is built around a sluggish stream, bordered by lilies and overhung with weeping willows, which serves as the backdrop to the main morning activity – washing clothes. Beneath a low **Romanesque bridge**, garments are spread to dry on the tall grass and soap suds run blue in the clear water. Houses clustered around the bridge are all of the small-town manor type, with granite steps and balconies and whitewashed plaster work. Topping this scene, a viaduct gracefully loops its way across the rooftops, while beyond it the Serras of Arada and Caramulo rise up, dark and green, to north and south.

Just off the main through-road, at the top of the lane down to the river, the **turismo** (Tues–Sun 10am–12.30pm & 2–5pm; ☎232 771 515) is housed in a former prison in the Largo Morais de Carvalho. On the floor above, there's a **museum** (free) offering insights into local preoccupations such as weaving, photography and painting. It contains a small, rather odd collection, ranging through anthropological and historical exhibits, traditional craftwork and Romanesque fragments, to an array of old dolls. Nearby, up in Praça da República, is the thirteenth-century **parish church** and the town **Pelourinho**, popularly referred to as the *forca* or scaffold, from its days as a site of executions during the Inquisition.

There's a **feira** on May 14 when flowers are strewn in the streets in honour of **São Frei Gil**, and everyone drives up into the hills to witness the blossoming of the rare *loendros*, a type of rhododendron peculiar to this area and which is now protected by law. Otherwise, note that there's a **street market** every first Wednesday in the month, a good time to be in town.

Practicalities

Buses drop you right in the centre, with the town square and **turismo** down the main road and off to the left. Finding a **room** shouldn't be much of a problem, either at *Casa Ferreira*, Rua Barão da Costeiro (☎232 771 650; ②), just off the main road, a little way up from the turismo, or at the *Pensão Marquês*, Rua Aires de Gouveia 76 (☎232 772 029; ②), which is signposted up a side street one minute from the turismo. *Casa de Fataunços* (☎232 772 697; ⑤), 3km from Vouzela in the village of the same name, is a beautifully restored manor house with lovely rooms, gardens and a pool.

The *Pensão Marquês* has a good **restaurant**, popular with local families. Otherwise, try the *Restaurante Chafariz* or *Restaurante Paulo*, both on Rua Mousinho de Albuquerque, off Praça da República.

There is a municipal **campsite** with fine views (☎232 771 847, fax 232 771 513), 4km up the road towards Mortágua and **Senhora do Castelo**, a low hill which is the location for much merrymaking and picnicking on the first Sunday after August 5. There's a signpost pointing the way from Praça da República.

Termas de São Pedro do Sul

Four kilometres northeast of Vouzela is the thermal resort area of **TERMAS DE SÃO PEDRO DO SUL**, possibly the oldest spa in Portugal. It was a great favourite with the Romans, a popular haunt of Portuguese royalty – Dom Afonso Henriques is said to have bathed his wounded leg here after the battle at Badajoz – and remains among the grandest and most attractive in the country. Its position beside the Vouga, and the pine trees all around, certainly lend it charm, and the resort makes for a pleasant stop between buses or an afternoon trip from Vouzela. Under the central span of the bridge, a small island teems with swans and ducks, while downstream, fishermen and young boys fool around on and in the water. The **spa** itself is open all year for those who want to sluice themselves in its foul-smelling waters and avail themselves of the usual range of treatments.

You can get here by **bus** from Viseu (Mon–Fri 4–5 daily, weekends 1–2) or Vouzela (Mon–Fri 2 daily); for information on onward bus travel ask at the Quiosque das Termas facing the spa. The **turismo** (Mon–Sat 9am–1pm & 3–6pm, Sun 9am–12.30pm, closed Sun in winter; ☎232 711 320), on Largo dos Correios, by the bridge, has a list of *pensões* and can help with **rooms** in private houses. If you plan to stay, you'd be wise to book ahead since the **hotels** and **pensões** stacked up above the river are frequently full. Among the best options – all easily found – are the modern, family-run *Pensão Romana* (☎232 711 524; ③; closed Dec & Jan), *Pensão Ultramarina* (☎232 723 011; ④), the *Hotel Vouga* (☎232 723 063, fax 232 723 500; ⑤), and the modern *Hotel do Parque* (☎232 723 461, fax 232 723 047; ⑤). In high season, these and the other places may insist on your paying for full board. The resort's brand-new **youth hostel** is situated in a big high-rise overlooking the centre (☎232 724 543, fax 232 724 541); it also has double rooms available (③). There's a **campsite** (☎232 711 793; June–Sept) on the eastern outskirts of town, signposted from the stone bridge.

The town of **SÃO PEDRO DO SUL** itself is another 3km to the northeast, an unremarkable spread of buildings either side of a busy main road, at the confluence of the Sul and Vouga rivers. You can pick up more bus connections here to Viseu and Lamego, if you're unlucky in Termas. For details of the extraordinary driving route between here and **Arouca** to the northwest, see p.214.

Figueira da Foz

FIGUEIRA DA FOZ is one of the liveliest towns on the west coast, a major resort and deep-sea fishing port. Sited at the mouth of the Mondego, roughly equidistant from Lisbon and Porto and just over an hour by train from Coimbra, it attracts people from all over the country to its superb beaches and surf. That said, it's not the most initially alluring of beach resorts: there's a somewhat industrial approach from the south, and the town itself is resolutely modern with its long promenade backed by a line of anonymous apartment blocks. But it's as close to a typical Portuguese resort as you'll find. Most of the action, in fact, takes place away from the sands in the atmospheric backstreets, where a bubbling good humour prevails, even when the town's packed to the gills.

Arrival, information and accommodation

The **train station** is a long 20- to 25-minute walk from the centre and beach. Keep walking along the river until you see the ocean and then cut into the town – a useful beachfront landmark is the concrete clock tower, close to the tourist office. AVIC **buses to Buarcos** – a fishing village at the northern end of the bay, which has become more or less part of Figueira – leave from directly outside the train station (Mon–Sat every 30min until 11pm; hourly on Sun). The **bus station** is slightly closer in, though it's still a fair walk down to São Julião church and the municipal gardens, from where the streets run straight to the beach.

If you need help with anything, the **main turismo** (daily: 9am–12.30pm & 2–5.30pm; July & August 9am–midnight; ☎233 422 610, fax 233 402 828) is in Edifício Atlântico on Avenida 25 de Abril and is even more helpful than most; there's another in Buarcos at Largo Tomás de Aquino (summer daily 9am–8pm; ☎233 422 610), which is served by regular buses along the seafront. If you stay some way out of town, you might want to **rent a bike** from the municipal campsite; it costs around 1500$00 per day; **car rental** can be arranged through Marco, Rua Maestro David de Sousa (☎233 425 113).

Accommodation

It can take time to find a room in Figueira in high season, but with persistence you should be able to get something. In high season, you might well be met at the train station by people offering **private rooms**, which – provided they're reasonably central – will be the best bargains in town. Otherwise, there are a couple of cheap *pensões* just in front of the train station on Rua Fernandes Tomás and Rua da República, but these are a long way from the beach. It's much better to head for the centre, where both **Rua Bernardo Lopes** and **Rua da Liberdade** are lined with possibilities, though many are booked well in advance. You'll also find that **prices** – already comparatively high in Figueira – tend to shoot through the roof in summer, particularly in July and August.

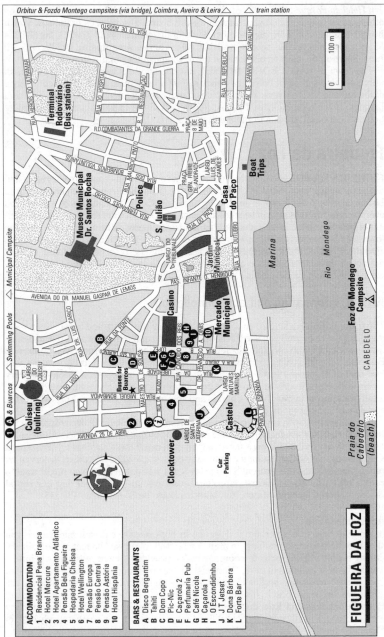

Orbitur & Fozdo Montego campsites (via bridge), Coimbra, Aveiro & Leira △   △ train station

FIGUEIRA DA FOZ

ACCOMMODATION
1 Residencial Pena Branca
2 Hotel Mercure
3 Hotel Apartamento Atlântico
4 Pensão Bela Figueira
5 Hospedaria Chelsea
6 Hotel Wellington
7 Pensão Europa
8 Pensão Central
9 Pensão Astória
10 Hotel Hispânia

BARS & RESTAURANTS
A Disco Bergantim
B Tahiti
C Dom Copo
D Pic-Nic
E Caçarola 2
F Perfumaria Pub
G Café Nicola
H Caçarola 1
I O Escondidinho
J J T Jetset
K Dona Bárbara
L Forte Bar

HOTELS AND PENSÕES

Hotel Apartmento Atlântico, Av. 25 de Abril (☎233 420 245, fax 233 422 420). Very good upmarket option in a modern high-rise with pool. En-suite rooms with all mod cons. Prices are higher on Fri & Sat. ⑥.

Pensão Astória, Rua Bernardo Lopes 45 (☎233 422 256). Not as nice as the *Central*, opposite, but a decent fall-back. It's above a restaurant. ③.

Pensão Bela Figueira, Rua Miguel Bombarda 13 (☎ & fax 233 422 728). Near the main beach and town centre. It can be noisy; many of the unremarkable rooms come with shower and TV. ③.

Pensão Central, Rua Bernardo Lopes 36 (☎233 422 308). Airy *pensão* approached up a flight of side-steps. Rooms have high ceilings and nice old furniture, and a couple share a grand street-facing balcony, though these are noisy. ④.

Hospedaria Chelsea, Rua Miguel Bombarda 8 (☎233 423 244). Good and reasonably priced with a range of rooms, the more expensive ones with bath or shower. ③.

Pensão Europa, Rua Cândido dos Reis 40 (☎233 422 265). Very central, near the casino and above a fish restaurant. Bare, adequate rooms with basin. ④.

Hotel Hispânia, Rua Dr. Francisco António Dinis 61 (☎233 422 164, fax 233 429 664). A rambling old hotel, one of the few right in the centre with private parking. Closed Nov–Feb. ④.

Residencial Pena Branca, Rua 5° de Outubro 42 (☎233 432 665, fax 233 421 892). In Buarcos, near the post office and turismo, and just outside the city wall. Splendid, high-quality set-up with private bathrooms, phone, TV, fridge and balcony; breakfast included. There's a good regional restaurant below. ④.

Hotel Wellington, Rua Dr. Calado 23 (☎233 426 767, fax 233 427 593). Three blocks from the beach, this is a genteel sort of place and less shabby than the exterior suggests, but rooms are rather small and it's overpriced in summer. ⑤.

CAMPSITES

Parque Municipal de Campismo (☎233 402 810). Large and well-equipped, with a swimming pool (though you have to pay to use it) and tennis courts. It's 2km inland – follow the signs from town and beach, or take a taxi from the station.

Foz do Mondego (☎233 402 740; closed mid-Dec to mid-Jan). Across the river mouth, and close to Cabadelo beach, this is by far the cheapest in the area.

Orbitur (☎233 431 492), Mata de Lavos, Gala, 4km to the south, across the estuary. The most expensive – though the ocean is much cleaner for swimming here. Take the AVIC "Cova Gala" bus (every 30min till 10.15pm, fewer at weekends) from the Mercado Municipal. *Carrossel*, at Largo da Beira-Mar near the campsite, serves good food.

The Town and beaches

The town doesn't offer much in the way of sightseeing – the most impressive sights are the beaches – but there are a couple of places to scout around once you tire of the sands. On the edge of the town park, Parque Abadias, the **Museu Municipal Dr. Santos Rocha** (Tues–Sun 9am–12.30pm & 2–5.30pm; free), Rua Calouste Gulbenkian, has an impressive archeological section, as well as a large number of photographs of nineteenth-century bathing belles. Meanwhile, the inside walls of the **Casa do Paço** (Mon–Fri 9.30am–12.30pm & 2–5pm; free), on the waterfront by the marina, are covered with thousands of Delft tiles, part of a ship's cargo which somehow got stranded in Figueira.

Apart from this, you can check out Figueira's central streets which form a tight little grid set back from the eastern end of the beach. Many are pedestrianized, brimming with pavement cafés and strolling holidaymakers, while back along the river, on Rua 5° de Outubro, is the **market** (summer Mon–Sat 7am–7pm; winter Mon–Fri 8am–5pm, Sat 8am–1pm), good for food and just about anything else you might need.

The beaches

Figueira's **town beach** is enormous, not so much in length as in width: it's a good five-minute walk across the sand to the sea and unless you wear shoes or stay on the wooden walkways provided, the soles of your feet will have been burned long before you get there. There are cafés along the whole length of the beach, but since the busy main road and promenade are set well back from the water, there's no great sense of place. Best spot is probably at the **Buarcos** end of the beach, 2km away, where a huddle of pastel-coloured fishermen's houses sit amidst a rash of new concrete high-rises behind what remains of the old defensive wall.

If it's **surfing** you're after, then just step around the promontory at Buarcos, where fans gather to admire the breakers. By contrast, **Cabadelo beach**, behind the mole on the Mondego river mouth's south bank, is small, sheltered and good for families – though to reach it you have to go right out through the town and over the bridge by bus.

The only problem in recent years has been that of pollution; the EU blue flag, denoting water acceptable to swim in, does not always fly over all of Figueira's beaches. If this concerns you, an up-to-date appraisal of the water quality at each of the beaches is posted outside the turismo – tests are carried out weekly in summer and monthly during the winter.

You can always have a dip instead in the fee-paying **swimming pools** on the north side of town: the nearest is Piscina de Santa Catarina, a fifteen-minute walk along Rua Joaquim Sotto Mayor, in a park on the right. Further along, there's another pool in the Ginásio Club next to the municipal stadium.

Eating

The centre of town is packed with **places to eat**, with any number of snack bars, cafés and seafood restaurants offering *ementas turísticas* at reasonable prices.

Aquário, Alto do Forno, Buarcos. One of several good seafood places in Buarcos, with a great *cataplana*, and fado on Fridays.

Bela Figueira, Rua Miguel Bombarda 13. The *pensão*'s restaurant serves fine Indian and Portuguese food. Try the shrimp and rice curry – and eat on the terrace (where prices are slightly higher). Around 2000$00.

Caçarola I, Rua Cândido dos Reis 65. Basement shellfish restaurant with daily specials chalked on the board. To keep costs down, you could just sit at the bar and have a plate of prawns and a beer.

Caçarola II, Rua Bernardo Lopes 85–87. Sister restaurant to *Caçarola I* and just as good, if not better. Open till 4am.

Dory Negro, Largo Caras Direitas 16, Buarcos. On the edge of Buarcos, this is a good place to come for fish, with dishes around the 1600$00 mark. It's hidden out of sight from the sea, but has a little covered patio. Closed Tues in winter.

O Escondidinho, Rua Dr. Francisco António Dinis 62. Hidden away (as the name suggests), this is worth seeking out for superb and inexpensive Goan food. Under 2000$00 if you pick and choose. Closed Mon.

Café Nicola, Rua Bernardo Lopes. At the corner with Rua Cândido dos Reis. A busy, modern, two-tier affair with reasonable snacks.

Pena Branca, Rua 5° de Outubro 42, Buarcos. With windows overlooking the beach at Buarcos, this is the best place for an *arroz de sardinha* and *caldeirada*. Other fish and meat specials, too, and full meals for 2500–3000$00.

Pic-Nic, Rua de São Lourenço, at junction with Rua David de Sousa. Well-priced menu (under 2500$00 for a full meal), with plenty of fish and a lovely roof-terrace to eat it on.

Tahiti, Rua da Fonte 86. Nice little backstreet restaurant, away from the central bustle, with friendly English-speaking staff, great prices and decent food – which extends to English breakfasts and fish and chips for the criminally unadventurous.

Nightlife, entertainment and events

Nightlife centres on the **casino** at Rua Bernardo Lopes 1 (3pm–3am; take your passport for entry), for which semi-formal dress and an initial outlay on chips are compulsory. The casino also houses a couple of **cinemas**, which generally have up-to-date releases. In the first couple of weeks of September the casino hosts an **International**

Film Festival – a little uneven in its organization, but always with a good selection of new films shown in their original language; ask at the turismo for more information.

Alternatively, there are several central **pubs** and **bars**, like *Perfumaria*, Rua Dr. Calado 37; *Dom Copo*, Rua São Lourenço 13; *J T Jet Set*, at the south end of Av. 25 de Abril; and *Dona Bárbara*, Rua A. Zagalo, all of which play the same kind of rock and pop until around 4am. However, for sheer location, *Forte Bar*, set in the castle's crumbling ramparts, is hard to match. Of the **discos**, *Disco Bergantim*, Rua Dr. Lopes Guimarães 28, is a long-standing favourite. If you have transport you could make a late-night trip out to *Flashen*, hidden in pine trees outside the village of Quiaios, 8km north of Figueira. Discos do not get going till around midnight, but they don't close till 4am and all-nighters are not unheard of in summer.

One of the best of the year's parties is **Saint John's Eve** (June 23 and 24) with bonfires on the beach and a "Holy Bathe" in the sea at dawn; while **bullfights** are often held during the summer season.

North of Figueira: to Praia de Mira

The coastline immediately **north of Figueira** is remarkable only for its air of total desertion. Beyond Buarcos, there's very little, and for long stretches hardly even a road. Off the main north–south road (N109) you can get to the coast at just three points before Aveiro: at **Quiaios, Tocha** and **Mira**, each with their respective beaches, all of them flying EU blue flags declaring them clean enough to swim in. If you're driving **on to Aveiro** (see p.208), stick with the minor coastal route beyond Praia de Mira, a pleasant run through farmland with dunes to one side and river to the other; this way, you'll pass through probably the nicest of this coast's small resorts, **Costa Nova** (see p.211).

Praia de Quiaios and Praia da Tocha

With a car you can find virtually empty beaches around either **QUIAIOS** or **TOCHA**, though the low-lying coastal plain offers no protection against the Atlantic winds. For more sheltered leisure pursuits, aim for the inland lakes between the two beaches, particularly the large, pine-fringed **Lagoa da Vela**, where there are scores of picnic areas, and windsurfing and sailing schools.

Buses run every hour or so from Figueira bus station up the N109, stopping at both Praia de Quiaios (25min) and Praia da Tocha (40min). There isn't any accommodation once you get to either beach other than the excellent **campsites**, *Praia de Quiaios* (☎233 910 499; June–Sept), which has its own swimming pool, and *Praia da Tocha* (☎231 441 143; mid-June to Sept).

Praia de Mira

Set on a small lagoon – the southernmost point of a system of waterways and canals centered around Aveiro – **PRAIA DE MIRA** is the focus of increasing development. Seven kilometres west of the inland town of Mira, it is rather more accessible than the beaches at Quiaios or Tocha, with half a dozen buses a day from either Figueira, Coimbra, or Aveiro. There's a lot more accommodation, too, the downside being that you may not want to stay. You couldn't exactly describe Praia de Mira as a beautiful place – its one extremely long main street, Avenida Cidade de Coimbra, spears towards the sea, lined by new apartments and dusty building sites. But the beach that stretches around it is seemingly endless and backed by dunes: ideal if your aims extend no further than beach-lounging and walks.

Many places offer cheap, basic *dormidas* along the main street – look out for the signs, or ask in any bar. The **turismo**, in the boathouse-like building beside the lagoon (☎231 472 566) may be able to help with rooms, but is itself often closed out of season.

Pensões aren't cheap and if you're going to stay in one, it might as well be one with a sea view from its balconies: immediately on the left at the end of the main street, the modern *Arco Íris* on Av. do Mar (☎234 471 202; ③) is a decent spot; a few hundred metres further along the seafront is the similarly pleasant but more expensive *Residencial do Mar* (☎ & fax 231 471 144; ④).

There are two official **campsites** a short way from the village – the municipal site (☎231 472 173; May–Sept) is closer and considerably cheaper, though less well-equipped, than the Orbitur site (☎231 471 234, fax 231 472 047; closed Dec and Jan), for which you go up the main street, turn left at the seafront and continue for a kilometre. Directly opposite the Orbitur site is a **youth hostel** with its own campsite (☎ & fax 231 471 275; hostel open all year; campsite June–Sept). The *A Cozinha* **restaurant**, one of several on Avenida Barrinha – the road backing the lagoon – has windows overlooking the water and, among other dishes, serves a buttery grilled squid and tasty *porco à alentejana*.

Aveiro and around

Most visitors to **AVEIRO** are intent on getting straight out again, to the series of excellent **beaches** to north and south and into what a tourist brochure describes as the "virile, iodine-bearing sea". However, Aveiro itself is also a place of some antiquity and interest. It was a thriving port throughout the Middle Ages, up until the 1570s, when the mouth of the Vouga silted up, closing its harbour and creating vast, fever-ridden marshes. Recovery began only in 1808 when a canal was cut through to the sea, reopening the port and draining much of the water; only the shallow lagoons you see today were left. These form the backbone of a modern economy based on vast **saltpans**, fishing, and the collection of seaweed (*molico*) for fertilizer. The occasional pungent odour wafting across town, seemingly from the lagoon, is actually from the large paper factory nearby.

The town's big annual event is the **Festa da Ria**, celebrated in the last two weeks of August with boat races, folk dances, and competitions for the best decorated *barcos moliceiro*, the flat-bottomed lagoon boats used to collect seaweed. The other major celebration is the **Festa de São Gonçalinho**, held in honour of the patron saint of fishermen and single women in the second week of January. Those who have made vows during the year, either for the safe return of a fisherman or for the finding of a husband, climb to the top of a chapel and throw down loaves of bread to the crowd below; the aim is to catch as much as possible.

The Town

Aveiro casts off its rather dowdy first appearances as soon as you reach the central praça and bridge over the main canal. The traditional industries here are celebrated by imposing statues of the local workers on the bridge – the *marnoto* and the *salineira*, the latter with her salt tray. Handsome, pastel-coloured houses (of which the turismo is one) line Rua João Mendonça, and in the narrow little streets behind the **fish market** tiled houses face each other across arms of the canal. Lagoon boats with raised prows lie tied up along the quaysides.

True, there's only one sight of real note, the fifteenth-century **Convento de Jesus**, across the central canal and five minutes' walk up on the right. This now houses the **town museum** (Tues–Sat 10am–5.30pm, Sun 10am–2pm; 250$00, free on Sun), whose finest exhibits all relate to Santa Joana, a daughter of Afonso V who lived in the convent from 1475 until her death in 1489. She was barred from becoming a nun because of her royal station and her father's opposition, and was later beatified for her determination to escape from the material world (or perhaps simply from an unwelcome arranged

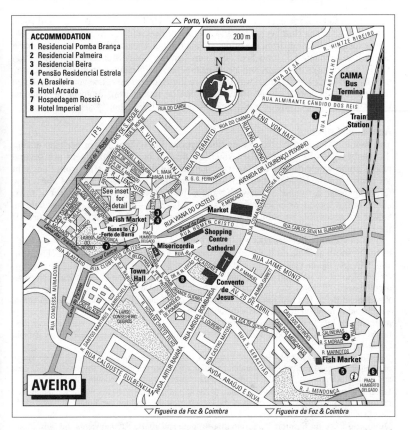

△ Porto, Viseu & Guarda

ACCOMMODATION
1 Residencial Pomba Branca
2 Residencial Palmeira
3 Residencial Beira
4 Pensão Residencial Estrela
5 A Brasileira
6 Hotel Arcada
7 Hospedagem Rossió
8 Hotel Imperial

0   200 m

N

CAIMA
Bus
Terminal

Train
Station

See inset
for
detail

Fish Market

Buses to ⓘ
Porto de Barra

Market

Shopping
Centre

Misericordia

Cathedral

Town
Hall

Convento
de
Jesus

Fish Market

AVEIRO

▽ Figueira da Foz & Coimbra   ▽ Figueira da Foz & Coimbra

marriage). Her tomb and chapel are strikingly beautiful, as is the convent itself, and there's a fine collection of art and sculpture – notably a series of naive seventeenth-century paintings depicting the saint's life.

Once you've seen this you may as well cross the road to the **cathedral**, whose exterior concrete loggia and interior breeze-block walls make it resemble a municipal swimming pool. Infinitely more pleasing is the **Misericórdia** church, back down towards the canal, whose seventeenth-century facade features blue snowflake-design tiles. The **town hall**, a century older, stands opposite, both buildings facing a declamatory **statue** of Aveiro's famous son, the nineteenth-century politician José Estevão Coelho de Magalhães.

Beyond these few attractions, the main local interest is in the surrounding beaches and lagoons, for which see p.211. There's a certain fascination, too, in hanging around in the **cafés**, watching life on the Ria: try some of the celebrated local sweets, especially *ovos moles*, candied egg yolks.

Practicalities

Aveiro is on the main Lisbon–Porto rail line, with the **train station** at the northeastern end of town; most **buses** (including services to and from Praia de Mira) use the train station forecourt and adjacent streets as their terminus. From the station, walk straight down the broad main street in front of you – Avenida Dr. Lourenço Peixinho – and you'll eventually hit Praça Humberto Delgado and the bridge, a fifteen-minute walk.

The **turismo** is just up from the bridge on the right in a beautiful Art Nouveau building at Rua João Mendonça 8 (June–Sept daily 9am–8pm; Oct–May Mon–Sat 9am–7pm; ☎234 420 760). It supplies free maps and local bus timetables and can help with finding accommodation. **Bicycles** are an ideal way to explore the lagoon area – once you've negotiated the first few kilometres of fast road – and can be rented from Agência de Viagens Culturália, near to the turismo at Rua João Mendonça 31, 1st Floor (☎234 423 142).

Accommodation

You shouldn't have much trouble finding a **room in Aveiro**, except perhaps during the Festa da Ria in August, when you'd be wise to book ahead. There are several places immediately down from the train station, but they're a little far from things; in the centre, try the backstreets around the fish market, particularly Rua das Marnotos, for inexpensive *dormidas*. Those with transport have the option of staying out of town at one of the lagoon- or beach-resorts (see pp.211–213) – although the beaches themselves are accessible by public transport, the nicer places to stay tend to be more off the beaten track.

The local **campsites** are also way out of town, at São Jacinto to the north (see p.212), or to the south at Praia da Barra, Costa Nova and Praia da Vagueira (see pp.211–212).

Hotel Arcada, Rua de Viana do Castelo 4 (☎234 423 001, fax 234 421 886). Small, unexciting rooms, though pleasant enough staff and a central location in a grand building by the bridge with views over the canal. All rooms with either shower or bath, breakfast and TV. ④.

Residencial Beira, Rua José Estevão 18 (☎234 424 297). Clean, welcoming place just off the praça, with breakfast included. It's often full – call ahead. ③.

A Brasileira, Rua Tenente Resende 47 (☎234 428 634). One of a handful of *dormidas* places near the fish market, this is a good bet for solo travellers, with small, clean rooms charged per person. English spoken. ②.

Pensão Residencial Estrela, Rua José Estevão 4 (☎234 423 818). An old, converted house whose plant-filled staircase and polished wooden corridor are rather grander than the smallish, but cool and comfortable, rooms. Friendly, English-speaking owners, and big discounts out of season. ④.

Hotel Imperial, Rua Dr. Nascimento Leitão (☎234 422 141, fax 234 424 148). Modern building, not far from the Convento, with fine views of the lagoon from the top-floor bar; breakfast included. At the top of its price range. ⑤.

Quinta do Paço da Ermida, 3km from Ilhavo, south and off the N109 to Vagos and Mira (☎234 322 496). A short distance from one of the lagoon arms, this magnificent Solares de Portugal manor house (with just four rooms) belongs to the family of the founder of the Vista Alegre porcelain company – one of the oldest in Europe. ⑥.

Residencial Palmeira, Rua da Palmeira 7–11 (☎234 422 521). Pretty, modern, tiled town house with attached dining room, in the old quarter between the praça and the Canal de São Roque. Bright rooms, some with shower or bath, and most with TV. ④.

Residencial Pomba Branca (also known as *Paloma Branca*), Rua Luís Gomes de Carvalho 23 (☎234 381 992, fax 234 381 844). Very comfortable rooms (with bath and TV) in a gracious, quiet town house, near the station and with its own parking. There are traditional features throughout, including a wood-panelled bar. ⑤.

Hospedagem Rossío, Rua Dr. Barbosa de Magalhães 24 (☎234 429 857). Good central location off the canalside park, and about as cheap as you'll find, though the fairly spartan rooms are as gloomy as the proprietor; separate bathrooms. ②.

Eating

There are some excellent restaurants in Aveiro, with **local specialities** including eels and shellfish from the lagoons and powerful Bairrada wine. The cheapest eats are in the little *casas de pasto* in the old town streets around the fish market, though there are also several regular restaurants in this area, too.

Alexandre, Cais do Alboi 14, near Largo Conselheiro Queirós. A short walk along the canal, this is a well-regarded snack bar and adjacent restaurant with good meals for around 2000$00. Closed July.

Neptuno, Rua Mendes Leite 1. Decent little grill house serving large portions of chicken, home-made sausage, chops or fish. Around 1200$00 for a *dose*. Closed Sun.

Salpoente, Canal São Roque 83. Ten minutes' walk north along the canal, this superior fish restaurant is set inside a renovated salt barn. Crabs, fish and eels at medium-to-high prices, served Mon–Sat noon–2.30pm & 7.30–10.30pm.

Sonatura, Rua Clube dos Galitos 6. Vegetarian wholefood self-service restaurant serving daily specials of varying size – the food isn't particularly good, but at least it offers veggies a change from omelette and chips. Mon–Fri 8am–7pm, Sat 9am–4.30pm, closed Sun.

O Telheiro, Largo da Praça do Peixe 20–21. Excellent *adega* with wooden benches and tiled tables, and food cooked any way you like as long as it's chargrilled. *Lulas grelhados* (grilled squid) is superb; add a fish soup, wine and coffee and you'll pay around 2500$00. Closed Sat.

O Terraço, Edifício 15, Av. Dr. Lourenco Peixnho, 7th Floor. Mediocre food but stunning views over the Aveiro and the Ria; get the lift to the sixth floor and walk the last flight.

Zé da Parreirinha, Trav. do Lavadouro 10. Rough-and-ready *casa de pasto* with full meals for under 1000$00. Just off Largo do Praça da Peixe. Closed Wed.

Zico, Rua José Estevão 52. Very popular local spot, with most dishes around 1400$00. Menu changes daily, but there are always grills, local fish and good wine. Closed Sun.

Drinking

Estrondo, Canal São Roque 73. Polynesian-style bar on the canal and just down from *Salpoente*, open till 2–3am for cocktails and drinks. Closed Mon.

Cervejaria Rossio, Largo da Rossio 8a. Central *cervejaria* serving beer and good steak sandwiches until 2am. Closed Mon.

Salpoente, Canal São Roque 83. The restaurant has an enjoyable late-opening bar with occasional live music (500$00 admission) at weekends. Open till 2am. Closed Sun.

Around Aveiro: the lagoon and beaches

There's no beach in Aveiro itself but the coast to north and south is a more or less continuous line of sand, cut off from the mainland for much of the way by the meandering **lagoon**. Although developers have long caught on, the whole sand bar is still little spoilt, and offers ample opportunity for beach lounging as well as fascinating walks along the lagoon's swampy edge, which boasts abundant birdlife. Note that the pine forests shelter several military bases, so stick to the roads and don't camp outside official sites.

From May to September, Turaveiro (☎ & fax 234 331 285), on Rua João Mendonça in front of the turismo, organizes two-hour **boat trips** by *moliceiro* along the lagoon (2000$00).There are also trips to Torreira (July & Aug only; 2400$00 return). At any time of year a group of people can rent a boat to tour the river; again, information is available from the turismo.

Praia da Barra and Costa Nova

The most easily accessible coastal points from Aveiro are **PRAIA DA BARRA**, at the mouth of the Vouga, and **COSTA NOVA**, a little further on; but be warned that both are enormously crowded on summer weekends. Local **buses** from Aveiro (hourly 8am–8pm) depart from outside the train station, also stopping on Rua Clube dos Galitos, across the bridge from the turismo and about 150m down the canal on the right. They call at Barra first, then Costa Nova.

Praia da Barra, though less charming than Costa Nova, has a greater choice of **accommodation**, as well as more restaurants and nightclubs, but prices in all three can be steep. The pick of the cheaper accommodation options is: *Residencial Farol* (☎234 390 600; ④), situated above a cool and pleasant café and billiards room at the end of the main road and overlooked by Portugal's tallest lighthouse; *Residencial Marisqueira*, Av. João Corte Real (☎234 369 262; ③); and the *Hotel Barra*, Av. Fernandes Lavrador 18 (☎234 369 156, fax 234 360 007; ⑤), which has a pool. There's also a municipal **campsite** (☎234 369 425; June–Sept). For **nightlife**, head for *EDP*, Rua Vasco da Gama 66 (closed Sun), popular with the locals in summer. It's about 9km east towards Aveiro.

Costa Nova is a highly attractive ensemble of candy-stripe wooden buildings, stuffed into the strip between beach and lagoon. There are two places **to stay**: the excellent *Residencial Azevedo*, Rua Arrais Ançã 16 (☎234 390 170, fax 234 390 171; ④), and the huge **campsite** 1km to the south (☎234 369 822, fax 234 360 008), complete with supermarket and disco.

Vagueira

Around 15km south of Aveiro but still accessible by bus, **VAGUEIRA** faces the lagoon, though it is actually situated on the mainland, just 1km from the ocean beaches. The summer **turismo**, on Largo Parracho Branco at the north end of the beach where the bus drops you, can help with **rooms**. Alternatively, there are bungalows for rent, 1500m to the south on the Mira road (☎234 797 732 or 234 797 754; ④) next to the entertaining Vaga Splash aqua park. There's also an excellent **campsite** here (☎234 797 618, fax 234 797 093) where you can rent bikes.

São Jacinto

If you want more than just a beach, then you need to head **north of Aveiro**, though the transport connections are a little more complex. Take the bus from Rua Clube dos Galitos to **Forte de Barra** (8–10 daily), a four-kilometre run through the saltpans and docks, from where a connecting boat (135$00; no cars) chugs the fifteen minutes across the lagoon to **SÃO JACINTO**. Unlike its neighbours along the coast, São Jacinto is not really a resort at all, but rather a thriving little port with a handful of dockside café-restaurants. With a military base at one end and a forest of cranes cluttering the skyline, it's not beautiful, but there is an enormous – and undeveloped – dune-fringed **beach** twenty minutes' walk away: off the boat, walk to the right past the post office and, at *Restaurant Ferraz* (the best place to eat), turn left. The beach is straight up the improbably long road ahead, where you'll also find the *Restaurante Marluci*, which has a few **rooms**, some with kitchens (☎234 331 074; ①, with kitchen ②). If your budget is a little higher, try the *Pousada da Ria*, Bico do Muranzel (☎234 838 332, fax 234 838 333; ⑥), a mid-priced *pousada* with swimming pool, tennis courts and lagoon-view balconies. There's a municipal campsite (☎234 331 220) 2.5km out on the Torreira road and a substantial Orbitur **campsite** (☎234 838 284, fax 234 838 122; Feb–Nov) with good facilities a further 2.5km on.

São Jacinto backs onto an extensive **bird reserve**, where you can join a five-kilometre (two-hour) guided tour (summer: Mon–Wed, Fri & Sat 9am & 2pm; winter hours erratic; 200$00), though this may depend on numbers; for more information and for times of tours in winter, contact the reserve office (daily 9am–noon & 1.30–5pm, closed Thurs & Sun; ☎234 331 282). It's 1km out of town, along the main road to Torreira: turn left at the post office, walk up to the main road and head right. Adjacent to the reserve office is a small scrap of beach overlooked by the *Portelas* bar-restaurant.

Torreira

In summer, buses run the 13km north from São Jacinto to **TORREIRA**, a lively little resort with several small *pensões*. The best hotel is the four-star *Estalagem Riabela*, at the north end of town (☎234 838 137, fax 234 838 147; ⑤); if you can't quite stretch to that, there's the slightly cheaper *Residencial Albertina*, Trav. Arraias Faustino (☎234 838 306, fax 234 838 206; ④), a popular, modern hotel by the beach with air-conditioned rooms and a bar. You can rent bikes here, too.

For **eating**, the restaurant *Casa Passoiera*, on the main road, is highly recommended. The *Copacabana* piano-bar in the *Estalagrem Riabela* also has a decent grill-restaurant and live music. The buses at this point loop back round to Aveiro; to head onwards to Furadouro (see below), you have to make a detour through Ovar.

Ovar, Furadouro and Santa Maria da Feira

The distinctive Ria countryside comes to an end around Ovar, 25km to the north of Aveiro, and there's no great reason to delay the drive or train ride straight to Porto. But Ovar itself is worth at least a coffee break, while the beach to the west at Furadouro is as good as anything that's gone before. Further inland, Santa Maria da Feira boasts a splendid castle and a good interactive science park.

Ovar and Furadouro

OVAR is on the main train line to Porto. If you're lucky, there'll be a bus waiting to take you into the centre of Ovar; failing that, it's a fifteen-minute walk. There are direct buses, too, from São Jacinto and Torreira.

An attractive market town, Ovar is 5km away from a fine beach at Furadouro, to which there's a regular bus. The **turismo** (daily: July–Sept 9am–9pm; Oct–June 9.30am–12.30pm & 2.30–5.30pm; ☎256 572 215) is off the main square, on Rua Dr. Manuel Arala. In the square itself you'll find the surprisingly good **Museu Etnográfica** (daily 10am–noon & 2–6pm; free), with an international collection of pottery, plus traditional clothing and the usual folklore displays. Perhaps more compellingly, while you're here try some of the local *pão-de-ló* sponge cake – every bit as good as it looks. The nicest **accommodation** in town is provided by the modern *Hotel Meia-Lua*, Quinta das Luzes (☎256 575 031, fax 256 575 232; ⑤), and the large, four-star *Albergaria São Cristóvão*, at Rua Aquilino Ribeiro 1 (☎256 575 105, fax 256 575 232; ⑥). At the budget end of the scale, the flash new **youth hostel** (☎ & fax 256 591 832) is about 2km out of town on Av. Dom Manuel I (the N327 "ring-road" around Ovar: to get on it, head towards Furadouro and turn right at the roundabout).

The rather unglamourous resort of **FURADOURO** marks pretty much the northern extent of the system of waterways, and like its neighbours to the south boasts a long stretch of pine-backed dunes. There may be a few **rooms** available at the basic *Pensão Avenida* (☎256 591 435; ①) above the *Café Amadeu* on the waterfront at the end of the pedestrianized Avenida Central, and there's a signposted **campsite** (☎256 596 010, fax 256 596 011), too.

Santa Maria da Feira

At **SANTA MARIA DA FEIRA** (or, more simply, Feira), easily reached by bus from Aveiro or Espinho (see p.279), one of the most spectacular castles in Portugal – the **Castelo da Feira** (daily: summer 9am–noon & 2–6pm; reduced hours in winter; 250$00) – towers above the town, its skyline a fanciful array of domes. A sunken gateway leads into the castle's interior, which has been rather zealously over-restored but provides a handsome indication of its erstwhile grandeur. Its principal room is the **Great Hall**, a magnificent Moorish structure, while, beyond the keep, a tunnel links the two parts of the castle in such a way that no direct or easy access can ever have been offered to intruders – arrow slits and hidden entrances emphasize the point. In some of the walls you may notice a few stones marked with Roman inscriptions, and you can make out the familiar straight Roman road through the wooded hills above. It's a fifteen-minute climb up the hill to the castle; outside, a little café dispenses drinks and sandwiches.

On the way down from the castle, you pass the grand **Convento de Loios** (now a conference centre), at the back of which you'll find an incredibly tacky cement grotto and garden of fake bridges and pebble-lined paths. Feira's newest attraction, the Europarque **Visionarium** (Mon–Fri 9am–6pm, Sat & Sun 10am–8pm; ☎256 370 609; 1300$00, discounted family tickets) is Portugal's largest science museum, located 3km out of town in the opposite direction to the castle. The enjoyable, impressive interactive displays (in both Portuguese and English) cover subjects ranging from the Portuguese voyages of discovery to the insides of microchips.

The best time to visit Feira is undoubtedly during the annual **Festa das Fogaceiras** (Jan 20), when files of little girls parade through the town carrying castle-shaped *fogaça* cakes. It's a custom – much revived in recent years – which dates back to the plague of 1750 when the Infante Pedro made a *vota* to Santa Maria that cakes in the shape of his castle would be baked in thanksgiving for those who survived.

Practicalities

If you want **to stay**, try *Residencial Tony*, Rua Jornal Correio da Feira 22 (☎256 372 593; ②), five minutes' walk from the bus station, which offers clean rooms with toilet and shower. With more money to spend, the best option is the outstanding *Casa das Ribas* (☎ & fax 256 373 485; ④), a lovely eighteenth-century manor house with gorgeous gardens, right next to the castle. Decent and inexpensive **meals** are to be had at the *Restaurante Churrasqueira Parque* and *Salvianos*, both on the street at the bottom of the road up to the castle, where there are several other little cafés, too.

Arouca and the Serra da Arada

Picking up the N224, it's a splendid drive from Feira to **Arouca**, 20km to the east, a winding route through forested hills and small terraced slopes of tumbling vineyards, the air heady with the scent of pine resin. There are regular buses from Feira, and although there are no public transport links south from Arouca, through the magnificent **Serra da Arada** (see below), buses do run on north to Porto.

Arouca

AROUCA is a small town entirely overshadowed by the vast **Convento da Arouca** (Tues–Sun 9.30am–noon & 2–5pm; 250$00), whose imposing walls loom across the busy main road that cuts through town. It was founded as early as 1091, though most surviving parts are from rather later medieval times. In the kitchen there are huge fireplaces along Alcobaça lines; the vast Baroque church (which you can see without buying a ticket; enter from the main road) holds richly carved choir stalls and a great organ with 1352 notes, played on rare occasions by one of the country's few experts; while off the central courtyard there's an airy Sala Capítula, where the abbesses once held court, lined with *azulejos*.

The convent peaked in importance when Queen Mafalda, of whose dowry it had formed a part, found her marriage to Dom Henriques I of Castile annulled and retired here to a life of religious contemplation. In the extensive **museum** upstairs, you can see some of Mafalda's most prized treasures, including an exquisite thirteenth-century silver diptych, along with a series of paintings by Josefa de Óbidos (see p.145) and Diogo Teixeira. In 1792, four centuries after Mafalda's death, villagers claimed to have witnessed her saving the convent from the ravages of a terrible fire. She was promptly exhumed and beatified.

The rest of town struggles to make a mark in the face of its prize exhibit, but it's a handsome little place away from the main road. The central square holds a couple of cafés with pavement seats, while in the medieval backstreets there are some beautiful old houses decked with wisteria. Stay for the night if you can: Arouca is at its quietest and best during the somnolent evenings or in the early morning when shrouded in rising mist from the surrounding hills.

Local heart rates increase slightly during the annual **Festa de Nossa Senhora da Mó**, when the whole town turns out for a picnic on the crown of the hill 8km east of the town. **Holy Week** processions are a big deal here, too, starting on the Wednesday and culminating on the Saturday night, when most of the inhabitants parade behind the local saints' statues to the Misericórdia church, with candles lit in all the town's windows.

Practicalities

Until the new bus station is completed, **buses** (from Porto and Feira) are stopping on Rua do A. Malafia. Opposite the entrance to the convent is the little main square, Praça Brandão de Vasconcelas, with the **turismo** (summer: daily 9.30am–1pm & 2–5pm; winter: same hours, closed Mon; ☎256 943 575).

There are two **places to stay** in town: *O Tranca*, Rua Alexandre Herculano (☎256 943 916, fax 256 943 054; ②), a little further up the road from the square and on the right, has simple, modern rooms above a restaurant; otherwise, keep right on to the top of the main road and take the left fork (there's a "*residencial*" sign) to the *Residencial São Pedro*, Av. Reinaldo de Noronha (☎256 944 580, fax 256 943 054; ④), five minutes' from the square. This has very smart rooms with bath, the front ones with balconies overlooking town and convent. For a more rustic setting, the *Quinta do Bóco* (☎256 944 169; ④) is a lovely old farmhouse with a pool; turn left at the town hall at the end of the main street.

For a **meal**, *O Tranco* serves marvellous and mountainous *churrasqueiria* dishes; the *Restaurante Parlamento*, Travessa da Ribeira 2 is a smarter and pricier option. There are a couple of *casas de pasto* around town, too, while *Residencial São Pedro* has a good restaurant.

The Serra da Arada

If you have your own transport, consult the turismo in Arouca for information on places to visit in the nearby **Serra da Arada**, whose beautiful countryside is terraced like the Minho and abundantly littered with dolmens, crumbling villages and waterfalls with ancient bridges. Whitewater rafting, mountain-biking and other mountain activities are on offer in the Serra – you'll need to contact the Arouca turismo in advance to arrange these activities.

Perhaps the most extraordinary route over the peaks is the drive **south**, heading for São Pedro do Sul and Vouzela (see p.202). Initially, you need to follow the minor road out of Arouca which climbs to the radio mast on the heights of **São Pedro Velho** (1100m), from where views of the valley are tremendous. Then head for Albergaria das Cabras, from where São Pedro do Sul is signposted. The route can be hard to find but you can get a map from the Arouca turismo. On the way, tiny hamlets cling to the hillside, vines grow on precipitous terraces, while the road snakes first through pine forest and then high across the heather-dotted moorland.

At **MANHOUCE**, a mean, medieval hamlet, the road disappears altogether for an instant and degenerates into cart-rutted cobbles worn by centuries of use. If you want to stay and enjoy the pine forests and rocky uplands of the Serra, the beautifully-restored *Quinta das Uchas* (☎232 700 800, fax 232 700 807; ⑤) about 1km from the village on the right, is the perfect base. They can supply information or organize trips around the Serra and also rent mountain bikes. Just before Manhouce, the attractive one-horse settlement of **ALBERGARIA DAS CABRAS**, with its **campsite** (☎256 947 723) and restaurant, makes another good base for exploring the Serra. Beyond Albergaria or Manhouce, there's another 12km of incredible bends and views before emerging onto the N227 – a 43-kilometre journey that takes ninety minutes to negotiate. It's a spectacular drive but be prepared to take evasive action along the whole route, against other drivers or, occasionally, against wandering cattle.

There is – incredibly – a bus service along this route, though it's geared towards market and school times and consequently isn't conducive to day-trips or connections to anywhere reasonable. However, if you fancied extensive **hiking** and camping in the forests, you could just strike out from any of these places, providing you were properly equipped: there are endless paths and tracks connecting all the hamlets along the way.

travel details

Trains

Aveiro to: Coimbra (at least hourly; 45min–1hr); Espinho (Mon–Fri 14 daily; 35–50min); Lisbon (13 daily; 2hr 40min–4hr 50min); Ovar (every 30min; 25–40min); Porto (every 30min; 50min–1hr 30min).

Coimbra to: Aveiro (at least hourly; 45min–1hr); Figueira da Foz (hourly; 1hr–1hr 20min); Guarda (8 daily; 3hr–3hr 20min); Lisbon (17 daily; 2hr–3hr 20min); Lousã (Mon–Fri 18 daily, Sat 12, Sun 8; 50min); Luso-Buçaco (5 daily; 45min); Ovar (hourly; 50min–1hr 30min); Porto (hourly; 1hr 20min–2hr).

Figueira da Foz to: Caldas da Rainha (7 daily; 1hr 25min–2hr 25min); Coimbra (hourly; 1hr–1hr 20min); Leiria (7 daily; 1hr 15min); Torres Vedras (4 daily; 2hr–3hr 25min).

Buses

Arouca to: Porto (Mon–Fri 10 daily, Sat & Sun 2; 1hr 30min); Santa Maria de Feira (Mon–Fri 10 daily, Sat & Sun 2; 40min).

Aveiro to: Arouca (Mon–Fri 6 daily; 2hr 50min); Figueira da Foz (6 daily; 1hr 15min); Ilhavo (8–10 daily; 30min); Lisbon (4–6 daily; 4hr); Porto (Mon–Fri 8 daily; 2hr 45min); Praia da Barra (every 30min; 30min); Praia de Mira (6 daily; 45min); Praia da Tocha (4–6 daily; 50min).

Coimbra to: Braga (6–7 daily; 2hr 40min–3hr); Caramulo (3 daily; 2hr); Condeixa-a-Nova (Mon–Fri 7am–11.30pm every 30min; reduced service weekends; 30min); Covilhã (4 daily; 3hr 25min); Fátima (4 daily; 1hr–1hr 25min); Figueira da Foz (10 daily; 1hr–1hr 45min); Guarda (4 daily;

2hr 40min); Leiria (4 daily; 1hr); Lisbon (16 daily; 2hr 20min); Luso (Mon–Fri 5 daily, Sat & Sun 2 daily; 45min); Mira (6 daily; 1hr); Montemor-o-Velho (3–9 daily; 1hr 10min); Penacova (3–5 daily; 45min); Peso da Régua (2–4 daily; 2hr 30min); Porto (7–10 daily; 1hr 30min–2hr 45min); Santa Maria de Feira (2 daily; 2hr 45min); Tondela (2–4 daily; 1hr 40min); Vila Real (2–4 daily; 3hr 20min); Viseu (2–5 daily; 1hr 20min–2hr 20min).

Figueira da Foz to: Aveiro (5 daily; 1hr 30min); Coimbra (Mon–Fri 10 daily, Sat & Sun 4–6 daily; 1hr–1hr 45min); Leiria (10 daily; 1hr 15min); Lisbon (3 daily; 2hr 45min); Mira (6 daily; 1hr); Montemor-o-Velho (Mon–Fri every 30min, Sat & Sun 4–8 daily; 30min); Tocha (7 daily; 40min).

Luso to: Coimbra (Mon–Fri 5 daily, Sat & Sun 2 daily; 45min); Viseu (Mon–Fri 5 daily, Sat & Sun 2 daily; 1hr 50min).

Penacova to: Coimbra (3–5 daily; 45min).

Praia de Mira to: Aveiro (6 daily; 45min); Coimbra (6 daily; 1hr); Figueira da Foz (6 daily; 1hr).

Santa Maria de Feira to: Arouca (Mon–Fri 10 daily, Sat & Sun 2; 40min); Coimbra (2 daily; 2hr 45min); Porto (every 30min; 35min).

São Pedro do Sul to: Sernada do Vouga (9–10 daily; 1hr 45min) for trains to Aveiro and Espinho; Viseu (9–10 daily; 1hr).

Termas de São Pedro do Sul to: Viseu (Mon–Fri 4–5 daily, Sat & Sun 1–2 daily; 1hr); Vouzela (Mon–Fri 2 daily; 10min).

Vouzela to: Sernada do Vouga (9–10 daily; 1hr 35min) for trains to Aveiro and Espinho; Varzielas (Mon–Fri 2 daily; 30min); Viseu (9–10 daily; 1hr 10min).

CHAPTER FOUR

MOUNTAIN BEIRAS

omposed of two provinces, the **Beira Alta** (Upper) and **Beira Baixa** (Lower), the **Mountain Beiras** region features some of the least explored country in the Iberian peninsula, as well as some of the most spectacular: the enormous boulders which are strewn across much of the region limit agriculture and have instead favoured a pastoral culture of rugged hamlets (*aldeias*). Arguably, it is also the most quintessentially Portuguese part of the country. Little touched by outside influence, it is historically the heart of **ancient Lusitânia**, where Viriatus the Iberian rebel (a symbol of the spirit of independence in Neoclassical literature) made his last stand against the Romans. You'll see many signs of this patriotism in the fine old town of **Viseu**, in Beira Alta, where every other café or hotel is called the *Viriato* or *Lusitânia*. Here, too, in the heights of the wild and beautiful **Parque Natural da Serra da Estrela**, lies the source of the **Rio Mondego**, that most Portuguese of rivers: the only one (bar the insignificant Zêzere) to run right to the sea without having its origins in Spain. The whole region in and around the park is excellent walking country, especially if you strike off from one of the two main routes which cross the range.

Guarda is perhaps the most fascinating of the Beira Alta towns. Though diminutive in size for somewhere of such renown, it has one of the highest locations of any provincial capital in the country and it bristles with life, especially on *feira* days. To the north and east stretch a whole series of high-sited castle-towns and some of the country's most remote villages, of which **Sortelha** is perhaps the outstanding example. Over to the south lies the more sombre plain of the **Beira Baixa** with its capital at **Castelo Branco** and, its most obvious highlight, the ancient hilltop town of **Monsanto**.

The whole Mountain Beiras region is little visited by tourists and travellers: if you've spent some days in the fleshpots of Lisbon, Porto, or the Algarve, you'll find a very different **atmosphere** here – and almost exclusively Portuguese company.

Viseu

From its high plateau, **VISEU** surveys the country around with the air of a feudal overlord; and indeed, this dignified little city is capital of all it can see. It's also a place of great antiquity. There was a Roman town here, and on the northern outskirts you can still make out the remains of an encampment claimed to be the site where Viriatus (Viriato

---

ACCOMMODATION PRICE CODES

All the accommodation prices in this book have been coded using the symbols below. The symbols represent the lowest prices you can expect to pay for a **double room in high season**; for a full explanation, see p.32.

① Under 4000$00   ④ 11,000$00–15,000$00   ⑦ 25,000$00–30,000$00
② 4000$00–7000$00   ⑤ 15,000$00–20,000$00   ⑧ 30,000$00–40,000$00
③ 7000$00–11,000$00   ⑥ 20,000$00–25,000$00   ⑨ Over 40,000$00

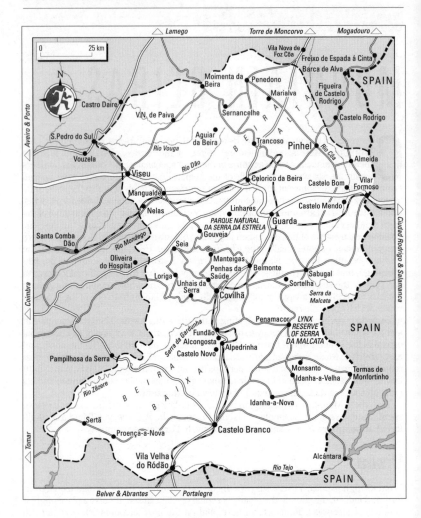

in Portuguese) fought his final battle. In fact, it was almost certainly a Roman fortification and, aside from a statue of Viriatus, there's not much there. The heart of the medieval city has changed little, though it's now approached through the broad avenues of a prosperous provincial centre. Parts of the walls survive and it is within their circuit, breached by two doughty gateways, that almost everything of interest lies.

The liveliest event in Viseu's calendar is the **Feira de São Mateus** which takes place from mid-August until its climax on September 21 (Dia do São Mateus) – it's largely an agricultural show, but is enlivened by occasional bullfights and folk-dance festivals. The showground is at the top end of Avenida Dr. António José de Almeida, beyond the bus station and across the Rio Paiva.

The Old City

A good place to start exploring the town is the old quarter around the **Praça da Sé**. The approach, from the central **Praça da República** (also known as Rossio), up through the Porta do Soar, or along the shop-lined Rua Dr. Luís Ferreira, exhibits a certain amount of pedestrianization and "beautification", but the jumble of alleys immediately behind the cathedral remains virtually untouched. You suddenly come upon sixteenth-century stone mansions proudly displaying their coats-of-arms in the middle of a street of rundown houses.

The cathedral square itself is lined with noble stone buildings, most striking of which is the **Igreja da Misericórdia** with its white Baroque facade. Silhouetted against a deep blue sky it looks like a film set without substance – you expect to walk around the back and find wooden props holding it up. There's some truth to that feeling: behind the symmetry of the facade, it's a very ordinary, rather dull church.

There's nothing two-dimensional, however, about the **Sé** (daily 8am–12.30pm & 2–7pm), a weighty, twin-towered Romanesque base on which a succession of later generations have made their mark. The granite frontage, remodelled in the seventeenth century, is stern and makes the church look smaller than it actually is – inside it opens out into a great hall with intricate vaulting, twisted and knotted to represent ropes. The cathedral's Renaissance **cloister**, of which you get no intimation from outside, is one of the most graceful in the country. The rooms of its upper level look out over the tangled roofs of the oldest part of the town and house the treasures of the cathedral's art collection, including naive sculptures, two thirteenth-century Limoges enamel coffers and a twelfth-century Bible.

Museu de Grão Vasco

The greatest treasure of Viseu is the **Museu de Grão Vasco** (Tues–Sun 9am–12.30pm & 2–5.30pm; 250$00; free Sunday mornings), right next door to the cathedral, in the Paço dos Três Escalões – once the Bishop's palace. **Vasco Fernandes** (known always as Grão Vasco, The Great Vasco) was born in Viseu and became the key figure in a school of painting which flourished here in the first half of the sixteenth century. The style of these "Portuguese primitives" was influenced heavily by Flemish masters and in particular by van Eyck, but certain aspects – the realism of portraiture and richness of colour – are distinctively their own. Vasco and his chief rival Gaspar Vaz have a fair claim to being two of the greatest artists Portugal has produced.

The museum is spread over three floors. The lower floor contains evocative historical paintings of Viseu and other Portuguese localities, while the works of the Viseu School are on the uppermost floor. The centrepiece of the collection is the masterly *Saint Peter on His Throne*, one of Grão Vasco's last works and painted, it is said, to rival Gaspar Vaz's treatment of the same theme for the church at São João de Tarouca (see p.301). It shows considerably more Renaissance influence than some of the earlier paintings but its Flemish roots are still evident, particularly in the intricately – and sometimes bizarrely – detailed background. Other works attributed to Vasco include a *Calvary* and a *Pentecost*, but there's considerable argument over what is actually his. Several pictures are clearly the fruits of collaboration – most obviously many of the fourteen panels of the former cathedral altarpiece. These, now exhibited in a room of their own, depict the life of Christ and some sections are clearly better executed than others – notice *The Adoration of the Magi* in which Balthazar, traditionally an African king, is depicted as an Indian from newly discovered Brazil.

Also worth a visit is the tiny **Museu Almeida Moreira** (Tues–Sun 9am–12.30pm & 2–5.30pm; 100$00) on the edge of the Jardim das Mães. This traditional house displays furniture and pottery from the seventeenth to nineteenth century, and is named after the founder of the Grão Vasco museum.

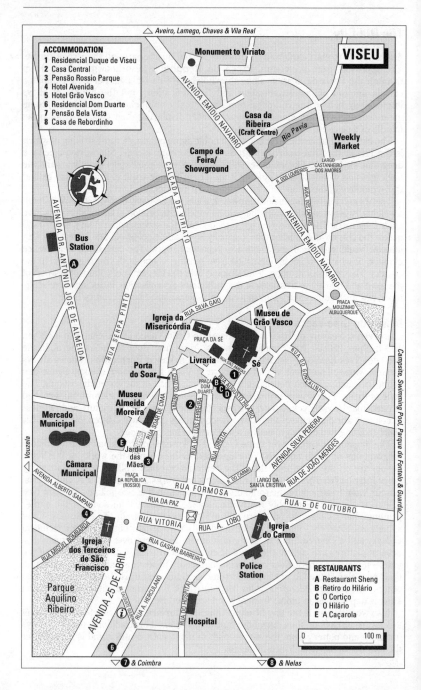

△ *Aveiro, Lamego, Chaves & Vila Real*

VISEU

ACCOMMODATION
1 Residencial Duque de Viseu
2 Casa Central
3 Pensão Rossio Parque
4 Hotel Avenida
5 Hotel Grão Vasco
6 Residencial Dom Duarte
7 Pensão Bela Vista
8 Casa de Rebordinho

Monument to Viriato

Casa da Ribeira (Craft Centre)

Rio Pavia

Weekly Market

Campo da Feira/ Showground

LARGO CASTANHEIRO DOS AMORES

Bus Station

PRAÇA MOUZINHO ALBUQUERQUE

Igreja da Misericórdia

Museu de Grão Vasco

PRAÇA DA SÉ

Livraria

Porta do Soar

Sé

Museu Almeida Moreira

PRAÇA DOM DUARTE

Mercado Municipal

Jardim das Mães

Câmara Municipal

PRAÇA DA REPÚBLICA (ROSSIO)

RUA FORMOSA

LARGO DA SANTA CRISTINA

RUA 5 DE OUTUBRO

RUA DA PAZ

RUA VITORIA

RUA A. LOBO

Igreja do Carmo

Igreja dos Terceiros de São Francisco

RUA GASPAR BARREIROS

Police Station

Parque Aquilino Ribeiro

AVENIDA 25 DE ABRIL

Hospital

RESTAURANTS
A Restaurant Sheng
B Retiro do Hilário
C O Cortiço
D O Hilário
E A Caçarola

0   100 m

△ *Vouzela*

Campsite, Swimming Pool, Parque de Fontelo & Guarda ▷

▽ **7** *& Coimbra*   ▽ **8** *& Nelas*

Practicalities

Viseu is no longer on the rail line, though CP **buses** still operate along the old routes, linking the town with Guarda, Coimbra and Lisbon on the Beira Alta line at Nelas (30min south of Viseu) and with the Coimbra–Aveiro–Porto line at Sernada do Vouga (2hr 45min west of Viseu). Coming from Porto, an alternative approach is to take the Douro train line to Peso da Régua (2hr) and then the bus via Lamego, Castro Daire and Carvalhal (2–3hr). The **bus station** in Viseu is on Avenida Dr. António José de Almeida, a short walk from the centre.

The **turismo** (Mon–Sat 9am–12.30pm & 2.30–6pm, Sun 9am–12.30pm; closed Sat & Sun Jan–March; ☎232 422 014) is situated just south of Rossio on Avenida Calouste Gulbenkian, and can provide maps and information on the Beira Alta region as a whole.

Accommodation

The best places to stay are in the old quarter, but Viseu is short on budget accommodation. Among **hotels and pensões**, pick from the list below. There's a well-equipped *Orbitur* **campsite** (☎232 436 146, fax 232 436 120; closed Dec & Jan) in the Parque do Fontelo, ten minutes' walk east from Rossio, and a municipal swimming pool 500m away, on Avenida José Relvas.

Hotel Avenida, Rua Miguel Bombarda 1 (☎ & fax 232 423 432). A fairly pleasant hotel near the Parque Aquilino Ribeiro, with a few cheaper rooms. ④.

Pensão Bela Vista, Rua Alexandre Herculano 510 (☎232 422 026). Functional *pensão* in a street up from the turismo; has some cheaper rooms without baths. ③.

Casa Central, Rua Dr. Luís Ferreira 65 (☎232 437 205). Basic, but the least expensive option in town, and in a good location. Book ahead. ②.

Casa de Rebordinho, Rebordinho (☎232 461 258). Situated 6km south on the N231 Nelas road, this ANTER property is in a converted seventeenth-century manor house on a farm estate. ⑤.

Residencial Dom Duarte, Rua Alexandre Herculano 214 (☎232 421 980, fax 232 424 825). Pleasant *residencial*; all rooms with bath and TV. ③.

Residencial Duque de Viseu, Rua das Ameias 22 (☎232 421 286). A converted town house right by the cathedral. Somewhat lacking in character and slightly expensive a/c. ③.

Hotel Grão Vasco, Rua Gaspar Barreiros (☎232 423 511, fax 232 426 444). Viseu's finest – a grand central hotel with bar and swimming pool, but overpriced. ⑤.

Pensão Rossio Parque, Praça da República 55 (☎232 422 085). An old hotel that has seen better days but it's in an excellent location. Some rooms are small and cramped; others have no window or shower – prices vary accordingly. ③.

Eating and drinking

Viseu is well known for its gastronomic delights, and wherever you eat, or drink, bear in mind that locally produced **Dão wines**, especially the reds, are some of the best you'll find in the country. For provisions, there's a **weekly market** on Tuesday, on the ring road by Largo Castanheiro dos Amores, and a weekday market in the **Mercado Municipal**, just west of Rossio. Most of Viseu's **nightlife** is to be found in the old town around Rua Augusto Hilário, Rua Dom Duarte and the Sé. The **restaurants** listed below are all very popular locally; you may have to wait for a table.

A Caçarola, Trav. Major Teles 3, just off Rossio. This place serves big and cheap portions of traditional fare and gets packed at lunchtimes.

O Cortiço, Rua Augusto Hilário 45 (☎232 423 853). In the old town near the cathedral, just down from the statue of Dom Duarte, this is popular enough for tables to be at a premium. Food and decor are *típicos*, but the service can be a bit sullen. Around 2500$00 a head.

O Hilário, Rua Augusto Hilário 35. Cheaper than *O Cortiço* and not bad for the money; try the *morcela casiera frita* (fried blood-pudding).

Retiro do Hilário, Rua Augusto Hilário 55 (☎232 426 499). This restaurant claims to be the only venue outside Lisbon to feature live fado every night – the owner is a musician himself. Good Portuguese food in a nice atmosphere.

Rodízio Real, Bairro Santa Eulália (☎232 422 232). Out in the suburbs in Repeses, on the N2 (Coimbra direction). Diners come from far and wide to sample its Brazilian cooking; up to 3500$00.

Restaurante Sheng, Av. Dr. António José de Almeida. A cheap and tasty Chinese option opposite the bus station.

East to Guarda

East of Viseu, the high and austere territory of the **Serra da Estrela** spreads itself as far as the eye can see: a landscape of great jagged boulders and rough, dry grass – often singed in patches by summer fires. The wilderness of the area, as so often in mountain regions, belies its inhabitants, who, though a little abrupt, have none of the suspicion of outsiders often encountered in Portuguese cities and coastal regions.

The fast IP5 highway from Aveiro cuts east through this region, skirting Viseu and running on to **Guarda**. Train travellers first have to backtrack south to Nelas from Viseu in order to follow the **Beira Alta rail line** from Santa Comba Dão to Guarda. By road or rail, the only realistic stop before Guarda is at **Celorico da Beira**, which lies at a nexus of routes, with bus connections to Linhares (p.234), perhaps the most attractive of the *serra* villages.

Celorico da Beira

CELORICO DA BEIRA, 50km east of Viseu, is an unprepossessing town; its one claim to fame is as the birthplace of the aviator Sacadura Cabral. It is certainly not the most attractive *serra* base – a major road and bus interchange for people heading to the *planalto* north of Guarda, the town is also split by heavy traffic along the east–west road from Spain and the north–south route to Lisbon. It does, however, have a pretty enough old town hugging the slopes around the fine castle and, if you're passing through at the right time, it's the best place to pick up a pungent *queijo da serra*, the famed round cheese of the Serra da Estrela district.

The **Castelo** is open intermittently but if it's closed you can get the key from the turismo (see p.223) or the Câmara Municipal. Put your trust in the rickety construction strung up outside the large keep and you can climb to impressive views from the roof. On a clear day the Sé and single tower of the castle at Guarda are both visible, while all around stretches the extraordinary wasteland of the mountains, split only by a small river and a couple of Portuguese highways. The castle has a long military history, forming, together with Trancoso and Guarda, a triangle of defensive fortifications against Spain. In its day, a garrison of three hundred, well equipped with arms and an ample supply of food, were able to hold out with relative ease against border skirmishes. Only on one occasion, in 1198, did they have to call for assistance, which was provided by the stout men of nearby Linhares.

Feiras – held on alternate Fridays for cheese, and on Tuesdays for the ordinary covered market – are the times to catch the town's cheery provinciality. You'll see some of the more rugged mountain types coming in to sell their *queijo da serra*, market-going being the only source of income to support their impoverished hilltop farms. If you miss the cheese market, visit the excellent old cheese shop on the main road through town, just down from the post office. A visit on June 13 will give you the chance to join in the Santo António **festivals** when the whole village enjoys a riverside picnic; ask at the turismo for details of other summer festivals, when locals indulge in the traditional game of climbing a greased pole to try and retrieve a flask of wine and some *bacalhau*.

Practicalities

Celorico's **train station** is 6km north of town at Celorico Gare; bus connections are erratic, so you'll probably need to take a taxi (if you can find one) or walk. If you find yourself walking from the station, look out for the forked rocks near Espinho – 1km west of the road – which were once used to hang criminals, and the megalithic stone necropolis at nearby São Gens. It's more convenient to arrive in Celorico by **bus** as many long-distance services pass through: there are bus stops outside the *Residencial Parque*. The *Café Central* on the town's main road has information about buses. There is a small, helpful **turismo** (Tues–Sat 9.30am–noon & 2–6pm; ☎271 742 109), on the edge of town on the Coimbra road.

If you want to **stay**, the town's best and most central *pensão* is the *Residencial Parque,* Rua Andrade Corvo 48 (☎271 742 197, fax 271 743 798; ③), located slightly south of the centre. There's also a hotel on the road to the turismo, the *Hotel Mira Serra,* Bairro de Santa Eufémia (☎271 742 604, fax 271 741 382; ⑤), with magnificent views from some of the bedrooms. Just beyond the turismo, on the same road, there are rooms above the *Nova Estrela* (☎271 741 241; ①), whose **restaurant** is excellent, as is the nearby *Boa-Hora.* There is a possible freelance **campsite** by the Rio Mondego, near the station. Seven kilometres further upstream, off the Guarda road, there's an official site, *Parque Ponte do Ladrão* (☎271 742 645; open April–Sept), at Lajeosa do Mondego.

Guarda

Twenty-two kilometres southeast of Celerico da Beira, **GUARDA**, at an altitude of over 1000m, is claimed by its inhabitants to be the highest city in Europe – an assertion to be taken with a pinch of salt. It is high enough, though, to be chilly and windswept all year round and to offer endless views, especially to the east into Spain. The city was founded in 1197 by Dom Sancho I, to guard (as the name implies) the borders against both Moors and Spaniards. It was a heftily fortified place and, despite the fact that castle and walls have all but disappeared, it still has something of the grim air of a city permanently on a war footing. Fortunately, nowadays, the presence of a polytechnic injects a fair amount of life into the town. Guarda is known in Portugal as the city of the four Fs: *Fria, Farta, Forte e Feia* – cold, rich, strong and ugly. However, in recent times, the city fathers – unhappy with the last of these – have launched a "five Fs" campaign to replace *Feia* with *Fiel* (loyal) and *Formosa* (beautiful). Oversensitive perhaps, though it is true to say that the centre of Guarda, with its arcaded streets and little *praças*, can be distinctly picturesque.

Numerous **festivals** take place in the Guarda area. The biggest events are the great **feiras** (June 24 and October 4), extended markets full of life and character. The **Festas da Cidade** (held during the summer months on different dates each year) are cultural affairs with exhibitions and folk-dancing, but a little too highly organized for their own good.

The Town

At the heart of it all and dominating the Praça Luís de Camões (or Praça Velha) is the dour grey **Sé** (Tues–Sun 9am–noon & 2.30–5pm), one of those buildings which took so long to complete (1390–1540) that several architectural styles came and went during its construction, all of them incorporated into the work somewhere. The castellated main facade, with its two heavy octagonal towers, looks like the gateway of some particularly forbidding castle, but around the sides the design is lightened by flying buttresses, fantastic pinnacles, and grimacing gargoyles – the ones facing Spain are particularly mean-looking. Inside, it's surprisingly long and lofty, with twisted pillars and vaulting influenced by the Manueline style of the later stages of its development. The huge carved stone **retábulo** is the work of João de Ruão, a leading figure in the sixteenth-century resurgence of Portuguese sculpture at Coimbra.

It's amazing, for a place of its size and historical importance, that apart from the cathedral, there's little else to see in Guarda: the displays of local archeology, art and sculpture in the **Museu da Guarda** (Tues–Sun 10am–12.30pm & 2–5.30pm; 250$00)

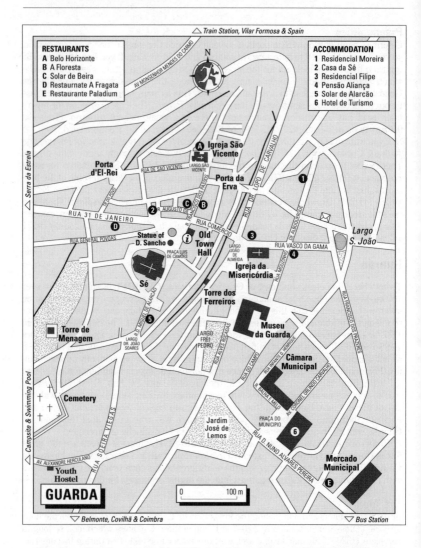

△ Train Station, Vilar Formosa & Spain

N

RESTAURANTS
A Belo Horizonte
B A Floresta
C Solar de Beira
D Restaurnate A Fragata
E Restaurante Paladium

ACCOMMODATION
1 Residencial Moreira
2 Casa da Sé
3 Residencial Filipe
4 Pensão Aliança
5 Solar de Alarcão
6 Hotel de Turismo

AV. MONSENHOR MENDES DO CARMO

Igreja São Vicente

Porta d'El-Rei

RUA DE SÃO VICENTE

LARGO SÃO VICENTE

Porta da Erva

R. DR. LOPO DE CARVALHO

RUA 31 DE JANEIRO

R. FRANCISCO DO PASSEIO

B. AUGUSTO GIL

RUA COMERCIO

RUA DE ALBUQUERQUE

Largo S. João

RUA GENERAL POVOAS

Statue of D. Sancho

PRAÇA LUIS DE CAMÕES

Old Town Hall

LARGO JOÃO DE ALMEIDA

RUA VASCO DA GAMA

R. MOUZINHO

RUA FRANCISCO DOS PRAZERES

Sé

Igreja da Misericórdia

R. MIGUEL DE ALARCÃO

Torre dos Ferreiros

Museu da Guarda

Torre de Menagem

LARGO DR. JOÃO SOARES

LARGO FREI PEDRO

RUA ALVES ROÇADAS

RUA DO CAMPO

RUA INFANTE D. HENRIQUE

Câmara Municipal

Campsite & Swimming Pool

Serra da Estrela

Cemetery

RUA SOEIRA VIEGAS

Jardim José de Lemos

PRAÇA DO MUNICIPIO

R. BAIXA E MELO

AV. CORONEL ORLINDO CARVALHO

RUA D. NUNO ÁLVARES PEREIRA

AV. ALEXANDRE HERCULANO

Youth Hostel

Mercado Municipal

GUARDA

0   100 m

▽ Belmonte, Covilhã & Coimbra

▽ Bus Station

on Rua Alves Roçadas are, frankly, dull, and of the castle, on a bleak little hill nearby, only the plain square keep, the **Torre de Menagem**, survives, while the walls are recalled by just three remaining gates – the most impressive of them the **Torre dos Ferreiros** (Blacksmiths' Tower). The cobbled streets of the old town, though, are fascinating in themselves, and the tangled area between the other two portals – the **Porta da Erva** and **Porta d'El-Rei** – can have changed little in the past 400 years.

Like Celorico, Guarda has a covered **market** on Rua D. Nuno Álvares Pereira, busiest on Saturdays, where you'll find delicious *queijo da serra*. On the other side of town, below Avenida Monsenhor Mendes do Carmo, is the open-air Feira Ao Ar Livre, held on the first and third Wednesday of every month and attracting agricultural folk from all around.

Practicalities

Guarda's **train station** is 3km north of the town centre but there's usually a bus to meet all the major arrivals. The **bus station**, alongside Rua D. Nuno Álvares Pereira, is fairly central and ultra-efficient. Services are operated by a variety of companies to most of the neighbouring villages, the only problem being that many buses leave early in the morning and often don't return until late in the afternoon. The **turismo** is in the old town hall building opposite the Sé on Praça Luís de Camões (daily 9am–12.30pm & 2–5.30pm; ☎271 222 251).

ACCOMMODATION

You should have no trouble getting a room at one of the **pensões** and **hotels** detailed below, or try the **youth hostel** on Avenida Alexandre Herculano (☎271 223 938). Guarda's *Orbitur* **campsite** (☎271 211 406, fax 271 221 911; closed mid-Nov to mid-Jan) is in a park a short way from the castle; beware that in spring and autumn the nights can get extremely cold. The town's heated swimming pool is 500m further on.

Pensão Aliança, Rua Vasco da Gama 8a (☎271 222 235, fax 271 221 451). Just down the hill from the *Filipe*, this welcoming place also has a restaurant. ②.

Casa da Sé, Rua Augusto Gil 17 (☎271 212 501). Recently renovated, characterful rooms. Good value and centrally located off the Praça Luís de Camões. ②.

Residencial Filipe, Rua Vasco da Gama 9 (☎271 223 659, fax 271 221 402). A more upmarket hotel, opposite the Igreja da Misericórdia. Some of the rooms are a little cramped, but all have TV and private facilities. Breakfast included. ③.

Residencial Moreira, Rua Mouzinho de Albuquerque 47 (☎271 214 131). Central and good-value option; all rooms have bathrooms. ②.

Solar de Alarcão, Rua Dom Miguel de Alarcão 25–27 (☎271 121 392, fax 271 121 275). Magnificent granite manor house dating back to the seventeenth century, with wonderful rooms. Highly recommended but you'll need to book ahead. ④.

Hotel de Turismo, Av. Coronel Orlindo Carvalho (☎271 223 366, fax 271 223 399). Guarda's grandest and part of the Best Western chain: big and reasonably well run but without the charm and character of the *Solar de Alarcão*. ⑤.

EATING

Most of the town's **restaurants** are to be found in the area between the Porta da Estrela and the Igreja de São Vicente.

Belo Horizonte, Largo de São Vincente 1. Specializes in local dishes such as rabbit and sausages, and also does an excellent *arroz de tamboril*. Closed first half of July.

Residencial Filipe, Rua Vasco da Gama 9. The first-floor dining room is a shade too florid, but there's no arguing with the generous portions of good food. You'll pay around 2000$00 for a meal.

A Floresta, Rua Franciso dos Passos 40. Reasonably priced and serves enormous portions – grills are the house speciality.

Restaurante A Fragata, Rua 31 de Janeiro 17. Near the cathedral and highly recommended, with an *ementa turística* at around 1400$00.

Restaurante Paladium, Rua Francisco dos Prezeres 23. On the way to the bus station (and near the *Hotel de Turismo*), this serves daytime snacks and a full menu in the evening. Meals for around 2000$00; the chicken dishes are especially good.

Solar da Beira, Rua Francisco dos Passos 9. Highly recommended option around the corner from Praça Luís de Camões with main courses for around 1100$00. Try the *cabrito de ensopado* (stewed kid goat) or *lombo grelhado* (grilled pork loin). Closed Thurs.

North of Guarda: the planalto of Beira Alta

North and east of Guarda stretches a rough and barren-looking territory known as the **Planalto** – tableland – of the Beira Alta. Villages here are spread far apart, with much of the land between untamed by agriculture, strewn with boulders and great slabs of granite.

There is the odd fertile valley, though, and a speciality of the local settlements is roast or dried chestnuts. Once a replacement for potatoes, and now a dessert, they come from vast, shady trees growing beside the roads on almost any approach to a village.

In medieval times, the region's Jewish settlements such as **Trancoso** and **Sernancelhe** prospered, though their merchant trade went into decline from the Age of Discovery onwards as business moved to the coast. In successive centuries, the *planalto* towns became closely associated with Portuguese independence from Spain, and in particular with Afonso Henriques's march south down the length of the country. Today, their **castles** are the highlight of the region. **Penedono's** Castelo Roqueiro is especially magnificent, with seventeenth-century reconstructions on top of the original article. Impressive, too, are the star-shaped fortress at **Almeida**, the site of the penultimate battle in the Peninsular Wars against Napoleon, and, in its own understated way, the town of **Pinhel**, evoking bygone ages in its atmosphere and unspoilt architecture.

If you're travelling in **winter**, take to heart the proverb that *"O frio almoça em Penedono, merenda em Trancoso e ceia na Guarda"* (The cold lunches in Penedono, takes tea in Trancoso and dines in Guarda), and come suitably prepared. You will at least be rewarded by some extraordinary landscapes: the frost (*sincelo*) can have an extraordinary effect on the *planalto*, with massive trees linked by boughs of crystal and metre-long icicles hanging from every house.

Trancoso

Forty-four kilometres north of Guarda, **TRANCOSO**, still largely contained within a circuit of medieval walls, is an atmospheric little town, full of dark alleyways and interesting architectural details. The presence of a large **Jewish community** during the Middle Ages is apparent from the facades of the more ancient homes. Each has two doorways – a broad one for trade and a narrow one (leading to the first floor) for the family – and above the carefully crafted and bevelled stonework, some have clumsy crosses, inscribed by the Inquisition to indicate the family's conversion to Christianity. The most striking is the former **rabbi's house** (known as the Casa do Gato Negro), near the restaurant *São Marcos*, which is decorated with the Lion of Judea, the Gates of Jerusalem, and a figure of *Preguiça,* which some translate as "Sloth".

At the centre of the fortifications is the **castle**, with its squat, almost triangular, tower – a distinctive silhouette visible from many miles away. It's a Moorish design and a reminder of the Saracen domination of the town in the tenth century, following the town's conquest by al-Mansur. The following two centuries saw frequent siege and battle, with the fortress taken by Fernando Magno in 1033, and finally by Afonso Henriques and Egas Moniz in 1139 – an event celebrated by the construction of the monastery at São João de Tarouca (see p.301). Trancoso's later military history includes the usual invasions and billeting during fourteenth-century Castillian troublemaking and the nineteenth-century Peninsular War – look out for the charming corner house with an open stone stairway on the central square, which has the tellingly British name, Quartel do General Beresforde.

An equally historic site is the small **Capela de São Bartolomeu**, on the side of the dusty avenue leading into town, where Dom Dinis married the twelve-year-old Isabel of Aragon in 1282; he later gave her the entire town as a gift. Outside the walls from here, in front of the law courts, **Celtic tombs** attest to very early origins indeed. Here and there a coffin-cover lies askew; the rest of the mound is a carved mass of human-shaped pits of varying sizes – one obviously for a child.

Feiras are held on Fridays, with the big annual bash, the **Feira de São Bartolomeu**, on August 8–14, followed by the **Festa de Nossa Senhora da Fresta** on August 15.

BANDARRA THE COBBLER'S PROPHECY

Trancoso takes its place in Portuguese history through the legend of one **Bandarra**, a shoemaker-prophet who lived in the town in the fifteenth century. The cobbler began his prophetic career with local horoscopes and poems, but after a while moved to more national matters – foretelling, among other things, the end of the Portuguese kingdom. In an age of religious dilemma and disillusionment with monarchical rule his prophecies struck a chord, and attracted the attention of the authorities. Their circulation was banned and Bandarra condemned to death – a sentence commuted after popular outcry to a punishment of walking barefoot around town carrying a massive candle until it burned to the wick.

There the matter might have rested, but twenty years after Bandarra's death, Dom Sebastião did indeed die (along with most of the Portuguese nobility) in the battle of Alcácer-Quibir in Morocco, leaving no heir to the throne. Portugal subsequently lost independence to Spain, and Bandarra was pronounced the Nostradamus of his time.

Practicalities

Buses to Lamego pass twice a day during the week, stopping in the square in front of the main gates. There are one or two buses daily to Lisbon via Coimbra and Celorica, where you can also catch connections to Viseu or Guarda. You can buy tickets from the café next to the **turismo** (Mon–Sat 9am–12.30pm & 2–5.30pm; ☎271 811 147); the latter is opposite the main gates to the walled town and can point you in the direction of **private rooms** (①).

The town offers a choice of three **pensões**: cheapest is the *Hospederia Portas d'El Rei* (☎271 811 411; ②), on the main street, Rua da Corredouro, just inside the gates to the old town – if no one is around, ask at the boutique beneath it. The newer *Pensão Vale a Pena* (☎271 811 951; ②) is a genial place above a garage, just outside the walls near the hospital on Largo Senhora da Calçada – breakfast is included in the rates. The *Residencial Dom Dinis* (☎271 811 525; ②) is a modern choice above the post office at Campo das Viúvas 2, also outside the walls. For **eating**, the *Café Bandarra*, near the main gateway, serves a wide range of dishes; more expensive, but value for money and very popular with the locals, is *O Brasão* on Rua Adriano Mountinho.

Sernancelhe

Sited 30km northwest from Trancoso, a couple of kilometres off the Guarda–Lamego road, **SERNANCELHE** is not exactly the hub of Beira Alta, but it's a quietly impressive place, in the manner of Trancoso, with further reminders of the area's Jewish past and a fine riverside location. The village is also said to produce the *planalto*'s finest chestnuts and its approach is dominated by the broad-boughed trees spreading across the road. Carnivals, love songs, recipes, and folk tales all centre on the fruit, and if you coincide with the **Festa de Nossa Senhora de Ao Pé da Cruz** on May 1 you'll witness a curious mixture of religious devotion, springtime merrymaking, and, above all, folkloric superstition. There's a dance of the chestnuts, a blessing of the trees, and the exchange of handfuls of blossom by local lovers, aside from the religious procession.

Should you want to know more about the town, the local cultural expert, Padre Cândido Azevedo, is more than pleased to welcome a stranger into his majestic, castle-like home overlooking the town. The walk up there takes you through the **old quarter** of town, now only semi-populated and coming alive only for the weekly Thursday market. En route, along the main road, you pass the **Igreja Matriz**, an attractive Romanesque church with a curious facade. Fixed into twin niches on either side of the main doorway are six weathered apostles – said to be the only free-standing sculptures of the period in the whole of Portugal. Inside the church are several sixteenth-century panels, including a magnificent *John the Baptist*.

A wander around the old quarter will also reveal the same features of medieval **Jewish settlement** as in Trancoso – canted lintels, pairs of granite doorways of unequal size, the occasional cross for the converted. Equally noticeable are a number of large **town houses**, dating from the sixteenth and seventeenth centuries. One of these is the supposed birthplace of the Marquês de Pombal, another is the birthplace of Padre João Rodrigues, an eminent and influential missionary who founded a series of mission houses in Japan in the sixteenth century. Japanese tourists often make the pilgrimage here to see the building.

There are basic **rooms** above the *Café Flora* (☎254 595 304; ②). Alternatively, you could put up a tent by the river, just outside Sernancelhe, or at the **Barragem do Tavora**, a man-made barrage 3km to the north. **Buses** on to Lamego (see p.297) leave from the N226, 4km away – there are two a day in the week, none at weekends. There are also buses (Mon–Fri) to Penedono and Trancoso, departing from the same place.

Penedono

Sixteen kilometres to the northeast of Sernancelhe, **PENEDONO** is another one-horse town, but again a likeable place, and with a fantastic **Castelo Roquiero** – visible from miles around. The *roqueiro* ("rock") part of the name is due to the castle's emergence from its granite base, as if the rock and the walls were one and the same. From the top, as you might imagine, there are grand views, with the village's old quarter laid out below. Keys are available from the village shop, who will warn you to rattle the castle doors first in order to get the pigeons in the air – rather than have them flying straight at your face.

The castle, in times of war, and the **Solar dos Freixos** (now the town hall), in times of peace, were supposed to have been home to Álvaro Gonçalves Coutinho, the legendary **King Magriço** ("Lean One"), sung of in Camões's *Os Lusíadas*. It's a claim fought over fiercely with the inhabitants of Trancoso, who likewise are prepared to swear he is their man. According to Camões, the Magriço led eleven men to England to champion the cause of twelve noble English ladies, who found themselves without knights, and fought a joust on their behalf. Such tales of chivalry made them the subjects of numerous allegorical murals and panels of *azulejos* around the country.

The village has one **pensão**, the clean *Residencial Flora* (☎254 504 411; ②), though you could also find **rooms** above the *Café Avenida* (☎254 504 473; ①) on the main road; the latter has excellent food. With a little more to spend, the new *Estalagem de Penedono* (☎254 509 120, fax 254 509 129; ⑤), directly opposite the castle, has excellent rooms and as good a **restaurant** as you'll find in this part of Portugal – their *bacalhau*, in particular, is superb. **Feiras** are held every other Wednesday, and there's a **romaria** on September 15–16. **Buses** continue (Mon–Fri) to Vila Nova de Foz Côa, and to Trancoso.

Marialva and Pinhel

If you've got your own transport, it's worthwhile driving from Penedono to Pinhel via the tiny village of **MARIALVA**, dominated by the crumbling remains of a massive ruined **castle** built by Dom Sancho I in 1200. Despite, or perhaps because of, its remoteness and state of disrepair, this is among the most atmospheric of all the region's many ruins, although it is currently being restored. A ruined and deserted old village is contained within the castle walls; the only intact building is the sixteenth-century Igreja Matriz (not open to visitors). There is no accommodation in the village.

PINHEL itself is big enough to run both a wine co-operative (producing an excellent red) and a cake factory (churning out *cavaca* sweetmeats). But, consumables apart, it's also small enough to have left the narrow lanes of the old centre of town virtually untouched inside its crumbling walls. From one corner of the walls you look down on the shell of a ruined **Romanesque church**, whose facade alone merits closer inspection. On another stretch sits what is left of the original **fortress**, a soaring tower with an intricately carved Manueline window, currently under restoration.

Down in the town further architectural pleasures are in store, with numerous **manor houses** clustered about magnificent gardens. One of the largest is now the **Câmara Municipal**, its hallway bedecked with a series of excellent photographs of local buildings of interest. An adjacent building houses the town **museum** (Mon–Fri 10am–noon & 2–6pm; free), with a pile of **Celtic tombstones** on the ground floor and, upstairs, remnants of a local convent.

Pinhel has two modest-priced **pensões**: the *Residencial Pinhelense* on Trav. do Sepulcro (☎271 412 373; ②), with superb meals, and the *Residencial Falcão*, Av. Carneiro Gusmão 25 (☎271 412 004; ③). The more upmarket *Hotel Paris*, 12km away in Pínzio on Rua Pínzio (☎271 947 121; ④) offers all the mod cons. If you want to **camp**, no one seems to object to tents being pitched around the castle walls. **Buses** leave from the centre of the municipal gardens – ask in the museum or nearby shop for schedules. One useful connection is the daily bus operated by Berrelhas, which you can flag down at about 4.15pm to go to Almeida or on to Figueira de Castelo Rodrigo (see p.295), and there's also a daily bus which connects Pinhel with Almeida and Guarda. The local **Festa de Santo António** is held on the Sunday closest to June 13.

Almeida

Perhaps the most attractive of all the fortified border towns, **ALMEIDA** is a beautifully preserved eighteenth-century stronghold. Its **walls** are in the form of a twelve-pointed star, with six bastions and six curtain walls within ravelins – a Dutch design, influenced by the French military architect Vauban. A four-kilometre walk around the walls – now overgrown with grass – takes in all the peaks and troughs. If you stay overnight, there's an irresistible charm in watching the sun go down and the lights come on in a hundred tiny villages across the plateau of the Ribacôa.

This was one of the last stretches of land to be recognized as officially Portuguese in the Treaty of Alcañices with the Spanish in 1297, and it's easy to see why boundaries were not clearly staked out in the broad, flat terrain. Indeed, it was occasionally reoccupied by Spain – the last time was in 1762, after which the present stronghold was completed. The original two double **gates** are among the town's most splendid features – long, shell-proof tunnels with emblazoned entrances and sizeable guardroom. In the outer guardroom of the São Francisco gateway there is a small **museum** (daily 9am–noon & 2–5pm), while the larger guardroom houses a **turismo** office. The **Casamatas** (daily 9am–noon & 2–5pm), or barracks, is second in size only to Elvas, with a capacity for five thousand men and their supplies. Its layout explains how it withstood lengthy sieges. With its own water supply, rubbish chute, breathing holes, hidden escape routes, munitions chamber (there's a range of cannonballs and gunshot still on view), and dormitory space, the possibilities were limitless.

One further curiosity, opposite the *pousada* gateway in the walls, is an inscription on the side of a small house declaring it to be the dumping ground for illegitimate children. At the **Rodo dos Eispostos** (literally the "Circle of the Deserted"), anyone could come and claim an unwanted child for themselves – a convenient arrangement for both mother and foster parent.

Inevitably, perhaps, tourism has been catching up with Almeida – the number of cafés in town has risen from three to twenty or more within the last decade, while the arrival of the *pousada* in 1987 necessitated the hacking out of a new gateway in Almeida's fortifications, though the result wasn't as outrageous as feared. The locals seem intrigued by the phenomenon of rich tourists turning up in their long-forgotten town to fork out more than a villager's daily earnings to ride in a souped-up pony cart, or to pay through the nose for a coffee on the balcony overlooking the humble

---

ALMEIDA IN THE PENINSULAR WAR

Almeida played a key role in the **Peninsular War** (1807–14). In January 1808 it fell to the French General Junot, whom Napoleon subsequently made Governor of Portugal. Later, when the French retreated unscathed following the infamous Convention of Sintra of August 1808, the Portuguese reoccupied the town. The Napoleonic army returned in 1810 and, en route to Buçaco and Torres Vedras, occupied Ciudad Rodrigo in Spain and besieged Almeida. The Luso-Britannic forces held out for seventeen days and then on July 26 the unforeseen happened. A leaky barrel of gunpowder, carried from the cathedral-castle in the centre of town to the Praça Alta (an artillery platform on the northern walls), left a fatal trail of powder. Once ignited, this began a fire which killed hundreds, and the survivors gave themselves up to the French. Wellington, on his victorious return from Torres Vedras, defeated the French on May 11, 1811, at Fuentes d'Onoro and subsequently took the fortress at Almeida with no bloodshed. The French army scuttled away during the night, probably making use of one of three *portas falsas* – narrow slits in the ramparts allowing for a discreet exit.

---

dwellings below. If you can possibly do so, try to visit during one of the twice-monthly **feiras** (on the eighth day and last Saturday) or – best of all – come at Pentecost (fifty days after Easter) for the grand picnic in the grounds of the **Convento da Barca**, a former Franciscan monastery with a distinctively Tuscan feel about its domed chapel and setting. It's the only time you can visit the convent grounds, which are now privately owned, but at other times of the year you can sample the excellent red wine, apples, peaches, nuts, and various other produce for which it is famous, at shops in town.

Practicalities

Apart from the luxurious (and ugly) *Pousada Senhora das Neves* (☎271 574 283, fax 271 574 320; ⑥), **staying** in the old town is a question of talking with the villagers. A good first stop is the *Casa da Amelinha*, where *ginginha* (morello cherry liqueur) has been served since 1883. It's an unofficial gathering place – ask here, or at any of the neighbouring cafés, whether there are any local rooms to let.

Otherwise, there are two modern *residenciais* by the crossroads outside the fort, both comfortable and friendly – *A Muralha* (☎271 574 357; ②) and *Morgado* (☎271 574 412; ③), alongside which, and under the same management, is the *Restaurante A Tertúlia*. A second good **restaurant**, just outside the main gate, is the *Portas de Almeida*. For **camping**, make your way to the Rio Côa, a two-kilometre stroll downhill on the Pinhel road. Just above the old Romanesque bridge (and its present-day equivalent), you'll find some idyllic spots.

Buses for the north come from Vilar Formoso twice daily (Mon–Fri) and go as far as Figueira de Castelo Rodrigo; the Berrelhas-operated bus stops on the main road, 200m from the gates to the old town, near the two *residenciais*, at about 5pm every afternoon. Going south there are local services as far as Vilar Formoso, which has trains to Guarda and Spain, and three daily buses to Sabugal and Castelo Branco. There is also one daily bus to Guarda (Mon–Fri) operated by Rodoviária Nacional, and a daily bus to Pinhel. Ask in either of the *residenciais* for bus information. At weekends, public transport is virtually non-existent.

Vilar Formoso, Castelo Bom and Castelo Mendo

From Almeida, it's 12km south to **VILAR FORMOSO**, an uninteresting town on the Spanish border that has good bus and rail connections to Guarda and elsewhere, as well as about a dozen hostels if you find yourself stuck there overnight. Seven kilometres west of Vilar Formoso, on the old N16 to Guarda, **CASTELO BOM** is a small village with some old fortifications and **rooms** available at *Restaurante Lurdes* (☎271 513 653; ①). There's also a **campsite** shortly before you reach the village, at Café Rio Côa on the N16 beside the river – a very pretty spot, although somewhat marred by the large bridge for the new IP5 highway. From Castelo Bom, it's a further 4km along the N16 to **CASTELO MENDO**, one of the prettiest of the region's fortified villages and well worth a visit if you have your own transport. Otherwise, the daily bus from Almeida to Guarda passes at about 9.50am, with the eastbound bus to Vilar Formosa and Almeida returning at 5.20pm. The walk along the N16 between the two villages is pleasant and there's very little traffic, as most cars take the newer IP5 instead.

The Serra da Estrela

The peaks of the **Serra da Estrela** – the highest mountains in Portugal and the last of the four central Iberian *serras* – rise to the southwest of Guarda. The range is basically a high plateau cut by valleys, from within which emanate two of Portugal's greatest **rivers**: the Rio Mondego, the longest Portuguese river to have its source in Portugal itself, flows north to Celorico da Beira before swinging southwest to Coimbra and the sea at Figueira da Foz; while the Rio Zêzere flows southwest from near Guarda until it joins the Rio Tejo at Constância. Over the last few decades the *serra* landscape has changed. Once, farmers lived in stone houses with straw roofs, dotted across the peaks and valleys, but they have now moved to more modern dwellings on the valley floor. Originally, too, the whole area was heavily forested, but these days the pines are widely cultivated for timber and shepherds now graze their sheep on the higher ground. Rye is grown lower down, where the land is more fertile.

For visitors, most of the interest is in the mountain region known as the **Parque Natural da Serra da Estrela**, established in 1976 to preserve the rural character of the *serra* villages and landscape. In 1990, all land over 1200m was designated "protected countryside", which means in effect that you're not allowed to camp wild, light fires or pick flowers. However, there are three major (and several minor) **trails** through the park, which take in various authorized campsites and villages with accommodation and other facilities. The best time to walk the trails is from May to October; some of them are featured in the box on p.233. If you're interested in staying in rural properties in the park, contact ADRUSE, Largo do Mercado, Gouveia (☎238 491 123, fax 238 402 50), who can provide details and handle reservations.

Park approaches and information

Public transport into the area is erratic at the best of times. **Buses** serve the main towns of Seia, Gouveia, Celorico, Guarda and Covilhã, which form a circle around the range, but since privatization almost all local services into the more interesting mountain villages have been cut back or axed completely. The best place to check for up-to-date bus times is at the turismo or the bus station in Guarda. However, **taxis** are not as prohibitive as you might expect; Covilhã–Penhas costs around 1000$00 and even the longest journey won't set you back more than 2500$00. **Hitching** is another possibility, especially in winter when Penhas de Saúde has Portugal's only skiing facilities.

If you're coming from the west and north **by car**, you can follow the N17 down from Celorico da Beira, branching off on minor roads to enter the park at the quirky village of **Linhares**, or via the larger (and less interesting) towns of **Gouveia** and **Seia** and the traditional settlement of **Sabugeiro**. Alternatively, from the east and south, the railway and N18 road (between Guarda and Castelo Branco) skirt the eastern slopes, with access to the park from **Belmonte** and **Covilhã**. If you're intent on serious hiking, the best base is **Penhas da Saúde**, just northwest of Covilhã. Penhas has the region's only youth hostel and offers easy access to the valleys north to **Manteigas** or south to **Unhais da Serra**.

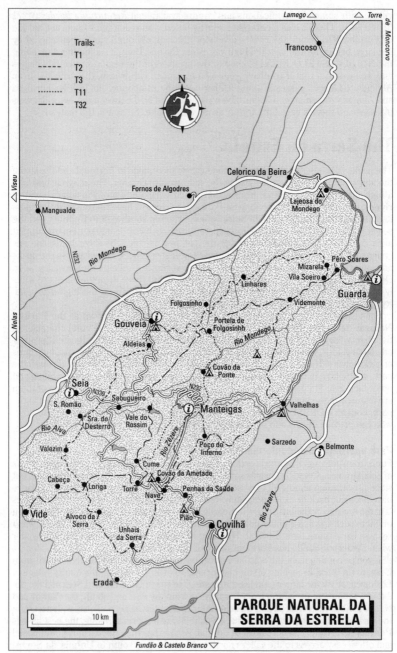

Lamego △   △ Torre

de Moncorvo

Trancoso

Trails:
- —— T1
- ----- T2
- —·—· T3
- ·········· T11
- —··—··— T32

N

△ Viseu

Celorico da Beira

Fornos de Algodres

Lajeosa do Mondego

Mangualde

N202

Rio Mondego

Péro Soares
Mizarela
Vila Soeiro

Linhares

Folgosinho

Videmonte

Guarda

△ Nelas

Gouveia ⓘ

Portela de Folgosinhh

Aldeias

Rio Mondego

Covão da Ponte

Seia ⓘ

N339

Sabugueiro

N202

Manteigas ⓘ

Valhelhas

S. Romão

Vale do Rossim

Rio Alva

Sra. da Desterro

Poço do Inferno

Sarzedo

Belmonte ⓘ

Valezim

Cume

Covão da Ametade

Cabeça

Torre

Penhas da Saúde

Loriga

Nave

Vide

Alvoco da Serra

Pião

Covilhã ⓘ

Unhais da Serra

Rio Zêzere

Erada

0   10 km

**PARQUE NATURAL DA
SERRA DA ESTRELA**

Fundão & Castelo Branco ▽

HIKING IN THE PARQUE NATURAL

Several waymarked **hiking trails** cut across the Parque Natural de Serra da Estrela. The map opposite shows the main trails, some of which are detailed here. Those described below would take between three and four days to complete, but shorter, alternative routes spin off from the main trails, while each is broken down into segments which could be tackled as half-day or day hikes. Always check with the **park information offices** (in Manteigas, Gouveia or Seia; see below, p.235 and 239) before setting off on hikes; and be properly prepared and equipped for what can be quite tough routes. Further details of **accommodation, campsites and facilities** en route can be found in the relevant town and village accounts.

● T1 (waymarked in red) runs **from Guarda to Vide** (on the N230). The route leads you across high land, first to Videmonte, an inhabited farming area, and then through Portela de Folgosinho on a forest road and to the dammed lake at Rossim. You then reach Torre (see "Penhas da Saúde", p.238), via Cume, after which the route ends either at Loriga (on the N231) or at Vide (N230). You'll need to be self-sufficient after Videmonte; there are no other settlements until you reach Vide.

An alternative route, the T11 (waymarked in red and yellow), leaves the trail at Portela de Folgosinho and cuts through pine woods and farm land to Covoa da Ponte, where there's a campsite. From there you can visit Manteigas (p.239) and return to the T1 at Cume. T14 leaves the trail at Torre instead and runs down to Penhas da Saúde and Covilhã, by way of the Pião campsite.

● T2 (waymarked in yellow) runs from west and then south, **from Vila Soeiro via Gouveia to Loriga**, along the western edge of the Serra da Estrela. Access to Vila Soeira is from Guarda along the T1, after which the route runs to Linhares (p.234) and the atmospheric mountain village of Folgosinho; there's a grocery store, medical centre, and rooms to rent above the restaurant. At Gouveia there's a campsite; then the route runs through Cabeça de Velha and on to Senhora do Desterro (grocery store), Castro de São Romão (superb vantage point), Valezim – a sizeable village on the N231 – and finally to Loriga.

● T3 (waymarked in yellow) runs **from Videmonte via Valhelhas to Loriga**, this time along the eastern slope of the *serra*, crossing the Mondego and Zêzere rivers. As above, you reach Videmonte from Guarda along the T1 and then walk on to Valhelhas (campsite). Next, at Poço do Inferno, there's a spectacular waterfall; the route then follows the Nave de Santo António, a sandy alluvial plain supporting cattle in the summer. Finally, you pass through Alvoco da Serra on the N231 and, from there, to Loriga.

Alternatively, T32 leaves the T3 at Poço do Inferno and takes the forest road to the Rio Zêzere, after which it passes through Manteigas to the Covão da Ametade (summer campsite), before rejoining the T3 at the Nave de Santo António.

For specific details about the *parque natural*, there are **information offices** in Manteigas, Gouveia and Seia; the details are given in the relevant sections below. At each, you'll be able to buy several useful English-language **guidebooks**, invaluable if you intend to delve into the region in any depth: *Discovering the Region of the Serra da Estrela* describes the hiking trails, while the Portuguese-only *Estrela: uma visão natural* ("A Natural Approach"), details all the major habitats and wildlife contained within park boundaries. The turismo in Guarda also has information and guidebooks on the park.

Linhares

LINHARES, 20km southwest of Celorico da Beira, perches on a slope overlooking the Rio Mondego valley, and is one of the most accessible of the *serra* villages, with a trio of attractions in its castle, series of troglodyte-like dwellings, and stretch of Roman road. To get here, take the Celorico da Beira–Gouveia **bus** and stop at Carrapichana, from where it's a two-kilometre walk to the village.

The lofty keep of the **Castelo** (9am–noon, 2–5.30pm; free) presides over its surroundings and for good reason: it dates from 1169 when Linhares, then more of a town, was claimed for Portugal. Afonso Henriques realized its potential as a defensive post, and soon the men of Linhares were trained up and equipped to carry out such feats of bravery as the rescue of Celorico da Beira from the Spaniards in 1198. In the walls are traces of the *cisternas* which gave the village a constant supply of water during times of siege. You can still see the course of the spring which now runs along the gully beneath the great slabs of rock on which the castle was constructed.

Although the stone houses of the village have been spruced up with neat, green street signs, Linhares still feels ancient. If you arrive in the early morning the village appears deserted; its only sounds of life are the animals grunting and kicking their stable doors to be let out. Later in the day you'll see the donkeys being brought in from the fields and, depending on the time of year, seeds laid out to dry in the sun, wine casks being washed for the next year's vintage and, whatever the season, village gossips on their doorsteps, keen as ever to meet a stranger.

A little-known secret of the village's **church** is that it contains three paintings almost certainly executed by **Grão Vasco** and belonging to a larger series which is now lost. Propped up behind vulgar wooden statues and, in one case, stuck in one of the side aisles, the panels, depicting the *Adoration of the Magi, Descent from the Cross* and *Annunciation*, shine out in the obscurity. They reveal all the qualities of the great painter – his skill as a portraitist and his deft handling of tone and colour, particularly in the depiction of clothing and folds of material.

Near the schoolhouse in Linhares a path branches off towards Figueiró da Serra. Following it, you'll soon realize that you are walking along an old **Roman road** – part of the one which ran to Braga – with heavy slabs of rock for paving stones looking like something out of an Asterix cartoon. The walk is a beauty, the hedgerows lined with flowers in the spring and blackberries in the autumn.

If you want to **stay**, ask at Linhares's only restaurant, *A Taberna* (☎271 776 608; ③), which has airy rooms and an English-speaking owner; to find it, turn left by the town pillory. Alternatively, see if the sporadically open **turismo**, attached to the Junta (☎271 776 612), can advise you where best to pitch your tent – most probably above the village near a football pitch.

Gouveia

Another 20km southwest of Linhares by road, **GOUVEIA** has lost the rural *serra* feel that once constituted its charm, as it has developed into a fair-sized provincial town.

However, it boasts several fine buildings, the most outstanding being the **Câmara Municipal**, on Avenida 25 de Abril. Open-air concerts are held in its courtyard during the summer months, but you are generally free to walk in. Incongruously, the town also has a modern art museum, in the same building as the Câmara Municipal, the **Museu de Abel Manta** (Tues–Sun 10am–12.30pm & 2–5.30pm), with a broad selection of contemporary Portuguese pictures donated by Gouveia-born artist Abel Manta (1888–1982).

You may have noticed a **statue** of a shepherd with his dog, at the entrance to the town, which is proudly illuminated at night. Though not perhaps the finest piece of sculpture, it is significant for what it represents. The people in the hills around here live a harsh and impoverished existence – there is never a break in the agricultural year, for when the summer is over and the harvest is stored away it is time to begin the cheese-making, an activity which brings in their only serious income. The shepherd's friend in this harsh lifestyle is his dog, the *Cão da Serra da Estrela* – a fearsome-looking breed said to be crossbred from wolves.

If you can, it's worth timing your visit to take in Gouveia's Thursday **market** and if you have your own transport or are happy to make the four-kilometre walk, the *Adega Cooperativa de São Pião* (Mon–Fri 9.30am–noon & 2–5pm; free; ☎238 492 101) welcomes visitors to try its Dão wines.

Practicalities

Buses drop you by the bridge; walk up and veer right and you'll reach the centre of town. The **turismo** (Tues–Sun 9am–12.30pm & 2–5.30pm; ☎238 492 185) is in Jardim Lopes da Costa (if there's no-one around try the helpful reception in the Câmara Municipal) and will hand out maps of the town. Walkers may also want to call in at the **information centre** of the *Parque Natural de Serra da Estrela*, around the corner at Rua dos Bombeiros Voluntários 8 (Mon–Fri 9am–12.30pm & 2–5.30pm; ☎238 492 411), which has further maps and leaflets on the area. For a hiking route in the park that passes through Gouveia, see the box on p.233.

Gouveia offers half a dozen **accommodation** possibilities, including *Pensão Estrela do Parque*, Rua da República 36 (☎238 492 171; ③), a dusty old hotel with modern prices, which has a **restaurant** with a good reputation. The town's most upmarket option is the *Hotel de Gouveia*, Avenida 1º de Maio (☎238 491 010, fax 238 494 370; ④), with decent if not very characterful rooms and a pool. The local **campsite** (☎238 491 008) is at Curral do Negro, around 3km from the centre of town; to get there, turn right immediately after the Câmara Municipal, then right again, before finally forking to the left for 2km.

Seia and Sabugeiro

Cut out **SEIA** (16km southwest of Gouveia) from your itinerary and you would miss little, but like Gouveia, it can be a useful jumping-off point, providing bus connections to Coimbra and access to the Estrela *parque natural*. If you stay, you could try one of the three upmarket **hotels**: the excellent *Hotel Camelo*, Rua 1º de Maio 16 (☎238 310 100, fax 238 310 101 *hotelcamelo@mail.telepac.pt;* ④); the *Estalagem de Seia*, Av. Dr. Afonso Costa (☎238 315 866, fax 238 315 538; ⑤); or the *Albergaria Senhora do Espinheiro*, Rua Senhora do Espinheiro (☎ & fax 238 312 073; ④). Less expensive options are the *Residencial Silva*, Rua 1º de Maio (☎238 312 305; ②), and the *Residência Serra da Estrela*, in the centre of town on Largo Marquês da Silva (☎238 315 566; ③).

With enough time, or transport, however, it's better to press on into the park, after first visiting the **information centre** at Praça da República 28 (Mon–Sat 9am–12.30pm & 2–5.30pm; ☎238 312 606). There's also a **turismo** in Praça da República (Tues–Fri 9am–noon & 2–6pm, Sat 9am–noon & 2–8pm; ☎238 312 272).

If you don't have the time for an extended trip, you can always make a fleeting visit to **SABUGUEIRO**, 10km east of Seia, said to be Portugal's highest village and one of the more interesting in the *serra*. As well as making a good base for walking, Sabugueiro offers the chance to see rye bread, local spice sausage and Estrela cheese being made, and plenty of Serra puppies for sale. There is a string of handicraft shops on the road in from Seia – most of which also rent out **rooms** – but the centre of the village remains essentially agricultural and traditional. Other options should you want to stay are the traditional country houses in the old village: the *Casa do Cruzeiro*, *Casa Nova* and *Casa da Sofia* (all on ☎238 312 825; ③). A less expensive option is the *Residencial Altitude* (☎238 315 895; ②), on the Seia road, which has a reasonable restaurant below it.

From Sabugeiro you can continue southeast on the N339 to Penhas da Saúde and Covilhã; or take the minor road northeast to the N232, which runs from Gouveia to Manteigas, Valhelhas and Belmonte – for all of which, see below. There is no regular transport on these routes, but you can usually make do with a mix of walking and hitching. Alternatively, buses cover the southern route to Covilhã, looping around the fringes of the park, via the little spa village of Unhais da Serra on the N230, on Mondays, Wednesdays and Fridays.

Belmonte

Twenty kilometres south of Guarda, the small and rather remote **BELMONTE** has the honour of being the birthplace of Pedro Álvares Cabral, the discoverer of Brazil, and is a village of considerable interest, commanded by a heavily restored thirteenth-century **castle**. Pedro Cabral was actually born in the castle when it was his family's residence; his tomb is next to the thirteenth-century **Igreja de São Tiago**, just below the walls. Inside the newer **Igreja Matriz**, at the foot of Rua 25 de Abril, there's an image of Nossa Senhora da Esperança, said to have accompanied Cabral on his first visit to Brazil. The castle is now equipped with a bar and modern amphitheatre for summer concerts; there are also plans for an archeological museum to display findings from recent excavations.

A little-known fact about Belmonte is that it has one of Portugal's largest Jewish communities, with up to 120 families living in the village. Records show there was a thirteenth-century synagogue in the town, but this fell into ruins after the Inquisition, when many Jews fled the country or were forced to convert to being "New Christians". However, many of the Jews continued to practise their faith in secret, using a town house on Rua Chafariz do Areal as a makeshift synagogue up until the 1970s. Only since the 1974 Revolution have the Jews felt secure enough to "out" their religion, and in the mid-1990s were finally able to build a brand-new synagogue on the site of the old town house.

Practicalities

Belmonte is a pleasant stopping-off point on the route south; for those with transport, it provides access to the *parque natural* as well as to the barren and medieval region of the Beira Baixa (covered later in this chapter). There are **bus** services to the two main Beira Baixa towns of Fundão and Castelo Branco, and a daily Rodoviaria Nacional bus (Mon–Fri) to Sabugal and the fortress-village of Sortelha. Most of the long-distance buses to Lisbon, Coimbra and Porto stop at Gingal junction, 2km below the town, at the foot of the hill. For details of times for onward connections, check in the café by the statue of Cabral, or the helpful **turismo** on Rua 1º de Maio (daily 9am–12.30pm & 2–5.30pm; ☎275 911 488), next to the reconstructed pillory.

If you want **to stay**, try the basic *Pensão Altitude* on Rua Pedro Álvares Cabral (☎275 911 170; ②), beyond the park at the western end of the village. For more comfort there's the *Hotel Belsol* (☎275 912 206; ④), which has a swimming pool – it's about 3km from town, back down on the main N18 road between the junction and the turn-off for Valhelhas and Manteigas (N232). A few kilometres further, at Valhelhas on the edge of the *parque natural*, there's a **campsite** (☎275 487 160; open mid-May to Sept). **Buses** for Manteigas, originating in Guarda, pass through at around 6pm daily.

Covilhã

Another 20km beyond Belmonte, **COVILHÃ** lies immediately below the highest peaks of the *serra*, and is the most obvious base for exploring the *parque natural*. In summer, weekend picnickers and campers spread across the hillsides; in winter, ski enthusiasts take over, using Covilhã as a base for trips to the slopes. It's a steeply terraced town

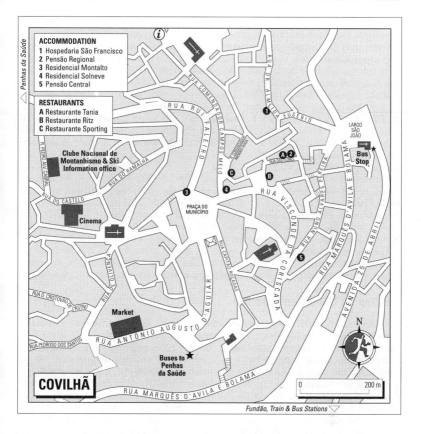

ACCOMMODATION
1 Hospedaria São Francisco
2 Pensão Regional
3 Residencial Montalto
4 Residencial Solneve
5 Pensão Central

RESTAURANTS
A Restaurante Tania
B Restaurante Ritz
C Restaurante Sporting

Clube Nacional de Montanhismo & Ski Information office

Cinema

PRAÇA DO MUNICÍPIO

Market

Buses to Penhas da Saúde

COVILHÃ

0   200 m

Fundão, Train & Bus Stations ▽

with every thoroughfare looking out across the plain below or up to the crags of the Serra da Estrela. A market town since the Middle Ages, it developed a textile industry in the seventeenth century using wool from the local sheep, who also provide the milk for the renowned local *queijo da Serra*. After industrialization, the woollen industry began to harness water power from the mountain streams; factories today, down on the plain below town, are powered by hydroelectricity.

Covilhã's favourite son is **Pêro de Covilhã**, who set out in 1487 on behalf of Dom João II, to search for Prester John (legendary Christian priest and king) in what is now Ethiopia. However, having reached Cairo, de Covilhã sailed instead to India before returning to Cairo and then heading south on his original errand. He never found Prester John and never returned to Portugal, though Vasco da Gama found his report about India useful when he made his own celebrated voyage there, around the Cape of Good Hope, in 1498. In front of the town hall there's a huge, polished granite slab depicting Pêro de Covilhã's voyages and a decidedly queasy-looking statue of the man himself.

Practicalities

The **train station** is 4km from the town, at the foot of the hill, as is the new **bus station**. From here, catch a local bus into town or take a taxi; otherwise, it's a stiff uphill walk. The

turismo (daily 9am–12.30pm & 2–5.30pm; ☎275 319 560), at Avda Heitor Pinto 438, is a five-minute walk from Praça do Munícipio along Rua Comendador Campos Melo.

Other than the campsite on the road to Penhas da Saúde (see below), the cheapest **accommodation** is to be found between Largo São João and Praça do Munícipio. Some good options include: *Pensão Central,* Rua Nuno Álvares Pereira 14 (☎275 322 727; ②), old, basic and as characterful as the perky old lady who runs it; *Residencial Montalto,* Praça do Munícipio 1 (☎ & fax 275 315 424; ③; rooms with bath ⑤), which has seen better days, but is in a brilliant position; *Pensão Regional,* Rua das Flores 4–6 (☎275 322 596 or 327 077; ③), a tranquil place tucked away in a side street and with an inexpensive restaurant underneath; the reasonably priced *Hospedaria São Francisco,* Rua Almeida Eusebio 35 (☎275 322 263; ①), downhill from the centre in a quiet street; and *Residencial Solneve,* Rua Visconde da Coriscada 126 (☎275 323 001, fax 275 315 497; ④), a smart option with its own garage parking.

For **food**, the *pensão* restaurants are usually the best bet. Alternatively, *Restaurante Tania,* in the same street as *Pensão Regional,* serves good, reasonably-priced meals, while *Restaurante Ritz,* above a bar of that name on Praça do Munícipio, is an excellent budget option. *Restaurante Solneve,* below the eponymous *residencial,* is another good choice with efficient, friendly service. *Restaurante Sporting,* on Rua Comendador Mendes Veiga, has a limited menu but its main attraction is its outdoor terrace.

Hikers or skiers intending to move on should contact the Club Nacional de Montanhismo, Rua Pedro Álvares Cabral 5 (office hours; ☎275 323 364), for up-to-date details of local conditions. Covilhã also has plenty of shops for stocking up on **provisions**.

Penhas da Saúde and around

PENHAS DA SAÚDE is another good base for hiking, being right at the heart of the *serra* and close to the highest and most spectacular ground. Getting here in the first place, however, is somewhat problematic. You can either hike the 11km up the glacial valley from Covilhã or catch the bus from beside Covilhã's market (August only, daily at 8.50am, the bus back leaves at 5.10pm; however, you should check bus times with the turismo before you travel, as they tend to change frequently. If you're hiking, after 4km you'll pass the *Pião* **campsite** (☎275 314 312; open all year), followed a couple of kilometres further on by the swanky *Hotel Varanda dos Carqveijas* (☎275 319 120, fax 275 319 124; ⑥), which offers breathtaking views over the Beira Baixa far below and has a restaurant (meals under 2000$00) and swimming pool. Further on, you pass the ruins of several large turn-of-the-century sanatoria, before reaching the rather desolate-looking Penhas da Saúde.

If you want to stay at Penhas, try the 112-bed **youth hostel** (daily: reception open 9am–noon, 6pm–midnight; ☎ & fax 275 335 375), at the crest of a rise as you enter Penhas on the Covilhã road and with superb views across the plain to the Serra de Malcata. For a little more comfort head further up the hill to *Pensão O Pastor* (☎275 322 810; ⑤), which has its own restaurant, or, just below the youth hostel, there's the overpriced *Hotel Serra da Estrela* (☎275 313 809, fax 275 323 789; ⑤). In July and August there's also large-scale unofficial **camping** across the hillside, but the site is unpleasant and litter-strewn and you're much better off staying at *Pião* (see above). Bear in mind that, despite the accommodation here, Penhas da Saúde is not really a village and, apart from a few cafés, there are not many facilities.

Torre

From Penhas, you are within striking distance of the chief beauty spots of the *serra,* with the highest peak in Portugal – **Torre** at 1993m – 10km up the road to the northwest. The stone *torre* (tower) here was added in the last century, on the orders of Dom

João VI, to raise the height to a more impressive 2000m. You can easily walk up from Penhas, but the road gets busy in summer so you may prefer to drive or hitchhike right to the top. However, any sense of natural beauty and grandeur at the summit has been severely reduced by the disfiguring array of buildings, litter and broken-down ski-lifts, all in various stages of decay. One, however, is a café, which may be welcome if you've walked up.

En route you will pass the vast statue of **Nossa Senhora da Boa Estrela**, carved into a niche in the rock, to which there's a massive procession from Covilhã on the second Sunday in August. A little northeast of Torre, on the road to Manteigas, is the narrow rock cone known as the **Cântaro Magro** (Slender Pitcher), which conceals the source of the Rio Zêzere; there's an excellent summer **campsite** below it at Covão d'Ametade. One of the park's hiking routes passes by Torre and through Penhas and Covilhã; see "Hiking in the Parque Natural" on p.233.

Caldas de Manteigas and Manteigas

A few kilometres beyond Penhas, you can strike **north** at Nave de Santo António, between Penhas and Torre, and follow the glacial **valley of the Rio Zêzere** down to the spa of **CALDAS DE MANTEIGAS**. Here the gushing spa waters run past a lovely old water mill (now a hotel training school), and the town spreads along the bottom of the river valley, where you'll find **places to stay**. *Residencial Miralapa* (☎275 982 098; ③) has modern comfortable rooms (each with a TV) and a decent restaurant. Further along the same road is the excellent *Do Manel* restaurant (☎275 981 104; ②), which also has rooms; and then, further still, the pine-clad, modern and well-run *Berne Albergaria* (☎275 981 351, fax 275 982 114; ④).

Caldas de Manteigas virtually merges with the larger *serra* village of **MANTEIGAS**, whose whitewashed houses and red roofs run along the contour above the Rio Zêzere. It is another good option as a base for exploring the *serra* and for hiking, with two of the *parque's* official walks passing through. Joalto run **buses** to and from Guarda, 45km to the northeast, passing through Belmonte and via the campsite at Valhelhas (see p.236), but check times with the turismo in Guarda. The bus stops on the main street, Rua 1º de Maio, setting you down outside the *parque's* **main information office** (Mon–Sat 9am–12.30pm & 2–5.30pm; ☎275 980 060), where you can buy guidebooks; nearby, next to the small park below the Galp service station, there's a regular **turismo** (Tues–Sat 9.30am–noon & 2–6pm; ☎275 981 129), which has a leaflet of circular walks from Manteigas, including the one detailed below.

As for **accommodation**, at the same end of the village as the turismo but high above the main street, is the *Pensão Estrela*, Rua Dr. Sobral 5 (☎275 981 288; ④), boasting fine views across the valley but overpriced, and with some poky rooms. A little way along Rua 1º de Maio, *Residencial Serradalto* (☎275 981 151; ②) has good simple rooms above a reasonable restaurant, while further on, and up a side street, is the *Casa de São Roque*, Rua de Santo António 51 (☎275 981 125; ③), a lovely turn-of-the-century property with a pretty courtyard and the friendliest of owners. Drivers (or energetic hikers) could continue beyond Manteigas, 12km to the west and all uphill, to the marvellous *Pousada de São Lourenço* (☎275 982 450, fax 275 982 453; ⑥); it has only 22 rooms, most with spectacular views, so don't turn up without a reservation.

Apart from the hotel **restaurants**, there's the reliable, but less ambitious, *O Olival*, on the way out of town away beyond the turismo; the upmarket but not too expensive *Antiga Casa Anita* near the Santa Maria church on Rua Dr. Sobral; and *A Cascata*, a cheap option with great views, located below the *Residencial Serradalto's* craft shop on Rua 1º de Maio.

A HIKE FROM MANTEIGAS TO THE POÇO DE INFERNO

There's a lovely round walk from **Manteigas** to the waterfall of **Poço de Inferno** and back via Caldas de Manteigas, which takes around five to six hours. Begin at the Galp petrol station, and take the small road which goes steeply down to the right of the main road, behind the turismo. Follow this road downhill, bearing right, until you cross a small bridge. Bear left and you will start to pick up the yellow marker arrows which head right into the woods. Keep your eyes peeled as these are not always easy to spot, but the arrows will eventually lead you to Poço de Inferno, 'hell's well', which is a great spot for a picnic and has good swimming potential. From here, continue along the paved road and you will arrive back in town at the top of Caldas de Manteigas.

Sabugal, Sortelha and Serra da Malcata

The area **east of Covilhã**, over towards the Spanish border, is worth exploring for the chance to visit **Sabugal** and, more particularly, **Sortelha**, whose amazing circuit of walls rises amid one of the bleakest locations in all Portugal – undulating highland plateau strewn with giant glacial boulders, desolate but for a few trees and the shepherds who make their living here. If you're dependent on buses, you'll need to pick up connections from Guarda or Belmonte, but with your own transport the two towns make an easy sidetrip from Covilhã, and you can continue into the **Serra da Malcata** – wild terrain which, believe it or not, harbours a **lynx reserve**.

Sabugal

SABUGAL, like most towns in Beira Alta, has a **castle**. It's a good one, too, with massively high walls, a vast hollow centre, and a pentagonal tower with three arched chambers piled one on top of the other. Trust the rickety staircase and you could be on top of the world; trust the wobbly stonework and you could walk right around the walls. Having explored the castle, there's little reason to hang around Sabugal but, should you need to stop over, the village has a couple of **pensões**: *Restaurante Robalo* (☎271 753 566; ②) by the roundabout 50m from the closed *Hotel Paliz*, with basic rooms; and the modern *Residencial Sol Rio*, down by the bridge (☎271 753 197; ②) which also rents out pedalos. There's no official campsite, but nobody should object if you put a tent up by the river, on its out-of-town stretch.

There's a **festa** (June 24) and a grand **feira** (June 29); at other times of year it's all pretty quiet. If you're heading for the Serra da Malcata (see p.241), pay a visit to the *Reserva Natural* office on Largo de São Tiago, near the castle.

Buses will leave from the main square, Largo da Fonte, until the completion of the new bus station behind the defunct *Hotel Paliz*. There are daily services to Guarda, Belmonte, Vilar Formoso, Penamacor and Castelo Branco on weekdays, but these buses are few and far between at weekends. Public transport **to Sortelha** is limited to the early-morning bus (Mon–Fri) to Belmonte. Otherwise, there are school buses, which run in the late afternoon (and, obviously, not during the holidays). You may have to walk, though that's no bad thing as the boulder-strewn scenery is as bizarre as it is breathtaking.

Sortelha

SORTELHA is isolated and rather eerie, especially when mist drifts down from the *serra*. It is an ancient town, with Hispano-Arabic origins, and was also the first *castelo roqueiro* ("rock fortress") to be built this side of the Côa. Mystery and legend have grown up with the castle and its fortifications (*sortelha* means "ring"), with stories spun around the figure of an old lady (*a velha*) whose profile you can see on rocks from outside the top gates. At first sight the town seems nothing special. Walk uphill from the new quarters, however, and you arrive at the fantastically walled old town. Within the grid, take a look at the **Igreja Matriz** (keys from the house next door) with its beautiful ceiling, executed by medieval Moors. Arabic script can be seen, too, on several house lintels near the top of town.

It's also worth taking time to browse around the **antique shop** on the road up to the castle, and the **carpet workshop** on the route back down towards Sabugal. Both offer insights into the way life used to be, but above all they show a healthy attitude to present-day tourism. Even if their continuing existence depends entirely on the foreign visitor, you never get the feeling that the show is laid on just for you. The chance to work with the fine materials and coloured wools seems to be enjoyed by all in the workshop, and the antique dealer is as happy to chat about the curious customs and folk tales as strike a bargain.

Sortelha's major event is a **bullfight**, which takes place on August 15, once every two or three years, when the local council has money to stage it. It retains the ancient and peculiar custom of the *forca* – a rudimentary defence against the bull, using branches – which has been handed down from generation to generation. The order of events for the day begins with a *forca* involving all the young boys of the village – at least 25 of whom are needed to carry the device to prevent it from being tipped up by the bull. Later, solo performers strut the stage with their red capes to take the bull's charges. Onlookers are also frequently involved – many a young bull has hopped up onto the terrace of rocks, only to find himself sniffing at discarded hats and bags while nervous laughter rises up from behind the safety of the nearest wall. In non-bullfight years there's still a **festa** on August 15, and a **romaria** in honour of Santo António takes place on June 13.

Practicalities

Sortelha has some superb traditional stone houses to stay in on the outskirts of the village: the *Casa do Vento Que Soa* (☎271 388 260; ④), *Casa do Pátio* (☎271 388 113; ④), *Casa Árabe* (☎271 388 283; ④) and, best of all, the *Casa da Palheiro* (☎271 388 182; ④); advance booking is recommended, especially in summer. Each of the houses is replete with massive walls, wooden furniture, hot baths, cobwebs – all in all, a splendid mix of modern comforts and medieval surroundings. If you want to stay in the old walled town itself, your best bet is to ask at the *Restaurante Alboroque* (see below) which sometimes has rooms to rent in nearby cottages and also acts as a kind of unofficial booking office for the houses mentioned above. The *Casa do Campanário* (☎271 388 198; ④), Rua Mesquita, at the top of the old village, also has rooms. There is a **turismo** signposted near the top of the village, but it's more often closed than open.

Alternatively, there are any number of promising areas to pitch **camp** above and beyond the old town, where the terrain is rocky and sheep take shelter beneath massive boulders. For **meals**, the wood-beamed *Restaurante Alboroque*, on Rua da Mesquita (☎271 388 129 or 271 388 283) is good value, or if your budget can stretch to it there's the classy but expensive *Restaurante Dom Sancho I*, around the corner, which often has *javali* (wild boar) on the menu.

Buses back to Sabugal leave at 7.30am on schooldays and 9am on Wednesdays and Thursdays – but its a good idea to check times the day before at one of the restaurants.

The Serra da Malcata

The **Serra da Malcata** has its reserve's headquarters at Penamacor, 33km south of Sabugal. They are full of advice about how to approach the area and where best to go at different times of the year. The **lynx** – a graceful spotted feline with the build of a domestic cat but the dimensions of a labrador – is notoriously difficult to see, especially without the aid of the park keepers, but the countryside is compensation enough if you don't get a sighting. If you're fortunate you might also see a wild boar disappearing into the forests of black oak. The reserve also contains a dam, currently a scar on the landscape, though it will hopefully heal in time; it has good swimming spots.

Penamacor

PENAMACOR's medieval **castle** may not be as impressive as those in Sabugal and Sortelha but it offers great views over the Serra da Malcata towards Spain, and the town itself makes a good base from which to explore the area. You can whet your appetite beforehand in the small municipal **museum** (daily 9.30am–12.30pm & 2.30–5.30pm; free) above *Café Caninhas* – look out for the stuffed lynx here as it's probably the only glimpse you'll get of one. There's also a comprehensive collection of other local fauna, agricultural tools, man-traps and the obligatory Singer sewing machine.

The **reserve's headquarters** can be found on Rua dos Bombeiros Voluntários (☎277 394 467) and there's a **turismo** in the main square at the lower end of town (Tues–Sun 9.30am–noon & 2–6pm, open till 8pm on Sat; ☎277 394 316) which has details of Solares de Portugal properties in the park. If you're making Penamacor your base, a good budget option is **to stay** in one of the rooms at *Café Caninhas*, Rua de São Estevão 26, just beyond the Galp station, or *Cervejaria Karika*, opposite (both ⓐ). The wonderful *Estalagem Vila Rica* (☎277 394 311, fax 277 394 321; ③), 500m west of the centre on the main road, offers a more sumptuous alternative; the views from this ivy-cloaked eighteenth-century *solar* are marvellous and the rooms comfortable.

Markets are held every first and third Wednesday of the month, and **feiras** on May 10, August 28, September 21, October 15 and November 30.

South from Covilhã: Serra da Gardunha

Fundão and the neighbouring villages of **Alpedrinha** and **Castelo Novo** lie sunk into a ridge, the **Serra da Gardunha**, south of Covilhã. All have magnificent views and are healthy, rural places, with delicious local fruit and, at Castelo Novo, healing waters. Without your own transport, a route through Fundão is an easier approach to Monsanto (see p.245) than cutting across country from Sabugal and Penamacor.

Fundão

FUNDÃO, 17km south of Covilhã by road or rail, is the largest town in the area and a pleasant place to stock up on supplies. As far as sights are concerned, though, even the local tourist pamphlet admits that the town has "no monuments of note". Fundão's rural tranquillity, however, does much to make up for its touristic shortcomings, as does its glorious abundance of fresh fruit and vegetables. The villages around the *serra* are celebrated for their produce and this is the local market centre. In season you'll find cherries, apples, pears, grapes and chestnuts – add to this a visit to the cheese and sausage shops in the Centro Comercial Cidade Nova, at the top of Avenida da Liberdade, and you've got an excellent picnic.

If you want to **stay overnight**, your only budget options are the rather run-down *Pensão 1º de Dezembro*, (☎275 752 384; ①), west of the Praça do Município at Rua da Cale 47, and the equally down-at-heel *Pensão Tarouca* at Rua 25 de Abril 37 (☎275 752 168; ②) – to find the latter turn left along Rua Jornal do Fundão off Avenida da Liberdade. Alternatively, you could try the five-storey *Hotel Samasa*, Trav. das Oliveiras (☎275 751 299, fax 275 751 809; ④), also off the avenida, or the eighteenth-century ANTER property *Casa dos Maias*, Praça do Município 11 (☎275 752 123; ⑤). The **turismo** on Avenida da Liberdade (Mon–Sat

9.30am–12.30pm & 2.30–5.30pm; ☎275 752 770) might be able to help with **rooms**; or there's a small all-year **campsite** (☎275 753 118), two kilometres west of town on the N238, with some shade and a swimming pool.

There aren't many **restaurants**, though the *Veneluso*, Trav. das Oliveiras 12, is well worth trying. The other options are the *Marisqueira* fish restaurant on the same road, or the flash and expensive *Hermínia Restaurante* at Av. da Liberdade 123. **Bars** are similarly limited: *Praça Velha*, off Rua Jornal do Fundão is open till late, as is the pleasant designer joint *O Alaúde Bar*, on Trav. das Oliveiras.

Most local **bus** services depart from the bus station at the bottom of the avenida; regional services operated by Rodoviária do Beira Interior leave from Rua Conde Idanha-a-Nova, parallel to the avenida and on the same side as the bus station.

Alpedrinha

ALPEDRINHA is set into the side of the *serra*, overlooking fields of olives and fruit trees and is easily reached by any bus from Fundão to Castelo Branco. In spring the hillside flowers, fruit-tree blossoms and springwater oozing from every crack in the road make it as idyllic a spot as you could hope to find – notwithstanding the rumbling lorries crashing through the village on the main road to the south.

A good first stop is at the museum in the former **Paços do Concelho**, which displays a collection of tradesmen's tools – from cobbler to baker to tinsmith – and traditional clothing, including a striking black wedding dress, the customary colour in this part of the world. A short way beyond, the **Capela do Leão**, in the courtyard of the Casa de Misericórdia, provides Alpedrinha with its current talking-point. Something of a mystery surrounds the present whereabouts of a series of valuable sixteenth-century panels that disappeared from the chapel during its renovation and which were last spotted at a Primitivist exhibition in Lisbon.

At the top of the same street, above the plain **Igreja Matriz**, is the elaborate fountain known as the **Chafariz de Dom João V**. When the king passed through in 1714 he found the water so good that he commissioned the *chafariz* as a sign of royal approval. The little village flourished and grand houses such as the now-deserted **Palácio do Picadeiro**, which towers above the fountain, were constructed during the eighteenth century. In front of this spectre of a palace, the old **Roman road** begins to wind its cobbled way up the side of the *serra* toward Fundão.

A further point of interest is the **furniture workshop**, situated below the main road on the way out of town toward Castelo Branco. Ask inside and someone will show you around António Santos Pinto's **sala de arte**, with some of the most consummate single-handed marquetry ever produced. Pinto moulded Louis XV chair legs to Napoleonic dressers and threw the odd carved African pageboy into his structures for good measure. There's even a set of tableaux depicting the first six cantos of Camões's *Lusíadas* – all in the most incredible detail.

Practicalities

Information on **buses** is available from the newspaper kiosk on the side of the main through-road. The Alpedrinha **train station**, on the plain below, is unstaffed but you can buy tickets on the trains.

Perhaps the best **accommodation** in town is the *Casa de Barreiro*, Largo das Escolas (☎275 567 120; ④), a turn-of-the-century house set amid rambling gardens at the north end of town and with magnificent views. Less grand in appearance, but equally luxuriant inside, is the ANTER property *Casa da Comenda* (☎275 567 161; ⑤), on the western edge of town – a seventeenth-century building with lovely gardens. Cheaper options include the recommended *Pensão Clara* (☎275 567 391; ②), run by a sprightly old lady of the same name (there's no sign, but it's on the right as you enter the village on the

E802 from the north), and *Pensão Sintra da Beira*, Rua Francisco Dias 14 (☎275 567 858; ①), which is reasonable enough and has a good restaurant. You can unofficially **camp** near the spectacularly situated swimming pool, which has its own bar (open June–Sept), about 1km north of town on the main Fundão road.

The town hosts a tremendous **feira** (market), on the first Sunday in every month, and a full-blown festival, the **Festa do Anjo da Guarda**, each August 3.

Castelo Novo

In northern Portugal **CASTELO NOVO** is best known as the source of *Alardo*, a bottled mineral water reputed to possess healing properties. At the **spa**, marked by just a single café-restaurant, the water gushes from every crack in the earth's surface. The only **accommodation** is the manor house, *Quinta do Ouriço* (☎275 567 236, fax 275 660 569; ⑤), but there's scope for camping – and no shortage of sparkling clear water.

The village proper, like Alpedrinha, has ancient origins, and a few crumbling remains to prove it: a **castle**, an attractive **Paços do Concelho** (above the main square), and a Manueline **pelourinho**. Off to the sides of the square, narrow alleyways and heavy stonework constitute the village's principal charm. Although there is no **bus** to the village, four daily run along the main N18 road (between Fundão and Castelo Branco); you can be dropped or picked up at the crossroads, 4km out.

Into the Beira Baixa

After the rugged beauty of most of Beira Alta, the flat plain of the lower province, **Beira Baixa**, can come as something of an anticlimax. Yet the monotonous, parched landscape has it's own slightly mysterious beauty, dotted with cork and carob trees or the occasional orchard. If you are here over Christmas, you may see burning logs outside each church; these are traditionally kept alight until Twelfth Night. From **Castelo Branco**, the capital of the Beira Baixa and its only sizeable town, you can make rewarding and fairly easy excursions to two strange and atmospheric villages – **Monsanto** and **Idanha-a-Velha**.

Castelo Branco

Not much of **CASTELO BRANCO** has survived the successive wars of this frontier area and today it appears as a predominantly modern town. Set out around wide boulevards, large squares, and small parks, it has an air of prosperity and activity in contrast to the somnolent villages round about.

What's left of its **old town** is confined within the narrow cobbled alleyways and stepped side streets leading up to the ruins of the **Castelo**. Around its twelfth-century walls, a garden-viewing point, the **Miradouro de São Gens**, has been laid out. Nearby is the **Palácio Episcopal** (daily: summer 9am–8pm; winter 9am–7pm; 200$00), the old bishop's palace, with its formal, eighteenth-century garden, a sequence of elaborately shaped hedges, Baroque statues, little pools, fountains and flowerbeds. The balustrades of the two grand staircases are peopled with statues – on one, the Apostles; on the other, the kings of Portugal. Two of the latter are much smaller than the rest: the hated Spanish rulers, Felipe I and II. Elsewhere in the gardens other statues represent months of the year, signs of the zodiac, Christian virtues and the then-known continents.

The palace itself houses the **Museu Tavares Proença Júnior**, a regional museum whose collections roam through the usual local miscellany, save for a large and splendid display of finely embroidered bedspreads, or *colchas*, a craft for which the town is known throughout Portugal. The museum has been closed for a few years for renovations but is due to reopen shortly. The same is true of the elegant sixteenth-century **Câmara**

Municipal in the Praça Luís de Camões, though you can still view the exterior and those of the several seventeenth- and eighteenth-century mansions in the streets around it.

Practicalities

There is a **turismo** (Mon–Fri 9.30am–6pm, Sat & Sun 10.30am–1pm & 2.30–6pm; ☎272 330 339) right in the centre of Castelo Branco, in a little park off the Alameda da Liberdade. The **bus station** is on the corner of Rua Rebelo and Rua do Saibreiro, the latter leading straight up to the Alameda. It's a little further to the **train station**, but equally simple – straight down the broad Avenida de Nuno Álvares.

As the regional capital, the town has a number of **pensões** (ten or more), though less than half of these merit recommendation. *Residencial Lusitânia* (☎272 344 214; ②) above a chemist shop at Rua Sidónio Pais 7, the northern extension of the Alameda, is the most central, though distinctly tattered. For more comfort, try the well-run *Residencial Arraiana*, Av. 1º de Maio 18 (☎272 341 634; ③); otherwise, the turismo can point you towards inexpensive *dormidas* behind the Alameda (①). The municipal **campsite** (☎272 341 615; closed Dec) is 3km north of town along the N18.

For somewhere decent to **eat**, head for the *Restaurante Arcadia*, Alameda da Liberdade 19 (near *Residencial Lusitânia*). It's open daily and particularly crowded with locals at the weekend, paying up to 2000$00 for a fine spread. Further up towards the castle (along Rua Sidónio Pais), there's an equally popular Chinese restaurant, *Grande Muralha*, at Rua da Sé 28. Opposite, *Café Beirão* has pleasant outdoor tables facing the cathedral. For your own supplies, there's a large covered **market** on Avenida 1º de Maio.

Monsanto

MONSANTO, 48km northeast of Castelo Branco (buses twice daily bound for Termas de Monfortinho), claims to be the most ancient settlement in Portugal. It is a claim easy enough to believe, for the old village – there's a newer settlement at the bottom of the hill where the bus drops you – looks as though it has barely changed in centuries. The houses cower beneath a huge fortified granite outcrop, the stone from which they are themselves constructed, and from a few hundred yards they disappear almost entirely into the grey, boulder-strewn background – bar the odd splash of whitewash, added in these more peaceful times. It's all incredibly basic and beautiful – flowers are everywhere and the streets, barely wide enough even for a mule, are simply carved out of the rock.

The **castle**, too, is impressive, though tumbledown. As you climb up through the village you're quite likely to meet someone who'll insist on guiding you up, showing you the views and expounding some of the legends. A big celebration takes place every May 3, when the village girls throw baskets of flowers off the ramparts. The rite commemorates an ancient siege when, in desperation and close to starvation, the defenders threw their last calf over the walls: their attackers, so disheartened at this evidence of plenty within, gave up and went home.

Practicalities

Adega Típica O Cruzeiro (☎277 314 528; ③), an attractive bar on Rua Fernando Namora 6, has a couple of lovely upstairs **rooms** with great views – but you'll almost certainly have to book ahead as the only other accommodation in town is the *Pousada de Monsanto* (☎277 314 471, fax 277 314 481; ⑤) with ten rooms. Otherwise, you could walk or take the twice-daily bus to Penha Garcia, 8km east, where the *Café Isaias* (☎277 366 171; ②), on Rua da Tapada, has rooms and good meals.

In Monsanto, the Pousada has a good **restaurant**, where you can taste delights such as stewed wild boar or braised kid goat with turnip sprouts for around 3500$00. *Restaurante Jovem*, just below the *pousada*, is cheaper but still good, whilst the *Adega Típica O Cruzeiro* is good for a drink and snacks.

Idanha-a-Velha

IDANHA-A-VELHA is another tiny backwater, situated a few kilometres from Monsanto. It sees two buses a day from Idanha-a-Nova, where there are connections to Castelo Branco; however, if you don't have transport, you could try the walk cross-country from Monsanto, but make sure you get good directions before heading off. The village is certainly worth a little effort to reach. It's possibly of a similar age to or even older than Monsanto, but has a considerably more illustrious history. Known as Igaetania, it was once a major Roman city, and subsequently, under Visigothic rule, was the seat of a bishopric – which endured even Moorish occupation. Wamba, the legendary King of the Goths, is said to have been born here. During the reign of Dom Manuel, however, early in the fifteenth century, it is said that a plague of rats forced the occupants to move to Monsanto or nearby Idanha-a-Nova.

The village looks much as it must have done when the rats moved in, and not far different to when the Romans left, either. It still retains a section of massive Roman wall, the **Roman bridge** is still in use, and odd Roman relics lie about everywhere. In the very ancient **Basilica**, which is at least part Visigothic, there's a collection of all the more mobile statues and lumps of inscribed stone found about the place; another small chapel contains an exhibition of coins, pottery, and bones, all found more or less by accident. Ask in the village café for the key to the basilica, if it is locked. Another oddity, whose history nobody seems to know, is a Moorish-inspired balconied mansion.

Termas de Monfortinho

Nestling among pine trees on the banks of the River Erges, **TERMAS DE MON-FORTINHO** is a tranquil wooded spa resort which, with your own transport, makes an attractive base for exploring the surrounding area and nearby Alcántara and Cáceres, over the border in Spain. It has been a popular resort since Roman times, though up until the 1930s it was not connected by road with the rest of Portugal and so was used mostly by the Spanish, who waded across the River Erges and camped among the pine trees. The town has a relaxed atmosphere and pleasant riverside walks, although since the construction of a bridge over the Erges in 1993, connecting the resort to Spain, things have become more lively.

The **thermal baths** (daily 8am–12.30pm & 4–7pm) are north of the turismo, hidden away down by the river and surrounded by woods; you may wish to try out one of the treatments or a massage as the waters are among the most mineral-rich in Portugal. The town also boasts three **swimming pools** and several **tennis courts**; **mountain bikes** are also available for hire from the *Hotel Fonte Santa*.

Practicalities

The **turismo** (☎277 434 223) is two blocks down on the main road, next to the municipal swimming pool. There's no shortage of places to **stay** in Monfortinho. In the modern part of town, the *Beira Baixa* (☎277 434 115; ②) on Rua das Fragueiras is comfortable and cheap but not particularly welcoming; while the friendlier *Pensão Boavista* (☎277 434 213; ③) has TV and telephone in all its rooms. In the old town, there's a cluster of inexpensive, attractive but slightly run-down *pensões* in the woods, by the river; take the road towards the thermal baths and turn right at the fork in the road. However, the best place to stay – if you can afford to splash out – is the peaceful *Hotel Fonte Santa* (☎277 430 300, fax 277 430 309; ⑤), with beautiful rooms and an attractive swimming pool set in landscaped gardens. There are plenty of **restaurants** and **cafés** along the Castelo Branco road, of which *O Garfo* is particularly good.

For onward transport, there are two **buses** daily to Monsanto and Castelo Branco, which leave early in the morning from outside the GALP petrol station near the turismo.

travel details

Trains

Castelo Branco to: Abrantes (5–6 daily; 1hr 20min–2hr); Covilhã (7 daily; 1hr 20min); Lisbon (5–6 daily; 4hr 5min).

Celorico da Beira to: Coimbra (5 daily; 2hr 50min); Guarda (5 daily; 50min); Lisbon (4 daily; 4hr 15min); Vilar Formoso (2 daily; 2hr).

Covilhã to: Abrantes (5 daily; 2hr 25min–3hr 15min); Castelo Branco (7 daily; 1hr–1hr 20min); Guarda (3 daily; 1hr 15min); Lisbon (5 daily; 3hr 20min–5hr 30min).

Fundão to: Castelo Branco (6 daily; 1hr 5min–1hr 30min); Covilhã (7 daily; 25min); Porto (6 daily; 4hr 15min–5hr 15min).

Guarda to: Coimbra (5 daily; 2hr 30min–3hr 40min); Covilhã (3 daily; 1hr 15min); Lisbon (5 daily; 5hr–7hr 50min); Vilar Formoso (4 daily; 50min).

Vilar Formoso (Spanish border) to: Guarda (4 daily; 50min); Lisbon (1 daily; 6hr 30min); Salamanca, Spain (2 onward connections from Portugal daily; 2hr 30min).

Buses

Almeida to: Guarda (1 daily; 2hr).

Alpendrinha to: Castelo Branco (Mon–Fri 5 daily; 30min); Covilhã (2–3 daily; 2hr 35min); Fundão (2–3 daily; 15–25min); Guarda (4 daily; 1hr 20min); Lisbon (5 daily; 4hr 30min).

Belmonte to: Guarda (3 daily; 45min).

Castelo Branco to: Coimbra (3–4 daily; 3hr); Covilhã (4 daily; 40min–1hr 5min); Guarda (hourly; 1hr 55min); Lisbon (2–6 daily; 3hr 45min–4hr 10min); Termas de Montefortinho (2 daily; 2hr 30min); Viseu (1–2 daily; 3hr 30min).

Celorico da Beira to: Coimbra (4 daily; 2hr 25min); Covilhã (4 daily; 1hr 15min); Guarda (4 daily; 1hr 30min); Lamego (Mon–Fri 3 daily; 3hr 5min); Lisbon (1 daily; 5hr); Viseu (4–6 daily; 50min–1hr).

Covilhã to: Castelo Branco (4 daily; 1hr 5min); Fundão (4 daily; 20min); Guarda (4 daily; 50min); Lisbon (2–4 daily; 5hr 30min); Penhas da Saúde (August only: Sat 2, Sun 3; 35min); Viseu (2 daily, 2hr 10 min).

Guarda to: Almeida (1 daily; 2 hr); Alpedrinha (4 daily; 1hr 20min); Belmonte (3 daily; 45min); Braga (3 daily; 4hr 20min); Castelo Branco (15 daily; 1hr 55min); Covilhã (10 daily; 50min); Fundão (4 daily; 1hr 5min); Lisbon (2–5 daily; 5–6hr); Pinhel (2 daily; 50min); Trancoso (3 daily; 1hr 30min); Vilar Formoso (4 daily, 50min); Viseu (2–5 daily; 2hr 15min).

Seia to: Celorico (4 daily; 45min); Coimbra (3–4 daily; 1hr 40min); Guarda (4 daily; 1hr 15min).

Trancoso to: Braga (1 daily; 4hr 10min); Bragança (2 daily; 3hr); Celorico da Beira (1–2 daily; 1hr 25min); Covilhã (1–2 daily; 1hr 45min); Guarda (1–3 daily; 1hr); Lamego (1–2 daily; 2hr); Lisbon (2 daily; 6hr 10min); Pocinho (2 daily; 1hr 20min); Viseu (2 daily; 1hr 50min).

Vilar Formoso to: Guarda (4 daily; 50min); Lisbon (4 daily; 5hr 40min–6hr).

Viseu to: Belmonte (Ginjal) (2 daily; 1hr 50min); Celorico da Beira (4–6 daily; 50min–1hr); Coimbra (5–10 daily; 1hr 25min); Covilhã (2–6 daily; 2hr 15min); Faro (6 daily; 11hr 35min–12hr 20min); Guarda (2–9 daily; 1hr 20min); Lisbon (5 daily; 4–5hr); Porto (1–3 daily; 1hr 50min); São Pedro do Sul (Mon–Fri 4–5 daily, 1–2 at weekends; 1hr); Sernancelhe (1 daily); Trancoso (2–3 daily; 1hr 25min).

CHAPTER FIVE

PORTO AND THE DOURO

P ortugal's second largest city, **Porto**, is magnificently situated at the mouth of the Douro River, its old quarters scrambling up the rocky north bank in tangled tiers. It's a massively atmospheric city, almost Dickensian in parts, though the attention of most visitors is focused firmly on the port-producing suburb of **Vila Nova de Gaia**, across the river. The coastal waters either side of the city are shockingly polluted these days, but you don't have to head that far north to find excellent beaches; those at the resorts of **Vila do Conde** and **Póvoa de Varzim** offer a taste of what's to come as you head into the Minho.

Above all, though, it's the **Rio Douro** ("river of gold") that dominates every aspect of this region: a narrow, winding gorge for the major part of its long route from the Spanish border, with port wine lodges dotted about the hillsides and a series of tiny villages, visited by few except for the seasonal wine trade workers. The valleys and tributaries form some of the loveliest and most spectacular landscapes in the whole of Portugal, and even though the wine no longer shoots down the river's rapids in barges, as it once did, a trip up the valley remains one of the best scenic routes in the country. The capital of the Alto Douro province is **Peso da Régua**, a perpetually developing town with more scope for visiting wine lodges; just 13km south of here is the delightful Baroque town of **Lamego**, the home of Portugal's champagne-like wine, Raposeira.

If you're driving, you can follow minor roads along the river practically all the way from Porto to the border crossings at Miranda do Douro (see p.239). Taking the **train**, though, is probably more fun, and certainly more scenic. The **Douro line** joins the course of the river about 60km inland from Porto and sticks to it from then on, cutting into the rock face and crisscrossing the water on a series of rocking bridges: one of those journeys that needs no justification other than the trip itself. To the east, narrow gauge rail lines follow the river's tributaries north into Trás-os-Montes: the **Tâmega line** runs to the beautiful riverside town of **Amarante**; the **Corgo line** connects with

---

ACCOMMODATION PRICE CODES

All the accommodation prices in this book have been coded using the symbols below. The symbols represent the lowest prices you can expect to pay for a **double room in high season**; for a full explanation, see p.32.

① Under 4000$00
② 4000$00–7000$00
③ 7000$00–11000$00

④ 11,000$00–15,000$00
⑤ 15,000$00–20,000$00
⑥ 20,000$00–25,000$00

⑦ 25,000$00–30,000$00
⑧ 30,000$00–40,000$00
⑨ Over 40,000$00

Vila Real, a useful bus terminal for exploring Trás-os-Montes; while the **Tua line** goes from Tua to Mirandela in central Trás-os-Montes, from where you can catch buses to Bragança in the northeast.

Porto

Although the capital of the north, **PORTO** (Oporto) is a very different city from Lisbon – unpretentious, inward-looking, and unashamedly commercial. As the local saying goes: "Coimbra studies; Braga prays; Lisbon shows off; and Porto works." The city's greatest sights are its five bridges: three modern, two nineteenth-century, and all of them spectacular. The older ones are the defunct metalwork Maria Pia railway link, designed by Eiffel, and the dizzying, two-tiered Ponte Luís I, which connects the city with **Vila Nova de Gaia**, home of the port wine lodges – all of which offer tours and tastings to visitors.

In the city proper, there is a handful of buildings around which to direct your wanderings: the landmark **Torre dos Clérigos** and the Sé, the ornate interiors of the **Bolsa** and church of **São Francisco**, and a clutch of good **museums**. But the fascination of Porto lies very much in the day-to-day life of the place, with its prosperous business core surrounded by both well-to-do suburbs as well as depressed housing estates, tempered by a heart of cramped streets and ancient alleys wholly untouched by the planners. This side of Porto comes into focus if you take a walk along the **quayside** between the the the old customs area of Alfândega and Ponte Luís I, this whole area known as the *Ribeira* (riverside) has been designated as a **Unesco World Heritage Site**.

It's hard not to like the city, or to respond to the crowds, tiny bars and antiquated shops. If you can, plan your visit to coincide with **Saint John's Eve** (the night of June 23–24), when the place is at its earthiest and finest for the riotous celebration of São João. On this night, seemingly the entire population takes to the streets, hitting each other over the head with squeaky, plastic hammers, or anything else to hand, letting off illuminated balloons. (See p.275 for more information on festivals.)

Arrival and information

Buses #56 and #87 (daily except Sun; every fifteen to thirty minutes; 160$00 one way) shuttle between the **airport**, 13km north of the city, and Jardim da Cordoaria, by the Universidade building; the journey usually takes forty minutes, but allow an hour at peak times of day. There's also the AeroBus (every 30 minutes from 8am–7.30pm; 500$00), which drops you off at your hotel if possible, or at an appropriate bus stop (the ticket remains valid for unlimited use on local buses until midnight). Taxis from the airport into the centre cost from 2500–3000$00. Airport **banks** are open daily 8am–8pm, and there's also an **information** counter (daily 8am–11.30pm; ☎229 412 534, fax 229 412 543).

Coming into Porto by train or bus, you'll find yourself deposited fairly centrally, though the various terminals can cause a little confusion (see p.254). Coming from the south, **trains** drop you at the **Estação de Campanhã**, a few kilometres east of the centre; change here for a local train into **Estação de São Bento**, in the heart of the city – it takes about five minutes and there should never be more than a twenty-minute wait. Most trains from the north run directly to São Bento, though narrow-gauge trains from Guimarães and from the north coast (Vila do Conde/Póvoa de Varzim) use the smaller **Estação da Trindade**, just to the north of Avenida dos Aliados.

Bus companies have no single terminal and a glance at the schedules shows that each company operates from a different street. Most, though, are fairly central, and

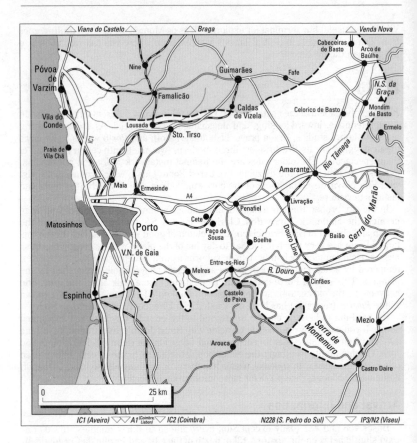

Viana do Castelo △ | △ Braga | △ Venda Nova

Cabeceiras de Basto, Arco de Baúlhe, Póvoa de Varzim, Nine, Guimarães, Fafe, N.S. da Graça, Famalicão, Caldas de Vizela, Celorico de Basto, Mondim de Basto, Ermelo, Vila do Conde, Lousada, Sto. Tirso, Praia de Vila Chã, Amarante, Rio Tâmega, Maia, Ermesinde, A4, Penafiel, Livração, Matosinhos, Porto, Cete, Paço de Sousa, Boelhe, Baião, Serra do Marão, V.N. de Gaia, Entre-os-Rios, Douro Line, Melres, R. Douro, Espinho, Castelo de Paiva, Cinfães, Mezio, Arouca, Serra de Montemuro, Castro Daire

0   25 km

IC1 (Aveiro) ▽ ▽ A1 (Coimbra/Lisbon) ▽ IC2 (Coimbra)   N228 (S. Pedro do Sul) ▽   ▽ IP3/N2 (Viseu)

many operate from a common terminal – Garagem Atlântico – on **Rua Alexandre Herculano** (just east of São Bento, off Praça da Batalha). See p.254 for information on Porto's various bus termini, and consult the "Travel details" at the end of this chapter for route details.

If you're hiring a rental car to explore the surrounding countryside, it might be better to wait until the day you leave Porto to pick one up. The downtown grid of one-way streets and Vila Nova de Gaia, are best negotiated on foot or in a taxi.

Information

Porto has two central **tourist offices**, where you can pick up large-scale city plans as well as information about train and bus departures. The most helpful is on Rua Clube Fenianos 25, facing the left side of the Câmara Municipal (July–Sept Mon–Fri 9am–7pm, Sat–Sun 9.30am–4.30pm; Oct–June Mon-Fri 9am–5.30pm, Sat–Sun 10am–5pm; ☎223 393 470), which has a useful noticeboard for visitors to leave messages on. The other partly privatized turismo is on Praça Dom João I, close to São Bento station (Mon–Fri 9am–7.30pm, Sat & Sun 9.30am–3.30pm; during Aug Sat & Sun 9.30am–7.30pm; ☎222 057 514, fax 222 053 212) and offers discounts on some of the more expensive hotels.

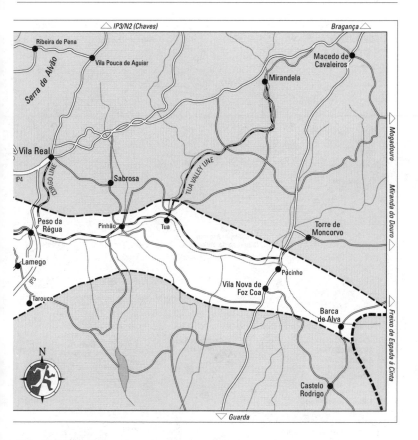

City transport

Although modern Porto sprawls for some miles along the north bank of the Douro, most sights are within the compact and very hilly centre, six kilometres from the ocean, and all are within **walking** – or perhaps more accurately climbing – distance. For trips further afield, there's a reliable network of local STCP **buses** – see the box below. **Information** on all routes, including night buses, can be had at the STCP office on Praça Almeida Garrett, facing São Bento station (freephone ☎800 200 166). The STCP provides an invaluable bus route map, the *mapa geral*; and also the *mapa da madruga-da*, which details the night buses.

Single **tickets** cost 160$00 on the bus, but only 80$00 in advance from local newsagents, stationers, or kiosks at all the main bus stops. The kiosks also sell ten-journey tickets for 750$00 (1050$00 including the suburbs). If you plan to travel a lot, however, you might consider buying a **travel pass** (available on the bus): a one-day city pass, Diário Porto, costs 370$00, and the Diário Geral, which includes Vila Nova de Gaia, costs 490$00. There's also a *turístico* pass, (available from kiosks) valid throughout the city (including Vila Nova de Gaia and the suburbs); prices range from 1900$00 for four days to 2500$00 for seven.

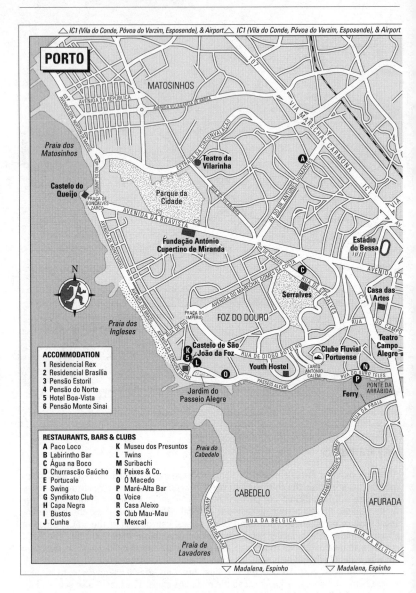

There are ten main bus terminals in the city centre for bus routes mentioned in the text (as listed in the box below). Services cease or are much reduced after around 9pm: those that also operate at night (usually hourly) are marked with asterisks. Buses to Rotunda da Boavista – 1.5km northwest of the centre – include #3, #20, #23, #34, #36, #52, #82 and #84. Note that until Boavista's new bus station is complete (circa 2001), buses stop at various points around and off the square, so you'll have to ask.

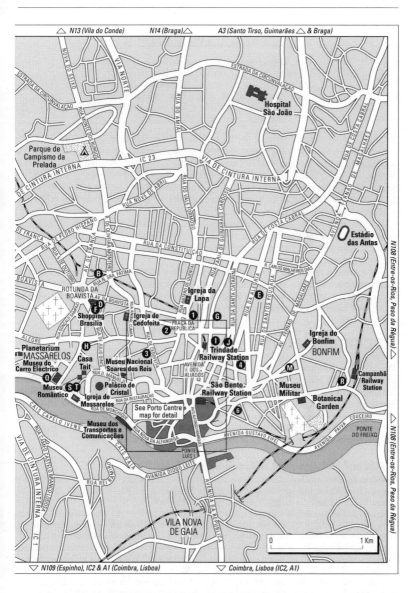

△ N13 (Vila do Conde)   N14 (Braga)△   A3 (Santo Tirso, Guimarães △ & Braga)

Hospital
São João

Parque de
Campismo da
Prelada

Estádio
das Antas

ROTUNDA DA
BOAVISTA

Igreja da
Lapa

Shopping
Brasília

Igreja de
Cedofeita

PRAÇA DA
REPÚBLICA

Planetarium
MASSARELOS

Museu do
Carro Eléctrico

Casa
Tait

Museu Nacional
Soares dos Reis

Trindade
Railway Station

Igreja do
Bonfim

BONFIM

Palácio de
Cristal

São Bento
Railway Station

Museu
Militar

Campanhã
Railway Station

Museu
Romântico

Igreja de
Massarelos

See Porto Centre
map for detail

Botanical
Garden

PONTE
DO FREIXO

Museu dos
Transportes e
Comunicações

PONTE
LUÍS I

VILA NOVA
DE GAIA

0   1 Km

△ N109 (Espinho), IC2 & A1 (Coimbra, Lisboa)   △ Coimbra, Lisboa (IC2, A1)

N108 (Entre-os-Rios, Peso da Régua) ▷

N108 (Entre-os-Rios, Peso da Régua) ▷

Central Porto has one surviving **tram route**, #18, which has a flat fare of 85$00 and is worth going on for the ride alone. It operates year round and leaves (Mon–Sat 8am–7pm; freephone 0800 200 166) from Rua do Carmo by Hospital Santo António and rattles along the river to the sea at Foz do Douro, where it heads up the coast to the diminutive Castelo do Queijo. You may wish to get off here and catch a tram back in the opposite direction, or you can continue for the full 45-minute ride which winds

BUS TERMINALS IN PORTO	
Avenida dos Aliados	Praça da Liberdade
Bolhão	Praça da República
Cordoaria	Rotunda da Boavista
Praça Almeida Garrett	Rua Nova da Alfândega
Praça da Batalha	Rua Sá da Bandeira

round to the shopping district at the eastern end of Avenida Boavista, from where it is a 25-minute walk back to the centre. Another option is to take an arranged tram trip or a sightseeing **tour** on a double-decker bus (April–Sept only). You have a choice of a hop-on, hop-off ticket, which gives you the option of spending time at the sights themselves, or a one-and-a-half-hour return trip with commentary in English. Tickets cost 1200$00 and are available from most travel agents, or call Diana Tours on ☎223 771 230. For details of **river cruises**, see p.278 (Listings).

In 1999 work began on an ambitious, partly underground, **metro** system, which is scheduled for completion in January 2003. The first line should be open by the end of 2001, connecting Trindade station with Senhora da Hora (home of the huge Norteshopping centre) in the northwest.

The easiest way to negotiate Porto is by **taxi**; they are cheap and there are ranks in most squares. Fares are metered, and shouldn't cost more than 800–1000$00 for a ride in the centre, often much less. The long-distance *carros de aluguer* – distinguishable by an "A" – do not run on a meter, so negotiate a price beforehand.

Accommodation

Porto's **accommodation** is generally good value. The least expensive rooms in the city are in the area south and east of São Bento station; for rather more salubrious places, your best bet is to ignore bargainers at the stations and head for the *pensões* and hotels detailed below, in areas west or east of the central thoroughfare, Avenida dos Aliados. In winter, it's worth investing in more expensive rooms than you might otherwise choose, or you'll freeze, as few budget hotels have any heating; turismos have lists of places with central heating.
All places are shown on the "Central Porto" map unless stated otherwise.

Hotels and pensões west of Avenida dos Aliados

Residencial dos Aliados, Rua Elísio de Melo 27–2º (☎222 004 853, fax 222 002 710). Just off Avenida dos Aliados, this very comfortable *pensão* fills quickly in summer; book ahead. It can be noisy, though, so try for a room at the back; breakfast included. ②.

Hotel da Bolsa, Rua Ferreira Borges 101 (☎222 026 768, fax 222 058 888). Marvellously located in the heart of the old city, this three-star hotel is one of the best, with pleasant service, good modern rooms (all with satellite TV, a/c and phone), and a bar. Lift access and rooms for disabled people. ④.

Pensão Residencial Duas Nações, Praça Guilherme Gomes Fernandes 59 (☎ & fax 222 081 616, *duasnacoes@mail.teleweb.pt*). Cheap and dependable budget hotel, but often full so it's best to ring ahead. English-speaking staff and a laundry service. ①.

Pensão Europa, Rua do Almada 396 (☎222 006 971). A bit gloomy, but with a lively bar and good restaurant. The cheaper rooms come without shower and use shared bathrooms. ①.

Hotel Infante de Sagres, Praça Dona Filipa de Lencastre 62 (☎222 008 101, fax 222 054 937). This opulent five-star hotel was built in the 1950s, and lavishly furnished with Chinese porcelain, Carrara marble, Persian carpets and stained glass windows. Today it also houses the Peruvian consulate. Has a good restaurant too. Recommended if your budget's up to it. ⑦.

Hotel Internacional, Rua do Almada 131 (☎222 005 032, fax 222 009 063). Modern three-star hotel, with a/c, TV, private bathroom and phones in all rooms. ⑤.

Hotel Residencial Malaposta, Rua da Conceição 80 (☎222 006 947, fax 222 006 295). Friendly and unpretentious modern place with good rooms; breakfast included. ③.

Pensão Monumental, Av. dos Aliados 151–4º (☎222 003 964, fax 222 005 794). A great, airy, family-run place situated on the fourth and fifth floors of a grand but decrepit building. It can get noisy when school groups are staying. ②.

Pensão Pão de Açucar, Rua do Almada 262 (☎222 002 425, fax 223 050 339). Stylish 1930s' hotel with quiet rooms and private bathrooms but it's getting overpriced; book ahead in summer. ③.

Pensão de Paris, Rua da Fábrica 27–29 (☎222 073 140, fax 222 073 149). Popular *pensão* with huge rooms and fine ceilings; however, it is beginning to show its age. More expensive rooms (②) have bathrooms. Breakfast is included and served in a restaurant overlooking a small garden. ①.

Residencial Porto Rico, Rua do Almada 237 (☎223 394 690). Small, adequate rooms, quieter at the back (if you prefer the noise of cats to cars). Rooms without facilities are cheaper; breakfast included. ②.

Pensão São Marino, Praça Carlos Alberto 59 (☎223 325 499 or 222 054 380) in a pleasant garden square near the Torre dos Clérigos. Efficient and friendly, all rooms with shower and most with a TV; breakfast included. ②.

Pensão Vera Cruz, Rua Ramalho Ortigão 14 (☎223 323 396, fax 223 323 421). Close to the tourist office, this represents a hike in quality, more of a hotel than a *pensão*. It's elegant, if a bit pricey, and breakfast is included. ③.

Hotels and pensões east of Avenida dos Aliados

Pensão Belo Sonho, Rua de Passos Manuel 186, facing the Coliseu (☎222 003 389, fax 222 012 850). Not the most salubrious but reasonable value and centrally placed. The more expensive rooms have en-suite bathrooms. ①–②.

Residencial Girassol, Rua de Sá da Bandeira 133 (☎222 001 891, fax 222 081 892). A good place up the street from the *Peninsular*; all rooms are self-contained and some have TVs. Also has a good restaurant. Breakfast included. ①.

Grande Hotel do Porto, Rua de Santa Catarina 197 (☎222 008 176, fax 222 051 061). Claiming to be the oldest hotel in Porto, this large three-star place still retains a touch of grandeur in the form of chandeliers, polished marble columns and staff uniforms. Rooms are a/c with TVs and phones. It's on the pedestrianized part of the street and car parking is available. ④.

Holiday Inn Garden Court, Praça da Batalha 127–130 (☎223 392 300, fax 222 006 009). An ugly pink edifice on Praça da Batalha opposite the cinema, modern and comfortable with TVs in its rooms. Facilities for the disabled. ④.

Hotel Mercure Batalha, Praça da Batalha 116 (☎222 000 571, fax 222 002 468). Similar standard to the *Holiday Inn*, with brighter rooms and common areas verging on kitsch. Disabled facilities and car parking too. ③.

Pensão Monte Sinai (*shown on the Porto map*), Rua Alexandre Herculano 146 (☎222 008 218, fax 222 018 861). Fairly big rooms, some with baths and TVs. This is extremely cheap – although it can be noisy. ①.

Pensão do Norte (*shown on the Porto map*), Rua de Fernandes Tomás 579 (☎222 003 503). On the junction with Rua de Santa Catarina (opposite an extravagantly tiled church), this pleasant, rambling old place has masses of rooms, with and without facilities. The best rooms have balconies overlooking the street, though these are undoubtedly noisy. ①.

Pensão Paulista, Av. dos Aliados 214–2º (☎222 054 692, fax 222 005 730). Well placed, and with good rooms, but you'll want one at the back if you're to sleep soundly. Breakfast included. ②.

Hotel Peninsular, Rua de Sá da Bandeira 21 (☎222 003 012, fax 222 084 984). Central (just uphill from São Bento station) and comfortable two-star pension with a range of rooms. Breakfast is included. The *azulejos* in the entrance reveal it to have once been the outbuilding of the nearby church. ③.

Hotels and pensões north towards Praça da República

Residencial Brasília (*shown on the Porto map*), Rua de Álvares Cabral 221 (☎222 006 095, fax 222 006 510). A really friendly hotel (the best of three in a row). Self-contained rooms have TVs, phones and a/c. Breakfast is included. There are only ten rooms, so ring ahead. Parking 800$00 per day extra. ②.

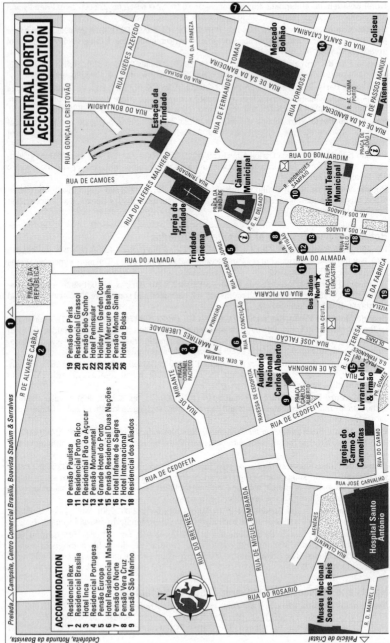

CENTRAL PORTO: ACCOMMODATION

ACCOMMODATION

1 Residencial Rex
2 Residencial Brasília
3 Hotel Inca
4 Residencial Portuguesa
5 Pensão Europa
6 Hotel Residencial Malaposta
7 Pensão do Norte
8 Pensão Vera Cruz
9 Pensão São Marino

10 Pensão Paulista
11 Residencial Porto Rico
12 Residencial Pão de Açucar
13 Pensão Monumental
14 Grande Hotel do Porto
15 Pensão Residencial Duas Nações
16 Hotel Infante de Sagres
17 Hotel Internacional
18 Residencial dos Aliados

19 Pensão de Paris
20 Residencial Girassol
21 Pensão Belo Sonho
22 Hotel Peninsular
23 Pensão Monumental
24 Holiday Inn Garden Court
24 Hotel Mercure Batalha
25 Pensão Monte Sinai
26 Hotel da Bolsa

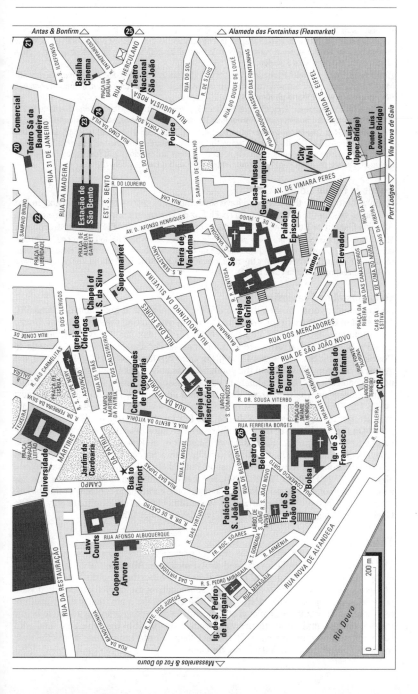

Pensão Estoril (*shown on the Porto map*), Rua de Cedofeita 193 (☎222 002 751, fax 222 005 152). Rooms of varying sizes (and sometimes odd shapes) in a friendly and well-maintained *pensão*, with a café on the ground floor for breakfast. Some rooms have balconies, all have TVs. It's on the pedestrianized section of the street, and overlooks a garden. ②.

Hotel Inca, Praça Coronel Pacheco 52 (☎222 084 151, fax 222 054 756, *hotelinca@mail.telepac.pt*). Modern and ugly hotel but well run, though not as plush as you'd expect for its four-star status. Rooms are a/c with TV and phones. ④.

Residencial Portuguesa, Trav. Coronel Pacheco 11, corner with Rua Martires da Liberdade (☎222 004 174). A converted house, some way out near Praça Coronel Pacheco, and consequently quiet. ①.

Residencial Rex (*shown on the Porto map*), Praça da República 117 (☎222 004 548, fax 222 083 882). At the top end of Rua do Almada, facing the garden square. It has the feel of a grand hotel, but was in fact a private house until relatively recently. Rooms are spacious and functional; breakfast is included. Private parking. Highly recommended, although it can be noisy. ②.

Hotels in Foz do Douro

If you want to stay by the **sea** – and have some money to spare – then you can stay in Foz do Douro, west of the centre. You can reach Foz do Douro on tram #18; bus #1 from Praça Almeida Garrett or Rua Nova da Alfândega, or alternatively bus #24 from the Cordoaria.

Hotel Boa-Vista (*shown on the Porto map*), Esplanada do Castelo 58, Foz do Douro (☎226 180 083, fax 226 173 881). Lovely old grand hotel at the mouth of the Douro, whose more expensive front rooms have magnificent views over the river, ocean and Castelo de São João da Foz. There's also a pool, good rooftop restaurant and bar. ⑤.

Youth hostel and campsites

Porto's popular **youth hostel**, the *Pousada da Juventude*), is at Rua Paulo da Gama 551, 4km west of the centre in the *bairro* of Pasteleira overlooking the mouth of the Douro (reception open 9–10am and after 6pm; ☎226 177 257, fax 226 177 247; ③); buses #35 from Praça Almeida Garrett, Cordoaria, or Praça da Batalha, and #36 from Rotunda da Boavista pass by, or catch buses #1 or #24 or tram #18 (as above for Foz do Douro) and get off at bus stop "Fluvial", and the youth hostel is only a 400m walk. In summer, you'll need to book ahead. There's a kitchen, bar, and disabled facilities; food is also available.

The closest **campsite**, *Parque de Campismo da Prelada*, Rua Monte dos Burgos; (☎228 122 616), is 3km northwest of the centre but – with 650 pitches – is not exactly intimate; get there on buses #6, #50, #54, #85 from the Cordoaria, or, #87 (from the airport). On the south side of the river, there are two sites near the mouth of the Douro: to get to the *Parque de Campismo de Salgueiros*, at Rua de Salgueiros, Canidelo (May–Sept; ☎227 810 500, fax 227 810 500), take a Santos and Irmãos bus marked "Paniceiro" from Rua Augusto Rosa, just off Praça da Batalha; for the Orbitur site (open all year; ☎227 122 520, fax 227 152 534), 500 metres from Praia da Madalena, which has a swimming pool, tennis and volleyball courts, some caravans to rent and a minimarket, take bus #57 from either the airport or Praça Almeida Garrett. Minimum stay for the Orbitur site is one week in July–August, two days at other times.

The City

The "centre" is perhaps best regarded as **Avenida dos Aliados**, the commercial hub of the city, fronted by banks and offices. **Praça da Liberdade** marks the bottom end of this sloping avenue and a little further south, across the busy road (reached via a pedestrian underpass), is the **Estação de São Bento**, the main train station. South of São Bento, a labyrinth of medieval streets and seedy-looking alleyways tumble below the **Sé**, or cathedral, down to the waterfront **Cais da Ribeira**, which is lined with restaurants, bars, clubs and cafés. Here, the two-tier **Ponte Luís I** runs across the river to the port wine suburb of **Vila Nova de Gaia**.

The streets leading off Avenida dos Aliados are the city's major shopping areas: to the west, the busy **Rua da Fábrica** with its stationers and bookshops; to the east, **Rua de Passos Manuel**, which runs into **Praça Dom João I**, and beyond into **Rua de Santa Catarina**, full of clothes and shoe shops. The only other areas of interest are to the west of the centre: you can walk as far as the **Jardim do Palácio de Cristal** and the *Solar do Vinho do Porto*, but you'll need to use public transport to reach Porto's world-class museum of modern art, **Serralves** (also called the Museu de Arte Contemporânea).

From Avenida dos Aliados to Cordoaria

The broad **Avenida dos Aliados** is as good a starting point as any for exploration, though other than a quick squint up the avenue to the Câmara Municipal at the very top and a coffee at the pavement tables of one of the cafés at the bottom, there's little reason to linger other than for a visit to the **Ateneu Comercial do Porto**, just east of the avenida at Rua de Passos Manuel 44. This opulent nineteenth century building is the headquarters of Porto's commercial association and houses temporary exhibitions of faience, postage stamps and paintings in its gloriously decorated halls (daily 2–7.30pm; free). If you didn't arrive by train, you may as well cut down briefly to the **Estação de São Bento**, one of the city's grandest buildings in its own right, with magnificent *azulejos* by Jorge Colaço in the entrance hall. These, somewhat arbitrarily, take on two great themes – the history of transport and the battle of Aljubarrota.

There's little reason to linger in this area though, other than for a visit to the **Mercado Bolhão** (Mon–Fri 8am–5pm, Sat 8am–1pm), three blocks east along Rua Formosa, a nineteenth century wrought-iron construction containing all the usual items, including food and flowers. On **Rua Formosa** itself, look for the few surviving **bacalhau and port wine shops**, delightfully antiquated places that hang their wares outside. The *bacalhau* (dried, salted codfish) is also bundled up in stacks all around the counter, alongside just about every type of port available. Two blocks south of Bolhão, the **Ateneu Comercial do Porto**, at Rua de Passos Manuel 44, is an opulent nineteenth century building housing the headquarters of Porto's commercial association, as well as temporary exhibitions of faience, postage stamps and paintings in its gloriously decorated halls (daily 2–7.30pm; free).

If you didn't arrive by train, you may as well cut down briefly to the **Estação de São Bento**, one of the city's grandest buildings in its own right, with magnificent *azulejos* by Jorge Colaço in the entrance hall. These, somewhat arbitrarily, take on two great themes – the history of transport and the battle of Aljubarrota.

The stifled streets of the old town rarely permit any sort of overall view of the city, so it's a good idea to climb the Baroque **Torre dos Clérigos** (summer Mon–Sat 10am–7pm, Sun 10am–noon & 2–7pm; winter Mon–Sat 10am–noon & Sun 2–5pm; 100$00), 400m west of São Bento, to get your bearings. This landmark was designed, like the curious oval church beneath it the Igreja dos Clérigos (10am–noon & 2–5pm; closed Wed), by the Italian architect Nicolau Nasoni and was once the tallest structure in Portugal. The dizzying vistas from the top take in the entire city, as well as south across the river to Vila Nova de Gaia and sometimes even to the distant mouth of the Douro and the coast.

The wonderful surroundings at the Livraria Lello & Irmão **bookshop**, off Rua dos Clérigos at Rua das Carmelitas 144, are certainly worth a visit. Behind the white Gothic facade, the Art Nouveau interior has been fully restored to its 1906 splendour – Gothic bookcases line the walls and a curved serpentine double staircase leads up to the antiquarian gallery (and a bar), lit by a stained-glass skylight.

The area immediately below the tower comprises the older sections of the university, and the gardens of the **Jardim da Cordoaria**. This area is a fairly prestigious quarter of town, housing, for example, most of the city's commercial **art galleries**, which are grouped together on Rua Galeria de Paris and Rua Miguel Bombarda, north of the Cordoaria. Worth a particular mention here is **Cooperativa Árvore,** Rua Azevedo de Albuquerque 1, west of Torre dos Clérigos (☎222 057 235); a co-operative of painters, sculptors and designers who run their own art school in close competition with the official Escola das Belas Artes (itself housed in a nearby mansion). They pride themselves on the vitality of the teaching and the freedom they allow their pupils – the results of which are on view in a punchy summer show in June/July.

The Sé and down to the Cais da Ribeira

Set on a rocky outcrop a couple of hundred metres south from São Bento station, Porto's cathedral, the **Sé** (Mon–Sat 9am–12.30pm & 2.30–6pm, Sun 2.30-6pm), is a bluff, austere fortress. Despite attempts to beautify it in the eighteenth century, it retains the hard, simple lines of its Romanesque origins – more impressive from a distance than close up. Inside it's depressing, even the vaunted silver altarpiece failing to make any impression in the prevailing gloom. For 250$00, however, you can escape into the neighbouring cloisters, and climb a Nasoni-designed staircase leading up to a dazzling chapterhouse, with more views from the casement windows over the old quarter. There are fine views, too, from the broad flagged courtyard in front of the cathedral.

Beside the Sé stretches the fine facade of the Archbishop's Palace (not open to the public), while around the back, at Rua Dom Hugo 32, is the beautiful **Casa-Museu Guerra Junqueiro** (Tue–Sat 10am–12.30pm & 2–5.30pm, Sun 2–5.30pm; 150$00, free Sat & Sun). This is the former home of the poet, who spent a lifetime collecting Islamic art, especially from Iberia – the fruits of his endeavours, such as Seljuk pottery, miniatures and glassware, are here to see.

Back at the Sé, Rua de Dom Hugo curls back around to the Sé to merge with the crumbling, animated old alleys which lead down to the riverside. From the prancing statue of Vimara Peres, **Calçada de Vandoma** plunges downwards through the most fascinating and atmospheric part of the city: a medieval ghetto of backstreets that would have been demolished or prettified in most other cities of Europe, although parts are now finally undergoing restoration. Tall, narrow, and rickety, the houses have grown upwards into every available space, adapting as best they can to the steep terrain.

Not much commerce goes on down at the waterfront since the big ships stopped calling here, but along the **Cais da Ribeira** old men still sit around as if they expect to be thrown a line or set to work unloading some urgent cargo, while local children cool off in the summer by leaping into the foul and filthy waters of the Douro. The iron *elevador* (150$00) at the eastern end of the Cais climbs up to a good viewing point achingly close to the top of the Bairro da Sé but as it's fenced in you won't be able to disembark. There's some bustle around the weekday fruit and vegetable market but otherwise it's at night that the riverfront comes alive, with dozens of cafés, clubs and restaurants (see p.267) to tickle the sensations. A Post-Modern cube of a fountain adds a slightly surreal air to the quarter.

Following the Cais westward, past the Praça da Ribeira, you reach Rua da Alfândega, which leads away from the water. If you double back along Rua Infante Dom Henrique you pass the **Casa do Infante** (Mon–Fri 8.30am–5pm; free), the house where Prince Henry the Navigator is said to have been born. It's an impressive mansion, which has in its time been the City Customs Hall and a Mint; it currently functions as the headquarters of the city's archives.

East of the Estação de São Bento

Compared to the area west of the station there's little of interest **east of the Sé**, however, the sunny **Praça da Batalha** is pleasant enough during the day; it's at the top end of Rua

31 de Janeiro, or up Rua da Madeira beside São Bento station (don't go there at night – it's a haunt of drug addicts). The square is dominated by the gorgeous **Teatro Nacional São João** (see p.274), which replaced an older theatre that burned down in 1909. At the north end of the Praça, the **Igreja de Santo Ildefonso** has some lovely *azulejo* panels in its Baroque facade, and inside conceals a *retábulo* attributed to the Italian master-carver, Nasoni. Heading east from the Praça along Avenida Rodrigues de Freitas, a ten-minute walk (or buses #35 or 80 from Praça da Batalha) brings you to the **Museu Militar do Porto**, Rua do Heroísmo 329 (Mon–Sat 2–5pm; 200$00 adults). Situated in the former headquarters of the hated political police (PIDE) – disbanded after the 1974 revolution – the museum contains firearms and vehicles from the fifteenth-century to the present day. If museum fatigue hits you, there is a very soothing **botanical garden** around the corner on Rua Barão de Nova Sintra 285 (Mon–Fri 9am–noon, 2–5pm; free); bus #35 from Praça da Batalha.

The Bolsa and around

Also on Rua Infante Dom Henrique, Porto's stock exchange – the **Palácio da Bolsa** – faces a statue of the Infante Henry himself, tucked into an eponymously named square. The building is a pompous nineteenth-century edifice with a vast Neoclassical facade and its keepers are inordinately proud of the place. On the **guided tours** (April–Oct Mon–Fri 9am–6.40pm, Sat–Sun 9am–12.30pm & 2–6.30pm; Nov–March daily 9am–12.30pm & 2–5.30pm; 750$00) they dwell, with evident glee, on the enormous cost of every item, the exact weight of every piece of precious metal, and the intimate details of anyone with any claim to fame ever to have passed through the doors; President Kennedy, apparently, was one. The tour's nadir is the "Arab" Hall, an oval chamber that misguidedly attempts to copy the Moorish style of the Alhambra; here the guide's superlatives achieve apotheosis. Should you not want to bother with the tour you can see the main courtyard, easily the most elegant part, without having to buy a ticket.

Adjoining the Bolsa is the **Igreja de São Francisco** (April–Oct daily 9am–5pm, Nov–Mar closed Sun; 500$00 ticket from the Bolsa), perhaps the most extraordinary (albeit deconsecrated) church in Porto. From its entrance on Rua de São Francisco it looks an ordinary enough Gothic construction, but the interior has been transformed by an unbelievably ornate eighteenth-century refurbishment. Altar, pillars, even the ceiling, drip with gilded Rococo carving which reaches its ultimate expression in an interpretation of the *Tree of Jesse* on the north wall. Don't miss the church's small **museum**, housed in the catacombs below, which consists of artefacts salvaged from the former monastery. Beneath the flags of the cellar is an *ossário* – thousands of human bones, cleaned up and stored to await Judgement Day.

Two other churches in this neighbourhood have small museums. Pride of the **Igreja da Misericórdia** (church: Sun 9am–noon; museum: Tue–Sun 9am–12.30pm & 2–5.30pm; 300$00 for both museum and church, students/children free), a couple of blocks to the north on Rua das Flores, is a remarkable *Fons Vitae*, depicting King Manuel I with his wife Leonor and eight children, richly clothed, kneeling before the crucified Christ. It's an exceptional example of fifteenth-century Portuguese realism – a style which was heavily influenced by Flemish painters like van Eyck and van der Weyden. Over to the west, in the **Igreja de São Pedro de Miragaia**, there's another fine fifteenth-century triptych; the church is kept locked but someone with a key is usually near at hand.

Northwest from Cordoaria

One hundred metres north of the Cordoaria on the corner of Rua do Carmo and Praça Carlos Alberto, lies the eighteenth-century **Igreja do Carmo** with its deliriously over-the-top *azulejos* (Mon–Fri 7.30am–noon & 2–5pm, Sat 8am–noon, Sun 8am–1pm). The older and rather more sober **Igreja das Carmelitas** (daily 8am–12.30pm & 2.45–7pm) is almost adjacent, but not quite, as a law stipulated that no two churches were to share the same wall (in this case perhaps to hinder amorous liaisons between the nuns of Carmelitas and the monks of Carmo). As a result, what is probably the **narrowest house in Portugal** – barely a metre wide – was built between them, which remained inhabited until the 1980s.

Heading west past Santo António hospital, you'll pass the **Museu Nacional Soares dos Reis**, on Rua de Dom Manuel II (Wed–Sun 9am–12.20pm & 1.30–6pm; 350$00), Portugal's first designated national museum – dating from 1933. It occupies the former royal Palácio das Carrancas, which served as the French headquarters in the Peninsular War. The museum contains excellent collections of glass, ceramics and a formidable display of Portuguese art of the eighteenth and nineteenth centuries. Highlights include the paintings by Henrique Pousão and sculptures by Soares dos Reis (*O Desterrado* – "The Exiled" – is probably his best-known work) and his pupil, Teixeira Lopes.

Follow the road for 100m or so past the Museu Soares dos Reis, or take a bus (#3, #20, #35 & #37 all go this way), and you reach the **Jardim do Palácio de Cristal**, a beautiful stretch of park dominated by a huge domed pavilion which sci-fi fans will adore; this was built to replace the original "Crystal Palace" and now serves as a sports arena. The park also houses a Quaker animal hospital and, in summer, hosts hockey matches, pop and classical concerts in its bandstand, and exhibitions. There is also a wealth of educational hands-on activities for children (daily 9am–5.30pm; free, except for adults to use the painting centre which costs 3000$00; information on all activities: ☎226 099 941 or 226 093 192); with an environmental theme, including a paper recycling centre, gardening, painting, a "sound centre" with interactive recordings of natural sounds and instruments, and the great Laboratório Micro-Mundo Vivo with its microscopic views of fungi, bacteria, bugs and algae. There's also a safe playground with climbing frames.

Around the back of the park, at the end of the cobbled Rua de Entre-Quintas, stands the **Quinta da Macieirinha**, which houses both the **Museu Romântico** (Tues–Sat 10am–noon & 2–5pm, Sun 2–5.30pm; 150$00, free on Sun and for children/students), a collection of mid-nineteenth-century furniture and art works, and – on the ground floor – the **Solar do Vinho do Porto** (Mon–Fri 10am–11.45pm, Sat 11am–11.45pm; ☎226 097 793, fax 222 080 465, *www.ivp.pt*). Here, in a comfortable lounge, whose terrace overlooks the river, you can sample one of hundreds of varieties of **port wine**, starting at around 200$00 a glass. The list is the same as at the *Instituto do Vinho do Porto* in Lisbon but the views are better, and the wine, after all, is at home. It's a good prelude to a visit to the port lodges across the river in Vila Nova de Gaia (see p.264).

Opposite the *Quinta*, at Rua de Entre-Quintas 219, is **Casa Tait** (Mon–Fri 10am–noon & 2–5pm, Sat & Sun 2.30–6pm; free), which as well as boasting attractive shaded botanical gardens, contains a **numismatic museum**, tracing the history of Portugal through the coins of successive invaders, from the Greeks and Romans to the Moors and Spanish.

Boavista and the Igreja de Cedofeita

From the Palácio de Cristal, the wide Rua de Julio Dinis runs north up to Praça Mouzinho de Albuquerque, popularly known as the **Rotunda da Boavista**. Buses to here include #3, 20, or 52 from Praca da Liberdade or Cordoaria, #23, #82 or #84 from Praça da Liberdade and #34, #82 or #84 from Bolhão, or Praça da República. This is overlooked by a huge column bearing a lion astride a much flattened eagle, erected to celebrate the victory of the Portuguese and British over the French in the Peninsular War. Three blocks to the east of the Rotunda, you pass the very simple **Igreja de Cedofeita** on Rua Aníbal Cunha (Mon–Sat 9am–12.30pm & 4–7pm, Sun 9am–12.30pm), whose name derives from *cedo feita* meaning "built quickly". It's reputed to be the oldest Christian building in the Iberian peninsula (though the people of Balsemão – p.300 – will dispute this) and was supposedly built by the Suevian king Theodomir in 556, though the current building is a twelfth-century Romanesque refashioning.

The Fundação de Serralves

The best of the museums outside the centre is the highly contemporary modern art museum, the **Fundação de Serralves** on Rua de Serralves, 2km west of the Rotunda da Boavista (Tue–Sun 10am–7pm, closes 10pm on Thurs; 800$00 museum and park, 500$00 park only, free Sun 10am–2pm), with exhibits from the 1960s to the present day including works by the likes of Warhol and Pollock. The exhibits are housed in an ultra-modern building, designed by renowned local architect Álvaro Siza. Temporary exhibitions are held in the nearby 1930s Art Deco Casa de Serralves. The grounds, both formal gardens and natural farmland, are worth a visit too, and are dotted with modern sculptures and usually some installations: there's also a tea shop. Don't miss the inventive scarecrows in the farm at the far end of the park, which appear towards the end of summer; made by schoolchildren from household garbage, they are cere-monially burned in October after the harvest period. Additionally, there's a summer sequence of jazz concerts held in the gardens, *Jazz no Parque*: (phone 226 180 057 for details). To get there take any of the buses #3, #35 or #78 from the Cordoaria; #19, #21 or #78 from Rotunda da Boavista; alternatively tram #18 stops at the top of the Avenida Marechal Gomes da Costa, from where its a 500m walk to the museum.

Tram museum and Planetarium

Near the Ponte de Arrábida, in an area known as Massarelos, is situated the **Museu do Carro Eléctrico** (Tram Museum), in the tram shed on Alameda de Basílio Teles 51 (Tue–Sun 9.30am–1pm & 3–6pm; 350$00; ☎226 064 054, ext 2295); buses #1 from Praça Almeida Garrett or Rua Nova da Alfândega; #23 from Praça da Batalha or Rua Nova da Alfândega, or #24 from Cordoaria. The museum will delight kids and enthusiasts. Almost all the trams were phased out in the 1970s – one exception being tram #18, see p.253 for details of its route – and it's only now that the authorities are phasing them back in; work has begun on new routes – some of which should be operational by 2001. In summer on Thursdays, the museum also hosts concerts known as the "Noites de Massarelos", these are mostly of classical chamber music but include some jazz too; ask at the museum or turismo for details. Don't bother with the museum's own tram trips – they run exactly the same route as the #18, but cost considerably more.

Close to the museum on the Rua das Estrelas is the **Planetarium** (☎226 089 863, fax 226 089 874, *www.astro.up.pt*); bus #31. Intended primarily for schoolkids, it has screen-ings for the public at weekends (Sat 4pm & 9pm, Sun & holidays 3pm & 4pm; 1200$00). There's also a bar and multimedia library.

West to the coast

Continuing 2km down Avenida da Boavista from Avenida Marechal Gomes da Costa, or 4km from Rotunda da Boavista, you come to the main entrance of the **Parque da Cidade** (daily: winter 9am–6pm; summer 9am–8pm) on the right, before hitting the coast at Castelo do Queijo. Although several buses pass down the Avenida from Rotunda da Boavista to Castelo do Queijo, tram ride #18 is definitely the way to travel (see p.253 for details). The park is the largest remaining public space in Porto and per-fect for an afternoon's ramble, with several duck ponds, woods and children's play-grounds. The other entrance is to the north, off Estrada da Circunvalação – the ring-road which divides Porto from Matosinhos. At the shore is the **Castelo do Queijo** (Tue–Sun 1.30pm–7pm; 50$00), which literally means "Cheese Castle", the reason being that apparently it was built upon boulders that looked like cheese. The castle is a typical star-shaped Vaubanesque fort and is still a military establishment but visitors are welcome. There's a small bar, and good views. South of here to the resort of Foz do Douro lies what remains of Porto's beaches; though you wouldn't want to swim in the polluted waters and the sand is rather coarse. You're more likely to be drawn here for the superb beachfront cafés and bars along the Avenida do Brasil, which become the hub of Porto's nightlife in summer.

Foz itself has a superb hotel (the *Boa-Vista*, see p.258), several nightclubs and classy restaurants (p.272); take tram #18, or bus #1 from Praça Almeida Garrett or Rua Nova da Alfândega, or #24 from Cordoaria. From here, the tram follows the river back to Rua do Carmo in the centre of town, passing close to the **youth hostel**, the **swimming pools** at Clube Fluvial (p.278), and several more restaurants, including some ultra-cheap *adegas* along Rua do Ouro.

Vila Nova de Gaia

The suburb of **Vila Nova de Gaia** (commonly just Gaia), which is actually a city in its own right, is taken over almost entirely by the port trade. As you walk across the **Ponte Luís I** from central Porto, the names of the old **port wine lodges**, spelled out in huge white letters across their roofs, dominate the views. The most direct route to the wine lodges is across the bridge's lower level from Cais da Ribeira, or take buses #32, from Avenida dos Aliados or Praça da Batalha, or #57 or #91 both from Praça Almeida Garrett. However, if you've a head for heights it's an amazing sensation to walk over the upper level some 60m above the river, or take buses #82 or #83 from Avenida dos Aliados or Praça Almeida Garrett, or #84 from Praça da Batalha or Praça Almeida Garrett. There's a beautiful view of the tiered ranks of Porto's old town from here and

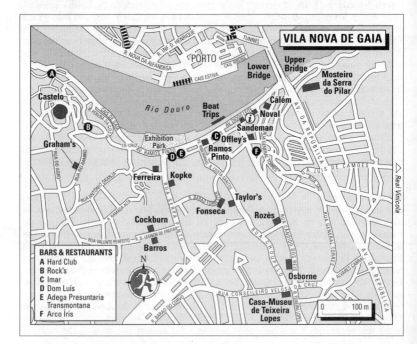

VILA NOVA DE GAIA

BARS & RESTAURANTS
A Hard Club
B Rock's
C Imar
D Dom Luís
E Adega Presuntaria
   Transmontana
F Arco Íris

an even better one from the terrace of the **Mosteiro da Serra do Pilar** high above the bridge. From this former convent, Wellington planned his surprise crossing of the Douro in 1809 and it's a barracks again today. The round church is open to the public on Saturday afternoon and Sunday morning, but sadly the unusual circular cloister rests in a sort of no-man's-land between church and army territory. Ask about details for visiting it at the **turismo** on the waterfront at Avenida Diogo Leite 242, by Sandeman (June–Sept Mon–Fri 10am–6pm, Sat–Sun 2–6pm; Oct–May closes 7.30pm weekdays; ☎223 703 735), who can also provide a useful map of Gaia port wine lodges.

Touring the lodges

Most of the **port wine lodges** were established in the eighteenth century, in the wake of the Methuen Treaty of 1703 (see box below), and although on the whole they have long since been bought by multinational companies, they still try hard to push a "family" image. Almost without exception, they offer **tastings and tours** (free except for Offley and Sandeman, where the 500$00 fee is redeemable against the price of a bottle), with a view to enticing you to buy their produce – worthwhile if you want top-quality stuff but you'll probably find it cheaper to buy the more basic ports in town. If you have the time, try to visit both a big name lodge and one of the smaller ones, where things are much less formal and the guides more likely to have time to explain things. If you're with children, a more fun way of doing the tour is via a forty-five-minute **mini-train ride**, which includes a visit to Offley's wine cellars (daily April–September, details from the turismo; 1000$00). The following are the companies which allow visits. Where no winter times are given, phone or check with the turismo.

It's interesting to contrast one of the large manufacturers, such as **Sandeman** (which has its own museum) or **Real Vinícola** (which operates virtually a production-line process), with the smaller, more traditional lodges such as **Cálem**. **Taylor's** – a bit of a hike uphill – gives a very informative talk on the processes and is happy to take just a couple of visitors at a time. There are distinct contrasts, too, between the "British" names and the Portuguese-founded establishments, such as **Ramos Pinto**. It was **Real Companhia Velha** who led the first Portuguese challenge to the British port monopoly

---

THE ORIGINS OF THE PORT WINE TRADE

The distinction between **port wine** and the other Portuguese wines was first made at the beginning of the eighteenth century. Many British merchants, engaged in importing English cloth and Newfoundland cod to Portugal, were already living in Porto and were familar with Portuguese wines. When Britain prohibited the import of French wines from 1679 to 1685 and later during the War of the Spanish Succession (1702–1714), Portuguese wines became increasingly popular in Britain, with wines from the Douro region being particularly fashionable.

The **Methuen Treaty** of 1703 between Britain and Portugal reduced the duty paid on Portuguese wine in return for the removal of Portuguese restrictions on British woollen goods. As a consequence, the port wine trade became so profitable and competitive that inferior wines, often adulterated and artificially coloured, were passed off as the genuine article – giving port itself a bad name. This led the future Marquês de Pombal to found the Companhia Geral de Agricultura dos Vinhos do Alto Douro in 1756 while, at the same time, demarcating the area from which port wine could legitimately come. The monopoly and demarcation were contentious for many years; the area was regularly extended, but only recently was permission granted for port to mature elsewhere than at the lodges at Vila Nova de Gaia. Even now, strictly speaking, the demarcated area lies on either side of the Douro from Barrô, 8km downstream of Peso da Régua, to the Spanish frontier at Barca de Alva and on the Portuguese bank north to Freixo de Espada à Cinta and beyond.

in the nineteenth century and their lodge contains numerous warehouses storing casks for the rich and famous (Generalísmo Franco's descendants among them), as well as a 6-kilometre tunnel, which was intended to form part of a rail link but, having turned out to be built at the wrong angle, now serves as a cold storage for Velha's famed sparkling wines and vintage ports.

Barros, Rua Dona Leonor de Freitas 182 (July–Sept Mon–Fri 9.30am–7pm; ☎223 752 395, fax 223 751 939).

Calém, Av. Diogo Leite 25–42 (Oct–May Mon–Sat 9am–noon & 2–5.30pm; June-Sept, daily 10am–12.30pm & 1.30–6.30pm; ☎223 746 660, fax 223 759 555). Founded in 1859; highly organized tours of this small and still traditional lodge.

Cockburn, Rua Dona Leonor de Freitas (Jan–Aug, Mon–Fri 9.30am–noon & 2–4pm; closed Sept–Dec; ☎379 40 31, fax 375 05 50). Founded in 1815, the most English (English-owned and run) of the lodges, personalized visits (1 hour), small groups only.

Ferreira, Rua da Carvalhosa 19–103 (April–Oct, Mon–Fri 9.30am–2pm & 2.30–5pm, Sat 9.30am–noon; Oct–June Mon–Fri 9am–1pm & 2–5pm; ☎223 700 010, fax 223 759 732). Founded in 1751 and worth a visit for its lovely *azulejo*-decorated tasting hall alone.

Graham's, Rua Rei Ramiro 514 (Apr–Aug Mon–Fri 9.30am–5.30pm; also Sat & Sun 9.30am–5.30pm in May; Sept–Mar Mon–Sat 9am–6pm; ☎223 796 330, fax 223 796 301). This lodge was founded in 1820; with an impressive stone-arched reception supporting a wooden roof. Tasting terrace overlooks river.

Ramos Pinto, Av. Ramos Pinto 380 (June–Sept Mon–Fri 10am–6pm, Sat 10am–1pm; Oct–May Mon–Fri 9am–5pm; ☎223 707 000, fax 223 793 121). Tastings of vintage wine, exhibits of photographs, trinkets and posters from the turn of the century, in this lodge founded in 1880.

Real Vinícola (Real Companhia Velha), Rua Azevedo Magalhães 314 (June–Sept Mon–Fri 9.30am–1pm & 2–6pm, Sat & Sun 9.30am–1pm; closed Oct–May; ☎223 775 100). Founded by Dom José I in 1756, exhibits of oil paintings from his reign: look for the one of the Marquês de Pombal.

Sandeman, Largo Miguel Bombarda 3 (April–Oct Mon–Sat 10am–12.30pm & 2–5.30pm, Sun 10am–12.30pm & 2–6pm; Nov–Mar Mon–Sat 10am–12.30pm & 2–5.30pm; 500$00 entrance fee redeemable against the price of a bottle; ☎223 706 807, fax 223 706 816). One of the largest companies, founded in 1790 by George Sandeman; includes a small museum of wine-related artefacts.

Taylor's, Rua do Choupelo 250 (All year Mon–Fri 10am–12.30pm & 2.30–6pm; July–Aug also Sat 10am–6pm; ☎223 719 999, fax 223 708 607). Founded in 1692. It retains a rustic-style tasting room and has panoramic views from the salon. The talk on the processes is very informative; happy to take just a couple of visitors at a time.

Casa-Museu de Teixeira Lopes

A more sober visit in Vila Nova de Gaia could be made to the **Casa-Museu de Teixeira Lopes** (Tues–Sat 9am–12.30pm & 2–5.30pm; July-Sept also opens Sun 3–7pm; free) – a very steep hike up Rua Cândido dos Reis from the waterfront, or, a taxi-ride of 500$00. Lopes was Soares dos Reis's principal pupil and formed the centre of an important artistic and intellectual set that lived in Gaia at the turn of the century. The circle is well represented in the second part of the museum's display, the first being devoted to Lopes's work – much of it preoccupied with the depiction of children. His masterpiece is considered to be the enigmatic portrait of an Englishwoman, *A Inglesa*.

Walks in and around Vila Nova de Gaia

To get a good feel of the town's historical past **walk** up Rua Costa Santos, turn right into Rua Barão de Forrester, then back to the river down Rua Serpa Pinto along cobbled streets and under trailing vines. Another rewarding excursion is the walk 3km **downriver** past the port houses to the small fishing village of **Afurada**, which used to be engaged in the *bacalhau* trade – with cod formerly strung out to dry in fields and along the shore all the way from here to the river's mouth at Cabedelo 2km away, where there's a huge sandbar across much of the river and strange boulders strewn around its edges. Small **ferries**, bedecked with Sandeman hoardings and pursuing

---

MAKING PORT WINE

Grapes from vines in the demarcated region are **harvested** from mid-September to mid-October and then crushed – mechanically nowadays and not by foot, whatever the various lodges say. The grape juice ferments for a couple of days and then, when the natural sugar level is sufficiently reduced, the **fermentation** process is arrested by the addition of grape brandy – in a ratio of four parts wine to one part brandy. The wine then stands in casks in the *armazém* (cellar) of the company **quinta** (estate) until the following March, when it's transported downstream to the shippers' lodges at Vila Nova de Gaia, where it matures.

There are four basic **types of port** – *branco* (white), *tinto* (red), *tinto aloirado* (ruby) and *aloirado* (tawny) – which spend varying times maturing. **Vintages** are only declared in certain years, when a *quinta*'s wine is deemed to be of a sufficiently high quality; when this happens, the wine spends only two years in the cask before being bottled and left to mature. A vintage wine is ready to drink between ten and fifteen years after bottling; it's a darker colour than the other wines, because of the time it spends in the bottle, and needs to be decanted to separate it from sediment. The label on the bottle will show the company, the vintage year, the year it was bottled, and sometimes the name of the *quinta*. **Late-bottled vintage wine** (LBV) is wine that's not of vintage quality, but still good enough to mature in bottles, to which it's transferred after five or six years in the cask when it is already good enough to drink. All other ports are made from blends of wines, and most are kept in the cask for much longer – at least seven years for a tawny. Wines designated 20-, 30- or 40-year-old port are also blended and spend, on average, that length of time in the cask, after which they lose much of their original red colour, becoming lighter the older they are.

---

erratic courses against the currents, cut across the rivermouth between Afurada and Rua do Ouro near the Porto suburb of **Foz do Douro** (fairly frequent throughout the day; tickets on board) – where you can pick up the #18 tram (p.253).

Eating

You may be shocked to discover that the city's speciality is *tripas* (tripe) and that the people are affectionately referred to by the rest of the country as *tripeiros* – tripe eaters. The story goes that the inhabitants gave away all their meat for the expeditions to Ceuta (Sebta) in North Africa in the late fourteenth century, leaving themselves only the tripe, and that it's been on the menu ever since. Don't let this put you off – there's always plenty of other choices and the cooking is as good as any in Portugal. Tripe aside though, another typical Portuense dish is the *francesinha* ("little French thing"), a hot sandwich containing beef, sausage and ham covered with melted cheese and peppery tomato sauce – quality varies depending on whether canned or real sausages and ham are used.

If you choose carefully, you can eat both well and cheaply, though for the best bargains (well under 1000$00 a head, including drinks) you have to be prepared to dig into less salubrious areas, notably along the riverfront west of Alfândega. At the basic level, Porto has **workers' cafés** galore, all with wine on tap and often with a cheap set menu for the day. They are mainly lunchtime places, though most serve an evening meal until around 7.30pm and a few stay open later; prime areas are the grid of streets north and south of the Cordoaria: especially Rua do Almada (north) and Rua de São Bento da Vitória (south). Moving more upmarket, into the **restaurant** league, the Cais da Ribeira is hard to beat for atmosphere or for its fish, with any number of café-restaurants installed under the arches of the first tier of dwellings, though prices have been moving steadily upwards and out of budget range.

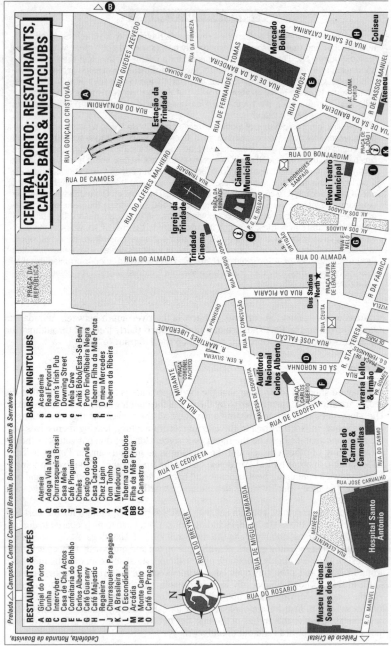

CENTRAL PORTO: RESTAURANTS, CAFÉS, BARS & NIGHTCLUBS

RESTAURANTS & CAFÉS

A Ginjal do Porto
B Cunha
C Intercyber
D Casa de Chá Actos
E Confeitaria do Bolhão
F Carlos Alberto
G Café Guarany
H Café Majestic
I Regaleira
J Churrasqueira Papagaio
K A Brasileira
L O Escondidinho
M Arcádia
N Monte Carlo
O Café na Praça
P Ateneia
Q Adega Vila Meã
R Churrasqueira Brasil
S Casa Meia
T Café Pinguim
U Chinês
V Postigo do Carvão
W Casa Cardoso
X Chez Lapin
Y Dom Tonho
Z Miradouro
AA Taberna de Bebobos
BB Filha da Mãe Preta
CC A Canastra

BARS & NIGHTCLUBS

a Academia
b Real Feytoria
c Ryan's Irish Pub
d Downing Street
e Meia Cave
f Aniki Bóbó/Está-Se Bem/
   Porto Fino/Ribeira Negra
g Taberna Filha da Mãe Preta
h O meu Mercedes
i Taberna da Ribeira

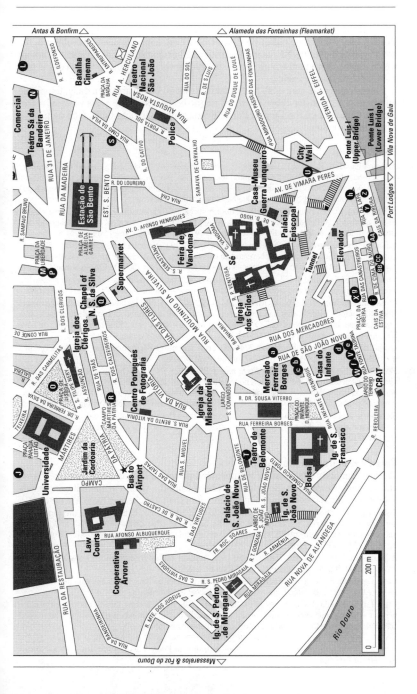

Antas & Bonfirm △

△ Alameda das Fontainhas (Fleamarket)

Massarelos & Foz do Douro ▽

Port Lodges ▽   ▽ Vila Nova de Gaia

Rio Douro

L

Comercial

N

Teatro Sá da Bandeira

Batalha Cinema

Teatro Nacional São João

Police

S

Casa-Museu Guerra Junqueiro

City Wall

Ponte Luís I (Upper Bridge)

Ponte Luís I (Lower Bridge)

U

Palácio Episcopal

Estação de São Bento

Feira de Vandoma

Sé

Igreja dos Grilos

Elevador

Tunnel

h

z

Q

M **P**

Chapel of N. S. da Silva

Supermarket

Igreja dos Clérigos

Centro Português de Fotografia

Igreja da Misericórdia

Mercado Ferreira Borges

a

c **b**

Casa do Infante

X **9**

88 **GG**

i

AA

w **f** **v** **e**

CRAT

O

R

Universidade

Jardim da Cordoaria

Bus to Airport

Teatro de Belomonte

J

Law Courts

Cooperativa Arvore

Palácio de S. João Novo

Ig. de S. João Novo

Bolsa

Ig. de S. Francisco

Ig. de S. Pedro de Miragaia

200 m

0

If you're **buying your own food**, check the central markets listed on p.278. Also worth seeking out is the **bakery** at Travessa de Cedofeita 20b, one of the oldest in the country, which uses traditional methods such as burning *carqueja* – a variety of broom which reaches high temperatures while producing very little ash. The speciality is *pão-de-ló*, a round sponge cake.

Unless otherwise stated, all the restaurants listed below are open daily; telephone numbers are given for those where it might be necessary to reserve in advance. Most are marked on the Central Porto: Restaurants, Bars and Cafés map on p.268 – exceptions are noted.

Central Porto

Adega Vila Meã, Rua dos Caldeireiros 62, near Clérigos (☎222 082 967). Modest old restaurant with a reputation for fresh and well-cooked food: various fish and *bacalhau* dishes, an exceptional *cozido à portuguesa* on Thurs (different meats stewed with root veg and cabbage), roast octopus (Tues), and roast veal (Fri). Under 2500$00. Closed Sun and August.

A Brasileira, Rua do Bonjardim 118. Next door to its café, this is one of the oldest and most elegant (if fast decaying) of Porto's restaurants, with an Art Deco interior, pavement café, stand-up bar and smallish dining room with attentive waiter service. Around 3000$00. Closed Sun.

Casa Aleixo (*see Porto map p.268*), Rua da Estação 216, by Campanhã train station (☎225 370 462). Long-established with good atmosphere and an excellent reputation; choose from fish fillets, octopus, roast veal, or roast pork chops. Half-portions (enough for one) under 1500$00. Closed Sun and August.

Cunha, Rua Sá da Bandeira 662–676 (*see Porto map p.268*). Famed traditional old pastry shop, also has a pretty decent snack-bar and restaurant – roast pork, roast chicken, dorado fillets. Around 2000$00.

O Escondidinho, Rua de Passos Manuel 144 (☎222 001 079). Hardly hidden (*escondidinho* means "the little hidden place"), this has a cluttered, country-house interior and excellent French-influenced cuisine, but it's expensive. Try the hake in Madeira sauce and a kirsch omelette if you have 3500$00 to spend; more like 6000$00 for a feast. Book ahead for evenings. Closed Sun.

Ginjal do Porto, Rua do Bonjardim 724–726. Tripe and other Portuguese specialities served in a no-frills setting. Cheap – under 1000$00 for the *prato do dia*.

Portucale, Rua da Alegria 598 (*see Porto map p.268*; ☎225 707 171). On top of a tower block with views over Porto. Dated 1960s interior, nonetheless sophisticated. Specialities include lobster gratin, *bacalhau*, kid goat, flambéed steak with mushrooms, partridge with chestnuts, wild boar and mango, pheasant in almond sauce. Good wine list, too. Expensive (mains 2500–5500$00) but recommended.

Regaleira, Rua do Bonjardim 87, around the corner from Praça Dom João I. One of the best places for fish and seafood, including platefuls of *perceves*, a weird-looking kind of barnacle. Mains cost from 1000 to 2500$00.

Cais da Ribeira and around

There are unfussy cheap eats at the unnamed places on Rua da Fonte Taurina nos. 44 and 78, and elsewhere in the sidestreets back from the river. For the following establishments, unless recommended, it's more often than not cheaper to go à la carte.

Taberna de Bebobos, Cais da Ribeira 24–25 (☎222 053 565). Established in the nineteenth century, this has a real old *tasca* feel, with its barrels of wine on the walls. Fish and regional specialities – try the pork with wine sauce. Very popular, so book ahead if possible. Full meals up to 3500$00. Closed Mon.

A Canastra, Cais da Ribeira 37 (☎222 080 180). Another highly recommended homely under-the-arches option, but cheaper and more local than its neighbours.

Casa Cardoso, Rua da Fonte Taurina 60. One of the cheaper options, with some excellent fish dishes – try the swordfish. Main dishes from 750 to 1650$00. Closed Sun.

Chez Lapin, Rua das Canastreiros 40 (☎222 006 418). Under the arches, this deceptively large place is not too cheap, but very popular locally, particularly on Sundays when many others are closed (reserve in advance then). And, yes, one house speciality is rabbit.

Chinês, Av. de Vímara Peres 38–40 (☎222 008 915). Some of the city's best Chinese food – served in a modern building by the top-level entrance to Ponte Luís I. Allow around 2000$00 for the *ementa turística*.

Dom Tonho, Cais da Ribeira 13–15 (☎222 004 307). Typical of the move upmarket for the Cais da Ribeira area is this high-class chrome-and-glass restaurant owned by *pimba* pop star Rui Veloso, overlooking the river. Mainly seafood with unusual specials like duck and goat. Bar on lower level. The tunnel entrance at the far end was a secret passage between the Sé and Ribeira.

Filha da Mãe Preta, Arcos do Douro 2–3, Cais da Ribeira (☎222 086 066). Built into the arches – the *azulejo*-decorated upper floor gives you a view over the river to Gaia. An excellent *ementa turística* features mackerel, sardines and all the business, though it's rather pricey. The name ("daughter of the black mother") comes from the original establishment, Mãe Preta, which was popular with charcoal makers from upriver. Closed Mon.

Miradouro, Cais da Ribeira, on the arches by the entrance to the bridge. Almost the only budget option left in Ribeira, and always bustling with locals. Serves up great pizzas, *bifanas*, *francesinhas* and huge salads. Its outdoor tables have as good an outlook as any. Closed Wed.

Postigo do Carvão, Rua da Fonte Taurina 24–26 (☎222 004 539). Restaurant and snack bar open to 2am with live music (fado, folklore, Brazilian). Good for cheap *pratinhos* (snacks: try the flame-grilled *chouriço assado*, cheese boards or smoked meats). They also do grilled lobster and fondue. Closed Mon.

Around Praça da Batalha

Casa Meia Lua, Rua Cimo da Vila 151. Small and friendly place where you can eat well for around 1000$00. You may have to share tables. Desserts aren't brilliant, but otherwise good.

Monte Carlo, Rua de Santa Catarina 17. Hidden away up on the second floor, this looks like a badly neglected 1930s' tearoom, but has views over Praça da Batalha, a buzzing television, food that veers from good to indifferent and, particularly at Sunday lunchtime, very noisy locals. Not everyone's cup of tea, but good value.

Suribachi, Rua do Bonfim 136–140, 800m east of Praça da Batalha (*see Porto map p.268*; ☎225 106 700). Cheap and cosy macrobiotic and vegetarian restaurant, accessed through a health food shop – not a greasy chip in sight. Inventive tofu dishes among others. Mon–Sat 8.30am–9.30pm.

Cordoaria to Praça de Carlos Alberto

Churrasqueira Brasil, Campo dos Mártires da Pátria 136. Very cheap workers' diner on the square immediately south of the gardens. Open until 10pm.

Carlos Alberto, Praça de Carlos Alberto 89. Friendly, cheap traditional restaurant, with excellent daily specials. Closed Sat.

Churrasqueira Papagaio, Trav. do Carmo 32. Appealing, tiled interior, with good grills and an inexpensive *ementa turística*.

West of the centre

The following are all shown on the Porto map on p.268.

Capa Negra, Rua do Campo Alegre 191, between Boavista and Palácio de Cristal; buses #35, #37, #78, #93 or #96 from Cordoaria. Huge, bright and busy operation with good local dishes; worried fish and lobsters ensconced in big bubbly tanks; famed city-wide for its *francesinha* meat sandwiches (1200–1600$00). Snacks from 800$00, full meals 1500–3000$00. Open to 2am, closed Mon.

Churrascão Gaúcho, Av. da Boavista 313 (☎226 091 738); buses #34 from Praça da República, or #82 or #84 from Bolhão or Praça da Batalha. Sophisticated Brazilian – speciality is both fish and *rodízio* (3400$00), which involves waiters carving slices off skewers of grilled lamb and beef onto your plate until you beg them to stop. Closed Sun.

Massarelos L'Entrecôte, Rua da Boa Viagem 3, Massarelos, behind the tram museum (☎226 008 732); buses #1 or 23 from Praça Almeida Garrett or Rua Nova da Alfândega, #24 from Cordoaria, or tram #18. Beautiful modernist conversion of the former headquarters of the Portuguese Legion, with balcony views over the Douro, and not as expensive as you might think: mains around 2500$00. Speciality is beef steak.

Museu dos Presuntos, Rua Padre Luís Cabral 1070, Foz do Douro (☎226 106 965); buses #1 from Praça Almeida Garrett or Rua Nova da Alfândega, or #24 from Cordoaria; tram #18. Surreal junk-shop-decorated place with a pub-like feel; popular with students. The decor aside (the dining room is hung with gilt-framed smoked hams), the main draws are the unusual *pratinhos* (small dishes), including stewed chicken innards, pickled *bacalhau* and smoked ham (*presunto*). Around 1000–1500$00 for a full meal.

Ó **Macedo**, Rua do Passeio Alegre 552, Foz do Douro (☎226 170 166); buses #1 from Praça Almeida Garrett or Rua Nova da Alfândega, or #24 from Cordoaria; tram #18. Pleasantly refined eating: onion tart, *bacalhau*, even English roast beef, and good wine list. Arrive early for the tables with views over the mouth of the Douro. Closed Sun, and for a fortnight in Aug.

Paco Loco, Av. do Dr. Antunes Guimarães 1217, 1km north of Av. da Boavista (☎226 189 480); bus #3 from Praça da Liberdade or Cordoaria. Hot Mexican and Texan food in suitably colourful surroundings, with music to match. Good Mexican wines, and live music on Thurs.

Peixes & Co., Rua do Ouro 133, on the river west of Arrábida bridge (☎226 185 655); buses #1 from Praça Almeida Garrett or Rua Nova da Alfândega, or #24 from Cordoaria; tram #18. Friendly and elegant atmosphere in a renovated house, with views over river. Lots of different kinds of fish, depending on the day's catch – expect to pay around 3000$00 for the works. Closed Sun.

Vila Nova de Gaia

The following are all shown on the Vila Nova de Gaia map on p.264.

Adega Presuntaria Transmontana, Rua Cândido dos Reis 132 (☎223 714 264). Lovely cool dining room with stone walls, and a dozen smoked hams hanging over the bar. Refined but expensive – a full meal costs over 3500$00.

Arco Íris, Rua Cândido dos Reis 75–79. Popular *pão quente* ("hot bread") place, which has fresh (warm) bread all day, as well as very reasonably priced snacks and full meals.

Imar, Av. Diogo Leite 56 (☎223 792 705). Highly recommended, with big portions, reasonable prices, and a predominantly local crowd.

Dom Luís, Av. Ramos Pinto. Has a good value *ementa turística*, or you can go à la carte and sample the speciality – tripe. Good value.

Cafés, tea and cake shops

Cafés in Porto rival Lisbon's, with some lovely old Art Deco survivors in the main shopping streets. All serve alcohol, snacks and cakes as well as coffee. There are also a handful of pavement cafés on Praça da Ribeira, packed with tourists in summer.

The following are on the Central Porto: Restaurants, Cafés, Bars and Nightclubs map on p.268, unless stated otherwise.

Arcádia, Praça da Liberdade 63. Long established sweet shop, famous for its chocolate bonbons, *ovos moles* (sticky UFO-shaped egg confectionery) and regional specialities.

Ateneia, Praça da Liberdade 58. For serious addicts: exquisite chocolates from the Costa Moreira company, quince *marmelada*, boiled sweets and cakes, with a cosy raised Art Deco seating area at the back in which to indulge your passion.

A Brasileira, Rua de Sá da Bandeira 75. A sister branch to the one in Lisbon, with pavement seats and a good stand-up bar for breakfast and refuelling during the day. Open till 8pm, closed Sun.

Café na Praça, Praça de Lisboa. Trendy chrome and glass place popular at all hours. The outdoor tables are a great place to sit and soak up the surroundings, and the *espetada de lulas* (squid kebab) is worth a try. DJs most weekend nights; daily 10pm–4am.

Casa de Chá Actos, Rua Sá Noronha 76-1°. Many teas, plus cakes, tarts and even scones. It has unusual hours 4–8pm shift for a genteel atmosphere, followed by 10pm–2am, when it plays host to students and more arty types. Hosts temporary exhibitions.

Casa de Chá da Boa Nova (not on maps), Leça da Palmeira, 1km north of Matosinhos port (☎229 951 785); buses #1 or #19 to Matosinhos, then walk or catch a cab. Famous café and restaurant by the ocean, designed by Álvaro Siza Vieira, with sweeping views and a small fishermen's chapel beside it. Closed Sun.

Confeitaria do Bolhão, Rua Formosa 339, opposite the entrance to the Bolhão market. Tranquil cake and coffee shop, kitschly repainted in Art Nouveau style, and rather popular with old ladies. They do good value *pratos do dia* in the restaurant above. Baffle the owner by asking for a *mazagrã* (cold coffee in a tall glass with water, sugar and lemon, which was popular in the 1950s). Open daily.

Guarany, Av. dos Aliados. Less stylish than *A Brasileira*, but bright and airy. Another one that's popular with old ladies at tea-time. Cheap food, but watch the overpriced soft drinks. Open till 10pm.

Intercyber, Praça General Humberto Delgado 291. Pleasant Internet café and bar near the Câmara Municipal, that charges 500$00 per hour for the Internet.

Majestic, Rua de Santa Catarina 112. The nicest and most expensive of the old Art Deco cafés, with perfectly preserved decor, outside tables and excellent coffee. The grand piano features in out-of-season recitals. Closed Sun.

Pinguim, Rua de Belomonte 65–67. A laid-back arty venue, with live Brazilian or Portuguese music Fridays evenings starting at 11pm, and poetry readings on Mondays at the same time.

Drinking, nightlife and entertainment

As with restaurants and cafés, you're spoilt for choice when it comes to drinking, clubbing or — given the attention being lavished on the arts in the run-up to 2001, when Porto becomes European Capital of Culture – entertainment.

Bars

Trendier than cafés, dozens of modish late-night **bars** are found in the streets around the Cais da Ribeira, as well as along the river in Gaia, in Foz do Douro and up the coast facing Praia dos Ingleses, the latter being the main evening drag in summer.

Most of the following are on the Central Porto: Restaurants, Cafés, Bars and Nightclubs map on p.268, unless stated otherwise.

Aniki Bóbó, Rua da Fonte Taurina 36–38, Ribeira. Cool and spacious; sometimes featuring live music. Occasional alternative happenings (eg theatre) on Thurs. Mon–Sat 10pm–4am. 500$00 cover charge.

Downing Street, Praça da Ribeira 10. A more refined ambience than most, mainly serving up glasses of port wine.

Está-Se Bem, Rua da Fonte Taurina 70–72, Ribeira. A nice little *tasca* where the arty crowd hang out, probably because it's cheap and there's no cover charge. It's also popular with the pre-club crowd. Mon–Sat 9pm–4am.

Taberna Filha da Mãe Preta, Rua das Canastreiros 26, Ribeira. A crusty place where the older locals congregate; wine straight from the barrel.

Labirintho, Rua Nossa Senhora de Fátima 334, off Rotunda da Boavista (*see Porto map p.268*; ☎226 063 665); night bus #76 to Rotunda. Very pleasant, friendly 1950s-style converted house, with a shaded back garden and unpretentious gallery space. Occasional live music, poetry recitals and drama (usually starting at midnight). Daily 10pm–4am.

O meu Mercedes é maior que o teu, Rua da Lada 30, Ribeira. Hands-down winner of the world's silliest bar name contest ("My Mercedes is bigger than yours") – although there's no name on the door – but happily, a small and friendly bar inside which tends to attract regulars. Evenings only.

Porto Fino, Rua da Fonte Taurina 52–54. Metallic modernist bar. Its art gallery is open from 4–10pm, followed by the bar until 2am. Ring the bell for admittance. Closed Sun.

Taberna da Ribeira, Praça da Ribeira. In a prime riverside location, this place has outdoor tables, *chouriço assada* (grilled with alcohol at your table) and home-made sangria to wash it down with. Open till 2am.

Ribeira Negra, Rua Fonte Taurina 66–68. Proof that Porto has it all: an *upmarket* grunge bar.

Ryan's Irish Pub, Rua do Infante Dom Henrique 18. Ain't no city in the world without one: Irish music, Guinness (bottled), Jamesons and Bushmills. Thur & Sun 10pm–2am, Fri 9pm–4am, Sat 5pm–4am. 500$00 entrance.

Solar do Vinho do Porto, Museu Romântico, Rua de Entre-Quintas (*see Porto map p.268*;). Laid-back venue for port-drinking in civilized surroundings, with views over the Douro; see p.268.

Syndikato Club, Rua do Bonjardim 836, two blocks east of Praça da República (☎222 084 383). The city's main gay bar, with drag acts for a discerning public. Also popular is *Bustos*, nearby at Rua Guedes de Azevedo 203-1º (☎222 054 876). Both are on the Porto map p.268.

Discos and clubs

Porto's discos are highly regarded, although most are way outside the centre – we've mentioned night buses (usually hourly) for these ones. As with Lisbon, most of the clubs really only get going well after midnight, and most stay open until 4–5am or later, with a standard 1000–1500$00 admission fee (fees are mentioned if cheaper); the entrance ticket acts as a voucher for drinks, not that it'll last long – with beers and soft drinks averaging 400–500$00, and spirits 800$00, most people drink in bars before hitting the clubs. Ring ahead to check weekday opening times, as these change frequently enough.

Unless stated otherwise, most of the following are on the Porto map on p.268.

Academia, Rua de São João Novo 80, Ribeira (*see the Central Porto: Restaurants, Cafés, Bars and nightclubs map on p.268*; ☎222 005 737). Modish disco-bar with pretensions, attracting students. Cover 400$00. Daily 10pm–2am.

Água na Boca, Rua Augusto Nobre 451, off Av. da Boavista (☎226 107 966); Night bus #19. Infectious Brazilian dance, occasionally live. Fri & Sat only, 11pm–4am.

Batô, Largo do Castelo 13, Leça da Palmeira, north of Matosinhos (off the maps; ☎229 953 405); night bus #76. High-camp pirates' galleon interior, just needs Errol Flynn sliding down one of the masts. Tue–Sun 11pm–4am.

Club Mau-Mau, Rua do Outeiro 4, west of Palácio de Cristal (☎226 076 660); night bus #1 from Praça Almeida Garrett to "Massarelos". Restaurant and pavement café Tue–Sat 8pm–4am, disco open Thur–Sat 11pm–6am. Weird mix of music, touching on punk and heavy metal, but still pretty friendly – usually has live music Thurs.

Hard Club, Cais de Gaia, Vila Nova de Gaia (*see Vila Nova de Gaia map p.264*; ☎223 753 819); night bus #91. Porto's main venue for DJs and live music, including a good number of British and Stateside acts. Fridays are more poppy. Worth ringing to see what's coming up.

Maré-Alta Bar, Alameda Basílio Teles, a floating teepee moored on the river bank west of Ponte da Arrábida (☎226 091 010); night bus #1 to "Gás". Trendy mix of music, leaning on Brazilian. Tue–Sun 2pm–6am. Sunday 'House Breakfast' (9am–5pm) is usually accompanied by a live band. 500$00 cover.

Meia Cave, Praça da Ribeira 6 (*see the Central Porto: Restaurants, Cafés, Bars and Nightlclubs map on p.268*; ☎223 323 214). Drum'n'bass and breakbeat. 10pm onwards with prices going up after 2am.

Mexcal, Rua da Restauração 39, next to *Mau-Mau* (☎226 009 188). Latin American music. Wed–Sat 10pm–4am; cover 700–1000$00 (women free on weekdays). Night bus #1 to "Massarelos".

Real Feytoria, Rua Infante Dom Henrique 20 (*see the Central Porto: Restaurants, Cafés, Bars and Nightclubs map on p.268*; ☎222 000 718). Daily 9pm–2am. In great location, with two floors, one with pop, rock and Brazilian, the other playing house. Cover 400$00.

Rock's, 228 Rua Rei Ramiro, Vila Nova de Gaia (*see Vila Nova de Gaia map p.264*; ☎223 751 208). Built in old port cellars, with a terrace overlooking the Douro, and barbecues in summer. Thur–Sat 10pm–4am. Night bus #91.

Swing, Rua Júlio Dinis 766, near Rotunda da Boavista (☎226 090 019). The disco-goers number one; five bars (one gay – the main venue in Porto) and lively clientele. Busiest Fri, also good on Mon. Open 12.30–6am. Night bus #19 or #76.

Twins, Rua do Passeio Alegre 994, Foz do Douro (☎226 185 740). Lively mix of music popular with a younger crowd. Wed to Sat, 10pm to 4am, later on Fri & Sat. Night bus #1 from Praça Almeida Garrett.

Voice, Rua da Boa Viagem 1, next to Museu dos Carros Eléctricos (☎226 097 889). An old customs warehouse attracting trendies Sat nights. 11pm–4am. Night bus #1 to "Massarelos".

Theatre, music, dance and cinema

Listings for the following venues are contained in the free monthly arts listings booklet, cultura.norte, and in the quarterly, Agenda do Porto, both available at the turismos, and on the Web site www.agendadoporto.pt.

After a shaky period following the 1974 revolution, during which time much of the underground dissident tradition of **theatre** lost ground to musicals, theatre is now undergoing a renaissance. Of the major venues there are: Rivoli Teatro Municipal (also known as "Culturporto") on Praça Dom João I (☎223 392 200); and Teatro Nacional São João on Praça da Batalha (☎222 086 392, *www.tnsj.pt*), as well as the Auditório Nacional Carlos Alberto (see below). Smaller, more intimate venues include the Teatro Universitário do Porto (TUP) Rua Jorge Viterbo Ferreira 120, off Rua Dom Manuel II (☎226 090 103); Teatro da Vilarinha, Rua da Vilarinha 1386 at the corner with Circunvalação (☎226 108 924), bus #52 from Cordoaria, and the superb auditorium at Teatro Campo Alegre, Rua das

PORTO FESTIVALS

POPULAR TRADITIONS – FEIRAS, FESTAS AND ROMARIAS

Passion Sunday (March/April; the second Sunday before Easter) is celebrated with a feast, special market and procession near Jardim de São Lázaro opposite the church of Nossa Senhora da Esperança, east of Praça da Batalha.

Easter Day (March/April), sees effigies of Judas burning in several locations around the Sé.

Corpus Christi (May/June), is marked by a procession of administrative and religious authorities through the centre of the city.

Santo António (closest Sat to June 13), religious services in the churches of Massarelos and Bonfim districts in honour of the protector of brides and newlyweds.

São João (June 23–24). The biggest popular tradition of festivals (São João is the patron saint of lovers), which sees performances of folk and choral music, a marathon, and *cascata* competitions (these are displays of dolls depicting Santo António, São João and São Pedro, usually arranged in terraced "cascades" in shop windows, complete with miniature houses, trains, cars and anything else at hand). The evening of June 23rd culminates with fireworks and riotous celebrations, especially in Ribeira.

São Pedro (June 29). Street decorations in many places, music and dance; dedicated to the first Christian Pope.

São Bartolomeu (Sunday after August 24). Procession in Foz do Douro of "puppets dressed in paper clothes", culminating in a health-giving bath (*banho santo*) in the nowadays rather polluted sea.

Senhora da Boa Fortuna (last weekend in August). In the parish of Vitória, west of Ribeira near Torre dos Clérigos/Rua de Ceuta, which sees a procession of young children dressed as angels carrying plastic baby dolls to the image of Nossa Senhora in Rua dos Caldeireiros.

Nossa Senhora de Campanhã (closest Sunday to September 8). Near Campanhã train station, market stalls and folkloric music.

Nossa Senhora do Ó (last Sunday of September), in honour of the *pregnant* Virgin, a solemn procession from the Capela Nossa Senhora da Piedade do Cais to the river west of Alfândega.

São Nicolau (Dec 6), children wait for Santa Claus's arrival by boat at the Cais de Estiva in Ribeira, who is then escorted by them along Rua da Alfândega to his welcoming ceremony at the Igreja de São Francisco.

Nossa Senhora da Conceição (Dec 8 – national holiday). Feast held in Foz do Douro, centred on the Capela da Nossa Senhora da Conceição, followed by a night procession though Foz's streets.

MODERN FESTIVALS

For details of exact dates, times and various venues, check with one of Porto's turismos.

February: Fantasporto international film festival at the Coliseu and other venues.

May: European Jazz Festival & Puppet Festival, both at the Auditório Nacional Carlos Alberto.

May–June: Book Festival at the Palácio de Cristal.

June: Beer festival at Jardim do Passeio Alegre, Foz do Douro.

July: World Music Festival at the Palácio de Cristal.

August: Rock Festival at the Palácio de Cristal.

September: Fado Festival at the Coliseu.

October–December: Contemporary Art Festival, various venues.

November–December: European Cinema Festival, various venues.

December: Crafts Festival (two weeks), at the Palácio de Cristal.

Estrelas (☎226 003 000), bus #31 from Rotunda da Boavista. Another smaller venue is the excellent Casa das Artes, Rua Ruben A 210 (or Rua António Cardoso), off Rua do Campo Alegre (☎226 006 153, fax 226 006 152), bus #78 from Cordoaria or Bolhão, which is the centre of the city's alternative arts scene, and screens art-house movies daily. Finally, the Teatro de Belomonte, Rua de Belomonte 57 (☎222 083 341) is a **puppet theatre** – ring for details of performances. Call the theatres directly or ask at the turismo for details.

Dance and other musical events, including major **pop and rock concerts**, usually take place in the Coliseu do Porto, Rua de Passos Manuel 137 (☎222 059 136, fax 222 011 386, *coliseu.do.porto@mail.telepac.pt*). The Balleteatro Auditório, is home to a professional ballet school and is located 2km north of Praça da República at Praça 9 de Abril 76 (☎225 508 918, fax 225 508 919, *info@ep-ballet-teatro.rcts.pt*); buses #7, #71, #92 or #95 from Praça da República.

Classical music concerts are held regularly in the Auditório Nacional Carlos Alberto, Rua das Oliveiras 43 (☎222 004 540, fax 222 087 952, *anca@portugalnet.com*), which also stages theatre and dance. The home of the Orquestra Nacional do Porto is the former monastery of São Bento da Vitória, Rua de São Bento da Vitória (☎222 006 549, fax 222 052 111).

Listings

Adventure sports Canoeing and kayaking: Associação Naútica do Douro, Av. Diogo Leite 150–2º, Vila Nova de Gaia (☎223 798 297), or the Federação Portuguesa de Canoagem, Rua António Pinto Machado 60–3º (☎226 097 350, fax 226 097 350). Mountain climbing: Clube Nacional de Montanhismo, Secção Região Norte, Departamento de Montanhismo, Rua Formosa 303–2º (☎223 321 295). Windsurfing: Clube Surf do Porto, c/o Sr. João Abreu (☎226 176 551, fax 226 178 436); Surf em Movimento, c/o Sr. Manuel Oliveira (☎ & fax 225 500 627). Sailing: Yate Clube do Porto, Molhe Norte, Leixões docks, Leça da Palmeira, Matosinhos (☎229 965 586). Horse riding: Centro Hípico do Porto e Matosinhos, Lugar de Gonçalves, Leça da Palmeira, Matosinhos (☎229 952 133), and the Centro Hípico de Vila Nova de Gaia, Rua Silva Tapada 200, Quebrantões, Vila Nova de Gaia (☎223 795 981).

Airlines Air France, Av. da Boavista 1203–4º (☎226 078 982, fax 226 078 989); Alitalia, airport (☎229 414 848, fax 229 416 851); British Airways, airport (☎229 449 989, or freephone 800 212 125); Ibéria, airport (☎229 419 316); KLM, airport (☎229 439 747, fax 229 486 433); Lufthansa, airport (☎229 410 183, fax 229 416 375); Portugália, Av. Boavista 1361–4º (☎226 004 766, fax 226 008 283); Sabena, airport (☎229 413 112, fax 229 413 111); Swissair, airport (☎229 413 893); TAP, Praça Mouzinho de Albuquerque 105 (☎226 080 227, fax 226 080 233).

Airport information Call ☎229 413 260. The airport bus, the *Aerobus*, leaves every half hour from 7am to 6.30pm, from Avenida dos Aliados (☎800 200 166; 500$00 one way).

American Express c/o Star Travel, Av. dos Aliados 210 (☎222 050 695).

Banks and exchange The main branches of the banks are concentrated around Praça da Liberdade (Mon–Fri 8.30am–3pm). All have ATMs for VISA and Eurocheque cards. Better commission and opening hours at Portocâmbios, Rua Rodrigues Sampaio 193, next to the Câmara Municipal (Mon–Fri 9am–6pm, Sat 9am–1pm), and at Intercontinental, Rua Ramalho Ortigão 10, around the corner from the main turismo office (Mon–Fri 9am–noon & 2–6pm, Sat 9am–noon).

Books There are English-language bookshops in Rua da Picaria and Rua José Falcão. Try also: Bertrand Livreiros, Rua 31 de Janeiro 65; Editorial Estampa, Rua Escola do Exercito 9; Livraria Clássica in Clérigos Shopping, next to the tower; or the lovely Livraria Lello & Irmão second-hand shop at Rua dos Carmelitas 144 (see p.259). Livraria Academica, Rua Martires da Liberdade 10, is a delightful antiquarian bookshop.

Buses Porto has many bus companies, most of which operate out of different terminals; check first with the turismo as to the timetable and departure point for your destination, and see the "Travel details" at the end of this chapter for destinations and appropriate companies. The main companies and their terminals are as follows: Asa Douro, Rua Alexandre Herculano 225; Auto Viação de Espinho, Rua Alexandre Herculano 366; Auto Viação do Minho, Praça Dona Filipa de Lencastre 218; Auto Viação do Tâmega, Rua Alexandre Herculano 68; Auto Viação Landim, Rua Gueses de Azevedo 218; Auto Viação Mondinense, Av. Rodrigues de Freitas 405; Auto Viação Pacense, Praça General Humberto Delgado 329; Caima, Rua Alexandre Herculano 366; EVA, Rua Alexandre Herculano 366; Internorte, Praça da Galiza 96; Joalto, Campo Mártires da Pátria 171; João Ferreira das Neves, Praça

D. Filipa de Lencastre 193-195; Linhares, Rua José Falcão 198-204; Marquês, Praça Guilherme Gomes Fernandes 71; Rede Expressos, to the north from Praça D. Filipa de Lencastre, to the south from Rua Alexandre Herculano 366; REDM (Rodoviária d'Entre Douro e Minho), Praça Dona Filipa de Lencastre; Renex, Rua das Carmelitas 32; Rodonorte, Central Shopping, Campo 24 de Agosto; Resende, Rua das Carmelitas 183; Santos de Freixo, Central Shopping, Campo 24 de Agosto; Turilis, Rotunda da Boavista/Rua da Meditação; Valpi, Praça General Humberto Delgado 339. See p.251 for further details.

Car rental Most companies maintain offices at the airport, where cars can usually be booked on the spot. Of the multinationals, Europcar is good value: Rua de Santa Catarina 1158 (☎222 057 737, fax 222 000 170) with saloons from 6535$00 per day including TW/CDW over a week. A cheap local company is Roditur, Rua Dr. Alfredo de Magalhães 114 (☎222 053 357, fax 222 087 724), offering the same from 5500$00 per day. Other companies include Hertz, Rua de Santa Catarina 899 (☎222 052 393, fax 222 081 287); Optima, Rua Visconde de Bóbeda 38 (☎225 103 427, fax 225 105 145); and Guerin, Rua do Bolhão 182 (☎222 084 704, fax 222 081 964).

Cinemas You're most likely to find Portuguese and Brazilian films at the Cinema Batalha (and Sala Bebé), Praça da Batalha (☎222 022 407). Art-house movies are screened at the Casa das Artes, Rua Ruben A 210, off Rua do Campo Alegre (☎226 006 153). Big-screen blockbusters are screened at Cinema Charlot, Centro Comercial Brasilia, Rotunda da Boavista (☎226 097 210); Cinema Passos Manuel, Rua Passos Manuel 137 (☎222 030 706); Nun'Álvares, Rua Guerra Junqueiro 45 85 (☎226 092 078); Trindade, Rua Dr. Ricardo Jorge, next to the Câmara Municipal (☎222 004 412); Central Shopping, Rua de Santos Pousada (six screens; ☎225 102 785); and Cidade do Porto, Shopping Centre Cidade do Porto, Rua Gonçalo Sampaio, Boavista (☎226 009 164). Film listings can be found in the weekly local edition of *Público*.

Consulates Austria, Praça General Humberto Delgado 267 (☎222 084 757); Brazil, Rua Fernão V. Dourado 62 (☎226 106 278); Cape Verde, Rua da Boavista 17 (☎222 031 077); Denmark, Rua Eugénio Castro 280 (☎226 094 584); France, Rua Eugénio Castro 352 (☎226 094 805, fax 226 064 205); Germany, Av. da Boavista 5004 (☎226 102 336); Italy, Rua da Restauração 409 (☎226 006 546); Morocco, Pátio das Japoneiras, Foz do Douro (☎226 107 009); Netherlands, Rua Reboleira 7 (☎222 000 061); Spain, Rua Dom João IV 341 (☎225 363 915); UK, Av. da Boavista 3072 (☎226 169 843); USA, Av. da Boavista 3523 (☎226 186 606, fax 226 186 625).

Crafts The best place for regional crafts is the Centro Regional de Artes Tradicionais (CRAT), on the riverside at Rua da Reboleira 33–37 (Mon–Fri 10am–noon & 1–6pm, Sat & Sun 1–7pm; ☎223 320 076). It also stages temporary exhibitions, and runs week-long arts courses (around 15,000$00). More touristy are Canjirão, Rua Santo Ildefonso 215 (☎222 008 523); the Artesanato dos Clérigos, next to the tower at Rua da Assunção 33–34 (☎222 000 257), and Fernando Dias Santos at Rua dos Clérigos 45 (☎222 006 053). For designer objects (including items by architect Álvaro Siza, among others), seek out the Casa de Ferragens Carvalho e Baptista on Rua do Almada 79–83.

Excursions and trips (see also "river cruises"). Diana Tours, Rua Francisco Alexandre Ferreira 96A, Vila Nova de Gaia (☎223 771 230, fax 223 791 508) runs: a two-hour combined cruise and trip by toy train at night in Porto (15 June–15 Sept only, daily except Sat; departs 9pm & 10pm from Gaia turismo office; 1800$00); a one-hour bus trip around Porto with commentary in English departing from the Sé (April–Sept Mon–Fri from Sé at 9am, 11am, 3pm & 5pm, Sat & Sun 9am & 11am; 1800$00); and a four-hour Porto and Gaia tour leaving from the turismo in Praça Dom João (Mon–Fri, 3pm; 4900$00) which includes a port wine lodge visit.

Football The city's principal soccer team, Futebol Clube de Porto (☎225 570 400, fax 225 570 498, *www.fcporto.pt*), play at the 90,000-capacity Estádio das Antas, off Av. Fernão Magalhães; take buses #6 or #78 from Cordoaria. Boavista F.C. (☎226 071 000), whose Estádio do Bessa is on Rua 1º de Janeiro, off Av. da Boavista, is also in the top flight (buses #3, #24 or #78, from the Cordoaria; tram #18).

Hospital Hospital Santo António, Largo Professor Abel Salazar (☎222 077 500 or 222 084 601). For emergencies call 112.

Internet cafés Internet access at: *Intercyber*, Praça General Humberto Delgado 291; inside the Rivoli theatre see p.274; and also at the Casa das Artes (p.276). The cost is approximately 250$00 for 30 minutes.

Left luggage The only coin-operated lockers are at Campanhã train station and cost 150$00 per 24 hours (maximum 72 hours).

Library Biblioteca Pública Municipal, Jardim de São Lazaro, Rua Dom João IV (☎225 198 480).

Maps Excellent topographic walking maps, published by the Instituto Geográfico do Exercito, are available from Porto Editora (☎222 007 681), at Praça Filipa Lencastre 42.

Markets The former fruit and flower market by Rua Ferreira Borges is now an exhibition space. There's a general daily market in the Mercado do Bolhão on Rua Sá da Bandeira, behind the main post office, a must for self-caterers and picnic buyers. On weekdays a fruit and veg market operates along the Cais da Ribeira. A weekly flea market is held on Saturday mornings along Rua das Fontainhas down to Alameda das Fontaínhas, at the east end of Rua Alexandre Herculano over-looking the river. A few of the stalls sell fruit or home-made foods, but most have a spread of unremitting if fascinating junk. There's a summer flower market on Sundays at Praça da Liberdade (April–Oct 9am–5pm). For crafts, there usually a few crafts stalls by the Igreja de Santo Ildefonso on Praça da Batalha every day (see also the Crafts listing above).

Newspapers English-language papers are available from Tabacaria Senador on Praça da Batalha; the subway kiosk below São Bento station; the kiosk next to *Café A Brasileira*; and Livraria Bertrand, Rua 31 de Janeiro 65. Porto's leading paper, the *Jornal de Notícias*, and the local edition of the weekly *Público*, are useful sources of information on cinemas, clubs and sports events.

Pharmacies Late-night and 24-hour pharmacies (both called *farmácias de serviço*) operate on a rota basis. Details in the rear of the *Jornal de Notícias*, or call ☎118 for information.

Police Main headquarters of the Polícia de Segurança Pública do Porto (PSP) are at Rua Augusto Rosa, off Praça da Batalha, next to the Teatro Nacional de São João (☎222 088 518 or 222 055 558). There's a station at the southwest corner of the Mercado Ferreira Borges, Rua Mouzinho da Silveira. Call ☎118 for information.

Post office The main post office is opposite the town hall in Praça General Humberto Delgado (Mon–Fri 8am–9pm, Sat 9am–6pm); poste restante mail is held here, and you can also make international phone calls.

River cruises (see also "Excursions and trips"). Short fifty-minute "five bridges" boat trips along the Douro leave from both the Cais da Ribeira and Cais de Gaia in Vila Nova de Gaia (1500-2000$00); details of schedules (much reduced in winter) are available from any turismo. Of these Via d'Douro, on the Gaia side (daily except 1–14 Jan; ☎229 388 816, fax 229 388 139) has the edge using a souped-up *barco rabelo*; it also runs one-day journeys to Peso da Régua and Entre-os-Rios. Longer trips are operated by Rota do Douro, Av. Diogo Leite 250–2º, Vila Nova de Gaia (☎223 759 042, fax 223 759 043), who run one-day trips to Régua (15,000$00), Pinhão (18,000$00), and Entre-os-Rios (13,000$00), and a two-day trip (40,000$00). In summer, they do a two-hour five bridges cruise at night (2000$00).

Swimming pools Piscina de Campanhã at Rua Dr. Sousa Ávides (☎225 372 041) and Piscinas da Constituição at Rua Almirante Leote do Rego (☎225 506 601); each has a gym as well. Better than either, but more expensive, is the pool at Clube Fluvial Portuense, Rua Clube Fluvial Portuense 13 (☎222 054 357), on the riverbank in Pasteleira district near the youth hostel on the way to Foz do Douro (#18 tram).

Taxis There are ranks all over the city; alternatively call Raditáxis (☎225 073 900).

Telephones You can make international calls at the post office in Praça General Humberto Delgado and at the Telecom office in Praça da Batalha. There's a further phone office at Praça Liberdade 62. Phonecards are widely available and card-phones can be found on most streets.

Trains See "Arrival and information" for destinations from the various Porto stations. São Bento station information office (9am–8pm) has timetables for all trains routed from Campanhã; they can tell you the connection you'll need to make from São Bento. Campanhã's own information office has the same hours. If you're leaving Porto on an international connection – Paris especially – in the summer, be sure to reserve a seat several days in advance. For general train information call ☎225 364 141 (8am–11pm).

Travel agencies Jumbo Expresso Viagens, Rua Ceuta 47 (☎223 393 320), is useful for budget/student travel. A good general travel agent is Star Turismo, at both Av. dos Aliados 210 (☎222 050 695) and Rua Manuel II (☎226 067 251).

Around Porto: the coast

The coastline immediately **south of Porto** remains one of the worst polluted in Europe, with industrial effluent and inadequate sewage facilities constituting a major health hazard. Outbreaks of hepatitis in Porto and Vila Nova de Gaia linked with bathing in these waters were common until recently, and though a major programme to clean up the Douro is currently underway (due to be completed some time in 2001), it's still not safe to swim until you reach Espinho, Esmoriz, or better still, Cortegaça or Furadouro. The coast **to the north** is little better and you should certainly not swim off Matosinhos, the country's second largest port. However, press on a few kilometres further north from Matosinhos to **Vila do Conde** or **Póvoa de Varzim** and you may be tempted to stay; indeed, in summer, you might prefer to visit Porto while based at one of these resorts.

South of Porto

Access to Espinho, Esmoriz and Cortegaça from Porto is either by **train** (hourly from São Bento) or **bus** (Auto Viação do Espinho departing from Rua Alexandre Herculano 366). En route it's well worth stopping at the small settlement of **MIRAMAR**, 10km south of Porto, to see the Capela do Senhor da Pedra, a seventeenth-century chapel bizarrely situated on a rocky, wave-beaten headland jutting out from the beach.

Espinho
ESPINHO, 18km south of Porto, is a major resort – though not a very attractive one. Windswept and overcrowded, it has a feeling of a suburb rather than a town, with a casino, golf course, a few high-rise hotels, hordes of tourist shops, a dull grid of numbered streets and a railway line right through the centre. You'll find the **turismo** at Rua 6, no. 709 (June–Sept Mon–Fri 9am–9pm, Sat & Sun 10am–noon & 3–6pm; Oct–May Mon–Fri 9.30am–12.30pm & 2–5.30pm, Sat 9.30am–noon; ☎227 340 911). **Surfing** is possible here – get advice from Omni Surf Shop in the Centro Comercial California. **Swimmers** might want to use the pool at the northern end of the esplanade; the Ministry of Health has blacklisted the Silvade beach to the south of town, although it is hoped that the recently constructed series of breakwaters will alleviate the pollution. If you'd rather steer clear of the water altogether, you can arrange horseback rides through the Sociedade Hípica de Espinho, Rua Professor Dias Afonso 129, Corredoura (☎227 344 958, fax 227 342 060).

Staying overnight can be expensive since the few remaining old buildings on the seafront, some of which were *pensões*, are being bulldozed to make way for apartments. The cheapest is the *Hotel Mar Azul*, Av. 8, no. 676 (☎227 340 824, fax 227 312 636; ②), with comfortable rooms and reasonable facilities. Under the same management is the older *Residencial Espinho*, Rua 19, no. 326 (☎227 340 002, fax 227 312 636; ③), which has a similar range of rooms at slightly higher prices. The plushest option is the modern, five-star *Hotel Solverde* at the northern end of town (☎227 313 144, fax 227 313 153; ⑥), which has its own pool and health club as well as a casino, or try the eight-storey *Hotel Praia Golfe* on Rua 6 (☎227 313 385, fax 227 313 397, *pgolfe@mail.telepac.pt*; ⑤). There's a **campsite**, *Lugar dos Mochos* (☎227 343 718), inland, on the northern edge of town.

You'll have no problem finding somewhere to **eat**, the most famous place being *Casa Marreta* on the esplanade at Rua 2, nos. 1355–61, which serves excellent fish and seafood dishes. The *Casa do Pescador* in the fisherman's quarter at the southern end of town, just beyond Rua 2, is more basic but does superlative seafood. There's surprisingly little to do in terms of **nightlife**. Espinho doesn't have any discos, though in summer you'll find a number of shoreline bars trying their best to fill the gap. However, the casino at the *Solverde* (☎227 313 154) stages a tacky cabaret as well as temporary art exhibitions – a more worthy option are the **poetry recitals** held every Wednesday at 9.30pm at *Livramar*, Rua 62, no. 136 (☎227 314 705).

Esmoriz and Cortegaça
The beaches at **ESMORIZ** (6km south of Espinho) and **CORTEGAÇA** (a further 2km south) offer a restful contrast to Espinho, primarily because the road and railway start to move inland as they head further south. This leaves you a walk of a couple of kilometres

or so to reach either beach, both of which are backed by sand dunes and groves of pine and eucalyptus; both also have all-year **campsites** – *Esmoriz* (☎256 752 709, fax 256 753 717) and *Cortegaça* (☎256 752 199, fax 256 755 177). Just to the north of Praia de Esmoriz there's a small lagoon – one of the reasons that the road and railway were forced inland in the first place – and here you can expect to see waders, ducks and, depending on the season, pigeons and doves. From both Esmoriz and Cortegaça, frequent trains continue south to Aveiro (see p.208).

North of Porto

The stretch of coast around the mouth of the Douro is severely polluted, and you need to head beyond Cabo do Mundo to **VILA CHÃ**, 18km north of Porto, for a dip in the ocean. Despite encroaching development, Vila Chã retains a fishing village identity, and has a fine sandy beach with pools at low tide. There's a **campsite** at Praia de Vila Chã (☎229 272 163), 3km west of the station and well signposted from the main N13 road. Trains run hourly from Porto's Estação da Trindade, and buses from Praça Filipa de Lencastre, to Vila Chã, before moving on to the larger resorts of Vila do Conde and Póvoa de Varzim.

Vila do Conde

VILA DO CONDE, 27km north of Porto, has become quite a significant resort over the last few years, but the town has lost refreshingly little of its character in the process. The old part of Vila do Conde remains an active fishing port, with a bustling Friday **market** selling everything from produce to shoes and crockery(and an antiques market on the third Sunday of every month) and an atmospheric medieval quarter, which juts towards the sea beside the Rio Ave. Here, workmen still construct wooden fishing boats with hulls that don't look too different from 15th century caravels.

Much of the compact centre has survived intact, helped along by some excellent restoration work on buildings that other town councils might simply have demolished. The narrow alleys, beautiful town houses and churches all make Vila do Conde an attractive place to wander. Dominating the **fishing quarter** is the white dome of the Capela do Socorro, built in 1603 and renovated in 1989 after a long period of decay. Inside, the *azulejos* depicting the Adoration of the Magi are notable for the presence of Moorish figures – further testament to the fact that here, as well as elsewhere in Portugal, many Moors chose to stay and convert to Christianity during the Inquisition. Vila do Conde's narrow streets are at their best on **saints' days**, when the little street-corner votive chapels are illuminated by candles.

Overlooking everything, on a rise behind, is the enormous bulk of the **Convento de Santa Clara** (daily 9am–noon & 2–5.30pm), now a reformatory for boys but still open for visits: just knock on the door. One of the inmates will be designated to show you around its early Gothic church, which contains fine relief carvings, especially on the tombs of the founders. There's an elegant cloister, too, with a fountain fed by the long aqueduct – now partly ruined – which stretches from here into the hills. Below, back in the centre of town, the sixteenth-century **Igreja Matriz** is a beauty, with a soaring, airy interior and – thanks to the Basque workmen who helped with its construction – an unusual but very effective mix of Spanish and Portuguese styles. Like the Capela do Socorro, the church sports a distinctly Moorish dome.

Vila do Conde is also known for its lace – you can visit the **lace-making school and museum** (Tues–Fri 10am–noon & 2–7pm, Sat & Sun 3–6pm; free) at Rua de São Bento 70, and there is work for sale in the turismo at Rua 5 de Outubro. If you're especially interested in Portugal's regional crafts, there's a bonus in the town's annual **Feira Nacional de Artesanato** (crafts fair), held in the last week of July and the first week of August. Vila do Conde also boasts the **Museu Vivo da Comutação Manual** (Telephone Exchange

Museum; Tues & Thurs 10am–noon & 2–4pm; free), on Rua Alberto Moreira Soutelo, which, unsurprisingly, claims to be the only one of its kind in Europe. The **Casa de José Régio**, at Av. José Régio 132 (Tues–Sat 10am–12.30pm & 2–6pm, Sun 2.30–6pm), is also worth a visit, displaying popular art collected by this famous writer. Another gallery, the **Auditório Municipal**, shows temporary exhibitions of photography and local arts and crafts as well as film, theatre and dance. It's housed in the renovated eighteenth-century Casa dos Vasconcelos on Praça da República (Tues–Fri 3–11pm, Sat & Sun 3pm–midnight) and also has a pleasant bar further to recommend it. For cinephiles, there's a six-day short-film festival held here (Festival Internacional de Curtas Metragens), which begins on the first Sunday of July. The other main cultural venue is the pink Centro Municipal de Juventude on Avenida João Graça, which hosts occasional music recitals; ask at the turismos for details of current performances.

Vila do Conde's **beaches** (and all their attendant development) are a couple of kilometres west of town. Here, long stretches of fine sand, with drinks, kiosks and restaurants to hand, have been steadily developed right up the coast to Póvoa do Varzim. **Guia** and **Cadeira** are the nearest places to swim, both a fifteen-minute walk from the centre with calm waters and a stumpy fortification – the Forte de São João (destined to become a *pousada*) – between the two. For a totally different tune, the revving of racing cars can be heard in the first weekend of June and the second weekend of July, as Vila do Conde gears up for the annual car races held in the town – streets are sheathed in red and white crash barriers and the beach sprouts grandstands.

PRACTICALITIES

Up to six daily Linhares and Auto-Viação **buses** from Porto arrive (and depart from) opposite the smaller turismo in Rua 5 de Outubro (Tues–Fri 10am–7pm, Mon & Sat 10am–1pm & 3–7pm, Sun 3–6pm; ☎252 642 700). There are 5–10 daily Linhares buses between Vila do Conde and Santo Tirso, and hourly services (Auto-Viação do Minho and Linhares) from and to Viana do Castelo. From the **train station** (☎252 631 404) it's a five-minute walk to the centre; follow the river down, past the convent, to the bridge. Two hundred metres further along the main road, turn left at the market and on the left you'll find the **main turismo**, an ivy-clad house at Rua 25 de Abril 103 (summer Mon–Fri 9am–6pm, Sat & Sun 2.30–5.30pm; winter Mon–Fri 9am–noon & 2–5.30pm; ☎252 642 700, fax 252 641 876). Both turismos have free maps and lists of hotels, and can provide information on day-trips in the region.

The main turismo may also have a list of private **rooms**, which is likely to be all you'll find in the summer when you're advised to book ahead for any of the following options. If you're on a strictly limited budget, try *Le Villageois*, Praça da República 94 (☎252 631 119; ①), with clean, well-furnished rooms, or failing that, the *Residencial Manco D'Areia*, Praça da República (☎ & fax 252 631 748; ①) – marked simply "Hospedes" – a rundown place with a mixed bag of rooms, most lacking private bathrooms. Mid-range options include: *Hospedaria Venceslau* (☎252 646 362; ②), at the junction of Rua das Mós and Rua 5 de Outubro, 1km north of the small turismo, which has modern, comfortable rooms, most with TVs; *Pensão Princesa do Ave*, Rua Dr. António José Sousa Pereira 261 (☎252 642 065, fax 252 632 972; ②) is another decent place, some way from the town centre but near the beaches and with satellite TV in every room; while *Pensão Patarata*, overlooking the waterfront at Cais das Lavandeiras 18 (☎252 631 894; ②), has big, pleasant rooms and a reasonable café and restaurant. The nicest hotel in town is the four-star *Estalagem do Brasão*, Avenida Dr. João Canavarro (☎252 642 016, fax 252 642 028; ④), a seventeenth-century town house with *pousada*-quality period furnishings, as well as satellite TVs in all rooms. Slightly cheaper is the *Motel Sopete Sant'Ana* (☎252 641 717, fax 252 642 693; ③), on the south side of the river by the bridge – its rooms all have en-suite bathrooms and river-view balconies, and there's an indoor swimming pool, sauna and solarium. The nearest **campsite** (☎252 63 3 225) is 3km south of town, near the beach at Árvore.

Of the **restaurants**, the most established is the one at *Le Villageois* (closed Mon), a pretty place serving huge portions and with a few tables outside. Expensive but recommended is *Restaurante São Roque* in Rua do Lidador (closed Mon); more reasonable is the *Restaurante Rendilheira* at no. 48, where regional specialities are served up within an odd modern art decor. Also good, with a value-for-money *prato do dia* (1200$00), is *Restaurante Ramon* (closed Tues), near the small turismo in Rua 5 de Outubro. The unnamed café at Rua de Santo Amaro 6, three doors down from the Casa de José Régio, used to be the favourite haunt of Régio and other artistic dissidents, and is still a good place for food at reasonable prices. There's not much **nightlife** to speak of, though *Tota Bar* – next to the *Estalagem do Brasão* on Avenida Dr. João Canavarro – is packed most nights from around 10pm. Try also *Danalf*, Rua de São Bento, which has a more studenty feel, or *Café Concerto* piano bar (7pm–2am), rather oddly placed in the Centro Municipal de Juventude on Avenida João Graça. Live music (anything from grunge to salsa) can be found at *Azenha Dom Zameiro Bar* (Thurs–Sat), a three-kilometre taxi ride out of town at Ponte d'Ave, Vilarinho.

Póvoa do Varzim

PÓVOA DO VARZIM is about 4km to the north of Vila do Conde (frequent buses along the main highway and coast road) but the two couldn't be more different. Although Póvoa, too, retains a small harbour, along with the ruins of an eighteenth-century fortress, it is very much an out-and-out resort. A casino and a line of concrete hotels open onto the eight-kilometre-long **beach** (partly pebbly, so bring flip-flops or sandals), which is crowded throughout the year with Portuguese holidaymakers.

That said, the local council seems well aware of Póvoa's shortcomings and has embarked on a series of projects to prettify the town, such as the state-of-the-art fountains in the Largo do Passeio near the *Grande Hotel*, which "dance" to music during the summer. In any case, the crowds here help to create a lively, enjoyable seaside feel, restaurants are plentiful and excellent value, there's plenty of nightlife, and there usually seems to be enough accommodation to go round. If you feel the need for culture, check out the **Museu Municipal de Etnografia e História**, on Rua Visconde de Azevedo (Tues–Sun 10am–12.30pm & 2.30–6pm; 200$00), which has well-presented displays of local archeological finds, including some from Terroso (see p.284), as well as an exhaustive collection of anything and everything connected to local seafaring through the ages.

An international classical music festival is held here in July, and there are a series of traditional **festivals** throughout the summer, the best of which is the Romaria de Nossa Senhora da Assunção on August 15, when local fishermen carry life-sized images of Our Lady of Assumption to the quayside to bless those who have perished at sea; the whole event is accompanied by fireworks let off from fishing boats. A similar event occurs at the end of September for Our Lady of Sorrows. Monthly details of cultural events are listed in the *Agenda Mensal*, available at the turismo. It may also be worth enquiring at the turismo about events at the newly constructed **marina**, Porto de Recreio, at the south end of town where a programme of tours and other touristic activities is planned.

PRACTICALITIES

The helpful **turismo** (July 15–September 15 daily 9am–9pm; Sept 16–July 14 Mon–Fri 9am–1pm & 2–7pm, Sat & Sun 9.30am–1pm & 2.30–6pm; ☎252 298 120, fax 252 617 870), in an unusual turretted building on Praça Marquês de Pombal on the way in from Vila do Conde, has maps, lists of rooms, and a leaflet detailing bus and train timetables. **Buses** operate from the central Praça do Almada; the **train station** is a few minutes' walk from here, along Rua Almirante Reis. To reach the beach from the train station – a ten-minute walk – turn right and, on reaching Praça do Almada, turn left and walk straight ahead. You can **rent cars** from OTM on Avenida dos Banhos (☎252 618 240) and Atlas on Avenida Vasco da Gama (☎252 682 922). **Bicycles** can be hired in summer from people who hang around the north end of the port at the south end of Passeio Alegre.

There are plenty of smart hotels around, while cheaper **pensões** are to be found mostly along Rua Paulo Barreto, which is the main Porto road and runs from Praça do Almada to Praça Marquês de Pombal, next to the market. The best inexpensive option is *Hospedaria Jantarada*, Rua Paulo Barreto 8 (☎252 622 789; ②), clean, friendly and above a popular restaurant. *Residencial Gett*, on the tree-lined Avenida Mouzinho de Albuquerque(☎252 683 206, fax 252 617 295; ③), is a pleasant, modern place, with friendly and efficient staff and satellite TV in all rooms, while *Pensão Avô Velino*, Avenida Vasco da Gama (☎252 681 628; ③), is a bit out of the way, on the Viana road, but otherwise a good choice. Functional but charmless comfort can be had at *Hotel Luso-Brasileiro*, Rua dos Cafés 16 (☎252 690 710, fax 252 690 719; ③), 100m from the beach, but if you can afford it, go for the oldest hotel in town, *Grande Hotel Sopete* (☎252 615 464, fax 252 615 565; ③), housed in a powder-pink 1930s building next to the casino on Largo do Passeio Alegre. It's worth paying the small (1200$00) supplement for a sea view. If you want somewhere with a swimming pool and several other facilities, your only choice is the expensive and ugly *Novotel Vermar*, a high-rise complex on Rua da Imprensa Regional, 2km north on the seafront (☎252 615 566, fax 252 615 115, *www.novotel.com*; ⑤). The nearest **campsite** is the *Orbitur* at Rio Alto, 8km to the north (☎252 615 699; open all year).

Póvoa is endowed with well over fifty **restaurants** ranging from Chinese to seafood or pizzas; most are within a block or two of the seafront. If you're into fish, Póvoa is a treat – there's huge choice and the competition keeps prices keen. The local speciality is *pescada à poveira* (slices of boiled whiting served with turnip leaves, eggs, potatoes and bread soused in olive oil, onion and paprika), while the adventurous might seek out *buchos de pescada* (boiled whiting stomachs stuffed with chopped whiting liver, onion and parsley), best eaten with olives. Good places for seafood include the *São José* on Largo do Passeio Alegre 118, which also has a fine view, the *31 de Janeiro* at Rua Tenente Valadim 58, which is otherwise strong on grills, or the *Belo Horizonte* at Tenente Valadim 63, which serves a great *açorda de marisco* (seafood soup). Alternatively, sample the local atmosphere and excellent marinated sardines and fish stews at the *Adega Firmino* at Rua Caetano de Oliveira 100, two blocks back from the beach off Avenida Mouzinho de Albuquerque. More sophisticated is *Brook's* on Praça Dom João XXIII (closed Sun), serving a wide variety of grilled fish, kid goat and other meats.

The liveliest **bars** are the youthful *J.B.* on Rua Caetano de Oliveira, *IT Bar* on Avenida dos Banhos and *Enseada Bar* on Passeio Alegre, in front of the *Grande Hotel*. The best **disco** is at *Novotel Vermar*, which hots up on Fridays and Saturdays. No surprises at the **Casino da Póvoa** (nightly dinner 8.30pm; floor show 11pm; ☎252 690 870), situated at the southern end of the esplanade – it's the usual concoction of tacky cabaret shows and games (minimum bet 200$00), but for many it remains the main reason to visit the town.

Around Póvoa de Varzim

There are four reasonably accessible sites located in or near villages close to Póvoa, which, given a spare day and rented bikes, or a car, would make a rewarding circuit – maps and information leaflets are available from the turismo in Póvoa de Varzim. **LAÚNDOS**, 7km to the northeast, is notable for the windmills which stand on São Félix hill. Further on is **RATES**, boasting a splendid eleventh-century Romanesque church built by the Benedictines in granite for Henry, Count of Burgundy. The three naves are timber-roofed, while inside, a series of fine pillars with carved capitals are lit by a colourful rose window. **RIO MAU**, 8km east of Póvoa, is the site of a smaller, but even better decorated, Romanesque church, also granite and completed in 1151. The carvings on the capitals are reminiscent of those in Braga cathedral and, in this case, are thought to illustrate the Song of Roland, an epic medieval French number glorifying Charlemagne (Charles the Great).

The oldest of the settlements on this circuit is **TERROSO**, just 5km northeast of Póvoa de Varzim. A *citânia* similar to the better-known ones at Sanfins (see below) and Briteiros (see p.313) was excavated at the beginning of this century and the double ring of ramparts can still be traced. The spring here once fed the eighteenth-century aqueduct which carried water over 999 arches to the Convento de Santa Clara in Vila do Conde (see p.280).

Santo Tirso and around

Travelling **northeast** by road or rail from Porto towards the southern Minho towns of Guimarães and Braga, you pass through attractive, rolling countryside: a mix of market gardening in the valleys, vines on the gentle slopes, and wooded hill tops. Santo Tirso is the minor capital of this area, a riverside town which serves as a base for visiting the Romanesque church at nearby Roriz and the *citânia* of Sanfins de Ferreira.

Santo Tirso

Just under 30km northeast of Porto, **SANTO TIRSO** lies on the steep southern bank of the River Ave, which flows west to meet the sea at Vila do Conde. At the foot of the slope, by the bridge linking the town to its train station, is the former Benedictine monastery and church of São Bento, which now houses an agricultural college and a small **municipal museum** (Mon–Fri 9am–12.30pm & 2–6pm, Sat 9am–12.30pm). This is less than gripping, fielding the usual motley collection of local archeological finds, but take the opportunity to visit the church, whose cloister features a fine double row of galleries dating from the fourteenth century. On the plateau cresting the slope is the town hall, a charmless, concrete block; the **turismo** (Mon–Fri 9am–12.30pm & 2–5.30pm; ☎252 830 411) occupies an annexe.

Santo Tirso is served by Linhares **buses** from Póvoa, and Mondinense and Landim buses from Porto; both drop you at the station on Rua Infante Dom Henrique. **Trains** (hourly, from Porto's Trindade station) stop on the other side of town, across the river. The train route continues from Santo Tirso to Guimarães. You're unlikely to need to stay – **accommodation**, in any case, is limited and expensive – but if you do, try the homely *Pensão Caroço* at Largo Coronel Batista Coelho 48 (☎252 852 823; ②), or the more expensive *Pensão Carvalhais* in the ugly modern block at the top of town on Praça Rodrigues Ferreira (☎252 857 894, fax 252 857 581; ③).

Roriz

RORIZ, 10km east of Santo Tirso, is much prettier, but poorly served by public transport. Any bus on the Santo Tirso–Guimarães route can set you down just after Rebordões, leaving a four-kilometre walk to the church of São Pedro, at the top of the village.

The village itself is a mixture of old, rough granite cottages, whitewashed houses and several fairly kitsch creations built by returned emigrants – one is straight out of Disneyland, a Seven Dwarfs' cottage with brown concrete thatch. The date of the elegant Romanesque **Igreja de São Pedro** is disputed, but it's said to stand on the foundations of a Roman temple, later destroyed by the Moors. It was originally the church of the Benedictine monastery that once stood alongside, of which only one building still stands – and that's in private hands. The fine west door is embellished with an early Gothic rose window, adjacent to the solitary bell tower.

The Citânia de Sanfins de Ferreira

Another 4km beyond the Igreja de São Pedro, along a track through shady woods and up a gentle slope (badly signposted), are the ruins of the Celtic **Citânia de**

Sanfins de Ferreira (Mon–Fri 9am–6pm, Sat & Sun 10am–7pm; free), dating from the second-century BC. It's a splendidly atmospheric place – perched atop its hill, the skyline to the south appears infinite and, at the height of summer, the only sound is that of the broom pods popping out their seeds. Though smaller than Briteiros, Sanfins is no less impressive, with several rings of protective walls and the foundations of 160 circular huts, arranged in family compounds and separated by wide streets. One of the compounds (the *núcleo familiar* or "family nucleus") has been rebuilt, complete with thatched roof. If you want to go inside, ask for the guardian at the café next to the site, who has the key. He's also happy to show you the site's other attractions – a replica *basto* statue of a warrior (the original is in the archeological museum in Lisbon) standing guard on the crest of the hill, and the ruins of a bathhouse at one of the sources of the Rio Leça, whose engraved *pedras formosas* ("beautiful stones") are housed in the site **museum**, a glorious seventeenth-century Baroque mansion inconveniently located 3km out of Sanfins, 1km from the village of Sanfins de Ferreira (summer: Tues–Sun 10am–noon & 2–6pm; winter Tues–Sun 10am–noon & 2–5pm; free). Aside from the *pedras*, and a much older slab engraved with a hunting scene, the museum's other draws include three gravestones engraved with Celtic crosses, identical to those found in Ireland.

Porto to Penafiel

One of the surviving northern inland train routes – the **Douro railway line** (Linha do Douro) – heads east, out of Porto, although for the initial 40km it runs alongside the Rio Sousa and not the Rio Douro. If you're on one of the slow trains, it will stop at Cête, a dozen stations out of Porto and just a kilometre or so away from the village of **PAÇO DE SOUSA,** which can also be reached by bus from Penafiel (Mon–Fri 6 daily, Sat 2 daily). This was the former headquarters of the Benedictines in Portugal and, set beside the Rio Sousa, is a popular picnic spot for Porto locals.

The principal sight, inevitably, is the old **abbey church**, a dank and dark medieval building in the process of restoration. In one corner is the **tomb of Egas Moniz**, tutor and adviser to the first king of Portugal, Afonso Henriques, and a great figure of loyalty in Portuguese histories. In 1127, shortly after Afonso Henriques had broken away from his grandfather, the king of León, Egas was sent to negotiate a settlement, thus enabling Afonso to concentrate his efforts on the Moors in the south. Within three years, the king of León considered the treaty to be broken on the Portuguese side and threatened all-out war. Egas made his way to León, presented himself and his family, and, as can be seen on the panels around the tomb, offered to receive the punishment due to his master. Mercy was granted and the king sent the loyal minister home unscathed.

There are a couple of **cafés** in the village and an excellent old-fashioned *adega*, *O Moleira*, which serves wine straight from the barrel. You'll find plenty of possible **camping** spots but should you prefer a bed, it's not much further down the line to Penafiel.

Penafiel and around

At Penafiel, 35km from Porto, you enter *vinho verde* country. The wine's origins lie with the Benedictine monks, who were famed in this region for their laborious terracing of the valley slopes. A further legacy of the Benedictine presence is a dozen of the finest **Romanesque churches** in the country, each gorgeously sited in hamlets hidden away in folds of the countryside. South of Penafiel, the Barragem de Torrão offers excellent swimming opportunities, or there's the more relaxing option of a river trip from Torrão itself.

Penafiel

Despite the motorway in the Sousa valley to the west, **PENAFIEL** itself is still split by main-road traffic, and getting to it involves a connecting bus (Mon–Fri only) from the train station, which is 3km down the hill; there are also regular buses from Porto, which stop by the kiosk outside Penafiel's turismo and further along by the Igreja Matriz. The town itself is a pretty place with a laid-back atmosphere and a fabulous local **wine**. You'll find it everywhere in bottles but to get it straight from the *cuba* (barrel) you'll either have to go to the *adega* facing the train station or to the charming **Quinta da Aveleda** (Mon–Fri 9.15–11.30am & 1–4.30pm; 400$00), where the stuff is made. To get there, go 2km down the Porto road, cross the motorway and turn right at the sign – it's 1km further on from this point. Their guided tours include wine and cheese tasting, and the gardens are delightful. Next to the turismo building on Avenida Sacadura Cabral, the **Museu Municipal de Penafiel** (Mon–Fri 9.30am–noon & 2–6pm) is worth a brief visit for its archeological and ethnological displays, mainly from the Celtic *castro* (fortified hilltop settlement) site at Mozinho, as well as some wonderful gold bracelets.

PRACTICALITIES

Accommodation is limited to the good-value *pensão*, the *Casa João da Lixa* (☎255 233 158; ①) in Largo do Padre Américo; *O Cedro*, Rua do Cedro (☎255 233 551; ②); and the *Penahotel* (☎255 711 420, fax 255 711 425; ③) in Parque do Sameiro, opposite the modern Santuário de Nossa Senhora da Piedade. If you are interested in exploring the area's churches, call in at the **turismo** at Av. Sacadura Cabral 90 (Mon–Fri 9am–12.30pm & 2–5.30pm; ☎255 712 561), and ask them to mark the locations on a map. Beneath the turismo, there's a fine covered **market** (Mon–Sat). Just downhill from here, at Rua Engenheiro Matos 67, *Restaurante Relógio do Sol* serves good **food** (for around 1500$00 a head) and has a fine view over the Sousa valley. *Churrasqueira Central* on Avenida Sacadura Cabral between the turismo and Igreja Matriz has tasty grilled chicken, and *O Cedro*'s *Churrascaria* is an equally lively place to eat. Popular **bars** include *Momentos* at Rua Zeferino de Oliveira 29, and for occasional live music, *Bar Jar d'Agua* at Avenida Sacadura Cabral next to Nova Rede bank. There's an **Internet café**, *Xafariz Net Café*, 50 metres from the Igreja Matriz on the main road.

For **onward transport**, VALPI runs buses to Amarante and Porto from its garage near the Igreja da Misericórdia; Santos, for services to Boelhe and Termas de São Vicente, has an office at Av. Egas Moniz 69–71; and Asa Douro at no. 125 operates services to Torrão and Paço de Sousa.

South of Penafiel

Most of the local **churches** are hard to reach without your own transport. The most accessible by bus (Mon–Fri 8 daily, Sat 4 daily, Sun 1 daily) from Penafiel is at **BOELHE**, some 10km southeast along the N312 minor road to Entre-os-Rios. This is reputedly the smallest Romanesque church in the country: a simple building, without much architectural detail, which gains its power from a stunning position on the brow of a hill overlooking the Tâmega valley. If it's closed, ask for the key at the nearest house. Note that the last bus back to Penafiel leaves Boelhe at 2.20pm. With your own transport, a few other diversions to Romanesque churches in the region become possible. At **ABRAGÃO**, 10km southeast along the N320 from Penafiel, all that survives of the Igreja de São Pedro is the vaulted chapel and transept arch with its rose window, while the Igreja de São Salvador or Cabeça Santa (Holy Head) at **GANDRA**, east off the N106 midway between Penafiel and Torrão, gets its name from the holy skull that used to be kept there.

A trip easily made by bus from Penafiel is to the tiny spa town of **TERMAS DE SÃO VICENTE** further along the N312 from Boelhe, where it meets the main N106. En route you'll pass the **Barragem de Torrão** and its reservoir (see below). The turn-of-the-century spa has all the usual treatments but hours vary so check with the turismo in

Penafiel before setting out. The last bus back leaves at 5.25pm or you can stay overnight in one of the good self-contained rooms at the *Pensão Regional* (☎255 612 311; ①).

Five kilometres from here, south along the N106, Entre-os-Rios faces **TORRÃO** across the confluence of the Douro and Tâmega. Buses regularly make the journey from Penafiel to Torrão (Mon–Fri 7 daily) and the last one back leaves at 6pm. A good way to see some of the area is to take a **river trip** from Torrão, (daily at 4pm & 5pm; 1hr; 1500$00), operated by the Quinta dos Agros (☎255 581 473): cross back over the bridge towards Entre-os-Rios, bear right and then turn right at the war monument – it's at the bottom of the road. Should you want to stay overnight, the best choice is the *Casa Defronte*, a beautiful *ANTER* town house on the N108 in Entre-os-Rios (☎255 613 484; ③), offering simple but comfortable stone-walled rooms and an ideal base from which to explore the area on foot.

The Tâmega: Amarante and beyond

At **LIVRAÇÃO**, about an hour east from Porto, the Tâmega train line cuts off for Amarante (see below), hugging the ravine of the **Rio Tâmega**, a tributary of the Douro. There is scarcely more than the station at Livração, so if you're intending to change trains, keep your eyes open. The Tâmega line trains terminate at Amarante, from where four buses daily run up into the Serra do Marão – following the course of the Rio Tâmega – to **Celorico de Basto** and on to the next crossroads at Fermil, where a local bus picks up passengers for **Mondim de Basto**. To explore the valley, the best idea is to take a bus to Celorico and walk, following the increasingly overgrown tracks, to Mondim: a pleasant two-hour hike, through woods and over viaducts.

If your time is limited, the half-hour trip from Livração to Amarante is worthwhile in itself. From the start it's an impressive, scenic ride, with pine woods and vines clinging to incredible slopes, and goats scrambling across the steep terrace walls to nibble at haystacks constructed to hang from the branches of trees, although the new motorway running alongside part of the rail line has spoilt it somewhat.

Amarante

AMARANTE is immaculately set in a gorge of the Tâmega River, with the wooden balconies of its old houses leaning over the water. It's a fine place to stop, with innumerable bars and cafés along the south side of the river. Sadly, the polluted river beaches can no longer be recommended for swimming – though in summer you'll see some brave souls risking it – but *guigas* (pedal boats) or rowing boats can be hired for an hour or two's dawdling and there's a swimming pool complex on the south bank with enough slides and water chutes to keep kids and adults happy for a while. There's also a year-round Wednesday and Saturday morning **market** held beside the river.

The church, and former monastery, of **São Gonçalo**, beside the very elegant town bridge, is Amarante's most prominent monument. It forms the heart of an ancient fertility cult – probably with pagan origins – which still persists here at the grand **Romaria de São Gonçalo**, celebrated on the first weekend (Fri–Sun) in June, with the large Sunday procession being the highlight of the festivities. At this time, traditionally, the local unmarried youth exchange phallic cakes as tokens of their love. In the church, the saint's tomb is said to guarantee a quick marriage to anyone who touches it – his face, hands and feet have been almost worn away by hopeful suitors. Another chapel, devoted to Gonçalo's healing miracles, is offered wax models of every conceivable part of the body along with entire artificial limbs and bottles full of gallstones, although the offerings are removed at the end of each day. Alongside São Gonçalo is another interesting Baroque church with a grand tower – **São Domingos** – which contains a small museum of sacred art (free entry).

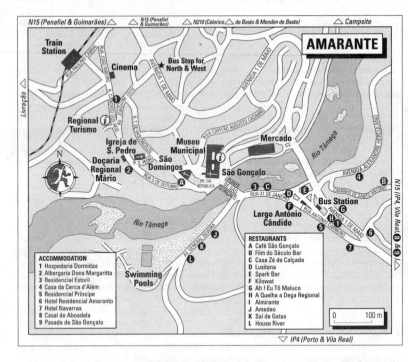

Around the side of the church, in the cloister of the former monastery, is the town's municipal library and the **Museu Municipal Amadeo de Souza Cardoso** (Tues–Sun 10am–noon & 2–5pm; 200$00). Dominated by the Cubist works of local boy Amadeo de Souza Cardoso (1887–1918), one of the few Portuguese painters of this century to achieve international renown, this is a surprising exhibition to find out in the sticks. Work by modern painters is displayed in the mini-gallery.

For **regional crafts**, Artesania, in Rua Teixeira de Vasconselos, is a good shop, selling shoes, rugs, weavings, and even string instruments.

Practicalities

The **train station** is ten minutes' walk northwest of the centre, while **buses** pull in a little closer but on the other side of the river at the bus station on Rua Antonio Carneiro. When leaving Amarante for the north and west you may find it easier to catch the bus from the stop on Avenida 1º de Maio (see map above) in the north of the town. For information, and help with accommodation during summer when rooms can be hard to come by, head for the **turismo** (daily 9am–12.30pm & 2–5.30pm; ☎255 432 259), housed in the Câmara Municipal, next to the Museu Municipal. There's also a **regional turismo** at Rua Cândido dos Reis 249 (Mon–Sat: summer 9.30am–noon & 2.30–6pm; winter 9am–noon & 2–5pm; ☎255 432 980).

ACCOMMODATION

There's a good range of accommodation in Amarante itself, as well as some lovely *turismo rural* places in the area – ask at the turismos for details. The municipal **campsite** is on the river bank 1.5km upstream at Penedo da Rainha (☎255 437 630).

Hotel Residencial Amaranto, Av. 1º de Maio (☎255 410 840, fax 255 410 849, *hotelamaranto@mail.telepac.pt/*). Large, modern and rather uninspiring hotel and restaurant on the south side of river, with satellite TV and a/c in all rooms. ③.

Casa da Cerca d'Além, Av. Alexandre Herculano, 200m east of the new bridge (☎255 431 449; or book via Privetur – details on p.299). The most atmospheric lodgings in town, in a converted manor house on the south bank of the Tâmega, beautifully fitted with antique furniture and with magnificent views. ③.

Casal de Aboadela, 9km east of town along the N15 at Aboadela (☎255 441 141). A homely, good-value farmhouse with central heating, real log fires and some self-catering apartments which carry a two night minimum stay. ③.

Albergaria Dona Margarita, Rua Cândido dos Reis 53 (☎255 432 110, fax 255 437 977). Comfortable and pleasantly situated hotel overlooking the river. Once the budget mainstay, this has acquired some pretentions as well as kitchens in all its rooms. ②.

Hospedaria Dormidas, at Rua Cândido dos Reis 288 (☎255 423 327). One of the cheaper places in town and perfectly adequate, with a range of basic rooms and shared bathrooms. ②.

Residencial Estoril, Rua 31 de Janeiro 49 (☎255 431 291, fax 255 431 892). A friendly place by the old bridge, and first choice for budget accommodation. Back rooms have superb views of the river. ②.

Hotel Navarras, Rua António Carneiro, beyond the *Príncipe* on the south side of the river (☎255 431 036, fax 255 432 991). The best modern option, friendly and with a good restaurant and a swimming pool on the roof. ③.

Residencial Príncipe, Largo António Cândido 53, on the south side (☎255 432 956). Cheap option in the modern part of town near the bus station, the front rooms here have balconies. ①.

Pousada de São Gonçalo, Curva do Lancete, Ansiães (☎255 461 123, fax 255 461 353). Twenty kilometres east of Amarante and just off the IP4 to Vila Real. Perched on a clifftop, the views over the nearby Serra do Marão (walking trips can be arranged) are unbeatable. However, service can be half-asleep, and it smells vaguely of antiseptic. ⑤.

EATING, DRINKING AND NIGHTLIFE

Local specialities include *empadas de frango* (chicken pasties) and *cozido à portuguesa* (boiled meats), but the town is most famous for its **egg pastries**: the charming *Doçaria Regional Mário* on Rua Cândido dos Reis (☎255 433 044) has the lot. For a more substantial meal, Amarante has many **restaurants**, with the most "typical" (and touristic) ones in the houses overlooking the river on the south bank. Washed down with jugs of heavy local red wine, the well-spiced dishes at *A Quelha Adega Regional*, Rua de Olivença, are a meat-eater's dream. On Rua 31 de Janeiro, *Casa Zé da Calçada* is decidedly pricey, but worth every escudo for its local specialities, good service and excellent wine list – the terrace at the back overlooks the river, while *Lusitana*, just up the road, is cheaper but still good – try the *bacalhau à Narcisa* or roast veal – and also has a river terrace. *Kilowat*, at Rua Cândido dos Reis, is a good cheap *tasca*, with main meals under 1000$00, while *Café São Gonçalo*, on Praça da República alongside the church and in view of the bridge, serves reasonably priced evening food and has outdoor tables for drinks and snacks. *Almirante* on Largo António Cândido is an upmarket place specializing in shellfish. Quirky Brazilian restaurant *Ah! Eu Tô Maluco* (the name translates as "Ah! I must be Crazy"), at Clube Residencial da Madalena on Avenida 1º de Maio, has live music some evenings and specializes in *rodízio* evenings, which involve stuffing your face with an unlimited quantity of roasted meat, while *Saí de Gatas* ("leave crawling"), on Avenida General Silveira, is a youthful restaurant and bar with – as its name suggests – a relaxed atmosphere.

For **nightlife**, try any of the bars and discos on the south side of the river, whose riverside terraces stay open till late in summer. Currently popular places are *House River* and *Amedeo* on Avenida General Silveira, *Spark Bar* on Avenida Alexandre Herculano, and *Fim do Século Bar* at Caminho de Santo António.

Into the Serra do Marão: the Basto villages

Beyond Amarante you really feel the climb into the **Serra do Marão** on the approach to the towns of Celorico and Mondim de Basto, both set astride the Tâmega with the Serra do Alvão rising immediately to the east. To the north – and technically in the Minho region – is the larger, provincial town of Cabeceiras de Basto, which provides a useful transport link to Braga and then the Peneda-Gerês national park (see Chapter Six). Together, these three towns and their districts form the **Terras de Basto**, a region of fertile countryside that produces a strong *vinho verde*. The name ("basto" meant "I claim") comes from a group of Celtic statues, symbols of power which were laid horizontally on warrior's graves and have been found in several local spots. Beautifully incised with Celtic emblems on its torso and the shield placed on its belly, the finest of these is in the Museu Nacional de Arqueologia in Lisbon (see p.87).

Celorico to Mondim de Basto

Thirty kilometres northeast of Amarante, **CELORICO DE BASTO** is proud of its neatly laid out lawns, formal flower beds, sweeping views into the Serra do Alvão and annual round of festivals: **Festa de São Tiago** (July 23–25), **Feira de São Caetano** (August 7), **Romaria de São Bartolomeu** (August 24) and **Feira de Santa Catarina** (November 25). Celorico de Basto has only a single **pensão** – the *Progresso* – in Praça Albino Alves Perreira (☎255 321 170; ①), and there's an excellent **restaurant** 1km north of town, the *Quinta do Forno*, set in an old farmhouse and specializing in homebred *vitela* (veal). For a brief foray into the woods, a labyrinth of paths head off from behind the village church, while in the distance lies the prospect of Monte Farinha, the highest peak in the region (see p.291). The mountain is more easily approached from the village of Mondim de Basto, which is accessible from Celorico on frequent Mondinense buses (the station is 200m north of *Pensão Progresso*).

On the main road, halfway between Celorico and Mondim lies the small, pleasant village of **Fermil**; buses on their way between Cabeceiras and Amarante pass through three to four times daily. The main attraction is a wonderful *turismo rural* property, *Casa do Barão de Fermil* (☎255 361 211; ⑤), a slightly decaying mansion with its own swimming pool and elderly, English-speaking owners.

MONDIM DE BASTO, 9km along the main road northeast of Celorico, is a little more exciting than Celorico, with a small, well-preserved old town in the centre of a modern sprawl. You might consider making Mondim de Basto a base for exploring the **Parque Natural do Alvão** (see p.371); there's an information office (☎255 381 209) 800m down the Celorico road by the Barrio primary school. **Guided walks** in the park can be arranged through Os Tamecanos (☎255 302 637), which also offers rafting, canoeing and canyonning. The **turismo** (daily: summer 9am–9pm; winter 9am–12.30pm & 2–5.30pm; ☎255 381 479) on Praça 9 de Abril provides maps, a list of hotels, information on local *turismo rural* properties and somewhat illegible handwritten sheets detailing local walking routes.

In town, **places to stay** include two modern, good-value options: the *Residencial Arcadia*, Avenida Dr. Augusto de Brito (☎255 381 410; ②), which can be a touch noisy as it's above a café and games arcade, and the very friendly *Residencial Carvalho (*also called *Residencial Sossego*), by the petrol station on the same road (☎255 381 057; ②), where the spotless, self-contained rooms come equipped with TV and minibar. There's also an excellent **campsite** (☎255 381 650; closed mid-Dec to mid-Jan) – about 1km from the centre along the N304 Vila Real road near the banks of the Rio Cabril; the river water is clean enough to swim in. Rua Velha is the main drag for both **bars** and **restaurants** – good, cheap options include the *Adega Santiago* and *Adega Sete Condes*, while *Restaurante Escondidinho* is more upmarket. On Avenida da Igreja, *Churrasqueira Chasslik* is a busy chips-with-everything sort of place, or try *O Transmontano* on the same road for specialities from beyond the Serra do Alvão; try the *feijoada* (bean stew with gristly bits of pork). The main **nightlife** focus is *Bar da Vinha* on Rua Velha, and *Koton Club* at Vilar de Viando, 1km out towards Vila Real. There's an **Internet café**, *Bar Net's*, on Avenida da Igreja.

Mondim's new bus station is by the central Mercado Municipal and there are regular **bus connections** to Vila Real, a spectacular ride, skirting the Parque Natural de Alvão (Mon–Sat 7am, 12.30pm & 5.30pm), as well as to Guimarães, Coimbra and Lisbon. Alternatively, you could catch a bus to Fermil, and then on to the lively provincial town of Cabeceiras de Basto (see below), from where there are regular buses to Braga.

Monte Farinha and the Cabril Valley

The 996-metre-high **Monte Farinha** is surprisingly easy to climb – less than three hours' easy walking – and, if the times coincide, you can get a head start by taking the bus to the foot of the ascent, three-and-a-half kilometres from Mondim. Walking, follow the N312 Cerva road east out of Mondim, then take a path up to the right shortly after Pedra Vedra. Once on the mountain, follow the road which zigzags to the summit (Mondim's turismo has a map). An alternative but more tiring route is to take the mountain track towards Carazêdo, turning left after 2km onto the path for Pegodinhas. At the hamlet of Campos, a further 2km on, turn left again and continue north to Pegodinhas, after which you've a good ninety-minute hike up steep terrain to join the zigzags to the top. The panoramic views well repay your efforts, though, and at the top is the attractive late eighteenth-century parish church of **Nossa Senhora da Graça**, centre of a major *romaria* on the first Sunday in September. Another *romaria* is held on July 24, in honour of São Tiago. There's also a **restaurant** next to the church, the *Alto da Sonhora da Graça* (☎255 381 404) – call ahead if you plan to eat here.

Another good hike from Mondim is into the **Cabril valley**. Only about twenty minutes beyond the village campsite, the Cabril – more a stream than a river – is crossed by a Roman bridge, impressive in itself and set near a little **waterfall** where there's a good swimming hole. From here, follow the Cabril upstream to a working watermill or take the stone track (about 200m upriver) along what must have been a Roman road. Follow this, cross a road, and you're at the start of a maze of small paths cutting between the fields and vineyards of the Cabril valley, and leading higher into the slopes.

Cabeceiras de Basto

At the heart of the Terras de Basto, **CABECEIRAS DE BASTO** is the largest and most interesting Basto village. If you can, time your visit to coincide with the **Monday feira**, when traders sell clothes and food, while the **Feira** and **Romaria de São Miguel** (September 19–30) centres on traditional choirs, dancing, and a market, with a colourful procession on the last day.

The town's old centre is dominated by the twin towers of the Baroque **Mosteiro de São Miguel de Refojos** (daily, roughly 7am–8pm), a former monastery that's now used as a church. Though you should be able to organize access if your Portuguese is good, staff at the **turismo** next door (Sept 15–June 14 Mon–Fri 9am–12.30pm & 2–5.30pm; June 15–Sept 14 daily 9am–12.30pm & 2–5.30pm; ☎253 669 100) may well be more successful in convincing the busy *padre* to let you visit the monastery's treasury (a collection of statues and religious garments) and access the clock tower, from which you can view the church's highlight – the *zimbório* (dome). The monastery was most likely founded early in the seventh century by the Visigoths, just before the first Moorish invasion.

Opposite the monastery, in the gardens of the Praça da República, is a rather curious *basto* figure that probably covered the tomb of one **Hermígio Romarigues**, who successfully defended Cabeceiras de Basto from three Moor attacks. The *basto's* original head disappeared somewhere along the line (no-one's sure where or when), and the figure stood headless for many years until 1892, when somebody added a dapper moustachioed head complete with French-style kepi hat and a new pair of legs and boots.

Most of Cabeceiras de Basto's **accommodation** is in the newer part of town, close to the bus station. A reliable, inexpensive option is the *Residencial São Miguel*, above the equally good restaurant on Largo Barjona de Freitas (☎253 661 034; ①) near the post office; more expensive are the rooms above *Restaurante A Cafrial* on Avenida General Humberto Delgado (☎253 662 690; ②). Four kilometres from Cabeceiras, off the road to Venda Nova at Riodouro, there's a small, thirty-pitch **campsite**, *Clube de Campismo Valsereno* (☎253 662 047). The site is close to a small river and has its own bar and swimming pool. More characterful accommodation can be found in a number of farmhouses in the region (all ③); ask at the turismo for details of *turismo rural* properties. Back in town, good cheap **meals** can be had at the *Cozinha Real de Basto*, Avenida Sá Carneiro, a short way up the road to Arco de Baúlhe from the monastery. Classier and more expensive is *Restaurante Barão*, at the narrow end of Praça da República and facing the monastery.

Leaving from the central terminus by the market in the new section of town, **buses** connect Cabeceiras with Celorico and Mondim de Basto, Póvoa de Lanhoso in central Minho, Braga and Porto (Mon–Sat only). Change in Arco de Baúlhe for Chaves. For details of **tours** in the region, pick up the beautifully produced *Guia das Aldeias* booklet from the turismo (free).

Along the Douro: to Peso da Régua and on to the Spanish border

Leaving Porto **by road** and heading for Peso da Régua and port wine country, there are two possibilities: either take the motorway eastwards, leaving it at Penafiel or Amarante, or – with more time – follow the N108 southeast. This road hugs the north bank of the Douro River until Entre-os-Rios (where the Tâmega meets the Douro), after which it forks, allowing you to drive along either river bank. The north bank road is quicker; the south bank more attractive. As for the Linha do Douro **train from Porto**, this shadows the motorway, and passes close to Penafiel, but shortly after Livração the line finally turns south to reach the Douro and then heads upstream. At Mesão Frio, the river temporarily leaves its confined channel and broadens into the little plain commanded by the port wine town of **Peso da Régua**. East of here, trains continue as far as **Pocinho**, though to travel any further – and to cross the border into Spain – you'll need to take buses or your own transport. You could always cut north from Régua instead, up the Corgo line, a brief excursion through marvellous vine and granite landscape to Vila Real (see p.365). Régua is also the jumping-off point for buses to the pilgrimage centre of **Lamego**, 13km to the south, at the tip of Beira Alta, and since this is by far the easiest link with the town, Lamego is covered here, along with its immediate region.

Peso da Régua

PESO DA RÉGUA (usually just Régua) is an expanding provincial town that has been known for over two centuries as the "Capital of the Upper Douro" because of its role in the port industry. In fact, the centre for quality port wines has shifted to Pinhão, half an hour further east; Régua is simply the junction and the depot through which all the wine must pass on its way to Porto. It's not a pretty place either, dominated by a semi-complete motorway (the enormous bridge and southern section are now open) that will eventually link Bragança with Viseu in Beira Alta. Nevertheless, the ornamental *barcos rabelos* anchored on the river, and the sombre Sandeman cutout on the horizon, are a reminder of Régua's previous importance as the first capital of Pombal's demarcated port-producing region.

The small **turismo** (Sept 1–June 30 Mon–Fri 9am–12.30pm & 2–5.30pm; July 1–Aug 31 daily 9am–12.30pm & 2–5.30pm; ☎254 313 846) is on Rua da Ferreirinha, 1km west of the train station on the river bank (buses stop right outside it) – turn right and head downhill along the river; it's right at the end of the river road at the junction near the petrol station. Staff will hand out an excellent map of wine-related sites along the Douro – the *"Rota de Vinho do Porto"* – which locate several dozen wine lodges and working *quintas* (farms) that are open to the public(see p.267 for more on port wine production). Turismo staff can also provide information about the local **port wine lodges** – the nearest is **Quinta de São Domingos** (Mon–Fri 9am–12.30pm & 2–5pm; free; ☎254 320 100), which offers a more personalized and interesting tour than its Vila Nova de Gaia equivalents. To get there, turn left from the train station and follow the signs. You can also visit the entrance hall of the Casa do Douro on Rua dos Camilos, the headquarters of the port growers' organization, to see the medieval-style stained-glass window by Lino António.

Apart from the alcoholic diversions, there's not much to do in Régua except wander through the upper town, take a **river trip** to some of the *quintas* around town (summer only; contact the turismo for more information), or book canoeing and mountain biking trips with Aventuridouro Rua do Souto (☎254 321 496).

You probably won't want to stay the night here, so be sure of your train connection or the next bus out. Leaving from outside the train station, **buses** to Lamego run every hour up until 8pm, and there are five trains daily to Vila Real (last one leaves at 6.44pm). If you do need **accommodation**, the high-rise *Residencial Império,* Rua Vasques Osório 8, at the corner of Largo da Estação (☎254 320 120, fax 254 321 457; ③), is close to the train station. Rooms are comfortable, with a/c, TVs, heating and minibar, and the excellent breakfasts are included. *Pensão Borrajo* on Rua dos Camilos (☎254 233 396; ①) is a basic option in an old tiled building above a restaurant. The classiest choice is the brand-new *Hotel Régua Douro,* on Avenida da Galiza by the train station (☎254 322 999 or 254 320 700; ④), which has an outdoor pool, jacuzzi and health club. There are plenty of **restaurants** along the riverfront; elsewhere, try *O Maleiro,* a friendly, bustling place on Rua dos Camilos. The understated, family-run *Restaurante Arco Íris* on Avenida Sacadura Cabral, west from the turismo, offers superlative cooking at good prices (up to 2000$00) and has a number of awards to its name.

RIVER, RAIL AND RIBBON LAKES

In the eighteenth century, when the port-producing area was first demarcated (see p.265), the **Rio Douro** could not be navigated by the traditional *barcos rabelos* (barges) beyond the rapids of Cachão de Valeira. By the end of the century, engineering works had circumnavigated the worst of the rapids and opened up the Douro as far east as Pocinho, but travel was still slow – it took three days to float wine down from Peso da Régua to Porto. The arrival of the **railway** at the end of the nineteenth century accelerated transport up and down the valley: the track reached Régua in 1880 and arrived at the Spanish border in 1887, with the branch lines up the river's tributaries completed by 1910. Later, road transport replaced rail and the river itself became something of a backwater until the 1970s, when dams were planned along the length of the Douro.

With the completion of the fifth dam in 1985, the river was turned into a series of **ribbon lakes** and, thanks to locks along the route, it's now possible to cruise via Régua from Porto to Barca de Alva on the Spanish border, a distance of just over 200km; for details, see Porto "Listings" p.278.

East to the border

Just beyond Régua, and past the massive dam of a hydroelectric power station, you begin increasingly to see the terraced slopes where the **port vines** are grown. They're at their best in August, with the grapes ripening, and in September, when the harvest has begun. Quotas for wine production have been in force around here since the mid-eighteenth century, and some terrace walls from that period have withstood the assault of the diggers and dynamite that are used nowadays to clear the way for the vineyard tractors. Grape-treaders and the traditional *barcos rabelos* have also been replaced by machines and cistern lorries, though there's still a demand for large groups of hand-pickers (*rogas*) when there's a bumper crop.

Pinhão to Pocinho

The country continues craggy and beautiful, with the softer hills of the interior fading dark green into the distance, past **PINHÃO**, the main centre for quality ports. Trains pull in at the east end of town near to the river. There are a couple of large *pensões* in Pinhão so **accommodation** shouldn't be a problem. *Pensão Douro*, facing the train station (☎254 724 404; ②), is the more modern of the two, with TVs and air-conditioning in the rooms. *Pensão Restaurante Ponto Grande* (☎254 732 456; ②), two doors down at Rua Central 103–105, offers the same in-room facilities but is fractionally cheaper and has a good restaurant. However, if your budget can stretch to it, opt for the *Quinta de la Rosa* (☎254 732 254, fax 254 732 346, *mail@quintadelarosa.com*; ⑤), a working wine estate 1.5km west of Pinhão, with six double rooms (breakfast is included) and a swimming pool as well as wonderful river views and the chance to see at first hand the early processes of port wine making.

From Pinhão, you could drive (or get a taxi) to the village of **Panascal** and visit the 250-year-old *Quinta do Panascal* (Mon–Fri 10am–7.30pm; ☎254 732 321), a Fonseca port wine company property which offers free tours of the grounds and a chance to sample some local port.

The Douro continues on its journey eastwards, through the village of **TUA**, where buses run up the Tua valley to Mirandela in Trás-os-Montes (see p.365). The train continues on to its terminus, 45km east of Pinhão, at the isolated station of **POCINHO**, where it is met by buses to Torre de Moncorvo, 10km northeast (see p.387).

Vila Nova de Foz Côa

Sitting high above the Côa valley eight kilometres south of Pocinho, **VILA NOVA DE FOZ CÔA** is a small and pleasant place, which, bizarrely, was recently awarded the status of a city. However, the main reason to visit is an astonishing collection of **Paleolithic rock art**, discovered in 1992 and rescued from imminent submersion under a proposed dam. The rock art sites are now open to the public (see the box opposite), and this in itself merits a night's stay. Other than the **Igreja Matriz**, with its impressive Manueline doorway, leaning walls and pillory outside, there's little else to Foz Côa. Good dates to coincide with include the self-explanatory Onion Fair (May 8), a municipal holiday on May 21 with parades and music performances, the *Festa de Nossa Senhora da Veiga* on August 8, and the *Feira de São Miguel* on September 29. A monthly market is held on the first Tuesday of each month, and the blossoming of almond trees draws the crowds in late February and early March.

PRACTICALITIES

Foz Côa is most easily reached by the Douro train to Pocinho, from where connecting **buses** pass through town on the way to Castelo Rodrigo (going back to Pocinho or Torre de Moncorvo, buses leave Mon–Fri at 9am & 4.30pm, Sat 9am & Sun 4.30pm). For information on other services to the Mountain Beiras and Lisbon, ask at *Café Luís* on Avenida Gago Coutinho, where the buses drop you. The new **turismo** (daily 9am–12.30pm & 2–5.30pm;

☎279 765 243), which supplies maps and can help with accommodation, is inconveniently situated 2km from the town centre on the road to Castelo Melhor and Vilar Formosa; from the archeological park office on Avenida Gago Coutinho in the centre of town (see box, p.296), walk down Rua da Portela opposite, and turn right on to Largo da Conceiçao, from where it's a 1.5km hike. **Hotels** in town include *Residencial Avenida*, Av. Gago Coutinho 8 (☎271 762 175; ②), the friendly *Residencial Marina* next door (☎271 762 112; ②), which has satellite TV in the rooms, and *Residencial Cifrão*, Rua do Mercado (☎271 762 452; ②), around the corner from the park office. There's also a brand new **youth hostel** (☎279 768 190, fax 279 768 191) on a windswept site with great views, 1.5km northwest of town off the Pocinho road: from the Igreja Matriz, walk down Rua Dr. Silverio de Andrade and turn right after 1km. There are washing machines, a kitchen, a restaurant and disabled facilities, and some double rooms (①). Good **food** can be had at *Restaurante A Marisqueira* on Rua Juiz Moutinho de Andrade 35, the eastern continuation of Avenida Gago Coutinho. For a little **nightlife**, karaoke beckons at *Gaitero Bar*, Av. Gago Coutinho 12; if you fancy a dance, try either *Pub Discoteca Visage* at Rua Carlos Lacerda 4, or *Discoteca A Rupestre* in Rua do Olho 35.

Onwards to Barca de Alva and the border

Following the last, uppermost reaches of the Portuguese Douro is impossible by road, as on both sides they veer well away from the river. However, the roads converge again over the bridge at Barca de Alva, where the river finally enters Portuguese territory after skirting the border for over 100km. Local Senhor Lopes buses run the two-hour journey to Barca de Alva from Pocinho (Mon–Fri 2pm & 6.30pm, Sat 2pm, Sun 6.30pm) passing through both Vila Nova de Foz Côa and the small, sleepy town of **FIGUEIRA DE CASTELO RODRIGO**, where you'll be dropped in the large Largo Mateus de Castro. There are a couple of basic **pensões** here, the better, but least characterful of which is *Pensão Figueirense* (☎271 312 517; ②), just south of the Largo on Avenida 25 de Abril, where breakfast is included. Slightly cheaper is *Pensão Transmontano da Beira*, Rua Osório de Vasconcelos (☎271 312 244, fax 271 312 237; ②). However, despite a glut of restaurants and a large but simple Romanesque church, the town itself isn't the main draw: nearby, on an isolated hill, is the much older, medieval settlement of **CASTELO RODRIGO** (500$00 by taxi), a site that has been permanently occupied since around 500 BC, when the Turdulos people arrived. It is now inhabited only by a few dozen families settled around the ruins of its castle and is a pleasant place to spend an afternoon – the views are superb and there's a very good restaurant, *O Cantinho dos Avós*, which also has rooms (☎271 312 643; ②). If you're heading south from Figueira de Castelo Rodrigo, there's currently one daily bus at 8.20am (except Sat) to Lisbon via Guarda, Viseu and Coimbra: information and tickets from the kiosk in the southwestern corner of the Largo, in front of the *Transmontano* café.

Twenty kilometres to the north and less than 2km from the Spanish border is the last Portuguese village along the Douro, **BARCA DE ALVA**. The route is a delight – defiantly unmodernized agricultural land dotted with boulders, storks' nests and conical, stone-roofed houses – and Barca itself is an attractive place, overlooked by mountains on all sides and with a row of whitewashed cottages facing the river. It is the final destination of some of the river cruises from Porto (see p.278), but it's looking a little neglected now since the railway line across the border was discontinued in the 1980s: if you're brave enough you can risk the rickety old metal railway bridge into Spain (beware of rotten sleepers and snakes).

Barca's main appeal is the tranquil atmosphere and attractive countryside, recently declared part of the new Parque Natural do Douro Internacional (see p.393), which also makes it a good local hiking base. A lovely walk along a quiet road starts by crossing the road bridge into Trás-os-Montes; then you can follow the Douro through olive and orange groves, and past the terraced vineyards still providing grapes for the port companies in Porto.

THE ROCK ART OF FOZ CÔA

The River Côa near Vila Nova de Foz Côa became the centre of one of Portugal's major controversies when plans to construct a massive dam coincided with the discovery in 1992 of what is now confirmed to be the **most extensive array of outdoor Paleolithic art in Europe**. Engravings of horses, deer, goats, and other animals (some extinct, such as the auroch bison), as well as later, Neolithic images of people, were found along 17km of the river's steep, rocky schist valley and subsequent interest gave rise to a flurry of further discoveries in nearby sites. The oldest engravings are estimated to be up to 22,000 years old and are particularly unusual in that they are not in caves but on exposed rock faces, invariably close to water. Unfortunately, more precise carbon-dating on paint samples (some of the engravings were also painted) has, for the most part, been made impossible by misguided chemical "cleaning" – intended to relieve the engravings of their moss and lichen covering, it also went a long way to removing most of the traces of paint. The hope is that future discoveries will provide a second chance to date the sites more accurately.

However, the fact that the sites have survived at all is testimony to a remarkable "people's **campaign**" against the proposed dam: if construction had gone ahead, the engravings would have been lost forever under 90m of water. Archeologists and environmental groups joined forces with local people (who also feared the loss of 16,000 hectares of prime-quality vineyards), and schoolchildren and students from across the country in pressurizing EDP, Portugal's then state-owned electricity monopoly, to abandon the project. Success came in 1995 when the sites were declared a National Monument. The **Parque Arqueológico do Vale do Côa** was created the following year, and in December 1998 became a UNESCO World Heritage site.

To arrange a guided visit, you must contact the park authorities in advance at Av. Gago Coutinho 19, 5150 Vila Nova de Foz Côa (Tues–Fri 9am–12.30pm & 2.30–5.30pm ☎279 764 317, *pavc@mail.telepac.pt; office/*). Three sites are open to the public (daily except Mondays; 500$00 per site): Canada do Inferno and Ribeira de Piscos can be visited in the morning (tours from 9.30am–noon), and Penascosa in the afternoon (tours 2–5pm). Without your own transport, Canada do Inferno – the site of the half-built dam – is the best option, as you're picked up from the park office in Foz Côa. For the other sites, you have to make your own way to the respective **interpretation centres**, each equipped with a cafeteria and computer terminals for surfing through the park's Internet site: *http://portugal.hpv.pt/fozcoa/index_e.htm*. For the Penascosa site, make your way to Castelo Melhor interpretation centre, on the road to the village of Castelo Rodrigo, which has a ruined castle and a couple of café-restaurants. The interpretation centre for Ribeira de Piscos is in Muxagata, off the road to Vis, with a bar and not much else. There are no helpful bus services to either site, so your only option is to take a taxi.

Bear in mind that it can get very hot in the sheltered valley, especially at Ribeira dos Piscos, and there's some walking involved, so it's a good idea to bring a hat and plenty of water. There's currently a waiting list of three to four days for weekday visits, and one to three weeks for weekends, although you might be lucky and find a place within a day or two.

Accommodation in Barca de Alva is at the *Baga d'Ouro* (☎279 315 126; ①), above the restaurant on the main road along the river; the *Casa de Pasto*, a few doors along, also has cheap rooms. The *Baga d'Ouro* is also a good place **to eat**, and does a fine set meal and excellent breakfasts of coffee, fresh bread and local honey. **Onward transport** is restricted as there are no bus services north to Freixo de Espada à Cinta; if you want to continue on to Trás-os-Montes your only option (unless you want to hitch the 20-odd kilometres to Freixo de Espada à Cinta) is to catch a Senhor Lopes bus back to Pocinho (Mon–Fri 7.30am & 4.30pm, Sat 7.30am, Sun 4.30pm), from where there are three daily buses to Torre do Moncorvo and beyond.

Lamego and around

Although technically in Beira Alta, **LAMEGO** is isolated at the tip of its mountain province, and much more accessible from Régua and the Douro. The town itself has more in common with the Douro region, too, spreading over gentle slopes of the rich agricultural land fed by the river, a terrain which the locals put to good use in the production of such delights as hams and melons, as well as *Raposeira* – the closest thing to champagne you will find in Portugal.

Lamego is a wealthy place, and long has been, as evidenced by the graceful white *quintas* and villas on the hillsides, and the luxuriant architecture of the centre, where Baroque mansions seem to stand on every corner and lavish decorations are found within the smallest chapel. Lamego also has one of the very greatest Baroque structures in Europe – the shrine of **Nossa Senhora dos Remédios**, which, with its monumental stairway, dominates the west–east axis of the town.

The Town

For all the architectural histrionics of the shrine, it's Lamego's **Sé** that clearly delineates the centre of town (daily 7.30am–1pm & 3–7pm). It's basically a Renaissance structure, though a thirteenth-century tower survives from a previous building. The mixture works well and the cloister is a beauty. Facing the cathedral, occupying an eighteenth-century palace, is the town's excellent **Museu de Lamego** (Tues–Sun 10am–12.30pm & 2–5pm; 250$00), whose exhibits include five of the remaining panels of a polyptych commissioned from Grão Vasco by the Bishop of Lamego in 1506. Judging by the lack of correlation between the various panels – for instance, the *Creation of the Animals* and the prodigiously executed *Annunciation* – some of the work must be attributed to the great man's school. Also on show are a series of huge sixteenth-century Flemish tapestries (including a marvellous *Life of Oedipus* sequence), three curious statues of a conspicuously pregnant Virgin Mary (a genre peculiar to this region), a fine assembly of *azulejos*, piles of ecclesiastical treasure from the Episcopal Palace, and a group of chapels rescued from the decaying sixteenth-century **Igreja das Chagas**.

Across the square, Rua da Olaria, a narrow street of tiny shops, leads into Rua de Almacave, which follows the walls of the old inner town. The route takes you past the **Igreja de Santa Maria Maior de Almacave** (daily 7.30am–12.30pm & 4–8pm), a very ancient foundation said once to have been a mosque, to Praça do Comércio. From here you can pass through the walls of the **Old Citadel** and climb up to the **Castelo** (mid-June to end September only: daily 9am–noon & 3–6pm; free), surrounded by a cluster of ancient stone houses. This has been pressed into service as the local scout headquarters and the boys do have a fairly legitimate claim on the place, having – so they say – cleared eighteen lorryloads of garbage away in the 1970s and saved the building from ruin. You can look around the castle, providing a spare scout is available to show you around – if the wigwams and scout banners inside don't grab you, climb the rickety stairs onto the roof for some stunning views. Nearby, the thirteenth-century **Cisterna** is one of the strangest buildings in the country. The interior of this ancient water source resembles a perfectly preserved Romanesque chapel, its walls still bearing the original stonemasons' marks – sadly, it's closed to the public.

Nossa Senhora dos Remédios

The celebrated shrine of **Nossa Senhora dos Remédios** (daily: summer 7.30am–8pm, winter 8am–5pm) is a major point of pilgrimage – a reputation for healing miracles draws devotees from all over the country. Standing on a hill overlooking the city, it's approached by a magnificently elaborate eighteenth-century stairway, modelled on the one at Bom

△ **①** ,Campsite, Castro Daire & Serra das Meadas   **②** △ Peso da Régua △

LAMEGO

ACCOMMODATION
1 Motel Turisserra
2 Vila Hostiling
3 Hotel Lamego
4 Albergaria do Cerrado
5 Residencial São Paulo
6 Café Abrigo
7 Residencial Solar da Sé
8 Pensão Império
9 Pensão Silva
10 Residencial Solar
   Espírito Santo
11 Hotel do Parque

RESTAURANTS & BARS
A Churrasqueira Londrina
B O Combinado
C Pizzaria O Groto
D Casa de Pasto Vitor Pinto
E Restaurante Novo
F Casa de Filipe &
   Adega Matos
G Jardim Popular
H Discoteca ETDS

N.S. da Esperança

Ig. das Chagas

Ig. da Graça

AVENIDA DO BOAVISTA

Chafariz

Porta dos Figi

Palácio Episcopal

Castelo

PR. DO COMÉRCIO

Ig. de Almacave

Old Citadel

Mercado

Cisterna

Law Courts

Bus Station

△ Castro Daire & Viseu (N2)

Porta do Sol

LG. DO CAMÕES

Museu de Lamego

Fire Station

RUA DE RAFEL

RUA PINHEIRO DE ARAGÃO

RUA COLUMELA

RUA JUSTINO PINTO DE OLIVEIRA

RUA DOS BANDEIRAS

Sé

Swimming Pool

AVENIDA DR. A. DE SOUSA

AV. DR. A. DE SOUSA

AV. P.E. HERCULANO

RUA DA SANTA CRUZ

RUA DIREITA

RUA TEIXEIRA

N

Recinto da Feira

Igreda de Santa Cruz

Capela do Desterro

Hospital

0   200 m

①① N.S. dos Remédios

Torouca, Guarda & IP3 (Viseu & Peso da Regua) ▽   Balsemão ▽

Jesus near Braga. Its seven hundred steps – which the most committed pilgrims ascend on their knees – are punctuated by a *via santa* of devotional chapels, *azulejos* and allegorical fountains and statues. After the approach, and its own facade, the church itself is simply a detail in the architectural ensemble: an assembly hall for the ever-present faithful.

The great **pilgrimage** here takes place on September 6–8, although the accompanying celebrations last several weeks, starting in the last week of August and continuing into mid-September. At 8am on September 6, the image of Our Lady leaves Remédios in procession to the Igreja das Chagas, where it stays in adoration for two days. The main procession takes place on September 8, with cavalcades of young children in white, and bulls pulling the carriage that transports Our Lady between the Igreja das Chagas and Igreja de Santa Cruz. In addition to the pilgrimage, there's a traditional "Battle of Flowers", torchlit parades, dances, car races, performances from some of the country's top rock bands and a fair on the Recinto da Feira, below the sanctuary. The turismo has details of other festivals which take place in May, June and November.

Practicalities

The **bus station** is behind the museum, right in the centre of town. In addition to the Régua connections (hourly until 8.15pm), there are daily services linking Viseu and other points in Beira Alta, as well as Lisbon and Porto. The very helpful **turismo** is on Avenida Guedes Visconde Teixeira (July–Sept daily 10am–12.30pm & 2–6pm; Oct–June Mon–Fri 10am–12.30pm & 2–6pm, Sat 10am–12.30pm; ☎254 612 005), just off the main square, Largo de Camões – staff will hand out a town map and lists of hotels and monuments. They also dole out photocopied sheets detailing walking trails in the region – see the box on p.301.

Accommodation

Accommodation in Lamego can be tricky to find and is on the expensive side. Booking ahead is strongly advised, though if you turn up on spec, the turismo may be able to sort you out a **private room**; possibilities include rooms at Rua de Santa Cruz 15 (①) or those above *Café Abrigo* on Rua dos Bancos (☎254 612 432; ②). Turismo staff can also provide you with details of *Solares de Portugal* and similar rural properties, though for these you'll need your own transport. The local **campsite** (☎254 612 090) is 4km north of town in Turisserra, by the *Motel Turisserra* (see below). There are no buses to the campsite; take the road marked to Avões until you see the campsite signs.

Albergaria do Cerrado, on the Régua road, 400m from the Sé (☎254 613 164, fax 254 615 464). Lamego's main business-class hotel, modern and well-equipped but a bit characterless. ③.

Pensão Império, Trav. dos Loureiros 6, off Av. Visconde Teixeira (☎254 612 742, fax 254 613 238). Above the restaurant of the same name, with pleasant if somewhat fusty rooms which can be noisy. ③.

Hotel Lamego, Quinta da Vista Alegre, about 2km out of town on the Régua road (☎254 656 171, fax 254 656 180). Modern, and well-run with two pools (one indoor), tennis courts and a health club including sauna and Turkish bath. Rooms have a/c, minibars, satellite TV and there are facilities for people with disabilities. ④.

Hotel do Parque, by the church of Nossa Senhora dos Remédios (☎254 609 140, fax 254 615 203). An unbeatable location and a lovely hotel, set in its own gardens. ③.

Residencial São Paulo, Av. 5 de Outubro 22 (☎254 613 114, fax 254 612 304). A modern building with friendly staff and its own parking spaces; breakfast is included in the rates. ②.

Pensão Silva, Rua Trás-da-Sé 26 (☎254 612 929). As this is next to the Sé, the bells might disturb. However, the rooms are decent, the French-speaking owner is friendly and it's the cheapest in town. ②.

Residencial Solar da Sé, Av. Visconde Teixeira (☎254 612 060, fax 254 615 928). Less characterful than *Silva* but smart, and a fraction further from the Sé clock – though still with fine views over the cathedral. ②.

Residencial Solar Espírito Santo, Rua Alexandre Herculano (☎254 655 391, fax 254 656 233). Comfortable, modern hotel with an amusing facade reminiscent of a giant meringue. Street-facing rooms have balconies. ③.

Motel Turisserra, 4km out on the Estrada Florestal (☎254 655 882, fax 254 656 152). A modest motel (and very good restaurant), occupying a lofty position on the Serra das Meadas, alongside the campsite. ③.

Villa Hostilina, 2km out off the Peso da Régua road in Almacave (☎254 612 394, fax 254 655 194, Web site: *www.minotel.com*). A well-signposted Privetur property set in vineyards and orchards, this is a grand nineteenth-century house furnished in Victorian-style clutter, contrasting oddly with its ultra-modern health club, tennis courts and pool. Food is available by arrangement. ④.

Eating, drinking and nightlife

At first glance, Lamego's **restaurants** may seem expensive, especially in the centre of town where guaranteed tourist trade has loosened standards, so you might consider assembling a **picnic**: from the turismo, head up the steep Rua da Olaria, where a selection of grocers sell excellent bread and cheese, as well as Lamego's famed *presunto* (ham) and smoked *salpicão* sausages. If you don't mind a more earthy ambience, there are a number of very cheap and characterful *adegas casas de pasto* scattered around.

Lamego's **nightlife** is somewhat limited; there's a saloon-door bar at the top of Rua de Almacave on the way to the castle, or try the *taberna* on Rua do Castelinho 25 – though both close at 9pm. There are more bars scattered along either side of Avenida Dr. Alfredo de Sousa, which forms the hub for summertime evening drinkers. For younger company, try *Discoteca ETDS* on Avenida Dr. Alfredo de Sousa, at the foot of the steps to the shrine.

Casa de Filipe and **Adega Matos**, Rua Virgílio Correia, immediately behind the Sé. Very basic *casas de pasto*, but highly recommended.

Casa de Pasto Vitor Pinto, Rua da Olaria 61. Very cheap eats, with fine *presunto* figuring strongly.

Churrasqueira Londrina, Rua de Fafel. Behind the fire station, an unassuming modern place with very reasonable prices and outstanding grills.

O Combinado, Rua da Olaria 84 (closed Sun). A good local *tasca* where you can eat well and plenty for under 1000$00. Try *lombos de porco* (grilled pork chops) or the trout.

Jardim Popular, Rua da Perreira. Around the corner from *Pensão Silva*, this is a rather strange construction in a walled garden but the grills and salads are good. Around 2500$00.

Pensão Império, Trav. dos Loureiros 6. Expensive and pretentious, and watch out for the "hidden" extras – bread and butter can add up to 1200$00. Coffee tables outside, with some live music in summer.

Pizzaria O Groto, Rua da Olaria. The menu of pizza, pasta and hamburgers is aimed mainly at tourists – you'll pay 1500–2000$00 a meal.

Restaurante Novo, Largo da Sé 9. Cheap and cheerful with a few outdoor tables overlooking the Sé.

Around Lamego: Balsemão and the Caves da Raposeira

At the hamlet of **BALSEMÃO**, a three-kilometre hike from the back of the Lamego cathedral, is a seventh-century chapel founded by the Suevi. The route requires three left turns in all: the first is at the Capela do Desterro down into the old quarters of town and across a bridge; the second, a fork on to the hillside road. The third comes a little later, taking you down into the valley and above a rushing river. After three large curves, a village school, a collection of outhouses and the **Capela de São Pedro** chapel appear (Tues 2–5.30pm, Wed–Sun 9.30am–12.30pm & 2–5.30pm, closed on the third weekend of the month). You might want to check the erratic opening hours with the turismo in Lamego. Some believe São Pedro to be on the site of the oldest Christian temple in the Iberian peninsula, erected by the Visigoths, though the present foundations were laid in the ninth century during the *Reconquista*. The undistinguished granite facade and dark interior give it the air of a family vault, an impression strengthened by the imposing fourteenth-century **sarcophagus** of the Bishop of Porto, Dom Afonso Pires, who was born in Balsemão. The florid capitals encircling the tomb make the few remaining Suevi curls on the archway into the choir seem subdued by comparison. Look out for the restored, profoundly pregnant statue of Nossa Senhora do Ó (that's Ó as in the shape of her belly, though others ascribe it to the exclamation uttered when seeing it: *Ó! Nossa Senhora, Mãe de Deus. . .*).

The other main attraction of Lamego is a visit to the **Caves da Raposeira** (☎254 655 003; Mon–Fri 10am–12.30pm & 2–4.30pm), 1km out of town on the Castro Daire road. These are open for free guided tours around the cellars and tasting of Portugal's "champagne".

South from Lamego

Continuing **south from Lamego**, in the direction of Guarda and Viseu, the country of the **Leomil** and **Montemuro** ranges is high, wild and sparsely inhabited. This territory was among the earliest to fall to Afonso Henriques, the first king of Portugal, in his march south against the Moors. It is said that he laid the first stone of the monastery of **São João de Tarouca** after his victories at Trancoso and Sernancelhe in Beira Alta. The region's three other rewarding sights – the monastery of **Salzedas**, the fortified bridge at **Ucanha** and the church at **Tarouca** – were also founded at this time.

THE INSTITUTE OF CULTURAL AFFAIRS

The **Montemuro** district, between Lamego and Castro Daire, suffers enormously from unemployment and depopulation, but sports a long tradition of local handicraft industries, including weaving, knitting, basketry, honey and cheese production, pottery and cape-making. There's still a thriving cultural life, too – from theatre and folk dance to religious festivals – which occupies a central place in Montemuro life.

The **Instituto dos Assuntos Culturais** (IAC) is an international development organization with a staff of foreign and Portuguese workers supporting the initiatives of local people. Some twenty villages, with a total population of about 11,000, are currently involved with the IAC's work. It's based at the village of **Mezio**, about 20km southwest of Lamego on the N2 Castro Daire road.

If you're interested in having a look at what the Institute does – and it seems there's not much it doesn't take an interest in – you might like to stop en route between Lamego and the Mountain Beiras and stay for a day or two: visitors are actively encouraged. Facilities are basic, but there are showers and toilets and plenty of organic food. Costs vary from 1500$00 per person for bed and breakfast or for camping with meals, to around 3000$00, which is pretty much all-inclusive. If you want to make enquiries in advance, contact the IAC at Rua Central 47, Mezio, 3600 Castro Daire (☎ & fax 254 689 246).

Whether or not you choose to stay, you may find the IAC pamphlet *Hiking Trails in the Montemuro* useful (the turismo in Lamego has photocopies). It describes ten half-day **walks** in the region (though they are pretty strenuous); the IAC can also provide guides and transport for arranged walking circuits for around 3000–4000$00 per person per tour.

São João de Tarouca

The small village of **SÃO JOÃO DE TAROUCA**, off the southeast route from Lamego to Guarda, was the site of the first Cistercian monastery to be founded in Portugal (1169). Only the **Romanesque church** remains fully intact, its simple and austere interior suffused with a subtle light. Inside, four large panels of early eighteenth-century *azulejos* depict the founding of the monastery, and the original painted Baroque choir pews are still in place. However, the highlight is Grão Vasco's celebrated painted altarpiece of Saint Peter, similar to the one in Viseu's Sé. There are usually students working on the site during the summer who might be persuaded to show you around. There's a pleasant spot for rest and recuperation – and a nice **café** – down by the river, not two minutes' walk from the church. Regular EAVT **buses** (Mon–Fri 9 daily, 3–4 at weekends) make the 25-minute journey here from Lamego's bus station.

Ucanha

In **UCANHA** – north of Tarouca, on the opposite side of the N226 – life revolves around the water. Down below the main road, two ingenious ducts have been made to tap the river upstream in order to provide adequate washing facilities in the centre of the village. The wash houses are practically in ruins, but the system of one tank for suds and another for rinses, common to the Mediterranean, has been preserved. Running below the pools, the river looks so tempting that on a sunny day, regardless of what trash might be floating by, village children are constantly nipping in and out.

The real beauty of the scene stems from the majestic **tollgate** and single-arched **bridge**. They date from shortly after 1163, when the diocese of Salzedas was awarded to Teresa Afonso, erstwhile nursemaid to Afonso Henriques's five sons and heirs and widow of Egas Moniz, the first king's tutor and closest adviser. Besides marking and protecting the border of her domain, these structures were also, of course, an ostentatious mark of manorial power. Today, clothes are hung out to dry under the arches.

THE ENTRUDO DE LAZARIM – SHROVE TUESDAY

A right turn off the Lamego–Tarouca road on the outskirts of Tarouca leads to the small and normally unremarkable village of **Lazarim**. Sleepy for 364 days of the year, it plays host to one of the oddest rituals to survive in Portugal, the **Entrudo dos Compadres**, or carnival, which has taken place every Shrove Tuesday since the Middle Ages. Revellers celebrate the end of winter and the beginning of spring (Lent in the Christian calendar) by taking to the streets wearing beautifully carved wooden masks, symbolic of the event's licentiousness. However, despite the lewd masquerades, Entrudo dos Compadres is also a time of castigation for the year passed: from a balcony on the Largo do Padrão, two colourful dolls loaded with fireworks are presented to the crowd – the *compadre*, carried by two young women, and *comadre*, toted by two young men. The couples proceed to recite insulting rhymes centring on sexual behaviour, which, in the manner of Punch and Judy, are often maliciously aimed at certain unnamed people in the crowd below. After the recital, the fireworks are lit and the dolls disintegrate in an explosive fury of smoke and flame, marking the end of the festival and the old year and the beginning of the new. A *feijoada* (bean and meat stew) is then served to the waiting crowd. If you like the masks, ask for the carpenter José António Costa: they cost upwards of 15,000$00.

Salzedas

SALZEDAS lies 4km further along the Ucanha road, past Murganheira, another "champagne" co-operative and a rival to Raposeira. The **Monastery** here was once the greatest of its kind, grander even than São João de Tarouca. In 1168, when the order was Augustinian, the complex was rebuilt with money donated by Teresa Afonso; it became Cistercian during a later period of administration from Alcobaça.

Unfortunately, eighteenth-century renovation has largely altered its original appearance into a clumsy mixture of Baroque and pseudo-Classical styles. The monastery's main facade presides over the small square of the diminutive village. As at Tarouca, students work here in the summer and, though they may seem surprised to see casual visitors, they will follow you around and open the relevant doors. The smell of decay is strong inside and the two dark and dusty **paintings** of *Saint Peregrine* and *Saint Sebastian* by Grão Vasco, either side of the choir, are easily overlooked. More conspicuous are the fifteenth-century tombs of the Coutinho family – dominant nobles in these parts in the early years of the Portuguese nation – near the entrance. Out through a side door, a succession of courtyards, once fronting formal gardens, bear the scars of a period of extensive pillage and decay, which began in 1834 with the dissolution of the monasteries.

---

travel details

Trains

Amarante to: Livração (7–9 daily; 25min); Porto (8–9 daily; 1hr 40min–2hr).

Espinho to: Coimbra (15–19 daily; 1hr 5min–1hr 40min); Lisbon (9 daily; 3hr 35min–4hr); Porto (15–19 daily; 20–40min).

Penafiel to: Livração (14–17 daily; 25min); Peso da Régua (12–13 daily; 1hr 20min); Pocinho (4 daily; 3hr 15min); Porto (15–18 daily; 45min–1hr 10min); Tua (5 daily; 2hr 10min).

Peso da Régua to: Pocinho (4 daily; 1hr 40min); Porto (14–15 daily; 2hr 10min–2hr 40min); Tua (6–7 daily; 45min); Vila Real (5 daily; 1hr).

Pocinho to: Penafiel (3–4 daily; 3hr 10min); Peso da Régua (4 daily; 1hr 40min); Porto (4 daily; 4hr 30min); Tua (6–7 daily; 45min).

Porto to: Coimbra (15–19 daily; 2hr); Espinho (15–19 daily; 20–40min); Faro (1 nightly Tues, Thurs & Sun, summer only; 9hrs); Lisbon (12 daily; 3hr–4hr 20min); Livração (15–18 daily; 1hr

15min–1hr 40min); Penafiel (15–18 daily; 45min–1hr 10min); Peso da Régua (14–15 daily; 2hr 10min–2hr 40min); Pocinho (4 daily; 4hr 30min–4hr 50min); Póvoa de Varzim (roughly every 30min; 1hr); Santo Tirso (11–17 daily; 50min); Tua (6–7 daily; 3hr 15min–3hr 35min); Viana do Castelo (9–10 daily; 1hr 45min–2hr 25min); Vila do Conde (roughly every 30min; 50min).

Tua to: Mirandela (5 daily; 1hr 50min).

Buses

NB: Destinations from Porto are followed by an abbreviation of the company who operates the service. Where more than one company is given, the order reflects frequency of service. For departure points of the various companies see "Listings" on p.276. Abbreviations are as follows: Asa Douro (AD); Auto Viação de Espinho (AVE); Auto Viação do Minho (AVMi); Auto Viação Mondinese (AVM); Auto Viação do Tâmega (AVT); Caima (C); EVA; Joalto (J); João Ferreira das Neves (JFN); Linhares (L); Marquês (M); Rede Expressos (RE); Renex (Rx); Resende (Rs); Rodonorte (R); Santos de Freixo (SF); Turilis (T); Valpi (V).

Amarante to: Braga (2–3 daily; 2hr 10min); Cabaceiros de Basto (3–4 daily; 1hr 35min); Celorico de Basto (Mon–Sat 5 daily; 40min); Fermil (3–4 daily; 1hr); Guimarães (Mon–Fri 7 daily; 1hr 15min); Porto (2–3 daily; 1hr 10min); Vila Real (10–12 daily; 2hr 40min).

Lamego to: Braga (1 daily; 2hr 50min); Celorico da Beira (Mon–Fri 3 daily; 3hr); Lisbon (2–4 daily; 6hr); Penafiel (3–5 daily; 1hr 40min); Peso da Régua (16 daily; 25min); Porto (4–6 daily; 4–4hr 30min); Sernancelhe (Mon–Fri 6 daily, Sat & Sun 2 daily; 2hr); Tarouca (Mon–Fri 9 daily, Sat & Sun 3–4 daily; 30min); Trancoso (1–2 daily; 2hr); Viseu (5–7 daily; 1hr 20min–2hr).

Penafiel to: Amarante (3–6 daily; 30min); Baúlhe (Mon–Fri 8 daily, Sat 4 daily; 1hr 45min); Entre-os-Rios (Mon–Fri 7 daily; 40min–1hr 25min); Lamego (3–5 daily; 1hr 40min); Porto (18 daily; 30min–1hr 20min); Torrão (Mon–Fri 7 daily; 45min–1hr 30min).

Peso da Régua to: Coimbra (1–2 daily; 3hr 40min); Guarda (1 daily; 2hr 30min); Lamego (16 daily; 25min); Vila Real (hourly; 40min); Viseu (Mon–Fri 6 daily, Sat & Sun 1–2; 1hr 30min).

Pocinho to: Bragança (2 daily; 1hr 40min); Celerico da Beira (2 daily; 1hr 45min); Coimbra (2 daily; 4hr 55min); Lisbon (2 daily; 7hr 25min); Torre de Moncorvo (3 daily; 30min); Trancoso (Mon–Fri 2 daily; 2hr 30min); Viseu (2 daily; 2hr 45min).

Porto to: Abrantes, R (1 daily; 4hr 35min); Amarante, AD, AVT, R (Mon–Fri 10 daily, Sat & Sun 5 daily; 1hr 10min–1hr 25min); Aveiro, C (4 daily; 2hr 30min); Barcelos, L (Mon–Sat 7 daily; 1hr 45min); Braga, Rx, Rs, RE, C (17 daily; 1hr 10min); Bragança, R (3 daily; 1hr 50min–3hr 50min); Caminha, AVMi (Mon–Fri 5 daily, Sat & Sun 1 daily; 2hr); Chaves, AVT, R (6–12 daily; 3hr 10min–5hr); Coimbra, RE, R, AVT (8–10 daily; 1hr 30min); Fátima, R (6 daily; 3hr 30min); Guarda, M, J, R (7 daily; 2hr 10min–3hr 20min); Guimarães, JFN (12 daily; 2hr); Lamego, AD (3–5 daily; 4hr–4hr 30min); Leiria, R (6 daily; 1hr 40min–2hr 30min); Lisbon, Rx, RE, EVA (hourly; 3hr–3hr 30min); Melgaço, AVMi (2 daily; 3hr); Mirandela, R, SF (2–4 daily; 2hr 45min); Monção AVMi, T, R (5 daily; 2hr 45min–3hr); Mondim de Basto, AVM (7 daily; 3hr 30min); Penafiel, V, AVT (24 daily; 55min–1hr); Póvoa de Varzim, L, AVMi (16 daily; 40–55min); Tomar, R (1 daily; 4hr); Valença do Minho, AVMi, T, R (5 daily; 2hr 30min–2hr 45min); Viana do Castelo, AVMi, L (12–14 daily; 2hr); Vila do Conde, AVMi, L (16 daily; 35–55min); Vila Real, AVT, R (9 daily; 2hr); Viseu, M, R, & J (8 daily; 2hr).

Póvoa de Varzim to: Barcelos (4–5 daily; 45min); Braga (9 daily; 1hr 15min); Esposende (9–12 daily; 40min); Guimarães (9–11 daily; 1hr 45min); Santo Tirso (Mon–Sat 12 daily, Sun 6 daily; 1hr); Viana do Castelo (Mon–Fri 24 daily, Sat 17 daily, Sun 11 daily; 1hr 5min); Vila do Conde (every 15min; 15min).

Domestic flights

Porto to: Funchal, Madeira (6 weekly; 2hr); Ponta Delgada, Açores (1 daily; 1hr 20min direct, 3hr indirect); Faro (2 daily; 2hr 15min–3hr); Lisbon (19 daily; 45min); Porto Santo, Madeira (2 weekly; 4hr 30min); Terceira, Açores (1 daily; 3hr 15min–4hr).

CHAPTER SIX

THE MINHO

With good reason, many Portuguese consider the **Minho** – the province north of Porto – to be the most beautiful part of their country. Its river valleys, wooded hills, trailing vines and barely developed coastline are given prominence in every travel brochure, while much is made of the Minho's traditional aspect, especially in the mountainous east, where you can still see wooden-wheeled ox-carts creak down cobbled lanes, while age-old conventions are maintained at dozens of huge country markets, *festas* and *romarias*. In summer especially, you're likely to happen upon these carnivals, though it's worth trying to plan your trip around the larger events if you're keen to experience Minho life at its most exuberant – the main markets and principal festivals are detailed where appropriate throughout the chapter. As you travel around the region, you'll see signs of new building in even the smallest and most isolated villages, accounted for by the new-found prosperity of returned emigrants: Minho, more than any other area of Portugal, suffered severe depopulation from the late 1950s onwards as thousands migrated to France, Switzerland, Germany and even as far afield as the United States in search of more lucrative work.

The largest towns are concentrated in the southern Minho and any trip should allow time to examine the competing historic claims of **Guimarães**, first capital of Portugal, and neighbouring **Braga**, the country's ecclesiastical centre. Between them lie the extensive Celtic ruins of the **Citânia de Briteiros**, one of the most impressive archeological sites in Portugal, while from Braga it's also easy to visit **Barcelos**, site of the best-known (and biggest) of the region's weekly markets. It takes place on Thursdays, though for the full experience reserve a room in advance and arrive on Wednesday evening.

At Barcelos, you're only 20km from the **Costa Verde**, the Minho coast, which runs north all the way to the Spanish border. This has some wonderful beaches along the way, though the sea here is cold – and the weather, too, can be uncertain, with cool temperatures even in midsummer. The principal resort is **Viana do Castelo**, an enjoyable and lively town with an elegant historic core, though if you're seeking isolation, there are strands to the north and south that scarcely see visitors. The coast ends at **Caminha**, beyond which the **Rio Minho** runs inland, forming the border with Spanish Galicia. This is a delightful region, featuring a string of compact fortified towns flanking the river on the Portuguese side, their fortresses, in various stages of disrepair, staring across at Spain.

ACCOMMODATION PRICE CODES

All the accommodation prices in this book have been coded using the symbols below. The symbols represent the lowest prices you can expect to pay for a **double room in high season**; for a full explanation, see p.32.

① Under 4000$00   ④ 11,000$00–15,000$00   ⑦ 25,000$00–30,000$00
② 4000$00–7000$00   ⑤ 15,000$00–20,000$00   ⑧ 30,000$00–40,000$00
③ 7000$00–11000$00   ⑥ 20,000$00–25,000$00   ⑨ Over 40,000$00

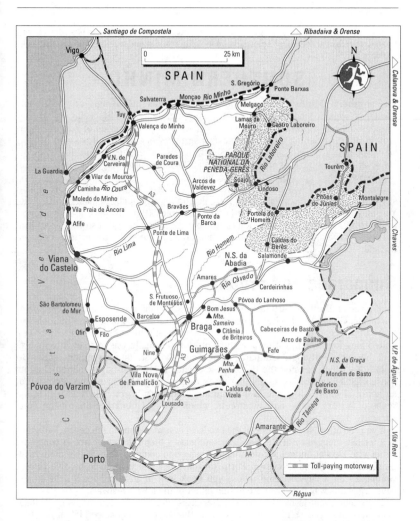

Inland from Viana, the Minho's other major river, the beautiful **Rio Lima**, runs east through a succession of gorgeous small towns where there's little to do but soak up the somnolent scenery. On the whole, much of the Minho is outrageously picturesque and full of quiet charm and interest. In fact it was in the Lima valley, and particularly around the town of **Ponte de Lima**, that Turihab first exploited the beauty of the countryside to the benefit of tourists by offering accommodation in local manor houses, old farms and country estates (see p.346). Further east, the gentle Minho scenery eventually gives way to the mountains, waterfalls, river gorges, reservoirs and forests of the protected **Parque Nacional da Peneda-Gerês**, Portugal's only national (as opposed to natural) park. This is superb camping and hiking territory, stretching from the main town and spa of **Caldas do Gerês** north as far as the Rio Minho and the Spanish border and east into Trás-os-Montes. It's possible to dip into the park from a couple of easily accessible towns, but you really need to devote several days if you're going to see the more isolated regions as bus services are limited; even by car the going's slow and on foot you could spend weeks exploring the trails.

SOUTHERN MINHO

The **southern Minho**'s two chief towns, **Guimarães** and **Braga**, are both small enough to walk around in a busy day's sightseeing, though a night's stay has greater rewards. This is especially true if you want to explore the series of religious sites around Braga, including the extraordinary pilgrimage site of **Bom Jesus do Monte**; while you'll need to set aside another half-day at least to see the **Citânia de Briteiros**. However, perhaps the best overnight stop is at **Barcelos**, provided you can find a room on a Wednesday night before the weekly market.

Guimarães and Braga are on separate branch lines of the main **train route**, which starts in Porto and passes through Barcelos on its way north to Viana do Castelo. You may need to change at Lousada for Guimarães (though there are also direct trains from Porto) and at Nine for Braga; but it's far quicker to use the direct **bus** between Braga and Guimarães rather than fiddle about with connections between the train lines.

Guimarães and around

Birthplace of Afonso Henriques in 1110, and first capital of the fledgling kingdom of Portucale, **GUIMARÃES** has a special place in the story of Portuguese nationhood. From here began the reconquest from the Moors and the subsequent creation of a united kingdom which, within a century of Afonso's death, was to stretch to its present borders. Although Guimarães subsequently lost its pre-eminent status to Coimbra – which became the Portuguese capital in 1143 – it never relinquished its sense of self-importance, something that's evident from the careful preservation of an array of impressive medieval monuments. There's a grandeur and a tangible sense of history in the narrow streets, which makes Guimarães one of the most attractive places in the country.

If you can afford to stay at one of the two local *pousadas* – one in the centre, the other in a former monastery at **Penha**, 5km southeast – then the experience is complete. Otherwise, decent budget accommodation is hard to come by, though this matters little since Braga (24km), or even Porto (55km), are close enough to be able to visit Guimarães on a day-trip. And unless you book well in advance, you'll have to see Guimarães this way if you're here during either of the town's festivals.

The major event is the **Festas Gualterianas** (for São Gualter, or Saint Walter), which has taken place on the first weekend in August every year since 1452. If you miss this you can catch most of the same stallholders, and something of the atmosphere, the weekend after in Caldas de Vizela, a spa town 10km south of Guimarães. Next in importance is the long-established *romaria* to **São Torcato**, 6km northeast of town, on the first weekend in July, which, in the curious language of the turismo leaflet, "includes a procession with archaic choirs of virgins". A well-timed visit in winter will enable you to see one or more of the **Nicolinas** (Nov 29–Dec 7), **Nossa Senhora da Conceição** (Dec 8) and **Santa Luzia** (Dec 13).

Arrival and information

Guimarães' **train station** is ten minutes' walk south of the centre; to get into town, bear left from the station and take the first right down Avenida Dom Afonso Henriques,

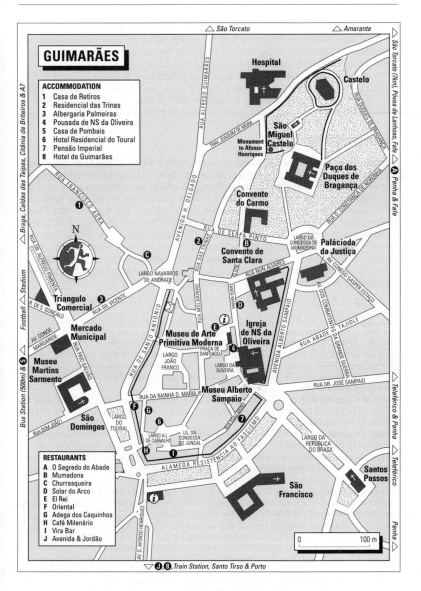

which takes you on to Alameda Resistência ao Fascismo – the main **turismo** is on your right (Mon–Fri 9.30am–12.30pm & 2–6.30pm; ☎253 412 450, *www.cm-guimaraes.pt*). There's a second turismo above an exhibition room at Praça de Santiago 37 (Mon–Fri 9.30am–6.30pm, Sat 10am–6pm, Sun 10am–1pm; ☎253 518 790). Both are helpful, and supply maps and informative colour booklets on museums and sights, as well as information on hotels and *turismo rural* properties.

The **bus station** is fifteen minutes' walk southeast of the town centre at the bottom of Avenida Conde Margaride – it's unmarked, but identifiable by the Continente supermarket or McDonald's sign above the entrance. To get from the bus station into the town centre, turn right and walk up Conde Margaride as far as the market (Mercado Municipal); from here you can continue along Rua Gil Vicente, or turn right towards Largo do Toural and the main turismo. There are express bus services from Porto and Lisbon, and regular weekday connections with Braga, Amarante, Cabeceiras and Mondim de Basto, and Póvoa do Lanhoso. **Taxis** can be hailed in the street, or called on ☎253 522 522.

Accommodation

Inexpensive **accommodation** is scarce in town, even more so during Guimarães' main festivals – nearby Braga (p.314) has a much better choice of budget accommodation. It's best to book ahead – especially if you're planning a splurge in the two *pousadas*, or in one of a number of superb manor houses in the vicinity: the turismo has details of these (ask for *turismo rural*). There are two **campsites** in the locality – the nearest is the *Parque de Campismo da Penha* (☎253 515 912, fax 253 516 569), a pleasant site with a small swimming pool and some bungalows for rent (②), on the slopes of Penha and accessible by the cable car. Though it's officially open between June and September, it's worth ringing ahead at other times. Seven kilometres northwest of Guimarães, *Caldas das Taipas* (☎253 576 274; June–Sept), by the banks of the Rio Ave off the N101, is pricier but arguably more attractive, with a swimming pool and a thermal spa nearby.

IN TOWN

Casa dos Pombais, Av. de Londres (☎253 412 917). Opposite the bus station, this eighteenth-century Solares de Portugal manor house is an oasis in a built-up part of town, a lovely old building with attractive gardens. There are only two guest rooms, so book well ahead. ④.

Casa de Retiros, Rua Francisco Agra 163 (☎253 511 515, fax 253 511 517). One of the cheaper places in town, this is a hostel run for pilgrims, which means it's sometimes booked up by groups. There's an 11.30pm curfew, fairly stark surroundings and spartan breakfasts. Rates are per person, and include breakfast. ②.

Hotel de Guimarães, Rua Dr. Eduardo Almeida, 100m from the train station (☎253 515 888, fax 253 516 234). The top modern choice with four-star comforts, including health club, jacuzzi, pool, sauna and restaurant. ⑤.

Pensão Imperial, Alameda Resistência ao Fascismo 111 (☎253 415 163). This rundown *pensão* is overpriced by any but Guimarães' standards, but offers some of the cheapest beds in town. ②.

Albergaria das Palmeiras, Centro Comercial das Palmeiras, Rua Gil Vicente (☎253 410 324, fax 253 417 261). Part of a commercial mall, which can make it difficult to find (and enter after shopping hours), but it's modern, with a restaurant and parking facilities. ③.

Pousada de Santa Maria da Oliveira, Rua de Santa Maria (☎253 514 157, fax 253 514 204). Converted from a row of sixteenth-century houses and right in the medieval centre, this sixteen-room *pousada* is beautifully furnished and worth every escudo. ⑦.

Hotel Residencial do Toural, Largo do Toural, entrance in Largo A.L. de Carvalho at the back (☎253 517 184, fax 253 517 149). Once an elegant town house, this has been completely renovated into an ultra-modern four-star establishment – not cheap, but very comfortable. ⑤.

Residencial das Trinas, Rua das Trinas 29 (☎253 517 358, fax 253 517 362). Situated in the old town, this has eleven spotless rooms, all with private bathrooms, satellite TV and telephone. Rooms at the back can be noisy, but the rates are good and include breakfast. ③.

OUTSIDE TOWN

Casa de Sezim, Nespereira, 6km south of Guimarães off the Santo Tirso road – turn right at Covas (☎253 523 000, fax 253 523 196). If money's not too tight, this aristocratic country estate – owned by the same *vinho verde*-producing family for over six centuries – is a delight. The buildings, plastered powder pink, are in a mixture of styles, and have six rooms in the main 18th-century *solar* (manor), each equipped with Murano chandeliers and varied objets d'art. There's a swimming pool, and walking and horse riding trips are offered. ⑤.

Paço de São Cipriano, Taboadelo, 6km south of Guimarães off the Santo Tirso road – turn left at Covas (☎253 565 337). Architecturally stunning 18th-century country palace, complete with chapel and medieval tower, which contains the five guest rooms. Gardens and a swimming pool complete the unforgettable ambience. ④.

Pensão da Penha, at the top of the *teleférico* (☎253 414 245, fax 253 512 952). A perfectly good option if you want to stay at the top of Penha. ③.

Pousada de Santa Marinha da Costa, at the foot of Monte Penha, 2km along Rua Dr. José Sampaio (☎253 514 453, fax 253 514 459). Occupying a convent, parts of which date from the ninth century, this is reckoned to be one of the top *pousadas* in the country; ask for one of the original rooms, not one of the new additions. ⑦.

The Town

The old centre of **Guimarães** is an elongated kernel of small, enclosed squares and cobbled streets, bounded at its southern end by the town gardens and overlooked from the north by the imposing castle, an enduring symbol of the emergent Portuguese nation. In between lie a series of medieval churches, convents and buildings that lend an air of dignity to the streets – two of the convents provide an impressive backdrop to a couple of the country's more illuminating museums. The presence of the University of the Minho gives the local cafés and bars a lively, student-orientated feel, particularly in the old town.

Around the Castelo

The imposing **Castelo** (June–Sept 9.30am–12.30pm & 2–7pm, Oct–May 9.30am–12.30 & 2–5pm; free) was built in the tenth-century by the countess of Mumadona to protect the people of Guimarães from attack by Moors and Normans. It was extended to approximately its modern size by **Afonso Henriques**, who established the first Portuguese court here in the twelfth-century. Afonso is reputed to have been born in the great square keep which is surrounded now, as then, by seven castellated towers. You can wander around the ramparts and check out the views of town, or climb the 77 steps to the top of the central **keep** (100$00), which opens out onto a narrow tower, but take care as the stonework is uneven and narrow in places. The castle's marvellous solidity is enhanced by its juxtaposition with the diminutive Romanesque chapel of **São Miguel do Castelo** (same hours; free), on the grassy slope below, in whose font Afonso was probably baptized.

Just across from the chapel, the **Paço dos Duques de Bragança** (July–Aug 9.30am–12.30 & 2–7pm, Sept–June 9.30am–12.30pm & 2–5pm; 400$00, free Sunday mornings), built in the fifteenth-century by Dom Afonso, was the medieval palace of the all-powerful Bragançan duchy. Under the Salazar dictatorship, its ruins were "restored" as an official residence for the president (the second floor is still reserved for this function), but today, with memories of the dictatorship fading, it looks rather ludicrous – like a mock-Gothic Victorian folly. Inside is an extensive collection of portraits (including a whole room of colourful paintings and sculptures by modern artist José de Guimarães), furniture and porcelain, around which lengthy guided tours perambulate. Free concerts are occasionally held here on summer weekends as part of the annual "Encontros da Primavera" season of concerts; enquire at the turismos for details.

Outside the castle, a number of shops sell **childrens' toys**, hammered out from old tin and no doubt lethal, but beautiful objects nonetheless; there's a café here, too.

Along Rua de Santa Maria

From the castle, **Rua de Santa Maria** leads down into the heart of the old town, a beautiful thoroughfare featuring iron grilles and granite arches. Many of the town's historic buildings have been superbly restored, and as you descend to the centre you'll pass one of the loveliest – the sixteenth-century convent of Santa Clara, with its Baroque facade, which today does service as the **Câmara Municipal**. Many of its furnishings were removed after the dissolution of the monasteries, and are now housed in the Museu Alberto Sampaio (see below).

On a much more intimate scale are the buildings ranged around the delightful central squares at the end of the street, **Praça de Santiago** and **Largo da Oliveira**. The latter is dominated by the **Igreja de Nossa Senhora da Oliveira** (Tues–Sun 7.15am–noon & 3.30–7.30pm; free), a convent-church built (like the great monastery at Batalha) in honour of a vow made by João I before his decisive victory over Castile. Its unusual dedication is to "Our Lady of the Olive Tree" and before it stands a curious Gothic **canopy-shrine**, erected in 1340 to commemorate the Battle of Salado, one of many encounters with the Castilians. It also marks the legendary spot where Wamba, unwillingly elected king of the Visigoths, drove a pole into the ground swearing that he would not reign until it blossomed. Naturally it sprouted immediately. João I, feeling this to be a useful indication of divine favour, set out to meet the Castilian forces from this very point.

Next door is the convent's simple Romanesque cloister with varied, naively carved capitals. This, and the rooms off it which formerly comprised the Colegiada (college), now house the **Museu Alberto Sampaio** (☎253 412 465; Tues–Sun 10am–12.30pm & 2–5.30pm; 300$00, free Sunday mornings), essentially the treasury of the collegiate church and convent but, for once, outstandingly exhibited and containing pieces of real beauty. The highlight is a brilliantly composed silver-gilt *Triptych of the Nativity*, said to have been found in the King of Castile's tent after the Portuguese victory at Aljubarrota in 1385. Close by this is displayed the tunic worn by João I in the battle.

Opposite the museum and housed in a heavy arched structure that was formerly the council chambers, the **Museu de Arte Primitiva Moderna** (☎253 414 186; Mon–Fri 9am–12.30pm & 2–5.30pm; free) contains over 300 works by self-taught artists which provide a fascinating excursion through daily, secular and ritual life and range from pure kitsch to the odd masterpiece.

The Museu Martins Sarmento and the Igreja de São Francisco

Across to the west, over the main Largo do Toural, the **Museu Arqueológico Martins Sarmento** (☎253 415 969; Tues–Sun 9.30am–noon & 2–5pm; 300$00) is another superb collection, also housed in a former convent. Here, finds from the neighbouring Celtic *citânia* of Briteiros (see p.312) are displayed in the fourteenth-century Gothic cloister of the Igreja de São Domingos. They include a remarkable series of bronze votive offerings (among them, a "coach", pulled at each end by men and oxen), and ornately patterned stone lintels and door jambs from the huts; while most spectacular of all are the **Pedras Formosas** ("beautiful stones"). Once taken to be sacrificial altars or the portals to funerary monuments, it's now agreed that these were most likely to have been taken from the interior of bath houses. The **Colossus of Pedralva**, a vast granite hulk of a figure with arm raised aloft and an oversized phallus, was formerly the museum's prize exhibit – it has now been relegated to the nearby pedestrian precinct outside the bus station. More enigmatic and considerably more ancient than the Pedras Formosas, it shares the bold, powerfully hewn appearance of the stone pigs found in Trás-os-Montes (see p.310), and, like them, may date from pre-Celtic fertility cults of around 1500 to 1000 BC.

Among the numerous other churches scattered about the centre of Guimarães, the finest is the **Igreja de São Francisco** (Tues–Sat 9.30am–noon & 3–5pm, Sunday 9.30am–1pm, Mass at 12.30pm; free), on the south side of the town gardens. It features a series of huge eighteenth-century *azulejos* of Saint Francis preaching to the fish, and an elegant Renaissance cloister and fountain. Once again, the church was attached to a monastery of considerable size until the 1834 dissolution.

Penha and Santa Marinha da Costa

Two kilometres southeast of Guimarães on the slopes of **Penha** (617m) stands the region's best-preserved medieval building, the former monastery – and now *pousada* – of **Santa Marinha da Costa**. It can be reached by taking the São Roque bus (Mon–Sat 6am–10pm, Sun 6am–8pm; every 30min) from the main turismo; get off at "Costa" and follow the signs.

The monastery was founded in 1154 by order of Dona Mafalda, the wife of Afonso Henriques, in honour of a vow to Santa Marinha, patron saint of pregnant women. Originally Augustinian, the foundation passed into the hands of the Order of Saint Jerome in the sixteenth century. In the **chapel** (official hours July–Sept 9am–1pm & 2–7pm but often inexplicably closed), Jerome's twin emblems of the skull and the lion are recurring motifs. They are surrounded by an oddly harmonious mixture of styles – tenth-century doorways on the south wall, sixteenth-century panels in the sacristy (including one depicting Jerome beating his breast with a stone against the temptation of women), and an eighteenth-century organ and stone roof in the choir. Strictly speaking, the rest of the monastic buildings are off limits except to guests of the *pousada* (see p.308 for details), but you can peek into the magnificent **cloister**, with its Mozarabic doorway, while the beautiful **gardens** are open to the public, too. For more of a look around it would be diplomatic to buy a meal, or at least a drink at the bar.

The peak of Penha is crowned by a statue of Nossa Senhora – by far the most fun way to reach it is to take the ingenious **Teleférico da Penha** cable car, whose hi-tech bubbles leave from the end of Rua de Doutor José Sampaio (Mon–Fri 11am–7pm, Sat & Sun 10am–8pm; 300$00 single, 500$00 return).

Eating and drinking

Guimarães has no shortage of places to **eat and drink**, mostly quite affordable. Local specialities to look out for – or avoid – include *chispalhada de feijão* (beans, sausage and pig's trotters), *papas de sarabulho* (a blood and bread stew), and *rojões de porco* (roast pork, sausages and potatoes). Desserts include *melindres* (honey cakes), *aletria* (like vermicelli) and *toucinho do céu* ("heavenly bacon", actually a super-sweet concoction of sugar, almonds, eggs and lemon).

Adega dos Caquinhos, between Largo A.L. Carvalho and Rua Rainha D. Maria III. A friendly, traditional *adega* whose name reflects its decor – walls covered in broken crockery (*caquinhos*). The food is good and reasonably priced, at around 1600$00 for a full meal and drinks.

Avenida, Av. Dom Afonso Henriques. Unassuming place near the main turismo. Eat at tables (you may have to share) or at the bar. No frills, and cheap: under 1500$00 for your meal and drinks.

Churrasqueira, Rua Francisco Agra 30. Excellent fresh grilled meat served in basic (and smoky) surroundings. Very cheap at under 1100$00 for a meal and drinks.

Jordão, Av. Dom Afonso Henriques 55, near the train station. Mid-range regional specialities such as roast veal and *rojões*. Closed Mon eves and Tues all day.

Café Milenário, Largo do Toural. Large and airy traditional café serving reasonable snacks; popular with young and old alike.

Mumadona, corner of Rua Serpa Pinto and Rua Santa Maria, near Largo Condessa de Mumadona. Reliable, inexpensive stand-by, with two-course set menus at 1500–2000$00.

Oriental, Largo do Toural. Excellent budget option serving very good regional specialities as well as more usual fare: try the *truta grelhada com presunto* (grilled trout stuffed with ham). Offers superb views over the square. Under 1500$00.

O Segredo do Abade, Lugar de Passos, Serzedelo (☎253 533 696). Seven kilometres north of town on the road to Fafe (there are regular buses from Guimarães), this sophisticated place has a verandah and swimming pool, and serves regional dishes such as roast kid goat or *arroz de marisco* (seafood with rice), and good home-made sweets. Closed Mon.

Pousada de Santa Maria da Oliveira, Rua de Santa Maria (☎253 514 157). When on form, this is the best restaurant in town, with traditional Minho dishes served in a wonderful antique dining room or at outside tables in summer. You'll need to reserve a table in advance. From 3500–5500$00 a head.

El Rei, Praça de Santiago 20a. Small cosy restaurant in a prime location, serving consistently good-quality food at moderate prices. Closed Sun.

Solar do Arco, Rua de Santa Maria 48–50, by the arch. Welcoming restaurant in a prime position, but priced accordingly. Try the unusual *feijoada de camarões* (bean stew with shrimps), or any of the home-made desserts. Around 2000–3000$00. Closed Sun.

Vira Bar, Alameda de São Domaso 25. A well-regarded, church-like place with stained-glass windows, stone walls, a barrel-vaulted ceiling and a subdued ambience. 2500–4000$00 will get you the full works. Closed Mon.

Entertainment and nightlife

Outside festival time, at the beginning of July and August, the only time the town erupts into spontaneous celebration is when the local **soccer** team, FC Guimarães (consistently one of Portugal's better teams), wins at home. The stadium is located to the northwest of the centre, along Rua de São Gonçalo. You'll find a number of **bars** in and around the central Praça de Santiago and the adjacent Largo da Oliveira, all with outdoor tables and very popular, particularly on summer nights. As for **clubs**, the two mainstays are *Penha Clube*, at the foot of the *teleférico,* which is busiest at weekends (10pm–4am) and has occasional live bands. Popular with all ages, *Seculo XIX* (Wed–Sun 10pm–4am) is 1.5km north of town on Rua Teixeira de Pascoais, just off the continuation of Rua Capitão Alfredo Guimarães (look out for the signs). Other clubs make mayfly-like appearances in the summer months, only to disappear without trace in winter – ask at the turismos for details, or – more reliably – collar a student at one of the Largo da Oliveira's many bars.

East towards Trás-os-Montes

Heading **east towards Trás-os-Montes**, the minor N206 runs across country towards the Rio Tâmega, a region covered in the previous chapter. Buses along this route are frequent as far as **FAFE** (up to 17 daily, run by Auto-Viação Landim), 14km away and little more than an overgrown bus station (you'll almost certainly need to change here for Trás-os-Montes destinations, and may have to stay the night). Fafe has three *pensões* and a large revolutionary statue of a worker violently clubbing his bowler-hatted boss.

Beyond Fafe lies some magnificent countryside, dotted with huge boulders, though you'll really need your own transport to get the most out of the region as bus services are less than regular. If you're driving, you might want to stop at **GANDARELA**, 17km east of Fafe, which is famed for its topiary, while at **ARCO DE BAÚLHE**, 10km further, a road leads 7km north to Cabeceiras de Basto (see p.291). A dozen kilometres or so further east you finally reach the Tâmega River itself, where you're just 30km from the main Vila Real–Chaves road.

The Citânia de Briteiros

Midway between Guimarães and Braga is one of the most impressive and exciting archeological sites in the country, the **Citânia de Briteiros**. *Citânias* – Celtic hill settlements – lie scattered throughout the Minho: remains of twenty-seven have been identified along the coast, plus sixteen more in the region between Braga and Guimarães alone. Most date from the arrival of northern European Celts in the Iron Age (c.600–500 BC), though some are far older, having merged with an existing local culture established since Neolithic times (c.2000 BC). The site at Briteiros was occupied from about 300 BC and seems to have been a last stronghold against the invading Roman forces, resisting colonization until around 20 BC.

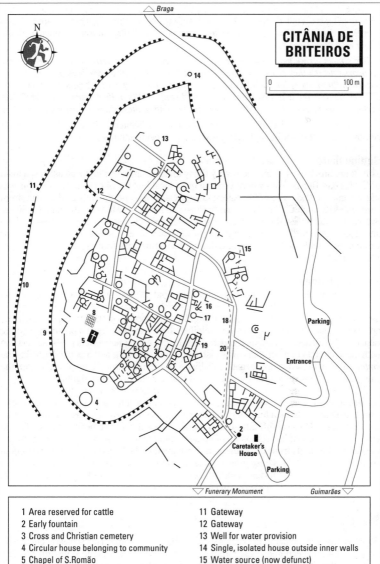

1 Area reserved for cattle
2 Early fountain
3 Cross and Christian cemetery
4 Circular house belonging to community
5 Chapel of S.Romão
6 House with helix
7 Houses reconstructed by Martins Sarmento
8 Small paved area
9 Inside wall
10 Second (of four) walls
11 Gateway
12 Gateway
13 Well for water provision
14 Single, isolated house outside inner walls
15 Water source (now defunct)
16 Houses with stone benches
17 Law courts (?), prisons (?)
18 Ingenious method of transporting water
19 House with various rooms
20 Cistern

The Roman historian Strabo gave a vivid description of the northern Portuguese tribes, who must have occupied these *citânias*, in his *Geographia* (c.20 BC). They organized mass sacrifices, he recorded, and inspected prisoners' entrails without removing them. Otherwise, they liked to:

> *live simply, drink water and sleep on the bare earth ... two-thirds of the year they live on acorns, which they roast and grind to make bread. They also have beer. They lack wine but when they have it they drink it up, gathering for a family feast. At banquets they sit on a bench against the wall according to age and rank ... When they assemble to drink they perform round dances to the flute or the horn, leaping in the air and crouching as they fall.*

Entrails aside – and they may have been literary licence – none of this seems far removed from the Minho and Trás-os-Montes of recent memory.

Getting there

The Braga **bus** leaves Guimarães every thirty minutes and stops in the pleasant spa town of Caldas das Taipas, from where you can get a local bus the 5km southwest to the *citânia* or take a taxi (1000$00). Alternatively, catch one of the buses that run from Guimarães through Caldas das Taipas to Póvoa do Lanhoso (Mon–Fri 10.45am & 1.30pm, Sat 9am) – which pass through Santo Estevão (Briteiros), just over 1km southeast of the site itself. Leaving the *citânia*, hitching a lift from other visitors, either to Braga or Guimarães, should be fairly easy, and there's also a bus back from Santo Estevão at 2pm (Mon–Sat).

The excavations

The site **excavations** (☎253 415 969; daily 9am–6pm; 200$00) have revealed foundations of over a hundred and fifty **huts**, a couple of which have been rebuilt to give a sense of their scale and design. Most of them are circular, with porches for their fires, though some are rectangular, among them a larger building which may have been a prison or meeting house – it is labelled the *casa do tribunal*. There's also a clear network of paved streets and paths, two circuits of town walls, plus cisterns, stone guttering and a public fountain (the *fonte*). Most of these features are identifiable as you wander around the place, though the site is more evocative in its layout and extent than for any particular sights.

One feature not to be missed, however, is the **bathhouse** or cistern (a fair walk down the hill to the left of the settlement), with its geometrically patterned stone doorway. This was believed to be a funerary chamber until recently, when it was pointed out that as much of the hill's run-off flowed into the site, it wouldn't have been the best place to put dead bodies. Similar remnants of construction, along with carved lintels from the huts and other finds from the *citânia*, are displayed at the Museu Martins Sarmento in Guimarães (see p.310). These indicate that the settlement was abandoned as late as 300 AD and – unlike Conímbriga, another Celtic site near Coimbra – show little Roman influence other than the presence of coins.

Braga

BRAGA, the turismo pamphlet claims, is the Portuguese Rome. This is clearly going a bit overboard – the Portuguese Canterbury might be more appropriate – though it neatly illustrates the city's ecclesiastical pretensions. One of the most ancient towns in Portugal, founded by the Romans in 27 BC, Braga was an important Visigothic bishopric before its occupation by the Moors. Reconquered early in the Christian campaigns, by the end of the eleventh century its archbishops were pressing for recognition as "Primate of the Spains", a title they disputed bitterly with archbishops of Toledo over the next six centuries.

The city is still Portugal's religious capital; look around and you'll soon become aware of the weight of church power, embodied by an archbishop's palace built on a truly

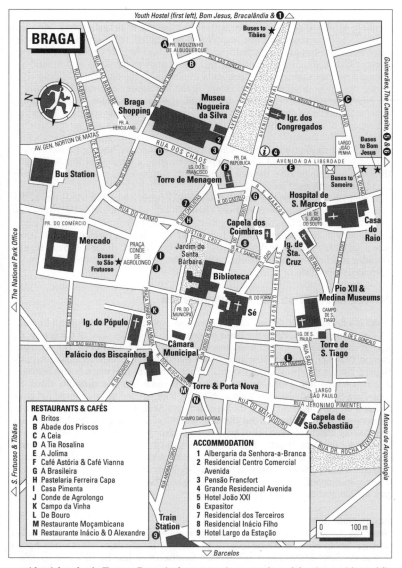

presidential scale. At **Easter**, Braga is the scene of spectacular celebrations, with torchlit processions and hooded penitents – while its outlying districts boast a selection of important religious buildings and sanctuaries, including that of **Bom Jesus**, one of the country's most extravagant Baroque creations. Braga also has a reputation as a bastion of reactionary politics. It was here, in 1926, that the military coup leading to Salazar's dictatorship was launched, while in the more recent past, after the 1974 Revolution, the Archbishop of Braga personally incited a mob to attack local Communist offices.

The city is an enjoyable place to stay and makes a decent base for touring the southern Minho. It seems recently, under the influence of Braga's mayor, Mesquita Machado, to have acquired a new energy that reflects less of the church and more of its position as a fast-growing commercial centre. However, the appearance of a network of fast roads, underpasses and big, modern tower blocks in and around the ancient town has angered many residents who feel that the old centre of Braga (the phrase "as old as the Cathedral of Braga" is the Portuguese equivalent of "as old as the hills") should have been better preserved. The uneasy alliance of old and new is never more apparent than when driving – the confused one-way system does its best to keep you in the town when you're trying to leave and to keep you out if you're trying to enter. But the most controversial action has been the digging up of the gardens around Praça da República and Avenida Central to make an underground car park. The excavations uncovered, and promptly destroyed, a number of Roman houses. However, on the plus side, the new fountain that dominates the Praça seems to have found favour with most locals.

In addition to the **Semana Santa** (Holy Week) celebrations, the whole city is illuminated for the **Festas de São João** (June 23–24), which provides the excuse for ancient folk-dances, a fairground and general partying. There's also a festival of *gigantones* (giant carnival figures) between June 18–20. The main **pilgrimage to Bom Jesus** (see p.321) takes place over Whitsun (six weeks after Easter). Braga also has a regular **Tuesday market**, held at the exhibition park in Avenida Pires Gonçalves, at the end of Avenida da Liberdade.

Arrival, information and accommodation

Braga is a fair-sized city, though the old town – an oval of streets radiating out from the Sé – is a compact area. From the **train station** (☎253 263 665), west of the centre, it's a 15–20 minute walk to the old town, reached down Rua Andrade Corvo. The main **bus station** (☎253 277 003) is 5–10 minutes' walk from the centre; turn right along Avenida General Norton de Matos, cross the small Praça Alexandre Herculano before following Rua dos Chãos into Praça da República. Here you'll find the **turismo** (Mon–Fri 9am–7pm, Sat 9am–12.30pm & 2–5pm; ☎253 262 550), housed in a wonderful Art Deco building on the corner of Praça da República and Avenida da Liberdade; it offers an impressive large-scale map of the city and has lists of bus and train timetables. Braga also has an unofficial **Web site**, *http://s700.uminho.pt/braga.html*. Finally, if you're heading for the Peneda-Gerês national park, it's worth calling in at the **national park headquarters** – a large, white house on Avenida António Macedo in the Quinta das Parretas suburb (Mon–Fri 9am–12.30pm & 2–5.30pm; ☎253 203 480, fax 253 613 169), a twenty-minute walk from the centre, where you can buy a useful map and booklet, and pick up information on walking trails (*trilhos*).

Accommodation

Braga has plenty of hotels and *pensões*, though it's unwise to turn up without a reservation during religious events and local festivals (see above). There's an excellent **youth hostel** at Rua de Santa Margarida 6, off Avenida Central (☎ & fax 253 616 163; reception 9am–noon & 6pm–midnight), which is very popular in summer with hikers and has some double rooms (①), as well as a good noticeboard, lockers for valuables and a kitchen. The **campsite**, *Camping Parque da Ponte* (☎253 273 355, April–October only), is a two-kilometre walk from the centre, down Avenida da Liberdade and right next to the municipal swimming pool. Officially, you need an international camping carnet. Alternatively, if none of the Braga options appeals, you can stay at Bom Jesus (see p.321), 4km from the centre.

Residencial Centro Comercial Avenida, Av. Central 27–37 (☎253 275 722, fax 253 616 363). On the second floor of the BragaShopping complex. Big, well-furnished rooms with TVs and baths, and handily located for the cinema below. ③.

Pensão Francfort, Av. Central 1–7 (☎253 262 648). Just across from Praça da República, this charming and friendly place dates from 1879 and is beginning to show its age – though the Art Deco dining room has recently been redecorated. Simple rooms, some with bath, make this one of the best bargains in town, although it can be noisy at the front. ①.

Grande Residencial Avenida, Av. da Liberdade 738–2º (☎253 609 020, fax 253 609 028). Fine old *pensão* in a great location. Once grand, it too is beginning to fade a little these days, but remains good value for money. Rooms at the rear are quieter than those overlooking the underpass and the Avenida. It fills quickly and reservations are advisable in summer. ②.

Residencial Inácio Filho, Rua Francisco Sanches 42–2º (☎253 263 849). Quirky, central, spotless *residencial*, cluttered with antique typewriters, cash registers and telephones. Most rooms come with a bath. It's to the left off Rua do Souto, heading down from the turismo. ②.

Hotel João XXI, Av. João XXI 849 (☎253 616 630, fax 253 616 631). Off Avenida da Liberdade, on the way out of town, this six-storey hotel has a top-floor restaurant and neat, en-suite rooms. Good value. ③.

Hotel Largo da Estação, Largo da Estação 13 (☎253 218 381, fax 253 276 810). According to the brochure, this modern block next to the train station will give you a "feeling of peace and eternity"; the jacuzzis in some rooms may go some way to achieving this. ④.

Albergaria da Senhora-a-Branca, Largo da Senhora-a-Branca 58 (☎253 269 938, fax 253 269 937). Facing a garden and attractively furnished, this is one of Braga's smarter choices – there's parking space too. It's about a kilometre from the centre; keep going out of town down Avenida Central. ③.

Residencial dos Terceiros, Rua dos Capelistas 85 (☎253 270 466, fax 253 275 767). A well-situated modern place; rooms have TV and private bathroom. ③.

The City

The obvious point from which to start exploring Braga is **Praça da República**, a busy arcaded square at the head of the old town. It's backed by the former town keep, the **Torre de Menagem**, while in the arcade itself you'll find two fine coffee houses which look out down the length of the long central square. From here, almost everything of interest is reached down narrow **Rua do Souto**, the main pedestrianized street which runs past the Sé. The street is also Braga's principal shopping district, though few commercial centres are like this one, where shoe shops rub shoulders with places selling candles, icons and other religious paraphernalia.

The Sé

The old town centre is dominated by the **Sé**, a rambling structure founded on the site of a Moorish mosque in 1070 after the Christian reconquest. The original Romanesque building encompasses Gothic, Renaissance and Baroque additions, though the cathedral's south doorway is a survival from the building's earliest incarnation, carved with rustic scenes from the legend of Reynard the Fox. The most striking element of the cathedral, however, is the intricate ornamentation of the roofline, commissioned by Braga's great Renaissance patron, Archbishop Diogo de Sousa, and executed by João de Castilho, later to become one of the architects of Lisbon's Mosteiro dos Jerónimos – the greatest of all Manueline buildings.

Inside, the cathedral complex is disorientating and, with the exception of the Baroque organs, somewhat disappointing: you enter through a courtyard fronting three Gothic chapels, a cloister and, most prominently, a ticket desk, where you can gain access to the **Museu de Arte Sacra** and Capela dos Reis (daily 8.30am–1pm & 2–6.30pm; 300$00). The *museu* is essentially the cathedral's treasury and one of the richest of such collections in Portugal, containing representative pieces from the tenth to the eighteenth century, but the items are unlabelled and confusingly arranged, and it all manages to look a little dull. Eventually you emerge alongside the magnificent Baroque twin organs in the **Coro Alto**, supported by life-sized figures of satyrs, mermen and monstrous fish. From here you can gaze down into the cathedral proper – unexpectedly small and, when you descend, remarkably uninteresting.

Of the three outer chapels, the fourteenth-century **Capela dos Reis** (King's Chapel) is the most significant, built to house the tombs of the cathedral's founders, Henry of Burgundy, first Count of Portucale, and his wife Teresa – the parents of Afonso Henriques. Exposed beside them is the mummified body of Archbishop Lourenço, found "uncorrupt" when his tomb was opened in the seventeenth century. He had fought in the great victory over the Castilians at Aljubarrota in 1385, riding around bestowing indulgences on the ranks, and there sustained a scar on his cheek – which he himself is said to have carved proudly on his effigy.

The rest of the old town

Opposite the cathedral, across Rua do Souto, you'll find the old **Archbishop's Palace**, a great fortress-like building, which in medieval times actually covered a tenth of the city. Today it easily accommodates the municipal **library** (Mon–Fri 9am–noon & 2–8pm) and various faculties of the university, and inside you can inspect the ornate ceilings of the medieval reading-room and the Sala do Doctor Manuel Monteiro. Unless you have an academic interest, you're unlikely to find Braga's other **churches** very inspiring: most, like the cathedral, were stripped and modernized in the late-seventeenth and eighteenth centuries. Probably the most interesting, architecturally, is the small Renaissance **Capela dos Coimbras**, another of Archbishop de Sousa's commissions, on Largo Carlos Amarante, further east up Rua do Souto and off to the right.

On the whole, more inspiring are the numerous **mansions** from earlier ages, with their extravagant Baroque and Rococo facades. The **Câmara Municipal** and **Casa do Raio** are both by André Soares da Silva, the archbishop's architect, and look out, too, for the apostle-clad roofline of the **Hospital de São Marcos**, adjacent to the Casa do Raio. Best of all, though, is the mid-seventeenth-century **Palácio dos Biscaínhos** (☎ & fax 253 217 645; Tues–Sun 10am–12.15pm & 2–5.30pm; 250$00), whose flagstoned ground floor was designed to allow carriages through to the stables. Nowadays, it houses a small museum of decorative arts, paintings and sculpture from the 17th–19th centuries, mostly Rococo and Baroque, in line with the decoration of the house. The pretty landscaped gardens out back, complete with a 200-year-old Virginian magnolia tree, were also designed by Soares da Silva.

On the southern side of town, in Campo de Santiago, a former seminary has been turned into the **Museu Medina e Pio XII** (Tues–Sun 9am–12pm & 2–5pm; 250$00), which consists of two distinct collections: the Pio XII, housing dusty religious regalia from the eleventh to seventeeth centuries, and the Medina, named after the Portuguese painter and donated on the understanding that it would be housed separately from any other exhibits. Save your energy for the collection of fonts and capitals gathered in a courtyard like standing stones, or for the small excavation of a first-century Roman water tank – and try persuading the guide to hold back on a few of the endless locked doors. There's also a small collection of stone and bronze age tools. Further archeological exhibits, from Paleolithic stone tools to Roman and medieval items, will be housed at the new **Museu de Arqueologia Dom Diogo de Sousa** when construction work is completed (only the library is currently open). It's situated beside some Roman excavations on Rua dos Bombeiros Voluntários, the southern continuation of Rua Jeronimo Pimentel (bus #7; ☎253 273 706, fax 253 612 366) – ask at the turismo for details.

Eating, drinking, entertainment and nightlife

The city's most characterful locales are its nineteenth-century **cafés** – busy throughout the day and into the evening. In all of these you can get sandwiches, snacks, and often full meals, though Braga is also well endowed with tempting **restaurants**; a selection of the best is listed below. Local specialities include *caldo de castanhas* (chestnut soup), or *charutos de chila* (cigar-shaped squash pastries) and *rabanadas* (fried slices of milk-soaked bread with a sweet cinnamon sauce) for dessert. We've noted phone numbers where it might be necessary to book ahead.

For details of local **cultural events**, get hold of a copy of the daily *Correio do Minho* newspaper; the turismo generally has one on the counter and is happy to offer advice. In particular, don't miss out on tickets to anything that's on at the Teatro Circo (☎253 262 403 or 253 217 167), at Avenida da Liberdade 697, opposite the Centro Comercial Gold. In addition to theatrical performances, **films** are shown here, as well as at the BragaShopping complex off Avenida Central (☎253 208 000; seven screens; showings daily at 3pm, 5.30pm, 9.45pm & 12.15am; 500–600$00). There are a number of commercial art galleries staging temporary **exhibitions**: try Galeria Belo Belo, Avenida Central 191 (☎253 217 656); or Galeria Sépia, Avenida da Liberdade 505 (☎253 277 447). Also worth a look-in is the city-run Museu da Imagem on Largo São Joaquim (Tues–Sun 9am–12.30pm & 2–5pm; free), which stages both permanent and temporary photography exhibitions.

During summer, there's popular entertainment in the **Bracalândia** theme park (10am–midnight; adults 1800$00, free for children under 4), 1km out of town on the Bom Jesus road (any bus to Bom Jesus will stop here), where you'll find the usual assortment of fairground rides, including a Ferris wheel and helter-skelter.

There's a fair **club scene** in Braga with most of the action taking place at the bottom end of Avenida da Liberdade, around the *Hotel Turismo*. Venues change hands and names reasonably regularly but the current favourites include: *84*, beneath the *Hotel Turismo*; the more fashionable *Praça Mayor* in Rua Gonçalo Sampaio; *Sardinha Biba Bar* (with a swimming pool), nearby at Rua dos Galos; and *Populum Bar* in the centre of Braga at Praça Conde de Agrolongo 115. All play a staple mix of 1980s disco interspersed with a little modern samba and 1990s techno sounds.

Cafés

Café Astória, Praça da República. By far the best of the old coffee houses, mahogany-panelled and with cut-glass windows, going very beautifully to seed. Occasional live music and invariably tasty snacks add to its attraction.

A Brasileira, Largo Barão de São Marinha. A superb old-style café, at the top of Rua do Souto, full of crusty old waiters dealing out brandies to a similarly aged clientele. In summer, you can sit in the open window-terrace – virtually on the street.

Pastelaria Ferreira Capa, Rua dos Capelistas 38–50. Tasty pastries and coffee.

Café Vianna, Praça da República. One of Braga's best, a gorgeous Art Nouveau turn-of-the-century establishment in a prime location, with outside tables and good beef sandwiches (*pregos*).

Restaurants

Abade dos Priscos, Praça Mouzinho de Albuquerque 7. Reliable and affordable Portuguese cuisine – try the *bacalhau* gratin or prawn curry. Closed Sun, Mon lunch, and all of July.

De Bouro, Rua Santo António das Travessas 30–32. Tucked away in the old centre, this pleasantly restored Cistercian monastic lodging house claims to continue the monks' tradition of serving food to "enhance spiritual and contemplative heights". All the traditional favourites mixed with a few Minho specialities. Around 2500$00.

Brito's, Praça Mouzinho de Albuquerque 49. Specializes in old-style cooking from ancient recipes, including *bacalhau* and salmon in shellfish sauce. Home-made desserts, and a good wine list. Closed Wed.

Campo da Vinha, Praça Conselheiro Torres de Almeida 5–6, just off Praça Conde de Agrolongo (☎253 214 359). Cheap, popular and cheerful: try the *frango*.

Casa Pimenta, Praça Conde de Agrolongo 46. A consistently good bet, especially for the fine set menu at around 2500$00. Specialities include *papas de sarabulho*, roast kid goat and veal.

A Ceia, Rua do Raio 331, off Av. da Liberdade. This excellent restaurant is always crowded with locals, so arrive early, especially at weekends, or you'll have to eat at the bar. Spit-roast chickens and steaks are served up in enormous portions at moderate prices, and there's a fine wine list. Closed Mon.

Conde de Agrolongo, Praça Conde de Agrolongo 74. Typical Portuguese restaurant serving good rice dishes for under 2000$00. Head for the large, cool basement rather than the deserted ground floor.

Expositor, Parques de Exposições, on the right at the end of Av. da Liberdade. Huge portions of traditional Minhota cooking, heavy on grilled meat and fish (displayed in window cases). Closed Tues.

O Inácio, Campo das Hortas 14. Through the town gate at the end of Rua do Souto and off to the left, this is a pricey and rather cosmopolitan restaurant that doesn't limit itself to Portuguese dishes. It's in an old stone house with rustic decor – and costs around 3000$00 a head and upwards. Closed Mon. A close alternative in food, price and location is *O Alexandre* at Campo das Hortas 10.

A Jolima, Av. da Liberdade 747, near the turismo. Cheap self-service cafeteria, from ice cream and pizza to local dishes. Around 700$00 a plate.

A Moçambicana, Rua Andrade Corvo 8. Moderately priced option just outside the town gate, at the end of Rua do Souto. As the name suggests, a spattering of African dishes feature on a menu that includes a rather rough house wine.

A Tia Rosalina, Rua dos Chaos 25–31. Long established purveyor of regional food with a good reputation and moderate prices.

Listings

Airline TAP, Rua Dr. Justino Cruz 154–2º (☎253 616 205, or freephone 800 213 141).

Ambulance ☎253 262 470 or 253 264 077.

Books and newspapers English-language books can be found at Livraria Bertrand, Rua Dom Diogo Sousa 113, and at Livraria Cruz, on the same street at no.129. International newspapers are available from the tobacconists at Rua Dr. Justina Cruz 149.

Exchange Caravela Travel on Rua Francisco Sanches 47 (☎253 200 500) offers reasonable rates of exchange and doesn't usually charge commission.

Hospital São Marcos, Largo Carlos Amarante (☎253 613 800).

Police ☎253 613 250.

Outdoor sports River canoeing and hiking tours are offered by Gota Verde, at the Instituto da Juventude, Rua de Santa Margarida 215, sala 8 (☎253 616 836, fax 253 616 835). Walking trips in Peneda–Gerês are run roughly once a week, and cost 5000$00 per person, including transport.

Swimming pools Both are 2km from the centre: the Complexo Desportivo da Rodovia, at the junction of the main ring road and Av. João Paulo II before Bracalândia (most easily reached down Av. Central, turning right onto Av. Padre Julio Fragata; ☎253 616 773); and the municipal Piscina da Ponte (July only) at the far end of Av. da Liberdade by the campsite (☎253 264 424).

Taxis Central Rádio Táxi, ☎253 614 019.

Travel agents Abreu, Av. Central 171 (☎253 613 100); Atlas, Praça Conde de Agrolongo 129 (☎253 613 731); Tagus, Praça do Município 7 (☎253 215 301).

Bom Jesus, São Frutuoso and Tibães

Having soaked up the religious atmosphere in Braga itself, there's a number of fascinating sites in its surroundings. The Baroque stairway and pilgrim church of **Bom Jesus do Monte**, 4km east of Braga, is a good enough reason to come in the first place and is within striking distance of the massive, if distinctly oppressive, **Santuário do Sameiro**; while a similar distance to the northwest is the Visigothic church of **São Frutuoso** and a ruined Benedictine monastery at **Tibães**.

Buses to Bom Jesus leave Braga at 10 and 40 minutes past the hour from Avenida da Liberdade, close to the post office. Those for São Frutuoso leave every thirty minutes from Praça Conde de Agrolongo (they are marked "Sarrido"); get off at the hamlet of São Jerónimo Real, from where it is a five-minute walk. For Tibães, hourly buses, marked "Padim da Graça", leave from Avenida Central. If you want to make things easy you could rent a **taxi** for a few hours (see above).

Bom Jesus do Monte and Santuário do Sameiro

BOM JESUS DO MONTE is one of Portugal's best-known images. Set in the woods high above the city, the glorious ornamental stairway of granite and white plaster is a monumental homage created by Braga's archbishop in the first decades of the eighteenth century. There is no particular reason for its presence – no miracle or vision – yet it remains the object of devoted pilgrimage, with many penitents climbing up on their knees. It is a very pleasant place to spend an afternoon or, best of all, early evening. There are wooded gardens, grottoes and miniature boating pools behind the church and, at the far end, just outside the park up the hill, horse rides.

Buses run the 3km from Braga to the foot of the stairway. At weekends they are packed, as seemingly half the city piles up to picnic in the woods. Most of the local families, armed with immense baskets of food, ride straight to the top in an hydraulic **funicular** (8am–8pm; every 30min and usually timed to coincide with buses; 100$00). If you resist the temptation to ride the funicular and make the climb up the stairway, Bom Jesus's simple allegory unfolds. Each of the **stairway** landings has a fountain: the first symbolizes the wounds of Christ, the next five the Senses, and the final three represent the Virtues. At each corner, too, are chapels with mouldering, larger-than-life wooden tableaux of the Life

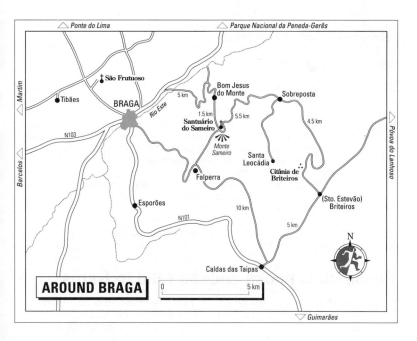

AROUND BRAGA

of Christ, arranged chronologically, leading to the Crucifixion at the altar of the church. As a design it's a triumph – one of the greatest of all Baroque architectural creations – and was later copied at Lamego.

In contrast, the domed **Santuário do Sameiro**, 2km up at the top of the hill, is impressive if only for its size and overtly ugly monumental stairway. It was built in the late nineteenth century but nowadays it bears the heavy mark of Salazar's regime – swathes of concrete and enormous statues. Like it or loathe it, it's a powerful monument to the power and authority of the Roman Catholic Church in Portugal, and the church is the second most venerated shrine in the country after Fátima (see p.162). There's a very good, if somewhat pricey, restaurant here too, the *Restaurante Sameiro*.

Practicalities

There's a good range of **places to stay** up on the mount, which makes a peaceful and attractive place to spend the night. At the budget end of the scale, the friendly *Pensão Águeda* (☎253 676 521; ①), behind the park at the back of the church, has basic rooms (separate bathrooms), but breakfast is included and the downstairs restaurant is good. There are several more expensive options, one of the best being the *Casa dos Lagos* (☎ & fax 253 676 738; ③), a lovely old Solares de Portugal house on the road just below the top of the steps, with a very hospitable owner and offering fantastic views; it also has three apartments for rent. The *Hotel Sopete Parque* (☎253 676 611, fax 253 676 679; ④) is another excellent option – a superb nineteenth-century pile furnished in 1920s style, situated next to the church and facing the amusing concrete grotto. The nearby *Hotel Elevador* (☎253 603 400, fax 253 676 679; ④), newly renovated and under the same management, is pretty similar.

There is a handful of lively **restaurants** on the Monte, which come into their own on Saturdays, when they're filled with parties from a constant stream of weddings. Note, however, that most open only at weekends during winter. A good option is *Restaurante Águeda*, beneath the *pensão* of the same name, which is cheap and serves large portions. *Restaurante Portico*, just beyond the bottom of the steps, is a traditional-style building serving quality food, but at high prices.

São Frutuoso and Tibães

Three and a half kilometres northwest of Braga is another worthwhile church excursion: to **São Frutuoso** (Tues–Sun 9am–noon & 2–5pm; keys are kept in a nearby house), built by the Visigoths in the seventh century, adapted by the Moors, and then restored to Christian worship after the reconquest. It's a gem of a church, flanked by an eighteenth-century chapel but unfortunately its previously tranquil setting has now been engulfed by Braga's ever-expanding suburbs. The approach is from São Jerónimo Real.

Half a kilometre beyond the São Frutuoso turning, to the left of the main road, a paved track leads to the monastery of **Tibães** (Tues–Sun 9am–noon & 2–5pm; free), formerly the grandest Benedictine establishment in the land. A vast and ruined hulk, its abandoned medieval buildings, cloisters and rambling gardens were once occupied by gypsy families. Now, however, it is state-owned, and extensive (and long-winded) renovation is currently underway to convert it into a museum and *pousada*. It is an evocative place and you can look around the **church**, which has been maintained. There are guided tours of the monastic buildings (Tues–Sun 10am–12.30pm & 2–6pm; 300$00).

Póvoa do Lanhoso and the road to Gerês

Heading **east from Braga** along the N103 to the Peneda-Gerês park (see p.350), after 16km you come to the turning for **Póvoa do Lanhoso**, which lies 3km south of the main road. If you have transport, and time to spare, this small provincial town is worth a detour for its castle and Romanesque church. Another sight, revered in Portugal though perhaps of more peripheral interest to visitors, is the shrine of **Nossa Senhora da Abadia**, to the north of the Braga–Gerês road, turning off at Santa Maria do Bouro.

Póvoa do Lanhoso

As you walk around **PÓVOA DO LANHOSO** you'll come across the many workshops (*ourivesarias*) that produce the gold jewellery for which the town is best known, much of it bearing clear traces of Moorish influence especially in the filigree work. This point of interest aside, the modern quarters of the town haven't much to offer, but they do lie sandwiched between two ancient sites. At the northern end of town (the approach from Braga), a steep mound – the Monte do Pilar – rises up to one of the smallest **castles** in Portugal and a scattering of chapels and picnic tables. In the fourteenth century, the lord of the shire was reported to have locked up his adulterous wife, her lover and their servants in the castle and ordered it to be burned; it was substantially rebuilt in the eighteenth century. The *Panorâmico* **restaurant** nearby keeps a set of keys and offers reasonable food and good views, if you can squeeze in between their regular parties of christening and wedding guests. In the opposite direction, 3km out of town, the small church of **Fonte Areada** is a short walk from the main road (past the white statue). The simple interior, characteristic of the Romanesque style, is in marked contrast to the complications of the doorway with its centrepiece relief of a large sheep. If you have your own transport or can hire a taxi, it's worth paying a visit to one of two local **Vinho Verde quintas** that welcome visitors and offer free tastings and tours: *Quinta do Minho* (contact Maria Teresa Martins on ☎253 633 240); or *Quinta Villa Beatriz* in Santo Emilião (☎253 631 523 or 253 631 292), an imposing blue-tiled four-towered mansion in the "Brazilian" style of the early twentieth-century, constructed by emigrants who made their fortune in the New World. There are superb gardens, as well as milk cows and horses for children to admire.

The town provides useful transport links to the east into Trás-os-Montes; south to the Douro, via Cabeceiras de Basto; and to Porto, via Famalição. Regular **buses** also connect with Braga, Caldas do Gerês and Guimarães. To pick up a bus to Montalegre and Chaves (5–7 daily), you have to walk the 3km north to Pinheiro, on the main N103.

Nossa Senhora da Abadia

With your own transport, an alternative route into Gerês is the minor N205–4 via Amares, after which the road becomes the N308. Some 13km along you come to **SANTA MARIA DO BOURO** (Bouro to the locals) – which has a shell of a monastery and a large Baroque church. Turning off from here, you arrive at the shrine of **Nossa Senhora da Abadia**. This is said to be the oldest sanctuary in Portugal and, like Bom Jesus, is a centre of pilgrimage: the main festival is on August 15. The focus of devotions is a twelfth-century wooden statue of the Virgin and Child, and while the church itself was largely rebuilt in the eighteenth century, outside are two earlier, elegant wings of monks' cells and, usually, some market stalls. There's no accommodation here but you can **eat** well with the pilgrims at the sizeable *Restaurante Abadia*, which can seat up to 500 people.

Barcelos

It's worth making plans to arrive in **BARCELOS**, 20km west of Braga, for the Thursday market, the **Feira de Barcelos**. The great weekly event of southern Minho, it takes place from around dawn until late afternoon on the Campo da República – also known as the Campo da Feira – a vast open square in the centre of town. There are traditional events at other times of the year, too: the Festa das Cruzes (Festival of the Crosses) on May 3, and, on the last Saturday of July, a renowned **folklore festival** in Barcelinhos, on the opposite bank of the river, with live music and fireworks.

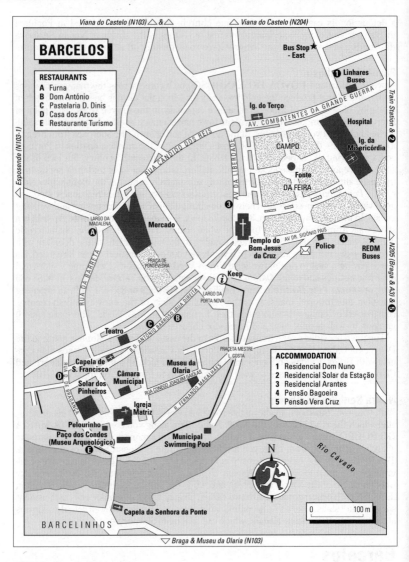

BARCELOS

RESTAURANTS
A Furna
B Dom António
C Pastelaria D. Dinis
D Casa dos Arcos
E Restaurante Turismo

ACCOMMODATION
1 Residencial Dom Nuno
2 Residencial Solar da Estação
3 Residencial Arantes
4 Pensão Bagoeira
5 Pensão Vera Cruz

The Feira de Barcelos

The Minho's markets are always interesting, and the **Feira de Barcelos**, one of the largest in Europe, is both a spectacle and a crash course in the region's economics. As well as row upon row of village women squatting behind baskets of their own produce, there are stalls selling virtually everything – yokes for oxen, sausage skins and superb fresh bread, whole avenues of ducks and rabbits. The Minho is made up of hundreds of tiny, walled smallholdings, rarely more than allotments, and many people here are just selling a few vegetables, some fruit, eggs, and maybe even cheese from the family cow. It all looks unbelievably wholesome.

Apart from produce, clothes and kitchen equipment, the *feira*'s big feature is local **pottery and handicrafts**, for Barcelos is at the centre of Portugal's most active *artesanato* region. The pottery ware – *louça de Barcelos* – is characteristically brown with distinctive yellow dots, and has been highly acclaimed since the 1950s when the imaginative earthenware figurines of Rosa Ramalho (marked RR) began to be collected throughout Europe. In comparison, most of today's pieces look as if they fell off a production line (some, indeed, are Far Eastern imports), but there are some good items to be found, sold at around half the price of outlets elsewhere. Look out for the work of Rosa's granddaughter, Júlia Ramalho, marked JR. Other crafts, too, are impressive – especially the basketwork, traditionally carved yokes (*cangas*) and wooden toys.

The Town

In addition to its festivities, Barcelos has a few more permanent sights worth visiting. At the southwest corner of the Campo is the town's most striking church, the **Templo do Bom Jesus da Cruz**, fronted by a Baroque garden of obelisks and box-hedges. Built in 1708, its distinctive exterior, created by a simple contrast of dark granite and white plasterwork, was to be influential in the design of churches throughout the region. It's an odd addition to the old part of town, though, which is essentially medieval in character – a small, hillside web of streets spun above the Rio Cávado. Heading south from the Campo, you'll soon end up at the **river**, as beautiful as any in the Minho, overhung by willows, fronted by gardens with Gothic pillories (*pelourinhos*), and spanned by a fifteenth-century bridge. Just above the bridge loom the ruins of the **Paço dos Condes**, the former Palace of the Counts of Barcelos, wrecked by the Great Earthquake of 1755 and now providing a shell for the outdoor **Museu Arqueológico** (daily: summer 9am–7pm; winter 9am–5.30pm; free). This is a miscellaneous assembly of gravestones, gargoyles and cornerstones, notable for a sixteenth-century crucifix locally famed for its connection with the legend of *Senhor do Galo* – the Gentleman of the Cock (see box below). Note also the religious tombstone emblems of the various peoples to have lived in Barcelos: both Celtic and Catholic crosses, six-point Jewish Stars of David, and five-point Islamic pentagrams. If you wanted to pursue an interest in the local ceramic wares, you could visit the **Museu de Olaria** (☎253 824 741; Tues–Sun 10am–12.30pm & 2–6pm, Thurs 10am–6pm; 200$00), in the Casa dos Mendanhas on Rua Conego Joaquim Gaiolas, 300m from the archeological museum.

Practicalities

The **train station** (☎253 811 243) is at the drab eastern edge of town; follow Avenida Alcaides de Faria straight ahead for fifteen minutes until it becomes Avenida Combatentes da Grande Guerra, and you'll emerge on the Campo da Feira. There are two main **bus** companies: Linhares, Av. Combatentes da Grande Guerra 46, for local

---

THE BARCELOS COCK

A stone cross in Barcelos's archeological museum depicts the legend of the **Galo de Barcelos**, a miraculous roast fowl which rose from the dinner table of a judge to crow the innocence of a Galician pilgrim he had wrongly condemned to the gallows. The pilgrim, having wisely proclaimed "I'll be hanged if that cock don't crow", got his reprieve. It's a story that occurs in different forms in northern Spain, but the Barcelos rooster has taken a special hold on popular folk art, becoming a national symbol of Portugal and now, usually in pottery form, the ubiquitous emblem of Portuguese tourism.

services within Minho and to Vila do Conde and Póvoa do Varzim; and REDM, Av. Dr. Sidónio Pais, facing the Campo, for main towns in the region and beyond (also agents for Rede Express, Renex, and Internorte for long-distance services). Both run frequent services to Braga. The **turismo** (March–Oct: Mon–Fri 9am–12.30pm & 2.30–6pm, Sat 10am–12.30pm & 2.30–5.30pm, Sun 2.30–5.30pm; Nov–Feb Mon–Wed & Fri 9am–12.30pm & 2.30–5.50pm, Thurs 9am–5.30pm, Sat 10am–5pm; ☎253 811 882) is housed in the old castle keep, the Torre da Porta Nova, just off the Campo. In addition to its information counter, it features a permanent display and sale of Barcelos handicrafts. The river is too polluted for **swimming** but there are municipal pools just upstream from the bridge.

Accommodation

There's nothing really cheap in Barcelos, so budget travellers should consider staying in Braga. You'll definitely need to book ahead if coinciding with the market (Wed & Thurs nights), as rooms fill up quickly.

Residencial Arantes, Av. da Liberdade 35–1º (☎253 811 326, fax 253 821 360). An eccentric mix of modern rooms in this family-run place on the west side of the Campo da Feira, above a good *pastelaria*; avoid the cell-like rooms overlooking a central well. Cheaper rooms are without facilities, but breakfast is included in all rates. ②.

Pensão Bagoeira, Av. Dr. Sidónio Pais 495 (☎253 811 236, fax 253 824 588). Facing the Campo, this is a real old market inn. The rooms, all with bathrooms, were being upgraded at the time of writing. ③.

Casa do Monte, Abade de Neiva, 3km west of Barcelos on the N103 Viana do Castelo road (☎253 811 519). Delightful country house belonging to the Solares de Portugal scheme, with large gardens and a verandah providing panoramic views over Barcelos and the valley. ③.

Residencial Dom Nuno, Av. Dom Nuno Álvares Pereira 76 (☎253 812 810). A fancy but characterless place, off to the right as you approach Campo da Feira from the station. All rooms have bath, telephone and TV. ③.

Residencial Solar da Estação, Largo da Estação (☎253 811 741). By the railway station, the large, spotless, modern rooms have shower and TV; rates include breakfast. ②.

Pensão Vera Cruz, Av. Dr. Sidónio Pais 371 (☎253 811 333). 100m from *Bagoeira* next to GALP, above a modern if not too salubrious café, this was rebuilding its rooms when we visited. ②.

Eating, drinking and nightlife

There is a row of three bargain-basement café-restaurants around the corner from the Campo, in the alleyway opposite the Templo; the central one is best value. The main **nightclub** is the trendy *Vaticano.Club*, Rua Cândido da Cunha 188 (☎253 812 962), with house and techno Thursdays, and more Latin sounds on Saturdays.

THE MIRACLE OF MOURE

If you want to witness a **miracle**, head for the **Igreja de Moure**, 7km southwest of Barcelos off the road to Vila Nova de Famalicão and reachable on REDM buses from Barcelos (see Practicalities below). The church has become a minor centre of pilgrimage since May 18 1996, when a ghostly "shadow of the top half of Christ" first appeared. The miracle has since returned every year on May 18, and during its 1998 appearance, the congregation entered "total delirium and nervosity" according to a newspaper report: some circled the image, others clapped, while others begged forgiveness for their sins. Sadly, the archbishop of Braga pooh-poohed the miracle, declaring to the press "it is a singular event generated from sentiments of faith and piety but explainable by the laws of optical physics". Further tests concluded that the "miracle" was caused by a mere trick of the light. However, science has not dissuaded the faithful, who still flock here every May to witness what the *Diário de Notícias* calls the "marvellous half-bodied manifestation of Moure".

Bagoeira, Av. Dr. Sidónio Pais 57 (☎253 811 236). Old market inn full of atmosphere – though it's open daily, be sure to have lunch here on market day, when a constant stream of stallholders bring in pots and pans for takeaways. It's open in the evening, too, and meals – mostly stews, steaks and grills – are excellent value.

Casa dos Arcos, Rua Duques de Bragança. Set in a traditional old stone house, and serving unusual regional specialities such as suckling pig. Expensive. Closed Mon.

Dom António, Rua Dom António Barroso. Friendly and well-priced despite being geared toward tourists, with huge portions sufficient for two. Wild boar from Montesinho features Thursdays, and boiled chestnuts are served in November. Good *rojões*. Under 2000$00.

Pastelaria Dom Dinis, Rua Dom António Barroso 100. Pleasant pastry shop with outdoor tables, serving very sweet egg-and-peanut sweets among other goodies.

Furna, Largo da Madalena. You'll see the queues for takeaway chickens stretching out of the door, which gives a good clue as to its best dish – superb chicken (650$00 for a whole bird). Closed Mon.

Restaurante Turismo, at the foot of Rua Duques de Bragança. This bar (despite its name), overlooking the river, is the perfect place for a beer while catching the last of the day's sun.

THE COSTA VERDE

Spurred by the flow of foreign currency into the Algarve, the Regional Tourist Board is energetically trying to promote the Minho's miles of sandy coastline as the **Costa Verde**. So far, the seaside element of the campaign hasn't quite worked, for despite the enticing promises of "unpolluted beaches with a high iodine content… health for the whole year", Costa Verde is green for a reason. It can be drizzly and overcast right through summer and the Atlantic here is never too warm. Still, if that doesn't bother you and the weather's looking good there's amazing potential; you can pick almost any road, any village, and find a great **beach** virtually to yourself.

The coast between Póvoa de Varzim and Caminha is virtually one long beach, with the road running, for the most part, 1km or so inland. There are at least four **buses** a day in each direction, most using the resort of **Viana do Castelo** – very much the main event on this coast – as an axis. In addition, there are regular **trains** from Porto, which cut inland to Barcelos before heading back to the coast at Viana do Castelo, from where they run up the coast to Caminha, then along the Rio Minho to Valença.

North from Porto to Viana

The coast immediately **north of Porto**, as far as Póvoa de Varzim, is accessible by train and covered on pp.278–284. Beyond Póvoa, the train doesn't touch the coast again until Viana do Castelo, but there are local (if slow) **buses**: six daily ones wend from Porto to Viana via Póvoa, Ofir, Esposende and São Bartolomeu do Mar. Much of this part of the Costa Verde is protected from development by law: 18km of coastline between Apúlia and the mouth of the River Neiva has been designated **Área de Paisagem Protegida do Litoral de Esposende** and afforded protected status. Along this stretch and beyond, the local people have perfected the art of dune agriculture. Small "fields" are created by digging out depressions in the sand dunes, which trap moisture from the Atlantic mists and protect crops from wind. Dried seaweed is used as fertilizer, which over the centuries has created a soil so fertile that many believe these dune fruits and vegetables to be among the best in the country. For more information on the coastal ecosystem, contact the reserve's headquarters in Esposende, at Rua 1º de Dezembro 65 (☎253 965 830, fax 253 965 330).

Esposende

The easiest place in the Costa Verde to reach by public transport is **ESPOSENDE**, a typical Portuguese seaside resort 20km north of Póvoa on the estuary of the Rio Cávado, and 2–3km from the ocean. Breezy and sun-bleached, it's a more intimate chill-out spot than tourist-packed Viana do Castelo (see p.329). Passing the rather drab sprawl of buildings on the town's outskirts, things brighten up in the compact centre, which has some lovely old buildings and squares, including a small **museum** on Rua Barão de Esposende (Tues–Fri 10am–noon & 2–8pm, Sat 3–6pm; free), which contains displays of local ethnography, items from nearby *antas* (megalithic Bronze Age tombs), and ceramics and tools from the 2000-year-old *castro* of São Lourenço, a Bronze Age settlement.

The town's **beach** is 2km to the north, accessed via the lighthouse which protrudes from the late-seventeenth-century Forte de São João Baptista. Much less enticing is the beach at **OFIR**, 6km by road on the south side of the estuary, whose impressive pine-backed dunes have been ruined by three ugly high-rise buildings.

Practicalities

Buses drop you at the Largo do Mercado on the riverfront beside the market. Two hundred metres south along the river is the **turismo** (summer: Mon–Sat 9.30am–12.30pm & 2.30–6pm, Sun 9.30am–12.30pm; winter same hours, closed Sun; ☎253 961 354), which gives out a good map that includes Ofir and Fão, as well as leaflets containing directions to various local *antas* and to the *castro* of São Lourenço. It also publishes an excellent guidebook to the district (the *roteiro*; free), whose amusing English-language version contains gems like the caption under a photo of two women entitled "One pair of Seaweeds". There's a modern **swimming pool** complex on the riverbank by the turismo (daily 10am–10pm; 200$00), with waves in its indoor pool and great views from the outdoor one. **Canoeing** and **rafting** are organized by the Associação de Defesa do Ambiente do Rio Neiva (☎253 872 562): rafting costs 5000$00 including transport. You can get **Internet access** (daily; 500$00 per hour) at Estúdio Internet's two branches: Rua Narciso Ferreira 88 (daily 9am–8pm, open until 1am in summer), and at the municipal swimming pools (daily 2.30–8pm).

ACCOMMODATION

The only really cheap accommodation is the **youth hostel** at Fão, 3km away on the south bank of the Cávado (☎ & fax 253 981 790), which has a kitchen, bar, disabled facilities, bicycles for rent, and can arrange canoeing trips – double rooms (①) are also available. Fão also has a decent **campsite** (open all year; ☎258 981 777). The turismo may be able to help you find rooms in private houses. Note that during the slow season, (September 15–June 14), room rates are often reduced by as much as fifty percent.

Residencial Acrópole, Praça Dom Sebastião, near the turismo (☎253 961 941, fax 253 964 238). The only cheapish option – the very comfortable rooms have TVs and telephones, and excellent breakfasts are included. ②.

Clube Pinhal da Foz, Rua João Ferreira da Silva, 1km north of the turismo (☎253 961 098, fax 253 961 275). Self-catering apartments with TVs, phones and use of a swimming pool. ③.

Estalagem Zende, on the EN13, 1km from the turismo (☎253 964 663, fax 253 965 018). Modern but not in the nicest position, but with a pleasant lounge, a good restaurant specializing in shellfish and a summer disco nonetheless. ④.

Residencial Mira Rio, on the N13, 1km south of the turismo (☎253 964 429). Ten rooms, each with bathroom, satellite TV and telephone, close to the river but a good 3km from the beach. There's a restaurant on site. ③.

Hotel Nélia, Av. Valentim Ribeiro (☎253 965 528, fax 253 964 820). Three blocks behind the turismo, a nondescript but well-facilitated 3-star hotel with AC in its rooms, an indoor swimming pool, gym, squash courts and nightclub. ③.

Hotel Suave Mar, Rua 27 de Maio (☎253 965 445, fax 253 965 249). Large resort hotel that's the closest of any to the beach (though still 1km away). Rooms have AC, satellite TV, balconies, safes and telephones, and there's a huge restaurant, outdoor swimming pool, tennis court and gym on site. ⑤.

EATING AND DRINKING

The main local speciality is *arroz de lampreia* (lamprey cooked with rice, *chouriço*, wine, onion, pepper and cloves). For dessert, try *clarinhas de Fão*, pastries filled with sweet marrow (*chila*) vermicelli. Recommended **restaurants** include *Dom Sebastião*, Rua Conde de Castro 3 near the *Residencial Acrópole*; and *Papa Fino*, also on Rua Conde de Castro. Set in Largo Fonseca Lima, a pleasant square facing the museum, *Adega Regional O Barrote* has outdoor tables and also serves snacks and drinks. Aside from the hotel nightclubs, the main **nightlife** venues are two late-night bars: *Quanto Baste* at Rua da Senhora da Saúde 34, and *Bar Bigosses* (also worth trying during the day), near Clube Pinhal da Foz.

São Bartolomeu do Mar

North of Ofir, you probably won't see another tourist all the way to the little fishing village of **SÃO BARTOLOMEU DO MAR**, on the N13 1km back from one of the best stretches of the Costa Verde. It's just 15km south of Viana do Castelo, but there is still refreshingly little to the place: just a church, shop and café (with a few **rooms** to let), and good unofficial camping amid the pines. As well as fishing, the local economy revolves around gathering **seaweed**. Traditionally, whole families harvest it on the beach using huge shrimping nets, which are then hauled across the sands by beautiful wooden carts pulled by oxen. Although the methods are changing and tractors are supplanting beasts, the seaweed is still stacked at the edge of the village to dry before being spread as fertilizer on the coastal fields.

If you're here on August 24, you'll catch the **romaria** that takes place at the end of the Festas de São Bartolomeu. The festivities draw thousands of people from the area, many of them families with sick children who come in the hope that they will be cured by taking the traditional Banho Santo – a bizarre ritual in which the child circles the church three times with a black cockerel tied to his or her head before being thrown into the ocean three times by an attendant. The **menhir** (standing stone; believed by many archeologists to be a fertility symbol) in the field immediately behind the church (it's hidden by corn in summer) is widely believed to have something to do with the roots of the ritual, as many Portuguese parish churches tended to be built adjacent to pre-Christian ritual sites, or else were constructed on top of them.

Viana do Castelo

VIANA DO CASTELO is the Minho's main resort town, and it's all the more appealing for it. A lively, attractive place, it has a historic old centre, above-average restaurants and, some distance from the town itself, one of the best beaches in the north. It's also beautifully positioned, spread along the north bank of the Lima estuary and shaped by the thick wooded hill of Monte de Santa Luzia, which is strewn with Celtic remains. If this wasn't enough of an incentive to come, Viana's **romaria** at the end of August (see p.331) is the biggest and most exciting festival in the Minho.

The Town

Viana has long been a prosperous seafaring town. It produced some of the greatest colonists of the "discoveries" under Dom Manuel and, in the eighteenth century, was

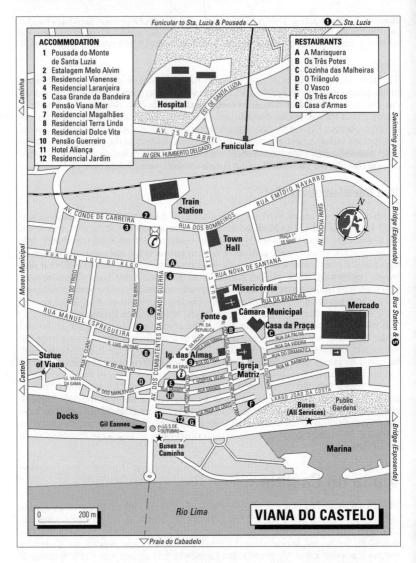

ACCOMMODATION
1 Pousada do Monte de Santa Luzia
2 Estalagem Melo Alvim
3 Residencial Vianense
4 Residencial Laranjeira
5 Casa Grande da Bandeira
6 Pensão Viana Mar
7 Residencial Magalhães
8 Residencial Terra Linda
9 Residencial Dolce Vita
10 Pensão Guerreiro
11 Hotel Aliança
12 Residencial Jardim

RESTAURANTS
A A Marisquera
B Os Três Potes
C Cozinha das Malheiras
D O Triângulo
E O Vasco
F Os Três Arcos
G Casa d'Armas

VIANA DO CASTELO

the first centre for the shipment of port wine to England. Many of the buildings reflect these times – unusually for the north, you'll notice Manueline mouldings around the doors and windows of Viana's mansions.

At the heart of Viana's old town is the distinctive **Praça da República**, a wonderful square enclosed by an elegant ensemble of buildings. You'll see copies of its showpiece Renaissance fountain in towns throughout the Minho, but few structures as curious as the old **Misericórdia** (almshouse) that lines one side of the square. Built in 1589, this is one of the most original and successful buildings of the Portuguese Renaissance, its upper storeys supported by deliberately archaic caryatids. The adjacent sixteenth-century **Câmara Municipal** has been brightly restored, and stands foursquare above a medieval arcade, while just off the square is the **Igreja Matriz**, Viana's parish church, which retains a Gothic door of some interest.

The **Museu Municipal** (Tues–Sun 9am–noon & 2–5pm; 155$00) adds further to these impressions of Viana's sixteenth- to nineteenth-century opulence; it is contained within an eighteenth-century palace and houses a notable collection of ceramics and furniture, as well as more modern temporary exhibitions. It stands near the end of Rua Manuel Espregueira, ten minutes' walk from the square, on the far side of the main Avenida Combatentes da Grande Guerra.

If you continue past the museum, you'll eventually reach the old **Castelo** by the sea, in an area known as Campo do Castelo. Outside the walls, on Fridays, Viana's **market** takes place; it's much smaller than the famous one at Barcelos but attracts many of the same stallholders.

Monte de Santa Luzia

Wherever you stand in Viana, the modern basilica atop **Monte de Santa Luzia** makes its presence felt. It's a great walk up, through the pines and eucalyptus trees (take the short cut over the railway tracks), or you can be hauled to the top by an old **funicular** (April–Sept daily; rest of year weekends, public holidays and third Friday of the month only; hourly 9am–noon, then half-hourly to 7pm; 100$00). This starts its run from just behind the train station: to reach it, walk through the station and cross the tracks. En route, there are tremendous views down the coast and along the River Lima.

At the summit, there's a café and plenty of wooded walks. While the **basilica** itself is of little interest, look for the side entrance (marked Zimbório; 70$00 entrance), where a narrow winding staircase climbs right through the building, past traffic lights laid on during the summer to keep the tourist hordes in check, and out on top of the dome itself. It's very narrow, very steep and – at the top – very scary if the wind has picked up, but the views are magnificent.

Behind the basilica, amid the woods and just below the luxury *Pousada do Monte de Santa Luzia*, lie the ruins of a Celto-Iberian **citânia** (Tues–Sun 9am–noon & 2–5pm; free), which include the foundations of dozens of small, circular stone huts, a thick village wall and partly paved streets. Occupied from around 500 BC, the settlement was only abandoned with the Roman pacification of the north under Emperor Augustus (c.26 BC).

THE VIANA ROMARIA

Viana's main *romaria*, dedicated to **Nossa Senhora da Agonía** – Our Lady of Sorrows – takes place for three days around the weekend nearest to August 20. A combination of carnival and fair, and fulfilling an important business function for the local communities, it's a great time to be in town.

Events kick off with an impressive **religious parade** on the Friday. But the best day is probably **Saturday**, when there's a massive parade of floats with every village in the region providing an example of a local craft or pursuit: a marvellous display of incongruities, with threshers pounding away in traditional dress while being pulled by a new Lamborghini tractor. If you want a seat in the stands, get a ticket well in advance.

On each of the three days there are lunchtime **processions** with *gigantones* (carnival giants), folk-dancing, remarkably loud drum bands, pipe bands and, needless to say, concerted drinking. The blessing of the fishing boats on Monday morning is quite moving – women in the fishing quarter decorate their streets with pictures in coloured sawdust on religious and quotidian themes. And there are nightly **firework displays** too, of immense brilliance and noise.

Praia do Cabedelo

Viana's town beach, **Praia do Cabedelo**, lies across the river, reached by a **ferry**, which leaves from the harbourside at the southern end of the main avenue (daily 8.45am–8pm, plus later crossings from mid-July to late August; every 30min–1hr; 200$00 return); it's a five-minute crossing. Road access from town to beach is over the bridge, east of the centre, a route served by frequent buses (May to mid-Sept).

Given sun, the beach is more or less perfect – a low, curving bay with good (but not wild) breakers and a real horizon-stretching expanse of sand. Praia do Cabedelo is idea for watersports – several companies rent out equipment (see Listings, p.335). In August, local authorities make the beach accessible to people with disabilities, laying on thick-wheeled buggies for the journey from sand to sea, amongst other things. There's a bar, *Aquario*, at the windsurf school, and a couple of others close to where the ferry docks, but beyond here there is nowhere to buy food or drink, so take a picnic. From Viana, the beach extends northwards, virtually unbroken, to the Spanish border at Caminha, and south to Póvoa de Varzim. For the energetic, either of these routes makes a memorable and enjoyable hike, and for details of the northern route, see p.335.

Practicalities

The **bus station** is at the top end of Rua da Bandeira, twenty minutes' walk northeast of the centre. Outside *festa* time, you might find it easier to catch services from more central bus stops along Avenida Combatentes da Grande Guerra, at the southern end of Largo 5 de Outubro, or further east by the marina. **Buses to Spain** head up the coast to Vigo in Galicia, and leave Monday–Saturday at noon and 5.30pm.The **train station** is at the north end of the main Avenida Combatentes da Grande Guerra, which runs right through the town and down to the river at Largo 5 de Outubro. There's a seasonal **turismo** stand at the station (June 20–Aug 20 Mon–Sat 9am–6pm, Sun 9.30am–12.30pm), but the main office is in the centre on Rua do Hospital Velho, off Praça da Erva(Mon–Sat 9am–12.30pm & 2.30–6pm, Sun 9.30am–12.30pm; ☎258 824 971 or 258 822 660): walk down the avenue and look for the sign pointing to the left. The building dates from 1468 and was first used by pilgrims travelling to Santiago de Compostela in Spain; later it became a hospital. Staff at the main office will hand out a good map-booklet and a pamphlet detailing **walks** between watermills in the Serra da Arga. There's also a **regional tourism office** in the Castelo (☎258 820 270, fax 258 829 798, *rtam@mail.telepac.pt*).

Accommodation

Pensões – mostly ranged down and off the main avenue – are easy enough to find, although in summer, and particularly during the *romaria*, private **rooms** offer the best deals; chances are you'll be offered rooms on arriving in Viana – otherwise, look for signs in the windows of houses, or try the turismo who have a limited list of *moradias turísticas*. During the actual festival, you can expect to pay between 5000$00 and 8000$00 for a private room, though they're more like 3000$00 for the rest of the year. Note that street-front rooms can be loud in summer, especially at weekends, thanks to mainly Viana's substantial motorbiking community. You might also ask the turismo about accommodation at **farms** and **manor houses** in the surrounding villages, an ideal way to get to know the countryside, provided you have transport; a couple are listed below. It might also be worth enquiring about what promises to be an excellent **youth hostel**, built into the *Gil Eannes*, Portugal's first hospital ship, currently moored in the dock off Largo 5 de Outubro.

The town's **campsite** (☎258 322 167, fax 258 321 946; closed Dec 1–Jan 15), run by Orbitur, is overcrowded in summer (there's a minimum stay of one week in July and August, and two days at other times) and overpriced for what you get (the facilities are no better than at other Orbitur sites). However, it does at least have the advantage of an attractive, pine-shaded location on the Praia do Cabedelo, and also has also some six-bed bungalows for rent (②). The summer bus (May to mid-Sept) to the beach passes the site, or you can take the ferry across the river and walk from there. The *INATEL* campsite is for members only.

Hotel Aliança, Av. Combatentes da Grande Guerra (☎258 829 498, fax 258 825 299). Eighteenth-century building that hasn't entirely lost its period charm. ③.

Casa Grande da Bandeira, Largo das Carmelitas 488, Rua da Bendeira (☎258 823 169). This charming seventeenth-century Solares de Portugal house near the bus station has a small garden and only three rooms – book ahead. ③.

Residencial Dolce Vita, Rua do Poço 44, opposite the turismo (☎258 824 860). Excellent value, spacious rooms, with shared bathroom, above a good pizza restaurant; breakfast is included. ②.

Pensão Guerreiro, Rua Grande 14–1º (☎258 822 099, fax 258 820 402). Down-at-heel place at the bottom of the main avenue. All rooms have shared bathrooms, but it's friendly, and the restaurant (see below) is good. ①.

Residencial Jardim, Largo 5 de Outubro 68 (☎258 828 915, fax 258 828 917). Overlooking the river, at the bottom of town, this has spotless, well-furnished rooms with bath and TV. Rooms with a balcony have good views but can be noisy in summer; excellent value, especially considering the huge breakfasts. ③.

Residencial Laranjeira, Rua General Luís do Rego 45 (☎258 822 261, fax 258 821 902). A reasonable choice, just off the main avenue, with small, but pleasant rooms, all with bath. Friendly, fresh and comfortable, and with breakfast included in the price. ③.

Residencial Magalhães, Rua Manuel Espregueira 62 (☎258 823 293). Twin and triple rooms, with or without bath, furnished in the best Minho tradition, with dark, carved headboards on the beds. Avoid the rooms at the back which can be noisy. ②.

Estalagem Melo Alvim, Av. Conde da Carreira 28 (☎258 808 200, fax 258 808 220). Sixteenth-century *solar* superbly renovated in modern minimalist style. Excellent service and a good restaurant too. ④.

Pousada do Monte de Santa Luzia, Monte de Santa Luzia (☎258 828 889, fax 258 828 892). Showpiece *pousada* at the top of the hill just behind the basilica, refurbished in Art Deco style. It's the priciest place in town, and the best equipped, though the restaurant is disappointing and it lacks the uncluttered style of *Melo Alvim*. ⑥.

Quinta do Paço d'Anha, Vila Nova de Anha (☎258 322 459, fax 258 323 904). A Solares de Portugal property 3km south of town on the N3 road to Esposende. The house is on an estate that produces and bottles its own wine; there are four apartments with kitchenette. ⑤.

Residencial Terra Linda, Rua Luís Jácome 11–15 (☎258 828 981). Average and adequate, but tries hard to please. Rooms without bath are cheaper. ②.

Pensão Viana Mar, Av. Combatentes da Grande Guerra 215 (☎ & fax 258 828 962). Another reasonably good place, with warm rooms in winter, and a sunken bar. More expensive rooms have baths; the summer overflow of guests is accommodated in two nearby annexes. ①–②.

Residencial Vianense, Av. Conde da Carreira 79 (☎258 823 118). Clean and close to the train station, with a somewhat surly reception and a restaurant that's best avoided. ②.

Eating

There's a wide choice of places to eat in town, as you might expect from a busy resort. Some are lunchtime workers' cafés, while there's also a full range of tourist **restaurants**, many of which serve extremely good food since they cater mostly for demanding Portuguese visitors rather than foreigners, but the service can be surprisingly slow and indifferent. There are a number of cheap **cafés** and restaurants with outdoor tables in Rua Prior do Crato, one road back from the river. Several of the *pensões* also incorporate restaurants, open to non-residents; a couple of them are definitely worth considering. For general provisions, there is a permanent **market** at the eastern end of town, on Rua Martim Velho.

Casa d'Armas, Largo 5 de Outubro 30. A quality restaurant in a lovely building, but high prices.

Cozinha das Malheiras, Rua Gago Coutinho 19 (☎258 823 680). Top-quality food and service, and not that expensive – main courses are 1500–2000$00. Try roasted wrasse, kid goat, *arroz de marisco* or *papas de sarrabulho* with fried pork (*rojões*). Closed Tues.

Dolce Vita, Rua do Poço 44. Consistently excellent pizzas and a good pasta and wine, too. Opens 7.30pm, and there are queues by 8pm.

Pensão Guerreiro, Rua Grande 14. This deceives with its unsubtle pictorial tourist menu; the food is actually very good and fairly inexpensive, and features a bumper serving of *porco à alentejana*. The goat in red wine is good too, as is the squid. Closed Thurs.

A Marisqueira, Rua General Luís do Rego 36. Carefully cooked, generous dishes – but service can be shoddy.

Neiva Mar, Largo Infante D. Henriques 1. Great for seafood, off the road on the seafront near the castle.

Os Três Arcos, Largo João Tomás da Costa 25. Facing the Jardim Marginal, this is perhaps the best restaurant in town, with excellent food, a full list of *vinhos verdes*, and a bar where you can eat much more cheaply from the same menu – it's mostly seafood, but the turkey is good. If you want a table, call in earlier to book. Closed Mon.

Os Três Potes, Beco dos Fornos 7 (☎258 829 928). Incredibly popular in high season, with national costumes and music at weekends. Good traditional food, but relatively pricey, with full meals running to at least 3000$00. Again, book ahead in summer. Closed Mon.

O Triângulo, Rua dos Manjovos 14. Quiet, pleasant seafood and snack joint.

O Vasco, Rua Grande. Simple, tasty Portuguese dishes at reasonable prices. Closed Sun.

Viana's Restaurante, Rua Frei Bartolomeu dos Mártires 179, off Av. Campo do Castelo. The place to pursue an interest in *bacalhau* dishes – simply superb.

Drinking, nightlife and entertainment

Romaria time aside, there's not an awful lot going on after dark in Viana. But a couple of **cafés** at the bottom of the main avenue are good places for a beer or late-night coffee, and if you're feeling energetic, there are a couple of clubs worth checking out.

For **cultural** events, consult the *Agenda Cultural*, a monthly diary issued by the Câmara Municipal; the turismo should have a copy, and can also provide information on regional events. There is one **cinema** in Viana, the Verde Viana (Praça 1º de Maio); and check the output of the Teatro do Noroeste **theatre company**, based at the Teatro Municipal Sá de Miranda, on Rua Major Xavier da Costa (☎258 822 644).

Pastelaria Brasileira, Rua Sacadura Cabral. Nearly 100 years old, this café-cum-pastry shop is good for a stand-up coffee.

Girassol Café, Jardim Marginal. A lovely spot for a *bica*; though it closes at 7pm.

Glamour, Rua da Bandeira 177–183. Very stylish and trendy bar-cum-nightclub with fittingly fashionable soul, blues and salsa.

Pastelaria Paris, Av. Combatentes da Grande Guerra. Great cakes, a pool room and decent toilets for a change!

Disco-Pub-Clube-Viana Sol, Rua dos Manjovos, off Largo Vasco da Gama by *Hotel Viana Sol*. A very youthful crowd packs into this place in summer. Open from the afternoon until 3am; 4am on Saturday nights.

Listings

Banks Main banks are on Praça da República and along the main avenue.

Boat trips Departures from the pier at the bottom of the avenue for trips up the Rio Lima; prices are negotiable but expect to pay around 3000$00 per person.

Books and newspapers English-language books are available at Livraria Bertrand, Rua Sacadura Cabral, and international newspapers are sold in the newsagents on the corner of Praça da República.

Car rental Avis, Rua do Gontim (☎258 823 598); Hertz, Av. Conde da Carreira (☎258/82 22 50).

Hospital Av. 25 de Abril (☎258 829 081).

Pharmacy Nelsina, Praça da República; Central, Rua Manuel Espregueira. The turismo has details of late-night openings.

Police Headquarters at Rua de Aveiro (☎258 822 022).

Post office Opposite the train station on Av. dos Combatentes da Grande Guerra; you can make phone calls from the Portugal Telecom office next door.

Sports Several companies rent **surfing gear** at around 5000$00/day with wetsuit; of these, try the Associação de Windsurf do Norte, which sets up a stand at Praia do Cabedelo on weekends; Omni Surf Shop, Rua do Poço 38–42 (☎258 820 024), which also rents mountain bikes; and the Surf Club de Viana, Centro Comercial 1º Maio, Praça 1º de Maio (☎966 221 092 (mobile)), which also offers individual lessons for 2000$00 per hour. **Sailing and canoeing** can be arranged through Amigos do Mar (Associação Cívica Internacional para a Defesa do Mar), Apartado 533, 4900 Viana do Castelo (3000$00 membership (bring two passport photos) entitles you to free activities – ring two days before to book; ☎258 827 427), and Clube Naútico de Viana, Lugar de Argaçosa, Meadela (☎258 842 165 or 258 827 652). **Biking trips** are run by Puraventura, Rua da Pedela, Vila Nova de Anha (☎253 251 287).

Swimming pool The municipal pool is at Av. Capitão Gaspar de Castro, 700m along the eastern continuation of Rua Emídio Navarro.

Taxis Available from ranks along Av. Combatentes da Grande Guerra.

Viana to Moledo

North of Viana the train line follows the coast all the way to Caminha. Two trains a day, in both directions, stop at all the villages en route – notably at Carreço, Afife, Gelfa, Vila Praia de Âncora and Moledo do Minho – offering easy access to a sequence of largely deserted beaches. Buses cover the same route with fourteen services daily (Mon–Fri) and five daily at weekends. It is possible to **walk** the same route, covering the whole stretch in a couple of days, camping overnight among the sheltered dunes at Afife, 10km north of Viana.

Carreço, Afife and Gelfa

The small village of **CARREÇO** lies a couple of kilometres east of its beach, where there's a café-bar, toilets and showers. **AFIFE**, another 2km further north, is also a good goal with a fort, several cafés and a casino. The modern *Residencial Compostela* (☎258 981 590, fax 258 981 244; ②) is on the main road just north of the turning to the beach; it also has a restaurant, although the two on the beach are preferable. If you're looking for a more dramatic place to stay, *Casa do Penedo* (☎258 981 474; ③) is a typical Minho home, an attractive stone property with a garden, 1km south of the station, up a hillside with sea views. The dunes – and a particularly wonderful expanse of beach – are fifteen to twenty minutes' walk from the village, the least frequented parts being to the south.

At **GELFA**, between Afife and Vila Praia de Âncora, there's a **campsite** in the pine woods (☎258 911 537; mid-March to mid-Oct daily; rest of year weekends only), but it's on the inland side of the train station and hence some distance from the beach.

Vila Praia de Âncora

Six kilometres up the coast from Afife, the next major stop on the train line is **VILA PRAIA DE ÂNCORA**, a large resort that's popular with locals at weekends and in summer. The beach, which is right alongside the train line, is again superb, sheltered by hills and drifting back into a beautiful river estuary, where you can swim enjoyably even when the Atlantic breezes are blowing towels around the sands. For good measure there are two **forts** guarding the bay: the Fortim de Cão, south of the estuary, and the better-preserved Forte de Lagarteira, recently restored, to the north by the little fishing harbour.

The **train station** for Vila Praia is called Âncora-Praia, and is the only station between Viana do Castelo and Caminha at which express trains stop. Just down the road on Largo da Estação, the well-signposted **bus station** also houses the **turismo** (Mon–Sat 9.30am–12.30pm & 2–6pm; ☎258 911 384), from where you can get leaflets detailing a 5km walking circuit to the **Cividade de Âncora**, the ruins of a first-century AD Bronze and Copper Age settlement; the walk starts from the main square of Santa Maria de Âncora, 2km inland. Finding **accommodation** for a few days here shouldn't be hard. The turismo has a list of **private rooms** (①–②), while other choices include the popular, mid-range *Hotel Meira*, at Rua 5 de Outubro 56 (☎258 911 111, fax 258 911 489, *hotel.meira@mail.telepac.pt*; ④) and the more reasonably priced *Albergaria Quim Barreiros*, on the seafront behind the train station Avenida Dr. Ramos Pereira (☎258 959 100, fax 258 959 109; ③). Apart from **camping** unofficially by the Fortim de Cão, there's the *Parque de Campismo do Paço* (☎258 912 697; reception open 8am–12.30pm & 2–10pm; closed Oct 15–March 15), 1.5km from town on the south bank of the Rio Âncora, which also has canoes and rafting.

Restaurants are plentiful, as is fresh fish. *Restaurante Fonte Nova*, along Rua Miguel Bombarda from the church, and the *Restaurante Central*, opposite the train station, are both good, serving meals for around 2000$00; while *Restaurante Mar Gelfa* (open July–Sept), twenty minutes' walk south down the beach, is recommended for both food (try the lamprey) and sunsets.

Moledo do Minho

North of Vila Praia de Âncora, **MOLEDO DO MINHO** is the train traveller's last chance to swim in the sea. Very much in the same mould as Vila Praia, it too has a fort – this time half-ruined, guarding the river from a long, sandy spit – and is predominantly a Portuguese family resort, with a reputation for attracting the nouveaux riches. If you're heading for Caminha, Valença, or even Spain, you could easily stop off here, wander down to the beach, and catch the next train. If you want **to stay**, the *Pensão Ideal*, Rua Eng. Sousa Rego 125 (☎258 721 505, fax 258 721 518; ②), might tempt you with its convenient location next to the train station and its well-equipped rooms; alternatively, the seafront **turismo** (Mon–Fri 9.30am–12.30pm & 2.30–6pm) might be able to help you find a room. You can **eat** at the good *Restaurante O Lagar* on the seafront, where you'll also find a number of bars serving snacks.

ALONG THE RIO MINHO

At Moledo, the train line finally leaves the coast to follow the south bank of the **Rio Minho**, which meanders northeastwards forming the country's border with Spain. **Caminha** is the first river town, a pleasant stopover, either for a night or for a meal between trains. Beyond here, several small fortified towns guard the Portuguese side of the river, with the Minho train line coming to a halt in perhaps the best of the lot, **Valença do Minho**. This is also the site of a splendid weekly market and a major crossing-point into Spain. However, the best section of the river route is from Valença east to **Monção** and **Melgaço**, which you can reach only by bus. Both towns are also minor border crossings, with buses onwards from the Spanish side.

Caminha

At the mouth of the Rio Minho, and straddling the Rio Coura, **CAMINHA** is a quiet river port with a few reminders of better days. These are principally in the main square, Praça Conselheiro Silva Torres (known locally as Largo Terreiro), which sports a battlemented town hall, a Renaissance clock tower and a large fountain. Caminha's most distinguished building, though, is the **Igreja Matriz**, a couple of minutes' walk from the main square towards the river; take the street through the arch by the clock tower, past the **turismo** (Mon–Sat 9.30am–12.30pm & 2.30–6pm; ☎258 921 952), which gives out good town maps. The church was built towards the end of the fifteenth century, when the town was reputed to rival Porto in trade, and it still stands within part of the old city walls. Try and find someone with a key, for it has a magnificent inlaid ceiling – a rare burst of Moorish inspiration in the north. Note also the figures carved on the two Renaissance doorways, one on the north side giving the finger to Spain across the river!

A couple of kilometres south of town, the island of **Fortaleza da Ínsua** makes an enjoyable trip – local fishermen run trips across on Sundays from the spit of sand at Foz do Minho, on the river side of its fine beach. If you want to arrange something during the week (for the next morning), ask in the *Café Valadares* for directions to António Garrafão's house. He will go only if there is a reasonably large – or affluent – group gathered. For **watersports**, contact Afluente Desporto e Natureza, Lugar da Sentinela, 5km east at Lanhelas (☎258 727 017), which offers boat trips, "canoe safaris" (daily at 10am & 3pm), mountain biking, rafting, sailing, and surfing – each activity costs 5000$00.

Practicalities

The town's best **accommodation** is in the new *Hotel Porta do Sol* (☎258 722 340, fax 258 722 347; ④), on Avenida Marginal at the southern entrance to town – a four-star resort with pools and tennis courts. Otherwise, there are a handful of **pensões** in the centre of town: the *Residencial Arca Nova* (☎258 721 590, fax 258 721 591; ③), near the train station in Largo Sidónio Pais but a little overpriced for what it offers; the older and better-value *Pensão Rio Coura* (☎258 921 142; ②), in Avenida Saraiva de Carvalho; and the friendly *Residencial Galo d'Ouro*, Rua da Corredoura 15 (☎258 921 160; ②), just off the main square. Alternatives include a few **private rooms** in houses (ask at the turismo or the *Pêro de Caminha* restaurant; see below), and the *Casa do Esteiró* (☎258 921 356; ③), a small Solares de Portugal property at the entrance to town which has two rooms to rent in lovely gardens.

There are two **campsites** nearby. The better of them is a little inland at *Vilar de Mouros* (☎258 721 595, fax 258 721 214, *pnvm.anta@cartaopostal.com*), which is nicely positioned by a small river gorge, and has a swimming pool, tennis court and some bungalows for rent (②–③); there are two buses daily (Mon–Fri) to the site from outside the café, 200m left out of the train station. The other, which tends to be crowded in summer, is an Orbitur site (☎258 921 295, fax 258 921 473; closed Dec 1–Jan 15), 2km to the south of town between the river and the sea, opposite the Fortaleza da Ínsua; three daily buses (Mon–Fri) from the town hall stop close by.

Several of the best **cafés** and **restaurants** are found in the main square: the *Sporting Clube O Caminhense* has superb regional specialities; the cheerful *Pêro de Caminha* serves pizzas amongst other things; and the *Confeitaria Colmeia* is the place for breakfast. There's good, if more expensive food, too, at the *Adega do Chico* on Rua Visconde de Sousa Rego 30 (head up the right-hand side of the main square, away from the clock tower).

The town has a **ferry** link to La Guardia in Spain, which leaves from beside the bridge over the Rio Coura. There are services daily throughout summer (hourly 8am–7pm; 120$00; cars are free) but winter times are variable.

Vila Nova de Cerveira

Up to seven daily trains run along the banks of the Rio Minho to **VILA NOVA DE CERVEIRA**, 11km to the northeast of Caminha. This small walled town has a car- and passenger-ferry – actually little more than a floating platform – which drifts every half-hour across the river to Goyan in Galicia. The **ferry** (summer 8.30am–8.55pm; winter

8.30am–7.25pm; passengers 60$00, cars 280$00) has turned the village into something of a shopping centre for Spaniards, but it remains a pleasant and accessible place and in many respects is more enticing than the bigger and better known Valença further upstream. The town is also home to an art school, hence the surprising prevalence of modern works around town.

The **Solar dos Castros** on Praça da Liberdade was once a manor house and now serves as a cultural centre. At the back, facing a beautifully well-kept garden, is the **turismo** (Mon–Sat 9.30am–12.30pm & 2.30–6pm; ☎251 795 787), while alongside, in a small garden, is a striking sculpture of a tripod holding aloft a rock. This has become the symbol of the **arts festival** held here every two years in August/September; the remarkable statue depicting men talking, which won first prize in 1984, is displayed just inside the front door of the Solar dos Castros.

Practicalities

If you want to stay, you'll find accommodation available in all price ranges. For budget travellers, the pleasant **youth hostel** at Largo 16 de Fevereiro 21 (☎ & fax 251 796 113) boasts its own kitchen and a terrace, and also has double rooms with private or shared bathroom (①). If you have money to burn, you can do no better than the excellent *Pousada de Dom Dinis* (☎251 795 601, fax 251 795 604; ⑦), built within the sixteenth-century fortress walls overlooking the ramparts. Although not a historic building itself, this would provide a memorable first or last night in Portugal; not surprisingly, it also has the best restaurant in town. In between these two extremes, standard accommodation is on offer at the *Residencial Rainha Santa Isabel*, Rua Herois do Ultramar (☎ & fax 251 796 227; ③), some of whose rooms have fine river views. For **food**, the *Café Restaurant Central*, on Largo 16 de Fevereiro, is one of several good places to eat, while *Barril Bar*, off the main square, is where much of the evening action takes place.

Valença do Minho and around

The border town of **VALENÇA DO MINHO** (usually just referred to as Valença) has become a bustling modern town, surrounding its absurdly quaint old town area clumped amid perfectly preserved, multi-layered seventeenth-century ramparts on a hillock above the river. There are great walks here, both down by the river and along the **ramparts** (watch out for hidden stairwells), the design of which was influenced by the work of the seventeenth-century French military architect, Vauban.

On foot, you're likely to approach the old town from the Largo da Esplanada round-about at the bottom of the hill, where Rua das Antas – which runs from the train station – enters the new part of town. Climb the hill straight ahead, turn right at the top, and you enter through the **Portas da Coroada**, further along from which a causeway leads over a dry moat to the **Portas do Meio**, the bastion's middle gates. An alternative approach is to turn right at the Largo da Esplanada, and left just before the turismo. Throughout the area around Largo de São João, you'll notice a rich diversity of buildings lining the narrow, cobbled streets, with sudden views of the surrounding countryside appearing over the lower reaches of the walls. During the day, these charms are exploited by a myriad souvenir shops, catering for the day-trippers who cross the border from Spain to pick up Portuguese linen, ceramics and electrical goods. Increasingly, the extent of this commercialism is reducing the appeal of the town – Tuy, across the river in Spain, is probably nicer. By late afternoon, though, the crowds are gone and at night the old part of Valença is almost a ghost town. Apart from the old town itself, the only visitable attraction here is the **Museu do Bombeiro**, Largo 7 de Julho, in the old town near the Praça da República (Tues–Fri 10am–12,30pm & 2–6pm; Sat & Sun 2–6pm; 200$00), which is full of old firefighting equipment and regalia.

The newer part of town, to the south of the ramparts, has nothing of interest but it's here that you'll track down all the basic necessities. Come on Wednesday and you'll encounter the huge weekly **market**, held on the wooded slopes below the walls. Apart from the rows of tourist shops in the old town, the best place for **shopping** is Garrafeira Vasco da Gama on Largo da Esplanada in the new town, to stock up on wines, cheeses, port or chocolate.

Practicalities

Now that European cross-border controls have been removed, arriving in Valença **from Tuy in Spain**, over the river, is a simple matter of staying on the train for another few minutes as it rattles over the bridge (there are three daily trains to and from Vigo to Valença), or simply walking over from Tuy. Domestic **trains** from Porto via Viana do Castelo end their run in Valença; to head further east or south you'll have to take a local **bus**, which arrives at and departs from in front of the train station. There are no obvious signs to the old town; turn right at the avenue that leads away from the station, then head uphill after the crossroads. You'll see the **turismo** (Mon–Sat 9.30am–12.30pm & 2.30–6pm (closes 5.30pm in winter), Sun 9.30am–12.30pm; ☎251 823 374) in a wooden building opposite a small park town; the free town map is helpful, and you can also buy an information pack (500$00) detailing Romanesque churches and monuments along the Rio Minho. A slightly more exciting way of seeing the region is via Minho Infernal (Lugar da Pedreira 6, Ganfei; ☎966 501 329 (mobile), fax 251 824 771), the town's main adventure sports operator, offering rafting, canyoning, biking, four-wheel-drive trips and even paint-balling.

Accommodation
Private rooms are available in the old town – ask at the restaurants. Otherwise try the following:

Casa do Poço, Trav. da Gaviarra 4 (☎251 825 235, fax 251 825 469). This former doctor's home has been converted into a luxurious Privetur property and is worth every escudo. It's in the old, walled town next to the *pousada*, which it equals for views and surpasses in atmosphere and furnishings. There are only five rooms so it's advisable to book ahead. ⑥.

Hotel Residencial Lara, Rua de São Sebastião, 300m uphill from Largo da Esplanada (☎251 824 348, fax 251 824 358). A smart, efficient place in the new town, facing the walls. All rooms have a balcony and TV. ③.

Hotel Valença do Minho, Av. Miguel Dantas, 500m from the train station (☎251 824 211, fax 251 824 321). Large and impersonal hotel with a restaurant and swimming pool, and TVs and telephones in its rooms. ③.

Residencial Ponte Seca, Av. Dr. Tito Fontes (☎251 822 580). To the east on the edge of the new town, this is spotless and good value, if awkwardly placed. Back rooms overlook fields with the mountains beyond. ③.

Residencial Rio Minho, Largo da Estação (☎251 809 240, fax 251 809 248). Opposite the train station, this is probably the cheapest option in town. with simple, airy, newly renovated rooms and a pleasant restaurant; breakfast is included. ②.

Pousada de São Teotónio (☎251 824 242, fax 251 824 397). Located inside the fortress itself, though much of the building is modern. Even if this is out of your price range, a drink in the bar – or lunch in the excellent restaurant (around 3000–4000$00 a head) – is money well spent. ⑥.

Residencial Val-Flores, Rua de São Sebastião, 200m uphill from Largo da Esplanada (☎251 824 106, fax 251 824 129). A friendly, modern high-rise with spotless rooms; all have baths and satellite TVs. ③.

Eating
You should be able to eat well in any of the old town's restaurants, where competition keeps prices down, though in summer, sharing the experience with the tourists hordes can make it anything but peaceful. **Specialities** include *lampreia* (lamprey), *cabrito à*

Sanfins (a goat dish prepared at Easter time), *sável frito* (fried shad), and *enguias à moda da Raposeira* (eels).

Restaurante Baluarte, Rua São José. Reasonably priced meals in the old town, with a fine range of *bacalhau* dishes.

Fortaleza, Rua Apolinário da Fonseca 5. Just outside the Portas do Meio, this is not as pricey as it looks. It specializes in goat, among other things, which you can enjoy at its outdoor tables.

A Gruta, just inside the Portas do Meio. Has an outside bar and an indoor restaurant under the vaults, where you can see your food being cooked.

Mané, Edifício São Sebastião, Av. Miguel Dantas, by Largo da Esplanada (☎251 823 402). Very good reputation but expensive. Try its *arroz de lampreia* (lamprey with rice).

Monumental, built into the walls, just inside the Portas da Coroada. Serves a wonderful, spicy *arroz de marisco* and is reasonably priced.

Crossing to Spain: Tuy

Just a mile from Valença, across an iron bridge designed by A.G. Eiffel, Spanish **TUY** is an ancient, pyramid-shaped town with a grand battlemented parish church. It, too, is partly walled and it looks far sturdier than Valença, though the first English guidebook to Portugal (*Murray's* in 1855) reported that "the guns of Valença could without difficulty lay Tuy in ruins". If you're not planning to go on to Spain, at least walk across the frontier bridge to explore Tuy's old quarter by the river. There's no passport control: walking from the centre of one old town to the other takes around thirty minutes. By **road** and **train** you can go direct from Valença to Vigo, which is within easy reach of Santiago de Compostela, the ancient and beautiful pilgrimage town of Galicia.

Inland: Paredes de Coura

PAREDES DE COURA, 28km south of Valença, claims to be the oldest village in Portugal, an assertion that's rendered a little hard to believe by the new emigrant-financed houses surrounding what's really quite a sizeable town. Still, if you're headed for Ponte da Barca or Ponte de Lima, it warrants a detour. You can climb up to the top of the town for views over an almost Swiss landscape, with chalet-style houses and white church spires, or follow the track down beyond the football field to the river for the town's best swimming spot. Every year, over the first weekend in August, there's a **festival** – the *Festas do Conselho* – featuring the usual Minho mix of dance, costumed procession and music.

On Mondays to Fridays, there is one daily **bus** to the town from Valença, one from Monção, and two to five daily from Ponte de Lima. The best **place to stay** is the *Pensão Miquelina*, Rua Miguel Dantas (☎251 782 103; ②). The **turismo** (Mon–Sat 9.30am–12.30pm & 2.30–6pm; ☎251 782 105) is housed in an old prison in Largo Visconde Mouzelos.

Monção and around

MONÇÃO, 16km east of Valença, preserves yet another **border fortress**, though it doesn't quite make the grade – there being little more than a doorway, a section of walling above the bus station and a high defensive walkway that runs along the northern, river-facing, side of town. Perhaps for this reason, Monção has escaped much of the daytime tourist attention that bedevils the towns to the west; the liveliest day to visit is Thursday, market day. But there's an attractive old centre, which always rewards a stroll as well as an old riverside spa bath popular with elderly holidaymakers – the town's history, in which two local women played a prominent part, provides a colourful backdrop to the surviving fortifications and buildings.

The principal figure in the town's history is **Deu-la-Deu Martins** (the name means "God gave her"), who is commemorated by a statue and fountain in Largo da Loreto. Her tale, similar to a number of other accounts across Portugal and Spain, recalls a crucial moment in the fourteenth century, when the Spanish troops had besieged the townspeople to the point of starvation. Deu-la-Deu baked some cakes, using much skill and next to no flour, and had them presented to the Spanish camp with an offer to "make more if they needed them". The psychological effect of this bluff was so great that the enemy promptly gave up and went away. Local *pãozinhos* (little bread cakes) are still baked in her honour; her birthplace is off the praça, above the butcher's shop on the arched side road.

A second Spanish siege, in the seventeenth-century Wars of Restoration, was relieved in 1659 when the **Countess of Castelo Melhor**, perhaps inspired by earlier example, resorted to psychological warfare once again. The story goes that, having negotiated a ceasefire on condition that full military honours be given to her men, the Countess relinquished her 236 surviving fighters to the Spanish army. Knowing nothing of the town's two thousand fatalities, the enemy assumed they had been kept at bay by this paltry platoon and duly retreated in shame.

In the town, there are a couple of interesting older places that reward a visit. The seventeenth-century **Igreja da Misericórdia** on Praça Deu-la-Deu contains some magnificent *azulejos*, as does the Romanesque **Igreja da Matriz** – at the centre of a maze of ancient streets – which houses various tombs, including that of Deu-la-Deu herself. The local **festivals** of Corpo de Deus (Corpus Christi; June 18) and Nossa Senhora das Dores (Sept 19–22) are interesting times to visit if you can manage it (though you are unlikely to be able to find any accommodation then). In the former, the procession is followed by a hilarious mock battle between an unconvincing St George and an elaborately painted wooden dragon manoeuvred by several locals.

Practicalities

The local **bus station**, for services to Melgaço, Valença and Viana do Castelo, is beside Monção's defunct train station, with the town centre straight ahead along Rua General Pimenta de Castro. AVIC (for Parades de Coura) are at Praça da República; Turilis (Mon–Fri, 3 daily), for services to Porto along the Rio Minho, are off Largo do Loreto at Rua da Independência 8; and Auto Viação do Minho services to destinations within Minho and to Porto depart from their office on the Arcos road by the Galp petrol station. There's a **turismo** (Mon–Sat: summer 9am–12.30pm & 2–7pm, winter 9.30am–12.30pm & 2–6pm; ☎251 652 757) in Praça Deu-la-Deu, further on from Praça da República. For travellers to Spain, there's a **road bridge** across to Salvaterra in Spain.

Accommodation

The turismo has details of reasonably priced **private rooms** to rent, including those above *Café-Restaurante Central* in Praça Deu-la-Deu (☎251 652 491; ②), and *Casa Constantino*, Rua da Independência 24 (☎251 653 624: ①), where a couple of the rooms overlook the river. The nearest **camping** is at the free riverside *Caldas de Monção* campsite (☎251 652 434), next to the spa, but facilities are somewhat basic: there's a pit latrine but no showers, no electricity and nowhere to eat or drink.

Albergaria Atlântico and Residencial Mané, Rua General Pimenta de Castro 15 (☎251 652 355 or 251 652 490, fax 251 652 376). The town's upmarket (if rather bland) modern choice, split into two separate hotels. Rooms in both have TVs, telephones and minibars. The *Atlântico* is more expensive on account of its air-conditioning, whilst the *Mané* has discos weekend nights. ③.

Casa de Rodas, just out of town at Lugar de Rodar (☎251 652 105). A lovely, low eighteenth-century *turismo rural* building with only four guest rooms. The turismo will find out if there's space and give you directions. ③.

Café Croissanteria Raiano, Praça Deu-la-Deu 34 (☎251 653 534). Modern, good-value rooms (some self-contained) above the café; the best ones look out over the square to Spain. ②.

Residencial Esteves, Rua General Pimenta de Castro (☎251 652 386). Near the station and reasonably priced, with smart, modern rooms – all have bathrooms and TVs. The entrance is on Rua de Santo António. ①.

Eating and drinking

The local wine from Monção and Melgaço, the finest *vinho verde* in the country, is available on draft in a couple of bars off the main square; the most delicious bottled variety is *Palácio da Brejoeira*, which, as a splendid Monção tourist leaflet one-liner puts it, "someone in France once classified as being the best in the world". It's made from the Alvarinho grape, which produces a full bodied wine with a much higher alcoholic content than other *vinhos verdes* (around 12.5 percent), and consequently has the ability to age. It goes well with strong-tasting fish, especially the local eels (*enguias*), shad (*savel*), and the rich, eel-like lamprey (*lampreia*) which is in season between January and March. Minho trout and salmon are always tremendous.

Probably the best bet for **food** in Monção is the *Café-Restaurante Central* on Praça Deu-la-Deu, which also has a good late-night bar at the front. Alternatively, the *Restaurante Terra Nova*, in Praça da República, does tasty trout and salmon at very reasonable prices.

The spa, Cortes and Lapela

The close proximity of a **thermal spa**, 1500m to the east of Monção (follow the walls), has turned the town into something of a resort for Spanish day-trippers and Portuguese weekenders. Aside from the dubious pleasures of the alkaline water, there's a park and a free campsite by the river. However, this is not exactly the most luxurious of spas, and the Victorian cells – each of which contains a cast-iron bath and assortment of frightening-looking equipment – are rather unsettling, though a new building currently under construction may change all this.

Further afield, to the west of the town, a pleasant **walk** trails off into the woods from the bus stop at Senhora da Cabeça to the hamlet of **CORTES**, which was Monção's medieval site. About 3km further west is **LAPELA**, whose **river beach** is safer for swimmers. The village is dominated by a lofty **tower**, all that remains of a fortress destroyed in 1706 to provide materials for the restoration of the battered walls of Monção.

East to Melgaço

An historic incident in Anglo-Portuguese relations took place on the fragile-looking bridge over the Rio Mouro just before **CEIVÃES**, 10km along the road from Monção to Melgaço. This is the spot where John of Gaunt, the Duke of Lancaster, arranged the marriage of his daughter Philippa to King Dom João I in 1386, an arrangement that resulted in the signing of the **Treaty of Windsor** between the two countries. It gave rise to an alliance lasting over six hundred years and to the naming of numerous public places in honour of "Filipa de Lencastre".

Thermal spa enthusiasts might want to stop at **PESO** (also known as **Termas de Melgaço**), another 10km to the east (and just 4km short of Melgaço). This is a tiny spa town, spread along the old main road (the new one passes just below) and looking down on a magnificent curve of the river. The **spa** (☎251 403 282; baths open summer Mon–Sat 8am–noon & 4–7pm) itself is a delight, with its shaded, landscaped gardens and fountain room. There's a **campsite** by the spa(☎251 403 282, fax 251 403 010; open all year), which also has bungalows (③) for rent. The only **hotel** is the plush, modern *Albergaria Boavista* (☎251 416 464, fax 251 416 350; ③), which has a swimming pool, fabulous views and a good **restaurant**. On the other side of the road, the *Adega do Sossego* (☎251 404 308; evenings only) is also an excellent place to eat.

Melgaço

MELGAÇO – the country's northernmost outpost – is a small border town sitting high above the Rio Minho. Though the town's rural origins are somewhat obscured by the modern developments that sprawl along the main road, at its heart, not much has really changed. Try to arrive for the **Friday market** when chickens, ducks, sticky buns, furniture, pottery, cabbages and corsets cover the stretch of road around the old walls. Otherwise, the only major event is the three-day *Festa da Cultura*, starting on the second Friday of August, when a display of tractors, an array of the town's long-reputed smoked hams (*presunto*), a craft exhibition and a performance from the school banjo band are organized.

At other times, the most probable reasons for visiting Melgaço are that it is so obviously off the tourist track, and that it gives easy access to the northern part of the Parque Nacional da Peneda-Gerês and to Spanish Galicia (see p.344 for access details). Its one historic feature is the ruined **fortress**, much fought over during the Wars of Restoration, but now little more than a tower and a few walls handy for hanging out washing.

Short **excursions** from Melgaço might include the two **Romanesque churches** of **PADERNE** (3km west, off the road to Monção) and Nossa Senhora da Orada (1km east, off the road to the border). Melgaço Radical (☎ 919 005 349 (mobile), fax 251 402 429) offer rafting, canoeing on the Rio Minho and canyoning in Peneda-Gerês National Park in addition to their rather over-subscribed walking trips. Costs are around 5000$00 per activity.

Practicalities

The town's helpful **turismo** (Mon–Sat 9.30am–12.30pm & 2.30–6pm; closed Wed in winter; ☎251 402 440) is just out of town on the road to Monção in the stone Casa Castreja. It has details on local *vinho verde quintas* (estates) which welcome visitors, leaflets detailing walks in Peneda-Gerês national park (pp.350–362), and can provide details of inexpensive **rooms** in private houses. Near the turismo on Rua Rio do Porto, those in the home of Maria Helena Morais are good (☎251 402 188; ①). The only **pensões** are *Pensão Pemba* on Praça Amadeu Abilio Lopes (☎251 402 555; ①), and the *Residencial Miguel Pereira* at Rua da Calçada 5, near the cinema (☎251 402 212; ①–②), which offers a range of budget and mid-range rooms. The nicest rooms around are at the old stone *Quinta da Calçada* (③), 1km from the turismo; you book through Solares de Portugal in Ponte de Lima (see p.346).

In the alleys below the fort, a couple of **café-restaurants** offer good food at reasonable prices; and there's a café in the attractive castle gardens overlooking the Minho valley. But best of all is *Restaurante Panorama* (☎251 400 400) in the Mercado Municipal, whose unexceptional decor belies top quality food (mains under 2000$00): try the roast pork leg with pineapple, or lamprey cooked in rice. Apart from fish, another local dish is *bifes de presunto de cebolada* (gammon steak fried with onions). For dessert, try *bucha doce*, made with eggs and port wine and traditionally served at carnival time.

Buses leave for Monção daily and connect with services to Braga, Coimbra, Porto and Lisbon. There are also direct services to Porto, Coimbra and Lisbon. Auto Viação Melgaço buses (Mon–Fri) to Lamas de Mouro and Castro Laboreiro for the Peneda-Gerês park leave at 7.30am (with an additional 12.50pm service on Fri). Their buses to São Gregório, for the Spanish border, leave four times a day, in the afternoon and early evening. All services leave from Largo da Calçada.

The Spanish border

The **Spanish border post** is at **PONTE BARXAS**, 1km east of **SÃO GREGÓRIO**, which itself is 10km east of Melgaço. Other than taking one of the buses outlined above in "Practicalities", the only way to get there is by taxi, which is reasonably inexpensive.

Across the frontier, buses leave twice daily (Mon–Fri) for Ribadavia and Orense. Ribadavia (along the Minho and with superb local red wine) and Celanova (on a different route to Orense and dwarfed by a vast medieval monastery) must be two of the most lovely and characteristic towns of Spanish Galicia. The Minho itself – or Miño as it becomes known – is more placid in the further reaches, as it is dammed shortly after the point when both of its banks are within Spain.

THE LIMA VALLEY AND PARQUE NACIONAL DA PENEDA-GERÊS

The **Rio Lima**, whose valley is perhaps the most beautiful in Portugal, was thought by the Romans to be the Lethe, the mythical River of Oblivion. Beyond it, they imagined, lay the Elysian Fields; to cross would mean certain destruction, for its waters possessed the power of the lotus, making the traveller forget country and home. The Roman Consul Decimus Junius Brutus, having led his legions across most of Spain, had to seize the standard and plunge into the water shouting the names of his legionaries from the far bank – to show his memory remained intact – before they could be persuaded to follow.

There are roads along both banks of the Lima from **Viana do Castelo** (see p.329), where the river meets the sea. Travelling from Viana on the main N202, regular bus services pass through two highly attractive towns – **Ponte de Lima** and **Ponte da Barca** – from either of which you could take fine walks into the hilly and wooded surroundings, perhaps exploring one or two of the many Romanesque churches in the region, such as that at **Bravães,** between the two towns.

Further east, the Lima runs into the heart of the astonishingly beautiful **Parque Nacional da Peneda-Gerês National Park**. The easiest points of access are from **Braga** to the central section of the park, **Arcos de Valdevez** and **Ponte da Barca** to the north of the park, and from **Melgaço** to the far north. Access to the eastern section is problematic, but probably simplest from Montalegre in Trás-Os-Montes. If you're planning a lot of hiking, you should visit the park offices located in Braga or Ponte da Barca (see p.348).

Ponte de Lima

An hour's ride east of Viana do Castelo, **PONTE DE LIMA** lies at the end of a low stone bridge, Roman in origin and said to mark the path of their first hesitant crossing. It's a delightful small town, whose old centre – as is often the way – has no specific attraction other than its air of sleepy indifference to the wider world. You might disagree if you visit in July or August, when Ponte de Lima begins to show worrying signs of midsummer tourist strain, which the local authorities have capitalized on with a new eighteen-hole golf complex. But at almost any other time of year, the town remains one of Portugal's most pleasing.

There's beautiful walking country all around Ponte de Lima, especially along both banks of the river west of the town. To the east, the recently constructed motorway sharply curtails any walking after a kilometre or so, but wandering through some of the

WALKS AROUND PONTE DE LIMA

This 12km, three- to four-hour walk from Ponte de Lima begins at the Roman bridge; cross over, and turn right just before the chapel. Two hundred metres on, you'll see a cobbled road to the left; bypass this and take the next left-hand track instead. This trail follows an old Roman road, used for centuries by pilgrims on their way to Santiago do Compostela in Spain; skirting around fields and squeezing between stone walls, it's overgrown in places. A kilometre or so further on, the route crosses a road and threads along a broad farm track. Take time to admire the gorgeous *Quinta do* Sabadão Solares de Portugal property on your right, then 400m further on, take the grassy track to the left, and turn left again on to a dirt track 100m later, passing the *Casa de Pomarchão*, another grand and lovely Solares de Portugal property that's worth a peek through its imposing gates.

The dirt track soon meets a Tarmacked main road; turn right here, passing a café and restaurant on your left, then in 300m turn left to follow the road signposted Santo Ovídio. Providing stunning views of the Lima valley, this road winds steeply for just over a kilometre to a tiny chapel dedicated to the patron saint of ears, where locals deposit rather grotesque wax models of their ailing ears, hoping for a saintly cure.

From the chapel, retrace your route down the road for about 500m, and turn left down a dirt track at a large right-hand hairpin bend. Veer left at a fork in the track 200m later, and left again onto the cobbled road 200m further on, walking through small hamlets and farms. After a kilometre or so, the road bends to the right; turn left at a crossroads soon afterwards. Half a kilometre further on, turn left at a T-junction to pass a shrine on your left and a stone cross on your right. Head straight down this road, passing cafés and an elaborate stone crucifix marking another stop on the route to Santiago, then cross over a main road. Keep straight ahead past a shady village green ideal for a picnic, and follow the narrow cobbled street until you reach the Ponte de Lima bridge.

villages on both sides of the river is still a joy. More energetic walkers can climb to Santo Ovídio chapel, a bizarre shrine to the patron saint of ears, for glorious views of the Lima valley, before ambling back to Ponte de Lima along cobbled and vine-covered lanes. The turismo in Ponte de Lima have a few illustrated leaflets detailing local trails, but as these have been rendered somewhat out of date since the construction of the motorway, staff are often reluctant to give them out. However, even without a leaflet, you should be able to follow the route detailed in the box below, though you should also take along a copy of the IGeoE 1:25,000 map (no. 28) available from the IGeoE in Lisbon (see p.23), or from Porto Editora in Porto (see p.23).

The river at Ponte de Lima would offer fine swimming were it not so polluted; however, you can still take to the water on a **canoe** (500$00 for two hours) rented from the Clube Naútico (☎258 952 610), 2km from the Alameda on the other side of the river by the new bridge). The river's wide sandbank beaches also provide the venue for the town's bi-monthly Monday **market**, the oldest in Portugal, held since a charter was first granted in 1125. Also held here are the curiously named **"New Fair"** (second and third weekend of September), a tremendous festival and market, seemingly attended by half of the Minho, with fireworks, a fairground, wandering accordionists, *gigantones* (enormous carnivalesque statues), and a large brass band competition. More tradition is on display in early June, with the **Vaca das Cordas** festival (see box, p.346).

The town's main focus is a long riverside **Alameda** (Passeio 25 de Abril), shaded by magnificent plane trees, leading to the rambling old convent of Santo António, which contains a small **museum** of treasures within its church. In the town, spare an hour to glance around at the handsome buildings: there are several sixteenth-century **mansions** with stone coats of arms, and interesting remains of the old fourteenth-century **keep** – the *Torre da Cadeia* – used up to the 1960s as a prison (the occupants were allowed to hang cups down from the windows for money and cigarettes). It now houses a small craft shop and the **turismo** (see below). Should the river not tempt you, there is a municipal **pool** in Rua Francisco Sá Carneiro (Mon–Fri 10am–10pm, Sat & Sun 9am–noon & 5pm–10pm; ☎258 900 412). Ponte de Lima also has a **cinema** (Fri–Mon) in the Centro Comercial Rio Lima. Six kilometres outside town, the *hipódromo* at Quinta das Velhas (☎258 762 784, fax 258 762 785) stages **horse races** once a month or so.

Practicalities

The **bus station** is behind the market, just a minute or so from the river. There are several daily services to Arcos de Valdevez, Viana do Castelo, Barcelos, Ponte da Barca, Paredes de Coura, Braga and Porto. A few minutes' walk along the riverbank, the **turismo**, in the Torre da Cadeia (Mon–Sat 9am–12.30pm & 2.30–6pm, Sun 9.30am–12.30pm; ☎258 942 335), is extremely helpful, and will provide a free map of the town as well as more information. The Solares de Portugal headquarters are located in the same building (see below).

Accommodation

Ponte de Lima is the birthplace of the **Turihab** scheme (now called *Turismo Rural*), founded in 1983 in order to promote and rent out top quality accommodation in local manor houses, farms and country estates around the region; it's now a country-wide operation (see pp.33–34 for further details). Solares de Portugal is the largest organization within the scheme, with twenty-five properties in the Ponte de Lima area and over ninety in the country as a whole. The Solares de Portugal office is at Praça da República (☎258 741 672, fax 258 741 444, *turihab@mail.telepac.pt*). A similar organization, offering

---

THE VACA DAS CORDAS

If you're in Ponte de Lima in early June (the day before Corpus Christi), you might witness the the rather odd spectacle of the **Vaca das Cordas** (literally, "Cow of the Ropes"), which involves an enraged bull being dragged down through the town's streets to the beach.

Like Pamplona's famous *Corrida*, this is one of many bovine-related Iberian traditions that stem back to pre-Christian times, with its origins in the ancient Egyptian cults brought to the Iberian peninsula by the Phoenicians a few centuries before Christ. Mythology has it that the beautiful Io was kidnapped by an amorous Jupiter; when repelled by Io's mother, Jupiter turned his love into a cow and commanded a bumble bee to repeatedly sting the unfortunate beast. Not terribly happy with this treatment, Io fled to Egypt, where she regained her human form, and promptly married the god Osiris. In her honour, the Egyptians erected altars to Isis in the image of an errant cow, a symbol which became a popular goddess of fertility in both Egypt and, later on, in Portugal. The Igreja Matriz in Ponte de Lima was presumably erected over such a temple, after which time the newly converted Christian citizens – to show their renunciation of idols – dragged their old bovine image around town until finally it fell into pieces. Since then, a live cow – actually now a bull – has been used.

Echoes of the original rite still remain: at around 3pm, the bull is led to the church, where it is stabbed with a small dart in order to madden it. At 6pm, two millers arrive, tie the bull by its horns and lead it three times around the church – a common feature of pre-Christian rituals – whilst jabbing it with goads in reference to the mythical bee described above. Following this, and depending upon whether anyone can keep a grip on its ropes, the unfortunate animal then stumbles or charges through the town's streets (mimicking Io's flight to Egypt) before finishing up at the beach. It is then led off to the abattoir, as the good people of Ponte de Lima prepare for the more sedate procession of **Corpo do Deus** the following day, which sees the streets covered with flowers carefully arranged into ornate patterns.

different properties, is Privetur, at Largo das Pereiras (☎258 743 923, fax 258 741 493, *privetur@mail.telepac.pt*). Some of the best options from both organizations are given below; note that you will need your own transport to reach them.

At the lower end of the price scale, there are plenty of good *pensões* in town; alternatively, you could **camp** (unofficially) just out of town on the riverbank, but be warned that the police will move you on if you go near the New Fairs site during the festival, when families wash clothes, auction cattle, and let off fireworks throughout the night. The nearest official site is at Viana do Castelo (see p.329).

IN TOWN

Pensão Beira Rio, on the Alameda (☎258 943 471). Cheap but somewhat gruff place on the waterfront, with grandstand views of the comings and goings for the Monday market. ①.

Casa das Pereiras, Largo das Pereiras (☎258 942 939, fax 258 941 493). Wonderful eighteenth-century stone *solar* (book through Privetur – see above) with a pool and splendid dinners served every Friday evening. The garden contains 100-year-old camellia shrubs. Open June–Oct. ③.

Albergaria Império do Minho, Av. Dom Luís Filipe (aka Av. dos Plátanos), on the riverfront (☎258 741 510, fax 258 942 567). Largest and most modern place in town. The fifty rooms all have TVs and private bathroom, and there's a swimming pool. ③.

Pensão Morais, Rua da Matriz 8 (☎258 942 470). Basic, traditional rooms, some with balconies overlooking a quiet street. Bed only ②.

Pensão São João, Largo de São João (☎258 941 288). Near the bridge, this is excellent value and serves good food downstairs in its restaurant. Most rooms have bathrooms. Front rooms can be noisy due to traffic. ②.

OUTSIDE TOWN

Casa de Crasto, 1km out of town along the N203 to Ponte de Barca (☎258 941 156). A seventeenth-century Solares de Portugal property, which – legend has it – was partly demolished by the owner in 1896 while looking for hidden treasure. ⑤.

Casa do Outeiro, Arcozelo, 2km from Ponte de Lima. This stately Solares de Portugal manor house dates from the sixteenth century and is surrounded by a garden and woods. Napoleonic forces were suitably impressed, too, when they decided to use it as their headquarters in 1809. Has three twin rooms. ⑤.

Moínho de Estorãos, Estorãos, 7km from Ponte de Lima. A Solares de Portugal property occupying a converted seventeenth-century water mill. The location is beautiful – next to a Romanesque bridge and with walking, fishing and swimming all at hand. If you want a double room, book in advance as there's only one. Open mid-May to mid-Oct. ⑤.

Paço de Calheiros, Calheiros, 7km from Ponte de Lima. This elegant seventeenth-century mansion is the country retreat of none other than the Count of Calheiros, original founder of the Turihab scheme (see above). Set in beautifully landscaped gardens with views over the Lima valley, it has nine tastefully decorated bedrooms and six apartments, and a swimming pool and tennis courts too. ⑤.

Quinta da Roseira, 1km out of town on the Darque road (☎258 941 354). A lovely nineteenth-century farm, set among vineyards and fruit trees, with its own swimming pool and horses. ⑤.

Eating and drinking

There are a few inexpensive **cafés** and **restaurants** along the riverfront, especially in Praça de Camões, by the old bridge. Local dishes include *arroz de sarabulho com rojões* (rice cooked with blood and pieces of roast pork), and lamprey (at its best Jan–March). For **sweets**, try *madalenas* or the dry *biscoito requife. Cervejaria Rampinha* and *Bar S.A. Galeria*, with its exhibitions, both at the foot of Rua Formosa, are popular evening **bars**. Good music can be heard at the two unnamed bars on the more northern of the two alleys off Largo das Pereiras. To sample *vinho verde* straight from the barrel, try either the *Tasca de Isac* in Largo São João, facing the hotel, or *Tasca de Gasparinho*, off the Largo on Rua do Arrabalde de São João.

Alameda, Largo da Feira, by the bridge on the town side of the river (☎258 941 630). In a nice position with splendid views, and photographs of Ponte de Lima at New Fairs time. Standards appear to be slipping of late, but it's still worth a try. Full meals are under 1700$00. Closed Wed.

O Brasão, Rua Formosa 1 (☎258 911 890). Good service in an old stone building. Delicious *arroz de marisco* and a long wine list. Closed Wed.

Encanada, on the Alameda (☎258 941 189). A good place to eat tasty, moderately priced local food such as *sarabulho*, close to the market and with a terrace overlooking the river. Closed Thurs.

Parisiense, on the Alameda. This simple *tasca* has a limited menu but a good view of the river from its first- and second-floor tables, and it's cheap.

Fu Man, Quinta do Olho Marinho (☎258 944 171). Chinese with weekday lunchtime menus under 1200$00, and take-away. Head south from Praça da República and follow the avenida as it forks to the left. Open daily from 11.30am to 3.30pm and 7pm to midnight

São João, Largo de São João. At lunchtime, this place is heaving with locals tucking into the huge, regional dishes, such as *rojões à minhota* – a very tasty mix of roast pork, sausages and roast potatoes.

East to Ponte da Barca

From Ponte de Lima, the N203 runs 18km east to **Ponte da Barca**, another Minho market town with a bridge so attractive it, too, has been incorporated into the town's name. On the way, call a halt at the small hamlet of **BRAVÃES**, 14km east of Ponte de Lima, home of the fine Romanesque **Church of São Salvador**, just to the left of the road. Its two sculpted doorways are perhaps the best in the country, filled with carvings of doves, griffins, monkeys and two of the local wide-horned oxen. If the church is locked ask at the cottage behind and the doors will be flung open for you, lighting up medieval murals of Saint Sebastian and the Virgin. The church is one of several in the Lima region that is simple and rustic in design but features beautiful, naive carvings on the doorways and columns. Most of these churches were built in the twelfth and thirteenth centuries under the supervision of Cluniac monks, who brought their architecture to Spain and Portugal along the pilgrimage routes to Santiago de Compostela in Galicia; the main Portuguese route ran through Braga and so Minho has the highest concentration.

There's a **bar** in Bravães where local transport-users can debate the chances of getting a bus going on to Ponte da Barca, 4km further east; it's probably quicker to walk.

Ponte da Barca

If you ignore the modern suburbs of **PONTE DA BARCA**, and head for the river, the old town quarters form a quintessential pastoral vision. The Lima is spanned here by a lovely, sixteenth-century bridge, beside which there's a superb fortnightly **Wednesday market** (it alternates with Arcos de Valdevez), spreading out by the river in an almost medieval atmosphere, and drawing hundreds of people from outlying hamlets. It's also worth noting that the town's annual **Feira de São Bartolomeu** takes place on August 19–24, with the big day on August 24; don't expect to get any sleep once the party starts. The whole period sees a crafts fair in Praça da República, and there's a linen festival and secular parade on August 23.

From the bridge, Rua Conselheiro Rocha Peixoto runs east to the triangular Praça da República, passing the small Largo da Misericórdia and its helpful **turismo** (June 15–Sept 14 Mon–Sat 9am–12.30pm & 2.30–6pm, Sun 9am–12.30pm; Sept 15–June 14 Mon–Sat 9am–12.30pm & 2.30–6pm; ☎258 452 899), where you can get a town map and lots of brochures. Next door is a **park information office** for the Peneda-Gerês National Park (☎ & fax 258 452 450, *aderepg@mail.telepac.pt*), where you can book accommodation in farmhouses (*casas abrigos*), and pick up leaflets detailing **walks** (*trilhos*) in the park. It also has details (there are photocopies at the turismo) of two circuits in Ponte de Barca district: one around Ermida, the other from São Miguel (Entre-Ambos-os-Rios) via Germil and the wonderfully unspoilt village of Sobredo. The instructions are somewhat out of date, so a compass and a good map would be useful, and you should bring your own food and drink.

Buses to and from all destinations drop you at the corner of Rua Diogo Bernardes and Rua Conselheiro Rocha Peixoto, by the bridge. There are connections to Lindoso (2 daily), Arcos de Valdevez and Braga (both hourly).

One of the nicest places to **stay** is the friendly *Pensão Maria Gomes*, Rua Conselheiro Rocha Peixoto 13 (☎258 452 288; ③), overlooking the river and bridge, where breakfast (250$00pp) is served on the balcony. It's worth phoning ahead to book. More expensive is *Residencial Fontaínhas*, further along on Rua António José Pereira at Praça da República (☎258 452 442; ②). *Pensão Os Poetas*, Jardim dos Poetas, in a converted townhouse near the bridge (☎258 453 578; ③), has plenty of cool marble and large clean rooms with TVs – some have river views. On the north bank of the river, opposite the town, the Solares de Portugal property *Quinta da Prova* (☎258 452 163; ⑤), has nine apartments with kitchenettes.

For **meals**, you could do far worse than eat upstairs at *Pensão Maria Gomes*, or try the pricier *Restaurante Bar do Rio*, close to the Praia Fluvial – a beach on the left bank of the river – which is an excellent place to dine while watching the sunset. Another good option is *Restaurante Varanda do Lima* (closed Thurs), near the bridge, which specializes in *rodobalho*, a type of flatfish, which you choose from the tank by the door; a meal here will set you back around 2500–3000$00. Cheaper eats at places doubling as **bars** can be found all along Rua Conselheiro Rocha Peixoto, notably at *Café Cantinho* at the corner with Rua Diogo Bernardes, which is very busy at lunchtimes (under 1000$00), and either of *Nicola* or *O Emigrante*, facing Praça da República. In addition to the workers' cafés along Rua Conselheiro Rocha Peixoto, other bars include *Pelourinho* (all day) and *Poetas*, which are open weekday evenings and all day at the weekends, and have occasional live music. Both are on the Jardim dos Poetas by the bridge. You could also try *Euzébius*, on Rua Conselheiro Rocha Peixoto, and *A Doca Bar*, Rua Dr. António Veloso, whose DJs attract a more youthful crowd on Friday and Saturday nights.

Arcos de Valdevez

As a diversion from the main Minho river route you might contemplate exploring the Rio Vez, which can be reached just 5km north of Ponte da Barca, at **ARCOS DE VALDEVEZ** (Arches of the Valley of the Vez). Like almost everywhere in this region, it's ordinarily a sleepy little place, though it shows its true Minho colours during the fortnightly Wednesday **market**. And, as at Ponte de Lima and Ponte da Barca, it only really comes alive during its annual festival, in this case the three-day **Festas do Concelho**, held over the second week in August, featuring *gigantones* (giant figures), *zés pereiras* (red-caped drummers), horse races and noisy fireworks. Traditionally these celebrations should take place on the last weekend of the holiday month, but they've been shifted to take account of local emigrants who return to work abroad at the end of August; one of the festival days is actually named the Dia do Emigrante.

Practicalities

The friendly and well-stocked **turismo** is 200m north of the bridge on the west bank of the river (June 15–Sept 14 daily 9.30am–12.30pm & 2.30–6pm; Sept 15– June 14 Mon–Sat 9.30am–12.30pm & 2.30–6pm; ☎ & fax 258 516 001). The staff will dole out maps (make sure you get the one with street names marked – the other is useless), brochures covering the Rota do Vinho Verde (wine-related attractions throughout the Minho) and information on *turismo rural* accommodation in the region, and there's also a room with local crafts for sale.

Like Ponte da Barca, Arcos de Valvedez is a useful point of departure for the Parque Nacional da Peneda-Gerês, and there's a **park information office** (☎258 515 338) at Rua do Padre Manuel Himalaia – turn uphill from the river at the new fountain – where you can buy a **map** (420$00). The turismo, however, has much more information, including leaflets (in Portuguese) detailing numerous walks.

For information on the **bus** service to Soajo and Lindoso (1–3 daily Mon–Fri), ask at the turismo, or try the Salvador office (☎258 521 504) on Rua Soares Pereira, off Largo da Lapa. Bear in mind, though, that the service isn't completely reliable and times change frequently. You can catch the Salvador buses to Soajo and Lindoso at the stops along Avenida Marginal, between the bridge and *Pensão Dom António*. The **bus station** itself is 2km northeast of town near the river, and has regular connections with Braga, Monção, Ponte de Lima and Viana do Castelo.

The town has a few reasonably priced **pensões**. In the best position, overlooking the river on the east side of the old bridge, is the newly rebuilt *Pensão Ribeira* (☎258 515 174; ②). On the west side of the river, are the characterful and inexpensive *Pensão Floresta* (☎258 515 163; ①) and *Pensão Brasileiro* (☎258 515 245; ①), both above boozy *casas de pasto*-cum-bars on Rua Amorim Soares, just up from the bridge. Neither are for the fussy, and they're often full around the time of the fortnightly market. More salubrious is the small and unpretentious *Flôr do Minho* in Largo da Valeta, at the end of Rua de São João off Largo da Lapa (☎258 525 216; ①), while expensive options include the *Residencial Tavares* (☎258 516 253; ③), just off Largo da Lapa on Rua Padre Manuel José da Cunha Brito, which has modern, if a bit gloomy, apartments with TV and kitchen; breakfast is included. The large *Pensão Dom António* (☎258 521 010, fax 258 521 065; ③), at the south end of Rua Marginal, has brighter rooms with TV; some have phones and minibars.

There's a cluster of reliable **restaurants** off Largo da Lapa in Rua de São João, notably *Churrascaria Arco dos Caneiros*, which is good and cheap, offering mainly pork and *bacalhau*, with *tripas à moda de Porto* (tripe) on Wednesdays. Other local places that recommend themselves include the *Minho Verde*, Rua Mário J.B. da Costa, up behind the turismo (try the grilled squid), and *O Lagar*, Rua Dr. Vaz Guedes, in the old quarter near Igreja da Misericórdia. For a real treat, though, visit *Casa Delfim*, a café 30m off Largo da Lapa facing the church tower, run by an ageing "world-famous" accordionist and stacked with his instruments, any of which are liable to be suddenly snatched up for an impromptu jam session.

Parque Nacional da Peneda-Gerês

The magnificent **PARQUE NACIONAL DA PENEDA-GERÊS** is hardly a secret. Caldas do Gerês (known simply as Gerês), the main centre of the park, attracts more tourists than anywhere else in the Minho, with the possible exception of Viana do Castelo, and at weekends, when Portuguese campers arrive in force, parts of it can seem a bit too close to civilization. The park as a whole, though, is large enough to absorb the great numbers of visitors. It's split into three distinct parts: the central area, based around the spa town of **Caldas do Gerês**, the wilder northern section around the **Serra da Peneda**, and the far eastern section of **Serra do Gerês** which continues into Trás-os-Montes. Both Serras remain largely undiscovered, especially in the eastern reaches of the Serra do Gêres where the spectacular mountain terrain feels largely impenetrable.

Vestiges of early human occupation are scattered around the park. Most common are *antas* (or dolmens), tombs constructed from upright stones that were topped with roof slabs and then covered with soil; unexcavated *anta* mounds are called *mamoas*. Less frequent are *menhirs* (tall standing stones with a phallic appearance that archeologists inevitably ascribe to fertility cults), *cromeleques* (stone circles) and *arte rupestre* (rock art, usually engraved symbols such as concentric circles, little cup-like depressions, possibly used for sorting or crushing seeds, boxed crosses and hand axes). The locations of some are marked, very approximately, on the park's maps.

Park practicalities

You can see a great deal of the park under your own steam, along a number of pretty decent roads, but note that **bus** services are limited and often non-existent at weekends. The main connections are: Melgaço to Lamas de Mouro and Castro Laboreiro in the north; Arcos de Valdevez and Ponte da Barca to Soajo and Lindoso in the centre; and Braga to Caldas do Gêres. For the far east of the park, the nearest buses run between Montalegre and Braga and vice versa.

Once in the park, **walking** is generally the only option for getting around. Trails and paths cover large areas, and there are dozens of hiking opportunities, from short strolls to two- and three-day treks across whole sections of the park. Some of the footpaths (*trilhos*) are detailed in an excellent series of leaflets, which along with the official park **map** are available from the **information centres** and **park offices** listed below. The map (420$00) details altitudes and all roads, but no footpaths. A more useful alternative (with footpaths listed) are the topographical maps produced by the Portuguese military, which you can buy in Lisbon and Porto. Maps and leaflets aside, if you plan a long hike, take good boots, warm and waterproof clothes, a compass, food and a water bottle – there are plenty of streams and the water is pretty clean, especially at higher altitudes, but if you're susceptible to stomach upsets, purify with iodine or chlorine tablets. Beware of fog in spring and winter. Picking flowers and – more importantly – **lighting fires** are forbidden in Gerês. The Portuguese have an alarming habit of lighting them whenever and wherever they picnic, with terrible consequences in the dry summers.

For **organized hikes** in the park, with vehicle transport there and back (around 5000$00 per person), contact Trilhos, Rua de Belém 94, Porto (✆ & fax 025 504 604, *trilhos@trilhos.pt*), which also offers canoeing, rafting, biking and caving trips. For **mountain climbing**, contact the Clube Nacional de Montanhismo, Secção Região Norte, Departamento de Montanhismo, Rua Formosa 303–2º, Porto (✆223 321 295). If you want to hire your own **guide**, contact the park office in Ponte da Barca, where there is a list of officially approved and generally excellent candidates. Fees are around 2000$00 per person, or 15,000$00 for a group (minimum five people). Although hiring a guide is not essential, those approved by the park are an invaluable source of information on local flora, fauna and history, and will be able to point out things to you that you'd otherwise miss; if you're trekking alone, it's also advisable to have someone accompanying you in case of an accident. With a decent map (see above) and a compass, you're unlikely to get lost, but do bear in mind that night falls a lot quicker in the mountains than on the coast, temperatures can drop quickly in fog, during rain and at night, and that in winter you're likely to find plenty of snow, which makes following trails a much riskier business.

Apart from the main centre of Caldas do Gerês (see p.354), **accommodation** is limited to a handful of *pensões* in other villages (which we detail in the relevant section of the guide), camping at designated sites run by the park and by private operators, and, if you can muster a group of eight, renting *casas abrigos*, four-bedroom converted farmhouses which must be booked and partly paid for well in advance at the park office in Ponte da Barca. Minimum stay is two nights, and you'll pay 7000–8000$00 in winter, and 12–13,000$00 in summer, including firewood.

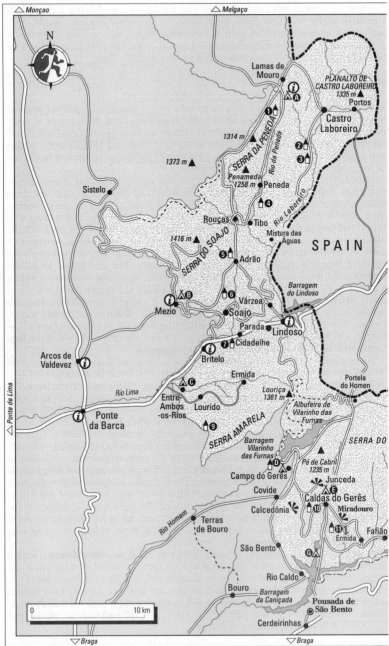

N

Lamas de
Mouro

PLANALTO DE
CASTRO LABOREIRO
1335 m ▲
Portos

Castro
Laboreiro

1314 m

SERRA DA PENEDA

Rio da Peneda

Rio Laboreiro

1373 m ▲

Penameda
1258 m
Peneda

Sistelo

Rouças
Tibo

Mistura das
Aguas

SPAIN

1416 m ▲

SERRA DO SOAJO

Adrão

Barragem
do Lindoso

Várzea
Soajo

Mezio

Parada
Lindoso

Arcos de
Valdevez

Britelo
Cidadelhe

Ermida

Portela
do Homen

Rio Lima

Louriça
1361 m

Albufeira de
Vilarinho das
Furnas

SERRA DO

Ponte
da Barca

Entre
Ambos
-os-Rios

Lourido

SERRA AMARELA

Barragem
Vilarinho
das Furnas

Pé de Cabril
1235 m

Junceda

Campo do Gerês

Covide

Caldas do Gerês

Calcedónia

Miradouro

Terras
de Bouro

Fafião
Ermida

Rio Homem

São Bento

Bouro

Barragem
da Caniçada

Rio Caldo

Pousada de
São Bento

Cerdeirinhas

0   10 km

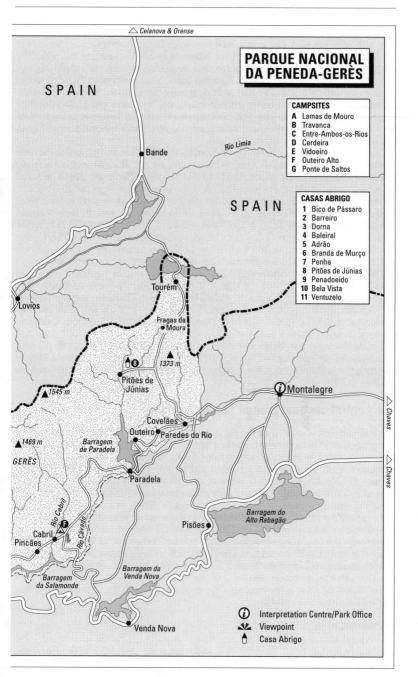

△ Celanova & Orense

SPAIN

● Bande

Rio Limia

**PARQUE NACIONAL
DA PENEDA-GERÊS**

SPAIN

CAMPSITES
A Lamas de Mouro
B Travanca
C Entre-Ambos-os-Rios
D Cerdeira
E Vidoeiro
F Outeiro Alto
G Ponte de Saltos

CASAS ABRIGO
1 Bico de Pássaro
2 Barreiro
3 Dorna
4 Baleiral
5 Adrão
6 Branda de Murço
7 Penha
8 Pitões de Júnias
9 Penadoeido
10 Bela Vista
11 Ventuzelo

● Tourém

Fragas da
● Moura

●Lovios

▲ 1373 m

Pitões de
Júnias

▲1545 m

ⓘ Montalegre

△ Chaves

▲ 1469 m

Covelães

GERÊS

Outeiro ●Paredes do Rio

△ Chaves

*Barragem
de Paradela*

● Paradela

Rio Cabril

*Barragem do
Alto Rabagão*

Pisões ●

Ⓕ

Rio Cávado

Cabril
Pincães ●

*Barragem da
Venda Nova*

*Barragem
da Salamonde*

ⓘ Interpretation Centre/Park Office

Viewpoint

Casa Abrigo

● Venda Nova

Information

Information on the park can be obtained both from Interpretation Centres situated at the park entrances, and at the four park offices in towns surrounding the park. The interpretation centres are geared toward their immediate vicinity, with photo displays and information on local agriculture, flora and fauna. Most have books for sale, but can be short on leaflets, and don't count on finding maps there either. The park offices are generally more useful, and better stocked with maps, brochures and leaflets detailing signposted walks. You can also find park information on the **Internet** at *www.adere-pg.pt* (the park's official site), and *www.di.uminho.pt/~esteves/turismo/parques1.html*, and *www.infocid.pt/areas/* (in Portuguese).

The main **park office** is in **Braga**, at Avenida António Macedo, Quinta das Parretas (Mon–Fri 9am–12.30pm & 2–5.30pm; ☎253 203 480, fax 253 613 169), and is especially useful for leaflets detailing walks. Also helpful is the one in **Ponte da Barca**, at Largo da Misericórdia 10 (Mon–Fri 9am–12.30 & 2.30–6pm; ☎258 452 450 or 258 452 250, *aderepg@mail.telepac.pt*), which is also the place to contact if you need to book *casas abrigo* accommodation. The office in **Arcos de Valdevez**, on Rua do Padre Manuel Himalaia (Mon–Fri 9am–12.30 & 2–5.30pm; ☎258 515 338, fax 258 522 707) is rather useless in comparison – you'll find more information at the town's turismo. There's also an office in **Montalegre**, at Rua do Reigoso 17 (Mon–Fri 9am–12.30pm & 2–5.30pm; ☎ & fax 276 512 281), which concerns itself with the eastern section of the park.

The **interpretation centres** all close on Wednesdays. In summer, they open Mon–Tues & Thurs–Fri 10am–12.30pm & 2–6pm, Sat 10am–noon & 2.30pm to 6pm, and Sun 10am–noon & 2.30–5pm. In winter, Mon–Tues & Thurs–Fri 9.30am–12.30pm & 2–5.30pm, Sat 10am–12.30pm & 2–5pm, Sunday 10am–12.30pm & 2–4.30pm. They are located at Britelo, on the road from Ponte da Barca (☎258 576 160); in Caldas do Gerês at Avenida Manuel Francisco da Costa (☎253 390 110, fax 253 391 496); and Lamas de Mouro, on the Melgaço–Peneda road (☎251 465 563); and Mezio, on the road in from Arcos de Valdevez (☎258 526 751); the Mezio office number is also a 24-hour emergency telephone service. You can also get limited park information at the castle in Lindoso (p.360).

The central section: around Caldas do Gêres

The national park is centred on the old spa town of **CALDAS DO GERÊS** (commonly known as Gerês), which can be reached easily from Braga by bus – a ninety-minute journey (operated by Empresa Hoteleira do Gêres). Weekends aside, when Portuguese picnickers arrive en masse, it's a relaxed and very elegant base. "The Spa of Gerês" became fashionable in the early years of the last century – an epoch convincingly evoked by a row of grand Victorian hotels (many now sadly rundown and boarded up) along the sedate old main street, Avenida Manuel Francisco da Costa. The **spa** (☎253 391 113) still functions, attracting the infirm in the summer season, though most visitors nowadays are younger and healthier, up from the northern cities to picnic in the woods or, in the case of eccentric foreigners, to hike. There's been a lot of recent development in town, but it's not all to the bad and you'll probably appreciate the public outdoor swimming pool (reached through the park), tennis courts, boating lake and countless cafés. Pick up information either at the **turismo** (9am–noon & 2–6pm; closed Tues & Sun; ☎253 391 133), at the top end of the main avenue, or at the national park office, a little further up (see above).

Accommodation

There is no shortage of **pensões** and some – even in the height of summer – are reasonably priced. Note, however, that many are open from May to October only;

Azulejo-covered church, Porto

Cais da Ribeira, Porto

Azulejos, São Bento station, Porto

Bragança citadel, Trás-os-Montes

Cove in Lagos, the Algarve

Castelo de Vide, Alentejo

SUSAN GRIMSHAW

PETER WILSON

Palácio do Visconde, Estói, the Algarve

Vila Nova de Milfontes, Alentejo

PETER WILSON

MATTHEW HANCOCK

Capela dos Ossos, Évora, Alentejo

Taking a break, Monsaraz, Alentejo

Espigueiro (grain house), the Minho

Tending the vineyards, Trás-os-Montes

Olive groves and cacti, the Algarve

WALKING IN PENEDA-GÊRES: THE TRILHOS

Most park offices and turismos can provide leaflets detailing the walking trails (*trilhos*) mentioned below. Each route has been assigned with an approved guide; their names and contacts are available from the office in Ponte da Barca (see p.354).

Percursos de Pequena Rota

These short (up to 10km) trails of slight to moderate difficulty follow ancient routes used by generations of villagers and herders through the northern and central sections of the park, and are particularly attractive as they pass through villages and hamlets, threading along age-old cobbled paths overhung with trellises and vines. The start of each route is signposted, and the tracks are rather poorly marked with parallel bars of paint (either green and yellow, or red and yellow) on rocks and walls: two horizontal bars mean you're on the right track, a cross means you're going the wrong way, and there are arrows for easily missed left and right turns. However, some marks have worn away completely or are hidden under vegetation; if you want a guide, contact the nearest interpretation centre or the park office in Ponte da Barca.

At present, the explanatory leaflets for these walks are printed only in Portuguese, and distribution is erratic – your best bet is the Ponte da Barca office. The adjacent turismo also has details of unsignposted circuits around Ermida, and from Entre-Ambos-os-Rios via Sobredo and Germil.

Trilho de Longo Curso

A long-distance footpath which was planned to run the breadth of park from west to east, the Trilho do Longo Curso is now sadly overgrown and park authorities have ceased publication of the leaflets which detailed parts of it. It may be worth enquiring at the Ponte da Barca office to see if improvements have been made, but in the meantime, your only option is to arm yourself with a compass and the region's military map and strike off cross-country.

prices are often halved at those open during the winter – however, their restaurants are usually closed. Much of the accommodation is along the main street, though there's a string of large, modernized *pensões* across the other side of the river in Rua do Amassó, which afford ever better views up the valley. The best-value options, however, are found strung out at reasonably regular intervals along the 8km down the valley to Rio Caldo. The closest **campsite** is *Vidoeiro* (☎253 391 289, fax 253 391 496; April–Oct but occasionally open all year) on the edge of town by the river – it's well-maintained and has good facilities. *Ponte de Saltos* campsite (☎253 391 394; July–Sept) is 3km south of Caldas by the reservoir at Vilar da Veiga, but it can get crowded – you'll find more room at the *Quinta dos Moinhos* (☎253 391 581), almost adjacent to it, which also sells its own *vinho verde*.

Pensão Adelaide, Rua do Amassó (☎253 390 020, fax 253 390 029). A good option, high up at the top end of the road; the balconies have correspondingly fine views. ③.

Pensão Casa da Ponte, Rua Boavista, turn right at the roundabout at the southern end of town (☎253 391 125). A long-established place by the river, friendly and welcoming if a bit faded. Breakfast is included in the rates. ③.

Casa Santa Comba, in the alley behind *Restaurante Pedra Bela*. Plyboard walls and views of rusting agricultural equipment, but the cheapest in town, and the rooms have TVs. ①.

Pensão Flôr de Moçambique, Rua do Amassó (☎ & fax 253 391 119). Clean and amiable. The modern rooms all have baths, TVs and balconies and there's a restaurant with an outdoor terrace. ③.

Pensão O Horizonte do Gerês, Rua do Amassó (☎253 391 260). Near the *Flôr de Moçambique*, with less impressive views but slightly cheaper rates; breakfast is included. ②.

Pensão São Miguel do Gerês, Rua do Amassó (☎253 391 360). This has large, airy rooms with bathrooms and stunning outlooks. Good value and breakfast is included. ②.

Hotel Universal, Av. Manuel Francisco da Costa (☎253 391 141, fax 253 391 102). Gerês' finest and one of the two surviving – albeit much renovated – old-style grand hotels. The other is its sister *Hotel das Termas* on the same street (☎253 391 143), similar if a little more downmarket. Both ③.

Eating

The restaurants attached to most of the *pensões* are usually good if unmemorable, with portions healthy enough to satisfy the most jaded hiker. Alternatively, try those below.

Casa Santa Comba. Part of the *pensão* (see above) and set in a small and charmingly rundown courtyard, with average food but an entertaining patron.

Churrasqueira Geresino, uphill on the left at the top of town. At last, an excellent place to eat. Unpretentious, with great food and outstanding barbecued chicken, which you can take away too (400$00 for half-chicken). Recommended.

Novo Sol, along the main street near the bottom of town. Service can be surly, but it serves a good *ementa turística*.

Restaurante Pedra Bela, on the main street on the corner of the turning to *Casa Santa Comba*. A limited but reasonable choice, with outdoor tables on the verandah.

Hiking in central Gerês

The main reason, of course, for staying in Caldas do Gerês is to explore the national park. From the spa town, there are several interesting and accessible hikes, though, frustratingly, the **central Gerês** section is not well equipped with footpaths and walking off the tracks can be difficult and painful, with small shrubs slashing the legs. For all the following routes, a good **map** is essential – see p.351. For the section between Caldas do Gerês and Campo do Gerês, get hold of the *Orienteering Map: Campo do Gerês* (200$00), available from the Gerês park office or the turismo.

SOUTHEAST TO THE MIRADOURO

An hour's walk to the southeast of Caldas do Gerês, the **Miradouro do Gerês** is *the* destination for Portuguese weekend picnickers. And small wonder, with its site overlooking the vast reservoir of Caniçada and a good part of the Gerês range. The only catch, if you're intent on following suit, is the extent of local enthusiasm. This is not a road to walk unless you're immune to inhalation of exhaust fumes and dust; it's better to hitch up and then start hiking. The quickest approach to the Miradouro is to follow the road behind the service station at Gerês, where it becomes an uphill path. The most obvious, and probably the most attractive, route to follow beyond the Miradouro is to **Ermida** (see p.361). Just before arriving here, there's a sign pointing you to the Cascata do Arado, left off the main track; follow this and a brief walk leads to the magnificent **Arado waterfalls**, with its refreshing pools for swimming.

NORTHWEST TO CAMPO DO GERÊS VIA VILARINHO DAS FURNAS

This is an exhausting and long day's hike (10–12hr) but a good one, taking you along the Roman road that began at Braga. The route also runs alongside the **Vilarinho das Furnas** reservoir, with obvious swimming potential. In the height of summer you can see the submerged village of Vilarinho das Furnas itself – turn right after crossing the dam.

Setting out from Caldas do Gerês, follow the road north towards **PORTELA DO HOMEM**, the Spanish/Portuguese border post where there's a café and a collection of Roman milestones. It's 13km from Gerês, and locals often hitch up here to swim in the nearby **river pool** at the bottom of the Minas dos Carris valley. However, to get to Campo do Gerês, you don't need to go as far as Portela de Homen; instead, veer left off the road beyond the defunct campsite at Albergaria after roughly 8km, following signs to Campo do Gerês and the reservoir. There is a path off to the reservoir, but the main track heads southwest along the water's eastern edge – first along gladed paths and then suddenly into the open, following stretches of the old Roman road. Staying with the road (past an old stone building housing a weaving project run by the park), you come into **CAMPO DO GERÊS** (to which there are daily buses from Braga, operated by Empresa Hoteleira do Gerês).

Here, the friendly *Residencial Stop* (☎253 351 291; ②) attracts a young and active crowd. The *Cerdeira* **campsite** (☎ & fax 253 351 005; open all year), also lets out bungalows which sleep up to eight people (roughly 2000$00 per person), and rents bicycles; it has its own restaurant, too. Nearby is the *Vilarinho das Furnas* **youth hostel** (☎253 351 3 39), named after the village which was submerged in 1972 under the nearby dam. The construction workers stayed here (some double rooms are also available; ②), and there's a swimming pool, tennis court and disco. Through any of these establishments you can contact Equicampo (☎ & fax 253 357 022) to organize local **horse-trekking** trips as well as canoeing, mountain biking and climbing.

South of Campo do Gerês and heading toward Rio Caldo, you come to the crucifix of São João do Campo. Turn left off the road here onto a dirt track which takes you around the southern tip of the mountain west of Gerês. Apart from the occasional obsessive car driver, you'll be pretty much alone – eerily so at times, amid the boulders. After about 3km, there's a signpost on your right for the 3km, two-hour *trilho* to **Calcedónia**, a Celtic and Roman *citânia* with an impressive cave, and boulders scattered all around. This stretch can be hard-going in the midday heat, as there is no shelter, so save it for the late afternoon. Retracing your footsteps to the sign, continue around the mountain in an anticlockwise direction, following the signs back to Gerês.

SOUTH: TO CANIÇADA RESERVOIR, RIO CALDO AND SÃO BENTO DA PORTA ABERTA

The best base for the **Caniçada reservoir** is the village of **RIO CALDO**, on its west bank and just 8km south of Caldas do Gerês; change here for buses from Caldas to São Bento. There are numerous **water sports** available locally at the reservoir, with possibilities for both windsurfing and waterskiing; swimming is fine, too. For water-sports equipment, contact the English-run AML (☎253 391 740 or 253 391 598), which rents canoes, motorboats, mountain bikes and walking gear. There are plenty of places to **stay** along the edge of the reservoir, as well as along the road to Caldas do Gerês – a good bet is the *Pensão Pontes do Rio Caldo* (☎253 391 540, fax 253 391 195; ②), a stone building with a garden bar at the road junction with the bridges. More modern, but in an unbeatable reservoir location, is the friendly *Casa Beira Rio* (☎253/39 11 97; ②), on the north side of the bridge to Gerês, where rooms have bathrooms and TVs. Alternatively, you could catch a bus uphill towards Cerdinhas to the *Pousada de São Bento* (☎253 647 190, fax 253 647 867; ⑥), in a superb position overlooking the reservoir from the east. This timber-beamed former hunting lodge has its own swimming pool and a superb restaurant, with great views.

Three kilometres beyond Rio Caldo, in the Covide direction, **SÃO BENTO DA PORTA ABERTA** is a small village, high above the reservoir, commanding superb views. Its austere sanctuary is a favourite spot with pilgrims, who gather here at the beginning of July and again a month later (and on most Sundays throughout the year) – at such times the traffic and fumes make it a place best avoided. The former monastery, hidden under an ugly modern facade, is now the *Estalagem de São Bento da Porta Aberta* (☎253 391 106, fax 253 391 117; ③), still a little severe inside but nevertheless comfortable and with a good restaurant. Cheaper **rooms** may be available in the *Restaurante Mira Serra* at the western end of the village (☎253 391 362; ②), and at the charming turn-of-the-century *Pensão São José*, halfway between São Bento and Rio Caldo (☎253 391 120; ②).

The northern section: Serra da Peneda

Thanks mainly to restrictive public transport and scant accommodation choices, the wild **Serra da Peneda**, in the north of the park, sees far fewer tourists than the central zone around Caldas do Gerês, and this sense of isolation can be an advantage. You'll often have the prehistoric sites, steep forested valleys, and exposed, wind-blown *planaltos* dotted with weird rock formations entirely to yourself – not to mention the marvellous views.

Weekday **buses** leave Melgaço for Lamas de Mouro and Castro Laboreiro at 7.30am (with an additional 12.50pm service on Fridays) and return at around 6.30pm – check times with the parcel depot in Melgaço, just around the corner from the *Pensão Pemba*, or ask at the turismo.

Lamas de Mouro, Castro Laboreiro and Peneda

LAMAS DE MOURO, 19km southeast of Melgaço, has a beautifully situated **campsite** just inside the park, past the interpretation centre (☎251 465 494; ring ahead in winter), one of four run by the park itself. It has hot showers, a bar, a nearby natural pool for swimming and a restaurant. There's also a good **guide** here, who covers the *Trilho da Peneda*, a four-hour, 8.2km circuit northwest of Peneda village (access by jeep), in addition to several other trails in the park. Other than the campsite, there's no other accommodation in town, although the owner of the *Café Restaurante Paysan* (☎251 465 223), at the junction 1km north of the campsite, has been planning rooms for years. For **food**, the *Churrasqueiria Vidoeiro* nearby is slightly expensive but has generous portions.

The left-hand fork at Lamas takes you up to the ancient village of **CASTRO LABOREIRO** (8km further), a place that's best known for the breed of mountain dog to which it gives its name. Before the arrival of tourism, the village was practically deserted every summer when the pastoral community would leave to find greener fields and build *brandas* (temporary homes with stone walls and "soft" roofs made of branches and twigs) elsewhere for the warmer months, returning in winter to their *inverneiras* (winter houses) in Laboreiro. There are some superb **walks** around here, especially to the east and south. The *Trilho Castrejo* leaflet, available from the turismo in Melgaço, is helpful here. The best **accommodation** is at *Miradouro do Castelo* (☎251 465 469; ①), at the far end of the village overlooking a magnificent valley and dominated by the castle. You'll also find good, modern rooms at *Casa São José* (☎251 465 134; ①), 500m out on the Lamas road. For **eating**, the *Miradouro do Castelo* has a good restaurant, or try the *cabrito serrano* (mountain kid goat) in the *Restaurante da Serra* opposite.

To reach the ruins of the town's **castle**, you have a steep twenty-minute walk: left at the roundabout on the other side of the village, then left up a path where the road drops to the right, past a large rock known as the *Tartaruga* (Tortoise), and through heather and between boulders, with sheer drops to each side and steps hacked out of the rock face.

Nine kilometres south of Lamas de Mouro, along a stunning forested valley topped on either side with vertiginous boulders, you arrive at the small village of **PENEDA**, most famous for the **Sanctuário da Nossa Senhora da Peneda**, a miniature version of Bom Jesus, and full of devotees at the beginning of September (especially on September 7 and 8), but pretty much deserted the rest of the year. The original focus of adoration was a curious stone which natural forces had sculpted into the form of a woman, who some say was pregnant. Come Christianity, the cult and its stone was adopted as the Virgin Mary, and was duly incorporated into the late eighteenth-century church. There she remained until the 1930s, when somebody stole her; a gaudy plastic replacement now stands in place of the original.

The village itself has cafés and religious artefact shops clustered around the main square. There are good **rooms** at a modern house 100m before Peneda: contact Isolina Domingues Fernandes at the *Casa de Artigos Religiosos*, in the main square (☎251 465

139; ②). Otherwise, ask at *Café Star* in the main square (☎251 465 568 or 251 465 275; ③), where there are dorm bunks usually used by pilgrims. There's also a classy *turismo rural* property, the *Anjo da Guarda* (no phone; ③), in the main square.

The moderately difficult four-hour, 8.2km *Trilho da Peneda* **walking circuit** takes you west up the side of the valley into the windblown Serra da Peneda and to the 1258m peak of **Penameda**, where there are freshwater lagoons and fine views across the whole of the park. From here, the track turns north and then east, eventually dropping back down to the Lamas de Mouro road, about 1km north of Peneda by the signpost for the same route in reverse.

Heading south from Peneda, there's a dramatic and attractive **walk** of 20km or so following the well-signposted and fairly quiet road that leads south; bear left at the fork in the road just before the village of Adrão and you'll eventually join the Soajo–Lindoso road.

Soajo, Lindoso and Parada

Midway between the northern and central sections of the park, the traditional villages of **Soajo**, **Lindoso** and **Parada** are fine centres for hiking, as well as attractive destinations in themselves. Soajo is reached most easily from Arcos de Valdevez; **buses** leave Arcos at 5.40pm from Monday to Friday, with extra services at 12.20pm on Mondays and Fridays, and at 8.30am and 2.10pm on Wednesdays. There are also buses from Arcos, via Ponte da Barca, to Lindoso and Parada (Mon–Sat noon, Sun–Fri 5.50pm, plus extra services Wed). Times for both routes change frequently, and you'd be wise to contact the Salvador office in Arcos before travelling (see p.350). A taxi to either place will set you back around 2500$00.

Approaching from Ponte da Barca, you enter the park at **ENTRE-AMBOS-OS-RIOS**, where's there's a **campsite** (☎258 588 361). From Arcos de Valdevez, you enter at **MEZIO**, which has an **interpretation centre** (see p.354) and a new campsite, 3km away at Travanca (no phone). There's an excavated *anta* tomb at the roadside, and the staff can give you details on a half-day excursion to see the prehistoric rock art in the vicinity. Horse-riding is offered at the Centro Hípico do Mezio, 1km into the park at Vilar de Suente (☎258 526 452, fax 258 526 088). Lessons cost 7500$00 for five sessions; trail riding 2000–7000$00, and a two-day guided ride costs 23,000$00 – the price includes food and accommodation.

SOAJO

SOAJO is a small village tucked into the folds of a hilly landscape. Its highlight is a collection of eighteenth- and nineteenth-century **espigueiros** (grain houses), over twenty of which are clumped together on a stony platform, their roof-crosses (intended to bless the annual crop) giving them the look of a graveyard. In addition to providing a ready-made, breezy threshing ground, the *espigueiros* site offers a degree of protection from rats, though the tall stone mushrooms that raise the houses from the ground do not appear to keep vermin entirely at bay. Their grouping together is a vestige of the days when the isolated village depended heavily on communal effort for its survival. Even now there are several flocks of sheep and goats that belong to the whole community and are tended by the village shepherds. If you set off on a hike at the crack of dawn you will walk up into the hills to the sound of small brass bells.

Changes are not accepted easily and the village takes its traditions very seriously. You'll notice that more women than usual observe the custom of wearing black after bereavement; widows wear it for the rest of their lives, while the death of a mother means four years of mourning, and that of children or siblings, two years. Folkloric groups are maintained by those who stay behind, while the emigrants all try to inculcate a sense of *minha terra* (my homeland) into their modern-minded (and in many cases American) offspring. The local **festival** (August 13–15) has a special feel, with the fun and games spontaneous. Owing to a lack of horses, the *corrida* is a race on foot – balancing blue plastic urns full of water on their heads, the contestants compete for the honour of being ceremoniously drenched by all the others. Large, home-made fireworks are set off all over the place without warning.

Staying in Soajo is no longer a problem since ten private homes joined together in a pioneering *Turismo de Aldeia* scheme. Each has its own character and costs upwards of 7500$00 for a double room or 14,000$00 for a two-bedroom house. You can book at the park office in Ponte da Barca (see p.354), or contact ADERE-Soajo (Mon–Fri 10am–7pm, Sat 10am–1pm; ☎ & fax 258 576 427) – ask at the supermarket. There's also a luxurious *turismo rural* property, the *Casa do Adro* (☎258 576 327; ③), offering rooms in a beautiful eighteenth-century house – book well ahead at festival time. Of the **restaurants**, try either *O Espigueiro*, which specializes in goat, or the *Vidreira*.

LINDOSO AND PARADA

Close to the Spanish border and set high above a hydroelectric reservoir on the Rio Lima, **LINDOSO** is one of the most attractive villages in Peneda-Gerês, and is most easily reached from Ponte da Barca. Like Soajo, Lindoso is dominated by a cluster of *espigueiros*, and again, life here is intensely traditional. The rearing of **livestock** is central; every morning starts with the lowing of cows or the clattering of the communally herded sheep and goats, and the smell of animals lies thick in the air. The traditional method of baking bread in these parts involved removing hot coals from the oven and sealing the door with an ash and dung mixture, and it's a technique still in use in the old part of the village. If you're at all interested, there's one of these ovens still in place in the heavily restored **Castelo** (summer Tues–Fri 10am–12.30pm & 2–6pm, Sat 10am–noon & 2.30–6pm, Sun 10am–noon & 2.30–6pm; winter Tues–Fri 9.30am–12.30pm & 2–5.30pm, Sat 10am–12.30pm & 2–5pm, Sun 10am–noon & 2–4.30pm; 200$00), whose museum details the results of local excavations – you can also get general park information from here.

The only **rooms** are at the *Lindo Verde*, 1km east of Lindoso on the road to Spain (☎258 578 010; ②), which has eight new rooms with bathrooms over its restaurant, notable for the somewhat bizarre speciality dish of crocodile. There's also a bar, which has a loud disco at weekends.

PARADA, clinging to the hillside 3km west of Lindoso, is perhaps an even more attractive place, with two clusters of *espigueiros*, and vines draped over its cobbled streets. There's a superb two-hour, 4km **walking circuit**, the *Trilho do Penedo do Encanto*, which heads uphill behind the village passing age-old houses and forests of chestnut and cork. For some of the way up, it follows a rocky stream bed, remarkable for the ruts worn into the stones over the centuries by ox-carts. After about 1km, with forest plunging down to your right, look for a rusty metal gate straight in front of you, and a wall to your right covered with bundles of branches. Hop over the wall some 40m before the gate, and walk 30m straight on through the bushes. The large flat boulders in the clearing (not visible from the track) are the **Peneda do Encanto** (the "enchanted rocks"), of which the largest is covered with numerous (but faint) Bronze Age engravings. Mainly concentric circles and circular depressions, these are most visible about two hours before sunset, when the shadows are long. No one knows for sure what they represent, though similar designs can be found elsewhere in Minho and in Trás-os-Montes. Further up, the track loses itself in an exposed rocky area with superb views. To descend back to Parada, hug the forest wall to your right.

Accommodation is limited to *Café Mó* (☎258 576 150; ①), on the main road 1km west of Parada, which has six modern but musty rooms with ancient TVs, shared bathrooms, and a macho ambience in the bar, though the owner and his family are friendly. Nearby is a natural pool for swimming, popular with local kids.

The eastern section: Serra do Gerês

Despite its proximity to Caldas do Gerês (2–3hrs on foot) and the Miradouro (30min on foot), **ERMIDA** has an air of isolation about it – be warned that driving there and beyond involves some extremely steep sections, in parts badly pitted by floods. If you're looking for a quiet base for hiking or else just soaking up the mountain atmosphere, this could be a good choice: there's good accommodation and food at *Casa do Criado* (☎253 391 390; ①; phone ahead), a scattering of *dormidas*, an orchard to camp in and a couple of cafés, but it is still very much a farming community.

Continuing **east from Ermida**, along a bramble-lined lane, you'll pass a gorgeous group of small waterfalls – paradise to swim in – and cross a distinctly unsafe-looking (and sounding) bridge before coming to **FAFIÃO**, a tiny farming hamlet. There's a restaurant here, the *Retiro do Gerês*, which also has rooms (①). Past here, the countryside becomes more fertile, terraced with vines and maize, the road winding down to another hamlet, **PINCÃES**, and through it (turn right at the end of the houses) to the slightly larger village of Cabril.

A lovely, isolated place, sat on the Rio Cabril and surrounded on all sides by mountains, **CABRIL** flaunts odd attempts at modernity, though its centre is still sauntered through by oxen, goats and flocks of sheep. Parts of the locality have been submerged because of the Salamonde dam near Fafião. Consequently, the old bridge is half under water and makes for great swimming, through the bridge arch. There's a **campsite** here, *Outeiro Alto* (☎253 659 860), 1km out on the Pincães road, which is fine provided it's not too busy – there are only two toilets. It also rents out bicycles and canoes and offers horse riding. You can get a good **meal** at the *Restaurante Ponte Novo*, by the bridge, which serves a warming meat stew; the *Café 1º de Maio*, further up the road, also serves food but usually needs advance warning.

On to Montalegre and the Trás-os-Montes: Paradela and Venda Nova

From Cabril, if you're hiking or driving, you could go on to Paradela, Outeiro, Paredes do Rio, Covelães and Pitões das Júnias, the latter with a decaying monastery nearby. Any of these settlements would make an ideal base for a leisurely exploration of this little-known corner of the Minho. With enough time, you could leave Portugal at Tourém, and hook back round through Spain to re-enter either at Portela do Homen (for Caldas do Gerês) or Lindoso for the northern section of the park. There's no public transport along this route, and infrequent traffic, but the gorgeous countryside is well suited for walking, and people are friendly.

In particular, the signposted path from Cabril to Paradela – around 23km – is stunningly dramatic, winding along the river valley through the handsome villages of Sirvozelo, Lapela and Xertola. At **PARADELA**, a particularly attractive mountain village whose cobbled streets are lined with vines, you're rewarded by fine views over the dam and mountains from a clutter of cafés and **hotels**. The modern *Restaurant Sol Rio* (☎276 566 167; ②) has ten rooms, most with views, bathrooms and TVs. More characterful and set in shaded gardens with views 200 metres down the road to Cabril, *Pensão Pousadinha* (☎276 566 165; ②) has the feel of an English B&B, with some self-contained rooms and excellent breakfasts included in the rates. The *Pousadinha* is also the base for **horse riding trips** run by Trote Gerês. A further 100m along the road is the cool and friendly *Hospedaria Restaurante Dom Dinis* (☎276 566 253; ②), where all rooms have views, TVs, showers and heating, and breakfast is included. The homely **restaurant** here is good, too, with Barrosã specialities like veal and *cozido* in winter.

The small village of **OUTEIRO**, 4km north of Paradela, has more upmarket accommodation in the form of the *Estalagem Vista Bela* (☎276 560 120, fax 276 560 121; ③), with sweeping views over the dam, and good meals (around 3000$00) – try the veal or roast goat for dinner (breakfast is included).

PAREDES DO RIO, 3km east, is the next stop, notable for the excellent *Hospedaria Rocha* (☎276 566 147; ②). All rooms have bathrooms, but the restaurant is the main draw, cooking meat from its own farm. Meals cost around 1200–1500$00 (breakfast is included in room rates): try the duck, or *cavidela de frango* – chicken cooked with blood and rice. In winter, go for the *feijoada* or *cozido*. They can also arrange 4–6 hour **walking trips** to Pitões de Júnias for the price of a picnic, or can lend you photocopies of maps with the route marked on. On the hill above the *hospedaria* is the rustic *Casa da Travessa* (☎276 566 121; or book via the park office in Ponte da Barca, see p.354; ③), which has only two rooms, offering bikes if your legs are up to it, horseriding and fishing.

After Paredes, **Covelães** is useful only for picking up the key for the *casa abrigo* (see p.351) in **PITÕES DE JÚNIAS**, 10km northwest, set in one of the remotest corners of Portugal, close to the Spanish border. This is lovely walking country, with a ruined monastery and waterfall nearby, and the jagged peaks (*pitões*) of Gerês tantalizingly close to the west. The monastery was founded in the ninth century, and the following century became part of the Cistercian Order; the Romanesque façade and most of the walls still stand. There's modern family-run accommodation at the *Casa do Preto* (☎276 566 158; ①), which also houses one of Pitões' two excellent restaurants, the other being the *Pitões do Gerês*.

Alternatively, from Cabril or Paradela you can move on to **Montalegre**, via another vast reservoir. Montalegre itself (see p.380) provides a suitably remote and dramatic link with the Trás-os-Montes region, and can be reached by bus from Venda Nova or from Braga. The appeal lies as much in the road there as in the place itself. Bumpy and narrow, it makes for one of those journeys that seem to trigger madness in bus drivers, simultaneously delighting and terrifying unaccustomed passengers.

This route takes you through **VENDA NOVA**, which has two rather pricey **accommodation** options: the better of the two is the purpose-built *Estalagem do Morgado*, 4km west of Venda Nova by the reservoir at Lugar de Padrões (☎253 659 906, fax 253 659 911, *mtempo@mail.telepac.pt*; ⑤), with a swimming pool, tennis courts, water sports marina and shaded gardens. Cheaper is the *Motel São Cristóvão* (☎253 659 387; ③), an ugly modern building at the corner of the reservoir, 1km beyond Venda Nova at the junction to Salto, which also has tennis courts, and rents out boats.

There are some lovely walks in the vicinity and exceptionally bracing swimming. Buses from Braga pass through Venda Nova to Montalegre and Chaves, passing the hydroelectric plant of **Pisões** – the largest dam in the country, and an unexpectedly modern development in this otherwise very remote region.

travel details

TRAINS

Barcelos to: Porto (10–15 daily; 1hr 5min–1hr 40min); Valença do Minho (5 daily; 1hr); Viana do Castelo (12 daily; 30min).

Braga to: Nine – change for Viana and Valença (12–15 daily; 12–28min); Porto (11–14 daily, some change at Nine; 1hr–1hr 45min).

Caminha to: Porto (5–8 daily; 1 hr 30min–3hr 10min); Valença do Minho (6–7 daily; 20–40min); Viana do Castelo (7–9 daily; 20–40min).

Guimarães to: Porto (11–15 daily; 1hr 45min); Santo Tirso (11–15 daily; 45min).

Valença do Minho to: Afife (3–5 daily; 1hr); Barcelos (5–6 daily; 1hr 15min–2hr); Caminha (6–8 daily; 20–45min); Nine – change for Braga (7 daily; 2hr 20min); Porto (5 daily; 2hr 10min–3hr 40min); Vigo, Spain (4 daily; 1hr 10min; connections to Santiago de Compostela and La Coruña); Vila Nova de Cerveira (6–8 daily; 12–18min); Vila Praia de Âncora (6–8 daily; 20min–1hr).

Viana do Castelo to: Afife (4 daily; 20min); Barcelos (12 daily; 25–45min); Caminha (7–9 daily; 20–40min); Porto (10–12 daily; 1hr 30min–2hr 15min); Vila Nova de Cerveira (6–8 daily; 30min–1hr); Vila Praia de Âncora (5–7 daily; 15–25min).

Vila Nova de Cerveira to: Porto (6–7 daily; 2hr 10min–3hr 30min); Valença do Minho (6–8 daily; 12–18min); Viana do Castelo (6–8 daily; 30min–1hr).

BUSES

Arcos de Valdevez to: Braga (2–4 daily; 1hr 15min); Lindoso (Mon–Fri 1–3 daily; 30min–1hr); Ponte de Lima (5–8 daily; 1hr); Porto (2–4 daily; 2hr); Soajo (Mon–Fri 1–3 daily; 30min); Viana do Castelo (5–8 daily; 1hr 45min).

Barcelos to: Braga (Mon–Fri every 30min, Sat & Sun hourly; 50min); Chaves (Mon–Fri 13 daily, Sat & Sun 3–6 daily; 6hr); Ponte de Lima (Mon–Fri 8 daily, 1–2 at weekends; 40–55min); Porto (Mon–Sat 9–12 daily, Sun 1–2; 1hr 45min).

Braga to: Arcos de Valdevez (2–4 daily; 1hr 30min); Barcelos (Mon–Fri every 30min, Sat & Sun hourly; 50min); Bragança (3–5 daily; 6hr); Cabaceiras de Basto (4–5 daily; 1hr 45min); Caldas do Gerês (Mon–Fri hourly, Sat & Sun 8–10 daily; 1hr 30min); Campo do Gerês (3–7 daily; 1hr 20min); Cerdeirinhas (5–9 daily; 45min); Chaves (5–7 daily; 4hr); Coimbra (1 daily; 3hr 15min); Covide (5 daily; 1hr 10min); Guimarães (every 30 min; 30min–1hr); Leiria (6–9 daily; 4hr 5min); Lisbon (8–11 daily; 5hr 30min); Monção (3–5 daily; 2hr 20min); Montalegre (4–5 daily; 2hr 40min); Pisões (4–5 daily; 2hr 15min); Ponte da Barca (4 daily; 1hr 15min); Ponte de Lima (Mon–Fri 9 daily, Sat 5, Sun 1; 1hr); Porto (hourly; 1hr 10min); Póvoa do Lanhoso (5–7 daily; 35min); Póvoa do Varzim (9 daily; 1hr); Terras do Bouro (7–9 daily; 55min); Venda Nova (5–7 daily; 1hr 50min); Viana do Castelo (4–10 daily; 1hr 40min).

Caldas do Gerês to: Braga (6–10 daily; 1hr 30min).

Campo do Gerês to: Braga (3–6 daily; 1hr 20min).

Guimarães to: Braga (every 30 mins; 30min–1hr); Cabeceiras de Basto (6–8 daily; 1hr 15min); Lisbon (4–6 daily; 5hr 30min–6hr); Mondim de Basto (2 daily; 1hr 5min); Porto (6–8 daily; 2hr 30min–3hr).

Melgaço to: Castro Laboreiro (Mon–Fri 1 daily; 1hr); Coimbra (1–3 daily; 5hr); Lamas de Mouro (Mon–Fri 1 daily; 40min); Lisbon (1–3 daily; 6hr); Monção (Mon–Fri 5 daily, Sat & Sun 1 daily; 40 min); Porto (1–3 daily; 3hr); São Gregório (Mon–Fri 3 daily; 30min).

Monção to: Braga (3–6 daily; 1hr 45min); Melgaço (Mon–Fri 5 daily, Sat & Sun 1 daily; 40 min); Viana do Castelo (5 daily, 1 hr 20 min).

Ponte da Barca to: Arcos de Valdevez (hourly; 15min); Braga (14 daily; 1hr); Lindoso (2 daily; 45min); Ponte de Lima (3–4 daily; 20–30min); Viana do Castelo (6–8 daily; 1hr 30min).

Ponte de Lima to: Arcos de Valdevez (5–8 daily; 50min); Barcelos (Mon–Fri 8 daily, 1–2 at weekends; 40–55min); Braga (Mon–Fri 10 daily, Sat 6, Sun 3; 1hr); Paredes de Coura (2–5 daily; 1hr 20min); Ponte de Barca (3–4 daily; 20–30min); Porto (7 daily; 2hr); Valença (1 daily; 1hr); Viana do Castelo (Mon–Fri 21 daily, Sat & Sun 9 daily; 50min).

Valença do Minho to: Lisbon (4 daily; 6hr 30min); Melgaço (8 daily; 40min); Monçao (10 daily; 20min); Ponte de Lima (1 daily; 1hr); Porto (7 daily; 2hr 30min); Viana do Castelo via Caminha (7 daily; 1 hr); Vila Nova de Cerveira (6 daily; 15min); to Spain: Sat to Vigo/Santiago (2hr/4hr 15min); Tues, Thurs, and Fri via Monção and Melgaço for Ponte Barxas.

Viana do Castelo to: Afife (5–14 daily; 15min); Arcos de Valdevez (3–7 daily; 1hr 50min); Braga (4–11 daily; 1hr 40min); Caminha (Mon–Fri 13 daily, Sat & Sun 5 daily; 35min); Esposende (Mon–Fri 10–15 daily, Sun 4; 40min); Lisbon (2 daily; 6hr); Moledo do Minho (Mon–Fri 13 daily, Sat & Sun 5 daily; 30min); Ponte da Barca (6–8 daily; 1hr 30min); Ponte de Lima (Mon–Fri 21 daily, Sat & Sun 7 daily; 50min); Porto (Mon–Sat 10–14 daily, Sun 4; 2hr 5min); Póvoa de Varzim (Mon–Sat 10–15 daily, Sun 4 daily; 1hr 5min); Vila do Conde (Mon–Sat 10–14 daily, Sun 4; 1hr 40min); Vila Praia de Âncora (Mon–Fri 13 daily, Sat & Sun 5 daily; 30min).

CHAPTER SEVEN

TRÁS-OS-MONTES

T RÁS-OS-MONTES – literally "Beyond the Mountains" – is Portugal's Lost Domain. For centuries this remote, rural province has been a place to hide and practise one's beliefs in peace: its peculiar traditions and dialects have been formed by a diversity of populations, from the prehistoric tribes who carved the *porcas* (stone pigs) to Jews who sought refuge here from the Inquisition.

A sharp natural divide cuts across the province. In the south is the fertile territory officially entitled the Upper Douro, but known unofficially as the **Terra Quente** (Hot Land), which encompasses the terraced stretches of the rivers Douro, Corgo and Tua, and produces peaches, oranges, melons and wine. By contrast, the bitter winters of the wild and rugged north have earned it the name of **Terra Fria** (Cold Land). The extremity of the climate – "Nine months of winter and three months of hell", as the local proverb puts it – and the aridity of much of its land have kept Trás-os-Montes well apart from the mainstream. Even today, with some industry coming to the major towns, the province has a population half the size of that of the Minho in almost twice the area. But change is approaching rapidly: a recent seven-year World Bank investment project saw over £400 million pumped into the area's agricultural sector, whilst an ongoing EU-funded road construction programme is creating one of the best and fastest road networks in the country.

Travelling into the province is easy, with fast daily bus services from Porto to the main towns of Vila Real, Chaves, Mirandela and Bragança, though travel within the region can be a slow business, with few remaining train services, and buses generally operating on weekdays only. However, almost any route in Trás-os-Montes has its rewards, and the fortified frontier towns of **Chaves** and **Bragança** should feature on any itinerary of northern Portugal. For the most part though, Trás-os-Montes' sights are defiantly rural: a succession of hardworking mountain or valley villages, and small, fortified settlements – **Mirando do Douro** (whose almond trees draw weekenders for their fleeting blossoming in late February and early March), **Mogadouro** and **Freixo de Espada à Cinta** – guarding the border with Spain, whose appeal lies above all in their isolation.

One of the few towns of any real size in the entire region is **Vila Real** – a good starting point for a tour of the province, especially for hikers, with its access to the dramatic granite scenery of the **Parque Natural do Alvão**. A second natural park hugs the border with Spain in the far north of the province, beyond Bragança, in the **Serra de Montesinho**, where walkers can experience Trás-os-Montes at its most rural and remote; while a third,

---

ACCOMMODATION PRICE CODES

All the accommodation prices in this book have been coded using the symbols below. The symbols represent the lowest prices you can expect to pay for a **double room in high season**; for a full explanation, see p.32.

① Under 4000$00	④ 11,000$00–15,000$00	⑦ 25,000$00–30,000$00
② 4000$00–7000$00	⑤ 15,000$00–20,000$00	⑧ 30,000$00–40,000$00
③ 7000$00–11,000$00	⑥ 20,000$00–25,000$00	⑨ Over 40,000$00

the **Parque Natural do Douro Internacional**, has recently been designated in the east of the region where the Douro and its tributary, the Rio Águeda, skirt the Spanish border.

Chaves can be reached, a little tortuously, from Braga and the Peneda-Gerês national park (see p.350), but the most obvious approach to the region is from the Douro, whose eastern reaches (covered in Chapter Five) are technically a part of the province. From the main Douro train line, which runs from Porto to Pocinho, the **Corgo line** branches off to the north through a spectacular winding gorge from Peso da Régua to **Vila Real**, from where you can catch buses north to Chaves and most other destinations; while the **Tua Valley line**, from Tua to **Mirandela** affords equally spectacular scenery, with the option of onward bus connections to Bragança and Chaves in the north, and Miranda do Douro and Torre de Moncorvo in the east.

Vila Real and around

VILA REAL is the one break from the pastoralism of the beautiful Rio Corgo, a tributary of the Douro which provides the first link from the Douro region to Trás-os-Montes. Its setting is magnificent, with the twin mountain ranges of **Marão** and **Alvão** (the so-called "Gateway to Trás-os-Montes") forming a natural amphitheatre behind the town. Walkers may well want to make Vila Real a base for a couple of days' exploration of these ranges, while, for more casual exploration, the town gives easy access to a Roman site at **Panóias** and to the **Solar de Mateus** – the country house featured on the Mateus Rosé wine label. Compared to the somnolent villages further north and east, Vila Real, which houses the University of Trás-os-Montes, is actually quite a lively place – especially during the major **festivals** of Santo António (June 13) and São Pedro (June 28–29), at which times you should book your accommodation well in advance. Other *feiras* to look out for include those of São Brás (February 3) and Santa Luzia (December 13), and there's also a procession for Corpus Deus on June 3. The *feiras* are the best time to buy the distinctive pewter-grey **earthenware crockery** made in the nearby village of Bisalhães.

The Town and its surroundings

The old quarter of Vila Real is attractive enough, built on a promontory above the confluence of the Corgo and Cabril rivers, with the main avenue running down its spine; the view from the fourteenth-century **Capela de São Brás** at its southern end is not one for vertigo sufferers. There's little else to see in town, save for the **turismo** building – formerly the palace of the Marquês of Vila Real, and fronted by four Manueline windows – and the **Sé**, over the way, which has modern stained-glass windows and a simple, fifteenth-century interior. Back at the bottom of town, by the **Câmara Municipal**, a plaque on the wall of the café opposite commemorates the birthplace of Diogo Cão, who discovered the mouth of the Congo River in 1482.

The Solar de Mateus and Panóias

Given the paucity of things to do in Vila Real itself, half-day **trips** out to the Solar de Mateus and the Roman remains at Panóias make good use of a night's stopover. Both are easily visited by car, and it's also it's quite feasible to see Mateus by public transport, with regular **bus** services along the Sabrosa road. Rodonorte buses run nine times daily, or you can catch a Cabanelas bus (Mon–Sat; four daily). To get to Panóias by public transport you'll need to take a Rodonorte bus bound for Sabrosa (Mon, Wed, Fri–Sun 12.10pm; Tues & Thurs 11.30am & 12.10pm), the birthplace of Magellan (Magalhães in Portuguese) but better known nowadays for its wine. The site is around 6km east of Mateus, signposted a few hundred metres north of the road. The last bus back to Vila Real leaves Sabrosa at 3pm, passing Panóias about fifteen minutes later; wait by the main road below the site.

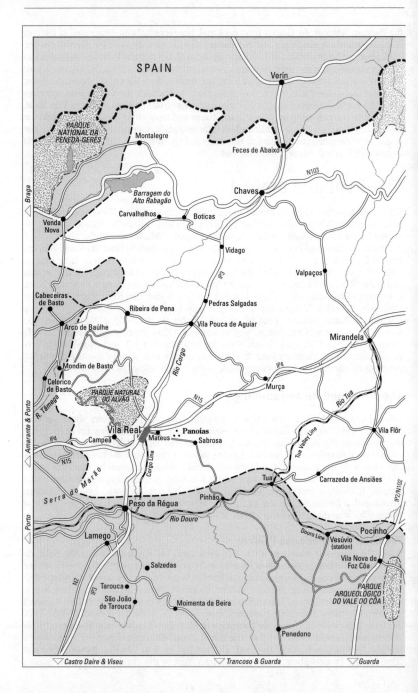

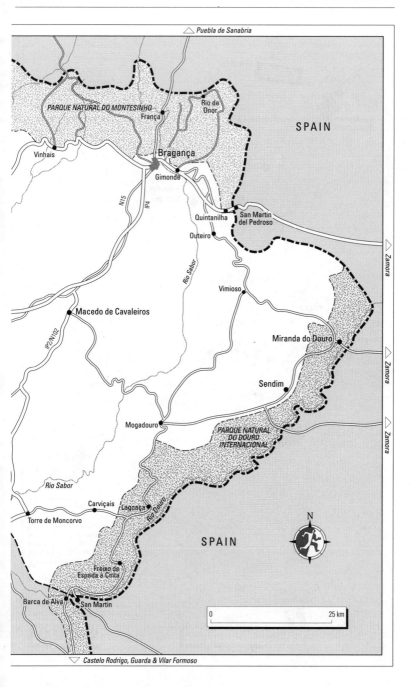

△ *Puebla de Sanabria*

PARQUE NATURAL DO MONTESINHO

Rio de Onor

França

SPAIN

Vinhais

Bragança

Gimonde

N15

IP4

Quintanilha

San Martin del Pedroso

Outeiro

Rio Sabor

Vimioso

▷ *Zamora*

Macedo de Cavaleiros

IP2/N102

Miranda do Douro

▷ *Zamora*

Sendim

Mogadouro

▷ *Zamora*

PARQUE NATURAL DO DOURO INTERNACIONAL

Rio Sabor

Carviçais

Lagoaça

Rio Douro

Torre de Moncorvo

N

SPAIN

Freixo de Espada à Cinta

Barca de Alva

San Martin

0   25 km

▽ *Castelo Rodrigo, Guarda & Vilar Formoso*

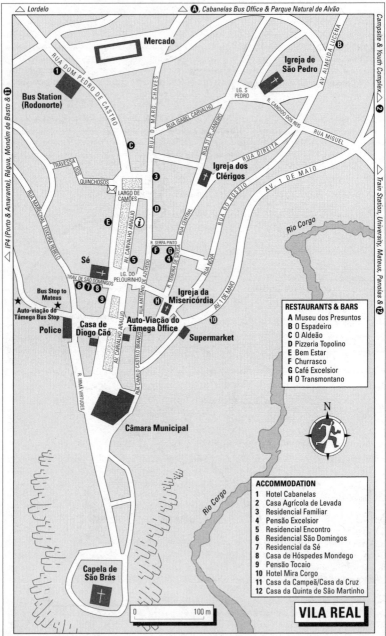

△ Lordelo

△ Ⓐ, Cabanelas Bus Office & Parque Natural de Alvão

Campsite & Youth Complex △ ②

△ Train Station, University, Mateus, Panóias & ⑫

◁ IP4 (Porto & Amarante), Régua, Mondim de Basto & ⑪

Mercado

Igreja de São Pedro

RUA DOM PEDRO DE CASTRO

Ⓐ

Bus Station (Rodonorte)

LG. S PEDRO

AV. ALMEIDA LUCENA

Ⓑ

R. CANDIDO DOS REIS

RUA D MARG CHAVES

RUA ISABEL CARVALHO

RUA 31 DE JANEIRO

RUA MIGUEL

Ⓒ

TRAVESSA DOS QUINCHOSOS

RUA DIREITA

Igreja dos Clérigos

AV. DO ROSSIO

AV. 1 DE MAIO

LARGO DE CAMÕES

③

Ⓓ

RUA CENTRAL

Rio Corgo

Ⓔ

ⓘ

AV. CARVALHO ARAUJO

R. SERPA PINTO

Ⓕ Ⓖ

Sé

⑤

④

RUA TEIXEIRA DE SOUSA

RUA NOVA

TRAV. DE SÃO DOMINGOS

⑥⑦⑧

LG. DO PELOURINHO

RUA ANTÓNIO AZEVEDO

Ⓗ

⑨

Igreja da Misericórdia

AV. 1 DE MAIO

Bus Stop to Mateus ★

★ **Auto-viação do Tâmega Bus Stop**

⑩

Police

Casa de Diogo Cão

AV. CARVALHO ARAUJO

Auto-Viação do Tâmega Office

Supermarket

R. IRMÃ VIRTUDES

RUA CAMILO CASTELO BRANCO

Câmara Municipal

Rio Corgo

N

RESTAURANTS & BARS
A Museu dos Presuntos
B O Espadeiro
C O Aldeão
D Pizzeria Topolino
E Bem Estar
F Churrasco
G Café Excelsior
H O Transmontano

Capela de São Brás

0   100 m

ACCOMMODATION
1   Hotel Cabanelas
2   Casa Agrícola de Levada
3   Residencial Familiar
4   Pensão Excelsior
5   Residencial Encontro
6   Residencial São Domingos
7   Residencial da Sé
8   Casa de Hóspedes Mondego
9   Pensão Tocaio
10 Hotel Mira Corgo
11 Casa da Campeã/Casa da Cruz
12 Casa da Quinta de São Martinho

VILA REAL

The **Solar de Mateus** (signposted "Palácio de Mateus") is just 4km east of Vila Real. Described by Sacheverell Sitwell as "the most typical and the most fantastic country house in Portugal", it's certainly the most familiar, being reproduced on each bottle of Mateus Rosé, one of Portugal's major wine exports. The facade fits in well enough with the wine's soft-focus image, its twin wings "advancing lobster-like", as Sitwell put it, across a formal lake. The architect is unknown, though most authorities attribute it to the Italian, Nicolau Nasoni, who built the landmark Clérigos church in Porto; the palace is dated around 1740 – the heyday of Portuguese Baroque.

Prices continue to spiral for a somewhat limited thirty-minute tour of the **interior** (daily: summer 9am–7pm; winter 10am–1pm & 2–5pm; house and gardens 1000$00, gardens only 600$00; ☎259 323 121, *www.utad.geira.pt/casa_mateus/*). Although there are no special treasures, the building is an enjoyable evocation of its period, full of draperies, aristocratic portraits and rural scenes. The **gardens**, too, are a delight, the spectacular box avenue forming an impressive tunnel about 50m long, and there's a small gift shop and café in the grounds. On summer weekends (mid-May to early September) classical **concerts** are held here: the turismo in Vila Real has the schedule, or contact the Solar itself. Performances usually begin late (9–10pm), so you'll need your own transport.

The Roman site of **PANÓIAS** (Tues 2–5pm, Wed–Sun 9.30am–12.30pm & 2–5pm; free, but plans to charge 200$00, including guided tour and brochure), 6km further along the Sabrosa road, is the sole remnant of the once powerful settlement of Vila de Constantim de Panoyas. It doesn't at first appear much of a site, consisting of a wire fence enclosing a few boulders with odd-shaped cavities, and for a long time it languished as something of a rubbish tip, though it's now been cleaned up. The site appears to have been the location of the temple of a particularly bloody pre-Roman cult, which was later adopted by the Romans and dedicated to Serapis (a cult of Egyptian origin), and possibly also to Jupiter. The rickety viewing tower at the top end gives you a good view of the three coffin-shaped **sacrificial cavities** on the largest boulder, which used to have a filter system for the blood and viscera created by the offerings; the much eroded inscriptions to this effect on nearby boulders are in a strange mixture of Greek and Latin, lending weight to the theory that the temple may have been constructed well before the Romans arrived.

Practicalities

Vila Real is the hub of Trás-os-Montes' regional transport. Rodonorte operates from their **bus station** beside the *Hotel Cabanelas* on Rua dom Pedro de Castro, just north of the centre (☎259 323 234); all other regional buses stop outside here. Cabanelas, who also act as agents for Santos (for services eastwards to Mirandela, Miranda do Douro and Torre de Moncorvo) have their office at Avenida Dom Dinis (☎259 325 256); while for services to Chaves and Bragança, Auto-Viação do Tâmega's office can be found at Avenida Carvalho Araújo 26, near the Camâra Municipal (☎259 322 928). The **train station** is 500m east of the centre, on the opposite bank of the river; to reach the town centre from here, follow the road into town, over the bridge, and turn left. From Vila Real there are five trains daily on the Corgo line to Peso da Régua (see p.292).

The **turismo** (summer Mon–Fri 9.30am–7pm, Sat & Sun 10am–noon & 2–5pm; winter Mon–Fri 9.30am–12.30pm & 2–5pm; ☎259 322 819, *www.cm-vilareal.pt*) is on the central Avenida Carvalho Araújo, at no. 94. Helpful as ever, it can provide transport and accommodation details, including advice on the various *turismo rural* properties in the area. More information on the region (including the Serra do Alvão and the Serra do Marão) is available from the **regional tourist office** at Avenida 1º de Maio 70–1º (Mon–Fri 9am–12.30pm & 2–5.30pm; ☎259 322 819, fax 259 321 712); while those planning a visit to the **Parque Natural do Alvão** (see p.371), should head for the park headquarters at Praceta do Tronco, Lote 17, Cruz das Almas (Mon–Fri 9am–12.30pm & 2–5.30pm; ☎259 324 138, fax 259 373 869).

Accommodation

The pick of the town's **pensões and hotels** is reviewed below but be warned that the more basic places can get distinctly chilly and damp in winter. The cheapest hostel-type accommodation is at the *Instituto da Juventude* youth complex on Avenida Dr. Manuel Cardona (☎259 323 551), and there's a pleasant **campsite** with a swimming pool down by the river (☎259 324 724). To get there from the centre, follow Avenida 1º de Maio; if you're coming from the train station, turn right after crossing the bridge. There's adequate shade, but arrive early if you want a riverside pitch.

IN TOWN

Hotel Cabanelas, Rua Dom Pedro de Castro (☎259 323 153, fax 259 323 028). Modern functional comforts next to the bus station, fractionally cheaper than the *Mira Corgo* but lacking a pool. ③.

Casa de Hóspedes Mondego, Trav. de São Domingos 11 (☎259 323 097, fax 259 322 039). Near the Sé, this has some of the cheapest rooms in town, but the plumbing is somewhat archaic, and it gets very hot in summer and cold in winter. ①.

Residencial Encontro, Av. Carvalho Araújo 76–78 (☎259 322 532). Family-run place, inexpensive with a mixed bag of rooms above a restaurant. It's near the turismo, and can be a bit noisy at night. Breakfast included. ②.

Pensão Excelsior, Rua Serpa Pinto (☎259 322 422). Next to the café of the same name, this has a few basic rooms, most without bathrooms. ①.

Residencial Familiar, Praça Luís de Camões 36 (☎259 322 100). Good cheap rooms, clean if a little basic, some with bathrooms. ①.

Hotel Mira Corgo, Av. 1º de Maio 76–78 (☎259 325 001, fax 259 325 006). Vila Real's swankiest hotel is an ugly modern block but its rooms overlook the stepped terraces of the Corgo, far below, and there's an indoor swimming pool and solarium. There's also a disco, guaranteed to disturb many a peaceful night. ③.

Residencial São Domingos, Travessa de São Domingos 33 (☎/fax 259 322 039). A nice, run-down but friendly *pensão*, operated by the same family as the *Mondego*, that makes an effort to be modern by putting TVs in the rooms. Gets stuffy in summer. ②.

Residencial da Sé, Trav. de São Domingos 19–23 (☎259 324 575). Next to the *Mondego*, this place has private facilities attached to most of the rooms, and a restaurant below. ②.

Pensão Tocaio, Av. Carvalho Araújo 45-55 (☎259 323 106, fax 259 371 675). Large and rather dark 1950s hotel, long since demoted to *pensão* status. All rooms come with a private bathroom (but not always hot water), and the reception area comes with a stuffed wild pig. ③.

OUTSIDE TOWN

Casa Agrícola da Levada, 2km northeast at Timpeira (☎259 322 190, fax 259 346 955; or reserve through Solares de Portugal, see p.33). Take the Mateus bus or follow Avenida 1º de Maio towards Bragança for 2km until the road descends towards a stone bridge; on the left you'll see this impressive farmhouse set in its own grounds and with an attached chapel. ④.

Casa da Campeã, 10km west, 2km before Campeã, just off the IP4 (☎259 979 640, fax 259 979 760). Modern chalet-cum-motel set-up with a pool and good restaurant, though the main attraction are the activities offered in the nearby Vale da Campeã (Serra do Marão), including rafting, paragliding, bungee jumping and of course hiking. ③.

Casa da Cruz, Campeã, 12km west along the road to Mondim (☎259 979 422, fax 259 972 995; or reserve through Privetur, see p.33). Three simple rooms with lovely carved beds in this eighteenth-century granite farmhouse, overlooking the Vale da Campeã. Rustic sitting room, and free use of kitchen. Fishing and cycling trips can be arranged. ③.

Casa da Quinta de São Martinho, 4km east at Mateus, 300m from the Solar de Mateus (☎/fax 259 323 986; or reserve through Privetur, see p.33). Seventeenth-century granite country house with a comfortable clutter of old and new furniture, nothing fancy but charming in its way. Two bedrooms, two apartments, and a pool. Also port wine tasting in the bar. ③.

Eating, drinking and nightlife

For inexpensive local **meals**, try any of the cafés in the streets behind the turismo. There's also a timeless (and nameless) *adega* – dark, cave-like and festooned with hams and plastic wine jars – at Travessa de São Domingos 17. If you're planning day-trips out of Vila Real you can stock up on your own **food supplies** at the weekday market opposite the Rodonorte bus station, or at the **supermarket** hidden in the shopping centre next to *Hotel Mira Corgo* on Avenida 1º de Maio. There's a good **wine shop** on Largo do Pelourinho.

The liveliest **nightspots** are the bars along Largo do Pelourinho and Rua Serpa Pinto, notably *Café Excelsior* at nos. 30–36 on the latter, which has a huge pool hall featuring the strangest timing meters for your game you'll ever see.

RESTAURANTS

Local dishes worth looking out for include roast kid goat and veal, *cozido à portuguesa*, and – if you hadn't eaten your fill in Porto – *tripas aos molhos* ("sheaves" of tripe, no less). For less gutsy bellies, **pastries** to ask for are *pastéis de Santa Clara* (stuffed with very sweet egg goo), *toucinho do céu* ("heavenly bacon", because it supposedly looks like it), and *tigelinhas de laranja* ("orange bowls").

O Aldeão, Rua Dom Pedro de Castro 70. Popular and very reasonably priced, with a changing daily menu of standards: meals upwards of 1500$00.

Bem Estar, Av. Carvalho Araújo, opposite the turismo. Family-run, basic, and inexpensive.

Churrasco, Rua António de Azevedo 24 (☎259 322 313). Simple place offering pretty much normal fare except for the wonderful spit-roast chicken. Around 1700$00. Closed Sun.

O Espadeiro, Av. Almeida Lucena (☎259 322 302). Highly reputed regional restaurant that's been going for over 30 years. Trout stuffed with ham, and the roast kid are both good, though the desserts lag behind; meals cost 2500$00 upwards. Good wine list. Closed Wed, and late Sept.

Museu dos Presuntos, Av. Cidade Orense 43 (☎259 326 017). Trendy place near the new teepee-styled church 1km to the north, great for *pratinhos* ("small dishes") – ham, cod-fish balls, grilled *chouriço*, chicken sweetmeats and tripe. Closed Tues.

Pizzeria Topolino, Rua António de Azevedo, off the Praça de Camões. A pleasant interior with good options for vegetarians.

O Transmontano, Rua da Misericórdia 37. Caters for big groups and can be a bit touristy, but good value nonetheless, specializing in *bacalhau*.

The Parque Natural do Alvão

Portugal's smallest natural park, the boulder-strewn and pine-covered **PARQUE NATURAL DO ALVÃO**, can be glimpsed when travelling by road between Vila Real and Amarante along the IP4, but you'll see more from the N304, which branches off the IP4 towards Mondim de Basto and goes through the park itself, around Ermelo. This route is served by buses (from Vila Real: Mon–Fri 8am, 1.20pm & 6pm, Sat 8am & 1.20pm; from Mondim de Basto: Mon–Fri 7am, 12.30pm & 5.30pm, Sat 7am & 12.30pm), and is the easiest approach if you're coming by public transport since there's none on the eastern side of the park. With a car, you might prefer to take the minor N313 from north of Vila Real to Mondim de Basto that cuts right through the park via Lamas de Ôlo.

Visits to the park aren't made any easier by the lack of **accommodation** (the turismo in Vila Real has a list of accommodation on the park's outskirts); camping is prohibited to avoid the very real risk of forest fires. Serious walkers intending to cross the whole reserve should obtain maps in advance from Porto or Lisbon and consult the **park headquarters** in Vila Real (see p.365) or the park office in Mondim de Basto (see p.290). For **organized tours**, contact Realvitur at Largo Pioledo 2 in Vila Real (☎259 321 800, fax 259 374 353), who offer tailor-made trips by Land Rover into the park; or Os Tamecanos in Mondim de Basto (☎255 302 637).

Despite these difficulties, the park itself is a delight, and one of the few places in Portugal where you really feel you're in the wild. There are only a handful of settlements, mostly constructed on rocky terrain to conserve the little arable land available, and almost everywhere you'll have your nostrils filled with the scent of pine, the sap of which is tapped to make solvents. Birds to look out for include royal eagles, round wing eagles, screech owls and the blue titmouse. Other **wildlife** isn't so easy to spot and you'd be extremely lucky to see any of the wolves, roe deer or wild boar that live in the park. You're unlikely to see snakes, as they tend to flee at the sound of approaching footsteps.

Without your own transport, the easiest **circuit** – giving you gorgeous views of mountains, pine trees and plunging valleys (allow 5–7 hours) – is in the west: catch the early morning bus from Vila Real or Mondim to the junction for **ERMELO** (1km off the main N304), a sleepy little hamlet that comes alive for two days a year (August 7–8) for the *Feira de São Vicente*, which also celebrates the annual return of Ermelo's emigrants from Porto and abroad. From here, a track leads up the mountain, running high above the left bank of the **Rio Ôlo** – a tributary of the Tâmega – past the hamlet of **Fervença** (a 3km detour from here takes you to **Barreiro**, with superb views westwards), before crossing the river at **Varzigueto**. From here a track runs back to Ermelo, where you can catch the late-afternoon bus back to Vila Real or Mondim (check at Vila Real or Mondim turismo for times). For an alternative circuit (also 5–7hr), take the track 1km west of Ermelo on the main Vila Real–Mondim road (signposted "Fisgas"), and head uphill along the forestry track, with the Rio Ôlo hidden in the ravine to your right. A couple of kilometres along, a right turn by a restaurant-café takes you on a 2km detour to a spectacular rocky ledge overlooking the waterfalls of **Fisgas de Ermelo**. Back at the restaurant, the track continues uphill among more rugged terrain for another 3km before joining the track from Varzigueto back to Ermelo.

To explore the eastern side of the park, catch a bus from Vila Real towards Chaves, getting off after 5km at the turning for the N313 to Mondim de Basto. From here it's a strenuous few hours hike to **LAMAS DE ÔLO**, a quiet rural hamlet around 1000 metres above sea level, notable for its peculiar granite houses with tent-like thatch roofs (many now abandoned) and, above the village, a watermill with a primitive aqueduct. It's a beautiful walk, though, and at weekends you may be able to hitch a lift with other visitors. A particularly attractive walking circuit (around 3hr) begins in **AGAREZ**, 4km from Lamas de Ôlo, looping anticlockwise via **Galegos da Serra** on the Arnal stream, with its working watermill and waterfall, past a school for ecologists (which may have **rooms** for the night – enquire at the park office in Vila Real), and upstream to **Arnal**, where a women's cooperative produces **linen** clothing and sheets which you can buy. From Arnal, there's a minor road back to Agarez.

Northeast: routes to Chaves and Bragança

Beyond Vila Real, Trás-os-Montes begins in earnest, with two main routes heading **northeast**, either to Chaves (64km) or to Bragança (136km). The IP3 (formerly the N2) to Chaves is a particularly fine route, the road constrained by the twists and turns of the **Corgo river valley**, though there's really only one worthwhile overnight stop, at the spa town of **Vidago**. The longer roads to Bragança (the N15 or the new, faster IP4) have more of interest to delay you, with a possible stopover halfway at medieval **Mirandela** in the **Tua valley** (from where the minor N213 cuts north to Chaves); from here, there are also diversions **south** along the N213/N214 to intriguing towns like Vila Flôr and Carrazeda de Ansiães.

The Corgo Valley and Vidago

From Vila Real, Auto-Viação do Tâmega buses run regularly along the IP3 through the spectacular **Corgo river valley**, where everything from cowsheds to vine posts is made from granite, and where the luscious green of the vines belies the apparent barrenness of the earth. En route, you'll also see the strange *espigueiros* or corn sheds, long and improbably thin granite constructions perched atop stone or wooden stilts. It's a less dramatic ride than that once provided by the old Linha do Corgo train line, long since abandoned to the elements, but it's handsome enough, the road following the valley fairly closely as far as the village of **VILA POUCA DE AGUIAR**, 28km from Vila Real, which is famous in the north for its bread. There's not much reason to stay here, though if you get stuck, there are a handful of *residenciais* along the main road (all ②). Beyond here, the road cuts through the edge of the Serra da Padrela, before reaching the upper valley of the Tâmega River at Vidago, which it then traces for the rest of the route to Chaves.

Vidago

The spa town of **VIDAGO** is easily the most interesting stop along the way, with some lovely walks in the vicinity and the opportunity to splash about in the local rivers. It's important to note, however, that the spa closes in winter, as do most of the hotels and *pensões*. Buses drop you by the summer **turismo** (9am–noon & 2–6pm; ☎276 907 470) on the main road and from here it's only a short walk to the spa and hotels – follow the flurry of signs.

The **spa** itself (mid-June to mid-Oct Mon–Sat 8am–noon & 4–7pm) is set in the beautiful grounds of the four-star *Vidago Palace Hotel* (☎276 907 356, fax 276 907 359; ⑥), an astonishingly opulent Edwardian pile and without doubt one of Portugal's finest hotels. The pump room is magnificent, and there's also a bandstand amid the trees, a boating lake and bikes for rent (for residents only), not to mention the pool, tennis courts and nine-hole golf course. Its restaurant is worth a visit, too, with less scary prices than you may imagine (under 3000$00). *Hotel do Parque*, Avenida Teixeira de Sousa (☎276 907 157, fax 276 909 666; ③), is a modern rival to the *Vidago Palace*, with tennis courts and a pool, but lacks its grace and character. The best of the less expensive options include *Pensão Alameda*, Rua Padre Adolfo Magalhães 2 (☎276 907 246; ③), a small, friendly, family-run place, with breakfast thrown in; and *Pensão Primavera*, at Avenida Conde de Caria 2, facing the *Vidago Palace* (☎276 907 378, fax 276 999 444; ③), a good-value and attractive place with a wide range of rooms and its own restaurant.

Mirandela and the Tua Valley

It's 71km along the N15 (or 65km along the fast IP4) from Vila Real to **MIRANDELA**, an odd little town with a few remnants of a medieval centre, a scattering of Baroque mansions and a modern art gallery, as well as some horrible concrete constructions. The town's most striking feature is undoubtedly its **Roman bridge**, renovated in the fifteenth century and stretching a good 200m across seventeen arches. It's open only to pedestrians, with traffic forced to use the new concrete bridge beside it, or the Ponte Europa upstream. Kayaks and pedalos splash up and down here, and the riverside gardens and lawns are pleasant places to loaf around.

Parts of the decaying **old town** have recently been renovated or demolished; the chapel near the Câmara Municipal, at the summit of the ancient citadel, simply fell down in 1985. Scavengers pilfered the best of the stonework, and what was left was rebuilt in a four-square style topped with an ugly glass pyramid that contrasts awkwardly with the grandiose **Câmara Municipal** itself. Formerly the Palácio dos Távoras, this was one of several flamboyant town houses associated with the **Távora** family, who controlled the town between the fourteenth and seventeenth centuries. The modern art gallery, the **Museu Armindo Teixeira Lopes** (Mon–Fri 10am–12.30pm & 2–6pm; free), is combined with the town's library and displays modern sculptures and paintings, with one section dedicated to local artist Armindo Teixeira Lopes's images of Mirandela and Lisbon.

The best time to visit Mirandela is during the **Festa da Senhora do Amparo** (July 25 to the first Sunday in August), one of the longest *festas* in Portugal. The final Saturday is the big day, with a procession and fireworks, although things also get hot on Friday night (the *Noite das Bombas*, or "Night of the Drums"), also with fireworks and a secular parade. Traditional music and dance can be sampled at the **Festa dos Reis** (January 6) at Vale de Salgueiro, 12km north on the Vinhais road, where a "king" visits the village's houses distributing *tremoços* (pickled beans) and wine to the sound of bagpipes. Weekday **markets** are held in Mirandela as close as possible to the 3rd, 14th, or 25th of every month.

Mirandela practicalities

Buses arrive at the terminal next to the train station. To get to the town centre turn right, then right again and with the river on your left it's a five-minute walk to the Roman bridge, from where the road veers into Rua da República. The **turismo** (Mon–Fri 9.30am–12.30pm & 2–6pm; ☎278 200 200 ext. 272) is located here in the market building, and has a handy free booklet containing information about the town and driving circuits in the area.

With half a dozen **pensões and hotels**, rooms in Mirandela are pretty easy to find, except during the *festa*. Cheapest are the reasonable *Pensão Sá Moreno*, off Rua da República at Rua das Amoreiras 71 (☎278 262 434; ①), with shared bathrooms; the characterful if basic *Pensão Praia*, Largo 1º de Janeiro 6, also off Rua da República (☎278 262 497; ①–②), which has a mixed bag of rooms (some en suite) and attractive lake views from its upper floor; and the self-contained rooms at the friendly pine-furnished *Pensão O Lagar*, Rua da República 120 (☎278 262 712; ②). *Residencial Globo,* Rua Cidade de Ortês (☎278 248 210, fax 278 248 871; ③), over the old bridge near the hospital, has better facilities and is good value, while *Residencial Mira-Tua*, at Rua da República 20 (☎278 265 003, fax 278 265 003; ③), is a decent and well-appointed high-rise. The local **campsite** (☎278 263 177) is 3km north of town on the Bragança road, and has a swimming pool (open to the public in summer).

For **meals**, try the good restaurant at *Pensão Sá Moreno*, or *O Pomar* on Avenida Dr. Francisco Sá Carneiro (closed Tues). You shouldn't miss trying Mirandela's famed *alheira* **sausages**, a legacy of the Jewish community that has since disappeared. Made primarily from chicken and bread (though pork is now also added), they're cooked quickly and served with rice or potatoes.

On to Bragança: Macedo de Cavaleiros

At Mirandela the Tua valley broadens and the Bragança road veers east along the Rio Azibo, past **MACEDO DE CAVALEIROS**. Unless the shooting and fishing parties at the exclusive *Estalagem do Caçador* on Largo Manuel Pinto de Azevedo (☎278 426 356 or 278 426 381; ④) are your bag, this is not much of a place to linger. If you want a lunch-stop from driving, or get stranded trying to make a bus connection southeast to Mogadouro, you might sample the delicious **pizzas** at the *Pizzaria d'Itália* at Rua Fonte do Paço 5. There are inexpensive **rooms** (with shared bath) at the central *Restaurante Residencial Flórida* (☎278 421 342; ①), facing the Câmara Municipal on Rua Dr. Francisco Sá Carneiro; more upmarket are *Residencial Nova Churrasqueira*, Rua Pereira Charula 8 (☎278 421 731; ②), with some en-suite rooms, and *Residencial Muchacha* opposite (☎278 422 658; ②, breakfast included). You can buy **bus tickets** from the kiosk outside the *Estalagem do Caçador*, and there's a small **turismo** on Praça das Eiras (Mon–Fri variable hours; ☎278 426 034).

Vila Flôr and Carrazeda de Ansiães

Travelling by road between Mirandela and the Douro, the main route (IP2) runs to the southeast of the Tua valley, past **Vila Flôr** and **Carrazeda de Ansiães**. Both are rewarding halts, and are connected by bus to each other, Tua, Mirandela and Torre de Moncorvo.

Vila Flôr

Twenty-four kilometres south of Mirandela, **VILA FLÔR** (Town of Flowers) was given its name in the thirteenth century by Dom Dinis, on his way to meet Isabel of Aragon. His favouritism was short-lived, though, for soon Vila Flôr was forced to contribute a third of its revenue to rebuilding the walls of rival Torre de Moncorvo, 30km to the south. Vila Flôr still has a piece of old wall known as the *Arco Dom Dinis* and a so-called "Roman" fountain.

With its tree-lined squares, attractive location and striking church, the town warrants at least a night's stay, and the eccentric **Museu Municipal de Berta Cabral**, just south of the main square (Mon & Wed–Sun 10am–12.30pm & 2–5.30pm; free), certainly merits a visit. Three eminent Vilaflôrians donated the contents of their houses to the museum when it was founded in 1946, and the result is an incredible hodge-podge: a much-glued stone *porca* and a few dusty pictures by Manuel Moura being the only items of value. The enveloping clutter includes typewriters, the town's first telephone, sewing machines, snake skins, a vicious set of walking sticks doubling as swords and guns, an embalmed Angolan rat, a set of broken percussion instruments, religious sculptures, teacups, stuffed animals and an ensemble of zebra-hide furniture. You'll have to ask the staff to open the rooms downstairs, which are normally kept closed.

An extensive **street market** is held on the weekday closest to the 15th and 28th of every month, and the town **festa** runs from August 22 to 28, with live music and open-air stalls on the last weekend: the main day is the 24th. There's also some activity on the night of São João (June 23–24), but the main event in the region is the **Romaria de Nossa Senhora da Assunção**, which takes place every August 15 at the hilltop sanctuary of Vilas Boas, 8km northwest of Vila Flôr. Held on the site of an apparition of the Virgin in 1673, this is one of the largest *romarias* in Trás-os-Montes, where ten saintly images are carried through the multitude, headed by an image of Nossa Senhora carried on the backs of over a hundred men.

PRACTICALITIES

The Carrazeda–Vila Flôr **bus station** is on Avenida Marechal Carmona; there are regular weekday services to Torre de Moncorvo and Mirandela, but weekends are very restricted with no Saturday service and only one or two buses on Sundays. The town's **turismo** (Mon–Fri only) is opposite the Museu Municipal, but is generally only open for a few hours in the afternoon.

There are two **pensões** at the new, upper end of town, of which *Pensão Campos,* on Avenida Marechal Carmona 43–45 (☎278 512 315; ②, breakfast included), is the most pleasant, with big rooms, most with bathrooms and TV. The *Casa Roças,* a little further up at Avenida Marechal Carmona 4 (①), is closer to the bus station, and cheaper too, with some balconied rooms over its café. With your own transport, head for the *Quinta da Veiguinha* (☎278 511 071, fax 278 511 041; ③), 6km northwest on the Mirandela road at Vilas Boas, close to the Rio Tua and with lovely views over its valley. In addition to the five rooms in the main house, there's also a three-bedroomed self-catering villa (60,000$00 per week) available. A stay here will also give you the chance to sample their home-made bread, cheese and sausages. Vila Flôr's **campsite** (☎278 512 350, fax 278 512 380), 2km to the southeast along the N215 Torre de Moncorvo road, is one of very few in this area, and is right next door to the municipal outdoor swimming pool (free) and a small zoo.

For **meals**, the best bet is the *Pensão Campos*, or *Restaurante Tony* next door; otherwise, you can find sustenance at one of the cafés down by the museum. The local red **wines** from the Adega Cooperativa are regarded as among the best in the country. For **nightlife**, try the modern *Sol da Noite* discotheque (Fri–Sun from 10pm), 1km down the Bragança road.

Carrazeda de Ansiães

CARRAZEDA DE ANSIÃES, 16km southwest of Vila Flôr, is a modern town of little intrinsic interest. However, three and a half kilometres to the south (a taxi should cost around 500$00 each way) are the intriguing ruins of a medieval **walled town**, known as Ansiães. Little remains within the perimeter of walls except rocks and boulders, but two chapels stand outside, the better preserved of which – the twelfth-century **São Salvador** – has a Romanesque portal, extravagantly carved with leaves, animals and human figures. Local myth has it that a tunnel connects Ansiães to another castle beyond the Douro, 12km away; a gaping, fly-ridden hole beneath an impressive slab is the principal piece of supporting evidence. What is undoubtedly true, however, is that the town was a base for five different kings, including the King of Léon and Castile, before Portuguese independence; they're listed by the gateway on a plaque unveiled by Mário Soares in February 1987.

The last inhabitants of old Ansiães left in the mid-eighteenth century. The gradual depopulation resulted from the decision, in 1734, of a gentleman named Francisco de Araújo e Costa, to transfer the official council seat to the new town below (known by then as Carrazeda de Ansiães). In response to local protests he ordered the castle *pelourinho* to be destroyed; with this symbol gone and deprived of a sufficient supply of water, the hill community had no hope of putting up effective resistance. The medieval town went into decline and was soon totally abandoned.

A good time to visit Carrazeda de Ansiães is on January 3 for the *Cantar os Reis* (night-long music and dance in honour of the Three Kings) or, in the summer, for the **Festa de Santa Eufémia** (August 15–16), in which pilgrims stuff themselves with weaned sow and the local wine, the latter famed for its supposed ability to be imbibed in vast quantities without the drinker falling over. If it reneges on its promise, you can always collapse at the *Pensão de Alfredo Pereira* (①), on Praça Dom Lopo Sampaio.

Chaves

CHAVES stands just 12km from the Spanish border and its name, which means "keys", reflects a strategic history of occupation and ownership. Between 1128 and 1160 the town was an Islamic enclave, and in the following seven centuries it was fought over in turn by the French, Spanish and Portuguese. One of its greatest overlords, **Nuno Álvares Pereira**, was awarded the "keys" of the north by João I for his valiant service at the battle of Aljubarrota, and from him the town passed into the steady hands of the House of Bragança. However, as recently as 1912, Chaves bore the brunt of a Royalist attack from Spain – two years after Portugal had become a republic.

Today, Chaves is considerably less significant, though it's still a market centre for the villages of the fertile Tâmega plain – the richest agricultural lands in the province – and regional capital for northern Trás-os-Montes. For visitors, its principal attractions are its **spa**, together with its splendid setting, a modest array of monuments, and its gastronomy: Chaves is famed in Portugal for its smoked hams, delicious meat cakes (*bolas de carne*), sausages and a strong red wine. The town centre also boasts a wonderful medieval jumble of streets, many of whose houses support wooden verandahs on their crumbling facades.

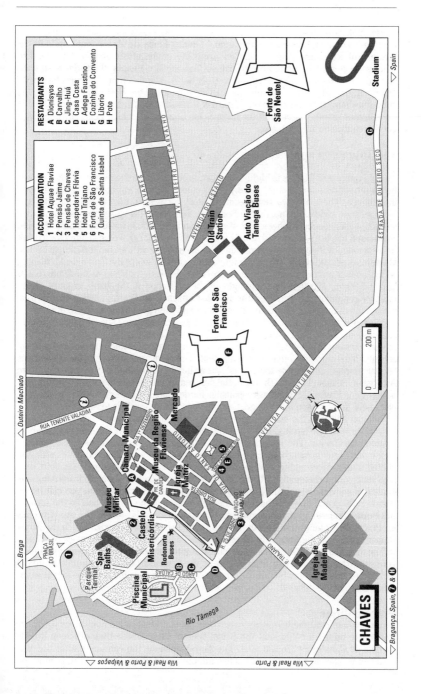

CHAVES

ACCOMMODATION
1 Hotel Aquae Flaviae
2 Pensão Jaime
3 Pensão de Chaves
4 Hospedaria Flávia
5 Hotel Trajano
6 Forte de São Francisco
7 Quinta de Santa Isabel

RESTAURANTS
A Dionisyos
B Carvalho
C Jing-Huá
D Casa Costa
E Adega Faustino
F Cozinha do Convento
G Liborio
H Pote

Festivals are another feature of Chaves; the town hosts an important winter fair, held on November 1, as well as the annual ten-day **Feira de Artesanato**, held in the Jardim Público in mid-August, and featuring the crafts, music and food of the Alto Tâmega region and neighbouring Spanish Galicia. The **Festas da Cidade** (July 8) coincide with the *Jogos do Eixo Altântico* (July 6–10), a kind of mini-Olympics for northern Portugal and Galicia. The turismo can give details of the **Feira de Velherias**, the antiquities fair that takes place one Saturday a month from May to November. Outside the summer months, check out the fixtures for Chaves FC, which generally puts out a good first-division soccer team.

The Town and spa

The old quarter of Chaves is highly compact, grouped above the river, with the spa just below the old walls to the west. Here, in the centre, the town's military past is still much in evidence. There are two seventeenth-century fortresses, built in the characteristic Vaubanesque style of the north: the **Forte de São Neutel** is closed for visits but occasionally hosts concerts (check with the turismo for details); while the **Forte de São Francisco** has been converted into a luxury hotel (see p.379), worth visiting for a drink or meal to enjoy its beautiful interior and the magnificent views from the ramparts. The **Castelo**, overlooking the spa, has a fourteenth-century keep, the Torre de Menagem, which houses a small **military museum** (Tues–Fri 9am–12.30pm & 2–5.30pm, Sat & Sun 2–5.30pm; 100$00). The highlight of the collection is the battle colours of the infantry regiment that repulsed the Royalist attack from Spain in 1912, but the real attractions of the place are the castle gardens and the views from the battlements.

The better town museum is the **Museu da Região Flaviense** (Tues–Fri 9am–12.30pm & 2–5.30pm, Sat & Sun 2–5.30pm; free) on Praça de Camões, a haphazard assortment of material tracing the history of the town and its customs, including quite an assembly of remains from the old Roman spa settlement. The town was known to the Romans as "Aquae Flaviae", after its spa waters, and was an important point on the imperial road from Astorga, in Spanish León, to Braga. In the first century AD it was the army headquarters under Aulus Flaviensis, who was responsible for developing the thermal stations here and elsewhere in the region – at Vidago, Carvalhelhos and Pedras Salgadas.

You can still take the waters at the Chaves **spa** (open all year; ☎276 332 445) built around the *nascente* (spring) below the city walls, towards the river, and offering a whole range of treatments. The water emerges at a piping 73°C and is not very tasty (loaded as it is with sodium bicarbonate), though the spa is generally full of old ladies with crocheted mug-holders taking a swig – it's reckoned to be particularly good for gout, obesity, senility and rheumatism. Unfortunately, the river itself is polluted, frustrating any chance of a swim, though the gardens are well kept and attractive, and you can take a pedalo ride up and down its banks to view the traces of the Roman past in the form of the **Ponte Trajano** – the Roman bridge – and its ancient milestones. The two churches in Praça de Camões are worth a look, too: the **Igreja Matriz**, which is partly Romanesque, and the **Igreja da Misericórdia**, distinguished by vast *azulejo* panels.

The area around Chaves boasts several **Paleolithic and Roman sites**; if you have your own transport, you may want to pick up the *Circuitos Turísticos* pamphlet from the turismo (see below) in which these sites and and other possible day-trips into the surrounding area are detailed.

Practicalities

Rodonorte **buses** for Vila Real and Braga operate from outside their office on Rua da Familia de Camões (☎276 333 491). The Auto-Viação do Tâmega bus station (for Vila Real and Bragança; ☎276 332 352) is five minutes' walk north of the centre around the back of the supermarket next to the old train station; if you're coming into town from here, follow the main road directly ahead, bear left at the roundabout, and you'll emerge near the **turismo** (Mon–Fri 9am–12.30pm & 2–7pm, Sat & Sun 9am–12.30pm & 2–6.30pm; closed Sun in winter; ☎276 340 661). The regional tourist board – **Região de Turismo do Alto Tâmega e Barroso** – is nearby at Avenida Tenente Valadim 39–1º (☎276 340 660, fax 276 321 419, *rturismoatb@mail.telepac.pt*).

Accommodation

Accommodation is plentiful but can be pricey in the summer months, when space is restricted, and intensely cold in winter if you're in an inexpensive, unheated room. At the cheaper end of the budget, *Casa Costa*, on Rua do Tabolado (☎276 323 568) can fix you up with rooms in **private houses** (①). The nearest **campsite** is *Quinta de Rebentão* in Vila Nova, 5km down the Vila Real road (☎276 346 805).

Hotel Aquae Flaviae, Praça do Brasil (☎276 309 000, fax 276 309 010). Adjacent to the spa itself, this is Chaves' largest (86 rooms) and ugliest hotel, four-star with pool and tennis courts. ④.

Pensão de Chaves, Rua 25 de Abril 25 (☎276 321 118). Late nineteenth-century hotel which retains a few trappings of grandeur from its better days, including a marvellous antiquated lift. Rooms with or without bath, and rather large price differences, depending on what you choose. ①–②.

Hospedaria Flávia, Trav. Cândido dos Reis 12 (☎276 322 513). Friendly but basic, opposite the *Hotel Trajano*, this has a pleasant, vine-draped courtyard. Same price for single and doubles. ①.

Forte de São Francisco (☎276 333 700, fax 276 333 701). Chaves' best luxury option has a superb setting in a seventeenth-century fortress with spectacular views. The conversion is a sensitive blend of old and new, with all the trappings you'd expect of a four-star hotel – pool, café, excellent restaurant, and even mini-golf. ⑥.

Pensão Jaime, Av. da Muralha (☎276 321 273). Closed at time of writing for extensive renovation, this well-placed hotel – just 50m from the spa – was good value at ①, but may well double in price when it reopens.

Quinta de Santa Isabel, Santo Estévão, 7km east of Chaves (☎/fax 276 351 818). A traditional Trás-os-Montes country house with vineyards, 500m off the N103 to Bragança. Queen Isabel is said to have slept here the night before she married Dom Dinis. ③.

Hotel Trajano, Travessa Cândido dos Reis (☎276 332 415, fax 276 327 002). Modern, comfortable and a bit dull, though some of the pleasant rooms have traditional local furniture and good views. There's a renowned restaurant in the basement (see below). ③.

Eating

Some of the *pensões* and hotels have reasonable **restaurants** attached, but wherever you eat you shouldn't have any difficulty finding good Chaves smoked ham, tasty local sausages and fine red wine. Over Christmas, look out for the traditional speciality of **octopus** (*polvo*), brought up dried from the coast, then boiled with potatoes and greens. For coffee and cakes try *Café Geraldes*, at Rua Santo António at the corner with Largo do Arrabaide.

Adega Faustino, Trav. Cândido dos Reis. Next to the *Hospedaria Flávia*, this old converted wine cellar, filled with huge wooden barrels, serves great bean salads and a selection of *petiscos*, which you can turn into an inexpensive meal. And, of course, it has terrific wine. There is also an art gallery in one corner.

Carvalho, Largo das Caldas. Some of Portugal's best food is served here, as testified by the numerous awards on the walls. Service is excellent – efficient and unobtrusive – and prices are keen: a meal costs 2000$00–2500$00. Recommended. Closed Thurs.

Casa Costa, Rua do Tabolado. Excellent place serving huge portions of good homely cooking; the speciality is *bacalhau à Costa*. Has a pleasant, vine-covered rear garden. Recommended.

Cozinha do Convento, at the *Forte de São Francisco* hotel. Offers the most elegant setting you'll find in Chaves and serves up a variety of unusual dishes including wild boar and partridge. Under 3500$00 per head.

Dionisyos, Praça do Município 2, opposite the Torre de Menagem. Serves huge portions at reasonable prices (with a cheap *prato do dia*). Try the local speciality, *folar*, an interesting and wholesome pork bread. There are tables outside in summer.

Hotel Trajano, Trav. Cândido dos Reis. A very slick operation in the basement and not too expensive; just the place for Chaves ham and local trout. Closes 9.30pm.

Jing-Huá, Rua do Tabolado (☎276 333 242). Reasonable Chinese food for around 1800$00.

Liborio, Estrada de Outeiro Seco. A good bet for decent Portuguese dishes, but it means trekking out to near the football stadium.

Pote, 1km out on the Bragança road. Serves up generously sized local dishes to an enthusiastic clientele. Closed Mon.

Bars and nightlife

Despite the number of elderly spa-clients in town, there are several trendy **bars** in Chaves. Many of them line the Largo das Caldas, including the *Pórtico Bar*, which plays mainly Latin music until 2am. Local students frequent the cosy *Sá Cristia Bar*, near the Castelo in Rua da Misericórdia, while for a more Stateside experience there's the *Bar Garage* on Travessa Cândido dos Reis, which has bits of cars protruding from the walls. Opposite, the town's only central **nightclub**, *Vanity*, is true to its name, attracting the town's fashion-conscious. *Triunfo*, the main club, is 4km out of town on the road to Valpaços – take a taxi or get a ride with other clubbers from around the Largo dos Caldas at around 10pm.

Routes on from Chaves: Montalegre and Vinhais

Chaves has useful bus connections west to Braga and the Peneda-Gerês national park via **Montalegre** (45km); east to **Vinhais** (65km) and Bragança; and southeast to Mirandela (53km). However, it's worth noting that Saturday services to Bragança are few and far between and that there is no bus from Chaves to Mirandela on Saturday. Heading **into Spain**, you could pick up an express bus to Orense, via Verin, on a Thursday or Sunday (originating in Porto, these pass through Chaves in the afternoon; book ahead at Chaves bus station if possible), or else, catch one of the frequent services (marked "Fronteira" – border), and then a Spanish bus on the other side. There is no currency exchange at the border post.

West to Montalegre

West of Chaves, **MONTALEGRE** – a ten-kilometre detour off the N103 – looms up suddenly, commanding the surrounding plains. Looking at its isolated position on the map, you might expect this frontier town, with a history rooted in past centuries, to be relatively untouched. In fact, there is a fair amount of modern development, caused by the nearby Pisões dam, and it's gradually encroaching on the medieval centre and fourteenth-century **castle** (Tues–Sun 9am–12.30pm & 2–5.30pm; free). However, it remains quite atmospheric place – especially in winter, when snow covers the Serra do Larouco to the north – and makes an enjoyable stopover of a night or two, being set amid good walking territory scattered with dolmens and the odd Templar and Romanesque church.

A ten-minute walk uphill from the **bus station** brings you to the main square, the Praça do Município, and the **turismo** (Tues–Fri 9am–12.30pm & 2–5.30pm, also Sat 9am–12.30pm & 2–5.30pm in summer; ☎276 512 254), which has a map of the district and booklets for sale on archeology (most in Portuguese). There's an office of the Peneda-Gerês National Park (see p.350) at Rua Reigoso 17 (Mon–Fri 9am–12.30pm & 2–5.30pm).

Montalegre has three good **hotels**, all with clean en-suite rooms with TV. Nearest the bus station on Rua Ponte do Moinho is the modern *Restaurante Hospedaria Girrasol* (☎276 512 715; ①–②, breakfast included), with some cheaper shared bathrooms, too.

More central are the large *Albergaria Pedreira*, two hundred metres off the Praça at Rua Dom Afonso III 41 (☎276 512 501; ②, breakfast included), and the friendly *Fidalgo*, uphill from the Praça at Rua da Corujeira 34 (☎276 512 462; ②), with good views over the valley. The **restaurant** at *Albergaria Pedreira* is excellent; order ahead for its specialities of wild boar, stuffed kid and *cozido à moda de Barroso* – a stew of different meats. Uphill from the *Fidalgo* is the *Restaurante Floresta*, where it's worth paying the higher than usual prices for good food and views. The *Brasilieiro*, on the southwest side of Praça do Município, and the charming *Restaurante Muralha Terra Fria* on Rua Reigoso, are also good bets for an excellent meal.

You might ask at the local bars about *Vinhos dos Mortos* – **Wines of the Dead** – so called because of the practice of maturing the wine in bottles buried underground at the nearby villages of the Serra do Barroso. Meat-eaters are also in for a treat – the Barroso region is famed for its **smoked meats** (*fumeiros*) and ham (*presunto*), best bought at the shop opposite GALP fuel station, down from Praça do Município, or at the **market** (Mon, Tues & Thurs) below the bus station. Montalegre's annual **Feira do Fumeiro e Presunto** takes place in the fourth week of January.

There's a minor border crossing into Spain north of Montalegre, at Tourém, which is also on the Trilho do Longo Curso (see p.355).

East to Vinhais

Heading eastwards from Chaves, Auto-Viação do Tâmega buses roll through the hills along a superb scenic route to Bragança, 96km away. The route becomes ever more barren as you climb and there are fabulous, if bleak, views from various tortuous bends in the road. Two thirds of the way along is the pleasant village of **VINHAIS**. Its main sight is the Baroque convent of **São Francisco**, a vast building incorporating a pair of churches in its facade. It is situated at the Chaves end of the main street, which runs for 1km or more, and offers staggering views away to the south at every turn.

Should you get stuck in Vinhais, there are a couple of good **places to stay**: *Pensão Ribeirinha*, Rua Nova 34 (☎273 771 490; ①–②), halfway between the main square and the convent, has lovely old en-suite rooms, some with TV and balconies overlooking the valley. More upmarket, and currently a bargain, is the brand-new *Residencial Dom Afonso*, 200 metres west of the *Ribeirinha* on the right (☎273 770 110; ②). For **food**, *Restaurante Comercial* at the corner of the main street and Rua da Corujeira has a good menu, as does the *Ribeirinha*, and there are several other restaurants as you head out of town on the Chaves road. If hiking hasn't tired you out, there's the weekend *Discoteca do Nordeste*, 1km from the centre on the Chaves road.

If you have the chance, try to coincide your visit with Ash Wednesday, or for the second weekend of February when Vinhais' *Festa das Fumeiros* takes place, with smoked meats and *presunto* ham galore.

For onward travel, the Auto-Viação do Tâmega **bus** office is on the main street, just west of *Restaurante Comercial*. If you have your own transport, you can take the minor road from Vinhais that leads into the Parque Natural de Montesinho (see p.386) – for more information on the park, ask at the Delegação do Parque at the Casa do Povo (Mon–Fri 9am–12.30pm & 2.30–5pm; ☎273 772 416).

Bragança

On a dark hillock above **BRAGANÇA**, the remote capital of Trás-os-Montes, stands a small circle of perfectly preserved medieval walls, rising to a massive keep and castle, and enclosing a white medieval village. Known as the Cidadela, this is one of the most memorable sights in Portugal, seemingly untouched by the centuries, with a hamlet whose size is wonderfully at odds with the royal connotations of the town's dynastic

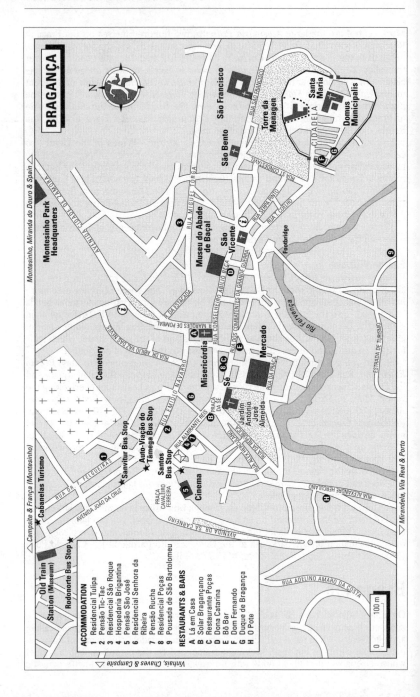

BRAGANÇA

△ Campsite & França (Montesinho)

Montesinho, Miranda do Douro & Spain △

▽ Vinhais, Chaves & Campsite

▽ Mirandela, Vila Real & Porto

ACCOMMODATION
1 Residencial Tulipa
2 Pensão Tic-Tac
3 Residencial São Roque
4 Hospedaria Brigantina
5 Pensão São José
6 Residencial Senhora da Ribeira
7 Pensão Rucha
8 Residencial Poças
9 Pousada de São Bartolomeu

RESTAURANTS & BARS
A Lá em Casa
B Solar Bragançano
C Restaurante Poças
D Dona Catarina
E Bô Bar
F Dom Fernando
G Duque de Bragança
H O Pote

name. The Braganças were the last line of **Portuguese monarchs**, ruling from 1640, when they replaced the Spaniards, until the fall of the monarchy in 1910. To the British, the name is most readily associated with Catherine, queen to Charles II. For the Portuguese, however, the town represents the defence of the liberty of the people, because the Bragançans were the first to muster a popular revolt against Junot in 1808, and have always defended their power to make their own decisions.

The citadel, along with an excellent museum, provides the principal reason for a visit to the town. However, for anyone interested in a bit of wilderness hiking, the nearby **Parque Natural de Montesinho** (see p.386) is an additional draw, while the **Festa de Nossa Senhora das Graças** (August 14–22) offers another very good reason to be in town, with lots of cultural events and traditional music. Shortly after, on August 24, there's the religious **Romaria de São Bartolomeu**. Other notable dates include the **Feira das Cantarinhas** (May 1–3), a crafts fair dedicated to the clay water jug (*cantarinha*) which was once used to store the gifts given to a bride on her wedding day; and **Ash Wednesday** (usually February or early March), when people dressed as devils run around whipping penitents – its origins probably lie in an ancient fertility cult, when it was believed that Pan impregnated women simply by smacking them.

The Cidadela

At the heart of the **Cidadela** stands the thirteenth-century council chamber, the **Domus Municipalis**. Very few Romanesque civic buildings have survived, and no other has this pentagonal form. Its meetings – for solving land disputes and the like – took place on the arcaded first floor; below was a cistern. Rising to its side is the **Igreja de Santa Maria** (10am–noon & 2–5pm), whose interior is distinguished by an eighteenth-century, barrel-vaulted, painted ceiling – a feature of several churches in Bragança.

Facing these buildings is the town keep, the **Torre de Menagem** (Mon–Wed & Fri–Sun 10am–noon & 2–5pm; 100$00, free Sun morning), which the royal family rejected as a residence in favour of their vast estate in the Alentejo. It was one of the first works of restoration by the Society of National Monuments in 1928, and now houses a collection of military odds and ends as well as offering great views from the top. At the side of the keep, a curious **pelourinho** (pillory) rises from the back of a prehistoric granite pig. The town's museum has three more of these crudely sculpted **porcas**, but their most famous representative is to be seen at Murça, halfway between Vila Real and Mirandela. They are thought to have been the fertility idols of a prehistoric cult, and it's easy to understand the beast's prominence in this province of wild boars and chestnut forests, where the staple winter diet is smoked sausage.

Look over the furthest walls of the castle and you'll see the Parque Natural de Montesinho stretching to Spain, a view which seems to stress the town's remoteness. One group who made the most of this isolation were the **Jews**, who escaped over the border in the sixteenth century from the terrors of the Inquisition in Spain. Despite the common rule by Spaniards over the two countries during this period, the Inquisition in Portugal was relatively inefficient – administered in municipalities, the organization spread slowly northwards with ever-decreasing zeal. The Jewish community has left its mark in the names of local families and in the town's cuisine (notably the *alheira* sausage), but the once-thriving synagogue is no more.

You can get a superb **view** of the Cidadela from the bottom of the steps of the church of São Bartolomeu; to get there, follow the signs to the *pousada*, which is next to the church – a half-hour walk from the town centre.

The rest of the town

Modern Bragança, set along the valley below the Cidadela, is a pleasant enough place, despite an eruption of concrete apartment blocks on the outskirts. From the Cidadela, the narrow, stepped Rua Serpa Pinto leads to the **Igreja de São Vicente**, where Dom Pedro I claimed to have secretly married Inês de Castro (see p.152); while a small diversion to the east along Rua São Francisco will bring you to the **Igreja de São Bento**, the town's finest church – a simple Renaissance structure with three contrasting ceilings.

On the way into town, along Rua Conselheiro Abílio Beça, you will find the **Museu do Abade de Baçal**, the town's distinguished museum (Tues–Fri 10am–5pm, Sat & Sun 10am–6pm; 250$00, free Sun morning), installed in the eighteenth-century former Bishop's Palace. In its gardens Celtic-inspired medieval tombstones rub shoulders with a menagerie of *porcas*; while inside, the collection of sacred art and the topographical watercolours of Alberto Souza are the highlights, along with displays of local costumes – especially the dress of the *Pauliteiros* ("stick dancers"), who still perform at festivals around Bragança and Miranda do Douro. Work is currently underway to expand the museum to include more furniture, paintings, and manuscripts. Further down the street is a fine Renaissance-style **Misericórdia** dating from 1873.

One last, incidental sight, which rail buffs will want to check out, is the tiny **transport museum** at the old train station (variable opening hours, check with the turismo; 250$00). This features the first steam train operative in northern Portugal, and the royal carriage of Portugal's penultimate king, Dom Carlos, both brought here from Arco de Baúlhe, following the closure of the upper reaches of the Tâmega train line.

Practicalities

Bragança is well connected with most major towns by public transport. The majority of **buses** operate from Avenida João da Cruz: Rodonorte (☎273 331 870), for services to Mirandela, Vila Real, and south of Trás-os-Montes, has a kiosk here next to the old train station; and Santos (☎273 326 552), which runs to Miranda do Douro and Mirandela, is based at no. 5 (also agents for Alfandeguense buses to Lisbon). Sanvitur (☎273 331 826) – agents for Rede Expressos services further afield – can also be found on the avenida. For onward travel to Vinhais or Chaves, Auto-Viação do Tâmega has an agent, Cabanelas Turismo, at Rua Guerra de Junqueiro 111 (☎273 323 582). For details of travel into the Parque Natural de Montesinho, see p.386, and for **crossing the border** into Spain, see p.385. You can **hire cars** at Nurocar, Rua 5 de Outubro (☎273 331 507).

From the Rodonorte bus stop it's a short walk south along Avenida João da Cruz to Praça da Sé, essentially the centre of town. From here it's a couple of hundred metres north to the very helpful **turismo** (July–Sept Mon–Fri 9am–12.30pm & 2–7pm, Sat to 6pm; Oct–June Mon–Fri 9am–12.30pm & 2–5pm; ☎273 381 273, *www.bragancanet.pt/braganca/*) on Avenida Cidade de Zamora, a wide boulevard split by gardens. Another 200m down the avenue, in a modern development on the left, is the head office of the **Parque Natural de Montesinho** at Apartamento 90, Lote 5, Bairro Salvador Nunes Teixeira (Mon–Fri 9am–12.30 & 2–5.30pm; also Sat & Sun noon–9pm during summer; ☎273 381 234), who can provide you with information about visiting the park.

Accommodation

Pensões and hotels are scattered around town. The nearest **campsite** (☎273 331 535; May–Oct) is 6km north of town, on the França road, and has pretty sparse facilities. Eight kilometres west of town on the N103 Vinhais road, there's a private campsite, *Cepo Verde* (☎273 999 371), with better facilities, including a pool.

Hospedaria Brigantina, Rua Almirante Reis, next to the post office (☎273 324 321). The cheapest option in Bragança and quite acceptable, with shared bathrooms. ①.

Residencial Poças, Rua Combatentes da Grande Guerra 200 (☎273 331 428). For many years a reliable and cheap city-centre option, though pick your room with care – some are very bare and in winter this place is freezing. Rooms with or without bathroom available. Prices are per person (2000$00 with shared bath), so very good value for singles. Check in at the restaurant next door. Breakfast included. ①.

Pensão Rucha, Rua Almirante Reis 42 (☎273 331 672). More of a family home than a *pensão*, run by an elderly couple and including a hearty breakfast; you'll have to look hard to spot the sign. Some of the eight rooms (with shared bath) are a bit airless, and it can be noisy. Breakfast included. Borderline ②.

Pousada de São Bartolomeu, Estrada de Turismo (☎273 331 493, fax 273 323 453). South of the river, about 1km by road from the centre – follow the signs off Rua Alexandre Herculano. Purpose-built in 1959, it's got wood panelling, cork ceilings, great views and a good restaurant. ⑥.

Pensão São José (formerly *Bragança*), Av. Dr. Sá Carneiro 11 (☎273 331 578, fax 273 331 242). Box-like concrete structure above the cinema, popular with visiting businessmen. Comfortable and well-run, most rooms with AC and TV. ③.

Residencial São Roque, Rua Miguel Torga 26–27, Zona da Estacada (☎273 381 481, fax 273 326 937). Large modern hotel with well-furnished rooms, attentive service and good views of the citadel from the dining room and upper floors. Breakfast included. ③.

Residencial Senhora da Ribeira (formerly *Cruzeiro*), Travessa do Hospital (☎273 300 550, fax 273 300 555). On an alley off Rua Almirante Reis, a recently renovated place (all rooms with bathroom) opposite a noisy games arcade – get a room at the back. ③.

Pensão Tic-Tac, Rua Emídio Navarro 85 (☎273 331 373, fax 273 331 673). Small and spotless modern rooms with TV and AC set above a reasonable restaurant. Breakfast included. ③.

Residencial Tulipa, Rua Dr. Francisco Felgueiras 8–10 (☎273 331 675, fax 273 327 814). Clean, simple but overpriced place near the train station with cramped rooms (with TV) that, nevertheless, is highly sought after in summer; arrive early or book ahead. It also has a reasonable restaurant. ②.

Eating, drinking and nightlife

Bragança has a promising array of **bars** and **restaurants** and the places listed below are all recommended. For the town's rather limited **nightlife**, the places to go are *Bô*, a late-night bar with good music on Rua Combatentes da Grande Guerra, and *Duque de Bragança*, a more upmarket but lively place inside the walled town, which sometimes has live music and is open until 2am.

Dom Fernando, Cidadela 197. Good-value restaurant, even without considering its location just inside the walls of the old town. There's a lively bar downstairs, too.

Dona Catarina, Rua Abílio Beça, facing Museu Abade Baçal. One of Bragança's top restaurants, with fine regional dishes at around 3000$00. Also has a *pastelaria* and tea room.

Lá em Casa, Rua Marquês de Pombal 7. A convivial place near the Igreja da Misericórdia. Don't be put off by the over-rustic decor. Full meals from 2500$00.

Restaurante Poças, Rua Combatentes da Grande Guerra 200. Excellent and inexpensive food in the restaurant below the *residencial* – family-run and popular enough to fill a couple of floors.

O Pote, Rua Alexandre Herculano. Good cheap *tasca*, also does *petiscos* of *chouriço*, ham, cheese, olives, and *bacalhau* fish balls.

Solar Bragançano, Praça da Sé 34 (☎274 323 875). An upmarket but excellent *casa típica*, where you dine in oak-panelled rooms to the accompaniment of classical music. Unusual specialities include hare (under 2000$00), and partridge cooked with grapes (under 4000$00). There's a nice bar, too.

Crossing to Spain

The easiest way to get to Spain is on the Internorte **express bus**, which runs to Zamora and Valladolid and on to Madrid, on Mondays, Tuesdays, Thursdays and Fridays; you can get tickets from the Rodonorte bus station. Failing that, take a Rodonorte bus to the Portuguese border post at **QUINTANILHA**, 34km away (1–2 daily). At the Spanish frontier village of San Martin del Pedroso, there's a single, combined *pensão* and restaurant, the *Evaristo*, and an early-morning bus to Zamora.

An alternative crossing is to take the road through the Parque Natural de Montesinho (see below), through the border villages of **PORTELO** (Portugal) and Calabor (Spain) to the Spanish town of Puebla de Sanabria, which has onwards bus and train services and accommodation. Using public transport, you can catch Rodonorte buses to Portelo (1–2 daily during school times only) and then irregular Spanish buses (Mon–Fri) between Calabor and Puebla de Sanabria, but you'll have to walk or hitch the 6km between Portelo and Calabor.

The Parque Natural de Montesinho

Occupying the extreme northeastern tip of Portugal, the **Parque Natural de Montesinho** is the only sector of the Terra Fria where the way of life and the appearance of villages have not yet been changed by the new wealth of the emigrant workers. The Terra Fria's predominantly barren landscape is here disrupted by micro-climates which give rise to the Serra de Montesinho's heather-clad hills, wet grass plains and thick forests of oak. Another curious feature of the region is the round *pombal* or pigeon house – a structure which, no matter how well-established its position, invariably seems to have dropped in from another world. The ethnographic museum in Miranda do Douro (see p.389) can fill you in on these and other aspects of traditional village life, such as the black cape and the cloaks of straw – as much a protection against heat as against cold.

For leaflets and advice for walkers, contact the **Montesinho park office** in Bragança (see p.384), which also has brochures on the local flora and fauna and maps for walkers. The office is also the place to ask about **renting traditional houses** (*casas abrigos*), which are scattered throughout the small villages in the park – prices range from around 5000$00 a night for a studio sleeping two, to 50,000$00 for a property that will hold 21, and all houses must be booked in advance. **Camping** in the park is prohibited and the only two official sites are located on the southern boundary of the park (see p.384).

The most useful **bus links from Bragança** are to França/Portelo, due north of Bragança (1–2 Rodonorte buses daily during school times only), and to Rio de Onor, to the northeast (2–3 STUB buses daily; see p.388). It is not too hard to hitch on the França road in summer, and walking beyond here, alongside the **Rio Sabor**, is idyllic, with wonderful and deserted spots for swimming. **Walking to Rio de Onor** is also an option.

Rio de Onor

RIO DE ONOR, hard by the Spanish border, 25km north of Bragança, provides perhaps the most fascinating insight into the village life of the Serra de Montesinho. There are in fact two Rio de Onors – one in Spain (called Riohonor de Castilla) and one in Portugal – but two stone blocks labelled "E" and "P", and a change from cobbles on the Portuguese side to smooth concrete on the Spanish, are all that delineate the frontier. The villagers have come and gone between the two for generations, intermarrying and buying goods; both sides spoke, until recently, a hybrid Portuguese-Spanish dialect known as *Rionorês*. Their extreme isolation encouraged systems of justice and mutual co-operation that are independent of the state and which still exist today, something for which Rio de Onor has become famous in Portugal. The ageing villagers (most of the youth have left for the cities) share land, flocks, winepresses, mills and ovens.

The two villages are set on either side of a stream: the granite steps and wooden balconies of rough schist houses line narrow alleyways, and straw creeps out across the cobbles. The bar in the Portuguese "half" of the village contains a long stick on which locals once marked the number of cattle and sheep they owned. Communal meetings fined troublemakers and miscreants in wine! Rio de Onor's *Festa dos Reis* – mainly an excuse to feast on *chouriços* – is on January 6. More traditional though

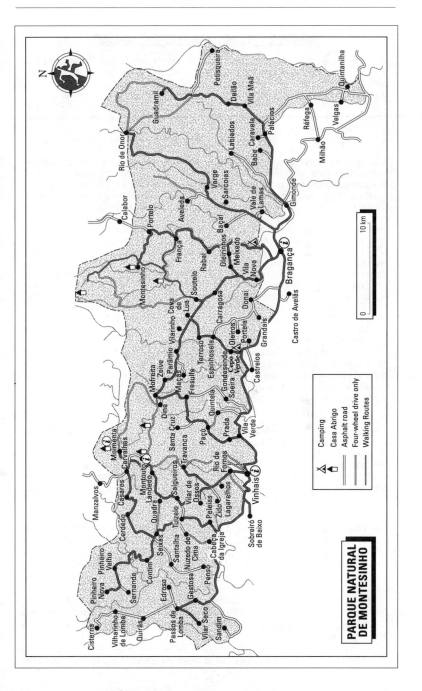

**PARQUE NATURAL
DE MONTESINHO**

WALKING IN MONTESINHO

One of the nicest places to start if you want to do some walking is the village of **França**, 10km north of Bragança and in the heart of the park. The village has a small shop, café and a bar, as well as a pony trekking and mountain bike rental centre, but no accommodation; the nearest official campsite is 6km south on the Bragança road (see p.384).

The best **trail** in the area is a moderately easy two-day walk beginning and ending at França. Start by turning left off the main road, just past a small bar, and walk along the track which follows the Rio Sabor. This track is rarely used by vehicles and winds through a steep gorge, where you can spot many species of birds and, in summer, maybe some wild boar. The track passes a hydroelectric power station and a trout farm (on your left), then after about 4km there's a turning off to the left marked Soutelo. If you have only a short time, take this track and follow it through the picturesque villages of **Soutelo** and **Carragosa**; it will lead you back to França within a few hours.

If you're doing the longer walk, ignore the turning and continue for about 6km along the track towards the isolated reservoir, **Barragem de Serra Serrada**, near the Spanish border. There's a mountain hut for spending the night – just past the reservoir take a right-hand path signposted *Lama Grande*. Alternatively, about 2km before the reservoir, there's a turning off to the left, signposted **MONTESINHO**: it's a worthwhile detour – signs clearly point the way – to see a traditional mountain village. Look out for the inscriptions on the doors of the houses, and the blacksmith's forge, which has been here since the sixteenth century and stopped working only fifteen years ago. There's also a good café here – the *Café Montesinho* (☎273 919 219) – which can do snacks, or meals if given enough notice, and which also has local honey for sale. There are also some nice rooms to rent (some with use of kitchen), all in traditional stone houses (doubles ③–④, or around 10,000$00 for a house sleeping four), though you'll need to book ahead: contact *Tia Maria Rita* (☎273 919 229), *Dona Constância (Casa da Eira)* (☎273 919 227), or the *Casa das Escaleirichas* (☎273 919 248) – or book through the *Café Montesinho*.

To rejoin the track to the reservoir, you can leave Montesinho via the road at the top of the village, next to the bar, and follow any of the narrow paths over the hills until you rejoin the main track; this should take around half an hour. However, many of the smaller paths are quite overgrown and difficult to navigate, so you may find it easier to retrace your steps back to the Montesinho junction and join the track there.

About 2km after the reservoir, the track splits in two; take the right-hand turning for the mountain hut (see above) and the left-hand turning – signposted França and Soutelo – to start the return journey to França. The track leads over a high plateau covered with expanses of heather and rock formations, and giving spectacular views over to Bragança in the distance. Follow the track, descending steadily for a few kilometres, then take a left-hand turning. A couple of kilometres further on, you'll see a right-hand turning – clearly signposted to França – take this turning and after about 4km you'll rejoin the track in França where the walk started.

is the **Lenha das Almas** ("Firewood of Souls") celebration on November 1, where the boys of the village gather firewood, which is then traditionally hauled into the village by ox carts (though more commonly now by tractors), and auctioned off, the proceeds going to the "souls" of the dead (ie the church). The ritual has its roots in a pre-Roman cult of ancestors, as well as marking the time when boys become adults, and ends with a communal feast and binge on roast chestnuts.

If you want to **stay**, there's the possibility of basic shelter in the *Casa do Povo* (parish rooms) provided you contact the village *presidente* on arrival, but don't count on it. STUB **buses**, fluctuating according to local school and market timetables, connect the village with Bragança: buses currently leave Bragança daily at 5.50pm (plus additional services on Sat at 1.35pm and schooldays at 2pm), returning from Rio de Onor at 7.10am, 2.40pm and 6.50pm (not Sat) – all of which means a day-trip by bus is not a real-

istic option. But you could always **walk** the 13km here from Varges, with its traditional stone houses; the Bragança–Varges bus leaves at 12.33pm daily. The route indicates
very clearly how isolated Rio de Onor is – the road has existed for only twenty years,
before which time the locals had to walk across open country to and from Bragança.

Southeast to Miranda do Douro

From Bragança, the N218 southeast to Miranda do Douro runs across the **Planalto
Mirandês**, a breathtaking journey in late February and early March, when the sudden
blossoming of the almond trees transforms the countryside. Some say that it was the
beauty of this vista – and Miranda do Douro itself – that decided Afonso Henriques, the
future first king of Portugal, to turn against his Spanish kinsmen, refortify the border
and begin his victorious sweep across Lusitânia at the start of the twelfth century. The
route offers the chance for stop-offs in some extremely attractive towns and villages on
the way; if you don't have your own transport, you can take one of the Rodonorte or
Santos buses that make the trip one to three times daily.

Seven kilometres out of Bragança is **GIMONDE**, a rural village of traditional wooden
houses beautifully sited on the edge of the Montesinho park which would make a fine base
should you want to stay somewhere even quieter than Bragança. The rivers Onor, Sabor
and Igrejas all meet here near a Romanesque bridge, a favourite spot for stork-watching in
early summer. There are **rooms** above the *Restaurante 4* (☎273 381 649; ①), slightly out
of town on the Bragança road, and more upmarket accommodation at *Dom Roberto* (☎279
302 510, fax 279 381 436; ③, breakfast included), which also has an excellent restaurant.

Fifteen kilometres beyond Gimonde, the N218 branches away from the main
cross-border road and runs another 10km south to **OUTEIRO**, a once-grand village with a disproportionately huge church, Santo Cristo, built in 1755. Outeiro's
erstwhile status as defender of Portugal's eastern tranches is confirmed by the
presence of a ruined **castle** on the hill above the village. The small bar on the
green by the church contains a sketch of this in its heyday, before it was destroyed
in the wars with Spain. The local water hereabouts is believed to cure breathing
problems, its miraculous powers supposedly enhanced after a visitation by Nossa
Senhora de Fátima on June 11, 1848. The **Festa de São Gonçalo** (January 10) is
a Christian version of an ancient bread cult, where an enormous bread "statue"
(the *Charolo*) is paraded through town. When it arrives outside the church, the
statue is auctioned off, and pieces are then distributed to the crowd by the buyer
to the sound of bagpipes.

Between Outeiro and **VIMIOSO**, 22km south, the countryside becomes ever more
mountainous and dramatic. The town itself is spectacularly set, with some pretty, traditional houses on the steep streets around the Igreja Matriz, though this aside,
there's little of interest in Vimioso, much of which is swamped by *emigrante*-financed
development. There are two *pensões*: the *Centro* (☎273 512 539, fax 273 512 254; ①)
and, signposted off the main Bragança road, the more upmarket *Charneca* (☎273 512
192; ①), both with a mix of shared bath and en-suite rooms – but you'd do far better
to press on to Miranda do Douro, only another 30km to the southeast.

Miranda do Douro

Facing Spain across the deep gorge of the Douro, **MIRANDA DO DOURO** played a
key role in all of the country's wars subsequent to Afonso Henriques' conquest of
Lusitânia in the early twelfth century. After valiant service in the Independence, Spanish
Succession, and Seven Years wars, it ended its fighting days in 1762 when an explosion
during a Spanish attack destroyed the castle and the town, and killed 400 inhabitants.

Today, the old town of Miranda seems scarcely more than a village. After the explosion of 1762 Miranda remained a neglected outpost for nearly two centuries until the huge Douro dam was built in 1955, breathing some new life into the town. Yet Miranda has the status of a city, and a sturdy sixteenth-century **Sé** (closed in winter) overlooks its cobbled streets and low white houses. This cathedral and the city status date from a decision by the Portuguese church authorities to make Miranda the capital of the diocese to counteract the feudal power of the House of Bragança in Trás-os-Montes. At the end of the eighteenth century, however, the see was transferred to the larger of the two towns, leaving Miranda cathedral as a cumbersome memento of past glory. To the bitter comment "The sacristy is in Bragança, but the cathedral is in Miranda", the astute Bragançans reply, "If ever you go to Miranda, see the cathedral and come home."

The cathedral aside, Miranda has a certain neat charm, despite its modern sprawling outskirts and a rather off-putting rash of frontier tourist shops. The tidied-up ruins of its Episcopal Palace, now a café, and the medieval facades along **Rua da Costanilha** set the tone, and there is a small medieval bridge, too, over the diminutive Rio Fresno. Beyond here you reach an eighteenth-century fountain, the Fonte dos Canos.

However, the main focus of interest in town is the **Museu da Terra de Miranda** on Praça Dom João III, just off Rua da Costanilha (summer Tues–Sun 10am–12.30pm & 2.30–6pm; winter Tues–Sat 10am–12.30pm & 2–5pm, Sun 10am–12.30pm; 150$00). Located in a seventeenth-century building which formerly housed the town hall and later the district prison, the museum is literally bursting with curiosities, from pistols to children's balloons made out of sheep's stomachs, and features a couple of reconstructed rooms in traditional Mirandês style – an illustration of local life that's inaccurate only in that the agricultural labourers of the region generally live, sleep and die in a single room.

If you can, try to time your visit to coincide with one of the local **festa** periods: *Santa Bárbara* on the penultimate weekend of August, which also has a crafts fair; *Romaria Nossa Senhora do Nazo* (September 7–8); or the *Festa dos Rapazes* (children's festival) on Christmas eve, held in honour of Santo Estêvão, in which firewood is collected in front of the cathedral and lit after midnight Mass. There's also a **feira** held on the first weekday of every month.

Practicalities

The **turismo**, on Largo do Menino Jesus da Cartolinha (summer Mon–Sat 9am–12.30pm & 2–8pm, Sun 2–8pm; winter Mon–Fri 9am–12.30pm & 2–5pm; ☎273 431 132), can provide details on river trips and will also help with **accommodation**. The only budget option is the characterful *Santa Cruz*, in the old town at Rua Abade de Baçal 61 (☎273 431 374, fax 273 431 335; ①), with a family atmosphere and a good restaurant. Other hotels are in the modern part of town, all with self-contained rooms and little to distinguish them, though the ones on Rua do Mercado have views over the reservoir: try *Residencial Morgadinha* at nos. 57–59 (☎273 438 050, fax 273 438 051; ②), *Residencial Flor do Douro* at nos. 7–9 (☎273 431 186; ②) or *Pensão Vista Bela* at no. 63 (☎273 431 054; ②). Of a similar standard, but lacking the views, are *Residencial Planalto*, Rua 1º de Maio 25 (☎273 431 362, fax 273 432 780; ②), and *Hotel Turismo*, Rua 1º de Maio 5 (☎273 438 030, fax 273 431 335; ③). The local *pousada*, Santa Catarina (☎273 431 005, fax 273 431 065; ④), is just off Largo Menino Jesus da Cartolinha; its twelve balconied rooms overlook the huge Miranda do Douro reservoir but the *pousada* itself is modern and unexceptional. There's a **campsite**, *Santa Luzia* (☎273 431 273, fax 273 431 075; June–Sept), on the southern side of town by the stadium and municipal swimming pools; it's run by the municipality and is free.

In addition to the hotel **restaurants**, you might like to check out the menus at *O Mirandês* (from 1500$00) on Largo do Moagem in the new town, or *Buteko* in the old town at Largo Dom João III, which serves excellent wine and a local *posta à mirandesa* (grilled veal steak) that will feed two or three. The *São Pedro* at Rua Mouzinho de Albuquerque 20 in the old town is also good value, serving excellent *tamboril* and prawn kebabs. For **nightlife**, try the *Taberna Fim do Seclo* just inside the west gate of the old town, or *Bar Atalaia* on Largo do Castelo.

Crossing to Spain

The Spanish border lies just three kilometres to the west of Miranda, across the **Barragem de Miranda**, at 528m the highest hydroelectric dam in the country and the last before the Portuguese Douro becomes the Spanish Duero. If you have your own transport, this crossing is a good point from which to approach Zamora.

Mogadouro, Torre de Moncorvo and Freixo de Espada à Cinta

For much of its journey southwest from Miranda do Douro to the border with Spain the N221 runs along the western fringes of Portugal's newest and largest nature reserve, the **Parque Natural do Douro Internacional** (see p.393), visible as tantalizing glimpses of water and forested valleys to the east. From **Mogadouro**, almost 50km away, there are onward travel options south to **Freixo de Espada à Cinta** – a good base from which to explore the natural park – or southwest to **Torre de Moncorvo** and Pocinho (see p.292).

Halfway between Miranda and Mogadouro is the pleasant, functional town of **SENDIM**, where the only real reason to stop off is to sample some great cooking at the *Restaurante Gabriela*. The restaurant is run by Alicia, an award-winning celebrity chef but sadly, if she's not there, the food can be average and overpriced (around 2000–2700$00). Should you strike lucky, and proceed to eat and drink your fill, you may be glad of the **rooms** at the restaurant (☎273 459 180; ①), or those around the corner at the *Galego* (☎273 459 202; ①).

Mogadouro

For an unkempt and authentic picture of town life in the Terra Fria, you need look no further than **MOGADOURO**, specifically its **castle**. This is unexceptional as a monument, but the ground in front is common land where children play and farmers sort out their produce. During the harvest period the area is stacked high with dried *tremoços* bushes, whose seeds are consumed as beer-time snacks and used in soups. The castle hill also commands terrific views over a long, low horizon and a patchwork of fields and *pombais*. The **Câmara Municipal** occupies a former convent, but is treated by the townspeople as their own backyard, for herding cows home in the evening and playing at tossing coins for hours at a time.

The main tree-lined Avenida Nossa Senhora do Caminho has a sports complex and views over the hills on one side, and a row of shops and cafés on the other. The avenue ends at Praça Duarte Pacheco and the adjacent Largo Trindade Coelho, where **buses** drop you, with the old town and ruined castle beyond. Should you want to stay, the best **hotel** is the three-star *Hotel Trindade Coelho* on the Largo (☎279 340 010, fax 279 340 011; ③), with a bar and restaurant. Several other places lie just off the square: there are reasonable balconied rooms – and a restaurant – at *Pensão Russo* (☎279 342 134; ①), the first of three *pensões* along Rua Francisco Antonio Vincente and its continuation, Rua das Eiras. Other choices include *Residencial A Lareira*, Av. N.S. do Caminho 58 (☎279 342 363; closed Jan ②;), with a renowned restaurant (closed Mon); *Residencial Nossa Senhora do Caminho*, nearby at no. 48 (☎279 342 771; ②); and the modern three-storey *Residencial Estrela do Norte*, Av. de Espanha 65 (☎279 342 726; ②). Apart from the hotel **restaurants**, *Restaurante Kalifa*, on Rua Santa Marinha, off the Largo, is recommended for its steak and superb red wine. Opposite, and with a second entrance on Rua da República, *Kalifa* **bar** serves as the main evening focus. Local **pastries** can be sampled at *Pastelaria Santa Cruz* on Rua da República.

Be warned that the town is busy (and rooms at a premium) in August, when the emigrants are back home with their families. There is an annual **festa** at this time, in honour of Nossa Senhora do Caminho (August 7–23), with a special *emigrante* weekend on the last weekend of August, before they leave the country again. There's more entertainment in mid-June, with processions, music and exhibitions for the **semana cultural**.

Onward travel

Twenty-five kilometres south of Mogadouro along the N221 is **LAGOAÇA**, a very old village whose houses feature Manueline stone-arched windows, and whose women still wear traditional dress. Pass through the village, beyond the cemetery, and there's a superb viewing platform, looking over the deep Douro valley into Spain. A further 6km along, the road divides: the N221 continues south to Freixo de Espada à Cinta, while the N220 branches off southwest to Torre de Moncorvo. If you're heading to Moncorvo with your own transport, stop off in **CARVIÇAIS** for one of Trás-os-Montes' best restaurants, *O Artur* (☎279 939 284), famed for its genuine *alheira* sausages – almost the only place left in Portugal which hasn't succumbed to mixing pork into the stuffing. They also have a few en-suite **rooms** available (②).

Torre de Moncorvo

Aside from its imposing sixteenth-century Igreja Matriz – the largest church in Trás-os-Montes, taking a century to build – there's little to see in **TORRE DE MONCORVO**, 58km southwest of Mogadouro, though its network of handsome, narrow medieval streets make the town a pleasant place to spend the night. The **turismo**, on Rua Manuel Seixas (Mon–Fri 9am–12.30pm & 2–5.30pm; ☎279 252 289), can advise you as to how to track down the remains of the old town walls. The town's other attraction is its almond trees, the blossoming of which draws crowds of Portuguese in late February and early March. Later, the nuts are gathered and sugared, and sold in local shops; a good place to try is Flormêndoa at Largo Diogo Sá 5–7, by the Igreja Matriz. Local festivities include the *Festa de Nossa Senhora da Assunção* (second weekend of August), the *Feira do Ano* (December 23), and the *Feira das Cerejas* (May 10), in honour of Moncorvo's locally produced cherries.

There are three **bus** connections a day from Mogodouro to Moncorvo (as it's known locally), which then continue on to Pocinho, 10km to the southwest, where they meet the trains running along the Douro line (see p.292). Buses also run from Moncorvo to Freixo de Espada à Cinta (see below) and there's a daily connection south to Vila Nova de Foz Côa, in Beira Alta, which continues to Lisbon. Buses to Porto run on Tuesdays and Thursdays. All these buses arrive in and depart from the bus station on Estrada 220, next to the telecom building near the hospital.

Accommodation should be no problem. The cheapest options are the *Residencial Café Popular*, Rua Tomas Ribeiro 66, off the main Praça Francisco Meireles (☎279 252 337; ①), and *Residencial Caçula* (☎279 254 218; ②), on Travessa das Amoreiras beside the Igreja Matriz. More upmarket are the unexciting *Residencial Campos Monteiro*, Rua Visconde de Vila Maior 55 (☎279 254 280, fax 279 254 055; ③), and *Residencial Brasília* (☎/fax 279 254 256; ③), 1km north on the N220, which has the benefit of a swimming pool. *Casa da Avó*, Rua Manuel Seixas 12, a cosy town house built in 1880, has much more charm, with four en suite rooms and a shaded garden (☎279 252 401; ③; Feb–Nov), while the lovely *Quinta das Aveleiras*, 300 metres from the bus station on the Pocinho road in a large estate (☎279 254 137, fax 279 252 652; ③), has spacious rooms in two old farmhouses, each with kitchenettes, and bicycles and horses for rent. They also make their own wine.

For **food**, good cheap options include *Restaurante Regional* at Rua do Hospital 16 (around 1500$00), and *Café Pizzaria Jardim*, Avenida Enginheiro Duarte Pacheco, in a small garden overlooking a vast and deep valley – the latter also does whole roast chicken with garlic potatoes and salad (1400$00). Much more expensive is the formal restaurant in *Campos Monteiro*.

Freixo de Espada à Cinta

The southernmost town in Trás-os-Montes, **FREIXO DE ESPADA À CINTA** is served by four daily buses operated by Santos (☎279 652 188), from Miranda do Douro and Mogadouro. The town feels end-of-the-worldish as the bus climbs down to its valley, hidden on each side by wild, dark mountains, a backdrop against which you might glimpse the occasional hawk or black kite. You're unlikely to come across any other travellers on the road; in fact the town was once considered so remote that prisoners who had been granted an amnesty were allowed to settle here – it's this sense of isolation that makes the town worth a visit.

Curiously, for such a remote outpost, there is a very rich parish church, the **Igreja Matriz** – part Romanesque, part Manueline – with a *retábulo* of paintings by Grão Vasco (see Viseu, p.217). The church is at the heart of the town's **Romaria de Sete Paços**, which takes place at midnight on Good Friday; a sombre cortege of hooded penitents dressed in black with their faces covered proceed from the church and wend their way through the town, chanting. Across the way from the church is a magnificent heptagonal **keep** (Mon–Fri 9am–12.30pm & 2–5.30pm; free), a landmark for miles around, which affords great views from its bell tower for those who brave the very steep steps. Another, unpublicized, attraction is a mansion in Largo do Outeiro that maintains a garden of mulberry bushes complete with worms for silk production; ask around and you may be taken for a look.

The town's small **turismo** (variable hours; ☎279 653 480) is on Avenida do Emigrante. Amongst the ring of dull new buildings surrounding the scene are some **places to stay**, such as the modern *Hospedaria Santo António* (☎279 653 104; ①), a little distance from Avenida 25 de Abril where the bus drops you and facing the Capela de Santo António. A more comfortable option is the *Quinta da Boa Vista* (☎279 632 145; ③), on the outskirts of town as you come in from Moncorvo, which has four bungalows for rent, a pool and pleasant views over the town; call in advance or you might find the place deserted. The *Cinta de Ouro* (☎279 652 550, fax 279 653 470; ②), opposite the new municipal market on the way out of town to the south, is very good (if a little bland) with TV and private bathrooms in each room. Its restaurant has an outdoor patio and is the place for **meals**, though you'll find there's a strong Spanish influence in the cooking. For typical Portuguese dishes try the *Bom Retiro*, 100 metres further along, which is also cheaper. There's a **campsite**, *Congida*, just over 4km east on the banks of the Douro (☎279 653 371); follow the signs or take a taxi. The complex also houses the municipal swimming pool, a couple of cafés and a restaurant.

To the south, the N221 follows a beautiful stretch of the Douro to Barca de Alva, 20km southwest (see p.295), but you'll need your own transport as there are no buses along this route.

The Parque Natural do Douro Internacional

Designated in September 1997, the **Parque Natural do Douro Internacional** covers a vast tract of land along the west bank of the Douro as it flows along the Spanish border from Miranda do Douro in the north (p.389) to Barca de Alva (p.295) – the point at which the river officially enters Portuguese territory – as well as a stretch of the Rio Águeda further south in Beira Alta.

The upper Douro is ecologically important owing to its Mediterranean microclimate, which contrasts markedly with the harsher, mountainous terrain of the Terra Fria which encloses it. The combination of mild winters and its isolation from both large human populations (the mountains saw to that) and the Mediterranean zone proper, has led to the survival of a number of animal and plant species now extinct in the south. To the visitor, this quirk of geology is most visible in the region's famous **almond trees**, explained in a legend of a Moorish prince who married a northern European princess. Though happy in summer, she grew sad and wistful in winter, and ached for the snow-clad hills of her homeland. The prince hurried to the Algarve, from where he brought back the almond trees, so that from then on, every February when the trees blossomed, the princess beheld white as far as the eye could see.

Despite some river pollution (mild in comparison with further downstream) and industrial sand extraction on the Spanish side, the area has been left largely untouched by the more damaging aspects of twentieth-century agriculture and industry, and preserves a rich, if endangered, local **flora and fauna**, including rare mammals such as wolves, wild cats and otters, as well as various species of bats and amphibians. The area is also an ornithologist's dream, home to over **170 bird species**, including rare peregrine falcons, black storks and Europe's largest population of Egyptian vultures.

In common with all natural parks, its success depends on achieving a fine balance between the encouragement of much-needed investment in the agricultural infrastructure on its margins, and the development of eco-tourism within the park itself to benefit the local population, which has one of the highest unemployment rates in the country. As the park is still in its infancy, there are no facilities, maps or brochures available, though a **park office** was recently set up outside the park in Mogadouro (Rua Santa Marinha 4; ☎279 340 030, fax 279 341 596), which may have **information** on wildlife, possible walking routes and camping spots. For the time being, **visiting the park** is a simple matter of choosing one of the towns in the area – Miranda da Douro, Freixo de Espada à Cinta or Barca de Alva are best – as a base (see the relevant accounts in the text for details of accommodation). You might also consider staying in Vila Nova de Foz Côa (see p.294), which has the added attraction of the Parque Arqueologico do Vale do Côa. Alternatively, **camping** in the park is permitted at present, although this is likely to be more strictly controlled in future.

travel details

Trains

Peso da Régua to: Livraçao (for Amarante; 11–13 daily; 1hr 10min); Pocinho (3–4 daily; 1hr 30min); Porto (11–13 daily; 2hr 30min); Tua (6–7 daily; 1 hr); Vila Real (5 daily; 1hr).

Pocinho to: Porto (3–4 daily; 3hr 45min–4hr 45min), via Tua (45min), Peso da Régua (1hr 30min) and Livraçao (2hr 30min–3hr 20min).

Tua to: Livraçao (6–7 daily; 2hr 30min); Mirandela (5 daily; 1hr 50min); Peso da Régua (6–7 daily; 1hr); Pocinho (3–4 daily; 45min); Porto (6–7 daily; 3hr 10min–4hr).

Vila Real to: Peso da Régua (5 daily; 1hr).

Buses

Hours of operation and journey times change frequently. It's advisable to check exact timetables with the turismos or relevant bus companies given in the accounts of each destination.

Bragança to: Braga (3–5 daily; 6hr); Chaves (Mon–Fri & Sun 3 daily; Sat 1 daily; 2hr); Coimbra (2–3 daily; 6hr 50min); Lamego (2–3 daily; 4hr); Lisbon (2–4 daily; 9–10hr); Macedo de Cavaleiros (5 daily; 35–45min); Miranda do Douro (1–3 daily; 1hr 30min–2hr 15min); Mirandela (10 daily; 1hr 25min–2hr 45min); Mogadouro (Mon–Fri 1 daily;

1hr 40min); Peso da Régua (2–3 daily; 3hr 45min); Porto (2–6 daily; 5hr–5hr 20min); Sendim (Mon–Fri 1 daily; 2hr 10min); Vila Nova de Foz Côa (2 daily; 2hr); Vila Real (Mon–Fri 7 daily; Sat & Sun 3 daily; 2hr 50min); Vinhais (2–3 daily; 35min); Viseu (2–4 daily; 5hr 15min).

Chaves to: Braga (4–5 daily; 2–4hr); Bragança (Mon–Fri & Sun 3 daily, Sat 1; 2hr); Coimbra (4–6 daily; 2hr 40min); Fronteira (3–6 daily; 1hr); Lamego (3–4 daily; 2hr); Lisbon (4–7 daily; 8–10hr); Mirandela (Mon–Fri & Sun 1–2 daily; 2hr); Montalegre (Mon–Fri 5 daily; 1hr 20min); Porto (3 daily; 3hr 20min); Vila Real (6–12 daily; 1hr 10min–2hr).

Freixo de Espada à Cinta to: Mogadouro (4 daily; 2–3hr).

Miranda do Douro to: Bragança (1–3 daily; 1hr 30min); Freixo de Espada à Cinta (4 daily; 3hr); Mirandela (1 daily Mon-Fri 2hr–2hr 30min); Mogadouro (3–4 daily; 2hr 20min).

Mirandela to: Bragança (10 daily; 1hr 25min–2hr 45min); Chaves (Mon–Fri & Sun 1–2 daily; 2hr); Miranda (1 daily Mon–Fri; 2hr–2 hr 30min); Vila Flôr (3 weekly; 40min); Vila Real (Mon–Fri 7 daily; Sat & Sun 3 daily; 1hr).

Mogadouro to: Freixo de Espada à Cinta (4 daily; 2–3hr); Miranda do Douro (3–4 daily; 2hr 20min); Pocinho (3 daily; 3hr); Torre de Moncorvo (3 daily; 2hr 40min).

Montalegre to: Braga (4–6 daily; 2hr 40min); Chaves (Mon–Fri 5 daily; 1hr 20min).

Vila Flôr to: Carrazeda (Mon–Fri 4 daily; Sun 2 daily; 1hr); Mirandela (4 weekly; 40min); Moncorvo (Mon–Fri 2 daily; 1hr); Tua (Mon–Fri 4 daily; Sun 1 daily; 1hr).

Vila Real to: Amarante (10–12 daily; 1hr 25min); Braga (2–4 daily; 3hr 10min); Bragança (Mon–Fri 7 daily; Sat & Sun 3 daily; 2hr 50min); Chaves (5–11 daily; 1 hr 20min–2hr); Coimbra (4–6 daily; 3hr 20min); Guimarães (Mon–Fri 7 daily; Sat & Sun 1 daily; 1hr 30min); Lamego (4–6 daily; 1hr 30min); Lisbon (2–4 daily; 7hr); Mirandela (Mon–Fri 7 daily; Sat & Sun 3 daily; 1hr); Peso da Régua (7–9 daily; 45min); Porto (10–12 daily; 2hr); Viseu (4–6 daily; 1hr 45min).

CHAPTER EIGHT

ALENTEJO

T he huge, sparsely populated plains of the **Alentejo** are overwhelmingly agricultural, dominated by vast cork plantations – the one crop that is well suited to the low rainfall, sweltering heat and poor soil. This is one of the poorest parts of the country (indeed, one of the poorest parts of Europe), much of whose sparse population still derives a living from the huge agricultural estates, known as *latifúndios*. However, despite the tedium of the interior landscape, there are unexpected surprises throughout the region, from the strong rural traditions still expressed in a variety of local festivals, to the wealth of ornithological interest – the Alentejo is home to hundreds of species of birds, from black storks to great bustards, all finely adapted to the mix of varied agriculture and marginal wilderness.

For most visitors, understandably, the region's major draws are its few towns and cities, with the outstanding attraction being historic **Évora**, whose Roman temple and medieval walls and cathedral have put it very much on the tourist map. Elsewhere in **Alto Alentejo** (Upper Alentejo), few towns see more than a handful of visitors in a day. Yet there is much to see and enjoy: the spectacular fortifications of **Elvas**; the hilltop sites of **Monsaraz**, **Évora Monte** and **Marvão**; and the marble towns of **Estremoz**, **Borba** and **Vila Viçosa**, northeast of Évora, where even the humblest homes are made of fine stone from the local quarries. This region is also scattered with **prehistoric remains**, including over a dozen megalithic sites with dolmens, standing stones and stone circles.

South of Évora, the plains of **Baixo Alentejo** (Lower Alentejo), have rather less appeal, and the towns, with the notable exception of **Beja** – once an important Moorish stronghold – can seem rather dull. But the Alentejo **coastline** is almost as extensive as the Algarve's and more than compensates for the lack of urban pleasures. Whipped by the Atlantic winds, its **beaches** can seem pretty wild, but in summer at least the sea is warm enough for swimming, and very few of the resorts attract more than weekend crowds. Particularly enticing are the lagoons of **Melides** and **Santo André** – between Setúbal and the eminently avoidable industrial port of Sines – and the long beaches further south at **Ilha do Pessegueiro**, **Vila Nova de Milfontes** and **Zambujeira do Mar**. If you want to head straight for these southern resorts, there are express buses in summer from Lisbon. Accommodation is somewhat limited, but there are plenty of campsites strategically positioned along the coast.

ACCOMMODATION PRICE CODES

All the accommodation prices in this book have been coded using the symbols below. The symbols represent the lowest prices you can expect to pay for a **double room in high season**; for a full explanation, see p.32.

① Under 4000$00   ④ 11,000$00–15,000$00   ⑦ 25,000$00–30,000$00
② 4000$00–7000$00   ⑤ 15,000$00–20,000$00   ⑧ 30,000$00–40,000$00
③ 7000$00–11,000$00   ⑥ 20,000$00–25,000$00   ⑨ Over 40,000$00

ALTO ALENTEJO

Unless you are heading south to the beaches, Évora provides the easiest starting point in Alentejo, with frequent and fast buses, or rather slower trains, from Lisbon. From here, you're within striking distance of **Estremoz** and the marble towns, beyond which, to the east, lie the superbly preserved walls of **Elvas**, close to the Spanish frontier. The northern part of Alto Alentejo is characterized by more fortified towns – **Portalegre, Castelo de Vide, Marvão** – any of which would make a splendid night's stopover on your way to points further north.

Évora

ÉVORA is one of the most impressive and enjoyable cities in Portugal, its relaxed provincial atmosphere forming a perfect setting for a range of memorable monuments. A Roman temple, Moorish alleys, a circuit of medieval walls, and a rather grand sixteenth-century ensemble of palaces and mansions are all in superb condition, spruced up by a long-term restoration programme and placed under UNESCO protection. Inevitably, they attract a great number of summer tourists but, despite the crowds, the city is far from spoiled. It still plays its part in the agricultural life of the region, with a morning produce market on the second Tuesday of the month; while the university, re-established here in the 1970s, adds an independent side to city life.

Évora's big annual event is the **Feira de São João**, a folklore, handicraft, gastronomic and musical festival, whose origins date from pre-Christian times and which takes over the city during the last ten days of June.

Arrival and accommodation

Évora's **train station** is 1km southeast of the centre; if you follow Rua da República, straight ahead, you'll reach **Praça do Giraldo**, the city's main square. CP **buses** to and from Estremoz, Vila Viçosa and Reguengos de Monsaraz use the train station as a depot; others operate from the new **bus terminal** which is about a kilometre out from the walls along the Lisbon road; there are regular green buses running from it to Praça

---

LAND REFORM IN ALENTEJO

The Alentejo's structure of **land ownership** has been in place since Roman times, when the new settlers established massive agricultural estates – *latifúndios* – on which they grew imported crops, such as wheat, barley and olives. Handed down from generation to generation, these estates remained feudal in character, employing large numbers of farm labourers with no stake in the land they worked. In the wake of the 1974 Revolution, much of the land in Alentejo – then a Communist stronghold – was collectivized. However, the workers possessed neither the financial means nor the technical know-how to cope with a succession of poor harvests, and increasingly the original *latifúndio* owners have been clawing back their estates at depressed prices. Jobs today are scarcer than ever, as mechanization has done away with much casual farm labour – a move hastened by European Community grants for modernization programmes and the introduction of new agricultural methods. Only the Beja district, known in Portugal as the reddest region of the country, has a government still controlled by the Communists, who have gradually lost sway in the rest of Alentejo.

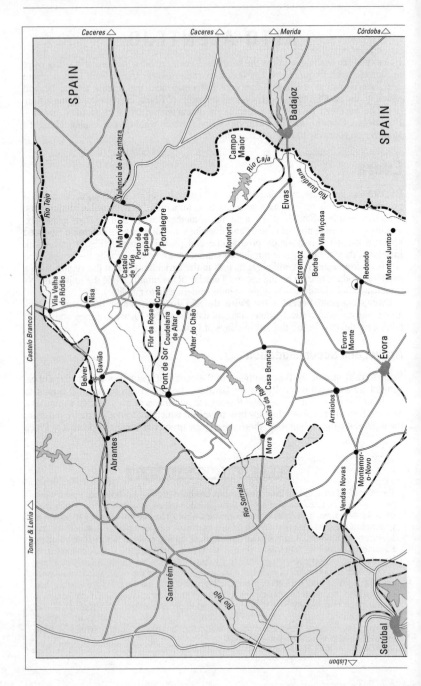

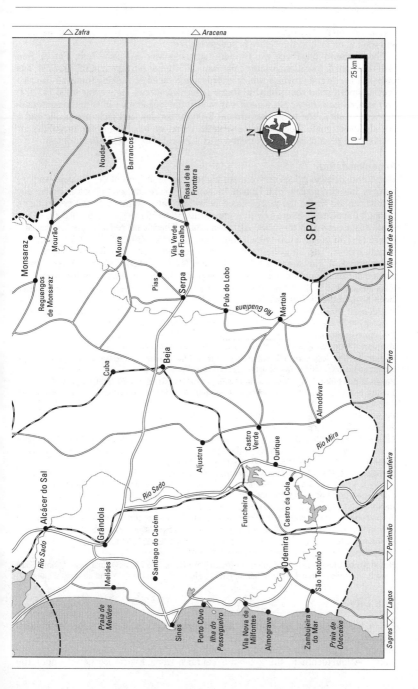

Giraldo. If you're **driving**, you'll have to park in one of the many car-parks at the walls and walk in on foot, as the centre is pedestrianized.

The **turismo** on Praça do Giraldo (summer Mon–Fri 9am–7pm, Sat & Sun 9am–12.30pm & 2–5.30pm; winter daily 9am–12.30pm & 2–5.30pm; ☎266 702 671), has maps of the city and province, which include some excellent walking routes. It can also provide information about **bicycle tours** (alternatively call Turaventur ☎266 743 134, *turaventur@mail.telepac.pt*), a good way to visit the megalithic sights in the surroundings (see p.404). The tours cost around 5700$00 per day, and include a picnic and a knowledgable guide. For the less energetic, there are bus trips to the megaliths for 3500$00 per person; ask at the turismo or call Policarpo ☎266 746 970 for details.

Accommodation

Hotel and pensão prices in Évora are higher than in the rest of the Alentejo, and are more or less comparable with Lisbon. In summer you're advised to book at least a day in advance for any of the places listed below; **private rooms** (②) can be arranged through the turismo. Évora's Orbitur **campsite** (☎266 705 190, fax 266 709 830) is 2km southwest of town on the N380 Alcáçovas road. There's no reliable bus service and you're best off taking a taxi (which should cost around 500$00) if you can't face the 45-minute trudge. The campsite itself is clean and well equipped, with a restaurant and swimming pool. The new **youth hostel** (☎266 744 848, fax 266 744 843; ②) is centrally located at Rua Miguel Bombarda 40 – though, as always, book well in advance.

Casa Palma, Rua Bernardo Matos 29A (☎266 703 560). First-floor rooms in a scrupulously clean family house stuffed with antiques and assorted china. ②.

Residencial Diana, Rua Diogo Cão 2 (☎266 702 008, fax 266 743 101). Adequate rooms in a house between the Sé and Praça do Giraldo; price includes breakfast. ③.

Pensão Giraldo, Rua dos Mercadores 27 (☎266 705 833). Very pleasant rooms, some with bath; also some "overspill" rooms available, which are not as nice but much cheaper. ②.

Pensão Invicta, Rua Romão Ramalho 37A (☎266 702 047). Évora's cheapest, with clean but dingy rooms; some have good views over the Igreja de São Francisco. ②.

Pousada dos Lóios, Largo do Conde de Vila Flor (☎266 704 051, fax 266 707 248). One of the country's loveliest *pousadas*, housed in the cloistered Convento dos Lóios (see p.404) and with a good open-air restaurant. ⑧.

Pensão Os Manuéis, Rua do Raimundo 35–1° (☎266 702 861). Decent rooms just west of Praça do Giraldo. There's a less preferable annexe across the road. ②.

Albergaria Solar Monfalim, Largo da Misericórdia 1 (☎266 750 000, fax 266 742 367). A restored summer palace formerly belonging to the Dukes of Monfalim – elegant, spacious and relaxed. Breakfasts are taken on the verandah with superb views. ④.

Pensão Monte das Flores, 2km south of the Orbitur campsite on the N380 (☎266 705 018, fax 266 707 564). A modern "activities guest house" in a rural setting offering horse riding as well as tennis courts, pool and a decent restaurant. ④.

Residencial Policarpo, Rua do Conde da Serra da Tourega 9 (☎266 702 424, fax 266 702 424). One of the best places to stay in Évora, this former ducal summer palace has beautiful views, a cosy lounge with a fire in winter, 16th-century *azulejos* and bags of charm; excellent value and highly recommended. ④.

Residencial Riviera, Rua 5 de Outubro 49 (☎266 703 304, fax 266 700 467). A reasonable if unexciting *pensão* between the Sé and Praça do Giraldo. ②.

Hotel Santa Clara, Trav. da Milheira 19 (☎266 704 141, fax 266 706 544). Just east of Santa Clara church, this modern hotel is bland but functional; all rooms with bath, TV and air-conditioning. ③.

The City

Évora was shaped by its **Roman** and **Moorish** occupations: the former is commemorated by a temple, the latter by a characteristic tangle of alleys, rising steeply among the whitewashed houses. Most of the city's other monuments, however, date from the fourteenth to the sixteenth century, when Évora prospered under the

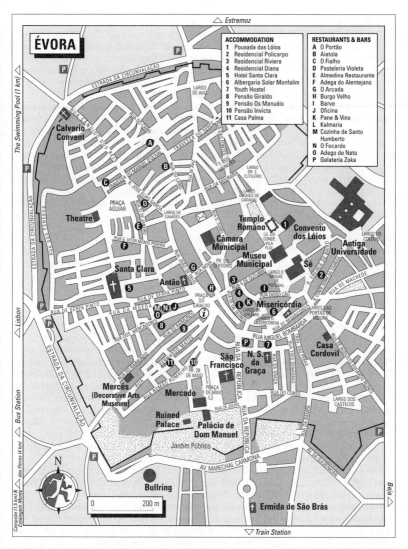

ÉVORA

ACCOMMODATION
1 Pousada dos Lóios
2 Residencial Policarpo
3 Residencial Riviera
4 Residencial Diana
5 Hotel Santa Clara
6 Albergaria Solar Monfalim
7 Youth Hostel
8 Pensão Giraldo
9 Pensão Os Manuéis
10 Pensão Invicta
11 Casa Palma

RESTAURANTS & BARS
A O Portão
B Aiatola
C O Fialho
D Pasteleria Violeta
E Almedina Restaurante
F Adega do Alentejano
G O Arcada
H Burgo Velho
I Barve
J Oficina
K Pane & Vino
L Kalmaria
M Cozinha de Santo Humberto
N O Focardo
O Adego do Neto
P Gelateria Zoka

patronage of the ruling **House of Avis**. To them are owed the many noble palaces scattered about the city; as are the Jesuit **university**, founded in 1559 by Cardinal Henrique, the future "Cardinal King"; and the wonderful array of Manueline and Renaissance buildings.

That the city's monuments have survived intact is due, in large part, to Évora's decline after the Spanish usurpation of the throne in 1580. Future Portuguese monarchs chose to live nearer Lisbon, and the university was closed down; for the next four hundred years, Évora drifted back into a rural existence as a provincial market centre. Even today, the 50,000-strong population is only half its medieval number.

The Templo Romano and Convento dos Lóios

The graceful **Templo Romano** stands at the very heart of the old city. Dating from the second century AD, it is the best-preserved temple in Portugal, despite (or perhaps because of) its use as an execution-ground during the Inquisition and a slaughterhouse until 1870. The stark remains consist of a small platform supporting fourteen granite columns with Corinthian capitals and a marble entablature. Its popular attribution to Diana is apparently fanciful; Jupiter is the more likely alternative.

Directly opposite the temple, the magnificent fifteenth-century **Convento dos Lóios** has been converted into a top-grade *pousada*. Its cloisters now serve as a dining area in summer, and the hotel staff can be sniffy about allowing in non-residents (or non-diners) to look around. However, dress up as formally as you can – a tie is a help for men – and walk in regardless. The dual horseshoe arches, slender twisted columns and the intricate carvings on the doorway to the chapter house are fine examples of the so-called Luso-Moorish style and have been attributed to Francisco de Arruda, architect of Évora's aqueduct and the Belém tower in Lisbon.

To the left of the *pousada* lies the former conventual church, dedicated to **São João Evangelista** (daily 9.30am–2.30pm & 2.30–5.30pm; 500$00). This is still the private property of the ducal Cadaval family, who occupy a wing or two of their adjacent ancestral palace. Just hang around for a few minutes and one of the three guides will let you in to see the floor-to-ceiling *azulejos* within, the masterpiece of one António Oliveira Bernardes and created early in the eighteenth century. Other highlights include a Moorish cistern (the church and convent were built over an old castle), a grisly ossuary containing the bones of the convent's monks, and a magnificent Manueline altar.

The Sé and Museu Municipal

Évora's cathedral, the **Sé** (daily 9am–12.30pm & 2–5pm), was begun in 1186, about twenty years after the reconquest of Évora from the Moors. The Romanesque solidity of its original battlemented towers and roofline contrasts sharply with the pointed Gothic arches of subsequent and less militaristic additions, such as the porch and central window. The interior is more straightforwardly Gothic, although the choir and high altar were remodelled in the eighteenth century by the German, Friedrich Ludwig, architect of the Convent at Mafra. For a nominal fee you can clamber onto a terrace above the west entrance and take an unusually close look at the towers and the *zimbório* (the lantern above the crossing of the transepts). Don't miss the cathedral **museum** (Tues–Sun 9–11.30am & 2–4.30pm; 350$00), either: it's stuffed with treasures and relics, the prize exhibits being a reliquary studded with 1426 stones and a carved statue of the Madonna whose midriff opens out to display layered scenes from the Bible.

Immediately adjacent to the Sé is the former archbishop's palace, now the **Museu Municipal** (Tues 2.30–5.30pm, Wed–Sun 9.30am–12.30pm & 2.30–5pm; 350$00), housing important collections of fifteenth- and sixteenth-century Flemish and Portuguese paintings assembled from the city's churches and convents. These provide a good illustration of the significance of Flemish artists in the development of the "Portuguese School", and reflect the strong medieval trade links between the two countries. Frei Carlos, probably the most important Flemish artist known to have worked in Évora, is well represented, but the centrepiece of the museum is a series of thirteen panels by an anonymous fifteenth-century Flemish artist, portraying scenes from the life of the Virgin. This was once the cathedral altarpiece.

Up behind the museum, a quick stroll to the north will take you to the beautiful entrance courtyard of the **Antiga Universidade**, with its brazilwood ceiling and *azulejos*, which you wander around at will. You can enter the inner courtyard by request (Mon–Fri 9am–6pm, Sat 9am–1pm; 350$00). The university was closed down by the Jesuit-hating Marquês de Pombal during the eighteenth century but since its re-opening in the 1970s it is now one of the liveliest corners of the city.

The Igreja de São Francisco and the Capela dos Ossos

Situated on the eastern side of Praça de Maio, the **Igreja de São Francisco** contains perhaps the most memorable monument in Évora – the **Capela dos Ossos** (Chapel of Bones; Mon–Sat 9am–1pm & 2.30–6pm; Sun 10am–1pm & 2.30–6pm; 100$00, plus another 50$00 for taking photos). A timeless and gruesome memorial to the mortality of man, the walls and pillars of this chilling chamber are entirely covered in the bones of more than 5000 monks. During the fifteenth and sixteenth centuries, there were 42 monastic cemeteries in town which took up much-needed space. The Franciscans' neat solution was to move all the remains to one compact, consecrated site. There's a grim humour in the ordered, artfully planned arrangement of skulls, tibias and vertibrae around the vaults, and in the rhyming inscription over the door which reads "*Nós ossos que aqui estamos pelos vossos esperamos*" (We bones here are waiting for your bones). Such macabre warnings can be encountered in a couple of other locations in Portugal – at Campo Maior, northeast of Évora, and at Faro in the Algarve.

Another interesting feature of this fifteenth-century church is its large **porch**, which combines pointed, rounded, and horseshoe arches in a manner typical of Manueline architecture. Appropriately enough, the restored **Palácio de Dom Manuel** – the king who gave his name to the style – lies no more than a minute's walk away, in the Jardim Público. Early sixteenth-century, it too incorporates inventive horseshoe arches with strange serrated edges.

Directly opposite São Francisco, on Praça 1º de Maio, the rich craft traditions of the Évora district are well displayed in the **Museu do Artesanato Regional** (daily 10am–noon & 2–5pm). The collections include pottery, weaving, tapestry and carvings in wood, cork and bone; modern pieces are on sale, too.

The rest of the city

As well as artists and writers such as Gil Vicente and Garcia, great Portuguese and European architects also gravitated to Évora, and the **Ermida de São Brás**, just outside the city walls on the road to the train station, has been identified as an early work by Diogo de Boitaca, pioneer of the flamboyant Manueline style. Its tubular, dunce-capped buttresses and crenellated roofline bear scant resemblance to his masterpieces at Lisbon and Setúbal, but they certainly foreshadow the style's uninhibited originality.

No less bizarre is the mid-sixteenth-century facade of the **Igreja Nossa Senhora da Graça**, out behind the bus station. At each of the corners of its Renaissance pediment, grotesque Atlas-giants support two globes – the emblem of Dom Manuel and his burgeoning overseas empire.

Other buildings worth seeing in Évora include the lavish Neoclassical **Theatre of Garcia de Redende** on Praça Aguiar; the **Misericórdia**'s baroque bas-reliefs and *azulejos*, on Largo da Misericórdia; the **Calvario Convent**, built by the Infanta Dona Maria in 1570, at the far end of Rua Candido dos Reis; and the **Church and Convent of Santa Clara**, on Rua Serpa de Pinto, for its beautiful gilded altar. Lastly, it's worth following **Rua do Cano**, north of the old centre, behind the Câmara Municipal. Here, you can travel the course of the medieval **Aqueduto do Água Prata** (Silver Water Aqueduct), into whose arches a row of houses has been incorporated.

Eating and drinking

When the students aren't around, Évora goes to bed pretty early, as if exhausted by the attentions of the tour groups. Finding a place to eat, however, is no problem, with a range of decent **restaurants** to suit most budgets located around the centre; below we've listed some of the best. For **picnic** supplies try the large market on the second Tuesday of every month in Rossio São Brás or Pastelaria Violeta, Rua José Elias Garcia 47 on the corner of Praça Aguiar, which sells a wide range of mouth-watering cakes and pastries.

For a late-evening **drink** in summer you'll find a couple of outdoor cafés in Praça do Giraldo, or, just off the praça on Rua João de Deus, there's the cavernous 1930s' *O Arcada*, and the very pleasant *Gelateria Zoka* at Rua Miguel Bombarda 10. Otherwise, try *Aiatola* at Ruo do Cano 11, an intimate, half-timbered joint that serves black beer – made from coffee to an African recipe – and plays an interesting range of relaxed sounds until 4am. *Oficin@*, at Rua da Moeda 27, is another easy-going place, with a more mature crowd, which plays jazz and blues and offers Internet access for 500$00 per hour. In term-time, you could try the student circuit which starts at *Barue* – the inexpensive union bar at Rua Diogo Cão 21 – and continues to Evoras's only **club**, *Kalmaria*, on Rua de Valdevinos (Mon–Sat until 7am; cover-charge of 500$00 Mon–Thurs includes three drinks, and 1000$00 cover charge Fri & Sat includes two drinks).

Adega do Alentejano, Rua Gabriel Vitor do Monte Pereira 21A. Traditional, well-cooked fare served in a delightful old *adega* adorned with giant amphorae. The à la carte menu is a bargain at 1750$00 including wine. Closed Mon.

Adego do Neto, Rua dos Mercadores 46. No-nonsense Portuguese cooking in intimate surroundings; always busy with locals. A meal with wine will set you back less than 1500$00.

Almedina Restaurante, Trav. de Santa Martha 5(off Praça Aguiar). In cosy Moorish-style surroundings, this restaurant serves excellent main courses for around 1300$00, including succulent *migas alentejanas* and *bacalhau almedina* (cod fried with marinaded onions).

Burgo Velho, Rua de Burgos 10. Serves a comprehensive range of the more common Alentejan dishes for under 1000$00, as well as a tasty shark soup.

Restaurante Cozinha de Santo Humberto, Rua da Moeda 39 (☎266 704 251). Top-notch establishment highly recommended by locals, this is on a street which runs downhill from Praça do Giraldo; there's only a small sign. Downstairs, in a converted cellar, you can eat from a fine menu of local dishes for around 4000$00 a head; try the *chispe assado de Santo Humberto* (knuckle of pork). Closed Nov.

O Fialho, Trav. das Mascarenhas 16. Up a cobbled alley off Praça Aguiar, this is reckoned to be one of the ten best restaurants in Portugal. Starters, particularly, are superb, the wine list is good and prices, unsurprisingly, are high.

O Focardo, Rua dos Mercadores 26. Best of a quartet of modestly priced restaurants in this central old city street; good prices and solid quality. The set menu costs 1550$00, while à la carte should set you back another 500$00.

Pane & Vino, Patio do Salema (entrance on Rua Diogo Focardo, visible from Rua 5 Outubro; ☎266 746 960). Once the stables of a town house, this restaurant serves up a wide range of Italian dishes – the pizzas are especially good – in a brick-walled, vaulted interior. There's a set menu for 2500$00. Very popular with the locals and booking is advised to avoid a long wait.

O Portão, Rua do Cano. Local haunt next to the aqueduct, popular with students for good, inexpensive food (it does a very decent *porco alentejana*). A full meal with wine will rarely cost more than 1500$00.

Pousada dos Lóios, Largo do Conde de Vila Flor. Elegant, upmarket, classic Portuguese dining in the monastery's cloisters. Meals from 4000$00 upwards.

Around Évora

The administrative district of Évora contains over a dozen **megalithic sites** dating from around 3000 BC. The dolmens, standing stones and stone circles found here have their origins in a culture which flourished in the peninsula before spreading north as far as Brittany and Denmark. Two of the most accessible sites lie to the west and northwest of Évora in the Serra de Monfurado, which makes them possible visits in conjunction with the carpet town of **Arraiolos**. For descriptions of – and directions to – sites other than the couple covered below, ask at the turismo in Évora for the *Guide to the Megalithic Monuments of the Évora Region* (1000$00). An additional attraction in the district, en route to Estremoz from Évora, is Évora Monte, with its superb Renaissance castle.

Os Almendres

One of the sites nearest to Évora is the **stone circle** and three-metre-high **menhir** (upright stone) at a cork plantation called **OS ALMENDRES**. It's located west of the city, about 3km out of Guadalupe, just south of the N114 Évora–Montemor road. Ask for directions in the village and expect a stiff uphill walk through wild country. The legend goes that this stone is the tomb of an enchanted Moorish princess, who appears once a year on the eve of São João and can be seen combing her hair. Those with ornithological interests will have the additional pleasure of seeing the **hoopoes** of the area.

Montemor-o-Novo

Back on the N114, 30km northwest of Évora, lies the white town of **MONTEMOR-O-NOVO**, birthplace of São João de Deus, patron saint of the sick. This large, sleepy town has a dearth of spectacular monuments though it does boast the **castle** (Mon–Sat 10am–5pm; free) where Vasco da Gama finalized his plans for opening up the sea route to India, and a **convent** founded at the end of the fifteenth century by São João de Deus. In the town's main square stands a statue of him carrying an injured beggar in need of care.

The **turismo** is on Largo Calouste Gulbenkian (Mon–Fri 9am–6pm, Sat 9.30am–12.30pm; ☎266 892 071). **Accommodation** is plentiful if unexciting. Pleasant and inexpensive **rooms** can be found at Rua do Poço do Paço 34 (☎266 892 357; ①); while the pick of the **pensões** includes the modern *Residencial Monte Alentejano*, Av. Gago Coutinho (☎266 899 630, fax 266 899 631; ③), the functional *Residencial Sampaio* at no. 12 on the same street (☎266 892 237, fax 266 890 195; ③), and the rather run-down *Pensão Ribetejo*, Rua do Passo 8 (☎266 892 362; ②). For **restaurants**, try any of the cluster along the Arraiolos road twenty minutes' walk north of town, or the more upmarket *Residencial Sampaio* restaurant, across the road from the *residencial*.

Twelve kilometres to the south of town are the Neolithic caves of **Escoural**, their weird leathery stalacmites alone worth the visit, and 6km east of the caves, at **São Brissos**, is another dolmen chapel similar to that of São Dinis at Pavia (see below), and just as impressive.

Arraiolos and Pavia

ARRAIOLOS, 22km north of Évora (and connected to it by bus twice a day), is the birthplace of Dom Nuno Álvares Pereira and home of the "noiva de Arraiolos", a legendary bride who took a fortnight to adorn herself only to appear at her wedding in a shepherd's cloak. But the real source of Arraiolos' fame, and fortune, lies with its superb carpets, which have been handwoven here since the thirteenth century. Based on elaborate Persian imports, the designs tend nowadays to be simpler and more brightly coloured; you can still see some of the originals at the **Casa de Artes e Ofícios** (Mon–Sat 9–11am & 2–5pm), in the village of Pelegrejinha 10km to the east of Arraiolos, while the most luxuriant eighteenth-century creations hang on the walls of Queluz Palace, near Lisbon (p.124).

Apart from the carpet shops – where the carpets are expensive, but a lot less so than elsewhere – Arraiolos is a typical Alentejo village with its ruined hilltop castle, white-washed houses and sixteenth-century pillory. While you're here you might as well visit the Quinta dos Lóios **carpet workshop** in Ilhas, just to the east of Arraiolos on the N370; it has an outlet in Évora itself, Castelo das Ilhas, at Rua 5 de Outubro 66, between Praça do Giraldo and the Sé. The **turismo** on Praça Lima e Brito (daily 10am–noon & 2–6pm; ☎266 499 105) can help with **accommodation**. For **food** try the excellent *Arco de Noe* restaurant, on Rua S. Condestavel 23.

In the hamlet of **PAVIA**, 20km north of Arraiolos along the N370, is a massive **dolmen**, within which the tiny sixteenth-century chapel of São Dinis was built. The effect is a bit grotesque and out of keeping with Pavia's traditional Alentejan architecture, but impressive nonetheless.

Évora Monte

Twenty-nine kilometres northeast of Évora, along the N18, the sixteenth-century **castle** at **ÉVORA MONTE** stands on fortifications going back to Roman times and occupies a spectacular position, atop a steep mound. Its keep is constructed in Italian Renaissance style, with four robust round towers, and is adorned with a simple rope-like relief of Manueline stonework. Within are three vaulted chambers, each displaying intricately carved granite capitals. The town – predominantly medieval in appearance – rings the castle mound.

It was here in 1834 that the regent Miguel was finally defeated and the convention signed that put Pedro IV on the Portuguese throne. Legend has it that the signing took so long that there was only stale bread left to eat, causing the invention of the well-known Portuguese dish *açorda* (a soup of bread, water, coriander, garlic and olive oil).

If you want to **stay** overnight, try *Monte da Fazenda*, (☎268 959 172; ④), an *ANTER* farmhouse (see p.33) by the castle; it has three apartments and two rooms for rent, all with private baths and use of the swimming pool. For **food**, the *Restaurante A Convento*, Rua de Santa Maria 26–30, is the town's best bet, with specialities including *bacalhau alentejana* and Brazilian-style pork with pineapple; a full meal costs upwards of 2500$00.

Estremoz and the marble towns

Northeast of Évora, quarry trucks and tracks announce your entry into marble country. Around **Estremoz**, 46km from Évora, the area is so rich in marble that it replaces brick or concrete as a building material, giving butchers' stalls and simple cottages the sort of luxurious finish you generally see only in churches and the grandest houses. Estremoz itself, and **Borba** and **Vila Viçosa**, are all distinctive marble towns, and the latter has an additional attraction in its ducal palace – the last residence of the Portuguese monarchy.

Estremoz

ESTREMOZ is the largest and liveliest of the three marble towns, and comes into its own every Saturday when the **market** takes over the Rossio, the main square of the **lower town**. This is a classic marketplace of huge dimensions, surrounded by bars, restaurants and churches, and selling – among other things – what are renowned as some of the best cheeses in Portugal, mainly made from ewe's and goat's milk. Estremoz's annual *feira* takes place in the Rossio on the first weekend in September, with bull-running, concerts and roll-baking contests. At the start of May it sees a cattle and handicraft fair, including displays of the **earthenware pottery** for which the town has been celebrated since the sixteenth century. The pottery is characterized by simple floral and leaf patterns, sometimes inlaid with marble chips, and is on sale at the weekly market; the most distinctive products are the porous water coolers known as *moringues*, globe-shaped jars with narrow bases, two short spouts, and one handle. Although nowadays largely ornamental, the pottery used to play an important role in gypsy weddings: the procession would march into town, whereupon the bride made a sudden dash for freedom across the market place, hotly pursued by the groom. When the groom finally caught up with his bride, a fine Estremoz dish was thrown into the air. The couple were pronounced man and wife at the moment that the dish fell to the ground in pieces.

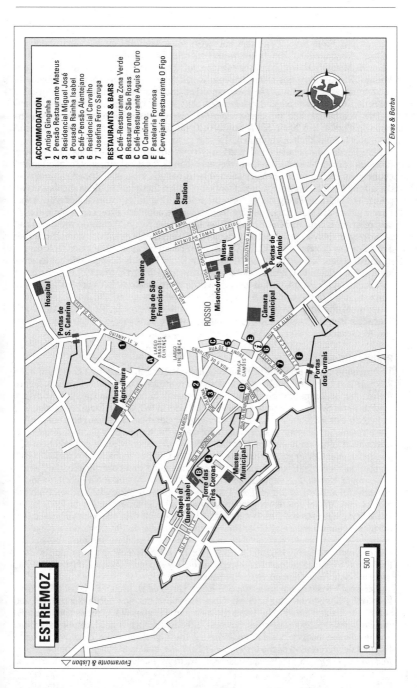

Evoramonte & Lisbon

Elvas & Borba

ESTREMOZ

ACCOMMODATION
1 Antiga Ginginha
2 Pensão Restaurante Mateus
3 Residencial Miguel José
4 Pousada Rainha Isabel
5 Café-Pensão Alentejano
6 Residencial Carvalho
7 Josefina Ferro Saruga

RESTAURANTS & BARS
A Café-Restaurante Zona Verde
B Restaurante São Rosas
C Café-Restaurante Aguis D'Ouro
D O Cantinho
E Pastelaria Formosa
F Cervejaria Restaurante O Figo

Hospital
Portas de S. Catarina
Theatre
Bus Station
Museu Agricultura
Igreja de São Francisco
ROSSIO
Misericórdia
Museu Rural
Câmara Municipal
Portas de S. António
Chapel of Queen Isabel
Torre das Três Coroas
Museu Municipal
Portas dos Currais

AVDA 9 DE ABRIL
AVENIDA CONDESSA DA CUBA
AVENIDA TOMAZ ALCAIDE
RUA MOUZINHO ALBUQUERQUE
AVDA 25 DE ABRIL
LARGO DRAGÕES OLIVENÇA
LARGO GEN. GRAÇA
RUA DE S. ANDRE
RUA 5 DE OUTUBRO
PRAÇA CAMÕES
RUA ALMEIDA
RUA SERPA PINTO
RUA 31 JANEIRO
R. 31 JANEIRO
R. JOÃO DE DEUS
RUA DAS ALMAS
RUA A. BONSO III
RUA VICTOR CORDON
RUA DA TRANQUILA
500 m
0

Arriving by bus, you'll be dropped in the east of town on Avenida 9 de Abril at the old train station. From here, it's a short walk west down Avenida Condessa da Cuba to the Rossio, dominated by the twin-towered marble facade of the eighteenth-century **Câmara Municipal**, which now houses the police station. At no. 62 on the Rossio, the **Museu Rural** (Mon–Sat 10am–12.30pm & 2–5.30pm; 100$00) features a display of earthenware figurines from the town potteries, and has an illuminating ethnographic collection of locally produced artefacts in clay, wood, rush, straw, cork, textile and metal. Nearby, at Rua de Serpa Pinto 87, is a **Museu Agricultura** (Mon–Fri 9am–12.30pm & 2–5.30pm, Sat & Sun 2–5.30pm; 200$00) with a surprisingly fascinating display of old kitchen equipment.

In its heyday, the population of Estremoz – currently around eight thousand – was ten times its current size and the town was once one of the most strongly fortified in the country. An army garrison is still stationed here, and the inner star-shaped **ramparts** of the **upper town** are well preserved. On the hill within these fortifications stands a white, prison-like building, easily visible from the Rossio; despite its external austerity, it was once a palace of Dom Dinis, the king famous for his administrative, economic and military reforms. It is now a *pousada* (see below for details), but you're free to wander in and look around; there's a splendid panoramic view from the thirteenth-century **Torre das Três Coroas** (Tower of the Three Crowns), so called because three kings took part in its construction, including Afonso III and Dom Dinis. With its Islamic-style battlements and Gothic balconies, it bears a close resemblance to the great tower of Beja, its exact contemporary. From this part of town the castle of Évora Monte is clearly visible on the horizon, 15km to the southwest. Opposite the tower, in an old almshouse, is a small **Museu Municipal** (May–Sept Tues–Sun 9am–12.30pm & 3–6.30pm; Oct–April Tues–Sun 9am–12.30pm & 2–5.30pm; 180$00), with more displays of Estremoz pottery and Alentejan life.

Practicalities

The **turismo** (Mon–Fri 9am–12.30pm & 2–6pm, Sat & Sun 10am–1pm & 3–6pm; ☎268 333 541) is at Largo da República 26. Unless you're stopping over on Friday night, before the market, **accommodation** should be easy enough to find; for inexpensive rooms try *Josefina Ferro Saruga*, Rua Brito Capelo 27A (☎268 332 463; ②), or *Antiga Ginginha*, Rua 31 Janeiro 4 (☎268 322 643; ①), run by an energetic elderly *senhora* who rents out her two spare rooms. In the same price range, there's also the wonderfully decrepit *Residencial Carvalho* at Largo da República 27 (☎268 339 370; ②). Slightly more upmarket but still good value are: *Café-Pensão Alentejano*, Rossio Marquês de Pombal 14–15 (☎268 322 834; ②; breakfast included), with a marble staircase and good views over Rossio; the *Pensão-Restaurante Mateus*, Rua Almeida 39–41 (☎268 322 226; ②) in the old quarter; and the characterful *Residencial Miguel José*, Travessa da Levada 8 (☎268 322 326; ③). Both the *Mateus* and *Miguel José* have good restaurants. The grandest option in town is the *Pousada de Santa Rainha Isabel* (☎268 332 075, fax 268 332 079; ⑧), occupying the lavish thirteenth-century palace of Dom Dinis in the old castle. Lastly, there are a couple of upmarket rural hotels just outside town, both with modern facilities: *Monte das Pensamentos* (☎268 333 166, fax 268 332 409; ④) is an *ANTER* property 4km west of Estremoz on Estrada da Estação do Ameixal; the less expensive *Monte Gil* (☎268 332 996; ③) is at Fonte Nova, 3km north on the Sousel road.

Estremoz's best **restaurant** is the *São Rosas*, Largo de D. Dinis 11, opposite the castle keep (☎268 333 345; booking advised). Once a medieval inn, now beautifully restored and run by the Cabaço family, this restaurant serves excellently cooked meals and a bargain *ementa turística* at 2900$00; wines, however, although uniformly good, can be expensive. For good-value budget *ementas turísticas* try the *Café-Restaurante Zona Verde*, Largo Dragões de Olivença 86, or the very basic *O Cantinho*, Rua do Marmelo 2. The *Cervejaria Restaurante O Figo*, Rua da Restauração 36, is worth visiting for its specialities (all priced at

1000$00), including an excellent *arroz de marisco*, and the *Café-Restaurante Aguias d'Ouro*, Rossio Marquês de Pombal 26–27, serves reasonably priced, hearty food, but is interesting principally for its eccentric mismatch of architectural styles. For **picnic** supplies, the place to go is the Saturday-morning market on the Rossio where a wide array of cheeses, spicy sausages and olives are on sale; for **snacks** and pastries, visit the Pastelaria Formosa, just off the Rossio at 16B Largo da República, which sells home-made specialities.

Borba

Eleven kilometres east of Estremoz is **BORBA**, a dazzlingly white little place, where just about anything not whitewashed is made of white marble. The town seems not to have exploited the wider commercial possibilities of its quarries, though, and with the exception of a fine eighteenth-century fountain there are no particular signs of wealth, no extravagant mansions or remarkable churches. All this only serves to make more extraordinary the extensive use of marble in even the most common-place cottages, shops and streets. Borba is an unassuming town with an unusually high concentration of antique shops where one might easily spend an afternoon's browsing. Its other main attributes are the magnificent **wines** produced by the local co-operative, which are receiving increasing plaudits from the rest of Europe; phone the *Adega Cooperative de Borba* (☎268 894 264), who speak little English but some Spanish and French, or, contact the **turismo**, Rua Convento das Servas (Aug & Sept 10am–1pm & 2–8pm; rest of year 10am–1pm & 2–6pm; ☎268 894 13), to arrange a tour of the winery. For **accommodation** try the *Residencial Inarmos*, just up from the bus stop, at Av. do Povo 22 (☎268 894 563; ②), or the spacious *Residencial Vila Borba*, Rua da Cruz 8 (☎ & fax 268 894 376; ②; breakfast included). Alternatively, **rooms** are available at the *Restaurante Lisboeta* at Rua de Mateus Pais 31 (☎268 894 332; ②), which also serves a decent *ementa turística* for 1800$00.

Vila Viçosa

The road from Borba to **VILA VIÇOSA**, 6km to the southeast, is lined on either side with enormous marble quarries, and in town everything from the pavements to the toilets in the bus station are made of the local marble. The town is justly famous, too, for its Paço-Ducal, the last palace-residence of the **Bragança dynasty**. The dukes of Bragança were descended from the illegitimate offspring of João I of Avis, and established their seat here in the fifteenth century. For the next two centuries they were on the edge of the Portuguese ruling circle but their claims to the throne were overridden in 1580 by Philip II of Spain. Sixty years later, while Spanish attention was diverted by a revolt in Catalonia, Portuguese resentment erupted and massive public pressure forced the reluctant João, eighth Duke of Bragança, to seize the throne; his descendants ruled Portugal until the foundation of the Republic in 1910.

The Paço Ducal and palace square

Despite a choice of sumptuous palaces throughout Portugal – Mafra, Sintra and Queluz are the most renowned – the Bragança kings retained a special affection for their residence at Vila Viçosa, a relatively ordinary country home, constructed in various stages during the sixteenth and seventeenth centuries. Dom Carlos spent his last night here before his assassination on the riverfront in Lisbon in 1908, and it was a favourite haven of his successor, Manuel II, the last king of Portugal.

The **Paço Ducal** (Tues–Sun 9am–1pm & 3–5.30pm; 1hr guided tour; 1000$00, 500$00 extra for the Castelo and coach house) has a simple, rhythmic facade. Inside, the standard regal trappings of the more formal chambers are tedious, but the private apartments and mementos of Dom Carlos and his wife Marie-Amélia have a *Hello!* magazine fascination. Faded family photographs hang on the walls, changes of clothing are laid out, and the table is set for dinner: the whole scene seems to await the royals' return. In reality, Dom Duarte, heir to the nonexistent throne, spends his days in experimental eco-farming at his estate near Viseu.

On the south side of the palace square stands the **Convento das Chagas**, used as a mausoleum for the duchesses of Bragança. Their husbands were buried opposite the palace in marble tombs in the chapel of the **Mostéiro dos Agostinhos**, adjacent to one of the most attractive of Vila Viçosa's 22 churches, **Nossa Senhora de Conceição**, worth a visit for its beautiful eighteenth-century *azulejos*.

The old town and castle

The **old town**, still enclosed within walls on its hilltop site, was built by Dom Dinis at the end of the thirteenth century and reinforced four centuries later. Originally the population of Vila Viçosa was based within these walls and a few of the cottages are still lived in. The **Castelo** (Tues–Sun 9am–1pm & 2–5.30pm; 45min guided tour; 500$00), in one corner of the town, was the seat of the Braganças before the construction of their palace. Its interior has been renovated beyond recognition and houses an indifferent archeological museum. However, from the roof there's a good view of the Braganças' old **Tapada Real** (Royal Hunting Ground), set within its eighteen-kilometre circuit of walls.

Practicalities

Buses park at the elongated Praça da República, from where the old town is straight ahead of you, and the Paço Ducal beyond. Vila Viçosa is a quiet town and despite its attractions there's very little available **accommodation**. Your best bet is to arrange **private rooms** through the **turismo** (☎268 881 101) by the town hall on Praça da República. Try those with Maria da Conceição Paixão at Rua Dr. Couto Jardim 7 (☎268 980 169; ③), just off the square. With more money, your options extend to the seventeenth-century mansion house *Casa dos Peixinhos* (☎268 980 472, fax 268 881 348; ⑤), 500m out of town (follow the signs for Alandroal), or, at the top of the price range, the new *Pousada de D. João IV*, on the south side of Terreiro do Paço (☎268 980 742, fax 268 980 747; ⑧), which is converted from a former convent dating from 1514. However, when all's said and done, it's probably simpler to make a day-trip from Évora or Estremoz or to stay in nearby Borba. The town has plenty of **restaurants** around the Praça da República and near the football field, the best of which is the *Ouro Branco* at Campo da Restauração 43, to the south of the football field.

Southeast to Monsaraz

The road **southeast from Vila Viçosa** provides great insights into the rural nature of the Alentejo, taking you past Moorish Alandroal and Terena, both quite prosperous villages set below a castle, before entering a region of scattered farming communities. A couple of buses cover the route daily, with numerous diversions along crumbling backroads.

Reguengos de Monsaraz

One of the better targets is the town of **REGUENGOS DE MONSARAZ** (which is also connected by the dull N256 with Évora, to its west). It's known for its fine local Terras del Rei white and red wines, and you can visit the *adega* just outside town where the wine is bottled: officially you need written permission, but if you just turn up you may find someone willing to take you around. For more information contact the **turismo** (Mon–Fri 9am–12.30pm & 2–5pm, Sat & Sun 10am–12.30pm & 2–5pm; ☎266 503 315 ext 121) in the Câmara Municipal on Rua 1º de Maio.

From Reguengos, there are two daily buses 17km further east to the dramatic fortified village of Monsaraz, as well as six daily buses to Évora, leaving from the square off Rua de São Marcos do Campo. Given this, it's unlikely you'd get stranded in Reguengos, but it's not a bad place to spend the night in any case. There are **rooms** at *Pensão Gato* (☎ & fax 266 502 353; ③) on the main Praça da Liberdade, and at the cheaper *Pensão Filhão* (☎266 519 266; ②), next door where the rooms are basic but clean. A better bet might be the rooms advertised in the beautiful old house at Praça de Santo António 1 (☎266 502 362; ②). Good-value **restaurants** include the *Café Central* on Praça da Liberdade, and *A Grelha*, on Rua do Covalinho, behind the church and on the left. The best place to sample the local wine is at the *Adega D'el Rei* **bar** opposite the market (up the road by the cinema); it's filled with huge barrels, from which the barman dispenses 75$00 glasses of wine.

Monsaraz

MONSARAZ – known to the locals as "Ninho das Águias" (Eagles' Nest) – is perched high above the border plains, a tiny village, fortified to the hilt and entirely contained within its walls. From its heights, the landscape of the Alentejo takes on a magical quality, with absolutely nothing stirring amid a sensational panorama of sun-baked fields, neatly cultivated and dotted with cork and olive trees. To the east, you can make out the Rio Guadiana, delineating the frontier with Spain.

There's something peculiarly satisfying, too, about such a small village. From the clock tower of the main gateway, the only real street, Rua Direita, leads past a bar (unmarked, on the left, next to the post office) to the village square. Here you'll find an unusual eighteenth-century pillory topped by a sphere of the universe.

The **Torre das Feiticeiras** (Witches' Tower) looms from the castle at the far end of the village, part of a chain of frontier fortresses continued to the south at Mourão, Moura and Serpa, and to the north at Alandroal, Elvas and Campo Maior. When the Moors were ejected in 1167 the village was handed over to the Knights Templar, and later to their successors, the Order of Christ; their fort has now been converted into a bullring.

Practicalities

The **turismo**, on Largo Dom Nuno Álvares (daily 10am–1pm & 2–5.30pm; ☎266 557 136), can help with **accommodation**. Alternatively, try the homely rooms along the main street with Dona Antonia (☎266 557 142; ②), or the attractive rooms at *Casa Dom Nuno*, Rua do Castelo 6 (☎266 557 146, fax 266 557 400; ③). All these places include breakfast in the price and fill up quickly in summer; out of season you can probably negotiate a reduction in the room rate. There's also a rather fancy **hotel**, the *Estalagem de Monsaraz*, with a pool and restaurant, at Largo São Bartolomeu 6 (☎266 557 112, fax 266 557 101; ⑤), in the settlement below the castle walls; while below the village, heading north towards the tiny village of Barrada, you'll find *Monte Saraz* (☎266 557 385, fax 266 557 485; ④) – a very pretty cluster of converted farmhouses with a swimming pool and ornamental gardens; advance booking is recommended. The *Lumumba*, opposite Dona Antonia's house, is the most reasonably priced **restaurant** with a nice patio and good views; a more upmarket option is the attractive, balconied *Casa do Forno*, on a side road between the lower and main roads.

Buses to Reguengos leave twice daily at 12.20pm and 3.30pm, while the three daily services to Évora currently leave at 6.45am, 8am and 3.20pm.

Menhirs around Monsaraz

There are two giant menhirs close by Monsaraz, just off the Reguengos road: at **Outeiro**, and at **Bulhoa**, where the stone is covered with symbolic engravings. Further menhirs lie at **São Pedro do Corval**, 12km west of Monsaraz along the Reguengos road, which is known by locals as the Lovers' Rock, and at **MONTE DO XAREZ**, between Monsaraz and the Guadiana River. This later one is four metres high, surrounded by a square of standing stones, and was probably the site of neolithic fertility rites.

Elvas

The hilltop town of **ELVAS**, 40km east of Estremoz, was long one of Portugal's mightiest frontier posts, a response to the Spanish stronghold of Badajoz, just 15km to the east across the Rio Guadiana. Its star-shaped walls and trio of forts are among the most complex and best-preserved military fortifications surviving in Europe. If you make a special detour to see just one Alentejo castle, Elvas is the natural choice; in addition, the town itself is a delight – all steep cobbled streets and mansions.

Elvas was recaptured from the Moors in 1230 and withstood periodic attacks from Spain throughout much of the following three centuries. It succumbed just once, however, to Spanish conquest, when the garrison was betrayed by Spanish bribery in 1580, allowing Philip II to enter and, for a period during the following year, establish his court. The town subsequently made amends during the war over the succession of Philip IV to the Portuguese territories. In 1644, the garrison resisted a nine-day siege by Spanish troops, and in 1658, with its numbers reduced by an epidemic to a mere thousand, saw off a fifteen-thousand-strong Spanish army.

During this period, the fortifications underwent intensive rebuilding and expansion, and they were later pressed into service twice more: in 1801, when the town withstood a Spanish siege during the War of the Oranges, and ten years later, during the Peninsular War, when the fort provided the base from which Wellington advanced to launch his bloody but successful assault on Badajoz. Perhaps out of tradition as much as anything, a military garrison is still stationed in the town.

Elvas's fortnightly event is its **Monday market** – a vibrantly chaotic affair attracting people from miles around, held just outside town behind the aqueduct. Otherwise, the town's big annual bash is its **Festa de São Mateus**, which lasts for six to eight days, starting on September 20, and encompasses a programme of agricultural, cultural and religious events, including the largest procession in southern Portugal. It's well worth coming at this time, although accommodation is at a premium.

Arrival & accommodation

The walls make Elvas a pretty easy place to get your bearings. Arriving by **bus**, you'll find yourself right in the centre of town, in Praça da República; the **turismo** (Mon–Fri 9am–6pm, Sat & Sun 9am–12.30pm & 2–5.30pm; ☎268 622 236) is next door. Shuttle buses also run from the local **train station**, 4km down the Campo Maior road at Fontaínhas to Praça da República; the station is on the Lisbon–Badajoz line. **Crossing from the Spanish city of Badajoz**, 15km to the east, is in fact easiest by train, with two daily services taking fifteen minutes. Buses from and to Badajoz arrive and leave from Praça da República four times daily, but take at least an hour and you'll have to change from a Spanish bus at the border.

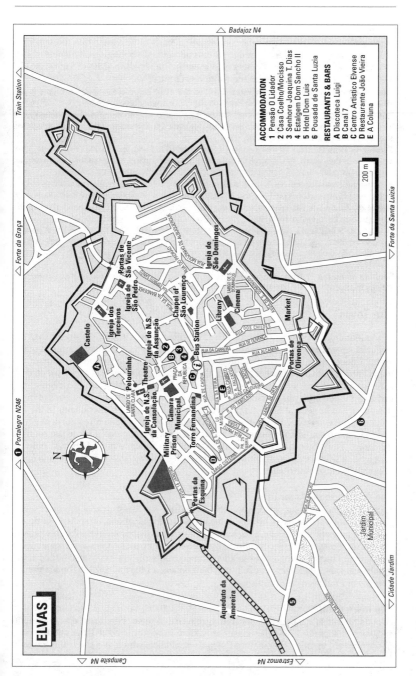

ELVAS

△ Badajoz N4

◁ Train Station ▷

◁ Forte da Graça △

◁ Portalegre N246 △

▽ Campsite N4

▽ Estremoz N4

▽ Cidade Jardim

▷ Forte da Santa Luizia

ACCOMMODATION
1 Pensão O Lidador
2 Casa Coelho/Mocisso
3 Senhore Joaquina T. Dias
4 Estalgem Dom Sancho II
5 Hotel Dom Luis
6 Pousada de Santa Luzia

RESTAURANTS & BARS
A Discoteca Luigi
B Canal 7
C Centro Artístico Elvense
D Restaurante João Vieira
E A Coluna

0   200 m

Aqueduto da Amoreira

Jardim Municipal

Portas da Esquina

Torre Fernandina

Military Prison

Câmara Municipal

Igreja de N.S. da Consolação

Pelourinho

Theatre

Castelo

Igreja dos Terceiros

Igreja de São Pedro

Portas de São Vicente

Igreja de N.S. da Assunção

Chapel of São Lourenço

Bus Station

Igreja de São Domingos

Library

Cinema

Market

Portas de Olivença

PRAÇA DA REPUBLICA

LARGO DE SANTA CLARA

RUA DA CADEIA

RUA DA FEIRA

RUA DA CARREIRA

RUA DE OLIVENÇA

RUA DOS CHILÕES

RUA ALCAMIM

RUA DA MUNICIPIO DE ABOBODA

RUA DO PÁDRO

RUA DE SANTO

LARGO DE S. DOMINGOS

AV. DE S. DOMINGOS

Accommodation

Most of the mid- to upper-range accommodation tends to be situated on the outskirts of Elvas, while in the old town budget rooms abound, of varying quality; some (listed below) are excellent value. There's also a **campsite**, *Piedade* (May–Sept; ☎268 628 997), on the outskirts of town on the N4 to Estremoz.

Casa Coelho/Mocisso, Rua Aires Varela 5 (☎268 622 126). Large, well-appointed rooms in the Moorish quarter, well-signposted from Praça da República; highly recommended. ②.

Hotel Dom Luís, Av. de Badajoz (☎268 622 756, fax 268 620 733). One of several modern hotels situated beyond the old walls on the major Spain-to-Portugal highway. The rooms are good, but the location has absolutely nothing going for it. ③.

Estalagem Dom Sancho II, Praça da República 20 (☎268 622 686, fax 268 624 717). The best bet for a hotel in the centre, this is a reliable place on the main square. Its restaurant has a beautiful inner courtyard for summer dining, though the food is nothing to write home about. ②.

Residencial Luso-Espanhola, Rua de Melo (☎268 623 092). Functional *residencial* a couple of kilometres out of town on the N246 towards Portalegre. Mainly has singles but a few doubles as well. ②.

Monte de Amoreira, Estrada de Barbacena (☎268 625 912). A small and reasonably priced rural property, 6km northeast of town. ③.

Pousada de Santa Luzia, Av. de Badajoz (☎268 622 194, fax 268 622 127). The country's first *pousada* (established 1942) but one of the more missable. A modern building, outside the town walls, on the fume-filled N4 – though in its favour, the rooms are comfortable enough and it has a good restaurant (see below) ⑥.

Senhora Joaquina T. Dias, Rua João d'Olivença 5 (☎268 624 722). Three rooms with showers, in a dingy but friendly family house. ②.

The Town

Any exploration of Elvas has to start with its **fortifications**. The earliest stretches of the walls date from the thirteenth century, but most of what you see today is a result of the Wars of Succession with Spain in the seventeenth century. Under the direction of the great French military engineer, Vauban, the old circuit of walls was supplemented by extensive moats and star-shaped ramparts, their bastions jutting out at irregular but carefully judged intervals to maximize the effects of artillery crossfire. Echoes of these designs are to be seen at Estremoz and throughout Portugal. Further chains in the fortifications were provided by the **Forte da Graça**, a couple of kilometres north of Elvas, and the superb star-shaped **Forte de Santa Luzia**, a few minutes' walk to the south of the town. The Forte de Graça is still used by the military and visits can only be arranged in advance by contacting the turismo (see below). Unfortunately, Santa Luzia is currently closed for repairs.

The Aqueduto da Amoreira

With its jagged and ungainly course, the **Aqueduto da Amoreira**, at the entrance to the town, looks at first like a bizarre extension of the fortifications. Despite its stark and awkward appearance, it is an imaginative and original feat of engineering: monstrous piles of masonry, distinctive cylindrical buttresses, and up to five tiers of arches support a tiny water channel along its seven-kilometre course, until it is finally discharged at the fountain in Largo da Misericórdia. It was built between 1498 and 1622 to the Manueline designs of Francisco de Arruda.

The town centre

Arruda was also responsible for the **Igreja de Nossa Senhora da Assunção** (9.30am–12.30pm & 2.30–7pm; closes at 5.30pm in winter; closed Tues, though days of opening are erratic), dominating Praça da República, which was the cathedral until

Elvas lost episcopal status in 1882. Alterations in the seventeenth and eighteenth centuries left a ragged hodge-podge of styles, but its original Manueline inspiration remains evident on the south portal and in the unusual painted conical dome above the belfry.

Behind the church lies **Largo de Santa Clara**, a tiny, cobbled square built on a slope around a splendid sixteenth-century **pelourinho**. Criminals were chained from the four metal hooks toward the top but, aside from the grisly technicalities, it's also a work of art, with a typically Manueline twisted column, and rope-like decorations. Directly opposite stands the strange and beautiful church of **Nossa Senhora da Consolação** (Tues–Sun 9.30am–12.30pm & 2.30–7pm; closes at 5.30pm in winter). From the outside, it's nothing more than a whitewashed wall with a mediocre Renaissance porch, but the interior reveals a sumptuous octagonal chapel: richly painted columns support a central cupola and virtually all the surfaces are decorated with magnificent seventeenth-century *azulejos*. The chapel was built between 1543 and 1557, on the site of a Knights Templar chapel – providing the inspiration for its octagonal design.

Largo de Santa Clara tapers upwards to a restored tenth-century archway flanked by fortified towers and surmounted by a **loggia**, or gallery. Originally part of the old town walls, this was built by the Moors, who occupied Elvas from the early eighth century until 1226. The street beneath the gateway leads to the **Castelo** (daily: summer 9am–1pm & 3–6pm; winter 9am–12.30pm & 2–5.30pm), also constructed by the Moors on an old Roman fortified site, but strengthened by Dom Dinis and João II in the late fifteenth century.

Eating, drinking and nightlife

Elvas has a good selection of restaurants, covering all price ranges; those in the old town tend to have the best atmosphere. If you want to put your own **picnic** together, the place to buy supplies is a small, early-morning food market held Monday to Saturday at the bottom of Rua dos Chilões.

Canal 7, Rua dos Sapateiros 16, off the main square. The best of the budget places, always popular; 1200$00 for a greasy fill-up.

Centro Artístico Elvense, Praça da República, next to the bus station. Reasonably priced café-restaurant with outdoor tables overlooking the *praça*; the *arroz de marisco* is very good.

Restaurante Chimarrão, 2km west off the Estremoz road. Pricey, but serves excellent quality Brazilian dishes.

A Coluna, Rua do Cabrito 11. Locally considered one of Elvas's best restaurants, and deservedly so. It's in an old stables, cavernous, whitewashed but still intimate, and specializes in cod dishes; the *ementa turística* (which invariably includes *bacalhau*) goes for 1700$00.

Restaurante João Vieira, Largo Cisterna 5. Very cheap, very friendly, family-run canteen-cum-restaurant. You'll be hard put to spend more than 800$00.

Pousada de Santa Luzia, Av. de Badajoz. Not the nicest of settings, but the food is worth every escudo of the 5000$00 or so it costs to eat here. Serves a range of typical local and Alentejano dishes such as a delicious *porco alentejana*.

Drinking and nightlife

Elvas is not a late-night town, but if you do want to make a night of it try the unnamed bar (first floor) on Rua São Pedro, on the left-hand side coming from the *praça* or the cosy *Não Sei* bar at Rua Sa da Bandeira 52a, which is open until 2am and also serves great Portuguese tapas. For something more energetic try *Discoteca Luigi,* in the square facing the castle, or *Cidade Jardim*, a complex of four bars and a disco – *Eric's* – a couple of kilometres out of the old town past the Jardim Municipal.

Campo Maior

Eighteen kilometres to the north of Elvas lies the fortress town of **CAMPO MAIOR**. The road from Elvas passes through olive groves and sunflower fields and it's a pleasant enough trip, though the town itself would be unremarkable were it not for the presence of its **Capela dos Ossos** (Mon–Sat 9am–7pm), a diminutive version of the Chapel of Bones in Évora. This stands immediately to the right of the large parish church just off Rua 1º de Maio: ask for the key in the church or try the door next to the chapel. Adding to the surreal effect, the entrance is through a neat local government office.

The walls and vaults in the claustrophobic chapel interior are completely covered in human bones, while two skeletons hang from the walls, and three rows of skulls are positioned on the window ledge to inspect passers-by. The chapel is dated 1766 and its purpose is indicated by two verses from the Book of Job traced out in collarbones near the window: "My bone cleaveth to my skin and to my flesh, and I am escaped with the skin of my teeth." Job is complaining of his horrific physical and mental suffering, but takes solace in the knowledge that "though after my skin worms destroy this body, yet in my flesh shall I see God".

The chapel may have been "furnished" following the disaster which devastated Campo Maior in 1732, when a gunpowder magazine in the town's castle was struck by lightning, killing 1500 people and destroying 823 houses. Today the castle is little more than a ruin, though with fine views over the borderlands.

Practicalities

The **bus** journey from Elvas takes just 35 minutes, making it an easy side-trip. There's a **turismo** on Rua Major Talaya (Mon–Fri 9am–12.30pm & 2–5.30; ☎268 688 936). If you want **to stay**, try *Pensão Ponto Final* on Av. da Liberdade (☎268 686 564; ②), near the bridge of the same name, or the more upmarket *Hotel de Santa Beatrice,* on Av. Combatentes da Grande Guerra off Praça da República (☎268 690 1040, fax 268 688 109, *www.guianet.pt/hotelsantabeatriz/pag.html*; ④). There's also Parque de Camping Barragal, a **campsite** (☎268 689 493) just a five-minute walk west of the town. For **food**, try *O Ministro*'s affiliated restaurant at Rua 13 de Dezembro 41, or the pleasant *O Faisão*, opposite the parish church.

Portalegre

PORTALEGRE is the capital, market centre and transport hub of Alto Alentejo. It is an attractive town, crouched at the foot of the Serra de São Mamede where there are good hiking possibilities (see box on p.418), and is endowed with the province's usual contingent of whitewashed and walled old quarters, along with some interesting reminders of its industrial history. These include a cork factory, whose great twin chimneys greet you on the way into town, and the Fábrica Real de Tapeçarias on Rua Gomes Fernandes – the town's single surviving tapestry factory and the last remnant of a great textile industry that peaked in the seventeenth and eighteenth centuries. In its studios and weaving hall over five thousand shades of wool are used in the reproduction of centuries-old patterns. At present the factory is not open to the public, although a new **tapestry museum** is due to open soon.

The wealth produced in the town's boom years, in particular from the silk workshops, has a further legacy in the collection of grand mercantile mansions and town houses, which give the town an air of faded affluence. It is especially apparent as you walk up Rua 19 de Junho – the main thoroughfare of the old town – which is lined by a spectacular concentration of late Renaissance and Baroque mansions. At the southern end of the street, and dominating the quarter, is the **Sé**, an austere building save for a flash of fancy in the

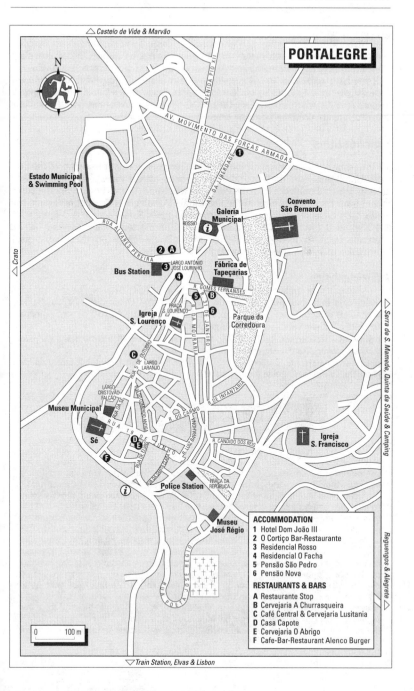

△ *Castelo de Vide & Marvão*

N

PORTALEGRE

AV. MOVIMENTO DAS FORÇAS ARMADAS

AVENIDA PIO XII

AV. DA LIBERDADE

Estado Municipal & Swimming Pool

RUA ALVARES PEREIRA

△ *Crato*

ROSSIO

Galeria Municipal

i

Convento São Bernardo

❷ ❶ A
Bus Station ❸
❹

LARGO ANTÓNIO JOSÉ LOURINHO

Fábrica de Tapeçarias

R. GOMES FERNANDES

❺ B
❻

31 DE JANEIRO

DA MOUARIA

PRAÇA S. LOURENÇO

Igreja S. Lourenço

Parque da Corredoura

C

RUA 5 DE OUTUBRO

LARGO LARANJO

LARGO CRISTOVÃO FALCÃO

RUA 19 DE

R. DE INFANTARIA

Museu Municipal

R. DO CARMO

Sé

D E

F

RUA DE ELVAS

R. CANDIDO DOS REIS

ELVASINHO

Igreja S. Francisco

i

Police Station

PRAÇA DA REPÚBLICA

△ *Serra de S. Mamede, Quinta da Saúde & Camping*

Reguengos & Alegrete △

Museu José Régio

R. POETA JOSÉ RÉGIO

ACCOMMODATION
1 Hotel Dom João III
2 O Cortiço Bar-Restaurante
3 Residencial Rosso
4 Residencial O Facha
5 Pensão São Pedro
6 Pensão Nova

RESTAURANTS & BARS
A Restaurante Stop
B Cervejaria A Churrasqueira
C Café Central & Cervejaria Lusitania
D Casa Capote
E Cervejaria O Abrigo
F Cafe-Bar-Restaurant Alenco Burger

0 ____ 100 m

▽ *Train Station, Elvas & Lisbon*

pyramidal pinnacles of its towers. To one side of this an eighteenth-century palace houses the **Museu Municipal** (10am–12.30pm & 2–6pm; closed Tues; 250$00). It's not exactly a compelling visit, with much routine furniture and fittings on display, though there are some lovely ceramics and ivories as well as some early Arraiolos carpets (see p.405).

If you have some time to kill in town, you may also consider a visit to the **Museu José Régio**, by the cemetery on Rua Poeta José Régio (Tues–Sun 10am–12.30pm & 2–6pm; 250$00), where you can see the poet's collection of over three hundred antique crucifixes, altarpieces and powder horns.

Practicalities

All the main roads converge on the **Rossio**, a large square at the centre of the new town. Uphill from here, the Rua 5º de Outubro runs into the walled **old town**. The **bus station** is just a few blocks from the Rossio on Rua Nuno Álvarez Pereira. Shuttle buses to and from here meet **trains** at the Estação de Portalegre, 10km out of town to the south, on the Lisbon–Badajoz line. The **turismo** (daily 9am–12.30pm & 2–5pm; ☎245 331 359) is at the far end of Rua de Elvas by the old town walls, and the Galerie Municipal (summer 10am–1pm & 3–7pm; winter 10am–1pm & 3–6pm) also dispenses information as well as staging temporary art exhibitions.

Accommodation

There is limited **accommodation** available, and it's advisable to book a day ahead to be sure of a bed. **Camping** is an attractive option; the Orbitur site (☎245 331 736; March–Oct) at *Quinta da Saúde*, 3km into the hills, on the N246-2, is well equipped, with electricity, showers and a few bungalows for rent.

O Cortiço Bar-Restaurant, Rua Dom Nuno Álvares Pereira 17 (☎24520 21 76). Has a few reasonable rooms upstairs; but the management can be surly. ③.

Hotel Dom João III, Av. da Liberdade (☎245 330 192, fax 245 330 444). A dull, functional hotel, opposite the Jardim Municipal in the new town. ③.

HIKING INTO THE SERRA DE SÃO MAMEDE: FROM PORTALEGRE TO MARVÃO

The sixteen-kilometre walk begins from the *Quinta da Saúde* campsite, 3km outside **Portalegre** on the N246-2. Turn right out of the campsite and follow the road for a few kilometres until you see a signpost to the left marked São Julião. Turn left here, then left again shortly afterwards, following signs to Porto Espada. You'll pass a reservoir on the left-hand side of the road after about 3 or 4km; you'll also see plenty of abandoned farmhouses and buildings, a result of the flooding caused by the construction of the reservoir. On reaching the small village of **Rasa**, turn right, then shortly afterwards, as the road bends sharply to the left, take the dirt track that leads straight ahead. This track emerges at a whitewashed stone bridge – turn right to go over this, then after about 50m turn left. Continue along here for about five minutes until you reach a main road; there are several cafés and restaurants here, where you can rest before tackling the long slog uphill to Marvão. If you're not up to the strenuous climb, which is best done early in the morning or late in the day, you can catch a bus from here up to Marvão. If you want to continue the walk, turn left onto the main road, then right straight after the bridge and right immediately afterwards. Follow this road for a few hundred metres, then turn left up a cobbled track soon after a group of houses. Follow the track upwards through the olive groves for roughly an hour and you will arrive just outside the walls of Marvão.

Residencial O Facha, Largo António José Lourinho 3–5 (☎245 203 161). Close to the Rossio, this place is rather rundown and should be tried only as a last resort. ②.

Pensão Nova, Rua 31 de Janeiro 28–30 (☎245 331 212, fax 245 330 493). Renovated, friendly hostel, with the same management as the nearby *Pensão São Pedro*, at Rua da Mouraria 14 (☎245 331 212). Both ②.

Quinta da Saúde, Estrada de São Mamede, 3km out of Portalegre next to the campsite (☎245 202 324, fax 245 207 234). An attractive property with a great view over the surrounding hills and a good rooftop restuarant. ③.

Residencial Rossio, Rua Dom Nuno Álvares Pereira 10, next to the bus station (☎245 201 975). The budget rooms on offer, some windowless, are somewhat small and stuffy but adequate for a night. ①.

Eating and drinking

By day the Rossio is the liveliest place for a drink, but in the evening the action, such as it is, switches to the old town; try the *Café Central* on Largo Frederico Laranjo or the *Cervejaria Lusitania*, close by at Rua Luís de Camões 43.

Café-Bar-Restaurante Alenco Burger, Rua 19 de Julho 38. 24-hour fast-food restaurant which serves inexpensive fried food and offers Internet access for 800$00 per hour (400$00 after 6pm).

Cervejaria O Abrigo, Rua de Elvas 74. Serves inexpensive Alentejan dishes; the *ementa turística* costs around 1500$00.

Casa Capote, Rua 19 de Junho 56. Friendly restaurant whose walls are hung with tapestries and paintings; a reasonable full meal will set you back around 2000$00.

Cervejaria A Churrasqueira, Rua Guilherme Gomes Fernandes 29, just off the Rossio. The cheapest option in town serves an excellent set menu for 800$00, with most main dishes between 250$00 and 650$00.

Residencial O Facha, Largo António José Lourinho 3–5. Wide choice of expensive dishes (more international than regional) served in glorious glass and brass Art Deco surroundings.

Restaurante Stop, 11–15 Rua Dom Nuno Álvares Pereira. One of the better options, just off the Rossio, serving typical Alentejan cuisine in pleasant surroundings; a slap-up meal will cost under 2000$00.

Crato, Flôr da Rosa and Alter do Chão

Directly to the west of Portalegre, **Crato** has small-town charms and, nearby, an impressive **dolmen**, as well as the beautiful honey-stone convent of **Flôr da Rosa**. Horse enthusiasts may also want to make the thirteen-kilometre detour south of Crato to **Alter do Chão**, home of a prestigious *coudelaria* (stud farm).

Buses run intermittently from Portalegre to both Crato and Alter do Chão, while the **Estação de Crato** gives access to the Lisbon–Badajoz train line, with connections west to Abrantes and east to Elvas.

Crato

CRATO – 21km west of Portalegre – is an ancient agricultural town which has clear-ly seen better days and larger populations. A trio of imposing, ornate churches and the elegant **Varanda do Grão Prior** in the main square attest, like Portalegre's monuments, to the textile boom years of the sixteenth century. The *varanda* is the most interesting of the structures – built for the outdoor celebration of Mass. Also worth a look is a town mansion a couple of streets away, by the public gardens, which houses a small **museum** (erratic hours) of Alto Alentejo handicrafts and domestic traditions. Well into this century, alms were handed out to the local poor from a balcony-chapel upstairs.

The town **castle** was once among the mightiest in the Alentejo, but today it's a pastoral ruin, overrun by farm animals, fig trees and oregano plants. It is normally locked, but keys are generally kept beneath an abandoned blue cart in the field in front; if they're not there, ask at one of the nearby farm dwellings. From the ramparts, there is a splendid view over the town and across the countless rows of olive trees to the hills of Portalegre.

For a good rural walk from Crato, follow the N363 northwest towards Aldeia da Mata. On the left-hand side of the road, about 5km from town, is what is reckoned to be the best-preserved **dolmen** in Portugal. On the corner of the road leading out of town, you'll find an excellent **adega**, with delicious home-cooking and a crowded bar where everyone plays *belho* – a kind of miniature version of *boules*.

The town has no accommodation, though the **turismo** in the Câmara Municipal (Mon–Sat 10am–noon & 2–5pm; ☎245 996 212) may be able to fix you up with rooms in private houses, though don't count on it. **Campers** can pick their own spots by the old Roman bridge near the train station, or up by the castle. If you arrive at the **train station**, 3km south of town, the station master will telephone for a taxi, which is not expensive.

Flôr da Rosa

Two kilometres north of Crato lies the village of **FLÔR DA ROSA**, traditionally a centre for **pottery**, with as many as seventy families engaged in the trade in the early part of this century. Today the distinctive *olaria* of the region is made in only two workshops, whose shared kiln is near the convent, high above the broad streets and low houses. Their methods of manufacture haven't changed in centuries, though the clay – yellow for waterproofing, grey for ovenware – has to be sought further and further afield. Purchases break easily, but it's nice to know that these functional (and inexpensive) pieces aren't designed for the tourist trade.

The **Convento de Flôr da Rosa**, founded in the fourteenth century and much endowed over the next two hundred years, was abandoned in 1897, due to leaking roofs and a decaying structure. After extensive state restoration (begun in 1940), the fortress monastery finally re-opened in 1995 as one of Portugal's most lavish *pousadas* (☎245 99 72 10, fax 99 72 12; ⑧). It is still possible to see inside, though, and to look round the adjoining church. Around the main building you can trace the plan of the gardens, laid out in the insignia of the Order of Malta, in honour of the warlord **Nuno Álvares Pereira**, whose father founded the monastery.

Father Pereira's tomb (dated 1382) is prominent in the narrow, soaring convent church. Adjoining it, on the ground floor, is the sixteenth-century **Sala do Capítulo**, distinguished by fine brickwork, fan-vaulting and a Gothic cloister. On the first floor are the monks' **dormitories**, whose open casements offer sweeping views across acres of olive trees.

If you need to stay in the village and can't afford the luxury of the *pousada*, the more cosy *Palacete Florida Rosa*, on Rua da Cruz (☎245 996 451, fax 245 997 286; ④), is a cheaper option.

Alter do Chão

ALTER DO CHÂO, 13km to the south of Crato, is another town that did well from textiles, particularly during the sixteenth century, as indicated by its attractive Renaissance marble fountain and an array of handsome town houses. There is a **castle**, too, whose central tower can be climbed for an overview of the region, but the chief reason for a visit is the Coudelaria de Alter-Real stud farm, 3km out of town.

The **Coudelaria de Alter-Real** was founded in 1748 by Dom João V of the House of Bragança, and remained in the family until 1910 when the War Office took it over. Today, maintained by the state, it is open for public visits (daily 9am–5pm), though to see the horses in action it's best to arrive in the morning: between 10am and noon when you can watch them filing in from the fields to feed, accompanied by the ringing of forty bells. In the town itself you may be lucky enough to see the Coudelaria coach and horses when they come to collect the mail.

The tours of the stud are also interesting, with a museum display of carriages and horse regalia, through which you are conducted at a stately pace by a cavalry officer. Alter-Real horses have been sought after since the stud's foundation – one is depicted in the equestrian statue of Dom José in Lisbon's Praça do Comércio, for example – and they remain the favoured breed of the Portuguese mounted police and the Lisbon Riding School at Queluz.

If you can time a visit, April 25 is the best day to be at the Coudelaria, when the **annual sale** takes place. The town's main festival – the **Festa de Nossa Senhora da Alegria** – occurs on the following day.

Practicalities

Several **pensões** are clustered in the road opposite the castle in Alter do Chão, including the *Pensão Ferreira* (☎245 612 254; ②). Alternatively, try the rooms above the *Snack Bar Avenida* on Avenida Dr. João Pestana (☎245 612 301; ①).

For **meals**, the *Café/Restaurante Lareira Alentejana*, Estrada Nacional 369, serves good local cuisine and has an *ementa turística* for 2000$00. *Café Oasis* is pretty good, and there are tasty cakes at the nearby Pastelaria Ateneia. **Buses** connect the town with Portalegre and Crato.

Castelo de Vide and Marvão

The upland district **north of Portalegre** is a bucolic landscape, with tree-clad mountain ranges and a series of gorgeous hilltop villages. Among these, the best targets are **Castelo de Vide** and **Marvão**, both with castles, and the former with a spa. Castelo de Vide is the most easily accessible, connected by bus five times daily with Portalegre; Marvão has three daily services, Monday to Friday only. Getting between the two, one morning and one late afternoon bus from Castelo de Vide to Portalegre connects with buses to Marvão at the main road junction of Portagem.

Castelo de Vide

CASTELO DE VIDE covers the slopes around a fourteenth-century castle, its blindingly white cottages delineated in brilliant contrast to the greenery around. Arriving by bus, you'll be dropped at the *pelourinho* outside the **turismo** (daily: summer 9am–7pm; winter 9am–12.30pm & 2–5.30pm; ☎245 901 361) in the centre of town. From here, half a dozen parallel streets make a sharp climb up to the aptly named **Praça Alta** on the edge of town. The main road, meanwhile, peters out into a narrow path, descending past a tranquil Renaissance fountain to the twisting alleyways of the **Judairia** – the old Jewish quarter. Amid the cottages, most of which still have Gothic doorways and windows, is a thirteenth-century **synagogue** (daily 9am–6pm), the oldest surviving one in Portugal. From the outside it doesn't look very different from the cottages, so you will probably need to ask for directions.

On a hill above the Judairia, the **Castelo** (daily: summer 8am–6pm; winter 9am–12.30pm & 2–5.30pm; free) squats within the wider fortifications of the original medieval village. While there, chat to the man at the castle door and he'll probably show you the elaborate moving wooden toys that he produces; his neighbour is a lacemaker who trains young women in the art.

Practicalities

Given its size, the town has a surprising amount of **accommodation**. Of the budget options, the best value is provided by the friendly, English-speaking *Casa de Hóspedes Melanie*, Largo do Paço Novo 3 (☎245 901 632; ②). Other options in the same price range include the *Pensão Cantinho Particular*, Rua Miguel Bombarda 9 (☎245 901 151; ②) – friendly if a bit on the basic side – and the *Residencial Xinxel* by the castle (☎245 901 406; ③); both include breakfast in the price. With more money, your best bet is one of the elegant rooms – breakfast included – in the *Albergaria El Rei Dom Miguel*, Rua Bartolomeu Álvares da Santa (☎245 919 191, fax 245 901 592; ③). The **restaurant** at the *Cantinho Particular* is basic but good, but for an expensive splurge (around 3000–4000$00) try the excellent *Restaurante Marino's* on Praça Dom Pedro (☎245 919 207), which specializes in Italian and regional dishes. The *Restaurante São João*, on the road to Portalegre, and *Don Pedro V*, Praça Dom Pedro V, are also very good. The perfect place for **snacks** is the *Pastelaria Sol Nascente* at Rua de Olivença 31, which has a wonderful selection of pastries.

Marvão

Beautiful as Castelo de Vide is, **MARVÃO** surpasses it. The panoramas from its remote eyrie site are unrivalled and the atmosphere even quieter than a population of less than a thousand would suggest. No more than a handful of houses – each as scrupulously whitewashed as the rest – lies outside the seventeenth-century walls. Originally the village seems to have been an outlying suburb of Medobriga, a mysterious Roman city which vanished almost without trace. Its inhabitants fled before the Moorish advance in around 715 but later returned to live under Muslim rule, when the place was renamed after Marvan, the Moorish Lord of Coimbra. It fell to the Christians in 1166 and the **castle** was rebuilt by Dom Dinis around 1229 as another important link in the chain of outposts along the Spanish border. The castle stands at the far end of the village, its walls blending into the sharp slopes of the *serra*. It's dauntingly impenetrable and was indeed captured only once, in 1833, when the attackers entered through a secret gate. Also worth a visit is the **municipal museum** in the Church of Santa Maria, which has an interesting range of Roman remains and other local finds.

The village makes a superb night's stop, as several houses within the walls are rented out under a scheme organized by the **turismo**, on Rua Dr. António Matos Magalhães (daily 9.30am–12.30pm & 2–5.30pm; ☎245 993 104). In some of these you can get just a room, while others are rented out as a unit; prices, consequently, are extremely varied. Additional **accommodation** is provided by *Restaurante Varanda do Alentejo* in Praça do Pelourinho, which rents out pleasant rooms (☎245 993 272; ②); *Pensão Dom Dinis* on Rua Dr. António Matos Magalhães (☎245 993 236, fax 245 909 159; ③); and the attractively converted *Pousada de Santa Maria* (☎245 993 502, fax 245 993 440; ⑦) on Rua 24 de Janeiro.

For **meals**, the *Restaurante Varanda do Alentejo* is good (see above) and you can also eat and drink at *Bar da Casa do Povo* or *Bar Marcelino*, both just off the square. The *pousada*'s restaurant serves meals at 4000–5000$00 per head which, even allowing for the grand views, is expensive.

Marvão-Beirã: on into Spain

Lisbon–Madrid trains stop at the station of **MARVÃO-BEIRÃ**, 9km north of Marvão village. Heading for Spain by public transport, this is the easiest way to go, although services, especially outside summer, can be infrequent; check with the turismo for current times. The road border at **GALEGOS**, 14km east of Marvão, is open to traffic but very few cars use it. In addition, there's one daily **bus** from Portalegre direct to the Spanish border town of Valencia de Alcántara.

Belver Castle

Travelling northwest from Portalegre, the N18/N118 roads take you up to the Tejo valley, and, of course, the Alentejo border. The most interesting targets on this route are the castles of Abrantes and Almourol in Ribatejo (see p.169), and **Belver**, which, although sited with its town on the north bank of the Tejo, is technically a part of Alentejo. If you are dependent on public transport, it is easiest to take a train or bus to Abrantes, and approach Belver from there.

BELVER CASTLE is one of the most famous in the country, its fanciful position, name and tiny size having ensured it a place in dozens of Portuguese legends. The name comes from *belo ver* (beautiful to see), the supposed exclamation of some medieval princess, waking up to look out from its keep at the river valley below. It dates from the twelfth century, when the Portuguese frontier stood at the Tejo, the Moors having reclaimed all the territories to the south, save Évora, that Afonso Henriques had conquered for his kingdom. Its founder was Dom Sancho I, who entrusted its construction and care to the knight-monks of the Order of Saint John.

The walls form an irregular pentagon, tracing the crown of a hill, with a narrow access path to limit attackers to virtual single file. If you find the castle locked, search out the guard who lives at no. 1 on the main square in Belver village. For a small fee, he will even unlock the **chapel** as well to show you its formidable fifteenth-century reliquary. All the pieces of bone were stolen during the French invasions in the nineteenth century, but fortunately for the villagers there was a casket of "spares" hidden away by the priest, and these substitutes are today paraded at the **Festa de Santa Reliquária**, held around August 18.

You're very likely to track down the castle guard sharing a few jokes over a glass of *bagaceira* (Portugal's cheapest hangover) in Belver's single **café-restaurant-pension**. Rooms (①) are usually available, outside the August festival times.

Buses leave from the praça or from the street above the **train station**, which is directly below the village beside the river. If you take the train north along the valley towards Castelo Branco, look out for the striking rock faces before Vila Velha de Ródão known as the **Portas do Ródão** (Gates of Ródão).

BAIXO ALENTEJO

The hot, dry inland routes of Baixo Alentejo have little to offer beyond a stop at **Beja** – the most interesting southern Alentejo town – en route to the Algarve, or, if you're heading for Spain, at the frontier towns of **Serpa** or **Mértola**. The coastline, however, is another matter, with resorts like **Vila Nova de Milfontes**, **Almograve** and **Zambujeira do Mar** providing an attractive alternative to the summer crowds on the Algarve. Their only disadvantage – and the reason for a very patchy tourist development – is their exposure to the Atlantic winds, which at times create huge breakers and dangerous swimming conditions. But as long as you're prepared to spend occasional days out of the water, they are enjoyable places to take it easy for a few days by the sea.

All the beaches are situated along minor roads, but there are local **bus services** from Santiago do Cacém and Odemira. Alternatively, coming from Lisbon, you can take the express bus direct to Vila Nova de Milfontes, Almograve and Zambujeira do Mar; it leaves Lisbon twice a day from the Campo Pequeno terminal (p.109) and, as with all *expressos*, it's wise to buy tickets in advance.

Southeast from Lisbon

Heading southeast into the Alentejo from Lisbon or Setúbal, the main road (and bus) loops around the **Rio Sado estuary**, through **Alcácer do Sal**, at the mouth of the river, and on through the agricultural town of **Grândola**. Heading **towards Beja**, drivers could travel instead directly east from Alcácer do Sal, cutting across a succession of country roads and past a couple of huge reservoirs before meeting the main Évora–Beja road.

Alcácer do Sal

Fifty-two kilometres from Setúbal, **ALCÁCER DO SAL** is one of Portugal's oldest ports, founded by the Phoenicians and made a regional capital under the Moors – whence its name (*al-Ksar*, the town) derives. The other part of its name, *do Sal*, "of salt", reflects the dominance of the salt industry in these parts; the Sado estuary is still fringed with salt marshes. Alcácer today is slightly seedy-looking, but quite attractively so, particularly along its waterfront promenade. A couple of roads back from the promenade at its western end is a charming quarter of mainly medieval houses, centred around Rua Rui Salem. Further uphill, above the town, stands the part-ruined Moorish **castle** (daily 10am–noon & 2–5pm; free), from where there are striking views of the lush green paddy-fields which almost surround the town, and of the storks' nests on the church rooftops.

The *Café-Restaurant Sado* is at the eastern end of the promenade, past the bus depot at Largo Luís de Camões – try the house speciality of prawns, beer and buttered toast. Here, too, or at one of the town's bakeries, you can sample *pinhoadas,* a honey and pine-seed toffee, or for a more substantial meal try *Restaurant O Campinho* on Avenida dos Aviadores. If you decide to **stay the night**, there are *dormidas* at Rua Periera 2 (☎265 622 355; ①), near the post office, but for a little more you can get a room at *Residencial Silvano*, Rua 1º de Maio 15 (☎265 622 590; ①).

At the beginning of October, for around three days, the town hosts a **regional fair** featuring an assembly of agricultural machinery, a couple of bullfights and acres of stalls. It's one of the most enjoyable fairs in the south.

Grândola

At **GRÂNDOLA**, 24km south of Alcácer do Sal, the roads diverge: southwest to the coast; east to Beja, Serpa and, ultimately, Spanish Andalucía. As well as the main road through Alcácer to Grândola, there's an enjoyable alternative approach for drivers from Setúbal who can take the ferry to Tróia and make their way down the long, sand-fringed **Peninsula de Tróia** along the N253. The town was made legendary through the song *Grândola vila morena*, the broadcasting of which was the pre-arranged signal for the start of the 1974 Revolution. There's precious little reason to stop in town, though it has a few decent restaurants – the pricey *Picapu* on Rua Dom Nuno Álvares Pereira has the best reputation – and a couple of average hotels, should you be stuck.

East towards Beja: Viana do Alentejo

Heading **east** instead from Alcácer do Sal, the minor N5 runs to Torrão, curving around the Rio Sado, past the **Barragem de Vale do Gaio**. Sited on the edge of the reservoir is the *Pousada de Vale do Gaio* (☎265 669 610, fax 265 669 545; ⑥), a fairly simple conversion of the lodge used by the dam engineers.

Continuing east, along the N383, you pass through **VIANA DO ALENTEJO**, a sleepy and typically southern Alentejan village which preserves a highly decorative **castle**, full of Mudejar and Manueline features (Tues–Sun 10am–12.30pm & 2–5pm;

closed Aug). The castle walls were built on a pentagonal plan by Dom Dinis in 1313, and the interior ensemble of buildings was expanded under Dom João II and Dom Manuel I in the late fifteenth century. To this latter period belong a sequence of elaborate battlements and the beautiful parish church, part of a striking group of buildings within the walls, encompassing a Misericórdia, town hall, cistern and *pelourinho*. Viana also boasts a very good restaurant, the expensive *Bernadino Santos Banha* at Rua António I Sousa 36 (☎266 953 116). **From Viana**, the N384 runs 30km east, past another huge reservoir, to meet the main Évora–Beja road.

Beja

On the inland route through southern Alentejo, **BEJA** appears as a welcome oasis amid the sweltering, featureless wheat fields. Commanding this strategic position in the centre of the plains, it has long been an important and prosperous city. Founded by Julius Caesar in 48BC it was named Pax Julia, in honour of the peace accord signed here between Rome and the Lusitanians, but later became Pax Augusta and then just Pax, from which it gradually corrupted to Paca, Baca, Baju, and finally Beja.

South of Évora, it's the most interesting stop on the way to the Algarve, and once past the modern suburbs Beja reveals an unhurried old quarter with a cluster of peculiar churches, a beautiful convent and a thirteenth-century castle. You can take in most of the sights in this compact historic centre in half a day, though in summer the heat will probably turn you towards a bar within an hour or so.

If you visit the town during May, you'll witness the town celebrating the **Festas da Cidade** – a month-long jamboree of music, dance, gastronomy and bullfighting.

The Town

In Portugal Beja is best known for the love affair of a seventeenth-century nun who lived in the **Convento de Nossa Senhora da Conceição**, just off Largo dos Duques de Beja. Sister Mariana Alcoforado is believed to have fallen in love with Count Chamilly, a French cavalry officer, and is credited with the notorious (in Portugal anyway) *Five Love Letters of a Portuguese Nun*, first published in Paris in 1669. The originals have never been discovered, and a scholarly debate has raged over the authenticity of the French "translation". Nonetheless, English and Portuguese editions soon appeared and the letters became internationally famous as a classic of romantic literature.

Sentimental associations aside, the convent is quite a building. Founded in the fifteenth century, it has a panoply of Manueline fripperies, with elaborate portals and a rhythmic roofline decorated with balustrades and pinnacles. The walls of the cloisters and chapter house are completely covered with multicoloured sixteenth- and seventeenth-century *azulejos*, and present one of the finest examples of this art form. The other highlight is a magnificent Rococo chapel, sumptuously gilded and embellished with flying cherubs. The convent was dissolved in 1834 and today houses the **Museu Regional** (Tues–Sun 9.45am–12.30pm & 2–5.30pm; 100$00, free on Sun). Compared to the architecture of the building, the museum pieces are comparatively lacklustre, though they include a wide-ranging display on the town's past eras – including items as diverse as Roman and Visigothic stone, fifteenth- to eighteenth-century Dutch and Portuguese painting, and the grille through which the errant nun first glimpsed her lover.

Beja's **Castelo** (Tues–Sun: summer 10am–1pm & 2–6pm; winter 9am–noon & 1–4pm) rises decoratively on the edge of the old quarter. It was built – yet again – by Dom Dinis and is remarkable for the playful battlements of its Torre de Menagem, which costs 200$00 to climb up. Similarly, an exaggerated horseshoe window halfway up hints at the architect's artistic intent.

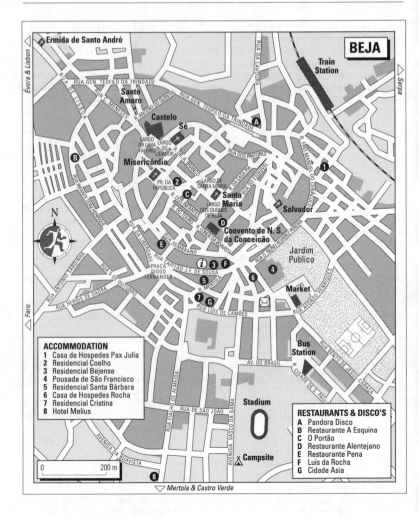

In the shadow of the keep stands the Visigothic basilica of **Santo Amaro**, today a small archeological museum. The building is a rare survival from pre-Moorish Portugal; the interior columns are carved with seventh-century geometric motifs.

Among other churches in Beja, the most distinctive is the mid-sixteenth-century **Misericórdia** in Praça da República; its huge projecting porch served originally as a meat market and the stonework is deliberately chiselled to give a coarse, "rustic" appearance. Earlier, fortress-inclined Gothic elements are to be seen on the church of **Santa Maria**, in the heart of the old quarter, and on the fifteenth-century **Ermida de Santo André**, on the road out to Lisbon, which is endowed with gigantic tubular buttresses.

Practicalities

The old quarter is a circular tangle of streets, enclosed within a ring road which has replaced the town walls. At its heart is a pair of interlocking squares – Largo de Santa Maria and Largo dos Duques de Beja. The **bus station** lies five minutes' walk south-east of this quarter; the **train station** five minutes northeast. A very helpful **turismo** (May–Sept Mon–Sat 9am–8pm; Oct–April Mon–Sat 10am–6pm; ☎284 311 913) is located just south of the central squares at Rua Capitão J. F. de Sousa 25.

Beja has good **transport connections** to the rest of central and southern Portugal, as well as a bus link to Seville in Spain. In most cases you have a choice of bus or train: for Lisbon and the western Algarve take the train, whereas for Évora, Vila Real de Santo António (for the eastern Algarve) and Santiago do Cacém (for the western Algarve) it's quicker to go by bus.

Accommodation

Most of the town's **accommodation** is to be found within a few blocks of the turismo. In summer and during the Festas da Cidade (see p.425) it is well worth booking ahead. The municipal **campsite** (☎284 324 328, fax 284 327 225) is located on the south side of town, past the stadium on Avenida Vasco da Gama. It's fairly pleasant and shaded, and adjoins the local swimming pool.

Residencial Bejense, Rua do Capitão J. F. de Sousa 57 (☎284 325 001, fax 284 325 002). Situated close to the turismo, this *residencial* has doubles (all with bath) and cheaper singles (without bath). Breakfast included. ②.

Residencial Coelho, Praça da República 15 (☎284 324 031, fax 284 328 939). Decent-value pension, with a few rooms overlooking the square; all rooms have private showers and breakfast is included. ③.

Residencial Cristina, Rua de Mértola 71 (☎284 323 035, fax 284 320 460). A rather soulless, modern hotel, but Beja's most comfortable, if it's comfort you're after. ③.

Hotel Melius, Ruá Fialho de Almeida (☎284 321 822, fax 284 321 825). Modern hotel on the edge of town, complete with gym and sauna. ③.

Casa de Hóspedes Pax Julia, Rua Pedro Victor 8 (☎284 322 575). One of the least expensive options in town, with clean, comfortable rooms. ②.

Casa de Hóspedes Rocha, Largo Dom Nuno Álvares Pereira 12 (☎284 324 271). Friendly, decrepit old hotel facing the *pousada* offering tatty but clean rooms. ②.

Residencial Santa Bárbara, Rua de Mértola 56 (☎284 322 028, fax 284 321 231). Reasonably priced modern rooms, with breakfast included. ②.

Pousada de São Francisco, Largo Dom Nuno Álvares Pereira (☎284 328 441, fax 284 329 143). Imposing *pousada* inside the convent of São Francisco, where rooms are in former monastic cells. Even if you can't afford to stay, you can wander in and have a look around anyway. ⑨.

Eating, drinking and nightlife

Although Beja has a relatively wide selection of restaurants, only a small number serve really good traditional Portuguese food. Beja has no less than four Chinese restaurants, which is rather unusual for Portuguese towns. At night, the Beja youth congregate at the enormous *Pandora* **disco** close to the train station at Rua General Teófilo da Trinidade 4 (Wed–Sat, 10pm–4am; 1000$00 cover charge), whose five dance-floors should have something to please every taste.

Restaurante Alentejano, Largo dos Duques de Beja 7. A popular, local restaurant. where most main courses come in at around 900$00.

Cidade Asia Rua Luís de Camoes 25. Moderately priced and the best of the Chinese restaurants in town. They have menus from 825$00, which include favourites such as sweet and sour pork, which will be as familiar as the flock-wallpaper-and-lantern decor.

Restaurante A Esquina, Rua Infante Dom Henrique 26. Located in the west of town and serving up good-quality, traditional food.

Luís da Rocha, Rua do Capitão J.F. de Sousa 63. An immensely popular café serving a wide range of Alentejan fare and a great selection of inexpensive wines. Specials include grilled squid and rack of lamb. There's an *ementa turística* for around 1700$00. Great pastries too.

Restaurante Pena, Praça de Diogo Fernandes de Beja 19a. Modest prices and dependable cooking, with fish a speciality. It's between the pedestrian shopping district and the castle.

Restaurante O Portão, Trav. da Audiença 1 (off Rua dos Infantes). Not an enormous choice, but excellent quality and great value – the *ementa turística* is 1500$00 – served in an old *adega*.

Pousada de São Francisco, Largo Dom Nuno Álvares Pereira (☎284 328 441, fax 284 329 143). The *pousada* offers by far the highest quality traditional Portuguese cuisine in town; though you'd expect it having to pay around 4000–5000$00 for a full meal.

Serpa and around

Thirty kilometres east of Beja, the small market town of **SERPA** offers the classic Alentejan attractions – a walled centre, a castle and narrow, whitewashed streets – and makes an enjoyable stop if you are heading towards Spain, or feel like a roundabout but scenic approach to the Algarve, via Mértola. The town has at various times been occupied by Celts, Romans, Moors and Spaniards, and inevitably is dominated by its **Castle** (Tues–Sun 9am–12.30pm & 2–5.30pm; free), predominantly Moorish, and with spectacular vistas of the plain to the north and the hills to the south. There is a tiny archeological museum in the keep and, close by, the thirteenth-century church of **Santa Maria**, containing an altarpiece of intricate woodcarving, surrounded by seventeenth-century *azulejos*.

From the castle, you can track the course of the well-preserved eleventh-century **aqueduct**. It is worth a look from close up, too, with the remnants of a chain-pump at one end. If you have time to fill, you might also wander down to the **Museu Etnográfico** (Tues–Sun 9am–noon & 2–5pm; free), near the hospital, which offers an interesting account of the changing economic activity of the area, with exhibits such as agricultural implements, olive presses and local costumes.

Practicalities

Serpa's **turismo** is at Largo Dom Jorge de Melo 2 (daily 9am–5.30pm; ☎284 543 727), and the **bus station** is on the Avenida de Paz in the southwest of town; there are six connections a day to Beja. The rail bus also connects with Beja (and Moura) three times a day, but drops you on the main road, well outside Serpa.

You may well find private rooms advertised around the largo but official **places to stay** in town are limited. There's the smart *Residencial Beatriz*, at Largo do Salvador 10 (☎ 284 544 423, fax 284 543 100; ②), near São Salvador church; the *Residencial Serpinia*, in the northwest of town on Rua de Santo António (☎284 544 628, fax 284 543 100; ③), though the disco below may put you off; or the centrally located *Casa da Muralha*, Rua das Portas de Beja 43 (☎ & fax 284 543 150; ③), a country house furnished with antiques. A good out-of-town option is the modern *pousada*, the *São Gens* (☎284 544 724, fax 284 544 337; ⑥), 2km to the south, on a hill known as Alto de São Gens; it has a swimming pool and wonderful views. Serpa's well-equipped **campsite** (☎284 543 290, fax 284 543 494) is at the southwest corner of town near the swimming pool complex.

Among Serpa's **restaurants**, the *Cervejaria Vila Branca*, Av. da Paz 4, is highly recommended for its excellent *cataplanas* and seafood, while *O Zé* at Praça da República 10 serves a decent *gaspacho* and delicious local cheese. Opposite, the Art Deco *Café Alentejano* has a very good, if slightly pricey, restaurant above it; alternatively there's a more reasonable, unnamed restaurant at the top of Rua Quente.

Around Serpa

Situated 15km and 30km to the north of Serpa respectively, the wine-producing village
of Pias and the spa town of Moura make for interesting destinations in the area, with
Moura offering the best options for an overnight stay. If you have your own transport,
it's also an easy half-day trip to the Pulo do Lobo waterfall, sited amid stark, rocky
scenery 18km south of Serpa.

Pias

The village of **PIAS** is well known hereabouts for its red wine, Margaça and Encostas
– the Sociedade Agrícola de Pias, Rua Santo António 8 (☎285 858 222), can arrange
tours of the vineyards and winery. There are no particular sights, and the local train
station has closed down, but if you're driving it makes a worthwhile detour for anyone
who wants to examine what is still a very traditional Alentejan village. Pias also has a
surprisingly good **restaurant**, the *Arroz Doce* in Rua Luís de Camões – try the *migas*.
If you just want a **drink**, head for the wonderful *Pias Bar* on Rua de João Tiágo
Coelho, or the *Taverna* next door. For a **room**, ask for Manuel Baião at the shop on
the main street at no. 79, or for Senhor José Carvalho Godinho on the road past the
Caixa de Credito Agricular bank, who has rooms (①) in a lovely old house.

Moura

A further 15km north, the thermal spa town of **MOURA** is an opulent place full of
grand mansions, houses and pretty squares. The Moors occupied the town from the
eighth century until 1233 – an Arabic well still survives in the old town – and the town
is named after a Moorish maiden, Moura Saluquia, who ostensibly threw herself from
the castle tower in despair when Christians murdered her betrothed and overran the
town. But it was the discovery of the **thermal springs** that prompted Moura's later
wealth; located beside the Jardim Doutora Santiago, they are still in use (Mon–Sat
10am–5pm; 60$00 a bath). The key to the adjacent **castle**, built by Dom Dinis over a
Moorish castle and largely destroyed by the Duke of Osuna in 1701 (though one
Moorish tower survives), is at the Câmara Municipal. Outside the gardens stands the
sixteenth-century Manueline **Igreja de São João Batista**, its chapel decorated with
Sevillian *azulejos*. Behind the castle lies the ruined Renaissance **Convento do Carmo**,
where you can still see statues and beautiful frescoes.

Moura is connected to Beja three times a day by **bus**, via Serpa, which drops you at
the southern end of town, and daily to Évora, arriving at the central Praça Cabral. The
turismo is on Largo Santa Clara (Mon–Fri 9am–1pm & 2–6pm; ☎285 251 375) and may
be able to help with private **rooms**. Alternatively, try the *Pensão Alentejana* at Largo
José Maria dos Santos 40 (☎285 250 080, fax 285 250 089; ③), which has large and rambling rooms but is often full, or *Residencial Mourense*, Largo Dr. Rodrigues Acabado (☎
& fax 285 251 264 ②), offering very pleasant, modern rooms. The town's upmarket
option is the *Hotel de Moura*, on the peaceful Praça Gago Coutinho (☎285 251 090, fax
285 251 091; ③), a superbly ornate building complete with *azulejos*, patios, mirrored
doors and a rambling garden. There are plenty of **restaurants** in town; *O Trilho*, Rua
5 de Outubro 5 (closed Mon), serves good regional dishes. In the upper town, try *O
Arco* by Porta Nova, with its huge range of *aguardiente* liquors. For **nightlife**, there's
Discoteca Shahazade by the ruined convent, and the pub *Caprixus* at 14 Rua da Mollejas
(just off Praça Cabral).

The Pulo do Lobo waterfall

The **Pulo do Lobo** (Wolf's Leap) waterfall lies in a deep gorge carved through the hills
by the river and the valley has some strikingly eerie rock formations. You'll probably

have the falls all to yourself; to get there from Serpa, follow the road which is signposted behind the Jardim Botanico. It's well surfaced as far as the village of **São Brás**
(6km) but as it climbs into the mountainous countryside, it deteriorates suddenly to a
rough track, which becomes narrow and vertiginous as it leads down, around the 16km
mark, to a stream – a tributary of the Guadiana. Following the track, after a couple of
kilometres you can turn left to arrive very close to the Pulo do Lobo.

South to the Algarve

There are three main routes **south from Beja to the Algarve**. The most interesting
and enjoyable is the **N122** to Vila Real de Santo António (two buses daily), on the eastern border of the province with Spain; this passes through the old Moorish fortress town
of **Mértola** and a scenic stretch of the Guadiana river valley. Alternatives, more convenient if you are heading for western or central Algarve, are to take the N391 across the
plains to **Castro Verde**, then the fast E1 to **Albufeira**, or the more mountainous N2 to
Faro (three buses daily).

Via Castro Verde

If you're a bird fancier, you may consider the route from Beja to **CASTRO VERDE**
(46km south) a must, for the chance to see **great bustards** winging across the
plains. This apart, the road has few attractions, with a handful of small agricultural
towns set amid interminable parched tracts of wheat fields. Following the N2, directly south of Castro Verde, the route continues in similar vein until you hit the lush
greenery of the **Serra do Malhão** and the **Serra do Caldeirão** around Ameixial –
just across the border in the Algarve.

To the west, the N264 provides faster access to the Algarve, as well as an interesting
detour in the **Castro da Cola**, the remains of a small, Romano-Celtic village, similar to
the *citânias* of the north. This is located to the west of the road, a few kilometres beyond
the village of Aldeia dos Palheiros. There is a pilgrimage to the site on September 7–8.

Via Mértola

The N122 gets a green edge on the Michelin map as it approaches **MÉRTOLA** – a sure
sign of rising gradients and an escape from the plains. The town is as beautifully sited as
any in the south, set high above the Rio Guadiana, around the extensive ruins of a Moorish
frontier castle. It's a quiet, isolated place, certainly worth a night's stopover – more if you
feel like a walking or bird-watching base. The region is home to the rare black stork.

The obvious focus for a visit is the **Castelo**, views from whose keep sweep across the
Guadiana valley. To the north, you may be able to make out the copper mines a few kilometres down the Serpa road at Mina de São Domingos. Until recent decades, these
were the principal source of the town's employment, and until World War II they were
owned by a British company, which employed a private police force and treated the
workers with appalling brutality. Back in town, take time to look around the **Igreja
Matriz**, which started life as a Moorish mosque and retains its *mihrab* (prayer niche)
behind the altar on the eastern wall. Also worth searching out is the little **Museu
Arqueológico** (Mon–Sat 9am–12.30pm & 2–5.30pm; 500$00), a well-presented collec-
tion of recoveries from local digs, notably Roman pottery, jewellery and needles, plus a
set of strange-looking religious figures retrieved from the castle.

PRACTICALITIES

Orientation is straightforward, with **buses** (to and from Beja and Vila Real de Santo
António) stopping at the bus station, a five-minute walk along Rua Dr. Ferreo Martins
from the **turismo**, on Largo Vasco de Gama (Mon–Fri 9am–12.30pm & 2–5.30pm, Sat

& Sun 10am–12.30pm & 2–5.30pm; ☎286 612 573). **Accommodation** options include the *Residencial Beira Rio*, Rua Dr. Afonso Costa 18 (☎286 612 340; ②), which has the edge on *Residencial San Remo*, Av. Aurelino Mira Fernandes (☎286 612 132; ②), in character and situation. For a little more, you could stay at the *Casa das Janelas Verdes*, Rua Dr. Manuel Francisco Gomes 38–40 (☎286 612 145; breakfast included; ③) – a traditional Alentejan house. The *Restaurante Boa Viagem*, opposite the bus stop, offers a good and inexpensive selection of **meals**.

Santiago do Cacém and around

Heading south on the main route from Lisbon or Setúbal, **Santiago do Cacém** is the first place that might, realistically, tempt you to stop. A pleasant little provincial town, it is overlooked by a castle, and has on its outskirts – half an hour's walk away – the fascinating Roman ruins of **Miróbriga**. In addition, it's only a short bus journey from the **Santo André** and **Melides lagoons**, forming two of the Alentejo's finest beaches.

Santiago do Cacém

The Moorish **Castle** (Mon–Fri 8.30am–4.30pm, Sat 8.30am–1pm) in **SANTIAGO DO CACÉM** was later rebuilt by the Knights Templar but now serves as a cemetery. There are splendid views over to the sea from the battlements, whose crumbling masonry provides the habitat for a curious species of large golden beetle. It's also worth making your way to the **Museu Municipal**, facing the municipal gardens off Avenida Pereira (Tues–Fri 10am–noon & 2–5pm, Sat & Sun 2.30–5pm; free), one of the most interesting of its kind and housed in one of Salazar's more notorious prisons in a small park just northeast of the centre. A suitably political strain pervades its display: one of the spartan prison cells has been preserved while two others have been converted into a "typical country bedroom" and "a rich bourgeois bedroom". Even a drawing in the section devoted to the local primary school shows a child's impression of the "Great Revolution" of 1974.

The archeological section in Santiago's museum should whet your appetite for a visit to Roman **Miróbriga** (Tues–Sun 9am–12.30pm & 2–5.30pm; closes at 4.30pm in winter; 300$00). From the centre, follow Rua de Lisboa (N120) for about 1km up the hill, then take the marked turning to the right, and, after another ten-minute walk, turn left at a sign marking the entrance to the site, which lies isolated amid arcadian green hills. At the highest point of the site a **Temple of Jupiter** has been partly reconstructed, overlooking a small forum with a row of shops built into its supporting wall. A paved street descends to a **villa and bath complex** whose underground central heating system is still intact.

Practicalities

Staying in Santiago is not a problem, but be warned that out of season, bus services to the coast can be annoyingly irregular. The **turismo** in Largo do Mercado (Mon–Sat 9am–6.30pm; ☎269 826 696) might be able to help with **rooms**, otherwise try *Porto das Covas* (☎269 822 766, fax 269 826 902; ②), a newsagent just off Largo 25 Abril. **Pensões and hotels** include: *Pensão/Restaurante Covas*, by the bus station, at Rua Cidade de Setúbal 8–10 (☎269 822 675; ③); *Residencial Hotelagoa*, Lagoa de Santo André (☎269 749 117; ③), both of which are comfortable enough; *Residencial Gabriel*, Rua Professor Egas Moniz 24 (☎269 822 245, fax 269 826 102; ③), with modern, comfortable rooms and helpful staff; and *Albergaria D. Nuno*, Av. D. Nuno Álvares Pereira (☎269 823 325, fax 296 823 328; ③), with swimming pool and parking. Best of all, however, is the *Pousada de São Tiago*, Estrada Nacional (☎ & fax 269 822 459; ⑤), 1km out of town on the Lisbon road – a simple but pleasant *pousada*, with a pool and a decent restaurant.

However, the best **restaurant** in Santiago is the *Pensão/Restaurante Covas*, which specializes in seafood and has a great-value *ementa turística* for 1300$00. Alternatively, try *O Retiro*, Rua Machado dos Santos 8 (off Av. Pereira), a cosy little place serving regional cuisine, or the friendly, modestly priced *Restaurante Praceta*, Largo Zeca Afonso (behind the bus station), serving fish and chicken cooked on coals outside. If you really want to push the boat out, the hearty regional specialities at the *Pousada de São Tiago* will set you back around 4500–5000$00 a head. There's also a fine covered **market** in the centre of town, next to the turismo, useful for stocking up for a stay at one of the beaches, as many have no facilities.

The Santo André and Melides lagoons

In summer there are five buses a day from Santiago do Cacém to **LAGOA DE SANTO ANDRÉ**, and it's a short walk from there along the shore to **LAGOA DE MELIDES**. These two **lagoon beaches**, separated from the sea by a narrow strip of sand, are named after the nearest inland towns, but each has its own small, laid-back community entirely devoted to having a good time on the beach. The **campsites** at both places are of a high standard and there are masses of signs offering rooms, chalets and houses to let. Space is at a premium in July and August, but at other times accommodation should be no problem at all.

At either place, the social scene centres around the beach-cafés and ice-cream stalls. Beyond these is the sand – miles and miles of it, stretching all the way to Comporta in the north and to Sines in the south. The sea is very enticing with high waves and good surf, but be warned and take local advice on water conditions: the undertow can be fierce and people drown here every year.

Sines and south to Pessegueiro

SINES – the cape just south of Santiago do Cacém – is the one place not to go to on this stretch of coast. Vasco da Gama was born here, but he'd probably turn in his grave if he could see the massive oil refinery and the sacrifice of the environment to new roads, railways, pipelines and wells. It's an ugly industrial town, with only a highly rated **seafood restaurant** to recommend it: *Varanda Oceano* on Largo Nossa Senhora Salvas in the old town, serving fresh shellfish in 1930s-style surroundings. Should you need the **turismo** (summer Mon–Sat 10am–6pm; winter Mon–Fri 9am–1pm & 2–6pm; ☎269 634 472), it's in the Discovery Gardens near the disused train station. In the unlikely event that you need to **stay the night** here, try the *Residencial Carvalho*, Rua Gago Coutinho 13 (☎269 632 019; ①), or the friendly *Pensão Fredemar*, Rua Cândido dos Reis 31–35 (☎269 632 122; ②).

The ugliness around Sines is short-lived and just south of here there's a whole set of untouched little beach settlements. The best of all of them is the furthest south, the area around Ilha do Pessegueiro, reached from the road heading down to Porto Côvo – which is served by three buses daily from Sines.

Porto Côvo

The centre of **PORTO CÔVO** is a simple, unassuming, whitewashed place with a small cove harbour, a few *pensões*, some rooms to let, a camping site . . . and a sewage plant right on the oceanfront. However, developers have discovered Porto Côvo with a vengeance over the last decade or so and the land behind the village has been engulfed into one large building site. Despite this, it remains a lively and pleasant place to base yourself, not least for the series of beautiful coves stretching along the coast and the Ilha do Pessegueiro within easy walking distance.

The summer-only **turismo** (10am–1pm & 2–5pm; ☎269 905 460) is on the main square. Buses connect Porto Côvo at least twice daily with Almograve, Vila Nova de Milfontes and Praia Zambujeira, and once or twice daily with Odemira and Santiago do Cacém. There are several services daily to and from Sines. **Accommodation** isn't a problem, except at the height of summer when advance booking is recommended – the *Pensão Boa Esperança*, Rua Conde Bandeira (☎269 905 109; ②), is the best and longest-established option. Apartments are for rent at nos. 6 and 7 Rua da Farmacía, with no. 6 (☎269 905 125; 10,000$00 for four people) having the edge owing to its congenial owner. Outside town is the bland, three-star *Porto Côvo Hotel* (☎269 905 017, fax 269 905 058; ④). There's not much to choose between the village's **restaurants**, though the *Herminio*, on Rua Vasco da Gama, distinguishes itself by also selling local honey. On the same road is *Restaurante Cácome*, popular with locals for its seafood: *arroz de marisco*, grilled squid and an excellent *cataplana royal*. For a good selection of **snacks** and pastries, you need look no further than the popular *Gelatería/Cafétería Marques* at the opposite end of the square to the turismo.

Ilha do Pessegueiro

ILHA DO PESSEGUEIRO (Peach Tree Island) can be reached from the Porto Côvo–Vila Nova de Milfontes road, but the nicest approach is to walk, following the coastal path south from Porto Côvo. It's only a couple of kilometres and en route you'll pass the remains of a Bronze Age burial site.

The resort's name actually applies to the mainland beach; the island itself is less than a kilometre offshore and reachable on local fishing boats. On the mainland, there's the wonderful *Restaurante A Ilha* (☎269 905 113), a small seaside **fort**, a rural hotel *Herdade Agro Turística do Pessegueiro* (apartments 10,000$00 for four people; bookings through *A Ilha*), and a **campsite** (☎269 905 178). Quite a few people – a good mix of Portuguese and foreign travellers – camp out on the island itself, and although there are no facilities here, it makes an excellent place to hole up for a while if the very simple life appeals. If you're feeling energetic you could even walk the 20km or so south from here to Vila Nova de Milfontes, a good half-day's walk along the beach and cliffs – take enough water for the whole journey.

Southern Alentejo resorts and Odemira

On the southern half of the Alentejo coast, **Vila Nova de Milfontes** is the main beach resort, with **Almograve** and **Zambujeira do Mar**, further south, being quieter, less developed seaside villages. **Odemira** – about 15km from the coast – makes a good inland base, and offers local bus connections to the coast.

Vila Nova de Milfontes

VILA NOVA DE MILFONTES lies on the estuary of the Rio Mira, whose sandy banks gradually merge into the coastline. It has an advantage of geography for sailors (the port is reputed to have harboured Hannibal and his Carthaginians during a storm) and swimmers: if the waves of the Atlantic are too fierce you can always swim in the estuary, though beware of very strong currents.

The resort is not exactly undiscovered – the Germans, especially, built villas here through the 1980s – and it is perhaps the most crowded and popular resort in the Alentejo. The old town, however, huddled around a striking, ivy-wreathed castle, remains a pretty enough place; while Portuguese families on holiday from the big cities of the north give it a homely atmosphere quite distinct from the cosmopolitan trendiness of the Algarve. If you want to escape some of the crowds, take the ferry from the little jetty to the far side of the estuary to beaches nearby.

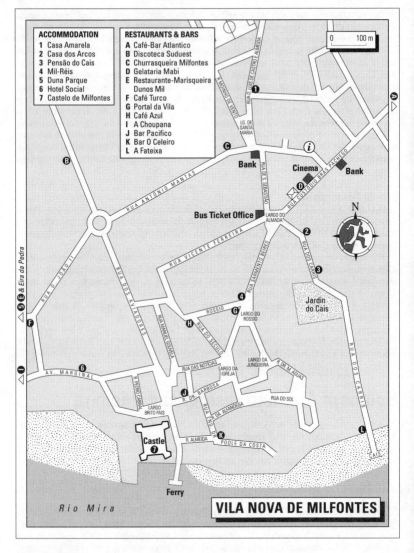

ACCOMMODATION
1 Casa Amarela
2 Casa dos Arcos
3 Pensão do Cais
4 Mil-Réis
5 Duna Parque
6 Hotel Social
7 Castelo de Milfontes

RESTAURANTS & BARS
A Café-Bar Atlantico
B Discoteca Suduest
C Churrasqueira Milfontes
D Gelataria Mabi
E Restaurante-Marisqueira
   Dunos Mil
F Café Turco
G Portal da Vila
H Café Azul
I A Choupana
J Bar Pacifico
K Bar O Celeiro
L A Fateixa

VILA NOVA DE MILFONTES

Practicalities

Arriving by **bus**, you'll be dropped off in a small lot near the **turismo** on Rua António Mantas (summer daily 10am–1pm & 2.30–7pm; ☎283 996 599). Buses run four times daily (Mon–Fri) and once daily at weekends to Odemira, Alcácer do Sal, Porto Côvo and Zambujeira do Mar. If you're Algarve-bound, catch the 10am bus to Cercal and transfer onto the Portimão express from Lisbon – the **ticket office** for all buses from Vila Nova is on Largo Almada. A range of activities can be arranged through the turismo. Alternatively, **horse riding** is offered by the English-run Companhia Caminhos do

Alentejo (☎283 998 106; 2000$00 per hour); **bike rental** is available from Corpo Vivo, in Rua do Pinhal opposite the *Quinta das Varandas* (☎283 997 198); while details of **river trips** to Casa Branca and Odemira can be obtained on ☎283 961 470.

ACCOMMODATION

Finding a place to stay should pose no problems out of season but it's advisable to book ahead in summer. If you turn up without a reservation ask at the turismo for a list of available **rooms** or look for others advertised in windows around town. Most of the newer **hotels** are situated in modern developments to the west of town – they usually have excellent facilities and can be very good value if you don't mind staying on a building site. Many of the new streets do not yet have names, but the hotels are well signposted. There are two **campsites** just north of town: the massive *Parque de Milfontes* (☎ & fax 283 996 104) has excellent facilities; more modest is the nearby *Campíférias* (☎283 996 409, fax 283 996 581; closed Dec).

Pensão do Cais, Rua dos Carris 9 (☎283 996 268). Very friendly hotel, full of Portuguese in summer (advance booking advised). Modern, spacious rooms, some with beautiful views over the estuary. ②.

Casa Amarela, Rua D. Luís de Castro e Almeida (☎283 996 632). A small pension with rooms for up to four people (11,000$00 for four). Most rooms come with bathroom and terrace.②.

Casa dos Arcos, Rua dos Carris (☎283 996 264, fax 283 997 156). A large 1960s' functional building; rooms are clean and breakfast is included. ③.

Castelo de Milfontes, (☎283 996 108, fax 283 997 122). Vila Nova's best lodgings, inside the fortress – cross the drawbridge to enter. The owner offers full board and is very picky about her guests, so dress well. Breakfast included. ⑥, full board ⑦.

Duna Parque, Rua Eira da Pedra (☎283 996 451, fax 283 996 459). A ten-minute walk from the centre is Milfontes' largest complex, with very well-equipped rooms; all rooms sleep up to four people and minimum stay is one week. ④.

Mil-Réis Actividades Hosteleiras Ltd, Largo do Rossio 2 (☎283 998 233, fax 283 998 328). On the corner with Rossio, an old-fashioned pension with kindly owners, offering smart, clean rooms with TV. ③.

Hotel Social, Av. Marginal (☎283 996 517, fax 283 996 517). Attached to the *Misericórdia de Odemira* and with a rather muted atmosphere. Friendly management, however, and good rooms, some with verandahs overlooking the estuary. Has an inexpensive, if institutional-looking, restaurant – a reasonable meal will set you back around 1500$00. ⑤.

Quinta das Varandas, Eira da Pedra (☎283 996 155, fax 283 998 102). Part of an uninspiring complex by the dunes, follow the coast up from *A Choupana*. Good value, though, in family-run apartments, all mod-cons with breakfast included. ③.

EATING

Restaurante do Cais, Rua dos Carris. Below the *pensão*, this good-value restaurant serves hearty Alentejan fare, with the *grelhados* (anything grilled) being particularly good.

A Choupana, Av. Marginal. At far western end on Praia do Farol. Serves excellent grilled fish, is good value and popular with the locals.

Restaurante-Marisqueira Dunas Mil, To the right off Av. Marginal. Top quality fish restaurant where a meal will set you back 3000$00 plus, but the food and service are well worth it. Especially recommended is the *açorda de marisco*.

A Fateixa, Rua dos Carris. Moderately priced, with a speciality of grilled fish. The quality here has slipped in the last few years but the location on the riverbank is superb.

Churrasqueira Milfontes, Rua António Mantas. Popular takeaway serving inexpensive, local fare.

Portal da Vila, Largo do Rossio. The Portuguese food in this family-run restaurant, served among greenery in a beautifully tiled interior, and is unbeatable for the price. The baked fish dishes are particularly good. A meal with wine will set you back about 2000$00.

DRINKING AND NIGHTLIFE

Café-Bar Atlantico, on the Porto Côvo road (follow Rua Custódio Brás Pachego). A friendly late-night drinking den.

Café Azul, Rossio 20. Relaxed bar playing a mix of jazz, rock and blues. Reasonably priced drinks include fine frozen tequila margaritas. Busy Fri and Sat and open till 4am.

Gelataria Mabi, Rua Custódio Brás Pachego, next to the Post Office. A combined ice-cream parlour and bar, attracting a mixed clientele.

Bar Pacífico, Rua Dr. Barbosa. New dance-bar playing a mixture of chart, techno and reggae music. Open 10pm–6am (closed Oct & Nov).

Discoteca Suduest, on northern continuation of Rua dos Aviadores. Plays the latest in rave and dance music.

Café Turco, Rua Dom João II. A place where it's easy to think you're in Lisbon; trendy, mock-Moorish café-bar with live acoustic music at the weekend when its full of Lisbonites (only open Sat & Sun in winter).

Almograve

The coast south of Vila Nova de Milfontes becomes ever more rugged and spectacular. At the tiny resort of **ALMOGRAVE**, 5km west of the Odemira–Vila Nova de Milfontes road, huge waves come crashing down on the rocks and for most of the day swimming is impossible. It can get very crowded at high tide, too, when the beaches are reduced to thin strips with occasional waves drenching everybody's belongings; but, for all that, it's an exhilarating place.

You could **camp** virtually anywhere back from the beach at Almograve, and there are a few cafés and bars, but the bus service from Odemira is just right for a day-trip. Should you need to stay overnight, however, the *Restaurante Torralta*, Av. da Praia (☎283 647 120; ①) has **rooms** available, or there's the *Pensão Paulo Campos*, Rua Antónia Pachecho 9 (May–Oct; ☎283 647 118; ③). If you can stretch to it, though, the best option is the pleasant, new *residencial*, *Duna Praia* (☎283 647 115, fax 283 647 112; ③), conveniently situated on the way to the beach and with a restaurant grill.

Odemira

In summer, the southern Alentejo resorts can get quite crowded, so you may prefer to stay in **ODEMIRA** and take day-trips to the seaside – be warned, though, that the bus services can be erratic. The town is pretty enough, set around the River Mira, and has several **pensões**, best of which are the very good *Casa Rita*, Largo do Poço Novo (☎283 322 531; ③), and *Residencial Idálio*, Rua Eng. Arantes Oliveira 28 (☎283 322 156; ②), both off to the left when you come out of the bus station. Alternatively, try the **rooms** above the *Restaurant Esperança*, Estrada de Circunvalação (☎283 322 270; ②), run by the same management. The **campsite** (☎282 947 145, fax 282 947 245) is out of town at São Miguel, but has good facilities including tennis and a pool. Among **restaurants**, try *O Tarro*, near the main road junction, where 1500$00 will get you a hearty meal, and for a drink head to *O Cais*, a terrace-bar down by the river, with live music at weekends (turn left over the bridge, then left again).

Zambujeira do Mar and on to the Algarve

At the village of **ZAMBUJEIRA DO MAR**, south of Odemira and 7km west of the main road, a large cliff provides a dramatic backdrop to the beach, which, like that of Vila Nova de Milfontes, can get very crowded in July and August. The scenery more than compensates for the winds and the sea – which can get positively chilly, even in summer – but can't disguise the rundown state of the village and the encircling villas. If you need to **stay** – and the bus schedule from Odemira makes a day-trip impossible – try any of these rather basic options: the *Residencial Mira Mar* (☎ & fax 283 961 352; ③); the modern *Residencial Ondazul* (☎283 961 450; ③); or the *Residencial Mar-e-Sol* (☎283 961 171; ②). There's also a reasonable **campsite** (☎283 961 172, fax 283 961 320), about

1km from the cliffs, which has showers and a café-bar. The best **restaurants** are the *Taverna Ti Vitório*, on Largo Mira Mar, which serves wonderful grilled fish, and the *Cervejaria A Marisqueira da Praia*, on Rua Mira Mar, which does a good *arroz de marisco* among other dishes. The popular and tacky late-night joint is the *Bar/Discoteca Clube da Praia*, on the beach.

Zambujeira is the southernmost Alentejo beach, and an attractive road twists its way into the hills of the Algarve from the river crossing at Odeceixe. For the most dramatic approach, however, take the road from Odemira through the **Serra de Monchique**, descending to the Algarve coast at Portimão.

travel details

Trains

Alcácer do Sal to: Lisbon (3 daily; 2hr–2hr 45min).

Beja to: Évora (5 daily; 1hr 15min–2hr 35min); Faro (2 daily; 3hr 5min–3hr 25min); Lisbon (6 daily; 2hr 40min–4hr 40min).

Belver to: Lisbon (5 daily; 2hr 35min–5hr).

Crato to: Lisbon (4 daily; 3hr 30 min–4hr).

Elvas to: Lisbon (4 daily; 4hr 45min–5hr 15min); Portalegre (3 daily; 50min).

Évora to: Beja (6 daily; 1hr 15min–2hr 55min); Faro (2 daily; 4hr 45min–5hr 20min); Lisbon (4 daily; 2hr 40min–3hr 10min).

Portalegre to: Crato (3 daily; 15min); Elvas (3 daily; 45min); Lisbon (4 daily; 3hr 55min–4hr 25min).

Buses

Alcácer do Sal to: Lisbon (3 daily; 1hr 30min).

Almograve to: Lisbon (3 daily; 4hr 10min); Porto Côvo (3–4 daily; 1hr); Vila Nova de Milfontes (2 daily; 35min).

Alter do Chão to: Lisbon (1 daily; 3hr 35min); Portalegre (1 daily; 35min).

Beja to: Albufeira (3–4 daily; 2hr 15min); Elvas (1 daily; 3hr 25min); Évora (7–9 daily; 1hr–1hr 20min); Faro (1 daily; 3hr 10min–4hr 30min); Lisbon (4–6 daily; 3hr 20min); Moura (3 daily; 1hr 25min); Portalegre (2 daily; 4hr); Serpa (5–11 daily; 45min).

Borba to: Elvas (4 daily; 30min); Estremoz (2 daily; 15min); Évora (2 daily; 1hr); Lisbon (3 daily; 3hr–3hr 30min).

Castelo de Vide to: Portalegre (2 daily; 20min).

Crato to: Lisbon (1 daily; 3hr 50min); Portalegre (1 daily; 20min).

Elvas to: Elvas train station (5 daily; 20min); Beja (1 daily; 3hr 25min); Borba (1 daily; 30min); Campo Maior (Mon–Fri 3 daily; 30min); Évora (5 daily; 1hr 35min–2hr 10min); Lisbon (5–6 daily; 3hr 30min–4hr 20min); Portalegre (Mon–Fri 2 daily; 1hr 30min).

Estremoz to: Borba (2 daily; 15min); Évora (hourly; 45min); Lisbon (2 daily; 3hr 20min); Portalegre (2 daily; 1hr).

Évora to: Albufeira (4 daily; 3hr 30min); Beja (7–9 daily; 1hr–1hr 20min); Borba (2 daily; 1hr); Coimbra (1 daily; 4hr 35min); Elvas (5 daily; 1hr 35min); Estremoz (hourly; 45min); Faro (4 daily; 4hr 35min); Lisbon (Mon–Fri 11 daily, Sat & Sun 6–7 daily; 1hr 45min); Monsaraz (2 daily; 55min); Moura (2–3 daily; 1hr 30min); Portalegre (4–5 daily; 1hr 45min); Santarém (2 daily; 2hr).

Mértola to: Lisbon (2 daily; 4hr 15min).

Moura to: Évora (1 daily; 1hr 30min); Lisbon (1 daily; 4hr).

Odemira to: Lisbon (4 daily; 3hr 50min–4hr 20min); Vila Nova de Milfontes (2 daily; 20min).

Portalegre to: Portalegre train station (3 daily; 15min); Alter do Chão (1 daily; 35min); Beja (2 daily; 3hr 50min); Castelo do Vide (2 daily; 20min); Crato (1 daily; 20min); Estremoz (2 daily; 1hr); Évora (4–5 daily; 1hr 45min); Lisbon (3 daily; 4hr 10min–4hr 25min); Viseu (2 daily; 5hr).

Porto Côvo to: Almograve (4 daily; 40min); Lisbon (6 daily; 3hr 35min); Santiago do Cacém (4 daily; 1hr); Vila Nova de Milfontes (7 daily; 30min).

Santiago do Cacém to: Lisbon (9 daily; 2hr 25min); Porto Côvo (5 daily; 1hr); Sines (5 daily; 35–45min); Vila Nova de Milfontes (6 daily; 1hr 25min).

Serpa to: Beja (2–3 daily; 35min); Lisbon (2–3 daily; 4hr).

Sines to: Beja (2 daily; 2hr 50min); Lisbon (6–8 daily; 3hr–3hr 20min); Odemira (1 daily; 1hr 10min); Porto Côvo (5 daily; 25min); Santiago do Cacém (5 daily; 35min); Zambujeira do Mar (3 daily; 1hr 30min).

Vila Nova de Milfontes to: Almograve (2 daily; 15min); Lisbon (3–7 daily; 3hr 35min–4hr 10min); Porto Côvo (2 daily; 25min); Zambujeira do Mar (2 daily; 40min).

Vila Viçosa to: Borba (3–4 daily; 10min); Elvas (2 daily; 35min); Estremoz (3 daily; 25min); Évora (3 daily; 1hr); Lisbon (2 daily; 3hr–3hr 50min).

Zambujeira do Mar to: Almograve (2 daily; 25min); Lisbon (1 daily; 4hr 45min); Porto Côvo (2 daily; 1hr 5min–1hr 15min); Santiago do Cacém (1 daily; 2hr 15min); Sines (3 daily; 1hr 40min); Vila Nova de Milfontes (2 daily; 40–45min).

CHAPTER NINE

THE ALGARVE

With its long, sandy beaches and picturesque rocky coves, the **Algarve** has attracted more tourist development than the rest of the country put together. In parts, this has all but destroyed the charms that it was intended to exploit. The strip of coast from Faro west to Lagos has suffered most, with its endless villa complexes creating a rather depressing Mediterranean-style suburbia. On the fringes, though, especially around Sagres and Tavira, things are far better, with small-scale and relaxed resorts and the odd undeveloped beach or island sandbank.

The coastline in fact has two quite distinct characters. To the **west of Faro** you'll find the classic postcard images of the province – a series of tiny bays and coves, broken up by weird rocky outcrops and fantastic grottoes. They're at their most exotic around the major resort towns of **Lagos** and **Albufeira**. For fewer crowds, alternative bases include the beach village of **Salema**, the historic cape of **Sagres** – site of Henry the Navigator's naval school – or one of the string of villages along the rougher west coast as far as **Odeceixe**.

East of Faro, there's a complete change as you encounter the first of a series of sandy offshore islets, the *ilhas*, which front the coastline virtually all the way to the Spanish border. Overall, this is the quieter section of the coast and it has the bonus of much warmer waters than those further west. First-choice bases along this stretch would be Faro itself, **Olhão** and **Tavira**, all of which offer access to sandbank-islands.

Inland, there are scattered attractions in the Roman ruins of **Estói** and the market town of **Loulé**, both north of Faro; and the old Moorish town of **Silves**, easily reached from Portimão. The outstanding area, however, is the **Serra de Monchique**, the highest mountain range in the south, with cork and chestnut woods, remote little villages and a beautiful old spa in **Caldas de Monchique**.

The Algarve is an all-year-round destination, with sunny and relatively mild winters. In many respects the region is at its best in **spring** or **winter**. Most *pensões* and restaurants stay open, so rooms are easy to find. Indeed, **off-season travel** in the Algarve will get you some of the best deals in the country, with luxury hotels offering all-in packages at discounts of up to seventy percent; check out the latest deals at the local tourist offices. May has the added attraction of the Algarve's **International Music Festival**, sponsored by the Gulbenkian Foundation and hosting major classical artists. If you come in the **summer**, without a booking, finding accommodation can be a real struggle, though you'll usually find something. Be prepared for very high summer

---

ACCOMMODATION PRICE CODES

All the accommodation prices in this book have been coded using the symbols below. The symbols represent the lowest prices you can expect to pay for a **double room in high season**; for a full explanation, see p.32.

① Under 4000$00	④ 11,000$00–15,000$00	⑦ 25,000$00–30,000$00
② 4000$00–7000$00	⑤ 15,000$00–20,000$00	⑧ 30,000$00–40,000$00
③ 7000$00–11,000$00	⑥ 20,000$00–25,000$00	⑨ Over 40,000$00

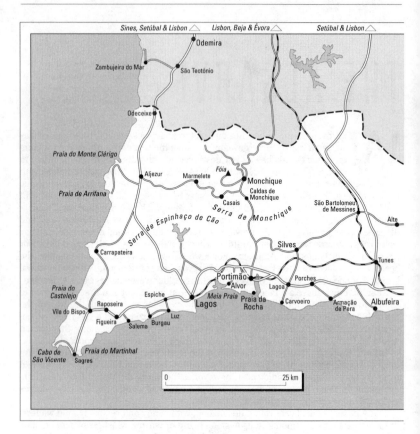

prices relative to the rest of the country. One of a dozen tourist-orientated Algarve home pages on the **Internet** worth investigating is *www.nexus-pt.com/index.htm*, with links to hotels, golf courses, general information and directories.

Transport

Getting around by **public transport** is easier here than anywhere else in Portugal, and since the coastline is only 240km long from east to west, you can see an awful lot in just a few days. The **Algarve rail line** runs from Lagos in the west to Vila Real de Santo António on the Spanish border, calling at most major towns en route; **buses** link all the resorts and main inland villages. The two main bus companies running services are EVA and Frota Azul, which link together in the western Algarve to offer a *Passe Turístico* (three days 2700$00; seven days 3950$00), giving unlimited bus travel between Lagos and Loulé, covering all the main resorts in between (though not Faro). You can buy a pass from any bus station in the region.

Driving is often more trouble than it's worth. It's undeniably useful if you want to reach the more out-of-the-way inland villages and inaccessible cove beaches (or head further into Portugal) but driving the main east–west N125 can be a pain since it's constantly being upgraded to cope with increasing traffic: expect road works, diversions and traffic jams.

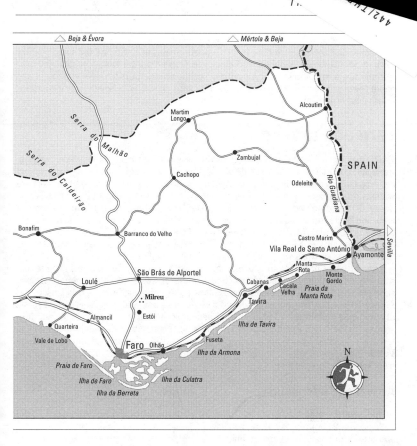

SPAIN

Alcoutim

Martim
Longo

Zambujal

Cachopo

Odeleite

Rio Guadiana

Bonafim

Barranco do Velho

Castro Marim

Vila Real de Santo António Ayamonte

Sevilla

São Brás de Alportel

Manta
Rota

Loulé

Cabanas

Monte
Gordo

.: Milreu

Cacela
Velha

Praia da
Manta Rota

Tavira

Almancil

Estói

Quarteira

Ilha de Tavira

Vale de Lobo

Fuseta

Faro Olhão

Ilha da Armona

Praia de Faro

Ilha de Faro Ilha da Culatra

Ilha da Berreta

N

THE EASTERN ALGARVE

All flights to the Algarve land at **Faro**, the administrative capital of the region and by far the largest town along the coast. Although no great holiday destination in itself, the centre of the town is considerably more attractive than the concrete suburbs might suggest; and there are some fine beaches and interesting local villages within easy reach. It's also not a bad place to start or finish a tour of the rest of the Algarve: Faro is connected with Lisbon by fast express coaches and offers efficient access to most Algarve towns by bus and – a little slower – on the Algarve rail line.

Faro marks a geographical boundary on the Algarve. The **coastline** east from here to Manta Rota, near the Spanish border, is protected by thin stretches of mud flats, fringed in turn by a chain of long and magnificent sandbanks, or *ilhas*. Often accessible only by boat, they're usually far less crowded than the small rocky resorts of the western Algarve. The towns of **Olhão**, **Tavira** and **Vila Real de Santo António** preserve a fair bit of character, while most of the resorts – with the exception of **Monte Gordo** – are fairly small-scale. Ornithologists should take binoculars, as the shores are thick with various types of wading bird in winter and spring.

Inland, the eastern Algarve offers few diversions, though a couple of day-trips provide some distraction: from Faro to the Roman remains at **Estói** and the small country town of **São Brás de Alportel**; and along the Spanish border from Vila Real de Santo António to **Castro Marim** and **Alcoutim**. With longer detours in mind, you might find equal rewards in travelling across the frontier **into Spain**, with Seville only a couple of hours from Vila Real.

Faro and around

FARO has been transformed from a sleepy provincial town into a centre of tourism, trade and commerce within three decades. However, although the international airport delivers visitors right to its door, the town has a job holding on to them, since most are whisked immediately away to the out-and-out resorts on either side of Faro. This is a little unfair: there's an attractive harbour, backed by a bustling, pedestrianized shopping area, and boats and buses run out to a couple of excellent local **beaches**. In summer, too, there's quite a **nightlife** scene, as thousands of travellers pass through on their way to and from the airport. There are certainly better places to spend a holiday on the Algarve, but for a night or two's stay at either end, it can be an enjoyable enough base.

Faro's Roman predecessor was 8km to the north, at Ossonoba (see p.447); the present city was founded by the Moors, under whom it was a thriving commercial port, supplying the regional capital at Silves. Following its conquest by the Christians, under Afonso III in 1249, the city experienced a chequered few centuries, surviving a series of conquests and disasters. Sacked and burned by the Earl of Essex in 1596, and devastated by the Great Earthquake of 1755, it is no surprise that the modern city has so few historic buildings. What interest it does retain is contained within the **Cidade Velha** (Old Town), which lies behind a series of defensive walls, across the harbour from the main part of town.

Arrival and information

In the summer months, flights land at Faro's international **airport**, 6km west of the town centre, 24 hours a day. Here, you'll find a police and first-aid post, bank, post office and tourist office (daily 10am–midnight; ☎289 818 582), but nothing much in the provisions line apart from a poor airport restaurant. A number of **car rental** companies (see "Listings", p.447) also have offices at the airport.

One of the quickest ways of getting into the centre is by **taxi**, which should cost about 1000$00, plus 300$00 for any luggage that goes in the boot; there's also a twenty percent surcharge between 10pm and 6am, and at weekends. There is now the direct **Aerobus** service operated by EVA, however, which takes only thirteen minutes. The aerobus runs between the airport and the bus station, and is free to flight ticket holders – simply show your ticket when taking the aerobus into the centre or coming back to the airport. It leaves the airport, and the bus station, at quarter past and quarter to the hour from 7.30am to 11.30pm. Two local buses also run from the airport to the centre, a twenty-minute ride costing 160$00: the #16 (roughly hourly 8am–9pm; July to mid-Sept until 11pm) and the rather less frequent #14 both stop outside the bus terminal in town (see below) and further on, at the Jardim Manuel Bivar (*Jardim* on the timetables) by the harbour. In the other direction, bus #16 runs to the beach and campsite at Praia de Faro, just 3km from the airport (see below). There are timetables posted at the airport bus stop; buy tickets on board.

The **bus terminal** is located on Avenida da República, behind the *Hotel Eva*, just across the harbour from the old part of town. The **train station** is a few minutes' walk further north up the avenue, facing Largo da Estação.

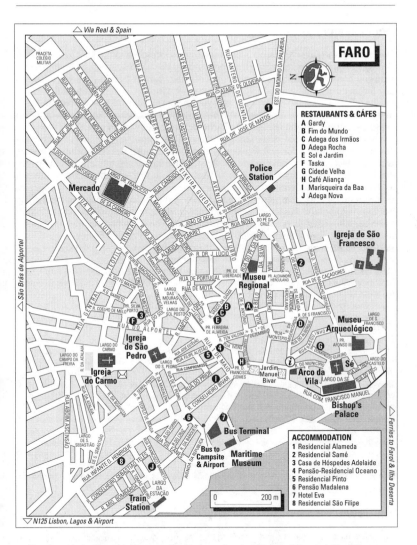

Faro's main **turismo** is close to the harbour front at Rua da Misericórdia 8 (summer daily 9.30am–7pm; winter Mon–Fri 9.30am–5.30pm, Sat & Sun 9.30am–12.30pm & 2–5.30pm; ☎289 803 604). The turismo provides maps of the town and has noticeboards which deal comprehensively with local and long-distance bus, boat and train timetables, too. The regional tourist office – **Região de Turismo do Algarve** – at Av. 5º Outubro (Mon–Fri 9.30am–12.30pm & 2–5.30pm; ☎289 800 400, *www.rtalgarve.pt*) is another source of information on the area as a whole.

The compact town centre is simple to negotiate **on foot**, and all the *pensões* and hotels are extremely central. There is a **town bus service**, but you'll need it only to get to the beach and campsite (for which, see below) and the airport.

Accommodation

Like most of the Algarve, Faro's accommodation is stretched to the limit in summer. If you fly in without a reservation, it's worth asking the airport tourist office to try and help you book you a place – though it's not officially part of their job and you'll have to pay for any calls they make on your behalf; otherwise the main turismo and regional tourist office in town (see above) can give you an idea of where to look for **rooms**. Most of the city's **pensões** and **hotels** – the best of which are picked out below – are concentrated in the area just north of the harbour. You might want to note that if sleep is a priority, you should avoid street-facing rooms on Rua Conselheiro Bivar – the bars (and street) are full until 3.30am at weekends. The town's **youth accommodation centre** is a quiet place, located next to the gardens at Rua do PSP, on the left past the police station (☎289 801 970, fax 289 801 413; ①), and you'd be advised to book well in advance as it's often filled with groups.

In summer, Faro's **campsite** at Praia de Faro is always full and very cramped; if you want to stay, phone or fax ahead (reception 8am–9.30pm; ☎289 817 876, fax 289 802 326). Take bus #16, either direct from the airport, or from the stop opposite the bus terminal in town; the site is a ten-minute walk from the bus stop at Praia de Faro.

Residencial Alameda, Rua Dr. José de Matos 31 (☎289 801 962, fax 289 804 218). Excellent rooms for the price, all with en-suite bathrooms and breakfast included. ③.

Casa de Hóspedes Adelaide, Rua Cruz das Mestras 7–9 (☎289 802 383, fax 289 826 870). Clean, basic rooms, though only a few have their own bathroom. Very friendly owner and several communal areas, including kitchen and lounge. ①.

Hotel Eva, Av. da República 1 (☎289 803 354, fax 289 802 304). The town's best hotel, with a superb harbour-front position and rooms whose balconies look across to the old town or the marina. There's a pool, too, and a courtesy bus to the local beach. Breakfast included. ⑥.

Pensão Madalena, Rua Conselheiro Bivar 109 (☎ & fax 289 805 806). One of the better budget places to stay – cool marble-and-tile decor, with mostly good, clean rooms, some overlooking the (noisy) street, and a friendly reception. Check first, though, as some of the rooms are a bit gloomy. ③.

Pensão-Residencial Oceano, Trav. Ivens 21–1° (☎289 823 349, fax 289 805 590). Centrally located just off Rua 1° de Maio, this clean – if fairly bland – *pensão* is ideally placed for the town's nightlife. Check the bathrooms first as in some rooms they are extremely cramped. ③.

Residencial Pinto, Rua 1° de Maio 27 (☎289 822 820). Small place with a few rooms sharing a common bathroom. It's a little past its sell-by date, but is cheap and friendly enough. ②.

Residencial Samé, Rua do Bocage 66 (☎289 824 375, fax 289 804 166). This clean, modern hotel is located in a quiet street east of the Sé; all rooms come with TV, bathroom and the price includes breakfast. ③.

Pensão São Filipe, Rua Infante Dom Henrique 55a (☎289 824 182). Clean, reasonable rooms and about as cheap as things get in town. ②.

The Town

The only part of town to have survived the various violent historic upheavals is the **Cidade Velha**, across the harbour, an oval of cobbled streets and brightly painted restored buildings set within a run of sturdy walls. It is entered through the eighteenth-century town gate, the **Arco da Vila**, next to the turismo. From here, Rua do Município leads up to the majestic Largo da Sé, flanked by the cathedral and a group of palaces – including the former bishop's palace – and lined with orange trees. The **Sé** itself (Mon–Sat 10am–noon & 2.30pm–5.30pm, Sun open for Mass at 10am & noon) is a squat, white mismatch of Gothic, Renaissance and Baroque styles, all heavily remodelled after the 1755 earthquake. It's worth looking inside, though, mainly for the fine eighteenth-century *azulejo* tiling.

More impressive is the **Museu Arqueológico** (Mon–Fri 9am–noon & 2–5pm; 110$00) installed in a sixteenth-century convent in nearby Praça Afonso III; in front of the building stands a forthright, crucifix-carrying statue of the conqueror Afonso himself, king between 1249 and 1279. The most striking of the museum's exhibits is a superb third-century AD Roman mosaic of Neptune surrounded by the four winds, unearthed near the train station. Other items include a collection of Roman statues from the excavations at Estói (see p.447), and a selection of local paintings, military artefacts and naive sixteenth-century multicoloured tiles, upstairs in the art gallery. In the rest of the old town, the streets have mostly been scrubbed clean of interest. However, it's well worth wandering around some of the cobbled side streets, whose houses are fronted by decorative balconies and tiling – the odd one serving as an antique shop or art gallery.

The **harbour** is the next most interesting area. The town gardens and a cluster of outdoor cafés overlook the moored yachts, while in the backstreets around **Rua de Santo António** shops, bars and restaurants do their best to keep you off the local beach. At the end of Rua de Santo António, on Praça de Liberdade, is the most intriguing of Faro's museums, the **Museu Regional** (Mon–Fri 9am–noon & 2–5pm; 300$00), which has a display of local crafts and industries, including reconstructions of typical cottage interiors, and models of the net systems still used for tuna fishing.

By far the most curious sight in town, however, is the twin-towered, Baroque **Igreja do Carmo** (Mon–Fri 10am–1pm & 3–5pm, Sat 10am–1pm, Sun only for mass at 9am), near the central post office on the Largo do Carmo. A door to the right of its altar leads to the sacristy where you buy a ticket (120$00) to view the macabre **Capela dos Ossos** (Chapel of the Bones), set in an overgrown garden out back. Like the one at Évora (see p.403), its walls are decorated with human bones – in this case disinterred from the adjacent monks' cemetery. Nearby, in Largo de São Pedro, the sixteenth-century **Igreja de São Pedro** is infinitely more attractive as a church, its finest decorative work an altar (to the left of the main altar) whose central image is a gilded, wooden *Last Supper* in relief.

The beaches

Faro's "town beach" – **Praia de Faro** – is typical of the sand-spit *ilha* beaches of the eastern Algarve; a long sweep of beautiful sand with both a sea-facing and a more sheltered land-facing side. It's less characteristic in being both overcrowded and overdeveloped, with bars, restaurants, villas and a campsite jammed onto a sandy island far too narrow to cope in the height of summer. Still, if you just want a few hours away from the centre of Faro, it's more than adequate; out of season you'll probably have the sands to yourself. The beach is situated on the Ilha de Faro, southwest of the town; bus #16 runs hourly (8am–8.40pm; until 9.40pm in summer) from the harbour gardens, or from the stop opposite the bus terminal, on a rather circuitous nine-kilometre trip that calls in at the airport first.

Alternatively, **ferries** shuttle through narrow marshy channels to a couple of other local sandbar beaches, between Faro and Olhão. They depart from the jetty below the old town, either to **Farol** on the Ilha da Culatra (June–Sept four daily; 500$00 return; 45min), which is described on p.450; or to the nearby **Ilha Deserta** (June–Sept four daily; 1000$00 return), part of the Parque Natural da Ria Formosa, where there's a bar-restaurant – *O Estaminé* – to cater for your needs.

Eating, drinking and nightlife

The heart of the town is a modern, pedestrianized shopping area on either side of Rua de Santo António, where you can find innumerable **restaurants, cafés and bakeries**

– the latter stocked with almond delicacies, the regional speciality. Most of the pavement restaurants have similar menus (and similar prices); if you're prepared to scout around the backstreets, you can often find cheaper, better food, though without the accompanying streetlife that makes central Faro so attractive. As you'd expect, the cuisine is predominantly seafood-based, including the ubiquitous and often expensive *arroz de marisco* (a stew of shellfish and rice).

Cafés and restaurants

Café Aliança, Rua F. Gomes 6–11. A down-at-heel coffee house – faded but rather appealing in its way – with seats outside in summer, and a full menu of breakfasts, burgers, salads, omelettes, pastries and ice cream. It also sells British newspapers.

Cidade Velha, Rua Domingos Guieiro 19 (☎289 827 145). Situated by the Sé, this is the only restaurant in the old town. It serves elegant French and Portuguese cooking in a fine eighteenth-century building. At least 4000$00 a head; booking essential. Closed Sat lunch & Sun.

Adega Dois Irmãos, Largo Terreiro do Bispo 13–15. Next to Praça Ferreira de Almeida, this is one of the oldest of the city's fish and seafood restaurants, a moderately priced place which specializes in tasty *cataplanas* (served for two only). Try the sardines, too. Upwards of 2500$00 a head.

Fim do Mundo, Rua Vasco da Gama 53. Poorly lit, barely welcoming *frango* joint. Don't go if you don't want chicken – if you do, you'll get half a bird, fries and wine for 1000$00. It's actually very good – ask for the *piri-piri* (hot chilli and olive oil seasoning) only if you have health insurance.

Gardy, Rua de Santo António 16. Popular local *pastelaria* where seats are always at a premium – excellent cakes, pastries and coffee.

Marisqueira da Baixa, Rua Conselheiro Bivar 12. A cool, spacious interior decorated with nautical memorabilia. This place has a good range of 800–900$00 *pratos do dia* that all come with salad. Also serves hefty two person *cataplanas* for around 2500$00 a head.

Adega Nova, Rua Francisco Barreto 24. Near the train station, this is an old-fashioned *adega* with classic Portuguese food and jugs of wine. An inexpensive choice – under 2000$00 for a filling meal.

Adega Rocha, Rua da Misericórdia 50. Up the road from the turismo, this check-tableclothed *adega* is just out of the central bustle and reassuringly good value – around 2000$00 for meat and fish grills.

Sol e Jardim, Praça Ferreira de Almeida 22–23. Associated with (and virtually next door to) the *Dois Irmãos*, this is a junk shop turned restaurant – flags of the world, football jerseys, old agricultural equipment, baskets and pots and pans suspended from the ceiling of a barn-like "garden" dining room. From around 1500$00 a head, though more like double that if you stray into the shellfish and specialities.

Taska, Rua do Alportel 38. Friendly place serving traditional Algarve fare to a mostly Portuguese crowd. House specialities include corn mash with cockles and prawns, and peanut mousse, accompanied by an excellent range of Portugese regional wines. Look at paying about 2500$00 a head.

Bars and discos

The best of Faro's **nightlife** is concentrated along two or three central pedestrianized and cobbled streets – in particular **Rua Conselheiro Bivar** with its café-bars with outdoor seating, and the parallel **Rua do Prior**, where many of the bars and clubs feature DJs, live bands and video screens. Things get going around midnight; soon afterwards, as the bars fill up, drinkers tumble out onto the cobbled alleys to party. Faro also occasionally hosts big-name rock and pop **gigs** at the football stadium – check posters around town, or ask at the turismo. There are no cover charges and all are open until midnight unless stated otherwise.

3rd Millenium, Rua do Prior 21. Large club with industrial-warehouse feel, playing all the latest sounds, good DJs and regular performances by local bands. One of the better venues. Open 11pm–5am.

24º Julho, Rua do Prior 38. Glitzy disco with high prices and a strict dress code – you'll need your best glad rags and definitely no trainers. Open until 7am.

Barracuda, Praia de Faro. The beach's most popular disco, with an outdoor first-floor bar. It's close to the campsite.

O Cofre, Rua Conselheiro Bivar 54. Café-*pastelaria* by day, youth hang-out by night with the tables hogged by locals fortifying themselves before a night spent shouting in the street.

Conselheiro, Rua Conselheiro Bivar 72–78. A bit more relaxed than most along here, with indoor tables, palms and some attempt at proper conversation by the patrons.

Diesel Bar, Travessa São Pedro. Chilled-out bar with Aztec-style decor, in a small, dark street off Ruo do Prior. Offers a wide selection of shots (150$00) and cocktails (500$00), and stays open late.

Gothic, Rua da Madelena 38, near the Igreja de São Pedro. As the name suggests, industrial/Gothic sounds and cheap beer in the dark. Unique on the Algarve.

Kingburger Bar, Rua do Prior 40. A small and relaxed bar, one of the first to open up along here, and one of the last to close. There is another branch on Conselheiro Bivar.

O Prior, Ruo do Prior 41. Run by the same management and with a similar clientele as *Universidade*, but less cheesy music in a slightly smaller venue, and no live bands.

Universidade, Rua de São Pedro 19–23. At the end of Rua do Prior – regular live bands and a post-11pm Happy Hour for cheap beer make this a popular student hang-out.

Versailles, Rua Ivens 7–9. Restaurant-bar that's good for a drink post-restaurant/pre-club, with outdoor seating and – later on at least – a youthful, local crowd. Open until midnight.

Listings_

Airlines British Airways (airport ☎289 818 476); Lufthansa (airport ☎289 800 751); TAP, Francisco Gomes 8 ☎289 800 200; (airport switchboard ☎289 800 800).

Airport Flight information on ☎289 800 801._

Bus terminal Av. da República 106 (bus information, ☎289 899 700). There's an English-speaking information office inside the terminal.

Car rental Auto Algarve, Rua Samual Gacon Vale Almas (☎289 825 711); Avis (airport ☎289 818 624, fax 289 818 540); Eurodollar/Globalrent (airport ☎289 817 100); Europcar (airport ☎289 818 777, fax 289 818 393); IPer Rent, Rua Fr. Lourenço S. Maria 30 (☎289 805 090, fax 289 801 782); Luso Rent, Av. 5 de Outubro 19 (☎289 812 277, fax 289 812 265).

Cinema In the Galerias Santo António shopping centre at Rua de Santo António 25.

Consulate The only British consulate in the Algarve is in Portimão (p.468), at Largo Francisco A. Maurício 7-1° (Mon–Fri 10am–noon & 3–4.30pm; ☎282 417 800). In Faro itself, there's a Canadian consulate (Rua Frei Lourenço de Santa Maria 1–1°; ☎289 803 757); a Dutch consulate (Rua Frei Lourenço de Santa Maria 2–1°; ☎289 820 903); and a German consulate (Av. da República 166–4°; ☎289 803 148).

Hospital Hospital Distrital (☎289 803 411). In emergencies ☎112.

Left luggage At the bus terminal (Mon 9am–1pm & 2–6pm, Tues–Thurs 9am–1pm & 2–6pm, Fri 8.30am–1pm & 2–6pm; 600$00 per day).

Police Rua da Policia de Segurança Pública 32 (☎289 822 022)._

Post office Largo do Carmo (Mon–Fri 8.30am–6.30pm, Sat 9am–12.30pm); also has *poste restante* facilities.

Taxis There's a rank in Praça Dr. Francisco Gomes, by the town gardens.

Telephones You can make international calls from the post office.

Travel agencies Abreu, Av. da República 124; Marcus & Harting, Rua Conselheiro Bivar 69 (☎289 805 335, fax 289 805 470); Space Travel, Rua Conselheiro Bivar 36 (☎800 204 443, fax 289 803 206).

North of Faro: Estói and São Brás de Alportel

Apart from the beach, other worthwhile day-trips from Faro are to the couple of villages in the gentle hills to the north. At Estói, you can divide your time between a delightful eighteenth-century country estate and the remains of a Roman settlement at Milreu, just below the village. Further north, the hilltop town of São Brás de Alportel also makes a pleasant excursion. Travelling by bus, unless you make a fairly early start, it's difficult to see both villages on the same day. However, if you feel reasonably energetic it's perfectly feasible to take the bus to São Brás and walk the 7km down to Estói, catching the late-afternoon bus back to Faro from there.

Estói

Regular buses make the twenty-minute journey 11km north of Faro to **ESTÓI,** which basically consists of a main street, a little square and a small white church. Buses drop you in the square, just off which is the delightful peach-coloured **Palácio do Visconde de Estói**, a diminutive version of the Rococo palace of Queluz near Lisbon (see p.124). At present, only the attractive grounds are open to the public (Mon–Sat 9.30am–12.30pm & 2–5.30pm; free); long-term renovations of the palace itself are still in progress.

The main reason for a visit to Estói, however, is the Roman site at **Milreu** (Tues–Sun 10am–12.30pm & 2.30–5pm; free), a ten-minute walk downhill from the square. Known to the Romans as Ossonoba, the town that once stood here predated Faro and was inhabited from the second to the sixth century AD. The surviving ruins are associated with a peristyle villa – one with a gallery of columns surrounding a courtyard – and dominated by the apse of a temple, which was converted into a Christian basilica in the third century AD, making it one of the earliest of all known churches. The other recognizable remains are of a bathing complex with fragments of mosaic; the *apodyterium*, or changing room, with its stone benches and arched niches below for clothes is clearly visible. The site was finally abandoned in the eighth century AD, after which date the Moors founded Faro to the south.

Back in the village, there's good **food** at *Victor's*, just off the square, where you'd be hard pushed to spend more than 1500$00 a head. There's also no fewer than eleven **bars** along and around the main street.

São Brás de Alportel

Seven kilometres north of Estói, **SÃO BRÁS DE ALPORTEL**, in a valley of the Serra do Caldeirão, also makes an appealing detour for those with a couple of hours to spare. Buses pull up in the main square, where, from its little circular booth, the **turismo** (Tues–Sat 9.30am–12.30pm & 2–5.30pm, Sun 9.30am–12.30pm; ☎289 842 211) will provide you with a map – though it's rather unnecessary given that everything lies within a three-minute walk.

Checking out the sights, therefore, doesn't take long: walk to the bottom of town to the church of **Senhor dos Passos** (signposted Igreja Matriz), for its views of the surrounding valleys. There's a fine open-air **swimming pool** (*piscina*) a couple of minutes along from here, from where you can cut up Rua Nova de Fonte to the main street, Rua Dr. José Dias Sancho. Here, the **Museu Etnográfico do Trajo Algarvio**, at no. 61 (Tues–Fri 10am–1pm & 2–5pm; Sat & Sun 2–5pm; 150$00), housed in an old mansion, is quite the best reason to come to São Brás, its alcoves and corridors full of traditional costumes and farming and domestic equipment. If you're the only person there (which is quite likely), you'll be given a personal tour, which consists of the ticket seller walking behind you saying "meat" and "cork" as you stare at various agricultural implements.

PRACTICALITIES

The quiet surroundings entice a few visitors to make the village their Algarve base. **Accommodation** isn't the good value it might be, but try for rooms (all with showers) at the *Residencial São Brás*, Rua Luís Bivar 27 (☎ & fax 289 842 213; ③), which runs off the main square, or at the slightly less expensive *Estalagem Sequeira* at Rua Dr. Evaristo Gago 9 (☎ & fax 289 843 444; ③), which provides modern en-suite rooms; both include breakfast in the price. Big spenders might want to stay at the very comfortable *Pousada de São Brás* (☎289 842 305, fax 289 841 726; ⑥), 2km north of town. The views from here are splendid, and there's an (expensive) restaurant, too; advance booking is essential in summer.

Bars and **restaurants** are sparse but try the excellent *Luís dos Frangos*, a five-minute walk up the Tavira road, or the *Savoy* (closed Sun lunch), on Rua Luís Bivar, past the *Residencial São Brás*. However, the best restaurant in the immediate area is the *Adega Nunes* (☎289 842 506; closed Sun), about 4km along the Faro road at Machados. It has a menu to suit most budgets and counts the President of Portugal among its customers.

Olhão and its ilhas

OLHÃO, eight kilometres east of Faro, is the largest fishing port on the Algarve and an excellent base for visiting the surrounding sandbank *ilhas*. It's an otherwise uneventful place, notwithstanding the rather surreal prose of a local brochure, which proclaimed Olhão home of the "amazing poodle of the Algarve. .. muscular and strong... [and] of valuable assistance to the fishermen for whom it dives into the water... to a depth of over four metres, to guide the fish into the nets". Unfortunately, the aquatic poodles were abandoned for more modern methods in the 1950s, though some are kept at the **Parque Natural** (daily 9am–12.30pm & 2–5.30pm; 250$00) around 3km east of town, signposted off the N125.

Once past the built-up outskirts, Olhão is quite an attractive town. There are no sights as such, but the flat roofs, outdoor stairways and white terraces of the old town are striking and give a North African look to the place. No surprise, then, that Olhão has centuries-old trading links with Morocco, as well as a small place in history for its uprising against the French garrison in 1808. Following the French departure, the local fishermen sent a small boat across the Atlantic to Brazil to transmit the news to the exiled king, João VI. The journey, completed without navigational aids, was rewarded after the king's restoration to the throne by the granting of a town charter.

The best view of the whitewashed cube-houses is from the bell tower of the seven-teenth-century parish church of **Nossa Senhora do Rosário** (Tues–Sun 9.30am–noon & 3–6pm), right in the middle of town. Outside, at the back of the church, an iron grille protects the chapel of **Nossa Senhora dos Aflitos**, where traditionally townswomen gather when there's a storm at sea to pray for their sailors amid candles and curious wax models of children and limbs.

The other obvious focus of the town is the **market**, held in the two modern redbrick buildings on the harbourside at the bottom of town. Open from the crack of dawn (Mon–Sat), there's meat, fruit and vegetables on one side, fish on the other, the latter hall full of such delights as swordfish heads propped up on the marble counters and squid ink running off the tables into the gutter.

Practicalities

The **train station** is at the northeastern edge of town, off Avenida dos Combatentes da Grande Guerra; the **bus terminal** is a few minutes away on Rua General Humberto Delgado. From either, it's a quick walk down to the main Avenida da República, a wide boulevard which leads into the city centre, a further five minutes' walk away. At the parish church, the avenue forks into two: follow Rua do Comércio, the main (pedes-trianized) shopping street, and when it rounds the corner you'll find the **turismo** (summer Mon 9.30am–12.30pm & 2–7pm, Tues 9.30am–1.30pm & 3–7pm, Weds & Sun 9.30am–12.30pm & 2–5.30pm Thur–Sat 9.30am–7pm; winter daily 9.30am–5.30pm, closed Tues; ☎289 713 936), which can provide a town map, advice on accommodation and sailing times of boats to the *ilhas*.

Accommodation

Accommodation can be hard to find in the height of summer, despite a fair scattering of **pensões**. Of these, first choice should be *Pensão Bela Vista*, Rua Teófilo Braga 65–67 (☎ & fax 289 702 538; ②), which has a range of bright rooms arranged around a tiled, flower-filled courtyard; from the turismo, turn left, then left again, and its sign is directly opposite. Second choice is the *Pensão Boémia*, slightly further out of the centre at Rua da Cerca 20, off Rua 18 de Junho (☎ & fax 289 714 513; ③); rooms come with shower and balcony. Nearer the sea the small and friendly *B & B City Lodge*, Rua da Verdade 6, off Av. 5 de Outubro (☎289 706 607, fax 289 723 709; ①), has some rooms with balconies overlooking the market as well as a communal kichen. Back in the centre, other options include two on Rua Vasco da Gama, the other fork off Av. da República: the *Pensão Bicuar* at no. 5 (☎289 714 816; ②), cheerful enough for the price and with smart communal areas; and the *Pensão Vasco da Gama* opposite, at no. 6 (☎289 702 785; ①). If all else fails, you should find room at the *Hotel Ria Sol*, Rua General Humberto Delgado 37 (☎289 705 267, fax 289 705 268; ③), an anonymous concrete hotel, by the bus station. The local **campsite** (☎289 700 300, fax 289 700 390) is at Marim, 3km east of town, and has a pool and good views of Armona. Buses from the Palace of Justice and Av. 5 Outubro run approximately hourly to Marim until 7.20pm during the week and also on Saturday mornings.

Eating and drinking

Rua do Comércio has its share of **cafés** with outdoor seating, and streets on either side harbour a few **restaurants**. For cheaper eating, there are two simple *casas de pasto* in the small square in front of the market, open for lunch and dinner, while the best places for local **fish** dishes are the nearby restaurants on Avenida 5 de Outubro, past the market towards the harbourside gardens. Here, *Santos* at no. 100, is the least touristy and most reasonably priced – its *arroz de marisco* is an enormous serving of prawns, crabs and clams for around 3000$00.

The ilhas: Armona and Culatra

Separate **ferries** leave for the *ilhas* of Armona and Culatra from the jetty at the eastern end of Olhão's municipal gardens, five minutes' walk from the market. There's a timetable posted at the kiosk; if it isn't open, you can buy tickets on the ferries. The **Ilha da Armona**, a fifteen-minute ride away, is reasonably accessible all year round (June & early-Sept 9–11 daily, July & Aug 14 daily; rest of year 3 daily; 150$00 one way), as are Culatra (35min) and Farol (45min), on the **Ilha da Culatra** (June & Sept 7 daily; rest of year 4 daily; 165$00 to Culatra, 210$00 to Farol one way), though in summer you may prefer to get the boat to Farol from Faro; see p.445.

Ilha da Armona

Ferries drop their passengers at the southern end of the single settlement on **Ilha da Armona** – a long, crowded strip of holiday chalets and huts that stretches right across the island on either side of the main path. It's a fifteen-minute walk to the ocean, where the beach disappears into the distance; a short walk will take you to attractive stretches of sand and dune – the further you go, the greater the privacy.

There are a few **bar-restaurants** by the jetty, while at the other end, the self-service *Santo António* has a terrace overlooking the beach where you can tuck into sardines, salad and beer. There are no *pensões* or hotels on Armona and camping on the beach is frowned upon, but Orbitur (☎289 714 173; ③) operates a series of holiday **bungalows** on the island – though you'll be lucky to find anywhere in high season.

Ilha da Culatra

The **Ilha da Culatra** is another huge sand spit, though very different in character from Armona, its northern shore dotted with a series of fishing settlements, mixed with an incongruous sprinkling of holiday chalets. The ferry's first port of call, **Culatra**, is the largest settlement, though **Farol**, the second stop, is far more agreeable. It's a rather commonplace, untidy village of holiday homes, but is edged by beautiful tracts of beach on the ocean side, though the mainland-facing beach is grubby. Once again, **camping** on the island is not encouraged, and in any case tends to be conspicuous among the fishing villages. In Faro, *À do João Restaurant* (☎289 702 001), serves some fine seafood dishes such as *cataplana*, which will set you back around 3500$00 per person. If you're considering staying, the best you can do is to ask around in the market where you might be able to pick up a private room for approximately 5000$00.

Tavira and around

Situated 30km east of Faro, **TAVIRA** is one of the most beautiful towns on the Algarve and a clear winner if you are looking for a base on the eastern stretch. It's sited on both sides of the broad Rio Gilão, which is overlooked by ancient balconied houses and straddled by two low bridges, one of Roman origin. This is an eminently attractive ensemble, which persuades many to stay longer than planned – particularly those intent on lounging around on the superb island beach of the **Ilha de Tavira**, which lies within easy reach of the town by year-round ferry. There are also several quieter spots in the area, such as **Pedras d'el Rei** a holiday village nearby, and, for some excellent seafood the tiny fishing village of **Santa Luzia**. In any case, Tavira itself is certainly worth visiting, at any time of the year. Despite ever-increasing numbers of visitors and encroaching development, it continues to make its principal living as a tuna-fishing port, and fish dinners at restaurants along the palm-lined river are in themselves a powerful incentive to stop.

The Town

Founded as long ago as 400 BC, Tavira's greatest period of prosperity came in the sixteenth to eighteenth century, the age that produced most of its graceful array of churches and mansions. In the old town streets on both sides of the river, numerous houses retain fine old doorways and coats-of-arms.

From the arcaded **Praça da República**, by the river, it's a short climb up into the old town following Rua da Galeria. Ahead of you stands the **Igreja da Misericórdia** with its once fine (now badly worn), carved stone doorway from 1541 depicting, among other decorative twirls, a couple of lute-playing figures. Inside there's a fine tiled interior and gilt altar, but unfortunately the church is almost always locked. Turn left here and a couple of hundred metres up the cobbled street are the ruins of the **Castelo** (Mon–Fri 9.30am–5.30pm; free), half hidden amid landscaped gardens on a low hill in the centre of town. From the walls you can look down over the peculiarly Oriental rooftops and the town's twenty other churches all of which are currently kept locked,

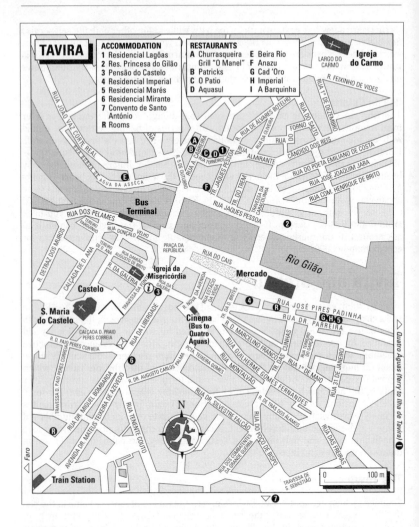

TAVIRA

ACCOMMODATION
1 Residencial Lagôas
2 Res. Princesa do Gilão
3 Pensão do Castelo
4 Residencial Imperial
5 Residencial Marés
6 Residencial Mirante
7 Convento de Santo
   António
R Rooms

RESTAURANTS
A Churrasqueira
  Grill "O Manel"
B Patricks
C O Patio
D Aquasul
E Beira Rio
F Anazu
G Cad 'Oro
H Imperial
I A Barquinha

although there is talk of opening up three or four during the summer months – ask at the tourist office for details. Adjacent to the castle, the whitewashed **Santa Maria do Castelo** contains the tomb of Dom Paio Peres Correia, who reconquered much of the Algarve, including Tavira in 1242, from the Moors. Fittingly, the church stands on the site of the former mosque.

The best part of Tavira is the **river**. Gardens lined with cafés run as far as the lively harbourside **market** (Mon–Sat mornings only), beyond which are moored the fishing boats that still operate out of the river port. This is a great place to wander, among the nets and marine clutter, stopping at one of the restaurants or more basic fishermen's bars, most of which serve up memorable meals, generally involving big tuna steaks.

Practicalities

Tavira's **bus terminal** is by the river, from where it's a two-minute walk to the old bridge and Praça da República. The **train station** is 1km from the centre of town, straight up the Rua da Liberdade and at the end of Avenida Dr. Mateus Teixeira de Azevedo. There's a **turismo** at Rua da Galeria 9 (summer Mon 9.30am–12.30pm & 2–7pm, Tues 9.30am–1.30pm & 3–7pm, Weds & Sun 9.30am–12.30pm & 2–5.30pm Thu–Sat 9.30am–7pm; winter Wed–Mon 9.30am–5.30pm; ☎281 322 511), up the steps just off Praça da República. **Bikes** and mopeds can be rented from Lorisrent (☎281 324 548, fax 281 324 548), next to the turismo, where you'll pay from around 800$00 a day for a bicycle, or Rent-a-Bike Rua do Forno, 22 (*exploratio@hotmail.com*, ☎281 321 973) on the other side of the river who also rent mountain bikes (1000$00 a day; delivered to your hotel) and organize cycling tours (2000$00 for a four-hour tour including bike and guide) to the Nature reserve of Ria Formosa and the countryside around Tavira. **Taxis** line up in the praça.

Accommodation

As throughout the Algarve, be warned that places are at a premium during the summer season; if a tout offers you a room, take it, at least for the first night, and look around on your own later on. The tourist office can help with **private rooms** if you have no luck at any of the *pensões* listed below. There are also informal rooms, which are part of a private house and have shared bathrooms (all ①), at Rua José Pires Padinha 44, opposite the market; Rua da Porta Nova 4, 300m north from the old bridge; and Travessa M. Bombarda 4, closer to the train station – these ones have access to a kitchen. The nearest **campsite** is on the Ilha de Tavira, for which see p.454.

Pensão do Castelo, Rua da Liberdade 22 (☎281 323 942). Very centrally located, with views of the castle and river. Recently renovated and extended, it's a rambling place and has clean rooms all with separate bathrooms; rates drop out of season. Also rents apartments from 12,000–16,000$00 adjoining the *pensão* which accommodates up to four people. ③.

Convento de Santo António, Atalaia (☎ & fax 281 325 632). Very elegant rooms in an old, converted convent with swimming pool and roof-terrace, located 1km out of Tavira on the Faro road. Breakfast is served in the arched courtyard. Minimum stay four nights in summer; three in winter. Booking essential. ③.

Residencial Imperial, Rua José Pires Padinha 24 (☎281 322 234). Small *residencial* next to the restaurant (see below); avoid the noisy street-facing rooms and go for one of those overlooking the gardens and river. Breakfast included. ②.

Residencial Lagôs, Rua Almirante Cândido dos Reis 24 (☎281 322 252). Situated on the north side of the river, this has attractive rooms and rooftop views. There's an added bonus in the top-notch budget restaurant, *Bica*, below – though the rooms above the kitchen can get uncomfortably hot. ①.

Residencial Marés, Rua José Pires Padinha 134–140 (☎281 325 815, fax 281 325 819). Extremely pleasant rooms with tiled floors, *azulejos* in the bathrooms, balconies over the river and a decent restaurant below. Breakfast included. Rates drop in the winter. ⑤.

Residencial Mirante, Rua da Liberdade 83 (☎281 322 255). Opposite the post office, and sporting a faded tiled facade, this place is all right, but some of the rooms overlooking the street are a bit noisy. ③.

Residencial Princesa do Gilão, Rua Borda d'Àgua de Aguiar 10–12 (☎ & fax 281 325 171). A modern, white building with *azulejo*-decorated interior, this friendly *residencial* stands right on the quayside. Go for a room at the front, with a balcony overlooking the river. Breakfast included. ③.

Eating, drinking and nightlife

A succession of **cafés** and **restaurants** front the gardens along the riverbank, while further down, on Rua José Pires Padinha, tables edge out on to the riverside. For some of the best cakes in town, try *Tavirense*, an old-fashioned *pastelaria* on Rua Marcelino Franco 19, opposite the cinema. As for **drinking**, there are a couple of cafés in the main square, plenty of nameless backstreet **bars** with matchstick-chewing old-timers for company, and a couple of trendier spots north of the river, including the *Arco Bar* on Rua Almirante Cândido dos Reis 67 – a gay-friendly place attracting a laid-back crowd. For something a bit different there's *Malfado,* at Rua Torneiros 22, where you can get down to African and Brazilian sounds on the small dance floor till 4am, fuelled by inexpensive drinks.

Tavira's only **disco**, *UBI*, is reached by following Rua Almirante Cândido dos Reis to the outskirts of town; it's housed in the huge shiny, metallic warehouse on the right. Playing a mix of house, Latin and techno grooves, (entrance is 1000$00 – which includes two drinks) it's open Friday and Saturday from 10pm–8 or 9am; the locals warm up with a few pre-clubbing drinks in the *Bubi Bar* in the same building.

RESTAURANTS

Anazu, Rua Jacques Pessoa 11–13. Large bar-restaurant on the riverfront – a good place to sit out at sunset. It also has Internet access for 800$00/hr.

Aquasul, Rua Torneiros 11–13. Serving excellent wood-oven-cooked pizzas, as well as a range of international dishes, this French-owned restaurant on the north side makes a pleasant change of cuisine. Although there are no vegetarian dishes on the menu, the owner will happily cook something up using organic ingredients. Expect to pay around 2000$00 for pizza and drinks. Closed Dec–Feb.

A Barquinha, Rua José Pires Padinha 142. This unpretentious bar-restaurant, along the riverfront from the market, has seats outside and serves a good tuna steak, with stewed onions and fries. A plateful, wine and coffee comes to 1900$00.

Beira Rio, Rua Borda da Àgua de Assêca 46–48. This riverside bar-restaurant with tree-shaded tables is a nice venue for a drink but the food's pricey. Situated on the west side of the bridge, opposite the bus station.

Bica, Rua Almirante Cândido dos Reis 22–24. Inexpensive, excellent Portuguese meals on the north side of the river, under the *Residencial Lagôas*. From around 1500$00 a head.

Cad'Oro, Rua José Pires Padinha 150. Upmarket riverfront fish restaurant with live music on certain summer evenings. Around 3000$00 and up for a full meal, while, outside of the summer months, there's a range of *pratos do dia* for between 750–1300$00.

Imperial, Rua José Pires Padinha 22. Just back from the riverside gardens, the *Imperial* is well known for its seafood, including clams and tuna. A decent meal here will cost around 3000$00.

Churrasqueira Grill "O Manel", Rua Almirante Cândido dos Reis 6. Reliable Portuguese grill restaurant near the *Bica* with most meals around 1500–2000$00.

O Patio, Rua Dr. António Cabreira 30. Pricey fish restaurant with French-influenced dishes and attractive summer roof-terrace. From 3000$00 and upwards.

Patrick's, Rua Dr. António Cabreira 25–27. Welcoming *adega*-style, English-run bar-restaurant with food to match. Full English breakfasts (990$00) served until 3pm – which even come with mugs of English tea. However, the speciality of the house is the mouthwatering *piri-piri* prawns; otherwise there's a daily changing menu that includes curries, and there's always a vegetarian option.

Ilha de Tavira

The **Ilha de Tavira** stretches southwest from Tavira almost as far as Fuzeta, some fourteen kilometres away. For most of its length the landward side of the island is a dank morass of mud flat, but at the eastern tip the mud disappears and the *ilha* ends in an expanse of sand and sea. The beach is enormous, backed by tufted dunes, and over the years its growing popularity has led to a certain amount of development: at the end of the main path, which runs from the jetty through a small chalet settlement, there are water-sports facilities, beach umbrellas and loungers, and half a dozen bar-restaurants facing the sea. But, rather than spoiling things, this has fostered something of a good-time feel at the beach. The **campsite** (☎281 324 455; May to mid-Oct), a minute from the sands and with a well-stocked mini-market, shelters a youthful crowd, and the bars pump out music into the night. The *Sunshine Bar* serves a tasty tuna steak, and has a full breakfast menu and vegetarian options, too.

Buses (July to mid-Sept hourly 8am–8pm; June Mon–Fri 5 daily, Sat & Sun hourly) leave from the bus station in Tavira, stopping outside the cinema, for the ten-minute trip to the jetty at **Quatro Águas**, 2km east of town. Here there's a snack bar and the very swish *Quatro Águas* seafood restaurant – highly regarded by locals. Out of season, you've the choice of a half-hour walk from the town (along the river, past the market, and just keep going) or a taxi. The boats to the island (summer every 15min; winter hourly; 200$00 return) take just five minutes and start running at around 8am – the frequency of departures depend a lot on the weather during winter. The last boats back from the island are at about 9pm in April, May and Sept, at 11pm in June, July and at midnight in August. In the winter ask the ferryman on your way over what time the last boat returns.

Less frequent boats to the island depart from the quayside just downstream from the fish market in town; up to six daily departures from July to mid-Sept (200$00 return).

Pedras d'el Rei, Santa Luzia and Barril

If you're after a little more space in summer, it's better to head 4km west from Tavira to **PEDRAS D'EL REI**, a holiday village, which, while a bit sterile, is not too big. Chalets can be hired on a short-term basis at reasonable prices for small groups, though the complex is usually full in July and August. Fairly regular **buses** (Mon–Sat only) connect the resort with Tavira on the main highway N125, alternatively, you can walk along the coastal road to Pedras in about an hour. Along the coastal road from Tavira to Pedras d'el Rei is the fishing village of **SANTA LUZIA**, a satisfying side-trip which has a trio of highly recommended seafood restaurants. Arguably the best of these is the friendly *Restaurante Baixamar* (closed Mon), which is directly opposite the quay. All three restaurants charge around 2500$00 to 3000$00 a head, including wine.

From Pedras, you cross a causeway and then catch a miniature train (200$00 return) which shuttles backwards and forwards across the mud flats to the beach of **BARRIL** on the Ilha de Tavira. It's a few minutes' walk right or left to escape the tourist facilities at the terminus, and there you are: miles of beautiful, peaceful, dune-fringed beach. Take your own food and drink, though, since the relative isolation means high prices in the couple of café-bars here. This whole area constitutes the **Parque Natural da Ria Formosa**, a nature reserve where you can watch tens of thousands of fiddler crabs, scuttling about and waving their claws at the sky.

East of Tavira: to Vila Real

Just to the east of Tavira, the sand spit that protects much of the eastern Algarve from the developers starts to thin out, merging with the shoreline beach at Manta Rota, 12km away. The result is predictable: **Cabanas**, **Manta Rota** and **Alagoa** have all been intensively developed, although the beaches at all three resorts are splendid, if crowded in summer; there are more alluring sandy stops at **Praia Verde** and **Monte Gordo**. However, there is one surprise on this part of the coast: for some reason, the small hamlet of **Cacela Velha** (not to be confused with Vila Nova de Cacela, 2km inland) is barely touched by tourism.

You can reach Cabanas and Monte Gordo by **bus** from Tavira; for Manta Rota, the only services are from Vila Real (or Monte Gordo); and for Praia Verde, the best you can do is get off any bus to Vila Real on the highway and walk down the side road. You can of course always **walk** along the beach: from Manta Rota it's around thirty minutes to Alagoa, another twenty minutes to Praia Verde, and forty more to Monte Gordo.

Cacela Velha

Ten kilometres from Tavira, **CACELA VELHA** is perched on a rocky bluff overlooking the sea, surrounded by olive groves, and home to an old church and the remains of a fort. It is spectacularly pretty – a reminder of how the Algarve must have looked half a century ago. Naturally enough, the hamlet is short on facilities, but it has a little restaurant, a tapas bar, a couple of cafés and a handful of **rooms** that are snapped up quickly in the summer. The beach below the village is a delight and it's possible to arrange a lift over to the sand bar just offshore.

To get here, you need to jump off the Tavira–Vila Real bus on the highway, just before Vila Nova de Cacela, from where it's a fifteen-minute walk down a side road to the village.

Manta Rota, Praia de Alagoa and Praia Verde

Two kilometres further along the coast at **MANTA ROTA**, a group of half a dozen restaurants cluster at the entrance to the beach, all serving platters of sardines and grilled swordfish and tuna. There's not much else to hang about for; the main road is a fifteen-minute walk up from the beach. **PRAIA DE ALAGOA** is more of a resort, backed by white villas and apartments. Here, there's a line of beach umbrellas and beach bars, drinks kiosks and water sports on hand. Just past Algoa, the once attractive hillside above the sands at **PRAIA VERDE** is starting to go the way of neighbouring resorts as building sites replace woodland. However, a walk up the hill will reward you with a splendid panoramic view from the lookout at the top, and the beach below, served by a couple of drinks kiosks-cum-beach-bars, is still much less crowded than others along the coast. Further east, towards Monte Gordo, the beach becomes more unkempt, backed by scrubby dunes, but the sands are much less likely to be crowded in summer.

Monte Gordo

MONTE GORDO is the last resort before the Spanish border and the most built-up of the eastern holiday towns. White hotels overlook the wide, clean sands, on which are scattered a profusion of beach café-restaurants with studiously similar menus and inflated prices; the *Mota* is not a bad choice. For something a little less expensive you could also try *O Jamie* on the main square, which does excellent lunchtime snacks.

From the casino on the seafront, the main Avenida Vasco de Gama leads back before turning into Rua Pedro Álvares Cabral, off which on the west side is the **bus stop**, by the parish church. There are **rooms** advertised at various bars in town; out of season, it's worth checking on discounts at the hotels with the **turismo** (summer daily 9.30am–7pm; reduced hours in winter; ☎281 544 495), next to the casino. If you want to stay right on the beach, then the *Vasco da Gama*, Av. Infante Dom Henrique (☎281 510 900, fax 281 510 901; ⑥), is probably your best bet, a nice place with lots of water sports and kids' facilities. Monte Gordo is also the site of the last – and largest – **campsite** (☎281 510 970, fax 281 511 932) on this stretch of the Algarve.

Vila Real de Santo António

The border town and harbour of **VILA REAL DE SANTO ANTÓNIO** has suffered a marked change in character since the completion of a bridge across the Rio Guadiana, 4km to the north of town. Fewer cars and tourists now clog the streets in summer since anyone bound for Spain can now drive (or catch a bus) straight there. Still, you may want to call in anyway, not least because it's one of the more architecturally interesting towns on the Algarve. The original town was demolished by a tidal wave at the beginning of the seventeenth century, and the site stood empty until it was revived in 1774 by the Marquês de Pombal. Eager to apply the latest concepts of town planning, Pombal used the same techniques he had already pioneered in the Baixa quarter of Lisbon and rebuilt Vila Real on a grid plan. The whole project only took five months – a remarkable achievement, but a startling waste of resources, as it transpired that the hewn stone that Pombal had dragged all the way from Lisbon could have been quarried a couple of miles up the road.

The Town

The central grid built by Pombal radiates out from the handsome square that bears his name, ringed by orange trees and low, white buildings, a couple of which are pleasant outdoor cafés. The **Museu Municipal Manual Cabanas** is currently being moved to the north side of the square; it's unclear at the moment what the new manifestation will be like, or when it will be open. Also on the square the **Centro Cultural** (Mon–Fri 10am–1pm & 2pm–8pm, Sat 10am–1pm & 4–8pm, Sun 4–8pm; ☎281 511 736; free) is dominated by reconstructions of local life in bygone days and hosts a changing programme of art exhibitions and music. Until the new **turismo** opens up next door, the centro is also the only source of tourist information. The surrounding streets have a certain low-key charm, bristling with linen shops, electrical retailers and grocers, though sadly the old central **market** – a couple of blocks up from the square – with its Moorish domes, is under restoration.

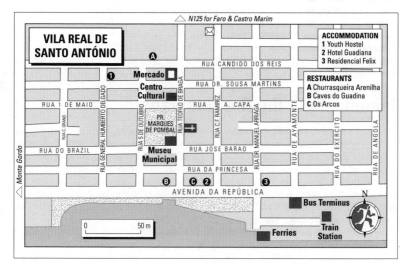

Admittedly, once you've had a beer and a wander around the shops there isn't a great deal else to do, though head down to the riverside **gardens** before you leave. There are more cafés here, an ice-cream stall or two, some rather touching public notices ("The garden is your friend – respect it"), and fine views across to the splash of white that is Ayamonte in Spain.

Practicalities

Vila Real is the eastern terminal of the Algarve railway, and **trains** pull up at Vila Real Guadiana – the tatty little station on the riverfront, while **buses** stop at a terminus just in front of here. If you're heading on to Spain (or elsewhere in Portugal come to that), you really shouldn't need to stay. Should you want to, **hotel** choices include the *Residencial Felix*, a block west of the bus terminal at Rua Dr. Manuel Arriaga 2 (☎281 543 791; ③), where the eager-to-please owners oversee little rooms with wooden floors and a clean separate bathroom; and the *Hotel Guadiana* at Av. da República 94, overlooking the gardens and river (☎281 511 482, fax 281 511 478; ④), which has a fine old Art Deco frontage and breakfast included in the price. Alternatively, there's a **youth hostel** in town at Rua Dr. Sousa Martins 40 (☎ & fax 281 544 565; ③); it's open all year round but fills up quickly in summer.

Among the **restaurants**, there's a line of half-a-dozen similarly priced places along the avenida (beyond Rua 5 de Outubro), all with outdoor seats overlooking the river. *Os Arcos* at Av. da República 45 is pretty good, at around 2000\$00 a meal. However, the *Caves do Guadiana*, at no. 90, has long been considered the best in town. It's got a nice tiled, vaulted interior and you'll pay under 3000\$00 for a full meal. Prices are much cheaper at the two or three modest places just off the riverfront avenue; while for grilled meats, try the *Churrasqueira Arenilha*, Rua Cândido dos Reis, opposite the market building, where a full meal will cost 2500\$00. **Drinks** and coffee are best taken in the bars on the square.

Crossing the border

Two daily **buses** (9.30am & 5.15pm) run from Vila Real across the bridge to Ayamonte in Spain (15min), continuing on to Huelva and Seville, the total journey taking three hours. **Coming from Spain**, two similarly timed services from Ayamonte run through Vila Real and on to Tavira and Faro. There are timetables posted at the bus terminus, and remember that, for most of the year, Spanish time is one hour ahead.

Inland: along the Rio Guadiana

North of Vila Real, the **Rio Guadiana** forms the border with Spain and provides a little-travelled diversion to some of the less spoiled parts of the region. **Buses** from Vila Real follow the N122, which runs inland of the river, calling at the tiny villages of Castro Marim, Odeleite and Alcoutim, each with a smattering of interest. Best of all, though, is a **boat trip** up the river itself. There are usually summer tourist charters offered in Monte Gordo or Vila Real: at around 7500\$00 per person they're not especially cheap, but you do get a barbecue lunch and plenty of swimming opportunities along the way. You should also be able to arrange river trips in Alcoutim, paying around 4000\$00 per hour for the boat – talk to the helpful turismo there.

Castro Marim

The little village of **CASTRO MARIM**, tucked away 5km north of Vila Real (several buses daily), was once a key fortification protecting Portugal's southern coast. Marim was the first headquarters of the Order of Christ (1319) and is the site of a huge **castle** (daily 9am–6pm; free) built by Afonso III in the thirteenth century. The massive ruins are all that survived the earthquake of 1755, as well as those of the smaller fort of São Sebastião across the village, but it's a pretty place with fine views of the impressive bridge to Spain. A small museum inside the castle walls (not always open) displays local archeological finds and the like. The **turismo** is in Praça 1º de Maio (Mon–Fri 9.30am–12.30pm & 2–5.30pm, Sat 9.30am–noon; ☎281 531 232), just below the castle.

The marshy area around Castro Marim has been designated as a nature reserve, the **Reserva Natural do Sapal**, so there's no danger of its being despoiled; the reserve office inside the castle has more information (Mon–Fri 9am–12.30pm & 2–5.30pm; ☎281 531 141). One of the area's most unusual and elusive inhabitants is the extraordinary, ten-centimetre-long, swivel-eyed, opposing-toed, Mediterranean chameleon – a harmless, slow-moving lizard that's severely threatened elsewhere by habitat destruction.

There are several **places to eat** in the village, including the *Eira Gaio*, just up Rua 25 de Abril from the turismo, or the nearby *Manuel de Agua* which serves excellent grilled fish from about 3000$00 per person. For drinks and snacks, try either the *Atlantis* or *Casa do Pasto Rodrigues*, both on Rua de São Sebastião, west of Praça 1º de Maio and the turismo.

Alcoutim

If you're feeling particularly energetic, you could walk the 15km north along the riverside road from Foz de Odeleite to **ALCOUTIM**, a beautiful route through unspoilt countryside. The village is extremely attractive, too, with a long history as a river port, dominated in turn by Greeks, Romans and Arabs who all fortified the heights with various structures over the centuries; the **castle** ruins date from the fourteenth century and offer fine views over the town and the River Guadiana. For further diversion, fishing boats ferry across the river to the **Spanish village of Sanlúcar**, a mirror image of Alcoutim, with its own ruined castle; the local boatmen will take you across for 100$00 or so.

A small **turismo** (summer Mon 9.30am–12.30pm & 2–7pm, Tues 9.30am–1.30pm & 3–7pm, Weds & Sun 9.30am–12.30pm & 2–5.30pm, Thu–Sat 9.30am–7pm; winter Wed–Mon 9.30am–5.30pm; ☎281 546 179) is located in the main square, Praça da República, right in the centre of the village. They're helpful people and can point you in the right direction for overnight stays: there are private **rooms** at *Casa D*, Edificio Turístico near the church (☎964 041 905; ③). There's also a rather nice fifty-bed **youth hostel** (☎ & fax 281 546 004) just out of the village, across the Ribeira Cadavais, with canoe rental among its attractions; cross the bridge beyond Praça da República and follow the signs. Alcoutim's **cafés** and **restaurants** cluster around the Praça: the *Afonso* and *Rogério* in the square, and *O Soeiro* a little way down Rua do Município are recommended.

One or two **buses** a day run back down to Vila Real, and there's a twice-weekly service north to Mertola (p.430) and Beja (p.425).

THE WESTERN ALGARVE

The **western Algarve** stretches for a hundred kilometres from Faro to Sagres and encompasses Portugal's most intense tourist developments. The most extreme section is between Faro and Lagos, where the beaches and coves are fronted by an almost continuous stretch of villas, apartments and hotels. The purpose-built resorts feature marinas, golf links and tennis centres – all fine if you've booked a holiday, but not especially inviting for casual visitors.

Albufeira is one of the biggest – and most enjoyable – resorts and other decent stops include **Portimão**, nearby **Praia da Rocha** and **Lagos**, the last of which still retains a bit of local character. All of these places are packed to the gills in summer and, particularly if you have transport, you might do better to seek a base inland at the old market towns of **Loulé** or **Silves**, and drive down to the nearest strip of beach. **Caldas de Monchique**, a nineteenth-century spa town, and neighbouring **Monchique** are other inland options, though these are a good forty minutes' drive from the sea.

Until recently, the coast **west of Lagos** was the place to escape the worst of the crowds, but development – in the shape of a fast road and burgeoning enclaves of holiday villas – has been horrifically quick. However, erstwhile fishing villages such as Burgau and Salema still teeter on the edge of complete exploitation. Beyond these villages the road cuts high above the sea, across a cliff-edged plateau, and down to **Sagres**, with its dramatic scenery and busy nightlife.

The coast **north of Sagres**, heading towards Alentejo, is the last undeveloped swathe of the Algarve – partly because the sea is distinctly colder and often pretty wild. If you can brave the climate, you might like to try low-key villages such as **Vila do Bispo**, **Carrapateira**, **Aljezur** and **Odeceixe**, all of which have magnificent local beaches. These attract a rather more youthful and "alternative" crowd than resorts on the Algarve proper; their combination of nude sunbathing, surf and parties is not everyone's idea of an idyll.

Quinta do Lago to Vilamoura

The coast immediately northwest of Faro is unremitting holiday village territory, with little promise for anyone simply in search of a quiet beach and an unsophisticated meal. This is territory for those into "Sportugal" – as the tourist board promotes the lesiure complexes – and none too fussy about a local environment. You have to head inland for even the barest whiff of the old Algarve, best encountered at the historic market town of **Loulé**.

Loulé makes for a pleasant lunchtime or evening break for those staying on the Quarteira strip of coast. Independent travellers may find it the best place for a night away from the crowds, though it's probably more realistic to stay in Faro and see the places below by **bus**; departures are roughly hourly throughout the day.

Quinta do Lago, Vale do Lobo, Almancil and Quarteira

The first of the resorts, **QUINTA DO LAGO** is a vast, luxury holiday village with its own golf course, sports complex and opulent hotel. There's a decent beach, too, the **Praia do Ançāo**, and more of the same at **VALE DO LOBO**, next door, with serious-money hotels, golf courses, a riding school, and the David Lloyd Tennis Centre.

Back on the highway, just before **ALMANCIL**, the church of **São Laurenço** (Mon 2.30–6pm, Tues–Sat 10am–1pm & 2.30–6pm; 200$00) comes as a surprise amid the development. Built in the eighteenth century, it survived the earthquake of 1755 and retains its superb fully tiled interior depicting the life of St Laurence – in particular, graphically illustrated panels of his martyrdom. In Almancil itself, the *Pensão Santa Teresa*, Rua do Comércio 13 (☎289 395 525, fax 289 395 364; ③), is one of the more reasonably priced places to stay in this entire area.

The first proper town west of Faro is **QUARTEIRA**, 22km away, with a good weekly market and an attractive stretch of sand – though development has overwhelmed most of what was once pleasant about Quarteira. The **bus terminus** (☎289 301 823) is a couple of blocks back from the beach, on Avenida Dr. Sá Carneiro, with the **turismo** on Praça do Mar by the beach (summer daily 9.30am–7pm; open July & Aug 9.30am–11pm; winter Mon–Sat 9.30am–5.30pm, Sun 9.30am–12.30pm & 2–5.30pm; ☎289 389 209). They should be able to help with finding accommodation, though if you want to scout around the cheaper **pensões** try the very pleasant *Pensão Miramar* at Rua Gonçalo Velho 8, off the seafront (☎289 315 225; ③), or the *Pensão Romeu*, on the same street at no. 38 (☎289 314 114; ③). There's also a **campsite** (☎289 302 821, fax 289 302 822) 1km east of town; any bus to or from Faro runs right past it.

Loulé

LOULÉ, 11km inland from Quarteira, has a history similar to most of the towns in southern Portugal – Roman and Moorish occupation – and **castle ruins** to match. The castle walls are the best point to begin a look around town. They have been restored as a walkway and enclose a **Museu Municipal** (Mon–Sat 9am–5.30pm; free) of vaguely diverting historical bits and pieces. Between the museum and the thirteenth-century Gothic parish church nearby, a grid of whitewashed cobbled streets reveals numerous handicraft shops in which you're free to watch the craftsmen at work – lacemaking, in particular, is a flourishing local industry. On Saturdays, the town is transformed as the whole region seems to arrive en masse for a busy **country market**.

Loulé's most curious sight is a beehive-shaped monument on a nearby hilltop, out in the direction of Boliqueime, which you can't help but notice as you arrive in town. It turns out to be the sanctuary of **Nossa Senhora da Piedade**; adjacent is a faded sixteenth-century chapel currently closed for much-needed restoration.

PRACTICALITIES

The **bus terminal** (☎289 416 656) is on Rua Nossa Senhora de Fátima, a couple of minutes' walk from the old town area; there are regular services from Quarteira and from Faro. The **turismo** (Tues–Sat 9.30am–12.30pm & 2–5.30pm, Sun 9.30am–12.30pm ; ☎289 463 900) is inside the castle walls, at Largo Dom Pedro I, and can help you find **accommodation**. The cheapest place in town is *Hospedaria Zé*, Rua Nossa Senhora da Piedade 64 (☎289 463 385; ②), or try the clean *Residencial Iberica* at Av. Marçal Pacheco 157 (☎289 414 100; ③), which is a continuation of Avenida 25 de Abril, on the other side of Largo Gago Coutinho. If you have the money, a clear first choice is the comfortable *Loulé Jardim Hotel* at Praça Manuel de Arriaga 23 (☎289 413 094, fax 289 463 177; ④), a block south of Rua Nossa Senhora da Piedade.

There's a good range of **places to eat**. Among a cluster of restaurants around the parish church, the Igreja da São Francisco, *Las Bons Enfants*, Rua Eng. Duarte Pacheco 116, is known for its carefully prepared and pricey French cuisine (dinner only; closed Sun). There's also the less pricey, intimate *Bica Velha* at Rua Martim Moniz 17 (closed Sun); or the *Cavaco*, up at Largo de São Francisco 44, where the *cataplanas* are popular. For grilled chicken the place to go is *O Rei do Churrasco* at Rua Assenção Guimarães 84, the street below the park.

Vilamoura

Back on the coast and based around a king-sized marina, **VILAMOURA**, 3km west of Quarteira, is a constantly expanding resort, with a bewildering network of roads signposted to upmarket new hotels and leisure facilities, including some highly exclusive

golf courses. The beach is impressive – as it should be considering all the development – and, if you're not bothered by the crowds, enjoyable enough. On the outskirts, opposite the Mobil garage on the Vilamoura–Albufeira road, *Kadoc* – the Algarve's biggest **disco** – pulls in up to eight thousand revellers a night, and often hosts guest DJs from all over Europe.

The bus drops you next to the casino, one block from the beach, the **Praia da Marina**. The enormous and luxurious *Vilamoura Marinotel* (☎289 389 988, fax 289 389 869; ⑨) is visible, two minutes away, overlooking the marina. Bristling with yachting hardware, the marina makes for an interesting stroll and is really the only other reason to stop off here; you can settle down at one of the cafés and watch the leisured set fooling around on their boats. If you want a go yourself, consider a **cruise** on the *Condor de Vilamoura* (☎289 314 070), a schooner which operates out of the marina daily during the summer: tickets cost around 4000$00 for a three-hour trip, more like 8500$00 for a full-day trip and barbecue, up to Albufeira and back.

Albufeira and around

Every inch a resort, **ALBUFEIRA** tops the list of package-tour – especially British package-tour – destinations in the Algarve. It was once an unusually pretty village, with narrow, twisting lanes of whitewashed houses criss-crossing the high grey-red cliffs above a beautiful spread of beaches. These still exist, but they are all but engulfed by hundreds of new apartment buildings strung across the local hillsides. If you're looking for unspoiled Portugal, this isn't it – whatever the brochures might say. Nevertheless, Albufeira is still one of the nicer resorts, attracting a varied mix of holidaymakers: an ageing, well-heeled clientele who frequent the more expensive restaurants, and a younger contingent who seem to devote themselves to downing as much beer as is humanly possible.

There's still a Moorish feel to parts of central Albufeira, as well as the more tangible remnants of a Moorish castle – the original Arabic name of the town, *al-Buhera*, means "Castle-on-the-Sea". But the 1755 earthquake did for much of the town, and most of the modern centre is nondescript, though enlivened somewhat by a small fishing harbour and by street stalls selling leather, copper, clothes and ceramics.

None of this is of any consequence whatsoever to the summer crowds, who sleep and eat in town but spend their days at one of a dozen excellent cove-beaches in the vicinity. The **beach** fronting Albufeira itself – reached through a tunnel from the main Rua 5 de Outubro – is as good as any of these, flanked by strange tooth-like rock formations. If it's too crowded here, a relatively short bus (or taxi) ride can open up a number of other possibilities, the best of which are detailed on p.465. At night, the focus switches to Albufeira's central, pedestrianized streets and squares, lined with pavement cafés, bars and restaurants fronted by eager touts and waiters keen to entice you in.

Practicalities

If you're in Albufeira on a package holiday, you might well not be staying in the town at all, but in one of the handful of small resort-villages on either side, like Montechoro, Areias de São João or Praia da Oura. However, all have access to their own beaches and are, in any case, within two or three kilometres of the town centre, which you can reach on regular local buses or by taxi. Everyone else will arrive in Albufeira at the

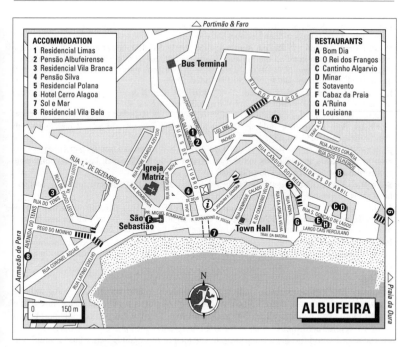

bus terminal (☎289 589 755) on Avenida da Liberdade, at the top of town, five minutes' walk from the central Largo Eng. Duarte Pacheco, just to the west of which is the
main street, Rua 5 de Outubro. At the end of here is the tunnel that's been blasted out
of the rock to give access to the town beach. Albufeira's "local" **train station** is actually 6km north of town at Ferreiras; a bus connects it with the bus terminal roughly
hourly (7am–8pm), or a taxi will set you back between 800$00 and 1000$00, depending on the time of day.

The **turismo** (daily: May & Sept 9.30am–7pm; July & August 10.30am–1pm & 5–11pm;
Oct–April 9.30am–12.30pm & 2–5.30pm; ☎289 585 279) is on Rua 5 de Outubro, close to
the tunnel. If you need to connect to the Internet, the friendly bookshop at Travessa dos
Telheiros 2B (next-door to *O Rei Dos Frangos*) can oblige for 1200–1600$00 per hour.

Accommodation
Finding a room can be difficult in high season since most of the **hotels and pensões** are block-booked by package holiday companies. Those listed below are a few
exceptions, which may have "independent" vacancies. Otherwise the tourist office
can help you find a **private room**, though they'll charge you for any phone calls they
make. Perhaps the best bet, when all is said and done, is to accept the offer of a room
from one of the touts who lurk around the bus station; you can always look around
on your own later if it's not up to scratch.

The finely appointed (and expensive) **Camping Albufeira** (☎289 587 629, fax 289
587 633) – complete with swimming pools, restaurants, bars, shops and tennis courts –
2km to the north of town, off the N396, has regular connections from the bus station
(any bus to Ferreiras passes it).

Pensão Albufeirense, Rua da Liberdade 16–18 (☎289 512 079). Comfortable but drab with fairly reasonably priced rooms, with and without bath. ②.

Hotel Cerro Alagoa, via Rápida, Apartado 2155 (☎289 583 100, fax 289 583 190). Extremely comfortable modern hotel on the hill above town, ten minutes' walk from the centre (take the steps at the eastern end of Av. 25 de Abril), with its own pool, gardens and gym, and courtesy bus to the local beaches. Buffet breakfast included. ⑦.

Residencial Limas, Rua da Liberdade 25–27 (☎289 514 025). A good, central choice, though the ten rooms fill quickly. Prices more than halve outside peak season. ④.

Residencial Polana, Rua Cândido dos Reis 32 (☎289 587 168, fax 289 586 850). A large, package-tour hotel, right in the thick of things – it's on a very noisy street full of bars. Rooms come with shower. Breakfast included. ④.

Pensão Silva, Trav. André Rebelo 18, off Rua 5 de Outubro (☎289 512 669, fax 289 514 318). Very close to the turismo, in an alleyway to the right as you face the beach. Small, just-about-comfortable rooms with shower, and a toilet down the hall. ③.

Sol e Mar, Rua Bernardino de Sousa (☎289 580 080, fax 289 587 036). Modern, low-slung, four-star hotel above the tunnel, overlooking the beach. ⑤.

Residencial Vila Bela, Rua Coronel Águas 32 (☎ & fax 289 512 101). Situated on the west side of the centre (at the junction with Av. do Ténis), this is an attractive *residencial* with it's own bar and balconied rooms overlooking a small swimming pool and the bay. Open April–Oct. ③.

Residencial Vila Branca, Rua do Ténis 4 (☎289 586 804, fax 289 586 592). A three-star *residencial* up in the new part of town, ten minutes from the beach. Modern, clean rooms with breakfast included. ③.

Eating

Albufeira has **restaurants** to match every budget – and most tastes. As well as Portuguese restaurants, there's also a whole range of places serving pizzas, Chinese and Indian food, even fish and chips. Naturally, you tend to get what you pay for (and prices here are ten percent higher than resorts further east), but for the better bargains head for the area behind the fishing harbour, to the east of the main beach. Stand around outside, perusing the menu, and you'll often be presented with enticements in the form of drinks vouchers and the like. The morning-after-the-night-before is well catered for in most restaurants and bars, with massive **English-style breakfasts** available until the sensible hour of 3pm.

Bom Dia, Rua Alves Correira 37–39. Modest little backstreet tourist restaurant with decent, mostly grilled Portuguese food, cheaper-than-usual prices and less predatory waiters than many. Affordable wine, too. Around 2000$00 for a full meal.

Cabaz da Praia, Praça Miguel Bombarda 7. Just up the hill from the main street and overlooking the beach, this serves excellent but expensive meals. The menu is mainly French-inspired, and the roof-terrace offers fine views – for which you're paying higher than usual prices, around 4000–5000$00 a head. Closed Thurs & lunchtime Sat.

Cantinho Algarvio, Trav. São Gonçalo de Lagos 3a. Mid-range restaurant with a large, varied menu where you can fill up on cuts of meat and other standard Portuguese dishes. A filling meal will cost around 2000–2500$00.

La Cigale, Olhos de Água (☎289 501 637). Nine kilometres east of Albufeira, and right on the beach, this renowned restaurant has a lovely terrace and high-quality food, including great seafood. Open for evening meals only; expect to pay around 4000$00.

Louisiana, Largo Cais Herculano 16–20. Drink cocktails on the terrace above the fishermen's beach and then retreat upstairs for selections from the grill menu.

Minar, Rua Diogo Cão, off Largo Cais Herculano. Surprisingly good Indian restaurant, where you'll eat for around 3000$00 – though you could get away with as little as 2000$00 if you stick to the vegetarian dishes.

O Rei dos Frangos, Trav. dos Telheiros 4, off Av. 25 de Abril. Common all over Portugal, but hard to pin down in resorts like Albufeira, here's a first-rate little *churrasqueira* – the chicken comes smothered in *piri-piri* and there's also grilled steak, swordfish and a speciality meat *cataplana*. Around 2000–3000$00 for a full meal.

A Ruina, Praia dos Pescadores, Largo Cais Herculano. Rustic old restaurant built into the hillside over the beach, serving fish fresh from the market. Eat on the beach, inside on one of two floors, or on the roof-terrace. Sardines and salad make a reasonably inexpensive lunch, but otherwise you're looking at 3500$00 and up for a full dinner.

Sotavento, Rua São Gonçalo de Lagos 16. Behind the fishing harbour, this small tiled bar-restaurant serves an affordable selection of Portuguese and international standards. Around 1500–2000$00.

Drinking and nightlife

Like the restaurants, Albufeira **bars** and **discos** are into promotion. There's not much to choose between them, and you may as well frequent those offering the cheapest drinks at the time – Happy Hour is an extremely flexible concept here. The main areas for carousing are along Rua São Gonçalo de Lagos, around Largo Eng. Duarte Pacheco and – for more of a late-night scene – along Rua Cândido dos Reis, Travessa Cândido dos Reis and Rua Alves Correira. Most bars stay open until around 3am, the discos until 4am or later in summer.

7/12, Rua São Gonçalo de Lagos 5. Central Albufeira disco on a street full of late-opening bars. The entry price of 1000$00 includes one drink and be warned it has a fairly strict dress code. Usually the last to close at around 6 to 7am.

Central Station, Largo Eng. Duarte Pacheco 44. Chic, modern bar which also doubles as a café/restaurant/*gelateria* depending on the time of day.

Classic Bar, Rua Cândido dos Reis 10. Loud and young, outside or in, with rudely named cocktails a speciality.

Jo Jo's, Rua São Gonçalo de Lagos 1. Friendly and easy-going family-run pub with British soccer and other sports on satellite TV. It also serves pub-style food which always includes a vegetarian option.

Kiss, Montechoro. Out of town, at the southern end of Montechoro, this is regarded as the best club around. The music is good, and the club often hosts foreign guest DJs, but it tends to be overcrowded and very glitzy; watch for posters advertising events.

Sir Harry's Bar, Largo Eng. Duarte Pacheco 36–37. Long-standing tourist institution on the square – though Sir Harry has long departed. The drinks here – including British beers – are over-priced and it's only really worth coming here for the nightly live music – you name it, the guitar-playing house musician can play it.

Sol Dourado, Largo Cais Herculano. A reasonably pricey grill-restaurant perched above the square, this has one of the nicer terrace-bars from which to watch the sun set over the water.

Zansi Bar, Rua Miguel Bombarda 7. Live music in the summer, karaoke and good-value international food served day and night. It's near the parish church.

The local beaches

The rocky red headlands just to the **west of Albufeira** are beautiful – and were largely inaccessible until the 1980s, when the development of a strip of villa resorts very much changed the landscape. There are no direct buses to these resorts, though the Albufeira–Portimão service drops passengers on the main road, a steep 2km walk distant. The main resorts – **SÃO RAFAEL**, **CASTELO** and **GALÉ** – spread back from small cove beaches with craggy, eroded rock faces, each place dominated by villa developments. At Praia de Galé is one of the Algarve's most exclusive hotels, the small, Moorish *Estalagem Vila Joya* (☎289 591 795, fax 289 591 201; ⑨), which sits right above the beach and includes dinner in its (extremely steep) prices.

Immediately **east of Albufeira**, ochre-red cliffs divide the coastline into a series of bays and beaches, all reached on local buses (6–9 daily) from the bus station. You can walk to the first, **PRAIA DA OURA**, just 2km from Albufeira, by heading up the steps at the end of Avenida 25 de Abril and following the road out of town; signposts point you down to the beach after 25 minutes. This, though, has been extensively developed and you might want to push on by bus to **OLHOS DE ÁGUA**, 7km further east, an erstwhile fishing village with a smaller beach (and *La Cigale* restaurant; see above). If this, too, is crowded, you can walk beyond it to other more isolated coves.

At **PRAIA DA FALÉSIA**, 10km east of Albufeira, and twenty minutes away by bus, the character of the coastline changes to produce one long tremendous stretch of sand, backed by unbroken red cliffs. Just before Falésia, the bus passes through Aldeia das Açoteias, a bewildering chalet and villa complex, from where four daily buses depart for Vilamoura and Quarteira (see pp.461–462).

Inland: São Bartolomeu de Messines and Alte

If you have transport, you can explore further **inland**, though you're not going to get much off the beaten track. Twenty kilometres to the north, the small town of **SÃO BARTOLOMEU DE MESSINES** preserves a sixteenth-century parish church, remodelled in Baroque style and incorporating interior columns decorated with twisted stone rope. There are buses here from Albufeira, Portimão and Silves, with enough services to provide for a day-trip.

From São Bartolomeu, it's 18km southwest to Silves, one possible lunch stop, or only about half that to the pretty village of **ALTE**, to the east, along the winding N124. Tacked across the hillside, a series of narrow, cobbled, mostly pedestrian streets lead up to the Fonte Grande, where there's a small rocky pool, artificially pumped full of water, a stream and an old mill, now converted into a restaurant that caters largely to the "safari" tours that stream out of Albufeira in jeeps into the surrounding countryside in search of the "real" Portugal. Notices by the water warn "No Fishing, Swimming or Washing", though you'd be hard pushed to attempt any in the first place. You can eat better at the *Café Central*, next to the church, back in the centre; and there are **rooms** available at the supermarket, close to the *fonte*, but no earthly reason to stay.

West towards Portimão

Heading west from Albufeira along the main N125, you'll pass through **PORCHES**, about halfway between Alcantarilha and Lagoa. This is where the most famous of the Algarve's hand-made **pottery** comes from. Thick, chunky and hand-painted, it has a good, heavy feel, and if you're looking for thoroughly impractical and ridiculously cheap presents to take home, this is the place to stop. Further on, **LAGOA** is best known for its wine; tours of the vineyards are arranged through local tourist offices.

Armação de Pêra and Praia da Marinha

Off the main road, down on the coast, is the resort of **ARMAÇÃO DE PÊRA**, which claims the largest beach in the Algarve (not a unique claim in these parts) and boasts caves and strange rock formations to the west, around which there are daily boat trips in the summer. It's not the greatest-looking of resorts by any means; modern buildings and apartments straggle along the town's main through-road, tempered only by the terraced gardens and cafés overlooking the central part of the sands. The remains of the town's fortified **walls** are at the eastern end of the seafront road; a terrace in front of a little white chapel provides sweeping views. The town **beach** is fine but if things are terribly crowded, head east along the beach for thirty minutes or so as far as the *Restaurante Salgados*, right on the sands and serving sardines and grilled fish and chicken – it's usually fairly quiet this far out.

There are good things to report about **Praia da Marinha**, too, reached from a turning south between Porches and Lagoa, 8km west of Armação (no bus services). A path leads from a parking area on the clifftop down to an immaculate sandy beach with a string of secluded coves, beautifully warm sea even in winter, and relatively few people with whom to share it. There's a café of uncertain hours on the sand by the path.

Practicalities

Armação de Pêra's **bus terminal** is at the eastern end of the town and there are regular services from Albufeira, Portimão and Silves. Walk up a block to the beach, at the fishing boats, and then head to the right along the seafront road, which changes its name two or three times as it makes for the centre. The **turismo** is along here (summer Mon–Sat 9.30am–9pm, Sun 9.30am–12.30pm & 2–9pm; winter daily 9am–1pm & 2.30–5.30pm; ☎282 312 145), around ten minutes' walk from the bus station, and is good for maps and accommodation information.

For **private rooms**, ask at *O Serol* restaurant, Rua da Praia (☎282 312 146; ②), overlooking the beach near the fishing boats – you'll pass it on the way in from the bus station – or at the butcher's shop, *Talho Caixinha* (☎282 312 886; ②), a couple of blocks back from here at the junction of Rua Dr. José António dos Santos and Rua Vasco da Gama. If you want something more upmarket, look no further than the *Hotel Garbe* (☎282 315 194; ⑧) – just up the seafront road from the turismo – which has a pool and terrace overlooking the beach and breakfast included in the price. The nearest **campsite**, *Praia da Armacão de Pera* (☎282 312 260, fax 282 315 379), is out of the centre, a kilometre back up the N269–1, towards highway N125.

There are countless **bars and restaurants**, all with more or less the same menus. For a bit more of a dining experience, two places that stand out are the *O Serol* restaurant itself, which sees a fair amount of local people tucking into its daily fish specials; and *A Santola*, in Largo 25 de Abril – adjacent to the old walls and terrace – which serves more expensive seafood accompanied by fine views; expect to pay 3000$00 plus here.

Carvoeiro and Estômbar

Further to the west, the small resort of **CARVOEIRO** can be reached by bus from Lagoa. Cut into the red sea cliffs, it remains quite an attractive place, despite a line of villa-apartments draped across the surrounding hills. The beach, however, is much too small to cope with the summer tourist influx, and rooms are virtually out of the question in high season. The resort also has quite a number of bars and restaurants, a tourist office situated on the beach, and boats offering fishing or beach trips.

Accessible by the coast road, a kilometre east, are the impressive rock formations of **Algar Seco**, where the cliffs form dramatic overhangs above narrow beaches – though there's a monstrous hotel a little further along. By way of contrast, a few kilometres inland is **ESTÔMBAR** (a stop for slow trains on the Algarve line), an unremarkable little town that was the birthplace of the eleventh-century Moorish poet Ibn Ammār. The town straggles down a steep hill in a confusion of narrow lanes – nothing very special, though at least you feel you're in Portugal.

Portimão, Praia da Rocha and around

Portimão is one of the largest towns on the Algarve, with a population of more than thirty thousand. It has made its living from fishing since pre-Roman times and with its site on the estuary of the Rio Arade, remains today a sprawling port, a major sardine-canning centre, and a base for the construction industries spawned by the tourist boom. Most visitors are just here for a day's shopping, taking time out from the resort of **Praia da Rocha**, 3km south of Portimão, which keeps a highly distinct identity of its own as a fairly upmarket resort. Just across the estuary to the east of Portimão is the workaday town of **Ferragudo**, which has a much smaller and less fancy beach. The coast road west of Praia da Rocha, towards Lagos, has been engulfed by a series of massive and graceless tourist developments of very little interest; only **Alvor** retains any of its original charm at all.

Portimão

As a town, **PORTIMÃO** is fairly undistinguished – most of the older buildings were destroyed in the 1755 earthquake – and it is pedestrianized shopping streets and graceless concrete high-rises that dominate. The mildewed **Igreja Matriz**, rebuilt after the earthquake, could do with a lick of paint, though the encircling streets are pleasant enough, filled with shops catering to the day-trippers – selling lace, shoes, jewellery, ceramics and wicker goods. However, the best part of town is undoubtedly the river-front gardens, with their outdoor cafés, and fishing **harbour** lined with open-air restaurants, serving grilled sardine lunches. Indeed, the streets just back from here – off Largo da Barca – are Portimão's oldest: narrow, cobbled and with more than a hint of their fishing-quarter past. Other reasons to come to town are the huge **market** on the first Monday of each month, held on the Estrada Velha de Praia da Rocha just out of town; and the **flea market** on the morning of the first and third Sunday of each month, which spreads along Avenida São João de Deus.

Practicalities

The **train station** is inconveniently located at the northern tip of town but the bus runs every 45 minutes (Mon–Fri) into the centre; a taxi costs about 600$00 or it's a fifteen-minute walk. **Buses** (including those to and from Praia da Rocha) pull up much more centrally, in the streets around the Largo do Dique, close to the river, from where it's a five-minute walk past the riverside gardens to the **quayside**, which stretches as far as the bridge over to Ferragudo. There's a **post office** in the main Praça Manuel Teixeira Gomes; and the Algarve's only **British consulate** further up the quayside at Largo Francisco A. Mauricio 7–1° (☎282 417 800).

The **turismo** (daily 9.30am–7pm; ☎282 419 131) is opposite the football stadium on Avenida Zeca Afonso – follow Rua do Pé da Cruz southwest off the map and take the first left – and might at least point you in the direction of **accommodation**, but it's scarcely worth staying when much nicer Silves or Lagos are so close. Still, if you do get stuck, the better-value options include the *Residencial O Pátio*, Rua Dr. João Vitorino Mealha 3 (☎ & fax 282 424 288; ③), or the spick-and-span *Pensão Arabi*, on Praça Manuel Teixeira Gomes 13 (☎282 460 250, fax 282 460 250; ④), the main river-side square. Another nice choice nearby is the *Residencial Roma*, at Rua Júdice Fialho 34 (☎ & fax 282 423 821; ③).

For **food**, any of the stalls that line the quayside, underneath the bridge, will serve half a dozen huge, charcoal-grilled sardines, with a plate of chips and half a bottle of the local wine for around 1000$00. On the other side of the road from the stalls, off Largo da Barca, there are a few very inexpensive workers' *tascas* – like *Taverna do Mar* – as well as some more elaborate fish restaurants, such as *Dona Barca*, in Largo da Barca. Otherwise, try the friendly *Bom Apetite Restaurant*, Rua Júdice Fialho 21, which serves authentic Portuguese cooking, including a splendid *arroz de marisco*. Or there's always the *Sateria Sambal*, Rua Santa Isabel 14 (closed Sun in winter), serving a nice range of Indonesian and Thai dishes from about 2500$00 a head. For **drinks**, *Casa Inglesa* in the main riverside praça is a thoroughly pleasant place with a bit of character unlike many of the tourist bars that infest the town.

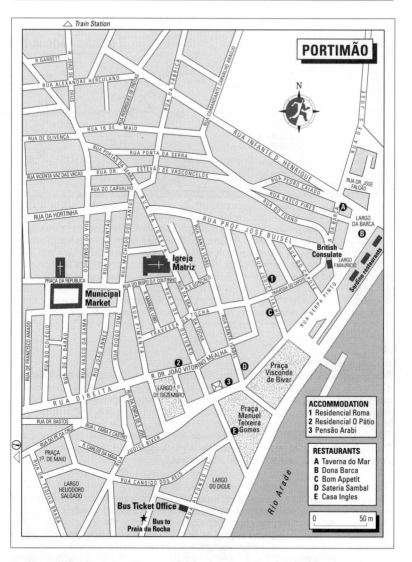

Praia da Rocha

PRAIA DA ROCHA, five minutes' south of Portimão by bus, was one of the first Algarve tourist developments and it's easy to see why. The **beach** is one of the most beautiful on the entire coast: a wide expanse of sand framed by jagged sea cliffs and the walls of an old fort built in 1691, the **Fortaleza da Santa Caterina**, that once protected the mouth of the River Arade. The fort itself now houses a café-restaurant, whose terrace offers splendid views at sunset – beach and ocean on one side, Ferragudo and river on the other.

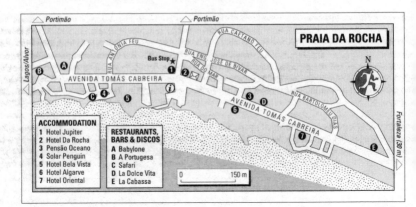

Despite the high-rise hotels, discos, sports complex and casino, the rest of Praia da Rocha is more appealing than many other Algarve resorts. Simply because it was one of the first strands to be developed, it looks less of a building site than most, and here and there among the hotel blocks sit *fin-de-siècle* villas that testify to the resort's rather upmarket reputation. Most of the development lies channelled in a strip just two blocks wide, with the beach reached down steep steps from the elevated main street, Avenida Tomás Cabreira; from virtually every bar, restaurant and hotel terrace, all the views are of the sands and sea. It isn't particularly Portuguese of course – there's nothing in town and little in the food offered in the restaurants to lead you to think it is – but it's thoroughly attractive all the same.

Arrival and information

Bus connections from Portimão are excellent, with a bus every fifteen to thirty minutes (7.30am–8.30pm); in Praia da Rocha it stops in front of the *Hotel da Rocha* (see below) on Avenida Tomás Cabreira. The **turismo** (summer 9.30am–11pm; winter 9.30am–7pm; ☎282 419 132) is in the hut opposite. You can pick up the **return bus to Portimão** from here (every 15–30min until 11.30pm; 190$00 one way), or from the stop on Rua Eng. José de Bivar, around the back of the *Hotel da Rocha*. If you plan to do much to-ing and fro-ing between Rocha and Portimão, buy a block of ten tickets from the kiosk in Portimão, which will save you around fifty percent.

Accommodation

Finding accommodation is rarely a problem; ask at the turismo for an array of **private rooms** to rent, or try one of the following **pensões** or (expensive) **hotels**. On the cliffs above the beach you'll find the eccentric *Solar Penguin* (☎282 424 308; closed mid-Nov to mid-Jan; ③), just off the main avenue on Rua António Feu – a delightful, old *pensão* with a few comfortable rooms overlooking the sea; it also has a restaurant. The place is a joy and in the antiquated lounge look out for the portrait of Queen Elizabeth which was painted by the late husband of the owner. Almost half the price but not as entertaining, and without the sea views, is the more basic *Pensão Oceano* on Avenida. Tomás Cabreira (☎282 424 309; ②). Of the **hotels** on Avenida Tomás Cabreira – all of which offer fine, sea-facing rooms, pools and heavily reduced winter room rates – the *Hotel Oriental* (☎282 413 000, fax 282 413 413; ⑤) wins hands down for its design, a Moorish-influenced extravaganza of arches, domes and gardens. Other main street choices include the luxurious five-star *Hotel Algarve* (☎282 415 001, fax 282 415 199; ⑨), which has an attached casino; and the *Hotel Jupiter* (☎282 415 041, fax 282 415 319; ⑤) and *Hotel da Rocha* (☎282 424 081, fax 282 415 988; ⑤) with comfortable rooms and the facilities you'd expect for the price. However, the most stylish place to stay is the seafront *Hotel Bela Vista* (☎282 450 480, fax 282 415 369; ⑥), a pseudo-Moorish mansion built in 1903 as a wedding gift by the wealthy Magalhães family; the interior is an exquisite mixture of carved woods, stained glass, and yellow, white and blue *azulejos*.

Eating, drinking and nightlife

Restaurants are plentiful and the half a dozen down on the beach mean that you don't have to leave the sands during the day. Up in town, the *Safari*, next to the *Solar Penguin*, overlooks the beach and serves mainly Portuguese dishes, a few with an Angolan influence – it's around 3000–4000$00 for a good meal, though you could eat for a lot less. The *Penguin* itself has a pleasing terrace-restaurant, serving freshly made dishes and snacks. Towards the fort on the Avenida, *La Dolce Vita* is owned and run by Italians, so the home-made pasta and pizzas are worth eating for once. However, even better Italian fare and surroundings can be had – strangely enough – at the Swedish-run *La Cabassa*, further along towards the fort in a quieter part of town. Here, they serve a mouth-watering array of authentic Italian dishes – though no pizza – for little more than you'll pay at *La Dolce Vita;* a meal with wine costs from about 2500$00.

For a civilized **drink**, the bar of the *Bela Vista* is open to the public (8.30pm–midnight). More rowdy venues include *Farmers*, behind the *Hotel Jupiter* and several on the Avenida: among them *On the Rocks* disco bar, *Tropicool* – the reps' favourite, and *Shaker Bar* (Happy Hour 4–8pm) are all loud and libidinous in varying degrees, at various times of the day or night. The *Katedral* **disco** is housed in a horrible futuristic building next to the *Penguin* but *Babylone*, in a basement just off the Avenida, makes better cocktails. If you want something a little more laid-back and less touristy, *A Portugesa*, towards the western end of the Avenida, plays relaxing music with live jazz every Friday and serves reasonable Portuguese food.

Ferragudo

FERRAGUDO, facing Portimão across the estuary, and connected by a regular bus service (hourly 7.30am–7.30pm), is very different in character from Praia da Rocha. Stuck on the side of a hill, it's a rundown little place of narrow streets and tiny houses that has only recently begun to be dressed up for tourists. It sprawls around a fort – the partner to that in Praia da Rocha – built in the sixteenth century to defend Portimão against attack. The town has a couple of small *pensões* and a few private rooms for rent through the local bars. There are a couple of lively bars and an excellent **restaurant**, *A Lanterna* (closed Sun), which is to be found just across the bridge from Portimão; the smoked swordfish is particularly tempting.

The Ferragudo **beach** is about a kilometre to the south of town. It is popular in a small-scale way, with a windsurfing school and a scattering of restaurant-bars. A large **campsite** (☎282 461 121) slouches next to the road ten minutes further to the south of the beach.

Alvor and Quinta da Rocha

Much of the appeal of the ancient port of **ALVOR**, 6km west of Praia da Rocha, has been washed away under a tide of tourists from the surrounding hotels and holiday villages: the town's narrow streets and its multitude of bars and restaurants can hardly cope. Whitewashed houses and lovely views of the estuary are the last vestiges of Alvor's charm. Nonetheless, the **beach** is enormous and, if it's a bit on the dull side, at least you can escape the crowds. The town's **turismo** is at Rua Dr. Alfonso Costa 51 (daily: summer 9am–11pm; winter 9.30am–5.30pm; ☎282 457 523). In season, **rooms** at Alvor are hard to come by, but there's a **campsite**: the *Campismo Dourado* (☎282 459 178), near the beach. The beach **café** *Rosamar* does good fish and basic meals. Back from the beach, try the *São João* restaurant on Rua Infante D. Henrique, or the more upmarket *Vagabondo*, Rua Frederico Mendes, which has a tree-filled terrace.

The **Quinta da Rocha nature area** lies in the peninsula between the mouths of the rivers Alvor and Odiáxere, northwest of Alvor's huge beach. It is an extensive area which, in the parts not given over to citrus and almond groves, consists of copses, salt marshes, sandy spits and estuarine mud flats, forming a wide range of habitats for different plants and animals – including 22 species of **wading bird**.

Silves

Eighteen kilometres northeast of Portimão, **SILVES** – the medieval residence and capital of the Moorish kings of *al-Gharb* – is one of the few inland towns in this province that really merits a detour. It has a superb castle and a highly dramatic approach, with its red ring of walls gradually revealing their course as you emerge from the wooded hills. Under the Moors, Silves was a place of grandeur, described in contemporary accounts as "of shining brightness" within its three dark circuits of guarding walls. Such glories and civilized spendours came to an end, however, in 1189, with the arrival of **Sancho I**, at the head of a mixed army of Portuguese and Crusaders. Sancho himself was a devout king, at least by the standards of his day, but, desperately in need of extra fighting force, had recruited a rabble of "large and odious" northerners, who had already been expelled from the holy shrine of Saint James of Compostela for their irreligious behaviour. The army arrived at Silves toward the end of June and the thirty thousand Moors retreated to the citadel. There they remained through the long, hot summer, sustained by huge water cisterns and granaries, until September, when, the water exhausted, they opened negotiations.

Sancho was ready to compromise, but the Crusaders had been recruited by the promise of plunder, and were not prepared to accept the king's financial inducements to forgo the pleasure of wrecking the town. The gates were opened after Sancho had negotiated guarantees for the inhabitants' personal safety and goods; all were brutally ignored by the Crusaders, who duly ransacked the town, killing some six thousand Moors in the process. Silves passed back into Moorish hands two years later, but by then the town had been irreparably weakened, and it finally fell to Christian forces in 1249.

The Town

The **Moorish Fortress** (daily: July–Sept 9am–8pm; Oct–May 9am–5pm; 250$00) remains the focal point of Silves, dominating the town centre with its impressively complete set of sandstone walls and detached towers. The interior is a bit disappointing: aside from the great vaulted water cisterns that still serve the town, there's nothing left of the old citadel, which is planted with modern gardens. However, you can circuit the walls for impressive views over the town and surrounding hills. There's a "traditional festival" held here on some Friday and Saturday nights in July, and a lively annual **beer festival** during the third week of July.

Silves's cathedral, or **Sé** (daily 8.30am–6.30pm, closes at 1pm on Sun), sits below the fortress, built on the site of the Grand Mosque. Flanked by broad Gothic towers, it has a suitably defiant, military appearance, though the Great Earthquake and centuries of impoverished restoration have left their mark within.

Below the Sé, in Rua das Portas de Loulé, is the town's **Museu Arqueologia** (Tues–Sun 10am–6pm; 300$00). It's engaging enough, despite a lack of English-language labelling, and romps through the history of Silves from the year dot to the sixteenth century with displays of local archeological finds. At the centre of the museum is an Arab water cistern, left in situ, which boasts a ten-metre-deep well. Strolling around the rest of Silves is a pleasure. There's a **market** (Mon–Sat 8am–1pm) on the riverfront, near the narrow thirteenth-century bridge. This is a fine place to sit out at one of the grill-cafés (see below) and watch life go by.

Practicalities

The **train station** – an easy approach from either Lagos or Faro – lies two kilometres out of town; there is a connecting bus, but it's a pleasant walk if you're not weighed down with luggage. Arriving by **bus**, you'll be dropped on the main road, next to the market near the riverfront at the foot of town.

The **turismo** on Rua 25 de Abril (summer Mon 9.30am–12.30pm & 2–7pm, Tues 9.30am–1.30pm & 3–7pm, Weds & Sun 9.30am–12.30pm & 2–5.30pm Thu–Sat 9.30am–7pm; winter Wed–Mon 9.30am–5.30pm; ☎282 442 255), in the heart of the town, will help arrange **private rooms**. Recommended are those with Isabel Maria da Silva at Rua Cândido dos Reis 36 (☎282 442 667; ②), which are spotless and share the use of a kitchen and a little outdoor terrace. Alternatively, there are a couple of **pensões**, including the comfortable old *Residencial Sousa*, Rua Samora Barros 17 (☎282 442 502; ②), and, across the river, the very pleasant *Restaurante Residencial Ponte Romana* (☎282 443 275; ③). Just over 5km out of town, on the road to São Bartolomeu de Messines, the *Quinta do Rio*, Sitio São Estevão, Apartado 217 (☎282 445 528, fax 282 445 528; ③), is a **country inn** with half a dozen en-suite rooms and garden set within a farm. Breakfast is included in the price and dinner can be arranged too. Closer to town, though on the same road (after the Galp service station), the *Vila Sodre* (☎282 443 441; ③) also has rooms and local wines and food on offer.

For **eating** in town, the *Restaurante Marisqueira Rui*, Rua Comendador Vilarinho (closed Tues), continues to attract locals and tourists from all over the Algarve; if you manage to squeeze in – and you should try – order shellfish, the restaurant's speciality. At the other end of the price scale, and just as enjoyable in its way, is the *U Monchiqueiro Casa de Pasto*, with a menu that changes daily; it's the best of a handful of grill-cafés on the riverfront road in front of the market. Sit outside and tuck into *piripiri* chicken, fries, salad and wine for 1500$00. The *Café Inglês*, by the fortress, sells delicious home-made snacks, ice cream and fruit juices, as well as full meals, and also has seats outside; while *Café Rosa*, in the Praça do Município, serves drinks and cakes all day (closed Sun).

Inland to the Serra de Monchique

Nine weekday buses – five at weekends – leave Portimão for the 24-kilometre, ninety-minute journey north to **Monchique** via **Caldas de Monchique**. Once clear of Portimão's ugly suburbs, the main road crosses the coastal plain, flanked by endless orchards of apples, pears, figs, almonds, pomegranates and citrus fruits. At Porto de Lagos the road divides, east to Silves and north into the foothills of the **Serra de Monchique**, a green and wooded mountain range of cork, chestnut and eucalyptus that provides the western Algarve with a natural northern boundary. It is ideal **hiking country**, or – with a bike or car – a superb route to take if you want to cut across afterwards to the wilder reaches of the western Algarve coast.

Caldas de Monchique

CALDAS DE MONCHIQUE, set in a ravine and surrounded by thick woods, has been a celebrated spa since Roman times. In 1495 Dom João II came here to take the waters (though he nevertheless died soon afterwards in Alvor), and in the nineteenth century the town became a favourite resort of the Spanish bourgeoisie. A casino from these times still stands in the main square, serving now as an excellent **handicraft centre** (summer daily 9.30am–8pm), surrounded by lovely, fading nineteenth-century buildings. The setting is as beautiful as any in the country, though the tiny village's peace and quiet is shattered daily by the busloads of day-trippers who stop for a wander around and a cup of coffee. At times, the buses queue nose-to-tail on the way into the village.

The modern Thermal Hospital sits below the main square, on the edge of a ravine, flaunting its well-kept gardens; below is the ugly Oficina de Engarrafamento where the famous water is bottled for sale around the country. But at least this maintains the town's tradition, and Caldas remains an active spa rather than being simply quaint. Climbing up from the spa, behind the square, you can follow the stream to sit under giant eucalyptus trees and picnic. Take along some of the local arbutus-berry-derived *aguardente* (fire water), on sale in the handicraft centre, which nicely complements the spring water.

The only reasonably priced **accommodation** in town is at the *Albergaria do Lageado* (open May–Oct;☎282 912 616, fax 282 911 310; ③), which has a pool and garden, and an excellent restaurant where you can eat for around 2500$00, and the *Albergaria Velha* (☎282 910 129, fax 282 973 920; ③), just off the square – both include breakfast in the price. A good place to **eat** is the *1692*, on the square, which serves up a range of Algarve fare in its cavern-like 1960s' interior; if you just want a **drink** you can either sit at its outside tables and watch the world go by or try the wine-bodega *O Tasco*, opposite the *Albergaria Velha*. Out of season you may well find most of these places closed.

Not all the **buses** from Portimão call into the centre of Caldas, stopping instead on the main road just out of town before continuing up to Monchique. Note, too, that there's a daily summer tourist service from Albufeira (with connections from Vilamoura, Quarteira and Faro) via Silves.

Monchique and around

MONCHIQUE, 6km to the north of Caldas de Monchique, and 300m higher up the range, is a small market town whose large market on the second Friday of each month is famous for its smoked hams, furniture and superabundance of emergency vehicles which are forced to double-park in the main square. There's not a great deal else to see, but it's a busy town and makes a nice enough excursion. Of the buildings, the most impressive is the **Igreja Matriz** (Mon–Sat 10am–5.30pm), the parish church, up a steep cobbled street from the main square, which has a Manueline porch and, inside, a little chapel with a facade of *azulejos*. The most evocative sight, though, is the ruined seventeenth-century monastery of **Nossa Senhora do Desterro**. Only a roofless shell of this Franciscan foundation survives, apparently quite uncared for, but it's in a great position overlooking the town and shows a beautiful blend of classical Renaissance facade with Moorish-influenced vaulting.

Buses arrive at the terminal in the main square at the bottom of town where Monchique's new **turismo** is located (Tues–Sat 10am–4.30pm, Sun 9.30am–noon; ☎282 911 189). There are a couple of **places to stay** in town (though it's difficult to see why you'd need to). First choice is the very welcoming *Estrela de Monchique*, Rua do Poço Fundo 46 (☎282 913 111; ②), a stone's throw to the right of the bus terminal. Otherwise, the *Bela Vista* (☎282 912 252; ①), in the main square, is cheaper but noisier and a bit

unappealing. Better by far are the **inns** on the road up to Fóia (s̄̄
need transport to reach them: the *Estalagem Abrigo da Montanha*,
(☎282 912 131, fax 282 913 660; ④), has a lovely garden and views as
ing room, while, four and a half kilometres out of Monchique, on the
Restaurant Quinta de São Bento is one of the best places in this part of the
high quality, reasonably priced Portuguese cooking including favourites such
piri-piri. The ambience is relaxed and meals, including wine, cost from around 2ŭ

Monchique itself also has a handful of **restaurants** which soak up the passing tou̇st
trade. *Restaurante A Charrete* on Rua Samora Gil is recommended, while *Café
Montanha*, Rua do Revez Quente, is fairly inexpensive, serving typical Algarvian meat
and fish dishes.

Fóia

Fóia, 8km west of Monchique, is – at nearly 900m – the highest of the Serra's peaks;
note that there are no bus services here. At the top there's a concrete obelisk, a radio
tower, a few stalls selling knick-knacks and knitwear (it can be cool up here), a *pensão*-
café, *O Planalto* (③), and a hotel, the *Estalagem de Santo António* (☎282 912 158, fax
282 912 878; ④). There are also lots of bus tours, all attracted by the panoramic view of
the Algarve which takes in Portimão, Lagos, the foothills stretching to the Barragem
da Bravura, and Cabo de São Vicente. The poet Robert Southey claimed to have caught
a glimpse of the hills of Sintra, beyond Lisbon, but that must have been one of those
legendary "clear days" – or maybe the air is never as clear now as it was in 1801.

Picota

Reaching 770m, **Picota** comes second in altitude to Fóia, though it's much more interesting in terms of its botany, and easier to reach without transport. You can reach the
peak from Monchique in around one and a half hours, a walk that takes in cork trees
(and cork collection points), eucalyptus and pines, peach, lemon and orange orchards,
and even wild goats scurrying about the heights. At the top there's nothing save a rickety watchtower occupied by a solitary guardian with a pair of binoculars. From here
you can see the coastline stretching all the way to Sagres, and take in another magnificent view of the Monchique mountain range.

West to the coast

Back down the road from Monchique towards Caldas, the minor N267 cuts west towards
the coast, passing through **MARMELETE** after 14km. There are two buses a day from
Monchique, but no real point in coming since, unless you're lucky enough to flag down a
lift, you won't get any further – and it's another 20km to Aljezur (p.487) and ten more to
the coast beyond that. In a car, though, it's a fine route, heading through tranquil countryside before swinging down through the hills and forests to the west coast.

North to Santa Clara

Heading north from Monchique, the N266 runs through forests of eucalyptus for 20km
before reaching the border with the Alentejo province, and then around 20km further on
arrives at the huge **Barragem de Santa Clara** – the largest artificial dam in Portugal. After
here, the route cuts across the flatlands of the Alentejo to a fork with turnings for Odemira
and the west coast, or Beja and the eastern Alentejo. Just west of the dam, **SANTA CLARA-
A-VELHA** makes a pleasant break in the journey, a compact little town with a Roman
bridge, rooms and a few café-restaurants where you can get a meal of fresh fish from the
lake. There's a **pousada** here, the *Santa Clara* (☎283 882 250, fax 283 882 402; ⑤), a tiny
place close to the dam, with just six rooms and a swimming pool. Alternatively, there's the
truly quiet, relaxing hideaway of *Quinta do Barranco da Estrada*, on the opposite side of the

...n and 12km from Santa Clara, just off the Cortelorique road (☎ & fax 283 933 901; ⑤). During the day you can mess about around the lake before enjoying the evening meal – costing 4000$00 – prepared by the proprietors. You'll need to book ahead for both places.

Lagos

LAGOS is one of the most ancient settlements in the Algarve, founded by the Phoenicians, who were attracted to its superb natural harbour. Under the Moors it became an important trading post until its reconquest by Christian armies in 1241. Its attractions today are less the historical associations – though there are a couple of fine churches and a circuit of medieval walls – than the fact that it remains a real town: a fishing port and market centre with a sense of independence and a life of its own. It has, of course, over the last two decades, also developed into a major resort (complete with huge new marina), and attracts the whole gamut of visitors, from backpackers to moneyed second-homers – during the summer the population of 20,000 people swells to more than 200,000. They come for some of the best beaches of the whole Algarve coast: to the east of the town is a long sweep of sand – Meia Praia – where there's space even in summer, while to the west is an extraordinary network of coves, sheltered by cliffs, pierced by tunnels and grottoes, and studded with weird and extravagantly weathered outcrops of purple-tinted rock.

Arrival, information and accommodation

Lagos is the western terminal of the Algarve railway line and its **train station** is across the river, fifteen minutes' walk from the centre via the new swing bridge in the marina; taxis are usually available if you can't face the walk. The **bus station** is a bit closer in, a block back from the main estuary road, Avenida dos Descobrimentos, and almost opposite the bridge to the train station.

The **turismo** (summer Mon 9.30am–12.30pm & 2–7pm, Tues 9.30am–1.30pm & 3–7pm, Weds & Sun 9.30am–12.30pm & 2–5.30pm Thu–Sat 9.30am–7pm; winter Wed–Sat 9.30am–12.30pm & 2–5.30pm; ☎282 763 031) is at Situo de São João, which is the first roundabout as you come into the town. This is fine if you're driving but if you haven't got your own transport you're looking at a twenty-minute walk from the centre of town and there's no bus stop nearby – a taxi will cost about 500$00 each way. From the centre walk out of town following the road to Portimão and Faro – just keep going. They can help in finding hotels and *pensões*, as well as dishing out maps, leaflets and timetables.

Accommodation

Most of the town's **hotels** and **pensões** are fully booked through the summer and, unless you turn up very early in the day, your only chance of a bed will be a **room** in a private house, for which you'll pay 3500–5000$00 for a double, depending on the time of year. The tourist office may phone around and try to find you a space in a private house, though they're reluctant due to an increasing volume of complaints about private rooms. Arriving early in the day, however, you'll probably be met by touts at the bus or train station, and it's a good idea to take whatever's going (as long as it's central), and look round later at your leisure. Out of season, or booking in advance, you could try for space at one of the established *pensões* and hotels, a selection of which are listed below. Prices are comparatively high in season; in winter, however, there are bargains to be had at many of the beach hotels west of town – ask at the tourist office for details. There's a **youth hostel** (see p.478) in town, while Lagos also has two **campsites**, both to the west of the centre, close by the Praia de Dona Ana, whose dramatic rock formations and clear waters provide a far more interesting place to relax than the more popular town beaches.

HOTELS AND PENSÕES IN TOWN

Pensão Caravela, Rua 25 de Abril 16 (☎282 763 361). Reasonable rooms on the town's main pedestrianized street. Doubles come with or without bath; breakfast included. ②.

Hotel de Lagos, Rua Nova da Aldeia (☎282 769 967, fax 282 769 920, *hotel-lagos@mail.telepac.pt*). The finest hotel in the centre and boasting a remarkable landscaped, "village-style" design – separate compounds of rooms, bars, restaurants and sports facilities joined by glassed-in corridors and walkways. There's a courtesy bus service to its own beach club at Meia Praia, too; and hefty off-season price reductions. ⑦.

Pensão Lagos-Mar, Rua Dr. Faria e Silva 13 (☎282 763 523, fax 282 767 324). Upmarket *pensão*, close to Praça Gil Eanes, and reliable enough for the money. All rooms have TV, telephone and private bathrooms. ④.

Residencial Marazul, Rua 25 de Abril 13 (☎282 769 143). The better establishment on this street, the rooms are comfortable and a few have a shower and terrace with sea view; breakfast is included. ③.

Hotel Riomar, Rua Cândido dos Reis 83 (☎282 763 091, fax 282 763 927). Smart, medium-sized hotel tucked into a central street. Most rooms have a balcony – the best overlook the sea on the far side of the hotel. Breakfast included. ⑤.

Pensão Rubi Mar, Rua da Barroca 70–1° (☎282 763 165, fax 282 767 749, *rubimar01@hotmail.com*). There are only nine rooms here, but if you can find space it's a treat; some rooms have sea views and breakfast in your room is included. ④.

HOTELS AND PENSÕES AT PRAIA DE DONA ANA

Pensão Dona Ana, Praia de Dona Ana (☎282 762 322). Small, white *pensão* situated at Lagos's finest beach, a 20-minute walk from town across the clifftops. In summer, you'll need to book well in advance for one of the 11 rooms. ②.

Hotel Golfinho, Praia de Dona Ana (☎282 769 900, fax 282 769 999). Modern hotel on the cliff set a hundred metres back from the beach. Attractive rooms, fine views and a courtesy bus into town. ③.

YOUTH HOSTEL

Pousada de Juventude de Lagos, Rua de Lançarote de Freitas 50 (☎282 761 970, fax 282 769 684, *pousadalagos@yahoo.com*). The modern youth hostel has a few double rooms with shower available (breakfast included), though you'll have to book well in advance. Dorm beds are 2000$00, which includes breakfast and sheets. Facilities include Internet access (600$00/hr) and a good-value currency exchange service. There's a nice central courtyard too. ②.

CAMPSITES

In season a bus marked "D. Ana/Porto de Mós" runs to the sites from the bus station, while the *Imulagos* site provides its own free bus from the train station (hourly 8am–10.30pm). On foot, follow the main Sagres road around the old town and it's about ten to fifteen minutes from the Forte Ponta da Bandeira to the sites.

Parque de Campismo Imulagos (☎282 760 031, fax 282 760 035). The larger of the sites – huge, in fact, with good facilities, lots of shade and access to a private beach.

Campismo da Trindade (☎282 763 893). Marginally closer to the town and beach, and much more cramped than the *Imulagos* (though it's only half the price).

The Town

Lagos was a favoured residence of Henry the Navigator, who used the town as a base for the new African trade, to which is owed the town's least proud relic – Europe's first **slave market**, whose arcades survive alongside the old **Customs House** in the **Praça da República** near the waterfront. On the other side of this square is the church of **Santa Maria**, through whose whimsical Manueline windows the youthful Dom Sebastião is said to have roused his troops before the ill-fated Moroccan expedition of 1578. Fired up by militant Catholicism, the dream-crazed king was to perish on the battlefield of Alcácer-Quibir (modern Ksar el Kbir, between Tangier and Fez) along with almost the entire Portuguese nobility. It was a disaster that enabled the Spanish to absorb Portugal for sixty years, but it did Dom Sebastião's reputation a world of good among the aggressively devout. He's commemorated in the centre of Lagos, in **Praça Gil Eanes**, by a fantastically dreadful modern statue – pink, ridiculous and looking like a flowerpot man.

Much of the old town was devastated by the 1755 earthquake, though one rare and beautiful church that survived is the **Igreja de Santo António**. Decorated around 1715, its gilt and carved interior is wildly obsessive, every last inch filled with a private fantasy of cherubic youths struggling with animals and fish. Next door is the **Museu Municipal** (Tues–Sun 9.30am–12.30pm & 2–5pm; 300$00), worth a look if only to discover the true meaning of the word eclectic. Alongside the usual barrowloads of Neolithic axeheads, pottery shards, statuary and terrible local religious art are jars containing misshapen animal foetuses, a display of models of Algarvian chimneys, stuffed animals, straw hats, lobster pots and fossils, a locked bookcase of novels, travelogues and English histories, the key to the city (literally), the 1504 town charter, and assorted muskets, swords and cannonballs.

The Praça da República, and the waterfront Avenida dos Descobrimentos, are the best vantage points for the remains of Lagos's once impregnable **walls** and fortifications, which include the squat seventeenth-century **Forte Ponta da Bandeira** (Tues–Sat 10am–1pm & 2–6pm, Sun 10am–1pm; 300$00), guarding the entrance to the harbour.

The beaches

The promontory **south** of Lagos is fringed by eroded cliff faces that shelter a series of postage-stamp-sized cove-beaches. All are within easy walking distance of the old town, though the beach tracks are increasingly confused by a multitude of paths leading to the hotels and campsites. In addition, the concentration of resort hotels near the beaches means that you may find the least crowded strand is the **town beach** itself, just beyond the Forte Ponta da Bandeira.

The easiest access on foot to the **cove-beaches** to the south and west is to follow the Avenida dos Descobrimentos up the hill (toward Sagres) and turn left just opposite the fire station, where you see signs to the tiny **Praia do Pinhão**. This is the first of the coves – around a twenty-minute walk from town. Five minutes further, across the cliffs, is the **Praia de Dona Ana** – one of the most photogenic of all the Algarve's beaches, with a restaurant, the *Mirante*, built into the cliffs.

Beyond here, despite the jostling hotels, you can follow a path around the cliffs and coast to **Praia do Camilo** – sometimes a bit less crowded – and right to the **Ponta da Piedade**, the point, where a palm-bedecked lighthouse makes a great vantage point for the sunset.

Beyond the point, the coast sweeps west again and you can continue to follow paths close to the cliff's edge to the beach of **Porto do Mós**, another 45 minutes' walk away, where the *Campimar* bar-restaurant overlooks the sands. The path then moves on as far as Luz (see p.482), another hour away; it's a splendid stretch, high above the ocean, until the obelisk above Luz comes into sight, from where you scramble down the hillside and into the town.

To the **east** of Lagos, flanked by the railway line, is **Meia Praia**, a vast tract of sand that extends for 4km to the delta of the rivers Odiáxere and Arão. The beach is particularly popular with backpackers who congregate at the *Bahia Beach Bar* – especially at sunset and for the live music on Sunday afternoons. A regular **bus service** leaves from the Avenida dos Descobrimentos and travels the length of the beach; alternatively, there's a seasonal **ferry** from Avenida dos Descobrimentos across the river, from which point the beach is a short walk away.

Eating

The centre of Lagos is packed with **restaurants**, most found along ruas Afonso d'Almeida and 25 de Abril. Where the Avenida dos Descobrimentos meets Rua das Portas de Portugal, there's a diverting **fish and vegetable market** (Mon–Sat mornings), in front of which is a line of good fish restaurants. Menus are of a similar standard and price almost everywhere, though Lagos does also have a couple of highly regarded places where it's worth pushing the boat out at least once.

Alpendre, Rua António Barbosa Viana 17. One of the oldest – and more formal – restaurants in the Algarve, serving memorable smoked swordfish and decent *arroz de marisco*. The crêpes are still the best reason to come though – flambéed at your table. At least 4000$00.

O Cantinho Algarvio, Rua Afonso d'Almeida 17. Popular for its wide range of modestly priced Algarvian food. Around 2500$00. Closed Sun lunch.

Casa do Zé, Av. dos Descobrimentos. On the corner with the market, this does filling fish dishes at very fair prices. Very much a locals' choice at lunchtime, with the outdoor seating soaking up a brisk trade – daily specials at 800–1000$00.

Casa Rosa, Rua do Ferrador 22. With substantial 600$00 fast food meals – though nothing particularly Portuguese – this is a backpackers' favourite.

O Cavaleiro, Rua Garret 23. Just off the Praça Luís Camões and open twenty-three hours a day, it makes a pleasant place to sit outside during the day and welcome refuelling stop in the small-hours. An inexpensive menu of drinks, meals, snacks and pizzas.

O Degrau, Rua Soeira da Costa 46 (☎282 764 716, *manuel@mail.telepac.pt*), The walls of this establishment are decorated with pages from the comment book that praise the international and Algarvian dishes as well as the comfortable and welcoming atmosphere. The menu includes a veg-etarian option, and a meal will cost you around 2500$00. Book in advance during the season to avoid queuing.

Dom Sebastião, Rua 25 de Abril 20–22. Arguably the town's finest restaurant, with outdoor seat-ing, a traditional, cobbled-floor interior, good seafood, and a fabulous selection of appetizers. A full meal runs to about 4000$00, though with careful selection you could get away for less.

O Franguinho, Rua Luís de Azevedo 25. Grilled chicken joint with a tiny, first-floor dining room – fine greasy chicken and daily specials. Good value at under 1500$00.

Galeão, Rua de Laranjeira 1. A little hidden away, but usually packed out with people who recognize good food when they taste it; you may have to wait for a table. All the Algarvian classics and superb steaks at eminently reasonable prices. Under 3500$00.

Galeria-Restaurante Cachoa. (☎282 782 822). A couple of kilometres out of Lagos just off the N125 to Sagres, this beautiful, rustic place has a large terrace set in well-kept gardens and a menu that includes Portugese, Mexican, Brazilian and Scandinavian dishes as well as a vegetarian option. The food is excellent and drinks inexpensive – a meal with wine costs around 2500$00. A taxi from Lagos will set you back about 750$00 each-way. Closed lunchtimes, Tues & Weds.

Italia, Rua Garrett 26–28, off Praça Luís Camões. Bright, cheery restaurant run by Italians: pizzas come from a wood-burning oven; there's Italian wine, pasta and a full menu besides. Around 2000$00 for a pizza or pasta meal, more if you eat the meat/fish specials. Closed Mon.

A Lagosteira, Rua Iº de Maio 20. Upmarket, blue-tiled restaurant with dishes at 1900$00, nice daily specials and pleasant staff.

O Patinhos, Rua Luís de Azevedo 10–12. Friendly, backstreet dining room, basic and local, with most dishes under 1000$00 and cheap wine. Try the baby squid in its own ink. Closed Sun.

Drinking and nightlife

There are lots of **bars** around town, many of them owned by expatriates – in particular Irish and British. Cocktails are unusually popular in Lagos and measures are almost universally generous; look out for the places offering two-for-one deals and special events. Most bars stay open until at least 2am, some even later if the party is in full flow.

Cervejaria Abrigo, Rua Marquês de Pombal 2. With outdoor tables under the orange trees – beer, cocktails, snacks and meals all day.

Doggy Style, Rua Cândido dos Reis 109. The appalling name ensures that you'll be lucky to meet another foreigner in its vaulted interior. The music is a typical mix of the latest Portuguese, Spanish and Brazilian sounds and the cocktails are among the best in Lagos.

Eddie's Bar, Rua 25 de Abril 99. Small, friendly bar with an extended Happy Hour from 5–9pm, a good selection of sounds and Internet access for 600$00/hr. Attracts a surf/bike/skate dude kind of crowd.

Hideaway, Trav. Iº de Maio 9, off Praça Luís de Camões. Cheap beer, more than fifty cocktails, laid-back sounds and food till 2am.

Joe's Garage, Rua Iº de Maio 78. Not for the faint-hearted, this joint throngs with Antipodeans drinking heavily and usually dancing on the tables. To cushion your stomach, a filling plate of food costs 500$00 and you know it's closing-time when they set fire to the bar and put it out with a fire-extinguisher.

Lords Tavern, Rua António Crisogono Santos 56. Opposite the *Hotel de Lagos*, this British-style pub has live music most nights (dismal crooners a speciality) and sports channel TV for the big games – probably the best reason to come. Open till at least 2am, more like 4am on occasions.

Mullens, Rua Cândido dos Reis 86. The most appealing late-night choice in town, this warehouse-like bar-restaurant serves excellent meals, has *vinho verde* on tap, plays jazz and soul on the sound system, and stays open until 2am.

Phoenix, Rua 5 de Outubro 11. The only club in Lagos; two dance floors play contemporary sounds. Stays open till 4am.

Roskos, Rua Cândido dos Reis 79. Down the road from *Mullens*, an Irish bar with an 8–10pm Happy Hour and fifty serious cocktails. Open till 2am.

Stones, Rua 25 de Abril 101. Split-level bar with a regular local crowd, loud rock and Happy Hour from 5–10pm.

Listings

Banks and exchange Banks are grouped around Praça Gil Eanes and you can exchange money in almost every travel agency, shop and general store.

Bike and motorbike rental *Eddie's Bar*, Rua 25 de Abril 99, organizes mountain bike excursions "from mellow glides to hardcore trailblazing" (☎282 768 329, *free_tours@hotmail.com*). For motorbikes try Motor Ride, Rua José Afonso 23 (☎282 761 720).

Boat trips Trips around the coast are easy to arrange with the fishing boats that gather around the Forte Ponta da Bandeira.

Buses Travel information for all destinations from the bus terminal (☎282 762 944). Note that buses to Portimão leave from Avenida dos Descobrimentos, while buses to most other destinations make a stop along here too.

Car rental Auto Jardim, Rua Vítor da Costa Silva 18 (☎282 769 486); Avis, Largo das Portas de Portugal 11 (☎282 763 691); LuzCar-Sociedade, Largo das Portas de Portugal 10 (☎282 761 016).

Consulate The only British consulate in the Algarve is in Portimão (p.467), at Largo Francisco A. Maurício 7 (☎282 417 800). All other consulates are in Faro (see p.442) or Lisbon.

Doctor For an English-speaking doctor, call MediLagos (☎282 760 181); you'll pay for the service.

Hospital Rua do Castelo dos Governadores, adjacent to the church of Santa Maria (☎282 763 034). In emergencies ☎112.

Police Rua General Alberto Silveira (☎282 762 930).

Post office Next to the town hall, just off Avenida dos Descobrimentos; open Mon–Fri 8.30am–6pm.

Taxis There are ranks in front of the post office or call Lagos Central Taxi ☎282 762 469 or 282 763 587.

Telephones It's easiest to make long-distance calls at the Telecom office, next to the post office (summer Mon–Fri 8.30am–10pm, Sat 9am–1pm & 5pm–midnight, Sun 6–10pm; winter Mon–Sat 8am–6pm).

Travel agency Tickets (including bus tickets) and tours from Clubalgarve, Rua Marreiros Netto 25 (☎282 762 337); and Tourlagos, Rua Infante de Sagres 31 (☎282 767 967).

Water sports There's a windsurfing school at Meia Praia (see above). For slides, pools and aquatic fun, take the bus from the bus station (at 9am or 12.15pm) to the Slide & Splash theme park, N125, Vale de Deus, Estômbar (adults 3000$00, children 1900$00; ☎282 341 685), 1hr away. Under your own steam, entrance is 2000$00 (children 1500$00).

West to Sagres

Once one of the least spoiled parts of the Algarve, the coast **west of Lagos**, to Vila do Bispo and Sagres, is currently facing a barrage of development. Villa development along the main highway continues apace and the erstwhile small settlements on the coast itself (Luz, Burgau and Salema) are also seeing an increasing amount of construction. Among them, **Salema** – with a superb beach and still recognizable as a former fishing village – promises most.

In summer there are frequent **bus** services from Lagos to Luz and Burgau, and a regular service to Salema. Connections are less frequent during the winter, but you should always be able to get to at least one of the villages and back in a day-trip, even if it means walking to the highway on occasion to pick up the bus. You could also plan a day that involved **walking** between the villages: Burgau to Luz to Lagos, in particular, is a nice, relatively easy, stretch.

Luz

Five kilometres west of Lagos, the mass of white chalets and villas that is the resort of **LUZ** swamps the old village entirely, disgorging multitudes in summer who, in turn, swamp the fine beach. For all this, it's a handsome enough place as long as you don't mind the crowds or the commercialization. The villas are at least low-rise and many have prime sea views; there's a palm-planted beachside promenade and any number of bar-restaurants with advantageous terraces. Sadly, the food everywhere is almost uniformly overpriced (and often distinctly average), though the *Restaurante Fortaleza*, above the west end of the beach, opposite the church, at least tries hard to match quality with high prices. It's the sort of place that serenades diners with Portuguese "folk music" most nights.

Unless you're booked in to Luz on a holiday, it's really not worth looking for **accommodation** here. There are rooms to be had, and doubtless the Lagos turismo could dig up an apartment vacancy, but you'll do better further west. **Campers** might want to use the large luxury *Valverde* site (☎282 789 211, fax 282 789 213), 1.5km or so from the seafront, close to the highway, with the full range of tourist facilities, but it's a charmless place.

Incidentally, the **path back to Lagos** starts at the eastern end of the beach. At the Algarve Sports Club, follow the private road uphill and make the obscenely steep scramble up to the obelisk on the cliffs, from where a gentle path careers along the tops to Porto do Mós, Ponte das Piedade and Lagos (see p.476).

Burgau

It's another five kilometres or so to **BURGAU**, another intensively developed holiday spot, though one which still retains vestiges of its former fishing-village life. The cobbled main street, with its side alleys and terraces, retains some charm, running right through the village and tumbling down to a wide sweep of sand backed by crumbling cliffs. Out of season, it's truly attractive, the beach deserted and the shutters down in most of the shops and restaurants, leaving the streets to echo to your own footsteps and little else. In summer, there's no mistaking Burgau for the out-and-out resort it is, packed day and night.

Again, unless you're here on a pre-booked holiday, you'll find it tough to locate a **room** in summer, though signs scattered around the village provide some hope. There are lots of bars and restaurants, though, including the *Beach Bar Burgau* with a splendid terrace-bar right on the beach (open till 2am). The food isn't all it could be (restaurant closed Mon), but the place also rents out water sports equipment.

Not all the **buses** from Lagos/Sagres call into Burgau itself, though all pass the turn-off on the highway, from where it's a two-kilometre (25min) walk to the village through arid farming country.

Salema

SALEMA, it seems, is still holding out against the worst of the local excesses. Just 20km west of Lagos, the turn-off from the N125 offers a brief respite from the barrage of development along the main highway, as the road snakes down a delightful, semi-cultivated valley, the sea creeping ever closer. The bus parks just above the fishing harbour, where the slipway is cluttered with brightly coloured boats and fishermen moping in and out of the fish warehouse. Of course, there has been apartment and villa construction, but for the most part it spreads back up the valley from the village in a fairly homogenous white splodge, leaving the sloping central street largely untouched. Here, white terraced houses are split by narrow alleys which run down to the rocky beach on the east side. The western **beach** – a wide, rock-sheltered bay – is magnificent: in winter, the sea comes crashing right up to the edge of the village.

Most of the **accommodation** in Salema is in apartments, though there is a fair-sized and quite attractive hotel, the *Salema* (open March–Oct; ☎282 695 328, fax 282 695 329; ④), plonked rather unceremoniously by the cobbled square just back from the beach, at Rua 28 Setembro. There are cheaper rooms at *A Mare* (☎282 695 165, fax 282 695 846, *www.algarve.co.uk*; ③), the white house on the hill, a few metres back up the road from the bus stop, where the rooms have bath, sea views and terraces with sun loungers. Alternatives are private **rooms** in the old village – ask at the bars and the post-office shop, or just stroll along the street and look for signs: you should be able to secure something with a terrace and kitchen. There's also a pleasantly landscaped **campsite**, *Quinta dos Carriços* (☎282 695 201, fax 282 695 122), 1.5km back up towards the main highway – the bus passes it on the way into the village.

Best of the **restaurants** is the *Mira-Mar*, signposted off the main street in the village (open 9am–midnight); this serves up barbecued fish and meat on a terrace above the beach. There are three or four others, too, with the *Atlantico* the best sited – right on the beach and with a cheapish menu incorporating sardines and all the usual dishes. The *Atabua*, also on the main street, is a late-opening **bar**.

Figueira and Raposeira

At the village of **FIGUEIRA** on the N125 (the point at which the highway most closely approaches the coast between Lagos and Sagres), there's the very welcoming *Bar Celeiro* by the bus stop. From here, paths lead off to the lovely **Praia da Figueira** (a 20–30min walk), which is often more or less deserted except for a few campers.

Two other worthwhile beaches are accessible by road from the village of **RAPO-SEIRA**, 5km further west, now positively overwhelmed by the speeding highway which cuts right through it. There is, though, a decent restaurant, the *Artisanale*, opposite a ceramic shop on the main road. The turn-off to the beach ("Ingrina") is signposted at the traffic lights on the highway: about 1km down the road, take the left fork that passes through Hortas do Tabual and after another 3km or so you'll reach two isolated, craggy beaches – **Praia do Zavial** and **Praia da Ingrina**. These have a minimum of tourist facilities, though there's a **campsite** (☎282 639 242) at Ingrina, 600m from the sea, and with its own bar-restaurant. Zavial is large and sandy, with tumbles of rock at either end and a café-restaurant open daily (except Wed) in season. Ingrina is sandy, too, and good for beach-combing amid the rock pools. There are no public transport connections from the main road.

West of Raposeira the road passes Vila do Bispo and the turn-off for the west coast, before heading across the flattened landscape for Sagres.

Sagres and Cabo de São Vicente

Wild and windswept, **SAGRES** and its cape were considered by the Portuguese as the far limit of the ancient and medieval worlds. It was on these headlands in the fifteenth century that Prince Henry the Navigator made his residence and it was here, too, that he set up a school of navigation, gathering together the greatest astronomers, cartographers and adventurers of his age. Fernão de Magalhães (Magellan), Pedro Álvares Cabral and Vasco da Gama all studied at Sagres, and from the beach at Belixe – midway between the capes of Sagres and **São Vicente** – the first long caravels were launched, revolutionizing shipping with their wide hulls, small adaptable sails, and ability to sail close to the wind.

Each year new expeditions were dispatched to penetrate a little further than their prede-cessors, and to resolve the great navigational enigma presented by the west coast of Africa, thereby laying the foundations of the country's overseas empire.

After Henry's death here in 1460, the centre of maritime studies was moved to Lisbon and Sagres slipped back into the obscurity from which he'd raised it. In the early 1980s, the forlorn one-street village began to attract a growing number of young backpackers and windsurfers from Europe and North America, drawn by the string of magnificent, isolated local beaches. Now, the main highway from Lagos has put Sagres within easy reach and the inevitable trail of villas and apartments is threatening to overwhelm the place entirely. It can still be a great place to stay, especially in winter, when the wind blows hard and there's a bleak, desolate appeal to the scenery, with hardly a tourist to be seen. Throughout the sum-mer, by contrast, the sprawling village draws quite a lively and oddball social scene: the young beachgoers still flock here, well catered for by an ever growing array of rooms for rent, restaurants and bars, rubbing shoulders these days though with families in villas and guests from one of the Algarve's two *pousadas*, which overlooks the village.

Sagres

Sagres village, rebuilt in the nineteenth century over the earthquake ruins of Henry's town, has nothing of architectural or historical interest and is little more than a line of houses connecting the fishing harbour and Praia da Baleeira at one end with the main square, Praça da Républica, at the other. Back from the main road, built to transport tourists straight to the headlands, a virtual new town of white villas and apartments spreads into the distance, much of it still under construction.

Henry the Navigator's **Fortaleza** (daily: May–Oct 10am–6pm; Nov-April 10am–8pm; 300$00) dominates the whole scene near the village, with Rua da Fortaleza, across the main square, running directly up the headland towards its massive bulk. An immense circuit of walls – only the north side survives intact – once surrounded its vast, shelf-like promontory, high above the Atlantic. With such explicit demands of secrecy and security, together with its wild remoteness, it must have seemed a kind of Aldermaston or Los Alamos of its day.

You enter through a formidable tunnel, before which is spread a huge pebble **Rosa dos Ventos** (wind compass), unearthed beneath a church in 1921 and said to have been used by Henry himself. Historians disagree – and are equally unimpressed by the claims of other surviving buildings to have been part of the prince's house. Still, it is a wonderful, wild setting and the simple, much-restored chapel of **Nossa Senhora da Graça** is at least contemporary with Henry's explorations. A shame, then, that long-term "development" here has done little to enhance the beauty of the site. New build-ings within the walls – housing an exhibition of maps of Portugal and other nautical memorabilia – are of ugly concrete, as is much of the reinforcement work done on the walls themselves. Parts of the grounds remain little more than flyblown wasteground, a situation that's barely changed for a decade or more.

Local beaches

However impressive the fortress, most people's days in Sagres are spent on one of the excellent nearby beaches, five of which are within easy walking distance of the village. Three of them are on the more sheltered coastline east of the fortress: **Praia da Mareta** is just below the square, and the **Praia da Baleeira** is by the harbour, from where it's a five-minute walk to the longest and best beach, the **Praia do Martinhal**, an ideal spot for windsurfing. West of the fortress, the beaches are longer and more impressive, and the one nearest the village is a good spot. It's a longer walk to the beau-tiful **Praia de Belixe**, 2km down the road from Sagres to Cabo São Vicente, where you are usually guaranteed plenty of sand to yourself.

Whichever beach you choose, the water is cold and swimming must be approached with caution – there are some very strong currents. Before setting off for the more distant strands, stock up with drinks and picnic supplies since there are virtually no facilities, especially out of summer. The village supermarket can oblige with most provisions, plus five-litre flagons of the local wine for evening parties.

Practicalities

Buses from Lagos stop on the main village road, just by the square, **Praça da República**, and continue to the harbour. The **turismo** (summer Mon 9.30am–12.30pm & 2–7pm, Tues 9.30am–1.30pm & 3–7pm, Weds & Sun 9.30am–12.30pm & 2–5.30pm Thu–Sat 9.30am–7pm; winter Wed–Mon 9.30am–12.30pm & 2–5.30pm; ☎282 763 031) is a lonely hut a couple of minutes walk – or one bus stop – along the village road from the Praça towards the fishing harbour. On the Praça there's also a privately run **information office**, *Turinfo* (daily 10am–7pm; ☎282 620 003, fax 282 620 004), which can arrange room rental, book you on a local jeep- or boat- tour, and rent out **mountain bikes** (500$00 per hour; 1200$00 per half-day; 1900$00 for a full-day), which isn't a bad way to get to the cape and far-flung beaches and back.

Accommodation

There are places to stay everywhere in and around Sagres village, and in high season, at least, it's basically a question of turning up and seeing what you're offered. Generally, you'll be approached by people offering **rooms** (from around 3500$00 a double) and, if you want it, access to a kitchen too. There's little point in giving specific recommendations, since there's not much difference as far as price and location goes. The only alternatives are a scattering of regular **pensões** and **hotels**; as with the private rooms, prices come down considerably out of season. *Residencial Dom Henrique* (☎282 620 000, fax 282 620 001; ④) is located right on the square – rooms here have bath and some have sea-facing balconies; while for harbour views, the *Hotel da Baleeira* (☎282 624 212, fax 282 624 425; ③) is the spot. But, best of all – if your budget will stretch to it – is the *Pousada do Infante* (☎282 624 222, fax 282 624 225; ⑦), an attractive clifftop mansion with Moorish elements and splendid views of the fortress from its bar-terrace. It's a wonderful location and offers special rates out of season. Equally upmarket is a small, four-room hotel, the *Fortaleza do Belixe* (☎282 624 124, fax 282 624 225; ⑤), an annexe of the *pousada*, perched high on the cliff edge, 2km out of town at Belixe.

The nearest **campsite** (☎282 624 351, fax 282 624 445) is 2km north of the village, along (and off) the main road; it is convenient for Praia do Martinhal. Camping rough on the beaches is definitely not an option; the local police don't like it and, given the number of rooms available, you can see their point.

Eating, drinking and nightlife

Sagres's main street, from Praça da República to the fishing harbour, is lined with restaurants and bars, catering for a range of tastes and budgets. For **breakfast**, either *Café Conchinha* or the next-door *pastelaria*, both on Praça da República, open fairly early. **Restaurants** run the gamut from travellers' cafés to more upmarket places specializing in fish. At the fishing harbour end, *A Grelha* is typical of the cheaper establishments, a simple place with a modest menu where you can eat for under 1500$00. Nearby, on the same stretch of road, *O Pescador* and the slightly cheaper *Atlântico* opposite – are both fish restaurants, the quality of whose dishes can be a bit hit and miss. At either, a full meal will cost around 2500–3500$00, while for the same price you can soak up the harbour views and tuck into the seafood or a *caldeirada* at *A Tasca*, down the steps to the port. At the other end of the village, nearer the square, *Dromedário*, opposite the kiosks on the main street, is an energetic bistro that serves drinks and snacks all day (open until 3am); while *Bossa Nova*, round the corner on Rua Comandante Matoso, is noted for its pizzas, pasta, salads and imaginative vegetarian meals. A short walk north of the village, on Rua dos Mortorios, *O Retiro do Pescador* serves delicious seafood at very reasonable prices. If you can afford it, however, try and eat at the *pousada* for a total dining experience in elegant surroundings with superb service. The *pousada* has French-Portuguese food, with coffee served on the terrace, for around 5000$00 a head. A cheaper option, on the way to the *pousada*, is the excellent *Vila Velha*, which serves a pleasant mix of Portuguese and Dutch dishes in a rustic-style interior.

Of the **bars**, two long-standing favourites, both packed with the travelling youth contingent, are *A Rosa dos Ventos*, on the village square – lively, loud, and drunken – and *The Last Chance Saloon*, around the corner, overlooking the Mareta beach. When it's falling-down time, everyone moves on to *Polvo's* bar (open until 4am), just off the square, or to one of the even later-opening **discos** such as *Topas*, just north of the village.

Cabo de São Vicente

The exposed **Cabo de São Vicente** – Cape Saint Vincent – across the bay from Sagres, was sacred to the Romans, who believed the sun sank hissing into the water beyond here every night. It became a Christian shrine when the relics of the martyred Saint Vincent arrived in the eighth century; watched over (some say piloted) by ravens, the remains were transferred by boat to Lisbon in 1173.

It was almost certainly at the cape that Henry established his School of Navigation, founded a small town, and built his Vila do Infante. Today only a **lighthouse**, flanked by the ruins of a sixteenth-century Capuchin convent, are to be seen. The other buildings, already vandalized by the piratical Sir Francis Drake in 1587, came crashing to the ground in the Great Earthquake of 1755, the monks staying on alone until the Liberal suppression of the monasteries in 1834.

The cape is nonetheless a dramatic and exhilarating six-kilometre walk from Sagres, a path skirting the tremendous cliffs for much of the way. This is a wonderful spot for **birdlife** and at the right time of year you should be able to spot blue rock thrushes and peregrines nesting on the cliffs. Walking on the road is easier– it'll take less than an hour and a half, with glorious views all the way. Try to be at the cape for sunset, which is invariably gorgeous, though frequently also very windy.

Vila do Bispo and the coast to Odeceixe

Unlike the southern stretches of the Algarve, the **west coast**, stretching north from Sagres to Odeceixe, is still relatively undeveloped. There are several reasons: the coast is exposed to strong Atlantic winds; the sea can be several degrees cooler; and swimming is dangerous. In addition, the designation in 1995 of the stretch of coast from Burgau to Cabo de São Vicente and up through the Alentejo as a nature reserve – the Parque Natural Sudoeste Alentejano e Costa Vincentina – should go even further to protect this dramatic and rugged scenery from potentially harmful development. If you can brave the climate, you might like to base yourself at low-key resorts such as **Vila do Bispo**, **Carrapateira**, **Aljezur** and **Odeceixe**, all of which have plenty of beach, plus an inexpensive network of private rooms and scope for freelance camping. Like Sagres, these resorts attract a predominantly young and/or alternative crowd. At a few resorts – Odeceixe, in particular – this can be overwhelming, with summer crowds of campervan-hippies strutting about nude on the beach.

Vila do Bispo

VILA DO BISPO, at the junction of the west and south coast roads, is a fairly scrappy little town whose kernel of old white houses centres on a lovely seventeenth-century parish **church** (summer Mon–Sat 10am–1pm & 2–6pm), every interior surface of which has been painted, tiled or gilded. If you drop enough in the plate in the sacristy, the old custodian on duty will point out the age of everything in the church – you'll get to see the collection of assorted carvings, chalices and ecclesiastical vestments too. That's about all the town has to offer in the way of diversions: have a look over the hills from the church terrace, a coffee in one of the bars by the adjacent town garden, a mooch around the supermarket and you'll be ready to move on.

Nothing much happens here, but the town could make a reasonable base if you have transport for day-trips to the beaches. The nearest beach, the cliff-edged **Praia do Castelejo**, is reached by a rough road – no buses and a tough hike – leading 5km west, across a stretch of bleak moors and hills. In summer, there's a little bar-restaurant here.

Buses from Sagres or Lagos drop you right at the bottom of the village, five minutes' walk from the church. There are **rooms** advertised here and there, or try the *Pensão Mira Sagres*, Rua do Hospital 3 (☎282 639 160; ②) – opposite the church – which has its own bar-restaurant downstairs. Not that Vila do Bispo lacks places to **eat**: down Rua 1º de Maio from the church, *Café Correira* (closed Sat) has a decent menu, while a block further down, along an alley on the left, is the much cheaper *Oasis*, a locals' haunt, where the house speciality is chicken. If neither appeals, Rua Comandante Matoso, the parallel downhill street, has three or four more choices, all modest and acceptable. And there's a small supermarket, bakery and even a couple of **bars** (summer only) that see some late-night action.

Carrapateira

Fifteen kilometres to the north of Vila do Bispo (connected by a week-day bus which leaves Vila do Bispo at 8.05am) is the village of **CARRAPATEIRA**, which is better positioned for the beach. It's possible to get a **private room** if you ask around the main square or at the *Bar Barroca*. However, the best accommodation is a couple of kilometres northeast of town at the *Residencial Casa Fajara* (☎282 973 123, fax 282 973 186; ④), a spruce modern villa with neat gardens, overlooking an empty river valley. It's in a great location, and is open all year round; breakfast is provided.

Carrapateira's local beach, a kilometre's walk from the *Casa Fajara*, is the **Praia da Bordeira**, a spectacular strand with dunes, a tiny river and crashing surf. The sand-banks provide shelter from the wind for a sizeable community of freelance campers, who seem to be tolerated by the local police. There is a restaurant on the beach, *O Sitio do Rio* (closed Nov; ☎282 997 119) which also offers horse-riding excursions. A second beach – quieter and with no facilities – is the **Praia do Amado**, 4km south of the Praia da Bordeira, around the Carrapateira headland.

Aljezur and around

The village of **ALJEZUR** (Mon–Fri 2 buses daily from Vila do Bispo; 2–5 daily from Lagos) is divided into two distinct halves: to the west of the river is a rather drab old quarter, Moorish in origin and straggling along the side of a hill below the scant ruins of a tenth-century **castle**, while across the river to the east lies a more modern settlement. More and more surfers are making their way here in summer, attracted by the local beaches; the **turismo** (Mon & Fri–Sun 9.30am–12.30pm & 2–5.30pm, Tues–Thurs 9.30am–7pm; ☎282 998 229), in Largo do Mercado, by the river, does its best to help with private **rooms**. There are also a couple of **pensões** scattered around the vicinity: in the Igreja Nova quarter, just to the northeast of the centre, try the

Residencial Dom Sancho, Largo 1º de Maio (☎282 998 119, fax 282 998 763; ②), or the rooms above the *Restaurante A Lareira*, Estrada da Cruz (☎282 998 440; ②) both of which have rooms reminiscent of a stay with an aged auntie. The bus from Lagos loops through Igreja Nova on its way out of Aljezur. There are two or three fairly simple **restaurants** in town, too, such as the *Primavera* and *Ruth*, both along the main Rua 25 de Abril.

A kilometre south of Aljezur, a road heads through to the local **beaches** of **MONTE CLÉRIGO** (8km) and **ARRIFANA** (10km). The latter is magnificent, though its small village, perched on the cliffs above, is a rather grubby affair, with a couple of lacklustre bars and restaurants and a supermarket. Midway between the beaches is the **VALE DA TELHA** tourist complex, which has planning permission for expansion to a site of 2500 chalets and villas. At present it's nowhere near that size, nor a great commercial success, with just a modest **hotel**, the *Hotel Vale da Telha* (☎282 998 180, fax 282 998 176; ③), and a **campsite** (☎282 998 444) up and running.

Odeceixe

ODECEIXE, hunched on a hill and cramped by the river, is the last village before the Alentejo. Situated near the head of a delightful curving estuary, it is a fairly quiet little place, at least outside July and August. At this time of year, it seems to attract just about every German hippy on the Algarve, a clientele that creates its own rather exclusive presence. If you hit town outside the hippy season, though, it could be very pleasant, with a couple of simple restaurants, a number of houses offering **rooms**, and some small villas for rent by the beach. There's a campsite here, too.

The beach – **Praia de Odeceixe** – is a high-cliffed cove, stretching north of the estuary. It is one of the most sheltered beaches on this stretch of coast, with a minimum of tourist development and wonderful surf.

travel details

Trains

The Algarve rail line runs from Lagos to Vila Real de Santo António, but only three or four services daily operate along the whole route; you may have to change at Tunes or Faro, depending on your destination. Note that reservations are compulsory on Intercidade and Rápido or "Alfa" trains. For journeys from one end of the rail line to the other, it's worth catching one of the express services rather than the slow local-stopping trains. Latest train times can be checked at www.cp.pt on the Internet.

Faro to: Albufeira (13 daily; 25–45min); Lagos (10 daily; 1hr 30min–2hr 5min); Monte Gordo (3–4 daily; 1hr–1hr 45min); Olhão (12–14 daily; 10min); Portimão (10 daily; 1hr 10min–1hr 40min); Silves (10 daily; 55min–1hr 25min); Tavira (12–14 daily; 35–45min); Vila Real de Santo António (10 daily; 1hr–1hr 10min).

Lagos to: Albufeira (8–11 daily; 1hr–2hr 5min); Faro (9 daily; 1hr 30min–2hr 30min); Loulé (11 daily; 1hr 20min–2hr 20min); Portimão (12 daily; 15–20min); Silves (12 daily; 30–40min); Tunes (12 daily; 50min–1hr).

Tunes to: Lisbon (4 daily; 3hr 40min–4hr 55min), add on 2hr or so for connections from Vila Real, one hour from Faro or Lagos; and to Beja (3 daily; 2hr 30min), with connections for Casa Branca (4 daily 3hr 25min–5hr 55min); Évora (2–3 daily; 4hr–7hr 5min).

Buses

Up-to-date information on routes and times is available on the Internet at www.eva-transportes.pt and rede expressos.pt/index_uk.htm both of which are available in English. Currently there is no Website for Frota Azul.

Albufeira to: Areias de São João (8–11 daily; 10min); Armacão de Pêra (Mon–Sat 9 daily, Sun 5; 25min); Faro (9 daily; 1hr 15min); Montechoro (8–11 daily; 15min); Olhos d'Água (hourly; 10min); Portimão (Mon–Fri 8 daily, Sat 7, Sun 4; 1hr 10min); Quarteira (Mon–Fri 15 daily, Sat & Sun 9 daily; 45min); São Bartolomeu de Messines (3–8 daily; 40min); Silves (3–7 daily; 45min).

Faro to: Albufeira (9 daily; 1hr 15min); Estói (Mon–Fri 14 daily, Sat & Sun 9 daily; 25min); Loulé (Mon–Fri hourly till 7.30pm, Sat 8 daily, Sun 6 daily; 40min); Monte Gordo (Mon–Fri 9 daily, Sat & Sun 4 daily; 1hr 35min); Olhão (Mon–Fri every 15–30min, Sat & Sun roughly hourly; 20min); Quarteira (Mon–Fri hourly, Sat & Sun 3 daily; 35min); São Brás de Alportel (Mon–Fri 10 daily, Sat 9, Sun 3; 35min); Tavira (7–11 daily; 1hr); Vilamoura (Mon–Fri hourly, Sat & Sun 9 daily; 40min); Vila Real (6–9 daily; 1hr 40min).

Lagos to: Albufeira (12 daily; 1hr 30min); Aljezur (Mon–Fri 4–5 daily, Sat 1 daily, Sun 1 in summer; 50min); Burgau (8–10 daily, only 4 on Sun in winter; 25min); Luz (8–10 daily, only 4 on Sun in winter; 15min); Odeceixe (Mon–Fri 3–4 daily, Sat 1; 1hr 20min); Portimão (hourly; 40min); Sagres (7–11 daily; 1hr); Salema (5–8 daily; 40min); Vila do Bispo (7–11 daily; 45min).

Portimão to: Albufeira (5–7 daily; 1hr 15min); Alvor (Mon–Fri hourly; Sat & Sun roughly every 2hr; 20min); Faro (Mon–Fri 2, Sat & Sun 4–5 daily; 1hr 45min–3hr); Ferragudo (hourly; 10min); Lagos (hourly; 40min); Monchique (Mon–Fri 9 daily; Sat & Sun 5 daily; 30–45min); Praia da Rocha (every 15–20min; 5min); São Bartolomeu de Messines (4–8 daily; 1hr 15min); Silves (Mon–Fri 9 daily, Sat & Sun 7 daily; 35–45min).

Sagres to: Lagos (Mon–Fri 7–11 daily; 1hr); Salema (Mon–Fri 6–7 daily, Sat & Sun 3–4 daily; 35min); Vila do Bispo (6–10 daily; 15min).

Vila do Bispo to: Aljezur (Mon–Fri 2 daily; 45min); Carrapateira (Mon–Fri 1 daily; 15min).

Vila Real de Santo António to: Alcoutim (Mon–Fri 2–3 daily, Sat 1; 1hr 15min); Ayamonte, Spain (2 daily; 1hr 15min); Castro Marim (Mon–Fri 8–13 daily, Sat 2 daily, Sun 2 daily in summer; 10min); Manta Rota (Mon–Fri 4–5 daily, Sat 2 daily; 30min); Monte Gordo (Mon–Fri at least half-hourly, Sat & Sun in winter 10–13 daily; 7min); Tavira (9–10 daily; 40min).

Long-distance buses

There's a long-distance Linha Litoral express service which connects Lagos to Vila Real/Ayamonte once daily on weekdays, the whole route taking four hours; on the Lagos–Albufeira leg of the route, there are more like seven weekday departures and four at weekends. Several companies also operate regular daily express buses between Lisbon and the Algarve, with approximate journey times as follows: Albufeira (3hr 35min); Faro (4hr 20min); Lagos (4hr 45min); Olhão (4hr 30min); Tavira (4hr 45min); Vila Real (4hr 30min). Ask at any travel agency or bus terminal for details, though note that the Rede Expressos buses are around 700$00 cheaper than the EVA bus.

International buses

EVA runs a number of international buses from the Algarve, the most useful being the twice daily service from Albufeira to Seville. Buses leave Albufeira at 7.20am and 2.30pm, continuing through Faro (8.10am/4.15pm) to Vila Real de Santo António (9.10am/5.15pm) and the Spanish border. The bus stops at Huelva (11.25am/7.30pm) before arriving in Seville (1.05pm/9.40pm) where you can pick up connections to Malaga, Cádiz, Algeciras and Granada. From Albufeira a single ticket is 2660$00, from Faro 2500$00 and Vila Real de Santo António 2100$00.

Flights

Faro to: Lisbon (5–6 daily); with connections to Porto.

PART THREE

THE CONTEXTS

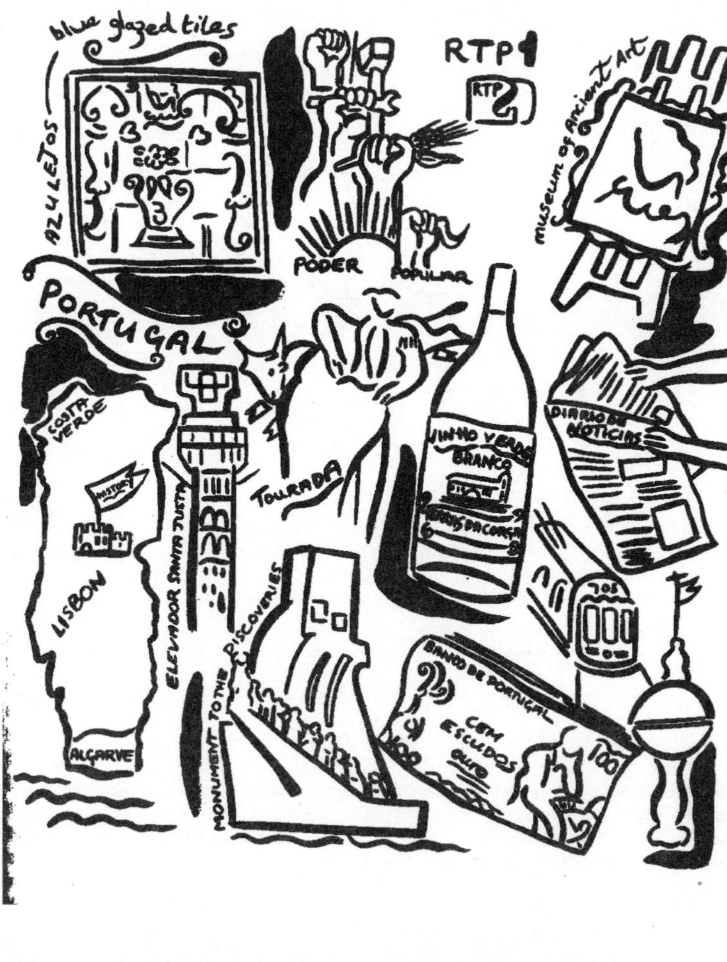

PORTUGAL'S HISTORY

The early history of Portugal – as part of the Iberian Peninsula – has obvious parallels with that of Spain. Indeed, any geographical division is somewhat arbitrary, independent development only really occurring following Afonso Henriques' creation of a Portuguese kingdom in the twelfth century.

EARLY CIVILIZATION

Remnants of pottery and cave burials point to tribal societies occupying the Tagus valley, as well as parts of the Alentejo and Estremadura, as early as 8000 to 7000 BC, and the recently discovered Paleolithic paintings near Vila Nova de Foz Côa in Beira Alta are thought to date back around 20,000 years (see p.294). More, however, is known of **Neolithic** Portugal and its Castro culture based on hilltop forts, a culture that was to be developed and refined after the arrival of Celtic peoples in around 700 to 600 BC. These forts, the first permanent settlements, were concentrated in northern Portugal, and particularly in the Minho, where excavations have revealed dozens of **citânias**, or fortified villages. The most impressive is at Briteiros (p.310), near Braga, with its paved streets, drainage systems and circuits of defensive walls; like many of the *citânias* it survived, remarkably unchanged, well into the Roman era. Settlements in neighbouring Trás-os-Montes, in contrast, reflect less of a defensive spirit –

but all that remains of this more pastoral **Verracos** culture are the crude granite *porcas*, stone figures venerating wild sows as objects of a primitive fertility cult.

The potential for new trading outlets and the quest for metals, in particular tin for making bronze, attracted a succession of peoples from across the Mediterranean but most of their settlements lay on the eastern seaboard and so fell within "Spanish" history. The **Phoenicians**, however, established an outpost at Lisbon around 900 BC and there were probably contacts, too, with Mycenaean Greeks. In the mid-third century BC, they were followed by **Carthaginians**, who recruited Celtic tribesmen for military aid against the Roman empire. Once again, though, their influence was predominantly on the eastern seaboard and in the south; with defeat in the Second Punic War (218–202 BC) they were to be replaced by a more determined colonizing force.

ROMANS, SUEVI AND VISIGOTHS

Entering the peninsula in 210 BC, the **Romans** swiftly subdued and colonized the Mediterranean coast and the south of Spain and Portugal. In the interior, however, they met with great resistance from the Celtiberian tribes and in 193 BC the **Lusitani** rose up in arms. Based in central Portugal, between the Tagus and Lima rivers, they were, in the words of the Roman historian Strabo, "the most powerful of the Iberian peoples, who resisted the armies of Rome for the longest period". For some fifty years, in fact, they held up the Roman advance, under the leadership of **Viriatus**, a legendary Portuguese hero and masterful exponent of the feigned retreat who, on several occasions, brought the Romans to accept his autonomous rule. He was betrayed after a successful campaign in 139 BC and within two years the Lusitani had capitulated as the legions of Decimus Junius Brutus swept through the north. Still, over a century later, their name was given to this most westerly of the Roman provinces, while in the northern Celtic villages Roman colonization can scarcely have been felt.

Integration into the Roman Empire occurred largely under Julius Caesar, who in 60 BC established a capital at Olisipo (Lisbon) and significant colonies at Ebora (Évora), Scallabis (Santarém) and Pax Julia (Beja). In 27 BC the Iberian provinces were further reorganized under Augustus, with all but the north of Portugal being governed – as Lusitania – from the great Roman city of Merida in Spanish Extremadura. The Minho formed part of a separate province, later added to northwest Spain to create Gallaecia, with an important regional centre at Bracara Augusta (Braga). In general, though, it was the south where Roman influence was deepest. Here they established huge agricultural estates (the infamous *Latifundia* which still survive in Alentejo) and changed the nature of the region's crops, as they introduced wheat, barley, olives and the vine to the area.

There are no great **Roman sites** in Portugal – at least nothing to compare with Spanish Merida, Tarragona, or Italica – though both Évora (p.397) and Conímbriga (p.195) have individual monuments of interest. The mark of six centuries of Roman rule consists more in a network of roads (used well into the Middle Ages) and bridges, many of them still in use today. There is a more basic legacy, too, the Portuguese language being very heavily derived from Latin.

The **decline of the Roman Empire** in Portugal echoes its pattern elsewhere, though perhaps with greater indifference, the territory always being something of a provincial backwater. **Christianity** reached Portugal's southern coast towards the end of the first century AD and by the third century bishoprics were established at Braga, Évora, Faro and Lisbon. But the state was already disintegrating and in 409 the first waves of barbarian invaders crossed the Pyrenees into Spain. Vandals, Alans, Suevi and Visigoths all passed through Portugal, though only the last two were of any real importance.

The **Suevi**, a semi-nomadic people from eastern Germany, eventually settled in the area between the Douro and Minho rivers, establishing courts at Braga and Portucale (Porto). They seem to have coexisted fairly peacefully with the Hispano-Roman nobility and were converted to Christianity by Saint Martin of Dume, a saint frequently found in the dedications of northern churches.

Around 585, however, the Suevian state disappeared, having been suppressed and incorporated into the **Visigothic** empire, a heavily Romanized yet independent force which for two centuries maintained a spurious unity and rule over most of the peninsula. The Visigothic kings, however, ruled from Toledo, supported by a small and elite aristocratic warrior-caste, so in Portugal their influence was neither great nor lasting. And by the end of the seventh century their divisions, exacerbated by an elective monarchy and their intolerance (including the first Iberian persecution of the Jews), resulted in one faction appealing for aid from Muslim North Africa. In 711 a first force of **Moors** crossed the straits into Spain and within a decade they had advanced and conquered all but the mountainous reaches of the Asturias in northern Spain.

THE MOORS AND THE CHRISTIAN RECONQUEST

In Portugal, Aveiro probably marked the northernmost point of the **Moorish advance**. The Moors met with little resistance but the dank, green hills of the Minho held little attraction for the colonizers-to-be and over the following century seem to have been severely depopulated. Most of the Moors were content to settle in the south: in the Tagus valley, in the rich wheat belts around Évora and Beja, and above all in the coastal region of **al-Gharb**. Here they established a capital at Shelb, modern Silves, and, by the middle of the ninth century, an independent kingdom, detached from the great Muslim emirate of al-Andalus which covered most of Spain.

The Moors in Portugal were a mix of ethnic races – for the most part consisting of Berbers from Morocco, but also considerable numbers of Syrians and, around Faro, a contingent of Egyptians, some of them probably Coptic Christians. In contrast to the Visigoths, the Moors were tolerant and productive, their rule a civilizing influence. Both Jews and Christians were allowed freedom of worship and their own civil laws, while under Muslim law small landholders continued to occupy lands that they themselves cultivated. For most of these **"Moçárabes"**– Christians subject to Moorish rule – life must have improved. Roman irrigation techniques were perfected and the Moors introduced the rotation of crops and cultivation of cotton, rice, oranges and lemons. Their culture and scholarship led the world – though less from al-Gharb than from Córdoba and Seville – and they forged important trade links, many of which were to continue centuries after their fall. Perhaps still more important, **urban life** developed, with prosperous local craft industries: Lisbon, Évora, Beja and Santarém all emerged as sizeable towns.

The Christian "**Reconquista**" began – at least by tradition – at Covadonga in 718, when Pelayo, at the head of a small band of Visigoths, halted the advance of a Moorish expeditionary force. The battle's significance has doubtless been inflated but from the victory a tiny kingdom of the Asturias does seem to have been established. Initially only 65 by 50 kilometres in extent, it expanded over the next two centuries to take in León, Galicia and the "lands of Portucale," the latter an area roughly equivalent to the old Swabian state between the Douro and the Minho.

By the eleventh century **Portucale** had the status of a country, its governors appointed by the kings of León. In 1073 Alfonso VI came to the throne. It was to be a reign hard-pressed by a new wave of Muslim invaders – the fanatical Almoravids, who crossed over to Spain in 1086 after appeals from al-Andalus and established a new Muslim state at Seville. Like many kings of Portugal after him, Alfonso was forced to turn to European Crusaders, many of whom would stop in at the shrine of Saint James in Compostela. One of them, Raymond of Burgundy, married Alfonso's eldest daughter and became heir-apparent to the throne of León; his cousin Henry, married to another daughter, Teresa, was given jurisdiction over Portucale. With Henry's death Teresa became regent for her son, **Afonso Henriques**, and began to try to forge a union with Galicia. Afonso, however, had other ideas and having defeated his mother at the battle of São Mamede (1128), he established a capital at **Guimarães** and set about extending his domains to the south.

The reconquest of central Portugal was quickly achieved. Afonso's victory at Ourique in 1139 was a decisive blow and by 1147 he had taken Santarém. In the same year Lisbon fell, after a siege in which passing Crusaders again played a vital role – though not sailing on to the Holy Land before murderously sacking the city. Many of them were English and some stayed on; Gilbert of Hastings became Archbishop. By now Afonso was dubbing himself the **first King of Portugal**, a title tacitly acknowledged by Alfonso VII (the new king of León) in 1137 and officially confirmed by the Treaty of Zamora in 1143. His kingdom spread more or less to the borders of modern Portugal, though in the south, Alentejo and the Algarve were still in Muslim hands.

For the next century and a half Afonso's successors struggled to dominate this last stronghold of the Moors. Sancho I (1185–1211) took their capital, Silves, in 1189, but his gains were not consolidated and almost everything south of the Tagus was recaptured the following year by al-Mansur, the last great campaigning vizier of al-Andalus. The overall pattern, though, was of steady expansion with occasional setbacks. Sancho II (1223–48) invaded the Alentejo and the eastern Algarve, while his successor **Afonso III** (1248–79) moved westwards, taking Faro and establishing the kingdom in pretty much its final shape.

THE BURGUNDIAN KINGS

The reconquest of land from the Muslims also incorporated a process of **recolonization**. As it fell into the king's hands, new territory was granted to such of his subjects that he felt would be able to defend it. In this way much of the country came to be divided between the church, the Holy Orders – chief among them the Knights Templar – and a hundred or so powerful nobles (*ricos homens*). The entire kingdom had a population of under half a million, the majority of them concentrated in the north. Here, there was little displacement of the traditional feudal ties, but in the south the influx of Christian peasants blurred the distinction between serf and settler, dependent relationships coming instead to be based on the payment of rent.

Meanwhile a **political infrastructure** was being established. The land was divided into municipalities (*concelhos*), each with its own charter (*foral*). A formalized structure of consultation began, with the first **Cortes** (parliament) being held in Coimbra in 1211. At first consisting mainly of the clergy and nobility, it later came to include wealthy merchants and townsmen, a development speeded both by the need to raise taxes and by later kings' constant struggles against the growing power of the church. The capital, which Afonso Henriques had moved to Coimbra in 1139, was transferred to **Lisbon** in about 1260 by Afonso III.

The Burgundian dynasty lasted through nine kings for 257 years. In the steady process of establishing the new kingdom, one name stands out above all others, that of **Dom Dinis**

(1279–1325). With the reconquest barely complete when he came to the throne, Dinis set about a far-sighted policy of stabilization and of strengthening the nation to ensure its future independence. During his reign, fifty fortresses were constructed along the frontier with Castile, while at the same time negotiations were going on, leading eventually to the Treaty of Alcañices (1297) by which Spain acknowledged Portugal's frontiers. At home Dinis established a major programme of forest planting and of agricultural reform; grain, olive oil, wine, salt, salt fish and dried fruit became staple exports to Flanders, Brittany, Catalonia and Britain. Importance, too, was attached to education and the arts: a **university**, later transferred to Coimbra, was founded at Lisbon in 1290. Dinis also helped entrench the power of the monarchy, forcing the church to accept a much larger degree of state control and, in 1319, reorganizing the Knights Templar – at the time being suppressed all over Europe – as the **Order of Christ**, still enormously powerful but now responsible directly to the king rather than to the pope.

Despite Dinis's precautions, fear of **Castilian domination** continued to play an important part in the reigns of his successors, largely owing to consistent intermarrying between the two royal families. On the death of the last of the Burgundian kings, Fernando I, power passed to his widow Leonor, who ruled as regent. Leonor, whose only daughter had married Juan I of Castile, promised the throne to the children of that marriage. In this she had the support of most of the nobility, but the merchant and peasant classes strongly opposed a Spanish ruler, supporting instead the claim of João, Grand Master of the House of Avis and a bastard heir of the Burgundian line. A popular revolt against Leonor led to two years of war with Castile, finally settled at the **Battle of Aljubarrota** (1385) in which João, backed up by a force of English archers, wiped out the much larger Castilian army.

The great abbey of **Batalha** (p.157) was built to commemorate the victory. **João I**, first king of the **House of Avis**, was crowned at Coimbra the same year, sealing relations with England through the 1386 Treaty of Windsor – an alliance which lasted into the twentieth century – and his marriage to Philippa of Lancaster, daughter of John of Gaunt, the following year.

DOM MANUEL AND THE MARITIME EMPIRE

Occupying such a strategic position between the Atlantic and the Mediterranean, it was inevitable that Portuguese attention would at some stage turn to **maritime expansion**. When peace was finally made with Castile in 1411, João I was able to turn his resources toward Morocco. The outpost at Ceuta fell in 1415, but successive attempts to capture Tangier were not realized until the reign of Afonso V, in 1471.

At first such overseas adventuring was undertaken partly in a crusading spirit, partly to keep potentially troublesome nobles busy. The proximity of North Africa made it a constant feature of foreign policy, giving a welcome boost to the economy of the Algarve. The first real advances in exploration, however, came about through the activities of **Prince Henry "the Navigator"**, third son of João and Philippa. As Grand Master of the Order of Christ, he turned that organization's vast resources towards marine development, founding a School of Navigation on the desolate promontory of Sagres (then regarded as the end of the world) and staffing it with Europe's leading cartographers, navigators and seamen. As well as improving the art of offshore navigation, they redesigned the caravel, making it a vessel well suited to long ocean-going journeys. **Madeira** and the **Azores** were discovered in 1419 and 1427 respectively, and by the time of Henry's death in 1460 the **Cape Verde Islands** and the **west coast of Africa** down to Sierra Leone had both been explored.

After a brief hiatus, overseas expansion received a fresh boost in the reigns of João II, Manuel and João III. In 1487 **Bartolomeu Dias** finally made it around the southern tip of Africa, christening it "Cabo da Boa Esperança" in the hope of good things to come. Within ten years **Vasco da Gama** had sailed on past it to open up the **trade route to India**. This was the great breakthrough and the Portuguese monarchy, already doing well out of African gold, promptly became the richest in Europe, taking a fifth of the profits of all trade and controlling important monopolies on some spices. The small cargo of pepper brought back by Vasco on his first expedition was enough to pay for the trip three times over. Meanwhile Spain was opening up the New World and by the **Treaty of Tordesillas** in 1494 the two Iberian nations divided the world between them along an imaginary line 370 leagues west of the Cape Verde Islands. This not only gave Portugal the run of the Orient but also, when it was discovered in 1500, Brazil (though its exploitation would have to wait nearly 200 more years). By the mid-sixteenth century Portugal dominated **world trade**; strategic posts had been established at Goa (1510), Malacca (1511), Ormuz (1515) and Macau (1557), and the revenue from dealings with the East was backed up by a large-scale **slave trade** between West Africa and Europe and Brazil.

The reign of **Manuel I** (1495–1521) marked the apogee of Portuguese wealth and strength. It found its expression at home in the extraordinary exuberance of the "**Manueline**" style of architecture – an elaborately decorative genre which found its inspiration in marine motifs. Notable examples can be seen in the Convent of Christ at Tomar and the monastery and tower of Belém in Lisbon (see pp.82–85), while the best examples of civil architecture are probably the extensions made by Manuel to the royal palace at Sintra.

Enormous wealth there may have been, but very little of it filtered down through the system, and in the country at large conditions barely improved. The practice of siphoning off a hefty slice of the income into the royal coffers effectively prevented the development of an entrepreneurial class and, as everywhere else in Europe, financial matters were left very much in the hands of the Jews, who were not allowed to take up most other professions.

Portugal had traditionally been considerably more tolerant than other European nations in its treatment of its **Jewish citizens** (and towards the Moorish minority who had been absorbed after the reconquest). However, popular resentment of their riches, and pressure from Spain, forced Manuel – who had initially welcomed refugees from the Spanish persecution – to order their **expulsion** in 1496. Although many chose the pragmatic course of remaining as "New Christian" converts, others fled to the Netherlands. This exodus, continued as a result of the activities of the **Inquisition** (from 1531 on), created a vacuum which left Portugal with an extensive empire based upon commerce, but deprived of much of its commercial expertise. By the 1570s the economy was beginning to collapse: incoming wealth was insufficient to cover the growing costs of maintaining an empire against increasing competition, a situation exacerbated by foreign debts, falling prices and a decline in the productivity of domestic agriculture.

SPANISH DOMINATION

In the end it was a combination of reckless imperialism and impecunity which brought to an end the dynasty of the House of Avis and with it, at least temporarily, Portuguese independence. **Dom Sebastião** (1557–78), obsessed with dreams of a new crusade against Morocco, set out at the head of a huge army to satisfy his fanatical fantasies. They were crushed at the battle of **Alcácer-Quibir** (1578), where the Portuguese dead numbered over eight thousand, including Sebastião and most of Portugal's nobility. The aged **Cardinal Henrique** took the throne as the closest legitimate relative and devoted his brief reign to attempting to raise the crippling ransoms for those captured on the battlefield.

The Cardinal's death without heirs in 1580 provided Spain with the pretext to renew its claim to Portugal. **Philip II** of Spain, Sebastião's uncle, defeated his rivals at the battle of Alcântara and in 1581 was crowned Felipe I of Portugal, inaugurating a period of Hapsburg rule which lasted for another sixty years. In the short term, although unpopular, the union had advantages for Portugal. Spanish wheat helped alleviate the domestic shortage and Spanish seapower helped protect the far-flung empire. Philip, moreover, studiously protected Portuguese autonomy, maintaining an entirely separate bureaucracy and spending long periods in Portugal in an attempt to win popular support. Not that he ever did – throughout his reign pretenders appeared claiming to be Sebastião miraculously saved from the Moroccan desert, tapping a strong vein of resentment among the people. And in the long run, Spanish control proved disastrous. Association with Spain's foreign policy (part of the Armada was prepared in Lisbon) meant the enmity of the Dutch and the British, Portugal's traditional allies, losing the country an important part of its trade which was never to be regained.

Philip's successors made no attempt at all to protect Portuguese sensibilities – cynical and uninterested, they attempted to rule from Madrid while raising heavy taxes to pay for Spain's wars. The final straw was the attempt by Philip IV (Felipe III of Portugal) to conscript Portuguese troops to quell a rising in Catalonia. On December 1, 1640, a small group of conspirators stormed the palace in Lisbon and deposed the Duchess of Mantua, Governor of Portugal. By popular acclaim and despite personal reluctance, the Duke of Bragança, senior member of a family which had long been the most powerful in the country, took the throne as **João IV**.

THE HOUSE OF BRAGANÇA

At first the newly independent nation looked pretty shaky, deprived of most of its trade routes and with the apparently imminent threat of invasion from Spain hanging over it. As it turned out, however, the Spanish were so preoccupied with wars elsewhere that they had little choice but to accept the situation, though they did not do so formally until 1668 under the **Treaty of Lisbon**. João IV used the opportunity to rebuild old alliances and although the Portuguese were often forced into unfavourable terms, they were at least trading again. Relations with Britain had been strained during the establishment of that country's Commonwealth, especially by Oliver Cromwell's particular brand of Protestant commercialism, but were revived by the marriage of Charles II to Catherine of Bragança in 1661.

At home Portugal was developing an increasingly centralized administration. The **discovery of gold and diamonds in Brazil** during the reign of Pedro II (1683–1706) made the crown financially independent and did away with the need for the Cortes (or any form of popular representation) for most of the next century. It was **João V**, coming to the throne in 1706, who most benefited from the new riches, which he squandered in an orgy of lavish Baroque building. His massive convent at **Mafra**, built totally without regard to expense, employed at times as many as fifty thousand workmen, virtually bankrupting the state. Meanwhile nothing was being done to revive the economy, and what little remained from João's grandiose schemes went mainly to pay for imports. The infamous **Methuen Treaty**, signed in 1703 to stimulate trade with Britain, only made matters worse: although it opened up new markets for Portuguese

wine, it helped destroy the native textile industry by letting in British cloth at preferential rates.

The accession of João's apathetic son, **José I** (1750–77), allowed the total concentration of power in the hands of the king's chief minister, the **Marquês de Pombal**, who became the classic "enlightened despot" of eighteenth-century history. It was the **Great Earthquake of 1755** that sealed his dominance over the age; while everyone else was panicking, Pombal's policy was simple – "bury the dead and feed the living".

Pombal saw his subsequent mission as to modernize all aspects of Portuguese life, by establishing an efficient and secular bureaucracy, renewing the system of taxation, setting up export companies, protecting trade and abolishing slavery within Portugal. It was a strategy that made him many enemies among the old aristocracy and above all within the Church, whose overbearing influence he fought at every turn. Opposition, though, was dealt with ruthlessly and an assassination attempt on the king in 1758 (which some say was staged by Pombal) gave him the chance he needed to destroy his enemies. Denouncing their supposed involvement, Pombal executed the country's leading aristocrats and abolished the Jesuit order, which had long dominated education and religious life in Portugal and Brazil.

Although Pombal himself was taken to trial (and found guilty but pardoned on the grounds of old age) with the accession of Maria I (1777–1816), the majority of his labours survived him, most notably the reform of education along scientific lines and his completely rebuilt capital, Lisbon. Further development, however, was soon thwarted by a new invasion.

FRENCH OCCUPATION AND THE MIGUELITE YEARS

With the appearance of **Napoleon** on the international scene, Portugal once more became embroiled in the affairs of Europe. The French threatened to invade unless the Portuguese supported their naval blockade of Britain, a demand that no one expected them to obey since British ports were the destination for most of Portugal's exports. Only the protection of the British fleet, especially after the victory at Trafalgar in 1805, kept the country's trade routes open. General Junot duly marched into Lisbon in November 1807.

On British advice the royal family had already gone into exile in Brazil, where they were to stay until 1821, and the war was left largely in the hands of British generals **Beresford** and **Wellington**. Having twice been driven out and twice reinvaded, the French were finally forced back into Spain in 1811 following the Battle of Buçaco (1810) and a long period of near starvation before the lines of Torres Vedras.

Britain's prize for this was the right to trade freely with **Brazil**, which, together with the declaration of that country as a kingdom in its own right, fatally weakened the dependent relationship that had profited the Portuguese treasury for so long. Past roles were reversed, with Portugal becoming effectively a colony of Brazil (where the royal family remained) and a protectorate of Britain, with General Beresford as administrator. The only active national institution was the army, many of whose officers had absorbed the constitutional ideals of revolutionary France.

In August 1820, with Beresford temporarily out of the country and King João VI still in Brazil, a group of officers called an unofficial Cortes and proceeded to draw up a new **constitution**. Inspired by the recent liberal advances in Spain, it called for an assembly – to be elected every two years by universal male suffrage – and the abolition of clerical privilege and the traditional rights of the nobility. The king, forced to choose between Portugal and Brazil, where his position looked even more precarious, came back in 1821 and accepted its terms. His queen, Carlota, and younger son **Miguel**, however, refused to take the oath of allegiance and became the dynamic behind a reactionary movement which drew considerable support in rural areas. With João VI's death in 1826, a delegation was sent to Brazil to pronounce Crown Prince Pedro the new king. Unfortunately Pedro was already Emperor of Brazil, having declared its independence some years earlier. He resolved to pass the crown to his infant daughter, with Miguel as regent provided that he swore to accept a new charter, drawn up by Pedro and somewhat less liberal than the earlier constitution. Miguel agreed, but once in power promptly tore up any agreement, abolished the charter and returned to the old, absolutist ways. This was a surprisingly popular move in Portugal, certainly in the countryside, but not with the governments of Britain, Spain,

or France who backed the liberal rebels and finally put Pedro IV (who had meanwhile been deposed in Brazil) on the throne after Miguel's defeat at Évora-Monte in 1834.

THE DEATH OF THE MONARCHY

Pedro didn't survive long. The rest of the century – under the rule of his daughter Maria II (1834–53) and his grandsons Pedro V (1853–61) and Luís (1861–89) – saw almost constant struggle between those who supported the charter and those who favoured a return to the more liberal constitution of 1822. In 1846 the position deteriorated virtually to a state of **civil war** between Maria, who was fanatical in her support of her father's charter, and the radical constitutionalists. Only a further intervention by foreign powers maintained peace, imposed at the Convention of Gramido (1847).

In the second half of the century, with relative stability and the two warring factions to some extent institutionalized into a revolving two-party system, the economy began at last to recover, with the first signs of widespread industrialization and a major public works programme under the minister Fontes Pereira de Melo. The monarchy, however, was almost bankrupt and its public humiliation over possessions in Africa – Britain and Germany simply ignored the Portuguese claim to the land between Angola and Mozambique – helped strengthen growing republican feelings.

Republicanism took root particularly easily in the army and among the urban poor, fuelled by falling standards of living and growing anger at government ineptitude. **Dom Carlos** (1898–1908) attempted to rule dictatorially after 1906, alienating most sectors of the country in the process, and was assassinated, along with his eldest son, following a failed Republican coup in 1908. Finally, on October 5, 1910, the **monarchy was overthrown** once and for all by a joint revolt of the army and navy. Dom Manuel went into exile and died, in Britain, in 1932.

THE "DEMOCRATIC" REPUBLIC

After a provisional government of Republican Unity, **elections** took place in 1911, showing a marked swing towards Afonso Costa's **Democratic Party**, which remained the most dominant political force in the country until 1926. However, the divisions among the Republicans, the cyclical attempts at violent overthrow of the new regime by the monarchists, and the weakening of the country's economic, social and political structures, kept the Republic in permanent turmoil. Political life was in chaos and the hopes, perhaps unrealistically high, of the Republic's supporters never began to be realized. There were 45 changes of government in sixteen years and several military uprisings.

The forces that had brought the Republic were supported largely by the urban and rural poor, yet new electoral laws based on a literacy test led to a smaller electorate than under the monarchy, disenfranchising most of the Republic's strongest supporters. Successive governments failed to fulfil the least aspirations. Anticlericalism had been a major plank of Costa's platform, arousing massive hostility in the countryside. Legalizing the right to strike merely gave workers a chance to voice their discontent in a massive wave of work stoppages, but the new regime proved to be less than responsive to workers' rights and the repression of union activities was a constant theme. Further fuel was given to the reaction by Portugal's economically disastrous decision to enter **World War I** on the side of the Allies in 1916 and by the vicissitudes of the postwar recession. By 1926 not even the trade unions were prepared to stand by the Republic, preferring to maintain "proletarian neutrality" in the face of what at first seemed no more significant a military intervention than any other.

SALAZAR AND THE "NEW STATE"

While the military may have known what they wanted to overthrow in 1926, they were at first divided as to whether to replace it with a new Republican government or a restored monarchy. From the infighting, a Catholic monarchist, **General Carmona**, eventually emerged as president (which he remained until his death in 1951) with the Republican constitution suspended.

In 1928 one **Dr. António de Oliveira Salazar** joined the Cabinet as Finance Minister. A professor of economics at Coimbra University, he took the post only on condition that he would control the spending and revenue of all government departments. His strict monetarist line (helped by a change in the accounting system) immediately balanced the budget for the first time since 1913 and in the short term the economic situation was visibly improved. From then on he effectively controlled the country, becoming prime minister in 1932 and not relinquishing that role until 1968.

His regime was very much in keeping with the political tenor of the 1930s and while it had few of the ideological pretensions of a **fascist** state, it had many of the trappings. Members of the National Assembly were chosen from the one permitted political association, the National Union (UN); "workers' organizations" were set up, but run by their employers; education was strictly controlled by the state to promote Catholic values; and censorship was strictly enforced. Opposition was kept in check by the PIDE – a secret police force set up with Gestapo assistance – which used systematic torture and long-term detention in camps on the Azores and Cabo Verde Islands to defuse most resistance. The army, too, was heavily infiltrated by PIDE and none of the several coups mounted against Salazar came close to success. Despite remaining formally neutral throughout the **Spanish Civil War**, Salazar had openly assisted the plotters in their preparations and later sent unofficial army units to fight with Franco. Republican refugees were deported to face certain execution at Nationalist hands.

At home Salazar succeeded in producing the infrastructure of a relatively modern economy but the results of growth were felt by only a few and agriculture, in particular, was allowed to stagnate. Internal unrest, while widespread, was surprisingly muted and apparently easily controlled; the New State's downfall, when it came, was precipitated far more by external factors. Salazar was an ardent imperialist who found himself faced with growing **colonial wars**, which proved costly and brought international disapprobation. India seized Goa and the other Portuguese possessions in 1961 and at about the same time the first serious disturbances were occurring in Angola, Mozambique and, later, in Guinea-Bissau. The regime was prepared to make only the slightest concessions, attempting to defuse the freedom movements by speeding economic development.

The government's reign came to an end in 1968 when Salazar's deck-chair collapsed, and he suffered brain damage. Incapacitated, he lived for another two years, deposed as premier – though such was the fear of the man, no one ever dared tell him. His successor, **Marcelo Caetano**, attempted to prolong the regime by offering limited democratization at home. However, tensions beneath the surface were fast becoming more overt and attempts to liberalize foreign policy failed to check the growth of guerrilla activity in the remaining colonies, or of **discontent in the army**.

It was in the African-stationed army especially that opposition crystallized. There the young conscript officers came more and more to sympathize with the freedom movements they were intended to suppress and to resent the cost – in economic terms and in lives – of the hopeless struggle. From their number grew the revolutionary **Movimento das Forças Armadas** (MFA).

REVOLUTION

By 1974 the situation in Africa was deteriorating rapidly and at home Caetano's liberalization had come to a dead end; morale, among the army and the people, was lower than ever. The **MFA**, formed originally as an officers' organization to press for better conditions, and which had become increasingly politicized, was already laying its plans for a takeover. Dismissal of two popular generals – Spínola and Costa Gomes – for refusing publicly to support Caetano, led to a first chaotic and abortive attempt on March 16. Finally on April 25, 1974, the plans laid by **Major Otelo Saraiva de Carvalho** for the MFA were complete and their virtually bloodless **coup** went without a hitch, no serious attempt being made to defend the government.

The next two years were perhaps the most extraordinary in Portugal's history, a period of continual **revolution**, massive politicization and virtual anarchy, during which decisions of enormous importance were nevertheless made – above all the granting of independence to all of the overseas territories. At first there was little clear idea of any programme beyond the fact that the army wanted out of Africa. Though the MFA leadership was clearly to the left and at first associated with the PCP (Portuguese Communist Party), the bulk of the officers were less political and **General Spínola**, whom they had been forced to accept as a figurehead, was only marginally to the left of Caetano and strongly opposed total independence for the colonies. Spínola's dream was clearly to "do a de Gaulle" in Portugal, while the army was above all determined not to replace one dictator with another.

In the event their hands were forced by the massive popular response and especially by huge demonstrations on May Day. It was clear that whatever the leadership might decide, the people, especially in the cities, demanded a rapid move to the left. From the start every party was striving to project itself as the true defender of the "ideals of April 25". Provisional governments came and went but real power rested, where it had begun, with the MFA, now dominated by Saraiva de Carvalho and Vasco Gonçalves. While politicians argued around them, the army claimed to speak directly to the people, leading the country steadily left. It was a period of extraordinary contradictions, with the PCP, hoping to consolidate their position as the "true" revolutionary party, opposing liberalization and condemning strikes as counter-revolutionary, while ultra-conservative peasants were happily seizing their land from its owners.

Sudden **independence** and the withdrawal of Portuguese forces from the former colonies – while generally greeted in Portugal with relief – did not always work so well for the countries involved. Guinea-Bissau and Mozambique, the first to go, experienced relatively peaceful transitions, but **Angola** came to be a serious point of division between Spínola and the MFA. When independence finally came, after Spínola's resignation, the country was already in the midst of a full-scale civil war. The situation was even worse in **East Timor**, where more than ten percent of the population was massacred by invading Indonesian forces following Portuguese withdrawal. In Portugal itself the arrival of more than half-a-million colonial refugees – many of them destitute, most bitter – came to be a major problem for the regime, though their eventual integration proved one of its triumphs.

At home, the first **crisis** came in September 1974, when Spínola, with Gonçalves and Saraiva de Carvalho virtual prisoners in Lisbon's Belém Palace, moved army units to take over key positions. The MFA, however, proved too strong and Spínola was forced to resign, General Costa Gomes replacing him as president. By the summer of 1975 more general reaction was setting in and even the MFA began to show signs of disunity. The country was increasingly split, supporting the Revolution in the south, while remaining deeply conservative in the north. The Archbishop of Braga summed up the north's traditional views, declaring that the struggle against communism should be seen "not in terms of man against man, but Christ against Satan". Nevertheless the Revolution continued to advance; a coup attempt in March failed when the troops involved turned against their officers. The Council of the Revolution was formed, promptly nationalizing banking and private insurance; widespread land seizures went ahead in the Alentejo; and **elections** in the summer resulted in an impressive victory for Mário Soares' Socialist Party (PS).

On November 25, 1975, elements of the army opposed to the rightward shift in the government moved for yet another **coup**, taking over major air bases across the country. Otelo Saraiva de Carvalho, however, declined to bring his Lisbon command to their aid; nor did the hoped-for mass mobilization of the people take place. Government troops under Colonel Ramalho Eanes moved in to force their surrender and – again virtually without bloodshed – the Revolution had ended.

DEMOCRACY AND EUROPE: THE 1980S

The period since November 1975 has been one of slow, and sometimes shaky-looking, **retrenchment**. The Socialist Party was still in power at the end of 1975 and won further ground in the elections that followed, helping to shape the post-revolutionary constitution – a mildly Socialist document, though providing for a fairly powerful president. Early fears of a right-wing coup led by Spínola failed to materialize, helped by the election of Colonel Eanes, a man whom the army trusted, as president. Saraiva de Carvalho came in second, despite the fact that no major party supported him – a token of the degree of popular following enjoyed by the MFA during the Revolution.

Although parties of the right and centre have consistently polled higher votes, the Socialists had effective control until 1980 when Dr. Sá Carneiro managed to create the **Democratic Alliance**, uniting the larger groupings on the right. But within a few months he died in a plane crash. His successor as prime minister, Francisco Pinto Balsemão, barely managed to maintain the coalition for the two years of the term remaining and then only because the rightist parties were united in their determination to amend the constitution "to eliminate clauses which were appropriate in the post-revolutionary atmosphere of 1976 but not to today's needs".

The most enigmatic figure throughout this period remained **President Eanes**, a career soldier who supported the MFA in its early days, later led the forces who ended the Revolution, and is now accused by the right of being a "Marxist sympathizer". He above all seemed to be the figure of stability, with enormous popular support though (at least until recently) apparently little ambition, being happy to concentrate on developing Portugal's links with Africa, Asia and Latin America and overseeing a gradual normalization process.

In **elections** held on the ninth anniversary of the Revolution, April 25, 1983, Mário Soares' Socialist Party again became the largest single party in the national assembly, though requiring the support of the Social Democrats to maintain a coalition government. Soares' premiership was dogged by the unpopularity of his **economic austerity measures** (in part insisted on by the IMF) and by constant delays and breakdowns in the talks over Portuguese and Spanish **entry into the European Community**. These problems did have one positive result, namely closer relations with the traditionally hostile government in Madrid. But the government's economic problems led eventually to the withdrawal of Social Democratic support and to the collapse of the coalition.

New elections in October 1985 were barely conclusive: the left-wing vote split three ways and the Socialists lost their position as largest party to the **Social Democrats** (PSD), whose flamboyant leader, **Dr. Aníbal Cavaco Silva**, became prime minister. But the main feature of the election was disillusionment with the government and the choices on offer to the electorate. There was massive, countrywide abstention and, in rural districts (where people worried most about the effects of EC membership), attacks occurred on polling booths.

In the months that followed, the revolutionary leader, Lt-Colonel Otelo Saraiva de Carvalho, was arrested and put on trial in Lisbon accused of being the leader of 73 suspected terrorists in the **FP-25** urban guerrilla group. Proceedings were postponed following the shooting of one of the key witnesses and it was not until 1987 that Saraiva de Carvalho was sentenced to 15 years' imprisonment (50 others also received prison sentences). He was later conditionally released after a Supreme Court ruling that there had been irregularities at his trial. In February 1990 he renounced the armed struggle and requested an amnesty.

President Eanes, meanwhile – the other great figure at the end of the Revolution – had been forced to resign the presidency on completion of his second term in January 1986. He was replaced by former Socialist Prime Minister **Mário Soares** who, with the reluctant support of the Communists, narrowly defeated the candidate of the centre-right, becoming the first civilian president for sixty years.

Portugal's entry into the **European Community** in 1986 brought with it the most important changes since the Revolution. With the help of a massive injection of funds to modernize infrastructure and increased foreign investment, Portugal enjoyed unprecedented **economic growth**, running at above four percent per year, greater than most of its European partners. For many Portuguese this resulted in greater material wealth, but behind the trappings of the new prosperity remained pockets of deeply entrenched poverty.

Prime Minister Aníbal Cavaco Silva's early attempts to introduce an economic reform programme were hampered by his lack of a majority, but in April 1987 a censure motion defeat caused the prime minister to resign, bringing about general elections. The PSD (Social Democrats) were returned to power in surprising numbers, enjoying the first absolute majority since the 1974 Revolution and the strength to implement real changes. The centre-right government's free enterprise drive for the removal of Socialist structures and privatization did not run unchallenged: the late 1980s were marked by **industrial unrest**. In March 1988, 1.5 million workers took part in a 24-hour general strike in protest against labour reform laws freeing up employers to lay off workers. The law was eventually approved by both the assembly and the president, but strikes continued throughout 1989 in various sectors of the workforce, attempting to bring wages in line with inflation. The government was also able to reach an eventual agreement with the opposition to remove Marxist-Leninist elements from the constitution in August 1989.

The Portuguese **Green Party** won its first seat in the **European Parliament** elections in Strasbourg in June 1989 and the ruling PSD was successful in retaining most of its own seats, but suffered an enormous set-back six months later in municipal elections. The socialist opposition gained control of the capital,

Lisbon; the northern industrial centre, Porto; and other significant cities. Four years of economic growth had benefited a new yuppie class, but voters were aware of accentuated social inequality and the continued inadequacy of health and education structures. Public opinion had also been influenced by **financial scandals** involving government ministers. Aníbal Cavaco Silva, however, avoided any dirt rubbing off on him personally and survived a motion of censure questioning the government's ethics. The ministers involved were summarily replaced in a surprise end-of-year reshuffle, along with three other ministers, in a move which was taken to indicate Cavaco Silva's firm grip on the reins.

THE 1990S – AND INTO THE NEW MILLENNIUM

Scandal was also in the air surrounding **President Mário Soares** in early 1990, when the Socialist governor of Portuguese-administered **Macau** (Hong Kong's enclave neighbour), a man personally appointed by Soares, was accused of receiving back-handers from a German company trying to secure the contract for the building of an airport. The incident called Soares' staff's integrity into question and strained relations with the prime minister, Cavaco Silva. But the president, popular for his down-to-earth image and his dislike of ceremony, retained his public support and won a landslide victory in presidential elections in January 1991. At Cavaco Silva's insistence, the PSD had not put forward a candidate for the presidency, partly in acknowledgement of a successful relationship between the government and the incumbent president and partly to avoid any further humiliation of a figure who was guaranteed to win. In turn, Cavaco Silva won a convincing mandate in the elections of October 1991, when the **PSD returned to government** with over fifty percent of the vote.

The new decade took Portugal into the second stage of its ten-year transition phase for EC entry and into its **presidency of the European Community** in 1992, the year when (on December 31) all remaining trade and employment barriers were removed and the EC became the EU. The country adopted its EU task with considerable imagination, and expense, staging a superb exhibiton of its culture – Europalia – in Brussels, and building a grand presidency HQ in the Lisbon suburb of Belém. On the domestic front, the PSD continued with privatization and forged plans for the conversion of state-run banks in preparation for joining the European Monetary System in the mid-1990s.

Dealing with **inflation** remained at the top of the government's agenda, during the early 1990s. It had to do this while coping with increased discontent over social issues, as the opposition called it to account for statistics that show Portugal had, and still has, the highest **infant mortality** and **illiteracy** rates in Europe. Unemployment figures, too, hide a high proportion of underpaid and part-time workers and disguise the fact that wages have failed to increase in real terms in spite of impressive economic growth. There are fears, too, that now the European Union has brought down its trade borders completely, fiercer competition is likely to force more Portuguese out of work. Portugal's social security system is incapable of assimilating large numbers of **unemployed**, something which could lead to social unrest.

The **opening up of Eastern Europe** has also exposed Portugal to fiercer competition for trade and investment, although a modernized infrastructure and improved transport networks mean that it continues to be attractive to foreign investors. **Tourism**, which accounts for nearly a tenth of the country's GNP and over a quarter of all foreign investment, has flourished and one challenge will be finding alternatives to the Algarve, where restrictions have been imposed to control the industry's all too disturbingly obvious side-effects.

One of the main headaches for the government, though, continues to be the inefficiency of **Portuguese agriculture**, which employs nearly one-fifth of the workforce but produces only a fraction of the country's wealth. So far, help from Brussels has buffered the less advantageous effects of EU membership, but the honeymoon period is over and although some modernization has taken place, there is still a huge gap between Portuguese **prices** and European Union prices – a gap that will tend to keep Portugal among Europe's poorest nations. A slightly alarming shift, too, has been the takeover of large areas of banking, real estate and the financial sectors by Spanish companies, while EU funds still play a dominant role in Portugal's development, thus blurring the true extent of real economic growth.

General elections in October 1995 brought ten years of Conservative rule to an end and the moderate Socialists came into power under the enthusiastic leadership of **António Guterres**. The Portuguese had tired of Cavaco Silva's austere, secretive style of government and were ready for a change. The Socialists fell just short of an absolute majority, but won a comfortable advantage against a divided opposition. Guterres' programme differed little from that of his conservative predecessors and caused few worries for the business world. He offered a touch more sympathy towards the social welfare budget and a tougher stance towards the European Union, but otherwise pledged to continue to liberalize and privatize the economy and keep the country on target for European monetary union (which was duly achieved on January 1, 1999).

A final nail was banged into the coffin of Cavaquismo by Cavaco Silva's surprise defeat in the presidential elections of January 1996. The leftwing former mayor of Lisbon, **Jorge Sampaio**, whose avuncular, paternalistic style reflects that of his predecessor, Mario Soares, won 54 percent of the votes, against Cavaco Silva's 46 percent. This result gave Portugal a head of state and prime minister from the same – Socialist – party for the first time since the 1974 Revolution.

In the **October 1999 general elections**, stability seemed the order of the day, with Guterres and the Socialists returned for a second consecutive mandate – the first since the revolution, with precisely fifty percent of the vote (which guarantees the liveliest parliament for years). Cavaco Silva, meanwhile, remains active in politics and, should he decide to stand in the next presidential elections (scheduled for 2001), would be considered a threat to Sampaio, although Sampaio has endeared himself greatly to the Portuguese and would be difficult to unseat.

As this book goes to press, Portugal's last colony – Macau – is about to be handed back to the Chinese, amid concerns that democracy be safeguarded. But of greater concern, as the old millennium drew to an end, was the situation in another former colony, **East Timor** (Timor Loro Sae). Following the 1974 revolution, the Portuguese abandoned the territory, leaving it unable to prevent its illegal annexation by Indonesia. Indonesia's bloody

24-year rule resulted in the genocide of over a third of the population, and only came to an end after a UN-organized referendum in August 1999 – for which the Portuguese had been pushing for two decades, and which voted overwhelmingly in favour of independence. As the UN prepared to leave, Indonesian-backed militias fulfilled their publicly stated promise to avenge the result, and embarked on a six-week orgy of killings which saw over half the population flee their homes, and the capital – Dili – almost completely destroyed. The news of the atrocities which followed prompted a popular movement in Portugal which found expression in the unlikeliest of places – posters of support displayed in buses and trains, vigils in many cities and towns, and an email and fax campaign (free numbers were set up by Portugal Telecom and others) to pressurize the United Nations into sending a peace-enforcing mission to East Timor. Although East Timor now barely functions as an independent state, and will be reliant on international donors and the UN for many years to come, the sense of relief in Portugal was palpable – the feeling was not one of success, but of a long-standing obligation which had finally been fulfilled.

The next major event on Portugal's calendar is the issuing of the common European currency – the euro – in 2002. Prices in most shops are now priced in both escudos and euros, in an attempt to habituate people to the new money. But the persistent worry is that the euro might slowly push up prices in a country which still earns much less per capita than its more industrialized partners. On the positive side the rural areas, which had remained untouched by the transformations of recent years, are beginning to see economic change, brought about partly by the new EU-funded motorways, but also out of fear of being caught lagging behind when the full effect of the unified currency hits home. However, with the EU's attention – and purse – now more attracted to eastern Europe, it seems likely that Portugal will have to shoulder more of its own financial burdens.

But for now, the political popularity of the left shows a desire for a framework of democratic stability and a leaning towards a fresher and more effervescent spirit, particularly among the young. Internationally, Portuguese self-esteem, already bolstered by the successful Lisbon Expo in 1998, will be further enhanced by Porto's becoming European Capital of Culture in 2001, and Portugal having been chosen to host the European Football Championships in 2004.

CHRONOLOGY OF MONUMENTS AND ARTS

2000 BC–1500 BC	**Neolithic** settlements in the north of the country – **Verracos Culture** in Trás-os-Montes.	*Porcas* (stone boars) of Bragança, Murça, etc.
700 BC–600 BC	**Castro Culture** of fortified hill-towns, or *citânias*, concentrated in the Minho; refined by the **Celtic** Iron Age invasions.	**Citânia de Briteiros** (near Braga) and other sites; best collection of artefacts in Museu Martins Sarmento, Guimarães.
210 BC	**Romans** enter peninsula and begin colonization; northern Portugal not finally pacified until 19 BC.	**Conímbriga**, 4th BC Celtic town near Coimbra, adapted to Roman occupation (survives until 5th c AD).
60 BC	Julius Caesar establishes a capital at Lisbon and towns at Beja, Évora, Santarém, etc.	Walls and other remains at Idanha, in Beira Baixa; temple and aqueducts of Évora; bridges at Chaves, Ponte de Lima, Leiria and elsewhere.
4th c AD	Bishoprics founded at Braga, Évora, Faro and Lisbon.	
409–411	**Barbarian** invasions: Suevi settle in the north.	
585	**Visigoths** incorporate Suevian state into their Iberian empire.	Isolated churches, mainly in the north, include 7th-c São Pedro de Balsemão (near Lamego) and São Frutuoso at Braga.
711	**Moors** from North Africa invade and conquer peninsula within seven years.	Fortresses/walls survive at Silves, Lisbon, Sintra, Elvas, Mértola, Alcácer do Sal, etc.
9th c	**Al-Gharb** (Algarve) becomes an independent Moorish kingdom, governed from Silves.	Moorish legacy also includes *azulejos* (ceramic tiles), later designed by Muslim (Mudejar) craftsmen for royal palace at Sintra, etc.
868	Porto reconquered by Christian kings of Asturias-León.	
11th c	Country of **Portucale** emerges and (1097) is given to Henry of Burgundy.	Cluniac monks, administering pilgrimage route to Santiago, bring Romanesque architecture from France. 12th-c churches at Bravães, Tomar, etc. Council chamber at Bragança.
1143	**Afonso Henriques** recognized as first king of Portucale at the Treaty of Zamora.	Guimarães castle built.
1147	Afonso takes Lisbon and Santarém from the Moors; followed in 1162 by Beja and Évora and in 1189 (temporarily) Silves.	Fortress-like **Romanesque cathedrals** of Lisbon, Coimbra, Évora, Braga and Porto.
1212	First assembly of the Cortes (parliament) at Coimbra.	1153: Cistercians found abbey of **Alcobaça**; in this and other Cistercian churches, notably at Coimbra, Gothic architecture enters Portugal.
1249	Afonso III completes reconquest of the Algarve.	

1385	Battle of Aljubarrota: João I defeats Castilians to become first king of **House of Avis.**	Abbey of **Batalha**, the great triumph of mature Portuguese Gothic, built in celebration of victory. Paço Real built at Sintra.
1415	**Infante Henriques** (Henry the Navigator; d 1460) active at Sagres. 1419: Madeira discovered. 1427: Azores discovered. 1457: Cape Verde Islands discovered.	Navigation School at Sagres; Lagos fort. Painters: Flemish-influenced "Portuguese Primitives" include Nuno Gonçalves.
1495–1521	Reign of **Dom Manuel I** ("The Fortunate"). 1497: Vasco da Gama opens up sea route to India. 1500: Cabral discovers Brazil. 1513: Portuguese reach China.	Late-Gothic **Manueline style** develops, with strong marine motifs and flamboyance anticipating Art Nouveau. Greatest examples at Tomar, Batalha, Lisbon (Belém) and Sintra. By 1530s Renaissance forms are introduced and merged.
1521–57	Reign of João III.	Painters include Grão Vasco (see Viseu).
1557–78	Reign of **Dom Sebastião**. 1578: Disastrous expedition to Morocco, loss of king and mass slaughter of nobility at Alcácer-Quibir.	Important sculptural school at **Coimbra** (1520–70) centred on French Renaissance sculptors Nicolas Chanterenne, Filipe Hodart and Jean de Rouen.
1581–1640	Philip II brings **Spanish** (Hapsburg) rule.	
1640	**João IV**, Duke of **Bragança**, restores independence.	Severe late-Renaissance style: São Vicente, Lisbon (designed by Felipe Terzi), etc.
1706–50	Reign of **Dom João V**. Gold and diamonds discovered in Brazil, reaching a peak of wealth and exploitation in the 1740s.	Baroque palace-monastery of **Mafra** (1717–35). Decoration of Coimbra University Library. High Baroque carved, gilt church interiors. Also simpler, more rustic Baroque style of plaster/granite – **Lamego** and **Bom Jesus**. Rococo Palace of **Queluz** (1752).
1755	**Great Earthquake** destroys Lisbon and parts of the Alentejo and Algarve.	"Pombaline" Neoclassical rebuilding of Lisbon (Baixa).
1843–53	Maria II holds throne with German consort, Fernando II.	**Pena Palace** folly built at Sintra.
1908	Assassination of Carlos I in Lisbon.	
1910	Exile of Manuel II ("The Unfortunate") and **end of Portuguese monarchy**.	Cubist painter Amadeu de Sousa Cardoso (d 1918); museum devoted to him at Amarante.
1910–26	"Democratic" Republic.	
1932–68	**Salazar** dictatorship. Goa is seized by India; colonial wars in Africa.	
1974	April 25 **Revolution**.	
1986	**Entry to European Community** (EC).	
1994	Lisbon is European City of Culture.	Permanent gallery of modern Portuguese artists at Lisbon's Gulbenkian Foundation.
1998	Lisbon hosts Expo 98.	

BOOKS

Portugal has been covered very sparsely by British and American writers and publishers, and many of the works that do exist in English are out of print (o/p) and available only from libraries or specialist book dealers. A reliable specialist source for out-of-print books on all aspects of Portugal is Keith Harris Books, PO Box 207, Twickenham, TW2 5BQ (☎ & fax 020 8 898 7789, *www.books-on-portugal.com*). For more contemporary publications, it's worth checking the latest books available from the UK publisher Carcanet Press, 4th Floor Conavon Court, 12–16 Blackfriars Street, Manchester, M3 5BQ (☎ 0161/834 8730, fax 832 0084, *www.carcanet.co.uk*), who have a fiction series entitled "From the Portuguese" and a non-fiction series entitled "Aspects of Portugal". Some of the titles in these series are reviewed below.

Where two publishers are given for the books listed below, they refer to the UK and US publishers respectively. Books published in one country only are followed by the publisher and UK, US or Portugal; if a book has the same UK and US publisher only the publisher's name is given.

GENERAL TRAVEL AND GUIDES

William Beckford, *Recollections of an Excursion to the Monasteries of Alcobaça and Batalha; Travels in Spain and Portugal (1778–88)* (Open Gate Press; Norwood Editions, o/p). Mad and enormously rich, Beckford lived for some time at Sintra and travelled widely in Estremadura. His accounts, told with a fine eye for the absurd, are a lot of fun.

Lord Byron, *Selected Letters and Journals* (Pimlico; Belknap). Only a few days of Portuguese travel but memorable ones – beginning with romantic enthusiasm, ending in outright abuse.

Almeida Garrett, *Travels in My Homeland* (Peter Owen; Dufour). A classic Portuguese writer, Garrett was exiled to Europe in the 1820s, came into contact with the Romantics and later returned to play a part in the liberal government of the 1830s. This is a witty, discursive narrative ramble around the country.

Paul Hyland, *Backwards Out of the Big World* (Flamingo, UK). A fascinating and sympathetic account of a journey through Portugal by a man who knows the country's people, history and literature as few foreigners do.

Manfredd Hamm and Werner Radasewsky, *Lisbon* (Nicolai, UK). The strength of this book is its wonderful photographs, which capture the atmosphere and light of the city, its people and its surroundings through all its varying moods.

Marion Kaplan, *The Portuguese: the Land and its People* (Penguin; Penguin, o/p). Published in 1991, this is a readable, all-embracing volume, covering everything from wine to the family, poetry and the land. The style is a bit old-fashioned, but it's the best general introduction to the country available.

Rose Macaulay, *They Went to Portugal, Too* (Carcanet, UK). The book covers British travellers to Portugal from the Crusaders to Byron, weaving an anecdotal history of the country in the process. A serious study if you take it as such; a good read if you just feel like dipping into the stories.

Fernando Pessoa, *Lisbon: What the Tourist Should See (O que o turista deve ver)* (Livros Horizonte, Portugal). Bilingual edition of the great poet's guide to Lisbon, which he wrote in English.

Oleg Polunin and B.E. Smythies, *Flowers of South-West Europe: A Field Guide* (Oxford University Press). The best available guide to the Portuguese flora.

Norman Renouf, *Spain and Portugal by Rail* (Bradt Publications; Globe Pequot). Fairly limited guide containing maps of major stations, lists of hotels near them, and background information on rail passes. Focuses largely on Spain.

Stuart Ross, *Portugal's Pousada Route* (Vista Ibérica Publicações, Portugal; Seven Hill, US, o/p). An informative book containing details about Portugal's state-owned hotels and some background history on the surrounding country-side; with photos by Marion Kaplan.

Sacheverell Sitwell, *Portugal and Madeira* (Batsford, UK o/p). Mix of art history, observation and rather pompous upper-class travelogue from the 1950s. Sitwell's great enthusiasm is Portuguese Baroque. He also "discovers" Mateus Rosé wine for the British.

Anne de Stoop, *Living in Portugal* (Flammarion; Abbeville). A glossy coffee-table tome filled with beautifully evocative photographs of Portugal's sights and architectural gems, from palaces and manor houses to rural houses, *pastelarias* and restaurants.

HISTORY AND POLITICS

David Birmingham, *A Concise History of Portugal* (Cambridge University Press). Recommended for the casual reader; concise indeed, but providing straightforward and informative coverage from the year dot to 1991.

Daniel J. Boorstin, *The Discoverers* (Dent o/p; Random House). Old, standard text on the Discoveries that you might find in libraries.

C.R. Boxer, *The Portuguese Seaborne Empire 1415–1825* (Carcanet Press, UK). Entertaining account by a prolific writer on the region.

António de Figueiredo, *Portugal: Fifty Years of Dictatorship* (Penguin, UK o/p). An illuminating study which takes as its starting-point the 1926 military coup that brought Salazar to power and goes through to the 1974 Revolution.

Lawrence S. Graham and Douglas L. Wheeler (eds), *In Search of Modern Portugal: the Revolution and Its Consequences* (University of Wisconsin Press). An academic study published in the early 1980s; heavy-going but ultimately rewarding.

Harold Livermore, *A New History of Portugal* (Cambridge University Press o/p). Covering events through to 1976, this is thorough, if not exactly inspiring, but was revised a little too soon after the 1974 Revolution to be authoritative.

A.H. de Oliveira Marques, *History of Portugal* (Columbia University Press). Accessible general history.

Dan L. Raby, *Fascism and Resistance in Portugal* (Manchester University Press, UK o/p). Scholarly account of the subject.

José Hermano Saraiva, *Portugal: A Companion History* (Carcanet, UK). The most recent of its kind, this is an accessible and concise history of the country written especially for non-specialist foreigners by the author of the bestselling Portuguese original. Includes useful easy-reference glossaries of historical figures and places.

ART AND ARCHITECTURE

Marcus Binney, *Houses and Gardens of Portugal* (Rizzoli, US). The excellent photos are the main reason to buy this solid volume.

Helder Carita and Homem Cardoso, *Portuguese Gardens* (Antique Collector's Club). A huge and beautiful tome, lavishly illustrated with photos and plans, with a scholarly text.

Miles Danby, *The Fires of Excellence* (Garnet Publishing, UK). Magnificent and detailed study of the Oriental architecture of Spain and Portugal, illustrated with specially commissioned photographs.

Júlio Gil and Augusto Cabrita, *The Finest Castles in Portugal* (Beaufort Publishing, UK o/p). A superb illustrated survey of Portuguese castles, let down a little by a highly pedestrian translation/text.

FICTION

António Lobo Antunes, *An Explanation of the Birds, The Natural Order of Things* and *Act of the Damned* (Secker & Warburg o/p; Grove-Atlantic); *South of Nowhere* (Chatto & Windus; Random House; both o/p). Many consider Antunes to be Portugal's leading contemporary writer, notwithstanding the increasing worldwide acclaim for José Saramago (see below). The two writers couldn't be more different, however. Antunes is a psychologist and writes helter-skelter prose, notably in the recent *Act of the Damned*, whose narrative voice changes ceaselessly.

Maria Isabel Barreno, Maria Teresa Horta and Maria Velho da Costa *New Portuguese Letters: The Three Marias* (Readers International). Published (and prosecuted) in 1972, pre-Revolution Portugal, this collage of stories, letters and poems is a modern feminist parable based on the seventeenth-century *"Letters of a Portuguese Nun"*.

José Cardoso Pires, *Ballad of Dog's Beach* (Dent o/p; Beaufort Books o/p). Ostensibly a detective thriller but the murder described actually took place during the last years of Salazar's dictatorship and Pires' research draws upon the original secret-police files. Compelling, highly original and with acute psychological insights, it was awarded Portugal's highest literary prize and made into a film.

Ray Keenoy, David Treece and Paul Hyland, *The Babel Guide to the Fiction of Portugal, Brazil and Africa* (Boulevard Books, UK). A tantalizing introduction to Portuguese literature, with a collection of reviews of the major works of Lusophone fiction since 1945.

Eugénio Lisboa (ed), *The Anarchist Banker and Other Portuguese Stories* and *Professor Pfiglzz and His Strange Companion and Other Portuguese Stories* (Carcanet, UK). A fabulous two-volume collection of twentieth-century short stories, mostly very modern, which gives more than a taste of the exuberance and talent currently proliferating in Portuguese literature. Stories by old favourites – Eça de Queiroz, Pessoa, José Régio and Miguel Torga – are included too, mostly for the first time in English.

Eugénio Lisboa and Helder Macedo (eds), *The Dedalus Book of Portuguese Fantasy* (Dedalus; Hippocrene). A rich feast of literary fantasy comprising short stories by the likes of Eça de Queiroz and José de Almada Negreiros.

José Rodrigues Miguéis, *Happy Easter* (Carcanet, UK). A powerful and disturbing account of the distorted reality experienced by a schizophrenic, whose deprived childhood leads him to a self-destructive and tragic life in Lisbon; evocatively written and a surprisingly gripping read.

Cees Nooteboom, *The Following Story* (Harvill; Harcourt Brace). Dutch author Nooteboom successfully evokes the Portuguese melancholy (*saudade*) in a tale of a Classics teacher who falls asleep in Amsterdam and wakes up in a hotel room in Lisbon, the scene of a romantic past that he realizes he can never fully recapture.

Fernando Pessoa, *The Book of Disquiet: a Selection* (Carcanet; Pantheon). The country's best-known poet (see below) wrote just this one work in prose (as Bernardo Soares, one of his six *noms de plume*): a kind of autobiography, set in Lisbon, and posthumously compiled from a trunkload of material. It is regarded as a modernist classic, with the book's admirers including Jorge Luís Borges.

José Maria Eça de Queiroz, *The Mandarin and The Relic* (Dedalus; Hippocrene); *The Sin of Father Amaro* (Penguin, UK); *The Maias* (Penguin, UK, o/p); *Cousin Bazilio* (Quartet, UK); *The Illustrious House of Ramires* (Quartet; New Directions). Queiroz is the classic Portuguese novelist, responsible for a string of nineteenth-century narratives, recently available in new translations. The two best are *The Illustrious House of Ramires* and *The Maias*, entertaining narratives which give a comprehensive account of nineteenth-century Portuguese society.

Mário de Sá Carneiro, *The Great Shadow* (Dedalus, UK). Sá Carneiro, who committed suicide at 26, writes with stunning intensity and originality about art, science, death, sex and insanity in this series of short stories.

José Saramago, *Baltasar and Blimunda* (Picador; Harvard University Press); *The Year of the Death of Ricardo Reis*, *The Gospel According to Jesus Christ*, *The Stone Raft* (Harvill; Harcourt Brace); and *Manual of Painting and Calligraphy* (Carcanet, UK). Saramago has been mooted as a Nobel winner and at last has a number of titles available translated into English. The one to start with is *Ricardo Reis*, a magnificent novel which won *The Independent* foreign fiction award. Its theme is the return of Dr. Reis, after sixteen years in Brazil, to a Lisbon where the Salazar dictatorship is imminent and where Reis wanders the streets to be confronted by the past and the ghost of the writer Fernando Pessoa. In *Baltasar and Blimunda*, Saramago mixes fact with myth in an entertaining novel set around the building of the Convent of Mafra and the construction of the world's first flying machine. In *The Stone Raft*, Saramago describes what happens when the Iberian peninsula begins to drift away from the rest of Europe, both literally and metaphorically.

Antonio Tabucchi, *Pereira Declares* (Harvill; New Directions); *Requiem: a Hallucination* (Harvill; New Directions). A highly-regarded Italian author who lived for many years in Portugal, Tabucchi has recreated in *Pereira Declares* the repressive atmosphere of Salazar's Lisbon, tracing the experiences of a newspaper editor who questions his own lifestyle under a regime which he can no longer ignore. The book has recently been made into a film by Roberto Faenza. *Requiem: a Hallucination* is an imaginative and dreamlike journey around Lisbon, with Tabucchi engaging in conversations with people as diverse as a barman in the Museu de Arte Antiga and a Pessoa-like writer. The unifying theme, however, is food and drink and the book even contains a note on recipes.

Miguel Torga, *The Creation of the World* (Carcanet, UK); *Tales from the Mountain* (Carcanet; QED Press). Twice nominated for the Nobel Prize before his death in 1995, Torga lived and set his stories in the wild Trás-os-Montes region. His pseudonym "Torga" is a tough species of heather which thrives in this rural, unforgiving landscape, where the fiercely independent characters of his books battle to survive in a repressed society. Torga's harsh views of rural life in *Tales from the Mountain* led to the book being banned under the Salazar regime.

Gil Vicente, *Gil Vicente: Three Discovery Plays: Auto da Barca do Inferno, Exortação da Guerra, Auto da Índia* (Aris & Phillips, UK). Three plays from the 16th-century scribe whom some consider the Portuguese equivalent of Shakespeare, with the original archaic Portuguese versions alongside English translations, and copious notes.

POETRY

Luís de Camões *The Lusiads* (Penguin, UK). Portugal's national epic, celebrating the ten-month voyage of Vasco da Gama which opened the sea route to India. This is a good prose translation.

Sophia de Mello Breyner *Log Book: Selected Poems* (Carcanet). Evocative selection of translated poems from one of the country's foremost writers, winner of the 1999 Prémio Camões.

Fernando Pessoa, *A Centenary Pessoa* (Carcanet; Sheep Meadow). This superlative anthology of poems, prose, letters and photographs is the most comprehensive selection of Pessoa's output yet published in English, and at the moment it's the only substantial in-print translation of the startling, lyrical verse on which his reputation rests.

FOOD AND WINE

Alex Liddell and Janet Price, *Port Wine Quintas of the Douro* (Philip Wilson, UK, o/p). Highly erudite account of the wines and history; superb photos put it beyond specialist interest.

Maite Manjon, *Gastronomy of Spain and Portugal* (Collins & Brown; Prentice Hall, o/p). A comprehensive collection of classic Iberian recipes, including a glossary of Portuguese and Spanish terms and explanations of traditional cooking techniques. Particularly good on regional specialities and wines, too.

Edite Vieira, *The Taste of Portugal* (Grub Street, UK). A delight to read, let alone cook from. Vieira combines snippets of history and passages from Portuguese writers (very well translated) to illustrate her dishes; highly recommended.

LEISURE AND SPORTS

Bethan Davies and Ben Cole, *Walking in Portugal* (Footprint Guides, UK). New and dependable guide to trekking in the national parks of Gerês, Serra da Estrela, Montesinho, and Serra de São Mamede. An excellent supplement to our own coverage.

Laurence Rose, *Where to Watch Birds in Spain and Portugal* (Hamlyn; Stackpole). Comprehensive guide to some of Europe's finest and most environmentally sensitive wildlife sites, with practical information on how to get there and when to go. Interesting reading for amateurs as well as being invaluable for ardent ornithologists.

John Russell and Nuno Campos, *Golf's Golden Coast* (Vista Ibérica Publicações, Portugal). An attractive, illustrated guide for anyone interested in the Algarve's clubs ∟ of the 18-hole variety.

RESIDENCE

Jonathan Packer, *Live and Work in Spain and Portugal* (Vacation Work; US). Invaluable handbook packed with details on permits, business, teaching, health, schools, renting and buying property, etc. Only downside is a heavy slant towards English ex-pats.

Sue Tyson-Ward, *How to Live and Work in Portugal* (How To Books, UK). Another detailed and practical guide on all aspects of living in the country, including info on how to start a business, open a bank account, find out about schools and, of course, track down ex-pat activities.

MUSIC

Portugal has a rich musical culture, with roots harking back to Provençal troubadours, North African ritual and folk song and Islamic court music, continuing through ballads and the unique "blues" of the fado and encompassing, more recently, the rhythms of the country's five former African colonies. Each of these elements has a currency in the sounds that you hear today – from the French Provençal strain in the folk music played at northern festivals, to the cosmopolitan rock and jazz of the larger cities. An additional element is added by the wealth of singer-songwriters, most of them from the highly political "New Song" movement fostered by the dramatic events of the 1970s, as the country threw off the 36-year dictatorship of Salazar and was forced to withdraw from its colonies.

INSTRUMENTS, VOICES AND RHYTHMS

There is a startling variety of Portuguese **folk instruments**: bagpipes, harmonicas, accordions, flutes, assorted drums (*caixas, bombos, adufes, pandeiros, sarroncas*), and countless percussion instruments (*reco-reco, ferrinhos, genebres, trancanholas*). But the country's pride and glory is strings, which include violins, the classic twelve-stringed "Portuguese guitar", and six varieties of **"viola-guitars"**, unknown elsewhere in Europe. Each of these has a character, tuning and design of its own. Best known

are the little four-stringed *cavaquinho* and the bigger *guitarra portuguesa*, the standard accompaniments to Lisbon fado. Others range through elaborate combinations of single, double and triple strings.

One of the most common combinations of instruments is the **zés-pereiras**, made up of a large *bombo*, a *caixa* and a bagpipe or fife (depending on whether you're in the Minho or Beiras region) and often used to announce grand occasions. Another traditional combination popular throughout the country is the **rancho**, made up of violins, guitars, clarinets, harmonicas and *ferrinhos*, with the later addition of the accordion.

If the folk traditions are rich in instruments, its **singers** are unrivalled. In every town and district there is an amateur choir. After a good meal someone will start an **à desgarrada** (a cappella) song, followed intuitively by the other guests. It is not at all unusual, if you go to a **fado** performance, to find the entire staff of the establishment taking part, from the owner to the cloakroom attendant. To listen to a vocal ensemble of three women from Manhouce, or a rural male choir from Alentejo, is to hear genuinely popular roots music. Alentejo is home also to the *saia*, sung by women accompanying themselves on the *pandeireta*.

Since Portugal remains for the most part a rural society, a great many **songs** that survive reflect the cycles of nature, such as *natal, reis* and *janeiras* – lullabies and tilling, sowing and harvesting songs. Until the 1970s they remained very much within living tradition, but one that has now in many areas changed beyond recognition – sadly, many songs now exist only in recordings. Equally traditional, if less harmonious, are the **singing contests** in which rival performers exchange improvizations on a theme, or the fandango, a dance where two men match their footwork. Among other popular **traditional dances** are *modas, despiques, chulas, rusgas, corridinhos, viras*, waltzes and the ritual steps of the *pauliteiros* (stick-dancers) of Miranda in the Douro region.

FADO

The fado is Portugal's most famous – though perhaps also its least accessible – music. Lyrical and sentimental, it is thought to have origins in African slave songs, though the influence of Portugal's own maritime and colonial past is equally apparent. After the 1974 Revolution, when the empire disintegrated, it went through something of a crisis. Today, it has come to be identified with a general sense of frustration and, some would have it, with an endemic and peculiarly Portuguese fatalism – *saudade*.

There are two versions of the fado. That of the humble **Alfama and Mouraria districts of Lisbon** (performed mainly in the Bairro Alto clubs, these days) is highly personal and full of feeling. The more academic strand from **Coimbra** reflects that city's ancient university traditions and is performed mainly by students and Coimbra graduates. In both versions, the theme is usually love, though fados have been composed on all kinds of subjects.

By far the most famous of the fado singers, and arguably its greatest performer was **Amália Rodrigues**, whose death in October 1999 saw three days of official mourning announced in Portugal.

Other big traditional names include Florencio Carvalho, Alberto Prado, José de Câmara and Castro Rodrigo. Recent performers have adapted the form to a more modern rhythm, including, most recently, Manuel Osório and (a name to look out for in the clubs) **Carlos do Carmo**. The singer-songwriters, too, have looked toward fado. Following the lead of José Afonso (see below), nearly all the stars have produced one or two of their own interpretations of the form.

THE BALLAD

It was an attempt to update the Coimbra fado that resulted in the modern Portuguese **ballad** and which in turn, in the last years of the dictatorship, gave way to "New Song" (see p.514). This, from the Revolution of April 25, 1974 onwards, became a genuine political song movement, broadening in recent years to a movement known as *Música Popular* – essentially contemporary folk music, composed and performed by an impressive roster of singer-songwriters.

The **lyrics** generated by this movement were – and are – as significant as the music. Many artists turned to modern poetry that dealt with contemporary social and cultural issues. They also drew on music rooted in popular tradition, both rural and urban, that reflected influences of various kinds – colonial, French, English, Spanish, or even North African – but avoided the easy rhythms of commercial pop.

One of the forerunners of the genre was the 1956 LP *Canções Heróicas – Canções Regionais Portuguesas* (*Heroic Songs – Portuguese Regional Songs*), arranged by Fernando Lopes Graça and performed by the Choir of the Amateur Musicians' Academy. Although the harmonizations are a long way from New Song, two basic elements are already present: committed lyrics and respect for genuine **regional music**.

Another LP, *Fados of Coimbra* by José Afonso and Luís Gois, appeared in May of the same year. The fado was out of favour in radical circles at the time. It had become just another branch of "national song", with overtones of vulgar soap-opera.

José Afonso gradually abandoned the Portuguese guitar for the Spanish, which allows for more freedom in the accompaniment. His first solo records came out in 1960, including *Balada do Outono* (*Autumn Ballad*), which gave its name to the new genre and made it respectable. He was soon joined by Adriano Correia de Oliveira and the **poets** Manuel Alegre, Ary dos Santos and Manuel Correia, whose work provided the text for numerous songs.

After the onset of the **colonial wars**, censorship began to wreak havoc. *Menino do Bairro Negro* (*Black Slum Kid*) and *Os Vampiros* (*The Vampires*), both by José Afonso, were withdrawn from the market and only instrumental versions allowed to be sold. Some singers chose to go into exile. Luís Cília released several records in Paris under the general title of *A Poesia Portuguesa de Hoje e de Sempre* (*Portuguese Poetry of Today and All Times*), on which he sung his own arrangements of poems by Camões, Pessoa, Saramago and others.

The release in 1968 of José Afonso's *Cantares do Andarilho* (*Songs of the Road*) marked the coming of age of the ballad. By now Adriano was making his first LPs, as were Manuel Freire, José Jorge Letria, José Mário Branco, Father Fanhais and soon afterwards Fausto, Pedro Barroso and the Angolan Rui Mingas. At the same time, the **social climate** was becoming increasingly suffocating. These singers were banned from television and hardly ever heard on the radio. There were very few venues and permits were granted sparingly, forcing them to take other jobs to make a living.

In today's uncensored climate, a contemporary performer of this style of music is Romantic singer **Paulo Gonzo**, whose ballads are always an instant hit.

NEW SONG

José Afonso's *Cantigas de Maio* (*Songs of May*), José Mário Branco's *Mudam-se os Tempos, Mudam-se as Vontades* (*Changing Times, Changing Wishes*) and Adriano Correia de Oliveira's *Gente d'Aqui e de Agora* (*People Here and Now*) showed an improvement in the quality of the material. The lyrics went further in their reflections on living conditions and were more open in their **protest**, while the music explored new forms, rhythms and means of expression. José Mário Branco made a key contribution as an arranger and producer. Pre-production **censorship**, however, continued to be strictly imposed and some singers stopped recording to avoid it. Others, like José Afonso, resorted to ever more cryptic lyrics.

This was how things stood on the night of **April 24, 1974**. At 10.55pm, João Paulo Dinis of the "Associates of Lisbon" radio programme played *E Depois do Adeus* (*After the Goodbyes*), Paulo de Caravalho's Eurovision Song Contest entry for the year. At midnight came the final signal – Leite Vasconcelos played *Grândola Vila Morena* on Radio Renascença's "Limit" programme. The army captains went into action and on the following day the coup was a reality: Portugal was returning to democracy.

There began an uncertain period during which it was unclear who held power. Singers such as Sérgio Godinho, Luís Cília, José Mário Branco and Father Fanhais returned from exile and, now that censorship had been lifted, New Song gave way to **political song**. Everyone had slogans, analyses and solutions to offer in the process of clarification which followed.

Singers were suddenly in constant demand for the political and cultural events being improvised with a minimum of technical resources all over the country, giving performances in factories, co-operatives and squatters' settlements. They set up various groups according to their political leanings: Free Song (Canto Livre), the October Group (Grupo Outubro), the Group for Cultural Action and Voices for the Cause (Grupo de Acção Cultural-Vozes na Luta, or GAC). The last of these, in mixing traditional songs with its sloganeering political ones, set an unconscious

pattern for future developments. Other artists slowly branched out into work with the numerous theatre groups of the time and on soundtracks for films. Some singers and musicians also formed co-operatives, such as Eranova (New Age) and Cantarabril (Sing of April).

FOLK GROUPS

As time passed and things returned to normal, **traditional music** enjoyed a revival, bringing with it the first commercial folk groups. In the 1960s, much work had been done in studying and recording traditional Portuguese music, most notably by Fernando Lopes Graça and Michel Giacometti, who produced a five-volume *Antologia de Música Regional Portuguesa*. Over the last decade, the group **Almanaque** of Lisbon has followed in their footsteps, producing a series of records from the oral tradition, as well as reworking the traditional themes in a more modern form.

The **Brigada Victor Jara** of Coimbra also began by collecting folk tunes but soon turned to new directions, adapting the work of other folk writers. Although none of its original members is still in the line-up, this group is one of Portugal's best, producing well-crafted work based on sound ideas. Other active folk groups, adopting similar approaches, include Raizes (Roots) from Vila Verde (Braga); the Grupo Etnográfico de Cantares e Trajes (Ethnographic Song and Costume Group) from Manhouce; Terra Terra (Land, Land); Vai de Roda, an ethnic arts co-operative from Oporto; Trigo Limpo (Clean Wheat) from Alentejo; and Ronda dos Quatro Caminhos (Crossroads) from Lisbon.

A more **contemporary** and ambitious folk music has also emerged over the last decade. **Trovante**, which was formed in 1975, is highly acclaimed in Portugal and has worked extensively with José Afonso and Fausto. Its work is full of uneven swayings and sudden changes of direction. Interesting, too, though less successful, are Charanga, Pedra d'Hera, Construção, Disto e Daquilo and Rosa dos Ventos.

Música Popular – as more recent folk has become known – owes much of its renewed popularity, however, to the work of some singer-songwriters who have dedicated themselves exclusively to it and to musicians who have made records devoted to individual folk instruments.

PORTUGUESE FOLK: THE KEY FIGURES

JOSÉ AFONSO The "father of modern Portuguese popular music" made a key contribution to song from the 1950s onwards and won fame far beyond his country's borders. He was born in Aveiro and as the son of a civil servant visited several colonies as a child, but it was not until later, when he made a trip to Angola as a student, that he became aware of the colonial realities.

His first records were collections of fado made with Luís Góis in 1956. In the 1960s he began to write songs on social issues. His records were censored and he was persecuted by the secret police. His whole life was dedicated to song and his personal crusade against fascism.

After the Revolution, he continued to work prolifically and to consistently high standards, composing music for films and the theatre as well as producing nearly twenty LPs. His work was constantly evolving, yet his first compositions are still fresh today. With their careful attention to music, lyrics, arrangement and voice, any of his records is a miniature work of art. He lived modestly and died after a long illness in 1987.

FAUSTO The work of this singer combines the most diverse influences – modern and traditional, Portuguese and African – with a marked urban slant and a lyrical delivery. His skill lies in the subtlety with which he links African rhythms to Portuguese melodies and instruments and the delicacy of his singing.

His early songs provide a poetic analysis of the uncertain post-revolutionary period. Later ones use tales of the deeds of *conquistadores*, sailors and other Portuguese heroes to reflect on the country's history.

SÉRGIO GODINHO Born in Porto, Godinho went into exile as an economics student to avoid military service in the colonial war. He travelled in France, Switzerland and Canada, working at one time as an interpreter for the musical *Hair* and at another as a member of Living Theatre.

Due to these influences he is one of the more modern, cosmopolitan singers of his generation. His songs are usually narrative and he has a particular knack for affectionate character sketches. When dealing more directly with political issues he employs a fine sense of humour. His music is both loud and cheerful, intimate and sophisticated.

LUÍS CÍLIA Of the new songwriters, Luís Cília is the one who has devoted most attention to setting his poems to music. His work is rigorous and serious, showing a pronounced French influence. He is good at capturing the essence and general atmosphere of a given political moment in his lyrics. Musically, he has worked in two apparently contrasting fields: traditional song and experimental work with synthesizers from which he has produced a solo album.

JOSÉ MÁRIO BRANCO Another native of Porto, Mário Branco's chief contribution has been as an arranger and producer of records, though he has made important records himself, both individually and as a member of the Grupo de Acção Cultural. His skill in the studios has given an added dimension to the records of Portuguese singers.

VITORINO The songs of Vitorino are inextricably linked with the Alentejo region and its farming co-operatives and rural communities, though recently he has made more contact with the city. His early records were uneven in their development, a mixture of Alentejo folk songs, revolutionary anthems and love songs. It is with the latter genre that he has had most success in his recent work.

JANITA SALOMÉ Brother of Vitorino, he also has links with the Alentejo, though he has concentrated increasingly on the Arab heritage there and in the Algarve. His music, full of percussion and gentle touches, also betrays the influence of José Afonso, with whom he worked closely in his last years.

Among **instrumentalists**, perhaps the most outstanding figure is the guitarist **Carlos Paredes**. He explores both the folk and the classical sides of the Portuguese guitar, with surprising results; his records are a rare treat. Pedro Cabreira Cabral, very much the next generation after Paredes, also continues the tradition of using indigenous instruments – apart from being an exceptional guitarist and learned musicologist, he also makes and restores instruments and has composed original pieces for the Portuguese guitar. Another excellent instrumentalist is **Júlio Pereira**, who began as a songwriter but became interested in traditional string instruments and has recently experimented to great effect in combining them with synthesizers, rhythm boxes and samplers in compositions inspired by folk tradition.

JAZZ AND AFRICAN

Though Portuguese jazz cannot even begin to match the maturity of its songwriting tradition, there have been some interesting developments in recent years. An intriguing figure, midway between jazz and "New Age", is the saxophonist **Rão Kyao**. As for jazz proper, there is the great vocalist **Maria João**, the **Lisbon Jazz Sextet**, the experimental trio **Shish**, and the ensembles led by **António Pinho Vargas** and **Mário Laginha**.

The appearance of groups from the former colonies of **Angola, Mozambique, Cabo Verde, Guinea-Bissau** and **São Tomé e Príncipe** has been another exciting development in the Portuguese music scene. Following the colonial wars and independence many African musicians have settled in Lisbon; others spend part of the year based in Portugal, recording and touring Europe, drawn by the comparatively high fees to be made. In recent years, Lisboans have embraced their musical styles with vigour, perhaps because the lively African beat is a complete contrast to the sad, nostalgic tradition of fado.

Staying in Lisbon, you're most likely to get a chance to see Cabo Verde groups, which include among their styles *morna*, similar to the Portuguese fado and the more danceable *moradeira*. The big star of the moment is **Cesaria Evora**, a fabulous diva with an international following. From **Guinea-Bissau** the sounds are an unusual mix of African and Latin, akin to zouk. Big names to look out for that may be in the country include **Justino Delgado, Super Mama Diombo, Manecas, Africa Libre** and **Jetu Katem**. Finally, two outstanding southern African groups to see are **Guem** from **Angola** and **Fernando Luís** from **Mozambique**.

Manuel Domínguez

ROCK, POP AND PIMBA

Two names that have been big for some time now are the pop singer **Mafalda Veiga** and the blues singer **Rui Veloso**. However, it wasn't until the beginning of the 1990s that the Portuguese rock and pop music scene started to take off. Up until then, a handful of groups and solo artists struggled to compete with the foreign music pumped out by cable TV and given almost exclusive airplay by radio stations. The national backlash came with the second generation of groups – formed largely of members of the old bands – who concentrated this time on establishing a cult following rather than achieving megastar status. Although slow to react initially, major record companies eventually realized that there was a market to exploit and set about

employing the modern marketing techniques of their foreign counterparts.

Although bands such as GNR and Xutos and Pontapes were strongly promoted, **Madredeus** has been the only group so far to achieve international recognition in countries as far afield as the USA and Japan. Other mainstream pop bands to keep an ear out for are **Delfins, Rio Grande** and **Santos e Pecadores**.

On a national level, however, it is not the likes of Madredeus but rap singer **Pedro Abrunhosa** who is idolized throughout the country. On its release, his first record, *Viagens*, broke sales records and opened the doors for many groups. One of the main achievements of his music was to make rap more acceptable and its decidedly jazzy feel has provided an alternative to a music scene previously dominated by FM-style hard rock. In fact Portuguese rap and hip-hop now dominate the underground music and club scene – **General D, Da Weasel** and **Cool Hipnoise** are the household names, their image and music rivalling anything coming out of the USA or Britain.

Dance music has taken a while to catch on, but in 1991 the first ever Portuguese house track, *Deep Sky* by **Matrix Run**, stimulated a wave of new talent and interest. House and techno rave parties are currently emerging all over the country, attracting thousands of young people to a new club culture.

You're unlikely to get through a visit to Portugal without hearing some **Música Pimba**, – a fashionably tacky music of the sort that usually enters the charts around Christmas time. Despite the wholesale snubbing of this style by the Portuguese media, *pimba* has succeeded in conquering the whole country as well as being big in countries with large Portuguese communities.

Mixing traditional and modern elements, its success was previously limited to the provinces, but the introduction of satirical jokes and sexual references to the lyrics found new support among college students and its popularity has now spread to the main cities. Today, *pimba* is firmly established and, to some extent, its humorous and satirical style reflects a lot of the national character.

The main exponent of *pimba* is the singer/songwriter **Marco Paulo**. Another seasoned performer is **Quim Barreiros**; if you get a chance to see him, take it. Even if you can't speak Portuguese, the atmosphere at the shows is contagious.

Michael Oliveira-Salac

RECORDS

Portuguese music is hard to obtain outside the country, save for a few fado recordings (including some excellent reissues of old classics), so our advice is buy when you're there. CDs are broadly similar in cost to those in the UK, and pricier than in the US; records, by contrast, are excellent value. The following is a personal selection of the most interesting. A highly recommended compilation is *Portuguese Folk Music* (5 volumes) Strauss/Portugalsom, an astonishing variety of recordings taken in the field by Michel Giacometti in the 1960s, much of which is now extinct.

FOLK
Almanaque Desafiando Cantigas; *Sementes.*
Brigada Victor Jara *Marcha dos Foliões.*
Ronda dos Quatro Caminhos *Fados Velhos.*
Vai de Roda *Vai de Roda.*

FADO
Amália Rodrigues *O Melhor.*
Carlos do Carmo *Um Homem na Cidade; Um Homem no País.*

PORTUGUESE GUITAR
Carlos Paredes *Guitarra Portuguesa; Movimento Perpétuo; Concerto em Frankfurt; Espelho de Sons.*
Pedro Caldeira Cabral *Encontros; A Guitarra Portuguesa nos Salões dos sec. XVIII.*

SINGER-SONGWRITERS
Adriano Correia de Oliveira *Memória de Adriano.*
Fausto *Madrugada dos Trapeiros; Por Este Rio Acima; Despertar dos Alquimistas.*
Janita Salomé *Lavrar em teu Peito; Olho de Fogo.*
José Afonso *Cantigas de Maio; Venham Mais Cinco; Coro do Tribunais; Com as Minhas Tamanquinhas; Fura Fura; Fados de Coimbra e Outras Canções; Como se Fora Seu Filho; Galinhas do Mato.*
José Maria Branco *Ser Solidário.*

Julio Pereira *Cavaquinho; Braguesa; Cadoí; Os Sete Instrumentos; Miradouro.*
Luís Cília *Cancioneiro; Penumbra.*
Sérgio Godinho *De Pequenino se Torce o Destino; Coincidências; Na Vida Real.*
Vitorino *Romances; Negro Fado; Frol de la Mar.*

ROCK/POP
G.N.R. *Os Homens não se querem Bonitos.*
Madredeus *Os Dias da Madredeus.*
Matrix Run *Deep Sky*
Pedro Abrunhosa *Viagens*
Rádio Macau *Rádio Macau.*
Sétima Legião *Mar d'Outubro.*
Trovante *Terra Firme.*

JAZZ
António Pinho Vargas *Variações.*
Maria João *Conversa.*
Rão Kyao *Fado Bailado; Danças de Rua.*
Sexteto de Jazz de Lisboa *Sexteto.*

AFRICAN
Cesaria Evora *Miss Perfumado; Café Atlantico* (Cabo Verde).
Kaba Mane *Kunga Kungake* (Guinea-Bissau).
Guem *Dans Voyage* (Angola).
Fernando Luís *Bassopa* (Mozambique).

LANGUAGE

If you have some knowledge of Spanish and/or French you won't have much problem reading Portuguese. Understanding it when it's spoken, though, is a different matter: pronunciation is entirely different and at first even the easiest words are hard to distinguish – the sound is more like that of an East European language than of the Romance tongues in which it has its roots. If you're stuck, most people will understand Spanish (albeit reluctantly) and in the cities and tourist areas French and English are also widely spoken. Even so, it's well worth the effort to master at least the rudiments; once you've started to figure out the words it gets a lot easier very quickly.

The pronunciation guide below and the box on p.519 will equip you with the basics. For more detail, check out the *Rough Guide Portuguese Phrasebook*, set out dictionary-style for easy access, with English–Portuguese and Portuguese–English sections, cultural tips for tricky situations and a handy menu reader.

PRONUNCIATION

The chief difficulty with **pronunciation** is its lack of clarity – consonants tend to be slurred, vowels nasal and often ignored altogether.

CONSONANTS

The **consonants** are, at least, consistent:
C is soft before E and I, hard otherwise unless it has a cedilla – *açucar* (sugar) is pronounced "assookar".

CH is somewhat softer than in English; *chá* (tea) sounds like Shah.

J is pronounced like the "s" in pleasure, as is **G** except when it comes before a "hard" vowel (A, O and U).

LH sounds like "lyuh" (Batalha).

Q is always pronounced as a "k".

S before a consonant or at the end of a word becomes "sh," otherwise it's as in English – Cascais is pronounced "Kashkaish", Sagres is "Sahgresh".

X is also pronounced "sh"– *caixa* (cash desk) is pronounced "kaisha".

VOWELS

Vowels are worse – flat and truncated, they're often difficult for English-speaking tongues to get around. The only way to learn is to listen: accents, ã, ô, or é, turn them into longer, more familiar sounds.

When two vowels come together they continue to be enunciated separately except in the case of **EI** and **OU** – which sound like a and long o respectively.

E at the end of a word is silent unless it has an accent, so that *carne* (meat) is pronounced "karn", while *café* sounds much as you'd expect.

The **tilde over Ã or Õ** renders the pronunciation much like the French -an and -on endings only more nasal.

More common is **ÃO** (as in *pão*, bread – *são*, saint – *limão*, lemon), which sounds something like a strangled yelp of "Ow!" cut off in mid-stream.

A FEW KEY WORDS . . .

Even if you speak no Portuguese at all there are **a few key words** which can help you out in an enormous number of situations.

Há (the H is silent) means "there is" or "is there?" and can be used for just about anything. Thus: "*Há uma pensão aqui?*" (Is there a pension here?), "*Há uma camioneta para…?*" (Is there a bus to…?), or even "*Há um quarto?*" (Do you have a room?).

More polite and better in shops or restaurants are **"Tem…?"** (Do you have…?) or "*Queria…*" (I'd like…).

And of course there are the old standards "Do you speak English?" (*Fala Inglês?*) and "I don't understand" (*Não compreendo*).

PORTUGUESE WORDS AND PHRASES

BASICS

sim; não	yes; no	*grande; pequeno*	big; little
olá; bom dia	hello; good morning	*aberto; fechado*	open; closed
boa tarde/noite	good afternoon/night	*senhoras; homens*	women; men
adeus, até logo	goodbye, see you later	*lavabo/quarto de banho*	toilet/bathroom
hoje; amanhã	today; tomorrow	*banco; câmbio*	bank; change
por favor/se faz favor	please	*correios*	post office
tudo bem?	Everything all right?	*(dois) selos*	(two) stamps
está bem	it's all right/OK	*sou Inglês/Inglesa*	I am English
obrigado/a*	thank you	*Americano/a*	American
onde; que	where; what	*Irlandês/Irlandesa*	Irish
quando; porquê	when; why	*Australiano/a*	Australian
como; quanto	how; how much	*Canadiano/a*	Canadian
não sei	I don't know	*Escocês/Escosesa*	Scottish
sabe . . .?	do you know . . .?	*Galês/Galesa*	Welsh
pode . . .?	could you . . .?	*Como se chama?*	What's your name?
desculpe; com licença	sorry; excuse me	*(chamo-me . . .)*	(my name is . . .)
aqui; ali	here; there	*Como se diz isto em*	What's this called in
perto; longe	near; far	*Português?*	Portuguese?
este/a; esse/a	this; that	*O que é isso?*	What's that?
agora; mais tarde	now; later	*Quanto é?*	How much is it?
mais; menos	more; less		

* *Obrigado* agrees with the sex of the person speaking – a woman says *obrigada*, a man *obrigado*.

GETTING AROUND

Para ir a . . .?	How do I get to . . .?	*A que horas parte?*	What time does it leave?
esquerda, direita, sempre em frente	left, right, straight ahead	*(chega a . . .?)*	(arrive at . . .?)
Onde é a estação de camionetas?	Where is the bus station?	*Qual é a estrada para. . .?*	Which is the road to . . .?
a paragem de autocarro para . . .	the bus stop for . . .	*Para onde vai? (Vou a)*	Where are you going? (I'm going to)
a estação de comboios	the railway station	*Está bem, muito obrigado/a*	That's great, thanks a lot
Donde parte o autocarro para . . .?	Where does the bus to . . . leave from?	*Pare aqui por favor*	Stop here please
É este o comboio para Coimbra?	Is this the train for Coimbra?	*bilhete (para)*	ticket (to)
		ida e volta	round trip

ACCOMMODATION

Há uma pensão aqui perto?	Is there a pension near here?	*É caro, não o quero*	It's expensive, I don't want it
Queria um quarto	I'd like a room	*Posso/podemos deixar os sacos aqui até . . .?*	Can I/we leave the bags here until . . .?
É para uma noite (semana)	It's for one night (week)	*Há um quarto mais barato?*	Is there a cheaper room?
É para uma pessoa (duas pessoas)	It's for one person (two people)	*Com duche (quente/frio)*	With a shower (hot/cold)
Posso ver?	May I see/look around?	*Pode-se acampar aqui?*	Can we camp here?
Está bem, fico com ele	OK, I'll take it	*chave*	key
Quanto custa?	How much is it?		

DAYS AND MONTHS

domingo	Sunday	*abril*	April
segunda-feira	Monday	*maio*	May
terça-feira	Tuesday	*junho*	June
quarta-feira	Wednesday	*julho*	July
quinta-feira	Thursday	*agosto*	August
sexta-feira	Friday	*setembro*	September
sábado	Saturday	*outubro*	October
janeiro	January	*novembro*	November
fevereiro	February	*dezembro*	December
março	March		

THE TIME

Que horas são?	What time is it?	*dez para as duas*	ten to two
é/são . . .	it's . . .	*meio-dia*	midday, noon
A que horas?	(At) what time?	*uma da tarde*	one in the afternoon
à/às . . .	at . . .		(1pm)
meia-noite	midnight	*sete da tarde*	seven in the evening
uma da manhã	one in the morning (1am)	*(dezanove)*	(7pm)
uma e dez	ten past one	*nove e meia da noite*	half past nine (pm)
uma e quinze	quarter past one	*(vinte e uma e trinta)*	
uma e vinte	twenty past one	*meio-dia e quinze*	quarter past noon
uma e meia	half past one	*meia-noite*	midnight
quinze para as duas	quarter-to-two	*meia-noite e dez*	ten past midnight

NUMBERS

1	*um*	10	*dez*	19	*dezanove*	90	*noventa*
2	*dois*	11	*onze*	20	*vinte*	100	*cem*
3	*três*	12	*doze*	21	*vinte e um*	101	*cento e um*
4	*quatro*	13	*treze*	30	*trinta*	200	*duzentos*
5	*cinco*	14	*catorze*	40	*quarenta*	500	*quinhentos*
6	*seis*	15	*quinze*	50	*cinquenta*	1000	*mil*
7	*sete*	16	*dezasseis*	60	*sessenta*	2000	*dois mil*
8	*oito*	17	*dezassete*	70	*setenta*	1,000,000	*um milhão*
9	*nove*	18	*dezoito*	80	*oitenta*		

PORTUGUESE WORDS AND TERMS: A GLOSSARY

ARCHITECTURAL, HISTORICAL AND RELIGIOUS TERMS

AFONSINO Relating to the reign of Dom Afonso Henriques, first king of Portugal.

ANTA Prehistoric megalith tomb.

AZULEJO Glazed and painted tile, in a style originating in North Africa; originally used as geometric decoration around the base of doorways of a church or mansion; by the late sixteenth century whole pictorial blocks were created. From the late seventeenth until the mid-eighteenth century – the main period – tiles were exclusively blue and white.

CAPELA Chapel; capela-mor is a chancel or sanctuary.

CAPELA DOS OSSOS Ossuary.

CITÂNIA Prehistoric/Celtic hill settlement.

CLAUSTRO Cloister.

CONVENTO Convent, though just as often an old church.

CORO Central, often enclosed, part of church built for the choir.

DOM, DONA Courtesy titles (sir, madam) usually applied to kings and queens. When used in common speech, it precedes the first name of the person referred to (e.g. Dona Helena).

ERMIDA Remote chapel – not necessarily a hermitage.

FORTALEZA Fort.

IGREJA Church; **igreja matriz** is a parish church.

INFANTA Princess.

INFANTE Prince.

MANUELINO Flamboyant, marine-influenced style of late Gothic architecture developed in the reign of Manuel I (1495–1521).

MOÇÁRABE Moorish-Arabic (usually of architecture or a design).

MOSTEIRO Monastery, or just as often an old church since most orders were suppressed in 1834–38.

MUDÉJAR Moorish-style architecture and decoration.

NOSSA SENHORA (N.S.) Our Lady – the Virgin Mary.

RETÁBULO Altarpiece – usually large, carved and heavily gilt.

SALA DO CAPÍTULO Chapter house.

SÉ Cathedral.

TORRE DE MENAGEM Keep of a castle.

GENERAL WORDS AND TERMS

ADEGA Wine cellar or winery, often also a wine bar or restaurant where wine is served straight from the barrel.

ALAMEDA Promenade.

ALBERGARIA Upmarket inn.

ALBUFEIRA Reservoir or lagoon.

ALDEIA Small village or hamlet.

ARTESANATO Handicraft shop.

BAIRRO Quarter, area (of a town); *alto* is upper, *baixo* lower.

BAIXA "Low"; used to mean commercial/shopping centre of town.

BARRAGEM Dam.

CACHOEIRA Waterfall.

CALDAS Mineral springs or spa complex.

CÂMARA MUNICIPAL Town hall.

CAMPO Square or field.

CASA ABRIGO "Open house"; a hut or shelter in natural and national parks for hikers and park staff (free); also "abandoned house" usually a farmhouse for rent.

CASA DE PASTO Cheap and simple place to eat.

CASTELO Castle.

CENTRO COMERCIAL Shopping centre.

CHAFARIZ Public fountain.

CHURRASQUEIRA (spelt variously) Grill house, usually serving chicken.

CIDADE City.

CORREIOS Post office, abbreviated CTT.

CRUZEIRO Cross.

DORMIDA Room in a private house.

ELÉCTRICO Tramcar.

ELEVADOR Elevator or funicular railway.

ESPIGUEIRO Grain shed on stilts, common in the north.

ESPLANADA Seafront promenade.

ESTAÇÃO Station.

ESTALAGEM One step up from an *albergaria*, usually in rural towns, formerly a coach inn.

ESTRADA Road; Estrada Nacional is a main road, designated EN on maps.

FARMÁCIA Pharmacy.

FEIRA Fair or market.

FESTA Festival or carnival.

FONTE Fountain or spring.

FREGUESIA Parish (*Junta da Freguesia* is the local council)

GRUTAS Caves.

HORÁRIO Timetable.

HOSPEDARIA Cheap and basic pension, usually with shared facilities (same as *casa de hóspedes*).

ILHA Island.

JARDIM Garden.

LAGO Lake.

LARGO Square.

MERCADO Market.

MIRADOURO Belvedere or viewpoint.

PAÇO Palace or country house.

PAÇOS DO CONCELHO Town hall.

PALÁCIO Palace or country house; *palácio real*, royal palace.

PARAGEM Bus stop.

PARQUE Park.

PARQUE DE CAMPISMO Camping site.

PARQUE NACIONAL/NATURAL National/Natural Park or Reserve.

PASTELARIA Bakery, pastry shop.

PELOURINHO Stone pillory, seen in almost every northern village.

POÇO Well.

POMBAL Pigeon house.

PONTE Bridge.

POUSADA Luxury state-run hotel, sometimes converted from a castle or monastery.

POUSADA DE JUVENTUDE Youth hostel.

PRAÇA Square.

PRAÇA DE TOUROS Bullring.

PRAIA Beach.

QUINTA Country estate, farm or villa.

RIA Narrow, open-ended lagoon where sand bars block a river's mouth.

RIBEIRO Stream.

RIO River.

ROMARIA Pilgrimage-festival.

SÉ Cathedral.

SENHOR Man, Sir, or Mr.

SENHORA Woman, Madam, Ms or Mrs.

SERRA Mountain or mountain range.

SOLAR Manor house or important town mansion.

SOLARES DE PORTUGAL (formerly "Turismo de Habitação"). A number of organizations use this term to market accommodation in often outstanding buildings, often of historical or architectural importance (see p.33).

TASCA No-frills local bar.

TERMAS Thermal springs or spa complex.

TOURADA Bullfight.

VILA Town.

INDEX

ROUGH GUIDES: Mini Guides, Travel Specials and Phrasebooks

MINI GUIDES

Antigua
Bangkok
Barbados
Big Island of
  Hawaii
Boston
Brussels
Budapest

Dublin
Edinburgh
Florence
Honolulu
Jerusalem
Lisbon
London
  Restaurants
Madrid
Maui
Melbourne
New Orleans
Seattle
St Lucia

Sydney
Tokyo
Toronto

TRAVEL SPECIALS

First-Time Asia
First-Time
  Europe
Women Travel

PHRASEBOOKS

Czech
Dutch

Egyptian Arabic
European
French
German
Greek
Hindi & Urdu
Hungarian
Indonesian
Italian
Japanese

Mandarin
  Chinese
Mexican
  Spanish
Polish
Portuguese
Russian
Spanish
Swahili
Thai
Turkish
Vietnamese

AVAILABLE AT ALL GOOD BOOKSHOPS

ROUGH GUIDES:
Reference and Music CDs

REFERENCE
Classical Music
Classical:
  100 Essential CDs
Drum'n'bass
House Music
Jazz
Music USA

Internet
Millennium

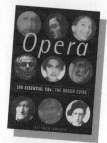

Music of Egypt
English Roots
  Music
Flamenco
India & Pakistan
Irish Music
Music of Japan
Kenya & Tanzania
Native American
North African
Music of Portugal

ROUGH GUIDE
MUSIC CDs
Music of the
  Andes
Australian
  Aboriginal
Brazilian Music
Cajun & Zydeco

Opera
Opera:
  100 Essential CDs
Reggae
Reggae:
  100 Essential CDs
Rock
Rock:
  100 Essential CDs
Techno
World Music
World Music:
  100 Essential CDs
English Football
European Football

Classic Jazz
Music of
  Colombia
Cuban Music
Eastern Europe

Reggae
Salsa
Scottish Music
South African
  Music
Music of Spain
Tango
Tex-Mex
West African
  Music
World Music
World Music Vol 2
Music of
  Zimbabwe

the perfect getaway vehicle

low-price holiday car rental.

rent a car from holiday autos and you'll give yourself real freedom to explore your holiday destination. with great-value, fully-inclusive rates in over 4,000 locations worldwide, wherever you're escaping to, we're there to make sure you get excellent prices and superb service.

what's more, you can book now with complete confidence. our £5 undercut* ensures that you are guaranteed the best value for money in holiday destinations right around the globe.

drive away with a great deal, call holiday autos now on **0990 300 400** and quote ref RG.

holiday autos miles ahead

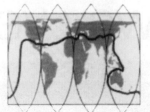
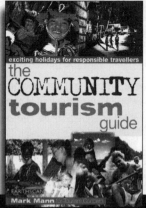